# Southwest

## a Lonely Planet travel survival kit

## Rob Rachowiecki

**Southwest USA – a travel survival kit**

**1st edition**

**Published by**
**Lonely Planet Publications**
Head Office:   PO Box 617, Hawthorn, Vic 3122, Australia
Branches:      155 Filbert St, Suite 251, Oakland, CA 94607, USA
               10 Barley Mow Passage, Chiswick, London W4 4PH, UK
               71 bis rue du Cardinal Lemoine, 75005 Paris, France

**Printed by**
Colorcraft Ltd, Hong Kong

**Photographs by**

| | |
|---|---|
| Wayne Bernhardson (WB) | Rob Rachowiecki (RR) |
| Nigel French (NF) | Robert Rayburn (RRb) |
| Kate Hoffman (KH) | Deanna Swaney (DS) |
| Carolyn Hubbard (CH) | Tony Wheeler (TW) |
| Maria Massolo (MM) | Bob White (BW) |
| Ann Neet (AN) | Gale Wrausmann (GW) |
| Ron Pickup (RP) | |

Front cover: Monument Valley, Navajo Reservation (Ric Ergenbright)
Title page: Arches National Park, Utah (Rob Rachowiecki)

**This Edition**
November 1995

**Although the author and publisher have tried to make the information as accurate as possible, they accept no responsibility for any loss, injury or inconvenience sustained by any person using this book.**

National Library of Australia Cataloguing in Publication Data

Rachowiecki, Rob.
    Southwest USA.

    1st edition.
    Includes index.
    ISBN 0 86442 255 5.

    1. Southwest, (U.S.) – Guidebooks.
    I. Title. (Series: Lonely Planet travel survival kit).

917.90433

## Rob Rachowiecki

Rob was born in London and became an avid traveler while still a teenager. He spent most of the 1980s in Latin America, traveling, teaching English, visiting national parks and working for Wilderness Travel, an adventure travel company. He is the author of Lonely Planet's travel survival kits for Ecuador and Peru, and he has contributed to Lonely Planet's shoestring guides for South America and Central America. He makes his home in Tucson, Arizona, which he found to be an ideal base from which to explore what he considers the most beautiful region of the USA. While researching this book, he traveled well over 20,000 miles and fixed three flat tires. He lives with his wife, Cathy, and three children: Julia (age 7), Alison (5) and David (2 ½).

## Dedication

To my son, David, who was conceived about when I was first planning this book and who is now a delightful, always cheerful toddler.

## From the Author

Staffers at chambers of commerce throughout the Southwest provided town maps and useful information. The Utah Travel Council provided extensive information on that state. National Park Service rangers and information officers were a great source of advice and background information about the many national parks and sites in the region. USFS rangers were very knowledgeable about the areas under their jurisdiction. Most of them helped me without knowing I was writing a book and would surely be as helpful to all travelers.

Jennifer Rasin was responsible for much of the research and writing of the Santa Fe and Taos chapter, and her input was very valuable in helping me finish up the book. Steve McLaughlin provided much of the Albuquerque information. The South American Explorers Club in Ecuador provided me with fax and computer facilities during the final proofing of the book. Dozens of Lonely Planet editors, cartographers, artists and other folks were involved at various times during the course of this massive project, and I thank them all.

Most of all, I thank my dear family for allowing me to work long hours without interruption, and I especially acknowledge my wife, Cathy, whose love and quiet encouragement in no small way helped get this book finished.

## From the Publisher

This travel guide is the result of many people's efforts and creativity. Kate Hoffman was the project editor, while Carolyn Hubbard, Michelle Gagne, Laini Taylor, Kim Haglund, Jacques Talbot and Sarah Lewis all poured over the many stages of editing.

Alex Guilbert, Cyndy Johnsen, Hayden Foell, Chris Salcedo, Blake Summers, Jack Kendrick, Julie Bilski, Patti Keelin, Scott Noren, Adina Nydstrom and Wayne Heiser all drew maps. Hugh D'Andrade, Hayden,

Jacques, JR Swanson and Mark Butler illustrated the book. Robert Arnold created the photo-collage state title pages. Hugh, Cyndy and Kitti Homme were responsible for layout. Hugh designed the cover. Scott Summers coordinated the production of the book.

Many thanks to Adrienne Costanzo, Tom Smallman, James Lyon, Richard Wilson, Sue Mitra and David Russ for their insight and help in production.

## Warning & Request

Things change – prices go up, schedules change, good places go bad and bad places go bankrupt – nothing stays the same. So if you find things better or worse, recently opened or long since closed, please write and tell us and help make the next edition better.

Your letters will be used to help update future editions and, where possible, important changes will also be included as a Stop Press section in reprints.

We greatly appreciate all information that is sent to us by travelers. Back at Lonely Planet we employ a hard-working readers' letters team to sort through the extensive correspondence we receive. The best ones will be rewarded with a free copy of the next edition or another Lonely Planet guide if you prefer. We give away lots of books, but, unfortunately, not every letter/postcard receives one.

# Contents

# Map Legend

## BOUNDARIES

| | |
|---|---|
| —·—·—·—·— | International Boundary |
| —·—·—·—·— | State Boundary |

## AREA FEATURES

| | |
|---|---|
| **City Park** | Park |
| **NATIONAL PARK** | National Park |
| **Indian Reservation** | Reservation |

## HYDROGRAPHIC FEATURES

| | |
|---|---|
| | Water |
| | Coastline, Beach |
| | Creek |
| | River, Waterfall |
| | Swamp, Spring |

## ROUTES

| | |
|---|---|
| | Freeway |
| | Major Road |
| | Minor Road |
| ======= ------- | Unpaved Road |
| 80 | Interstate Freeway |
| 70 | US Highway |
| 99 | State Highway |
| | Bicycle Trail |
| ............ | Foot Trail |
| — — — — | Ferry Route |
| | Railway, Railway Station |
| —M— | Metro, Metro Station |
| | Ski Lift |

## SYMBOLS

| | | | |
|---|---|---|---|
| ◉ **State Capital** | 🏦 Bank, ATM | ✚ Hospital, Clinic | ✉ Post Office |
| ● City | Baseball Diamond | 🕯 Lighthouse | Skiing, Nordic |
| ● Town | ✕ Battlefield | ☀ Lookout | Skiing, Alpine |
| | ⚊ Buddhist Temple | ⚒ Mine | ⛩ Shinto Shrine |
| ■ Hotel, B&B | Bus Depot, Bus Stop | Monument | Shipwreck |
| ▲ Campground | Castle, Chateau | Mosque | ❖ Shopping Mall |
| Hostel | Cathedral | ▲ Mountain | Stately Home |
| RV Park | Cave | 🏛 Museum | ✿ Synagogue |
| ▼ Restaurant | † Church | ← One-Way Street | ☎ Telephone |
| Bar (Place to Drink) | Dive Site | Observatory | Taoist Temple |
| Cafe | Fishing, Fish Hatchery | P Parking | Tourist Information |
| | Garden | ▲ Park | Tomb, Mausoleum |
| ✝ Airfield | Gas Station | Picnic Area | Trailhead |
| ✈ Airport | Golf Course | ★ Police Station | Winery |
| Archaeological Site, Ruins | Hindu Temple | Pool | Zoo |

Note: not all symbols displayed above appear in this book.

# Introduction

Mention the Southwest, and distinct images leap to mind: thick arms of the saguaro cactus, towering red-rock outcrops of Monument Valley, howling coyotes, stunning Anasazi Indian ruins tucked against cliffs, the changing colors of the Grand Canyon. Deserts, grasslands, mountain ranges and high mesas and plateaus are all engulfed in the vast sky. Yet, more than a magnificent geographical terrain, the Southwest also exists as a cultural phenomenon.

The first people in the region were the ancestors of today's Native Americans. Archaeologists have excavated fragments of their villages, hunting sites and irrigation ditches, and have found petroglyphs and pictographs – many of which can been seen in protected national monuments and in museums. Today's Southwestern tribes – the Navajo, Apache, Pueblo and Tohono O'odham, among others – relate oral histories that shed light on their ancestors, and their vibrant cultures and languages reveal traces of their forebears.

The first Europeans in the region were Spanish conquistadors and missionaries, searching for gold, land, slaves and converts. But the Indian tribes had no gold and held land communally. They rebelled against forced labor and resented the new religion. After centuries of overt and covert resistance, many tribes succeeded in maintaining their own cultural identity, and learned the lessons they would rely on when they confronted the next wave of newcomers – the Anglo Americans.

After Mexico won its independence from Spain, the USA was quick to fight for the

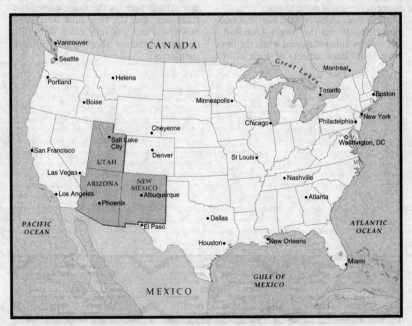

new territory. After the Mexican-American War of 1846 to 1847, the USA assumed control over what was to be called the New Mexico Territory, including most of Arizona and New Mexico. Traders continued to travel west from Missouri to New Mexico along the Santa Fe Trail, but the best route to California lay south of the territorial border. In 1853 the Gadsden Purchase brought southern Arizona into US hands. The government soon sent troops to 'clear' the lands of the Native Americans, establishing massive reservations that cover large parts of the Southwest.

Meanwhile to the north, members of a new Christian sect, the Church of Jesus Christ of Latter-Day Saints (LDS), had reached the Great Salt Lake, where their leader, Brigham Young, announced that 'this was the place' where they would settle. Under Young's orders, small bands of Mormons, as LDS members were called, established communities throughout present-day Utah. The progeny of those pioneers still form the majority in most of those towns.

These three cultures – the Native American, Hispanic and Anglo American – live side by side today, and while the three have assimilated aspects of each other's cultures, they remain distinct. The large cities of Phoenix, Tucson, Santa Fe and Albuquerque all have districts where one culture or another is more prevalent, and many smaller towns still reflect the ethnicity of their founders in their residents and architecture. In Salt Lake City, the Mormon influence is still strong, but even there economic growth has lured newcomers of various races and religions.

As you raft through the Grand Canyon on the Colorado River or mountain bike on slickrock trails outside Moab, watch for the evidence of other eras: lacy fossils of sea creatures, footprints of dinosaurs, pottery shards and rusting mining rigs. As you hike through Canyon de Chelly or Monument Valley, contemplate the peaceful life of the Indians disrupted by the Spaniards and US Cavalry. When you drive in the warmth of your car to ski slopes covered in Utah's world-famous snow, imagine Mormon pioneers digging their wagons out of those deep drifts. A visit to any Indian reservation affords perhaps the finest contrast of traditions: the US flag flies over most powwows, and you may catch sight of a ceremonial dancer slipping on Ray Ban sunglasses.

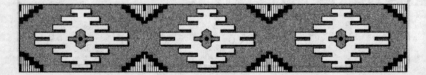

# Facts about the Southwest

## HISTORY
### The First Americans

The history of the sun-baked Southwest begins not with sun but with ice. For it was during the last Ice Age, roughly 25,000 years ago, that the first people reached the North American continent from Asia by way of the Bering Strait. These first Americans were hardy nomadic hunters who, armed with little more than pointed sticks and the courage born of hunger, pursued Ice Age mammals such as mammoths, cave bears and giant sloths.

As the climate began to warm, the glaciers that had covered much of North America receded and the nomads began to move south. It is not known, however, when the first people appeared in the canyons and plateaus of the Southwest. In fact, until the late 1920s, archaeologists believed that the continent had been inhabited for a mere 4000 years. Then workers in Folsom and Clovis, New Mexico, began studying stone spear points fashioned by paleolithic hunters. They found these artifacts embedded in the bones of extinct large mammals that were dated to over 11,000 years ago. This is the earliest current evidence of the first inhabitants of the Southwest, although people may have populated the area before then. By the time of the Clovis hunters, people had spread from Asia and Alaska throughout most of North, Central and South America.

Even though the above scenario is a widely accepted one, there are other descriptions of the arrival of the first Americans. Some archaeologists claim that people crossed from Asia perhaps 35,000 or more years ago, while others suggest no more than 15,000. Indian oral histories offer various other depictions. One cosmic origin myth describes how the first arrivals, four men and three women, came from the Man Carrier (an Indian name for the Big Dipper constellation) 50,000 years ago. There are many other tribal beliefs.

Theories on the descent of Native Americans from East Asians point to the two groups' dentition patterns. Among other similar features, Native Americans and East Asians have a pronounced curved shape (termed shovel-shaped by anthropologists) on the backs, fronts or both sides of their incisor teeth, while people of European, African and West Asian heritage have almost flat incisor surfaces. (Check your teeth to see if you can support this evidence.)

Soon after the end of the last Ice Age, the large game mammals abruptly and mysteriously became extinct, and people began to hunt the smaller animals we know today, such as deer and rabbits. They used a throwing device called an *atlatl* to propel hunting spears and also built simple traps.

In addition, gathering of wild food crops (berries, seeds, roots and fruits) bolstered the diet and became as important as hunting. Baskets were used to collect food and stone metates were developed to grind hard seeds and roots. The baskets were so tightly woven that they held water and were even used for cooking by the process of dropping heated stones into the basket. Archaeological sites in or near Cochise County in southeastern Arizona have yielded the remains of basket and stone cooking implements, and thus the Southwestern hunter-gatherers of this early period (approximately 7000 BC to 500 BC) have been named the Cochise people.

After about 3000 BC, contacts with early farmers from further south (in what is now central Mexico) led to the beginnings of agriculture in the Southwest. The first crops were minor additions to the Cochise people's diets, and they continued their nomadic hunter-gatherer lifestyles. Eventually, people started reusing the same plots of land for their crops and spending more

time in these areas. Primitive corn was one of the first crops. By about 500 BC, beans, squash and, later, cotton were also being cultivated. Finally, around 300 BC to 100 AD, distinct groups began to settle in semi-permanent villages in the Southwest.

## Ancient Southwestern Cultures

Most archaeologists agree that, by about 100 AD, three dominant cultures were emerging in the Southwest: the Hohokam of the desert, the Mogollon of the central mountains and valleys, and the Anasazi of the northern plateaus. In addition, several other groups were either blendings of or offshoots from the three main cultures – these smaller groups are still the subject of controversy among archaeologists. Examples are the Hakataya, Fremont, Salado and Sinagua traditions.

These groups are all discussed below, but remember that there is still debate and disagreement about these matters. Clearly, neither of the three dominant cultures nor the smaller ones existed in isolation, and much blending and fusion of lifestyles took place. By the mid 1400s, and earlier in some cases, most of these cultures had disappeared, their villages abandoned. The reasons for this are unclear, although many theories have been suggested. Most likely it was a combination of factors including a devastating drought near the end of the 12th century, climate changes, overhunting, soil erosion, disease and the arrival of new groups. The overview I offer here is a traditional one, but it is not the only interpretation.

**Hohokam** This culture existed in the southern and central deserts of Arizona from about 300 BC to 1450 AD. These people created an advanced irrigation system based on the Gila, Salt and Verde Rivers and became extremely well adapted to desert life. Apart from farming, they collected wild desert food such as the fruit of the giant saguaro cactus and the beans of the mesquite tree – a tradition that can still be observed today among desert Indians such as the Tohono O'odham tribe.

The irrigation system was quite incredible. Using stone tools the people dug many miles of canals, some of which were 15 feet deep and twice as wide.

The people lived in simple shelters of mud or sticks over a shallow depression in the earth. As time passed, this culture developed low earthen pyramids, which may have been temples, and sunken ball courts with earthen walls in which games were played. These features clearly point to the Hohokam connection with the cultures of Mexico and Guatemala. Burials were by cremation, and so archaeologists today learn comparatively little by excavating burial sites. A rich heritage of pottery, however, attests to Hohokam craftsmaking and their ceramics and other artifacts can be seen in places such as the Arizona State Museum in Tucson, Arizona. Hohokam ruins can be visited in Pueblo Grande Museum and Cultural Park, Phoenix, Arizona, and the Casa Grande National Monument, between Phoenix and Tucson.

During the middle of the 15th century, the Hohokam disappeared. Why? We don't know. Today's Pima and Tohono O'odham, (formerly Papago) Indians appear to be descended from the Hohokam, but the links are not clear. This is but one of the many mysteries that make the Southwest a fascinating place to travel in.

**Mogollon** The Mogollan (pronounced 'muggy-un') culture is named after the mountains of the same name in western New Mexico and the Mogollon Rim in eastern Arizona. The region south of these mountainous areas as far as the Mexican border and east to the Llano Estacado flatlands of eastern New Mexico was the province of the Mogollon Culture, which existed here from about 200 BC to 1450 AD.

The Mogollon people settled in small communities, often elevated on an isolated mesa or ridge top. The houses were simple pit dwellings. They did some simple farming, but they depended much more on hunting and foraging than did their contemporaries of other cultures. As the Mogollon people developed, their villages

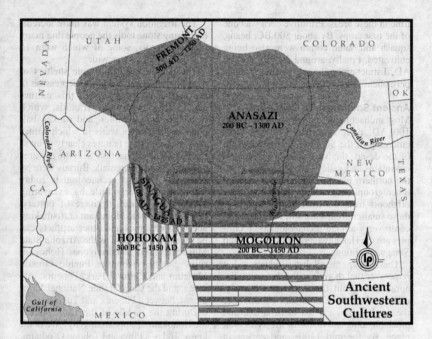

NEVADA · UTAH · COLORADO · OK
FREMONT 500 AD – 1250 AD
Colorado River · ARIZONA · NEW MEXICO · TEXAS
ANASAZI 200 BC – 1300 AD
Canadian River
Rio Grande
SINAGUA 1100 AD – 1425 AD
HOHOKAM 300 BC – 1450 AD
MOGOLLON 200 BC – 1450 AD
Gulf of California · MEXICO

**Ancient Southwestern Cultures**

grew bigger and often featured a *kiva* (a circular, underground chamber used for ceremonies and other purposes).

As time progressed, the Mogollon people began to depend on farming to a greater extent. By about the 1200s and 1300s, however, there were many signs that the Mogollon were being peacefully incorporated into the Anasazi groups from the north. The beautiful black-on-white Mimbres pottery (from the Mimbres River area in southwestern New Mexico) has distinctive animal and human figures executed in a geometric style reminiscent of Anasazi ware. The Gila Cliff Dwellings National Monument, near the Mimbres area, is a late Mogollon ruin with Anasazi pueblo features. In fact, most of today's Pueblo Indians trace their ancestry to the Mogollon or Anasazi Cultures.

**Anasazi** The Anasazi inhabited the Colorado Plateau (also called the Four Corners area and comprising northeastern Arizona,

northwestern New Mexico, southwestern Colorado and southeastern Utah). This culture left us by far the richest heritage of ruins and archaeological sites in the Southwest. The word Anasazi comes from a Navajo term that was first interpreted as 'ancient ones' but can also be translated as 'enemy ancestors'. As there is not direct translation of word, but rather a Navajo myth, it is difficult to pinpoint the exact meaning.

Like the Hohokam and Mogollon Cultures, the earliest Anasazi were hunter-gatherers who slowly brought farming into their repertoire of methods of obtaining food. Food was gathered in baskets, and the excellence of their basket weaving has led archaeologists to refer to the early period of Anasazi Culture as the Basket Maker periods. The people lived in simple pit houses and, towards the end of Basket Maker III period (400 AD to 700 AD), pottery became increasingly important.

The Pueblo periods, which followed the

Basket Maker periods, saw much development in pottery and architecture. Larger villages, some with over 100 rooms, were built, many (but not all) of them in shallow caves under overhanging cliffs. Important and impressive Anasazi pueblo ruins can be seen at Mesa Verde National Park, Colorado; Navajo National Monument, Arizona; Canyon de Chelly National Monument, Arizona; Bandelier National Monument, New Mexico; Aztec Ruins National Monument, New Mexico; Chaco Culture National Historic Park, New Mexico; and in many other sites.

Today, descendants of the Anasazi are found in the Pueblo Indian groups along the Rio Grande in New Mexico, and in the Acoma, Zuni and Laguna Pueblos of New Mexico's northwestern corner. The most ancient links with the Anasazi are found among the Hopi tribe of northern Arizona. Here, perched on a mesa top, the village of Old Oraibi has been inhabited since the 1100s, the oldest continuously inhabited settlement in North America.

By about 1450 AD, the Hohokam had mysteriously disappeared and the Mogollon people had been more or less incorporated into the Anasazi. The Anasazi themselves also began to leave many of their ancient pueblos in the 1400s and, by the 1500s, had mainly moved to the pueblos now found along the Rio Grande.

**Smaller Groups** The Hakataya is the term given to several small groups who once lived in western and central Arizona and were contemporaries of the Anasazi. The best known of these groups is the Sinagua, who left a variety of interesting and attractive ruins such as those at the Montezuma Castle, Tuzigoot, Walnut Canyon and Wupatki National Monuments in central Arizona. Lesser known groups existed west of the Sinagua and included the Prescott, Cohonina, Cerbat and Laquish peoples.

The Salado Culture exhibits influences from both the Anasazi and Mogollon peoples, and the culture appears to have influenced some late Hohokam sites. Salado remains are found in central Arizona, in the area where all three of the major cultural groups overlapped to some extent. The best Salado ruins can be seen at the Tonto National Monument, Arizona.

The Fremont Culture took hold north of the Anasazi, in south and central Utah. The Fremont were marginally related to the Anasazi but with several distinct features. Among these are a unique form of pottery made from a coarse sand/clay mixture and a greater reliance on hunting. A good place to see their artifacts is in Fremont Indian State Park, Utah.

**Later Cultures**
The cultures described above can generally be traced back in the Southwest for two millennia or longer. Many of the tribes living in the Southwest today, however, are comparatively recent arrivals. Nomadic bands of Indians from two distinct language groups, the Shoshonean and the Athapaskan, straggled into the Southwest from the north between about 1300 AD and 1600 AD.

Shoshonean tribes found in the Southwest today live mainly in Utah and make up only a small part of the population. They include the Shoshone in northern Utah (and into Idaho and Wyoming), Utes in central and eastern Utah (and into Colorado), Goshutes in western Utah (and into Nevada), and Southern Paiutes in southwestern Utah (and into Nevada and Arizona).

The Navajo and a variety of Apache tribes are of Athapaskan descent; they now make up a substantial part of Arizona's and New Mexico's populations. The Navajos moved into the Four Corners area, especially the northwestern part of Arizona. The Apaches consisted of several distinct groups, of which the most important were the Jicarilla Apaches in the north-central mountains of New Mexico, the Mescalero Apaches in New Mexico's south-central mountains and various other groups, together referred to as the Western Apaches, in southeastern Arizona.

These late arrivals did not conquer the Pueblo and Hopi descendants of the

Anasazi but rather co-existed with them. Certainly, there were occasional skirmishes and raids, but generally the Pueblo peoples took advantage of the hunting skills of the newcomers, while the Apache and Navajo learned about pottery, weaving and agriculture from the Pueblo tribes. Then the Europeans arrived in the Southwest, bringing a lifestyle completely foreign to the Native Americans. Mother Earth and Father Sky, bows and arrows, ritual dances and sweatlodges, foot travel, spiritual oneness with the land – all these were to be challenged by the new concepts of Christ and conquest, gunpowder and sword, European civilization and education, horses, and a grasping desire for land.

## The Spaniards

For the next three centuries, it was the Spanish who wrought the greatest changes in the region. Most of what is now Arizona and New Mexico became a Spanish colony and, much later, part of Mexico. It was not until the 1840s that the Southwest became part of the USA. Utah, however, remained almost unexplored until the arrival of the Mormons in the 19th century.

After brief incursions into the Southwest by small Spanish groups in 1536 and 1539, a major expedition was launched in 1540 under the leadership of Francisco Vásquez de Coronado. He set off from Mexico City with 336 Europeans, 1000 Indians and 1100 pack and riding animals. The expedition's goals were the fabled, immensely rich 'Seven Cities of Cíbola'.

For two years, they traveled through Arizona, New Mexico and as far east as Kansas, but instead of gold and precious gems, the expedition found Indian pueblos of mud bricks and wooden sticks. Some of the leaders took contingents to explore the Hopi mesas and the Grand Canyon, among other areas. During the harsh winters, the expedition expropriated some of the pueblos for its own use, burnt one, and killed dozens of Indians. This ferocity was to prove typical of the behavior of many of the Europeans who were yet to come. Finally, the expedition returned home, penniless and broken. Coronado had failed to become rich or find the fabled cities, and for the next half century, Spanish exploration focused on areas outside the Southwest.

The dreams of fabulously rich cities were revived periodically by small groups making minor forays, especially along the Rio Grande. Then, in 1598, a large force of 400 European men and an unknown number of Indians, women and children, accompanied by a reputed 7000 head of various livestock and 83 ox carts, headed north from Mexico and up the Rio Grande. Their leader was a fortune-seeker named Juan de Oñate, a Spaniard who had been born in Mexico and whose deceased wife had been a descendant of both the conquistador Hernán Cortés and the Aztec emperor, Moctezuma. Oñate was accompanied by his 12-year-old son and two of his nephews.

Near what is now El Paso, the Texan city by the tri-border of Texas, New Mexico and Mexico, Oñate stopped. He called the land to the north New Mexico, claimed it for Spain and became governor of this land. Then he headed north and, as the Rio Grande began to swing westward, he continued north through the dry and inhospitable desert that became named *Jornada del Muerto* or the 'Journey of the Dead'. (This region is where the USA chose to detonate the first nuclear bomb – which gives you an idea of how desolate this Jornada del Muerto is.)

After a desperate journey, Oñate reached the pueblos near the confluence of the Rio Chama and Rio Grande, and here he set up the first capital of New Mexico, San Gabriel. This route along the Rio Grande and Jornada del Muerto became known as *El Camino Real* (the royal road) and was the standard trail linking Mexico with northern New Mexico. For most of the 1600s, there was little European exploration of other parts of the Southwest.

During the Spaniards' first few years in northern New Mexico, they tried to subdue the pueblos, which led to much bloodshed. The fighting started in Acoma Pueblo, when a Spanish contingent of 30 men led by Juan de Zaldívar, one of Oñate's nephews, demanded payment of taxes in the form of food. The Indians of Acoma responded by killing Zaldívar and about half of his force. Oñate then sent 70 soldiers led by his other nephew, Vicente de Zaldívar, to punish the inhabitants of Acoma. This was accomplished with the Spaniards' usual ruthlessness – several hundred Indians were killed, and hundreds more were taken prisoner and subjected to punishments ranging from amputation of a foot to slavery. By 1601, three other pueblos were ransacked and many hundreds of Indians were killed or enslaved.

Meanwhile, San Gabriel fared poorly as the capital of New Mexico. Tense relationships with the Indians, poor harvests, harsh weather and accusations of Oñate's cruelty led to many desertions among the colonizers. By 1608, Oñate had been recalled to Mexico and, on the journey south, lost his son to an attack by Indians. On his return, he was stripped of his governorship.

A new governor, Pedro de Peralta, was sent north to found a new capital, which he did in 1609. This was Santa Fe, and it remains the capital of New Mexico today, the oldest capital in what is now the USA. In 1610, Peralta built the Palace of the Governors on the Plaza in Santa Fe – this building is the oldest non-Indian building in the USA still in use today. (Meanwhile, the first British colony had been founded in Jamestown, Virginia, in 1607. The second British colony was founded in 1620 at Plymouth, Massachusetts, by the famous Pilgrims.)

A steady trickle of colonists, accompanied by soldiers and Franciscan priests, moved from Mexico to the Santa Fe area over the next 50 years. Their aim was to settle and farm the land and bring the pagan Indians into the Catholic Church. Most of the Pueblo groups had little interest in being converted, although some blended Catholicism with their own beliefs. Neither were the Indians much inclined to help the Spanish build churches in their pueblos nor to work for the new colonists. For the most part, the Spanish treated the recalcitrant Pueblo people brutally at any sign of resistance – prison, beatings, torture and executions were common.

A particularly destructive Spanish campaign in 1675 was aimed at destroying the Pueblo kivas and powerful ceremonial objects such as prayer sticks and kachina dolls. The horrified Indians tried to protect their heritage but were punished harshly. This was the last straw for them. By 1680, the united northern Pueblos rose up in the 'Pueblo Revolt' and succeeded in driving some 2400 Spaniards back down the Rio Grande to El Paso. The Pueblo people took over Santa Fe's Palace of the Governors and held it until 1692.

The northern Pueblo people were, of course, a mix of many different tribes, languages and beliefs, and so they didn't remain united for very long. In 1692, the Spaniards, led by Diego de Vargas, once again took over Santa Fe and, over the succeeding years, subdued all the pueblos in the area. During the 1700s, the colony grew slowly but steadily, and the Spaniards lived uneasily but relatively peacefully alongside the Pueblo peoples.

Meanwhile, less brutal incursions were being made into Arizona by the Jesuit priest Eusebio Kino, who has garnered almost mythical status as the bringer of God to what is now (mainly) southern Arizona. He began his travels in Mexico in 1687 and spent over two decades in the Arizona-Sonora area. His approach to being a missionary was, certainly by the standards of the day, humane, and this, at least, distinguished him from many of his contemporaries. He established missions at Tumacacori and San Xavier del Bac (both between Tucson and the Mexican border); these sites can be visited today, although the present buildings were erected about a century after Kino was there.

After Kino's departure, conditions for the Indians in what is now Arizona deteriorated and led to the short-lived Pima Revolt of 1751 and the Yuma Massacre of 1781, when the Yumans killed colonizers in their area.

Throughout the Southwest, Apaches, Comanches, Navajos and Hopis were alternately fighting with one another or with the Spaniards, and it was this warfare that limited further Spanish expansion in the area during the 18th century.

In an attempt to link Santa Fe with the newly established port of San Francisco and to avoid Indian raids, the Spanish priests Francisco Atanasio Dominguez and Silvestre Velez de Escalante led a small group of explorers into what is now Utah, but they were turned back by the rugged and arid terrain. The 1776 Dominguez-Escalante expedition was the first to survey Utah, but no attempt was made to settle there.

Although the historically important events outlined above provide a sketch of Hispanic-Indian relations during the 16th to the 18th century, one crucial point has not been discussed. The Europeans brought with them diseases to which the Indians had no resistance and which caused terrible epidemics within the tribes. By some accounts, 80% of the Native Americans died from disease in the 16th century, and the history of North America may have been very different if epidemics had not taken such a terrible toll.

## The Anglos

In 1803, the USA bought the Louisiana Purchase (which stretched from Louisiana to the Rocky Mountains) from the French, thereby doubling the size of the young country. The Spanish colonies of the Southwest now abutted, for the first time, US territory, and the two countries maintained an uneasy peace.

During the winter of 1806-1807, a small contingent of US soldiers led by Lt Zebulon Montgomery Pike reached the upper Rio Grande and were taken by Spanish soldiers to Santa Fe for lengthy interrogation before being allowed to return to the USA. In 1810, Pike published a book about his experiences. He described New Mexican life, including details of the high cost of merchandise in Santa Fe because of the great distances from the rest

of New Mexico. This induced several groups of US traders and entrepreneurs to make the difficult journey to Santa Fe with trade goods, but the Spanish repudiated their efforts, jailing the Americans and confiscating their goods.

This situation changed in 1821, when Mexico became independent from Spain. The next party of US traders who arrived in Santa Fe were welcomed by the newly independent Mexicans, and a major trade route was established. This was the famous Santa Fe Trail between Missouri and Santa Fe, a trail traversed by thousands of people until the coming of the railway in 1879.

Politically, the Southwest had changed, but the reality was that, for a couple of decades, life continued much as before. The Spanish soldiers and missionaries left and were replaced by a Mexican army. Santa Fe grew and thrived, but the Hispanic inhabitants continued to be hampered by raiding Indians, especially Apaches and Comanches (a nomadic prairie tribe known for their skills in buffalo hunting and horseback riding). Few Anglos (as the non-Hispanic Whites from the USA were called) ventured beyond the Santa Fe Trail. Those that did were the 'mountain men' – hunters and trappers who explored all over the West. These men were the first Europeans to explore Utah since the Dominguez-Escalante expedition in 1776.

In 1846, the USA declared war on Mexico, and two years later, Mexico gave up all the land between Texas and the Pacific. The border more or less followed the present one, with the exception of 30,000 sq miles in southern Arizona and New Mexico, which the USA bought from the Mexicans in 1853 in what was to become known as the 'Gadsden Purchase'. The Mormons, led by Brigham Young, founded Salt Lake City, still technically part of Mexico, in 1847. A Mormon battalion was sent to help in the Mexican War effort, although they saw no action.

## The Territory Years

After the Mexican-American War, most of present-day Arizona and New Mexico became the New Mexico Territory of the United States, while most of Utah and Nevada became the Utah Territory. It was not until 1861 that Nevada became a separate territory, and in 1863 Arizona became a separate territory.

Territories differed from states in that they were not allowed to elect their own senators and representatives to the US Congress in Washington, DC. Territories were headed by an elected governor, who had little real power in the nation's capital.

Utah's territorial capital was briefly in Fillmore but was relocated to Salt Lake City in 1858, where it has remained. Arizona's first capital was Prescott, but was moved quickly to Tucson in 1867, returned to Prescott in 1877 and finally moved to the present location, Phoenix, in 1889. New Mexico's capital has been Santa Fe since its foundation in 1609. Statehood came first to Utah in 1896, and much later to New Mexico and Arizona in 1912.

The history of the Southwest during the territory years and the gaining of statehood is complex and colorful. It is beyond the scope of this book to probe deeply into it, and readers are directed to the Books section in Facts for the Visitor for suggestions for further study. Following are brief overviews of some fo the more important historical topics.

**Indian Wars & Reservations** The Americans proceeded to settle the new territories much more aggressively than the Spaniards had. For decades, US forces had pushed west across the continent, killing or forcibly moving whole tribes of Indians who were in their way. This continued in the Southwest as the West was 'won'.

The best-known incident was the forceful relocation of many Navajos in 1864. US forces, led by Kit Carson, destroyed Navajo fields, orchards and houses and forced the people into surrendering or withdrawing into remote parts of the Canyon de Chelly in Arizona. Eventually, they were starved out and a total of about 9000 Navajos were rounded up and marched 400 miles east to a camp at Bosque Redondo,

near Fort Sumner in New Mexico. Hundreds of Indians died from sickness, starvation or gunshot along the way. The Navajos call this 'The Long Walk', and it remains an important part of their history.

Life at Bosque Redondo was harsh with inadequate resources for 9000 people; over 2000 Navajos died. Even from the Anglo point of view, this relocation was not working and, after four years, the surviving Navajos were allowed to return to their lands in northeastern Arizona and allotted over 5000 sq miles for their reservation. Since the 1868 treaty, the reservation has grown to encompass over 20,000 sq miles in Arizona, New Mexico and Utah; it is the largest in the USA and the Navajo people are the largest tribe.

Every one of the many tribes in the Southwest resisted the westward growth of the USA to a greater or lesser extent.

The last serious conflicts were between US troops and Apaches. This was partly because raiding was the essential and honorable path to manhood for Apaches – any young Apache man had to demonstrate raiding skills in order to marry well, and then to provide for his extended family and to be considered a leader. As the US forces and settlers moved into Apache land, they became obvious targets for the raids that were part of the Apache way of life. These continued under the leadership of Mangas Coloradas, Cochise, Victorio and, finally, Geronimo, who surrendered in 1886 after being promised that he and the Apaches would be imprisoned for two years and then allowed to return to their homeland. As with many promises made during these years, this one, too, was broken. The Apaches spent 27 years as prisoners of war.

By the time of Geronimo's surrender, there were many Indian reservations in the Southwest, each belonging to one or sometimes a few tribes. Although the wars were over, Indian people continued to be treated like second-class citizens for many decades. Non-Indians used legal loopholes and technicalities to take over reservation land. Many children were removed from reservations and shipped off to boarding schools where they were taught in English and punished for speaking their own languages or behaving 'like an Indian' – this practice continued into the 1930s. Older Indians were encouraged to lose their culture and customs. Despite the history of cultural oppression, Indians today still practice spiritual customs and other beliefs that predate US expansion. Many Native languages are still spoken, and a majority of Navajos learn their tribal language before English.

Indians fought alongside Americans in WW I but were not extended US citizenship until 1924 and were not given voting rights until 1948 in Arizona and New Mexico, and 1957 in Utah. Most tribes have their own government and laws that are applicable to people living on or visiting their reservations. Federal laws are also applicable to reservations, but normally state and other local laws do not apply.

WW II saw the first large exodus of Indians from the reservations; they went to join the US war effort. One of the most famous units was the Navajo Code Talkers – 420 Navajo marines who used a code based on their language for vital messages in the Pacific arena. This code was never broken by the Japanese. Today, the surviving code talkers are among the most revered of Navajo elders and are often honored in public events. Currently, about half of US Indians live off reservations, but many of these maintain strong ties with their tribes.

**Transportation** The history of the Southwest during the 19th century is strongly linked to the development of transportation in the region. During early territorial days, movement of goods and people from the east to the Southwest was very slow. Horses, mule trains and stage coaches were state-of-the-art transportation in those days.

Major trails included the Santa Fe Trail, which linked Missouri with Santa Fe from the 1820s to the 1870s, and the Old Spanish Trail from Santa Fe into central Utah and across Nevada to Los Angeles, California. Regular stagecoach services along the Santa Fe Trail began in 1849.

The Mormon Trail reached Salt Lake City in 1847. In succeeding years, thousands of Mormon settlers followed this route, many pulling their possessions for hundreds of miles in handcarts.

The Butterfield Overland Mail Company opened in 1858 and linked St Louis, Missouri, with San Francisco, California, via southwestern New Mexico, Tucson and Yuma. Butterfield offered two stagecoaches a week that completed the journey in 25 days – an incredibly exhausting trip.

Cattle trails, along which cowhands drove many thousands of head of cattle, letting them feed as they went, sprung up in the 1860s and 1870s; among these, the most important were the Goodnight-Loving Trail for moving cattle from Texas through eastern New Mexico into Colorado, and the Chisum Trail, which branched of from the Goodnight-Loving Trail near Roswell, New Mexico, and directed cattle west into Arizona. Clearly, ranching was already important business and has remained so.

More people arrived with the advent of the railroads. The first transcontinental line was completed in northern Utah in 1869 and led to an influx of non-Mormons into Utah. The Atchison, Topeka and Santa Fe Railroad reached Santa Fe in 1879, linking that city with the east. Meanwhile, the Southern Pacific Railroad had been pushed inland from Los Angeles through Yuma and Tucson as far as Deming. A few years later, this was linked up to the Santa Fe line. The Atlantic and Pacific Railroad, built in 1883, went from near Albuquerque across northern Arizona to Los Angeles.

The arrival of more people and resources on the railroad led to further exploration of the land, and deposits of minerals were frequently being discovered. The 1870s and 1880s saw the foundation of many mining towns; some of these are now ghost towns, while others (for example Tombstone and Silver City) remain active today. Gold, copper and silver mining all boomed, although silver mining busted suddenly with the crash of 1893. Mining, particularly copper, continues to be an significant part of the Southwest's economy today.

**The Wild West** Desperate tales of gun-slingers and cattle rustlers, outlaws and train robbers, are all part of the legend of the Wild West. The good guys and the bad guys were designations often in flux – a tough outlaw in one state might become a sheriff in another. New mining towns, mushrooming overnight near the richest mines, often had more saloons and bordellos than any other kind of building. Newly rich miners would come into town to brawl, drink and gamble, sometimes being fleeced by professional card sharks. It was no surprise that law and order was practically nonexistent in many parts of the Southwest during the latter part of the 19th century.

Some of the most legendary figures in the Southwest include Billy the Kid and Sheriff Pat Garrett, who were involved in the infamous Lincoln County War in New Mexico in the late 1870s. Billy the Kid shot and killed over 20 men in a brief career as a gunslinger – he himself was shot and killed by Garrett when he was but 21 years old. In 1881, Wyatt Earp, along with his brothers Virgil and Morgan and Doc Holliday, shot dead Billy Clanton and the McLaury brothers in a blazing gunfight at the OK Corral in Tombstone – the whole thing took less than a minute. Both sides accused the other of cattle rustling, but the real story will never be told. Today, re-enactments of the gunfight take place regularly in Tombstone.

In fact, reenactments are the closest you'll get to those lawless frontier days, and several towns have them during various festivals. Old Tucson Movie Studios outside of Tucson is as good a place as any to see some Wild West action. One chilling event that you won't see reenacted is the hanging of notorious train robber Black Jack Ketchum in Clayton in 1901 – an error by the hangman literally caused Ketchum to lose his head. Other names inextricably linked with the Southwest are Butch Cassidy and the Sundance Kid, who roamed over much of Utah and other parts of the West. Cassidy was a Mormon, and during the 1890s he and his Wild Bunch gang robbed banks and trains, but he never killed anyone.

Wyatt Earp

By the turn of the century, some semblance of law and order had arrived in the Southwest, and the days of gangs and gunslingers were over.

**Drought & Deluge** The history of the modern settlement of the arid Southwest is closely linked with the development of water use. The Colorado River is 1450 miles long, the ninth longest in North America and the most important river in the Southwest. The Rio Grande, at 1900 miles, is longer but has less water. Other important rivers are the Salt, Gila, Green and Little Colorado, all tributaries of the Colorado, and the Pecos River.

The climate – dry for months and then subject to sudden storms of very heavy rain – made the rivers difficult to control. Reduced to a trickle or drying completely during the dry months, rivers could change into tremendous torrents in a matter of hours after a monsoon storm. Interestingly enough, the ancient Hohokam people had learned how to irrigate large parts of central and southern Arizona, but their system is long forgotten and silted up.

From the 1870s until the early 1900s, Mormon pioneers along the Little Colorado River, ranchers along the Salt and Pecos rivers and settlers along river valleys throughout the Southwest built makeshift dams in attempts to control and divert the waters for irrigation. Time after time, floods would sweep away the dams and they would be rebuilt. In 1905, a huge flood along the lower Colorado River resulted in a permanent alteration of its course.

At the time, it was clear that something needed to be done to control the rivers, and so the Reclamation Act of 1902 was passed, which led to the building of huge federally funded dams, constructed to resist even the wildest of floods. The first was the Theodore Roosevelt Dam on the Salt River, completed in 1911, soon followed by the Strawberry River Dam in Utah in 1913, the Rio Grande's Elephant Butte Dam in 1916 and the Coolidge Dam, finished in 1929 on the Gila River.

There were constant disagreements and rancorous debates within each state as to who should be allowed to use the water of these rivers. Colorado River water rights, however, were a much bigger matter – seven different states had claims to the water. In 1922, US Secretary of Commerce (later President) Herbert Hoover brought the states together in the Colorado River Compact and engineered a scheme to divide up the water rights, with California getting the largest share.

Disagreements continued, however, with Arizona refusing to ratify the compact until 1944. Despite this, the 1922 compact laid the groundwork for a series of major dams on the Colorado River, particularly the Hoover Dam, built between 1931 and 1936, then the largest ever built and still the second highest in the USA. Hoover Dam's reservoir, Lake Mead, has the largest capacity in the USA, closely followed by Lake Powell, which was formed in 1966 by the construction of Glen Canyon Dam, also on the Colorado River.

Despite this seeming bounty of water created by modern technology, there were and are many water problems, of which not the least were ethical ones – the huge lakes formed by the dams flooded canyons containing hundreds of ancient Indian ruins that are now lost forever. Technical problems have included the inaccurate measurement of water flow by early gauges; it is now thought that the original estimates of available water were 20% too high. Other technical problems include what to do with the silt that drops out of the water when it comes to a halt behind a dam. And some problems have no solution – dams built to withstand the biggest floods can do nothing when there is a drought, as has occurred during several years of the last decade.

Nevertheless, water has become available in the Southwest and, with it, towns have grown. More water meant more people who needed more water still – a vicious cycle that has reached crisis proportions. Phoenix is the most noteworthy example. Founded in 1870, the city had 5,500 inhabitants in 1900 and has about one million today, the ninth largest in the country. There is simply not enough water for all these people.

Recent additions to the Southwest's water supply are underground water reserves, or aquifers, which have been discovered in west-central Arizona, southwestern Utah and, most importantly, the Ogallala Aquifer of the Great Plains, which provides moisture for large parts of New Mexico and five other plains states.

These aquifers are being 'mined' – in other words, water is being extracted from them at a much faster rate than it can naturally be replenished. Recent legislative action is attempting to halt this exploitation to avoid losing the aquifers by early in the next century. Southwesterners can only hope that this will be successful. Providing water to the ever-growing population of the Southwest remains the region's most serious problem, and some groups have been eyeing rivers as far away as the Pacific Northwest and Canada as possible sources of water.

## GEOGRAPHY & GEOLOGY

Travelers will find that vast canyons and steep bluffs, buttes, mesas and mountains often make it difficult to get from here to there. Although the varied topography may hinder travel, it is also one of the attractions that lures travelers to the region in the first place. The scenery is literally breathtaking.

The central part of the Southwest is the **Colorado Plateau**, which covers most of northern Arizona, southeastern Utah, northwestern New Mexico and southwestern Colorado. The center of the Colorado Plateau is often called the Four Corners region, because all four of these states share a common boundary point at Four Corners, the only place where four US states meet. Much of this area is part of the Navajo Indian Reservation, the largest in the USA, and the Hopi Indian Reservation.

The Colorado Plateau is actually a series of plateaus between 5000 and 8000 feet in elevation. They are separated by deep canyons, among them the world-famous Grand Canyon. The plateaus are not flat

**Petroglyphs**
Throughout the Southwest, rocks, boulders and cliffs may be darkened with a blue-black layer called desert varnish. The dark color is caused by iron and manganese oxides that leach out of the rock over many centuries, leaving a thin and slightly shiny polish that sometimes streaks cliffs from top to bottom. Ancient Indians chipped away the varnish to expose the lighter rock beneath, thus creating the rock art known as petroglyphs. (RR) ■

but rather are topped by distinctive buttes, mesas and other topographical features that give the landscape its Southwestern character. Erosion has played with these features, resulting in natural arches, bridges, spires and towers. These, combined with the canyons, led to the foundation of the region's many national parks and other scenic sites.

The Colorado Plateau is more or less surrounded by mountainous regions. Southwest of the plateau, Arizona's country drops in a rugged cliff called the Mogollon (pronounced 'muggy-un') Rim, which is as high as 2000 feet in some places and stretches about a third of the way across that state. Beyond lies a broad belt of mountain ranges, getting progressively lower towards the southwest.

The southwestern and south-central parts of Arizona belong to the desert basin and range country. Flat desert basins alternate with mountain ranges, many topped by forests and almost all running north to south. It's in these arid basins that Arizona's major cities, Phoenix and Tucson, are found, supported by massive irrigation projects from the Colorado, Gila and Salt Rivers. This is part of the **Arizona-Sonora Desert**.

Basin and range country continues northwest into Nevada and swings back into Utah. In Utah, northwest of the Colorado Plateau, the basin and range country is part of the **Great Basin Desert**. Where the Great Basin Desert abuts the Wasatch Mountains (part of the Rocky Mountain Region) in north-central Utah lies a fertile valley where Salt Lake City and other important Utahan towns are found. The northeastern corner of Utah pertains more to the Rocky Mountains than to the Southwestern deserts. This region includes the unusual Uinta Mountains, one of the few US mountain ranges that trends from west to east, and the largest of those that do so in the lower 48 states.

Southeast of the Colorado Plateau, heading into New Mexico, the traveler again encounters the Rocky Mountains, whose Continental Divide snakes through the western part of the state. The Southwest's highest peaks belong to the Rocky Mountains in north-central New Mexico, including Wheeler Peak at 13,161 feet. These highland areas are home to many of the state's inhabitants, both in earlier centuries, with the Anasazi and Pueblo Indians, and today. The biggest city, Albuquerque, is on the edge of the Rockies, and the state capital of Santa Fe is, at 6950 feet, easily the highest capital in the nation.

Further south, the Rockies are split by New Mexico's most important river valley, that of the Rio Grande. To the west is the beginning of the basin and range province (see above).

East of the Continental Divide are the high plains of the 'Llano Estacado', the westernmost parts of the Great Plains. About a third of New Mexico falls into this area, which is mainly pancake-flat ranching country with some oil production in the south. This area is watered by the Pecos River and the recently discovered underground Ogallala Aquifer.

By way of comparison, the Southwest lies at about the same latitudes as Spain, Greece, Turkey, northern China and Japan.

## CLIMATE

The Southwest conjures up images of searing desert heat, and this is certainly true in many parts of the region. An excellent rule of thumb, however, is to gauge the climate by the altitude. The lower you are, the hotter and drier it will be. As you climb, temperatures drop about 3 to 5°F for every 1000 feet of elevation gain.

The southwestern and south-central parts of Arizona are below 3000 feet in elevation and are often the hottest places in the USA. High temperatures exceed 100°F for weeks on end and go over 120°F several times each year. The humidity is low, however, and evaporation helps to cool the body. As the locals say, 'It's a dry heat'. Dry air does not hold heat like humid air does, and so nighttime temperatures drop by 20 or 30°F, or even more. Winter temperatures occasionally will drop below freezing but only for a few hours. Yuma, in the southwestern

corner of Arizona, averages about two inches of rain a year, making it the driest part of the region covered in this book. The rest of Arizona is higher and cooler, and the state has an average elevation of 4100 feet.

Almost 90% of New Mexico is over 4000 feet, with the exception being the lower Rio Grande and Pecos River valleys, which are the hottest parts of the state. The average elevation of New Mexico is 5700 feet, rather higher and slightly cooler than the 5000 feet at Albuquerque. Utah is generally higher and cooler still, with an average elevation of 6100 feet (the third highest state in the USA). The far southwestern corner of Utah is the lowest and hottest part of that state.

Over 90% of the Southwest receives well under 20 inches of precipitation annually and about 30% receives less than 10 inches a year. In the driest areas of southwestern Arizona, almost no rain falls from April to June. The highest rainfall here is during the monsoons of July and August, but then rains tend to be brief, with heavy downpours falling mainly in the afternoon. In the less dry areas, it can rain at any time, but even so, few areas have more than five wet days in any month.

Those areas receiving more than 20 inches are generally the high mountain areas of central Arizona, the Wasatch and Uinta Mountains of northern Utah and the mountains north of Albuquerque in New Mexico – these areas also receive the most snowfall in winter and have excellent skiing.

Conditions can be extreme, and every year, people die in weather-related accidents such as lightning, dehydration and flash floods. See Dangers & Annoyances in Facts for the Visitor for more information on such conditions.

## FLORA & FAUNA

The wildlife of the Southwest is unique and fascinating, and much of it can easily be seen and experienced. Forests of the giant saguaro cactus cover many slopes of southern Arizona. The roadrunner, the state bird of New Mexico, and the coyote, the wily trickster of Navajo legend, are often seen darting across the highways or skulking off the road. Vultures wheel through the air, poisonous lizards and venomous snakes are occasionally glimpsed, tarantulas and scorpions scuttle along the ground and jackrabbits bound along with prodigious leaps. Southeastern Arizona is a mecca for birders, with 16 species of hummingbirds recorded (eight are commonly seen). This area also has many other exotic species and people fly thousands of miles to record an unusual bird here.

Clearly, there is plenty of life in this desert – the question is, which desert? What was once called the Great Southwestern Desert by early travelers is now divided into four different deserts. Each has a characteristic flora, fauna, climate and physical geography to distinguish it from the others, although some features are common to all

Coyote

four deserts as well as other areas. In addition, highland regions in all three Southwestern states and the plains of eastern New Mexico are other ecological regions with unique plants and animals.

A brief overview of these regions introduces you to the diversity of plants and animals in the Southwest. Note that many of the species mentioned below are found, to a greater or lesser extent, in areas other than those under which they are mentioned.

For information about poisonous creatures (snakes, spiders, scorpions, etc) see the sections on Health and Dangers & Annoyances in Facts for the Visitor.

### The Arizona-Sonora Desert

This area covers most of southern Arizona and much of the northern part of Mexico's state of Sonora, most of Baja California and the southeastern corner of California. It is a subtropical desert with two distinct wet seasons: the summer monsoons and the winter rains. Generally low-lying and extremely hot, it has a greater diversity of wildlife than the other deserts. This is partly because the biseasonal rainfall allows for two flowering seasons and also because tropical regions have many more species than do temperate ones. The spring flowering season, in particular, can sometimes be incredibly spectacular, though short-lived.

### Packrats – Today's Pest, Yesterday's Historian

Packrats (or, more properly, woodrats, genus *Neotoma*) are large rodents related to mice that have an incredible ability to dig and burrow through the hard desert soil. The nickname packrat arose out of their habit of collecting and hoarding almost anything in large and often inaccessible nests. Plants or pennies, bones or bottle caps are all collectibles for the packrat. Tales abound in the Southwest of packrats ruining air-conditioning systems or collapsing patios with their endeavors. I once left a refrigerator in storage for six months, returning to find a packrat nest inside and the wiring stripped away.

The dry conditions of the Southwest preserve packrat nests remarkably well. Scientists have discovered nests thousands of years old. Microscopic scrutiny of the contents have revealed much about the ancient history of the region. Plant materials found inside the nests show that the environment was much wetter and greener when the first people arrived in the Southwest, at least 11,000 years ago. ■

If winter rainfall and temperature are just right, yellow, orange, blue, violet and pink flowers bloom by the millions.

More than any other region, the Arizona-Sonora Desert is characterized by cacti, especially by the giant saguaro cactus that is found here but nowhere else in the USA. These huge columnar cacti with their uplifted arms are part of almost everyone's image of the Southwest. (You can see these cacti in the Saguaro National Park near Tucson.) Several other species of giant columnar cacti are found in the Arizona-Sonora Desert, too, but they are mainly on the Mexican side. Exceptions are the organ pipe cactus and the senita cactus found especially in the Organ Pipe Cactus National Monument in southern Arizona. Dozens of other species are here too - prickly pear, barrel, fishhook, hedgehog and teddybear cholla are a few of the typical cacti of this desert.

The Arizona-Sonora Desert also has the greatest variety of trees, which tend to be short and spiny with small leaves. The Arizona state tree, the blue paloverde, as well as the yellow and Mexican paloverdes are common here. *Paloverde* is Spanish for 'green stick' and refers to the color of the bark that is capable of photosynthesizing. The ironwood, a tree with very dense wood that sinks in water, is also typical of this desert. Mesquite trees are common but not confined to this region.

Animals are easily seen, especially many species of lizards and, sometimes, several

Gambel's quail

snake species including various rattlesnakes and the highly venomous Arizona coral snake. Commonly seen mammals are coyotes, several species of rabbits and various species of ground, rock and antelope squirrels. (These mammals are common throughout most of the Southwest.) Birds include the quaint Gambel's quail, with its question-mark-shaped head plume, the roadrunner and the ubiquitous cactus wren.

The superb Arizona-Sonora Desert Museum in Tucson provides visitors with an excellent introduction to this region.

## The Chihuahuan Desert

This desert is found in southern New Mexico, western Texas, the extreme southeastern corner of Arizona and the Mexican state of Chihuahua. Although at a similar latitude to the Arizona-Sonora Desert, it lies at a generally higher elevation and is therefore cooler. On average, more rainfall occurs in summer, and most flowers bloom in late summer and early fall.

The desert's most striking plants are agaves and yuccas. The agaves, of which there are several species (some found in the other desert regions), have a rosette of large, spiny, tough, swordlike leaves out of which shoots an amazing flowering stalk, often 15 feet high, covered with thousands

Cholla flower

**Tumbleweeds**

Huge twiggy balls rolling across the desert seem as much a part of the Southwestern landscape as the cowboy. However, both are recent imports to the Southwestern scene. The tumbleweed, also called the Russian thistle (*Salsola kali*), arrived in the 19th century with immigrant farmers from Eastern Europe.

Tumbleweeds are annuals that grow quickly in disturbed areas and soon become a large ball of tough branches attached to the ground by a single stem. Summer winds uproot the dried plants and send them tumbling eerily across the desert. ∎

of tiny flowers. This stalk can grow as much as a foot in a day you can literally watch it grow. The energy required to produce this huge reproductive body is so great that it is a one-time occurrence. After flowering for a few weeks, the plant dies.

Some yuccas resemble agaves with rosettes of tough leaves and tall plant stalks; others are more shrublike. Unlike the agave, however, the yucca flowers annually. There are some 15 species of yucca in the Southwest; the soaptree yucca is New Mexico's state flower. The flowers are pollinated at night by yucca moths, which lay their eggs inside the flowers. The moth larvae then feed on the developing fruit and thus both plant and animal benefit. The most interesting aspect of this mutualism is that each species of yucca is pollinated by its own species of yucca moth that has co-evolved with it.

Creosote bush dominates the ground cover of the Chihuahua Desert, and it is found in the Arizona-Sonora and Mojave Deserts as well. Although this low, straggly bush is not much to look at, it produces complex oils and resins, which make it taste bad to just about any creature that might consider making a meal of it. When it rains, many of these chemicals are released and give the air an astringent but not unpleasant smell.

The ocotillo is a common plant of both the Chihuahuan and Arizona-Sonora Deserts. During dry months, this plant looks like a bunch of skinny, spiny stems that become covered by many tiny green leaves after rain. They are tipped by clusters of small, bright red flowers.

Both the Chihuahuan and Arizona-Sonora Deserts are home of mammals that are typical of Mexico but not frequently seen by visitors to the USA. If you enjoy hiking and backcountry camping, however, you may well see javelina or coati. Javelinas, also called collared peccary, are truly wild pigs and travel in small groups or occasionally herds of up to 60, feeding on cacti and making quiet grunting sounds. They are most easily seen in early morning or late afternoon. If you're lucky, you might catch sight of them in the suburbs of towns – I've seen them crossing the road on the outskirts of Tucson. Coatis are subtropical members of the raccoon family and are sighted fairly often both in the deserts and in the mountains as far as the Mogollon Rim in Arizona.

One of the best places to learn more about this area's biology is the Living Desert State Park in Carlsbad, New Mexico.

**The Mojave Desert**

This desert covers parts of southern Nevada, southeastern California, northwestern Arizona and the extreme southeast of Utah, and so only a small portion falls within the area covered by this book. The Mojave is the smallest, driest and hottest of the country's deserts, and it is also thought of as a transition desert between the Arizona-Sonora and Great Basin Deserts.

Much of this desert is low-lying, and it includes Nevada's Death Valley at 282 feet below sea level. The low areas, usually the hottest and driest, are characterized by widely spread shrubby vegetation or empty sand dunes and dry lake beds. In Arizona and Utah the elevations are higher and the dominant plants are the eerie Joshua trees. These 30- to 40-foot-high plants, which are believed to live as long as 1000 years, are the largest species of yucca and are members of the lily family.

## Cacti of the Southwest

My mother always had a couple of small cacti surviving desperately in tiny pots on the sunless windowsills of our suburban London house. I'll never forget the spring day when one of those hopelessly decrepit specimens suddenly burst into a florid bloom, exotically overwhelming all the surrounding houseplants. And exotic it certainly was – every one of the world's over 2000 species of cactus are native to the Americas.

Researchers cannot agree on exact numbers, but over 100 of the approximately 2000 species of cactus are found in the Southwest and are superbly adapted to survival in these arid environments. The succulent pads that form the body of the plant are actually modified stems, and their waxy 'skin' helps retard moisture loss. The leaves, which in other plants normally allow a lot of water to escape through transpiration, have been modified into spines that not only lose little moisture, but also protect the plant against herbivores looking for water. Evaporation is further reduced by the plant keeping its pores closed during the day and open only at night. These remarkable plants are further enhanced by their often splendid flowers.

**Identification** It is fairly easy to identify at least the six most common types of Southwestern cactus. The six types are prickly pear, pincushion, cholla, giant columnar, barrel and hedgehog cacti.

Prickly pears are often of the genus *Opuntia* and are distinguished by the flattened cross-section of their pads. If the pads are cylindrical, read on.

Pincushion cacti, often of the genus *Mammilaria*, are small and cylindrical in cross-section, and don't have ribs running from top to bottom. Spine clusters grow out of nipplelike bumps on the stems – hence the scientific name. Many species have hooked spines.

Cholla cacti are also cylindrical and lack ribs, but are much taller and have branches. Like the prickly pears, they belong to the genus *Opuntia*. They can range from pencil chollas, with extremely thin branches; to teddybear chollas, which look warm and fuzzy but have wickedly barbed spines; to large jumping chollas, which have fruits hanging in loose chains. Brushing a jumping cholla lightly often results in part of the chain becoming attached to your body – almost as if it had jumped on you. Jumping chollas often grow in thick stands. The chollas have some of the sharpest and most difficult to remove spines – if you are stuck, it may be easier to cut the spines with scissors and then remove them one by one with tweezers.

After the right amount of rainfall in winter, when it rains the most, spring can bring a carpet of flowers, including around 250 species of which 80% are endemic to the Mojave Desert. Cacti are quite common, although they are generally smaller than the ones of the Arizona-Sonora Desert. Creosote bushes are also seen in great and odorous quantities. Large numbers of lizards and desert birds are also present.

### The Great Basin Desert

This is the continent's most northerly desert, covering most of Nevada, western Utah and the Colorado Plateau, and stretching on into Idaho and Oregon. The name 'Great Basin' is not very accurate, because this region contains many basins in the basin and range country. This is generally a high desert, with most of the basins at over 4000 feet. The high latitude and elevation make this a cooler desert than the others, and also one that has less wildlife. There are few of the cacti, agaves and yuccas that are so noticeable in the hot deserts, and those that are present tend to be small. Instead, miles of low, rather nondescript shrubs such as saltbrush and sagebrush cover the ground.

Here, the big sagebrush, which can reach over six feet in height, replaces the creosote of the hot desert. It is very widespread in the Great Basin Desert and, like creosote, has volatile oils to make it less appetizing to potential herbivores. It also gives off a pleasantly pungent odor after

The remaining three main types are all cylindrical in cross-section, and ribbed. If they are also very tall (from 15 to 50 feet high), they are giant columnar cacti and most likely to be a saguaro cactus *(Cereus giganteus)*, which has branches high off the ground (and is found only in southern Arizona and northern Mexico). In a few places in southern Arizona, you might see large cacti branching from the ground. These are either organ pipe or senita cacti. (Organ pipes have 10 or more ribs, and lack the white or gray hairs of the senita. You can see them at Organ Pipe Cactus National Monument.) There are many more species of columnar cacti across the border in Mexico.

Barrel cacti

Finally, smaller cylindrical cacti with ribs are likely to be hedgehog or barrel cacti. Hedgehog cacti, often of the genus *Echinocereus*, are small, with the main pad less than four inches in diameter and with flowers growing from the sides. Barrel cacti, often of the genus *Ferocactus*, are over five inches in diameter and have flowers growing from their top. The largest examples can grow to 10 feet in height, although this is unusual.

All six types are commonly found in southern Arizona. The other Southwestern deserts lack the giant columnar cacti. The Great Basin Desert tends to have just the smaller species.

**Protection** Cacti are legally protected. You need a permit to collect any kind of cactus from the wild. It is also illegal to damage or destroy a cactus. A famous (and true) story you may hear is of a man who was shooting at a saguaro from close range. One of the huge arms of the cactus toppled over and killed him. ∎

rain or when crushed. (This sagebrush is no relation to the sage herb used in cooking.) So pervasive is the big sagebrush that, in some areas, it provides 70% of the ground cover and an astonishing 90% of the plant biomass.

Generally, wildlife is either scarce or hard to observe. A bird that is closely associated with big sagebrush is the sage grouse, which eats twice as much of this plant as all other food combined. Males make a resonant booming call and dance around in specific places (called leks) to attract females during the early spring breeding season, when they are the most easy to observe. Various other birds associated with big sagebrush (sage sparrow, sage thrasher) are small, secretive and hard to spot.

Raptors are seen fairly often, particularly red-tailed hawks and kestrels. They feed on lizards and snakes which, although less common than in other deserts, are still numerous. Otherwise, rabbits are the most likely animals to catch your eye. If you're lucky, though, you never know what you may run into (or over if you're not careful). My best sighting of a badger was in the Great Basin Desert, and you may see pronghorns browsing among the sagebrush.

### Grasslands

Grasslands once covered extensive areas of the Southwest, particularly in the river basins of Arizona and New Mexico. Millions of head of cattle and sheep were introduced into these fine grazing areas in the

1870s and 1880s. The animals overgrazed the grasslands, and many of these areas quickly became extensions of the deserts. Today, the grassland areas are found in eastern New Mexico, especially in the northeastern part of the state. Here, the observant traveler can spot small herds of pronghorn grazing. The pronghorn is also known as the pronghorn antelope because of its antelope-like horns and graceful body, but it is unrelated to the antelopes of Africa and Asia.

### Higher Life Zones

As you climb into the mountain ranges, you'll pass plants and animals recalling the northern parts of the continent. A very rough rule of thumb is that a 1000-foot elevation gain is equivalent to a drive of several hundred miles to the north; in other words, the vegetation of the Southwest's high mountains is comparable to that of Canada.

Biologists divide the elevations of the mountains into a series of life zones that, despite being somewhat arbitrary and imprecise in regards to their altitude, are useful tools for making sense of the sudden and bewildering changes in flora and the associated fauna. The following is a popular zonation.

The lower elevations (below 4500 feet) are called the Lower Sonoran Zone, followed by the Upper Sonoran Zone (4500 to 6500 feet). These encompass most of the deserts discussed above. The Upper Sonoran Zone also supports evergreen trees such as small junipers and the piñon pine.

The Transition Zone (6500 to 8000 feet) falls between the desert basins and the high mountains. Much of the Colorado Plateau appears to be in this zone, although many biologists include it in the Great Basin Desert. The most notable vegetation is the ponderosa pine, of which there are large stands, especially in New Mexico where it is extensively logged. The cacti, agaves, yuccas, creosote and sagebrush of lower elevations are no longer common in this zone. Other plants found here are Gambel's oak and various shrubs. There are fewer species of reptiles, but squirrels and chipmunks are common. Black bears and mountain lions live here, but you are unlikely to see them. White-tailed deer are more often spotted, and in some places, you may see elk.

From about 8000 to 9500 feet, the predominant trees are Douglas firs and aspens in what is called the Canadian Zone (also called the Montane Forest Zone). Other trees include white fir and juniper, and the shading of these thick forests precludes the growth of many other plants. From 9500 to 11,500 feet, in the Hudsonian Zone (also called Subalpine Forest Zone), other conifers tend to predominate, including Engelmann spruce, subalpine fir and bristlecone pine, among others. This zone receives very heavy snow in winter, and few mammals are found here except during the summer months. The treeline begins at about 11,500 feet, and the zone above the treeline is called the Alpine Zone. There are only a few areas in the Southwest that reach these elevations, which are characterized by small tundra-like plants.

## GOVERNMENT

The USA has a republican form of government, which is popularly defined as government 'of the people, by the people and for the people'. The US Constitution, passed in 1789 and amended 26 times since then, provides the fundamental laws for the running of the national government and the relations between the national and state governments.

US citizens over the age of 18 are eligible to vote (criminals may lose this right, depending on their crime). Elections are hotly contested, and politicians and parties spend many millions of dollars on political campaigns that can become very acrimonious. Despite this, barely half of the eligible voters cast a ballot in recent elections.

There are two main political parties – the Republicans (called the GOP for Grand Old Party) and the Democrats. Independent politicians occasionally provide a third choice. Other parties do exist, but they are too small to play a significant part in

The saguaro cactus blossom is the Arizona state flower. (RR)

Prickly pear cactus flower (RR)

Flowering hedgehog cactus (RR)

Pincushion cacti (RR)

The dried bloom of the yucca (RRb)

Ocotillo flower (RR)

Joshua trees, which look like a cross between a cactus and a palm, grow throughout the desert regions of the Southwest. (RR)

Saguaro cacti, bearing edible red fruit, grow in the Southwest and northern Mexico. (RR)

The author's son, David, measures up to a barrel cactus. (RR)

government. Traditionally, Republicans are conservative, and Democrats are liberal. Often, the President and his Cabinet are of one party, while the Congress may have a majority of the opposing party.

In so far as generalizations can be made, Republicans favor cutting taxes; shrinking nationally funded (federal) programs of health care, education, welfare and so forth; and minimizing or eliminating national funding for items such as arts programs and abortion. Republicans believe such programs are better handled at the state level. Democrats prefer higher taxation and more federal funding of these programs. However, Republicans support spending a larger proportion of the federal budget on the military than do Democrats.

## National Government

The government has three branches: the legislative branch makes the laws of the land, the executive branch executes (or carries out) these laws, and the judicial branch studies and interprets both the Constitution and the laws.

The legislative branch is made up of the bicameral Congress, which is composed of the Senate and the House of Representatives. The 100-member Senate has two senators from each of the 50 states, while the 435-member House has one or more members from each state, depending on the size of each state's population. States are constitutionally equal, and so those with small populations are overrepresented in the Senate, but this influence is diluted in the House. Senators are elected for six years, and representatives are elected for two.

The fact that two parties with opposing views are both strongly represented in Congress means that it is sometimes difficult to pass laws that are seen as beneficial to the country by one party but not by the other.

The executive branch consists of the President, the Cabinet and various assistants. The 14 members of the President's Cabinet are each appointed by the President but must be approved by the Senate. The President has the power to veto the laws passed by Congress, although a law can still be passed if two-thirds of the members vote for it the second time, overriding the President's veto.

The judicial branch is headed by the Supreme Court, which consists of nine justices who are appointed for life by the President and approved by the Senate.

The President, whose term is four years, is chosen by an Electoral College consisting of a number of individual electors from each state equivalent to its number of senators and representatives, who vote in accordance with the popular vote within their state. To be elected, the President must obtain a majority of 270 of the total 538 electoral votes (the District of Columbia has no voting representatives in Congress, but nevertheless has three electoral votes). The President may serve only two terms. The 104th Congress (1995 to 1997), has a Republican majority in both houses, the first time they have had such a majority since WW II.

## State Government

Each of the 50 states has its own government, run along similar lines to the national government with some differences, mainly regarding how long an elected representative remains in office. The head of the executive branch of state government is the governor, and the bicameral legislature consists of a senate and a house delegation.

National (federal) laws apply to all states, although there are often conflicts between federal and state interests. In addition, each state enacts its own laws that visitors should be aware of. States have different laws about driving, alcohol use and taxes, which are discussed in Facts for the Visitor.

Traditionally, most Western states (including the Southwest) support the Republican party. Utah and Arizona are generally conservative, New Mexico is more middle of the road. In a land where water is a scarce resource and the population is increasing much more rapidly than in the country as a whole, it is not surprising that the most contentious issues in the region concern water and land use.

## ECONOMY

The USA has a GNP of $6,350 billion, making it the richest country in the world. However, the national debt, created by a truly breathtaking spate of overspending that began in the early 1980s, stands at a rough $4,350 billion and keeps growing. A trade deficit of $254 billion has also been a point of concern.

US citizens pay income tax on a sliding scale, with the poorest paying around 15% of personal earnings and the richest fifth paying around 40%. The average American can expect to pay out 20% of his or her earnings.

While TV programs and Hollywood movies may show the flashy, wealthy side of the USA, the country is as diverse in its economic circumstances as it is in its cultures. Whole areas of the USA are wealthier than others, and within a city the standard of living can vary considerably from neighborhood to neighborhood.

The lowest 20% of the population in income only receives 4.4% of the national income distribution, while the top 5% receive 17.6%.

Traditionally, mining and agriculture (especially ranching) have been the backbone of the Southwest's economy. Ranching, of course, is more than just a meat and dairy industry – it is a way of life, a tradition. *Gunsmoke* reruns on TV, cowboys riding into purple sage sunsets, rodeos, roundups, lassos and wide open plains, are all part of the psyche of the American West. Traditions die hard, and although ranching today is a far cry from the rough and tumble 1800s, it still sparks the interest of many visitors who stay on 'dude ranches' or take part in cowboy-led horse packing trips.

Mining and ranching were major factors in the settling of the Wild West. Laws were enacted in the 1800s to regulate these industries, some of which are still in force today. Recent moves to modernize this legislation have met with strong resistance from the industries involved. Miners and ranchers consider the old laws to be reasonable; others find that current concerns about fair price for the use of public lands, conservation, water quality and pollution necessitate a modernization of the laws. One of the most contentious issues is that of ranchers' traditional rights to graze on public land for which they pay only about 25% of the current cost of a grazing lease on private land.

### Arizona

Historically, Arizona's economy is based on the 'Four Cs' – copper, cattle, cotton and citrus. For many years, copper mining was the most important industry (Arizona is the nation's leading producer), and it is the main product of the almost three billion dollar annual mineral production in Arizona.

Citrus and cotton in the midst of the Southwestern desert is more of a surprise – irrigation from the Gila River has provided the necessary moisture. Cotton continues to be the most important crop, but citrus appears to have been replaced by several other 'C' crops – carrots, cauliflower, corn and celery – as well as other vegetables. The annual value of all farm marketings is almost two billion dollars.

Today, all these have been surpassed by both manufacturing and tourism. Major products include aircraft and missiles (Hughes Missile System Co employs many thousands in Tucson), electronics, metals, clothes and the printing and publishing industry. Tourism now brings in over eight billion dollars annually.

For Arizonans, over 70% of jobs are in the service, trade and government sectors. The per capita income is over $18,000 per year.

### New Mexico

New Mexico's petroleum and natural gas production is worth about three billion dollars annually and non-fuel minerals, especially copper, are worth an additional billion. Agricultural products, predominantly livestock, are worth about 1.6 billion dollars. New Mexico is the nation's largest producer of chiles – this crop is worth about 200 million dollars annually.

Logging is a more significant part of the state's economy than for the other Southwestern states.

As in Arizona and Utah, manufacturing industries are experiencing strong growth, and production of electrical goods, food, transportation equipment, machinery and clothing are important. The tourist industry is worth 2.5 billion dollars annually.

The government sector and service industries are the state's major employers, providing about 53% of New Mexico's jobs. Per capita income is over $16,000 per year.

### Utah

The pioneering Mormons based their economy on agriculture. Although this continues to be important, other industries, especially ranching, are now the mainstay of Utah's economy. Agricultural products were worth over 800 million dollars to Utah in 1993. Copper, oil and natural gas supply Utah's main mineral wealth, although many other substances are also mined – minerals are worth two billion dollars to the state annually. Tourism also brings in over two billion dollars annually.

About 70% of the population are employed in the service, trade and government sectors. In addition, construction and manufacturing, especially electronic and computer goods, guided missiles, metals and food products, are major industries. Per capita income in 1993 was under $16,000, which is one of the lowest in the USA. This reflects the large size of many Mormon families rather than overall poverty.

### POPULATION

The US Census Bureau takes a census of the population every 10 years. The last census was in April 1990, and the figures given below are estimates for 1993. Persons are asked to classify their race by choosing the one with which they most closely identify. Five main race categories are available: White, African American, Native American, Asian or Pacific Islander, and Other. In addition, persons may also identify themselves as Hispanic, but this is not considered a race category because Hispanic people can be of any race.

The populations of the Southwestern states are shown in the table, and figures for the USA are given for comparative purposes.

The table demonstrates that New Mexico and Arizona have a rich Hispanic heritage. These states also have large populations of Native Americans, over half of which are Navajo. Other tribes include various Apache groups, Havasupai, Hopi, Hualapai, various Pueblo tribes, Tohono O'odham, Ute and a host of smaller groups. Arizona and New Mexico have the third and fourth largest Native American populations of the

## US Census Figures (1993 estimates)

| State | W | AA | NA | API | O | H |
|---|---|---|---|---|---|---|
| **USA** 257,907,937 | 80.3% | 12.1% | 0.8% | 2.9% | 3.9% | 9% |
| **Arizona** 3,936,142 | 80.8% | 3% | 5.6% | 1.5% | 9.1% | 18.8% |
| **New Mexico** 1,616,483 | 75.6% | 2% | 8.9% | 0.9% | 12.6% | 38.2% |
| **Utah** 1,859,582 | 93.8% | 0.7% | 1.4% | 1.9% | 2.2% | 4.9% |

**W** White, **AA** African American, **NA** Native American,
**API** Asian or Pacific Islander, **O** Other, **H** Hispanic

50 states (Oklahoma and California have the largest). The Southwest's African American population, on the other hand, is very small, as is the Asian-Pacific Islander group. Utah, with its strong Mormon heritage, is very predominantly White.

The Southwestern states are sparsely populated. Arizona's comparatively high population density is skewed by the presence of the greater Phoenix metropolitan area, which accounts for half of the state's inhabitants. Similarly, the Salt Lake City region accounts for over half of Utah's population. The Southwest is one of the fastest growing regions in the USA, with the warm weather attracting large numbers of retirees. From 1990 to 1993, Arizona's population grew by 7.4%, New Mexico's by 6.7% and Utah's by 7.9%, compared to 3.7% for the nation as a whole. Since 1950, Arizona's population has increased five-fold – one of the greatest increases of any state.

## PEOPLE

The Southwest is commonly perceived as having a tri-cultural mix of Indian, Hispanic and Anglo cultures. Only in north-western and north-central New Mexico can you see clear evidence of all three cultures – ancient Indian pueblos, historical Hispanic churches and Anglo atomic bomb laboratories coexist in an intricate and unique alliance.

In the rest of the Southwest, all three cultures make their mark in differing degrees depending on the region. The Indians predominantly live on the reservations in the Four Corners area, especially the Navajo and Hopi Reservations of northeastern Arizona, and in the pueblos of northwestern New Mexico. There are also the large Apache reservations in mountainous eastern Arizona and the Tohono O'odham Reservation in the desert south of Arizona as well as a scattering of smaller reservations elsewhere in the region. With the exception of the pueblo areas, none of these places can be considered tri-cultural! However, reservation culture is definitely bicultural – Indian and Anglo – in most respects.

New Mexico has the highest proportion of Hispanic people, with the Rio Grande Valley and Santa Fe being historically the center of that culture. Southern Arizona, too, has much Hispanic influence as can be seen by the huge number of Mexican restaurants in Tucson and the fact that telephone directories and government documents have Spanish sections or translations. Architecture in parts of southern Arizona, and especially along the Rio Grande and in Santa Fe, is an attractive blend of Hispanic and Indian styles.

Anglos dominate the scene in most of Mormon Utah and in the fast-growing cities of Arizona, particularly the Phoenix metropolitan area and the towns along the Colorado River in western Arizona. In rural areas of the Southwest, many off-reservation ranches and mines are Anglo-owned, although workers may be Hispanic or Indian.

But it is not simply the tri-culturalism of the Southwest that gives it its unique flavor. It must be combined with the land and climate – beautifully desolate, splendidly harsh, incredibly varied and rarely forgiving. People's survival in these extreme conditions has shaped what may be perceived as the culture of the Southwest.

## ARTS

New Mexico and Utah both have symphony orchestras at Albuquerque and Salt Lake City respectively, and Phoenix and Tucson have their own symphony orchestras. Major opera companies in the Southwest include the Arizona Opera Company, which performs in Tucson and Phoenix; the Santa Fe Opera; and the Utah Opera in Salt Lake City. The famous Mormon Tabernacle Choir has performed in weekly radio broadcasts since 1929. Notable dance companies include Ballet Arizona in Phoenix; Ballet West and the Repertory Dance Theater in Salt Lake City; and the Maria Benitez Teatro Flamenco in Santa Fe. Every city of any size has many theaters, art galleries and museums. Performers from all over the world are regularly hosted in venues of major Southwestern cities – you

Zuni bowl

can hear and see anything from Japanese kodo drummers to Ukrainian folk dancers.

In addition, strong Hispanic and Native American influences have helped create a distinctive local arts scene. Much of this Southwestern aesthetic is evident in the region's pottery, paintings, weavings, jewelry, sculpture, wood carving and leather working. Southwestern art can be very traditional or cutting-edge contemporary.

Perhaps the region's most famous artist is Georgia O'Keeffe (1887-1986), whose Southwestern landscapes and motifs are found in major museums throughout the world. Also highly regarded is the Navajo artist R C Gorman (born 1932), whose sculptures and paintings of Navajo women are becoming increasingly famous worldwide. Gorman has made his home in Taos for many years – both Taos and nearby Santa Fe have large and active communities of artists and are considered seminal places in the development of Southwestern art.

Many visitors are anxious to see Native American art. The Southwest certainly has a wide variety – Navajo rugs, Hopi kachina dolls, Zuni silverware, Tohono O'odham basketry and Pueblo pottery are some of the best known. Maria Martinez (1887-1980) of the San Idelfonso Pueblo led a revival of traditional pottery making during the 1920s – her 'black on black' pots are considered some of the finest ever made and are now worth thousands of dollars. Excellent examples of Southwestern Native American art can be seen in many museums, of which the Heard Museum in Phoenix is one of the best.

Contemporary Native American art is eminently buyable, and both traditional and modern work is available in hundreds of galleries throughout the region.

The music scene, too, has its Hispanic and Native American influences. Of course, you can hear anything from jazz to hip hop in the major cities, but you can also catch *mariachis* (Mexican street bands typically dressed in dark, ornately sequinned, body-hugging costumes and playing predominantly brass instruments and guitars), especially in the towns close to the Mexican border. Native American dances and music are performed throughout the Southwest. A couple of noteworthy ones are Carlos R Nakai and Perry Silver Bird, both flute players. Nakai is a Navajo-Ute who has played his traditional cedar flute with a variety of musicians, ranging from his own ethnic jazz ensemble, called Jackalope, to the Tucson Symphony Orchestra.

## RELIGION

The US Constitution mandates separation of church and state, and tolerance is the norm. However, issues like prayer in public schools and abortion have brought theological issues onto the secular stage. Nominal allegiance is more widespread than church attendance, but many churchgoers are extremely devout.

The USA is predominantly Christian – one source claims that 85% of the population professes some kind of Christianity (approximately 40% Roman Catholic, 40% Protestant and 20% other denominations). Over 9% are nonreligious or atheists, 2.5% are Jewish and the remaining 3.5% are a diverse mix of other beliefs. Other sources give figures of 55.1% Christian (of which over 60% are Protestant) and 2.1% Jewish. These figures are probably both 'right' – it depends on the definition of how religious a person has to be.

## Native American Dance & Music

Swirling dancers bedecked in headdresses and facepaint, wearing intricately beaded clothing and stomping in time to a circle of drummers – this spectacle is one that many travelers to the region want to see. Here are suggestions on how to best enjoy the various dances, which are held many times throughout the year all over the Southwest.

From the visitors' point of view, Native American dances can be grouped into three categories, although there is certainly overlap between them.

**Religious** First, there are the ceremonial or ritual religious dances that take place on Indian reservations at traditionally specified times of the year. Some of these are celebratory occasions that mark stages of life (for instance, a girl's puberty rite), and others, such as rain dances, revere specific gods. Precise dates and locations vary from year to year and are often not known until a few weeks before the event. Because of the strong religious and traditional motive, access to ceremonial dances is usually strictly controlled.

Some ceremonials are open to the public, but photography or recording of any kind is completely prohibited. It is important for tourists to respect this rule. Occasionally, a tourist might try to sneak a quick and unobtrusive photo – in this case, a tribal policeman may confiscate the camera, or an irate tribal elder may simply grab the camera and hurl it over the nearest cliff! Other rules for watching ceremonial dances are refraining from applauding and asking many questions, following instructions about where to stand or sit, wearing appropriate clothing (no shorts or tank tops) and generally behaving in a quiet and respectful way. Alcohol is not permitted during dances or anywhere on most Indian reservations. Increasing numbers of ceremonial dances are being closed to the general public because the Indians are fed up with non-Indians' behavior.

For details of which dances are performed when, contact the tribal offices listed in the relevant parts of the text.

**Social** Social dances can be very traditional or relatively modern, and are danced for competition, display, to tell a story, as an honor, or just for plain fun and getting together with other families, clans or tribes. The dancers are accompanied by drum groups and singers. Usually, songs are in one of the Native American languages, or they are vocables (songs made up of sounds that are not words). An emcee calls each dance, often

Considering the inconsistencies above, I hesitate to give exact numbers for those of you who want to know. In fact, I simply won't do it! The overall picture is that Christians make up the religious majority in the Southwest, with Catholics having the numerical edge in New Mexico and Mormons being by far the majority in Utah. New Mexico and Utah have very few Jews, while Arizona's Jewish population is about the national average.

The oldest religions in North America are those of Native American tribes, greatly modified since contact with Europeans, however. Some, like the Native American Church, which uses hallucinatory peyote buttons as a sacrament, are in part pan-Indian responses to encroachment by the politically dominant culture imposed on them.

Various Native American religions are closely followed by tens of thousands of people. In any discussion of Indian religious beliefs, several points are worth bearing in mind. First, different tribes often have very different creation stories, rituals and practices, which means that there are dozens of unique and carefully prescribed spiritual ways of life. Second, Indians usually maintain a strict sense of privacy about their most important ceremonies and thus books written by even the most respected anthropologists usually contain some inaccuracies when describing Indian religion. Third, the Indian ways are beliefs that Indians feel and know essentially

Hopi dancer

with an inside joke or two, and usually at least some of the dances are called in English, especially the intertribals, when anyone, including members of the tourist tribe, can go out and dance.

For visitors, these are the best kinds of dances because you can enjoy them, participate if you wish, and let go of your worries about interfering in a religious ceremony. Social dances occur throughout the Southwest during powwows or at various festivities with names like 'Indian Days'. They also occur during fairs, rodeos and other gatherings in Indian reservations. Details are given under the relevant places in the text.

Often, a small admission fee is charged; Indian food, arts & crafts, and cassettes or CDs are sold; and photography may be permitted. Photographers can usually take general pictures of the festivities but should always ask permission to take photographs of individuals. A small tip may be requested in this case.

**Performances** The third category of dances is purely performance dancing, where you sit in a theater (often outdoors) and watch. These dances are usually of the social kind and are very colorful – it's performance art, but it's also authentic – the dancers don't just make up non-Indian dances for tourists! One of the best places to see dance performances is during the summer at Red Rock State Park just outside of Gallup, New Mexico. ■

because they *are* Indians – it's not something that non-Indians can properly understand or convert to.

Travelers will find that members of almost every religion, belief, faith or sect can be found in major cities. Even small towns have several religious groups to choose from. For further information, look in the telephone yellow pages under Churches, Mosques or Synagogues.

## LANGUAGE

Although American English is spoken throughout the USA, there are regional variations. According to the most recent census, 35.5% of New Mexico's population (over the age of five) speaks a language other than English at home – this is the highest percentage of any state (compare this to the USA as a whole with 13.8%). In Arizona, 20.8% speak a language other than English at home, but in Utah it's only 7.8%. In New Mexico and Arizona, the languages spoken at home (other than English) are usually Spanish or one of numerous Indian languages.

For the traveler, however, this is not of major concern. Almost every Mexican restaurant or Native American art gallery will have English-speaking staff, and you don't need to brush up on your Spanish or learn Navajo. If you are interested in hearing speech or music in these languages, you'll find plenty of Spanish-speaking radio stations in the southern parts of New Mexico and Arizona, many broadcasting from Mexico. In the Four Corners area, KTTN radio station, broadcasting out of Window Rock on 660 AM, has many programs in Navajo. One word you might hear frequently in this area is the Navajo greeting *ya-ta-hey*.

Visitors to Indian reservations should bear in mind that silence is almost like a statement. If you say something to an Indian and are met by silence, this doesn't indicate that the person you are talking to is ignoring you. Indians speak their minds when they disagree with the speaker and may remain silent when they agree with the speaker or have no special opinion. This can be strange to non-Indians, who are used to interjecting 'uh huh' and 'really' after almost every sentence they hear.

Finally, visitors to the major national parks will often find introductory brochures printed in Spanish, German, French or Japanese. Although speakers of these languages are among the most frequent foreign visitors to the Southwest, they will find that few Americans here speak these languages.

Hopi dancer

highest percentage of any state (compare this to the USA as a whole with 13.8%). In Arizona, 20.8% speak a language other than English at home, but in Utah it's only 7.8%. In New Mexico and Arizona the languages spoken at home (other than English) are usually Spanish or one of numerous Indian languages.

For the traveler, however, this is not of major concern. Almost every Mexican restaurant or Native American art gallery will have English-speaking staff, and you

because they are Indians – it's not something that non-Indians can properly understand or convert to.

Travelers will find that members of almost every religion, both of faith or sect, can be found in major cities. Even small towns have several religious groups to choose from. For further information, look in the telephone yellow pages under Churches, Mosques or Synagogues.

LANGUAGE

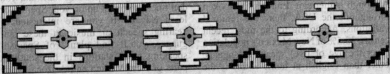

# Facts for the Visitor

## VISAS & EMBASSIES

Canadians must have proper proof of Canadian citizenship, such as a citizenship card with photo ID or a passport. Visitors from other countries must have a valid passport and most visitors also require a US visa.

However, there is a reciprocal visa-waiver program in which citizens of certain countries may enter the USA for stays of 90 days or less without first obtaining a US visa. Currently these countries are the UK, New Zealand, Japan, Italy, Spain, Austria, the Netherlands, Belgium, Switzerland, France, Germany, Norway, Denmark, Sweden, Finland, Iceland, San Marino, Andorra, Luxembourg, Liechtenstein and Monaco. Under this program you must have a roundtrip ticket that is non-refundable in the USA and you will not be allowed to extend your stay beyond 90 days.

Other travelers will need to obtain a visa from a US consulate or embassy. In most countries the process can be done by mail.

Your passport should be valid for at least six months longer than your intended stay in the USA and you'll need to submit a recent photo (37 x 37 mm) with the application. Documents of financial stability and/or guarantees from a US resident are sometimes required, particularly for those from Third World countries.

Visa applicants may be required to 'demonstrate binding obligations' that will insure their return back home. Because of this requirement, those planning to travel through other countries before arriving in the USA are generally better off applying for their US visa while they are still in their home country – rather than while on the road.

The validity period for US visitor visas depends on what country you're from. The length of time you'll be allowed to stay in the USA is ultimately determined by US immigration authorities at the port of entry.

Incidentally, the infamous prohibition against issuing visas to people who 'have been members of communist organizations' has been dropped. An anachronism of the Cold War, it still appears on the visa applications although most consular offices have penned a line through the item.

## US Embassies & Consulates

US diplomatic offices abroad include the following:

Australia
US Embassy: 21 Moonah Place, Yarralumla ACT 2600 (☎ (6) 270 5900)
American Consulate General: Level 59 MLC Center 19-29 Martin Place, Sydney NSW 2000 (☎ (2) 373 9200)
There are also consulates in Melbourne, Perth and Brisbane.

Austria
Boltzmanngasse 16, A-1091, Vienna (☎ (1) 313-39)

Belgium
Blvd du Régent 27, B-1000, Brussels (☎ (2) 513 38 30)

Canada
US Embassy: 100 Wellington St, Ottawa, Ontario 1P 5T1 (☎ (613) 238-5335)
US Consulate-General: 1095 West Pender St, Vancouver, BC V6E 2M6 (☎ (604) 685-1930)
US Consulate-General: 1155 rue St-Alexandre, Montreal, Quebec (☎ (514) 398-9695)
There are also consulates in Toronto, Calgary and Halifax.

Denmark
Dag Hammarskjold Allé 24, Copenhagen (☎ 31 42 31 44)

Finland
Itainen Puistotie 14A, Helsinki (☎ (0) 171-931)

France
US Embassy, 2 rue Saint Florentin, 75001 Paris (☎ (1) 42.96.12.02)
There are also consulates in Bordeaux, Lyon, Marseille, Nice, Strasbourg and Toulouse.

Germany
Deichmanns Aue 29, 53179 Bonn (☎ (228) 33 91)

Greece
91 Vasilissis Sophias Blvd, 10160 Athens (☎ (1) 721-2951)

India
     Shanti Path, Chanakyapuri 110021,
     New Delhi (☎ (11) 60-0651)
Indonesia
     Medan Merdeka Selatan 5, Jakarta
     (☎ (21) 360-360)
Ireland
     42 Elgin Rd, Ballsbridge, Dublin
     (☎ (1) 687 122)
Israel
     71 Hayarkon St, Tel Aviv
     (☎ (3) 517-4338)
Italy
     Via Vittorio Veneto 119a-121, Rome
     (☎ (6) 46 741)
Japan
     1-10-5 Akasaka Chome, Minato-ku, Tokyo
     (☎ (3) 224-5000)
Korea
     82 Sejong-Ro, Chongro-ku, Seoul
     (☎ (2) 397-4114)
Malaysia
     376 Jalan Tun Razak, 50400 Kuala Lumpur
     (☎ (3) 248-9011)
Mexico
     Paseo de la Reforma 305, Cuauhtémoc,
     06500 Mexico City (☎ (5) 211-00-42)
Netherlands
     US Embassy: Lange Voorhout 102, 2514 EJ
     The Hague (☎ (70) 310 92 09)
     US Consulate: Museumplein 19, 1071 DJ
     Amsterdam (☎ (20) 310 9209)
New Zealand
     29 Fitzherbert Terrace, Thorndon,
     Wellington (☎ (4) 722 068)
Norway
     Drammensvein 18, Oslo
     (☎ (22) 44 85 50)
Phillipines
     1201 Roxas Blvd, Ermita Manila 1000
     (☎ (2) 521-7116)
Russia
     Novinskiy Bul'var 19/23, Moscow
     (☎ (095) 252-2451)
Singapore
     30 Hill St, Singapore 0617 (☎ 338-0251)
South Africa
     877 Pretorius St, Box 9536, Pretoria 0001
     (☎ (12) 342-1048)
Spain
     Calle Serrano 75, 28006 Madrid,
     (☎ (1) 577 4000)
Sweden
     Strandvagen 101, S-115 89 Stockholm
     (☎ (8) 783 5300)

Switzerland
     Jubilaumsstrasse 93, 3005 Berne
     (☎ (31) 357 70 11)
Thailand
     95 Wireless Rd, Bangkok
     (☎ (2) 252-5040)
UK
     US Embassy, 5 Upper Grosvenor St, London
     W1 (☎ (71) 499 9000)
     US Consulate-General, 3 Regent Terrace,
     Edinburgh EH7 5BW (☎ (31) 556 8315)
     US Consulate-General, Queens House, Bel-
     fast BT1 6EQ (☎ (232) 328 239)

## Foreign Embassies and Consulates

There are a few foreign embassies in the
Southwest. Albuquerque has a Mexican
and a German consul; Salt Lake City has a
Mexican, Swiss, Danish, French and Italian
consul; and Tucson has a Mexican consul.
These can be found in the yellow pages of
a telephone directory under 'Consulates'.

Most nations' main consuls or embassies
are in Washington, DC. To find out the telephone number of your embassy or consul,
call Washington, DC information (☎ (202)
555 1212).

## Visa Extensions

If you want, need or hope to stay in the USA
longer than the date stamped on your passport, go to the local Immigration & Naturalization Service (INS) office (look in the
local white pages telephone directory under
'US Government') *before* the stamped date
to apply for an extension. Anytime after that
will usually lead to an unamusing conversation with an INS official who will assume
you want to work illegally. If you find yourself in that situation, it's a good idea to bring
a US citizen with you to vouch for your
character. It's also a good idea to have some
verification that you have enough money to
support yourself.

## DOCUMENTS

All foreign visitors (other than Canadians)
must bring their passport. US citizens and
Canadians may want a passport as well, in
the event they're tempted to extend their
travels into Mexico or beyond. All visitors

should bring their driver's license and any health-insurance or travel-insurance cards.

You'll need a picture ID to show that you are over 21 to buy alcohol or gain admission to bars or clubs (make sure your driver's license has a photo on it, or else get some other form of ID). A good idea is to make a couple photocopies of all your travel documents including airline tickets, your passport and international ID. Keep one copy separate from the originals and use the other to carry around instead of the originals. There's nothing worse than losing your identity on a trip.

### International Driving Permit

An International Driving Permit is a useful accessory for foreign visitors in the USA. Local traffic police are more likely to accept it as valid identification than an unfamiliar document from another country. Your national automobile association can provide one for a nominal fee. They're usually valid for one year.

### Automobile Association Membership Cards

If you plan on doing a lot of driving in the USA, it would be beneficial to join your national automobile association. Members of the American Automobile Association (AAA) or an affiliated automobile club may get car rental and sightseeing admission discounts with membership cards. More importantly, it gives you access to AAA road service in case of an emergency (eg locking your keys in the car or having major blow-ups).

### Hostelling International Card

Most hostels in the USA are members of Hostelling International/American Youth Hostel (HI/AYH). HI is managed by the International Youth Hostel Federation or IYHF. You can purchase membership on the spot when checking in, although it's probably advisable to purchase it before you leave home.

### Student Identification

If you're a student, get an international student ID or bring along a school or university ID card to take advantage of the discounts available to students.

## CUSTOMS

US customs allows each person over the age of 21 to bring one liter of liquor and 200 cigarettes duty-free into the USA. US citizens are allowed to import, duty-free, $400 worth of gifts from abroad while non-US citizens are allowed to bring in $100 worth. Should you be carrying more than $10,000 in US and foreign cash, traveler's checks, money orders and the like), you need to declare the excess amount. There is no legal restriction on the amount which may be imported, but undeclared sums in excess of $10,000 may be subject to confiscation. Agriculture inspection stations at the Arizona-California border may ask you to surrender fruit when entering California, in an attempt to halt the spread of pests associated with the fruit.

## MONEY
### Currency

The US dollar is divided into 100 cents (¢). Coins come in denominations of 1¢ (penny), 5¢ (nickel), 10¢ (dime), 25¢ (quarter) and the seldom seen 50¢ (half dollar). Notes come in $1, $2, $5, $10, $20, $50 and $100 denominations (you'll only occasionally come across $2 bills – they're perfectly legal). There is also a $1 coin that the government has tried unsuccessfully to bring into mass circulation; you may get them as change from ticket and stamp machines. Be aware that they look similar to quarters.

### Exchange Rates

If you plan to carry money in the form of traveler's checks, you will save yourself quite a bit of trouble and expense if you buy them in US dollars. While you may lose out on blips in the foreign exchange rates, the hassle of having to exchange money at banks and other facilities makes

## HIV & Entering Customs

Everyone entering the USA who is not a US citizen is subject to the whim and authority of the Immigration & Naturalization Service (INS), regardless of whether that person has legal immigration documents. The INS can keep someone from entering or staying in the USA by excluding or deporting them. This is especially relevant to travelers with HIV (Human Immunodeficiency Virus). Though being HIV positive is not a ground for deportation, it is a 'ground of exclusion' and the INS can invoke it to refuse to admit visitors to the country.

Although the INS doesn't test people for HIV at customs, they may try to exclude anyone who answers yes to this question on the non-immigrant visa application form: 'Have you ever been afflicted with a communicable disease of public health significance?' INS officials may also stop people if they seem sick, are carrying AIDS/HIV medicine or, sadly, if the officer happens to think the person looks gay, though sexual orientation is not legally a ground of exclusion. Because the INS can refuse or delay admission to anyone they suspect of being HIV positive, your best protection is not to tip them off.

It is imperative that visitors know and assert their rights. Immigrants and visitors should avoid contact with the INS until they discuss their rights and options with a trained immigration advocate. For legal immigration information and referrals to immigration advocates, contact The National Immigration Project of the National Lawyers Guild (☎ (617) 227-9727), 14 Beacon St, Suite 506, Boston, MA 02108, or Immigrant HIV Assistance Project, Bar Association of San Francisco (☎ (415) 267-0795), 685 Market St, Suite 700, San Francisco, CA 94105. ■

up for the savings. Restaurants, hotels and most stores accept US dollar traveler's checks as if they were cash, so if you're carrying traveler's checks in US dollars, odds are you'll never have to use a bank or pay an exchange fee.

All branches of several regional banks will exchange foreign currency or travelers checks at regular teller windows. However, banks in outlying areas aren't asked to exchange money very often. You will probably find it less of a hassle and waste of time if you change your money at larger cities. Nearly all banks will buy and sell Canadian currency; some businesses near the border will offer to accept Canadian dollars 'at par', meaning that they will accept Canadian dollars at the same rate as US dollars.

At the main branch of banks money can be wired and currency exchanged. Additionally, Thomas Cook, American Express and exchange windows in airports offer exchange (although you'll get a better rate at a bank). At press time, exchange rates were:

| | | |
|---|---|---|
| A$1 | = | $0.74 |
| C$1 | = | $0.74 |
| DM1 | = | $0.75 |
| HK$10 | = | $1.34 |
| NZ$1 | = | $0.69 |
| UK£1 | = | $1.64 |
| ¥100 | = | $1.17 |

### Credit & Debit Cards

Major credit and charge cards are widely accepted by car-rental agencies and most hotels, restaurants, gas stations, shops and larger grocery stores. Many recreational and tourist activities can also be paid for by credit card. The most commonly accepted cards are Visa, MasterCard and American Express. However, Discover and Diners Club cards are also accepted by a fair number of businesses.

You'll find it hard to perform certain transactions without one. Ticket buying services, for instance, won't reserve tickets over the phone unless you offer a credit card number, and it's virtually impossible to rent a car without a credit card. Even if you loathe credit cards and prefer to rely on traveler's checks and ATMs, it's a good idea to carry one (best bets are Visa or MasterCard) for emergencies.

Places that accept Visa and MasterCard are also likely to accept debit cards. Unlike a credit card, a debit card deducts payment directly from the user's savings account. Instead of an interest rate, users are charged a minimal fee for the transaction. Be sure to check with your bank to confirm that your debit card will be accepted in other states – debit cards from large commercial banks can often be used worldwide. For telephone numbers to call in case your card is lost or stolen, see the Emergency section.

## Automatic Teller Machines (ATMs)
ATMs are another plastic alternative. Most banks have these machines which are usually open 24 hours a day. There are various ATM networks and most banks are affiliated with several. Some of the most common are Cirrus, Plus, Star Systems and Interlink. For a nominal service charge, you can withdraw cash from an ATM using a credit card or a charge card. Credit cards usually have a 2% fee with a $2 minimum, but using bank cards linked to your personal checking account is usually far cheaper. Check with your bank or credit card company for exact information.

In addition to traditional bank locations, you can also find ATMs at most airports, large grocery stores, shopping malls and in a growing number of convenience stores.

## Costs
The highest cost of traveling around the Southwest is likely to be transportation. The best way to get around is by car, because intercity buses, trains and planes are not very cheap, nor do they go to the out-of-the-way places. Car rental is available in most towns of any size, and rates can be as cheap as under $100 a week for the smallest (sub-compact) cars – these are off-season rates. More often, though, rentals begin around $130 for a week. Insurance, if you are not already covered by a credit card or personal insurance policy, is usually another $7 a day. Gas (gasoline or petrol) is cheap, ranging from about $1.05 to $1.50 for a US gallon, depending on the location and grade of fuel. A few out-of-the-way places may charge as much as $2 for a gallon, so fill

up in towns before heading for remote areas. For more information on rentals and purchasing a car, see the Getting Around chapter.

How much you pay for accommodations depends on where you want to stay. If you are on a very tight budget, you can camp for free in many places and cook for yourself in these campgrounds. Some full-service campgrounds charge up to about $20 a night for a site with RV (recreational vehicle) hookups, but most are cheaper.

Youth hostels exist, but they are few and far between and charge around $10 per person. Cheap and basic motels for about $20 a double are often a better deal for the budget traveler. Some towns, for example, Gallup, Tucumcari and Flagstaff, are known for their motel strips full of places advertising rooms for about $20 or less. Most other towns have basic motels beginning in the mid-$20s for a double room and going on up from there.

Travelers looking for more than a basic room can find satisfactory mid-range accommodations for $40 to $80 a double in most places, and some towns have luxury hotels with rooms over $100. There are also world-class resorts and dude ranches where you can pay over $200 a day. Some towns in the Southwest are relatively expensive – Sedona, Santa Fe and Taos are among these. Lodges in national parks are also pricey – there is a high demand for these rooms, which start at about $70. B&Bs are not for budget travelers; they start at about $40 for a double, but most are in the $60 to $100 range. There is more information about accommodations later on in this chapter.

Meals also vary tremendously in price. Even the smallest town will have one of the ubiquitous fast-food restaurants where you can get a large hamburger, soft drink and french fries for about $3 or $4. Many towns have all-you-can-eat restaurants where the starving budget traveler can fill up for about $5. This is eating to live, not living to eat! But penurious travelers needn't be limited to junk food or unappetizing selections of all-you-can-eat buffets. Mexican restaurants abound in the Southwest and offer great meals for under $10, and a large pizza – enough for two – can be had for $10 and up. You can eat very well any night in any town for under $25 per person. If you are looking for a splurge, bigger cities have 1st-class restaurants where you can spend $100 on dinner for two. More details on food are given later in this chapter.

Entrance into National Park Service (NPS) areas (parks, monuments, historical sites) costs $3 to $10 a vehicle (irrespective of whether there are six people or just a driver), but the entrance fee is sometimes valid for seven days with in and out privileges. Some less frequently visited NPS areas are free. You can buy a Golden Eagle Passport, which allows unlimited entry into all NPS sites for a year for $25 from any NPS site. The pass covers one person plus the people in that person's car. US citizens over 62 can get Golden Age Passport and those who are blind or disabled can get Golden Access Passport. These are free at any NPS site and allow free entrance to all NPS sites. Entrance fees do not cover the costs of camping or some special tours. Golden Eagle, Age and Access Passports are not valid in state-run parks, where entrance is often $3 per car. There is more information about these passes under Useful Organizations later in this chapter.

First-run movies are usually $6 or $7, but you can pay under $2 in budget theaters showing movies that have been out for a few months. A 12-oz bottle of domestic beer can range from $1.50 to $2.50 in a bar or restaurant (though airlines and airports charge an exorbitant $3 or $4). A six-pack of domestic beers costs $3 to $4 in the supermarket, while a six-pack of soft drinks is $1 to $2, depending on the brand. A cup of coffee is usually 50¢ to $1. Museums can range from free to as much as $8 to visit.

## Tipping

Tipping is expected in restaurants and better hotels, as well as by taxi drivers, hairdressers and baggage carriers. In restaurants, wait staff are paid minimal wages and rely upon tips for their livelihoods. Tip 15% unless the service is terrible (in which case a complaint to the manager is warranted) or up to 20% if the service is great. There is no need to tip in fast-food, take-out or buffet-style restaurants where you serve yourself.

Taxi drivers expect 10% and hairdressers get 15% if their service is satisfactory. Baggage carriers (skycaps in airports, bellboys in hotels) receive $1 for the first bag and 50¢ for each additional bag carried. In budget hotels (where there aren't bellboys anyway) tips are not expected. In 1st class and luxury hotels, tipping can reach irritating proportions – doormen, bellboys, parking attendants, chambermaids are all tipped at least $1 for each service performed. However, simply saying 'thank you' to an attendant who merely opens the door when you could just as easily have done it yourself is OK.

In hotels, beware of grossly inflated charges for some services, especially telephones and laundry. To avoid unpleasant surprises, ask about these before you incur any expenses. Many expensive hotels have pay phones in their lobbies which are much cheaper than calling from your room, and cheap coin-operated laundries outside the hotel are an alternative to expensive hotel laundry charges.

## Special Deals

The USA is probably the most promotion-oriented society on earth. Everything has an angle and with a little detective work and a lot of gumption, the traveler stands to find some worthwhile bargains.

Off-season hotel prices, for example, are frequently negotiable. 'You know, I'd love to stay at your fine establishment, but Joe Bob's Hotel down the street is much cheaper.' Be confident, but don't be rude.

One of the newer retail trends is the bulk warehouse store. These are huge buildings that sell everything you could possibly want at a discount. Items tend to come in ungainly institutional-sized units, so you probably need a strong liking for a certain product to ensure you don't get sick of it.

These are good places for items like batteries and film. Sometimes you can even find bargains on computers.

Sunday newspapers typically have discount coupons for local supermarkets and advertising circulars for sales at department stores.

Supermarkets also run specials on tickets for local attractions, especially 'family' attractions, like amusement parks or professional sporting events (usually baseball). If there is skiing within a two-hour drive, cheap lift tickets are often available at supermarkets as well.

Enterprising local publishers often put together coupon books for local merchants that can be purchased at independent book shops. They're usually on display at the front counter and typically offer discounts at local cafes and restaurants. Tourist offices and chambers of commerce usually have something similar.

If you plan to rent a car, rental agencies sometimes offer discounts in tandem with national motel chains. Since the deregulation of the US airline industry, airlines have been jockeying to provide the most appealing premiums for potential flyers. If you belong to any frequent-flyer programs, be sure to ask what discounts they entitle you to.

The granddaddy of discount programs is something called *Entertainment Publications*. This is a thick tome of coupons used in conjunction with a membership card that allows discounts for everything from restaurants and hotels to baseball games. They're available for specific geographic regions of the USA and Canada and cost $40 for a year's membership. They're ideal if you plan to spend more than a few months in the USA. Call (☎ 1 (800) 285-5525) for information.

### Taxes

Almost everything you pay for in the USA is taxed. Occasionally, the tax is included in the advertised price (eg, gas, drinks in a bar and entrance tickets for museums or theaters). Transportation (taxi, bus, train and plane tickets) taxes are usually included in the advertised price. Airport taxes of up to $3 per airport are added to the ticket price, not paid at the airport. Restaurant meals and drinks, motel rooms and most other purchases are taxed, and this is added to the advertised cost.

The tax rates are bewildering. For meals, rooms and other purchases, there are both state and local (city or county) taxes as well as lodging, restaurant and car rental taxes. This means that as you move around the Southwest, you'll pay different taxes in every town. Basic state sales taxes are 5% in Arizona and Utah, and 5.75% in New Mexico, but most restaurants add 6% to 8% to the bill, most hotels add 8% to 13%, and most car rental companies add 7% to 13%. The prices given in this book do not reflect local taxes.

### WHEN TO GO

The best season to visit the Southwest is January to December.

In northern Arizona, New Mexico and Utah, summer is the high season, coinciding with school vacations in both North America and Europe. Traditionally, Memorial Day weekend (end of May) to Labor Day weekend (beginning of September) is the vacation season, and you can expect higher prices and more crowds except in hot southern Arizona, when luxury resorts cut their prices in half.

Winter visitors flock to the highlands for great skiing. Utah, especially, has world-class skiing, but New Mexico and Arizona also have good ski areas. If you don't like the idea of hurtling down snow covered mountains, head down to southern Arizona. Hotels in Phoenix, Tucson and other southern Arizonan towns consider winter (Christmas to May) their high (and more expensive) season. While the rest of the country is buried under snowdrifts, southern Arizonans enjoys T-shirt weather (you might have to put on a sweater some days, but you won't need a down jacket).

I enjoy the spring and fall when there are fewer people, but some services may be closed then.

## WHAT TO BRING

The Southwest generally has a casual attitude, and people's clothing reflects that. Clean jeans and cowboy boots are seen in symphony halls and good restaurants, although you can certainly dress up if you want. Very few restaurants expect men to wear ties and, in those, a bola tie is fine. (A bola tie is a leather cord fastened with a semiprecious stone and/or metal clasp; it is Arizona's state neckwear.) Utah, with its Mormon influence, appears to be the most formal, but even here, clean casual attire is just fine.

Your clothing will depend on season and elevation. Southern Arizonans wear shorts and T-shirts all summer long, but if you are heading into the highlands, you'll need some warmer clothes for the evening, even in midsummer. The climate charts in this book will help you decide.

Beware of the extreme sunshine. For much of the year, severe sunburn is a real possibility, so bring plenty of sunblock or wear light, long pants or skirts and long-sleeved shirts. A broad-brimmed hat and sunglasses are important, too. Bring a water bottle if you plan on doing any walking outside of towns; the heat will dehydrate you very quickly. Don't forget prescription medicines, spare contact lenses or glasses, and copies of your prescriptions.

If you are staying in the cheapest motels, a travel alarm clock is useful. (Wake-up calls can be arranged in better hotels.) Some travelers bring a small immersion heater and a cup to heat up water for instant coffee or soup in their room.

If you forget something, you can usually buy it without much hassle in any town of any size.

## TOURIST OFFICES

Many towns don't have tourist offices per se – this function is often performed by the chamber of commerce in each town. They can provide you with local information about what to see and where to stay. The address and telephone number of each chamber of commerce or other tourist office is given in the Orientation & Information headings under each town.

### Tourist Offices Abroad

US Embassies will often have tourist information (see the preceding entry US Embassies & Consulates Abroad). The United States Travel & Tourism Administration (USTTA) has the following offices abroad:

Australia
    Level 59, MLC Centre, King & Castlereagh Sts, Sydney, NSW 2001 (☎ (2) 233-4666)
Canada
    480 University Ave, Suite 602, Toronto, Ontario, M5G 1V2 (☎ (416) 595-5082)
    1253 McGill College Ave, Suite 328, Montreal, Quebec, H3B 2Y5 (☎ (514) 861-5040)
    1095 West Pender St, Vancouver, BC VBE 2M6 (☎ (604) 685-1930)
France
    2 Ave Gabriel, 75382 Paris Cedex OB (☎ (1) 42.60.00.66)
Germany
    Platenstrasse 1, 60320 Frankfurt (☎ (69) 95-67-90-0)
Italy
    Via Principe Amedeo 2/10, 20121 Milano (☎ (2) 2900-2657)
Japan
    Kokusai Building,3-1-1 Marunouchi, Chiyoda-ku, Tokyo 100 (☎ (3) 3212-2124)
Mexico
    Edificio Plaza Comermex, 402, Blvd M Avila Camacho No1, Colonia Polanco Chapultepec,11560 Mexico, DF (☎ (5) 520-3010)
UK
    24 Grosvenor Square, London, England W1A 1AE (☎ (171) 495-4466)

### State Tourist Offices

State tourist offices can send you an informative, colorful brochure about the main attractions of each state. These brochures, which are usually free, are updated annually and contain addresses and telephone numbers of chambers of commerce, hotel lists and other useful information. If you have specific needs or questions, state tourist offices may be able to answer them or refer you to the appropriate office. The Utah Travel Council also publishes an annual *Ski Utah* brochure with detailed information about each ski area.

Arizona Office of Tourism
   1100 W Washington, Phoenix, AZ 85007
   (☎ (602) 542 8687, 1 (800) 842 8257, fax
   (602) 542 4068)
New Mexico Department of Tourism
   Lamy Building (Office 106), 491 Old Santa
   Fe Trail, Santa Fe, NM 87503 (☎ (505) 827
   7400, 1 (800) 545 2040)
Utah Travel Council
   Council Hall/Capitol Hill, Salt Lake City, UT
   84114 (☎ (801) 538 1030, 1 (800) 200 1160,
   fax (801) 538 1399)

## USEFUL ORGANIZATIONS
### American Automobile Association
The AAA, with offices in all major cities and many smaller towns, provides useful information, free maps and routine road services like tire repair and towing (free within a limited radius) to its members. Members of its foreign affiliates, like the Automobile Association in the UK, are entitled to the same services; for others, the basic membership fee ranges from $39 to $41 per annum, plus a one-time initiation fee of $17 (still an excellent investment for the maps alone, even for non-motorists). Its nationwide toll-free roadside assistance number is 1 (800) AAA-HELP or 1 (800) 222-4357.

### National Park Service (NPS) & US Forest Service (USFS)
The NPS and USFS administer the use of parks and forests. National forests are less protected than parks, allowing commercial exploitation in some areas (usually logging or privately owned recreational facilities).

National parks most often surround spectacular natural features and cover hundreds of sq miles. A full range of accommodations can be found in and around national parks. Contact individual parks for more specific information. National park campground and reservations information can be obtained by calling 1 (800) 365-2267 or writing to the National Park Service Public Inquiry, Department of the Interior, 18th and C Sts NW, Washington, DC 20013.

Current information about national forests can be obtained from ranger stations which are also listed in the text. National forest campground and reservation information can be obtained by calling 1 (800) 280-2267 or write to National Park Service Public Inquiry, Dept. of Interior, 18th & C Sts NW, Washington, DC 20013. General information about federal lands is also available from the Fish & Wildlife Service and the Bureau of Land Management (see below) and from the following agencies:

National Forests Southwestern Region
   Public Affairs Office, 517 Gold Ave SW,
   Albuquerque, NM 87102 (☎ (505) 842
   3292). This office covers Arizona as well.
National Forests Intermountain Region
   324 25th St, Ogden, UT 84401 (☎ (801) 629
   8600)

### Golden Passports
Golden Age Passports are free and allow permanent US residents 62 years and older unlimited entry to all sites in the national park system, with discounts on camping and other fees.

Golden Access Passports offer the same to US residents who are medically blind or permanently disabled.

Golden Eagle Passports cost $25 annually and offer one-year entry into national parks to the holder and accompanying guests. You can apply in person for any of these at any national park or regional office of the USFS or NPS or call 1 (800) 280-2267 for information and ordering.

### Bureau of Land Management (BLM)
The BLM manages public use of federal lands, including grazing and mining leases. They offer no-frills camping, often in untouched settings. Each state has a regional office in the state capital. Look in the white pages under 'US Government', or call the Federal Information Directory (☎ 1 (800) 726-4995).

### US Fish & Wildlife Service (USFWS)
Each state has a few regional offices that provide information about viewing local wildlife. Their phone numbers can be

found in the white pages phone directory under the Department of Interior 'US Government' or you can call the Federal Information Directory (☎ 1 (800) 726-4995).

## State Fish & Game Departments

Unlike the above organizations, the Fish & Game departments are run by state government. Information about seasons, licenses and other regulations is available from the following agencies:

Arizona Game & Fish Department
   2222 W Greenway Rd, Phoenix, AZ 85023
   (☎ (602) 942 3000)
New Mexico Department of Game & Fish
   Villagra Building, State Capitol, Santa Fe,
   NM 87503 (☎ (505) 827 7911)
Utah Division of Wildlife Resources
   1596 W North Temple, Salt Lake City, UT
   84116 (☎ (801) 596 8660)

## BUSINESS HOURS & HOLIDAYS

Generally speaking, business hours are from 9 am to 5 pm, but there are certainly no hard and fast rules. In any large city, a few supermarkets, restaurants and the lobby of the main post office are open 24 hours a day. Shops are usually open from 9 or 10 am to 5 or 6 pm, but are often open until 9 pm in shopping malls, except on Sundays when hours are noon to 5 pm. Post offices are open from 8 am to 4 or 5:30 pm Monday to Friday, and some are open from 8 am to 3 pm on Saturday. Banks are usually open from either 9 or 10 am to 5 or 6 pm Monday to Friday. A few banks are open from 9 am to 2 or 4 pm on Saturdays. Basically, hours are decided by the individual branch so if you need specifics give the branch you want a call.

National public holidays are celebrated throughout the USA. Banks, schools and government offices (including post offices) are closed and transportation, museums and other services are on a Sunday schedule. Holidays falling on a Sunday are usually observed on the following Monday.

January
   *New Year's Day*, 1 January
   *Martin Luther King, Jr Day* – held on the

third Monday of the month, it celebrates this civil rights leader's birthday (15 January 1929).
February
   *Presidents' Day* – held on the third Monday of the month, it celebrates the birthdays of Abraham Lincoln (12 February, 1809) and George Washington (22 February, 1732).
March/April
   *Easter* – observed the first Sunday after a full moon in March or April.
May
   *Memorial Day* – held on the last Monday in the month, it honors the war dead (and is also the unofficial first day of the summer tourist season).
July
   *Independence Day* – 4 July, celebrates the adoption of the Declaration of Independence on that day in 1776; parades, fireworks displays and a huge variety of other events are held throughout the country.
September
   *Labor Day* – held on the first Monday of the month, it honors working people (and is also the unofficial end of the summer tourist season).
October
   *Columbus Day* – held on the second Monday of the month, it commemorates the landing of Christopher Columbus in the Bahamas on 12 October, 1492. Though it is a federal holiday, many Native Americans do not consider this day a cause for celebration.
November
   *Veterans Day* – 11 November, honors war veterans.
   *Thanksgiving* – held on the fourth Thursday of the month, it's a day of giving thanks and is traditionally celebrated with a big family dinner, usually turkey, potatoes and other fall harvest vegetables.
December
   *Christmas* – 25 December

## CULTURAL EVENTS

The USA is always ready to call a day an event. Retailers remind the masses of coming events with huge advertising binges running for months before the actual day. Because of this tacky overexposure some of these events are nicknamed 'Hallmark Holidays' after the greeting card manufacturer. In larger cities with diverse cultures, traditional holidays of other countries are also celebrated with as much, if not more, fanfare. Some of these are also public holidays (see above) and therefore banks, schools and government buildings are closed.

January

*Chinese New Year* – begins at the end of January or the beginning of February and lasts two weeks. The first day is celebrated with parades, firecrackers, fireworks and lots of food.

February

*Valentine's Day* – 14 February. No one knows why St Valentine is associated with romance in the USA but this is the day of roses, sappy greeting cards and packed restaurants. Some people wear red and give out 'Be My Valentine' candies.

March

*St Patrick's Day* – 17 March. The patron saint of Ireland is honored by all those who feel the Irish in their blood, and by those who want to feel Irish beer in their blood. Everyone wears green (or you can get pinched), stores sell green bread, bars serve green beer and towns and cities put on frolicking parades of marching bands and community groups.

April

*Easter* Those who observe the holiday may go to church, paint eggs, eat chocolate eggs or any mixture of the above. Travel during this weekend is usually expensive and crowded. Incidentally, Good Friday is not a public holiday and often goes unnoticed.

*Passover* – celebrated either in March or April, depending on the Jewish calendar. Families get together to honor persecuted forebears, partake in the symbolic seder dinner and eat unleavened bread.

May

*Cinco de Mayo* – the day the Mexicans wiped out the French army in 1862. Now it's the day on which all Americans get to eat lots of Mexican food and drink margaritas.

*Mothers Day* – held on the third Sunday of the month with lots of cards, flowers and busy restaurants.

June

*Fathers Day* – same Sunday, same idea, different parent.

July

*Independence Day* – more commonly called Fourth of July. Lots of flags are flown, barbecues abound, parades storm the streets of many towns, fireworks litter the air and ground.

October

*Halloween* – 31 October. Kids and adults dress in costumes, in safer neighborhoods. Children go 'trick-or-treating' for candy and adults go to parties to act out their alter egos.

November

*Day of the Dead* – observed in areas with Mexican communities on 2 November. This is a day for families to honor dead relatives, and make breads and sweets resembling skeletons, skulls and such.

*Election Day* – held on the second Tuesday of the month. This is the chance for US citizens to perform their patriotic duty and vote. Even more flags are flown than on 4 July and signs with corny photos of candidates decorate the land.

*Thanksgiving* – held on the last Thursday of the month. The most important family gathering is celebrated with a bounty of food and football games on TV. The following day is declared by retailers as the biggest shopping day of the year with everyone burning off pumpkin pie by running shopping relays through the malls.

December

*Christmas* – The night before the 25th is as much of an event as the day itself with church services, caroling in the streets, people cruising neighborhoods looking for the best light displays and stores full of procrastinators.

*Kwanzaa* – held from 26 to 31 December. This seven-day African American celebration give thanks to the harvest. Families join together for a feast and practice seven different principles corresponding to the seven days of celebration.

*New Year's Eve* – 31 December. People celebrate with little tradition other than dressing up and drinking champagne, or staying home and watching the festivities on TV. The following day people stay home to nurse their hangovers and watch college football.

## SPECIAL EVENTS

From highbrow arts festivals to down-home country fairs, from American Indian ceremonials to chili-cooking competitions, from duck races to hot-air balloon ascents, the Southwest has literally hundreds of holidays, festivals and sporting events. Entire books have been written describing Southwestern festivals – only a selection of the most important or unusual events can be given below.

As dates for many events vary slightly from year to year, it's best to check local papers or chambers of commerce for precise dates.

## January

*Various Dances* are held on 1 and 6 January at most Indian pueblos in New Mexico.

*Sundance Film Festival* takes place the second half of January in Park City, Utah.

*Animal Dances* are held on the evening of 22 and throughout 23 January in San Idelfonso Pueblo, New Mexico.

*Winter Carnival*, on the last weekend of January (or first of February), features skiing, dogsledding, a torch parade and Western fun in Red River, New Mexico.

## February

*Quartzsite Gem & Mineral Show and Swap Meet*, held in late January to mid-February in Quartzsite, Arizona, draws thousands of gem fans to this small town – be prepared to camp.

*Candelaria Day*, 2 February, brings ceremonial dances to Picuris and San Felipe Pueblos, New Mexico.

*Tucson Gem & Mineral Show*, held during the first two weeks in Tucson, Arizona, is one of the biggest in the country.

*Tubac Festival of the Arts*, which occurs in early February in Tubac, Arizona, is one of the state's most important arts & crafts festivals. *O'odham Tash*, held at Casa Grande, Arizona, in mid-February, involves major Indian festivities – dances, a rodeo, a parade, food and arts & crafts.

*Winter Arts Festival*, which takes place over two weeks starting mid-month in Silver City, New Mexico, has art shows, music (especially jazz) and other events.

*La Fiesta de los Vaqueros*, celebrated from the last Thursday to Sunday of February in Tucson, Arizona, begins with the world's largest non-motorized parade, followed by a rodeo and other cowboy events – even the city's schools are closed for the last two days of what is locally called 'Rodeo Week'.

## March

*Wa:k Powwow Conference*, hosted in early March by the Tohono O'odham tribe in San Xavier del Bac Mission, near Tucson, Arizona, is attended by members of many Southwestern Indian tribes. Highlights include several days of dances, singing, food and other entertainment.

*St Patrick's Day*, 17 March, celebrates the feast of the Irish patron saint with parades and parties in most cities.

*Easter* (sometimes in April) is celebrated with masses, races, dances and parades in many Indian pueblos and at the Indian Pueblo Cultural Center in Albuquerque, New Mexico.

## April

*Albuquerque Founder's Day*, 23 April, involves a parade and street fair in Albuquerque's Old Town Plaza during the third or fourth weekend.

*American Indian Week*, the week before the Gathering of Nations Powwow below, includes lectures, audiovisual presentations, dances and art displays, that celebrate Indian traditions. Events are held at the Indian Pueblo Cultural Center in Albuquerque, New Mexico.

*Gathering of Nations Powwow*, a weekend in late April (or early May), consists of a Miss Indian World contest, dances and arts & crafts at University of New Mexico Arena in Albuquerque.

*Annual Square Dance Festival*, held three days over the third or fourth weekend (Friday to Sunday), includes workshops, performances and public dances (spectators welcome) at Red Rock State Park, Gallup, New Mexico.

## May

*San Felipe Day*, on 1 May, is celebrated with dances at San Felipe, Cochiti and Taos Pueblos, New Mexico.

*Santa Cruz Day*, on 3 May, is celebrated with dances at Cochiti and Taos Pueblos, New Mexico.

*T & C Fiesta*, on the first weekend in May has taken place annually for almost half a century in Truth or Consequences, New Mexico. It features an old-time fiddlers contest as well as a rodeo, parade and street booths.

*Tularosa Rose Festival*, held over the first weekend in May in Tularosa, New Mexico, features music, arts, crafts and food as well as roses.

*Cinco de Mayo* is a Mexican holiday that is celebrated in many Southwestern towns, especially those with a strong Hispanic heritage. Parades, dances, music, arts & crafts, street fairs and Mexican food are the order of the day.

*Golden Spike Anniversary*, on 10 May, is remembered with a reenactment of the joining of the first east-to-west railroad in

1869. It takes place in Golden Spike National Historic Site, Utah.

*Taos Spring Arts Festival*, two or three weeks in May to June, is held in Taos, New Mexico.

June

*Billy the Kid Tombstone Race* is held in mid-June at Fort Sumner, New Mexico.

*St Anthony's Day*, 13 June; *San Juan Day*, 24 June; and *St Peter's and St Paul's Day*, 29 June, are celebrated with dances and other events at several Indian pueblos and villages in New Mexico.

*Northern Pueblo Artist and Craftsman Show*, the third weekend, draws hundreds of Indian artisans who display their work. It was held in San Idelfonso Pueblo for many years, but it has recently been celebrated in Santa Fe, New Mexico.

*Utah Arts Festival* is held in late June in Salt Lake City, Utah.

*Festival of Native American Arts*, which occurs from late June through all of July, and *Hopi Artists Exhibition*, which takes place from late June to early July, both happen in Flagstaff, Arizona.

July

*Utah Shakespearean Festival*, from July to early September, takes place in Cedar City, Utah.

*Ute Indian Powwow*, in early July (or late June), happens in Fort Duchesne, Utah.

*Fourth of July* is celebrated in most South-western towns with a variety of events including races, rodeos, arts & crafts fairs, ceremonial Indian dances, pageants, music festivals, pancake breakfasts, barbecues, picnics and country & western dancing. These are in addition to parades and fire-works.

*Days of '47*, two weeks up to 24 July, cele-brates the arrival of pioneering Mormon leader Brigham Young on 24 July 1847 (also called Pioneer Days). It's celebrated in Salt Lake City and other towns in Utah.

*Mormon Miracle Pageant* is held in mid-July in Manti, Utah.

*Santiago and Santa Ana Days*, on 25 and 26 July, is celebrated with dances at several Indian pueblos and a big traditional fiesta in Taos, New Mexico.

*Loggers/Sawdust Festival*, held in late July, lures loggers who compete in various events – bucking, cutting, stacking and birling – in Payson, Arizona.

*Spanish Market*, held during the last week-end, includes arts & crafts and entertainment in the Santa Fe's Plaza in New Mexico.

*Ruidoso Art Festival*, over the last weekend, showcases arts & crafts of a high standard in Ruidoso, New Mexico.

August

*Park City Arts Festival*, is held on the first weekend in Park City, Utah.

*Old Lincoln Days*, during the first weekend, includes the Last Escape of Billy the Kid pageant. It takes place in Lincoln, New Mexico.

*Festival of the American West* takes place the first week in Logan, Utah.

*Inter-Tribal Indian Ceremonial*, during the second week, draws members of dozens of tribes who participate in this huge annual event, which includes rodeos, dances, pow-wows, parades, races, food, arts & crafts, and much more. It's held in Red Rock State Park, Gallup, New Mexico.

*San Lorenzo Day*, 10 August, is celebrated with dances at Acoma, Laguna and Picuris Pueblos, New Mexico.

*Indian Market*, on the third weekend, offers a chance to buy high-quality Indian arts & crafts. It has occurred annually since 1922 in Santa Fe, New Mexico.

*Great American Duck Races* are held on the last weekend in Deming, New Mexico.

September

*Peach Days*, on the first weekend, celebrates the local harvest in Brigham City, Utah.

*Fiesta de Santa Fe*, held on the second week-end in Santa Fe, New Mexico, is one of the oldest annual fiestas in the country.

*Navajo Nation Fair*, held mid-September in Window Rock, Arizona, offers a rodeo, parade, dances, songs, arts & crafts, food and more.

*New Mexico State Fair and Rodeo*, held mid-September in Albuquerque ranks as one of the largest state fairs in the USA.

*Utah State Fair* is celebrated in mid-Septem-ber in Salt Lake City, Utah.

*Old Taos Trade Fair*, on the fourth weekend in Taos, New Mexico, celebrates life in the 1820s at Martínez Hacienda.

*Taos Fall Arts Festival* takes place in late September to early October in Taos, New Mexico.

October

*Whole Enchilada Festival*, which takes place the first weekend in Las Cruces, New Mexico, showcases the world's biggest enchilada. Other draws include local food, entertainment, arts & crafts and races.

*Arizona State Fair* is held the last two weeks in Phoenix, Arizona.

## Visitors' Etiquette in Pueblos & on Reservations

Indian pueblos and reservations are legislated both by federal and tribal law. Each tribe is independent, and visitors should be aware that what is permitted on one reservation may be banned on another. Language, customs and religious ceremonies differ from one reservation to the next. Many Indians prefer to speak their own language, and some don't speak English. Privacy is cherished, both on an individual and community level. Visitors to pueblos and reservations are generally welcome, but they should behave in an appropriately courteous and respectful manner. Tribal rules are often clearly posted at the entrance to each reservation, but here are a few guidelines.

**Photography & Other Recording** Many tribes, notably the Hopi but others as well, ban all forms of recording be it photography, video-taping, audio-taping or drawing. Others permit these activities in certain areas only if you pay the appropriate fee. If you wish to photograph a person, do so only after obtaining his or her permission. This also holds true for children. A posing tip is usually expected. Photographers who disregard these rules can expect tribal police officers to confiscate their cameras and then escort them off the reservation.

**Private Property** Do not walk into houses or climb onto roofs unless invited. Do not climb on ruins. Kivas are always off-limits to visitors. Do not remove any kind of artifact. Off-road travel (foot, horse or vehicle) is not allowed without a permit.

**Verbal Communication** It is considered polite to listen without comment, particularly when an elder is speaking. Silent listening does not mean that the listener is ignoring the speaker; to the contrary, intent listening is considered respectful. Be prepared for long silences in the middle of conversations; such silences often indicate that a topic is under serious consideration.

**Ceremonials & Powwows** These are either open to the public or exclusively for tribal members. Ceremonials are religious events. Applauding, chatting, asking questions or trying to talk to the performers is rude. Photography and other recording are rarely permitted. While powwows also hold spiritual significance, they are usually more informal. Many ceremonials and powwows don't have a fixed date and are arranged a couple of weeks ahead of time. The tribal office can inform you of upcoming events.

**Clothing** Modest dress is customary. Especially when watching ceremonials, you should dress conservatively. Halter or tank tops and miniskirts or short shorts are inappropriate.

**Alcohol** Most reservations ban the sale or use of alcohol. The Apache reservations are notable exceptions. Drugs are banned on all reservations.

**Eating** There are few restaurants. Especially during public ceremonials, visitors may be invited into a house for a meal. Courteous behavior includes enjoying the food (of course!) but not lingering at the table after your meal, because others are waiting. Tipping is not customary.

**Recreation** Activities such as backpacking, camping, fishing and hunting require tribal permits. On Indian lands, state fishing or hunting licenses are not valid. ■

*All Hallows Day* and *All Saints Day*, on 31 October and 1 November, is celebrated with ceremonies and dances at most Indian pueblos in New Mexico.

November
*San Diego Day*, on 12 November, involves ceremonial dances at Tesuque and Jemez Pueblos, New Mexico.
*Christmas Lighting of Temple Square* takes place the last weekend in Salt Lake City, Utah.

December
*Fiesta of Our Lady of Guadalupe*, from 10 to 12 December, is celebrated with traditional dances and a pilgrimage in Tortugas, Las Cruces, New Mexico.
*Christmas* festivities occur all month, including Nativity pageants and festivals of lights in many Southwestern towns.

## Sporting Events

From football to rodeos to mountain-bike races, the Southwest has many sporting events.

January
*Fiesta Bowl*, which takes place on 1 January in Tempe, Arizona, is a major post-season college football game.
*Utah Winter Games* are held throughout the state over the first two weeks.
*Tucson Open*, held in mid-January in Tucson, Arizona, is a men's PGA (Professional Golfer's Association) tournament.
*United States Ski Association Ski Week* occurs during the third week in Park City, Utah.
*Phoenix Open*, held in late January in Scottsdale, Arizona, is a men's PGA tournament.

February
*Mount Taylor Winter Quadrathlon*, no fixed date, invites teams of one to four athletes to compete in bicycling, running, cross-country skiing and snowshoeing near Grants, New Mexico.
*Chama Chili Classic*, over President's Day weekend, consists of cross-country ski races near Chama, New Mexico.

March
*Tucson Open*, held in mid-March in Tucson, Arizona, is a women's PGA tournament.
*Turquoise Classic*, held in Phoenix, Arizona, in late March, is a women's PGA tournament.
*Jeep Safari* takes place over Easter Week in Moab, Utah.

April
*La Vuelta de Bisbee*, held over four days in

late April in Bisbee, Arizona, ranks as Arizona's biggest bicycle race.

May
*Great Rio Grande Raft Race*, held in mid-May in Albuquerque, New Mexico, features homemade boats as well as more conventional canoes, kayaks and rafts.

June
*Tour of the Gila*, around the second weekend, is a premier bicycle stage race that takes place in Silver City, New Mexico.
*Utah Summer Games* are held in late June in Cedar City, Utah.
*Annual PRCA and WRPA Rodeo* is hosted the fourth weekend in Raton, New Mexico.

## Gearing Up for 2002

Since 1966, Salt Lake City has put in bids to be the host city of the Winter Olympics. The city's persistence has been rewarded with 2002 Winter Olympic Games.

Eight new state-of-the-art sports facilities have been constructed (the skiing events will be held in Park City) and the University of Utah will house the Olympic Village. Over 80 countries are expected to be represented and estimates show this may be the most attended Winter Games yet. New events will include snowboarding and women's hockey.

While 2002 is still a ways off, hotels are already taking reservations and construction of facilities will continue. The Games will be held from February 9 to 24 and tickets will go on sale about a year before that. At press time, there was no information on ticket sales (tickets are estimated to range in price from $35 to high capacity events, like cross-country, to $300 for the opening and closing ceremonies and hockey). For more information contact the Salt Lake Olympic Organizing Commitee (☎ (801) 322 2002) 215 S State St, No 2002, Salt Lake City, UT 84111; the Salt Lake City Chamber of Commerce (☎ (801) 364 3631) 175 East 400 South, Suite 600, Salt Lake City, UT 84111; or the US Olympic Commitee (☎ (719) 632 5551) 1750 East Boulder St, Colorado Springs, CO 80909. ∎

## Rodeo: A Western Ritual

Rodeo, from the Spanish word meaning roundup, began with the cowboys of the Old West. As they used to say, 'There was never a horse that couldn't be rode – and never a rider that couldn't be throwed'. Naturally, cowboys riding half-wild horses eventually competed to determine who was the best. The speed with which they could rope a calf also became a competitive skill.

Rodeo as we know it today began in the 1880s. The first rodeo to offer prize money was held in Texas in 1883, and the first to begin charging admission to the event was in Prescott, Arizona, in 1888. Since then, rodeo has developed into both a spectator and professional sport under the auspices of the Professional Rodeo Cowboys Association (PRCA). Despite its recognition as a professional sport, very few cowboys earn anywhere near as much as other professional athletes.

For the first-time spectator, the action is full of thrills and spills but may be a little hard to understand. Within the arena, the main participants are cowboys and cowgirls, judges (who are usually retired rodeo competitors) and clowns. Although the clowns perform amusing stunts, their function is to help out the cowboys when they get into trouble. During the bull riding, they are particularly important if a cowboy gets thrown. Then clowns immediately rush in front of the bull to distract the animal, while the winded cowboy struggles out of the arena.

While men are the main contenders in a rodeo, women also compete, mainly in barrel racing, team roping and calf roping.

Each rodeo follows the same pattern, and once you know a few pointers, it all begins to make sense. The first order of the day is the grand entry, during which all contestants, clowns and officials parade their horses around the arena, raise the US flag and sing the national anthem. The rodeo then begins, usually including seven events, which are often in the following order.

**Bareback Bronc Riding** Riders must stay on a randomly assigned bucking bronco (a wild horse) for eight seconds, which might not seem long from a comfortable seat in the stands, but from the back of a horse it can seem like an eternity. The cowboy holds on with one hand to a handle strapped around the horse just behind its shoulders. His other hand is allowed to touch nothing but air, otherwise he's disqualified. His spurs must be up at the height of the horse's shoulders when the front hooves hit the ground on the first jump out of the chute, and he must keep spurring the horse during the ride. Two judges give 25 points each to the horse and the rider, for a theoretical total of 100. A good ride is one in which the horse bucks wildly and the rider stays on with style – a score of over 70 is good.

**Calf Roping** This is a timed event. A calf races out of a chute, closely followed by a mounted cowboy with a rope loop. The cowboy ropes the calf (usually by throwing the loop over its head, although a leg catch is legal), hooks the rope to the saddle horn, dismounts, keeping the rope tight all the way to the calf. Watch the horse as the cowboy

July

Frontier Days, held during first week in Prescott, Arizona, hosts one of the world's oldest professional rodeos plus other entertainment.

August

Connie Mack World Series Baseball Tournament, held during the second week in August in Farmington, New Mexico, is an opportunity for the country's best amateur teams to compete.

Payson Rodeo, the world's other oldest rodeo, is held in mid-August in Payson, Arizona. Expect to see plenty of top-ranking cowboys.

Bonneville Nationals Speed Week, takes place during the third week in Bonneville Salt Flats, Utah.

September

All American Futurity, held on Labor Day in Ruidoso Downs, New Mexico, is a quarter horse race worth about $2.5 million.

goes to the calf. A well-trained horse will stand still and hold the rope taut to make the cowboy's job less difficult. When he reaches the calf, the cowboy throws the animal down, ties three of its legs together with a six-foot-long 'piggin string' and throws up his hands to show he's done. A good roper can do the whole thing in just a few seconds.

**Saddle-Bronc Riding** This has similar rules to the bareback event and is scored the same way. In addition to starting with the spurs up above the horse's shoulders and keeping one hand in the air, the cowboy must keep both feet in the stirrups. Dismounting from the saddle of a bucking bronco is not easy – watch the two pickup men riding alongside to help the contestant off. This demands almost as much skill as the event itself.

**Steer Wrestling** In this event (also called bull-dogging), a steer that may weigh as much as 700 pounds runs out of a chute, tripping a barrier line, which is the signal for two cowboys to pursue the animal. One cowboy – the hazer – tries to keep the steer running in a straight line, while the other cowboy – the wrestler – rides alongside the steer and jumps off his horse trying to grip the steer's head and horns – this at speeds approaching 40 miles per hour! The wrestler must then wrestle the steer to the ground. The best cowboys can accomplish this in under five seconds.

**Barrel Racing** Three large barrels are set up in a triangle, and the rider must race around them in a clover shape. The turns are incredibly tight, and the racer must come out of them at full speed to do well. There's a five-second penalty for tipping over a barrel. Good times are around 15 to 17 seconds.

**Team Roping** A team of two horseback ropers pursues a steer running out of the chute. The first roper must catch the steer by the head or horns and then wrap the rope around the saddle horn. The second team member then lassos the steer's two rear legs in one throw. Good times are as low as five seconds.

**Bull Riding** Riding a bucking and spinning 2000-pound bull is wilder and more dangerous than bronc riding, and it is often the crowd's favorite event. Using one heavily gloved hand, the cowboy holds on to a rope that is wrapped around the bull. And that's it – nothing else to hold on to, and no other rules apart from staying on for eight seconds and not touching the bull with your free hand. Scoring is the same as for bronc riding.

**Books** For a full overview on rodeo, consult Kristine Fredriksson's *American Rodeo from Buffalo Bill to Big Business* (College Station: Texas A&M University Press, 1985), Clifford P Westermeier's *Man, Beast, Dust: The Story of Rodeo* (Lincoln: University of Nebraska Press, 1987; originally published in 1948), Teresa Jordan's *Cowgirls: Women of the American West* (Lincoln: University of Nebraska Press, 1992) and Mary Lou LeCompte's *Cowgirls of the Rodeo: Pioneer Professional Athletes* (Chicago: University of Illinois Press, 1993). ■

**October**

*International Balloon Fiesta*, held the second week in Albuquerque, New Mexico, is the biggest gathering of hot-air balloons in the world.

*World Senior Games* are held in mid-October in St George, Utah.

*Fat Tire Festival*, sometime in late October, includes mountain-bike races in and around Moab, Utah.

**November**

*Indian National Finals Rodeo* is hosted in mid-November in Albuquerque, New Mexico.

*Thunderbird Balloon Race* is held in mid-November in Glendale, Arizona.

**December**

*Red Rock Balloon Rally* takes place the first weekend in Red Rock State Park, Gallup, New Mexico.

## POST & TELECOMMUNICATIONS
### Postal Rates
Postage rates increase every few years. The next increase is expected in 1997, when postage rates will probably go up by about 10%. Currently, rates for 1st-class mail within the USA are 32¢ for letters up to one ounce (23¢ for each additional ounce) and 20¢ for postcards.

International airmail rates (except Canada and Mexico) are 60¢ for a half-ounce letter, 95¢ for a one-ounce letter and 39¢ for each additional half ounce. International postcard rates are 40¢. Letters to Canada are 46¢ for a one-ounce letter, 23¢ for each additional ounce and 30¢ for a postcard. Letters to Mexico are 35¢ for a half-ounce letter, 45¢ for a one-ounce letter and 30¢ for a postcard. Aerogrammes are 45¢.

The cost for parcels airmailed anywhere within the USA is $3 for two pounds or less, increasing by $1 per pound up to $6 for five pounds. For heavier items, rates differ according to the distance mailed. Books, periodicals and computer disks can be sent by a cheaper 4th-class rate.

### Sending Mail
If you have the correct postage, you can drop your mail into any blue mail box. These are found at many convenient locations including shopping centers, airports, street corners etc. The times of the next mail pickup are written on the inside of the lid of the mail box. This sign also indicates the location of the nearest mail box with later or more frequent pickup.

If you need to buy stamps or weigh your mail, go to the nearest post office. The addresses of each town's main post office is given in the text. In addition, larger towns have branch post offices and post office centers in some supermarkets and drugstores. For the address of the nearest office, call the main post office listed under 'Postal Service' in the 'US Government' section in the white pages of the telephone directory.

Usually, post offices in main towns are open from 8:00 am to 5 pm Monday to Friday and 8 am to 3 pm on Saturday, but it all depends on the branch. The major cities have a 24-hour Express Mail service (at a higher cost) in the city's main post office.

### Receiving Mail
You can have mail sent to you care of General Delivery at any post office that has its own zip (postal) code. It's best to have your intended date of arrival (if the sender knows it) clearly marked on the envelope. Mail is usually held for 10 days before it's returned to the sender. Alternatively, have mail sent to the local representative of American Express or Thomas Cook, which provide mail service for their clients.

### Telephone
All phone numbers within the USA consist of a three-digit area code followed by a seven-digit local number. If you are calling locally, just dial the seven-digit number. If you are calling long distance, dial 1 + the three-digit area code + the seven-digit number.

Area codes for the Southwest are 801 for all of Utah, 505 for all of New Mexico, and 520 for all of Arizona except Maricopa County (ie, Phoenix and surrounding towns), which has a 602 area code. If you're calling from abroad, the international country code for the USA is '1'.

The 800 area code is designated for toll-free numbers within the USA and sometimes from Canada as well. Some can be called from anywhere in the USA, others are only used within the state. Those that are state specific are indicated in the text.

The 900 area code is designated for calls for which the caller pays at a premium rate. They have a reputation of being sleazy operations – a smorgasbord of phone sex at $2.99 a minute is one of many offerings.

Directory assistance can be reached locally by dialing 411. For directory assistance outside your area code, dial 1 + the three-digit area code of the place you want to call + 555-1212. For example, to obtain directory assistance for a toll-free number, dial 1 (800) 555-1212. Area codes for places outside the region are listed in telephone directories.

Many businesses use letters instead of

numbers for their telephone numbers in an attempt to make them snappy and memorable. Sometimes it works, but sometimes it's difficult to read the letters on the dial pad. If you can't read the letters, here they are: 1 doesn't get any; 2 – ABC, 3 – DEF, 4 – GHI, 5 – JKL, 6 – MNO, 7 – PRS, 8 – TUV, 9 – WXY. Sorry no Qs or Zs.

**Rates** Local calls usually cost 25¢ at pay phones, but watch out for occasional private phones which may charge more. Many hotels (especially the more expensive ones) add a service charge of 50¢ to $1 for each local call made from a room phone and they also have hefty surcharges for long-distance calls. Public pay phones, which can be found in most lobbies, are always cheaper. You can pump in quarters, use a phone card, or make collect calls from pay phones. A new long-distance alternative is phone debit cards, which allow purchasers to pay in advance, with access through a 800 number. In amounts of $5, $10, $20 and $50, these are available in airports and from Western Union and some other sources.

When using phone credit cards, be aware of people watching you, especially in public places like airports. Thieves will memorize numbers and use them to make large numbers of international calls. Shield the telephone with your body when punching in your credit card number.

Long-distance rates vary depending on the destination and which telephone company you use – call the operator (0) for rates information. Don't ask the operator to put your call through, however, because operator-assisted calls are much more expensive than direct-dial calls. Generally, nights (11 pm to 8 am), all day Saturday and from 8 am to 5 pm Sunday are the cheapest times to call (60% discount). A 35% discount applies in the evenings from 5 to 11 pm Sunday to Friday. Daytime calls (8 am to 5 pm Monday to Friday) are full-price calls within the USA.

**International Calls** To make an international call direct, dial 011, then the country code, followed by the area code and the phone number. You may need to wait as long as 45 seconds for the ringing to start. International rates vary depending on the time of day and the destination. For example, the cheapest rates to London are between 6 pm and 7 am, while when calling Melbourne, the cheapest rates are from 3 am to 2 pm. Again, rates vary depending on the telephone company used and the destination. Call the operator (0) for rates. The first minute is always more expensive than the following extra minutes.

### Fax, Telegram & E-mail
Fax machines are easy to find in the USA, at shipping companies like Mail Boxes, Etc, photocopy services and hotel business service centers, but be prepared to pay high prices (over $1 a page). Telegrams can be sent from Western Union (☎ 1 (800) 325-6000). E-mail is quickly becoming a preferred method of communication; however, unless you have a laptop and modem that can be plugged into a telephone socket, it's difficult to get on-line. Hotel business service centers may provide connections, and trendy restaurants and cafes sometimes offer internet service as well.

### TIME
The Southwest is on mountain time, which is seven hours behind Greenwich Mean Time. Daylight-saving time begins on the first Sunday in April, when clocks are put forward one hour, and ends on the last Sunday in October, when the clocks are turned back one hour.

Arizona does not use daylight-saving time, and so during that period it is eight hours behind Greenwich Mean Time and one hour behind the rest of the Southwest. The Navajo Indian Reservation, most of which lies in Arizona, does use daylight-saving time (but the small Hopi Indian Reservation, which lies surrounded by the Navajo Indian Reservation, doesn't).

### ELECTRICITY
The entire USA uses 110 V and 60 cycles and the plugs have two (flat) or three (two

flat, one round) pins. Plugs with three pins don't fit into a two-hole socket, but adapters are easy to buy. Two-pin plugs, especially ones with equal dimensions, can easily slip out of the socket. Should this happen a quick remedy is to stretch the prongs apart a bit for a tighter fit.

## LAUNDRY

There are self-service, coin-operated laundry facilities in most towns of any size and in better campgrounds. Washing a load costs about $1 and drying it another $1. Coin-operated vending machines sell single-wash size packages of detergent but it's usually cheaper to pick up a small box at the supermarket. Some laundries have attendants who will wash, dry and fold your clothes for you for an additional charge. To find a laundry, look under 'Laundries' or 'Laundries – Self-Service' in the yellow pages of the telephone directory. Dry cleaners are also listed under 'Laundries' or 'Cleaners'.

## RECYCLING

Traveling in a car seems to generate large numbers of cans and bottles. If you'd like to save these for recycling, you'll find recycling centers in the larger towns. Materials accepted are usually plastic and glass bottles, aluminum and tin cans and newspapers. Some campgrounds and a few roadside rest areas also have recycling bins next to the trash bins so look out for those.

Perhaps better than recycling is to reduce your use of these products. Many gas stations and convenience stores sell large plastic insulated cups with lids which are inexpensive and ideal for hot and cold drinks. You can usually save a few cents by using your cup to buy drinks.

Despite the appearance of many large cities, littering is frowned upon by most Americans. Travelers need to respect the places they are visiting even though it may seem that some locals think it's OK to trash their territory. Some states have implemented anti-littering laws (which impose fines for violation) to try to curb the problem. When hiking and camping in the wilderness, take out everything you bring in – this includes *any* kind of garbage you may create.

## WEIGHTS & MEASURES

Despite the evangelical exhortations of metric missionaries and concerted efforts on the part of federal authorities since the 1970s, Americans continue to resist the imposition of the metric system.

Distances are in feet (ft), yards (yds) and miles (m). Three feet equal one yard, which is .914 meters; 1760 yards or 5280 feet equal one mile. Dry weights are in ounces (oz), pounds (lbs) and tons (16 ounces are one pound; 2000 pounds are one ton), but liquid measures differ from dry measures. One pint equals 16 fluid ounces; two pints equal one quart, a common measure for liquids like milk (which is also sold in half gallons (two quarts) and gallons (four quarts). Gasoline is dispensed by the US gallon, which is about 20% less than the imperial gallon. Pints and quarts are also 20% less than imperial ones. Drivers in the southern parts of Arizona and New Mexico may note distances are also marked in km near the Mexican border. This aids Mexican drivers on trips into the USA. The most significant exception to the use of Imperial measures is the wine industry, whose standard size is 700 ml, but the labels of canned and liquid supermarket foods usually list both imperial measures and their international equivalents. There is a conversion chart at the back of the book to make this all easier.

## BOOKS

Many thousands of books have been written about the Southwest, and here I can introduce only a few. Many of these, however, have comprehensive indexes that will lead you as far as you want to go. If you feel I missed one of your favorite books, write and tell me. I'll read it and include it – if I like it!

### Travel Guidebooks

There are many guidebooks about the Southwest; they are updated every couple of years and so I don't give dates. Ask your bookseller or librarian to check the date of the most recent edition.

The following are standard guides from the travel series of well-known publishers. Moon Publications has the most exhaustive treatment in its *Arizona Traveler's Handbook* by Bill Weir & Robert Blake; *New Mexico Handbook* by Stephen Metzger; and the *Utah Handbook* by Bill Weir. Prentice Hall's *Frommer's Arizona* by Karl Samson and *Frommer's New Mexico* by John Gottberg are also good references. Fodor's Travel Publications has the multi-authored *Fodor's Arizona* and *Fodor's New Mexico*. Both Frommer's and Fodor's have guides to Albuquerque, Santa Fe and Taos. There is also the *Berlitz Travelers Guide to the American Southwest*. If you have used any of these series before, you know what to expect.

More independent guides include the very readable *Journey to the High Southwest* by Robert L Casey (Globe Pequot Press). This reads like a travelogue but is full of useful background to Santa Fe and the Four Corners area. Another breezy guide is *The New Mexico Guide* by Charles L Cadieux (Fulcrum Publishing). Bill Jamison's *The Insider's Guide to Santa Fe* (Harvard Common Press) is also useful.

Specialty guides, dealing with history, flora and fauna and other topics are listed under the specialty heading.

## Outdoor Recreation

Of the hundreds of books available about hiking, climbing, river running, canyoneering, bicycling and other activities in the Southwest, I present some general ones here. Books about a specific place are mentioned in the appropriate parts of the text. Most of the books below have extensive bibliographies.

*Hiking the Southwest* by Dave Ganci (Sierra Club Books, 1983) covers hikes in Arizona, New Mexico and west Texas. For suggestions about hiking the desert as safely and comfortably as possible, read Ganci's *Desert Hiking* (Wilderness Press, 1987) and *Desert Survival* (ICS Books,

1991). Falcon Press in Montana publishes a series of hiking guides including *The Hiker's Guide to Arizona* by Stewart Aitchison & Bruce Grubbs (1991), *The Hiker's Guide to New Mexico* by Laurence Parent (1991), and *The Hiker's Guide to Utah* by Dave Hall (1991).

*Adventuring in Arizona* by John Annerino (Sierra Club Books, 1991) gives a selection of hikes, car tours, river expeditions, climbs and canyoneering adventures all over the state. *Utah's National Parks: Hiking, Camping and Vacationing in Utah's Canyon Country* by Ron Adkison (Wilderness Press, 1991) is a thorough and useful book with good historical background.

*Mountain Bike Rides of the West* by Dennis Coello (Northland Publishing, 1989) details 20 classic tours of which a dozen are in the Southwest. Also look for *Bicycle Touring Arizona* (1988) and *Bicycle Touring Utah* (1988) from the same author and publisher.

*Rivers of the Southwest: A Boater's Guide to the Rivers of Colorado, New Mexico, Arizona and Utah* by Fletcher Anderson and Ann Hopkinson (Pruett Publishing, 1987) is an introduction. There are plenty of books about individual rivers.

## General Overviews

Compass American Guides publishes *Arizona* by Larry Cheek (1991), *New Mexico* by Nancy Harbert (1991) and *Utah* by Tom & Gayen Wharton (1991). Each is well illustrated with both old and new photos and drawings and gives great background information. Their travel information for hotels and restaurants is limited to a few pages of brief listings. Beautiful photographs and standard background essays are the hallmark of the Insight Guides Series – their *American Southwest* book, edited by Hans Hoefer (1989), is no exception.

Great photos and insightful essays by some of the region's best writers are found in *Arizona, the Land and the People*, edited by Tom Miller (University of Arizona Press, 1986). Detailed writings about many aspects of New Mexico appear in *New*

*Mexico: A New Guide to the Colorful State* by L Chilton et al (University of New Mexico Press, 1984). Neither offers hotel or restaurant information.

## Archaeology & History
*Those Who Came Before* by Robert H & Florence C Lister (Southwest Parks and Monuments Association, 2nd edition, 1994) is my favorite source of readable information about the prehistory of the Southwest and about the archaeological sites of the national parks and monuments of this area. It is extensively indexed.

*Indians of the American Southwest* by Steven L Walker (Camelback/Canyonlands, 1994) is a slim, large-format book with introductory essays to the ancient inhabitants of the area, illustrated by some of the Southwest's premier photographers. An expanded version by the same author/publisher is *The Southwest: A Pictorial History of the Land and Its People* (1993).

The best general history is *The Southwest* by David Lavender (University of New Mexico Press, 1980). It has a detailed (if dated) index. *The Smithsonian Guide to Historic America – The Desert States* by Michael S Durham (Stewart, Tabori & Chang, 1990) is a beautifully illustrated guide to the historical sites of the region.

*New Mexico – An Interpretive History* by Marc Simmon (Norton, 1977) was originally subtitled 'A Bicentennial Guide' and is reprinted by the University of New Mexico Press (1988). It offers an easy-to-read general overview of the state's history from 1776 to 1976. Others in this series are *Utah – A Bicentennial History* by Charles S Peterson (Norton, 1977) and *Arizona – A Bicentennial History* by Lawrence Clark Powell (Norton, 1976).

## Geology
*Basin and Range* by John McPhee (Farrar, Straus & Giroux, 1981) is as much a journey as a popular geological text. It covers Nevada as well as Utah, but is a recommended read.

*Roadside Geology of Arizona* (1983), *Roadside Geology of New Mexico* (1986) and *Roadside Geology of Utah* (1990), all by Halka Chronic (Mountain Press), are good guides for the curious non-geologist. They describe the geology along major roads and are well illustrated. *Geology of Utah* by William L Stokes (Utah Museum of Natural History, 1986) is a more technical overview of that state's geology.

Useful and readable geology books about the national parks include *A Guide to Grand Canyon Geology along the Bright Angel Trail* by Dave Thayer (Grand Canyon Natural History Association, 1986). This will take you back 2000 million years in time as you descend to the bottom of the Grand Canyon. Another choice is *The Sculpturing of Zion – With Road Guide to the Geology of Zion National Park* by Wayne L Hamilton (Zion Natural History Association, 1984). An introduction for the nonspecialist is *The Colorado Plateau: A Geologic History* by Donald L Baars (University of New Mexico Press, 1983).

## Natural History
A tremendous variety of books will help you identify Southwestern plants and animals, tell you where you can see them and give you insight into their biology.

The Peterson Field Guide Series has almost 40 excellent books including *(A Field Guide to the) Mammals* by William H Burt and Richard P Grossenheider (3rd edition, 1976), *Western Birds* by Roger Tory Peterson (3rd edition, 1990), *Western Reptiles and Amphibians* by Robert C Stebbins (1985), *Western Butterflies* by Tilden & Smith and *Southwestern and Texas Wildflowers* by Niehaus, Ripper & Savage. All are published by Houghton Mifflin.

An excellent series of pocket books published by the Southwest Parks & Monuments Association in Tucson helps you identify the region's plants. Titles include *Flowers of the Southwest Deserts* by Natt N Dodge & Jeanne R Janish (1985), *Flowers of the Southwest Mountains* by Leslie P Arnberger & Janish (1982), *Flowers of the Southwest Mesas* by Pauline M Patraw & Janish (1977), and *Shrubs and Trees of the Southwestern Uplands* by

Francis H Elmore & Janish (1976). Also from this publisher is *Mammals of the Southwest Deserts* by George Olin & Dale Thompson (1982), which is less a field guide and more a description of the mammals illustrated with full-page drawings.

There are numerous other field guides. The series of *Audubon Society Field Guides* (Alfred A Knopf) covers birds, plants and animals, arranged by color and using photos – a departure from the standard field guides, which are arranged in biological sequence and are illustrated by color paintings. The Audubon Society Nature Guide *Deserts* by James A MacMahon (Alfred A Knopf, 1985) gives a fine overview of all four Southwestern deserts as well as being a field guide to the most important plants and animals of these regions. The *Golden Field Guide* series (Western Publishing Company) is known for its simple approach and is often preferred by beginners. The National Geographic Society's *Field Guide to the Birds of North America* (2nd edition, 1987) is well done and one of the most detailed.

Birders may want to supplement their field guides with *Birds in Southeastern Arizona* by William A Davis & Stephen M Russell (Tucson Audubon Society, 4th edition, 1995). This book describes the seasonal distribution and abundance of birds in what is one of the premier birding 'hot spots' in the country, and gives directions on how to travel to scores of the best birding areas.

*Utah Wildlife Viewing Guide* by Jim Cole (1990), *Arizona Wildlife Viewing Guide* by John N Carr (1992), and *New Mexico Wildlife Viewing Guide* by Jane S MacCarter (1994), all from Falcon Press, list scores of places to see wildlife. Access information and descriptions of the probability of seeing the most important species at specific sites are given.

Several excellent books about Southwestern natural history are designed to be read rather than used as field guides. I recommend all the following. *The Great Southwestern Nature Factbook* by Susan J Tweit (Alaska Northwest Books, 1992) is full of interesting details about anything from Gila monsters to the Grand Canyon. *The Desert Year* by Joseph Wood Krutch (1951, reprinted by University of Arizona Press, 1985) is a classic account of nature in the Sonoran desert. More detailed are John Alcock's excellent and very readable *Sonoran Desert Spring* (University of Chicago Press, 1990) and *Sonoran Desert Summer* (University of Arizona Press, 1990). *Gathering the Desert* by Gary Paul Nabhan (University of Arizona Press, 1985) describes in splendid and fascinating detail 12 desert plants and their importance to Native Americans.

Ann Zwinger writes eloquently in *The Mysterious Lands: A Naturalist Explores the Four Great Deserts of the Southwest* (Dutton, 1989). Her *Run, River, Run: A Naturalist's Journey down One of the Great Rivers of the American West*, reprinted by the University of Arizona Press, 1984 describes her journey down the Green River from its headwaters in Wyoming to its confluence with the Colorado River in southeastern Utah. And her *Wind in the Rock* (Harper & Row, 1978) explores the natural history of the Four Corners region.

## Native Americans

The best introduction for the serious student is the 20-volume *Handbook of North American Indians* (Smithsonian Institution). The volumes that cover this region are *Volume 9: Southwest* edited by Alfonso Ortiz (1979); *Volume 10: Southwest* edited by Alfonso Ortiz (1983); and *Volume 11: Great Basin* edited by Warren L D'Azevedo (1986).

An even better introduction for the generalist is *The People: Indians of the Southwest* by Stephen Trimble (School of American Research Press, 1993). The author traveled among the area's many tribes, photographing and interviewing them for almost a decade. Much of the book is the words of the Indians themselves – a remarkable and satisfying book. The excellent 14-page annotated bibliography will lead you to many other books.

Some introductions to Southwestern

Indian arts & crafts include *Navajo Rugs: How to Find, Evaluate, Buy and Care for Them* by Don Dedera (Northland Publishing, 1990); *Hopi Kachinas: The Complete Guide to Collecting Kachina Dolls* by Barton Wright (Northland Publishing, 1977); and *Hopi Silver: A Brief History of Hopi Silversmithing* by Margaret Wright (Northland Publishing, 1989).

Native American novelists and writers are mentioned in the section on fiction.

### Fiction

It comes as some surprise that one of the earliest novels about the Southwest is Arthur Conan Doyle's first Sherlock Holmes mystery, *A Study in Scarlet* (1887). Half the book is set in the 'Alkali Plains' of Mormon Utah. Another surprise is that the author of *Ben Hur* (1880) was New Mexico Governor Lew Wallace. Other early novels of note include Zane Grey's westerns, of which *Riders of the Purple Sage* (1912) is the best known. Grey spent years living in Arizona. *Death Comes for the Archbishop* (1927) by Willa Cather is a novel based on the life of Bishop Jean Baptiste Lamy, who was the first archbishop of Santa Fe. It gives insights into New Mexican life during territorial days. Oliver La Farge won a Pulitzer prize for his *Laughing Boy* (1929), a somewhat romantic portrayal of Navajo life.

*House Made of Dawn* (1969, various reprints) won Native American novelist and poet N Scott Momaday a Pulitzer prize. His theme of a Pueblo Indian's struggle to return physically and spiritually to his home after fighting in WW II is echoed in another superb book, *Ceremony* by Leslie Marmon Silko (Viking Press, 1977). Silko, herself a Pueblo Indian, is one of the best Southwestern novelists. Other critically acclaimed novels by Silko include *Almanac of the Dead* and *Storyteller*.

Tony Hillerman, an Anglo, writes award-winning mystery novels that take place on the Navajo, Hopi and Zuni Reservations. Even Indians find his writing to be true to life. Following the adventures of Navajo policemen Jim Chee and Joe Leaphorn is a lot of fun, particularly when you are driving around the reservations of the Four Corners area. Hillerman's first mystery novel was *The Blessing Way* (1970), and he has written about a dozen since then.

*The Monkey Wrench Gang* by Edward Abbey (1975, various reprints) is hugely fun to read, which is more than can be said of many classic novels, and this one certainly is a classic. It's a fictional and comic account of real people who become 'eco-warriors' – their plan is to blow up Glen Canyon Dam before it floods Glen Canyon. You don't have to believe in industrial sabotage to enjoy this book – or any of his others. *The Milagro Beanfield War* by John Nichols (1974, various reprints) tells the story of bean growers trying to protect their New Mexican lands against developers. It's a good book, and a good movie, too (directed by Robert Redford, same title).

My favorite recent Southwestern novelist is Barbara Kingsolver, whose novels are superb portrayals of people living in the Southwest. *The Bean Trees* (Harper & Row, 1988) echoes the author's own life – a young woman from rural Kentucky moves to Tucson. *Animal Dreams* (Harper & Row, 1990) gives wonderful insights into the lives of people from a small Hispanic village near the Arizona-New Mexico border and from an Indian pueblo. Don't miss these books.

### Miscellaneous

The first book I remember reading about the Southwest was *Desert Solitaire: Season in the Wilderness* by Edward Abbey (1968, various reprints). I read it in 1974 during my first visit to the Southwest, and it has remained one of my favorite books. It describes the author's job as a park ranger in Arches National Park in the 1950s, when the park was still a monument reached by a dirt road and locals easily outnumbered tourists in nearby Moab. Abbey shares his philosophy and passions about the desert, the mismanagement of the Southwest, and the problems of mass tourism – which he foresaw with striking clarity. This book is a classic.

Indian dance at the Inter-Tribal Ceremonial in Gallup, New Mexico (RR)

Morning Singer kachina doll by B David, Navajo Nation (RR)

White House ruin, Canyon de Chelly, Arizona (EB)

Richly decorated altar in San Xavier del Bac Mission near Tucson, Arizona (RR)

Paul Bunyan stands tall in Tucson, Arizona. (RR)

Roy Purcell's cliff murals outside of Chloride, Arizona (RR)

Hornos (ovens) are used for baking throughout New Mexico. (RR)

Other important books are *Grizzly Years: In Search of the American Wilderness* by Doug Peacock (Henry Holt & Co, 1990). Peacock was a friend of Edward Abbey's (one of the Monkey Wrench Gang members was based on Peacock) and is one of the world's experts on grizzly bears. Although much of the action takes place in the northern Rockies, with Vietnam flashbacks, the narrative occasionally returns to Tucson, where the author lives. Another Abbey protégé is Charles Bowden, who wrote eloquent essays about Arizona in *Blue Desert* (University of Arizona Press, 1986) and *Frog Mountain Blues*. More insightful essays on the Southwest are found in *The Telling Distance* by Bruce Berger (Breitenbush Books, 1990).

Also consider reading *Cadillac Desert: The American West and Its Disappearing Water* by Marc Reisner (Penguin, 1986), which is a thorough account of how the exploding populations of Western states have utilized every possible drop of available water. *The Man Who Walked Through Time* by Colin Fletcher (Random House, 1972) tells the story of the author's many weeks backpacking the length of the Grand Canyon – the first account of such a trip.

## MAPS

Free state maps are available from state tourist information offices and welcome centers. Members of the American Automobile Association (AAA) can receive free state maps from their local AAA office. Also ask your AAA about their recommended *Indian Country* map, which covers the Four Corners area in excellent detail. The AAA also has maps of major cities – Albuquerque, Phoenix, Tucson, Santa Fe and Salt Lake City – which are available to nonmembers for a few dollars. City maps are often provided at the appropriate chamber of commerce for free or at a low cost.

Colorful national park maps are free at each national park after you pay the entrance fee. USFS ranger stations sell maps of their national forest for a few dollars.

Hikers and backpackers can purchase topographical maps from the US Geological Survey, Map and Book Sales, Denver, CO 80225 (☎ (303) 236 7477). A list of maps is available upon request. Many camping stores, US National Park visitors centers and US National Forest ranger stations sell USGS maps of their immediate area. The maps most useful for hikers are the 1:62,500 scale (approximately one inch to one mile).

## Atlases

Visitors spending a significant amount of time in the region should try to acquire the appropriate state volume of the DeLorme Mapping series of atlases and gazetteers, which contain detailed topographic and highway maps at a scale of 1:250,000 as well as very helpful listings of campgrounds, historic sites, parks, natural features and even scenic drives. Readily available in good bookstores, these are especially useful off the main highways and cost about $20 each.

## MEDIA

The media is a huge industry in the USA as is illustrated by the fact that advertisers spent over $44,000 million on ads in newspapers, magazines, TV and radio during 1994. The USA supports a wide spectrum of newspapers, magazines and book publishers, both nationally and regionally.

Radio and TV also support a wide variety of news programs, though most of the reporting tends to center on the USA.

### Newspapers & Magazines

There are over 1500 daily newspapers published in the USA, with a combined circulation of about 60 million. The newspaper with the highest circulation is *Wall Street Journal* followed by *USA Today*, *New York Times* and *Los Angeles Times*, which are all available in major cities.

### Radio & TV

All rental cars have car stereos and travelers can choose from hundreds of radio stations. Some general suggestions for radio listening from your car are as follows. Most stations have a range of less than 100 miles, so you'll have to keep changing stations as you drive. In the southern parts of the region, stations broadcasting from Mexico (in Spanish) can easily be picked up. In and near major cities, you'll have scores of stations to choose from with a wide variety of music and entertainment. In rural areas, be prepared for a predominance of country & western music, Christian programming, local news and 'talk radio'.

There are many talk radio stations, especially on the AM dial, and they have gained much popularity. They can be entertaining, but don't believe most of what you hear. As Bill Watterson's cartoon character Calvin describes it: 'I'll spout simplistic opinions for hours on end, ridicule anyone who disagrees with me, and generally foster divisiveness, cynicism, and a lower level of public dialog!'

National Public Radio features a more level-headed approach to news, discussion, music and more. NPR normally broadcasts on the lower end of the FM dial.

For listings of all the radio stations in the country, complete with their broadcasting frequency and description of the type of music or show, consult the *Broadcasting and Cable Yearbook* from Bowker Publishing.

All the major TV networks have affiliated stations throughout the USA. These include ABC, CBS, NBC, FOX and PBS. Cable News Network (CNN), a cable channel, provides continuous news coverage.

## PHOTOGRAPHY & VIDEO
### Film
Print film for amateur photography is widely available at supermarkets and discount drugstores throughout the Southwest. Color print film has a greater latitude than color slide film; this means that print film can handle a wider range of light and shadow than slide film. However, slide film, particularly the slower speeds (under 100 ASA), has better resolution than print film. Like B&W film, the availability of slide film outside of major cities is rare or at inflated prices when found.

For certain subjects, like Indian petroglyphs, carry high-speed (400 ASA) film to avoid using flash, which is not permitted at these sites.

Film can be damaged by excessive heat, so don't leave your camera and film in the car on a hot summer's day and avoid placing your camera on the dash while you are driving.

It's worth carrying a spare battery for your camera to avoid disappointment when your camera dies in the middle of nowhere. If you're buying a new camera for your trip do so several weeks before you leave and practice using it.

Drugstores are a good place to get your film cheaply processed. If it's dropped off by noon, you can usually pick it up the next day. A roll of 100 ASA 35 mm color film with 24 exposures will cost about $6 to get processed.

If you want your pictures right away, you can find one-hour processing services in the yellow pages under 'Photo Processing'. The prices tend to creep up to the $11 scale, so be prepared to pay dearly. Many one-hour photo finishers operate in the larger cities, and a few can be found near tourist attractions.

### Technique
Many parts of the Southwest experience over 350 days of sunshine annually, so there's plenty of light for photography. However, when the sun is high in the sky, photographs tend to emphasize shadows and wash out highlights. It's best to take photos during the early morning and the late afternoon hours when light is softer. This is especially true of landscape photography. Always protect camera lenses with a haze or ultraviolet (UV) filter. At high altitudes, a UV film may not adequately prevent washed-out photos; a polarized filter can correct this problem and, incidentally, dramatically emphasizes cloud formations in mountain and plains landscapes.

## Airport Security

All passengers on flights have to pass their luggage through X-ray machines. Technology as it is today doesn't jeopardize lower speed film, but it's best to carry film and cameras with you and ask the X-ray inspector to visually check your camera and film.

## Video Systems

Overseas visitors who are thinking of purchasing videos should remember that the USA uses the National Television System Committee (NTSC) color TV standard, which is not compatible with other standards (Phase Alternative Line or PAL; Système Electronique Couleur avec Mémoire or SECAM) used in Africa, Europe, Asia and Australasia unless converted. It's best to keep those seemingly cheap movie purchases on hold until you get home.

## HEALTH

Generally speaking, the USA is a healthy place to visit. There are no prevalent diseases or risks associated with traveling here, and the country is well-served by hospitals. However, because of the high cost of health care, international travelers should take out comprehensive travel insurance before they leave. If you're from a country with socialized medicine, you should find out what you'll need to do in order to be reimbursed for out-of-pocket money you may spend for health care in the USA.

Also, if you should fall ill in the USA, avoid going to emergency rooms. Although these are often the easiest places to go for treatment, they are also incredibly expensive. Many city hospitals have 'urgent care clinics', which are designed to deal with walk-in clients with less than catastrophic injuries and illnesses. You'll pay a lot less for treatment at these clinics. If you know someone in the area, consider asking them to ring their doctor: often private doctors are willing to examine foreign visitors as a courtesy to their regular patients, but a fee, often around $100 may still be applied.

## Travel Health Guides

There are a number of books on travel health.

*Staying Healthy in Asia, Africa & Latin America*, Dick Schroeder (Chico: Moon Publications, 1994), though not specifically oriented toward North American travel, this is probably the best all-round guide. It's compact but very detailed and well organized.

*Travelers' Health*, Dr Richard Dawood (New York: Random House, 1994), is comprehensive, easy to read, authoritative and highly recommended, but rather large to lug around.

*Where There is No Doctor*, David Werner (Macmillan, 1994), is a very detailed guide, more suited to those working in undeveloped countries than to travelers.

*Travel with Children*, Maureen Wheeler (Lonely Planet Publications, 1995), offers basic advice on travel health for younger children.

## Predeparture Preparations

**Health Insurance** A travel insurance policy to cover theft, loss and medical problems is a good idea, especially in the USA, where some hospitals will refuse care without evidence of insurance. There are a wide variety of policies and your travel agent will have recommendations. International student travel policies handled by STA Travel or other student travel organizations are usually good value. Some policies offer lower and higher medical expenses options, but the higher one is chiefly for countries like the USA with extremely high medical costs. Check the small print.

- Some policies specifically exclude 'dangerous activities' like scuba diving, motorcycling and even trekking. If these activities are on your agenda avoid this sort of policy.
- You may prefer a policy which pays doctors or hospitals directly, rather than your having to pay first and claim later. If you have to claim later, keep all documentation. Some policies ask you to call back (reverse charges) to a center in your home country for an immediate assessment of your problem.
- Check whether the policy covers ambulance fees or an emergency flight home. If you have to stretch out you will need two seats and somebody has to pay for it!

**Medical Kit** It's useful to carry a small, straightforward medical kit. This should include:

* Aspirin, acetominophen or panadol, for pain or fever
* Antihistamine (such as Benadryl), which is useful as a decongestant for colds, and to ease the itch from allergies, insect bites or stings or to help prevent motion sickness
* Antibiotics, which are useful for traveling off the beaten track, but they must be prescribed and you should carry the prescription with you
* Kaolin preparation (Pepto-Bismol), Immodium or Lomotil, for stomach upsets
* Rehydration mixture, to treat severe diarrhea, which is particularly important if you're traveling with children
* Antiseptic, mercurochrome and antibiotic powder or similar 'dry' spray, for cuts and grazes
* Calamine lotion, to ease irritation from bites or stings
* Bandages, for minor injuries
* Scissors, tweezers and a thermometer (airlines prohibit mercury thermometers)
* Insect repellent, sun-screen lotion, chapstick and water purification tablets.

**Note** Antibiotics are specific to the infections they can treat. Ideally they should be administered only under medical supervision and never taken indiscriminately. They are only available under medical prescription in the USA. Take only the recommended dose at the prescribed intervals and continue using it for the prescribed period, even if symptoms disappear earlier. Stop immediately if there are any serious reactions and don't use the antibiotic at all if you are unsure if you have the correct one.

**Health Preparations** Make sure you're healthy before you start traveling. If you are embarking on a long trip, make sure your teeth are in good shape. If you wear glasses, take a spare pair and your prescription. You can get new spectacles made up quickly and competently for well under $100, depending on the prescription and frame you choose. If you require a particular medication, take an adequate supply and bring a prescription in case you lose your supply.

**Immunizations** Vaccinations provide protection against diseases you might meet along the way. For some countries no immunizations are necessary, but the further off the beaten track you go the more necessary it is to take precautions.

It is important to understand the distinction between vaccines recommended for travel in certain areas and those required by law. Essentially the number of vaccines subject to international health regulations has been dramatically reduced over the last 10 years. Currently yellow fever is the only vaccine subject to international health regulations. Vaccination as an entry requirement is usually only enforced when coming from an infected area.

On the other hand a number of vaccines are recommended for travel in certain areas. These may not be required by law but are recommended for your own personal protection. All vaccinations should be recorded on an International Health Certificate, which is available from your physician or government health department.

Plan ahead for getting your vaccinations: some of them require an initial shot followed by a booster, while some vaccinations should not be given together. It is recommended you seek medical advice at least six weeks prior to travel.

Most travelers from Western countries will have been immunized against various diseases during childhood but your doctor may still recommend booster shots against measles or polio, diseases still prevalent in many developing countries. The period of protection offered by vaccinations differs widely and some are contraindicated if you are pregnant.

In some countries immunizations are available from airport or government health centres. Travel agents or airline offices will tell you where. Vaccinations include:

*Smallpox* Smallpox has now been wiped out worldwide, so immunization is no longer necessary.

*Tetanus & Diphtheria* Boosters are necessary every 10 years and protection is highly recommended.

*Hepatitis A* The most common travel-acquired illness which can be prevented by vaccination. Protection can be provided in two ways – either with the antibody gamma globulin or with a new vaccine called Havrix, which provides long term immunity (possibly more than 10 years) after an initial course of two injections and a booster at one year. It may be more expensive than gamma globulin but certainly has many advantages, including length of protection and ease of administration. It is important to know that as a vaccine it will take about three weeks to provide satisfactory protection – hence the need for careful planning prior to travel.

Gamma globulin is not a vaccination but a ready-made antibody which has proven to be very successful in reducing the chances of hepatitis infection. Because it may interfere with the development of immunity, it should not be given until at least 10 days after administration of the last vaccine needed; it should also be given as close as possible to departure because it is at its most effective in the first few weeks after administration, and the effectiveness tapers off gradually between three and six months.

## Basic Rules
Care in what you eat and drink is the most important health rule; stomach upsets are the most likely travel health problem (between 30% and 50% of travelers in a two-week stay experience this) but the majority of these upsets will be relatively minor. Don't become paranoid; trying the local food is part of the experience of travel, after all.

**Water** Bottled drinking water, both carbonated and non-carbonated, is widely available in the USA.

**Water Purification** The simplest way of purifying water is to boil it thoroughly – vigorous boiling for ten minutes should be satisfactory even at a high altitude (where water boils at a lower temperature and germs are less likely to be killed).

Simple filtering will not remove all dangerous organisms, so if you cannot boil water it should be treated chemically. Chlorine tablets (Puritabs, Steritabs or other brand names) will kill many pathogens, including giardia and amoebic cysts, but is not 100% affective. Iodine is very effective in purifying water and is available in tablet form (such as Potable Aqua), but follow the directions carefully – too much iodine can be harmful.

If you can't find tablets, tincture of iodine (2%) or iodine crystals can be used. Four drops of tincture of iodine per liter or quart of clear water is the recommended dosage; let the treated water stand for 20 to 30 minutes before drinking. Iodine crystals can also be used to purify water, but this is a more complicated process, as you must first prepare a saturated iodine solution (iodine loses its effectiveness if exposed to air or damp, so keep it in a tightly sealed container). Flavored powder will disguise the taste of treated water and is a good idea if traveling with children.

**Food** If a place looks clean and well run and if the vendor also looks clean and healthy, then the food is probably safe. In general, places that are packed with travelers or locals will be fine, while empty restaurants are questionable.

*Nutrition* If your food is poor or limited in availability, if you're traveling hard and fast and therefore missing meals, or if you simply lose your appetite, you can soon start to lose weight and place your health at risk.

Make sure your diet is well balanced. Eggs, tofu, beans, lentils and nuts are all safe ways to get protein. Fruit you can peel (bananas, oranges or mandarins for example) is always safe and a good source of vitamins. Try to eat plenty of grains and bread. Remember that although food is generally safer if it is cooked well, overcooked food loses much of its nutritional value. If your diet isn't well balanced or if your food intake is insufficient, it's a good idea to take vitamin and iron pills.

In hot climates make sure you drink enough – don't rely on feeling thirsty to indicate when you should drink. Not needing to urinate or very dark yellow urine is a danger sign. Always carry a water bottle with you on long trips (see also Weather under Dangers & Annoyances). Excessive sweating can lead to loss of salt and therefore muscle cramping. Salt tablets are not a good idea as a preventative, but in places where salt is not used much adding salt to food can help.

### Everyday Health

Normal body temperature is 98.6°F or 37°C; more than 2°C or 4°F higher indicates a 'high' fever. The normal adult pulse rate is 60 to 80 per minute (children 80 to 100, babies 100 to 140). It is important to know how to take a temperature and a pulse rate.

Respiration (breathing) rate is also an indicator of illness. Count the number of breaths per minute: between 12 and 20 is normal for adults and older children (up to 30 for younger children, 40 for babies). People with a high fever or serious respiratory illness (like pneumonia) breathe more quickly than normal. More than 40 shallow breaths a minute usually means pneumonia.

### Medical Problems & Treatment

Potential medical problems can be broken down into several areas. Firstly there are the problems caused by extremes of temperature, altitude or motion. Then there are diseases and illnesses caused through poor environmental sanitation, insect bites or stings, and animal or human contact. Simple cuts, bites and scratches can also cause problems.

Self-diagnosis and treatment can be risky, so wherever possible seek qualified help. Although we do give drug dosages in this section, they are for emergency use only. Medical advice should be sought where possible before administering any drugs. An embassy or consulate can usually recommend a good place to go for such advice.

### Climatic & Geographical Ailments

**Sunburn** In the desert or at high altitude you can get sunburned surprisingly quickly, even through cloud cover. Use a sunscreen and take extra care to cover areas not normally exposed to sun. A hat provides added protection, and you should also use zinc cream or some other barrier cream for your nose and lips. Calamine lotion is good for mild sunburn.

**Heat Exhaustion** Dehydration or salt deficiency can cause heat exhaustion. Take time to acclimatize to high temperatures and make sure that you get enough liquids. Salt deficiency is characterized by fatigue, lethargy, headaches, giddiness and muscle cramps. Salt tablets may help. Vomiting or diarrhea can also deplete your liquid and salt levels. Anhydrotic heat exhaustion, caused by the inability to sweat, is quite rare. Unlike the other forms of heat exhaustion it is likely to strike people who have been in a hot climate for some time, rather than newcomers. Always carry – and use – a water bottle on long trips.

**Heat Stroke** Long, continuous periods of exposure to high temperatures can leave you vulnerable to this serious, sometimes fatal, condition, which occurs when the body's heat-regulating mechanism breaks down and body temperature rises to dangerous levels. Avoid excessive alcohol intake or strenuous activity when you first arrive in a hot climate.

Symptoms include feeling unwell, lack of perspiration, and a high body temperature of 102°F to 105° F (39°C to 41°C). Hospitalization is essential for extreme cases, but meanwhile get out of the sun, remove clothing, cover with a wet sheet or towel, and fan continually.

**Hypothermia** Changeable weather at high altitudes can leave you vulnerable to exposure: after dark, temperatures in the mountains or desert can drop from balmy to below freezing, while a sudden soaking and high winds can lower your body temperature too rapidly. If at all possible, avoid traveling alone; partners are more likely to avoid hypothermia successfully. If you must travel alone, especially when hiking, be sure someone knows your route and when you expect to return.

Seek shelter when bad weather is unavoidable. Woolen clothing and synthetics, which retain warmth even when wet, are superior to cottons. A quality sleeping bag is a worthwhile investment, although goose down loses much of its insulating qualities when wet. Carry high-energy, easily digestible snacks like chocolate or dried fruit.

Get hypothermia victims out of the wind or rain, remove their clothing if it's wet and replace it with dry, warm clothing. Give them hot liquids – not alcohol – and high-calorie, easily digestible food. In advanced stages it may be necessary to place victims in warm sleeping bags and get in with them. Do not rub victims but place them near a fire or, if possible, in a warm (not hot) bath.

**Fungal Infections** Fungal infections, which occur with greater frequency in hot weather, are most likely to occur on the scalp, between the toes or fingers (athlete's foot), in the groin (jock itch or crotch rot) and on the body (ringworm). You get ringworm (which is a fungal infection, not a worm) from infected animals or by walking on damp areas, like shower floors.

To prevent fungal infections wear loose, comfortable clothes, avoid artificial fibres, wash frequently and dry carefully. If you do get an infection, wash the infected area daily with a disinfectant or medicated soap and water, and rinse and dry well. Apply an antifungal powder and try to expose the infected area to air or sunlight as much as possible, and wash all towels and underwear in hot water as well as changing them often.

**Altitude Sickness** Acute Mountain Sickness (AMS) occurs at high altitude and can be fatal. In the thinner atmosphere of the high mountains, lack of oxygen causes many individuals to suffer headaches, nausea, shortness of breath, physical weakness and other symptoms which can lead to very serious consequences, especially if combined with heat exhaustion, sunburn or hypothermia. Most people recover within a few hours or days. If the symptoms persist it is imperative to descend to lower elevations. For mild cases, everyday painkillers such as aspirin will relieve symptoms until the body adapts. Avoid smoking, drinking alcohol, eating heavily or exercising strenuously.

There is no hard and fast rule as to how high is too high: AMS has been fatal at altitudes of 10,000 ft, although it is much more common above 11,500 ft. It is always wise to sleep at a lower altitude than the greatest height reached during the day. A number of other measures can prevent or minimize AMS:

- Ascend slowly – take frequent rest days, spending two to three nights for each climb of 3000 ft (1000 meters). If you reach a high altitude by trekking, acclimatization takes place gradually and you are less likely to be affected than if you fly direct.
- Drink extra fluids. The mountain air is dry and cold and you lose moisture as you breathe.
- Eat light, high-carbohydrate meals for more energy.
- Avoid alcohol, which may increase the risk of dehydration.
- Avoid sedatives.

**Motion Sickness** Eating lightly before and during a trip will reduce the chances of motion sickness. If you are prone to motion sickness, try to find a place that minimizes disturbance, for example, near the wing on aircraft, near the center on buses. Fresh air usually helps, while reading or cigarette smoke doesn't. Commercial anti-motion sickness preparations, which can cause drowsiness, have to be taken before the trip commences; when you're feeling sick it's too late. Ginger, a natural preventative, is available in capsule form.

**Jet Lag** Jet lag is experienced when a person travels by air across more than three time zones (each time zone usually represents a one-hour time difference). It occurs because many of the functions of the human body (such as temperature, pulse rate and emptying of the bladder and bowels) are regulated by internal 24-hour cycles called circadian rhythms. When we travel long distances rapidly, our bodies take time to adjust to the 'new time' of our destination, and we may experience fatigue, disorientation, insomnia, anxiety, impaired concentration and loss of appetite. These effects will usually be gone within three days of arrival, but there are ways of minimizing the impact of jet lag:

- Rest for a couple of days prior to departure; try to avoid late nights and last-minute dashes for traveler's checks, passport, etc.
- Try to select flight schedules that minimize sleep deprivation; arriving late in the day means you can go to sleep soon after you arrive. For very long flights, try to organize a stopover.
- Avoid excessive eating (which bloats the stomach) and alcohol (which causes dehydration) during the flight. Instead, drink plenty of noncarbonated, nonalcoholic drinks such as fruit juice or water.
- Avoid smoking, as this reduces the amount of oxygen in the airplane cabin even further and causes greater fatigue.
- Make yourself comfortable by wearing loose-fitting clothes and perhaps bringing an eye mask and ear plugs to help you sleep.

## Infectious Diseases

**Diarrhea** A change of water, food or climate can all cause the runs; diarrhea caused by contaminated food or water is more serious. Despite all your precautions you may still have a mild bout of travelers' diarrhea but a few rushed toilet trips with no other symptoms is not indicative of a serious problem. Moderate diarrhea, involving half a dozen loose movements in a day, is more of a nuisance.

Dehydration is the main danger with any diarrhea, particularly for children where dehydration can occur quite quickly. Fluid replacement remains the mainstay of management. Weak black tea with a little sugar, soda water, or soft drinks allowed to go flat and diluted 50% with water are all good. With severe diarrhea a rehydrating solution is necessary to replace minerals and salts. Commercially available ORS (oral rehydration salts) are very useful; add the contents of one sachet to a liter of boiled or bottled water. In an emergency you can make up a solution of eight teaspoons of sugar to a liter of boiled water and provide salted cracker biscuits at the same time. You should stick to a bland diet as you recover.

Lomotil or Imodium can be used to bring relief from the symptoms, although they do not actually cure the problem. Only use these drugs if absolutely necessary – eg if you *must* travel. For children Imodium is preferable, but under all circumstances fluid replacement is the most important thing to remember. Do not use these drugs if the person has a high fever or is severely dehydrated.

In certain situations antibiotics may be indicated:

- Watery diarrhea with blood and mucous. (Gut-paralyzing drugs like Imodium or Lomotil should be avoided in this situation.)
- Watery diarrhea with fever and lethargy.
- Persistent diarrhea for more than five days.
- Severe diarrhea, if it is logistically difficult to stay in one place.

The recommended drugs (adults only) would be either norfloxacin 400 mg twice daily for three days or ciprofloxacin 500 mg twice daily for three days.

The drug bismuth subsalicylate has also been used successfully. It is not available in Australia. The dosage for adults is two tablets or 30 ml and for children it is one tablet or 10ml. This dose can be repeated every 30 minutes to one hour, with no more than eight doses in a 24-hour period.

The drug of choice in children would be co-trimoxazole (Bactrim, Septrin, Resprim) with dosage dependent on weight. A three-day course is also given. Ampicillin has been recommended in the past and may still be an alternative.

**Dysentery** This serious illness is caused by contaminated food or water and is characterised by severe diarrhea, often with blood or mucus in the stool. There are two kinds of dysentery. Bacillary dysentery is characterized by a high fever and rapid onset; headache, vomiting and stomach pains are also symptoms. It generally does not last longer than a week, but it is highly contagious.

Amoebic dysentery is often more gradual in the onset of symptoms, with cramping abdominal pain and vomiting less likely; fever may not be present. It is not a self-limiting disease: it will persist until treated and can recur and cause long-term health problems.

A stool test is necessary to diagnose which kind of dysentery you have, so you should seek medical help urgently. In case of an emergency the drugs norfloxacin or ciprofloxacin can be used as presumptive treatment for bacillary dysentery, and metronidazole (Flagyl) for amoebic dysentery.

For bacillary dysentery, norfloxacin 400 mg twice daily for seven days or ciprofloxacin 500 mg twice daily for seven days are the recommended dosages.

If you're unable to find either of these drugs then a useful alternative is co-trimoxazole 160/800 mg (Bactrim, Septrin, Resprim) twice daily for seven days. This is a sulpha drug and must not be used by people with a known sulpha allergy.

In the case of children the drug co-trimoxazole is a reasonable first-line treatment. For amoebic dysentery, the recommended adult dosage of metronidazole (Flagyl) is one 750-mg to 800-mg capsule three times daily for five days. Children aged between eight and 12 years should have half the adult dose; the dosage for younger children is one-third the adult dose.

An alternative to Flagyl is Fasigyn, taken as a two gram daily dose for three days. Alcohol must be avoided during treatment and for 48 hours afterwards.

**Giardiasis** Commonly known as Giardia, and sometimes 'Beaver Fever', this intestinal parasite is present in contaminated water. Giardia has even contaminated apparently pristine rushing streams in the backcountry.

Symptoms are stomach cramps, nausea, a bloated stomach, watery, foul-smelling diarrhea and frequent gas. Giardia can appear several weeks after exposure to the parasite; symptoms may disappear for a few days and then return, a pattern which may continue. Tinidazole, known as Fasigyn, or metronidazole (Flagyl) are the recommended drugs for treatment. Either can be used in a single treatment dose. Antibiotics are useless.

**Hepatitis** Hepatitis is a general term for inflammation of the liver. There are many causes of this condition: drugs, alcohol and infections are but a few. The discovery of new strains has led to a virtual alphabet soup, with hepatitis A, B, C, D, E and a rumored G. These letters identify specific agents that cause viral hepatitis. Viral hepatitis is an infection of the liver, which can lead to jaundice (yellow skin), fever, lethargy and digestive problems. It can have no symptoms at all, with the infected person not knowing that they have the disease.

Travelers shouldn't be too paranoid about this apparent proliferation of hepatitis strains; hep C, D, E and G are fairly rare (so far) and following the same precautions as for A and B should be all that's necessary to avoid them.

Viral hepatitis can be divided into two groups on the basis of how it is spread. The first route of transmission is via contaminated food and water, and the second route is via blood and bodily fluids.

**Hepatitis A** This is a very common disease in most countries, especially those with poor standards of sanitation. Most people in developing countries are infected as children; they often don't develop symptoms, but do develop life-long immunity. The disease poses a real threat to the traveler, as people are unlikely to have been exposed to hepatitis A in developed countries.

The symptoms are fever, chills, headache, fatigue, feelings of weakness and aches and pains, followed by loss of appetite, nausea, vomiting, abdominal pain, dark urine, light colored feces and jaundiced skin, and the whites of the eyes may turn yellow. In some cases you may feel unwell, tired, have no appetite, experience aches and pains and be jaundiced. You should seek medical advice, but in general there is not much you can do apart from resting, drinking lots of fluids, eating lightly and avoiding fatty foods. People who have had hepatitis must forego alcohol for six months after the illness, as hepatitis attacks the liver and it needs that amount of time to recover.

The routes of transmission are via contaminated water, shellfish contaminated by sewerage, or foodstuffs sold by food handlers with poor standards of hygiene. Taking care with what you eat and drink can go a long way towards preventing this disease. But this is a very infectious virus, so if there is any risk of exposure, additional cover is highly recommended. This cover comes in two forms: Gammaglobulin and Havrix. Gammaglobulin is an injection where you are given the antibodies for hepatitis A, which provide immunity for a limited time. Havrix is a vaccine, where you develop your own antibodies, which gives lasting immunity.

**Hepatitis B** Hepatitis B, which used to be called serum hepatitis, is spread through contact with infected blood, blood products or bodily fluids, for example through sexual contact, unsterilized needles and blood transfusions. Other risk situations include having a shave or tattoo in a local shop, or having your ears pierced. The symptoms of type B are much the same as type A except that they are more severe and may lead to irreparable liver damage or even liver cancer.

Although there is no treatment for hepatitis B, a cheap and effective vaccine is available; the only problem is that for long-lasting cover you need a six-month course. The immunization schedule requires two injections at least a month apart followed by a third dose five months after the second. Persons who should receive a

hepatitis B vaccination include anyone who anticipates contact with blood or other bodily secretions, either as a health-care worker or through sexual contact, particularly those who intend to stay in the country for a long period of time.

**Hepatitis C** This is another recently defined virus. It is a concern because it seems to lead to liver disease more rapidly than hepatitis B. The virus is spread by contact with blood – usually via contaminated transfusions or shared needles. Avoiding these is the only means of prevention, as there is no available vaccine.

**Hepatitis D** Often referred to as the 'Delta' virus, this infection only occurs in chronic carriers of hepatitis B. It is transmitted by blood and bodily fluids. Again there is no vaccine for this virus, so avoidance is the best prevention. The risk to travelers is certainly limited.

**Hepatitis E** This is a very recently discovered virus, of which little is yet known. It appears to be rather common in developing countries, generally causing mild hepatitis, although it can be very serious in pregnant women. Care with water supplies is the only current prevention, as there are no specific vaccines for this type of hepatitis. At present it doesn't appear to be too great a risk for travelers.

**Rabies** Dogs are noted carriers of rabies. Any bite, scratch or even lick from a warm-blooded, furry animal should be cleaned immediately and thoroughly. Scrub with soap and running water, and then clean with an alcohol solution. If there is any possibility that the animal is infected medical help should be sought immediately. Even if the animal is not rabid, all bites should be treated seriously as they can become infected or can result in tetanus.

A rabies vaccination is now available and should be considered if you are in a high-risk category – eg if you intend to explore caves (bat bites can be dangerous) or work with animals.

**Tetanus** Tetanus is difficult to treat but is preventable with immunization. Tetanus occurs when a wound becomes infected by a germ which lives in the feces of animals or people, so it is vital to clean all cuts, punctures or animal bites. Tetanus is also known as lockjaw, and the first symptom may be discomfort in swallowing, or stiffening of the jaw and neck; this is followed by painful convulsions of the jaw and whole body.

**Sexually Transmitted Diseases** Sexual contact with an infected sexual partner spreads these diseases. While abstinence is the only 100% preventative, using condoms is also effective. Gonorrhoea and syphilis are the most common of these diseases; sores, blisters or rashes around the genitals, discharges or pain when urinating are common symptoms. Symptoms may be less marked or not observed at all in women. Syphilis symptoms eventually disappear completely but the disease continues and can cause severe problems in later years. The treatment of gonorrhoea and syphilis is by antibiotics.

There are numerous other sexually transmitted diseases, for most of which effective treatment is available. However, there is no cure for herpes and there is also currently no cure for AIDS.

**HIV/AIDS** HIV, the Human Immunodeficiency Virus, may develop into AIDS, Acquired Immune Deficiency Syndrome. HIV is a major problem in many countries. Any exposure to blood, blood products or bodily fluids may put the individual at risk. Infection can come from practicing unprotected sex or sharing contaminated needles. Apart from abstinence, the most effective preventative is always to practice safe sex using condoms. It is impossible to detect the HIV-positive status of an otherwise healthy-looking person without a blood test.

HIV/AIDS can also be spread through infected blood transfusions; most developing countries cannot afford to screen blood

for transfusions. It can also be spread by dirty needles – vaccinations, acupuncture, tattooing and ear or nose piercing can potentially be as dangerous as intravenous drug use if the equipment is not clean. If you do need an injection, ask to see the syringe unwrapped in front of you, or better still, take a needle and syringe pack with you overseas – it is a cheap insurance package against infection with HIV.

Fear of HIV infection should never preclude treatment for serious medical conditions. Although there may be a risk of infection, it is very small indeed. A good resource for help and information is the US Center of Disease Control AIDS hotline (☎ 1 (800) 343-2347).

### Insect-Borne Diseases

**Ticks** Ticks are a parasitic arachnid that may be present in brush, forest and grasslands, where hikers often get them on their legs or in their boots. The adults suck blood from hosts by burying their head into skin, but are often found unattached and can simply be brushed off. However, if one has attached itself to you, pulling it off and leaving the head in the skin increases the likelihood of infection or disease such as Rocky Mountain spotted fever or Lyme disease.

Ticks are not common in the Southwest, but to avoid one use insect repellent or rub on petroleum jelly, alcohol or oil to induce ticks to let go, or press a very hot object like a match (the lighted end of a cigarette works well, if you have one). The tick should back out and can then be disposed of. Always check your body for ticks after walking through a tick-infested area. If you get sick in the next couple of weeks, consult a doctor.

### Cuts, Bites & Stings

**Cuts & Scratches** Skin punctures can easily become infected in hot climates and may be difficult to heal. Treat any cut with an antiseptic such as Betadine. Where possible avoid bandages and Band-aids, which can keep wounds wet.

**Bites & Stings** Bee and wasp stings are usually painful rather than dangerous. Calamine lotion will give relief, and ice packs will reduce the pain and swelling. Some spiders have dangerous bites, and scorpion stings are very painful, but neither is likely to be fatal. Bites are best avoided by not using bare hands to turn over rocks or large pieces of wood. Bites from snakes do not cause instantaneous death, and antivenins are usually available. Seek medical help, if possible with the dead snake for identification. Don't attempt to catch the snake if there is even a remote possibility of being bitten again.

The best course is to avoid being bitten or stung. The Arizona Poison Control System reports that about half of reported snake bites are caused by people picking up the snake, either out of bravado or mistakenly assuming that the animal was dead. Keep a healthy distance away from any snakes you might see and watch where you step.

If you are bitten or stung, call Poison Control. The numbers are given below. In the case of snake bite, avoid slashing and sucking the wound, avoid tight tourniquets (a light constricting band above the bite can help), avoid ice, keep the affected area below the level of the heart and move it as little as possible. Do not ingest alcohol or any drugs. Stay calm and get to a medical facility as soon as possible.

In the case of spiders and scorpions, there are no special first-aid techniques, but you should call Poison Control for advice. A black widow spider bite may be barely noticeable, but their venom can be dangerous, and if you're bitten you should seek medical attention immediately.

For Gila monster bites, make sure to disengage the jaws quickly – these animals bite and clamp on for several minutes while delivering their poison. Call Poison Control and obtain medical assistance immediately.

Conenose bug bites may require medical assistance; call Poison Control for advice.

Bites from a centipede, bee, wasp or ant bites may be relieved by application of ice (but don't use ice for the other critters mentioned above). Again, call Poison Control if an unusual reaction develops.

If you are hiking a long way from the nearest phone or other help, and you are bitten or stung, you should hike out and get help, particularly in the case of snake and spider bites. Often, reactions are delayed for up to 12 hours and you can hike out before then. It is recommended to hike with a companion. For more information on some of these bugs and reptiles see Dangers & Annoyances later in this chapter.

**Poison Control** These centers are staffed 24 hours a day. They can advise about bites and stings as well as ingested poisons of all kinds. If you have trouble reaching a Poison Control Center, dial 911 or 0 and ask to be connected.

Arizona
    In Phoenix (☎ (602) 253 3334); in Tucson (☎ (520) 626 6016); in the rest of Arizona (☎ 1 (800) 362 0101)
New Mexico
    In Albuquerque (☎ (505) 843 2551); in the rest of New Mexico (☎ 1 (800) 432 6866)
Utah
    In Salt Lake City (☎ (801) 581 2151); in the rest of Utah (☎ 1 (800) 456 7707)

**Bedbugs & Lice** Bedbugs live in various places, but particularly in dirty mattresses and bedding. Spots of blood on bedclothes or on the wall around the bed can be read as a suggestion to find another hotel. Bedbugs leave itchy bites in neat rows. Calamine lotion may help.

The venomous female black widow got her name from the habit of eating her mates.

All lice cause itching and discomfort. They make themselves at home in your hair (head lice), your clothing (body lice) or in your pubic hair (crabs). You catch lice through direct contact with infected people or by sharing combs, clothing and the like. Powder or shampoo treatment will kill the lice and infected clothing should then be washed in hot water.

## Women's Health

Poor diet, lowered resistance due to the use of antibiotics for stomach upsets and even contraceptive pills can lead to vaginal infections when traveling in hot climates. Maintaining good hygiene and wearing skirts or loose-fitting trousers and cotton underwear will help to prevent infections.

Yeast infections, characterized by a rash, itch and discharge, can be treated with a vinegar or lemon-juice douche, or with yogurt. Nystatin suppositories are the usual medical prescription. Trichomoniasis is a more serious infection; symptoms are a discharge and a burning sensation when urinating. Male sexual partners must also be treated, and if a vinegar-water douche is not effective medical attention should be sought. Metronidazole (Flagyl) is the prescribed drug.

## WOMEN TRAVELERS

Women often face different situations when traveling than men do. If you are a woman traveler, especially a woman traveling alone, it's not a bad idea to get in the habit of traveling with a little extra awareness of your surroundings.

The USA is such a diverse and varied country that it's impossible to give advice that will fit every place and every situation. People are generally friendly and happy to help travelers, and you will probably have a wonderful time unmarred by dangerous encounters. To ensure that this is the case, consider the following suggestions, which should reduce or eliminate your chances of problems. The best advice is to trust your instincts.

In general, you must exercise more vigilance in large cities than in rural areas. Try to avoid the 'bad' or unsafe neighborhoods or districts; if you must go into or through these areas, it's best to go in a private vehicle (car or taxi). It's more dangerous at night, but in the worst areas crime can occur even in the daytime. If you are unsure which areas are considered unsafe, ask at your hotel or telephone the tourist office for advice. Tourist maps can sometimes be deceiving, compressing areas that are not tourist attractions and making the distances look shorter than they are.

While there is less to watch out for in rural areas, women may still be harassed by men unaccustomed to seeing women traveling solo. Try to avoid hiking or camping alone, especially in unfamiliar places. Hikers all over the world use the 'buddy system,' not only for protection from other humans, but also for aid in case of unexpected falls or other injuries, or encounters with rattlesnakes, bears or other potentially dangerous wildlife.

Women must recognize the extra threat of rape, which is a problem not only in urban but also in rural areas, albeit to a lesser degree. The best way to deal with the threat of rape is to avoid putting yourself in vulnerable situations. Conducting yourself in a common-sense manner will help you to avoid most problems. For example, you're more vulnerable if you've been drinking or using drugs than if you're sober; you're more vulnerable alone than if you're with company; and you're more vulnerable in a high-crime urban area than in a 'better' district.

If despite all precautions you are assaulted, call the police; in any emergency, telephoning 911 will connect you with the emergency operator for police, fire and ambulance services. In some rural areas where 911 is not active, just dial '0' for the operator. The cities and larger towns have rape crisis centers and women's shelters that provide help and support; these are listed in the telephone directory, or if they're not, the police should be able to refer you to them.

Carry your money (and only the money you'll need for that day) somewhere inside your clothing (in a money belt, a bra or your socks) rather than in a handbag or an outside pocket. Stash the money in several places. Most hotels and hostels provide safekeeping, so you can leave your money, passport and other valuables with them. Hide, or don't wear, any valuable jewelry.

Men may interpret a woman drinking alone in a bar as a bid for male company, whether you intended it that way or not. If you don't want the company, most men will respect a firm but polite 'no thank you'.

Don't hitchhike alone, and don't pick up hitchhikers if driving alone. If you get stuck on a road and need help, it's a good idea to have a pre-made sign to signal for help. At night avoid getting out of your car to flag down help; turn on your hazard lights and wait for the police to arrive. Be extra careful at night on public transit, and remember to check the times of the last bus or train before you go out at night.

To deal with potential dangers, many women protect themselves with a whistle, mace, cayenne pepper spray or some self-defense training. If you do decide to purchase a spray, contact a police station to find out about regulations and training classes. Laws regarding sprays vary from state to state, so be informed based on your destination. One law that doesn't vary is carrying sprays on airplanes – because of their combustible design it is a federal felony to carry them on board.

The headquarters for the National Organization for Women (NOW; ☎ (202) 331 0066), 1000 16th St NW, Suite 700, Washington, DC 20036, is a good resource for any woman-related information and can refer you to state and local chapters. Planned Parenthood (☎ (212) 541 7800), 810 7th Ave, New York, NY 10019, can refer you to clinics throughout the country and offer advice on medical issues. Check the yellow pages under 'Women's Organizations & Services' for local resources.

## GAY & LESBIAN TRAVELERS

There are gay people throughout the USA, but by far the most established gay communities are in the major cities. In the cities and on both coasts it is easier for gay men and women to live their lives with a certain amount of openness. As you travel into the middle of the country it is much harder to be open about your sexual preferences and many gays are still in the closet. This matches the prevailing attitude of the country, which prefers that gay people are neither seen nor heard. Gay travelers should be careful, *especially* in the predominantly rural areas – holding hands might get you bashed.

San Francisco and New York have the largest gay populations, but larger cities often have a gay neighborhood or area. Examples are Hillcrest in San Diego, West Hollywood in LA, Capitol Hill in Seattle and the South End in Boston.

A couple of good national guidebooks are *The Womens' Traveler*, providing listings for lesbians, and *Damron's Address Book* for men, both published by the Damron Company (☎ 1 (800) 462 6654, (415) 2550404) PO Box 422458, San Francisco, CA 94142-2458. Ferrari's *Places for Women* and *Places for Men* are also useful, as are guides to specific cities (check out *Betty & Pansy's Severe Queer Reviews* to San Francisco, New York City and Washington, DC). These can be found at any good bookstore.

Another good resource is the Gay Yellow Pages (☎ (212) 674 0120), PO Box 533, Village Station, NY 10014-0533, which has a national edition as well as regional editions.

The club scene is ever changing, and most cities have a gay paper or alternative paper that will list what's happening or at least provide phone numbers of local organizations.

For people with online capabilities America Online (AOL) hosts the Gay & Lesbian Community Forum. This is also the on-line home of National Gay/Lesbian Task Force (NGLTF), Gay & Lesbian Alliance Against Defamation (GLAAD), Parents-Friends of Lesbians & Gays (P-FLAG) and other regional, state and national organizations. Michelle Quirk, host of AOL's Gay & Lesbian Community Forum, can be contacted at quirk@aol.com.

National resource numbers include the National AIDS/HIV Hotline (☎ 1 (800) 342 2437), the National Gay/Lesbian Task Force (☎ (202) 332 6483 in Washington, DC) and the Lambda Legal Defense Fund (☎ (212) 995 8585 in New York City, (213) 937 2727 in Los Angeles).

## SENIOR TRAVELERS

When retirement leaves the time clock behind and the myriad 'senior' discounts begin to apply, the prospect of rediscovering the USA elicits a magnetic draw for foreigners and the native-born alike. Though the age where the benefits begin varies with the attraction, travelers from 50 years and up can expect to receive cut rates and benefits unknown to (and the envy of) their younger fellows. Be sure to inquire about such rates at hotels, museums and restaurants.

Visitors to national parks and campgrounds can cut costs greatly by using the Golden Age Passport, a card that allows US citizens aged 62 and over (and those traveling in the same car) free admission nationwide and a 50% reduction on camping fees. You can apply in person for any of these at any national park or regional office of the USFS or NPS or call 1 (800) 280 2267 for information and ordering.

Some national advocacy groups that can help in planning your travels include the following:

American Association of Retired Persons
The AARP (☎ 1 (800) 227 7737), 601 E St NW, Washington, DC 20049, is an advocacy group for Americans 50 years and older and is a good resource for travel bargains. A one-year membership is available to US residents for $8.

Elderhostel
Elderhostel (☎ (617) 426 8056), 75 Federal St, Boston, MA 02110-1941, is a nonprofit organization that offers seniors the opportunity to attend academic college courses throughout the USA and Canada. The programs last one to three weeks. They include

meals and accommodations, and are open to people 55 years and older and their companions.

Grand Circle Travel
This organization offers escorted tours and travel information in a variety of formats and distributes a free useful booklet, *Going Abroad: 101 Tips for Mature Travelers*. Contact them at 347 Congress Street, Boston, MA 02210 (☎ (617) 350 7500, fax 350 6206).

National Council of Senior Citizens
Membership (you needn't be a US citizen to apply) to this group gives access to added Medicare insurance, a mail-order prescription service and a variety of discount information and travel-related advice. Fees are $13/30/150 for one year/three years/lifetime. The council is based at 1331 F Street NW, Washington DC, 20004 (☎ (202) 347 8800).

## DISABLED TRAVELERS

Travel within USA is becoming easier for people with disabilities. Public buildings (including hotels, restaurants, theaters and museums) are now required by law to be wheelchair accessible and to have available restroom facilities. Public transportation services (buses, trains and taxis) must be made accessible to all, including those in wheelchairs, and telephone companies are required to provide relay operators for the hearing impaired. Many banks now provide ATM instructions in Braille and you will find audible crossing signals as well as dropped curbs at busier roadway intersections.

Larger private and chain hotels (see Accommodations for listings) have suites for disabled guests. Main car rental agencies offer hand-controlled models at no extra charge. All major airlines, Greyhound buses and Amtrak trains will allow service animals to accompany passengers and will frequently sell two-for-one packages when attendants of seriously disabled passengers are required. Airlines will also provide assistance for connecting, boarding and deplaning the flight – just ask for assistance when making your reservation. (Note: airlines must accept wheelchairs as checked baggage and have an onboard chair available, though some advance notice may be required on smaller aircraft.) Of course, the more populous the area, the greater the likelihood of facilities for the disabled, so it's important to call ahead to see what is available.

There are a number of organizations and tour providers that specialize in the needs of disabled travelers:

Access
> The Foundation for Accessibility by the Disabled, PO Box 356, Malverne, NY 11565 (☎ (516) 887 5798).

Information Center for Individuals with Disabilities
> Call or write for their free listings and travel advice. Fort Point Place, 1st Floor, 27-43 Wormwood Street, Boston, MA 02210 (☎ (617) 727 5540, TTY 345-9743 or 1 (800) 248 3737).

Mobility International USA
> Advises disabled travelers on mobility issues and runs an exchange program. Contact PO Box 3551, Eugene, OR 97403 (☎ (503) 343 1284).

Moss Rehabilitation Hospital's Travel Information Service
> 1200 W Tabor Road, Philadelphia, PA 19141-3099 (☎ (215) 456 9600, TTY 456 9602).

SATH
> Society for the Advancement of Travel for the Handicapped 347 Fifth Ave No 610, New York, NY 10016 (☎ (212) 447 7284).

Twin Peaks Press
> Publishes several handbooks for disabled travelers and can be contacted at PO Box 129, Vancouver, WA 98666 (☎ (202) 694 2462, 1 (800) 637 2256).

*Handicapped Travel Newsletter*
> Nonprofit publication with good information on traveling around the world and US government legislation. Subscriptions are $10 annually. Contact PO Drawer 269, Athens, TX 75751 (☎ /fax (903) 677 1260).

## DANGERS & ANNOYANCES
### Crime
The cities of the Southwest generally have lower levels of violent crime than the larger, better known cities such as Washington, DC, New York and Los Angeles. Nevertheless, violent crime is certainly present, and you should take the usual precautions, especially in the cities.

Always lock cars and put valuables out of sight, whether leaving the car for a few minutes or longer, and whether you are in towns or in the remote backcountry. Rent a car with a lockable trunk. If your car is bumped from behind, it is best to keep going to a well-lit area, service station, or even a police station.

Be aware of your surroundings and who may be watching you. Avoid walking dimly lit streets at night, particularly if you are alone. Walk purposefully. Exercise particular caution in large parking lots or parking structures at night. Avoid unnecessary displays of money or jewelry. Split up your money and credit cards to avoid losing everything, and try to use ATM machines in well-trafficked areas.

In hotels, don't leave valuables lying around your room. Use safety deposit boxes or at least place valuables in a locked bag. Don't open your door to strangers – check the peephole or call the front desk if unexpected people are trying to enter.

### Weather
Summer storms can be dangerous in the Southwest. Lightning is common and you should avoid being in the open, especially on canyon rims or hilltops, or next to tall or metallic objects.

During heavy rain, flash floods occur regularly. A dry river bed can become a raging torrent in minutes, strong enough to sweep a person, or even a vehicle, away. Don't camp in washes (dry river bottoms) or up in dry arroyos (river courses) if it's raining hard in the mountains or nearby. Don't attempt to cross a flooded road or wash unless there's plenty of other traffic driving through.

The Southwest is very dry and people die of dehydration every year. Dehydration occurs rapidly in 100°F weather. Tourists on short day hikes have become disoriented and lost – what starts off as an hour or two of hiking can turn into a fatal accident without water. Don't attempt any hike, however short, without carrying plenty of water. A minimum of four quarts per person per day is needed in the summer.

Also remember to carry containers of water in the car, in case you break down on a rural road.

Dust storms are brief but can be temporarily blinding. If caught in a dust storm while driving, pull over as far to the side of the road as you can and wait it out. It shouldn't take more than a few minutes to blow over.

## Wildlife Big & Small

Drivers should watch for stock on highways, especially on Indian reservations, which are generally unfenced, and in areas signed as 'Open Rangelands' or words to that effect. Hitting a cow (or a deer) at 55 mph will total your car, kill the animal and might kill you as well.

Despite the large numbers of snakes, spiders, scorpions and other venomous creatures in the Southwest, fatalities are very rare. This is partly because these animals tend to avoid humans and partly because their venom is designed to kill small animals rather than big ones like ourselves. If you are bitten or stung by one of these critters, refer to the Health section under Cuts, Bites & Stings.

The descriptions below are more for interest than because large numbers of readers are likely to be bitten. Note that most animals described below can be found in urban as well as rural areas.

**Snakes** When hiking, watch where you are stepping, particularly on hot summer afternoons and evenings when rattlesnakes like to bask in the middle of the trail. They are also often active at night. There are many species of rattler, most easily identified by the 'rattle' of scales at the tip of the tail. These emit a rapid rattling sound when the snake is disturbed. Most rattlesnakes have roughly diamond-shaped patterns along their backs and vary in length from two to six feet. They are found all over western USA. If you are bitten, you will experience rapid swelling, very severe pain and possible temporary paralysis, but rarely do victims die. Antivenin is available in Southwestern hospitals.

Rarer than the rattlesnake, but much more poisonous, is the Arizona coral snake, found from central Arizona to southwestern New Mexico. This small snake, usually 13 to 21 inches in length, is easily identified by a pattern of glossy bands – wide black, narrow yellow, wide red, narrow yellow – repeated along its length. This snake tends to burrow underground but emerges after warm night rains. It is unlikely that you will see one. Few people have been bitten, but of those victims, some have required hospitalization. Antivenin is available.

Spiders The most dangerous spider in the area is the black widow, a species that has gained notoriety because the venomous female eats her mate after sex. The female has a small, round body marked with a red hourglass shape under its abdomen. She makes very messy webs, so avoid these, as the widow will bite if harassed. Bites are very painful but rarely fatal, except in young children. Antivenin is available.

The brown spider, of which there are several species, occasionally hides in closets and may bite when you put on some clothing in which it is hiding. The bite may become large and painful and flu-like symptoms are reported, but long-term problems are unlikely.

The large (up to six inches in diameter) and hairy tarantula looks much worse than it is – it bites very rarely and then usually when they are roughly handled. The bite is not very serious, although it is temporarily quite painful. There are over a dozen species in the Southwest.

**Scorpions** About 20 species of scorpions are found throughout the Southwest. They spend their days under rocks or woodpiles, so use caution when handling these. The

Gila monster

long stinger curving up and around the back is characteristic of these animals. The stings can be very painful but are almost never fatal; again, small children are at highest risk.

**Gila Monster** This is one of only two venomous lizards in the world. It is found in most of Arizona except the northwestern plateau, and also dwells in extreme southwestern Utah and southwestern New Mexico. This large and slow lizard, which can reach two feet in length, has a bizarre, multicolored, beaded appearance. Although a bite could be fatal, it's very hard to get bitten. You pretty much have to pick the monster up and force-feed it your finger. There have been no fatalities in the last several years. Gila monsters are legally protected and should not be handled.

**Other Creatures** Centipedes bite occasionally, resulting in a painfully inflamed wound that lasts for about a day. Bees and wasps deliver sharp and painful stings, which may cause severe reactions if you are allergic to these. Some ants may also give painful stings. Conenose bugs (also called kissing or assassin bugs) are from one-half to one inch long and have elongated heads. The winged bodies are oval and brown or black with lighter markings (sometimes orange) around the edges. Bites are painful and can result in severe allergic reactions.

## EMERGENCY
If you need any kind of emergency assistance, such as police, ambulance or fire station, call 911. This is a free call from any phone. A few rural phones might not have this service, in which case dial 0 for the operator and ask for emergency assistance – it's still free.

### Credit Card Numbers
If you lose your credit cards or they get stolen contact the company immediately. Following are toll-free numbers for the main credit cards. Contact your bank if you lose your ATM card.

| | |
|---|---|
| Visa | ☎ 1 (800) 336 8472 |
| MasterCard | ☎ 1 (800) 826 2181 |
| American Express | ☎ 1 (800) 528 4800 |
| Discover | ☎ 1 (800) 347 2683 |
| Diners Club | ☎ 1 (800) 234 6377 |

## LEGAL MATTERS
If you are stopped by the police for any reason, bear in mind that there is no system of paying fines on the spot. For traffic offenses, the police officer will explain your options to you. Attempting to pay the fine to the officer is frowned upon at best and may lead to a charge of bribery to compound your troubles. Should the officer decide that you should pay up front, he or she can exercise their authority and take you directly to the magistrate instead of allowing you the usual 30-day period to pay the fine.

If you are arrested for more serious offenses, you are allowed to remain silent and are presumed innocent until proven guilty. There is no legal reason to speak to a police officer if you don't wish. All persons who are arrested are legally allowed (and given) the right to make one phone call. If you don't have a lawyer or family member to help you, call your embassy. The police will give you the number upon request.

### Driving & Drinking Laws
Each state has its own laws and what may be legal in one state may be illegal in others.

Some general rules are that you must be at least 16 years of age to drive (older in some states). Speed limits are 65 mph on interstates and freeways unless otherwise posted. You can drive five mph over the limit without much likelihood of being pulled over, but if you're doing 10 mph over the limit, you'll be caught sooner or later. Speed limits on other highways are 55 mph or less, and in cities can vary from 25 to 45 mph. Watch for school zones which can be as low as 15 mph during school hours – these limits are strictly enforced. Seat belts must be worn in most states. Motorcyclists must wear helmets.

The drinking age is 21 and you need a photo ID to prove your age. Stiff fines, jail time and penalties could be incurred when caught driving under the influence of alcohol. During festive holidays and special events, road blocks are sometimes set up to deter drunk drivers.

For more information on other car-related topics, see the Getting Around chapter.

## WORK

Seasonal work is possible in national parks and other tourist sites, especially ski areas; for information, contact park concessionaires or local chambers of commerce.

If you're coming from abroad and want to work in the USA, you'll need to apply for a work visa from the US embassy in your home country before you leave. The type of visa varies depending on how long you're staying and the kind of work you plan to do. Generally, you'll need either a J-1 visa which you can obtain by joining a visitor-exchange program, or a H-2B visa which you get when being sponsored by a US employer. The latter is not easy to obtain (since the employer has to prove that no US citizen or permanent resident is available to do the job); the former is issued mostly to students for work in summer camps.

## ACCOMMODATIONS

The Southwest has a comprehensive range of accommodations including free camping, developed campsites for tents and RVs, youth hostels, cheap and mid-priced motels, B&Bs, expensive hotels, guest ranches and luxury resorts. For information on lodging taxes see Taxes earlier in this chapter.

## Camping
**Public Campgrounds** These are on public lands such as in national forests, state and national parks and BLM land.

Free dispersed camping (meaning you can camp almost anywhere) is permitted in many public backcountry areas. Sometimes you can camp right from your car along a dirt road, and sometimes you can backpack your gear in. Information on where camping is permitted and detailed maps are available from many local ranger stations (addresses and telephone numbers are given in the text) and may be posted along the road. Sometimes, a free camping permit is required, particularly in national parks, less so in forest and BLM areas. The less developed sites are often on a first come, first served basis, and can fill up on Friday nights. More developed areas may accept or require reservations; details are given in the text.

Camping in an undeveloped area, whether from your car or backpacking, entails basic responsibility. Choose a campsite at least 100 yards from water, and wash up at camp, not in the stream. Dig a six-inch-deep hole to shit in. Burn your toilet paper (unless fires are prohibited because of high forest fire danger). Carry out all trash. Use a portable charcoal grill or camping stove; don't build new fires. If there already is a fire ring, use only dead and down wood or wood you have carried in yourself. Leave the campsite as you found it.

Developed areas usually have toilets, drinking water, fire pits (or charcoal grills) and picnic benches. Some don't have drinking water. At any rate, it is always a good idea to have a few gallons of water with you if you are going to be out in the boonies. These basic campgrounds usually cost about $7 to $10 a night. More developed areas may have showers or recreational vehicle (RV) hookups. These will cost several dollars more.

Costs given in the text for public campgrounds are per site. A site is normally for up to six people (or two vehicles). If there are more of you, you'll need two sites.

Public campgrounds often have seven or 14-night limits.

**Private Campgrounds** These are on private property and are usually close to or in town. Most are designed with recreational vehicles (RVs) in mind; tenters can camp but fees are several dollars higher than in public campgrounds. Also, fees given in the text are for two people per site. There is usually a charge of $1 to $3 per extra person and state and city taxes apply. However, they may offer discounts for week or month stays. Private campgrounds often have many facilities lacking in public ones. These include hot showers, a coin laundry, a swimming pool, full RV hook-ups, a games area, a playground and a convenience store. Kampgrounds of America (KOA) is a national network of private campgrounds. You can get its annual directory of sites by calling or writing: KOA (☎ (406) 248-7444), PO Box 30558, Billings, MT 59114-0558.

**Hostels**
The US hostel network is less widespread than in Canada, the UK, Europe and Australia, and is predominately in the north and coastal parts of the country. Not all of them are directly affiliated with Hostels International/American Youth Hostels (HI/AYH; HI is managed by International Youth Hostel Federation or IYHF). Those that are offer discounts to HI/AYH members and usually allow nonmembers to stay for a few dollars more. Dormitory beds cost about $10 to $12 a night. Rooms are in the $20s for one or two people, sometimes more.

HI/AYH hostels expect you to rent or carry a sheet or sleeping bag to keep the beds clean. Dormitories are segregated by sex and curfews may exist. Kitchen and laundry privileges are usually available in return for light house-keeping duties. There are information and advertising boards, TV rooms and lounge areas. Alcohol may be banned. Reservations are accepted and advised during the high season – there may be a limit of a three-night stay then. You can call HI/AYH's national toll-free number (☎ 1 (800) 444-6111) to make reservations for any HI/AYH hostel.

Independent hostels may offer a discount to AYH or IYHF members. They often have a few private single/double rooms available, although bathroom facilities are still usually shared. Kitchen, laundry, notice board and TV facilities are available.

Dormitory beds cost about $10 to $12 a night. Rooms are in the $20s for one or two people, sometimes more.

**B&Bs**
If you've only ever experienced B&Bs in Britain, then you're probably in for a surprise when you stay at most US B&Bs. B&Bs all have breakfast included in their prices, but similarities stop there. The cheapest establishments, with rooms in the $30s and $40s, may have clean but unexciting rooms with a shared bathroom. Pricier places have rooms with private baths and, perhaps, amenities such as fireplaces, balconies and dining rooms with enticingly super breakfasts. Other places may be in historical buildings, quaint country houses or luxurious urban homes.

Most B&Bs fall in the $50 to $100 price range, but some go over $100. The best are distinguished by a friendly attention to detail by owner/hosts who can provide you with local information and contacts and a host of other amenities. One place I stayed whipped up a homemade chocolate birthday cake for my wife – no extra charge. Another might dig out a bike for you to ride or lend you a pair of binoculars for a bird-watching trip. B&B hosts should, and usually do, lend a personal touch to your stay.

However, B&Bs come and go quickly (some are only seasonal), so call ahead to make sure the inn is still in operation; check with the local chamber of commerce to find out what new B&Bs might have opened. Most B&Bs don't take walk-in customers; you're expected to have a reservation. Many B&Bs don't accept children or smokers, and pets are usually not welcome; some will have prohibitions like no alcohol or try to enforce a curfew.

## Motels & Hotels

The cheapest motel rooms rent for under $20 for a double room. This is, perhaps, one reason why there are few youth hostels in the Southwest and more in the coastal cities where cheap motels are harder to find.

Motel and hotel prices vary tremendously in price from season to season. A hotel charging $40 for a double in the high season may drop to $25 in the low and may raise its rates to $55 for a special event when the town is overflowing. A $200-a-night luxury resort may offer special weekend packages for $79 in the low season. So be aware that prices in this guide can only be an approximate guideline at best. Also, be prepared to add room tax to prices. I give rates for one or two people; extra people are charged anywhere between $3 and $10 per person.

Although I give dates of high seasons and special events (when prices may rise) in the text, you never know when something out of the ordinary may happen to ruin your plans. I pulled into St George, Utah, one afternoon when nothing much was supposed to be happening and found almost every hotel full and the remainder overpriced. The reason was that an Amway convention had taken over several hundred rooms.

Children are often allowed to stay free with their parents, but rules for this vary. Some hotels allow children under 18 to stay free with parents, others allow children under 12 and others may charge a few dollars per child. You should call and inquire if traveling with a family.

The prices advertised by hotels are called 'rack rates' and are not written in stone. If you simply ask about any specials that might apply you can often save quite a bit of money. Booking through a travel agent also saves you quite a bit of money as well. Members of the AARP and the AAA can qualify for a 'corporate' rate at several hotel chains.

Making phone calls directly from your hotel room is usually a losing proposition. Hotels charge around 75¢ for local calls vs 20¢ or 25¢ at a pay phone. Long distance rates are inflated up 100% to 200%! The best plan of action is simply to carry a fistful of quarters or a phone card and use a pay phone for all your calls.

**Bottom-End Motels** Motels with $20 rooms are found especially in small towns on major highways and the motel strips of larger towns. A quick drive through one of these will yield a selection of neon-lit signs such as '$19.95 for Two'. Take your pick. A few towns which may currently be experiencing great popularity just won't have rock-bottom budget motels. Therefore what may be a bottom-end motel in one town may pass for a middle hotel in another. These towns include Santa Fe, Taos, Moab and Sedona, where a room close to $40 is rock-bottom budget. Therefore, what I may call a bottom-end motel in one town may pass for a middle hotel in another. Utah, on the whole, has budget rooms starting in the low $20s rather than under $20 (although the cheapest room I stayed in during the research of this book was $14.95 in Utah!).

I list cheap and very basic motels as information for budget travelers, not because the rooms are anything special. They're not! Rooms are usually small, beds may be soft or saggy, but the sheets should be clean. A minimal level of cleanliness is maintained, but expect scuffed walls, atrocious decor, old furniture and strange noises from your shower. Even these places, however, normally have a private shower and toilet and a TV in each room. Most have air-conditioning and heat. Some of even the cheapest motels may advertise kitchenettes. These may cost a few dollars more but give you the chance to cook a simple meal for yourself if you are fed up with restaurants. Kitchenettes vary from a two-ring burner to a spiffy little mini-kitchen and may or may not have utensils. If you plan on doing a lot of kitchenette cooking, carry your own set.

In smaller towns, I find cheap rooms to be acceptable 'mom and pop' type places, but in larger towns, the cheap motels may be in the least salubrious areas. Don't leave valuables out in your car and exercise caution. However, I've spent several weeks worth of nights in rock-bottom hotels and have never had serious problems. If you're on a budget, don't shun these $20-a-night cheapies. Many readers will have read the preceding paragraphs thinking 'Saggy beds? Strange shower noises? Twenty bucks? This guy's gotta be kidding!' Well, no, I'm not. These accommodations are out there for those travelers who want them, but there are plenty of nicer places detailed in the text. Read on!

**Motel & Hotel Chains** There are many motel and hotel chains in the USA. These offer a certain level of quality and style which tend to be repeated throughout the chain. People may say 'If you've stayed in one, you've stayed in them all!'. This is partially true, but there are certainly individual variations in both standards and, especially, prices depending on location. Some travelers like a particular chain and stay there repeatedly, expecting and generally receiving the level of comfort they want. These travelers should investigate the chain's frequent-guest program – discounts and guaranteed reservations are offered to faithful guests.

The cheapest national chain is Motel 6. Rooms are small and very bland, but the beds are usually OK, every room has a TV and phone (local calls are free) and most properties have a swimming pool. Rooms start in the $20s for a single in smaller towns, in the $30s in larger towns. They usually charge a flat $6 for each extra person.

Several motel chains compete with one another at the next price level, with rooms starting in the $30s in the smaller towns or in the $40s in larger or more popular places. The main difference between these and Motel 6 rooms is the size of each room – more space to spread out in. Beds are always reliably firm, decor may be a

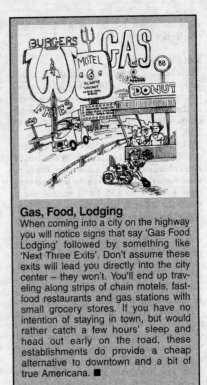

**Gas, Food, Lodging**
When coming into a city on the highway you will notice signs that say 'Gas Food Lodging' followed by something like 'Next Three Exits'. Don't assume these exits will lead you directly into the city center – they won't. You'll end up traveling along strips of chain motels, fast-food restaurants and gas stations with small grocery stores. If you have no intention of staying in town, but would rather catch a few hours' sleep and head out early on the road, these establishments do provide a cheap alternative to downtown and a bit of true Americana. ■

little more attractive, a 24-hour desk is often available and little extras like free coffee, a table, cable or rental movies, or a bathtub with your shower may be offered. If these sorts of things are worth an extra $10 or $15 a night, then you'll be happy with the Super 8 Motels, Days Inn or Econo Lodge. Not all of these have pools, however – Super 8 Motels especially have a good number of properties lacking a pool.

Stepping up to chains with rooms in the $45 to $80 range (depending on location), you'll find noticeably nicer rooms, cafes, restaurants or bars may be on the premises or adjacent to them and the swimming pool may be indoors with a spa or exercise room also available. The Best Western chain consistently has properties in almost every town of any size and offers good rooms in this price range. Often they are the best available in a given town. Less widespread but also good are the *Comfort Inns* and *Sleep Inns*. *Rodeway Inns* fall at the lower end of this category.

**Private Hotels** There are, of course, non-chain establishments in these price ranges. Some of them are funky historical hotels, full of turn-of-the-century furniture. Others are privately run establishments which just don't want to be a part of a chain. In smaller towns, complexes of cabins are available – these often come complete with fireplace, kitchen and an outdoor area with trees and maybe a stream a few steps away.

**Top-End Hotels** Full-service hotels, with bellhops and doormen, restaurants and bars, exercise rooms and saunas, room service and concierge, are found in the main cities. These are also in the text, but they are of limited interest to travelers wanting to see a lot of the Southwest because there are so few of them outside of the (few) big cities. For travelers wanting the most comfort possible, Best Westerns or B&Bs are often the best choices.

**Lodges**
In national parks, you can either camp or stay in park lodges operating as a concession. Lodges are often rustic-looking but are usually quite comfortable inside. Restaurants are on the premises and tour services are often available. National park lodges are not cheap, with most rooms going for close to $100 for a double during the high season, but they are your only option if you want to stay inside the park without camping. A lot of people want to do that, and therefore, many lodges are fully booked months in advance. Want a room the day after tomorrow? Call anyway – you might be very lucky and hit on a cancellation. But your best bet for national park lodges is to make reservations months in advance if you are arriving during the high seasons.

**Resorts & Guest Ranches**
Luxury resorts and dude ranches really require a stay of several days to be appreciated and are often destinations in themselves. Guests at a luxury resort can start the day with a round of golf, then continue with a choice of tennis, massage, horseback riding, shopping, swimming, sunbathing, hot tubbing, drinking and dancing. Guest ranches may be even more 'whole vacation'-oriented with a busy schedule of horseback riding and maybe cattle roundups, rodeo lessons, cookouts and other Western activities. Ranches in the desert lowlands may close in summer, while those in the mountains may close in winter or convert into skiing centers.

There is decent skiing in all three Southwestern states, with Utah definitely offering the best. Skiing resorts may charge $200 or so for a condo in mid-season, and drop prices to less than half in the snowless summer.

**Reservations**
The cheapest bottom-end places may not accept reservations, but at least you can call them and see if they have a room – even if they don't take reservations, they'll often hold a room for you for an hour or two.

Chain hotels will all take reservations days or months ahead. Normally, you have to give a credit card number to hold the room. If you don't show and don't call to cancel, you will be charged the first night's rental. Cancellation policies vary – some let you cancel at no charge 24 hours or 72 hours in advance; others are less forgiving. Find out about cancellation penalties when you book. Also make sure to let the hotel know if you plan on a late arrival – many motels will rent your room if you haven't arrived or called by 6 pm. Chains often have a toll-free number (see below), but their central reservation system might not be aware of local special discounts. Booking ahead, however, gives you the peace of mind of a guaranteed room when you arrive.

Some places, especially B&Bs and some cabins, won't accept credit cards and want a check as a deposit before they'll reserve a room for you.

**Motel Chains** The chains with widespread representation in the Southwest are listed below. Other US chains with only a few hotels in the Southwest are excluded.

| | |
|---|---|
| Best Western | ☎ 1 (800) 528 1234 |
| Comfort Inn | ☎ 1 (800) 221 2222 |
| Days Inn | ☎ 1 (800) 329 7466 |
| Econo Lodge | ☎ 1 (800) 424 4777 |
| Motel 6 | ☎ 1 (505) 891 6161 |
| Sleep Inn | ☎ 1 (800) 221 2222 |
| Super 8 Motel | ☎ 1 (800) 800 8000 |

## FOOD

Whatever your eating preference, you'll be able to find it in the Southwest. From fast food to fancy French, it's all here. The predominant pleasure, for me at least, is Mexican (or New Mexican) cooking. There are plenty of authentic, inexpensive restaurants serving delicious Mexican fare. In small towns, your choice is often between Mexican and American food – only in the bigger cities and resort areas will you find large varieties of ethnic dining and fine Continental cuisine. Here, I discuss only Southwestern food, but rest assured that you can eat Italian, Greek, Chinese, Thai, Indian, French, Japanese and less obvious ethnic choices such as Guatemalan, Russian or Hungarian. These other options are listed in the text.

Mexican food is often hot and spicy – but it doesn't have to be. If you don't like spicy food, go easy on the salsa and you'll find plenty to choose from (see the glossary below). There are distinct regional variations. In Arizona, Mexican food is of the Sonoran type, with dishes like *carne seca* being a specialty. Meals are usually served with refried beans, rice and flour or corn tortillas, and the chiles used are relatively mild. Tucsonans call their home the 'Mexican food capital of the universe', which, although hotly contested by a few other towns, is a statement with at least some ring of truth to it.

New Mexican food is different from, but reminiscent of, Mexican food. Tortillas may be made from blue corn, pinto beans are served whole instead of refried, and *posole* may replace rice. Chiles are used not so much as part of a condiment (like salsa) but more as an essential ingredient in almost every dish. Some can be eye-wateringly hot – ask your waiter for advice if you want a mild meal. One dish that is more likely to be found here than in other parts of the Southwest is *carne adovada*.

And then, of course, there's *nouvelle* Southwestern cuisine, an eclectic mix of Mexican and Continental (especially French) traditions. This is rightly called '*nouvelle*' – it didn't begin to really flourish until the 1970s and early 1980s. This is your chance to try innovative combinations such as chiles stuffed with lobster or barbecued duck tacos. But don't expect any bargains here. Mexican and New Mexican cooking is usually very inexpensive, but tack on nouvelle, and you'll pay big bucks for your gourmet meal.

What about non-nouvelle Southwestern cooking? Head into one of the many steak houses and get a juicy slab of beef with a baked potato and beans. There won't be much here for a vegetarian dining companion.

Native American food is not readily available in restaurants. More often, you'll be able to sample it from food stands at state fairs, powwows, rodeos and other outdoor events in the region. The variety is quite limited. The most popular is fry bread (deep-fried cakes of flattened dough), which may be topped with honey or other delights. Navajo tacos are fry bread topped with a combination of beans, cheese, tomato, lettuce, onion or chile – and sometimes with ground beef.

Generally speaking, Arizona and New Mexico have the most Mexican and nouvelle Southwestern restaurants. Utah doesn't have a tradition of Mexican-influenced food. Here, the influence is mainly Mormon – good, old-fashioned American food like chicken, steak, potatoes and vegetables, homemade pies and ice cream. Salt Lake City, of course, is large and cosmopolitan enough to have a good range of ethnic restaurants. The other, smaller towns have less variety.

The restaurant listings in this book provide a good cross-section of possibilities for everybody. I don't stick to just the best, prizewinning places. I also list 24-hour restaurants, places open at 6 am for an early breakfast, all-you-can-eat joints for starving students on a tight budget, family restaurants where you can eat fairly bland American food inexpensively, funky local places, ice cream parlors, restaurants with an interesting history, and, of course, the various ethnic, Mexican, nouvelle Southwestern and uptown possibilities as well. I don't mention fast-food places, but you can be sure that every town that has a restaurant will have one of the many fast-food franchises, usually on the main drag and with their neon-lit logos visible from many blocks away.

## Southwestern Food Glossary

The items listed below have regional variations – if you like Mexican food, part of the fun of traveling around the Southwest will be figuring out the variations.

*Burrito* (or *burro*) A soft flour tortilla folded around a choice of chicken, beef, chile, bean or cheese filling. A breakfast burrito is stuffed with scrambled eggs, potatoes and ham. (A burro is a large burrito.)

*Carne adovado* Pork chunks marinated in hot chile sauce and baked.

*Carne seca* Beef that has been dried in the sun before cooking.

*Chile relleno* Chile stuffed with cheese and deep-fried in a light batter.

*Chimichanga* A burrito that is deep-fried to make the tortilla crisp.

*Enchilada* A rolled corn tortilla stuffed with a choice of sour cream and cheese, beans, beef or chicken, and smothered with a hot red (or green) sauce and melted cheese.

*Fajitas* Marinated beef or chicken strips, grilled with onions and bell peppers, and served with tortillas, salsa, beans and guacamole.

*Flauta* Similar to a burrito but smaller and tightly rolled rather than folded, and then fried.

*Guacamole* Mashed avocado seasoned with lime juice and cilantro, and optionally spiced with chopped chiles and other condiments.

*Huevos rancheros* Fried eggs on a soft tortilla, covered with chile sauce and melted cheese, and served with beans.

*Menudo* Spicy tripe soup – supposedly a hangover remedy.

*Mole* A mildly spicy, dark sauce of chiles flavored with a hint of chocolate, usually served with chicken.

*Nachos* Tortilla chips covered with melted cheese and/or other toppings.

*Posole* A corn stew (similar to hominy in other states).

*Refried beans* A thick paste of mashed, cooked pinto beans fried with lard.

*Salsa* A cold dip or sauce of chopped chiles, pureed tomatoes, onions and other herbs and spices.

*Sopaipilla* Deep-fried puff pastry served with honey as a dessert.

*Taco* A crispy, fried tortilla, folded in half and stuffed with a combination of beans, ground beef, chiles, onions, tomatoes, lettuce, grated cheese and guacamole.

*Tamale* Slightly sweet corn dough (*masa*) stuffed with a choice of pork, beef, chicken, chile, an olive or plain and wrapped in a corn husk before being steamed.

*Tortilla* A pancake made of unleavened wheat or corn flour. They stay soft when baked, become crisp when fried, and form the basis of most Mexican dishes. Small pieces, deep-fried, become the crispy tortilla chips served with salsa as an appetizer (often at no extra cost) in many Mexican restaurants.

*Tostada* A flat taco.

## Mealtimes

Usually served between about 6 am and 10 am, standard American breakfasts are large and filling, often including eggs or an omelette, bacon or ham, fried potatoes, toast with butter and jam and coffee or tea.

Lunch is available between 11 am and 2 pm. One strategy for enjoying good restaurants on a budget is to frequent them for lunch, when fixed-price specials for as little as $5 or slightly more are common.

Dinners, served anytime between about 5 and 10 pm, are more expensive but often very reasonably priced, and portions are usually large. Specials may also be available, but they will usually be more expensive than lunch specials. Some of the better restaurants will require reservations. Restaurants are often closed on Mondays.

## DRINKS
### Non-Alcoholic
Most restaurants will provide customers with free ice water – tap water is safe to drink. All the usual flavors of soft drinks are available, although you may be asked if you'll drink Coke instead of Pepsi and vice versa. Many restaurants offer milk or juices; a few will have a wide variety of fruit juices. British travelers should remember that 'lemonade' is a lemon-sugar-ice water mix rather than the carbonated variety. (If you want the fizzy kind, ask for a Sprite or Seven-Up, mate.)

Coffee is served much more often than tea. Most restaurants will offer several free coffee refills to customers eating a meal. Drinkers of English-style tea will be disappointed. Tea is usually a cup of hot water with a tea bag next to it – milk is not normally added but a slice of lemon often is. Herb teas are offered in better restaurants and coffee shops.

### Alcoholic
The laws for obtaining alcoholic drinks vary from state to state and are outlined in the introductions to each state in the Southwest.

Bland and boring 'name brand' domestic beers are available everywhere alcohol is sold. Most stores, restaurants and bars also offer much tastier but lesser known local brews, many of which I mention in the text. These may cost more than a Bud, but I think they are worth it. Imported beers are also easily available and, although a little more expensive, offer a wider choice of flavors than domestic brands. Mexican beers, of course, are easy to find everywhere, but UK, European, Canadian and Australian brews are common.

Wine drinkers will find that Californian wines compete well with their European and Australian counterparts. For those interested in experimenting, there are little known wineries in Arizona and New Mexico. A few of these may offer tours and wine tasting and are mentioned in the text.

### Alcohol & Drinking Age
In all three states, persons under the age of 21 (minors) are prohibited from consuming alcohol in the USA. Carry a driver's license or passport as proof of age to enter a bar, order alcohol at a restaurant, or buy alcohol. Servers have the right to ask to see your ID and may refuse service without it. Minors are not allowed in bars and pubs, even to order non-alcoholic beverages. Unfortunately, this means that most dance clubs are also off-limits to minors, although a few clubs have solved the under-age problem with a segregated drinking area. Minors are, however, welcome in the dining areas of restaurants where alcohol may be served.

## ENTERTAINMENT
### Cinemas
The drive-in cinema once seemed to be a part of US culture. Clearly, that is now in the past. Today, just about every town of any size has multiscreen cinemas showing a variety of flicks on two to eight screens. Only the bigger towns have one or two cinemas screening foreign, alternative or underground films.

### Bars & Nightclubs
In small Southwestern towns, a bar might be the best place in town to have a beer, meet some locals, shoot a game of pool or listen to a country & western band. Patrons are usually interested in hearing a foreign accent, so if you have one take advantage of this opportunity to meet locals. Bars in bigger towns offer anything from big TV screens showing sporting events to live music of various genres.

### Theater & Performances
The main cultural centers are mentioned under Arts in Facts about the Southwest chapter. In addition, smaller towns may have local amateur theatrical performances. These include Indian pageants, Mormon pageants, vaudeville shows with audience participation (boo the villain, cheer the hero), mystery crime weekends (where a hotel becomes the scene of a hideous

'crime' and guests are both suspects and sleuths) as well as standard dramatic performances.

## Spectator Sports

Sports in the USA developed separately from the rest of the world, and baseball (with its clone, softball), football and basketball dominate the sports scene, both for spectators and participants. Football and basketball, in particular, are huge. Both are sponsored by high schools and universities, which gives them a community foundation that reinforces their popularity. Basketball has the additional advantages of requiring only limited space and equipment, making it a popular pastime among inner-city residents.

Baseball is so embedded in the country's psyche that, despite its complex rules, the difficulty and expense of maintaining playing fields with an irregular configuration, and labor-management problems at the highest professional levels, it continues to flourish. Many of the most meaningful metaphors in American English and even political discourse – such as 'getting to first base' or the recently debased 'three strikes and you're out' – come from the sport. Softball, which requires less space than baseball, draws more participants, both men and women, than any other organized sport in the country.

Soccer has made limited inroads, mostly among immigrants, but it has failed as a spectator sport and is likely to remain a minor diversion for at least a few years.

The Southwest has a few nationally ranked teams playing the big three US professional sports. Tickets for these events are very hard to get, although you might be lucky. Scalpers sell overpriced tickets outside the stadiums before a game. The only Southwestern major league football team is the Arizona Cardinals of Phoenix. There are no major league baseball teams in the Southwest, but several come from the wintry north in February and March for training seasons in the warm climate of Arizona. Professional basketball is better represented with the Phoenix Suns (who have been hot in recent seasons) and the Utah Jazz (out of Salt Lake City). College basketball is always popular – fans seem to enjoy watching the students as much as the pros. Currently, the University of Arizona Wildcats (from Tucson) are the highest ranked Southwestern team, consistently placing among the top 25 college teams in the nation.

Rodeo is popular in the Southwest – after all, rodeo as a paying spectator sport started here. From late spring to early fall, there are rodeos almost every week somewhere in the Southwest. Rodeo circuits sponsored by the Professional Rodeo Cowboy Association (PRCA) draw competitors from many western states.

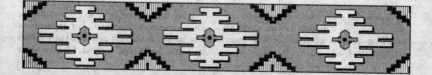

# Getting There & Away

Whether coming from another part of the USA or from abroad, the easiest way to travel is by airplane. Within the USA you can also travel by bus, train or car but this could take up all your vacation time! This chapter focuses on getting to the major transport hubs in the Southwest from the major US ports of entry and other parts of the world. Because of the proliferation of routes into and out of the USA and the complexity of air travel, much of this information is general.

## TRAVEL INSURANCE

No matter how you're traveling, make sure you take out travel insurance. This not only covers you for medical expenses and luggage theft or loss, but also for cancellation or delays in your travel arrangements (you might fall seriously ill two days before departure, for example), and everyone should be covered for the worst possible case, such as an accident that requires hospital treatment and a flight home. Coverage depends on your insurance and type of ticket, so ask both your insurer and your ticket-issuing agency to explain the finer points. STA Travel offers a variety of travel insurance options at reasonable prices. Ticket loss is also covered by travel insurance. Make sure you have a separate record of all your ticket details – or better still, a photocopy of it. Also make a copy of your policy, in case the original is lost.

Buy travel insurance as early as possible. If you buy it the week before you fly, you may find, for instance, that you're not covered for delays to your flight caused by strikes or other industrial action that may have been in force before you took out the insurance.

If you're planning to travel a long time, the insurance may seem very expensive – but if you can't afford it, you certainly won't be able to afford a medical emergency in the USA.

# Within the USA

Most travelers arrive by air, bus or private vehicle. Train service is a little-used fourth option. The landlocked Southwest can't be reached by sea, but the lack of ports has been remedied somewhat by naming the Phoenix International Airport 'Sky Harbor'.

The *New York Times*, *Los Angeles Times*, *Chicago Tribune*, *San Francisco Examiner* and other major newspapers all produce weekly travel sections with numerous travel agents' ads. Council Travel (☎ 1 (800) 226 8624) and STA Travel have offices in major cities nationwide.

The magazine *Travel Unlimited* (PO Box 1058, Allston, MA 02134) publishes details of the cheapest air fares and courier possibilities.

## AIR

Phoenix International Airport (Sky Harbor) is between the seventh and 12th busiest in the USA (depending on which kind of data is used), and it's by far the most important airport in the Southwest. Salt Lake City is the next most important, and Tucson and Albuquerque airports vie for a fairly distant third place. The many other airports are mainly for regional transportation.

Denver International Airport in Colorado is busier than Phoenix, and Las Vegas in Nevada is almost as busy. If you rent a car in Denver, you can be in New Mexico in four hours, and if you rent one in Las Vegas, you can reach Arizona in under an hour, so both Denver and Las Vegas can be considered gateways to the Southwest. El Paso, Texas, a few miles from the New Mexico border, is also a possible gateway.

Fares are incredibly varied. For example, an economy roundtrip ticket from Tucson to San Francisco can cost (as I write) between $128 and almost $400 with a

21-day advance purchase requirement – it depends on which airline you fly. Sometimes the fare increases if you don't spend a Saturday night at your destination (although this was not a requirement for the $128 fare). If you book less than 21 days in advance, fares go up. Still, nothing determines fares more than demand, and when things are slow, regardless of the season, airlines will lower their fares to fill empty seats. There's a lot of competition, and at any given time any one of the airlines could have the cheapest fare.

The most expensive fares are those booked at the last minute – cheap standby fares are not normally offered. Some airlines price their one-way tickets at half the price of their cheapest roundtrip; others may charge much more than half of a roundtrip ticket for a one-way ticket.

Phoenix is a major hub for America West and Southwest Airlines. Salt Lake City is a Delta hub. Denver is a hub for both Continental and United Airlines. The cheapest tickets are often nonrefundable and require an extra fee for changing your flight, so plan ahead carefully. Many insurance policies will cover this loss if you have to change your flight for emergency reasons.

See Buying Tickets in the To/From Abroad section for more air-travel hints.

## Major US Domestic Airlines

Major domestic airlines include the following:

| | |
|---|---|
| Alaska Airlines | ☎ 1 (800) 426 0333 |
| America West | ☎ 1 (800) 235 9292 |
| American | ☎ 1 (800) 433 7300 |
| Continental | ☎ 1 (800) 525 0280 |
| Delta | ☎ 1 (800) 221 1212 |
| Hawaiian Airlines | ☎ 1 (800) 367 5320 |
| Northwest | ☎ 1 (800) 225 2525 |
| Southwest | ☎ 1 (800) 531 5601 |
| TWA | ☎ 1 (800) 892 4141 |
| United | ☎ 1 (800) 241 6522 |

## Visit USA Passes

Almost all domestic carriers offer Visit USA passes to non-US citizens. The passes are actually a book of coupons – each coupon equals a flight. The following airlines are representative of the kinds of deals available, but it's a good idea to ask your travel agent about other airlines that offer the service.

Continental Airlines' Visit USA pass can be purchased in conjunction with an international airline ticket anywhere outside the USA except Canada and Mexico. All travel must be completed within 60 days of the first flight into the USA or 81 days after arrival in the USA. You must have your trip planned out in advance. If you decide to change destinations once in the USA, you will be fined $50. High-season prices are $479 for three coupons (minimum purchase) and $769 for eight (maximum purchase).

Northwest offers the same deal, but it gives you the option of flying standby.

American Airlines uses the same coupon structure and also sells the passes outside of the USA, excluding Canada and Mexico. You must reserve flights one day in advance, and if a coupon only takes you halfway to your destination, you will have to buy the remaining ticket at full price.

Delta has two different systems for travelers coming from abroad. Visit USA gives travelers a discount, but you need to have your itinerary mapped out to take advantage of this. The other option is Discover America, in which a traveler buys coupons good for standby travel anywhere in the continental USA. One flight equals one coupon. Only two transcontinental flights are allowed – Delta prefers that your travels follow some sort of circular pattern. Four coupons cost about $550, 10 cost $1250. Children's fares are about $40 less. Coupons can only be purchased in conjunction with an international flight, Canada and Mexico excluded.

When flying standby, call the airline a day or two before the flight and make a 'standby reservation'. Such a reservation gives you priority over all the others who just appear and hope to get on the flight the same day.

## Getting Bumped

Airlines try to guarantee themselves consistently full planes by overbooking and counting on some passengers not showing up. This usually involves 'bumping' passengers off full flights. Getting bumped can be a nuisance because you have to wait around for the next flight, but if you have a day's leeway, you can really take advantage of the system.

When you check in at the airline counter, ask if they will need volunteers to be bumped, and ask what the compensation will be. Depending on the desirability of the flight, this can range from a $200 voucher toward your next flight to a fully paid roundtrip ticket. Be sure to try and confirm a later flight so you don't get stuck in the airport on standby. If you have to spend the night, airlines frequently foot the hotel bill for their bumpees. All in all, it can be a great deal, and many people plan their trips with a day to spare in order to try for a free ticket that will cover their next trip.

However, be aware that, due to this same system, being just a little late for boarding could get you bumped with none of these benefits.

## LAND

The Southwest is well served by several interstate freeways that connect with the rest of the USA. During the winter, however, even the interstates can be closed or slowed by snow. Interstate 8 from San Diego and I-10 from Los Angeles into southern Arizona and southwestern New Mexico, continuing into Texas, are normally spared weather closures.

## Bus

Greyhound is the main bus system in the USA and plays an important transportation role in the Southwest. Parts of New Mexico are served by the TNM&O (Texas, New Mexico & Oklahoma) bus line. These companies serve major cities and minor towns that happen to be on the routes between major cities. They do not serve places off the main routes, so you won't find many buses to most national parks or important tourist towns such as Moab. For this reason, traveling by car is definitely recommended as more convenient, although details of most every bus route will be given in the text if you have the time or inclination to see the Greyhound side of travel. However, a long-distance bus ride can get you to the region, and then you could rent a car.

Bus travel, of course, gives you the chance to see some of the countryside and talk to some of the inhabitants that air travelers might miss. Meal stops are made on long trips; you pay for your own simple food in an inexpensive and unexciting cafe. Buses have on-board lavatories. Seats recline for sleeping. Smoking is not permitted aboard Greyhound buses. Because buses are so few, schedules are often inconvenient, fares are relatively high and bargain air fares can undercut buses on long-distance routes; in some cases, on shorter routes, it can be cheaper to rent a car than to ride the bus. However, very long distance bus trips are often available at bargain prices by purchasing or reserving tickets three days in advance.

For more fare details, see Buses in the Getting Around chapter.

## Train

The Amtrak train system crosses the south, central and northern part of the Southwest. The trains are used more as a means of getting to or through the area than for touring around the region.

Train travel can be an experience in itself: meals on wheels, being rocked to sleep and, of course, splendid vistas from special carriages with large viewing windows. Sleeping cabins are available, ranging from inexpensive family cabins with bunks sleeping four, to double cabins with private baths and hot showers. You can also sleep in your ordinary reclining seat. Dining and lounge cars serve meals and alcoholic and soft drinks; meals are included in the cost of tickets for the sleeping cabins. Long-distance trains provide entertainment such as movies (and cartoons for kids), bingo and other games. Smoking is not permitted on most routes; however, on some routes smoking is allowed in private rooms and in the lounge car during specific times.

The *Southwest Chief* has daily service between Chicago and Los Angeles via Kansas City, Albuquerque, Flagstaff and Kingman. The *Desert Wind* runs daily between Chicago and Los Angeles via Denver, Salt Lake City and Las Vegas. There are also daily *California Zephyr* trains between Salt Lake City and San Francisco. The *Sunset Limited* train runs three times a week on the southern route from Los Angeles through Phoenix, Tucson and El Paso to New Orleans.

On some journeys, local guides get on the train to talk about the area you are going through; particularly popular are the Indian guides on the *Southwest Chief* train between Gallup and Albuquerque. These run daily in the morning eastbound and in the evening westbound.

All tickets should be booked in advance. Amtrak arranges a variety of train-based tours and discounts. The best value overall is their All Aboard America fare. This costs $278 for adults and enables you to travel anywhere you want. There are limitations, however. Travel must be completed in 45 days, and you are allowed up to three stopovers. Additional stopovers can be arranged at extra cost. Your entire trip must be reserved in advance, and the seats are limited so book as far ahead as possible. Travel between mid-June and late August is $338. These tickets are for reclining seats; sleeping cars cost extra.

If you want to travel in just the eastern, central or western parts of the country, $178 All Aboard America fares are available. The west is considered to be El Paso, Albuquerque and Denver and all points west. The central region lies between El Paso, Albuquerque and Denver, and New Orleans and Chicago. The east is points east of New Orleans and Chicago. Thus you can travel from Chicago to Albuquerque and back for $178, including three stopovers (this is cheaper than the one-way fare!) Travel between two adjoining regions is $228. Fares go up from mid-June to late August. A sample fare not using the All Aboard America system is Los Angeles to Flagstaff for $87 one-way or $94 roundtrip.

For further travel assistance, call Amtrak (☎ 1 (800) USA RAIL, 872 7245) or ask your travel agent. Note that most small train stations don't sell tickets; you have to book them with Amtrak over the phone. Some small stations have no porters or other facilities, and trains may stop there only if you have bought a ticket in advance.

### Car

For information on buying or renting a car, or using a drive-away (driving a car for someone else) see the Getting Around chapter.

### TOURS

Tours of the USA are so numerous that it would be impossible to attempt any kind of comprehensive listing; for overseas visitors, the most reliable sources of information on the constantly changing offerings are major international travel agents like Thomas Cook and American Express. Probably those of most interest to the general traveler are coach tours that visit the national parks and guest ranch excursions; for those with limited time, package tours can be an efficient and relatively inexpensive way to go.

A number of companies offer standard guided tours of the Southwest, usually by bus and including hotel accommodations. Any travel agent can tell you about these and arrange air, train or bus tickets to get you to the beginning of the tour.

Some more specialized tours include the following. Green Tortoise (☎ (415) 956 7500, 1 (800) 867 8647), 494 Broadway, San Francisco, CA 94133, offers alternative bus transportation with stops at places like hot springs and national parks. Meals are cooperatively cooked, and you sleep on bunks on the bus or camp. This is not luxury travel, but it is fun. The company's National Parks Loop from San Francisco is 16 days, eight of which are in Utah. The cost is $499 plus $121 toward the food fund. The nine-day Grand Canyon trip from San Francisco spends seven days in northern Arizona and southern Utah – $349 plus $61 food fund. These trips run from May to September only.

Roundtrip van camping tours of the Southwest (and other areas of the country) are offered by Trek America (☎ (908) 362 9198, 1 (800) 221 0596, fax (908) 362 9313), PO Box 470, Blairstown, NJ 07825. In England, they are at Trek House (☎ 01 869 38777, fax 01 869 338846), The Bullring, Deddington, Banbury, Oxon OX15 0TT. These tours last from one to nine weeks and are designed for small, international groups (13 people maximum) of 18- to 38-year-olds. Tour prices vary with season, and July to September are the highest. Sample prices including food and occasional hotel nights are about $1000 for a 10-day tour of the canyonlands of northern Arizona and southern Utah to $3500 for a nine-week tour of the entire country including a week in the Southwest. Some side trips and cultural events (cowboy cookouts!) are included in the price, and participants help with cooking and camp chores.

Similar deals are available from Suntreks (☎ (707) 523 1800, 1 (800) 292 9696, fax (707) 523 1911), Sun Plaza, 77 West Third St, Santa Rosa, CA 95401. Suntreks also has offices in Australia (☎ 02 281 8000, fax 02 281 2722), 62 Mary St, Surry Hills, Sydney NSW 2010; Germany (☎ 089 480 2831, fax 089 480 2411), Swdanstrasse 21, D-81667 Munich; and Switzerland (☎ 01 462 6161, fax 01 462 6545), Birmensdorferstr 107, PO Box 8371, CH-8036, Zurich. They also have representation in many other countries. Suntreks also has longer tours, up to 13 weeks, and offers motel-based as well as camping tours. Their tours are for the 'young at heart' and attract predominantly young international travelers, although there is no age limit. Prices range from about $1600 for the three-week Navajo Trail trek (northern Arizona, Utah and Colorado), to about $4500 for their 13-week around America treks.

Road Runner USA/Canada (☎ (800) 873 5872), 6762A Centinela Ave, Culver City, CA 90230, organizes one- and two-week treks in conjunction with Hostelling International to different parts of the USA and across country. They also have offices in England (☎ (892) 542010), PO Box 105, Kelly House, Warwick Rd, Tunbridge Wells, Kent TN1 1ZN and in Australia (☎ (2) 299 8844) Wholesale Pty Ltd, 8th Floor, 350 Kent St, Sydney, NSW 2000.

AmeriCan Adventures (☎ (800) 864 0335), 6762A Centinela Ave, Culver City, CA 90230, offers seven- to 21-day trips to different parts of the USA, usually following a theme like Route 66 or Wild West. For worldwide sales contact them at their UK headquarters (☎ (892) 511894) 45 High St, Tunbridge Wells, Kent TN1 1XL.

# To/From Abroad

## AIR
### Buying Tickets

Numerous airlines fly to the USA, and a variety of fares are available; in addition to a straightforward roundtrip ticket, it can also be part of a Round-the-World ticket or Circle Pacific fare. So rather than just walking into the nearest travel agent or airline office, it pays to do a bit of research and shop around first. You might start by perusing travel sections of magazines like *Time Out* and *TNT* in the UK, or the Saturday editions of newspapers like the *Sydney Morning Herald* and *The Age* in Australia. Ads in these publications offer cheap fares, but don't be surprised if they happen to be sold out when you contact the agents: they're usually low-season fares on obscure airlines with conditions attached.

The plane ticket will probably be the single most expensive item in your budget, and buying it can be intimidating. It is always worth putting aside a few hours to research the current state of the market. Start shopping for a ticket early – some of the cheapest tickets must be bought months in advance, and some popular flights sell out early. Talk to other recent travelers – they may be able to stop you from making some of the same old mistakes. Look at the ads in newspapers and magazines, consult reference books and watch for special offers.

Note that high season in the USA is mid-June to mid-September (summer) and the one week before and after Christmas. The best rates for travel to and in the USA are found November through March.

Call travel agents for bargains (airlines can supply information on routes and timetables; however, except at times of fare wars, they do not supply the cheapest tickets). Airlines often have competitive low-season, student and senior citizens' fares. Find out the fare, the route, the duration of the journey and any restrictions on the ticket.

Cheap tickets are available in two distinct categories: official and unofficial. Official ones have a variety of names including advance-purchase fares, budget fares, Apex and super-Apex. Unofficial tickets are simply discounted tickets that the airlines release through selected travel agents (not through airline offices). The cheapest tickets are often nonrefundable and require an extra fee for changing your flight. Many insurance policies will cover this loss if you have to change your flight for emergency reasons. Return (roundtrip) tickets usually work out cheaper than two one-way fares – often *much* cheaper.

Use the fares quoted in this book as a guide only. They are approximate and based on the rates advertised by travel agents and airlines at press time. Quoted airfares do not necessarily constitute a recommendation for the carrier.

If traveling from the UK, you will probably find that the cheapest flights are being advertised by obscure bucket shops whose names haven't yet reached the telephone directory. Many such firms are honest and solvent, but there are a few rogues who will take your money and disappear, to reopen elsewhere a month or two later under a new name. If you feel suspicious about a firm, don't give them all the money at once – leave a deposit of 20% or so and pay

the balance on receiving the ticket. If they insist on cash in advance, go elsewhere. And once you have the ticket, ring the airline to confirm that you are booked on the flight.

You may decide to pay more than the rock-bottom fare by opting for the safety of a better-known travel agent. Established firms like STA Travel, which has offices worldwide, Council Travel in the USA or Travel CUTS in Canada are valid alternatives and they offer good prices to most destinations.

Once you have your ticket, write down its number, together with the flight number and other details, and keep the information somewhere separate. If the ticket is lost or stolen, this will help you get a replacement.

Remember to buy travel insurance as early as possible.

### Arriving in the USA

Even if you are continuing immediately to another city, the first airport that you land in is where you must carry out immigration and customs formalities. Even if your luggage is checked from, say, London to Phoenix, you will still have to take it through customs if you first land in Chicago.

Passengers aboard the airplane are given standard immigration and customs forms to fill out. The cabin crew will help you fill them out if you have any questions, but the forms are quite straightforward. After the plane lands, you'll first go through immigration. There are two lines: one is for US citizens and residents, and the other is for nonresidents. Immigration formalities are usually straightforward if you have all the necessary documents (passport and visa). Occasionally, you may be asked to show your ticket out of the country, but this doesn't happen very often.

After passing through immigration, you collect your baggage and then pass through customs. If you have nothing to declare, there is a good chance that you can clear customs quickly and without a luggage search, but you can't rely on it. After passing through customs, you are officially in the country. If your flight is continuing to another city or you have a connecting flight, it is your responsibility to get your bags to the right place. Normally, there are airline counters just outside the customs area that will help you. Also see the information under Customs in Facts for the Visitor.

### Travelers with Special Needs

If you have special needs of any sort – a broken leg, dietary restrictions, dependence on a wheelchair, responsibility for a baby, fear of flying – you should let the airline know as soon as possible so that they can make arrangements accordingly. You should remind them when you reconfirm your booking (at least 72 hours before departure) and again when you check in at the airport. It may also be worth ringing round the airlines before you make your booking to find out how they can handle your particular needs.

Airports and airlines can be surprisingly helpful, but they do need advance warning. Most international airports can provide escorts from check-in desk to plane where needed, and there should be ramps, lifts, accessible toilets and reachable phones. Aircraft toilets, on the other hand, are likely to present a problem; travelers should discuss this with the airline at an early stage and, if necessary, with their doctor.

Guide dogs for the blind will often have to travel in a specially pressurized baggage compartment with other animals, away from their owner, though smaller guide dogs may be admitted to the cabin. Guide dogs are not subject to quarantine as long as they have proof of being vaccinated against rabies.

Deaf travelers can ask for airport and in-flight announcements to be written down for them.

Children under two travel for 10% of the standard fare (or free, on some airlines), as long as they don't occupy a seat. (They don't get a baggage allowance either.) 'Skycots' should be provided by the airline if requested in advance; these will take a child weighing up to about 22 pounds. Children between two and 12 can usually occupy a seat for half to two-thirds of the full fare, and do get a baggage allowance. Strollers can often be taken on as hand luggage.

### Baggage & Other Restrictions

On most domestic and international flights you are limited to two checked bags, or three if you don't have a carry-on. There could be a charge if you bring more or if the size of the bags exceeds the airline's limits. It's best to check with the individual airline if you are worried about this. On some international flights the luggage allowance is based on weight, not numbers; again, check with the airline.

If your luggage is delayed upon arrival (which is rare), some airlines will give a cash advance to purchase necessities. If sporting equipment is misplaced, the airline may pay for rentals. Should the luggage be lost, it is important to submit a claim. The airline doesn't have to pay the full amount of the claim, rather they can estimate the value of your lost items. It may take them anywhere from six weeks to three months to process the claim and pay you.

**Smoking** Smoking is prohibited on all domestic flights in the USA. Many international flights are following suit. Incidentally, the restriction applies to the passenger cabin and the lavatories but not the cockpit. Many airports in the USA also restrict smoking, but they compensate by having 'smoking rooms'.

**Illegal Items** Items that are illegal to take on a plane, either checked or as carry-on, include aerosols of polishes, waxes, etc; tear gas and pepper spray; camp stoves with fuel; and divers' tanks that are full. Matches should not be checked.

### Major International Airlines

Major international airlines include:

| | |
|---|---|
| Air Canada | ☎ 1 (800) 776 3000 |
| Air France | ☎ 1 (800) 237 2747 |
| Air New Zealand | ☎ 1 (800) 262 1234 |
| American Airlines | ☎ 1 (800) 433 7300 |
| British Airways | ☎ 1 (800) 247 9297 |

| Canadian Airlines | ☎ 1 (800) 426 7000 |
| Continental Airlines | ☎ 1 (800) 525 0280 |
| Delta Air Lines | ☎ 1 (800) 221 1212 |
| Japan Air Lines | ☎ 1 (800) 525 3663 |
| KLM | ☎ 1 (800) 374 7747 |
| Northwest Airlines | ☎ 1 (800) 447 4747 |
| Qantas Airways | ☎ 1 (800) 227 4500 |
| TWA | ☎ 1 (800) 221 2000 |
| United Airlines | ☎ 1 (800) 241 6522 |
| USAir | ☎ 1 (800) 428 4322 |

## Round-the-World Tickets

Round-the-World (RTW) tickets have become very popular in the last few years. Airline RTW tickets are often real bargains and can work out to be no more expensive or even cheaper than an ordinary return ticket. Prices start at about UK£850, A$1800 or US$1300.

The official airline RTW tickets are usually put together by a combination of two airlines, and permit you to fly anywhere you want on their route systems as long as you do not backtrack. Other restrictions are that you must usually book the first sector in advance and cancellation penalties apply. There may be restrictions on the number of stops permitted, and tickets are usually valid from 90 days up to a year. An alternative type of RTW ticket is one put together by a travel agent using a combination of discounted tickets.

Although most airlines restrict the number of sectors that can be flown within the USA and Canada to four, and some airlines black out a few heavily traveled routes (like Honolulu to Tokyo), stopovers are otherwise generally unlimited. In most cases a 14-day advance purchase is required. After the ticket is purchased, dates can be changed without penalty and tickets can be rewritten to add or delete stops for $50 each.

The majority of RTW tickets restrict you to just two airlines, British Airways and Qantas Airways offer a RTW ticket called the Global Explorer that allows you to combine routes on both airlines to a total of 28,000 miles for US$2999 or A$3099.

Qantas also flies in conjunction with American Airlines, Delta Air Lines, Northwest Airlines, Canadian Airlines, Air France and KLM. Qantas RTW tickets, with any of the aforementioned partner airlines, cost US$3247 or A$3099.

Canadian Airlines offers numerous RTW combinations, such as with Philippine Airlines for C$2790 that could include Manila, Dubai, Pakistan and Europe; another with KLM that could include Cairo, Bombay, Delhi and Amsterdam for C$3149; and a third with South African Airways that could include Australia and Africa for C$3499.

Many other airlines also offer RTW tickets. Continental Airlines, for example, links up with either Malaysia Airlines, Singapore Airlines or Thai Airways for US$2570. TWA's lowest priced RTW, linking up with Korean Air, costs US$2087 and allows stops in Honolulu, Seoul, Tel Aviv, Amsterdam and Paris or London.

## Circle Pacific Tickets

Circle Pacific tickets use a combination of airlines to circle the Pacific – combining Australia, New Zealand, North America and Asia. Rather than simply flying from point A to point B, these tickets allow you to swing through much of the Pacific Rim and eastern Asia taking in a variety of destinations – as long as you keep traveling in the same circular direction. As with RTW tickets there are advance purchase restrictions and limits on how many stopovers you can take. These fares are likely to be around 15% cheaper than RTW tickets.

Circle Pacific routes essentially have the same fares: A$2999 when purchased in Australia, US$2449 when purchased in the USA and C$3309 when purchased in Canada. Circle Pacific fares include four stopovers with the option of adding additional stops at US$50 each. There's a 14-day advance purchase requirement, a 25% cancellation penalty and a maximum stay of six months. There are also higher business class and 1st-class fares. Departure and airport-use taxes, which will vary with the itinerary, are additional.

Qantas Airways offers Circle Pacific routes in partnership with Delta Air Lines, Japan Air Lines, Northwest Airlines or Continental Airlines. In the off-season (the

## Air Travel Glossary

**Apex** – Apex, or 'advance purchase excursion' is a discounted ticket that must be paid for in advance. There are penalties if you wish to change it.

**Bucket Shop** – An unbonded travel agency specializing in discounted airline tickets.

**Bumping** – Just because you have a confirmed seat doesn't mean you're going to get on the plane – see Overbooking.

**Cancellation Penalties** – If you must cancel or change an Apex ticket there are often heavy penalties involved, but insurance can sometimes be taken out against these penalties. Some airlines impose penalties on regular tickets as well, particularly against 'no show' passengers.

**Check In** – Airlines ask you to check in a certain time ahead of the flight departure (usually two hours on international flights). If you fail to check in on time and the flight is overbooked the airline can cancel your booking and give your seat to somebody else.

**Confirmation** – Having a ticket written out with the flight and date you want doesn't mean you have a seat until the agent has checked with the airline that your status is 'OK' or confirmed. Meanwhile you could just be 'on request'.

**Discounted Tickets** – There are two types of discounted fares – officially discounted (see Promotional Fares) and unofficially discounted. The lowest prices often impose drawbacks like flying with unpopular airlines, inconvenient schedules or unpleasant routes and connections. A discounted ticket can save you other things than money – you may be able to pay Apex prices without the associated Apex advance booking and other requirements. Discounted tickets only exist when there is fierce competition.

**Full Fares** – Airlines traditionally offer 1st class (coded F), business class (coded J) and economy class (coded Y) tickets. These days there are so many promotional and discounted fares available from the regular economy class that few passengers pay full economy fare.

**Lost Tickets** – If you lose your airline ticket an airline will usually treat it like a travelers' check and, after inquiries, issue you with another one. Legally, however, an airline is entitled to treat it like cash and if you lose it then it's gone forever. Take good care of your tickets.

**No Shows** – No shows are passengers who fail to show up for their flight. Full-fare passengers who fail to turn up are sometimes entitled to travel on a later flight. The rest of us are penalized (see Cancellation Penalties).

**On Request** – An unconfirmed booking for a flight; see Confirmation.

**Open Jaws** – A return ticket where you fly to one place but return from another. If available this can save you backtracking to your arrival point.

Australian winter), Qantas occasionally offers hefty discounts on tickets that use Qantas as the primary carrier.

United Airlines flies in conjunction with Cathay Pacific, Qantas, Ansett, Malaysia Airlines or British Airways. Canadian Airlines has Circle Pacific fares from Vancouver that include, in one combination or another, virtually all Pacific Rim destinations. Canadian's partners include Qantas, Air New Zealand, Singapore, Garuda, Cathay Pacific or Malaysia Airlines.

**Overbooking** – Airlines hate to fly empty seats and since every flight has some passengers who fail to show up they often book more passengers than they have seats. Usually the excess passengers balance those who fail to show up but occasionally somebody gets bumped. If this happens guess who it's most likely to be? The passengers who check in late.

**Promotional Fares** – Officially discounted fares like Apex fares which are available from travel agents or direct from the airline.

**Reconfirmation** – At least 72 hours prior to departure time of an onward or return flight you must contact the airline and 'reconfirm' that you intend to be on the flight. If you don't do this the airline can delete your name from the passenger list and you could lose your seat. You don't have to reconfirm the first flight on your itinerary or if your stopover is less than 72 hours. It doesn't hurt to reconfirm more than once.

**Restrictions** – Discounted tickets often have various restrictions on them – advance purchase is the most usual one (see Apex). Others are restrictions on the minimum and maximum period you must be away, such as a minimum of 14 days or a maximum of one year. See Cancellation Penalties.

**Standby** – A discounted ticket where you only fly if there is a seat free at the last moment. Standby fares are usually only available on domestic routes.

**Tickets Out** – An entry requirement for many countries is that you have an onward or return ticket, in other words, a ticket out of the country. If you're not sure what you intend to do next, the easiest solution is to buy the cheapest onward ticket to a neighboring country or a ticket from a reliable airline which can later be refunded if you do not use it.

**Transferred Tickets** – Airline tickets cannot be transferred from one person to another. Travelers sometimes try to sell the return half of their ticket, but officials can ask you to prove that you are the person named on the ticket. This is unlikely to happen on domestic flights, but on an international flight tickets may be compared with passports.

**Travel Agencies** – Travel agencies vary widely and you should ensure you use one that suits your needs. Some simply handle tours, while full-service agencies handle everything from tours and tickets to car rental and hotel bookings. A good one will do all these things and can save you a lot of money but if all you want is a ticket at the lowest possible price, then you really need an agency specializing in discounted tickets. A discounted ticket agency, however, may not be useful for things like hotel bookings.

**Travel Periods** – Some officially discounted fares, Apex fares in particular, vary with the time of year. There is often a low (off-peak) season and a high (peak) season. Sometimes there's an intermediate or shoulder season as well. At peak times, when everyone wants to fly, not only will the officially discounted fares be higher but so will unofficially discounted fares or there may simply be no discounted tickets available. Usually the fare depends on your outward flight – if you depart in the high season and return in the low season, you pay the high-season fare. ■

## To/From Canada

Travel CUTS has offices in all major cities. The *Toronto Globe & Mail* and *Vancouver Sun* carry travel agents' ads; the magazine *Great Expeditions* (PO Box 8000-411, Abbotsford BC V2S 6H1) is also useful.

Most connections between the Southwest and Canada are through Vancouver, BC. Both Phoenix and Salt Lake City have frequent and inexpensive flights to/from Vancouver, BC, which is serviced by Air Canada and Canadian Airlines. Airlines flying to the Southwest include Alaska Airlines, United and Delta.

## To/From the UK & Ireland

Check the ads in magazines like *Time Out* and *City Limits*, plus the Sunday papers and *Exchange & Mart*. Also check the free magazines widely available in London – start by looking outside the main railway stations.

Most British travel agents are registered with the ABTA (Association of British Travel Agents). If you have paid for your flight to an ABTA-registered agent who then goes out of business, ABTA will guarantee a refund or an alternative. Unregistered bucket shops are riskier but sometimes cheaper.

London is arguably the world's headquarters for bucket shops, which are well advertised and can usually beat published airline fares. Two good, reliable agents for cheap tickets in the UK are Trailfinders (☎ 071-938-3366), 46 Earls Court Rd, London W8 6EJ, and STA Travel (☎ 071-937-9962), 74 Old Brompton Rd, London SW7. Trailfinders produces a lavishly illustrated brochure including air fare details.

Virgin Atlantic has a roundtrip high-season fare from London to New York for £448 (US$734), which allows a one-month maximum stay and requires a 21-day advance purchase. Off-season (winter) flights from London to New York range from £240 (US$393) to £508 (US$833), and to Los Angeles starting at £280 (US$460).

The Globetrotters Club (BCM Roving, London WC1N 3XX) publishes a newsletter called *Globe* that covers obscure destinations and can help you find traveling companions.

## To/From Continental Europe

It is definitely worth flying straight to the West Coast instead of transfering from New York or Chicago. Flights from Copenhagen, Paris and Amsterdam often stop in London before continuing on to Los Angeles or San Francisco. Vancouver, BC is also convenient, and has links to Frankfurt. San Francisco has direct links to Paris. There are no direct flights to the Southwest from Europe.

It takes about 10 hours to fly non-stop between from Amsterdam to Los Angeles. Compare this with the total travel time if West Coast-bound travelers from Europe hub out of New York or Chicago. The primary European airlines serving the West Coast are British Air, SAS and Air France. Fares fluctuate wildly, but are usually around $900 to $1000 roundtrip between Los Angeles and London during high season; off-season fares can drop as low as $550 roundtrip. Martin Air, out of Amsterdam, offers discounted tickets and flies non-stop to Denver.

In Amsterdam, NBBS is a popular travel agent. In Paris, Transalpino and Council Travel are popular agencies. The newsletter *Farang* (La Rue 8 á 4261 Braives, Belgium) deals with exotic destinations, as does the magazine *Aventure du Bout du Monde* (116 rue de Javel, 75015 Paris, France).

Virgin Atlantic flights from Paris to New York are substantially cheaper than other carriers; a ticket with seven-day advance purchase ranges from FF3790 (US$773) to FF4530 (US$924).

## To/From Australia & New Zealand

In Australia, STA Travel and Flight Centres International are major dealers in cheap air fares; check the travel agents' ads in the Yellow Pages and call around. Qantas flies to Los Angeles from Sydney, Melbourne (via Sydney or Auckland) and Cairns. United flies to San Francisco from Sydney and Auckland (via Sydney) and also flies to Los Angeles.

In New Zealand, STA Travel and Flight Centres International are also popular travel agents.

The cheapest tickets have a 21-day advance-purchase requirement, a minimum stay of seven days and a maximum stay of 60 days. Qantas flies from Melbourne or

Sydney to Los Angeles for A$1470 (US$1088) in the low season and A$1820 (US$1346) in the high season. Qantas flights from Cairns to Los Angeles cost A$1579 (US$1168) in the low season and A$1919 (US$1420) in the high season. Flying with Air New Zealand is slightly cheaper, and both Qantas and Air New Zealand offer tickets with longer stays or stopovers, but you pay more. Full-time students can save A$80 (US$59) to A$140 (US$103) on roundtrip fares to the USA. United also flies to Los Angeles.

Roundtrip flights from Auckland to Los Angeles on Qantas cost NZ$1720 (US$1186) in the low season. (This is the quoted student fare.)

### To/From Asia

Hong Kong is the discount plane ticket capital of the region, but its bucket shops can be unreliable. Ask the advice of other travelers before buying a ticket. STA Travel, which is dependable, has branches in Hong Kong, Tokyo, Singapore, Bangkok and Kuala Lumpur. Many if not most flights to the USA go via Honolulu, Hawaii.

**To/From Japan** United Airlines has three flights a day to Honolulu from Tokyo with connections to West Coast cities like Los Angeles, San Francisco and Seattle. Northwest and Japan Air Lines also have daily flights to the West Coast from Tokyo; Japan Air Lines also flies to Honolulu from Osaka, Nagoya, Fukuoka and Sapporo.

**To/From Southeast Asia** There are numerous airlines flying to the USA from Southeast Asia; bucket shops in places like Bangkok and Singapore should be able to come up with the best deals. Tickets to the US West Coast often allow a free stopover in Honolulu.

Northwest Airlines flies to Honolulu from Hong Kong, Bangkok, Manila, Seoul and Singapore, with connections to the West Coast. Korean Air and Philippine Airlines also have flights from a number of

Southeast Asian cities to Honolulu, with onward connections.

### To/From Central & South America

Most flights from Central and South America go via Miami, Houston or Los Angeles, though some fly via New York. Most countries' international flag carriers (some of them, like Aerolíneas Argentinas and LANChile, recently privatized) as well as US airlines like United and American, serve these destinations, with onward connections to cities in the Southwest. Continental has flights from about 20 cities in Mexico and Central America, including San Jose, Guatemala City, Cancún and Mérida.

### LAND

Drivers of cars and riders of motorbikes will need the vehicle's registration papers, liability insurance and an international drivers permit in addition to their domestic license. Canadian and Mexican drivers licenses are accepted.

### LEAVING THE USA

You should check in for international flights two hours early. During check-in procedures, you will be asked questions about whether you packed your own bags, whether anyone else has had access to them since you packed them and whether you have received any parcels to carry. These questions are for security reasons.

### Departure Taxes

Airport departure taxes are normally included in the cost of tickets bought in the USA, although tickets purchased abroad may not have this included. There's a $6 airport departure tax charged to all passengers bound for a foreign destination. However, this fee, as well as a $6.50 North American Free Trade Agreement (NAFTA) tax charged to passengers entering the USA from a foreign country, are hidden taxes added to the purchase price of your airline ticket.

# Getting Around

Once you reach the Southwest, traveling by car is generally considered the best way of getting around. A car will get you to rural areas not served by air, bus or train. However, you can use public transport to visit the towns and cities, then you can hire a car locally to get to places not served by public transport. This option is usually much more expensive than just renting a car and driving yourself everywhere, but it can cut down on long-distance driving trips if you don't relish them.

## AIR

Phoenix is the hub of America West Express, which serves small towns throughout Arizona, northwestern New Mexico and southwestern Colorado. Albuquerque is the hub of Mesa Air, which serves small towns throughout New Mexico. Salt Lake City is the hub for Delta Connection, serving St George, Cedar City and Vernal in Utah. These flights tend to be used mainly by local residents and business people. Fares for these short hops are not very cheap, but are an option for tourists with money.

America West, Southwest, Delta and Arizona Airways are the main carriers linking Phoenix, Salt Lake City and Albuquerque. Regular fares on these routes can be expensive if you don't have advance booking, but fares can drop by about half if you are able to fly very early in the morning or late at night, or on specific flights. Ask about special fares when making reservations.

If you are arriving from overseas or another major airport in the USA, it is usually much cheaper to buy a through ticket to small airports as part of your fare rather than separately, unless your travel plans are so spontaneous as to preclude doing so.

Another alternative is an air pass, available from the major airlines that fly between the USA and Europe, Asia and Australia. Air passes are particularly valuable if you're flying between widely separated destinations. (See Visit USA Passes in Getting There & Away.)

## Regional Carriers

The following list includes both major airlines and smaller commuter carriers.

| | |
|---|---|
| American | ☎ 1 (800) 433 7300 |
| America West Express | ☎ 1 (800) 235 9292 |
| Arizona Airways | ☎ 1 (800) 274 0662 |
| Delta Connection | ☎ 1 (800) 221 1212 |
| Horizon Air | ☎ 1 (800) 547 9308 |
| Mesa Air | ☎ 1 (800) 637 2247 |
| Reno Air | ☎ 1 (800) 736 6247 |
| Southwest Airlines | ☎ 1 (800) 466 7747 |

## BUS

Greyhound (☎ 1 (800) 231 2222 for fares and schedules, 1 (800) 822 2662 for customer service) is the main carrier in the Southwest. They run buses several times a day along major highways between large towns, stopping at smaller towns that happen to be along the way. Greyhound has reduced or eliminated services to smaller rural communities it once served efficiently. In many small towns Greyhound no longer maintains terminals, but merely stops at a given location, such as a grocery store parking lot. In these unlikely terminals, boarding passengers usually pay the driver with exact change. Buses have air conditioning, on-board lavatories and reclining seats. Smoking is not permitted on Greyhound buses. The buses do stop for meals, usually at fast-food restaurants or cafeteria-style truck stops.

Towns not on major routes are often served by local carriers. Greyhound usually has information about the local carriers – the name and phone number and, sometimes, fare and schedule information as well. Information about the many local bus companies is given in the text.

## Greyhound Fares

Tickets can be bought over the phone with a credit card (MasterCard, Visa or Discover) and mailed to you if purchased 10 days in advance, or picked up at the terminal with proper identification. Greyhound terminals also accept American Express, traveler's checks and cash. All buses are nonsmoking, and reservations are made with ticket purchases only.

Fares vary tremendously. Sometimes, but not always, you can get discounted tickets if you purchase them seven or 21 days in advance. Sometimes a roundtrip ticket costs twice the price of a one-way ticket; at other times roundtrips are cheaper than two one-ways. Special fares are sometimes offered (eg, 'Anywhere that Greyhound goes for $99'). These details depend on where and when you are traveling and can change from season to season. (At the time of writing this, for example, there is no $99 ticket.) It's best to call Greyhound for current details.

Fares do not necessarily depend on the distance traveled. The 260-mile trip from Tucson to Flagstaff was recently $41 one-way, while the 470-mile trip from Phoenix to Albuquerque was $45 and the 725-mile Salt Lake City to Phoenix trip (via Las Vegas) was $59. Bus passes are currently available for seven days ($259), 15 days ($459) and 30 days ($559). Children's fares are half price for two- to 11-year-olds. Student discounts are available occasionally on specific routes during certain times of the year – in other words, call Greyhound. Student bus passes at a discount may be available for foreign students in their home country – ask your travel agent specializing in student travel.

**Ameripass** Greyhound's Ameripass is potentially useful, depending on how much you plan to travel, but the relatively high prices may impel you to travel more than you normally would simply to get your money's worth. There are no restrictions on who can buy an Ameripass; it costs $179 for seven days of unlimited travel year round, $289 for 15 days of travel and $399 for 30 days of travel. Children under 11 travel for half price. You can get on and off at any Greyhound stop or terminal, and the Ameripass is available at every Greyhound terminal.

**International Ameripass** This can be purchased only by foreign tourists and foreign students and lecturers (with their families) staying less than one year. These prices are $89 for a four-day pass for unlimited travel Monday to Thursday, $149 for a seven-day pass, $209 for a 15-day pass and $289 for a 30-day pass. The International Ameripass is usually bought abroad at a travel agency or can be bought in the USA through the Greyhound International depot in New York City (☎ (212) 971 0492) at 625 8th Ave at the Port Authority Subway level, open Monday to Friday from 9 am to 4:30 pm. New York Greyhound International accepts MasterCard and Visa, traveler's checks and cash, and allows purchases to be made by phone.

To inquire about regular fares and routes call Greyhound International at 1 (800) 246 8572. Those buying an International Ameripass must complete an affidavit and present a passport or visa (or waiver) to the appropriate Greyhound officials.

There are also special passes for travel in Canada that can be bought only through the New York City office or abroad.

## TRAIN

Amtrak (☎ 1 (800) USA RAIL or 872 7255) fares vary greatly, depending on different promotional fares and destinations. Reservations (the sooner made, the better the fare) can be held under your surname only; tickets can be purchased by credit card over the phone, from a travel agent or at an Amtrak depot.

The three main train routes through the Southwest run more or less east to west, and these parallel lines are not very convenient for touring the region. The All Aboard America fares are not very useful for touring the Southwest unless you include other regions as well.

If you want to take a train just for the ride, you'll find that a roundtrip ticket, when reserved in advance, is not much more than a one-way ticket. For example, the one-way fare from Albuquerque, New Mexico, to Flagstaff, Arizona is $82, and the roundtrip fare is $90. (Restrictions apply; mainly, no stopovers are allowed, except at your destination.) This particular route is interesting because an Indian Country Tour Guide narrates the section between Albuquerque and Gallup, New Mexico. The Getting There & Away chapter has more information on train routes and fares.

## CAR & MOTORCYCLE

The US highway system is very extensive, and, since distances are great and buses can be infrequent, traveling by automobile is worth considering despite the expense. Officially, you must have an International or Inter-American Driving Permit to supplement your national or state driver's license, but US police are more likely to want to see your national, provincial or state driver's license.

### Safety

Read the Dangers & Annoyances section in the Facts for the Visitor chapter for general safety rules regarding driving and traveling in the Southwest, and the Legal Matters section for information on drinking and driving laws.

Also bear in mind that Gallup, New Mexico, has built up an unfortunate reputation for careless and drunken driving. Hwy 666 north to Shiprock has an especially high accident rate. New Mexico has one of the highest ratios of fatal car accidents to miles driven in the whole country. Be extra defensive while driving in the Southwest, especially in New Mexico.

### American Automobile Association (AAA)

The American Automobile Association (known as 'Triple A') has hundreds of offices throughout the USA and Canada. Membership in Arizona costs $40 (there's also a $17 one-time initiation fee) for one driver and $20 for each additional driver in the same household. Rates in other states may be higher. Reciprocal member services for residents of one state are available in all other states. Members also receive free road maps and tour books of any state they wish.

Free city maps and advice are also available, and AAA will help you plan your trip. If you break down, get a flat tire, or have a dead battery, call their toll-free number and they will send out a reputable towing company at costs lower than if you had called the towing company yourself. The AAA travel agency will also book car rentals, air tickets and hotel rooms at discount prices.

The main full-service offices in the Southwest are in Phoenix and Salt Lake City. Maps and many other services are available at the smaller branches. Hours are 8:30 am to 5 pm, Monday to Friday. The Albuquerque and Santa Fe offices are also open from 9 am to 1 pm on Saturday. Emergency towing services are available 24 hours a day.

Here's a list of some of the offices in the Southwest:

**Arizona**
Mesa (☎ (602) 834 8296), 262 E University Drive, 85201
Peoria (☎ (602) 979 3700), 7380 W Olive Ave, 85345
Phoenix (☎ (602) 274 1116, 1 (800) 352 5382), 3144 N 7th Ave, PO Box 33119, 85067
Scottsdale (☎ (602) 949 7993), 701 N Scottsdale Rd, 85257
Tucson (☎ (520) 885 0694), 6950 N Oracle Rd, 85704; or (☎ (520) 296 7461), 8204 E Broadway, 85710
Yuma (☎ (520) 783 3339), 1045 S 4th Ave, 85364

**New Mexico**
Albuquerque (☎ (505) 291 6611), 10501 Montgomery Blvd NE, PO Box 16000, 87191
Las Cruces (☎ (505) 523 5681), 225 E Idaho, Suite 21, 88005
Santa Fe (☎ (505) 471 6620), 1644 St Michael Drive, 87501

## A Crash Course

Accidents do happen – especially in such an auto-dependent country as the USA. It's important that a visitor knows the appropriate protocol when involved in a 'fender-bender'.

- DON'T TRY TO DRIVE AWAY! Remain at the scene of the accident; otherwise you may spend some time in the local jail.
- Call the police (and an ambulance, if needed) immediately, and give the operator as much specific information as possible (your location, if there are any injuries involved, etc). The emergency phone number is 911.
- Get the other driver's name, address, driver's license number, license plate and insurance information. Be prepared to provide any documentation you have, such as your passport, international driver's license and insurance documents.
- Tell your story to the police carefully. Refrain from answering any questions until you feel comfortable doing so (with a lawyer present, if need be). That's your right under the law. The only insurance information you need to reveal is the name of your insurance carrier and your policy number.
- Always comply to an alcohol breathalyzer test. If you take the option not to, you'll almost certainly find your driving priveleges automatically suspended.
- If you're driving a rental car, call the rental company promptly. ∎

Utah

Ogden (☎ (801) 399 1116), 685 25th St, 84401

Orem (☎ (801) 225 4801), 1110 S State, 84058

Salt Lake City (☎ (801) 364 5615, 1 (800) 541 9902), 560 E 500 South, PO Box 1079, 84110

### Rental

Major international rental agencies like Hertz, Avis, Budget and A-1 have offices throughout the region. To rent a car, you must have a valid driver's license, be at least 25 years of age and present a major credit card or else a large cash deposit.

Exact details vary from city to city, company to company and depend on the time of year, so call around. Also try calling some of the smaller, lesser known agencies, which are more likely to allow people under 25 to rent a car with no age surcharge. If you are under 21, your options are to travel with someone who is older, to buy a car or to use some other form of transport.

Many rental agencies have bargain rates for weekend or week-long rentals, especially outside the peak summer season or in conjunction with airline tickets. Prices vary greatly in relation to the region, the season and the type or size of the car you'd like to rent. In the off-season, I have rented compact cars as cheaply as $89 a week, but rates of $129 to $169 a week are more common in the high season. Larger, more comfortable cars are available at higher rates. Taxes are extra and average around 10%. If you rent a car for a week and return it sooner, many rental companies will recalculate the rate you were charged at a daily rate, rather than prorate the weekly rate, and you may end up spending more than you were originally quoted.

If you want to rent a car for less than a week, daily rates will be more expensive. Thirty dollars a day is a good price but closer to $40 is not unusual. Monthly rates, on the other hand, don't offer much change from four times the weekly rate. You can get discounts if you are a member of AAA or another travel club. Although $150 or more a week may seem high for travelers on a tight budget, if you split the rental between two or three (or squeeze in a fourth!), it works out much cheaper than going by bus.

Rates usually include unlimited mileage, but check this. If there is a mileage charge, your costs will go up disconcertingly as you drive the long distances of the Southwest. You are expected to return the car to the same place where you picked it up. You can arrange to drop the car off elsewhere, but there is a large surcharge. Be aware that the person who rents the car is the only legal driver, and in the event of an accident, only the legal driver is covered. However, when you rent the car, additional drivers may be signed on as legal drivers for a fee, usually $3 per day per person.

Basic liability insurance, which will cover damage you may cause to another vehicle, is required by law and comes with the price of renting the car. Liability insurance is also called third-party coverage.

Collision insurance, also called the Liability Damage Waiver, is optional; it covers the full value of the vehicle in case of an accident, except when caused by acts of nature or fire. For a mid-sized car the cost for this extra coverage is around $15 per day. You don't need to buy this waiver to rent the car. Agencies also tack on a daily fee per each additional driver in the car.

Some credit cards, such as the MasterCard Gold Card, will cover collision insurance if you rent for 15 days or less and charge the full cost of rental to your card. If you opt to do that, you'll need to sign the waiver, declining the coverage. If you already have collision insurance on your personal policy, the credit card will cover the large deductible. To find out if your credit card offers such a service, and the extent of the coverage, contact the credit card company.

Be aware that some major rental agencies no longer offer unlimited mileage in non-competitive markets – this greatly increases the cost of renting a car.

The following companies rent cars throughout the Southwest. The large cities have the best selection of companies, cars and rates. You can rent subcompact to luxury cars, pickup trucks, 4WDs, vans or moving trucks. Smaller cities have less selection and often charge a little more. Small companies serving just one or two towns are not listed below.

| Advantage | ☎ 1 (800) 777 5500 |
| Alamo | ☎ 1 (800) 327 9633 |
| Avis | ☎ 1 (800) 331 1212 |
| Budget | ☎ 1 (800) 527 0700 |
| Dollar | ☎ 1 (800) 800 4000 |
| General | ☎ 1 (800) 327 7607 |
| Hertz | ☎ 1 (800) 654 3131 |
| National | ☎ 1 (800) 227 7368 |
| Rent-A-Wreck | ☎ 1 (800) 421 7253 |
| Sears | ☎ 1 (800) 527 0770 |
| Thrifty | ☎ 1 (800) 367 2277 |

## Purchase

If you're spending several months in the USA, purchasing a car is worth considering; a car is more flexible than public transport and likely to be cheaper than rentals, but buying one can be very complicated and requires plenty of research.

It's possible to purchase a viable car in the USA for about $1500, but you can't expect to go too far before you'll need some repair work that could cost several hundred dollars or more. It doesn't hurt to spend more to get a quality vehicle. It's also worth spending $50 or so to have a mechanic check it for defects (some AAA offices have diagnostic centers where they can do this on the spot for its members and those of foreign affiliates). You can check out the official valuation of a used car by looking it up in the *Blue Book*, a listing of cars by make, model and year and the average resale price. Local public libraries have copies of the *Blue Book*, as well as back issues of *Consumer's Report*, a magazine that annually tallies the repair records of common makes of cars.

If you want to purchase a car, the first thing to do is contact AAA (☎ (800) 222 4357) for some general information. Then contact the Department of Motor Vehicles to find out about registration fees and insurance, which can be very confusing and expensive. As an example, say you are a 30-year-old non-US citizen and you want to buy a 1984 Honda. If this is the first time you have registered a car in the USA, you'll have to fork over some $300 first and then about $100 to $200 more for general registration.

Inspect the title carefully before purchasing the car; the owner's name that appears on the title must match the identification of the person selling you the car. If you're a foreigner, you may find it very useful to obtain a notarized document authorizing your use of the car, since the motor vehicle bureau in the state where you buy the car may take several weeks or more to process the change in title.

**Insurance** While insurance is not obligatory in every state, all states have financial responsibility laws and insurance is highly desirable; otherwise, a serious accident could leave you a pauper. In order to get insurance some states request that you have a US driver's license and that you have been licensed for at least 18 months. If you meet those qualifications, you may still have to pay anywhere from $300 to $1200 a year for insurance, depending on where the car is registered and the state. Rates are generally lower if you register it at an address in the suburbs or in a rural area, rather than in a central city. Collision coverage has become very expensive, with high deductibles, and is generally not worthwhile unless the car is somewhat valuable. Regulations vary from state to state but are generally becoming stringent throughout the USA.

Obtaining insurance, however, is not as simple as walking into an agency, filling out a form and paying for it. Many agencies refuse to insure drivers who have no car insurance (a classic Catch-22!); those who will do so often charge much higher rates because they presume a higher risk. Male drivers under the age of 25 will pay astronomical rates. The minimum term for a policy is usually six months, but some insurance companies will refund the difference on a prorated basis if the car is sold and the policy voluntarily terminated. It is advisable to shop around.

**Drive-Aways**

Drive-aways are cars that belong to owners who can't drive them to a specific destination but are willing to allow someone else to drive it for them. For example, if somebody moves from Boston to Portland, they may elect to fly and leave the car with a drive-away agency. The agency will find a driver and take care of all necessary insurance and permits. If you happen to want to drive from Boston to Portland, have a valid driver's license and a clean driving record, you can apply to drive the car. Normally, you have to pay a small refundable deposit. You pay for the gas (though sometimes a gas allowance is given). You are allowed a set number of days to deliver the car – usually based on driving eight hours a day. You are also allowed a limited number of miles, based on the best route and allowing for reasonable side trips, so you can't just zigzag all over the country. However, this is a cheap way to get around if you like long-distance driving and meet eligibility requirements.

Drive-away companies often advertise in the classified sections of newspapers under 'Travel'. They are also listed in the yellow pages of telephone directories under 'Automobile Transporters & Drive-away Companies'. You need to be flexible about dates and destinations when you call. If you are going to a popular area, you may be able to leave within two days or less, or you may have to wait over a week before a car becomes available. The routes most easily available are coast to coast, although intermediate trips are certainly possible.

**Shipping a Car or Motorbike**

In general, because good used cars are cheap in the USA, it is usually unnecessary to ship a car, but a surprising number of people take their own transport to the USA and beyond. Jonathon Hewat, who drove a VW Kombi around the world, wrote a book called *Overland and Beyond* (Roger Lascelles, 47 York Rd, Brentford, Middlesex TW8 0QP, UK), which is a worthwhile read for anyone contemplating such a trip.

Air-cargo planes do have size limits, but a normal car or even a Land Rover can fit. For motorcyclists, air is probably the easiest option; you may be able to get a special rate for air cargo if you are flying with the same airline. Start by asking the cargo departments of the airlines that fly to your destination. Travel agents can sometimes help as well.

## TAXI

Taxis are especially expensive for long distances, but aren't so outrageous if shared among two or three people. Check with the service before setting out regarding fares per-person, roundtrip fees and taxes. Check the yellow pages under 'taxi' for phone numbers and services. Drivers often expect a tip of about 10% of the fare.

## BICYCLE

Cycling is a cheap, convenient, healthy, environmentally sound and, above all, fun way of traveling. A note of caution: Before you leave home, go over your bike with a fine-toothed comb and fill your repair kit with every imaginable spare. You may not be able to buy that crucial gizmo for your machine when it breaks down somewhere in the back of beyond as the sun sets. Carry and use the toughest bicycle padlock you can get.

Bicycles can travel by air. You can take them apart and put them in a bike bag or box, but it's much easier simply to wheel your bike to the check-in desk, where it should be treated as a piece of baggage. You may have to remove the pedals and turn the handlebars sideways so that it takes up less space in the aircraft's hold; check all this with the airline well in advance, preferably before you pay for your ticket.

If you'd rather rent a bike when you get there, look under 'Bicycles – Rental' in the telephone directory yellow pages. There are several places to choose from in larger towns. In smaller towns, I mention bicycle rentals in the text. For a long-term rental, you might want to consider buying a new or used bike and then selling it back. Call around the bike stores in the town where you want to start from and explore these options.

Bicycles are generally prohibited on interstate highways. However, where a suitable frontage road or other alternative is lacking, bicyclists are permitted on some interstates. Call the local police to find out about this possibility. Note that some scenic areas have cycling restrictions.

## HITCHHIKING

Hitching is never entirely safe in any country in the world. Travelers who decide to hitch should understand that they are taking a small but serious risk. You may not be able to identify the local rapist/murderer before you get into his vehicle. People who do choose to hitch will be safer if they travel in pairs and let someone know where they are planning to go. Ask the driver where they are going rather than telling them where you want to go.

Hitching is illegal on the interstates, but you can stick out your thumb at the bottom of the on-ramp. Police routinely check hitchhikers IDs, so be prepared for this. You may be asked to show the police some money to prove you aren't destitute. (The police won't continue to hassle you if you have an ID and act in a reasonable manner.)

## LOCAL TRANSPORT

There are no urban train systems in any Southwestern city.

Cities and many larger towns have local bus systems that will get you around. These generally run a very limited schedule on Sundays and at night. Telephone numbers of urban bus systems are given in the text.

Taxis will get you around, but they are not cheap. Expect to pay around $2 a mile.

## TOURS

Hundreds of companies offer a huge variety of tours of the Southwest. You can hike, camp, bike, run or float rivers, learn about archaeology, watch birds, go on photo workshops and take advantage of many more possibilities. Many companies are listed in the text under the appropriate towns or areas. Read the information on tours in the Getting There & Away chapter as well.

Adventure Source (☎ (206) 328 4426, 1 (800) 249 2885), 1111 E Madison Suite 302, Seattle, WA 98122, provides listings of thousands of adventure travel and eco-tour companies that organize tours all over the world (including the Southwest). Call or write to them and tell them the type of tour you are interested in, the region you want to visit, the time of year you want to tour and your budget limitations. They will send you a list of operators fitting your criteria, and they will also contact the operators and ask them to send you a brochure.

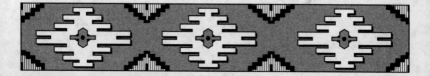

Utah

# Facts about Utah

Utah's world-famous red-rock scenery comprises an astonishing array of canyons, cliffs, mesas, buttes, plateaus, pinnacles, hoodoos, spires, towers, faults, uplifts, folds, bridges and arches, covering the land in a bewilderingly beautiful maze. Much of this land was not settled until recently. Today's roads through red-rock country remain winding and narrow, forcing travelers to cover large distances slowly.

Many visitors spend their time in the southern half of the state, where the majority of the national parks and monuments are. The northern half, however, offers an opportunity to explore the unique culture of the Mormons, based in attractive Salt Lake City. Just to the east of the city, the splendid Wasatch Mountains give access to forested hiking and camping in summer and wonderful skiing in winter. And northeastern Utah draws travelers with the lure of dinosaurs – you can watch workers in the process of excavating fossils and examine complete skeletons in various museums.

### Recent History

Utah petitioned for statehood six times, the first as far back as 1856, but these petitions were consistently rejected because of the Mormon practice of polygamy. Church leaders considered the practice protected by the First Amendment (which guarantees freedom of religion), but the Supreme Court ruled against them in 1879. Over the next decade, over 1000 Mormon men were imprisoned for practicing polygamy. The relationship between the largely Mormon territory and the federal government deteriorated steadily, and some members of Congress even proposed a bill to withdraw the voting rights of all Mormon men.

The tense situation was suddenly settled in 1890 when Mormon Church President Wilford Woodruff announced that God had told him that Mormons should abide by US law, and polygamy was discontinued. Soon

**Utah Trivia**
**Statehood:** 4 January 1896 (45th state)
**Area:** 84,904 sq miles
(13th largest state)
**Highest Point:** Kings Peak, 13,528 feet
**Lowest Point:** Beaverdam Creek
(SW Utah), 2000 feet
**Population (1993):** 1,859,582
(34th most populous state)
**Population under 18 Years:** 36.42%
(1st in nation)
**Average Lifespan:** 75.76 years
(3rd in nation)
**Literacy Rate:** 94% (1st in nation)
**Nickname:** Beehive State
**State Capital:** Salt Lake City
**State Bird:** California gull
**State Mammal:** Rocky Mountain elk
**State Flower:** Sego lily

after, Utah's sixth attempt at statehood was successful; it was admitted to the Union in 1896. The young state was still very much Mormon, but it resolutely supported US policies at home and abroad. By the early 1900s, politics began to run along party lines rather than religious ones. In general, Mormons tended to vote conservatively, and to this day Republicans have been elected more often than Democrats.

Mormons still remain in the majority, although the margin is slimmer now than it ever has been, with about 70% of the state practicing the religion. They continue to

UTAH

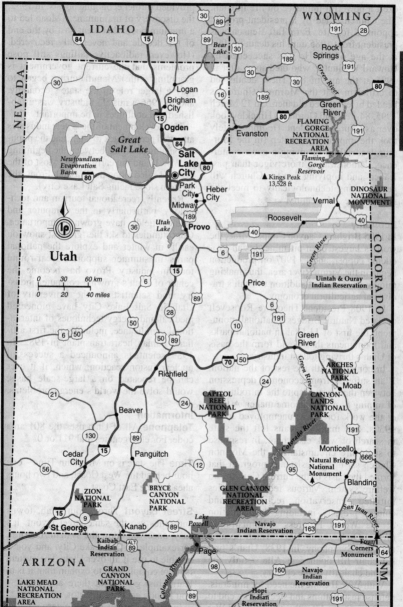

## Utah

0   30   60 km
0   20   40 miles

exert a powerful influence on life in Utah. The Church is led by a president-prophet appointed for life. Ezra Taft Benson was president from 1985 until his death in 1994 at the age of 94. He was succeeded by Howard W Hunter, who died soon after in 1995 at the age of 87. These deaths led to criticism that the Mormon Church is headed by enfeebled old men. On 12 March 1995, 84-year-old Gordon B Hinckley took over as Church president. He immediately took the unprecedented step (in the Mormon leadership) of giving a news conference, demonstrating more vigor than past leaders and implying that the Church will be advancing technologically to meet the needs of the 21st century.

## Economy

In 1905 Brigham Canyon Copper Mine, the world's largest open-pit mine, began producing copper, and in 1907 oil production began in the Virgin River area, thus making mining an important addition to Utah's traditional agricultural economy.

In 1908 President Theodore Roosevelt declared Natural Bridges a national monument, the first of 11 Utahan national parks and monuments that would form the basis of Utah's thriving tourist industry.

In common with the rest of the nation, Utah suffered from economic depression between the wars, despite the introduction of mining as a new income maker. A third of the work force was unemployed in the 1930s, and many Utahans left the state in search of work elsewhere. In response to such dire circumstances, the Mormon Church set up an assistance program that formed the basis of the current Church-run welfare system. Various federal agencies initiated conservation, reclamation and cultural projects, including the formation of the Works Progress Administration (WPA) Orchestra in 1935, which became the Utah Symphony. In 1938, Utah's first ski chair lift opened at Alta – only the second chair lift in the country.

With WW II came the need for minerals, defense installations and steel and an end to the Depression. After the war, the Cold War provided further economic boosts. In 1952, the discovery of uranium near Moab led to a uranium boom that went bust by the end of the decade and never fully recovered. (However, radioactive tailings still pose problems that the current government is grappling with.) Manufacturing began to play a larger role in the state's economy, and in 1956 a missile industry was established that continues to be important.

The development of these new industries attracted people back to Utah, and the population almost tripled between the beginning of WW II and the early 1980s. Most of the people settled along the Wasatch Front (the western slope facing Salt Lake City).

Recently, recreational tourism and technology, particularly in the computer and medical fields, have grown in importance. Opportunities to ski the 'greatest snow on earth' in winter and explore the national parks in summer support a year-round tourism industry. Provo has become the center of Utah's growing computer industry, and scientists at the University of Utah in Salt Lake City have pioneered medical and energy techniques of international significance, including the first artificial human heart transplant in 1982. In 1989 scientists announced a successful nuclear fusion reaction, which, if it ever can be repeated on a large-scale basis, would solve the world's energy problems.

## Information

**Telephone** All of Utah uses the 801 area code. For emergencies dial 911 or 0.

**Time** The state is on Mountain Time – one hour behind the West Coast, and two hours ahead of the East Coast.

**Street Layout** Throughout Utah, towns and cities use the same street layout. It's easy, once you know the system. Learn it, for example, in Salt Lake City, and you'll be able to use it all over Utah. The system is more complicated to explain than it is to learn. Just go on out there and use it – you'll soon get the hang of it.

In Salt Lake City, there is a zero point in

the town center, at the intersection of S Temple and Main St. S Temple runs east to west; Main St runs north to south. Addresses are given from this zero point with 100 being equivalent to one city block. Thus an address of 500 South 400 East (**A**) will be at the intersection of 500 South St and 400 East St, or five blocks south and four blocks east of the zero point. The first cardinal point is usually abbreviated, but the second cardinal point is abbreviated less often – 500 S 400 East would be the most likely designation. An address such as 270 S 300 East (**B**) is a building on 300 East St between 200 South and 300 South St.

Not all streets are named 100, 200, etc. In Salt Lake City, the street at 100 W (or parallel to and one block west of Main St) is W Temple, followed by 200 West St, 300 West St, and so on. Heading east, it's State St at 100 E, followed by 200 East St, 300 East St, etc. (The 'St' is often dropped.)

Heading north from S Temple, at 100 N you cross N Temple, at 200 N you cross 200 North St, then 300 North and so on. Heading south of S Temple, at 100 S you cross 100 South St, followed by 200 South, etc. 300 South is also called Broadway.

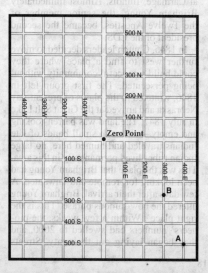

Just to complicate things, there are areas where streets don't follow the same pattern, but the general numbering system remains the same. 500 N 600 East will always be to the northeast of the zero point.

Note that a few maps might use 1st North, 2nd North, etc, instead of 100 North, 200 North. It means the same thing.

**Driving Laws** You must be at least 16 years old to obtain a driver's license. Drivers and front-seat passengers are required to wear a safety belt. Children under age eight must use child restraints. You must be over 16 to obtain a motorcycle license; motorcycle helmets are required for rider and passenger if they are under 18. The blood alcohol concentration over which you are legally considered drunk while driving is 0.08 (lower than the 0.10 of most other states). It is illegal to have an open container of alcohol in your car while driving.

**Drinking Laws** As in all of the USA, you must be 21 to buy a drink in a store, bar or restaurant. Beyond that, liquor laws in Utah differ noticeably from the rest of the country. Grocery stores can sell beer of not more than 3.2% alcohol content every day of the week. Stronger beer, wine and spirits are sold in state-run liquor stores (also called package stores) that are closed on Sundays. Hours on other days vary from town to town.

Lounges and taverns sell only 3.2% beer – stronger drinks are sold in 'private clubs'. Temporary visitor's membership to any private club costs $5 and is valid for two weeks. All members (including temporary ones) can invite in up to five guests. If you ask at the door of a private club, you can often get one of the staff or other patrons to invite you in as their guest.

Restaurants must have licenses to serve alcohol. Servers are not permitted to offer you a drink or even show you a menu with drinks unless you specifically ask for one. You must order food to buy a drink, but it can be just a snack shared between several people. Alcohol is prohibited on Indian reservations.

# Salt Lake City

Salt Lake City, the capital of Utah, is by far the largest city in the state. It is also the headquarters of the Mormon Church. The Great Salt Lake and the impressive architecture and culture of the Mormon Church are the two most famous attractions for visitors. There is much more to see, however, not the least of which is the city's spectacular setting at the foot of the Wasatch Mountains. The mountains offer great recreational opportunities for the residents of the city: beautiful hiking in the summer and some of the best skiing in North America in the winter.

The population of Salt Lake City is a seemingly modest 170,000, but almost 1.2 million people live in the Salt Lake City-Ogden metropolitan area – well over half of the population of Utah. The region's elevation of 4300 feet ensures a relatively mild climate year-round, with summer highs occasionally rising into the 90°s F and winter highs usually staying above freezing.

## HISTORY

The history of Salt Lake City is linked inextricably with the remarkable history of the Mormons. During the 1820s a New York farmer by the name of Joseph Smith had a series of angelic visitations in which the word of God, in the form of writings on golden tablets, was revealed to him. During these visions, Smith was told that he was a prophet who would lead the Church. Smith translated the writings, which were written in some ancient but unknown language, using 'stone spectacles' provided by the angel Moroni. After Smith finished the translations, the golden tablets were taken away by the angel and have not been seen since.

Smith's translation, published in 1830 as the *Book of Mormon*, recounts the epic story of the arrival of the first Americans from the Old World about 4000 years ago

and of the teachings of Jesus Christ in America. Later that year, he founded The Church of Jesus Christ of Latter-day Saints (LDS), appointing himself the first president of the Church.

Confronted with strong opposition to the new sect, Smith and a small group of followers decided to leave New York in 1831. They built their first church in Kirtland, Ohio, and some Mormons pushed on as far as Missouri. But confrontation continued; most of the citizens of Ohio and Missouri felt their way of life was being threatened by this strange new denomination, and the Mormons were continually harassed and persecuted. Within a few years, they had pushed on to Illinois, where they founded the Mormon community of Nauvoo.

But many non-Mormons opposed the Mormon newcomers, particularly their teachings of polygamy and religious superiority. Mormons were persecuted, attacked and killed, and in 1844 Joseph Smith and his brother Hyrum were murdered in a jail at Carthage, Illinois. Almost immediately Brigham Young, the senior member of the Twelve Apostles, became the second president of the LDS.

In 1845, Church leaders decided to move further west to find a place where they could build a peaceful community without being persecuted. The first group left in 1846, wintered in the plains of present-day Nebraska and arrived at the Great Salt Lake in July 1847. The land was barren-looking and empty – although small bands of Ute Indians traveled and hunted here, no large Indian tribes lived permanently in this area. This was the place that Brigham Young had been looking for, remote and unwanted. A few days after their arrival, Brigham Young uttered the now-famous phrase 'This is the right place'. Within a few weeks, the pioneers' numbers had swelled to 2000, and they began laying out their city. Streets

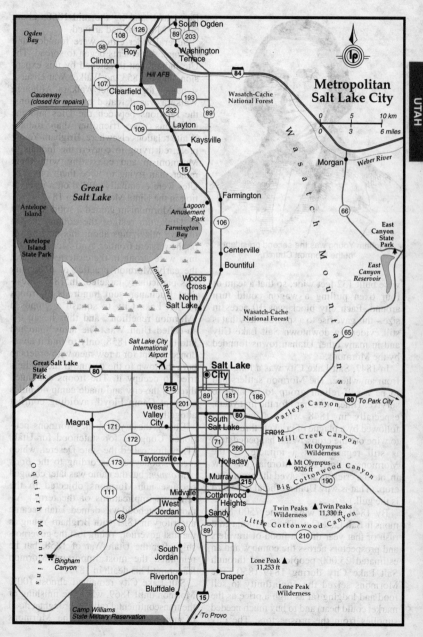

# Metropolitan Salt Lake City

UTAH

Brigham Young was the second president
of the Mormon Church.

were built 132 feet wide, so that a team of
four oxen pulling a wagon could turn
around. Each city block was 10 acres in
size – this gave rise to a spaciousness that is
still evident in downtown Salt Lake City
and in many other Utahan towns founded
by the Mormons.

In 1847, Salt Lake City was a long way
from anywhere. The Mormon settlers had
to be a self-reliant group to be able to
survive. Times were hard for the first years,
especially in 1848 when a late frost
followed by a plague of crickets threatened
to wipe out the crops. What happened next
is still regarded as a miracle by the
Mormons; a flock of California gulls flew
in, ate the crickets and saved the remaining
crop. (That is why Utah's official state bird
is the gull.)

By 1849, there were some 7500 Mormons in Salt Lake City. The California gold
rush of that year drew a flood of travelers
and prospectors across the country, and an
estimated 25,000 people passed through
Salt Lake City during 1849-1850. The
Mormons seized the opportunity to sell
food and lodging (at as high a price as the
market could bear) and to buy much needed
supplies from the prospectors. The city

flourished, and by the mid-1850s about
60,000 Mormons had arrived.

Several other cities were founded and
Mormon settlements began to spread. The
Ute Indians felt threatened by this expan-
sion, and in 1853 the Walker War ensued,
so named for Ute Chief Walkara. Although
Walkara was defeated by the Mormons,
the relations between the Utes and the
Mormons were friendlier than Indian-
White relations elsewhere. Brigham Young
preferred trying to convert the Indians to
Mormonism and coexisting with them
rather than trying to wipe them out. The
Utes were eventually settled on a reserva-
tion in the Uinta Mountains in 1872.

As Mormonism gained a solid foothold
in Utah, the rest of the country began
to have misgivings about this new power
on the western frontier. Anti-Mormon feelings were strong in the eastern USA, and
the early Mormon practice of polygamy
was particularly targeted. In 1857, President Buchanan sent hundreds of troops
to Salt Lake City to squash a supposed
'Mormon rebellion', and thus began the
so-called Utah War. The army marched
into the city in 1858, only to find it abandoned except for a few men with orders to
burn the town to the ground if the soldiers
tried to occupy it. The troops continued
through the city and made camp 40 miles
away at Camp Floyd, avoiding conflict
altogether.

During these years, the Mormons petitioned Congress for statehood for Utah.
(They first called the state Deseret, which
means 'honeybee' according to the *Book
of Mormon*, but the name was later changed
because non-Mormons objected to the
religious implications of the term.) Although statehood was denied, Utah became
a territory in 1851 with Brigham Young as
the first governor. Young lost the governorship after the Utah War of 1858, but he
remained the most important Mormon
leader until his death in 1877.

Salt Lake City remained almost 100%
Mormon until 1869, when the finishing of
the transcontinental railway brought a flood
of non-Mormons (which the Mormons

called 'Gentiles') to northern Utah. By the late 1800s, only half of the inhabitants of Salt Lake City were Mormons, and today the figure is about 40%.

Polygamy had been outlawed by the US government in 1862, but the law was not enforced by the Mormons. With the coming of Gentiles to Utah, the polygamy issue became more difficult to ignore, and over 1000 Mormon men were jailed in the 1880s for the practice. Finally, in 1890, polygamy was abolished by the Mormon Church, and from 1890-1893 Salt Lake City was controlled by a Gentile government.

Throughout the latter half of the 19th century, Utah continued to petition frequently for statehood. Polygamy had been a major stumbling block to statehood, but the abolishment of the practice, combined with the increasing sharing of political control with Gentiles, led to Utah becoming the 45th state in 1896, with Salt Lake City as the state capital. The magnificent capitol building was finished in 1915.

The history of the 20th century in Salt Lake City follows a similar pattern to that of many other US cities. A period of economic growth in the first decades of the century was followed by the Depression in the 1930s. The economy revitalized after WW II and industry blossomed. Then prices and production of minerals fell, but a new economic mainstay was found: tourism and related industries. Today, these play a vital part in Utah's economy.

Today, Mormons largely follow the early teachings of Joseph Smith, with the exception of polygamy, which the LDS abandoned in 1890. The teachings of the Bible are also followed, along with the *Book of Mormon*, which is available in many Mormon tabernacles – just ask.

## ORIENTATION

Salt Lake City (as with most Mormon towns) is laid out in a spacious grid with streets pointing north to south or east to west. The most important block is Temple Square, bounded by North Temple, West Temple, South Temple and Main St

---

**Bees in the Beehive State**

Utah's nickname is the Beehive State, and state road signs clearly show the beehive logo. The original, short-lived name of the Utah Territory was 'Deseret', which means honeybee in the *Book of Mormon*. The honeybee, communal and hardworking, is an apt representation of the strong Mormon influence on the state.

However, the honeybee is not a Utah native. Honeybees *(Apis mellifera)* were introduced to North America in the 1600s from Europe. The Southwest is home to several thousand species of native bees, which are extremely important as pollinators. These native bees, with the exception of the bumble-bee, don't live in colonies. They are solitary, with each female nesting in a small hole in the ground or in natural cavities elsewhere. ∎

---

(formerly East Temple). These are all important downtown streets. N Temple becomes Hwy 186 to the west and heads for the airport. Hwy 186 eastbound turns south of N Temple at 300 West St, then heads east on 400 South St until 900 East St, where the Hwy 186 jiggles over to 500 South and Foothill Drive. Other important thoroughfares are State St (which becomes Hwy 89 to the south) and 300 West (which becomes Hwy 89 to the north).

Two major interstates intersect at Salt Lake City. Interstate 15 heads north-south and I-80 east-west. Interstate 215 is a loop that skirts the city to the east, south and west.

## INFORMATION
### Visitors Centers

Salt Lake Convention & Visitors Bureau (☎ 521 2868), 180 S West Temple, 84101, has information about both the city and the state. Hours are 8 am to 5:00 pm (7 pm in summer) from Monday to Friday, 9 am to 4 pm on Saturday. The bureau publishes the useful *Salt Lake Visitors Guide*, which is free.

The Utah Travel Council (☎ 538 1030),

UTAH

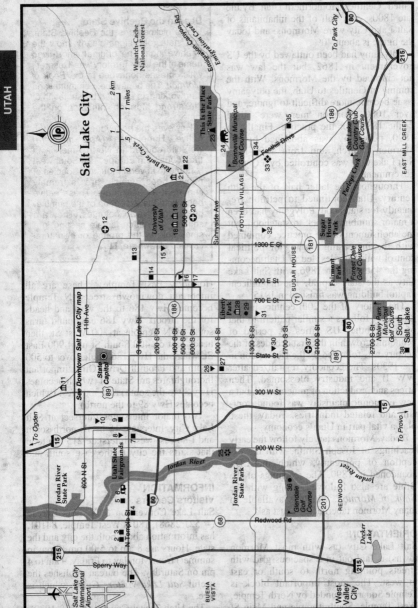

# Salt Lake City

Wasatch-Cache
National Forest

Emigration Creek

Emigration Canyon Rd

Red Butte Creek

This is the Place
State Park ▲ 23

Bonneville Municipal
Golf Course
24 ♦

● 35

34 ▦

Salt Lake City
Country Club
Golf Course

Foothill Drive
33 ♦

EAST MILL CREEK

FOOTHILL VILLAGE

Parleys Creek

♦ 12

University of Utah
18 ▦ ▦ 19
500 S St
▦ 20

21 ▦
22 ■

Sunnyside Ave

Sugar House
Park

Forest Dale
Golf Course

181

▶ 32

1300 E St

SUGAR HOUSE

Fairmont
Park

■ 13

15 ▼

■ 14

▼ 16
▶ 17

900 E St

700 E St

Liberty
Park
▦ 28
● 29

▶ 31

71

South
Salt Lake

Nibley Park
Municipal
Golf Course

2700 S St

See Downtown Salt Lake City map

11th Ave

186

S Temple St

200 S St

400 S St
500 S St
600 S St

900 S St

1300 E St

1700 S St

2100 S St

37 ♦

38 ■

80

89

State St

▼ 30

State
Capitol
89

■ 26
■ 27

300 W St

To Ogden
15

To Provo

▦ 11

▼ 10
■ 9

■ 8 ▶
■ 7

Utah State
Fairgrounds

600 N St

Jordan River
State Park

25 ✚

Jordan
River

900 W St

Jordan River
State Park

36 ●
Glendale
Golf Course

Redwood Rd

201

REDWOOD

Jordan River

Decker
Lake

■ 5 ◉ 6
■ 4

80

68

Redwood Rd

215

West
Valley
City

215

To Park City

80

215

186

■ 2
■ 3

N Temple St

Sperry Way

■ 1

Salt Lake City
International Airport

BUENA
VISTA

2 km
1 miles
1
.5
0

LP

| PLACES TO STAY | | | |
|---|---|---|---|
| 1 | Radisson Hotel |
| 2 | Nendel's Inn |
| 3 | Days Inn |
| 4 | Holiday Inn - Airport |
| 5 | Overniter Motor Inn |
| 6 | Camp VIP, Salt Lake Campground |
| 7 | Econo Lodge, Continental Motel |
| 9 | Se Rancho Motel |
| 13 | Brigham Street Inn |
| 14 | Saltair B&B |
| 22 | University Park Hotel |
| 27 | Ramada Inn |
| 34 | Scenic Motel |
| 35 | Skyline Inn |
| 38 | Holiday Motel |

| PLACES TO EAT | |
|---|---|
| 5 | Diamond Lil's |
| 8 | Red Iguana |
| 10 | Cordova's El Rancho |
| 15 | Gepetto's |
| 16 | Old Salt City Jail |

| | |
|---|---|
| 17 | The Dodo Restaurant |
| 26 | Cafe Trang |
| 30 | Thai House Restaurant |
| 31 | The Park Cafe |
| 32 | Fresco Italian Cafe |

| OTHER | |
|---|---|
| 11 | Children's Museum of Utah |
| 12 | Hospital |
| 18 | Utah Museum of Natural History |
| 19 | Utah Museum of Fine Arts |
| 20 | Veterans Hospital |
| 21 | Fort Douglas, Military Museum |
| 23 | This Is the Place Monument, Old Deseret |
| 24 | Hogle Zoo |
| 25 | International Peace Gardens |
| 28 | Chase Home Museum of Utah Folk Art |
| 29 | Tracy Aviary |
| 33 | Foothill Village |
| 36 | Raging Waters |
| 37 | County Hospital |

Council Hall, Capitol Hill, 84114 (at the corner of 300 North and N State St), is open from 8 am to 5 pm from Monday to Friday, and from 10 am to 5 pm on weekends. The council publishes the helpful *Utah! Travel Guide*, also free and available from the visitors bureau.

### National Forest Offices
The National Forest Service (USFS) (☎ 524 5030), 8th Floor, Federal Building, 125 S State St, 84138, has maps and information about all of Utah's national forests. Hours are 7:30 am to 4:30 pm from Monday to Friday. The local Wasatch National Forest Ranger Station (☎ 524 5042), 6944 S 3000 East, is open from 8 am to 4:30 pm from Monday to Friday. The US Geological Survey (☎ 524 5652) is also on the 8th floor of the Federal Building; here you'll find the best selection of topographic and other maps in the Southwest. Hours are 8 am to 4 pm from Monday to Friday.

### Money
You can change money at the airport and downtown. If you need to change foreign currency, do so in Salt Lake City because it is difficult in other parts of Utah. Downtown, you can go to First Security Bank (☎ 246 6600), 15 E 100 South; Zions First National Bank (☎ 524 4711), 1 South Main St; or American Express (☎ 328 9733), 175 S West Temple.

### Post
The main post office (☎ 974 2200) is at 1760 W 200 South. The downtown post office is more convenient at 230 W 200 South, and there are about a dozen other branches.

### Books & Periodicals
The Main Library (☎ 524 8200) is at 209 E 500 South. There are five branch libraries.

The two city newspapers are the morning *Salt Lake Tribune* and the conservative, Mormon-run, afternoon paper, the *Deseret News*. *The Event*, which is published every two weeks, describes upcoming arts and entertainment. Utah's independent weekly, *Private Eye*, has good local events coverage and is published every Wednesday; it's free.

UTAH

### Recycling

Do your environmental duty at Recycling Corporation of America (☎ 973 0333), 2600 W 900 South, or at Utah Recycling (☎ 972 0220), 3100 S 900 West.

### Medical Services

There are 33 hospitals scattered throughout the Salt Lake City Area. The nearest hospital to downtown is the LDS Hospital (☎ 321 1100 or 321 1180 in an emergency), 8th Ave and C St. It provides 24-hour emergency service and charity medical care to those in need. For quick answers to your health-care questions or to find a doctor, call Ask-A-Nurse (☎ 972 8488 or 1 (800) 444 8488 outside of Salt Lake City).

### Police

The police station (☎ 799 3000 or 911 in an emergency) is at 315 E 200 South.

### Parking

Parking downtown costs $2 to $5 in all-day parking lots or 25¢ for 30 minutes at parking meters. You can usually find a spot without too much problem. There is an all-day lot by the visitors bureau, 180 S West Temple, which costs $3. The visitors bureau itself has a free parking zone for up to 30 minutes. Merchants in the downtown shopping malls provide validation for mall parking if you make a minimum purchase of $5, and many restaurants also provide validated parking – just ask.

### Dangers & Annoyances

Utah is not considered a dangerous state to visit, and Salt Lake City is safer than most large cities in the USA. There are no areas that should definitely be avoided, although you should, as in any city, exercise the normal precautions as outlined in the Facts for the Visitor chapter.

### DOWNTOWN
### Temple Square

The city's most famous sight, Temple Square (☎ 240 2534), is enclosed by white walls 15 feet high, which surround a 10-acre block bounded by N Temple,

W Temple, S Temple and Main Sts. Within are some of the most important Mormon buildings, visitors centers, exhibits and tours. Even if you are not interested in the LDS (Mormon) religion, you'll find that the visit is very worthwhile for the architecture and culture.

Enter either from S or N Temple. Near either entrance Mormon guides will advise you on where to go, what to see and how to hook up with a free **guided tour** led by Mormon missionaries. Tours leave several times an hour, last about 40 minutes and are available in several languages. Questions are welcome.

You are also free to walk around at your own pace – there are plenty of information signs. The **South Visitor Center** (by the south entrance) houses paintings of church history and an exhibit about the *Book of Mormon*. Photos of the inside of the Temple (which non-Mormons cannot enter) are also on display. The **North Visitor Center** (by the north entrance) has

The angel Moroni stands atop Salt Lake City Mormon Temple.

many religious paintings and murals, as well as a small theater with audio-visual presentations.

Temple Square is open daily from 9 am to 9 pm and from 8 am to 10 pm in the summer. Admission to the square, buildings and performances is free.

**The Temple** The most impressive building inside Temple Square is the 210-foot-high Temple; atop the tallest spire stands a golden statue of the angel Moroni, who appeared to LDS founder, Joseph Smith. Built between 1853 and 1893, the Temple was opened upon completion to all visitors for a few days and then closed to everybody except practicing Mormons engaged in secret religious ceremonies. (The practice of opening a new temple to visitors for a few days and then closing it to all but worshipping Mormons is one that still occurs whenever a new temple is

### The Mormon Church

About 70% of Utah's population is Mormon, so it's worth learning a little about this religion. In the 1820s, Joseph Smith, a New York farmer, experienced a series of angelic visitations during which the word of God was revealed to him in the form of writings on golden tablets, which he eventually translated into the *Book of Mormon*. Smith derived Mormon Church doctrine from this book, and most of these tenets remain integral to Mormon life today. Mormon leadership is through the Church president and 12 elected laymen called the Twelve Apostles. Members are required to be strongly supportive of their families, and the families supportive of one another. A woman marries a man into eternity, and all their relatives (including deceased) and offspring automatically become Mormons – hence, the Mormon interest in genealogy. In keeping with this sense of family Mormons referred to each other as sister or brother. Hard work, tithing (donating 10% of one's annual income) and a strict obedience to Church leaders were also important. Smoking and drinking alcohol, tea or coffee are forbidden, because they do not promote a healthy or moral lifestyle. During the early decades of the Church, polygamy was encouraged, particularly within the upper rank, but this practice was discontinued in the 1890s.

The LDS has attracted large numbers of followers who like the strong sense of community, the healthy lifestyle and the fact that Mormons consider themselves God's chosen people. Mormons consider the LDS the one rightful Christian Church; they believe other Christian denominations are defective or corrupt.

The religion is practiced in public and in private. Public services, complete with hymns and sermons, are often held in tabernacles. Private ceremonies, including weddings and baptisms, are usually held in temples and are open only to practicing Mormons who vow to keep the secrets of the faith. Apparently, ceremonies performed in the temples require the attendees to wear special temple undergarments. Talking to non-Mormons about these 'secret ceremonies' leads to excommunication, and generally, the Mormons are a close-mouthed bunch when questioned about these details. Temples are only open to non-Mormons when they are new and then only for a few weeks.

The Church of Latter-Day Saints is very conservative. African-American men were not allowed to become Church leaders until 1978. Women are still not allowed to take on leadership roles and, until 1990, had to pledge to obey their husbands. In Mormon schools and colleges, dress codes are very strict – no shorts or skirts above the knee, for example. Mormon men are not allowed to grow beards. The LDS Church is strongly supportive of the conservative Republican Party.

In recent decades, young adults perform a voluntary missionary service to spread the faith around the world. Women, called Sisters during their service, spend 18 months, while the men, called Elders, spend two years. There are now over eight million Mormons worldwide, and the number is growing rapidly. ■

UTAH

completed.) When worshipers enter the building for these ceremonies, they must be clothed entirely in white.

**The Tabernacle** You should make every effort to enter the Tabernacle, opposite the Temple, when the world-famous Mormon Tabernacle Choir is singing or an organ recital is being given. This domed building, constructed between 1863 and 1867, has stunning acoustic properties. Guides leading tours will demonstrate that you literally can hear a pin drop on the stage even when sitting in the back row of the tabernacle. The organ has almost 12,000 pipes, and recitals are given 12 to 12:30 pm from Monday to Saturday and 2 to 2:30 pm on Sunday. The Mormon Tabernacle Choir rehearses every Thursday at 8 pm and gives a live radio/TV broadcast at 9:30 am every Sunday (arrive by 9 am for seats). This radio broadcast, which has been airing continuously since 1929, is now heard all over the world. The Mormon Youth Chorus rehearses at 8 pm on Tuesday, and the Youth Symphony rehearses at 8 pm on Wednesday. (It's worth checking times as there are occasional changes if the choir is on tour.)

**The Assembly Hall** South of the Tabernacle lies Assembly Hall, built between 1877 and 1882. It houses a smaller organ. A concert series (☎ 240 3318 for details) is performed here at 7:30 pm every Friday and Saturday, and more frequently in June, July and December. Outside the Assembly Hall is the **Seagull Monument**, built in honor of the state bird (see History above for details).

### Adjoining Temple Square

The two blocks flanking Temple Square to the west and east have several other important Mormon buildings and monuments. The **Museum of Church History and Art** (☎ 240 3310), 45 N West Temple, has impressive exhibits of pioneer history and a large selection of fine art. A log cabin built in 1847 is nearby. Guided tours are available only if you make a reservation at

least one week in advance. Hours are 9 am to 9 pm, Monday to Friday, from April to December; 10 am to 7 pm weekends and holidays and during January to March (to 9 pm on Mondays and Wednesdays). Admission is free.

Next door is the **Family History Library** (☎ 240 2331), 35 N West Temple, 84150, the largest genealogical library and research facility in the world. Genealogy is of great importance to the Mormons because they believe that all family members are united within the LDS Church and therefore ancestors can be baptized and saved. Non-Mormons are permitted to use the facilities to research their own roots. An orientation center instructs visitors on how to use the library. Genealogical information is arranged by geographic location and then by date, so you should know in advance where your family came from. Library hours are 7:30 am to 6 pm on Monday, to 10 pm from Tuesday to Saturday. Admission is free.

At the intersection of South Temple and Main St is the **Brigham Young Monument** marking where the street numbering system for Salt Lake City originates. At the northeast corner of this intersection stands the elaborate old **Utah Hotel**, which housed guests from 1911 to 1987 and is now being renovated and converted into LDS office space. The 28-story **LDS Office Building**, nearby at 50 E North Temple, is the tallest building in Salt Lake City; this is where the day-to-day running of the Church is coordinated. Free 30-minute tours begin in the lobby and go up to the 26th floor observation deck – great views. Hours are 9 am to 4:30 pm from Monday to Friday, plus Saturday from April to September.

The **Beehive House** (☎ 240 2671), 67 E South Temple, was built in 1854 for Brigham Young, who lived here until his death in 1877. At the time, it was the most elegant house in Salt Lake City, and it has been meticulously maintained with period furnishings and artwork. An ornate reception room, bedrooms, dining room,

**Peregrine Falcons**
Peregrine falcons have been observed nesting on the Utah Hotel and LDS Office Building – watch out for these birds from mid-May to late June, when eggs are hatching and the young are being fed. The Utah Wildlife Resources Division (☎ 596 8660, 538 4730), 1596 W North Temple, has information on exact nesting locations and viewing opportunities during each breeding season. ■

kitchen, children's playroom (polygamist Young had at least 44 children!) and so forth can all be inspected. The name of the house derives from the hard-working qualities of bees; symbolic beehives appear on the roof and throughout the house. (Utah is nicknamed the Beehive State.) Free guided tours leave several times an hour from 9:30 am to 4:30 pm, Monday to Saturday (extended to 6:30 pm on summer weekdays), and 10 am to 1 pm on Sunday and holidays.

Next door to the Beehive House is the **Lion House**, 63 E South Temple, which was built in 1855 as additional living space for Brigham Young's many wives. The building is closed to public touring, but the Lion House Pantry restaurant on the lower level is open for public dining (see the Historic Restaurants aside in Places to Eat). At the intersection of State St and S Temple, just east of the Beehive House, stands the arching **Eagle Gate**, originally the entrance to Brigham Young's property. Walking the short block north on State St and turning east at 1st Ave brings you to **Brigham Young's Grave**, where he and several family members are buried. Here, you'll also find the Mormon Pioneer Memorial Monument.

### Hansen Planetarium
A good stop for stargazers of all ages, the Planetarium (☎ 538 2098), 15 S State St, has a museum, gift shop and theater. Among the museum's two floors of exhibits, you can see a rock from the moon. Museum admission is free. Hours are 9 am to 9 pm, Monday to Saturday. The domed theater offers a variety of astronomical, laser/music and live performances costing $4 to $7.50 for adults and $3 to $6 for children, depending on the performance.

### Salt Lake Art Center
Changing shows at the Art Center (☎ 328 4201), 20 S West Temple (in the Salt Palace complex) cover the art spectrum, and classes, lectures, demonstrations, readings, discussions and performances are offered. Call to learn about upcoming events. Hours are 10 am to 5 pm from Monday to Saturday, and 1 to 5 pm on Sunday. Admission is free.

### Symphony Hall
The splendidly ornate but modern home of the Utah Symphony (☎ 533 6407), 123 W South Temple (in the Salt Palace complex), lays claim to the best acoustics of any modern concert hall in the world. Tours are offered on Tuesday and Friday at 1:30, 2 and 2:30 pm – call to confirm times.

### Utah Historical Society
Housed in the old Rio Grande Railroad Depot, the Historical Society (☎ 533 3501)

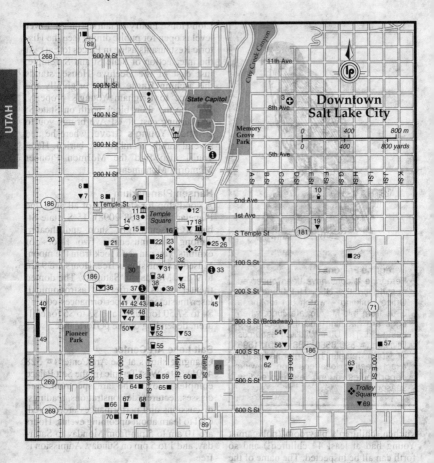

is at 300 S Rio Grande St (just west of 300 S 400 W). There are exhibits about local and state history, an excellent bookshop with regional books, and a research and historic photo library. Hours are 10 am to 5 pm from Tuesday to Friday and 10 am to 2 pm on Saturday. Admission is free.

## South Temple St

In addition to the buildings and monuments at adjoining Temple Square, many other interesting buildings line historic South Temple St. The following is a selection.

The grand old **Union Pacific Railroad**

**Depot**, 400 W South Temple, was completed in 1909. The Roman Catholic **Cathedral of the Madeleine** (☎ 328 8941), 331 E South Temple, has elaborate stained-glass windows and marble altars. The Gothic-style building, which dates from 1900, was renovated in 1992. The **First Presbyterian Church** (☎ 363 3889), 347 E South Temple, also has beautiful stained-glass windows. The **Enos A Wall Mansion**, 411 E South Temple, which houses the LDS Business College, has an ornate turn-of-the-century exterior. **Kearns' Mansion** (☎ 538 1005), 603 E

UTAH

| PLACES TO STAY | | |
|---|---|---|
| 1 | Kendell Motel |
| 6 | Royal Executive Inn |
| 8 | Covered Wagon Motel |
| 9 | Travelodge - Temple Square |
| 10 | Avenues Youth Hostel |
| 15 | Howard Johnson |
| 21 | Doubletree Hotel |
| 22 | The Inn at Temple Square |
| 28 | Marriott Hotel |
| 29 | Anton Boxrud B&B |
| 43 | Shilo Inn |
| 44 | Red Lion Inn |
| 48 | Peery Hotel |
| 57 | Residence Inn by Marriott |
| 58 | Salt Lake Hilton |
| 59 | Deseret Inn |
| 60 | Emerald Inn |
| 64 | Travelodge - City Center |
| 65 | Little America Hotel |
| 66 | Ramada Inn |
| 67 | Quality Inn - City Center, Motel 6 |
| 68 | Embassy Suites Hotel |
| 70 | Super 8 Motel |
| 71 | Best Western Olympus Hotel |

**PLACES TO EAT**
7  China Place
17  Lion House Pantry Restaurant
19  Pagoda
26  Nino's Restaurant
31  Mikado
32  Brackman Bros Bagels
35  Lamb's Restaurant
38  Benihana of Tokyo
40  Rio Grande Cafe
41  Green Parrot
42  Marianne's Delicatessen
44  Maxi's
45  Cedars of Lebanon

46  Baci Trattoria, Cafe Pierpont
47  Broadway Deli & Bandaloop's Coffee Bar
48  Shenanigan's
50  Squatter's Pub Brewery
52  New Yorker, Market Street Oyster Bar, Market Street Grill
53  Shogun
54  Ristorante della Fontana
56  Sizzler
62  Le Parisien
63  Bill & Nada's Cafe
65  Little America Dining Room
69  Trolley Square, Don Felipe's, Ferantelli's

**OTHER**
2  Marmalade District
3  LDS Hospital
4  Pioneer Memorial Museum
5  Utah Travel Council
11  Museum of Church History & Art
12  LDS Office Building
13  Family History Library
14  Greyhound Bus Depot
16  Brigham Young Monument/Meridian Marker
18  Beehive House
20  Union Pacific Railroad Depot
23  Crossroads Plaza
24  Eagle Gate
25  Hansen Planetarium
27  ZCMI Shopping Center
30  Salt Palace
33  National Forest Service (Federal Building)
34  Dead Goat Saloon
36  Post Office
37  Salt Lake Convention & Visitors Bureau
39  Capitol Theater
49  Rio Grande Depot & Utah Historical Society
51  Zephyr
55  Port-O-Call
61  City & County Building

South Temple, was built in 1902 by mining magnate and Utah Senator Thomas Kearns. These days, the lavish mansion is usually the official residence of the governor; however, a recent serious fire caused extensive damage, and repairs are under-way. Tours should resume in late 1996.

## Pioneer Memorial Museum

This museum (☎ 538 1050), 300 N Main St, is run by the Daughters of Utah Pioneers (DUP). You'll find many DUP museums and monuments as you travel around the state, but this is the organization's best museum. Four floors and 38 rooms are filled with carefully labeled and well-displayed historical memorabilia, pains-takingly and proudly collected by the DUP. You can see old photographs and por-traits, locks, crafts, furniture, toys, kitchen implements, clothing, firearms, walking sticks – you name it and you'll probably find it. An adjoining building contains pioneer wagons and farm machinery. Hours are 9 am to 5 pm, Monday to Saturday. Admission is free.

As you walk from Temple Square to the Pioneer Memorial Museum, don't forget to stop into the excellent Mormon Handicraft store at 105 N Main St (see Things to Buy).

### Marmalade District

Just north of the Pioneer Memorial Museum and west of the State Capitol is an area of steep little streets angled away from the grid pattern of the city. The triangular area, bounded by 300 North St to the south, 500 North St to the north, Center St to the east and Quince St to the west, is a residential area with many late 19th-century buildings. Several of the streets are named after the fruit bearing trees planted in the area – hence the district's name. There are no particular houses to visit; just explore the area at your leisure.

### Utah State Capitol

This impressive structure (☎ 538 3000), 350 N Main St stands at the north end of State St on the appropriately named Capitol Hill. It is a worthwhile walk up here (you can also easily take in the Pioneer Museum and the Marmalade District). The impressive legislative building is modeled after the national Capitol in Washington, DC. The exterior is Utah granite topped by a shining copper dome. Inside, the rooms are spacious and elegant; lined with huge columns, the walls are covered with murals of Utah's history. The beautifully landscaped gardens contain some superb monuments, particularly of the Indian Chief Massasoit on the south side and the Mormon Battalion on the southeast side. Look for a stairway behind this monument leading to **Memory Grove**, where statues honor Utah veterans. The Grove, situated in **City Creek Canyon**, is open during daylight hours. It's a favorite spot for local walkers, runners and bicyclists.

From the Capitol grounds there are good views of the city. Across the street on the south side, at the corner of 300 North and State St, is **Council Hall**. This structure, originally built downtown in the 1860s, used to be the city hall; the entire structure was moved to its present location in 1960 and now houses the Utah Travel Council (see Information for hours). Some rooms have been furnished in 19th-century style. Next door is the **White Memorial Chapel**, which was also moved here from downtown.

The Capitol is open daily from 8 am to 8 pm in the summer and 8 am to 6 pm during the rest of the year. Free tours are given during summer. They depart on the half hour from 9 am to 3 pm from Monday to Friday. Call 538 1563 for tour information.

## AROUND DOWNTOWN

### University of Utah

The university (☎ 581 7200) is two miles east of downtown. Head out on 200 South St to 1300 East, and you'll find University St just beyond. The university, the oldest and largest in Utah, spreads over two sq miles. Within the grounds are two museums and an arboretum.

The **Utah Museum of Natural History** (☎ 581 4303) is on President's Circle, just east of 200 South and University St. This

Chief Massasoit, an ally to the Pilgrims, was never in Utah.

fine two-story museum, which has a few very good exhibits, is small enough to visit in a couple of hours. Biology, geology, anthropology and the ever-popular paleontology (dinosaurs!) are featured. There is a gift shop. The museum is fun for children as well as adults. Hours are 9:30 am to 5:30 pm from Monday to Thursday and Saturday, 9:30 am to 8:00 pm on Friday, and noon to 5 pm on Sunday and holidays; closed New Year's Day, the Fourth of July, 24 July, Thanksgiving and Christmas. Admission is $2 for adults, $1.50 for children; university faculty and students with ID go for free. Parking outside is free if you ask for a pass inside the museum.

The **Utah Museum of Fine Arts** (☎ 581 7332) is just off S Campus Drive (the eastern extension of 400 South St). Although small, the museum has exhibits from all over the world and from many periods. Changing shows are also featured. Hours are 10 am to 5 pm from Monday to Friday and 2 to 5 pm on weekends. Admission is free and there is a metered parking lot outside.

The **Arboretum** (☎ 581 5332) spreads out throughout the campus and beyond to **Red Butte Gardens**, east of the university along S Campus Drive. The gardens are open from 9 am to dusk daily and feature thousands of trees. Self-guiding trail brochures are available from the Museum of Natural History.

A free campus shuttle bus operates several times an hour from 6 am to 6 pm from Monday to Friday during the school year. Call 581 4189 for information.

### Fort Douglas & Military Museum

The museum (☎ 588 5188) is on the grounds of Fort Douglas, just east of the university. Built in the 1860s, the fort contains several impressive red sandstone buildings. The museum has exhibits pertaining to Utahan military history, and a self-guiding leaflet describing some of the historic buildings is available. (The fort is still in use and some sections are off limits.) Hours are 10 am to noon and 1 to 4 pm from Tuesday to Saturday all year

except during holiday weekends. Admission is free.

### This Is the Place State Park

This historic state park (☎ 584 8391), 2601 E Sunnyside Ave (eastern extension of 800 South St), is for day use only. Picnicking in the summer and cross-country skiing in the winter are popular activities. This is the closest area to downtown where you can do some bird-watching and maybe see mule deer, raccoons or red foxes. The huge **This Is the Place Monument** looms over the park – it was dedicated in 1947 to mark the 100th anniversary of the arrival of the Mormons. Three walls of the nearby visitors center are covered with murals depicting the Mormon odyssey, and audio narration describes the events.

Within the park is **Old Deseret**, which is a living-history museum with actors in mid-19th-century clothes working among buildings typical of the early Mormon settlements. Some buildings are replicas; others are renovated originals, including Brigham Young's farmhouse.

Park hours are 8 am to 8 pm. The visitors center is open 10 am to 4:30 pm (or 6 pm in the summer). Old Deseret is open from 11 am to 5 pm from Memorial Day to Labor Day only. Admission is $1.50 for adults and $1 for children, six to 15.

### Hogle Zoo

No real surprises here – this zoo (☎ 582 1631), 2600 E Sunnyside Ave (opposite Pioneer Trail State Park), has the usual collection of animals from all over the world, well displayed in appropriate settings. There is a children's petting zoo and a miniature train ride (summers only). The zoo is open daily, 9 am to 6 pm, from Memorial to Labor Day, 9 am to 4:30 pm the rest of the year. Admission is $4 or $2 for children (five to 14) and seniors over 65.

### Liberty Park

This extensive park (☎ 972 7800) is bounded by 500 and 700 East, and 900 and 1300 South. During the summer you'll find

**UTAH**

## Kids' Stuff

**Children's Museum of Utah** Interactive exhibits at this museum (☎ 328 3383), 840 N 300 West St, encourage children to 'work' as archaeologists, TV producers, surgeons, artists, pilots, performers and more. Other exhibits introduce children to the difficulties of physical handicaps. Hours are 9:30 am to 5 pm from Monday to Saturday (until 9 pm on summer Mondays) and from 12 to 5 pm on Sunday. Admission is $3 for adults and $2.75 for children under 13.

**Raging Waters** If you're traveling with children who threaten to throw up if they have another museum or historic building inflicted upon them, head to Raging Waters (☎ 973 9900), 1700 S 1200 West, for a cool time. Youngsters of all ages can go wild on the world's first water roller coaster, body surf in a giant wave-making pool, splash down over 20 water slides (totaling 3000 feet) or simply swim in one of 10 heated pools, including a pool for small children. There are picnic areas and food concessions. From Memorial Day to Labor Day, the park is open 10:30 am to 8 pm from Monday to Saturday and 10:30 am to 6:30 pm on Sunday. Admission is $11.95 for kids over 10, $8.95 for kids three to nine, and free for those two and under or 60 or over.

**49th St Galleria** Kids will head with glee to this indoor fun mall (☎ 263 2987, 265 3866), 4998 S 360 West, which includes a video arcade, mini golf, baseball cages, roller-skating rink, bowling lanes, rides, entertainment and plenty of food. Take I-15 south to the 5300 South exit, head west to 700 West and then north to the Galleria. It's open daily from noon till late. Admission is free, but bring plenty of change and small bills for the attractions. ■

displays of hundreds of birds from all over the world. Kids can feed the ducks. Hours are 9 am to 6 pm in summer, and 9 am to 4:30 pm the rest of the year. Admission is $3 for adults and $1.50 for children.

The **Chase Home Museum of Utah Folk Art** is in Isaac Chase's adobe house, built in the 1850s. The museum displays quilts, saddles, rugs, needlework, woodcarving, etc. Hours are noon to 5 pm during weekends from mid-April to mid-October and daily from Memorial Day to Labor Day. Admission is free. Researchers can make an appointment to see the museum archives of books, photographs and recordings of Utah folk art.

### Wheeler Historic Farm

The farm (☎ 264 2212), 6351 S 900 East, which dates from 1887, used to be south of the city – now it is surrounded by suburbs. The farm is worked in a traditional manner – see (and maybe help) farmhands milk cows, churn milk into butter, feed animals, collect chicken eggs, etc. Hay rides and sleigh rides are offered. You can fish in the duck pond or tour the historic farmhouse and farm buildings where demonstrations are given. There is no admission charge, but some activities and rides have small fees. The farm is open daily year-round.

### Jordan River State Park

This state park (☎ 533 4496), 1084 N Redwood Rd, 84116, follows both banks of the Jordan River from 1700 South northward for about 8.5 miles. To reach the ranger station, take N Temple to 900 West, go north on 900 West to 1000 North, then head west to 1084 N Redwood. Station hours are 8 am to 5 pm, Monday to Friday. Activities in the park include canoeing (put in at the south end and take out at the ranger station). At the ranger station, you can get maps showing boating and fishing areas, picnic sites, jogging, bicycling, equestrian and wheelchair exercise trails, the golf course and a model airplane field. Also ask about the best places to see shorebirds and waders during migrations,

a swimming pool, tennis courts, children's amusement park, playground, pond with rental boats, horseshoe pits and formal flower gardens.

The **Tracy Aviary** (☎ 322 2473) is in the southwest corner of Liberty Park. Bird lovers will enjoy wandering through the and watch birds and wildlife year-round. Beavers have been spotted here in summer. Most activities (golf and model plane field excepted) are free. There is no overnight camping.

### International Peace Gardens
Nearby on the east bank of the river lies the Peace Gardens (☎ 972 7800), 1000 S 900 West. Floral displays pay tribute to the culture of countries from all over the world. Hours are dawn to dusk from mid-May through November.

### OUTSIDE THE CITY
### Great Salt Lake State Park
The park (☎ 250 1822), Box 323, Magna, 84044, is in Magna on the south shore of the lake about 16 miles west of the city along I-80. It was badly flooded in the '80s and has only recently been reopened as a camping area. Depending on current lake levels, it may be a longish walk to the water's edge. Before the floods, people used to float in the saline waters just to see what it felt like to be unsinkable. You can still do this, though the buoyancy of the water is not what it once was. In a few years, it may return to its former state.

The main attractions are bird-watching and enjoying the lake, which is, after all, quite unique. There is also a marina (recovering from flooding) and a small visitors center, both left (west) of the park entrance after taking exit 104 (Magna) from I-80.

---

**Ruins from an Elegant Era**
Near the entrance of Great Salt Lake State Park is Saltair, a strange structure that was a fashionable resort in the 1890s and was restored in the early 1980s – just before the floods hit. Now it lies in ruins. In front of it, tourist concessions dispense information and sell snacks, souvenirs and gifts including what they proudly proclaim to be 'Without a doubt the most delicious saltwater taffy that the world has ever known!' ■

---

To the right of the entrance is a picnic and camping area. The gate is open from 8 am to 10 pm. Day use is $3 per car and camping is $7. There are freshwater showers (cold when I was there). You can continue east on the Frontage Rd to 7200 West (exit 111 on I-80) as an alternative lakeshore return to Salt Lake City.

### Antelope Island State Park
This 15-mile long island, the largest in the Great Salt Lake, used to be connected with the mainland by a seven-mile causeway, which was completely flooded in the 1980s. There are plans to reopen it in the mid-1990s. The entrance to the causeway is about 35 miles northwest of Salt Lake City. Contact the park (☎ 451 3397, 580 1043), Box 618, Farmington, 84025, or Utah State Parks Information (☎ 538 7221) for current information.

There used to be picnicking and camping areas (which were also destroyed by floods). The main attractions were the buffalo herds roaming the island (the antelope are gone). Deer, coyotes, bobcats and many birds are also reported.

### Lagoon Amusement Park & Pioneer Village
This is the second oldest amusement park (☎ 451 8000) in the country (opened in 1886), and it has several roller coasters and dozens of other rides. The Lagoon 'A' Beach water park offers plenty of water slides and pools. Live musical entertainment occurs daily in the summer. Pioneer Village has many historically accurate 19th-century buildings, and visitors can ride stagecoaches or steam trains and watch gunslingers shooting it out. There is an old-time restaurant, modern food booths and picnic areas, pleasant gardens and a camping site.

The park is open during weekends from mid-April to early October and daily from Memorial to Labor Day. Hours are 11 am to midnight on busy days, earlier on quiet days. All-day amusement park passes for adults and children over four feet, three inches (1.29 meters) tall are $17.95 and water park passes are $11.50; combination

## The Great Salt Lake

The huge lake that gave the city its name lies about 10 miles northwest of downtown. It is the largest lake in the USA west of the Great Lakes. So how big is the Great Salt Lake? That's hard to answer, because between 1873 and the present the lake has varied in size from 900 to 2500 sq miles. Maximum lake depths have varied from 24 to 45 feet – it is a large but shallow lake. The high figure was recorded in 1873, the low figure in 1963. Variations are caused by spring run-off raising lake levels and summer heat evaporating the water. A series of dry winters and hot summers will cause extremely low levels, and, conversely, wet winters and cooler summers will lead to high water levels. Evaporation rather than drainage is the main cause of water loss, so the lake has attained extremely high salinities of over 20% (compared to 3.5% in seawater).

The prehistoric variation in lake levels was much greater. Sixteen thousand years ago the lake was part of Lake Bonneville, which was 900 feet higher and covered almost 20,000 sq miles. Then it suddenly dropped 350 feet when it burst through Red Rock Pass into the Snake River in Idaho. It receded to its present size about 8000 years ago. If you look at the nearby mountains, you can see terraces marking these ancient levels etched into the slopes about 900 and 550 feet above present lake levels.

In the 1980s the Great Salt Lake underwent devastating changes. In 1963, the record low depth of the lake left the surface only 4191 feet above sea level. During that time, several miles of I-80, the main interstate west of Salt Lake City, were built at 4207 feet above sea level. During the '60s and '70s the level rose slowly, but in the '80s, levels increased suddenly and dramatically. The winters of 1982-1983 and 1983-1984 both had record-breaking snowfalls. Skiers call it 'the greatest snow on earth', but the ensuing snowmelts flooded the interstate. Crews worked feverishly to raise the freeway seven feet to 4214 feet above sea level. By the winter of 1986-1987, lake levels had reached

passes are $22.95. Children under four feet pay a few dollars less but cannot go on the wilder rides. Children under three and seniors pay $8.50 and can swim but not ride. Pioneer Village and entertainment are included.

The campground (☎ 451 8100) is open from mid-April to 31 October. Sites are $13 without hookups, $17 with full RV hookups. Showers and a coin laundry are available, and guests get a discount on park passes.

To get there, take I-15 north to the Lagoon Drive exit, 17 miles north of downtown Salt Lake City. The park is actually in the sizable town of **Farmington**, which is the seat of Davis County. Because of its proximity to Salt Lake City, Farmington doesn't have any hotels, though there are fast food restaurants and gas stations.

### Bingham Canyon Copper Mine

Billed as 'The Richest Hole on Earth', this open-air mine (☎ 322 7300) is also the largest excavation that humans have ever dug. The gigantic 2.5 mile wide and half a mile deep gash in the earth's surface has yielded millions of tons of copper and other metals. It is also an environmental disaster. The hazardous waste water it has emitted over decades poses a threat to Salt Lake City's drinking water. The mine is operated by Kennecott Corporation, which has recently announced plans to clean up the area and has agreed to improve its mining practices. Government and other authorities, however, worry that the corporation will be unable to do a satisfactory clean up.

The visitors center, which includes a museum, film presentation and overlook of the mine, is open 8 am till dusk daily from April to October. Admission (donated to charity) is $2 per car, $1 per motorcycle.

The mine is 25 miles southwest of Salt Lake City. Take I-15 south to exit 301, then follow Hwy 48 west to the mine.

4212 feet, breaking the 1873 record by several inches. Then, barely averting disaster, the lake began to recede.

For the time being, the interstate is safe again. But many other changes resulted from the sudden increase of water. The salinity dropped from 20% to 6% in some parts of the lake – still saltier than seawater but not much. The hard-working Utahans spent countless volunteer hours sandbagging creeks and rivers, building dikes and fighting the floods. Nevertheless, farmlands surrounding the lake were flooded and washed away. Evaporation ponds used for potash production were inundated. Many beaches, state parks, bird and wildlife refuges, and shoreline buildings were damaged or destroyed. If not for the timely actions of the locals, however, the toll would have been far greater.

The lake's wildlife was also hard hit. Before the flood, the lake had always been too saline for fish (except for a few areas near the mouths of rivers). Bacteria and small green algae grew in the salty water and became food for brine shrimp. Brine flies lived in great clouds on rotting vegetation in the marshes along the shoreline. The shrimp and the flies attracted great numbers of migrating birds, and these migrations were one of the natural spectacles of the lake. However, the flooding of coastal marshes caused a huge decline in the shrimp and fly populations, which in turn, led to a massive decline in the number of migratory birds. Fortunately, in the last few years, the lake and its wildlife are beginning to show signs of recovery.

The Great Salt Lake has been declared a World Heritage bird sanctuary. Spring and summer migrants include many shorebirds, waders, gulls, terns and waterfowl. Some 80,000 California gulls, Utah's state bird, nest here. In good years, about a million Wilson's phalaropes feed here between mid-June and mid-August on their way south for the winter. Fall migrants are mainly ducks and geese, and during the winter, numerous ducks, gulls and occasionally bald eagles can be seen. White pelicans nest on islands in the lake. ■

## ACTIVITIES
### Skiing & Snowboarding

An entire book could be written about Utah's skiing – this guide isn't it. Your best bet is to get a hold of a *Utah Winter Vacation Planner*. This free and recommended booklet is published each winter by Ski Utah (☎ 534 1779, fax 521 3722), 150 W 500 South, Salt Lake City, 84101. Available from the visitors bureau, it lists up-to-date prices and details of all nearby resorts and amenities, plus hotel packages in Salt Lake City. For current ski conditions, call 521 8102.

The Wasatch Range overlooking Salt Lake City provides great winter (and summer – see below) outdoor recreation. The snow is excellent and skiing is world-class. Four alpine ski resorts are less than 30 miles from Salt Lake City and are mentioned below. Several others are within an hour's drive, especially near Park City (see Park City in the Wasatch Region chapter). You can use Salt Lake City as a base and ski in a different resort every day of the week. Skiers driving to the resorts should note that snow tires or chains are required from November to May.

A few ski lodges stay open in summer with much reduced room rates (see Ski Resorts under Places to Stay). In the winter, room rates increase dramatically. The ski season stretches from mid-November to early May. If you stay at a ski lodge during the peak season (around Christmas and during February to early March) expect to pay $40 to $100 per person for a dormitory room and several hundred dollars for a private room (single or double occupancy) or for an apartment sleeping up to eight people. Some places may include meals and/or lift passes in the rates. Remember, though, that much cheaper rooms can be had in Salt Lake City, and public transport (with ski racks) is available from downtown to the four closest ski resorts. The lodges that are not right at the ski resorts are also cheaper.

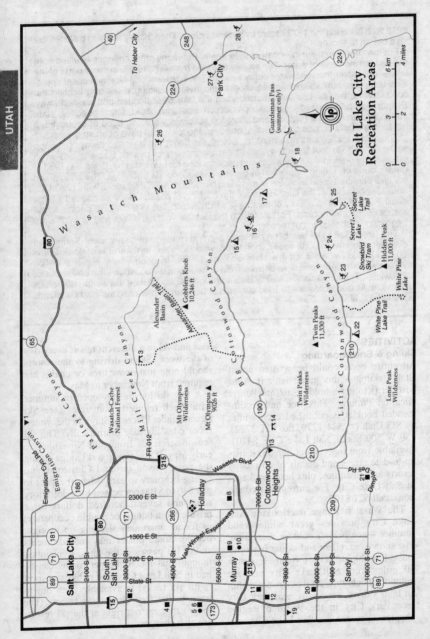

**Salt Lake City Recreation Areas**

To Heber City

Park City

Guardsman Pass (summer only)

Wasatch Mountains

Emigration Canyon

Emigration Canyon Rd

Parley's Canyon

Mill Creek Canyon

Wasatch-Cache National Forest

Alexander Basin

Alexander Basin Trail

Gobblers Knob 10,246 ft

Big Cottonwood Canyon

Mt Olympus Wilderness

Mt Olympus 9026 ft

Twin Peaks Wilderness

Twin Peaks 11,330 ft

Little Cottonwood Canyon

Snowbird Ski Tram

Hidden Peak 11,000 ft

White Pine Lake

White Pine Lake Trail

Secret Lake

Secret Lake Trail

Lone Peak Wilderness

Salt Lake City

South Salt Lake

Holladay

Murray

Cottonwood Heights

Sandy

Wasatch Blvd

Van Winkel Expressway

Dell Rd

Dimple

2100 S St
2300 E St
1300 E St
700 E St
State St
4500 S St
3300 S St
5600 S St
7000 S St
7800 S St
9000 S St
9400 S St
10600 S St

FR 012

LP

0    1    2    3    4 miles
0    2    3    6 km

**PLACES TO STAY**

|   |   |
|---|---|
| 2 | Days Inn Central |
| 4 | Quality Inn - South |
| 6 | Reston Hotel |
| 8 | Log Cabin on the Hill B&B |
| 9 | The Spruces B&B |
| 11 | Discovery Motor Inn, Best Western Executive Inn |
| 12 | La Quinta Motor Inn, Motel 6 |
| 15 | Spruces |
| 17 | Redman |
| 20 | Comfort Inn |
| 21 | Mountain Hollow B&B |
| 22 | Tanner's Flat |
| 25 | Albion Basin |

**PLACES TO EAT**

|   |   |
|---|---|
| 1 | Ruth's Diner, Santa Fe Restaurant |
| 13 | Fong Ling Restaurant |
| 19 | Archibald's Restaurant |

**OTHER**

|   |   |
|---|---|
| 3 | Terraces Picnic Area |
| 5 | 49th St Galleria |
| 7 | Cottonwood Mall |
| 10 | Wheeler Historic Farm |
| 14 | Oak Ridge Picnic Area |
| 16 | Solitude Ski Area |
| 18 | Brighton Ski Area |
| 23 | Snowbird Ski Area |
| 24 | Alta Ski Area |
| 26 | Park West Ski Area |
| 27 | Park City Ski Area |
| 28 | Deer Valley Ski Area |

UTA Ski Buses (☎ 262 5626) collect passengers from several downtown hotels to the above ski areas. Service begins at 7 am, and buses depart every 10 minutes between 8 am and 9 am. One-way fare is $5. UTA buses also go from resort to resort.

**Snowbird** This ski area (☎ 742 2222, 1 (800) 453 3000, fax 742 3300) is the closest to Salt Lake City, only 24 miles away in Little Cottonwood Canyon. It is also the highest in northern Utah at 11,000 feet, dropping to 7900 feet at the base. The 2000-acre ski area has 47 runs serviced by seven double chairs and a tram,

which carries up to 250 skiers to the top in about eight minutes. About 25% of the runs are beginner and 30% are intermediate. Snowboarding is allowed on 80% of the slopes.

Adult all-day chair lift passes (9:30 am to 4:30 pm) are $40 including the tram or $33 for chairs only. Kids under 13 and seniors over 62 pay $26 or $21 for all-day passes; seniors over 70 ski free. Adult half-day passes are $33 or $27; kids and seniors pay $21 or $18. The Chickadee Lift (for beginners only) costs $10 for the whole day. Ski rentals (skis, boots and poles) cost $16 for a full day, and snowboards are available for $27.80 per day. Child care, children's programs and a ski school are available.

**Alta** Alta, an 1870s mining town, became Utah's first ski resort in 1937. Only two miles beyond Snowbird, Alta (☎ 742 3333) has 2200 acres dropping from 10,650 to 8550 feet. Eight chair lifts and four tows service 39 runs of which 25% are for beginners and 40% for intermediate skiers. All-day chair lift passes (9:15 am to 4:30 pm) are $25 for all chair lifts or $18 for beginner chair lifts. People over 80 ski free. Half-day passes are $19 or $13 for beginners. Skis rent for $17 for a full day and $12 for half. There is child care and a ski school.

**Solitude** This area (☎ 534 1400, 1 (800) 748 4754, fax 649 5276) is 27 miles from Salt Lake City in Big Cottonwood Canyon. There are 1100 skiable acres between 10,030 and 8000 feet. Seven chair lifts service 69 runs of which 20% are for beginners and 50% for intermediate skiers. Snowboards are allowed on the slopes only Monday through Wednesday. All-day lift passes (9 am to 4:30 pm) are $30 or $26 per day if you buy a two- or three-day pass. Kids and seniors pay $18, and those over 75 ski free. Half-day passes are $22. There is a ski school. Ski rentals cost $16 for a full day and $12 half-day.

Just beyond the downhill area is the **Solitude Nordic Center** (☎ 536 5774,

1 (800) 748 4754) at 8700 feet. There are 13 miles of prepared cross-country ski trails of which 30% are for beginners and 60% for intermediate skiers. All-day trail use is $8, and skis cost $10 for a full day, $8 for half. Lessons are available.

**Brighton** Just two miles beyond Solitude, Brighton (☎ 943 8309, 1 (800) 873 5512) has 850 acres between 10,500 and 8755 feet. Seven chair lifts service 64 runs of which 21% are for beginners and 40% are for intermediate skiers. Snowboarding is allowed on the runs. All-day passes (9 am to 4 pm) are $26, and children under 10 ski free with an adult (two kids per adult). Seniors over 70 also ski free. Brighton offers night skiing from 4 to 9 pm for $11. Ski rentals cost $16 for a full day and $11 for half. Snowboard rentals are also available for $25 for a full day and $20 for half. Both skiing and snowboarding lessons are available.

### Hiking

Summer hikers and campers head in droves for **Little Cottonwood Canyon**. Take exit 7 off the southeastern corner of the I-215 loop, follow Hwy 190 south to Hwy 210, which climbs up into the canyon. This steep and spectacular road gains over a mile in elevation in the 11-mile drive to the top – don't try it unless your car is in good shape. The USFS operates two campgrounds in the canyon: Tanner's Flat (7100 feet), just over four miles along the canyon road, and Albion Basin (9700 feet), at the end of the road. Snowbird and Alta lie between these two sites.

Good hiking trails include the **White Pine Lake Trail**, which begins almost a mile along the road beyond Tanners Flat. Several other trails also leave from this trailhead and go to different alpine lakes. White Pine Lake (10,000 feet) is just over three miles away. Watch rocky slopes around the lake for the unique pika, a small, short-eared, tailless lagomorph (a member of the rabbit order of mammals). Pikas can be found in high rocky areas throughout the Wasatch Mountains. Mar-

The pika sun-dries different grasses to create a kind of hay, which it stores in a den.

mots, ground-squirrels and a variety of birds may also be seen and the summer wildflowers are abundant.

At the end of the road is the **Secret Lake Trail** (also called Cecret Lake), along which you can view spectacular summer wildflowers (July and August). A one-mile trail leads from the Albion Basin Campground to Secret Lake – which isn't visible until you're there. It's not very steep, except for the last section up to the lake.

If you don't fancy climbing at these breathless elevations, take the ski tram at Snowbird, which operates daily during the summer. Rides cost $7/4 for adults/children and take you to Hidden Peak (11,000 feet). You can enjoy the views and then hike down via the Peruvian Gulch Trail – it's a 3.5-mile descent to 8100 feet – or return by tram.

Another favorite spot for summer hikers is **Big Cottonwood Canyon**. Take exit 7 off the I-215 loop and follow Hwy 190 into the canyon. The USFS maintains nine picnic areas and two campgrounds along Hwy 190. The first picnic area, Oak Ridge (5100 feet), is open from May to October; the last one, Brighton (8800 feet), is open from June to September. The campgrounds are Spruces (7400 feet) and Redman (8300 feet), open from June to September. The paved road ends at Brighton, but an unpaved road goes over a 9800-foot pass and continues to Park City or Heber City.

This road is closed by snow from October to May. Many hiking trails leave from various trailheads along Hwy 190. Look for trailhead signs.

The next canyon north of Big Cottonwood Canyon is **Mill Creek Canyon**. Take exit 4 off the I-215 loop and follow the signs for Mill Creek. (There are no skiing resorts here.) The USFS maintains nine summer picnic areas along this road. If you hike in from some of the picnic sites or along a trail, camping is permitted. Several hiking trails leave from the road, including the Alexander Basin Trail, which climbs 3000 feet in 1.75 miles up to Gobblers Knob mountain (10,246 feet). Alternatively, a trail from the Terraces picnic area climbs just over 4000 feet in 5.5 miles to Gobblers Knob. All these places are signed.

These brief descriptions will get you started on walking in the Wasatch. Both day hikes and overnight backpacking trips are possible. See the Books & Maps section in Facts for the Visitor if you want in-depth information. Also, the Wasatch National Forest Ranger Station can provide plenty of details.

### Golf & Tennis
There are dozens of public and private golf courses in the Salt Lake City Area – the Salt Lake City Visitors Bureau or the telephone yellow pages can give an exhaustive list. The following official Salt Lake City Municipal Golf Courses are easily accessible. Forest Dale (☎ 483 5420), 2375 S 900 East, has nine holes. Nibley Park (☎ 483 5418), 2780 S 700 East, has nine holes and a driving range. The remainder in this list have 18 holes and a driving range: Bonneville (☎ 596 5041), 954 Connor; Glendale (☎ 974 2403), 1630 W 2100 South; Mountain Dell (two courses, ☎ 582 3812), Parleys Canyon; Rose Park (☎ 586 5030), 1386 N Redwood Rd; and Wingpointe (☎ 575 2345), 3602 W 100 North.

The Salt Lake City Parks & Recreation Department (☎ 972 7800) has information about tennis and other activities in the city's many parks. Their biggest selection of tennis courts in one spot is by the Liberty Park pro shop (☎ 596 5036) – see the section on Liberty Park.

### Professional Sports
The Delta Center (☎ 325 7328), 301 S West Temple (just west of the Salt Palace), hosts both National Basketball Association (NBA) and International Hockey League (IHL) games. The NBA Utah Jazz and the IHL Golden Eagles are the home teams. Seats for the most important games are sold out well in advance but call anyway – you might get lucky. Otherwise, scalpers may be found near the center offering tickets for the best games at exorbitant prices.

Derks Field (☎ 484 9900, 484 9901), 1301 S West Temple, hosts the Salt Lake Trappers baseball team and the Salt Lake Sting soccer team. Tickets are easier to come by for these less well known teams.

### ORGANIZED TOURS
Various companies offer narrated city tours as well as tours to outlying sites like the Great Salt Lake or Bingham Copper Mine. Old Salty (☎ 359 8677) has 1½-hour city tours in open-air wagons pulled by trainlike contraptions. Their tours run 1 April to 31 October and cost $8/4 for adults/children. Gray Line (☎ 521 7160) has 2½-hour city tours that cost $14/7 for adults/children. Innsbruck Tours (☎ 534 1001) has three-hour city tours for $15. These last two will pick you up and also run longer tours. Scenic West Tours (☎ 572 2717) has half-day tours starting at $20. The visitors bureau (☎ 521 2868) can provide names of other operators of short and long tours.

### SPECIAL EVENTS
As in any big city, there are a variety of happenings each week – the Salt Lake City Visitors Bureau can bring you up to date. The following is a selection of the most important annual events.

**June Arts** Held in the last week of June, the festival has hundreds of entries for the juried event. Entertainment, ethnic food and children's art are featured. The unique Pageant of the Arts is held throughout most of June. Actors present tableaux re-creating famous works of art; in past years, this has been held either in Salt Lake City or in other nearby towns, so check on the venue. Also held either in the city or in a nearby town in mid-June is the Highlands Festival with Scottish dancing, bagpipes, crafts, food booths and highland games.

**Pioneer Day** Held on 24 July, this celebration commemorates the arrival of Brigham Young's band of Mormon pioneers in 1847. For several days before the 24th, there are rodeo competitions and an arts festival. Pioneer Day itself is celebrated with fireworks, picnics and a huge parade, which organizers claim to be the third largest in the country.

**Utah State Fair** The fair occurs in mid-September at the fairgrounds on N Temple just east of the Jordan River. For over a week there are rodeos, carnival rides, agricultural and livestock shows, arts and crafts displays and entertainment.

**Oktoberfest** During September weekends, Oktoberfest comes to the Snowbird resort with beer, live music and dancing.

**Christmas Festivities** Christmas season begins in late November with the Christmas Lighting of Temple Square, during which about a quarter of a million light bulbs are switched on to illuminate the square. In December, various Christmas cultural events take place, such as performances of the *Nutcracker Ballet* or Dickens' *A Christmas Carol*.

## PLACES TO STAY

There are over 100 places to stay in Salt Lake City and the immediate surroundings. The following represents a large selection – but there are more. Summer and winter are the high seasons, and prices may be lower in spring and fall. Winter rates in the middle and top-end price ranges may

include access to UTA buses to the ski slopes and various ski packages.

## PLACES TO STAY – CAMPING

There are two campgrounds just two miles west of Temple Square. Both provide coin laundry, pool, recreation room and showers. *Camp VIP* (☎ 328 0224), 1350 W North Temple, charges $15/20 for sites without/with RV hookups. The *Salt Lake Campground* (☎ 355 1214), 1400 W North Temple, charges $21/23 for sites without/ with RV hookups.

Away from the center, Great Salt Lake State Park and Lagoon Amusement Park (see the above sections) offer camping.

The USFS (☎ 524 5042) maintains four campgrounds in the Wasatch Mountains. In Little Cottonwood Canyon there is *Tanner's Flat* (7100 feet), with 59 sites and fishing nearby. Sites are $8 and open from late May to early October. *Albion Basin* (9700 feet) has 28 sites for $6, open from late June to early September. In Big Cottonwood Canyon, *The Spruces* (7400 feet) has 61 sites for $8, open from late May to late September. *Redman* (8300 feet) has 76 sites for $8, open from early June to early October. Both Spruces and Redman have fishing nearby. All four campgrounds have water; none have showers or RV hookups. RVs over 22 feet are not recommended. Open and closing dates depend on snow conditions.

## PLACES TO STAY – BOTTOM END

**Near Downtown** The *Avenues Youth Hostel* (☎ 363 8137), 107 F St and 2nd Ave, has dormitory rooms for $11/15 for youth hostel members/nonmembers, and private rooms for $22/33 for singles/ doubles. (There are only two doubles.) A kitchen, laundry and message board are available, and the guests are mainly young international travelers. Registration hours are 8 to 11 am and 5:30 to 10 pm – no registration after 10 pm. Credit cards are not accepted.

The following cheap places don't offer

much – check the rooms to avoid dissatisfaction. The *Stratford Hotel* (☎ 328 4089), 169 E 200 South, is old, cheap and very basic, but it's right in downtown. Rooms start at $15 for a single and $50 to $70 per week – they fill up fast. Otherwise, the cheapest motels within one mile of Temple Square are the following. The *Covered Wagon Motel* (☎ 533 9100), 230 W North Temple, has rooms starting at $26 single. The *Se Rancho Motel* (☎ 532 3300), 640 W North Temple, starts at $25 for a room with one bed (single or double). Some rooms have kitchenettes. The *Allstar Motel* (☎ 531 7300), 754 W North Temple, has rooms from $29. The *Continental Motel* (☎ 363 4546), 819 W North Temple, charges $40/45 for singles/doubles. The *Kendell Motel* (☎ 355 0293), 667 N 300 West, looks clean and charges $40/45 for singles/doubles (some rooms have kitchenettes). The downtown *Motel 6* (☎ 531 1252), 176 W 600 South, offers rooms for $35/41 and has a pool. This last is one of the best cheap hotels near the center.

**Beyond Downtown** Heading further west on North Temple (towards the airport) brings you to the *Overniter Motor Inn* (☎ 533 8300), 1500 W North Temple, which has rooms for $26/29 for singles/doubles. The airport *Motel 6* (☎ 364 1053), 1990 W North Temple, has a pool and charges $40/45. Opposite is the *Chateau Motel* (☎ 596 7240), 1999 W North Temple, which has rooms starting at $26 single.

The *Regal Inn* (☎ 364 6591), 1025 N 900 West, charges from $27/36. On the east side of downtown, the *Scenic Motel* (☎ 582 1527), 1345 Foothill Drive, charges $30/38. *Holiday Motel* (☎ 466 8733), 3035 S State, charges about the same and has a pool. The Midvale *Motel 6* (☎ 561 0058), 496 N Catalpa Rd (near exit 301 off I-15 at 7200 South), and the Woods Cross *Motel 6* (☎ 298 0289), at exit 318 off I-15, are about nine miles south and north of downtown respectively. Both charge $35/41 and have a pool.

## PLACES TO STAY – MIDDLE
### Hotels
**Near Downtown** The *Emerald Inn* (☎ 533 9300), 476 S State, has a pool and queen-size beds; it charges $35/45 for singles/doubles. The *Royal Executive Inn* (☎ 521 3450), 121 N 300 West, has nice rooms for $45 single and $60 for a family of four in two beds. Both prices include continental breakfast. The inn has a courtesy van to the airport and a pool. The *Econo Lodge* (☎ 363 0062), 715 W North Temple, has a pool, laundry facilities and airport transportation; rooms are about $46/50. Another good choice is the *Deseret Inn* (☎ 532 2900), 50 W 500 South, which has large, clean rooms with queen- and king-size beds and a writing desk; amenities include a restaurant and a spa. Rooms with one bed are $40; rooms with two beds are $37 to $42; and two-room suites are $50.

The *Travelodge at Temple Square* (☎ 533 8200), 144 W North Temple, has clean rooms starting at $45 single or double – it's nothing special, but the Temple Square location is good. Six blocks south is the *Travelodge – City Center* (☎ 531 7100), 524 S West Temple, which charges from $50; amenities include a pool and hot tub. Nearby is the *Super 8 Motel* (☎ 534 0808), 616 S 200 West, with rooms beginning at $40.88/48.88 for singles/doubles.

The *Shilo Inn* (☎ 521 9500), 206 S West Temple, opposite the visitors bureau, is a good value. This 12-story hotel has queen- or king-size beds in the spacious rooms, many of which have balconies. Facilities include free van to the airport (bus and train station too), a restaurant with room service, pool, sauna, exercise room, coin laundry and gift shop. Rooms are $100 for one or two people and include a free continental breakfast.

*Howard Johnson* (☎ 521 0130, 1 (800) 366 3684), 122 W South Temple, is conveniently adjacent to Temple Square and a block away from the Family History Library. If you are spending several days in Salt Lake researching your family history, ask for a discount – you'll get it. Room rates start at $52/60 for singles/doubles and go up to about $90. Suites are about $150.

The better rooms, which include refrigerators and king-size beds, are in quieter parts of the hotel. Cheaper rooms have queen-size beds. Facilities include a restaurant, airport van, pool, spa, exercise room and coin laundry.

The *Peery Hotel* (☎ 521 4300, 1 (800) 331 0073), 110 W 300 South, is an old hotel dating from 1910 and restored in 1985. The lobby is old-fashioned, the rooms are comfortable, and one of the city's favorite bars is on the premises. Other amenities include a restaurant, exercise room, spa and airport van. Room rates, which include continental breakfast, are $90 to $120 – rates are discounted on weekends.

Several other modern, full-service, downtown hotels with nice rooms in the $80 to $100 range are found about six blocks south of Temple Square. These include the Best Western *Olympus Hotel* (☎ 521 7373), 161 W 600 South; the *Ramada Inn* (☎ 364 5200), 230 W 600 South; the *Quality Inn – City Center* (☎ 521 9230), 154 W 600 South; and the huge 17-story *Little America* (☎ 363 6781), 500 S Main St, which has nearly 900 rooms and suites ranging from $60 to $120, depending on the size, views and amenities.

**Beyond Downtown** There are several hotels in the airport area. The *Days Inn* (☎ 539 8538), 1900 W North Temple, has nice rooms at $50/55 for singles/doubles or $57/60 with queen-size beds. Continental breakfast is included, and there are restaurants nearby. *Nendel's Inn* (☎ 355 0088), 2080 W North Temple, has a cafe, pool and coin laundry. Rooms are $48/54 and include continental breakfast. The *Comfort Inn – Airport* (☎ 537 7444), 200 N Admiral Byrd Rd, has similar amenities and spacious rooms at $55/65. The *Holiday Inn – Airport* (☎ 533 9000), 1659 W North Temple, with laundry, pool and restaurant, charges $75/85. The *Quality Inn – Airport* (☎ 537 7020), 5575 W Amelia Earhart Drive, is similar.

A fairly new and very comfortable full-service hotel, the *Holiday Inn – Downtown* (☎ 359 8600, 1 (800) 933 9678), 999 S Main St, is set in beautifully landscaped grounds 1.5 miles south of Temple Square. The hotel offers all standard facilities and has spacious rooms with king-size beds from $75/85 for singles/doubles and from $110 for suites with kitchenettes. Almost two miles south of the university on the east side of town, the *Skyline Inn* (☎ 582 5350), 2475 E 1700 South, is a small, clean, moderately priced motel with a pool and spa; rates are $45/50 including continental breakfast.

Other mid-range hotels lie well south of town. The *Days Inn – Central* (☎ 486 8780), 315 W 3300 South (just east of I-15 exit 306), has a sauna, exercise room and rooms with queen-size beds for $45/50. The *Quality Inn – South* (☎ 268 2533), 4465 S Century Drive (near I-15 exit 304), has a 24-hour restaurant nearby (but not in the hotel). There are laundry facilities, pool, spa and exercise room. Large, comfortable rooms are about $65/70 in the high season; add $15 for rooms with kitchenettes. The *Reston Hotel* (☎ 264 1054), 5335 College Drive (near exit 303 off I-15), has a pool, spa and restaurant. Good, comfortable rooms are $62/67.

The following hotels are near exit 301 off I-15, about 11 miles south of Temple Square. All have large, comfortable rooms with queen- or king-size beds. The *La Quinta Motor Inn* (☎ 566 3291), 530 Catalpa St, charges $55/63. A 24-hour restaurant is nearby. The *Discovery Motor Inn* (☎ 561 2256), 380 W 7200 South, and the *Best Western Executive Inn* (☎ 566 4141), 280 W 7200 South, both have adjacent restaurants and rooms for about $57/69. All these hotels have pools; the latter two have a spa. Further south, near I-15 exit 298, is the *Comfort Inn* (☎ 255 4919), 8955 S 255 West, with a pool and spa. A restaurant is next door. Comfortable rooms go for around $60/65 including continental breakfast.

### B&Bs

The B&B tradition is catching on in Utah, with new ones opening every year in Salt

Lake City. These accommodations in private homes should be reserved in advance – though a phone call may sometimes yield same-day accommodations.

The closest B&B to downtown is the *Anton Boxrud B&B* (☎ 363 8035, 1 (800) 524 5511), 57 S 600 East, 84102. This historic 1901 home, furnished with antiques, has five rooms, two with private baths. Rates are $50/60 for single/double with shared bath and $70 with private bath. Just a little further east is the *Saltair B&B* (☎ 533 8184, 1 (800) 733 8184), 164 S 900 East, 84102. Built in 1903, this historic home was Salt Lake's first B&B. The five rooms have period furnishings; two have private baths. Rooms start at $50/60 and go up to $80. Both these homes have no-smoking policies.

The most luxurious B&B is the *Brigham Street Inn* (☎ 364 4461), 1135 E South Temple, 84102. Just under two miles east of Temple Square, this elegant Victorian mansion has nine attractive rooms, most with queen-size beds and private baths. Some rooms have fireplaces. Most rooms rent for $110; one room with a twin bed is $80, and a suite with kitchen and double whirlpool bathroom is $150.

The *Spruces B&B* (☎ 268 8762), 6151 S 900 East, 84121, is a 1903 ranch that was refurbished in 1985. The decor is Southwestern. There are four suites with private baths and private entrances. Two small suites are $55 double. A larger suite sleeps four and has a whirlpool bathtub – it was originally a fruit cellar. The largest has three bedrooms, a living room and kitchen; it rents for $100. Rates are higher during ski season. No smoking allowed.

The *Pinecrest B&B* (☎ 583 6663, 1 (800) 359 6663), 6211 Emigration Canyon Rd, 84108, is a 1915 country residence in the Wasatch foothills, about 12 miles east of downtown. The large and peaceful garden has a stream running through it. There are six rooms, all with private bath, two with spa/sauna, and two with fireplace and kitchen. Two of the 'rooms' are cabins, which can sleep a family, and a huge suite can also accommodate a family. Rates are

$70 to $175 double, depending on the room. No smoking allowed.

The *Log Cabin on the Hill B&B* (☎ 272 2969), 2275 E 6200 South, 84121, has rooms with shared bath for $45/55 and one room with a private bath for $75. The inn has a hot tub for guests. The *Mountain Hollow B&B* (☎ 942 3428), 10209 Dimple Dell Rd, Sandy, 84092 (five miles east of I-15, exit 297, via 10600 South) has eight rooms with private baths from $60 double. There is a hot tub, and the inn is eight miles from Snowbird and Alta skiing areas. No smoking is allowed. *Quail Hills B&B* (☎ 942 2858), 3744 E Little Cottonwood Canyon Rd, Sandy, 84092, is just six miles from the skiing areas and has double rooms with private bath for $70. No smoking.

## PLACES TO STAY – TOP END
### Hotels
**Near Downtown** *The Inn at Temple Square* (☎ 531 1000, 1 (800) 843 4668), 71 W South Temple, is in a 1930 Edwardian building refurbished for the 1990s. It offers the closest luxury lodging to Temple Square (which is across the street), and many rooms have good views of the square; some rooms have whirlpool bathtubs. The approximately one hundred rooms or suites are attractively furnished and elegantly old-fashioned. Mini-refrigerators with complimentary soft drinks are inside the rooms. Nearby pool and health club privileges are available. Smoking is not permitted throughout the hotel, and no liquor is served. Rates include breakfast and range from $90 to $150 a room, and $150 to $225 for a suite. Weekend discounts are available.

Two other luxury hotels just a block away from Temple Square are the *Marriott* (☎ 531 0800, 1 (800) 228 9290), 75 S West Temple, and the *Doubletree* (☎ 531 7500, 1 (800) 528 0444), 215 W South Temple. Both are large, full-service hotels with hundreds of rooms, a few expensive suites, and swimming, sauna and exercise facilities. The Marriott has three restaurants and a lounge. Smaller rooms start at about $90; larger rooms with concierge service and breakfast are about $140. Substantial weekend discounts are available. The Doubletree has one restaurant and a lounge. Spacious rooms, many with excellent views, range from $100 to $140, but discounts of about 30% can easily be arranged for AAA members, seniors, etc. Breakfast is included. Children stay free with parents at these hotels.

Large, full-service luxury hotels a few blocks from Temple Square include the following: the *Red Lion* (☎ 328 2000), 255 S West Temple; the *Salt Lake Hilton* (☎ 532 3344), 150 W 500 South; and the *Embassy Suites Hotel* (☎ 359 7800), 600 S West Temple. All have the usual athletic, restaurant and lounge facilities. Rooms range from $95 to $135, including breakfast. Weekend discounts are available. The *Residence Inn by Marriott* (☎ 532 5511), 765 E 400 South, is well away from the hotel area and offers one- and two-bedroom apartments with kitchens for $120 to $160, including daily breakfast and a free happy hour on weekday evenings. Apartments sleep four to six people. Many rooms have fireplaces, and there are three hot tubs and a pool.

**Beyond Downtown** The *Airport Hilton* (☎ 539 1515), 5151 Wiley Post Way, and the *Radisson Hotel* (☎ 364 5800, 1 (800) 333 3333), 2177 W North Temple, are the most luxurious lodgings close to the airport. Both are large, full-service hotels with all the usual amenities. The Hilton boasts a small lake with boats and a putting green nearby. Rates are in the $80 to $120 range; more expensive suites are available.

The *University Park Hotel* (☎ 581 1000), 500 S Wakara Way, just east of the university, is a modern and luxurious full-service hotel with good views of downtown or the mountains. Rooms are about $110, and suites are about $150, with weekend and other discounts available.

**Ski Resorts**
Both the Snowbird/Alta area in Little Cottonwood Canyon and the Solitude/Brighton area in Big Cottonwood Canyon have ski resorts, condos and lodges. Of the ski areas, Snowbird/Alta offers the greatest choice of accommodations. Some of these remain open in summer, when they offer cheaper accommodations than in winter. During the summer, they make good bases for hiking, mountain biking, rock climbing and other outdoor activities.

The ski season rates vary during low, regular and holiday periods. The low periods are normally the first and last few weeks of the ski season, when snow conditions are the most erratic. The regular season runs from January to March. The holiday season, from about 18 December to New Year's Day, is the most expensive. There is often a post-holiday season lull in January, when slopes are the least crowded of the regular season, and low-season prices may be offered by many resorts, some of which may require a minimum stay of several days. Note that a sales tax of about 10% is added to the prices given and that lodges offering meals-inclusive packages add a further 15% service charge.

Ski resorts and airlines often join together to offer package deals that are cheaper than paying for flights and rooms separately. Ask your travel agent about these.

Budget travelers will not find any bargains at the ski resorts. To save money, stay in Salt Lake City and take a bus up to the resorts. The free and very useful annual *Utah Winter Vacation Planner*, available

from the Utah Travel Council and many information centers (see Information) provides both skiing and accommodations information.

**Snowbird** The *Snowbird Ski & Summer Resort* (☎ 1 (800) 453 3000, fax 742 3300), Snowbird 84092-9000, operates the 532-room *Cliff Lodge*, as well as three condo complexes: the *Lodge at Snowbird*, the *Iron Blosam Lodge* and the *Inn at Snowbird*. These places house the majority of skiers as all are within walking/skiing distance of the chair lifts, ski rental and repair shops and skiing school. They require a four-night stay if the rental dates include a Thursday, Friday or Saturday night during the regular and holiday seasons. These lodges are generally newer and a little more upscale than most of the lodges in Alta.

The Cliff Lodge has a full-service spa with everything from herbal wraps to a giant whirlpool (adults only), child care, three restaurants, room service, bars and dancing. Other restaurants are nearby. The lodge offers single-sex dormitories at $37/53 per person in low/regular season; rooms from $110 to $160 in the low season and $190 to $310 in the regular season; and suites from $270 to $425 in the low and $510 to $780 in the regular season. Rates are for one or two people.

The Lodge at Snowbird, the Iron Blosam Lodge and the Inn at Snowbird have restaurants, child care, pools, saunas and spas. There are a total of 360 units in the three complexes, and about 60% have kitchens. Some have fireplaces and balconies. Units (in increasing order of size and price) include studios, bedrooms, efficiencies, studio lofts and one-bedroom condos with lofts ranging from $76 to $275 in the low season and from $159 to $532 in the regular season.

**Alta** There are over a dozen places to stay near Alta, and many can be reserved through *Alta Reservation Service* (☎ 942 0404), 3332 East Little Cottonwood Road, Sandy, 84092.

All the following are a short walk or ski

from the chair lifts. *Alta Lodge* (☎ 742 3500, 1 (800) 707 2582) offers over 50 rooms ranging from dormitories at $88 per person to deluxe rooms, some with fireplaces, for $300 double (regular season). Prices include breakfast and dinner (add 10% tax and 15% service charge). They have a sauna and spa, as well as a children's program. *Alta Peruvian Lodge* (☎ 742 3000, 1 (800) 453 8488, fax 742 3007) has a swimming pool but no child care; otherwise it is similar to the Alta Lodge at prices from $81 in dorms to $290 a double. *Goldminer's Daughter Lodge* (☎ 742 2300, 1 (800) 453 4573) has a hot tub, sauna and exercise room. Dorm rooms cost $79 per person; bedrooms cost from $115 to $129 for singles and $178 to $190 for doubles; and suites from $220 a double to $390 for quadruple occupancy, including breakfast and dinner. Discounts of 10 to 20% are offered in the low season.

The most comfortable of the Alta base lodges is the 56-room *Rustler Lodge* (☎ 742 2200, 1 (800) 451 5223, fax 742 3832). It has child care, a pool, sauna and spa. Regular season rates are $85 per person in dorms, and range from $200 to $430 a double in rooms and suites. Low-season rates drop to $75 in dorms and $170 to $330 in rooms and suites. Rates include breakfast and dinner. Next door, the 20-room *Snow Pine Lodge* (☎ 742 2000) offers dorms for $72 per person, and rooms, some with shared baths, range from $160 to $236 a double (regular season) including breakfast and dinner. It has a hot tub.

If you want more elegant accommodations and don't mind walking a few hundred yards to the chair lifts, *Canyon Services* (☎ 943 1842, 1 (800) 562 2888), PO Box 920025, Snowbird 84092-0025, has several dozen two- and three-bedroom condos and townhouses, some with lofts, sleeping four to 10 people. Most come with private hot tubs, parking garage and full kitchen, and many have laundry facilities, balconies and fireplaces. Regular season rates range from $325 for two bedrooms to $500 for three bedrooms and a loft. Holiday-season rates run about 10%

higher, and low-season rates around 30% lower.

Other small places (under 20 units) close to but not right by the lifts include the following, all with kitchen facilities. *Blackjack Condominium Lodge* (☎ 742 3200, 1 (800) 434 0347), with two person studios for $155 and one-bedroom apartments sleeping four for $245, is a short ski from Snowbird. Half a mile from either Alta or Snowbird, *Hellgate Condominiums* (☎ 742 2020) has units ranging from studios for $150 to four-bedroom condos for $460. *View Condominiums* (☎ 277 7172, 1 (800) 274 7172), a short walk from Alta, offers one- to three-bedroom condos for $270 to $445. (All prices are regular season.)

**Brighton/Solitude** The Brighton/Solitude ski areas have far fewer places to stay. The *Brighton Lodge* (☎ 649 7908, 1 (800) 873 5512) is right by the lifts. It has 22 rooms, a hot tub and a pool. Double rooms are about $85 during regular season. A quarter mile from the slopes, *Brighton Chalets* (☎ 942 8824, 1 (800) 748 4824) features five cabins of various sizes complete with kitchen and fireplace and suitable for families. Regular season rates go from about $100 to $300. *Home Away from Home* (☎ 272 0965, fax 277 4496) has a variety of cabins and houses (one sleeping two dozen people!) for $100 to $800, all within a few hundred yards of the slopes. *Das Alpen Haus* (☎ 649 0565), Star Route, Brighton, 84121, is a B&B with a sauna, library and TV room about 200 yards from the lifts. There are four rooms with private bath (two have spas) renting for $110 to $180 a double during the regular season.

## PLACES TO EAT
### Budget
Starving travelers with huge appetites and limited funds might try the following 'all-you-can-eat' establishments – none of which I have eaten in (have to watch my waistline when researching places to eat!). *China Place* (☎ 364 1546), 320 W North

### Historic Restaurants
Apart from the Rio Grande Cafe and Cordova's El Rancho (see Mexican) and the Ristorante della Fontana (see Italian), there are several eateries with a sense of history, especially the *Lion House Pantry* (☎ 240 2977), 63 E South Temple. This is on the ground floor of the Lion House, built in 1855 as quarters for some of Brigham Young's many wives. Hearty American food is served for weekday lunches (11 am to 2 pm). Meals are $4 to $10. It also has a buffet dinner from 6 to 9 pm on Friday and Saturday.

*Lamb's Restaurant* (☎ 364 7166), 169 S Main, founded in 1919, is Utah's oldest continually operating restaurant. It moved to its present location in 1939 and has maintained a 1930s atmosphere – it feels as if you are in a Bogart movie. And the food is good and fairly inexpensive, too. Hours are 7 am to 9 pm daily, except Sunday.

The *Old Salt City Jail* (☎ 355 2422), 460 S 1000 East, housed in what used to be a jail house, has a 'singing sheriff' and other early Western touches. It's OK, though a bit touristy. The food is mostly meat, and main courses are in the $10 to $20 range. Seafood and a children's (Little Cowboy's) menu are available. Hours are 5:30 to 10 pm from Monday to Thursday, 5 to 11 pm on Friday and Saturday, and 5:30 to 9 pm on Sunday.

*Archibald's* (☎ 566 6940), 1095 W 7800 South, is well south of town in the historic mill built by Archibald Gardner in 1853. (There are many gift shops and a small museum – see Things to Buy.) American food is served and there is a patio for summer dining. Main courses are in the $6 to $15 range. Hours are 11 am to 9 pm on weekdays, and 8 am to 9 pm on weekends. ■

Temple, has lunches for $4 and dinners for $6. *Chuck-A-Rama* (☎ 531 1123), 744 E 400 South, has buffet lunches for $5 (11 am to 4 pm, Monday to Saturday) and dinners for $6 (4 to 9 pm, Monday to Saturday, and 11 am to 8 pm on Sunday). The upmarket *Cedars of Lebanon* (see Middle-

Eastern & Asian below) has midweek lunch specials for $5, as does the *Star of India* across the street – both advertised all-you-can-eat when I visited. *Sizzler* has several locations: 371 E 400 South (☎ 532 1339); 435 S 700 East (☎ 359 3355); and 3600 S State (☎ 266 7381). They offer fruit, salad, soup, pasta, tostada and dessert all-you-can-eat buffets along with any main course.

My favorite budget place is *Bill & Nada's Cafe* (☎ 359 6984), 479 S 600 East. This is an unpretentious and basic American diner – but the service is friendly, the food is satisfactory, the prices are low and the hours are perfect. This locally popular cafe provides good value 24 hours a day. Apart from the usual – full breakfasts, sandwiches, grilled chicken, liver 'n onions, etc – you'll find some off-beat dishes like scrambled eggs with brains (which I last ate in Peru!).

The *Student Union Cafeteria* (☎ 581 7256) in the University of Utah's Olpin Union Building (☎ 581 5888) serves cheap meals and offers a chance to meet students. The Union is in the middle of the campus.

Chinese, Vietnamese and Thai restaurants also offer inexpensive dining (see Middle-Eastern & Asian below).

### Deli

Other good budget choices include *Brackman Brothers Bagel Bakeries* with three locations: 859 E 900 South (☎ 322 4350); 1520 S 1500 East (☎ 466 8669); and the new downtown spot at 147 S Main St. They are open daily from 7 am to 7 pm and offer a wide variety of tasty bagel sandwiches for under $5, as well as other deli items like soups, salads and coffee. Bagels are baked fresh all day long. Another deli where you can eat for under $5 is *Marianne's Delicatessen* (☎ 364 0513), 149 W 200 South, which specializes in German food. It's open for lunch (11 am to 3 pm) from Tuesday to Saturday or for take-out from 9 am to 6 pm (4 pm on Saturday). *Broadway Deli & Bandaloops Coffee Bar* (☎ 322 3138), 172 W 300 South, has American-style sandwiches and specialty coffees. It is open from 8 am to 10 pm during the week and 10 am to midnight on weekends.

### Mexican

Salt Lake City lays claim to many 'authentic' Mexican restaurants. While they are generally not quite up to the standards of Mexican fare in Tucson, Arizona, they are certainly more authentic than the Mexican restaurant I once tried in Fargo, North Dakota.

I like the food at the *Red Iguana* (☎ 322 1489), 736 W North Temple. Come here for the low prices and good Mexican dishes – not for the ambiance, which is cheap and undistinguished. Hours are 11 am to 9 pm, Monday to Thursday, and to 10 pm on Friday and Saturday. The *Rio Grande Cafe* (☎ 364 3302), 270 S Rio Grande, is inexpensive and fun – it is housed in the historic Rio Grande railway depot. Lunch is served from 11:30 am to 2:30 pm and dinner from 5 to 10 pm daily (no lunch on Sunday). *La Frontera* is at 1236 W 400 South (☎ 532 3158) and at 1434 S 700 West (☎ 974 0172); both serve good-sized meals at reasonable prices. Hours are 10 am to 11 pm daily except Friday and Saturday, when they close at 1 am. Also reasonably priced is *Don Felipe's* (☎ 537 1919), 459 Trolley Square Shopping Center, which has an outdoor patio for dining.

*Cafe Pierpont* (☎ 364 1222), 122 W Pierpont Ave, has a more extensive and expensive menu, though you are paying for the surroundings and wider selection rather than better Mexican food. You can eat on the outdoor sidewalk or inside accompanied by festively loud Mexican music and surrounded by piñatas and other south-of-the-border touches. Combo plates are in the $6 to $9 range; specialty dishes can be up to twice that. The cafe is open 11:30 am to 10 pm from Monday to Friday and 4 to 10 pm on weekends. Also fancier and more expensive is *Cordova's El Rancho* (☎ 355 1914), 543 W 400 North, which has been here since 1939 and claims to be the city's first Mexican

UTAH

restaurant. Hours are 5:30 to 10 pm from Wednesday to Saturday only – reservations are a good idea.

Finally, I can't resist mentioning the delightfully named *Guadalahonky Mexican Restaurant* (☎ 571 3838), 136 E 12300 South. I can only wonder what the food is like.

## Italian

For pizza, *Gepetto's* (☎ 583 1013), 230 S 1300 East, is popular, especially with students from the nearby university. Hours are from 11 am to about 11 pm or midnight from Monday to Saturday. Around the corner is the *Pie Pizzeria* (☎ 582 0193), 1373 E 200 South – another popular college hangout and open daily. Both places may have live entertainment on weekends.

There are several good, upscale Italian restaurants. A particularly distinctive one is the *Ristorante della Fontana* (☎ 328 4243), 336 S 400 East, which is housed in a converted 1892 church. The baptismal font is now a fountain (hence the name) and stained-glass windows provide unusual lighting. The restaurant serves a wide variety of Italian six-course dinners in the $9 to $16 range, a little more for steak. A la carte meals and lunches are less. Hours are 11:30 am to 9:30 pm daily except Sunday.

*Nino's* (☎ 359 0506), 136 E South Temple, is also distinctive – on the 24th floor of the University Club Building, it is the highest dining spot in Salt Lake City. The views, of course, are excellent and the ambiance is candle-lit – a good place for that special date. The food is very good and the selection varied. Main dinner courses are in the $11 to $21 range; lunches are less expensive and include daily specials for $5. Hours are 11:30 am to 2:30 pm from Monday to Friday and 5 to 10:30 pm from Monday to Saturday. Early-bird dinner specials are $13 for a four course set meal before 7 pm.

*Fresco Italian Cafe* (☎ 486 1300), 1513 S 1500 East, offers yet a different Italian dining experience. The small but neat dining room is inside a house, and diners spill out onto a courtyard outside during warm weather. A no-smoking policy is enforced. Pasta and other Italian dishes are flavored with some unusual sauces – not necessarily to everyone's taste, but local cognoscenti think highly of the unique offerings. Main courses are in the $10 to $20 range, and hours are 11:30 am to 2:30 pm from Tuesday to Friday and 5:30 to 9:30 pm from Tuesday to Sunday.

Other top-quality Italian restaurants worth trying include the *Baci Trattoria* (☎ 328 1500), 134 W Pierpont Ave, which has a modern but beautiful decor; next door is the Club Baci – a popular private club. The same tasty food is served in both places. It's open from 11:30 am to 10 pm from Monday to Thursday and to midnight on Friday and Saturday. Also very good is *Rino's Italian Ristorante* (☎ 484 0982), 2302 Parley's Way (at 2100 S & 2302 East), which is open only for dinner 6 to 10 pm from Monday to Thursday, 5:30 to 10:30 pm on Friday and Saturday, and 5 to 9 pm on Sunday. The food is recommended, but the prices are high. If you are in Trolley Square, a good choice is *Ferantelli's* (☎ 531 8228), 300 Trolley Square. Prices are a little more reasonable here, and the food is good. Hours are 11:30 am to 10 pm, to 11 pm on Friday and Saturday.

## French

Despite its name, *Le Parisien* (☎ 364 5223), 417 S 300 East, serves both French and Italian food at slightly more modest prices than most French restaurants. The restaurant has several private booths for which a reservation is a good idea. Hours are 11 am to 10 pm from Monday to Thursday and to 11 pm on Friday and Saturday; 5 to 10 pm on Sunday.

It's a fair drive to *La Caille at Quail Run* (☎ 942 1751), 9656 Wasatch Blvd (near the beginning of Little Cottonwood Canyon), but it's worth the drive to this beautiful restaurant. Set in 22 acres of landscaped gardens, the place bills itself as an 18th-century French chateau and does a nice job of fulfilling the promise. The food is very good at prices commensurate with the high quality and elegant surroundings. Reservations are required. Dinner is served from 6 to 10 pm daily (11 pm on Friday and Saturday). There is a Sunday brunch from 10 am to 1 pm.

## Middle-Eastern & Asian

Lebanese, Indian, Thai, Vietnamese, Chinese or Japanese – you have a good choice of Asian restaurants in a city where the population is very predominantly Caucasian. The *Cedars of Lebanon* (☎ 364 4096), 152 E 200 South, has inexpensive lunches and pricier dinners with a good variety of Middle-eastern and vegetarian dishes. Middle-eastern carpets and music add to the ambiance, and belly dancers entertain on Friday and Saturday nights. Dinner entrees range from $8 to $16. Hours are 11 am to 10 pm, Monday to Saturday. Across the street, the *Star of India* (☎ 363 7555), 177 E 200 South, offers medium-priced curries and other Indian dishes.

The *Thai House Restaurant* (☎ 486 8043), 1499 S State, serves good food at inexpensive prices. Hours are 11:30 am to 3 pm and 5 to 10 pm from Monday to Saturday. Also good and inexpensive is the *Cafe Trang* (☎ 539 1638), 818 S Main St, which serves tasty Vietnamese cuisine 11 am to 9 pm from Tuesday to Sunday. The *Shanghai Cafe* (☎ 322 1841), 145 E 1300 South, has cheap Vietnamese and Chinese specials. There are dozens of other Chinese restaurants including the *Pagoda* (☎ 355 8155), 26 East St (north of the 500 East block of South Temple), which has been here since 1946 and must be doing something right. It's open from 5 pm to 11:30 pm from Tuesday to Thursday and to 12:30 am on Friday and Saturday. Sunday hours are 3 to 10:30 pm. Another Salt Lake City favorite is *Fong Ling* (☎ 943 8199, 943 4999), 3698 E 7000 South, open daily from 5 to 11 pm.

Japanese food has recently become popular in the city, and there are several good places to choose from. *Kyoto* (☎ 487 3525), 1080 E 1300 South, has authentic food at moderate prices and offers private

dining rooms where guests sit on mats around a low table, Japanese style. Lunches are $5 to $9, dinners $9 to $15. Reservations for the private rooms are recommended. Lunch is served 11:30 am to 2 pm from Monday to Saturday; dinner is served daily 5:30 to 9:30 pm. (It may close on Mondays.)

The well-recommended *Mikado* (☎ 328 0929), 67 W 100 South, which has been open since the 1960s, has authentic Japanese dining in a traditional ambiance – private *zashiki* dining rooms are available and there is a good sushi bar. Dinners are served 5:30 to 9:30 pm from Monday to Thursday and to 10:30 pm on Friday and Saturday. Dinner prices range from $12 to $18, and a children's menu is available.

*Benihana of Tokyo* (☎ 322 2421), 165 S West Temple, entertains diners by cooking food to order right by their table – and the food is very good. Lunches are $6 to $14; dinners are $14 to $25. Hours are 11:30 am to 2 pm from Monday to Friday; 5:30 to 10:30 pm from Monday to Thursday; and to 11:30 pm on Friday and Saturday. Sunday hours are 5 to 10 pm. Similar cooking is available at *Hibachi* (☎ 364 5456), 238 E South Temple. Prices here are more moderate – around $6 for lunch and $12 to $17 for dinner. Hours are 11:30 am to 3 pm from Monday to Friday and 6 to 9:30 pm from Monday to Saturday.

*Shogun* (☎ 364 7142), 321 S Main St, has one of the better sushi bars in town, as well as a wide variety of other Japanese dishes. Its downtown location makes it popular with business people. Lunch combos are in the $5 to $8 range; dinners go from $8 to $20, plus a special sushi combo for $25. Hours are 11:30 am to 2:30 pm from Monday to Friday, 6 to 10:30 pm from Monday to Thursday and to midnight on Friday and Saturday.

## American (well, kind of . . . )

If you feel like a burger and brew, the best place is the *Squatter's Pub Brewery* (☎ 363 2739), 147 W 300 South. The Salt Lake Brewing Company has a microbrewery on the premises (right behind the bar), and you can down a pint of draught pale ale, cream stout, best bitter or one of the brew master's seasonal ales along with your meal. The beer is the best in Utah. The food is good and plentiful too – not just burgers but a satisfying choice of soups, salads, sandwiches, pizza, chili and pub food like fish & chips or curry. Almost everything is under $8.50. The ambiance is pub-like and friendly – a good place to hang out. Fireplaces blaze in winter and there's a beer garden for summer. Hours are 11:30 am to midnight (1 am on Friday and Saturday) – but you have to be 21 to get in.

The *Green Parrot* (☎ 363 3201), 155 W 200 South, is a private club, but out-of-town visitors are welcome to eat here and the management will sponsor you. Dining booths have wall-mounted jukeboxes so you can listen to your favorite tunes. The menu is divided into 'Ballads' (lunch), 'Ditties' (appetizers), 'Old Standards' (dinner) and 'Closing Riffs' (dessert – what else?). Lunch is served 11 am to 5 pm and runs $4 to $7; dinner is served from 5 to 10 pm (11 pm on weekends) and features steak, seafood, chicken, pasta and a couple of Mexican plates in the $7 to $17 range. Appetizers are served all day and night. This is a popular place in the evenings with live music (jazz, acoustic, etc) and dancing.

Good value has not gone the way of the dinosaurs in the nicely named *Dodo Restaurant* (☎ 328 9348), 680 S 900 East, which serves excellent and moderately priced food. The varied selection is interesting, and the ham and turkey used in the delicious sandwiches ($5 to $6) is smoked right on the premises. There is a pleasant outdoor patio. Lunches run about $5 to $9, and dinner entrees are in the $10 to $15 range. Hours are 11 am to about 9 pm from Monday to Thursday and to 10:30 pm on Friday and Saturday. A Sunday brunch is served from 10 am to 2 pm.

Other American food choices include the following. *Shenanigan's* (☎ 364 3663), 274 S West Temple, in the Peery Hotel Building, has a wild menu with burgers, steaks, sandwiches, seafood, and salads; Hawaiian, Mexican, and Italian food; and triple-decker chocolate fudge cake. Prices are $5 to $13. Hours are about 11 am to 11 pm daily. The *Park Cafe* (☎ 487 1670), 604 E 1300 South, just south of Liberty Park, has great breakfasts for $5 to $7; lunch sandwiches, soups, quiches and salads for $6 to $9; and delicious pasta, meat and seafood dinner entrees for $8 to $15. Hours are 7 am to 3 pm daily, and 5 pm to 9 pm from Monday to Thursday and to 10 pm on Friday and Saturday.

You get Western food in an Old Wild West setting at *Diamond Lil's* (533 0547), 1528 W North Temple. The food is appropriate – prime rib, steak and barbecue are the big sellers, though seafood is available too. Meals range from $8 to $25. It's open 11:30 am to 10 pm from Monday to Saturday.

For more upmarket American food, head for the fancy *Market Street Grill* (☎ 322 4668), 48 Market St (at 350 South), which specializes in seafood. It's open for breakfast and lunch from Monday to Saturday (6:30 am to 3 pm) and dinner daily from 5 pm. Excellent breakfasts are $4 to $7 (crab omelets and broiled halibut or trout are among the many choices). Lunch salads, sandwiches, pasta and seafood plates are in the $5 to $10 range. Dinners include meat and seafood entrees ranging from linguine with clams ($14) to filet mignon with Alaskan king crab legs ($28). Come in before 7 pm to take advantage of the early bird special – prime rib or halibut for $12. Next door is the *Market Street Oyster Bar* (☎ 531 6044), 54 Market St, a private club with similar food for lunch and dinner – temporary club membership is $5 for two weeks.

Next to the above pair is the *New Yorker* (☎ 363 0166), 60 Market St. This, too, is an elegant and upmarket restaurant in a private club. Dinner entrees include pheasant at about $30 and abalone for around $40, though there is also a good selection of meat and seafood entrees for around $20. Daily fixed-price lunches are

$7. Lunch is served from 11:30 am to 2:30 pm from Monday to Friday and dinner from 6 pm daily except Sunday. Reservations are recommended. Adjoining the main restaurant is a cafe that is open 2:30 to 11 pm from Monday to Friday and 6 to 11:30 pm on Saturday. It serves lighter meals for lighter prices.

For dining out in the nearby countryside, head up to Emigration Canyon, northeast of the city. Here, there are three good restaurants to choose from. First is *Ruth's Diner* (☎ 582 5807), 2100 Emigration Canyon, about four miles east of the university. Once a diner, Ruth's is now a pleasant cafe with outdoor gardens and live musicians most evenings when the weather is warm. The place is popular and packed with locals who want to eat well-prepared and reasonably priced food out-of-doors – or inside in winter. The menu is varied but tends towards Mexican and American (sandwiches, salads, burgers, chicken, etc). Prices are in the $5 to $15 range for most items. Hours are 9 am to 10 pm daily.

Right next door to Ruth's is the *Santa Fe Restaurant* (☎ 582 5888). High ceilings, wooden beams, fireplaces, picture windows and Southwestern decor make this one of the more distinctive and popular restaurants in the Salt Lake area. It also has an outdoor patio. The menu is American with a Southwestern and Mexican flair. Lunches are in the $4 to $10 range; main dinner entrees from $10 to $23. Hours are 11:30 am to 2:30 pm from Monday to Friday; 5:30 to 10 pm from Monday to Saturday; and from 10 am to 2:30 pm for Sunday brunch.

*Crompton's Roadside Attraction* (☎ 583 1869), is a few miles further up at 5195 Emigration Canyon. This friendly American cafe is simple inside, has a nice patio outside, and is a good lunch and dinner choice for those watching the budget – meals are in the $4 to $8 range and include innovative omelets as well as the usual American standards. Hours are 9 am to 10 pm daily, except Friday and Saturday when

it stays open till midnight and features live acoustic entertainment.

## Other Restaurants

The main shopping malls have good food courts with a variety of fairly inexpensive dining – pizzas, burgers, sandwiches, Chinese, Mexican, Greek, etc. These are handy for lunch downtown. The biggest selection is at the *Crossroads Plaza*, 50 S Main St, right by Temple Square. Other malls with plenty of places to eat include *ZCMI*, 36 S State, and *Trolley Square*, 600 S 700 East. Besides the food court, Trolley Square stands out among the malls for its good restaurants (some of which have been described above).

Many of the city's better hotels have good restaurants open to the public. A few especially noteworthy ones include the following.

The *Peery Pub & Cafe* (☎ 521 8919), in the Peery Hotel at 110 W 300 South, serves relatively inexpensive continental cuisine in one of the city's most popular and traditional-looking pubs. Dinners in the $10 to $15 range are served from 6 to 10 pm, and the pub serves lighter meals and good sandwiches from 11:30 am to 10:30 pm. It's closed on Sundays.

Somewhat more upmarket dining is available at *L'Abeille* (☎ 531 0800), which serves French and continental food in the Marriott at 75 S West Temple. *Maxi's* (☎ 328 2000), a relative newcomer to the hotel dining scene, serves American and continental food, including pheasant, at the Red Lion Inn, 255 S West Temple. *Little America Dining Room* (☎ 363 6781), 500 S Main St in the Little America Hotel, is known for its hugely varied menu and especially for its Sunday brunch served from 9 am to 2 pm.

## ENTERTAINMENT
### Cinemas

There are dozens of movie theaters all over town – look in the entertainment sections of the city newspapers for cinema addresses, phone numbers and movie times. Note the discounted prices (as low as $1) if you go to afternoon matinee performances midweek.

For alternative movies, call the *Avalon Theater* (☎ 266 0258), 3605 S State, which shows old classics at 7:30 pm from Monday to Saturday, or *Cinema in Your Face* (☎ 364 3647), 45 W 300 South, which screens foreign flicks. You could also try the *Utah Media Center* (☎ 534 1158) in the Salt Lake Art Center at 20 S West Temple, which could be showing just about anything.

## Nightlife

The best listing of bars, concerts and nightclubs is in the free *Private Eye Weekly*, published on Wednesday and available at hundreds of outlets, including many of the bars themselves. The free biweekly *Event* is also a good information source. The Friday editions of the two city dailies have entertainment listings.

Many nightclubs are private clubs – you can buy a temporary two-week membership for $5 (which allows you to bring five guests), or you can hang out at the entrance and find a member to sponsor you for one night. You have to be 21 to get in to most places everywhere – and IDs are often checked. If you can't find a newspaper listing, call before showing up – nightclubs don't last forever!

There are dozens of popular night spots, catering to a wide variety of tastes. Some popular ones include the following (all along S West Temple). The *Dead Goat Saloon* (☎ 328 4628), 165 S West Temple, is more or less underground, down a funky-looking iron stairwell and behind a formidable wooden door. This has been a popular drinking spot for both young locals and travelers since 1965. There is live blues or rock & roll with a $3 to $6 cover most nights. Pub lunches are served and there are pool tables. Hours are 11:30 am to 1 am during the week and 6 pm to 1 am on weekends. Also popular with live rock & roll, blues, folk and alternative music is the hip private club *DV8* (☎ 539 8400), 115 S West Temple. The young crowd is cool, and the

cover can wander into the double digits. Decide for yourself whether it's worth it. *Zephyr* (☎ 355 2582), 301 S West Temple, is a friendly private club sticking to fairly mainstream rock & roll every night. It serves pizza and Italian food until late at night, and the dance floor is usually packed (with dancers, not pizzas).

Other places include *Corona Rock 'n R* (☎ 269 9555), 4410 S State, which calls itself 'Utah's largest rock & roll playground' and tends towards the heavy metal side of things. For alternative music, try the innocuously named *Bar & Grill* (☎ 533 0341), 60 E 800 South. It advertises industrial music and 'hard-dance-weirdo-music' (no joke) with bands like Scabs On Strike and the always popular Sex Gang Children. The good folks at the Bar & Grill, mindful of the under 21 crowd, present All Ages Shows on Sundays. Another place that caters to below drinking age audiences is *Club Starzz* (☎ 355 2446), 740 S 300 West. *Port-O-Call* (☎ 521 0589), 78 W 400 South, is a private club with a variety of live music – it is popular with the college crowd. *Pete's Pool & Cinema Club* (☎ 359 1200), 45 West Broadway (300 South), offers industrial and technopop.

For country and western bands and dancing, head on over to the *Westerner Club* (☎ 972 5447), 3360 S Redwood Rd, which claims the largest dance floor in Utah and offers free dance lessons on Monday, Tuesday and Wednesday nights. Pool tables and ranching paraphernalia contribute to the Western ambiance.

Don't forget to read Places to Eat above. Gepetto's, Pie Pizzeria, Squatter's Pub Brewery, Green Parrot, Crompton's Roadside Attraction and the Peery Pub are all popular watering holes, some with live music. Other good bars with no cover charge include *Junior's Tavern* (☎ 322 0318), 200 E 500 South, which is your basic beer bar with a jukebox and pool table – small and cheap, it draws a mildly wild clientele of all ages and races. *X Wife's Place* (☎ 532 2353), 465 S 700 East, serves cheap beer to a young pool-playing crowd. Many of the better hotels have good clubs attracting people of all ages. These include the clubs at the Marriott, Embassy Suites, Red Lion, Holiday Inn Airport and Shilo Inn.

## Performing Arts

See Nightlife for entertainment information sources. The semiprofessional City Rep, one of Salt Lake's favorite theater companies, presents various plays and family performances at either the Jester or Court auditoriums in the *Old Utah Theater* (☎ 532 6000), 148 S Main St. Good plays or musicals are also presented by the Salt Lake Acting Company (☎ 363 0525), 168 W 500 North; Pioneer Theater Company (☎ 581 6961), 300 S 1340 East at the university, with performances throughout the September to May school year; and the *Broadway Stage* (☎ 359 1444), 272 S Main St. The *Promised Valley Playhouse* (☎ 364 5696), 132 S State, is a charming turn-of-the-century theater presenting squeaky clean productions.

Several professional and acclaimed companies share the elegant *Capitol Theater* venue at 50 W 200 South. These include the Utah Opera Company (☎ 534 0888, 534 0842) and Ballet West (☎ 355 2787, 363 9318), each of which stages four classical productions during the season (fall to spring). Modern dance is presented by the Repertory Dance Theater (☎ 581 6702) and the Ririe-Woodbury Dance Company (☎ 328 1062).

The Utah Symphony Orchestra (☎ 533 5626, 533 6407), 123 S West Temple, performs at frequent intervals around the year in the acoustically superb *Symphony Hall*.

The Salt Lake City Arts Council (☎ 596 5000) has information about various local cultural events. One particularly popular event is the Brown Bag Concert Series, which presents a free downtown concert at lunchtime, Monday to Friday, from June to August. Bring your own lunch (it doesn't *have* to be in a brown bag) and listen to anything from Celtic music to hip hop, from Egyptian cabaret to fusion, from Brazilian music to boogie-woogie. Each day it's something different.

## THINGS TO BUY

One place stands out for its typical handicrafts. Simply called Mormon Handicrafts (☎ 355 2141), 105 N Main St, it sells beautiful handmade quilts, dolls and stuffed animals, clothes (especially baby clothes) and a host of other painstakingly made articles reminiscent of pioneer days. Quilt making supplies are available.

More conventional shopping is available at a number of good shopping malls. ZCMI (Zions Cooperative Mercantile Institution) (☎ 321 8743, 321 8745), 36 S State, is the oldest in Utah, though the approximately one hundred stores and restaurants within are all thoroughly modern. Opposite is the Crossroads Plaza (☎ 531 1799), 50 S Main St, with about one hundred and fifty shops and restaurants. Free validated parking is available if you spend over $5 at one of the establishments in these two malls.

There are a number of good bookstores. Deseret Book (☎ 328 8191), 36 S State in the ZCMI center has the best selection of books for and about Mormons. Sam Weller Books (☎ 328 2586), 254 S Main St, carries many books on the West and is the city's biggest bookstore. Waking Owl Books (☎ 582 7323), 208 S 1300 East, is a readers' bookstore with a good choice of titles and an easy browsing atmosphere. A Woman's Place (☎ 583 6431), 1400 S Foothill Drive in Foothill Village and (☎ 278 9855), 4835 S Highland Drive in Cottonwood Mall, has books by, for and about women. The Children's Hour (☎ 359 4150), 928 E 900 South, has the best selection of books for kids. Experienced Books (☎ 467 0258), 1390 S 1100 East, buys, sells and trades used books. Central Book Exchange (☎ 485 3913), 2017 S 1100 East, trades paperbacks. The Magazine Shop (☎ 359 3295), 267 S Main St, carries the best selection of magazines and out-of-town or foreign newspapers.

REI (☎ 486 2100), 3285 E 3300 South, is a reliable source of high quality outdoor guidebooks and gear – everything from climbing ropes to sleeping bags. Rentals are available for your trip into the backcountry.

Trolley Square (☎ 521 9877), 600 S 700 East, is housed in what used to be the trolley car depot, which went out of use after WW II. There are plenty of signs of the old days – a restaurant in a trolley car, stores in car barns, a photography exhibit, etc. This mall has a good selection of restaurants as well as shops.

## GETTING THERE & AWAY
### Air
Salt Lake City International Airport, about six miles west of downtown, is by far the most important airport in Utah. Several major carriers including America West, American, Continental, Delta, Southwest, Sky West, TWA and others fly out of state; Sky West (☎ 575 2510, 1 (800) 453 9417) flies to the Utahan cities of St George, Cedar City and Vernal. The local Alpine Air (☎ 575 2839, 1 (800) 748 4899) has flights to Manti, Moab, Mt Pleasant, Nephi, Price, Provo, Richfield and Salina; it also arranges charters to several other Utahan destinations.

The airport has two terminals. Facilities include a tourist information office, money exchange, restaurants, car rentals, left luggage lockers, shops, etc. A taxi downtown will cost about $10. The UTA Bus 50 goes downtown for 65¢ (exact change required) between about 6 am and 7 pm. There are 19 trips a day from Monday to Friday, 13 trips on Saturday and five on Sunday. UTA Bus 150 has five night buses from Monday to Saturday until midnight. There is no holiday service. Call 287 4636 for local bus information. Super Shuttle (☎ 566 6400) has an office at the transportation desk in the airport. Shuttles can take you to and from anywhere in the Salt Lake City area.

### Bus
Greyhound-Trailways Bus Lines (☎ 355 4684), 160 W South Temple, provides long-distance bus service. There are several buses a day heading south on I-15 through Provo, St George, and Cedar City to Las Vegas, Nevada, and Los Angeles, California. There are also several buses a day west to San Francisco, California, east to Denver, Colorado, and north to Portland, Oregon, and Seattle, Washington.

UTA (Utah Transit Authority) (☎ 287 4636) provides services to the nearby cities of Provo, Tooele, Ogden, and the towns and suburbs in between. Fares are a very reasonable $1.50. Sunday services are limited to three buses each to Ogden and Provo, but there are frequent departures during the rest of the week.

### Train
Amtrak (☎ 1 (800) 872 7245) provides services to and from the Rio Grande Depot at 300 S Rio Grande near downtown. There is a daily service via Cedar City and Las Vegas, Nevada, to Los Angeles, California; via Helper, Thompson and Denver, Colorado, to Chicago, Illinois; and to San Francisco, California, or Seattle, Washington. Some of these trips might involve a bus transfer to nearby Provo or Ogden.

## GETTING AROUND
### Bus
UTA (☎ 287 4636) provides services throughout Salt Lake City and the surrounding areas. There are dozens of routes with 30 or 40 departures a day on the busier lines. Sunday services are limited to buses to the airport, Provo and Ogden. There is no holiday service.

Fares in the city are a flat 65¢ (subject to change – exact change required) and free transfers are available on request. There is a free fare zone from 400 South to North Temple (continuing along N Main St to the State Capitol) and from West Temple to 200 East. If you enter and exit the bus between these streets, the ride is free. The most useful free fare bus is the No 23, which goes from 355 S Main St to the State Capitol 30 times between 6:40 am and 6 pm from Monday to Friday and 23 times on Saturday. During June, July and August, the UTA Trolley runs from Temple Square via the hotel district (West Temple and 600 South) to Trolley Square. During the ski season, a ski bus goes to four nearby ski areas (see Skiing & Snowboarding under Activities).

Detailed bus maps and timetables are available from the visitors bureau, public libraries, shopping malls, and city and municipal buildings.

## Taxi

The three main taxi companies, all with 24-hour service, are Yellow Cab (☎ 521 2100), Ute Cab (359 7788) and City Cab (363 5014).

## Car Rental

All the major car rental companies have offices in Salt Lake City and at the airport. Reserve a car in advance for the best rates.

## Bicycle

Utah Ski Rental & Sales (355 9088), 134 W 600 South, rents mountain bikes for $12/18/89 per half day/day/week including a helmet.

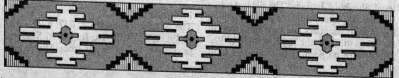

# Wasatch Mountains Region

Salt Lake City is but one of several towns running north to south along the western front of the Wasatch Mountains. The towns combine into an urban chain stretching roughly from Ogden, 35 miles north of Salt Lake City, to Provo, 45 miles south – this area is home to well over half of Utah's residents. The steep-sided, forested mountains form a splendid backdrop to the urban areas and, perhaps more to the point, provide a reliable source of water for the area. Historically, nomadic Ute and Shoshone Indians roamed this well-watered area, and it became the first region to be settled by the Mormon pioneers.

Today, the Wasatch Mountains provide the winter visitor with 11 ski resorts within an hour's drive of Salt Lake City. Four are best reached from Salt Lake City itself, and three others are most accessible from Park City to the east. Yet another three are found northeast of Ogden, and the last is north of Provo.

The summer visitor can enjoy the beautiful scenery by hiking, camping, fishing, visiting underground caves, sightseeing and relaxing. The towns themselves have interesting historical buildings, museums, festivals and plenty of good places to stay and eat. In fact, a visitor could spend months enjoying the area without venturing more than 60 miles from Salt Lake City.

This chapter first covers the Ogden area in the north, continues with Park City and Heber City to the east, and finishes with the Provo area south of Salt Lake City.

## OGDEN

The city is named after Peter Skene Ogden, a trapper who arrived in the Ogden river valley in 1826 and traded with the local Shoshone Indians. The pleasant area was the site of multiple rendezvous among the Indians, trappers and mountain men of the area during the 1820s and 1830s. There were no permanent structures until

Miles Goodyear built a cabin in the 1840s (reputedly the oldest non-Indian building in Utah). In 1846, he built Fort Buenaventura. Goodyear was bought out by the Mormons soon after, and under Brigham Young's direction, founded the town in 1850.

After the completion of the first transcontinental railway in 1869, Ogden became an important railway town. The railway brought many non-Mormon settlers, and Ogden quickly developed a large non-Mormon population, whose frontier town excesses often created tension with the sober Mormon inhabitants.

Since then, Ogden has seen the opening of Weber State University (in 1889) and Hill Air Force Base (in 1939). Today, Ogden is an important agricultural and manufacturing center. The military base is also an economic mainstay. The population of Ogden itself is about 70,000, but along with the surrounding communities, it is Utah's third most populous urban area. Ogden is the seat of Weber County. Its elevation of 4500 feet gives it a similar climate to Salt Lake City.

### Orientation

Although laid out by Mormons in their typical wide-avenued grid pattern, the city's street names differ somewhat from most Mormon towns. The east-west streets begin at 1st St in the north and continue to about 40th St in the south; the north-south streets are named mainly after famous people. The most historic east-west street is 25th St, and the most important north-south street is Washington Blvd, also called Hwy 89. Interstate 15 skirts the city to the west.

### Information

The visitors bureau (☎ 627 8288, 627 8289), 2501 Wall Ave (in Union Station), is open 8 am to 5 pm from Monday to

UTAH

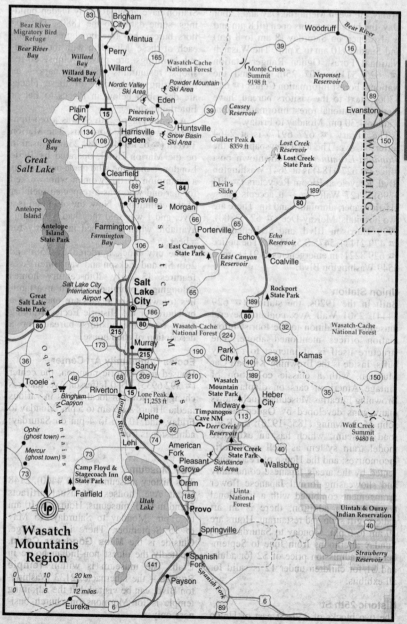

Wasatch
Mountains
Region

0   10   20 km
0     6    12 miles

Friday. Between Memorial Day and Labor Day, the bureau remains open till 8 pm and is also open on Saturday (8 am to 8 pm) and Sunday (10 am to 5 pm). The Wasatch National Forest Ogden Ranger Station (☎ 625 5112), 507 25th St, and the National Forest Information Center (☎ 625 5306), next to the visitors bureau, have maps and national forest information from 8 am to 4:30 pm, Monday to Friday.

The library (☎ 627 6917) is at 2464 Jefferson Ave. The local newspaper is the *Standard-Examiner*. The downtown post office (☎ 627 4184) is at 2641 Washington Blvd. Recycle at Bloom Recyclers (☎ 393 5396), 2127 Wall Ave – it accepts glass, plastic, paper, aluminum and tin. There are two hospitals: McKay-Dee (☎ 627 2800), 3939 Harrison Blvd, and St Benedict's (☎ 479 2111), 5475 S 500 East. The police (☎ 629 8221; in emergencies ☎ 911) are at 2549 Washington Blvd.

### Union Station

Built in the 1920s, the station (☎ 629 8444), 2501 Wall Ave, contains several museums in addition to the tourist information offices mentioned above. The structure itself is of interest to railway buffs. Inside is the Browning-Kimball Car Museum, with a classic collection of vintage American cars on display; the Browning Firearms Museum, which shows many guns developed by Ogden native, John M Browning (1855-1926); the Railroad Museum, which has an extensive model train system as well as historic locomotives; and the House of Peace, presented by the area's Japanese community and showcasing formal Japanese flower arrangement combined with a traditional tea room. In addition, there is an art gallery, gift shop and restaurant. Hours are 10 am to 6 pm, Monday to Saturday plus Sunday afternoons from June to September. One admission price of $2 for adults and $1 for children under 12 is valid for all exhibits.

### Historic 25th St

The two blocks of 25th St east of Union Station have about 10 early Ogden buildings, some dating to the 1880s. The visitors bureau has free brochures detailing each of these. Mixed in with the historical buildings are private clubs, coffee shops, restaurants and dive bars – an interesting mix! Some of these places are described below in Places to Eat or Entertainment.

A century ago, 25th St was a red-light district with many bordellos. The Marion Tavern (☎ 621 9448), 184 25th St, used to be the Marion Hotel, operated by Belle London, a madame who made her mark as a champion of the women who worked for her and who was a respected member of the community. Now, the old hotel is a dive, and I was told they had $10 rooms available when I stopped in recently for a beer.

The city block bordered by 25th and 26th Sts and Jackson and Van Buren Aves features 13 early 20th-century homes belonging to prominent Ogden area families (of which the Eccles are one). Get a brochure for the Historic Eccles Walking Tour from the visitors bureau for a description of each house.

### Eccles Community Art Center

Housed in a historic mansion, the center (☎ 392 6935), 2580 Jefferson Ave, features changing shows of local artists in various media. Hours are 9 am to 5 pm, Monday to Friday, and 10 am to 4 pm on Saturday; admission is free.

### DUP Museum

This history museum (☎ 393 4460), 2148 Grant Ave, houses the usual artifacts found in DUP museums. Hours are 10 am to 5 pm, Monday to Saturday, 15 May to 15 September. There is no charge. Outside is the **Miles Goodyear Cabin**, reputedly the oldest non-Indian house in Utah. The museum is within **Temple Square** – the tabernacle, 2133 Washington Blvd, can be visited, but the adjoining temple is for Mormons on church business only.

UTAH

## Fort Buenaventura State Park
On the grounds of this park (☎ 621 4808), 2450 A Ave, is an accurate, full-size replica of the original fort built in 1846. Guides in period dress will show you around and a 'mountain-man rendezvous' occurs over Labor Day weekend. Other programs are scheduled throughout the summer.

Outside the fort is a picnic site, a pond for fishing, canoeing or ice-skating (depending on season), and a campsite for pre-registered large groups. Daily hours are 8 am to 5 pm, March to November, and until dusk from April to September. Admission is $1 per person or $3 per carload.

## Weber State University
This university, pronounced 'weeber', (☎ 626 6975), 3750 Harrison Blvd, offers a variety of events and destinations for visitors. On campus is a **Natural History Museum** (☎ 626 6160) with a small but varied collection (including a dinosaur skeleton) and a planetarium with star shows (small admission) on Wednesday nights. Hours are 8 am to 5 pm, Monday to Friday, during the school year (closed during summer break). Admission is free.

The **Collett Art Gallery** (☎ 626 6455) has changing shows during the school year. Hours are 8 am to 10 pm, Monday to Thursday, and to 4 pm on Friday. There is no charge.

The **Shepherd Student Union** (☎ 626 6367) has restaurants, a bookstore, entertainment and an information center where you can find out about sports events and performing arts on campus. The **Browning Center for the Performing Arts** (☎ 626 7000, 626 6800) features Ballet West and Utah Symphony performances during the winter season. The **Musical Theater** (☎ 626 8500) has musical revues in summer. The **Swenson Gymnasium** (☎ 626 6466) has sports facilities (swimming, track, gym) open to the public.

## Treehouse Children's Museum
The hands-on museum (☎ 394 9663), 2255 B, Ogden City Mall (23rd St and Washington Blvd), features literacy experiences in which kids can read, write, pretend, listen, act, draw and discover the world of books through a variety of interactive programs. Hours are 4 pm to 9 pm, Monday; 10 am to 6 pm, Tuesday to Thursday; 10 am to 9 pm, Friday; noon to 7 pm, Saturday; noon to 5 pm, Sunday. Admission is $2 for kids under 15, $1 for adults.

## Ogden Nature Center
This private reserve (☎ 621 7595), 966 W 12th St, has trails through a variety of habitats. An exhibit room and naturalist guides are on the premises, and there is a picnic area. Raccoons, muskrats, porcupines, mule deer and various bird species may be seen, especially in spring and fall. Hours are 10 am to 4 pm, Monday to Saturday. Admission is $1.

## Hill Air Force Base Museum
For anyone interested in planes or the history of flight, this museum (☎ 777 6868), four miles south on I-15 to Roy exit, follow signs, has dozens of historic aircraft on display outside and an indoor museum. Hours are 9 am to 3 pm, Tuesday to Friday, 8 am to 5 pm on Saturday and Sunday. There is no admission charge.

## Ogden River Parkway
Following the banks of the Ogden River from near downtown to the mouth of Ogden Canyon, the parkway offers opportunities for picnicking, bicycling, playing tennis and golf, and running. **Eccles Dinosaur Park** (☎ 393 3466), 1544 E Park Blvd, has replicas of over 20 dinosaurs.

## Ogden Canyon & Monte Cristo Summit
The scenic, steep-walled canyon east of Ogden through the Wasatch Mountains and continuing on to Monte Cristo Summit (9148 feet), about 40 miles to the northeast, is especially attractive in late September and early October for the fall colors. The Monte Cristo Summit is closed in winter due to heavy snow. The road is best reached by taking 12th Ave and driving east.

UTAH

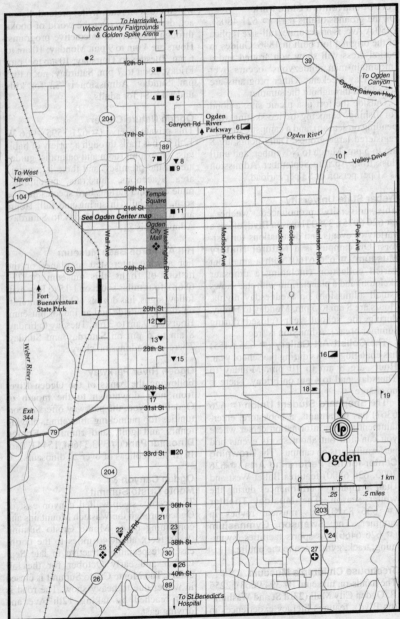

To Harrisville,
Weber County Fairgrounds
& Golden Spike Arena

▼ 1

To Ogden Canyon

● 2

12th St

3 ■

39

Ogden Canyon Hwy

(204)

4 ■    5 ■

Canyon Rd

Ogden
River
Parkway

6

Park Blvd

Ogden River

17th St

89

10

Valley Drive

7 ■   ▼ 8

■ 9

To West
Haven

(104)

20th St

Temple
Square

21st St

(204)

■ 11

See Ogden Center map

Ogden
City
Mall

Washington Blvd

Madison Ave

Jackson Ave

Eccles

Harrison Blvd

Polk Ave

(53)

24th St

Fort
Buenaventura
State Park

Wall Ave

26th St

Weber River

12

▼ 14

13 ▼

28th St

▼ 15

16

30th St

▼
17

31st St

18

19

Exit
344

79

Ogden

0        .5     1 km

0    .25    .5 miles

33rd St

■ 20

(204)

203

36th St

▼
21

23
▼

24

22

38th St

25

(30)

Riverdale Rd

● 26

40th St

27

(26)

89

To St Benedict's
Hospital

**PLACES TO STAY**

| 3 | Colonial Motel |
|---|---|
| 4 | Motel 6 |
| 5 | Millstream Motel |
| 7 | Ogden River Motel |
| 9 | Budget Inn |
| 11 | Ogden Travelodge |
| 20 | Holiday Inn |

**PLACES TO EAT**

| 1 | El Rancho Mexicali |
|---|---|
| 8 | Prairie Schooner Steak House |
| 13 | China Nite |
| 14 | Western Sunrise Cafe |
| 15 | Lee's Mongolian Bar-B-Q |
| 17 | Paisano's |
| 18 | Grounds for Coffee |
| 21 | Ye Lion's Den |
| 22 | Windy's Suki-Yaki |
| 23 | Eastern Winds |

**OTHER**

| 2 | Ogden Nature Center |
|---|---|
| 6 | Lorin Farr Park & Swimming Pool |
| 10 | El Monte Golf Course |
| 12 | Post Office |
| 16 | Ogden Community Swimming Pool |
| 19 | Mount Ogden Golf Course |
| 24 | Weber State University |
| 25 | Riverdale Mall |
| 26 | Country Club Theatre |
| 27 | McKay-Dee Hospital |

## Activities

There are three ski resorts east of Ogden; see the information in Ski Resorts below. **Cross-country skiing** on groomed tracks is available at the Mount Ogden Golf Course in town. You can rent Nordic skis at Alpine Sports (☎ 393 0066) between 30th and 31st, just off Harrison; Fly Line Sports (☎ 394 1812), 2943 Washington Blvd; and Ogden Mountaineering (☎ 399 9365), 3701 Washington Blvd.

You can **golf** a round at various nearby courses. The closest golf courses to central Ogden are the Mount Ogden Golf Course (☎ 629 8700), 1787 Constitution Way (east end of 30th St), which has 18 holes, and the nine-hole El Monte Golf Course (☎ 629 8333), 1300 Valley Drive, at the mouth of Ogden Canyon. There are about 10 more

courses in the suburbs and surrounding communities – ask the visitors bureau or look in the yellow pages for more choices.

Ogden City Recreation (☎ 629 8253) can inform you about city parks with public tennis courts. If you'd like to **swim**, the city also runs the Lorin Farr Park & Swimming Pool (☎ 629 8691), 1691 Gramercy Ave, and the Marshall White Center Pool (☎ 629 8346), 222 28th St. Others are Ben Lomond Pool (☎ 625 1100), 1049 7th St, and Ogden Community Pool (☎ 625 1101), 2875 Tyler Ave. The Deseret Gymnasium (☎ 399 5861, or 621 0147 for court reservations), 550 25th St, has racquetball courts, a swimming pool, a gym and other activities for the public.

Summer hiking and winter cross-country skiing and snowshoeing are popular activities in the nearby Wasatch National Forest. The ranger station is listed in Information above.

### Special Events

There are several events every month in Ogden, especially in the summer – the visitors bureau has precise dates and a full list. The most notable events are the following.

Pioneer Days, in the week leading up to 24 July (but not Sunday), includes a rodeo, fireworks, music, antique cars, a parade and other events. The Weber County Fair, held in mid-August, takes place at the Weber County Fairgrounds and Golden Spike Arena (☎ 399 8544), 1000 N 1200 West, about four miles north of town.

There is an Autumnfest the weekend after Labor Day – arts, crafts, food, and entertainment are found downtown. More of the same in a winter atmosphere occurs during January's Winterfest.

### Places to Stay – camping

*Century Camping Park* (☎ 731 3800), 1399 W 2100 South, near exit 346 off I-15, has tent/RV sites for $14 or RV sites for $19 with full hookups. There is a coin laundry, hot showers, store, playground and (in summer) a swimming pool.

There are many more camping areas about 10 to 20 miles east of town along

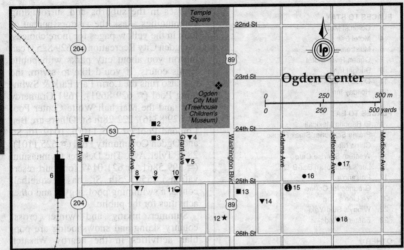

**Ogden Center**

PLACES TO STAY
2  Western Colony Inn
3  Best Western Ogden Park Hotel
13  Radisson Suite Hotel

PLACES TO EAT
4  Chick's Cafe
5  Bamboo Noodle Parlor
7  Star Noodle Parlor
8  La Ferrovia Ristorante
9  The Daily Grind
10  Delights of Ogden
14  El Matador

OTHER
1  Toones Club
6  Visitors Bureau, National Forest Information Center, Union Station, Museums
11  Greyhound Bus Depot
12  Police
15  Ranger Station
16  Deseret Gymnasium
17  Library
18  Eccles Community Art Center

scenic Ogden Canyon (Hwy 39) as it cuts through the Wasatch Mountains. Maps and details are available from the Wasatch

National Forest Ranger Station (☎ 625 5112), 507 25th St, which is open 8 am to 4:30 pm weekdays. These sites are open only in the summer, cost about $6 to $8, have water but no showers, and, though RVs are accepted, they have no hookups. Many of these sites fill up with locals during summer weekends. Reservations can be made through Mistix (☎ 1 (800) 283 2267); you will incur a $6 reservation fee in addition to site fees.

Distances given below are from the beginning of Ogden Canyon Rd at 12th St and Harrison Blvd. *Anderson Cove*, nine miles east of Ogden, has access to fishing and swimming in Pineview Reservoir, as does *Jefferson Hunt*, 10 miles east of Ogden. Between 17 and 19 miles east of Ogden are a slew of sites – *Magpie, Hobble, Botts, South Fork, Perception, Meadows* and *Willows*. All are along the Ogden River and offer fishing. Tiny Hobble lacks drinking water and is free (though often full). There is also *Maples*, 12 miles southwest of Anderson Cove near the Snowbasin Ski Resort – this site also lacks drinking water and is free. *Monte Cristo Campground*, just below

Monte Cristo Summit, 40 miles northeast of Ogden, has sites open from July to September.

Also see Willard Bay State Park (below) for other camping options.

**Places to Stay – bottom end**

Rates may be slightly higher in summer. Some hotels have larger rooms with kitchenettes, which cost a few dollars more. Many offer weekly discounts. Ogden provides alternative accommodation to Salt Lake City, 35 miles away.

Hotels charging about $25 for a double include the following. The *Mt Lomond Motel* (☎ 782 7477), 755 N Harrisville Rd, has some rooms with kitchenettes, as does the *Colonial Motel* (399 5851), 1269 Washington Blvd. The *Budget Inn* (☎ 393 8667), 1956 Washington Blvd, has a pool and some rooms with kitchenettes. The *Ogden River Motel* (☎ 621 8350), 1825 Washington Blvd, has a pool, spa and some kitchenettes.

For rooms around $30, the *Big Z Motel* (☎ 394 6632), 1123 W 21st St, has nice rooms, some with kitchenettes, and a restaurant on the premises. The (almost) downtown *Motel 6* (☎ 627 4560), 1455 Washington Blvd, charges $28/34 for singles/doubles and has a pool. The *Western Colony Inn* (☎ 627 1332), 234 24th St, also has rooms in the low $30s.

**Places to Stay – middle**

The *Super 8 Motel* (☎ 731 7100), 1508 W 21st St, charges $33.88/37.88 for singles/doubles and has a cafe on the premises. The Riverdale *Motel 6* (☎ 627 2880), 1500 W Riverdale Rd (near exit 342 from I-15), is one of the fancier members of the Motel 6 chain, offering a pool, restaurant, private club with dancing and a tennis court; rooms are $34/40. The *Millstream Motel* (☎ 394 9425), 1450 Washington Blvd, has a restaurant, antique car museum and a garden. Rooms start around $30, though there are more expensive rooms with kitchenettes or a spa.

The *Flying J Motel* (☎ 393 8644), 1206 W 21st St (near exit 346 on I-15), is good

value with nice rooms in the low $40s. The pleasant grounds have a pool, and the motel features a restaurant, cafe, private club (occasional entertainment) and exercise room. Geared to freeway travel, the hotel has 24-hour service in the restaurant and in the adjoining gas station and convenience store. The *Ogden Travelodge* (☎ 394 4563, 1 (800) 255 3050), 2110 Washington Blvd, also with good rooms and a pool, is similarly priced. The *Sleep Inn* (☎ 894 5000, 1 (800) 221 2222), 1155 S 1700 West, has a pool, spa, restaurant and lounge; rooms are $40 to $50.

The Best Western *High Country Inn* (☎ 394 9474, fax 392 6589), 1335 W 12th St, charges from about $47/51 for singles/doubles and has a pool, spa, coin laundry and restaurant. It offers ski packages in winter. The *Holiday Inn* (☎ 399 5671, fax 621 0321), 3306 Washington Blvd, has an Olympic-size pool, spa, exercise and game room, restaurant with room service and private club with occasional entertainment; rooms are $60 to $70.

**Places to Stay – top end**

The Best Western *Ogden Park Hotel* (☎ 627 1190, fax 394 6312), 247 24th St, is a full-service hotel with an indoor pool, spa, games and exercise rooms, beauty salon and concierge. There is a restaurant with 24-hour room service, and a private club with occasional entertainment. Rooms are about $75/85 for singles/doubles, $10 more with king-size beds. Suites with refrigerators and balconies range from $100 to $140 double. A full breakfast is included, and substantial weekend discounts are available.

The *Radisson Suite Hotel* (☎ 627 1900, fax 394 5342), 2510 Washington Blvd, is a centrally located older hotel on the National Register of Historic Buildings. Most of the units are suites ranging from about $80 to $140 – they have refrigerators and wet bars. A few smaller rooms for $60/70 are available. Rates include full breakfast. The hotel has a sauna, spa, exercise room, two restaurants and a private club with weekend entertainment.

**UTAH**

## Places to Eat

Ogden has well over 100 restaurants, so there's plenty to choose from – here's a selection.

If you like to start the day with a jolt of coffee, *The Daily Grind* (☎ 629 0909), 252 25th St, features an espresso bar and specialty coffees, as well as pastries, sandwiches and light lunches. This building is one of the oldest in Ogden. Hours are 7:30 am to 8 pm weekdays, 9 am to 10 pm on Saturday and 10 am to 2 pm on Sunday. Other coffee shops include the nearby *Delights of Ogden* (☎ 394 1111), 290 25th St, open 7:30 am to 5 pm weekdays, and 7 am to 9 pm on Saturdays; and *Grounds for Coffee* (☎ 621 3014), 3005 Harrison Blvd, open 7 am to 10 pm weekdays, and 8 am to 10 pm on weekends.

Small local restaurants open early for breakfast and lunch include *Chick's Cafe* (☎ 621 9159), 319 24th St (closed Sunday) and the *Western Sunrise Cafe* (☎ 392 6603), 1071 E 27th St (closed Sunday and Monday). For 24-hour dining, head over to the *Tamarack Restaurant* (☎ 393 8691), 1254 W 21st St, adjoining the Flying J Motel. All the motels with restaurants mentioned under Places to Stay above are decent choices for breakfast, lunch and dinner.

Good American food (steak and seafood) is served at the recommended *Ye Lion's Den* (☎ 399 5804), 3607 Washington Blvd, which has been here for over three decades. It's open 11:30 am to 2:30 pm from Monday to Friday, 5 to 9:30 or 10 pm from Monday to Saturday and noon to 7 pm on Sunday. Also recommended is the attractive 50-year-old *Gray Cliff Lodge* (☎ 392 6775), five miles up Ogden Canyon Rd. The menu features local trout. It's open 5 to 10 pm from Tuesday to Friday, to 11 pm on Saturday, and 10 am to 2 pm for Sunday brunch and 3 to 8 pm for Sunday dinner. Both these places are rather pricey but worth it.

A slightly cheaper possibility for American food in a pioneering atmosphere is the *Prairie Schooner Steak House* (☎ 392 2712), 445 Park Blvd. Here you have the pleasure of dining in covered wagons – yyeeee haaaa! Hours are 5 to 10 pm from Monday to Thursday, to 11 pm on Friday and Saturday, and 4 to 9 pm on Sunday. Or try the *Timber Mine* (☎ 393 2155), 1701 Park Blvd, with an old Western mine atmosphere. Hours are 5 am to 10 pm from Monday to Thursday, to 11 pm on Friday and Saturday, and to 9 pm on Sunday. The ravenous can try the all-you-can-eat specials at *The Shed* (☎ 479 5559), 440 E 4400 South. Hours are 5 to 10 pm daily and to 11 pm on Friday and Saturday.

There are several good Italian restaurants, including *La Ferrovia Ristorante* (☎ 394 8628), 210 25th St, in a 1908 'Commercial Victorian' building restored in 1985. Hours are 11 am to 9 pm, Tuesday to Thursday, and to 10 pm on Friday and Saturday. *Paisano's* (☎ 392 9701), 3050 Grant Ave, is a good choice, open 11 am to 2:30 pm, Tuesday to Saturday, 5 to 10 pm, Tuesday to Thursday, and to 11 pm on Friday and Saturday. *Berconi's* (☎ 479 4414), 4850 Harrison Blvd, is also good; it's open 11 am to 10 pm, Monday to Thursday, to 11 pm on Friday and Saturday, and 4:30 to 9:30 pm on Sunday.

Here are a few Asian food options. *Lee's Mongolian Bar-B-Q* (☎ 621 9120), 2866 Washington Blvd, serves good Mongolian and Chinese; it's open for lunch and dinner daily except Sunday. *China Nite* (☎ 393 1031, 621 9233), 2783 Washington Blvd, has inexpensive lunch and dinner specials daily except Tuesday. *Eastern Winds* (☎ 627 2739), 3740 Washington Blvd, has a huge menu of Mandarin and Cantonese cuisine with daily specials. Hours are from 11 am to 10 pm, Monday to Thursday, to 11 pm on Friday and Saturday, and 4 to 10 pm on Sunday. *Star Noodle Parlor* (☎ 394 6331), 225 25th St, has been serving Chinese and American dinners in the historic district for over 50 years (closed on Monday). *Bamboo Noodle Parlor* (☎ 394 6091), 2426 Grant Ave, is one of Ogden's oldest restaurants (opened in 1923) and serves Asian and American food daily except Tuesday. *Windy's Suki-Yaki* (☎ 621 4505), 3809 Riverdale Rd, serves a full

Japanese menu, with many dishes prepared at your table. It has private tea rooms and Japanese gardens. It's open for dinner at 5 pm daily except Sunday.

*El Matador* (☎ 393 3151), 2564 Ogden Ave, is considered the best Mexican restaurant by local cognoscenti. It is open daily for lunch and dinner. Also try *El Rancho Mexicali* (☎ 393 7227), 924 Washington Blvd.

### Entertainment
*Country Club Theater* (☎ 393 5864), 3930 Washington Blvd, has movies at very low prices. The following all have four screens: *Mann Theaters* (☎ 392 1122), 23rd St and Grant Ave; (☎ 627 1061), 4109 Riverdale Rd; and *Newgate Cinema* (☎ 394 4283), Wall Ave and Riverdale Rd.

Ballet, theater, symphony recitals and other performing arts are featured at Weber State University (see above). Also call the Ogden Symphony Ballet Association (☎ 399 9214, 399 0453), 2580 Jefferson Ave, for performance schedules and information.

The private clubs in the hotels above provide entertainment or are just a place for a quiet drink. Other choices include the *City Club* (☎ 392 4447), 264 25th St, in a 'Commercial Victorian' 1898 brick building – the club has an extensive Beatles collection. There are other bars in the area – some less salubrious. *Toones* (☎ 399 5792), 2410 Wall Ave, features pool, darts, Foosball and dancing on weekends.

### Getting There & Away
**Air** Ogden Municipal Airport (☎ 629 8251) is southwest of exit 344 on I-15. There are no commercial flights (though planes can be chartered). Air travelers use the Salt Lake City airport.

**Bus** Greyhound (☎ 394 5573), 2501 Grant Ave, has an early morning and an evening bus to Salt Lake City and on down I-15 to Las Vegas, Nevada. It also has buses north, east and west out of the state.

UTA (☎ 621 4636) has local services to Salt Lake City and intermediate points as well as services around Weber County. UTA bus No 70 leaves from 21st St and Washington about 30 times a day between 4 am and 11:30 pm Monday to Friday for Salt Lake City; buses from Salt Lake City leave from 355 S & Main St between 5 am and 11:15 pm. There are about 25 buses on Saturday, three on Sunday and none on holidays. Bus No 55 has about eight departures a day between Ogden and Salt Lake City Monday to Friday only. An important UTA bus stop is at 25th St and Washington Blvd – there is an information booth here.

**Train** Union Station (☎ 627 3330) has Amtrak trains (☎ 1 (800) 872 7245) leaving daily to Idaho, Oregon and Washington in the evening and to Wyoming, Denver, Colorado and points east in the morning. Amtrak also provides bus service to connect with trains from Salt Lake City.

## WILLARD BAY STATE PARK
Willard Bay State Park (☎ 734 9494, 734 2404), 650 N 900 West, PO Box A, Willard, 84340, lies on a small bay on the northwest shore of the Great Salt Lake. The park includes mud flats hosting thousands of migrating shorebirds in March to May and September to November. In summer, the birding is also good, and there is boating and fishing. Ice fishing is possible in winter.

The park has two sections. To reach the north unit, take exit 360 off I-15 (at Willard, 14 miles north of Ogden) and head a short way west; to reach the south unit, take exit 354 from I-15 and head three miles west – there are signs.

The north unit is larger and more popular for boating and fishing; the south unit is less developed but perhaps better for birding. Both have boat launch areas. There are over 60 campsites in the north (showers available) and about 30 in the south. Rates are $9 for camping (tents or RVs – no hookups) and $3 for day use.

Adjoining the western side of the south unit is the Harold S Crane Waterfowl Management Area administered by the Utah Division of Wildlife Resources

(UDWR) in Ogden (☎ 479 5143). South of here is the Ogden Bay Waterfowl Management Area (☎ 773 1398, in Hooper), also administered by the UDWR. To get there, take exit 347 off I-15 in Ogden, head west on Hwy 39 for eight miles, then go a couple of miles south on 7500 W or 9500 W. There are no camping or boating facilities, but birders will enjoy these areas. 500,000 birds have been reported in Ogden Bay during the migratory peak in September!

## SKI RESORTS

There are three ski resorts in the mountains east of Ogden, all accessed via the steep-walled Ogden Canyon. You can stay at the ski resorts or in Ogden, or Eden and Hunts ville. Eden and Huntsville are on the banks of Pineview Reservoir, a popular spot for boating, fishing, swimming and water-skiing in summer. All the resorts have ski shops, instructors and places to eat.

### Nordic Valley

This very tiny, 85-acre resort (☎ 745 3511) is the closest to Ogden (15 miles). The nearest accommodation is in Eden (one mile) or Huntsville (12 miles). The elevation goes from 5500 to 6400 feet, and there are two double lifts and 12 runs – 30% is designated for beginners and 50% for intermediate skiers. All-day (9 am to 4:30 pm) lift passes are $15/11/2 for adults/kids and free for those over 65. Lighted night skiing from 5 to 10 pm is $11. Snowboarding is permitted.

### Powder Mountain

This resort (☎ 745 3772) is 19 miles from Ogden, six from Eden and 16 from Huntsville. The elevation goes from 7600 to 8900 feet, and the 1600 acres of skiing include 33 runs serviced by two double lifts and one triple, and three tows. Only 10% of the terrain is for beginners and 60% is for intermediate skiers. All-day (9:30 am to 4:30 pm) lift passes are $22/13 for adults/kids. Lighted night skiing (4:30 to 10 pm) is $10.50. Snow-

boarding is allowed. The season is mid-November to early May.

The newly opened *Columbine Inn* (☎ 745 1414) provides five rooms at Powder Mountain.

### Snowbasin

This 1800-acre resort (☎ 399 1135) is a possible host for downhill skiing in the 2002 Winter Olympics. Accommodation is available in Huntsville (six miles), Eden (16 miles) and Ogden (17 miles). The elevation is 6400 to 8800 feet, a vertical drop of 2400 feet – Utah's third largest. There are four triple lifts and one double servicing the 39 runs. Terrain is 20% for beginners and 50% for intermediate skiers. All day (9 am to 4 pm) lift passes are $24/17 for adults/kids and $14 for adults over 65.

### Places to Stay & Eat

**Eden** The *Vue de Valhalla B&B* (☎ 745 2558), 2787 Nordic Valley Rd, Box 136, Eden, 84310, has just two rooms and a spa. Rates are about $40. The *Snowberry Inn B&B* (☎ 745 2634), 1315 N Hwy 158, Box 795, Eden, 84310, has five rustic rooms with private bath and a spa. Rates are $50 to $75. *Wolf Creek Village* (☎ 745 0222, fax 745 3732), 3900 N Wolf Creek Drive, Box 475, Eden, 84310, has one- and two-bedroom condos (some sleeping up to eight), a restaurant, pool and spa. Rates are $90 to $130. Similar facilities are available in the larger *Skinners Inc Condos* (☎ /fax 745 2621, 1 (800) 345 8824), 3720 N Wolf Creek Rd. These places are north of Eden.

For camping near Pineview Reservoir, see Places to Stay – camping in Ogden.

**Huntsville** *Jackson Fork Inn B&B* (☎ 745 0051), 7345 E 900 South, 84317, has eight rooms, five with private spa. There is a restaurant for complimentary breakfast and for dinner. Rates are $50/90 without/with the spa for two people. They rent snowmobiles for about $100 a day.

The *Shooting Star Saloon* (☎ 745 2002), 7350 E 200 South, has been in operation since 1879, making it Utah's oldest continually running saloon. It serves beer and burgers, and has pool tables.

For a light snack, try the homemade bread and honey sold by the Trappist monks at the *Abbey of Our Lady of the Holy Trinity* (☎ 745 3784), four miles east of Huntsville.

For camping in the Huntsville area, see Places to Stay – camping in Ogden.

## OGDEN TO PARK CITY

Thirty-nine-mile-long I-84 runs from I-15 just south of Ogden, to I-80 to the southeast. Another 23 miles south on I-80 brings you to the Park City exit. Along this drive there are two county seats and access to three state parks – none of major importance to travelers.

### Morgan Area

The town of **Morgan**, 23 miles southeast of Ogden on I-84, is the seat of Morgan County. The county fair is held annually in August. There are no hotels, but there are a few places to eat.

Seven miles east of town on the north side of I-84 is the **Devil's Slide** geological formation. Just past this is the exit for **Lost Creek State Park** (☎ 829 6866, or 829 3838), 15 miles northwest of the interstate. The park, which surrounds a small reservoir, offers boating, fishing (ice fishing in winter) and primitive camping – drinking water and pit toilets are available. The fee for overnight camping is $6.

**East Canyon State Park** (☎ 829 6866, 829 3838) is 10 miles south of Morgan along Hwy 66 (there are three other access routes). This park, too, surrounds a reservoir and has a marina (summer only, boat rentals available), fishing, boating and camping (showers available, but no hookups). Bald eagles overwinter by the reservoir. In winter the road may get snowed in. There is a $6 to $9 camping fee, depending on the site. Day use is $3.

### Coalville

Coalville, the Summit County seat, is midway between Morgan and Park City. The coal fields discovered in the 1850s are

no longer mined. The county fair here is also in August; call the City Hall (☎ 336 5981) for information.

The very small motels on Main St charge about $30 to $50 for a double (more in winter) and could provide accommodations for Park City skiers. Call the *Blonquist Motel* (☎ 336 2451), the *Moore Motel* (☎ 336 5991), or the *Kozy Cafe & Motel* (☎ 336 5641), five miles north in Echo. *Dean's Coffee Shop* serves decent meals.

### Rockport State Park

Yet another state park around a reservoir with the usual fishing, boating, camping. This one is popular for windsurfing as well. The campground ($9 per day) has showers but no RV hookups. There is primitive camping too ($6). Day use is $3. Rockport State Park (☎ 336 2241) is five miles east of I-80 exit 156.

### PARK CITY

At the foot of Utah's largest ski resort and with two other resorts nearby and five more within an hour's drive, Park City is the Southwest's most important skiing town. The skiing is world-class – Park City is even the headquarters of the United States ski team.

It was not always this way, of course. After silver was discovered here in 1868, Park City became a booming mining town. Most of it burnt down in 1898 but was quickly rebuilt. When the mining boom went bust in the early 20th century, the town faded in importance until the state governor suggested shutting it down in the 1950s – it was almost a ghost town. But the locals persevered and began building the first ski areas in the 1960s. Today, the town has grown into a sprawl of condos and apartments catering to skiers, but fortunately the turn-of-the-century downtown area has been well preserved and forms an attraction in itself.

At 6900 feet elevation, the town has plenty of winter snow. Summer daytime temperatures average in the upper 70°F range, but nights can be chilly.

UTAH

UTAH

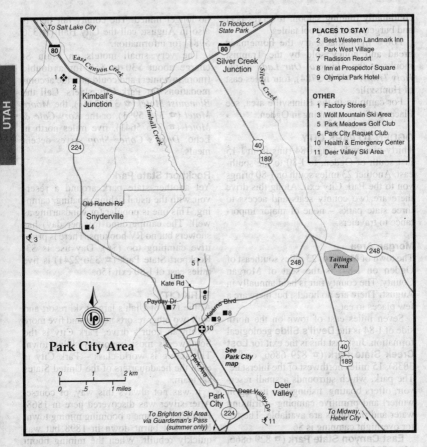

PLACES TO STAY
2  Best Western Landmark Inn
4  Park West Village
7  Radisson Resort
8  Inn at Prospector Square
9  Olympia Park Hotel

OTHER
1  Factory Stores
3  Wolf Mountain Ski Area
5  Park Meadows Golf Club
6  Park City Raquet Club
10  Health & Emergency Center
11  Deer Valley Ski Area

## Orientation & Information

Park City is five miles south of I-80 exit 145 and 32 miles west of Salt Lake City.

The Visitor Information Center (☎ 649 6104, 649 1000, 1 (800) 453 1360) is at 528 Main St (in the museum). During the summer (Memorial Day to Labor Day) and ski season (mid-November to mid-April), it is open 10 am to 7 pm daily, except Sunday noon to 6 pm. During off-season months, hours are noon to 5 pm daily. The library (☎ 645 5140) is at 1255 Park Ave. The local weekly newspaper is the *Park Record* – continuously published for over a century. The post office (☎ 649 9191) is at

450 Main St. The Health & Emergency Center (☎ 649 7640) is at 1665 Bonanza Drive. The police (☎ 645 5050; in emergencies ☎ 911) are at 445 Marsac Ave.

## Park City Museum

This small museum (☎ 649 6104), 528 Main St, which keeps the same hours as the visitors center, has exhibits of mining and local history, and you can visit the old Territorial Jail in the basement. It is free.

## Main St Walking Tour

The visitors center has brochures describing the historic town center for self-guided walks. Locals in period dress lead walking tours in the summer.

## Art Galleries

There are over a dozen commercial galleries along Main St and Park Ave. The most interesting is the spacious **Kimball Art Center** (☎ 649 8882), 638 Park Ave, which has changing exhibits in various media by regional artists, as well as pieces from other countries.

## Downhill Skiing

The free and recommended *Utah Winter Vacation Planner*, published each winter, is available from visitors bureaus and information centers. It gives up-to-date prices and details of Utah's ski resorts and accommodations.

The **Park City Ski Area**, Utah's largest ski area (☎ 649 8111, fax 647 5374), offers 2200 skiable acres, 14 lifts (one of which begins from downtown Park City) and 89 runs. It can handle over 22,000 passengers an hour, so lift lines tend to be short! Elevations range from 6900 to 10,000 feet. 16% is beginner terrain, and 45% is intermediate. All-day adult lift passes (9 am to 4 pm) are $45, kids under 12 $20, 65 to 69 years $22.50 and those over 70 years ski free. Half-day adult passes (1 to 4 pm) are $32. Night skiing (4 to 10 pm) is $10 for adults, $5 for kids. Ski rentals are $14.

On the southeastern outskirts of Park City, **Deer Valley** (☎ 649 1000) strives to be the most luxurious ski resort in the USA. Thirteen lifts service 66 carefully groomed runs covering 1100 acres between 7200 and 9400 feet. 15% of the terrain is for beginners and 50% is intermediate. All-day adult passes (9 am to 4 pm) are $47 ($49 on holidays), children twelve and under $26 ($29 on holidays), and those over 65 are $32. Half-day (1 to 4 pm) adult passes are $34. Ski rentals are $26 for a full day, $17 for half.

Four miles north of Park City (there are buses), **Wolf Mountain** (☎ 649 5400, 1 (800) 754 1636, fax 649 7374) provides good skiing at reasonable prices. Seven lifts service 58 runs on 850 acres between 6800 and 9000 feet – 22% is for beginners and 30% for intermediate skiers. All-day adult passes (9 am to 4 pm) are $25, $15 for kids, $9 for those over 62 and free for those over 70. This is the only Park City resort to allow snowboarding. Both skiing and snowboarding lessons are available.

Sundance also offers ski facilities not far from Park City (see the Sundance Resort section later in this chapter).

## Cross-Country Skiing

White Pine Touring (☎ 649 8701), 363 Main St, provides ski rentals, instruction and guides for its 11 miles of groomed trails in and around Park City (60% beginner, 20% intermediate). Day passes are $6 for 12- to 65-year-olds, free to others.

## Sledding

The Park City Ski Area (☎ 649 7150) keeps a lift ($4.50, $3 for kids six to 12) and a gondola ($6, $5 for kids) open in summer. You can descend thousands of feet on a wheeled sled within cement tracks winding back down the mountain or ride the lift back down.

## Ballooning

Hot-air balloon rides are offered throughout the year and cost about $150 per person per hour. Call one of the following companies for information: Balloon Affaire (☎ 649 1217), Balloon Biz (☎ 278 3051), Great Balloon Escape (☎ 645 9400) or Sunrise Fantasy Balloons (☎ 649 9009).

## Fishing

Jans (☎ 649 4949), 1600 Park Ave, and the Fly Shop (☎ 645 8382), 632 Main St, have fly-fishing equipment for sale or rent. Lessons and guides are available.

## Golf

Play 18 holes of golf at the Municipal Golf Course (☎ 649 8701) or the highly rated Park Meadows Golf Club (☎ 649 2460), designed by Jack Nicklaus. Both are near the city – other courses are a short drive away.

## Mountain Biking

Jans (☎ 649 4949), 1600 Park Ave (and at the Deer Valley and Park City Resorts), and White Pine Touring (☎ 649 8710), 363 Main St, offer bicycle rentals (about $25 a day), local information, maps and tours. Deer Valley Resort (☎ 649 1000) has one ski lift open for cyclists ($5 a ride, $10 all day).

## Other Activities

Park City Racquet Club (☎ 645 5100), 1200 Little Kate Rd, and Prospector Athletic Club (☎ 649 6670), in the Inn at Prospector Square, offer indoor/outdoor recreation year-round. Both have racquetball and tennis courts, swimming pool, spa and gym. Park City Stables (☎ 645 7256), 1700 Park Ave, rents horses for guided trail rides.

## Special Events

The week-long Sundance Film Festival in mid- to late January showcases independent filmmakers. (Despite the festival's name, the majority of the films are actually screened in Park City, not at the resort.) The US Ski Association's Ski Week is held the third week in January. Winterfest in late February or early March features a snow sculpture contest and other events. Symphony, chamber music, bluegrass, jazz and other music events take place during various summer concert series. The Art Festival in early August features over 200 artists. Miners Day with a parade and contests is held over Labor Day weekend, and the Hot Air Balloon Festival happens in the second week of September. Contact the visitors center to find out about other events that will be going on.

## Places to Stay

The hundred or more places to stay in the Park City area cater mainly to skiers. This is a booming ski town, and new places are opening every year, so I can give only a selection below. Studios usually include a kitchenette, condos have a full kitchen and may have a fireplace, laundry room and other amenities.

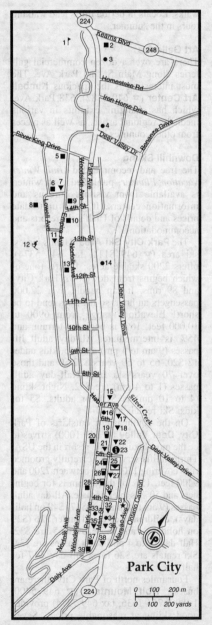

Park City

**PLACES TO STAY**
2   The Yarrow
5   Silver King Hotel
6   Shadow Ridge Resort
8   Resort Center Lodge & Inn
9   Edelweis Haus
10  Chamonix Lodge
13  Chateau Après Lodge
20  Washington School Inn
28  Blue Church Lodge
37  Treasure Mountain Inn
39  Imperial Hotel, Star Hotel B&B,
    Alpine Prospector's Lodge

**PLACES TO EAT**
7   Stew Pot
11  Baja Cantina
15  Utah Coal & Lumber
17  TCBY
18  Legends Cafe
19  The Claimjumper
21  Main St Deli
22  Pizza & Noodle Ranch
27  Irish Camel, Szechwan Chinese
    Restaurant, Texas Red's, Alex's

30  Mileti's, Cafe Terigo, Ichiban Sushi,
    PC Pizza Co
32  Barking Frog Grill
35  The Eating Establishment
36  Cisero's, Red Banjo Pizza Parlor
37  El Cheepo
38  Wasatch Brew Pub, Morning Ray
    Cafe/Evening Star Dining

**OTHER**
1   Municipal Golf Course
3   Holiday Village Cinemas 3
4   Jans
12  Park City Ski Area
14  Library
16  Kimball Art Center
19  DownUnder Club
23  Visitor Information Center,
    Park City Museum
24  The Club
25  Post Office
26  The Alamo
29  Z-Place Club
31  Police Station
33  White Pine Touring
34  Egyptian Theatre

**UTAH**

Rates are high, especially during the peak season around Christmas and New Year's, when vacationers have to pay premium prices and commit to a minimum stay of several nights. The top rates given below are for this short period; at other times rates drop 20% or more.

The cheapest winter rates begin in mid- or late November when skiing begins and run to mid-December, and then again 1 April to when the skiing stops which is usually mid- to late April. From early January to the end of March are the mid-rates, though there is often a brief low season during the slack period immediately after the Christmas/New Year's peak season. Thus early to mid-January represents the best prices and snow conditions for the budget-conscious skier.

However, keep in mind that during the Sundance Film Festival (see Special Events above), some hotels are fully booked, so if your trip coincides with the festival, plan to book a room early.

Many lodgings have a variety of accommodations ranging from economy rooms to expensive multi-bedroom condos with a kitchen and perhaps a spa. Make precise requests to get what you want. Because prices vary so much from month to month and from unit to unit within one establishment, use the prices given below only as an approximate guide.

Some lodgings close altogether in summer and others offer rates as much as half off the winter prices. The cheapest times to stay here are May and October, when not much is going on.

**Vacation Packages** Deciding where to stay among the many choices depends partly on what's available (many lodges run at full or almost full capacity in winter). Skiers may want to use a ski tour operator who can put together entire packages – accommodation, lift passes, ski rentals, flights, car rentals or transfers and other services.

Operators specializing in the Park City area include the following:

Avenir Adventures
(☎ 649 2495, 1 (800) 367 3230, fax 649 1192), PO Box 2730, 84060
Condo Destinations
(☎ /fax 645 9132, 1 (800) 444 9104), 3014 W Fawn Drive, 84060
Deer Valley Central Reservations
(☎ 649 1000, 1 (800) 424 3337), PO Box 3149, 84060
Inter-Mountain Lodging
(☎ 649 2687, 1 (800) 221 0933, fax 649 2688), PO Box 2909, 84060
Park City Ski Holidays
(☎ 649 0493, 1 (800) 222 7275, fax 649 0532), PO Box 4409, 84060
Reservations, Etc
(☎ 1 (800) 342 5754, fax 273 1311), PO Box 682169, 84060
Ski Reservation Headquarters of Utah
(☎ 649 2526, 1 (800) 522 7669, fax 645 8666), PO Box 3868, 84060
Utah Ski Reservations
(☎ 649 6493, 1 (800) 882 4754, fax 645 8419), PO Box 3000, 84060
Zauber Ski Holidays
(☎ 649 8392, 1 (800) 333 1400, fax 649 2622), PO Box 1715, 84060

**Reservation Services** The following services specialize mainly in finding places to stay for visitors to the Park City area. They also arrange lift tickets, air fares, etc, on request. Rates given are per night and range from low winter rates in budget rooms to peak winter rates in the most comfortable luxury lodgings. The cheapest places go fast, so make reservations early. Don't forget to add the 10.25% lodging tax to all rates. Summer rates are cheaper.

Because the services listed below have rooms all over the area, skiers should check carefully about the distance from the room to the nearest resort (you can ski or walk in from some places), bus line or parking area, and exactly what facilities are offered – kitchen, laundry, fireplace, spa, views, maid service, front desk, restaurant and so on. The following services are all in Park City.

Acclaimed Lodging
(☎ 649 3736, 1 (800) 552 9696), PO Box 3629, 84060, has studios ($95 to $170) to five-bedroom condos ($300 to $850).
Alpenhaus Lodging
(☎ 649 3551, 1 (800) 627 0381), PO Box 208, 84060, has one- to four-bedroom condos and private homes from $150 to $350 (five-night minimum).
Around Town Lodging
(☎ /fax 645 9335, 1 (800) 347 3392), PO Box 682548, 84068, has budget to deluxe accommodations starting at $45.
Blooming Enterprises
(☎ 649 6583, 1 (800) 635 4719), PO Box 2340, 84060, has one-bedroom units ($70 to $200) and two-bedroom ($185 to $460) to five-bedroom ($275 to $1050) condos and houses. There are four- to seven-day minimums.
Budget Lodging
(☎ 649 2526, 1 (800) 522 7669, fax 645 8666), PO Box 3868, 84060, has hotel rooms sleeping one to four ($50 to $120) to three-bedroom condos sleeping 10 ($120 to $275) and four-bedroom condos ($300 to $525).
Chamonix Groupe and Chalets
(☎ 649 2618, 1(800) 443 8630, fax 649 2618), 2228 Evening Star Drive, 84060, offers condos, chalets and a home 150 to 375 yards from the skiing. Studios to a chalet with kitchen and three bedrooms ($190 to $230) are among the places offered.
Deer Valley Lodging
(☎ 649 4040, 1 (800) 453 3833, fax 645 8419), PO Box 3000, 84060, has deluxe accommodations near luxurious Deer Valley Resort. One-bedroom ($225 to $700) to four-bedroom ($500 to $1965) condos require a four- to seven-day minimum stay.
Deer Valley Resort Central Reservations
(☎ 649 1000, 1 (800) 424 3337), PO Box 3149, 84060, lists hundreds of rooms from $75 to $1750.
Identity Properties
(☎ 649 5100, 1 (800) 245 6417), PO Box 779, 84060, has studios ($135 to $250) to four-bedroom townhouses and condos ($390 to $810).
PMA Lodging
(☎ 649 8800, 1 (800) 645 4762, fax 649 8876), PO Box 4650, 84060, has one-bedroom ($100 to $650) to five-bedroom ($500 to $1600) condos requiring four-night minimums.

Park City Reservations
(☎ 649 9598, 1 (800) 453 5789), PO Box 680128, 84060, has 400 properties ranging from one-bedroom chalets ($105 to $170) to five-bedroom condos and houses ($500 to $960). Three- to seven-day minimums are required.

R&R Properties
(☎ 649 6175, 1 (800) 348 6759), PO Box 827, 84060, has rooms and studios ($60 to $100) to four-bedroom homes or condos ($300 to $475).

## Places to Stay – camping

The nearest campsite is the *Hidden Haven Campground* (☎ 649 8935), 2200 Rasmussen Rd, one mile west of exit 145 from I-80 along the north frontage road (six miles north of Park City). Tent sites are $12, and RV sites are $15 to $20 depending on hookups used. There are showers, a playground, and fishing in the stream.

Also see Rockport State Park (above) and Wasatch Mountain State Park (below).

## Places to Stay – bottom end

*Chateau Après Lodge* (☎ 649 9372), 1299 Norfolk Ave, PO Box 579, 84060, is a two-minute walk from the Park City lifts. There are men's and women's dormitories ($20 per person) and 32 rooms with bath for $62/72/82 for two/three/four people.

*Alpine Prospector's Lodge* (☎ 649 4383), 151 Main St, PO Box 4198, 84060, is in a historic building. Twelve rooms range from $29 (summer) to $90. Some rooms share baths; there is a spa, restaurant and bar. The *Star Hotel B&B* (☎ 649 8333), 227 Main St, PO Box 777, 84060, has 10 rooms in a family house. Most rooms share baths. Rates are $30 (summer) to $55, including breakfast.

## Places to Stay – middle

**B&Bs** The *Imperial Hotel* (☎ 649 1904, 1 (800) 669 8824, fax 645 7421), 221 Main St, PO Box 1628, 84060, in a restored building dating from 1904, has both antiques and modern amenities. Rooms are $80 to $120 in summer, $130 to $200 in winter, including continental

breakfast. There is a spa. The *Old Town Guest House* (☎ 649 2642), 1011 Empire Ave, PO Box 162, 84060, has four rooms and a spa. Rates are $60 to $160 with full breakfast.

The *Old Miners' Lodge* (☎ 645 8068, 1 (800) 648 8068, fax 645 7420), 615 Woodside Ave, PO Box 2639, 84060, which dates from 1893, is decorated with period pieces. There are seven rooms and three suites, a spa, fireplace and full breakfast included. Rates run $45 to $85 in summer, $85 to $200 in winter.

The *Washington School Inn* (☎ 649 3800, 1 (800) 824 1672, fax 649 3802), 543 Park Ave, PO Box 536, 84060, is a B&B in a renovated stone school dating to 1889. You'll find both period furnishings and modern amenities, including a spa and sauna. The 15 rooms (some with fireplaces) go for $200 to $300 in winter with full breakfast. Summer rates are $125 to $175.

**Hotels & Condos** *Edelweis Haus* (☎ 649 9342, 1 (800) 438 3855, fax 649 4049), 1482 Empire Ave, PO Box 495, 84060, is less than a quarter mile from Park City lifts and requires a six-night minimum in winter. A pool, spa and sauna are available. Simple rooms run about $40 in summer, $90 to $135 in winter. Condos are up to $95 in summer, $140 to $325 in winter.

The Best Western *Landmark Inn* (☎ 649 7300, fax 649 1760), 6560 N Landmark Drive, 84060, (I-80 exit 145) is five miles north of Park City, but it has a shuttle to ski areas. There is a pool, spa, exercise room and 24-hour restaurant. Rates are $57 to $77 in summer, $80 to $140 in winter. The *Chamonix Lodge* (☎ 649 8443, 1 (800) 443 8630, fax 649 2618), 1450 Empire Ave, has hotel rooms with refrigerators for $55 in summer and $85 to $135 in winter. Other amenities include a sauna and spa.

The *Blue Church Lodge & Townhouses* (☎ 649 8009, 1 (800) 626 5467, fax 649 0686), 424 Park Ave, PO Box 1720, 84060, offers hotel rooms for $90 to $150 and one- to four-bedroom condos (opposite the hotel) for $125 to $475, three-night minimum. *Park West Village* (☎ 649 8023, 1 (800) 421 5056), 3819 N Village Round Drive, PO Box 1655, 84060, has hotel rooms for $45 to $75 and one- or two-bedroom condos for $75 to $225, less in summer. The *Radisson Resort* (☎ 649 5000, 1 (800) 333 3333), 2121 Park Ave, PO Box 1778, 84060, has a pool, spa, sauna and exercise equipment; hotel rooms go for $85 to $170 in winter. *Treasure Mountain Inn* (☎ 649 7334, 1 (800) 344 2460, fax 649 5758), 255 Main St, PO Box 639, 84060, has a pool, spa, fireplace and games area; studios ($82 to $170) to two-bedroom condos ($165 to $300) are available in winter.

The *Olympia Park Hotel* (☎ 649 2900, 1 (800) 234 9003, fax 649 4852), 1895 Sidewinder Drive, PO Box 4439, 84060, is a good full-service hotel (pool, spa, sauna, exercise room, massage, two restaurants, bar, room service, concierge, ski shop and rental, lift ticket sales, car rental, etc). Rooms are about $90 in summer, $150 to $200 in winter. Nearby is the *Inn at Prospector Square* (☎ 649 7100, 1 (800) 453 3812, fax 649 8377), 2200 Sidewinder Drive, which has a restaurant, bar and complete athletic club. Rooms are $70 to $100 in summer, $100 to $180 in winter. Studios and one-, two- and three-bedroom condos are $80 to $200 in summer and $110 to $480 in winter.

The *Resort Center Lodge & Inn* (☎ 649 0800, 1 (800) 824 5331, fax 649 1464), 1415 Lowell Ave, PO Box 3449, 84060, is right at the base of the Park City lifts. It offers pool, spa, sauna, massage, and a restaurant and bar. There is tennis and mini-golf in summer. Hotel rooms are $60 to $160, studios are $110 to $300 and one- to four-bedroom condos run from $160 to $1285; five-day minimums are preferred in winter, and lower rates are available in summer.

*Shadow Ridge Resort* (☎ 649 4300, 1 (800) 451 3031, fax 649 5951), 50 Shadow Ridge Rd, PO Box 1820, 84060, is a block from the ski area. Amenities include a pool, spa, sauna, exercise room and restaurant with room service. Hotel rooms are $70 to $230; studios to three-bedroom condos go for $80 to $580.

*The Yarrow* (☎ 649 7000, 1 (800) 327 2332, fax 649 4819), 1800 Park Ave, PO Box 1840, 84060, a full-service resort hotel and conference center opposite a golf course, is only 500 yards from the Park City ski area. It offers a pool, spa, sauna, restaurant, bar, room service, concierge, ski -rental/repair shop, ticket sales and so on. Hotel rooms, studios and one-bedroom condos cost $90 to $350 in winter.

The *Goldener Hirsch Inn* (☎ 649 7770, 1 (800) 252 3373, fax 649 7901), 7570 Royal St East, PO Box 859, 84060, is an Austrian-style hotel with 20 double rooms located at mid-mountain in Deer Valley ski area. There is a good restaurant and bar with après ski entertainment. Bedrooms and suites range from $195 to $575, and a penthouse is $410 to $660, with continental breakfast.

The *Silver King Hotel* (☎ 649 5500, 1 (800) 331 8652, fax 649 6647), 1485 Empire Ave, PO Box 2818, 84060, is two blocks from the Park City ski area. Amenities include two pools, spa, sauna, exercise area and concierge. Studios and one- or two-bedroom condos have kitchens, and some have fireplaces, laundry areas or private hot tub. Rates are $135 to $240 for a studio, $340 to $600 for a two-bedroom penthouse spa suite. The hotel also runs the nearby *Silver Cliff Village* with two-bedroom condos for $220 to $445.

### Places to Stay – top end

Most of the last few places described in the previous section fit in the top-end category, especially their most expensive suites and condos. For the very best top-end places, either of the Deer Valley reservation services mentioned earlier will be able to help.

One lodge stands out above the rest, however. The *Stein Eriksen Lodge* (☎ 649 3700, 1 (800) 453 1302, fax 649 5825), 7700 Stein Way, PO Box 3177, 84060, is at 8200 feet, mid-mountain on the slopes of the Deer Valley ski area. Amenities include two restaurants, including the best in the area (the Glitretind), room and pool-side service, bar with music, pool, spa, sauna, exercise room, massage service, games, shops, concierge and a huge fireplace in the lobby. Summer guests can use mountain bikes and enjoy the extensive grounds. Most rooms have superb views; suites may include kitchen, fireplace, laundry area, private hot tub and balcony. Winter rates are $265 to $600 for bedrooms, $500 to $1000 for suites and $520 to a cool $2000 for the Grand Suite! Summer rates are $100 to $275 for rooms and suites, and $215 to $500 for the Grand Suite.

## Places to Eat

Scores of places to eat do a thriving business in winter. Most cut back operations in the summer. Call ahead to check on hours.

**Hotel Restaurants** Many places to stay have restaurants open to the public. The most famous is the elegant *Glitretind* (☎ 645 6455, 649 3700), serving fresh continental cuisine in the Stein Eriksen Lodge. You don't get a choice of french fries or mashed potatoes here – it's 'crisped bliss potatoes' or 'garlic potato puree'. The restaurant is open for breakfast, lunch and dinner, and Sunday brunch costs $16 – which gives an idea of the prices. Reservations are recommended.

Other hotel restaurants worth visiting even if you're not a guest include the following. The *Goldener Hirsch Inn* (☎ 649 0010) serves breakfast, lunch and dinner during winter and dinner from Thursday to Saturday in summer – reservations recommended. The menu is continental with a strong Austrian/German influence – entrees around $20. *Mr G's* (☎ 649 2900) in the Olympia Park Hotel is open for breakfast, lunch and dinner daily in winter, Wednesday to Saturday in summer. It serves Italian food ranging from pizza and pasta (under $10) to veal, seafood and chicken ($15 to $20). The *Grub Steak Restaurant* (☎ 649 8060) in the Inn at Prospector Square is named for its excellent steaks ($14 to $20), and it's famous for a huge salad bar. It offers chicken ($11 to $14) and seafood ($15 and up) as

well. It's open for lunch, dinner and Sunday brunch and has live music on weekends.

The *1800 Park Ave Cafe & Pub* (☎ 649 7000) in The Yarrow is open for American-style breakfast, lunch and dinner at prices lower than other top hotels. Check out their daily specials and all-you-can-eat prime rib buffet on Friday and Saturday evenings. *Radigan's* (☎ 649 5000) in the Radisson Hotel has a good breakfast, lunch and dinner selection at reasonable prices, as does the *Columbine* (☎ 649 7062) in the Resort Center Lodge & Inn, which features American food including fresh seafood. The *Alpine Prospector's Restaurant* (☎ 649 7482) has good $4 to $8 lunches and $8 to $20 steak and seafood dinners in the historic lodge at 'The Top of Main Street' (151 Main St in the Alpine Prospector's Lodge).

**Main St** This street is the historic heart of Park City, along which restaurants abound. Browse the following selection (there are many others), arranged from south to north. Many places have outdoor dining areas.

The *Wasatch Brew Pub* (☎ 649 0900), 250 Main St, is a microbrewery producing at least five unpasteurized beers for all tastes – ask about brewery tours. Its slogan is 'We drink our share and sell the rest'. Open at 11 am, it serves soups, salads, sandwiches and specialties for lunch ($3 to $8) and a variety of dinners ($7 to $15). There's a sports bar and dart board.

*El Cheepo* (☎ 649 0883), 255 Main St, is a family-style restaurant with Southwestern food (chili, fajitas, quesadillas, chicken, etc) in the $2 to $10 range. The *Morning Ray Cafe/Evening Star Dining* (☎ 649 5686), 268 Main St, has good breakfasts and lunches in the cafe and dinner specials ($8 to $15) in the 'Star' – the menu includes gourmet organic and vegetarian selections.

*Cisero's* (☎ 649 5044) 306 Main St, is a reasonably priced Italian restaurant. *The Eating Establishment* (☎ 649 8284), 317 Main St, serves hearty breakfasts ($4 to $7) all day and a good selection of sandwiches and specialties for lunch ($4 to $7) and dinner ($6 to $14). The *Red Banjo Pizza Parlor* (☎ 649 9901), 322 Main St, serves pizza, spaghetti and salads. The *Barking Frog Grill* (☎ 649 6222), 368 Main St, serves more upmarket Southwestern food for lunch and dinner.

The 400 block of Main St is the heart of the restaurant district. Family-run *Mileti's* (☎ 649 8211), 412 Main St, has been a favorite for over two decades (a long time in this ski town). It serves good pastas ($8 to $11) and Italian specialties (around $16) for dinner only. The popular *Cafe Terigo* (☎ 645 9555), 424 Main St, serves American cafe cuisine (salads, sandwiches, pastas, pizzas and specials) for lunch and dinner ($7 to $16). Upstairs is *Ichiban Sushi* (☎ 649 2865), with a good sushi bar and fine selection of traditional Japanese dinners.

*PC Pizza Co* (☎ 649 1591), 430 Main St, is open 11 am to 11 pm, and they deliver – pizzas, what else? No surprises either at *Szechwan Chinese Restaurant* (☎ 649 0957), 438 Main St, serving lunch specials ($5 to $6) and dinners ($9 to $17). The oddly named *Irish Camel* (☎ 649 6645), 434 Main St, is open daily for dinner and for lunch on weekends. It serves good Mexican meals (entrees $6 to $16) and humped potatoes with blarney on the side. *Texas Red's* (☎ 649 7337), 440 Main St, serves chili ($3 to $6), barbecue ($8 to $16) and Texan-style catfish and chicken-fried steak for lunch and dinner in a Western setting. Don't like cowboy cookin'? Next door is *Alex's* (☎ 649 6644), 442 Main St, a French dinner restaurant with entrees in the $13 to $24 range.

The *Main St Deli* (☎ 649 1110), 525 Main St, open from 7:30 am to 9 pm, has an excellent selection of inexpensive breakfasts, sandwiches and baked goods. Also a good value for the budget-conscious is the *Pizza & Noodle Ranch* (☎ 645 8878), 530 Main St, with lunches and dinners for $5 to $9. *The Claimjumper* (☎ 649 8051), 573 Main St, is open for hearty breakfasts or steak and seafood dinners (about $10 to $20). *Legends Cafe* (☎ 649 9229), 580

Main St, serves reasonably priced American fare for breakfast, lunch, dinner and late-night snacking till midnight or 2:30 am some nights. *TCBY* (☎ 649 4000), 632 Main St, a national chain, serves tasty frozen yogurt desserts. *Utah Coal & Lumber* (☎ 649 8072), 201 Heber Ave (just off Main St), has Mexican dinners and, during winter, lunches as well. Entrees run $5 to $10.

**Other Restaurants** The *Baja Cantina* (☎ 649 2252), 1284 Empire Ave, next to the Park City ski resort, serves reasonably priced Mexican lunches and dinners.

The *Stew Pot* (☎ 645 7839), 1375 Deer Valley Drive South (in Deer Valley Plaza) serves soups, salads, sandwiches and daily specials from 8 am to 9 pm in winter. Not only does it have good views from the deck, but it's one of the cheaper places to eat in the Deer Valley area. Another Stew Pot (☎ 649 5997), adjacent to the Shadow Ridge Resort, is open 7 am to 10 pm.

*Dining Express* (☎ 649 3233) does home (or rented condo) deliveries from a number of local restaurants.

**Entertainment**
During the summer, concerts of all kinds take place in the various resorts around town. Park City Performances (☎ 649 9371) puts on plays or musicals during summer in the historic *Egyptian Theater*, 328 Main St.

*Holiday Village Cinemas 3* (☎ 649 6541), 1776 Park Ave, screens movies year round.

There are plenty of private clubs; to gain admission, you must either obtain a guest membership or be sponsored by a member, but both are easy to do. There are more live performances in winter. *Z-Place* (☎ 645 9722), 427 Main St, the largest club in the area (with a capacity of about 1000), features live rock & roll, country and other music genres. *The Club* (☎ 649 6693), 449 Main St, is very popular – get there early. Next door, *The Alamo* (☎ 649 2380), 447 Main St, is another good possibility. You can catch blues at *Cisero's* (649 6800), 306 Main St. The *DownUnder* (☎ 649 9971),

573 Main St, hosts local country talent. *Mileti's* (☎ 649 8211), 412 Main St, has jazz on occasion. There are plenty of other venues, including several in the better hotels. Check out the Diversions section of the *Park Record* on Thursday for detailed listings.

### Things to Buy

The Factory Stores at Park City (☎ 645 7078), near exit 145 on I-80, has dozens of factory outlet stores selling everything from boots to books.  .

### Getting There & Away

Lewis Bros Stages (☎ 649 2256 in Park City, 1 (800) 826 5844, in Salt Lake City 359 8677), 549 W 500 South, Salt Lake City, specializes in transportation for skiers going between the Salt Lake City airport, Park City, and other ski areas. It runs a limited summer service. Park City Transportation (☎ 649 5466, in Salt Lake City 364 8472) has year-round bus service between Park City and Salt Lake City. One-way fares are about $20, depending on season.

### Getting Around

Park City Transit (☎ 645 5130) runs free buses two or three times an hour throughout the day along Main St and Park Ave to most areas of town. Schedules and bus maps are available from the Visitor Information Center or ask any bus driver.

### HEBER CITY & MIDWAY AREA

An agricultural center founded in 1859, Heber City makes a good base from which to visit the surrounding valley and mountains. At an elevation of almost 5600 feet, Heber City is the seat of Wasatch County and has a population of 5000.

Midway is a small town (population 1500) three miles west of Heber City. It has a few good places to stay, some of which have natural hot springs.

### Orientation & Information

Main St (Hwy 40) is Heber City's main commercial street and runs north-south. 100 S westbound takes you to Midway.

The area's Information Center (☎ 654 3666) is at 475 N Main St, PO Box 427, Heber City, 84032. Hours are 9 am to 5 pm, Monday to Friday plus weekends in summer. (There is limited information available at the Midway City Offices (☎ 654 3223), 140 W Main St, Midway.) The Uinta National Forest Heber Ranger Station (☎ 654 0470), 125 E 100 North, PO Box 190, 84032, is open 8 am to 5 pm, Monday to Friday. The library (☎ 654 1511) is at 188 S Main St. The local weekly newspaper is the *Wasatch Wave*. The post office (☎ 654 0881) is at 125 E 100 North. The County Hospital (☎ 654 2500) is at 55 S 500 E. The police (☎ 654 3040; in emergencies ☎ 911) are at 75 N Main St.

### Things to See & Do

The **Heber Valley Historic Railroad** (☎ 654 5601, 1 (800) 982 3257), 450 S 600 West, uses a steam locomotive built in 1904 and two old diesel engines for sightseeing trips. Roundtrips to Deer Creek Dam last two hours and to Vivian Park 3.5 hours. They leave once or twice daily from June to October. Trains to Deer Creek leave at 11 am and sometimes 2 pm as well; to Vivian Park at 10 am and sometimes 2:30 pm. Call for exact schedules and engines used. Roundtrip fares on the steam train to Deer Creek are $14 for adults, $12 for seniors and $8 for two- to 10-year-olds; to Vivian Park it's $16, $14 and $10. Fares on diesel trains are $2 less.

The **State Fish Hatchery** (☎ 654 0282), on Hwy 113 a mile south of Midway, is one of the world's biggest trout hatcheries. Visitors are welcome between 8 am and 4:30 pm.

About 15 miles southwest of Heber City along Hwy 189 is the beginning of scenic and steep-walled **Provo Canyon**, which you can drive through en route to Provo. A few miles after the canyon begins, the 600-foot-high double **Bridal Veil Falls** can be seen on the south side. An **aerial tramway** (☎ 225 4461, summer only) climbs 1753 feet to the top of the canyon with great views of the falls. Locals say this is the world's steepest tramway. It operates

**UTAH**

UTAH

Heber City & Midway Area

To Skyline Drive

To Park City, Salt Lake City

Wasatch Mountain State Park & Golf Course

Mountain Spaa Resort

Homestead Resort & Simon's Restaurant

600 N

200 N

Main St

Midway

113

500 S

850 S

970 S

State Fish Hatchery

Cascade Springs Drive

To Cascade Springs

Tate Lane

113

Heber City & Midway Area

0    1    2 km

0   .5   1 miles

Charleston

Deer Creek Reservoir

Daniels Creek

To Deer Creek State Park, Bridal Veil Falls, Provo

1800 N

1200 N

525 W

Westside - 1750 W

See Heber City map

500 N

400 N

Center St

Midway Lane

300 S

650 S

600 S

Heber City

1200 S

2400 S

189

3000 S

Heber Valley Airport

Daniel

To Strawberry Reservoir, Roosevelt

Daniels Creek

Charleston Rd

40

189

40

Main St

Mill Rd

Daniels Canyon Rd

Industrial Pkwy

Heber Creeper

S. Field Rd

1200 W

Provo River

Memorial Day to Labor Day (or slightly longer, weather permitting); fares are about $6/3 for adults/children. Bring binoculars or spotting scope if you want to watch the Rocky Mountain goats that are often seen in the area.

On the north side of Hwy 189 near the entrance to Provo Canyon is the **Alpine Loop Road** (Hwy 92), one of the most scenic, steep, narrow and twisting roads in the area – not recommended for long RVs or trailers. Parts of the loop are closed by snow in winter. The road passes Sundance Resort and Timpanogos Cave National Monument, both described below. Along the way, you can take in impressive vistas of 11,750-foot **Mt Timpanogos**. The mountain can be climbed by trails leaving from either Mt Timpanogos or Timpooneke Campgrounds, both on Hwy 92 and described under Places to Stay. It's about nine miles to the summit, but the trails are closed by snow from late October to early July – there is a permanent snowfield near the summit. To learn about the many other summer hiking possibilities in the area, contact the Uinta National Forest ranger stations in Heber City (☎ 654 0470), Provo

(☎ 377 5780) or Pleasant Grove (☎ 785 3563) for maps, camping regulations and hiking information.

During winter, Heber City makes a good base for skiing in Park City or Sundance – both just under 20 miles away. Likewise, you can cross-country ski or snowshoe in the Uinta National Forest.

The **High Valley Aviation** (☎ 654 5831), at the Heber Airport (a mile south of town), offers glider rides and instruction.

Other area excursions include driving to Wasatch Mountain and Deer Creek State Parks and Strawberry Reservoir, all described below.

### Special Events
Early February sees dogsled and snowmobile racing. Wasatch County Fair is held in Heber City in mid-August. Midway celebrates its European heritage during Swiss Days held Labor Day weekend (the dates vary for this).

### Places to Stay – camping
The RV park next to the *High Country Inn* (see below) allows campers to use some inn facilities. Fees are $8 for tents and $14 for RVs with hookups. The *Mountain Spaa Resort* (see below) also has tent camping for $6 and RV hookups for $13.

There are about three dozen camping areas operated by the Uinta National Forest, which are open during the summer only. Several lie along or just off the Alpine Loop Drive (Hwy 92), and some can be reserved either through Mistix (1 (800) 283 2267) or by calling Pleasant Grove Ranger Station (☎ 785 3563), 390 N 100 East, Pleasant Grove. From east to west along Hwy 92, camping areas are as follows: *Mt Timpanogos* (6800 feet elevation), *Altamont* (reserved groups only), *Timpooneke* (7400 feet), *Echo* (6000 feet, only four sites), *Little Mill* (6000 feet), *North Mill* (reserved groups only) and *House Rock* (5800 feet). These all have water, no RV hookups, and charge $7 per night. Other areas are reached by forest roads off the main loop.

The state parks and reservoir (See Around Heber City below) also offer camping.

### Places to Stay – bottom end to middle
Hotel prices tend to be a little higher in summer and can get rather expensive during summer weekends. Weekly discounts and ski packages are often available. Addresses given below are in Heber City, unless otherwise indicated.

The simple *Cottage Inn B&B* (☎ 654 2236), 830 S Main St, 84032, has only two rooms (no smoking) and charges about $22/28 for singles/doubles including continental breakfast. *Mac's Motel* (☎ 654 0612), 670 S Main St, charges in the low $30s for a room. *Aloma Whispering Pines Motel* (☎ 654 0231), 90 N Main St, also has rooms in the $30s, and some more expensive suites with kitchenettes.

All the following have rooms in the low to mid $30s for a single, or the low $40s for a double. The *Hy Lander Motel* (☎ 654 2150), 425 S Main St, is well run and a good value. Rooms all have queen- or king-size beds, and some have refrigerators. A few larger rooms have kitchenettes, which are more expensive. There is a restaurant and pool. The *High Country Inn* (☎ 654 0201), 1000 S Main St, has a pool and spa, and restaurant next door. Rooms are pleasant, all with queen- or king-size beds, and some have kitchenettes. There is RV camping and a small play area for children. A laundry room is available. The *Danish Viking Lodge* (☎ 654 2202), 989 S Main St, has a pool, spa, sauna, playground and coin laundry. Most rooms have refrigerators, and there are a few suites with kitchens and private spas, which go for up to $70. *Swiss Alps Inn* (☎ 654 0722), 167 S Main St, has a pool, spa, sauna and playground. There is a restaurant opposite the motel.

In Midway, the *Mountain Spaa Resort* (☎ 654 0721, 654 0807), 800 N Mountain Spaa Lane (at 600 N 200 E), has rustic cabins starting around $40. There is a restaurant. They have two naturally heated mineral water swimming pools and horse rental, but are open only in summer.

UTAH

UTAH

## Places to Stay – top end

The *Inn on the Creek B&B* (☎ 654 0892, fax 654 5871), 375 Rainbow Lane, Midway, 84049, is an attractive steep-roofed building offering eight suites, each with fireplace, spa and view from the balcony. Smoking is not allowed in the rooms. A full breakfast is included in the rates of $80 (summer), $95 (winter), $125 (Christmas season). A dining room and local tours are available.

The 130-room *Homestead Resort* (☎ 654 1102, 1 (800) 327 7220, fax 654 5087),

700 N Homestead Drive, PO Box 99, Midway, is the area's premier year-round resort. Some buildings date to the 1880s (though most are modern), and the attractive grounds are extensive. There are (depending on the season) an 18-hole golf course or 12.5 miles of cross-country ski tracks; golf or ski lessons; horse, mountain bike, cross-country ski or snowmobile rentals; horse-drawn buggy or sleigh rides; tennis courts, mineral water bath, swimming pools, spa, sauna, lawn games, play area, gift shop, coffeeshop and the best

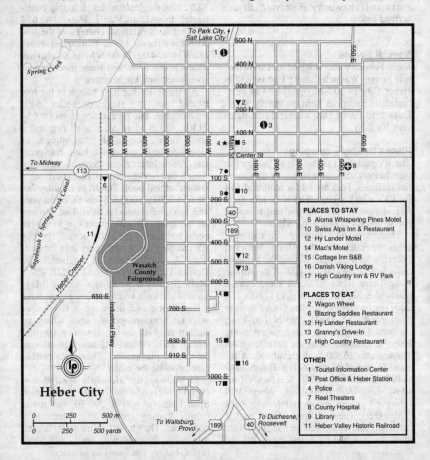

**Heber City**

```
0    250    500 m
0    250    500 yards
```

To Park City,
Salt Lake City

To Midway

To Wallsburg,
Provo

To Duchesne,
Roosevelt

Spring Creek

Sagebrush & Spring Creek Canal

Heber Creeper

Wasatch County Fairgrounds

Industrial Pkwy

**PLACES TO STAY**
5 Aloma Whispering Pines Motel
10 Swiss Alps Inn & Restaurant
12 Hy Lander Motel
14 Mac's Motel
15 Cottage Inn B&B
16 Danish Viking Lodge
17 High Country Inn & RV Park

**PLACES TO EAT**
2 Wagon Wheel
6 Blazing Saddles Restaurant
12 Hy Lander Restaurant
13 Granny's Drive-In
17 High Country Restaurant

**OTHER**
1 Tourist Information Center
3 Post Office & Heber Station
4 Police
7 Reel Theaters
8 County Hospital
9 Library
11 Heber Valley Historic Railroad

restaurant in the area. (Some facilities are available to the public.) Rates are $75 to $125 for rooms, $135 to $210 for suites and $185 to $285 for condos for up to eight people. Some rooms and suites come with one or more of these amenities: fireplace, antique furnishings, and private hot tub, sun deck or patio. The highest rates are mid-December to early January (three-night minimum required) and summer weekends. All-inclusive one-week ski or golf vacation packages are available.

### Places to Eat

The *Wagon Wheel* (☎ 654 0251), 220 N Main St, is a family-style restaurant serving American food from 6 am to 10 pm. *Blazing Saddles Restaurant* (☎ 654 3300), 605 W 100 South, is convenient for the historic railway rides. It serves American and Mexican lunches and dinners. For a decent burger and milk shake while avoiding the fast-food chains, there's *Granny's Drive-In* (☎ 654 3097), 511 S Main St. *Song's* (☎ 654 3338), 930 S Main St, serves good Chinese and American lunches and dinners.

Several hotels have good restaurants – the *Hy Lander Restaurant, High Country Inn* and *Swiss Alps Inn* are all good. The best is *Simon's* (☎ 654 1102) at the Homestead Resort. Their Sunday brunch (10 am to 3 pm, $14) attracts people from as far as Salt Lake City, especially during fall when the drive over is very pretty. Dinners are served nightly, and reservations are advised, especially on weekends.

### Entertainment

*Reel Theaters* (☎ 654 1181), 94 S Main St, shows movies. For a beer, head over to *The Other End* (☎ 654 2645) on Hwy 40 at the north end of town.

### Getting There & Away

Greyhound (☎ 355 4684 in Salt Lake City) passes through Heber City on its daily run along Hwy 40 to and from Denver, Colorado. There may be two runs a day in summer. Most people drive.

## AROUND HEBER CITY
### Wasatch Mountain State Park

This large state park (34 sq miles) offers fine mountain views, a good 27-hole golf course (which becomes a cross-country ski track in winter), hiking and horse trails (which become snowmobile trails in winter), a visitors center and developed camping with showers. These amenities make it one of the most popular state parks in the area, and reservations for summer weekend camping are advised.

The park (☎ 654 1791), PO Box 10, Midway, 84049, is two miles northwest of Midway and can be reached in summer via scenic but partly unpaved Guardsman Pass (Hwy 224) south of Park City. Camping reservations can be made at 1 (800) 322 3770. Camping costs $7 or $13 with full hookups; day use is $3. The golf course can be reached at 654 0532.

### Deer Creek State Park

As usual in the area, this state park (elevation 5417 feet) surrounds a reservoir and offers fishing, boating and windsurfing in the summer, and ice fishing in winter. In addition, there are fine mountain views.

The park (☎ 654 0171), PO Box 257, Midway, 84049, is nine miles southwest of Heber City via Hwy 189. Camping is available from April to October; there are showers, a grocery store and a boat launch. A marina rents boats in summer. Day use is $3, camping is $9 and weekend reservations (☎ 1 (800) 322 3770) are a good idea in summer – there are only about 30 sites.

### Strawberry Reservoir

By far the biggest reservoir in the area, it offers the usual water attractions. Its 7600-foot elevation in high-plains country ensures cool summers and icy winters when cross-country skiing, snowmobiling and ice fishing are popular.

The area is managed by the Uinta National Forest, Heber Ranger Station (☎ 654 0470). The reservoir is 26 miles southeast of Heber City along Hwy 40.

There is a visitors center at the northwest end of the reservoir.

Camping from May to October costs $7, and water is available. There are over 350 sites at *Strawberry Bay* on the west side of the reservoir, over 150 sites at *Soldier Creek* on the east side, and *Aspen Grove* has 23 sites on the south side. All three have boat launch areas. Day use and boat launching is free.

There are marinas at Strawberry Bay (☎ 548 2261) and Soldier Creek (☎ 548 2696) in season. Both offer boat rentals, gas station, dock rental, fishing supplies and a convenience store. There is a cafe at Strawberry Bay.

## Sundance Resort

Owned and developed by actor/director Robert Redford, this year-round resort offers a rustic getaway in a scenic wilderness setting. Tucked under Mt Timpanogos, the resort offers excellent skiing in winter and an arts program, hiking and mountain biking during summer. The resort is 2.5 miles along Hwy 92 from the north end of Provo Canyon (Hwy 189).

Skiing goes from mid-December to April. Four lifts service 41 runs in 450 acres between 6100 and 8250 feet. 20% is for beginners and 40% for intermediate skiers. All-day lift passes (9 am to 4:30 pm) are $29 for adults, $18 for children under 12 and free for over 65s. Half-day passes are $23/16 for adults/children. The charge for using the resort's nine miles of groomed cross-country ski tracks is $7 (all day) or $5 (after 2 pm); free for children and those over 65. Ski rentals cost $18.

Mountain bikes can be rented in summer. The ski lifts run weekends and holidays (occasionally midweek) in summer and can lift mountain bikes, so you can either hike or bike back down. Rides are $3. Horses are available for rent, and guided day rides are an option.

Outdoor theater programs (☎ 225 4100 for reservations) for adults and children are scheduled from mid-June to August each year. Performances take place every evening except Sunday. Tickets are about $12 for adult performances, $5/3 for adults/children for children's theater. Other events occur through the summer season. During the rest of the year, weekend theatrical performances and special film screenings are presented.

From mid-June to August there are activities for kids – theater, crafts, games, riding, hiking and so on.

**Places to Stay & Eat** *Sundance* (☎ 225 4107, 1 (800) 892 1600, fax 226 1937), RR 3, Box A-1, Sundance, 84604, has about 70 rustic wooden cottages for rent. Winter rates range from $150 for a standard room to $550 for a three-room cottage. (Rates may be higher over the Christmas period.) The comfortable and attractively decorated cottages have fireplaces, laundry areas and decks or patios; the larger units have kitchens. Summer rates are about a third lower and include breakfast. Long stay lodging and recreational packages are available. Sundance also manages some four- and five-bedroom mountain homes for about $575 to $900 a night, depending on the season.

There are two restaurants. The *Tree Room*, the most elegant and expensive, features Redford's private Indian art collection. Dinner reservations are recommended. The *Grill* serves breakfast, lunch and dinner in a more casual atmosphere. In addition, fast-food is served at *Creekside* and at *Bearclaw's Cabin* at the bottom and top of the ski area respectively – great views.

**Getting There & Away** Lewis Bros Stages (☎ 1 (800) 826 5844, in Salt Lake City 359 8677, in Park City 649 2256), 549 W 500 South, Salt Lake City, has buses from Salt Lake City and Park City to and from Sundance and other ski areas. The company runs a limited summer service. Jet Express (1 (800) 272 5533, in Salt Lake City 375 5533) has airport shuttles (vans or cars) from Salt Lake City airport to and from Sundance and other ski areas.

## Timpanogos Cave National Monument

The three beautiful caves of this national monument, at an elevation of 6730 feet in the foothills of Mt Timpanogos, are a popular stop for those driving the Alpine Scenic Loop. Lovely geological formations and underground pools make the mildly strenuous access very worthwhile.

The caves are reached by a 1.5-mile trail leaving the visitors center in American Fork Canyon. The climb to the caves is over 1000 feet, and there is no wheelchair or stroller access. All cave visitors must be accompanied by a park ranger, and guided tours are limited to 20 people. The trail is closed by snow for most of the year, and the caves are open only from mid-May to early October.

Tour tickets must be bought at the visitors center and cost $5, or $4 for six- to 15-year-olds. Tours depart from the cave entrance every 10 minutes, and you will be assigned a specific time to be at the entrance. Visitors center hours (in summer) are 7 am to 5:30 pm, but afternoon tours are often filled by late morning, especially during midsummer weekends. Therefore arrive early, preferably midweek, for the shortest waits. Allow an hour for the 1.5-mile trail climb to the entrance. Each tour lasts just under an hour, and cave temperatures are 43°F year-round, so bring a sweater. In the visitors center, exhibits, slide show and a gift shop help pass the time, or ask rangers for suggestions about local trails.

Tickets can be purchased in advance for any day at the visitors center or by mail, prepaid, two weeks in advance. Call to check for price changes. Special tours are occasionally given. Information and tickets are available from Timpanogos Cave National Monument New Mexico, (☎ 756 5238), RR 3, Box 200, American Fork, 84003.

There is a snack bar and picnic area, but no overnight camping.

## PROVO

Provo, about 43 miles south of Salt Lake City along I-15, is the seat of Utah county and the second largest city in the state. Although the city population is only about 91,000, it combines with its neighbors **Orem** to the north (70,000 inhabitants) and **Springville** to the south (15,000 inhabitants) to make a sizable metropolitan area. These two towns are included in the following account.

Provo is named after Canadian fur trapper Etienne Provost, who trapped here in 1824-1825. The earliest European visit, however, was the Spanish Dominguez-Escalante missionary expedition, which spent a few days in the area in 1776, preaching to the Ute inhabitants. Despite these brief incursions, the land remained under Ute control until Brigham Young sent 150 settlers to the valley in 1849. Short wars were fought between the Mormons and the Utes, but the settlers prevailed and several more towns were quickly founded nearby.

Provo rapidly became the leading Mormon town in the area. In 1875, the Brigham Young Academy (now Brigham Young University) opened, and it has grown into the world's largest church-established university. Most of the nearly 30,000 students are strict Mormons, and the school and city have a squeaky-clean feel to them. More than other Utahan cities, Provo has held on to its early Mormon heritage; the population is largely white, conservative and middle class. The university and schools are the town's biggest employers, but the computer industry is a fast-growing second economic contributor as well.

The many late 19th- and early 20th-century buildings, the university, the several excellent museums, the proximity of skiing at Sundance (15 miles), beautiful mountain scenery along the Alpine Loop Drive (see Heber City & Midway Area) and the attractions of nearby Utah Lake (the state's largest freshwater lake) make Provo a tempting destination for travelers.

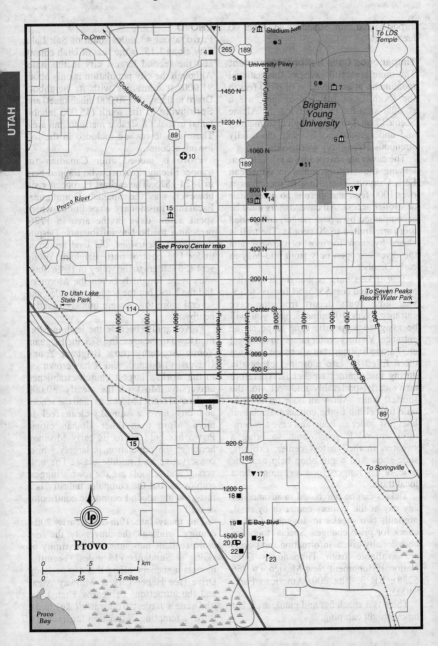

To Orem

To LDS Temple

▼1

2 🏛 Stadium Ave

● 3

4 ■

265

189

University Pkwy

Columbia Lane

5 ■

1450 N

6 ● 🏛 7

Brigham Young University

1230 N

89

▼8

1060 N

189

⊕10

9 🏛

Provo River

● 11

800 N

15 🏛

13 🏛 ▼14

12 ▼

600 N

See Provo Center map

400 N

To Utah Lake State Park

200 N

To Seven Peaks Resort Water Park

114

900 W

700 W

500 W

Freedom Blvd (200 W)

University Ave

Center S

200 E

400 E

600 E

700 E

900 E

S State St

200 S

300 S

400 S

600 S

16

89

920 S

189

To Springville

▼17

1200 S

18 ■

19 ▼  E Bay Blvd

1500 S

20 🔲

21 ■

22 ■

23

Provo

0        .5        1 km
0   .25   .5 miles

Provo Bay

**PLACES TO STAY**
4   Days Inn
5   Comfort Inn
18  Best Western Rome Inn, Super 8 Motel, East Bay Inn
19  Holiday Inn, National 9 Colony Inn Suites
20  Silver Fox RV Resort
21  Marriott Fairfield Inn
22  Motel 6

**PLACES TO EAT**
1   Viva Spaghetti
4   Magleby's
8   Formosa Garden Restaurant
12  El Azteca
14  Brick Oven
17  Chuck-A-Rama

**OTHER**
2   Earth Science Museum
3   Cougar Stadium
6   Marriott Center
7   Monte L Bean Life Sciences Museum
9   Harris Fine Arts Center
10  Utah Valley Medical Center
11  Eyring Science Center & Planetarium
13  Museum of Peoples & Cultures
15  Pioneer Museum
16  Amtrak Station
23  East Bay Golf Course

In addition, the quality and reasonable prices of hotels make this a cheaper base than Salt Lake City and Park City.

## Orientation & Information

University Ave (Hwy 189), running north from I-15 exit 266, is the main drag through town. Center St, running east from I-15 exit 268, crosses University Ave at Provo's meridian (or zero) point. Don't confuse University Ave with University Parkway, which crosses University Ave at about 1600 N and leads to the university.

The Utah County Travel Council (☎ 370 8393), in the historic courthouse at 51 S University Ave, is open 8 am to 8 pm, Monday to Friday, and 10 am to 6 pm on weekends from Memorial Day to Labor Day. During the rest of the year, hours are 8 am to 5 pm, Monday to Friday. The Uinta National Forest Provo · Ranger Station (☎ 377 5780), 88 W 100 North, is

open 8 am to 5 pm, Monday to Friday. The city library (☎ 379 6650) is at 425 W Center St. The local newspaper is the *Daily Herald*. The post office (☎ 374 2000) is at 95 W 100 South. The medical center (☎ 373 7850) is at 1034 N 500 West. The police (☎ 379 6210; in emergencies ☎ 911) are at 351 W Center.

## Brigham Young University (BYU)

This campus (☎ 378 4636) is huge and has much of interest, not least of which is the sober appearance mandated by the student dress code – no cutoffs, long hair, bikinis or beards here! Visitors' parking is south of the Marriott Center, reached from University Parkway along 450 East. Near here is a Host Center (8 am to 5 pm, Monday to Friday) with campus information and tours (☎ 378 4678), 11 am and 2 pm, Monday to Friday. Campus highlights are described below.

The following museums are on campus and are all free. Most will give tours by appointment. Some restructuring of BYU museums is being planned – call ahead to confirm locations and hours. The **Harris Fine Arts Center** (☎ 378 2881) has two art galleries as well as interesting collections of rare musical instruments. Hours are 8 am to 5 pm, Monday to Friday. The **Monte L Bean Life Sciences Museum** (☎ 378 5051) has dioramas of Utahan and other wildlife. Hours are 10 am to 5 pm daily except Monday (to 9 pm) and Sunday (closed). The **Museum of Peoples & Cultures** (☎ 378 6112), located at the very southwest corner of campus, concentrates on Native Americans (including South Americans) and people of the Near East. Hours are 9 am to 5 pm, Monday to Friday. The **Earth Science Museum** (☎ 378 2232), at the northwest corner of campus, has an extensive dinosaur exhibit as well as others. Hours are 9 am to 9 pm on Monday, 9 am to 5 pm from Tuesday to Friday, and noon to 4 pm on Saturday. The **Eyring Science Center & Planetarium** (☎ 378 5396) has a free geology museum and occasional public planetarium programs. The entrance fee varies.

The university sponsors many artistic and athletic events including concerts (☎ 378 7444), theater (☎ 378 7447), dance (☎ 378 3384) and football, basketball, baseball and other sports (☎ 378 2981).

## McCurdy Historical Doll Museum

In addition to thousands of dolls in all kinds of costumes, this museum (☎ 377 9935), 246 N 100 East, has a doll shop and doll hospital. Hours are noon to 5 pm, Tuesday to Saturday, and admission is $2, or $1 for three- to 11-year-olds.

## Pioneer Museum

This historical museum (☎ 377 7078), 500 W 600 North, has Western art and local Indian and pioneer artifacts. Hours are 1 to 4 pm, Monday to Friday from Memorial Day to Labor Day. Call for other hours. Admission is free.

## Historic Buildings

Utah County Travel Council has a free brochure/map describing over 20 buildings. Among these is the **Utah County Courthouse**, 100 E Center St (within which the travel council office is located). Built in the 1920s, it's one of Utah's finest public buildings. There are several historic buildings along Center St and in Provo Town Square (Center St at University Ave) – the storefronts here retain a realistic early-20th century appearance. Construction on the **Mormon Tabernacle**, 100 S University Ave, began in 1883; the tabernacle is the site of organ recitals. Only Mormons on church business can enter the impressive, modern, sparkling white Mormon Temple that dominates the city to the northeast at 2200 N Temple Drive.

## Springville Museum of Art

This is considered one of Utah's best art museums with some galleries tracing the history of art in the state and others with a variety of changing exhibits. The grounds hold many sculptures. To reach the museum (☎ 489 2727), 126 E 400 South, Springville, go seven miles south on Hwy

89 (S State St). Hours are 10 am to 5 pm, Tuesday to Saturday, and 2 to 5 pm on Sunday; it may stay open till 9 pm on Wednesdays. Admission is free.

## Provo Bay

The bay is on the east side of Utah Lake, southwest of Provo. The marshes on the south side of the bay attract wetland birds such as white pelicans, white-faced ibis, ducks, geese and herons. They are also seen in the waterfowl management area on the north shore, just east of the municipal airport. The birds take up residence from March to November; April and November are the best months.

For the south side, drive west from I-15 exit 263 for about four miles on Hwy 77. At the Spanish Fork River bridge, a dirt road leads north to the marsh. There are trails. For the north side, go west on W Center St, then south on 1600 W or 3110 W.

## Seven Peaks Resort Water Park

At the east end of Center St, this park (☎ 377 7717, 373 8777) has dozens of wave makers slides, tubes, twists, and pools – even the world's tallest water slide. There are picnic areas and sports facilities,

The great blue heron can be as tall as four feet.

including an ice-skating rink and an 18-hole golf course. It's open from Memorial Day to Labor Day and charges $12 for 10- to 60-year-olds, $9 for four- to nine-year-olds. Babies and seniors are free. Hours are 10:30 am to 8:30 pm Monday to Saturday and to 6:30 pm on Sunday.

### Utah Lake State Park
The largest body of freshwater in the state, Utah Lake offers fishing, boating and swimming in its 150 sq miles. The state park includes several hundred yards of shoreline and has boat launching areas; it also encompasses the mouth of the Provo River, where canoeing is popular. In winter, there is an ice-skating rink, ice fishing and cross-country skiing.

The state park (☎ 375 0733, 375 0731) is at 4400 W Center St (the west end of Center St). There is a visitors center and showers. Day use is $3; camping from March to October costs $7 to $9. Make reservations at 1 (800) 322 3770.

### Golf
You can play a round at several public courses: Seven Peaks Resort (☎ 375 5155, see above); East Bay Golf Club (☎ 379 6612), 434 E 1860 South (27 holes); and Cascade Fairways (☎ 225 6677), 1313 E 800 North, Orem (nine holes).

### Special Events
The year's main event is Freedom Days, which begins about the third week in June. Festivities include sports contests, a carnival, music and arts events, a parade and a grand fireworks display on the Fourth of July. Other events of note are an important national art show in April and a quilt show in June – both at the Springville Museum of Art.

### Places to Stay
If you want to camp near Provo, you have a variety of private and public sites to choose from. In addition to the campgrounds listed, also see the state parks in this chapter. Hotel prices tend to be a little higher in summer. The following prices are approximate.

### Places to Stay – camping
*Provo KOA* (☎ 375 2994), 320 N 2050 West, charges from $13.50 for tent sites to $19.25 for RV sites with full hookups, and has two Kamping Kabins for $25 a double. Amenities include a pool, showers, grocery store and coin laundry. *Lakeside Campground* (☎ 373 5267), 4000 W Center St (near Utah Lake, see above), charges from $12 for tents to $17 for RVs with hookups. Fee includes use of a pool, showers, play areas, grocery store, coin laundry and canoe rental. *Silver Fox RV Resort* (☎ 377 0033), 101 W 1500 South, charges $12 to $16 and has showers, a pool and coin laundry.

The Uinta National Forest Pleasant Grove Ranger Station (☎ 785 3563), 390 N 100 East, Pleasant Grove, 84062, 10 miles north of Provo, administers most of the local USFS campgrounds northeast of Provo. The nearest is *Hope Campground*, six miles northwest on Hwy 189, then four miles south on USFS Rd 27. It's open late May to late September, has water but no showers or hookups and costs $5.

The Spanish Fork Ranger Station (☎ 798 3571), 44 W 400 North Spanish Fork, 84660, eight miles south of Provo, administers four USFS campgrounds along USFS Rd 058 and other roads in Hobble Creek Canyon east of Springville. They are open in summer only and have water. Fees are $5 to $7; distances are seven to about 30 miles east of Springville.

### Places to Stay – bottom end
*Hotel Roberts* (☎ 373 3400), 192 S University Ave, is a funky but decent old hotel dating from the late 1800s. Basic rooms are about $19/24 for singles/doubles with bath, or $12/15 with shared bath down the creaky hall. The hotel won't take reservations for the cheapest rooms, which are often full.

All the following provide simple but clean budget rooms and (with the exception

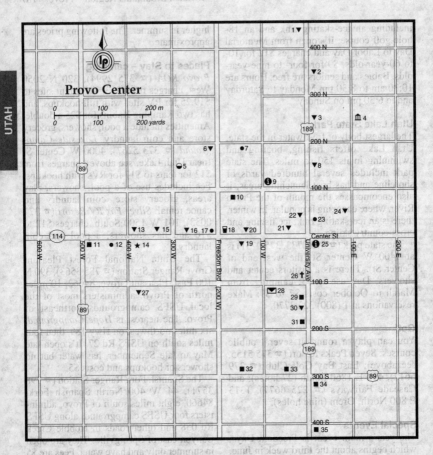

**Provo Center**

of the Super 8 Motel) have pools. *Motel 6* (☎ 375 5064), 1600 S University Ave, charges $27/33 for singles/doubles. The *Uptown Motel* (☎ 373 8248), 469 W Center St, is quite nice and charges $28/36 for singles/doubles or $5 more with a kitchenette. The *Super 8 Motel* (☎ 375 8766, 1 (800) 800 8000, fax 377 7569), 1288 S University Ave, charges $32.88/36.88 for singles/doubles. Others in the low $30s include the *City Center Motel* (☎ 373 8489), 150 W 300 South, and the *Best Value Western Inn* (☎ 373 0660, fax 373 5182), 40 W 300 South. Both have some

rooms with kitchenettes. The *Travelodge* (☎ 373 1978, 1 (800) 255 3050), 124 S University Ave, is about the same as the preceding places but charges several dollars more.

Other bottom end places to try are the following, both in Orem: the *Hillcrest Motel* (☎ 224 0824), 1675 S State, and the *L&L Motel* (☎ 225 3784), 963 N State.

### Places to Stay – middle

The *National 9 Colony Inn Suites* (☎ 374 6800, 1 (800) 524 9999, fax 374 6803), 1380 S University Ave, provides a good

**PLACES TO STAY**

| 10 | Provo Park Hotel |
|----|------------------|
| 11 | Uptown Motel |
| 29 | Travelodge |
| 31 | Hotel Roberts |
| 32 | City Center Motel |
| 33 | Best Value Western Inn |
| 34 | Best Western Columbian Motel |
| 35 | Whitney House B&B |

**PLACES TO EAT**

| 1 | Paris/New York Grill |
|---|---------------------|
| 2 | JB's |
| 3 | Govinda's Buffet |
| 6 | Coachman's Diner & Pancake House |
| 8 | Clair's Cafe |
| 10 | Mingles |
| 13 | Mi Rancherito |
| 15 | El Salvador Restaurant |
| 16 | Cafe Viet Hoa |
| 19 | Sensuous Sandwich |
| 20 | Deb's Deli |
| 21 | Los Hermanos, Osaka |
| 22 | The Torch, The Underground |
| 24 | La Dolce Vita |
| 27 | Victorian Rose |
| 30 | Annie's Pantry |

**OTHER**

| 4 | McCurdy Historical Doll Museum |
|---|-------------------------------|
| 5 | Greyhound Bus Depot |
| 7 | Mann 4 Central Square Theater |
| 9 | Ranger Station |
| 12 | Library |
| 14 | Police |
| 17 | LeMars Nightclub |
| 18 | ABG's Libation Emporium |
| 23 | Academy Theater |
| 25 | Utah County Courthouse & Travel Council |
| 26 | LDS Tabernacle |
| 28 | Post Office |

value considering its amenities. There are kitchenettes in the rooms, as well as a pool, spa, sauna, coin laundry and an adjacent restaurant. Comfortable rooms with one bed are about $36/40, or $50 with two beds, and you can arrange weekly discounts. The *East Bay Inn* (☎ 374 2500, 1 (800) 326 0025, fax 373 1146), 1292 S University Ave, is also about this price range and offers a pool, spa, restaurant, games and exercise area. The similarly priced *Safari Motel* (☎ 373 9672), 25 S

University Ave, has a pool, sauna and spacious rooms, some with kitchenettes.

The following places have comfortable, pleasant rooms and charge in the $50s or $60s for a double room in summer. All have a pool. The small Best Western *Columbian Motel* (☎ 373 8973, 1 (800) 321 0055), 70 E 300 South, offers in-room coffee. The Best Western *Rome Inn* (☎ 375 7500, fax 373 9700), 1200 S University Ave, offers a free continental breakfast. The *Days Inn* (☎ 375 8600, 1 (800) 325 2525, fax 374 6654), 1675 N 200 West, also includes continental breakfast. The *Marriott Fairfield Inn* (☎ 377 9500, fax 377 9591), 1515 S University Ave, has a spa and exercise room and includes continental breakfast. The *Holiday Inn* (☎ 374 9750, fax 373 4451), 1460 S University Ave, has a kids' pool and a restaurant with room service.

The *Whitney House B&B* (☎ 377 3111), 415 S University Ave, 84601, which dates from 1898, is on the National Register of Historic Places. There are four rooms, three upstairs with queen- or king-size beds and antique claw-foot tubs (with shower). The fourth room is the basement 'Hideaway', which has a double bed, private bath and sitting room with private rear entrance. Upstairs rooms are $60, and the 'Hideaway' is $55; there are discounts for midweek or multi-night stays. A full breakfast is included, and no smoking is allowed inside the house.

The *Kearns Hotel* (☎ /fax 489 0737), 94 W 200 South, Springville (six miles south of Provo) is another historic building, built in 1892 and also on the Historical Register. The hotel has four rooms, plus two mini-suites and three full suites with kitchenettes. The decor is Victorian. Rates (including continental breakfast) are $60 to $70 for a room, $85 for a mini-suite and $105 to $125 for a full suite.

### Places to Stay – top end

The *Comfort Inn* (☎ 374 6020, 1 (800) 221 2222, fax 374 0015), 1555 N Canyon Rd, is set in pleasant grounds next to BYU. Facilities include a pool, spa, gift shop and coin

UTAH

laundry, and the $60/70 room rates (which go up for special BYU events) include continental breakfast. There are a few honeymoon suites with private spa for $125. Restaurants are nearby, though none are on the premises.

The Best Western *Cotton Tree Inn* (☎ 373 7044, fax 375 5240), 2230 N University Parkway, is set in attractively landscaped grounds along the Provo River. Some rooms have balconies and river views. There is a pool, spa, coin laundry and restaurant. Rooms are $65/75, and there are a few suites for up to $150.

The *Provo Park Hotel* (☎ 377 4700, 1 (800) 777 7144, fax 377 4708), 101 W 100 North, is easily the most comfortable hotel in town. Hotel facilities include a pool, spa, sauna, exercise room, restaurant, lounge bar/nightclub and gift shop. Rates are about $75/90 for single/double rooms; suites range from $125 to $300.

## Places to Eat

Many Provo restaurants are closed on Sundays. The area around Provo Town Square (Center St at University Ave) has interesting early buildings with many restaurants to choose from.

**American (more or less)** *Annie's Pantry* (☎ 373 3900), 150 S University Ave, is a small family restaurant open from 6 am daily – a good choice for American breakfast. It also serves lunch and dinner. If you like breakfast at the counter of a basic hole-in-the-wall diner, try *Clair's Cafe*, 154 N University Ave, open from 7 am to 2:30 pm, Monday to Friday. You may prefer breakfast (or any other meal) served by attentive waiters in an elegant setting, which you'll find at *Mingles* (☎ 377 4700), in the top-end Provo Park Hotel. It has a varied American menu, is open daily from 6:30 am to 10 pm and does a good Sunday brunch for $11.

If you just want reasonably priced American food in a family restaurant, try *Coachman's Dinner & Pancake House* (☎ 374 1265), 175 N 200 West, which is open daily from 7:30 am to 10:30 pm (to 8:30 pm on

Sunday) and serves breakfast anytime. *Waldon Cove* (☎ 375 1345), 2230 N University Parkway in the Best Western Cotton Tree Inn, is handy for the BYU area and serves steaks and seafood for lunch and dinner (closed Sundays). Or there's always unremarkable but affordable *JB's* (☎ 375 1133), 366 N University Ave, which is open from 6:30 am to midnight daily (or later on Friday and Saturday). Starving? Economizing? Fill up at *Chuck-A-Rama* (☎ 375 0600), 1081 S University Ave, which has a variety of all-you-can-eat specials.

For lighter fare, *Deb's Deli* (☎ 373 9811), 110 W Center St, makes sandwiches from 9 am to 10 pm daily. Another good sandwich shop is the *Sensuous Sandwich* (☎ 377 9244), 163 W Center St, which is closed on Sundays. The *Victorian Rose* (☎ 373 5356), 383 W 100 South, serves soups, salads, sandwiches and dessert for lunch only – it's located in a shop that sells gift items for women. *Govinda's Buffet* (☎ 375 0404), 260 N University Ave, serves vegetarian and organic meals from 11 am to 2 pm and 5 to 8:30 pm, Monday to Saturday.

A local favorite is *The Underground* (☎ 377 5044), 55 N University Ave. The underground setting is reminiscent of a Prohibition-era speakeasy – there's even dining in a couple of antique cars. It has inexpensive soup 'n sandwich lunch specials and a variety of American, Italian and Mexican dinners in the $9 to $15 range. It's open from 11 am to 10:30 pm, Monday to Thursday, and to midnight on Friday and Saturday.

The *Paris/New York Grill* (☎ 377 4545), 463 N University Ave, is a little more upscale and presents a French/American menu with some Italian dishes. It's open from 11 am to 10 pm, Monday to Friday, and 4 to 10 pm on Saturday. *Magleby's* (☎ 374 6249), 1675 N 200 West in the Days Inn, is also upscale and handy for BYU. It specializes in fresh seafood, though it serves meat as well from 11 am to 10 pm, Monday to Thursday, to 11 pm on Friday, and 4 to 11 pm on Saturday. For desserts, head up to the *Carousel Ice Cream Parlor* (☎ 374 6667), 2250 N University Parkway. It's open from 11 am to midnight, Monday to Saturday.

**Latin American** I like *The Torch* (☎ 374 0202), 43 N University Ave, which serves Cuban food. Lunches are about $3 to $6, dinners are $6 to $12; it is open 11 am to 11 pm from Monday to Saturday (to midnight on weekends). Cheaper is the *El Salvador Restaurant* (☎ 377 9411), 332 W Center St. It serves the typical and inexpensive El Salvadoran snack, *pupusas*, which are thick corn tortillas stuffed with cheese or beans or occasionally something else – I love them. Other El Salvadoran and Mexican food is also served from 11:30 am to 10 pm, closed Sunday.

There are plenty of Mexican restaurants. *Los Hermanos* (☎ 375 6714), 16 W Center St, open from 11 am to 11 pm, Monday to Saturday, is the obvious Provo Town Square choice. It has musicians occasionally. Another good choice is *El Azteca* (☎ 373 9312), 746 E 820 North, which has been serving authentic Mexican food for over 30 years. Hours are 5 to 10 pm daily except Sunday. Also worth trying is *Mi Rancherito* (☎ 373 1503), 368 W Center St, open 11 am to 9:30 pm, Monday to Thursday, to 11 pm Friday and Saturday.

**Italian** *La Dolce Vita* (☎ 373 8482), 61 N 100 East, is one of the best. It is open 11 am to 10 pm daily except Sunday. Most meals are about $10 or less. Other Italian choices are the inexpensive *Viva Spaghetti* (☎ 374 5906), 1718 N University Parkway, handy for BYU visitors. It is open 11 am to 10 pm, Monday to Thursday, and to midnight on Friday and Saturday. The *Brick Oven* (☎ 374 8800), 150 E 800 North, is a good choice for pizza and has some pasta dishes. Its hours are 11 am to 11 pm, Monday to Thursday, and to 12:30 am on Fridays and Saturdays.

**Asian** *Cafe Viet Hoa* (☎ 373 8373), 278 W Center St, is a locally popular place serving both Vietnamese and Chinese meals. Lunch specials are around $4, with dinners in the $5 to $9 range. It's open from 11 am to 9:30 pm, Monday to Thursday, and to 10:30 pm on Friday and Saturday. Closer to BYU, there's *Formosa Garden Restaurant* (☎ 377 5654), 265 W 1230 North, specializing in Mandarin Chinese and Mongolian barbecue. Hours are 11 am to 9 pm, Monday to Thursday, to 10 pm on Friday and Saturday. Similar food is served at the simple *Taiwan Cafe* (☎ 373 0389), 2250 N University Parkway, from 11 am to 9:30 pm Monday to Thursday, to 11 pm Friday and Saturday, and 1 to 7 pm on Sunday. There are a dozen other Chinese restaurants in town.

More upscale dining is available at *Osaka* (☎ 373 1060), 46 W Center St, which serves traditional Japanese food and has 'shoji rooms' (private dining areas partitioned by sliding rice-paper screens). It has lunch specials from 11:30 am to 2:30 pm, dinners from 5 to 9:30 pm, closed Sunday.

### Entertainment
See a film at *Academy Theater* (☎ 373 4470), 56 N University Ave; *Mann 4 Central Square Theater* (☎ 374 6061), 175 W 200 North; or *Movies 8* (☎ 375 5667), 2424 N University Parkway.

See Brigham Young University above for telephone numbers to call for performing arts events on campus.

Because almost all BYU students are strict Mormons, bars aren't a big part of the entertainment scene. *ABG's Libation Emporium* (☎ 373 1200), 190 W Center St, is a tavern/restaurant open Monday to Saturday and with live music on Friday and Saturday. *LeMars Nightclub* (☎ 373 9014), 210 W Center St, is open daily and has live music from Thursday to Saturday nights.

### Getting There & Away
**Bus** Greyhound/Trailways (☎ 373 4211), 124 N 300 West, has two to four buses a day north and south along I-15. UTA (☎ 375 4636 or BUS INFO) has buses along University Ave going to Salt Lake

City and other local towns at least every hour during the week, but only three times on Sundays, and none on holidays.

**Train** Amtrak (1 (800) 872 7245) has an early morning train to Denver, Colorado, and points east, and a late evening train to Salt Lake City with connections to Los Angeles and San Francisco, California. The train station is at 600 S 300 West.

### Getting Around
You can rent bikes at the Highlander (☎ 377 3969), 1155 N Canyon Rd, Provo, and at Guy's Bike Shop (☎ 798 9479), 410 N Main St, Spanish Fork.

### LEHI
This small town is at the north end of Utah Lake. Most visitors stay in Provo (14 miles to the south) or Salt Lake City (30 miles to the north).

### Hutchings Museum of Natural History
The varied exhibits at this museum (☎ 768 8710), 685 N Center, offer a bit of everything – Indian and pioneer artifacts, art, fossils, minerals, bird and egg collections, etc. Hours are 9:30 am to 5:30 pm Monday to Saturday. Admission is $2, $1 for kids under 14.

### Saratoga Resort
Five miles southwest of Lehi, this resort (☎ 768 8206) is well suited to families. Several swimming pools are fed by warm mineral springs ($4 all day, $3 for three- to 12-year-olds). There is a huge water slide ($3 all day), children's carnival rides (all under $1), mini golf and boat launching areas.

The resort is open from Memorial Day to Labor Day. Facilities include a picnic area, snack bar and camping with showers ($8 to $11).

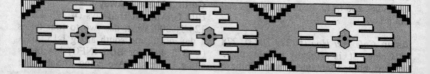

Assembly Hall in Salt Lake City, with the
Mormon Temple looming behind (TW)

A statue of Chief Massasoit in front of the
Utah State Capitol, Salt Lake City (RR)

Abandoned homestead in the New Harmony
Mountains (BW)

Phantom Valley in Zion National Park (BW)

Antique railcars at Golden Spike NHS (RR)

Fall colors ablaze in Rock Canyon (DS)

A summer storm descends upon Bryce Canyon National Park. (BW)

Vermillion Cliffs in southwestern Utah near Kanab (BW)

A magnificent formation in Kolob Canyon at the north end of Zion National Park (RR)

# Northern Utah

This chapter covers the area north of Ogden and the Great Salt Lake, and bordered by Idaho to the north. Geographically, the area has two distinct regions – one dry and desolate, the other mountainous and forested.

North and northwest of the Great Salt Lake, the land is very arid, saline and extremely barren with very few inhabitants – human or otherwise. This is some of the most desolate scenery in the southwestern USA, and even desert lovers are stunned by the sheer unlivability of the terrain. The remote area does attract visitors, however – they come to see where America's first transcontinental railroad was finally linked.

The countryside northeast of the Great Salt Lake, by contrast, is a scaled down continuation of the Wasatch Mountains region described in a previous chapter. Today, two small Mormon towns dominated by beautiful temples are overlooked by forest-clad mountains reaching over 9000 feet in elevation. Snow sports in winter, and camping, hiking and water sports in summer are the big attractions for northern Utahans. Visitors to the small towns of Brigham City and Logan will find them quintessential, old-fashioned American communities with strong Mormon ties.

# Brigham City & the Northwest Corner

## BRIGHAM CITY
Settled in 1851 by Mormons and originally named Box Elder, the town was soon renamed to honor Brigham Young, who gave his last public speech here before his death in 1877. Brigham City (population approximately 20,000) remains staunchly Mormon and today serves as an agricultural center, especially for the local orchards.

Brigham City is a pleasant town dominated by mountains rising immediately to the east. Although the region seems related more closely to this green and mountainous region, it is, in fact, the seat of Box Elder County, which encompasses the desolate region to the west. This odd pairing occurred simply because there are no (Utahan) settlements of any size west of Brigham City.

## Orientation & Information
Brigham City is two miles east of I-15 about 50 miles north of Salt Lake City. Main St runs north-south and is the main thoroughfare; its intersection with east-west Forest St forms the meridian, or zero, point.

The chamber of commerce (☎ 723 3931), 6 N Main St, is open from 9 am to noon and 1 to 4 pm, Monday to Friday. The library (☎ 723 5850) is at 26 E Forest St. The local weekly newspaper is the *Box Elder News & Journal*, appearing on Wednesday. The post office (☎ 723 5234) is at 16 S 100 West. The hospital (☎ 734 9471) is at 950 S 500 West. The police (☎ 723 3421; in emergencies ☎ 911) are at 20 N Main St.

## Brigham City Museum Gallery
This museum (☎ 723 6769), 24 N 300 West, has changing art shows and permanent exhibits of local history. Hours are 11 am to 6 pm, Tuesday to Friday, and 1 to 6 pm on Saturday. Admission is free.

## Mormon Tabernacle
If you're passing Brigham City on I-15, it's worth taking the short detour to see the city's tabernacle, built in 1896 to replace one destroyed by fire. With 16 spires and a steeple sweeping skywards, this church (☎ 723 5376), 251 S Main St, is considered one of the finest in Utah. It's open daily from 9 am to 9 pm; free tours are given from May to October.

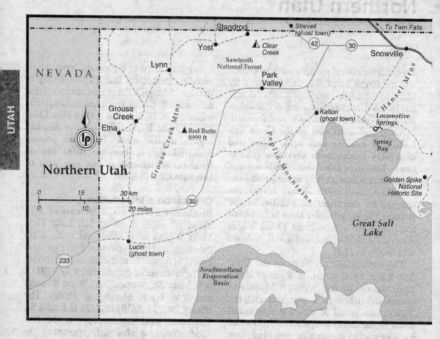

## Bear River Migratory Bird Refuge

A must for bird watchers, this refuge encompasses marshes on the northeastern shores of the Great Salt Lake, about 16 miles west of Brigham City via Forest St. The area is extremely important for many thousands of waterfowl, shorebirds and other birds that use the refuge, especially from August to November. Birds banded here have been recovered as far away as Siberia and Colombia.

Floods topped dikes in 1983 and subsequently destroyed all the buildings within the refuge. These are being rebuilt, but visitor facilities are still minimal. A 12-mile loop road is open for birding and photography, daily from 8 am to dusk.

Further information is available from the headquarters (☎ 723 5887), 866 S Main St, Brigham City, 84302.

## Scenic Drive

Take Hwy 89 east to the small community of Mantua (three miles), and ask for directions to USFS Rd 84, a dirt road heading south to Inspiration Point in the Wasatch-Cache National Forest. The road climbs the northern flanks of 9764-foot Willard Peak, reaching Inspiration Point (9422 feet, 17 miles from Brigham City), which offers fine views over the Great Salt Lake and, weather permitting, into Nevada and Idaho. 4WD is recommended, though high-clearance vehicles make it in dry weather.

## Crystal Springs

Built around natural hot springs, this facility includes a pool, water slide and a picnic area. The springs (☎ 279 8104), 10 miles north at 8215 N Hwy 69 in Honeyville, are open daily from late morning to evening; hours vary. Admission is $8, or less if you don't use the water slide. There is a campground open April to September with showers and a spa. Sites are $9 or $13 with hookups.

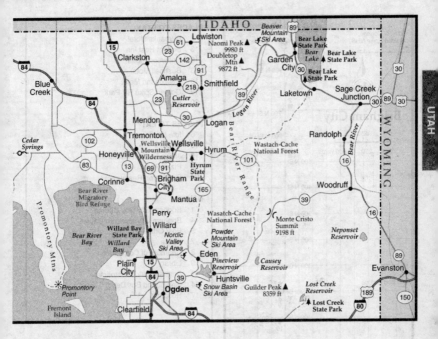

## Activities

Play **golf** at nine-hole Brigham City Golf Course (☎ 723 5301), 900 N Main St, or 18-hole Eagle Mountain (☎ 723 3212), 960 E 700 South. Just east of Mantua, the Mantua Reservoir is locally popular for **boating, water-skiing** and **fishing**.

## Special Events

From July to September, Hwy 89 south of Brigham City almost as far as Ogden becomes the Golden Spike Fruitway with scores of fruit stands lining the highway. Local orchards produce delicious fruit and give rise to Peach Days – the main annual event of the area, held since 1904. Peach Days happens the weekend after Labor Day and celebrates the end of the harvest with a parade, carnival, antique car show, arts and crafts, entertainment and so on.

Golden Spike Days is held locally during the first weekend in June with similar events.

## Places to Stay

**Camping** *Golden Spike RV Park* (☎ 723 8858), 1025 W 975 South, charges $11 a site or up to $16 for full hookups. There are a few 'cozy cottages' for $15. Facilities include a spa, showers, playground and coin laundry. *KOA* (☎ 723 5503), four miles south on Hwy 89, is open March to mid-November and charges $15 to $24 for none to full hookups. There are two Kamping Kabins for $24. Facilities include showers, pool, playground, coin laundry and a store. The USFS runs *Box Elder Campground* (☎ 753 2772, or 1 (800) 283 2267 for reservations), two miles south of Mantua. It's open mid-May through September. Sites are $6; there is water but no hookups or showers. Also see Crystal Springs above.

**Motels** Rates go up during special events. The run-down *Burbanks Motel* (☎ 723 7011), 759 N Main St, and the better

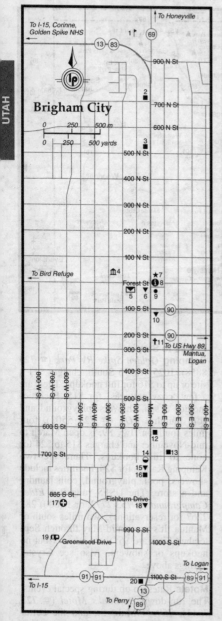

**PLACES TO STAY**

| | |
|---|---|
| 2 | Burbanks Motel |
| 3 | Budget Host Inn |
| 12 | Driftwood Motel |
| 13 | Bushnell Motel |
| 16 | Galaxie Inn Motel |
| 19 | Golden Spike RV Park |
| 20 | HoJo Inn |

**PLACES TO EAT**

| | |
|---|---|
| 6 | Idle Isle |
| 10 | Arturo's |
| 15 | J&D's Family Restaurant |
| 18 | Pizza Press |
| 20 | Red Baron Restaurant |

**OTHER**

| | |
|---|---|
| 1 | Brigham City Golf Course |
| 4 | Brigham City Museum Gallery |
| 5 | Post Office |
| 7 | Police |
| 8 | Chamber of Commerce |
| 9 | Library |
| 11 | Brigham City Tabernacle |
| 14 | Greyhound Bus Depot |
| 17 | Hospital |

*Driftwood Motel* (☎ 723 2218), 605 S Main St, are tiny, basic motels with only four or five rooms all in the $20s. The larger *Bushnell Motel* (☎ 723 8575), 115 E 700 South, has some rooms with kitchenettes and charges in the upper $20s and $30s.

The modern *Galaxie Motel* (☎ 723 3439), 740 S Main St, is next door to a family restaurant, has some units with kitchenettes, and charges in the $30s. The clean *Budget Host Inn* (☎ 723 8584), 505 N Main St, has rooms in the $30s or low $40s. The best in town is the *HoJo Inn* (☎ 723 8511, 1 (800) 446 4656, fax 723 8511), 1167 S Main St, which has a pool, spa, refrigerators in many rooms and an adjoining restaurant. Rates include continental breakfast and are about $43/47 for singles/doubles in summer and a few dollars less in winter.

About 10 miles northeast on Hwy 89/91, near Wellsville, is the *Sherwood Hills Resort* (☎ 245 6424, 1 (800) 772 4209, fax

245 6581). Amenities include three pools, spas, saunas, horse rental, golf and tennis. There is a good restaurant open daily for breakfast, lunch and dinner. During the summer, the resort presents outdoor theater and musical revues and regularly hosts murder mystery dinners – call for dates and details. Rooms range from the $50s to the $80s; honeymoon and other suites are about $120.

### Places to Eat
A fun stop for inexpensive breakfast, lunch or dinner is the family-run *Idle Isle* (☎ 734 9062), 24 S Main St. It has an old-fashioned soda fountain and homemade desserts and candies. The *Red Baron Restaurant* (☎ 723 3100), 1167 S Main St in the HoJo Inn, is a decent family restaurant open from 7 am to 10 pm, or 8 am to 8 pm on Sunday. It may close on Tuesdays out of season. *J&D's Family Restaurant* (☎ 723 3811), 720 S Main St, has a varied American and kid's menu and is open 6 am to 9 pm. *Pizza Press* (☎ 723 7900, 723 5752), 868 S Main St, offers pizza and a salad bar from 11 am to 10 pm Monday to Thursday, and to 11 pm Friday and Saturday. It offers delivery service to your room. *Arturo's* (☎ 723 1304), 131 S Main St, serves Mexican lunches and dinners daily except Sunday.

The best in town is not in town – it's in Perry, two miles south on Hwy 89. *Maddox Ranch House* (☎ 723 8545), 1900 S Hwy 89, serves chicken, steak and seafood in a Western ranch setting from 11 am to 9:30 pm Tuesday to Saturday. There's a kids' menu and sometimes entertainment on weekends.

### Entertainment
See a movie at the *Capitol Theater* (☎ 723 3113), 53 S Main St, or *Walker Cinemas IV* (☎ 723 6661), 1776 S Hwy 89, in Perry.

Also in Perry, the *Heritage Theater* (☎ 723 8392), 2505 S Hwy 89, presents plays and musicals.

### Getting There & Away
The Greyhound bus (☎ 723 8519), 704 S Main St, comes through two or three times a day on its runs up and down I-15.

## TREMONTON
This small agricultural town (population 5000), about 14 miles northwest of Brigham City, is at the intersection of I-15 (north to Pocatello, Idaho) with I-84 (northwest to Boise, Idaho). It has a small museum and is host to the Box Elder County Fair & Rodeo held the fourth weekend in August. The County Fair Office (☎ 257 5366) has more information or call the community center (☎ 257 3371), 150 S Tremont St, for city information.

The tiny *Marble Motel* (☎ 257 3524), 116 N Tremont St, has adequate singles/doubles for about $25/30. The better *Sandman Motel* (☎ 257 5675, 257 5676), 585 W Main St, charges $30/35 in summer, less in winter. The best is the *Western Inn* (☎ 257 3399), 2301 W Main St, which charges $36/40. Nearby, *Denny's* (☎ 257 1919), 2341 W Main St, serves breakfast, lunch and dinner. Two local cafes are *The Bear's Den* (☎ 257 7428), 40 N 1600 East, and *Western Trail Cafe* (☎ 257 3323), 59 W Main St. *Saigon Towers* (☎ 257 0443), 26 S Tremont St, serves Chinese food.

## GOLDEN SPIKE NATIONAL HISTORIC SITE
Between the 1830s and early 1860s, over 30,000 miles of railway track were laid in the USA – all east of the Missouri River. In 1863, work began on a transcontinental system. The Union Pacific Railroad was built westwards from Omaha, Nebraska, and the Central Pacific Railroad pushed eastwards from Sacramento, California. On 10 May 1869, the two railroads met at Promontory Summit and were linked by ceremonial golden spikes – now the nation could be crossed by train. The face of the American West was changed forever.

New tracks bypassed the site in 1903, and modern trains take a different route, but the historic site contains almost two miles of track laid on the original roadbed where the railroads were linked. Visitors can watch exact replicas of the original steam engines chugging along the tracks, and various talks and demonstrations of track-laying and life in the 1860s are given by folks in period costume. A 1.5-mile self-guided walk and a nine-mile self-guided auto tour are good opportunities for taking closer looks at the area. The visitors center has booklets describing the tours, audio-visual programs and exhibits about the history of the transcontinental railroad. There is a gift and book shop.

### Information

The headquarters (☎ 471 2209), PO Box 897, Brigham City, 84302, can confirm open dates and times, as well as those of special events.

The visitors center is open from 8 am to 6 pm from late May to early September and to 4:30 pm otherwise. It is closed on New Year's Day, Thanksgiving and Christmas.

Bob Dowty, chief engineer of
the locomotives, gives talks on the
railroad at Golden Spike NHS. (RR)

Steam train demonstrations happen at 10:30 am, 1:30, 3:30 and 5:30 pm from late May to early September and at 9:30 am, 1:30 and 4 pm in early May and September to mid-October. There are also steam demonstrations during the last weekend of the year. The rest of the year the trains don't run – it may be possible to look at them in the engine house with a ranger.

Admission is $4 per car or $2 per person, and there's no charge during special events and when the trains aren't running. Golden Age and Eagle passes are honored.

There are no camping sites nor restaurants. Picnic sites are available. Food vendors attend the special events.

The site is 32 miles west of Brigham City along paved and signed roads.

### Special Events

There is an annual reenactment of the Golden Spike Ceremony every 10 May. The annual Railroader's Festival takes place on the second Saturday of August with reenactments and a variety of events ranging from spike-driving contests to buffalo-chip throwing contests. (No, a buffalo chip is not a large french fry – it's an authentic, sun-dried buffalo turd especially imported from the herd in Antelope Island State Park.) The last weekend of the year sees the annual Railroader's Film Festival and Winter Steam Demonstration, with classic Hollywood railroading films.

From mid-March to mid-April, especially just after dawn, you may see sage and sharp-tailed grouse performing court-ship rituals in the sagebrush areas near the visitors center.

### AROUND GOLDEN SPIKE NHS

About five miles east of Golden Spike, a turnoff to the south leads to **Promontory Point**. A 40-mile road, half paved and half gravel, follows the eastern coast of the Promontory Mountains Peninsula – the biggest land mass jutting into the Great Salt Lake. There are fine views of the lake and the Wasatch Mountains behind. The road has no facilities, and the southernmost point is private.

Adventurous drivers can follow the old **Central Pacific Railroad** bed for about 90 miles to the west through uninhabited desert. A dirt and gravel road heads west from Golden Spike NHS and passes Locomotive Springs National Waterfowl Management Area, goes through the ghost town Kelton, climbs over the steep Peplin Mountains, and emerges at the ghost town Lucin near the Nevada border. Parts of the drive (particularly over the Peplin Mountains) require 4WD; some parts may be passable to cars in good weather. The section in the best condition is between Locomotive Springs and Kelton, both of which can be reached by decent gravel roads from the north. The area is remote; it's rarely traveled (not marked on many maps), and drivers must carry emergency food and water, spare tires, fuel, etc. Occasional 'Scenic Backway' signs point the way.

The small community of **Corinne** is about five miles before Brigham City on the way back from Golden Spike NHS. Corinne used to be an important railroad town, and several 19th-century buildings can be seen, including the Methodist Church built in 1870 and considered Utah's oldest non-Mormon church.

If, instead of returning to Brigham City, you take Hwy 83 north to I-84, you'll see **Thiokol**, a rocket manufacturing plant spread out over several square miles. Windowless buildings, countless 'No Trespassing' signs, occasional glimpses of rockets and miles of forbidding fencing give the area a somewhat menacing air.

## THE NORTHWESTERN MOUNTAINS

From Snowville, Utah's northernmost town on I-84, paved Hwy 30 cuts across the northwestern corner of the state on its 90-mile run to the Nevada border, passing several mountain ranges. Rock hounds roam some slopes, looking for variquoise in the Hansel Mountains south of Snowville and variscite in the Grouse Creek Mountains north of Lucin.

In the Raft River Mountains, there's a free campground in the Sawtooth National Forest at Clear Creek, open from June to October. Water is available from springs. Reach the campground from Strevell on Hwy 42, a mile into Idaho, from where there is a signed gravel road for Yost and Clear Creek, about 10 miles south of Strevell. Hiking, exploration by 4WD vehicle and wildlife observation are all possible activities. Most of the Sawtooth National Forest is in Idaho; for more information, contact the USFS at (☎ (208) 737 3200), 2747 Kimberley Rd East, Twin Falls, Idaho 83301-7976.

Tiny **Snowville** (population 250) has the *Outsiders Inn* (☎ 872 8293, fax 872 8183), 60 S Main St, with a restaurant, spa and rooms for around $30. The only settlement along Hwy 30 to Nevada is even tinier **Park Valley**, where there is the simple *Overland Trail Motel* (☎ 871 4755), with rooms also about $30. There is a cafe open from Monday to Saturday, and a gas station/convenience store.

After Hwy 30 crosses into Nevada, it becomes Hwy 233 and continues another 35 miles to I-80, from where it is another 32 miles back to Utah at Wendover, which is described in the chapter on western Utah.

# Bridgerland

## LOGAN

Logan, with a population of nearly 40,000, is the Cache County seat and the largest town in northern Utah. The drive northeast of Logan through Logan Canyon is very scenic and especially popular in the fall for the beautiful colors. Legend has it that the local Shoshone Indians called it 'the house of the Great Spirit' long before the White man recognized the valley's beauty.

Founded by Mormons in 1859, the city quickly became an important agricultural center. In 1888, Utah State University was founded here, although it was originally known as the Agricultural College of Utah. During the late 1800s, many other important buildings were constructed and can still be seen by the curious visitor. Not the least of these is the magnificent Mormon Temple, which dominates the city.

Agriculture continues to fuel the economy. Ranching and dairy farming are important, and Cache Valley cheeses can be bought in the supermarkets of many western states. There is also a meat packing plant and some light industry. The tourist industry is growing; visitors come for the beautiful scenery, historical setting and local cultural activities.

## Orientation & Information

Main St (Hwy 91), the main thoroughfare, runs north-south. Center St is the east-west intersection at the meridian point. 400 N (Hwy 89) eastbound leads into scenic Logan Canyon.

The chamber of commerce (☎ 752 2161), 160 N Main St, 84321, is open 8 am to 5 pm from Monday to Friday and Saturday in summer. The Wasatch-Cache National Forest Logan Ranger Station (☎ 753 2772), 860 N 1200 East, 84321, is open 8 am to 4:30 pm from Monday to Friday. The library (☎ 750 9870) is at 225 N Main St. The local newspaper is *The Cache Citizen*. The post office (☎ 752 7246) is at 151 N 100 West. The hospital (☎ 752 2050) is at 1400 N 500 East. The police (☎ 750 9900; in emergencies ☎ 911) are at 45 W 200 North.

## Historic Main Street

Many turn-of-the-century buildings are found on or just off the three blocks of Main St between 200 N and 100 S. The building at 160 N Main St was originally the US

Federal Building but now houses both the chamber of commerce (which has self-guided walk leaflets for 14 or more buildings on the street) and the **DUP Museum** with local historical exhibits. They are open on summer afternoons, Tuesday to Friday, and other times by arrangement; call the chamber for information.

Opposite, at 179 N Main St, is the **County Courthouse**, built in 1883 and Utah's oldest county building still being used for its original purpose. Its cupola has been restored.

A block south, in a park-like setting, is the Mormon **Tabernacle**, built between 1865 and 1891. The building has been restored, and the public is welcome; tours are given in summer. The thrifty and dedicated Mormon community was using the building for meetings two decades before its completion.

The **Capitol Theater**, 43 S Main St, dates from 1923, and once again is being used for performances, after other uses in its past. Similarly, the **Lyric Theater**, 28 W Center St, dates from 1913 and boasts a ghost as well as repertory arts. A favorite building on the walk is the **Bluebird Restaurant**, 28 N Main St, which was begun in 1914 and has been operating since 1923. It is described under Places to Eat.

## Mormon Temple

Built between 1877 and 1884, the temple is Utah's third oldest; reputedly 25,000 people worked on it. Although it is open only to Mormons on church business, the visitor cannot miss the massive, 170-foot tall, twin-towered building, which is perched on a green hilltop and visible from many parts of Logan. You are welcome to walk the grounds around the temple at 175 N 300 East.

## Utah State University

About 16,000 students and 2000 staff enliven Logan's cultural scene. The campus is famous for **Old Main**, the late 19th-century center of university life. The **Taggart Student Center** has an informa-

---

**Jim Bridger**

This area is locally nicknamed 'Bridgerland' after the exploits of Jim Bridger (1804-1881), a mountain man who trapped in this area well before the arrival of the Mormons and who, in 1824, was the first White man to see the Great Salt Lake. His interactions with the local Indians were unusual in that he learned to speak the Ute language as well as several others.■

tion desk (☎ 750 1710), restaurants serving the locally popular student-made Aggie Ice Cream and other meals, a movie theater and other services. The **Nora Eccles Harrison Museum of Art** (☎ 750 1412) has both permanent exhibits and changing shows in various media. It is open on most days; call for hours. Admission is free.

The university has many concerts, festivals and sports events; call 750 1657 for date and ticket information.

### Alliance for the Varied Arts

This art space (☎ 753 2970), 43 S Main St, has changing shows of regional and national artists. Receptions with refreshments, free to the public, are held every few weeks at the start of each new show.

### Willow Park Zoo

The small zoo and aviary (☎ 750 9893), 400 W 700 South, are open daily from 8 am to dusk. Admission is free. Picnic and playground areas are available.

### Cheese Factories

The Logan area produces most of Utah's cheese, and some factories are open for tours. See Things to Buy below.

### Activities

You can **golf** a round at the new Logan River Golf Course (☎ 750 0123), one mile south on Hwy 89/91. The 18-hole Birch Creek Golf Course (☎ 563 6825) is seven miles north in Smithfield. The Community Recreation Center (☎ 750 9877), 195 S 100 West, has tennis, racquetball, gym, sauna and so on. **Swim** at the Municipool (☎ 750 9890) at 114 E 1000 North. **Snowmobiling** is popular in the Logan area. Rent or buy snowmobiles at Time Rental Sales & Service (☎ 752 8652), 925 N Main St.

### Special Events

**Festival of the American West** This major annual event is an eight-day happening beginning the last Friday in July. Sponsored by Utah State University, the festival includes a historical pageant held every evening (except Sunday) with acting,

---

### How the West Was Named

The town and the river that flows through it were named after Ephraim Logan, a trapper who worked this area in the 1820s. The trappers used to cache their pelts until it was time to trade or sell them, and so the area became known as Cache Valley.■

---

dancing and singing. There is also a fair open daily (except Sunday) from 2 to 9 pm with Western entertainment, craft demonstrations, mountain men and Indians, food stands, etc. Admission is about $14 (half price for children) and includes one night at the pageant and two days at the fair. Advance tickets are sold at the university ticket office (☎ 750 1657).

**Other Events** Summerfest Art Fair brings arts & crafts booths to the tabernacle lawn every June. The Fourth of July is celebrated with many events on or close to the date, including a fireworks show in Logan and rodeos in neighboring Hyrum (seven miles south) and Lewiston (20 miles north). The Cache County Fair & Rodeo is held the first Thursday through Saturday in August; it has been held in Logan since 1892.

### Places to Stay – camping

*Bandit's Cove* (☎ 753 0508), 590 S Main St, which has showers, a coin laundry and mini golf, charges about $15 with hookups, $10 without, and less for a tent. *Riverside RV Park* (☎ 752 9830), 445 W 1700 South (east of Hwy 89/91), has showers and coin laundry and charges about $16 with hookups or $10 without. *Western Park* (☎ 752 6424), 350 W 800 South (enter via 600 South), has showers and charges a little less.

Hardware Ranch Rd, which leaves east from Hyrum as Hwy 101, enters Blacksmith Canyon after a few miles, and nine miles from Hyrum, it passes *Pioneer Campground*, run by the Wasatch-Cache National Forest. Open from May to October, the campground provides water and toilets for a $6 fee. Just west of

UTAH

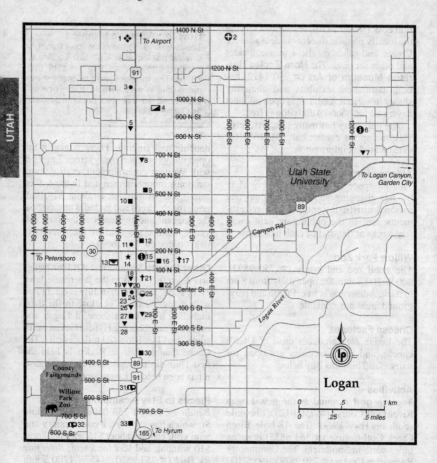

Logan

0        .5        1 km

0    .25        .5 miles

Pioneer, USFS Rd 055 heads north along the Left Fork of the Blacksmith, where there are two free USFS campgrounds, *Friendship* and *Spring*, which have toilets but no drinking water. Also see Hyrum State Park and Logan Canyon (detailed in Around Logan below).

### Places to Stay – bottom end

Many hotels have higher summer rates. The *Alta Motel* (☎ 752 6300), 51 E 500 North, has simple rooms in the low $30s in summer, $20s in winter. The *Zanavoo*

*Lodge* (☎ 752 0085), 2.5 miles up Logan Canyon, has rustic basic rooms (no TVs or telephones) for about $30. The motel recently opened some much nicer B&B rooms for about $100. The *Super 8 Motel* (☎ 753 8883, fax 753 2577), 865 S Main St, has clean rooms from $32.88/38.88 for singles/doubles.

### Places to Stay – middle

**B&Bs** *Center Street B&B* (☎ 752 3443), 169 E Center St, 84321, has 12 rooms and suites for adults in a totally nonsmoking

**PLACES TO STAY**

| | |
|---|---|
| 9 | Alta Motel & Alta Manor Suites |
| 10 | Comfort Inn |
| 12 | Weston Inn |
| 16 | Logan House Inn |
| 22 | Center Street B&B |
| 27 | Baugh Motel |
| 30 | Days Inn |
| 31 | Bandit's Cove Campground |
| 32 | Western Park Campground |
| 33 | Super 8 Motel |

**PLACES TO EAT**

| | |
|---|---|
| 5 | El Sol |
| 7 | Mildred's Restaurant, Frederico's Pizza |
| 8 | Angie's |
| 18 | Copper Mill |
| 19 | Glauser's Restaurant |
| 20 | The Bluebird |
| 26 | Gia's Restaurant, Pizza Factory |
| 28 | Cottage Restaurant |
| 29 | Garcia's |

**OTHER**

| | |
|---|---|
| 1 | Cache Valley Mall (Excellence Theaters) |
| 2 | Hospital |
| 3 | Mountain Farms Cheese |
| 4 | Municipool |
| 6 | Ranger Station |
| 11 | Library |
| 13 | Post Office |
| 14 | Police |
| 15 | Chamber of Commerce, DUP Museum |
| 17 | Logan Temple |
| 21 | Tabernacle Square |
| 23 | Country Friends, The White Owl |
| 24 | Capitol Theater (Ellen Eccles Theater) |
| 25 | Greyhound Bus Depot (Conoco Gas Station) |

environment. Part of the property dates to the 1800s; some rooms are decorated with period furniture, and others are modern. Rates include full breakfast. Rooms are about $45, and suites are $70 to $150. This is Logan's oldest B&B.

Two recently opened B&Bs that I haven't seen are the *Alta Manor Suites* (☎ 752 0808), 45 E 500 North, 84321, with eight large rooms for $75, and *Logan House Inn* (☎ 752 7727), 168 N 100 East, 84321, with five rooms from $80 to $150. Both advertise a spa.

**Hotels** The *Days Inn* (☎ 753 5623, fax 753 3357), 364 S Main St, has pleasant rooms for about $35/42 for singles/doubles and suites around $50. Some suites have kitchenettes and/or spas. The hotel has a pool, spa, coin laundry and free continental breakfast. The *Comfort Inn* (☎ 752 9141, fax 752 9273), 447 N Main St, has a pool, spa, exercise area and coin laundry. Spacious rooms are $40/48; suites with refrigerators and hydrojet tubs are $55.

The Best Western *Weston Inn* (☎ 752 5700, fax 752 9719), 250 N Main St, has a pool, spa, sauna, exercise room and coin laundry. It is at the north end of the most historic area of downtown. Good rooms are about $40/50.

The Best Western *Baugh Motel* (☎ 752 5220, 1 (800) 462 4154, fax 752 3251), 153 S Main St, located at the southern end of the historic district, is set in agreeable gardens with a pool, sun deck and picnic area. There is a restaurant open from 6 am to 10 pm daily, except on Sunday (8 am to 2 pm). Most rooms are about $40/50. A few suites with fireplaces, refrigerators or spas are about $60.

Also see the *Sherwood Hills Resort*, located between Logan and Brigham City and described under Brigham City.

**Places to Eat**
There are plenty of places to eat – the chamber of commerce has a handout listing over two dozen places on Main St alone. If you like a drink with your meal, be warned that most of Logan's restaurants don't serve booze. Many don't allow smoking either. Call ahead if you require these.

The favorite of many visitors is the 1920s-style *Bluebird Restaurant* (☎ 752 3155), 19 N Main St, which almost transports you into an early Hollywood movie. The back room has a wraparound mural of Logan's history and various antiques on display. It's not all hype – the building dates from 1914 and has been a restaurant since the 1920s. Hours are 8 am to 8 pm, Monday to Thursday, and to 10 pm on Friday and Saturday. It may be open 11 am to 4 pm on summer Sundays. Lunches are

$4 to $10; dinners are $8 to $15. Predictably, it serves traditional American fare.

Many locals favor *Angie's* (☎ 752 9252), 690 N Main St. Its atmosphere is the converse of The Bluebird – large, modern, squeaky clean and a little plastic looking, but it offers a decent selection of very reasonably priced American food. It is open 6 am to 8 pm every day, sometimes later in summer. A more atmospheric place for very inexpensive American family dining is *Glauser's Restaurant* (☎ 752 1681), 25 W Center, open 6 am to 9 pm, Monday to Saturday. *Mildred's* (☎ 753 7781), 1351 E 700 North, advertises 50 different hamburgers, from buffalo to vegetarian, as well as other meals. Hours are 11 am to 10 pm, Tuesday to Sunday.

The *Cottage Restaurant* (☎ 752 5260), 51 W 200 South, serves good American food ranging from sandwiches to steak and seafood in a old-fashioned, homey atmosphere. Prices range from $4 to $20; hours are 6 am to 10 pm daily except on Sunday (8 am to 2 pm). The *Copper Mill* (☎ 752 0647), 55 N Main St (top of the Emporium Building), specializes in prime beef and seafood (entrees in the teens) and some cheaper choices. There's a decent salad bar. It is open 11:30 am to 9:30 pm from Monday to Thursday, and to 10:30 pm on Friday and Saturday.

The best choices for Italian food are *Gia's Restaurant* (☎ 752 8384) and the *Pizza Factory* (☎ 752 9384), both at 119 S Main St. Gia's serves fine Italian lunches and dinners daily – but call about Sunday; the Factory has pizza from 11 am to 11 pm, Monday to Thursday, till midnight on Friday and Saturday, and shorter hours on Sunday. *Frederico's Pizza* (☎ 752 0130), 1349 E 700 North, is convenient to the university; it's open from 11 am to 10 pm daily, to 11 pm on Friday and Saturday.

If you want to try something a little more exotic, there's *Garcia's* (☎ 753 0777), 130 S Main St, which serves Mexican food and sometimes advertises an all-you-can-eat lunch buffet. It is open daily from 11 am to 11 pm, shorter hours on Sunday. *El Sol* (☎ 752 5743), 871 N Main St, is another inexpensive, daily Mexican choice. There are several Chinese restaurants along Main St as well.

Two out-of-town restaurants deserve a mention. The *Zanavoo Lodge* (☎ 752 0095), 2.5 miles out of town into Logan Canyon, serves satisfying American dinners in a rustic setting; open daily except Sunday. *Mendon Station Restaurant* (☎ 752 2570), 95 N Main St in Mendon, eight miles west of Logan, serves good steak and seafood dinners from Tuesday to Saturday. Enjoy the old train station surroundings after a hike in the Wellsville Mountains (see Around Logan below).

### Entertainment

Catch a movie at the *Excellence Theaters* (☎ 752 7762), 1300 N Main St, in the Cache Valley Mall or the *Cinema Theater* (☎ 753 1900), 60 W 100 North. Utah State University shows 'alternative' movies at the Student Union (☎ 750 1710) during the school year.

Also call the university ticket office (☎ 750 1657) for details of cultural events throughout the year – during the summer some of these are held at the 1913 *Lyric Theater*, 28 W Center St. The almost as old *Capitol Theater* (also known as the Ellen Eccles Theater) (☎ 753 6518), 43 S Main St, presents a variety of performing arts during the summer.

For a beer, head over to *Country Friends* (☎ 753 9943), 22 W Center St, or, almost next door, *The White Owl* (☎ 752 4059), 36 W Center St. The Owl has a pool table.

### Things to Buy

Utah produces 10% of the USA's hard cheese, and this is Utah's major cheese manufacturing area. *Mountain Farms Cheese* (☎ 753 8658), 1124 N Main St, advertises over 100 varieties. Cheese factories that both welcome visitors and sell cheese and dairy products include *Gossner Foods* (☎ 752 9365), 1000 W 1000 North, and *Cache Valley Cheese*

(☎ 563 3281, 563 3550), in Amalga, about 10 miles north of Logan. Both can arrange tours – call ahead.

## Getting There & Away

**Air** Logan Cache Airport (☎ 752 5955) can arrange charters or rentals; no commercial flights.

**Bus** Greyhound (☎ 752 4921), 18 E Center St (in the Conoco Gas Station), has a daily evening bus to Salt Lake City (1.5 hours, $10) and a couple of buses a day up to Idaho.

## AROUND LOGAN

### R V Jensen Living Historical Farm

This 'American Family Farm – 1917' (☎ 245 4064) lies six miles southwest of Logan on S Hwy 89/91 in Wellsville. Run by university students in period clothing, the farm operates as it would have in 1917. Visitors are welcome to tour the historic buildings, watch the daily use of antique farm implements and enjoy the animals.

There are scheduled special events such as sheepshearing by hand, horseshoeing, threshing grain with a steam engine, etc. Events are also scheduled for many Saturdays during the year – call for dates. The farm is open 10 am to 4 pm, Tuesday to Saturday, June through August. Adult admission is $2, $1 for seniors and students, and 50¢ for kids under 14.

### Wellsville Mountains

This is reputedly the highest range in the world rising from such a narrow base, so there are no roads and only a few steep trails up the almost vertical sides. The area is in the Wasatch-Cache National Forest (call Logan Ranger Station for information and maps). Hikers must carry water and know what they are doing. There are no campsites, and wilderness camping is permitted but not recommended, due to scarcity of flat areas and water, and the high exposure.

Access is from the small town of **Mendon** (elevation 4435 feet), 10 miles west of Logan. From Mendon, drive two miles west on 300 North to park at the trailhead (5400 feet). The trail switchbacks three miles up to the ridge (8100 feet) with excellent views. From here a trail goes northwest for about a mile to a vista point (8585 feet) that is one of Utah's best hawk-watching spots during fall migration, which peaks in September. Golden eagles and many other raptors have been recorded.

Alternatively, follow the ridge southeast two miles to Stewart Pass (8400 feet) from where a trail drops eastwards to the Coldwater Lake trailhead (6000 feet, about two miles) from where a dirt road returns to Mendon (3.5 miles). Or from Stewart Pass continue south along the ridge to the highest points, Wellsville Cone (9356 feet, about 1.5 miles) and Box Elder Peak (9372 feet, a further mile). Many fossils, especially coral, have been found at Wellsville Cone.

### Hyrum State Park

Seven miles south of Logan near the small town of **Hyrum** (places to eat, but no hotels) is this park on Hyrum Reservoir, locally popular for fishing, boating, waterskiing and camping in summer. In winter, ice fishing and snowmobiling are the things to do.

The Ranger Station (☎ 245 6866) is at 405 W 300 South, Hyrum, 84319. There are picnic areas, boat launch areas, and campsites with toilets and water, but no showers. Day use is $3, camping is $7 from April to November. Reservations for busy summer weekends can be made by calling 1 (800) 322 3770.

### Hardware Ranch Rd

This road, which leaves east from Hyrum as Hwy 101, is a designated 'Scenic Backway'. After a few miles it enters Blacksmith Canyon, where there are spots to fish for trout along the Blacksmith Fork of the Bear River. Just west of Pioneer Campground, USFS Rd 055 heads north along the Left Fork of the Blacksmith, where the USFS runs two free campgrounds, *Friendship* and *Spring*. There are many primitive roads and hiking trails in the area. During fall, the brilliant foliage colors make Blacksmith Canyon a popular and attractive drive.

In winter, there are **snowmobile trails** in the canyon. The paved road is plowed for the 18 miles between Hyrum and Hardware Ranch, which is a game management area and the center of an extensive snowmobile trail network. With the arrival of snow, 700 head of elk (Utah's state animal) are fed at the ranch, and there are sleigh rides to view the animals from January to March. A visitors center (☎ 245 3131) has information, exhibits and a snack bar. In spring, the elk move off into the forest.

Forest service roads north of Hardware Ranch lead to Bear Lake Summit on Hwy 89 (see Logan Canyon below), a distance of about 25 miles. Follow USFS Rd 054 and USFS Rd 055, but be aware that these dirt roads become impassable after wet weather or spring thaw. Fall colors are lovely along here too. The roads become groomed snowmobile trails in winter.

The male elk has an antler span of up to five feet.

## LOGAN CANYON SCENIC DRIVE

Logan Canyon (Hwy 89) northeast of Logan is one of Utah's best-known scenic areas: Indians, mountain men, fur trappers and Mormon pioneers all noted its beauty. Today, Hwy 89 is used by countless drivers in the summer to visit Bear Lake and/or continue to Yellowstone and Grand Teton National Parks in Wyoming. Likewise, fall travelers admire spectacular foliage colors splashing the steep limestone walls of the canyon. In the winter, many take this road to ski, snowmobile or continue on to the famous ski resort of Jackson Hole, Wyoming. Many hiking trails, dirt roads, fishing spots, campgrounds and picnic areas line the 40 mile drive through Logan Canyon to Bear Lake.

The drive begins as Hwy 89 crosses the Logan River at the east end of town and enters the canyon. There are several geological and historic markers along the road – just pull over to read them. There are also plenty of fishing and picnicking spots. Good stopping places include the following:

**Riverside Nature Trail** This locally popular bird-watching trail follows the south side of Logan River from the canyon entrance for almost five miles. There are seven entry/exit points to Hwy 89. The section between Springer and Guinavah campgrounds (four and five miles) is the most popular – moose have been seen here.

**Wind Caves Trail (five miles)** Caves and arches eroded by wind and ice, 900 feet above the canyon floor, are reached by a one-mile trail.

**Jardine Juniper Trail (10 miles)** This is reputedly the world's oldest juniper tree – over 3000 years. A five-mile trail leaves Wood Camp and climbs almost 2000 feet to the tree. Good views and spring flowers in May and June, fall colors in September.

**Logan Cave (12 miles)** The cave is about a third of a mile long and can be explored with flashlights – there are no facilities.

**Naomi Peak Trail (19 miles)** After 19 miles, go west on USFS Rd 003 for seven miles. The trail leaves Tony Grove Lake and climbs about 2000 feet in three miles to reach Naomi Peak – at 9980 feet, it's the highest in the Bear River Range. The peak is surrounded by meadows awash with spring flowers in July and August – spring comes late at this elevation! Several other trails leave from Tony Grove Lake and campground.

**Beaver Mountain Ski Area (25 miles)** Hwy 89 exits Logan Canyon. Near Beaver Mountain turnoff is **Stump Hollow Ranch** (☎ 753 1707), which has horse and mountain bike rental. The ski area is described below.

**Bear Lake Summit (30 miles)** This is the highest point on the drive at 7800 feet. Nearby is the relatively flat, one-mile long **Limber Pine Nature Trail**, with views of Bear Lake and many flowers in June and July. The Hardware Ranch Road drive exits near the trailhead.

**Bear Lake Overlook (31 miles)** The overlook is on the right of the road. Great views and interpretive signs make this an essential pullout. Beyond the lake you can see Bear River, which is the longest US river that does not empty into the sea. Instead, it rises in Utah's Uinta Mountains and passes through Wyoming and Idaho before discharging into the Great Salt Lake.

**Places to Stay – camping**
The Wasatch-Cache National Forest operates 10 small campgrounds along Hwy 89 northeast of Logan. Most open in May and close in September/October; those over 6000 feet have shorter seasons. Actual dates vary depending on weather conditions. All campgrounds have pit or flush toilets, and all have drinking water. Sites cost $6 to $8, except Wood Camp, which is free but has no water. Sites fill up on summer weekends; arrive early or reserve by calling 1 (800) 283 2267.

The campgrounds are *Bridger* (5000 feet elevation, three miles into Logan Canyon); *Spring Hollow* (5100 feet, four miles); *Malibu-Guinavah* (5200 feet, five miles, which has an amphitheater with weekend evening presentations); *Preston Valley* (5500 feet, eight miles); *Lodge* (5600 feet, nine miles plus 1.5 miles to right); *Wood Camp* (5600 feet, 10 miles); *Lewis M Turner* (6000 feet, 19 miles); *Tony Grove Lake* (8100 feet, 19 miles plus seven to left); *Red Banks* (6500 feet, 20 miles); and *Sunrise* (7800 feet, 31 miles, six miles before Garden City).

## BEAVER MOUNTAIN SKI AREA
This small (464 acres) ski area (☎ 753 0921) is 25 miles up Logan Canyon and 1.5 miles to the left (or 13 miles from Garden City). Garden City has the closest overnight accommodations for skiers. A day lodge has food, ski rentals and instruction. Three lifts service 16 runs between 7200 and 8840 feet elevation. Thirty-five percent is for beginners, 40% for intermediate skiers. A full-day (9 am to 4 pm) lift pass is $18 or $14 for a half day. Children and those over 65 pay $14 for all day; seniors over 70 ski free. Ski rentals are $12 for a full day, $9 for half. Snowboarding is permitted on most runs.

Near the ski area turnoff is Stump Valley Ranch (☎ 753 1707), which rents snowmobiles. Both cross-country ski and snowmobile trail systems are found in the area.

## GARDEN CITY & BEAR LAKE
Despite its name, Garden City is just a village of 200 inhabitants on the west shore of Bear Lake at 5890 feet above sea level. The village provides lake visitors with places to stay and eat and is very busy in summer. The lake extends into Idaho, covers 112 sq miles and supports four endemic fish species, which are sought after by anglers. The lake's deep blue color is caused by limestone particles suspended in the water.

## Information

Bear Lake Visitors Bureau (☎ (208) 945 2072) is a few miles north in Idaho. There is a tourist information center in Garden City open during the summer.

## Things to See & Do

Three areas on the west, south and east sides of the lake are all administered as the **Bear Lake State Park** (☎ 946 3343, 1 (800) 322 2770 for camping reservations), PO Box 184, Garden City, 84028.

The **marina**, one mile north of Garden City, is open all year. There is a picnic area, swimming and boat launch, but low water levels in the early 1990s meant that many facilities were high and dry – call ahead for current conditions. A very small campground with showers charges $9 per site – reservations are recommended in summer. Day use is $3. During the January spawning season, anglers dip nets through the ice to catch the endemic Bonneville cisco.

The **Rendezvous Beach** area is eight miles south of Garden City on the south end of the lake. The season runs April to October. There are boat rentals, picnic areas and a sandy beach. The campground (with showers) has about 140 campsites for $9 to $13 (with hookups). Day use is $3.

The **Eastside** area is 12 miles north of Rendezvous Beach and offers boat launches and picnic areas all year. The shore slopes steeply here, and scuba divers use the area. Day use is $3 and campsites are $5 – drinking water is available but limited.

Garden City is the center of a large network of **snowmobile trails**. Bear Lake Funtime (☎ 946 3200, 1 (800) 516 3200), 1217 S Bear Lake Rd, rents snowmobiles and gives tours.

## Special Events

The popular Raspberry Days festival is held the first Thursday to Saturday in August with parades, entertainment and, of course, raspberries. Garden City is known throughout Utah for its raspberries, which (in summer) are served in several locations as delicious sundaes and almost solid shakes.

Bear Lake Music Festival attracts classical music fans from northern Utah, southern Idaho and western Wyoming during the last half of July.

During the third Thursday to Saturday in September, the Mountain Man Rendezvous, with reenactments of the old fur-trapping days, is held at Rendezvous Beach (camp reservations suggested).

## Places to Stay – camping

Apart from Bear Lake State Park (above), there is the *KOA* (☎ 946 3454), three-quarters of a mile north of Garden City. Open May through October, it offers showers, adults' and kids' pools, a playground, store and coin laundry. Sites are $14.50 to $18.50 (with hookups) and $23 to $34 for a few Kamping Kabins, which sleep up to four.

## Places to Stay – bottom end

High summer demand and few hotels means you won't find any bargains here. The eight-room *Greek Goddess Motel* (☎ 946 3233), 205 N Bear Lake Blvd, looks the cheapest at $25 to $45 per room depending on demand. There is a restaurant.

## Places to Stay – middle

*Bear Lake Motor Lodge* (☎ 946 3271), 50 S Bear Lake Blvd, has a restaurant and charges $40 to $70 for rooms; some have kitchenettes. The *Blue Water Beach Motel* (☎ 946 3333), 2126 S 250 East, charges $50 to $80 for rooms with kitchenettes. The *Inn of the Three Bears* (☎ 946 8590), 135 S Bear Lake Blvd, PO Box 197, 84028, is a three-roomed B&B with a hot tub for guests. Rates are $50 to $60.

*Harbor Village at Bear Lake* (☎ 946 3448, 1 (800) 324 6840), 900 N Bear Lake Blvd, has a restaurant, bar, swimming pool, spa and one- and two-bedroom units with kitchenettes. One-bedroom units are $109 a double, and two-bedroom units are $200 a double – $10 for each additional adult.

*Sweetwater* (☎ 531 1666 in Salt Lake City, 1 (800) 272 8824, fax 531 9011),

757 N Bear Lake Blvd, rents fully furnished one- and two-bedroom townhouses with kitchens. Rates are $325 for the one-bedroom and $390 for the two-bedroom units, per half week. It has a restaurant, pool and spa on the premises. The *Ideal Beach Resort* (☎ 946 3364), 2176 S Bear Lake Blvd, has similar facilities as well as boat rentals, and will rent rooms by the night as well.

New places are being built. Also call the Bear Lake Visitors Bureau for places to stay a few miles north in Idaho.

### Places to Eat
Apart from the resorts mentioned above, stop by *La Beau's* (☎ 946 8821), 69 N Bear Lake Blvd, or one of the other little drive-ins nearby for a raspberry shake.

### Entertainment
*Pickleville Playhouse* (☎ 946 2918 or 753 1944 in Logan), 2049 S Bear Lake Blvd, showcases local theatrical talent during their late June to early September season. Show time is at 8 pm most days, and there is a steak barbecue at 6:30 pm before the show.

## SOUTH OF BEAR LAKE
Hwy 30 and Hwy 16 lead 65 miles southeast of Garden City to connect with I-80 at Evanston, Wyoming, by the Utah border. Tiny **Randolph**, seat of Rich County, is halfway – no hotels. From Evanston, Hwy 150 leads 90 miles south to Kamas – this scenic route (called the Mirror Lake Hwy) provides access to the Uinta Mountains and is described in the chapter on northeastern Utah.

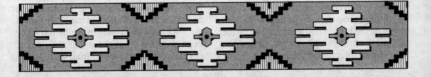

# Northeastern Utah

High wilderness terrain dominates northeastern Utah. The few small towns are all a mile above sea level, and the highest mountains in the state, the rugged Uintas, rise a further 8000 feet above the towns. These mountains are relatively undeveloped – camping, backpacking, fishing and hiking are prime activities. East of the Uintas, the Flaming Gorge National Recreation Area provides record-breaking fishing, and the Green River is known for good river running.

Near the Colorado border lies Vernal, the region's largest town with a population of just 8000. A short drive leads to Dinosaur National Monument, one of the largest dinosaur fossil quarries in the West, where fascinating exhibits show fossilized dinosaurs still being worked on. Northeastern Utah capitalizes on its dino-attraction; local tourist brochures dub the region 'Utah's Dinosaurland'.

This chapter begins with the western edge of the Uinta Mountains and continues through the Uintas to the area around Vernal.

## MIRROR LAKE HIGHWAY

The highway begins in the small community of **Kamas**, 16 miles southeast of exit 156 on I-80. Kamas is the western gateway to the Uinta Mountains – information about camping and so on can be obtained from the Wasatch-Cache National Forest **Kamas Ranger Station** (☎ 783 4338), 50 E Center St, PO Box 68, 84036. It is open from 8 am to 4:30 pm daily from July to September, and Monday to Friday the rest of the year.

The scenic route covers 65 miles to the Wyoming border, climbing from Kamas (6400 feet) over Bald Mountain Pass (10,678 feet and 30 miles along) and continuing at elevations of over 8000 feet into Wyoming. Evanston, Wyoming, is 23 miles north of the border and has hotels; a further 65 miles north brings you to Garden City (see the chapter on northern Utah).

Snow closes this high mountain road for most of the year. Snowplows clear the first 15 miles from Kamas to give access to cross-country skiing and snowmobiling, but Bald Mountain Pass is open only from June to October – exact dates depend on weather conditions. The road provides beautiful vistas of the western Uintas and passes by scores of lakes for fishing and trailheads for both short hikes and extended backpacking trips.

Travelers should visit or call the Kamas Ranger Station to obtain detailed information about outdoor recreational opportunities. The USFS operates over two dozen campgrounds along the approximately 40 miles of highway that lie within the national forest. Most campgrounds cost $6 to $8 and provide outhouses and water; none have RV hookups. Many campgrounds have hiking or nature trails or fishing. The few that don't provide drinking water are free. Campgrounds can fill up on summer weekends – either arrive early or make a reservation (☎ 1 (800) 283 2267).

## THE UINTA MOUNTAINS

These mountains are unusual in that they run east-west; all other major mountain ranges in the lower 48 states run north-south. Several peaks rise to over 13,000 feet, including Kings Peak (13,528), which is the highest point in Utah – and in Arizona or New Mexico for that matter. But before you start driving there, bear in mind that this is not one of those peaks which can be reached by car! The shortest route requires a 32-mile roundtrip hike with over 4000 feet elevation gain.

Utah's highest mountain, 13,528-foot Kings Peak, was named after Clarence King, who worked as a surveyor in Utah and other Western states in the latter part of the 19th century. The apostrophe has since been dropped from the mountain's name, perhaps to add a touch of majesty to it.

UTAH

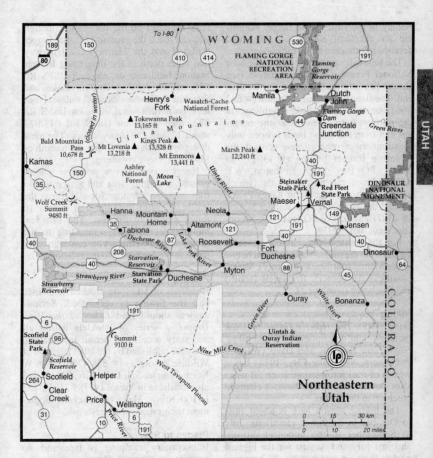

The climb to Kings Peak begins to give you an idea of how wild the Uintas are. There is no national park here, no visitors centers, scenic overlooks, snack bars or lodges. The central summits are within the High Uintas Wilderness Area, which covers almost 800 square miles in which no logging or development are allowed. There are no roads – not even mountain bikes are permitted. You have to hike or ride a horse; the choice depends on whether you prefer a sore butt or aching feet.

There are hundreds of lakes in the high country. Over 600 of these are stocked with trout and whitefish each year (some are stocked by airplane), and the fishing is considered to be some of the best in the West. Alpine wildlife is plentiful – deer are the most commonly seen animals, but moose and elk are also often spotted. Lucky hikers may glimpse martens, black bears, mountain lions and other mammals.

## Information

The Uintas fall into two national forests – the Wasatch-Cache in the west and the

Ashley in the east. Forest ranger stations are an excellent source of maps and detailed information about the entire range.

The following are for the Wasatch-Cache National Forest. The Kamas station (see above) has information about the western end. The Bear River Ranger Station (☎ 642 6662) on the Mirror Lake Highway (in the northwestern corner near the northern exit from the forest land) is open only in summer; at other times, contact the Evanston Ranger Station (☎ (307) 789 3194), PO Box 1880, Evanston, WY 82931. From the northern side (which offers the shortest access to Kings Peak), contact the Mountain View Ranger Station (☎ (307) 782 6555), PO Box 129, Mountain View, WY 82939.

For the Ashley National Forest, refer questions to the ranger stations listed below under Manila (northeastern corner), Vernal (southeastern corner), Roosevelt (south) and Duchesne (southwest).

### Hiking

Dave Hall's *The Hiker's Guide to Utah* includes eight descriptions of Uinta hikes. *High Uinta Trails* by Mel Davis (Wasatch Publishers, Salt Lake City, 1974) has a wealth of trail information. Even 20 years after publication, things haven't changed much up in the Uintas.

The hiking season here is about June to October in the lower elevations, July to September in the upper elevations, and just July and August for the highest peaks. Even in midsummer, be prepared for cold, drenching rain – you need warm and waterproof gear. Bugs can be a problem – bring repellent. Many trails are remote and not recommended for beginners. Experienced backpackers should carry an emergency kit.

Trips can range from day hikes to extended backpacking trips of many days. About 20 trailheads give access to a huge variety of trails from all sides of the Uintas. Generally speaking, the west is more crowded than the east.

Those wishing to climb **Kings Peak** will find the shortest access is from Henry's

Fork trailhead on the north side (though you can reach the summit via other longer trails). From the Mirror Lake Highway two miles north of the Bear River Ranger Station, head east on unpaved USFS Rd 058, which reaches Bridger Lake and Stateline Reservoir (about 40 miles). From here go north several miles on USFS Rd 072, then south on USFS Rd 017/077 about 12 miles to Henry's Fork. The most direct approach is a 32-mile drive south of Mountain View, Wyoming.

Henry's Fork has a primitive campground, a parking area and a sign with a trail map, though none for sale. From the trailhead (9400 feet) the trail climbs 16 miles almost to the top. The last few hundred feet involve scrambling to the rocky summit, where you can sign your name in the logbook. Congratulations!

### Fishing

Hundreds of lakes are stocked with fish, and the fishing is very good. Serious anglers should read *Lakes of the High Uintas*, a series of booklets listing all necessary access and permit information. They are published by the Utah Division of Wildlife Resources (☎ 538 4700), 1596 W North Temple, Salt Lake City, 84116, and also available in Vernal (☎ 789 3103), 152 E 100 North. Many backpackers supplement their rations with fresh fish.

### Places to Stay

Backcountry camping is free and no permits are required. Ranger stations can suggest areas in which to camp. They also have lists of drive-in campgrounds on all sides of the range, most of which provide drinking water, toilets and fire pits; they cost $6 to $8. Because of snow, most drive-in campgrounds operate from about May to October.

### DUCHESNE

Pronounced 'Do-sheyn', this small town of 1500 is the seat of Duchesne County (although Roosevelt, 28 miles east, is larger and has more facilities). Duchesne is a southern gateway to the Uintas.

## Orientation & Information

Main St (Hwy 40) is the main thoroughfare.

The city hall (☎ 738 2464), 165 S Center St, provides basic visitor information. The Ashley National Forest Duchesne Ranger Station (☎ 738 2482), 85 W Main St, 84021, is open 8 am to 5 pm from Monday to Friday, plus Saturday in summer.

## Starvation State Park

This park (☎ 738 2326), PO Box 584, 84021, is four miles northwest of Duchesne. The Starvation Reservoir has a boat launch area and boat rentals in summer. Water-skiing, windsurfing, sailing and fishing are popular. A campground (with showers and a playground) is open all year – sites range from $5 to $9. Day use is $3.

## Special Events

The Duchesne County Fair & Rodeo (☎ 738 2435) is held in the third week in August.

## Places to Stay & Eat

There are three basic motels. *Ell's Motel* (☎ 738 2215, 738 2216), 220 E Main St, has rooms for about $30. *Rio Damian Motel & RV Park* (☎ 738 2217), 23 W Main St, has rooms in the $30s; prices depend on the size. Some have kitchenettes. RV spaces are $11 with hookups. *Sportsman's Inn* (☎ 738 5733), 145 E Main St, also has rooms in the $30s.

*Cowan's Cafe* (☎ 738 5609), 57 E Main St, serves daily breakfast, lunch and dinner. *Well's Club* (☎ 738 9693), 47 E Main St, is a bar that serves reasonable food. There are also a few drive-in places.

## Getting There & Away

The Greyhound bus stops at the Conoco Gas Station (☎ 738 5961), 432 W Main St, on its twice daily run between Salt Lake City and Denver, Colorado.

## NORTH OF DUCHESNE

**Altamont,** 22 miles northeast of Duchesne, has the cheap *Altamont Motel* (☎ 454 3341) and the small but comfortable *Falcon's Ledge Lodge* (☎ 454 3737, fax 454 3392), which has a restaurant and spa. Rooms are about $100.

Further north, there are many campgrounds in the Ashley National Forest and trailheads leading into the high Uintas. You need a USFS map to find the roads.

USFS Rd 131 leads to **Moon Lake**, 45 miles north of Duchesne, which has a USFS campground and resort. The campground is open Memorial Day to Labor Day and costs $8. The *Moon Lake Resort* (☎ 454 3142 in summer), Mountain Home, 84051, has inexpensive cabins from Memorial to Labor Day. There is a grocery store, and horses (with guides if required) and boats are available for rent. About 12 miles before Moon Lake, USFS Rd 119 to the northeast runs into USFS Rd 124 and passes five more USFS campgrounds.

USFS Rd 134 leads northwest from Mountain Home to *Rock Creek Resort* (☎ 637 1236), PO Box 1736, Price, 84501. Here, there are cabins for about $40 to $50, RV hookups, a restaurant, and horse-riding trips from May to November. Three USFS campgrounds lie along this road.

Hwy 35, northwest of Duchesne, passes through **Tabiona**, 26 miles away, where there is the small *Sagebrush Inn* (☎ 848 5637). Hwy 35 continues through Hanna to USFS Rd 144, which leads to the *Defas Dude Ranch* (☎ 848 5590), Hanna, 84031, about 50 miles from Duchesne. The ranch offers inexpensive cabins and horseback trips; facilities include a restaurant and RV hookups. It is open May to October. Three USFS campgrounds are on this road, too.

Trails lead into the Uintas from the ends of all of these roads, which are passable in ordinary vehicles in good weather.

## ROOSEVELT & AROUND

Roosevelt (population 4000) was founded in 1905 and named after President Theodore Roosevelt who once camped nearby. It is the largest town in Duchesne County and the center of the region's cattle and oil industries. Driving north of Roosevelt and Duchesne, you'll see occasional oil pumps.

## Information

The chamber of commerce (☎ 722 4598), 48 S 200 East, is open from 8 am to 5 pm, Monday to Friday. The Ashley National Forest Roosevelt Ranger Station (☎ 722 5018), PO Box 338, 84066, is at 244 W Hwy 40. The post office (☎ 722 3231) is at 81 S 300 East. The hospital (☎ 722 3971) is at 250 W 300 North. The police (☎ 722 4558; in emergencies ☎ 911) are at 255 S State.

## North of Roosevelt

With USFS maps, you can find several campgrounds and trailheads into the Uintas. Hwy 121 north through Neola runs into USFS Rd 118, which reaches two USFS campgrounds and the *U-Bar Ranch* (☎ 722 3560). The ranch, located about 30 miles from Roosevelt, has cabins and horses for rent in the summer.

There are several other remote campgrounds in the Ashley National Forest north of Roosevelt.

## Nine Mile Canyon

A gravel and dirt road leaves Hwy 40, 11 miles southwest of Roosevelt and heads about 80 miles southwest over the West Tavaputs Plateau to Hwy 191/6, about eight miles southeast of Price. About halfway along this signed backcountry road is Nine Mile Canyon, known for many petroglyphs and pictographs dating from the Fremont Indian culture. The road is passable to cars in dry weather; several side canyons have tracks for which 4WD is advised. Further information is available from the Roosevelt or Price tourist or BLM offices.

## Ouray National Waterfowl Refuge

The refuge includes marshlands along the Green River that form an oasis for migrating ducks and geese flying over the desert. At least 15 species of waterfowl nest on the refuge in summer, but numbers peak in October and April during migrations.

Refuge headquarters (☎ 789 0351) are at 1680 W Hwy 40, Vernal. To reach the refuge, take Hwy 40 (16 miles east of Roosevelt or 14 miles west of Vernal) and then drive 14 miles south on Hwy 88. There is a self-guided auto-tour covering nine miles within the refuge, which is open year-round.

## Special Events

During Rough Rider Days, the first or second Thursday to Saturday in June, the town celebrates the great outdoors with a rodeo and events of interest to horse riders, anglers, hunters and other enthusiasts.

Uinta Basin in Celebration, the first Thursday to Saturday in August, includes rural events ranging from parades to pig chasing, food stands to fireworks. This is the area's biggest fair.

Also see the section on the Uintah and Ouray Indian Reservation, below.

## Places to Stay & Eat

Prices for accommodations go up for special events weekends. At other times, simple rooms with kitchenettes at the *Regal Motel* (☎ 722 4878), 160 S 200 East, are about $25 to $30. The *Western Hills Motel* (☎ 722 5115), 737 E 200 North, charges

PLACES TO STAY
7   Frontier Motel
9   Regal Motel

PLACES TO EAT
3   Driftwood Lounge
7   Frontier Grill

OTHER
1   Hospital
2   Uinta Theater
4   Roosevelt Theater
5   Chamber of Commerce
6   Greyhound Bus Depot
8   Post Office
10  Police
11  Ranger Station

To Fort Duchesne, Vernal

300 N St
200 N St
100 N St
Lagoon St
100 S St
200 S St
300 S St
400 S St

121
40  191

Roosevelt

To Duchesne

0   100   200 m
0   100   200 yards

about $30 a room. It has a cafe serving breakfast, lunch and dinner daily.

The *Frontier Motel* (☎ 722 2201, fax 722 3640), 75 S 200 East, charges in the mid-$30s for decent rooms. Attached is the *Frontier Grill* (☎ 722 3669), 65 S 200 East, a nice family restaurant and bar open from 6 am to 9:30 pm daily.

The *Best Western Inn* (☎ 722 4644, fax 722 0179), one mile east of town on Hwy 40, has a swimming pool and pleasant rooms in the low $40s. The *Green Briar Restaurant* (☎ 722 2236) next door serves good breakfast, lunch and dinner every day. A short walk away is the *Cow Palace* (☎ 722 2717), which serves cows (OK, OK – steaks) from 11 am to 9 pm, Monday to Saturday. The Palace has a salad bar.

The tribe operates *Bottle Hollow Motel* (☎ 722 3941), on Hwy 40 in Fort Duchesne. Simple rooms are $25/30 for singles/doubles. Facilities include a swimming pool, restaurant and gift shop selling beadwork items typical of the Utes. The restaurant closes on Sunday; the motel closes in winter.

In addition, there are about a dozen small hamburger, sandwich or pizza places in town.

### Entertainment
The *Roosevelt Theater*, 21 S 200 East, and the *Uinta Theater*, 41 N 200 East, show movies. Call 722 2095 for show times.

For a beer, a game of pool, and maybe some live weekend music, head over to the *Hilltop Lounge* (☎ 722 9603) near the Best Western Inn. For a beer downtown, there's the *Driftwood Lounge* (☎ 722 2571), 23 N 200 East.

### Getting There & Away
The Greyhound bus office (☎ 722 3342) is at 23 S 200 East. Buses stop here on the run between Salt Lake City and Denver, Colorado.

### UINTAH & OURAY INDIAN RESERVATION
Much of the land around Roosevelt belongs to the Ute tribe. At one time, Roosevelt itself and many other areas were part of the reservation, but in the late 19th and early 20th centuries the reservation was cut in size, and homesteaders and oil prospectors moved in. There is still talk of increasing the reservation area again. Today, about 3000 Utes live on the reservation.

### Information
The Ute Tribal Offices (☎ 722 5141) are in Fort Duchesne, PO Box 190, 84026, about a mile south of Hwy 40 and eight miles east of Roosevelt. Non-Utes can freely travel the reservation by road. Tribal permits (obtainable in Fort Duchesne or in sporting or fishing stores) are required for fishing, hunting, camping, boating or backcountry use.

A Tribal Museum (☎ 722 4992) is next to the Bottle Hollow Motel on Hwy 40. Ute history, customs and crafts are explained and displayed. Hours are from 9 am to 4 pm, Monday to Friday.

### Special Events
The main public Indian event in northeastern Utah is the Northern Ute Powwow and Rodeo held on the Fourth of July. A smaller Indian Rodeo is held in September.

Other events, held throughout the year, are more tribal in nature, and no photography or other recording devices are allowed. Contact the tribal offices for information about the Bear Dance (in April or May) and the Sun Dance (in July or August).

### VERNAL
Northeastern Utah's mineral wealth (oil, natural gas, Gilsonite and other deposits) as well as stock grazing make Vernal an important industrial and agricultural center. Tourism has also become an important industry in recent years, and the town has the best motel selection in the area.

There are two major tourist attractions in this far northeastern corner of Utah. To the north lies the geological and scenic splendor of Flaming Gorge, and to the east lies the fascinating Dinosaur National Monument. In addition, river running on the Green River and its tributaries is increasingly popular.

UTAH

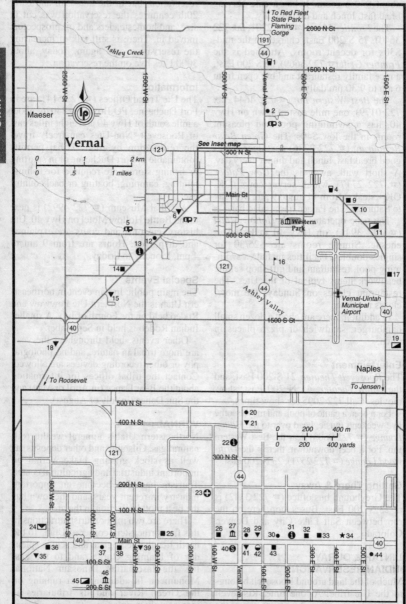

To Red Fleet
State Park,
Flaming
Gorge

Ashley Creek

Maeser

**Vernal**

0        1        2 km
0    .5    1 miles

See inset map

Main St

Western
Park

Ashley Valley

Vernal-Uintah
Municipal
Airport

Naples

To Roosevelt

To Jensen

UTAH

**PLACES TO STAY**

| | |
|---|---|
| 3 | Campground Dina |
| 5 | KOA |
| 7 | Fossil Valley RV Park |
| 9 | Split Mountain Lodge |
| 14 | Weston Plaza |
| 17 | Lazy K Motel |
| 25 | Days Inn |
| 26 | Sage Motel |
| 32 | Best Western Dinosaur Inn |
| 33 | Econo Lodge |
| 36 | Dine-a-Ville Motel |
| 38 | Best Western Antlers Motel |
| 43 | Weston Lamplighter Inn |

**PLACES TO EAT**

| | |
|---|---|
| 1 | Office Lounge |
| 4 | Gateway Saloon & Social Club |
| 6 | Golden Corral Family Steak House |
| 9 | Split Mountain Restaurant |
| 10 | Crack'd Pot Restaurant |
| 15 | Casa Rios |
| 18 | La Cabaña |
| 21 | Naples Deli & Pizza |
| 26 | Sage Restaurant |
| 29 | Seven Eleven Ranch Restaurant |
| 35 | Jerry's Pizza Barn |
| 39 | Main St Pizza |
| 41 | Great American Cafe |

**OTHER**

| | |
|---|---|
| 2 | Vernal Athletic Club |
| 8 | Western Heritage Museum, County Fairgrounds |
| 11 | AquaNoodle |
| 12 | Tri Cinema |
| 13 | Ouray National Waterfow Refuge Headquarters |
| 16 | Golf Course |
| 19 | Naples Hydrosaurus Waterslides |
| 20 | Basin Sports, Saw & Cycle |
| 22 | Ranger Station |
| 23 | Hospital |
| 24 | Post Office |
| 27 | Thorne Museum |
| 28 | Hatch River Expeditions |
| 30 | First Ladies of the White House Doll Collection (in library) |
| 31 | Utah Field House of Natural History State Park (Museum & Visitor Information) |
| 34 | Police |
| 37 | Basin Sports |
| 40 | Bank of Vernal |
| 42 | Vernal Theater, Greyhound Bus Depot |
| 43 | Dina Peak Cycle & Tour |
| 44 | Dinosaur River Expeditions |
| 45 | Swimming Pool |
| 46 | DUP Museum |

Vernal was settled in 1878. In the late 1800s, outlaws used to hide out in the area, because it was remote and inaccessible. Today, Vernal (population of 8000) is the seat of Uintah County and the cultural and commercial center of 'Dinosaurland'.

### Information

The Welcome Center (☎ 789 4002), in the state park at 235 E Main St, is open daily from 8 am to 9 pm in summer, and 9 am to 5 pm during the rest of the year. The center provides both local and regional information for travelers arriving from Colorado or Wyoming. Also call Dinosaurland Travel Board (☎ 789 6932, 1 (800) 477 5558) for area information.

The Ashley National Forest Vernal Ranger Station (☎ 789 1181) is at 355 N Vernal Ave, 84078. The local newspaper is the *Vernal Express*. The post office (☎ 789 2393) is at 67 N 800 West. The hospital

(☎ 789 3342) is at 151 W 200 North. The police (☎ 789 5835, or 911 in emergencies) are at 437 E Main St.

### Utah Field House of Natural History State Park

This park and its museum (☎ 789 3799), 235 E Main St, is well worth a visit. Kids will enjoy encountering the life-size dinosaurs in the gardens outside; inside are exhibits of geology, paleontology, natural history and local area history. A gift shop sells dino-treasures. Museum hours are from 8 am to 9 pm June to August, and 9 am to 5 pm the rest of the year (closed on New Year's Day, Thanksgiving and Christmas). Admission is $1.50, or $1 for six- to 15-year-olds.

### Museums

The **DUP Museum** (☎ 789 3890), at the corner of 500 West 200 South, has an

Life-size but none-too-lively, this replica of a triceratops stands
guard at the Utah Field House of Natural History State Park. (RR)

extensive, free display of local pioneering artifacts. The museum entry was a tithing house built in 1887. Hours are 1 to 7 pm Monday to Saturday, June to September, and at other times by arrangement.

The **Thorne Museum** houses a private collection of local pioneering and Indian artifacts. The museum (☎ 789 0392), 18 W Main St, is located in a photography studio and is open 9:30 am to 6 pm Monday, Tuesday, Thursday and Friday. Admission is free.

Located in the library (☎ 789 0091), 155 E Main St, is a **doll collection** comprised of representations of the wife of each president of the USA dressed in the gown she wore during the inaugural ball. It's open from 10 am to 8 pm, Monday to Thursday, and to 6 pm on Friday and Saturday.

On the grounds of Western Park (☎ 789 7396), 302 E 200 South, you will find the County Fairgrounds and the **Western Heritage Museum** (☎ 789 7399), which curates local history and art shows. There is

a gift shop. Summer hours are 9 am to 6 pm, Monday to Saturday; the rest of the year hours are 10 am to 5 pm, Monday to Friday.

Built over 70 years ago, the Bank of Vernal at 3 W Main St (today called Zions First National) was constructed with bricks that came from Salt Lake City. At the time, mailing the bricks cost much less than freighting them, so they arrived by US mail – and prompted a change in mailing regulations soon after!

### River Running

The Green and Yampa Rivers are the main waterways in the area, and both have rapids to satisfy the white-water enthusiast as well as calmer areas for gentler rafting and float trips. Several companies organize trips ranging from one to five days at costs of about $60 to $600. A friendly and experienced local company is Hatch River Expeditions (☎ 789 4316, 1 (800) 342 8243), 55 E Main St, PO Box 1150, 84078. Other companies are listed under the Mountain

Biking (see below) and Flaming Gorge sections. You might also try Adrift Adventures (☎ 789 3600, 1 (800) 824 0150) in Jensen, 13 miles east of Vernal.

If you have your own boat and need a vehicle or passenger shuttle at the end of a float trip, call River Runners Transport (☎ 781 1180), 126 S 1500 West. The outfit will also rent rafts.

## Mountain Biking
The Welcome Center has brochures detailing various rides in the area. Basin Sports, Saw & Cycle (☎ 781 1226), 450 N Vernal Ave, offers info and bike rentals. Dina Peak Cycle & Tour (☎ 781 2453), 120 E Main St, has bike tours, rentals and repairs. Dinosaur River Expeditions (☎ 781 0717, 1 (800) 247 6197, fax 649 8126), 540 E Main St, has river tours and bike tours or combinations thereof, and will also rent mountain bikes.

## Other Activities
The Municipal Course (☎ 781 1428) has 18 holes of **golf** at 675 S 200 East. Play minigolf or use the water-slide and pool at AquaNoodle (☎ 789 5281), 1155 E Hwy 40. **Swim** indoors at the public pool (☎ 789 5775), 170 S 600 West, or outdoors at Naples Hydrosaurus Water Slides (☎ 789 1010), 1701 E 1900 South. Expect to pay about $5 for a day at the water-slide pools.

Basin Sports (☎ 789 2409, fax 789 2219), 511 W Main St, rents **fishing** equipment. Fishing boats can be rented or repaired at Blue Mountain Motor & Marine (☎ 789 5661), 2217 N Vernal Ave. Vernal Athletic Club (☎ 789 5816), 1180 N Vernal Ave, rents all you need and has information about local **cross-country skiing** areas.

## Special Events
The Outlaw Trail Festival, from late June to late July, is centered on Western Park. Events include a western musical performed on a dozen or more evenings, the Dinosaur Roundup Rodeo held in mid-July and all sorts of other Western stuff ranging from cowboy poetry contests to Wild West shootouts.

The Uintah County Fair is held in early

August. In mid-August, the Utah Field House of Natural History presents special programs for kids and adults during Dinosaur Days. The Vernal Balloon Races are held at the airport in mid-September, and an Indian Rodeo takes place at Western Park at the end of the month. At the end of November the dinosaurs outside the Utah Field House are decorated with Christmas lights – they are switched on the Friday after Thanksgiving.

## Places to Stay – camping
I couldn't find any Vernal campgrounds open in winter. *Fossil Valley RV Park* (☎ 789 6450), 999 W Hwy 40, has showers and a coin laundry; it is open April to November. Sites are $14 with hookups or $10 for a tent space. *Vernal KOA* (☎ 789 8935), 1800 W Sheraton Ave, has a pool, playground, showers, store, recreation area and coin laundry; it's open from May to September. Sites are $13 or $17 with hookups and Kamping Kabins go for $22. *Campground Dina* (☎ 789 2148), 930 N Vernal Ave, has similar facilities plus minigolf for $10 to $16.

In Jensen, 13 miles east of Vernal, the *Dinosaur Village Campground* (☎ 789 1997) has showers and charges $8 to $11. Other campgrounds are listed below in Around Vernal.

## Places to Stay – bottom end
Vernal is growing as a tourist center, and prices are rising accordingly; summer prices can be $10 or $20 higher than the rest of the year.

The clean and well-run *Sage Motel* (☎ 789 1442), 54 W Main St, has fairly large rooms starting around $30 during the summer. There is a family restaurant attached. The small *Lazy K Motel* (☎ 789 3277), 1500 E 775 South, and the *Dine-a-Ville Motel* (☎ 789 9571), 801 W Hwy 40, which has a pool, are similarly priced.

## Places to Stay – middle
**B&Bs** *Hillhouse B&B* (☎ 789 0700), 75 W 3300 North, 84078, has three nonsmoking rooms with private entrance, patio and bath

for about $50. Rooms have queen-size beds and will sleep up to four people; discounts are offered for stays of over three nights.

**Hotels** The *Split Mountain Lodge* (☎ 789 9020), 1015 E Hwy 40, has nice rooms starting at $35/40 for singles/doubles in the summer. The *Econo Lodge* (☎ 789 2000, fax 789 0947), 311 E Main St, is conveniently located downtown; it has a restaurant next door and provides complimentary morning coffee. Clean rooms start at $38/42. The *Days Inn* (☎ 789 1011, fax 789 0172), 260 W Main St, has a pool and free continental breakfast included in its rates, which start in the $40s in the summer.

The *Weston Lamplighter Inn* (☎ 789 0312, fax 789 4874), 120 E Main St, has almost 200 rooms and is the biggest place in town. Amenities include a pool, a restaurant and a play area for kids. It is a good value for about $46 a double in summer. The *Weston Plaza* (☎ 789 9550, fax 789 4874), 1684 W Hwy 40, has a pool, spa, coin laundry, restaurant and bar (with occasional music and dancing). Rooms are good-sized and go for $48/56 for singles/doubles.

Best Western has two good hotels in Vernal. The *Antlers Motel* (☎ /fax 789 1202), 423 W Main St, has a restaurant, pool, spa, exercise room and play area for kids. Pleasant rooms are $55 to $70 in summer, $15 less off-season. The *Dinosaur Inn* (☎ 789 2660, fax 789 2467), 251 E Main St, is convenient to downtown and has a pool, spa, playground, restaurant and bar. Attractive rooms are $60 to $75 in summer, $20 less off-season.

### Places to Eat
The locally popular *Crack'd Pot Restaurant* (☎ 781 0133), 1089 E Hwy 40, is open 24 hours in the summer and 5 am to 10 pm at other times. It offers a wide variety of American meals ranging from inexpensive daily specials to steak and seafood.

Starving budget travelers can fill up at the *Seven Eleven Ranch Restaurant* (☎ 789

1170), 77 E Main St, which advertises all-you-can-eat meals. Another inexpensive choice is the *Great American Cafe* (☎ 789 1115), 13 S Vernal Ave, which serves breakfasts any time from 6 am to 11 pm and features local catfish, hamburgers and sandwiches for lunch and dinner.

For steaks, the *Golden Corral Family Steak House* (☎ 789 7268), 1046 W Hwy 40, is a good value; it serves chicken and fish as well. The hotel restaurants are all reasonable. The *Sage Motel* has inexpensive family dining; the *Split Mountain Lodge* features both American and Chinese menus; the *Weston Plaza* is one of the best in town.

For Mexican food, there are two decent choices west of town: *Casa Rios* (☎ 789 0103), 2015 W Hwy 40, and *La Cabaña* (☎ 789 3151), 2750 W Hwy 40. Both are closed on Sunday.

Grab a pizza at *Main St Pizza* (☎ 789 8303), 389 W Main St, *Naples Deli and Pizza* (☎ 789 6558), 420 N Vernal Ave, or *Jerry's Pizza Barn* (☎ 789 2030), 831 W Main. All three places will deliver to your room. Jerry's also serves steaks, seafood and Mexican food.

### Entertainment
Catch a movie (☎ 789 6139 for schedules) at *Tri Cinema*, 1400 W Hwy 40, or *Vernal Theater*, 40 E Main.

For a beer, the *Gateway Saloon & Social Club* (☎ 789 9842 or 789 5075), 773 E Main St, is a private club featuring live entertainment or karaoke on some nights. The *Office Lounge* (☎ 789 4008), 1678 N Vernal Ave, has live music on weekends. The *Last Chance Saloon & Cafe* (☎ 789 5657), 3340 N Vernal Ave, will rustle up a burger or breakfast to go with your beer; it's about three miles north of downtown.

### Getting There & Away
**Air** The airport is at 830 E 500 South. Skywest Airlines (1 (800) 453 9417) has two or three flights a day to and from Salt Lake City. The fare is about $100 roundtrip with advance purchase.

**Bus** The Greyhound bus office (☎ 789 0404), 38 E Main St, sells tickets for buses on the Denver, Colorado-Salt Lake City run and on to other points. There are one or two buses a day in either direction.

## AROUND VERNAL
### State Parks
Seven miles northwest of Vernal, **Steinaker State Park** (☎ 789 4432) is a popular fishing, boating and water-skiing area during the summer. There is a sandy beach, boat ramp, picnic area and campground with water, but no showers. Camping costs $7; day use is $3.

**Red Fleet State Park** (☎ 789 6614) has nearly the same attractions and facilities as Steinaker. In addition, a 1.5-mile hike (roundtrip) passes fossilized dinosaur tracks. The park, located 12 miles northeast of Vernal, is not marked on all maps – head north on Hwy 191 for about 10 miles, and you'll see a sign for the park to your right.

### Driving Tours
The Welcome Center in Vernal has several brochures giving details of driving tours. The two most popular are outlined below – ask at the Welcome Center for other suggestions.

**Drive through the Ages** From about four miles north of Vernal on Hwy 191 to the entrance to Flaming Gorge, 32 miles further, the road passes many different geological strata and formations. About 20 signs along the way explain the scientific significance of the phenomena – the signs are designed to be read by northbound drivers.

**Petroglyphs & Red Cloud Loop** Leave Vernal westbound on 500 North. After about three miles go through the community of Maeser, then turn right on Dry Fork Canyon Rd. About seven more miles brings you to the McConkie Ranch, where there are hundreds of Indian petroglyphs spread over a mile along a canyon wall. A small admission fee is charged – note that this

is private property, so follow the owners' signed instructions.

After the petroglyphs, the road continues northwest into the Ashley National Forest as USFS Rd 018. Low-slung cars may want to turn back at this point. This is the scenic Red Cloud Loop, along which several dirt sections may require high clearance or 4WD – ask at the ranger station for details. The road is closed by snow in winter. USFS Rd 018 loops around for about 45 miles through beautiful high forests and alpine meadows with Uinta mountain views before emerging at Hwy 191, 21 miles north of Vernal. Many people do the loop starting at Hwy 191 and emerging at Dry Fork, because the signs are easier to follow.

There are many possibilities for hiking, fishing, camping and picnicking along this route – the ranger station has maps and details.

### Bonanza
The 40-mile drive southeast of Vernal along Hwy 45 to Bonanza passes through remote country with herds of antelope, deer and wild horses. This is also mineral country, and there are oil wells, pipelines, mines and industrial workings to be seen. The Deseret Generation and Transmission Bonanza Power Plant (☎ 789 9000) and Chevron's American Gilsonite Mine (☎ 789 1921) can be visited, with guided tours given usually on Tuesdays and Thursdays around noon – call for details.

The road is paved as far as Bonanza. Beyond, a network of unpaved roads lead to Watson, Rainbow and Dragon ghost towns to the south. Further south still, 4WD vehicles can reach the remote and poorly explored East Tavaputs Plateau and Book Cliffs areas, emerging finally at I-70. This is not an area for casual exploring – bring plenty of extra food, water and maps, and don't expect to see anyone else if you break down.

## FLAMING GORGE NATIONAL RECREATION AREA
Flaming Gorge was named by John Wesley Powell, who explored the area in 1869

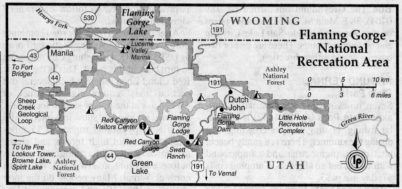

during his historical first descent of the Green and Colorado Rivers. Between 1957 and 1964, the Bureau of Reclamation built the Flaming Gorge Dam across the Green River, which backed up for over 90 miles to form the present reservoir. This straddles the Utah-Wyoming state line, but the visitors center and most of the best scenery, campsites and other facilities are on the Utah side.

As with many of the artificial lakes of the Southwest, fishing and boating are prime attractions. The lake is stocked with half a million fish annually, and the fishing is some of the best in the Southwest. Various fishing records have been set here, and the season is year round.

Flaming Gorge, however, provides more than just fishing and boating. The scenery is quite spectacular, and there are plenty of hiking, camping, picnicking and backpacking opportunities in the summer. In winter, cross-country skiing, snowshoeing and snow camping are all possible. Wildlife, including big game such as moose, elk, pronghorn antelope and mule deer are quite common, and bighorn sheep, black bears and mountain lions are occasionally seen. Hunting is allowed in season with the appropriate permits.

Admission to Flaming Gorge National Recreation Area is free. The main season is May to October. At other times, most services are shut down, though there are still places to stay and eat, and the main roads are kept open with snowplows.

The elevation of the lake is 6040 feet above sea level, which ensures pleasantly warm but not desperately hot summers – daytime highs average about 80°F.

## Orientation & Information

A 36-mile drive due north from Vernal on Hwy 191 leads to Greendale Junction at the entrance of the recreation area. From the junction, Hwy 191 continues six miles to the east past the Flaming Gorge Dam and Visitor Center, then a further three miles through the small community of Dutch John (population 300) and on up the east side of the area into Wyoming. Heading west from Greendale Junction, Hwy 44 passes the Red Canyon Visitor Center (four miles, plus two on a side road) and goes on to the small town of Manila (about 30 miles), continuing up the west side of the lake into Wyoming. All these roads are paved.

The recreation area is part of the Ashley National Forest, and information is available from the ranger station in Vernal or at the Flaming Gorge Headquarters (☎ 784 3445), PO Box 278, Manila, 84046. The Manila office is open from 8 am to 4:30 pm, Monday to Friday, plus weekends in summer. There is also the Ashley National Forest Dutch John Ranger Station (☎ 885 3315), PO Box 157, Dutch John, 84023.

The Flaming Gorge Dam Visitor Center

(☎ 885 3135) is open from 8 am to 8 pm, Thursday to Saturday and to 7 pm, Sunday to Wednesday in summer, or 9 am to 5 pm the rest of the year. The Red Canyon Visitor Center (☎ 889 3713) is open from 9:30 am to 5 pm daily from mid-May to October. Audio-visual displays, exhibits about the area and a bookstore are all here. The views from the center are impressive; even better views are possible from a short, paved interpretive trail to various overlooks. Both visitors centers have schedules of nature walks, fireside talks and similar events led by rangers.

### Flaming Gorge Dam
Free guided tours leave from the visitors center between 9 am and 4:30 pm during the summer. An elevator within the dam will drop you 42 floors to the base of the structure, which rises 502 feet above bedrock. At other times, you can walk along the top of the dam. The visitors center has exhibits, audio-visual displays and a store selling maps and books.

### Swett Ranch National Historic Site
Half a mile northeast from Greendale Junction on Hwy 191 brings you to a signed road to Swett Ranch, 1.5 miles away. This ranch dates to the early 1900s and provides a glimpse of what life was like before roads opened up the area. Hours are 9 am to 5 pm Thursday to Monday, Memorial Day to Labor Day.

### Sheep Creek Canyon
A 13-mile paved loop road leaves Hwy 44 about 15 miles west of Greendale Junction, returning to Hwy 44 about seven miles further north. The loop road goes through Sheep Creek Canyon Geological Area; brochures from the visitors centers and roadside signs interpret the geology of the area. The scenery is dramatic, and there are picnicking areas but no campgrounds. Snow closes the loop road in winter.

### Spirit Lake Rd
Two miles along the Sheep Creek Canyon loop road, unpaved USFS Rd 221 branches

to the west and leads about 20 miles to Spirit Lake, where you can camp (no water or fee) or stay at the *Spirit Lake Resort* (☎ 783 2339), which has inexpensive cabins, a cafe and horse and boat rentals. It is open June to October. Though unpaved, USFS 221 is passable to cars in good weather.

Near the beginning of USFS Rd 221, a sign for **Ute Mountain Tower** points the way up two-mile long USFS Rd 005, a steep dirt road leading to the only fire tower left standing in Utah. A hike will bring you to the top (8834 feet above sea level), where you can take in great views and read signs explaining what being a fire lookout here was like in the 1930s. A couple of miles after the Ute Tower turn, USFS Rd 096 leads about two miles to Browne Lake, where there is a free USFS campground (no water). These roads are all closed by snow in winter.

### Hiking & Backpacking
In addition to the hike to the Ute Mountain Tower (above), there are a number of day hikes in the area. These range from short day hikes such as the popular five-mile walk along the Canyon Rim Trail to a strenuous climb up Leidy Peak, the highest point in Flaming Gorge at 12,028 feet.

The **Canyon Rim Trail** begins at the Red Canyon Visitor Center and ends at the Greendale overlook a mile west of Greendale Junction off Hwy 44. The terrain is gently rolling and elk are sometimes seen. Several campgrounds are close to parts of the walk.

The **Leidy Peak Trail** leaves Browne Lake (see Spirit Lake Rd above) from the southeast corner and climbs almost 4000 feet in eight miles to Leidy Peak.

Rangers at the visitors centers or forest ranger stations can suggest several more hikes, as well as overnight backpacking trips. Permits are not required.

### Fishing
You can fish at any time in Flaming Gorge Lake, which has produced record-breaking trout, salmon, bass and other fish. You need

a permit, available from ranger stations, marinas or lodges in the area. Day permits are $5; season permits cost $40.

**Fly-fishing** for trout is excellent on the Green River (below the dam for obvious reasons!) and some of its tributaries. These rivers are carefully managed with occasional closures and various catch-and-release and other regulations designed to maintain the high quality of fishing – ask about current conditions at the ranger stations or you risk being fined for breaking the rules.

The very best fishing is had by local experts. If you're not one, then local guides can be hired who'll show you the places to go and the lures to use. Guides aren't cheap – over $100 per day per person in small groups – but they get you the best fishing. See the Places to Stay section for lodges with guides.

**Boating & River Running**
In this case, 'boat' describes everything from fishing boats, pontoons and power/ski boats on the lake to rafts and canoes on the river. Fishing boats rent for around $60 a day, pontoon boats for about $120 and ski boats for about $170. Raft rentals range from $30 to $70, depending on size, and inflatable kayaks for one person are about $20. Half-day and hourly rates are available.

The lake has two marinas on the Utah side and another in Wyoming. All offer lake boat rentals, gas, camping, boat launch area, store and guided fishing trips. **Lucerne Valley** (☎ 784 3483, fax 784 3433), PO Box 356, Manila, 84046, is seven miles east of Manila on the Lucerne Peninsula. It has the longest season, with limited boat rentals beginning sometime in March and ending in November (depending on weather). It also has a few house boats to rent in the summer. **Cedar Springs** (☎ /fax 889 3795), PO Box 337, Dutch John, 84023, a little over a mile west of Flaming Gorge Dam, is open from about April to October. There is also **Buckboard Marina** (☎ (307) 875 6927), 23 miles northeast of Manila in Wyoming. In addition to the marinas, there are several other boat launch areas for privately owned boats.

River rafts and kayaks can be rented from Flaming Gorge Lodge (☎ 889 3773,

In the spring, fields of wildflowers can appear almost overnight in southeastern Utah. (RR)

One of the many canyons at Canyonlands National Park (BW)

A double arch at Arches National Park (RP)

Delicate Arch, in Arches National Park, is 45 feet high. (RR)

You won't find much shade at Arches National Park. (DS)

see Places to Stay); **Flaming Gorge Flying Service** (☎ 885 3338 or 885 3370), PO Box 368, Dutch John, 84023, at the Dutch John airport; and **Flaming Gorge Recreational Services** (☎ 885 3191), Dutch John, 84023. All these can provide fishing guides as well as shuttle vehicles to pick you up at the end of a raft trip. There are raft launch areas for privately owned boats on the Green River a short way below the dam. Life jackets must be warn by all boaters, but permits are not required.

The most popular rafting section is the first seven miles below the dam, pulling out at Little Hole about three hours after entry. A shuttle bus (up to eight passengers) will meet you and bring you and your raft back for $25, if arranged in advance. There are several minor (class I and II) rapids; for more experienced rafters, bigger rapids are found below Little Hole. Summer weekends are very popular – reserve a raft rental in advance or come midweek.

### Winter Activities

Solitude is what the locals say you'll find in winter. Cross-country skiers will find marked trails following the Canyon Rim Trail (see Hiking & Backpacking) and also around Swett Ranch. Plenty of unmarked possibilities exist for the adventurous skier.

Snowmobilers use the forest roads to the east; the Dowd Springs picnic area just south of the Sheep Creek Canyon loop road is the base for snowmobiling, but there are no facilities apart from a plowed parking area and restrooms.

If you get up to the highland lakes (for example, Browne and Spirit Lakes), you'll find a few anglers on the ice. You can join them. Brrr!

### Places to Stay & Eat

**Camping** The Ashley National Forest (☎ 784 3445) operates about two dozen campgrounds in the Flaming Gorge area or just outside it. Campgrounds are open May to October in lower elevations, and for a briefer period up higher. Reservations (☎ 1 (800) 283 2267) for some of the more popular campsites are suggested.

Free USFS campgrounds (bring your own water) are available at Spirit Lake and Browne Lake and Deep Creek (three miles along unpaved USFS Rd 539, leaving Hwy 44 about three miles south of the Sheep Creek Loop). In addition, there are several free USFS campsites on the lake that can be reached by boat only.

Over a dozen other campgrounds scattered around the south end of the area provide drinking water and toilets, but no showers or hookups. These cost $7 to $10. Lakeside campgrounds have boat launch ramps. A favorite campground is *Lucerne Valley*, near to the marina, where over 150 sites are available at $10 a night, open April to October. A herd of pronghorn antelope roams the Lucerne Peninsula, and visitors often see them. *Antelope Flat*, 10 miles west of Dutch John on the east side of Flaming Gorge Lake, is another popular campground with over 100 sites at $8 each. *Firefighters Memorial* campground has over 90 sites conveniently located between Greendale Junction and the dam, but not on the lake. Sites cost $10 a night. Other campgrounds are smaller.

There is a private campground in Manila. The *Flaming Gorge KOA* (☎ 784 3184), a quarter mile east on Hwy 43 from Hwy 44, is open from May to mid-November, and facilities include a pool, showers, play area, grocery store and coin laundry. Sites are $14.50 or $19 with hookups.

**Cabins & Motels – Flaming Gorge** The *Red Canyon Lodge* (☎ 889 3759) is near the Red Canyon Visitor Center. It provides simple rustic cabins with shared bathrooms for $26 (one queen-size bed) or $36 (two queen-size beds in two rooms). Cabins with private bathrooms are $10 more. Each cabin has an outdoor picnic table and fire ring. Luxury cabins with two queen-size beds and a queen-size sofa, a kitchenette, private bath, and covered porch rent for $90. All cabins have a wood-burning stove. The lodge has a full restaurant and a grocery and tackle store. It is next to small Green Lake, where there is private fishing and boat rental; fishing guides are available. The lodge is open from April to October.

The *Flaming Gorge Lodge* (☎ 889 3773, fax 889 3788) is just off Hwy 191 between Greendale Junction and the dam. Motel rooms go for $48 to $66 (one to four people), and condominiums run $85 to $110 – these come with a kitchen. From December to February, rates are $10 lower. Facilities include a restaurant, cafe, store and river-raft rentals. Guided fishing trips are available.

A simple restaurant (hamburgers, etc) in Dutch John near the Recreation Service is open in summer only.

**Hotels & Motels – Manila** With a population of about 300, Manila manages to be the Daggett County seat. It is just outside the west end of Flaming Gorge and has a few small hotels.

The *Flaming Gorge Cafe & Motel* (locally called Grubbs' after the friendly owners) (☎ 784 3131) has simple but adequate rooms for about $30/40 in the summer, less in winter. The cafe serves good home-cooked meals. *Steinakers' Motel* (☎ 784 6520) has five cheap and basic rooms. *Niki's Inn* (☎ 784 3117) has decent rooms around $40 and a restaurant. The *Vacation Inn* (☎ 784 3259, fax 263 3404) is the biggest place with two dozen rooms with kitchenettes going for about $48. It may close in winter.

## DINOSAUR NATIONAL MONUMENT

Dinosaurs have inspired people's imaginations perhaps more than any other animal group – it is hard to believe that they have been extinct for tens of millions of years. Although dinosaurs once roamed over much of the earth, in only a few places have the right geological and climatic conditions combined to preserve the beasts as fossils. One of the largest dinosaur fossil beds in North America was discovered here in 1909, and the site was protected by national monument status in 1915.

Today's visitor can wander through a dinosaur quarry in which over 1600 bones have been exposed and left in plain sight. This productive quarry has been completely enclosed within a building to protect the fossils from weathering. Apart from dinosaur bones, the starkly eroded canyons of the national monument provide the visitor with scenic drives, hiking, camping, backpacking and river running.

### Orientation & Information

The monument straddles the Utah-Colorado state line and is best reached from Hwy 40. The park headquarters and most of the land is within Colorado, but the dinosaur quarry (which is the only place that such fossils can be seen in the site where they were found) is in Utah. Reach the quarry by driving north from Jensen (13 miles east of Vernal) on a seven mile paved road. The headquarters is just off Hwy 40, 25 miles east of Jensen and about four miles into Colorado.

Information is available from Dinosaur National Monument Headquarters (☎ (303) 374 2216), PO Box 210, Dinosaur, CO 81610. The visitors center at the headquarters has an audio visual program, exhibits, book shop and information. It is open from 8 am to 4:30 pm, Monday to Friday, plus weekends in summer, and closed New Year's Day, Thanksgiving and Christmas. Entrance to this visitors center is free; entrance to all other parts of the monument (including the dinosaur quarry) is $5 per (private) vehicle or $2 per cyclist/bus passenger. Golden Age and Access cards are accepted.

Summer daytime temperatures average in the mid to upper 80°s F – carry drinking water if hiking. Snow during the winter may close some of the areas described below, though the road to the quarry is usually open.

### Dinosaur Quarry

This educational spot (☎ 789 2115) is open daily from 8 am to 7 pm from Memorial Day to Labor Day, and 8 am to 4 pm the rest of the year (closed New Year's Day, Thanksgiving and Christmas). The Jurassic rock layer that holds the fossils is well-worth seeing – it gives an idea of how hard paleon-

Although T Rex has been shown standing upright for years, recent evidence suggests that it traveled nearly horizontal to the ground.

tologists work to transform the solid rock into, on the one hand, the beautiful skeletons seen in museums and, on the other hand, the scientifically accurate interpretation of what life was like for the dinosaurs.

Rangers, brochures, audio-visual presentations and exhibits are here to help you understand what you see. Rangers also have information about the rest of the monument, and there is a schedule of ranger-led events (walks, talks, tours). There is a gift and book shop.

During the busy summer, park your car in the lower lot and either walk about a half mile to the quarry or wait for the frequent and free shuttle bus. Disabled visitors can drive all the way to the small parking lot at the quarry, as can the general public during off-peak periods.

### Scenic Drives & Hiking Trails

Several drives with scenic overlooks and interpretive signs lead to various trailheads for short nature trails or access to the backcountry.

The paved **Cub Creek Rd** goes east of the dinosaur quarry for 10 miles, ending at Josie Morris' Cabin. Josie Morris was a tough woman who lived here for some 50 years – legend has it that Butch Cassidy was among her many suitors. Along the road, you can stop at a couple of **nature trails** (each about two miles long), see

Indian petroglyphs, learn about geology, have a picnic or camp at one of the two campgrounds here.

The paved **Harpers Corner Rd** leaves Hwy 40 at the park headquarters and heads north for 31 miles into the heart of the backcountry, crossing the Utah-Colorado state line a couple of times. This scenic and popular drive has several pullouts with vistas and interpretive signs, picnic areas and trailheads but no campgrounds. Trails include the very short **Plug Hat Butte Nature Trail** (four miles from the headquarters), the four-mile (one way) **Ruple Point Trail** (25 miles from headquarters) and the one-mile (one way) **Harpers Corner Trail** at the end of the road. Both the Ruple Point and Harpers Corner Trails lead to dramatic views of Green River canyons.

The unpaved **Echo Park Rd** leaves the Harpers Corner Rd 25 miles north of the headquarters. Vehicles with high clearance or 4WD are recommended for this 13-mile drive, which drops steeply down to Echo Park at the confluence of the Yampa and Green Rivers. The steep road can get very slick after rain – beware. There is a primitive campground in a splendid setting at Echo Park, and hiking is encouraged, though there are no maintained trails. The road is not passable to large motor homes or trailers, though ordinary cars can make it in dry weather – check at the visitors center first. People with trucks or 4WDs could also explore the rough **Yampa Bench Rd**, which leaves Echo Park Rd about eight miles from Harpers Corner Rd. The 38-mile-long Yampa Bench Rd has views of the Yampa River and comes out on Hwy 40 at Elk Springs, Colorado, about 34 miles east of monument headquarters.

The paved but narrow **Jones Hole Rd** leaves from four miles south of the dinosaur quarry and goes 48 miles around the west and north sides of the monument to Jones Hole Fish Hatchery (☎ 789 4481). The hatchery is open to the public daily from 7 am to 3:30 pm. The **Jones Hole Trail** from here descends four miles to the Green River. Along the way, the trail passes Indian petroglyphs and crosses Ely Creek, where backcountry camping (with a permit) is allowed.

The unpaved **Island Park Rd** leaves from about 15 miles along the Jones Hole Rd and descends 12 miles to Rainbow Park or another five miles to Ruple Ranch, both on the Green River and both with primitive campgrounds. The warnings for the Echo Park Rd apply here as well.

Other paved roads lead to **Deerlodge Park** on the Yampa River at the east end of the monument and the scenic **Gates of Lodore** on the Green River at the northeast end of the monument. Both places have campgrounds and ranger stations; they are open in summer and are accessed by roads from Colorado.

### Backpacking

Most hikers take one of the trails described above. A few prefer to backpack into remote areas. There are designated backcountry campsites only on the Jones Hole Trail (see above). Otherwise, wilderness camping is allowed anywhere that is at least a quarter mile from an established road or trail. Backpackers must register with a ranger at one of the visitors centers or ranger stations – they receive free permits and can review the best routes with a ranger.

### River Running

The Yampa River is the only major tributary of the Colorado River that has not had its flow severely impounded by major dams. Both the Yampa and Green Rivers offer excellent river-running opportunities, with plenty of exciting rapids and white water amidst splendid scenery. Trips range from one to five days and normally go from mid-May to early September. Two excellent local companies are listed under

Vernal and about 10 others are authorized by the National Park Service to do tours – call the monument for a current list.

Experienced rafters wishing to do it themselves need a permit obtainable from the River Ranger Office (☎ (303) 374 2468) between 8 am and noon, Monday to Friday. Permits are limited, and most are issued many months in advance (especially for multiday trips), so plan well ahead.

### Fishing

Fishing is permitted only with the appropriate state permits, available from sports stores or tackle shops in Vernal, or Dinosaur, Colorado. Check with park rangers about limits and the best places.

### Places to Stay

There are no lodges or restaurants in the monument, so camping is your only option. The main campground is *Green River*, five miles east of the dinosaur quarry along Cub Creek Rd. Open from May to September, it has bathrooms and drinking water but no showers or hookups. Camping is $6 and reservations are not taken. The campground may fill on summer weekends but rarely fills midweek.

During the winter, Green River campground is closed, but you can stay at the nearby *Split Mountain* campground, which has no water and is free (but closed in summer). Free camping is permitted at *Rainbow Park, Ruple Lodge, Deerlodge Park, Gates of Lodore* and *Echo Park*. Only the last two have drinking water, and all are closed in winter. See the Scenic Drives and Hiking Trails section above for descriptions of how to get to these places, and call the visitors centers to check on dates and availability.

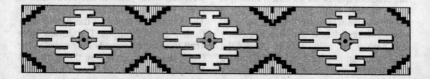

# Western Utah

The grim names on local maps describe western Utah: Snake Valley, Black Rock Desert, Skull Valley, Little Sahara, Blood Mountain, Disappointment Hills, Skull Rock Pass, Confusion Range. This is harsh desert country. The map shows few settlements or paved roads southwest of the Great Salt Lake, but the many dirt roads crisscrossing the area indicate that, even in this difficult land, people have tried – and continue to try – to eke out an existence through mining and ranching. A large portion of western Utah is inaccessible even to the hardiest desert rat – military testing, training and proving grounds allow no public access.

Western Utah was never home to many people. Small bands of nomadic Indians hunted through the area, and today, there are two small Goshute Indian reservations, which offer little of interest to non-Indians.

The inhospitable terrain did not deter the famous Pony Express riders, who galloped across western Utah in the 1860s. The Pony Express Trail can still be followed, and it is one of the area's most interesting excursions for drivers of good vehicles. Other attractions are stark scenery, the Bonneville Salt Flats (famed as the site of many land speed records), the occasional museum in one of the small towns on the edges of the region or gambling on the Nevada/Utah border.

This chapter begins in the north along I-80 and then moves south.

## WENDOVER

Two hours (125 freeway miles) west of Salt Lake City, Wendover straddles the Nevada/Utah border and provides northern Utahans with a taste of the glitter and gambling that Nevada is famous for. There are hotels on both sides of the state line, but only those on the Nevada side can legally operate a casino. But not all visitors come

for gambling – the Bonneville Salt Flats are only a short drive away.

### Orientation & Information

Wendover Blvd, parallel to and south of I-80, is the main (and almost only) thoroughfare. Utah addresses are E Wendover Blvd; Nevada addresses are W Wendover Blvd.

The Welcome Center (☎ (702) 664 3414, 1 (800) 426 6862), 937 W Wendover Blvd, is open from 8:30 am to 5 pm daily. There is also a visitors bureau in the Bonneville Speedway Museum (see below). The Wendover Clinic (☎ (702) 644 2220) handles medical emergencies. Wendover is on Utah time, but the rest of Nevada is one hour behind Utah.

### Things to See & Do

The **Bonneville Speedway Museum** (☎ 665 7721), 1000 E Wendover Blvd, on the east edge of town, is full of classic American cars. In addition to classic models, the collection includes some of the cars that set land speed records on the salt flats (see Around Wendover below). There are also photos, trophies and other racing mementos, as well as a souvenir shop. Hours are flexible, though the museum is open daily in summer. Admission is $2 or $1 for six- to 12-year-olds.

For **gambling**, catch the shuttle bus that runs along Wendover Blvd linking hotels with casinos on the Nevadan side. There is complete 24-hour gambling action and occasional entertainment, but the few casinos are subdued compared to those in most Nevadan gambling towns. Play at the Red Garter Casino, the Peppermill Casino, the Silver Smith Casino or the Nevada Crossing Hotel & Casino, all along W Wendover Blvd.

There is a **golf course** south of Wendover Blvd at the west end of town.

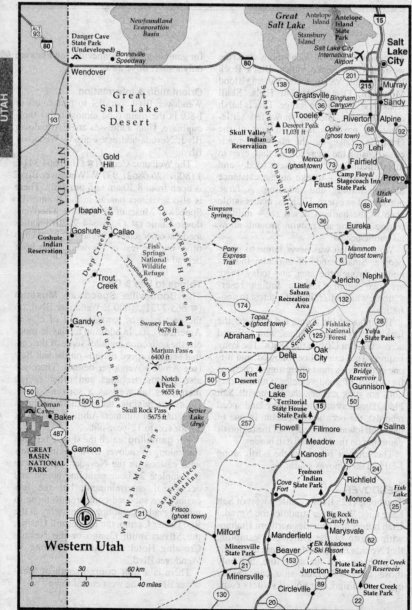

Western Utah

## Places to Stay – camping

*State Line RV Park* (☎ (702) 664 2221) is just off Wendover Blvd at the state line. It has RV sites with hookups for $16 on weekends, less midweek. There is a coin laundry, and guests can use facilities at the nearby State Line Inn.

On the Nevada side, the Red Garter Casino has a free RV parking area (no facilities) for RV folks who want to park and play. Behind the casino is a *KOA* (☎ (702) 664 3221) that has showers. Fees range from $13 (no hookups) to $22 (full hookups).

## Places to Stay – bottom end

Because gamblers often opt to descend on the town on weekends, many hotels raise their prices on Fridays, Saturdays, holidays and for special events. Summer rates may also be higher.

The *Motel 6* (☎ 665 2267), 561 E Wendover Blvd, charges $26/30 for singles/doubles midweek, $10 more on weekends. It has a pool. The *Western Ridge Motel* (☎ 665 2211), 895 E Wendover Blvd, also has a pool. Midweek rooms range from $26/30 to $34/36, depending on room size. Weekend rates can go up by $10 to $30 depending on the room and demand.

Other decent places to try in this price range are the *Bonneville Motel* (☎ 665 2500), 389 E Wendover Blvd, which has a pool; the *Heritage Motel* (☎ 665 7744, 1 (800) 457 5927, fax 665 2975), 505 E Wendover Blvd; and the *Western Motel* (☎ 665 2215), 645 E Wendover Blvd, which has a pool and an adjacent restaurant.

## Places to Stay – middle

The *State Line Inn* (☎ 665 2226, 1 (800) 848 7300, fax 531 4090), 295 E Wendover Blvd, has a pool, spa and 24-hour coffee shop. From the inn, a glassed-in bridge across the state line leads into the Silver Smith Casino, outside which stands the giant figure of Wendover Will waving you in. Rooms are pleasant and reasonably sized; there are some larger rooms and a few suites. Doubles start from $34 midweek and from around $40 on weekends; suites are twice as expensive.

The Best Western *Salt Flat Inn* (☎ 665 7811), 999 E Wendover Blvd (near I-80 exit 2), features a pool, sauna, spa and exercise room. It includes a continental breakfast in the rates, but it's a half mile to the nearest restaurant. Large rooms are in the $40s midweek from mid-September to mid-May, in the $50s midweek in summer, and $60 to $70 on weekends.

The *Super 8 Motel* (☎ /fax (702) 664 2888) is on W Wendover Blvd in Nevada next to the Red Garter Casino, where there is a bar and 24-hour restaurant. Summer midweek rates are $39.88/42.88 for singles/doubles with one bed, $46.88 for doubles with two beds. Rates are lower from October to March, higher on weekends.

The *Nevada Crossing Hotel & Casino* (☎ (702) 664 2900, 1 (800) 537 0207), 1035 W Wendover Blvd, has a pool, spa and casino next door (with restaurant, bar and occasional entertainment). Rooms are in the $40s midweek, in the $50s on weekends. This place is popular with truck drivers because of the service station next door. The *Silver Smith Casino* (☎ (702) 664 2231) is the oldest of Wendover's casinos, but it's kept up very well and has rooms around $50. The *Peppermill Casino* (☎ (702) 664 2255) has slightly cheaper rooms.

## Places to Eat

The casinos have the food scene wrapped up. The *Peppermill* features all-you-can-eat buffets – lunch is about $6 and dinner about $8 from Monday to Friday. The other casinos have 24-hour restaurants or coffee shops. There are several fast food places as well.

## Getting There & Away

The Greyhound bus (☎ 665 2322) stops in Wendover on its runs between Salt Lake City and San Francisco, California.

## AROUND WENDOVER
### Bonneville Salt Flats

The salt flats are the remnants of ancient Lake Bonneville, which once covered all of northern Utah and beyond. Today, all that remains is the Great Salt Lake – and the thousands of acres of salt flats that create a super smooth surface for car racing. Unfortunately, problems of salt deterioration and shrinkage blamed partially on natural cycles and partially on local mining activities have resulted in the flats shrinking by approximately 1% each year since the 1960s. The area is managed by the BLM, which plans to pump salty waste water from a potash mining plant in an attempt to retard salt loss from the flats.

The salt flats are visible from I-80 a few miles northeast of Wendover. A paved side road leads to a parking area – you can continue beyond and drive on the hard-packed salt yourself and camp if you wish. There are no facilities, and it is a little eerie to sleep out in the middle of the vast flat whiteness. Obey all signs – parts of the flats are very thin and can trap vehicles in the mud beneath.

Cars, tents, and entire garages mushroom on the flats periodically, especially in the third week of August during the **Bonneville National Speed Trials**. Other speed trials occur periodically, especially from July to November – call the Welcome Center or museum in Wendover for details. The speed trials are threatened by the salt deterioration – locals hope that the BLM's plans to retard the salt loss will work.

One of my childhood heroes was English racing driver Sir Malcolm Campbell, who was the first person to drive over 300 mph. He did this in his *Bluebird Special* on 3 September 1935 over a perfectly groomed one-mile course laid on the salt flats of Bonneville. Since then, American Craig Breedlove, driving *Spirit of America*, has broken the 400, 500 and 600 mph barriers – the last on 15 November 1965. Rocket-powered cars are slowly pushing the present record of 633 mph.

### Danger Cave State Park
This cave was used by prehistoric Indians 10,000 years ago. It lies a couple of miles northeast of Wendover, but despite being marked on many maps, there are no facilities at all.

### Ibapah
Ibapah is about 60 miles south of Wendover via paved roads through Nevada and Utah. Ibapah is the end of the Pony Express Trail, described later in the chapter.

## TOOELE
Tooele (pronounced 'too-ill-uh') was settled by Mormon pioneers in 1849 and is the Tooele County seat. Agriculture has been overtaken by industry as the main economic base – mining, a military munitions depot and proving grounds, and landfills are important.

Tooele is the area's largest town. A pleasant place with 16,000 inhabitants, it provides accommodations for people wishing to visit the local museums, nearby ghost towns and surrounding countryside. The area can also be visited on day trips from Salt Lake City, only 35 miles away.

### Orientation & Information
Hwy 36 (Main St) is the main street and runs north-south; Vine St is the main east-west street.

The chamber of commerce (☎ 882 0690), 50 E 100 North, is open from 9 am to 4 pm Monday to Friday. The library (☎ 882 2182) is at 47 E Vine. The post office (☎ 882 1429) is at 65 N Main. The medical center (☎ 882 1697) is at 211 S 100 East.

### Things to See & Do
The **Tooele County Museum** (☎ 882 2836), 35 N Broadway (four blocks east of Main St), is in the old railway station, which dates to 1909. Exhibits deal mainly with local mining history and the railway. Outside, there are vintage carriages, a steam engine and a replica mine. A miniature railway operates on Saturdays. Hours are 1 to 4 pm Tuesday to Friday, and 11 am to 4 pm on Saturday, Memorial Day to Labor Day. Call for an appointment at other times.

Another historical museum, the **DUP Museum** at 39 E Vine St, is housed in an 1867 stone courthouse and an older log cabin alongside. Inside are pioneer photographs and artifacts. Hours are from 11 am to 3 pm on Saturdays in July and August. At other times, call the curators for an appointment – their phone numbers are posted in the window.

Play nine holes of **golf** at Oquirrh Hills Course (☎ 882 4220), 700 East and Edgemont St.

## Special Events

Tooele County Arts Festival is held the last weekend in May or the first in June. Tooele County Fair & Rodeo is held in mid-August.

## Places to Stay

The small *Villa Motel* (☎ 882 4552), 475 N Main St, has simple rooms for about $30 or a few dollars more with a kitchenette. The *Valley View Motel* (☎ 882 3235), 594 Canyon Rd at the south end of town, has 10 rooms with kitchenettes for about $36.

The *Comfort Inn* (☎ 882 6100, fax 882 6102), 491 S Main St, offers a pool, spa, exercise room and coin laundry. Most rooms have a refrigerator and microwave; rates start around $40/44 for singles/doubles – a few dollars more in summer. Suites and larger rooms with kitchenettes go up to $75. Rates include a breakfast coupon redeemable in a nearby restaurant.

The *Best Western Inn* (☎ 882 5010, fax 882 5746), 365 N Main St, has a indoor, glassed-in pool, spa (fee) and coin laundry. Pleasant rooms with refrigerators run about $45/50 singles/doubles in summer, a few dollars less at other times. Rates include continental breakfast.

## Places to Eat

The local favorite is the *Glowing Embers Restaurant* (☎ 882 0888), 494 S Main. It serves reasonably priced American meals from 6 am to 9 pm daily (to 10 pm on Friday and Saturday). Sensibly priced American lunches and dinners are also served at the *Golden Corral Steak House* (☎ 882 6579), 411 N Main. These two are convenient to the Comfort and Best Western Inns.

A decent little Mexican restaurant is *Los Laureles* (☎ 882 2860), 23 N Main St, open from 11 am to 10 pm except Sunday. *Tooele Pizza & Restaurant* (☎ 882 8035),

21 E Vine, is open from 10 am to 10 pm, Monday to Saturday, and has eat-in or takeout pizzas and other fare.

## Getting There & Away

UTA (☎ 882 9031), 100 E 200 South, runs bus 38 to Salt Lake City and bus 51 to Grantsville – no Sunday service.

## AROUND TOOELE
### Benson Grist Mill

This grist (grain) mill was built around 1860 using wooden pegs and leather to hold the timbers together. It operated until about 1940 and has recently been restored. Inside, the original machinery remains on display; outside are several period buildings. The mill is usually open summer afternoons, Tuesday to Saturday. Call 882 7137 for information. The mill is eight miles north of Tooele, just west of Hwy 36 on Hwy 138.

### Grantsville

Settled in 1850 by Mormon pioneers, this small town is 11 miles northwest of Tooele. The chamber of commerce (☎ 884 3411), corner of Park and Main St, has area information.

The main attraction is the **Donner-Reed Memorial Museum** (☎ 884 3348, 884 6674, or call the chamber of commerce), 90 N Cooley St (two blocks west of the chamber) in an adobe house dating from the 1860s. Inside, exhibits describe the Donner-Reed party's wagon train, which was caught by winter snows in the Sierra Nevada in 1847. Almost half the group died, and the survivors resorted to cannibalism to survive – a famous story of the early Western frontier. The museum is opened on request. Outside, Grantsville's first **jail** can be seen – a small, portable, iron-grill box. Photograph your traveling companions languishing inside – the jail remains open even if the museum is closed!

Grantsville has no hotels, but the *Skyline Restaurant* (☎ 884 3272), 58 W Main St, serves meals, and the *Bluebird* (☎ 884 6503), 148 W Main St, sells ice cream and sandwiches.

### Stansbury Mountains

These mountains are just west of Grantsville and include 11,031-foot Deseret Peak. They are part of the Wasatch-Cache National Forest (☎ 524 5042 in Salt Lake City). Drive five miles south of Grantsville and then head west another four miles to South Willow – there are several free USFS campgrounds along this road, but they lack drinking water and are closed October to May.

At the end of the road past the campgrounds (12 miles from Grantsville) is a parking area and trailhead at 7400 feet. From here, a six-mile trail reaches **Deseret Peak**, which offers superb views.

### Bingham Canyon
### Copper Mine Overlook

This gives good views of the world's largest open-pit mine (described in the chapter on Salt Lake City). To reach the overlook, head east of Tooele on Vine St and follow signs along Middle Canyon Rd. The first seven miles are paved, but then the road becomes dirt; it is passable to cars (high-clearance recommended) in good weather. The overlook is about four miles beyond the end of the paved road.

Vehicles with high clearance or 4WD can continue past the turnoff to the overlook, down Butterfield Canyon, and finally reach paved roads in the Salt Lake Valley. These roads are closed by snow in winter and are not recommended after heavy rains.

### Ghost Towns

Head south from Tooele on Hwy 36 for 12 miles, then east on Hwy 73 for five miles to signs for **Ophir**, where you'll find deserted mining buildings and a few houses – please respect the residents' property. There's little to see unless you are interested in old mining towns.

Four miles beyond the Ophir turnoff on Hwy 73 is a sign for **Mercur**. There is a small mining museum open daily from 10 am to 8 pm from May to September.

### PONY EXPRESS TRAIL

Over 130 miles of the original Pony Express Trail, passing through the ruins of several stations, can be followed on a backcountry byway operated by the BLM (☎ 977 4300 in Salt Lake City). Most of the road is maintained as gravel or dirt and is passable to ordinary cars in good weather. In winter, snow may close the route or necessitate the use of 4WD; in summer, heavy rains may bog down vehicles. Spring and fall are the best traveling times. There are no services, and drivers should carry extra food and water, fill up with gas and check tires and spares before departing. Primitive camping is allowed along the trail, which is well signed.

The trail begins at **Fairfield**, about 25 miles southwest of I-15 at Lehi along Hwy 73. Here, you'll find the **Camp Floyd/Stagecoach Inn State Park** (☎ 768 8932,

---

### Delivering Mail by Trusty Steed

Those who complain that mail delivery is too slow would not have been happy in the mid-1800s, when a letter took two months to reach California from the East Coast of the USA. Delivery was by boat to Caribbean Panama, by mule to the Pacific Coast, and by boat again up to San Francisco, California.

The Pony Express was founded in 1860 to speed mail across the country. Expert horsemen who weighed under 120 pounds were hired to ride the almost 1900 miles from St Joseph, Missouri, to Sacramento, California. This was done in relays, passing through home stations roughly 60 miles apart where riders changed, and through swing stations about 12 miles apart where horses were changed. Speeds averaged 190 miles per day, though 'Buffalo Bill' (William C Cody) rode a record 322 miles in less than 22 hours, using 21 different horses. The fastest run was the delivery of President Lincoln's Inaugural Address, which took just seven and a half days. The service lasted only 19 months – its end came with the completion of a transcontinental telegraph system in 1861. ∎

254 9036), where thousands of troops were housed in the 1850s and 1860s. The 12-room inn dates from 1858 and has been restored (no accommodations). The park and inn are open from Easter to October; there is a picnic area and small museum. Hours are 11 am to 5 pm; admission is $1.50 or $1 for six- to 12-year-olds.

A sign near the inn points the way to the Pony Express Trail. **Faust Junction**, about 15 miles west, is where the trail intersects Hwy 36, about 30 miles south of Tooele; this is another easy access point to the trail. There is an interpretive marker here – one of many which can be read by the curious traveler. The road continues past the Onaqui Mountains, where wild horses are often seen, and climbs over 6100-foot-high Lookout Pass, the highest point on the trail. **Simpson Springs Station**, 25 miles west of Faust Junction, is the best restored of the Pony Express stations along the route. Nearby is a small *BLM campground* with drinking water and toilets ($3 a night).

West of Simpson Springs, the trail passes the Dugway Range to the north and the Thomas Range to the south, both good rock hounding areas. A small sign indicates a rough road into the Dugways, which are known for geode beds. Topaz Mountain in the Thomas Range is known for topaz. About 40 miles west of Simpson Springs is the **Fish Springs National Wildlife Refuge** (☎ 831 5353), an oasis in the desert where 220 species have been recorded. Ducks, geese, herons and other waterfowl flock to the refuge, especially during spring and fall migrations. Tundra swans overwinter here from late December to early March. No camping is permitted, but daylight visits are allowed along an 11-mile loop road giving views of the marshes, springs and dikes of the refuge. Bird checklists and information are available at the entrance.

A sign interprets the few rocks that remain of **Boyd Station**, halfway between the refuge and **Callao**, 25 miles west. Callao is home to about 200 people who work in local agriculture.

A road south of Callao goes 15 miles to Trout Creek; there is a picnic area (no drinking water, free camping allowed) about four miles along this road. Side roads from the Trout Creek Rd head west into the 12,000-foot **Deep Creek Mountains** – a remote, high and rarely visited wilderness. The forested mountains are the haunts of mountain lions, bobcats, elk, mule deer, bighorn sheep and other wildlife. Climbing and hiking is best from June to October – the peaks are snowbound during the rest of the year. Access is best from the Trout Creek Road side – access from the west requires permits from the **Goshute Indian Reservation** (☎ 234 1138, fax 234 1162), PO Box 6104, Ibapah, 84034. The west side is much drier. Trail descriptions are found in *Hiking the Great Basin* by John Hart (Sierra Club Books, 1992). The dirt road continues south of Trout Creek for about 50 miles to intersect paved Hwy 6/50 just across the state line in Nevada, near Great Basin National Park.

Bighorn sheep (TW)

The Pony Express Trail continues 13 miles northwest of Callao to the signed remnants of **Canyon Station** and on through Clifton Flats, from where a signed dirt road heads north to **Gold Hill**, a few miles from the trail. Gold Hill is one of the largest ghost towns in Utah – a few people still live here, but the town is largely deserted. The Pony Express Trail ends at **Ibapah**, 28 miles from Callao. Here, there is a gas station, store and a paved road leading north into Nevada and emerging at Wendover, 60 miles away. South of Ibapah is the Goshute Indian Reservation, most of which requires a permit to visit.

## EUREKA

This small mining town (population 700) is the gateway to Hwy 6/50, which slashes southwest across the deserts of western Utah, reaching Great Basin National Park just across the state line in Nevada. Once, thousands of people lived in Eureka – today, the mining boom is over and the town has shrunk. It calls itself 'The Friendliest Town on America's Loneliest Highway'.

### Orientation & Information

The city hall (☎ 433 6915), in a historic building at 241 W Main St, has tourist information. The medical clinic (☎ 433 6905) is at 330 W Main St.

### Things to See

Upstairs in the city hall and next door in the old railway station, informative exhibits of the **Tintic Mining Museum** deal mainly with the mining history of the area. The museum is open weekends in summer and erratically or on request at other times; curators' phone numbers are posted in the window or call the Tintic Historical Society (☎ 433 6842), PO Box 218, 84628. The society gives **walking tours** of the area.

Booklets available at the Tintic Mining Museum describe a few **ghost towns** within a short drive of Eureka. Silver City and Mammoth are the best known.

### Special Events

The annual Tintic Silver Festival takes place the third weekend in August. Mining tours by the Tintic Historical Society are the highlight.

### Places to Stay & Eat

*Little Valley*, about 10 miles south of Vernon, has free camping in the Wasatch-Cache National Forest – almost 30 miles from Eureka. Bring drinking water. The campground is open May to October. There is also camping at Little Sahara Recreation Area.

The five-room *Carpenter Station* (☎ 433 6311), 202 W Main St, has rooms for about $30 a double, as well as a general store, coin laundry and gas station.

The *Gold Diggers Restaurant* (☎ 433 6675), 301 W Main St, is the best place to eat – closed Monday.

## LITTLE SAHARA RECREATION AREA

The BLM manages almost 95 sq miles here, of which almost half are sand dunes. Little Sahara is a mecca for ORV (off-road vehicle) users who roar around the dunes. The BLM brochure states 'Each year several people are seriously injured or killed in the dunes through negligence. Always check for steep drop-offs before powering over the crest of a dune'.

Naturalists should keep their eyes open for the herd of pronghorn antelope that roams the area. There is also a unique species of giant fourwing saltbush that grows here – it grows twice as fast and has half the chromosomes of regular saltbush.

Information is available from the BLM (☎ 743 6811), 15 E 500 North, Fillmore, 84631. A visitors center (with exhibits) is open from 1 to 4 pm Monday to Friday, and 9 am to 4 pm on weekends from March to October, and shorter hours during winter.

There are three campgrounds, two of which have designated safe areas (no ORVs) for kids to play in the sand. The campgrounds have picnic tables, charcoal grills, toilets and drinking water from March to October only. In winter, toilets and water are available at the visitors center.

Day-use fees are $5 per vehicle from

March to October – this allows the use of a campsite if you wish. There is no charge in winter. Spring and fall are the most heavily used periods, especially on weekends.

Little Sahara is 21 miles south of Eureka or 35 miles north of Delta.

## DELTA

This town of 3500 people is an agricultural center for the farms irrigated by the Sevier River – alfalfa and grain crops are important. Industry is not absent, however. The Intermountain Power Plant is 18 miles north of town – it is the largest coal-fired power plant in the known universe. Delta's main importance for travelers is as the 'Gateway to Great Basin National Park', which lies almost 100 miles west. Delta has the best selection of hotels and services west of I-15 (in Utah).

### Orientation & Information

The chamber of commerce (☎ 864 4316), 80 N 200 West, is open from 9 am to 4 pm, Monday to Friday. The library (☎ 864 4945) is at 76 N 200 West. The post office (☎ 864 2811) is at 86 S 300 East. The medical center (☎ 864 5591) is at 126 S White Sage Ave.

### Things to See & Do

The **Great Basin Museum**, a small regional museum (☎ 864 5013), 328 W 100 North, has pioneer, mining and historical exhibits. One exhibit describes the Topaz War Relocation Center (see Around Delta below). Hours are 10 am to 4 pm, Tuesday to Saturday.

You can take a guided tour of the cheese-making plant at the **Delta Valley Farms Cheese Company** (☎ 864 2725), 1365 N 1250 East – call for hours. It also has a restaurant.

Play a nine-hole round of golf at Sunset View Course (☎ 864 2508), 3000 E 1500 North. Or visit West Millard Recreation (☎ 864 3133), 201 E 300 North, which has an indoor pool, outdoor kids pool, racquetball court and gym equipment. Call for times – the swimming pool has strange hours.

### Places to Stay – camping

The oddly named *B Kitten Klean Trailer Park* (☎ 864 2614), 181 E Main St, has showers and sites with hookups for $12, without hookups for $6.

The Fishlake National Forest (☎ 743 5721 in Fillmore) runs the *Oak Creek Campground*, 17 miles east of Delta or four miles east of Oak City on paved roads. Drinking water and toilets are available from mid-May to October. Overnight use is $6, and there is trout fishing in Oak Creek.

### Places to Stay – bottom end

Summer rates (given below) are a few dollars more than at other times. The cheapest places charge about $26/30 for basic single/double rooms and include the following: the *Willden Motel* (☎ 864 2906), 127 W Main; the *Rancher Motel & Cafe* (☎ 864 2741, fax 864 5507), 171 W Main; and the *Starglo Motor Lodge* (☎ 864 2041), 234 W Main St, which has a coin laundry.

Slightly better rooms for a few more dollars are available at *Deltan Inn – Super 5 Motel* (☎ 864 5318), 347 E Main. The *Killpack Motor Lodge* (☎ 864 2734), 201 W Main St, has basic but clean rooms for $28/32, and a couple of larger rooms with kitchenettes for a few dollars more. The *Budget Motel* (☎ 864 4533, fax 864 4533), 75 S 350 East, is the largest of the cheap hotels, with 29 rooms. Rates are $30/34 or about $40 for seven larger rooms with kitchenettes.

### Places to Stay – middle

The Best Western *Motor Inn* (☎ 864 3882, fax 864 4834), 527 E Topaz Blvd (near the intersection of Hwy 6 and Hwy 50) is by far the best and largest (82 rooms) place in town. Facilities include swimming and kids' pools, an exercise room, and a coin laundry. The Jade Garden Restaurant is across the street. Rooms are about $45 to $70 in summer, depending on room size.

### Places to Eat

The restaurant selection is limited and American food predominates, but meals are reasonably priced and quite good. *Top's*

*City Cafe* (☎ 864 2148), 313 W Main St, serves simple, inexpensive meals all day. For steak and seafood, both the *Rancher Motel & Cafe* (☎ 864 2741), 171 W Main St, and *Chef's Palace* (☎ 864 2421), 225 E Main St, are locally recommended. The Rancher also serves Mexican food and is open all day, while the more upscale Chef serves dinners only (closed Sunday) and has a salad bar. The *Jade Garden Restaurant and Lounge* (☎ 864 2947), 540 E Topaz Blvd, is a good family restaurant open daily for breakfast, lunch and dinner. The *Pizza House* (☎ 864 2207), 69 S 300 East, serves soups, salads and sandwiches as well as pizza and pasta (closed Sunday).

Two miles north of town is the *Delta Valley Farms Restaurant* (☎ 864 3566), 1365 N 1250 East, which is a local favorite family restaurant serving lunches from 10 am to 4 pm (closed Sunday). It is next to a cheese-making plant (see Things to See & Do above).

### Entertainment
The *T&T Twin Theaters* (☎ 864 4551) are at 420 E Topaz Blvd. The *Wagon Wheel Tavern* (☎ 864 4006), 347 W Main St, has dancing on weekends.

### AROUND DELTA
A maze of paved and gravel roads serving the local farming community surrounds Delta. Apart from ranches, the roads reach several sites of interest. These are not easy to find – ask at the chamber of commerce for directions if you are interested.

The Great Basin Museum and the city park near the chamber of commerce have memorials to the **Topaz War Relocation Center**, about 14 miles northwest of Delta. This is where thousands of US citizens of Japanese descent were 'relocated' during WW II – today it is a ghost town of streets and a few ruins.

**Fort Deseret** is about 10 miles southwest of Delta. Some maps describe it as a state park – it's no more than a picnic area near the crumbling remains of a fort built by Mormon pioneers in the 1860s. A few miles west is the **Great Stone Face** – a

rock outcrop that locals claim resembles Joseph Smith, founder of the Mormon church. (Use faith, imagination or hallucinogens to see the prophet.)

Two state waterfowl management areas offer birding opportunities, especially during spring and fall migrations. These are **Topaz** (15 miles northwest) and **Clear Lake** (20 miles south).

Gunnison Bend Reservoir, five miles west of town, has a boat ramp, swimming beach, fishing and water-skiing.

The **Fishlake National Forest** (see Fillmore & Around in Central Utah) is about 15 miles east of Delta. There is camping, fishing and hiking in the small Canyon Mountains, which reach over 9000 feet.

About halfway between Delta and the Nevada state line are the **House Range** mountains, with several gravel or dirt roads leading to rock hounding sites. The **Notch Peak Rd**, 43 miles west of Delta along Hwy 6/50, is a good gravel road giving access to the area – a 50-mile loop brings you back to Hwy 6. Locals say that Notch Peak is the largest limestone mountain in Utah. Swasey Peak (9678 feet), north of Notch Peak, is known for trilobite fossils. Much of the area is managed by the BLM (☎ 743 6811), 15 E 500 North, Fillmore, 84631, which administers over 40% of Utah's lands. It can provide further information about this remote area.

### GREAT BASIN NATIONAL PARK
This park is 100 miles west of Delta, just over the state line in Nevada, and features two main attractions – Lehman Caves and Wheeler Peak. Although the park lies just beyond the states covered in this book, a brief description follows.

### Information
Get National Park Service information from the Superintendent (☎ (702) 234 7331), Great Basin NP, Baker, NV 89311. Entrance is free. There is a visitors center, open daily except New Year's Day, Thanksgiving and Christmas. Summer hours are 7:30 am to 6 pm, 8 am to 5 pm the rest of the year.

Bristlecone pine cone

For descriptions of the backcountry, read *Hiking and Climbing in Great Basin National Park* by Michael Kelsey (Kelsey Publishing, Utah, 1988).

### Lehman Caves

Most visitors come for these caves, which have beautiful geological formations. Entrance to the cave is from near the visitors center and only allowed if you go on a ranger-led tour. Tours last 90 minutes, cover over half a mile and include a few stairways. The cave temperature is a constant 50°F – bring a sweater. Tours are offered hourly from 8 am to 6 pm from Memorial Day to Labor Day; the 6 pm tour is conducted by candlelight. More frequent departures are available on weekends. Four tours a day are offered the rest of the year. Tours cost $4, or $3 for children ages six to 15 and $2 for seniors over 62. Buy tickets at the visitors center as soon as you arrive.

### Wheeler Peak

At 13,061 feet, Wheeler Peak is Nevada's second highest mountain and the only one that has a year-round ice field. A scenic road climbs 12 miles to Wheeler Peak Campground at about 10,000 feet. From here a strenuous four-mile (one-way) trail climbs to the summit. Apart from the ice field, see the bristlecone pines, which are about 4000 years old and said to be the world's oldest living species. There are various other trails. The entire road is open from about June to September, depending on snow conditions. Hiking is difficult because of snow in winter and spring, when cross-country skiing is a possibility.

### Places to Stay & Eat

This is one of the more remote areas in the National Park System, and there are far fewer visitors than in the more famous parks of southern Utah or the Grand Canyon. The nearest town of any size is Ely, almost 70 miles to the west, with about 20 hotels. Delta (100 miles) and Beaver (124 miles) offer lodging choices on the Utah side. Milford (94 miles) has just one hotel. The little town of Baker, Nevada, just outside the park, has a motel and a couple of places to eat. Also try the *Border Inn* (☎ (702) 234 7300) on the state line along Hwy 6/50, which has simple rooms in the $30s and a restaurant serving meals all day.

Within the park there are small campgrounds that may fill during the summer, especially on weekends, though many visitors simply pass through on day trips. *Lower Lehman Creek Campground*, two miles beyond the visitors center along the Wheeler Peak Rd, is the only one open all year. Three other campgrounds are open in summer only. Fees are $5, and there are toilets and water but no showers. Free backcountry camping is permitted in most of the park – ask at the visitors center for recommendations.

There is a cafe at the visitors center, which is open from Easter to October. A picnic area is nearby.

### HWY 21

This is another lonely road crossing western Utah, running 112 miles from I-15 at Beaver to Garrison near the Utah-Nevada line, and another 12 miles to Great Basin National Park. It offers the fastest link between Great Basin and the national parks of southwestern Utah. Rock hounds claim that this is one of the best areas in the state to prospect for semiprecious stones – a brochure describing rock hounding in Beaver County is available from the county travel council (see Beaver in Southwestern Utah).

Starting from the state line, you drive through Garrison, a 'blink and you'll miss it' town with no tourist facilities. The road continues through almost uninhabited and sparsely vegetated desert and climbs over a 7000-foot pass in the eerily named **Wah Wah Mountains** about 50 miles into Utah. Near mile marker 54, a gravel road heads south for about 15 miles into the Wah Wahs, providing access to remote hiking and camping possibilities – bring water.

Another 15 miles brings you to the San Francisco Mountains, once important for silver. **Frisco** is a ghost town visible from Hwy 21 near mile marker 63; a historical marker tells the story near a turnoff that leads into the remains.

Frisco once had a population of several thousand and was served by a railway, but its mining heyday came to a dramatic end in 1885 when the main silver mine quite literally caved in.

Today, several buildings still stand. Be careful when exploring the area as some buildings are nearing a state of collapse, and there are mine shafts nearby. Other ghost towns can be found close by.

## Milford

This small town is 82 miles from the state line and 30 miles before Beaver. It offers one hotel and several places to eat, but is otherwise of little interest. Information is available from the Milford City Office (☎ 387 5070, 387 2711), 302 S Main. The Amtrak trains (☎ 1 (800) 872 7245) that run between Salt Lake City and Los Angeles, California, stop here in the middle of the night.

The *Station Motel* (☎ 387 2481), 485 S 100 West, has about two dozen simple but clean rooms in the low $30s for a double. The attached *Station Restaurant* (☎ 387 2804) serves American and Chinese food from 9 am to 10 pm daily. Also try the *Hong Kong Cafe* (☎ 387 2251), 433 S Main St, or the *Old Hickory Inn* (☎ 387 5042), 485 W Center.

## Beyond Milford

You have the choice of heading north on Hwy 257 to Delta (almost 80 miles) or continuing south on Hwy 21 to **Minersville**, 13 miles away. The town comes alive in mid-August with the Beaver County Fair. Minersville has *Pryor's Cafe* (☎ 386 2487) but nowhere to stay. From Minersville, Hwy 21 continues east five miles to Minersville State Park (see Beaver in Southwestern Utah) and on another 12 miles to Beaver. Alternatively, Hwy 130 goes south from Minersville to Cedar City, 40 miles away and the fastest route to Zion National Park (see Southwestern Utah).

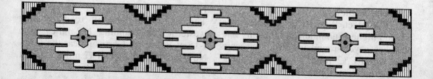

# Central Utah

The area in this chapter falls into a rough triangle delineated by I-15, I-70 and Hwy 6 between Spanish Fork and Green River. Interstate 15 runs along the west side of the San Pitch Mountains and Pavant Range, which are high, forested and scenic extensions of the Wasatch Mountains. A 7000-foot pass at the south end of the Pavant Range allows I-70 to take off eastward through Utah and on across the continent. Interstate 70 soon intersects with Hwy 89, which follows the east side of the San Pitch and Pavant Mountains.

Interstate 15 and Hwy 89 trace historically significant routes, and the towns found along them were among the first settled by the Mormon pioneers in the 1850s. There were several minor 'wars' between the Mormon pioneers and the Ute Indians as well as between Mormons and 'gentiles' (non-Mormon Whites). These altercations are described in the various museums in the area.

The towns along I-15 have been changed and modernized as freeway towns tend to be, but those along Hwy 89 have a definite early Mormon feel to them suggested by their turn-of-the-century Main St architecture, magnificent temples and traditional, clean-living, friendly inhabitants. The whole area is a mountainous one, and with few exceptions, the towns below are all between 5000 and 6000 feet above sea level with warm summers and cool winters. Thus, Mormon history and splendid mountain scenery are the major attractions along these important highways.

The next range east of Hwy 89 is wider and lower – so much so that it is known as the Wasatch Plateau. Although it is called a plateau, the area is far from flat; comprising many small ranges, it is rugged and almost roadless. This is scenic country, with plenty of remote outdoor recreation opportunities for people looking to get away from the national park crowds. A skyline drive follows the crest of the 'plateau' at elevations in excess of 10,000 feet – this drive is about 100 miles long, requires 4WD and is one of the most spectacular wilderness roads in the state.

East of the Wasatch Plateau is the Castle Valley, traversed by Hwy 10, which links a number of small towns infrequently visited by tourists. They give access to the Wasatch Plateau from the east. North of Castle Valley is Carbon County, which is important for coal mining. The towns of Price and Helper have interesting museums.

This chapter is arranged in three sections, each following the principal north-south thoroughfares outlined above.

# Central I-15 Corridor

This section covers I-15 for 130 miles from south of Provo to the intersection with I-70.

## SPANISH FORK

Spanish Fork is eight miles south of Provo. The Escalante-Dominguez expedition passed through in 1776, praising the beauty of the area. Mormons settled here in 1850, and soon after, Mormons from Iceland formed the first Icelandic settlement in the USA. Monuments to these events are found in the city park at 51 S Main St (Escalante-Dominguez) and at 895 E 300 South (Icelandic tower). The town has a population of about 11,500.

The main reason most people stop here is to visit the Spanish Fork Ranger Station (☎ 798 3571), 44 W 400 North, 84660, which has information about USFS campgrounds and the Nebo Loop, described below. The chamber of commerce (☎ 798 8352), 40 S Main St, also has visitor information.

The *Escalante B&B* (☎ 798 6652), 733

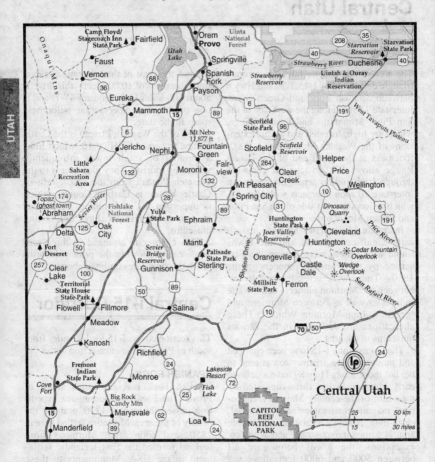

**Central Utah**

N Main St, 84660, charges about $50 for the two rooms and has a hot tub. Most visitors stay in Provo.

A locally popular place to eat is the *Trails End Cafe* (☎ 798 6212), 500 S Main St. There are several other places along Main St.

## NEBO LOOP SCENIC BYWAY

This beautiful road climbs from the old Mormon settlement of Payson at 4500 feet to over 9000 feet before dropping to 5100 feet at Nephi, about 40 miles away. The paved road is open from June to October and provides lovely views of 11,877-foot Mount Nebo and many other peaks. Elk and bighorn sheep roam the area, and the fishing is good. During the winter, the roads are open part of the way and give access for snowshoers, cross-country skiers and snowmobilers. Reach the loop by taking 600 East southbound in Payson. For more tourist information, stop by the Payson city hall (☎ 465 9226) at 439 W Utah Ave.

There are many good hiking trails in the area. From the north side of Payson Lakes, a 5.5-mile trail climbs to **Loafer Peak**

(10,687 feet) and continues a couple of miles to **Santaquin Peak** (10,685 feet). A tougher hike starts from Bear Canyon (two miles east of Ponderosa Campground), where a 6500-foot trailhead gives access to **Mount Nebo**, only five miles away but over a mile higher than the trailhead. Views from this summit are fantastic. See Dave Hall's *The Hiker's Guide to Utah* for a full description of these hikes. A much easier walk is the quarter-mile trail leaving the loop 28 miles from Payson and heading to the strangely eroded red sandstone formation called the **Devil's Kitchen**. There are many other trails along the way as well.

### Places to Stay & Eat
Uinta National Forest Service (☎ 1 (800) 283 2267 for reservations; get information in Spanish Fork or Nephi) operates several campgrounds along the loop during summer. They are *Maple Bench* (eight miles from Payson, 5800 feet elevation); *Payson Lakes* (12 miles, 8000 feet); *Blackhawk* (16 miles, 8000 feet); and *Ponderosa* (36 miles, 6200 feet). These have water and toilets and cost $5 to $7. There are also picnic sites. Free backcountry camping is also permitted.

In Payson, the *Comfort Inn* (☎ 465 4861, fax 465 4861), 830 N Main St (just off I-15 exit 254), has over 60 spacious rooms in the $60s, including continental breakfast. A few rooms with kitchenettes cost more. Rates drop from November to April. Facilities include a pool, spa, sauna, exercise room and coin laundry. Next door, the *Cobblestone Family Restaurant* (☎ 465 9283), 840 N Main St, is open 24 hours. There are a couple of other places to eat. The only other place to stay is the much cheaper *Terry's Motel & Service* (☎ 465 2582), 240 E 100 North, with 10 modest rooms at $26/31 a single/double.

### NEPHI & AROUND
As the Mormon pioneers pushed further south, they settled area after area. Nephi, named after a Mormon prophet, was established in 1851. It is about 40 miles south of Provo – far enough away to have several hotels of its own, even though it is a small town of only 3,500 inhabitants. It is the Juab County seat.

Hwy 132 east of Nephi passes the end of the Nebo Loop after six miles and continues through **Fountain Green** to **Moroni**, 21 miles away. Both are early Mormon towns founded in 1859, the latter named after an angel. Both have a couple of restaurants but no hotels. As you drive through, note the many sheep and turkey farms in the vicinity – this is one of the most important sheep and turkey-raising regions in the West. (Foreign visitors might remember that the US Thanksgiving holiday is traditionally celebrated with a turkey dinner.) Fountain Green (☎ 445 3340) celebrates Lamb Days in mid-July with a parade, games and entertainment. Eight miles south of Moroni, Hwy 132 intersects with Hwy 89 just north of Ephraim (see Central Hwy 89 Corridor, below).

### Orientation & Information
Nephi is west of I-15 between exits 228 in the north and 222 in the south. Follow signs from either exit to Main St, which is the primary thoroughfare – the south exit is the closest to services.

The chamber of commerce (☎ 623 2411), 146 N Main St, or city hall (☎ 623 0822), 21 E 100 North, have tourist information. The Uinta National Forest Nephi Ranger Station (☎ 623 2735), 740 S Main St, 84648, has information about the Nebo Loop. The medical center (☎ 623 1242) is at 549 N 400 East.

### Yuba State Park
Twenty-five miles southwest of Nephi along I-15, this park (☎ 758 2611), PO Box 159, Levan, 84639, centers on the Sevier Bridge Reservoir, which has a boat launch area for fishing and boating. The campground is open all year, has showers and a swimming area (you can swim in January if you want to hack through the ice), and charges $9 for each of its 19 sites – reservations (☎ 1 (800) 322 3770) are recommended for summer weekends. There are primitive camping areas

available around the reservoir; they have lower rates but no showers. Day use is $3.

## Special Events
The annual Ute Stampede held during the second Thursday to Saturday in July at the county fairgrounds (☎ 623 0591) has been held for over 60 years. It is a major event featuring rodeo, parades, crafts, contests, cooking, carnivals, concerts and car shows. The Juab County Fair takes place in August.

## Places to Stay – camping
The *KOA Kampground* (☎ 623 0811) is six miles east of town along Hwy 132, near the exit for the Nebo Loop. Open from mid-May to mid-October, it has a pool, game room, grocery store and coin laundry, and charges $13 without hookups, $18 with full hookups. There are Kamping Kabins for $23 a double. In Nephi itself, there is *High Country RV Park* (☎ 623 2624), 899 S Main St. See also the Nebo Loop Scenic Byway and Yuba State Park (above).

## Places to Stay – bottom end
Prices go up during the Ute Stampede. October to April rates are often lower. The *Safari Motel* (☎ 623 1071), 413 S Main St, which has a pool surrounded by a lawn and shade trees, is a good-value hotel. Singles are in the upper $20s and doubles in the $30s. Cheaper rooms are available at the *Starlite Motel* (☎ 623 1937), 675 S Main St, which has a pool, and at *Shepherd Lodge* (☎ 623 2334), 940 N Main St. Both have some rooms with kitchenettes. The *Super 8 Motel* (☎ 623 0888, fax 623 5025), 1901 S Main St, charges $33.88/36.88 for singles/doubles or $39.88 for doubles with two beds.

## Places to Stay – middle
**B&Bs** The *Whitmore Mansion* (☎ 623 4047), 110 S Main St, PO Box 73, 84648, is the most interesting place to stay. This Victorian house dates from 1898 and features antiques and elegant period decor including a turret around one of the suites. The rooms lack TVs and phones but are comfortably furnished and have private baths. Apart from a full breakfast, rates include afternoon (nonalcoholic) refreshments. Meals are served by prior request. There is no smoking, and children under 12 are not allowed. Four rooms are about $50 a double; two suites are $70.

**Hotels** *Roberta's Cove – Budget Host Motor Inn* (☎ 623 2629), 2250 S Main St, lacks a pool but has very pleasant rooms ranging from $30 to $40 a single, $35 to $45 a double and $40 to $50 for a double with two beds. The Cedar Hollow Restaurant is just over a block away. The Best Western *Paradise Inn* (☎ /fax 623 0624), 1025 S Main St, has an indoor pool and good rooms with one queen- or king-size bed for $40 to $48 and $4 more for two beds – a little less in winter.

## Places to Eat
The best restaurant is the *Cedar Hollow* (☎ 623 2633), 2087 S Main St. It is open from 6 am to 10 pm and is inexpensive – dinners cost around $10, lunches and breakfasts much less. It also has a hamburger place with takeout if you're just passing through. There are several other restaurants along Main St.

## Getting There & Away
Greyhound buses (☎ 623 0823) stop at 563 N Main St on their two or more daily runs up and down I-15 (Salt Lake City to Las Vegas, Nevada).

## FILLMORE & AROUND
Fillmore is pretty close to being the geographical center of Utah and, perhaps for that reason, became the territorial capital in 1851, even before the town was settled. A statehouse was built, but Fillmore's capital status lasted only till 1856.

Today, Fillmore is the seat of Millard County, both named after Millard Fillmore, 13th president of the USA, who was supportive of the Mormons. It has 2500 inhabitants and is the center of agriculture in the region. Fillmore is clearly a rural town. Although the statehouse is near the town center, I found a horse in the backyard of a house just two blocks away. Another house had peacocks strutting around the garden. Walk around and enjoy the small town.

## Orientation & Information

Fillmore is east of I-15 between exits 167 in the north and 163 in the south. Main St is the main drag through town.

Millard County Tourism (☎ 743 7803), 195 N Main St, has area information. Fillmore has a tourist information booth in North Park, 500 N Main St, open in summer. The Fishlake National Forest Fillmore Ranger Station (☎ 743 5721), 390 S Main St, 84631, is open 8 am to 5 pm, Monday to Friday. The BLM (☎ 743 6811), 35 E 500 North, is open from 8 am to 4:30 pm, Monday to Friday; it provides information about BLM areas west of Fillmore. The library (☎ 743 5314) is at 25 S 100 West. The post office (☎ 743 5748) is at 60 E Center. The medical center (☎ 743 5591) is at 674 S Hwy 99. The police (☎ 743 5302, or 911 in emergencies) are at 750 S Hwy 99.

## Territorial Statehouse State Park

This park (☎ 743 5316), 50 W Capitol Ave, (off 100 S Main St) lays claim to Utah's oldest government building. Rooms are furnished with period pieces, and there are exhibits of old photos and other Indian and pioneer memorabilia. Outside is a rose garden, an 1867 stone school, 1880s log cabins and a picnic/play area. Call ahead for guided tours. Hours are 9 am to 5 pm daily (to 6 pm in summer), and admission is $1.50 or $1 for six- to 15-year-olds.

## Fishlake National Forest

Head east on 200 South to reach the Fishlake National Forest along Chalk Creek Rd – the many fishing and picnic places here are popular with the locals in summer.

About seven miles south of Fillmore, Hwy 133 intersects with I-15. Take Hwy 133 south through the pioneer Mormon villages of **Meadow** and **Kanosh**, settled in the 1850s and largely undisturbed by freeway traffic. Kanosh is named after

Paiute Indian Chief Kanosh, who is buried in the village cemetery. From Kanosh, Corn Creek Rd heads east into the Pavant Range of the Fishlake National Forest, which offers many camping, hiking and fishing opportunities. The **Paiute ATV Trail** (All Terrain Vehicles) also takes off from here and heads many miles into the wilderness – information is available at Millard County Tourism in Fillmore. The trail can also be accessed at Richfield, Marysvale and other places.

## Flowell Lava Beds

Drive west on Hwy 100 (400 North) to Flowell, six miles away. From there head south for three miles to the end of the paved road, and continue on dirt roads into lava beds caused by eruptions thousands of years ago. There are many interesting geological formations within this natural devastation – the BLM in Fillmore has maps and information.

## Cove Fort

Thirty miles south of Fillmore is Cove Fort, built in 1867 on the spot indicated by Brigham Young. Restoration of the solid-looking structure was completed by the Mormon Church in 1994, and Mormon guides in period dress tell interesting stories of the fort's history. One of several forts built along the Mormon corridor between Salt Lake City and St George, it is the only one that has been fully restored. The 12 rooms are furnished with antiques. The site is just northeast of the intersection of I-15 and I-70 and can be reached from exit 135 on I-15 or exit 1 on I-70.

Interstate 15 south of here is described in the chapter on southwestern Utah. Interstate 70 east reaches Fremont Indian State Park (15 miles) and intersects with Hwy 89 (23 miles), both described in the next section.

## Places to Stay – camping

*Wagons West RV Camp* (☎ 743 6188), 545 N Main St, has showers and a coin laundry and charges $10 without hookups, $15 with hookups. The *KOA* (☎ 743 4420),

800 S 270 West, has showers, coin laundry and store; fees are $14/19 without/with hookups.

The Fishlake National Forest has campgrounds – the nearest is 14 miles southwest to Kanosh, then six miles southeast to *Adelaide Campground*. This is open from mid-May to October, has drinking water and toilets, and costs $5 a night. You can fish nearby.

### Places to Stay – bottom end

The *Spinning Wheel Motel* (☎ 743 6260), 65 S Main St, has simple but clean rooms with one or two beds, some with kitchenettes, for $23 to $33. The clean *Fillmore Motel* (☎ 743 5454), 61 N Main St, charges about $24 for a double or $34 for a double with two beds. Other basic places in this price range are the *El Ana Motel* (☎ 743 5588), 50 N Main St, and the *Economy Inn* (☎ 743 5588), 1100 N Main St. Even cheaper rooms may be found at the *Capitol Motel* (☎ 743 6633), 40 E Center.

### Places to Stay – middle

The Best Western *Paradise Inn* (☎ 743 6895, fax 743 6892), 800 N Main St, features a pool, spa and restaurant next door. Good rooms with one bed are in the $40s; spacious rooms with two beds are around $50 a double.

### Places to Eat

The *Garden of Eat'n* (☎ 743 5414), next to the Best Western Paradise Inn, is the best restaurant in town. It features American fare, a salad bar and a cocktail bar; the prices are reasonable – dinners are around $10. Hours are 6 am to 10 pm (to 11 pm in summer).

*Deano's Pizza* (☎ 743 6385), 96 S Main St, features soups, sandwiches, salads and pizzas to eat in or take out. Hours are 10 am to 10 pm, Monday to Saturday. The *Cowboy Cafe* (☎ 743 4302), 31 N Main St, features local home cooking from 6 am to 10 pm. The *Truckstop Cafe* (☎ 743 6876), 590 N Main St, serves breakfast, lunch and dinner; it is also the bus terminal.

### Entertainment

The *Avalon* (☎ 743 6918), 41 N Main St, shows movies. For a beer, stop by *Room 24* (☎ 743 8005), 280 W 500 South.

### Getting There & Away

The Greyhound bus (☎ 743 6876) stops by the Truckstop Cafe on its two or more daily runs between Salt Lake City and Las Vegas, Nevada.

# Central Hwy 89 Corridor

This section follows Hwy 89 for about 140 miles as it parallels I-15 east of the San Pitch Mountains and Pavant Range. The historic road passes through some of Utah's most traditional Mormon towns, several of which have early Western buildings lining their main streets. Hwy 89 avoids freeway traffic, which makes it a fine alternative to I-15 if you have extra time.

## SKYLINE DRIVE

This gravel and dirt road parallels Hwy 89 and traverses about 90 miles of the Wasatch Plateau from Hwy 6 in the north to I-70 in the south. The scenic but difficult drive reaches 10,900 feet and is passable to vehicles only in summer and fall. Wildflowers in early summer and fall attract drivers. 4WD vehicles are needed to complete the drive, although easier sections passable to cars can be accessed from towns along Hwy 89 or Hwy 10. Most of the drive is within the Manti-La Sal National Forest, and information is obtainable from ranger stations in Price, Ephraim and Ferron.

The drive begins near the Tucker Rest Area, about 30 miles east of Spanish Fork along Hwy 6. It follows USFS Rd 150 for most of its length except the final few miles, which run along USFS Rd 001 and USFS Rd 009 in the Fishlake National Forest. There are campgrounds at *Gooseberry* about a third of the way along the drive, and at *Ferron Reservoir* and *Twelve-mile Flat*, two-thirds of the way. These have drinking water, toilets and fire pits; they are open from about June to September. Fees are about $7. The first is also reachable from Fairview or Huntington along Hwy 31, the second area from Ferron or Gunnison along forest roads. Free primitive camping is allowed, and there are plenty of hiking trails. There's mountain wildlife, especially mule deer and elk, and more for observant naturalists. Other campgrounds and recreation opportunities are available in the lower reaches of the national forest. During the winter, many parts of the area attract cross-country skiers and snowmobilers.

### FAIRVIEW

Settled by Mormons in 1859, Fairview is a minor agricultural center for the surrounding sheep and turkey farms. The town's Mormon roots are strong, as they are in most towns in the area. Barely 1000 people live here, yet the town attracts visitors with its excellent museum. It is also an important gateway to the Skyline Drive. The **city hall** (☎ 427 3858), 85 S State, has visitor information.

### Fairview Museum of History & Arts

Housed in a school built in 1900, this small-town museum (☎ 427 9216), 85 N 100 East, is one of my favorites. Apart from a fine collection of Indian and pioneer memorabilia, there's a replica of the woolly mammoth unearthed under Huntington Reservoir dam, period art, models of Goldilocks and the three bears, and the work of Fairview's Lyndon Graham, a sculptor and wood carver who has produced wonderfully detailed miniatures of stagecoaches, trains and even Cinderella's carriage. Outside, old farm implements are scattered about. Something for everyone and it's free; donations welcomed. Hours are 10 am to 6 pm, Monday to Saturday, and 1 to 6 pm on Sunday, from roughly May to September. Hours may be extended in summer. Call for out-of-season hours.

### Skyline Drive

Hwy 31 east of Fairview intersects with the Skyline Drive after nine miles. The paved road is kept open in winter and provides access to cross-country skiers and snowmobilers. The Gooseberry campground is a short way north along the drive.

### Special Events

Pioneer Days in the week leading up to 24 July (anniversary of Brigham Young's arrival in Salt Lake City) is celebrated with rodeos, a demolition derby, food, arts & crafts and entertainment.

### Places to Stay & Eat

The small *Skyline Motel* (☎ 427 3312), 35 E 200 North, has doubles in the $30s. The *Travel Inn Cafe* (☎ 427 3466), 44 S State, has been the place to eat since 1937. There's also *Stew's Home Plate Restaurant*.

### MT PLEASANT

Settled by Danes in 1859, the town retains much of its early character. Main St has many old buildings and is on the National Historic Register. The small **Old Pioneer Museum**, 150 S State, is open from 9 am to 4 pm, Monday to Friday. The **Wasatch Academy**, 120 S 100 West, is Utah's oldest continuously operating secondary school – it dates from 1875.

Mt Pleasant is five miles south of Fairview and has about 2000 inhabitants. Hwy 116 leads west to Moroni (see Nephi & Around above). The city hall (☎ 462 2456), 115 W Main St, has local information – the police are here, too. The area's hospital (☎ 462 2411) is at 1100 S Medical Drive.

### Places to Stay & Eat

The *Mt Pleasant City Park* (☎ 462 2456) allows tents and RVs during the July celebrations here and in Manti.

*Mansion House B&B* (☎ 462 3031), 298 S State, 84647, is a splendidly restored 1890s building with stained-glass windows and hand-painted designs on the ceiling. Four rooms with private bath rent for about $60 a double with full breakfasts served in your room. The owner is a photographer and has a studio on the premises. There is no smoking; no kids under 12 allowed. Another possible B&B (☎ 462 3333) is at 2581 N Hwy 89.

There are several places to eat around Main and State Sts – the town's major intersection. The *Backroads Restaurant* (☎ 462 3111), 70 N State, serves American fare from 7:30 am to 10 pm daily.

## SPRING CITY

Spring City is about six miles south of Mt Pleasant. Named after a spring that flows year-round, this village was settled in 1852 and has about 800 inhabitants. The whole town is on the National Historic Register. The **city hall** (☎ 462 2244, 462 3029), 46 N Main St, was built in 1893; you can get information and buy booklets describing the town's buildings there. There is a small **DUP Museum** in the 1899 schoolhouse at 40 S 100 East. The *Horseshoe Mountain Inn* (☎ 462 2871), 310 S Main St, has three rooms for about $40 including breakfast. Nearby is the Horseshoe Mountain Pottery, where you can buy locally made ceramics.

## EPHRAIM

Ephraim, with over 3000 inhabitants, is the biggest town in the area. It's also a major turkey-farming center. The town was settled in 1854 and has several historic buildings.

## Information

The city offices (☎ 283 4631), 5 S Main St, have local information. The Manti-La Sal National Forest Ephraim Ranger Station (☎ 283 4151), PO Box 692, 84627, is at 150 S Main St. The library (☎ 283 4544) is at 30 S Main St. The post office (☎ 283 4189) is at 45 E 100 North. The police (☎ 283 4602, or 911 in emergencies) are at 11 S Main St.

## Things to See & Do

The late-19th-century **Mercantile Co-op Store**, 100 North and Main St, has been restored and is Ephraim's best known historic building. Another is the Homestead

B&B (see below). Others can be seen just walking around.

**Snow College**, a junior college (☎ 283 4021) at 150 E 100 North, of over 200 students dates to 1888 and provides much of the area's cultural life with concerts, plays and other performances – call for a schedule.

## Special Events

The Scandinavian Festival held over Memorial Day weekend celebrates the Scandinavian heritage of Sanpete County – now you know why so many of the locals are blond.

## Places to Stay

**Camping** *Century Trailer Court* (☎ 283 4468), 158 N 300 East, has RV sites with hookups.

*Lake Hill Campground*, nine miles away in the national forest, is reached by heading east on 400 South and following Hwy 29. The campground is at 8500 feet, has water and toilets but no showers, and is open about June to October. Overnight use is $5. The road continues past an agricultural experimental station (with self-guiding trail) and on to the Skyline Drive about five miles away.

**Motels** Two small motels charge in the $30s for a double but raise their prices during special events in the area. Call the *Iron Horse Motel* (☎ 283 4223), 670 N Main St, or *Travel Inn Motel* (☎ 283 4071), 330 N Main St.

*Ephraim Homestead B&B* (☎ 283 6367), 135 W 100 North, 84627, is a small opportunity to live in pioneer surroundings – small because there are only two units, with a third planned. The Granary, an 1860s log cabin furnished with period pieces (spinning wheel, wood stove, antique beds and claw-footed tub) is available year-round. The 1880s Victorian house (with 19th-century furnishings) is available in summer. A barn will be made into living quarters, too. Old fashioned – but comfortable and the bathrooms work! Outside, attractive grounds include swings for kids and porches for adult relaxation. No smoking or liquor is allowed, but children are welcome and the owners are friendly. Rates vary and discounts are available for longer stays – up to $80 for a one-night double in winter and a less in summer. Units can sleep families – call to arrange a stay.

There is also the *W Pherson House B&B* (☎ 238 4197), 224 S Main St, with three rooms in the $60s.

## Places to Eat

There are half a dozen places to eat along Main St – they satisfy the college crowd and will satisfy you, too, if you're hungry. (Hunger is the magic ingredient that is never seen in cookbooks but which can elevate a hot dog to heaven – or a pizza to paradise.)

## MANTI

This is one of Utah's earliest towns, settled in 1849. It is overlooked and dominated by a magnificent temple dedicated by Brigham Young in 1877 and completed in 1888. Manti is the Sanpete County seat and has over 2000 inhabitants – not a large town. Mention Manti to a Mormon, and the town gets bigger. The annual Mormon pageant is a major highlight that attracted 167,000 visitors during its 25th anniversary in 1991. Otherwise, there's little to do apart from looking at the old buildings, or maybe taking a balloon ride at Yogi Bear's Camp (see below).

## Information

The History House Visitor Center (☎ 835 8411), 402 N Main St, is a block from the temple and provides both local and church information during the summer. The library (☎ 835 2201) is at 2 S Main St. The post office (☎ 835 5081) is at 140 N Main St. The medical clinic (☎ 835 3344) is at 159 N Main St. The police (☎ 835 2191, or 911 in emergencies) are at City Hall, 50 S Main St.

## Palisade State Park

This park (☎ 835 7275, or 1 (800) 322 3770 for reservations), PO Box H, Manti, 84642, offers opportunities for swimming, fishing and nonmotorized boating. Canoes can be rented. There is a nine-hole golf course

with pro shop (☎ 835 4653). Cross-country skiing, skating, tubing and ice fishing are winter activities. The park is five miles south of Manti (or one mile north of **Sterling**, which has a store and gas station) then two miles east on Palisade Lake Rd. Day use is $3. There's a campground.

## Special Events

**Mormon Miracle Pageant** The pageant (☎ 835 3000) is a major Mormon Church event held annually since 1967. About 600 performers tell the story of Mormon beginnings and migration to Utah, and the spectacle attracts over 100,000 visitors during a 10-day run in mid-July. The pageant takes place on the grassy slopes of the hill below the Manti Temple (which is open only to Mormons on church business). The many visitors somewhat overwhelm the small town, and although the community copes valiantly, there has been talk of moving the pageant to a bigger location – inquire first before making reservations.

**County Fair** The Sanpete County Fair, featuring a rodeo, square dance, carnival, parade and other activities, is the last weekend in August.

## Places to Stay

**Camping** *Yogi Bear's Jellystone Camp Park Resort* (☎ 835 267), on Hwy 89 at north end of Manti, has showers, pool, playground, game room, coin laundry, store and various activities including Yogi Bear (in person to meet the kids) and hot-air balloon rides. Sites are $14/18 without/ with hookups.

*Manti Community Campground*, seven miles east along 500 South and Manti Canyon, has seven sites operated by the Manti-La Sal National Forest (☎ 283 4151 in Ephraim) from June to October. There are toilets and drinking water. The fee is $5. The road continues eight miles further to the Skyline Drive and provides access to cross-country skiing and snowmobiling in winter.

At Palisade State Park, there's a campground open from April to October that has hot showers. Fees are $9 for camping ($5 for winter without services). Campsites often fill on summer weekends.

**Hotels** Manti has only about 70 rooms – book in advance and expect higher rates during the pageant. Towns with more rooms are Salina (200 rooms, 33 miles), Richfield (nearly 500, 55 miles) and Nephi (nearly 200, 45 miles).

*Manti Motel* (☎ 835 8533), 445 N Main St, and *Temple View Lodge* (☎ 835 6663), 260 E 400 North, have rooms in the $30s. The Manti Motel has kitchenettes in some rooms. *Manti Country Village* (☎ 835 9300), 145 N Main St, is the biggest (23 rooms) and most comfortable motel, with large rooms, a spa and a restaurant a few steps away. Rates begin in the upper $30s.

Just outside Palisade State Park, the *Cedar Crest Inn* (☎ 835 6352), 819 Palisade Lake Rd, has about 10 rooms. There is a hot tub and a restaurant (reservations essential); some rooms have refrigerators and microwaves. Rooms are $50 to $60; one two-bedroom unit is about $80.

On Hwy 89 near its intersection with Palisade Lake Rd is the *Palisade Lodge* (☎ 835 4513), a resort with swimming pools, spas, a water slide, sauna, gym and racquetball. It has over 40 rooms ranging from motel-style to family cottages to deluxe rooms, renting from the $30s to over $100. Camping areas are also available. There are barbecue and picnic areas, but no restaurant.

**B&Bs** The B&Bs are all historic Mormon buildings with attractive period furniture, but they're renovated so that all units have private bathrooms. Each place has a spa and a no smoking rule. (The zip code for all of these B&Bs is 84642.)

The oldest is the *Old Brigham House Inn* (☎ 835 8381), 123 E Union, which was built in the 1860s and 1870s; it has four rooms in the $40 to $60 range. The *Manti House Inn B&B* (☎ 835 0161), 401 N Main St, has a restaurant open on weekends and sometimes midweek – advance reservations required. Its four rooms run around $50 to

$60; two suites are $60 to $90. One suite has an in-room spa and balcony. The *Yardley B&B* (☎ 835 1861), 190 W 200 South, has five rooms for about $40 to $60 and a more expensive suite – many rooms have four-poster beds. The *Old Grist Mill Inn B&B* (☎ 835 6455), 780 E 500 South, has eight rooms in a converted mill; rates are $55 and up.

**Places to Eat**

The *Country Village Restaurant* (also called Kay's; ☎ 835 9550), 115 N Main St, serves American meals all day. There are also a couple of fast-food places and the restaurant at the Manti House Inn B&B.

During the pageant only, food concession stands appear near the temple. In addition, the church serves dinners at the tabernacle, 100 South and Main St, or Manti Stake Center, 295 S Main St.

**GUNNISON**

When settled in 1860, this town was originally given the delightful name of Hogs Wallow, but it was renamed in honor of Captain John Gunnison, who was killed near here by Indians. A park at the north end has a tourist information booth in summer, as well as a pool and playground. Gunnison is 17 miles south of Manti.

*Lunds Campground* (☎ 528 3366), 230 S Main St, has RV hookups. Simple rooms for about $30 are available from the 13-room *Gunnison Motel* (☎ 528 7840), 12 N Main St, or the smaller *Country Paradise Motel* (☎ 528 7521), 395 S Main St.

For food, try the *Golden Spur* (☎ 528 3713), 512 N Main St, open daily for breakfast, lunch and dinner; *Mama Butch's Pizza* (☎ 528 3792), 191 S Main St; or the *Wisteria Restaurant* (☎ 528 7690), a mom 'n pop type place at 50 S Main St.

**SALINA**

Hwy 89 intersects with I-70 at Salina, 33 miles south of Manti, and the two highways continue together to the southwest for 30 miles. Settled in 1863, Salina is known for its salt deposits (hence the name, which is Spanish for 'salt mine' – one can be seen in operation a few miles north of town). Locals find prime snowmobiling in Salina Canyon, along I-70 southeast of town. There are a few 19th-century buildings in Salina, but otherwise, there's little of interest in this town of 2000 apart from the several hotels serving travelers passing through the intersection of the highways.

### Orientation & Information

Salina itself is two miles north of I-70, and there are hotels both in the center and at the freeway.

The chamber of commerce (☎ 529 7839), 60 E Main St, has area information. The library (☎ 529 7753) is at 90 W Main St. The post office (☎ 529 7221) is at 135 N 100 East. The medical clinic (☎ 529 7411) is at 310 W Main St. The police (☎ 529 3311, or 911 in emergencies) are at 90 W Main St.

### Places to Stay – camping

*Butch Cassidy Campground* (☎ 529 7400), 1100 S State, has a pool, playground, showers and coin laundry. It is open from March to October and charges $15 with hookups, less without. *Salina Creek RV Camp* (☎ 529 3711), 1385 S State, has showers and coin laundry and is similarly priced. *Don's Texaco Trailer Park* (☎ 529 3531), 215 W Main St, has RV sites only.

The nearest USFS campground is *Maple Grove* (☎ 743 5721), 11 miles northwest on US 50, then four miles west. The campground is open mid-May to October and has toilets and water. Sites cost $4.

### Places to Stay – bottom end

Most hotels raise their prices from May to October – summer rates are given. The *Lone Star Motel* (☎ 529 3642), 785 W Main St, has simple, clean rooms in the low $30s. The *Wasatch Motel & Cafe* (☎ 529 7074), 395 W Main St, and the *Ranch Motel* (☎ 529 7789), 80 N State, also offer budget rooms.

### Places to Stay – middle

The *Ho Jo Inn* (☎ 529 7467, fax 529 3671), 60 N State, has a pool, spa, coin laundry

and restaurant/bar. Rooms are $40/45 for singles/doubles with one bed, $55 with two beds.

Out near I-70, the *Budget Host Scenic Hills Motel* (☎ 529 7483, fax 529 3616), 75 E 1500 South, has reasonably sized, clean rooms, some with kitchenettes, for about $35/45 for a single/double. Nearby is the *Safari Motel & Restaurant* (☎ 529 7447), 1425 S State, which has a pool and good rooms for about $40/50. The Best Western *Shaheen's Motel & Restaurant* (☎ 529 7455, fax 529 7257), 1225 S State, has a pool and comfortable rooms for $49/57.

The *Victorian Inn B&B* (☎ 529 7342), 190 W Main St, 84654, is a recently restored 1896 house with three large rooms, each with king-size bed and antique bathtub. Rates are $75 to $90 including full breakfast. Smoking is not permitted.

### Places to Eat

*Mom's Cafe* (☎ 529 3921), 10 E Main St, has been in Salina since 1929 and is locally popular. 'Mom' serves up home cooking at reasonable prices from 7 am to 10 pm.

The *Safari Restaurant* (☎ 529 7696) is a truck stop and service station – big meals for hungry drivers are served from 6 am to midnight (24 hours in summer). *Shaheen's Restaurant* (☎ 529 7600, 529 7455), 1229 S State, is a coffee shop and steak house, open from 5:30 am to 10 pm.

The restaurant at the *Ho Jo Inn* is open from 7 am to 10 pm and has a lounge bar. The *Watering Hole* (☎ 529 7897), 43 E Main St, is a local spot for a beer.

### RICHFIELD

Richfield was settled in 1864; now its an important agricultural center as well as the largest town for 100 road miles in any direction. It has over 6000 inhabitants and is the Sevier County seat.

### Information

An information booth is in an 1880s building in the City Park at 400 N Main St; it is open in the summer daily (except Sunday) from 10 am to 7 pm. At other times call the chamber of commerce (☎ 896 4241), 15 E

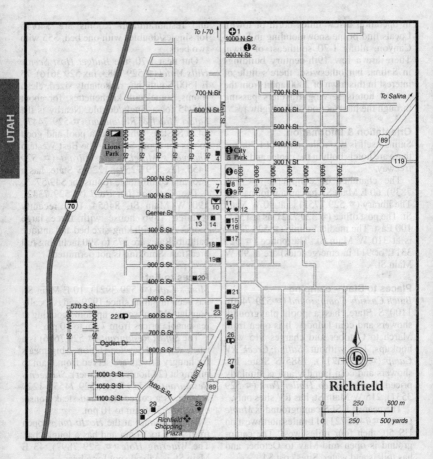

100 North; the County Travel Council
(☎ 896 8898, 1 (800) 662 8898), 220 N 600
West; or Panoramaland Travel Region
(☎ 896 9222, 1 (800) 748 4361), 250 N
Main St. The Fishlake National Forest
Richfield Ranger Station (☎ 896 9233),
115 E 900 North, 84701, is open from 8 am
to 5 pm, Monday to Friday. The post office
(☎ 896 6231) is at 93 N Main St. The
library (☎ 896 5169) is at 83 E Center. The
hospital (☎ 896 8271) is at 1100 N Main St.
The police (☎ 896 8484, or 911 in emergencies) are at 75 E Center.

**Things to See & Do**

**Historic Buildings** The information
booth has a brochure detailing the town's
historic buildings. Highlights include the
**Ramsay Home**, 57 E 200 North, built in
1873 and now housing a small museum,
open 11 am to 5 pm, Monday to Friday.
Others to see include the **post office**,
built in 1917; the **library**, built by the
Carnegie Foundation in 1913; the **Valley
Community Church**, 200 South and
Main St, built in 1880; and several
others.

| PLACES TO STAY | | 7 | Little Wonder Cafe |
|---|---|---|---|
| 4 | Days Inn | 13 | Ideal Dairy |
| 14 | Wagon Wheel Motel | 16 | John & Jan's |
| 15 | Budget Host Knight's Inn | 30 | Topsfield Steakhouse |
| 17 | Best Western Appletree Inn | | |
| 18 | Mountair Motel | **OTHER** | |
| 19 | Jensen's Motel | 1 | Hospital |
| 20 | Old Church B&B | 2 | Ranger Station |
| 21 | New West Motel | 3 | Municipal Pool |
| 22 | KOA | 5 | Tourist Information Booth |
| 23 | Quality Inn | 6 | Panoramaland Travel Region |
| 24 | Grand Western Motel | 8 | The Detour |
| 25 | Weston Inn | 9 | Chamber of Commerce |
| 26 | JR Munchies RV Park | 10 | Post Office |
| 29 | Romanico Inn | 11 | Police |
| 30 | Topsfield Lodge | 12 | Library |
| | | 24 | Greyhound Bus Depot |
| PLACES TO EAT | | 27 | K-C Water Slide |
| 4 | Days Inn Restaurant | 28 | Reel Theater |

As you enter or leave town at the north end, watch for the giant metal **dinosaur sculptures**.

**Golf** nine holes at the municipal course (☎ 896 9987), in the southwest corner of town. **Swim** at the municipal pool (☎ 896 8572), 600 W 500 North, or K-C Water Slide (☎ 896 5334), 950 S 100 East.

Richfield is also an access point for the **Paiute ATV Trail** (see Fillmore & Around or ask at Richfield information offices).

**Places to Stay – camping**
*Richfield KOA* (☎ 896 6674), 600 W 600 South, has a pool (summer only), showers, playground, game room, store and coin laundry. Sites are $14 or $20 with full hookups. *JR Munchies* (☎ 896 9340), 745 S Main St, is an RV Park (no tents) with hookups for about $15, less without. It has showers and a coin laundry.

**Places to Stay – bottom end**
Rates from about May to October (given below) are several dollars higher than the rest of the year. The *Wagon Wheel Motel* (☎ 896 4486), 59 W Center, looks worn but has some of the cheapest rooms – in the low to mid $20s, some with kitchenette. Simple rooms in the $20s are also available at *Jensen's Motel* (☎ 896 5447), 290 S

Main St; the *Grand Western Motel* (☎ 896 6948), 575 S Main St; and the *Mountair Motel* (☎ 896 4415), 190 S Main St. This last one has a pool and a few more expensive rooms with kitchenettes. The *New West Motel* (☎ 896 4076), 447 S Main St, has nicer rooms in the low $30s. *Topsfield Lodge & Steak House* (☎ 896 5437, 896 5438), 1200 S Main St, has adequate rooms in the $30s – the steaks are better.

**Places to Stay – middle**
The *Old Church B&B* (☎ 896 6705), 180 W 400 South, 84701, is mildly bizarre – it offers space for weddings, receptions and honeymoons all in the same building! The owners are friendly and have two rooms for about $40.

The attractive *Romanico Inn* (☎ 896 8471, fax 896 8228), 1170 S Main St, is a good deal with pleasant rooms for $32/38 a single/double. There is a spa and coin laundry, and some rooms have a kitchenette. Another decent choice for rooms under $40 is the *Budget Host Knight's Inn* (☎ 896 8228), 69 S Main St, which has a pool and a restaurant next door. With 50 rooms, this is easily the largest place listed so far.

The *Super 8 Motel* (☎ 896 9204), 1575 N Main St, has nice rooms for $38.88/42.88

for singles/doubles with one bed – more for two beds. Restaurants are close by. The *Weston Inn* (☎ 896 9271, fax 896 6864), 647 S Main St, has similar prices and satisfactory rooms. Facilities include a restaurant, pool and spa.

The remaining hotels all have over 50 rooms and belong to reputable chains. The Best Western *Appletree Inn* (☎ 896 5481, fax 896 9465), 145 S Main St, has a pool, and rates include continental breakfast. Spacious rooms are about $45/55 for singles/doubles, more with two beds. A few two-room units are about $70 to $90. Both the *Days Inn* (☎ 896 6476), 333 N Main St, and the *Quality Inn* (☎ 896 5465), 540 S Main St, have a pool, spa, and exercise room. The Days Inn has a restaurant and bar; its rooms have refrigerators and rent for about $58/68 for singles/doubles. The Quality Inn has some rooms with kitchenettes or a few suites with private spas. Rates, which include continental breakfast, range from $40/50 for standard rooms to $50 to $80 for larger units.

### Places to Eat

The *Little Wonder Cafe* (☎ 896 9483), 101 N Main St, is a basic but locally popular small diner serving cheap breakfasts and lunches from 6 am to 5 pm. Somewhat more upscale is the family restaurant by the *Days Inn*, which is open from 6 am to 10 pm. Also good, with the same hours but a little cheaper, is *John & Jan's* (☎ 896 4330), 89 S Main St, next to the Budget Host Knight's Inn. It has American meals and a salad bar. The *Topsfield Lodge Steak House* (☎ 896 5437), 1200 S Main St, is open from 5:30 to 10 pm, Monday to Saturday. The fireplace makes this a homey restaurant, with reasonably priced, good steaks and seafood. *Ideal Dairy* (☎ 896 5061), 151 W Center, features a homemade ice cream parlor.

### Entertainment

The *Reel Theater* (☎ 896 4400), 1150 S Hwy 89, shows movies. *The Detour* (☎ 896 9947), 160 N Main St, is a private club and bar – a local will often sponsor a traveler.

### Getting There & Away

The Greyhound bus stops at Grand Western Motel (☎ 896 6948), 575 S Main St, on its four daily runs each way along I-70 between Denver, Colorado, and Las Vegas, Nevada. Most visitors drive.

## MONROE

This small town of 1500 inhabitants was first settled in 1864 and retains several early buildings. Monroe is 10 miles south of Richfield on minor roads. Just east of town are **hot springs** (☎ 527 4014), with a soaking pool open all year, heated swimming pool open in summer, and tent/RV camping with showers. *Peterson's B&B* (☎ 527 4830), 95 N 300 West, 84754, has three rooms for $50 to $60 a double, with full breakfast. No smoking is allowed, and it's open from April to October only.

## FREMONT INDIAN STATE PARK

The Fremont Indians were related to the Anasazi people, who dominated the Four Corners area and northern Arizona during the roughly 1000 years leading up to the 15th century. The Fremont Culture is poorly understood – this recently opened state park outlines some of our current knowledge of these people.

Although the park includes a prehistoric village site, it's not much to see. Instead, stop by the visitors center (☎ 527 4631), where there are good exhibits. Then take two very short trails (wheelchair accessible) to view petroglyphs on nearby cliffs. There is a longer nature trail as well. Rangers lead interpretive walks and give talks in summer. Bicycles are available for rent – brochures giving recommended local cycling trips are available. The center is open 9 am to 5 pm daily (to 6 pm in summer) except New Year's Day, Thanksgiving and Christmas. Entrance to the park is $1.50 or $1 for ages five to 16.

There are two picnic sites nearby. You can stay at *Castle Rock Campground*, a few miles west of the visitors center. Sites cost $5; there are toilets and drinking water, and the area is open from April to October.

The park is best reached from exit 17 on

UTAH

I-70 – follow the signs. From a short way west of the park, USFS Rd 113 heads south to the remains of the old mining town of **Kimberly** and continues east to Marysvale. Alternatively, after Kimberly, take USFS Rd 123 south, emerging at Beaver Canyon (Hwy 153 east of Beaver). Between 6000 and 11,000 feet above sea level, these Fishlake National Forest roads are packed dirt but are often passable to cars in dry weather; all are closed by snow in winter and spring. Summer wildflowers, fall colors, fine views of 12,000-foot peaks in the Tushar Range and glimpses of wildlife make this a good way to leave or access the Fremont Indian State Park.

### MARYSVALE

This small town of 400 is an access point for the Paiute ATV Trail (see Fillmore & Around) and has a few small hotels. Local businesses rent ATVs and horses – guides are available. Marysvale hosts a rodeo in July. The town is on Hwy 89, 11 miles south of I-70. Hwy 89 continues south for 16 miles to Junction (see the Southwestern Utah chapter).

#### Places to Stay & Eat

Four miles north of Marysvale is the *Wildflower RV Camp* (☎ 326 4301), open from April to October for RVs only.

The *4-U Motel* (☎ 326 4388, 326 9996) and the *Sportsman's Lodge & Cafe* (☎ 326 4258), both in the town center, each have seven basic rooms in the $20s. *Our Bar & Grill* serves food and beer.

Six miles north on Hwy 89 is the *Big Rock Candy Mountain Resort* (☎ 326 4263). The mountain is a not-very-exciting multicolored massif on the west side of the road. The supposedly therapeutic mineral waters from the mountain are bottled and sold. The small resort has modest motel rooms with doubles in the low $30s, a restaurant and a campground with drinking water but no showers. It is open from March to October. One-hour float trips on the Sevier River ($10 per person) are offered when there is a demand; there is a grocery and souvenir store.

# East of the Wasatch Plateau

This section begins with the coal-mining towns of Carbon County and then continues southeast along Hwy 10 through the towns of the Castle Valley. This colorful but dry region was settled relatively late in the 1870s and 1880s, after pioneers had arrived in the moister valleys west of the Wasatch Plateau. The many massive buttes and eroded geological formations in the area led to it being locally called 'Castle Country'.

The discovery of coal and the arrival of the railway in 1883 attracted many immigrants from diverse backgrounds to Carbon County, and the Mormon heritage that predominates in the valleys west of here is lacking. The towns in this area, of which Price is the most important, are between 5000 and 6000 feet above sea level.

### HELPER

Named after the 'helper' locomotives that once pulled coal-laden trains over the steep Soldier Summit nearby, Helper was a major railroad and coal-mining center. Today, many historic buildings along Main St are boarded up or for sale. Nevertheless, almost 3000 people still live here, the train continues to stop every day, and a good museum is worth the visit. Price, a bigger town about 10 miles to the southeast, has information and other visitor services.

#### Things to See & Do

The **Western Mining & Railroad Museum** (☎ 472 3009), 296 S Main St, is a good introduction to the area. Models, photographs, artifacts, paintings and audiovisual displays describe anything from mining disasters to Butch Cassidy holdups. Outside is a collection of antique mining and railroad equipment. The museum is open 9 am to 5 pm Monday to Saturday, from May to September. At other times,

**Butch Cassidy**
Local historians tell how Butch Cassidy, along with two others, pulled off a major bankroll heist in Castle Gate (a now defunct mine just north of Helper) in 1897. One of Cassidy's accomplices was shot the next year by a posse who thought that they had killed Cassidy. When the robber was buried, Cassidy himself is said to have shown up to watch the proceedings. ∎

call 472 3393 for hours (usually in the afternoon). A donation is suggested.

The museum is in a 1914 hotel; other turn-of-the-century buildings along Main St have put Helper on the National Historic Register.

The **Bristlecone Ridge Hiking Trail** at Price Canyon Campground (see below) leads up into the mountains nearby, gaining almost 700 feet in two miles and reaching an area where bristlecone pines can be seen – the oldest living things on earth.

### Places to Stay & Eat
The BLM (☎ 637 4584 in Price) runs the *Price Canyon Campground* about eight miles north of town. It is open from June to October, has water but no showers and costs $6. There is a picnic area and deer are often seen.

The *Balance Rock Motel* (☎ 472 9942), at the north end of town, has a few rooms in the $20s. Most people stay in Price. There are a couple of places to eat near the museum. *Jimbo's Steak House and Lounge* (☎ 472 9903), 330 S Main St, is pretty good if you like steak and beer.

### Getting There & Away
**Bus** The Greyhound bus has a flag stop (bus stops on demand only) as it passes Helper between Price and Provo (see Price below).

**Train** Amtrak (☎ 1 (800) 872 7245) has a daily train through Denver, Colorado, to Chicago, Illinois. There is also a daily train to Provo with connections to Salt Lake City and beyond. The train station is near the museum.

### SCOFIELD STATE PARK
At almost 7600 feet above sea level, Scofield Reservoir is one of the highest in the state. The park on its shores offers a short summer season of boating, fishing and water-skiing. During winter, ice fishing, cross-country skiing and snowmobiling are popular. Campgrounds on the north and east sides of the reservoir are open from May to October; they offer showers, boat launch facilities and fish cleaning areas. Day use is $3, camping is $9.

Information is available from PO Box 166, Price, 84501-0166. Call 448 9449 in summer or 637 8497 in winter, or write for information. Trail maps showing snowmobile trails climbing up to the Skyline Drive are available in winter. The park is about 14 miles north of Helper on Hwy 6, then 12 miles southwest on Hwy 96. It can also be reached from Fairview via Hwy 31 and Hwy 264 – a steep route that crosses the Skyline Drive and is closed in winter.

The tiny mining town of Scofield, just south of the reservoir, was the site of Utah's most disastrous mining accident (described at the museum in Helper). Tombstones of victims can still be seen in the town cemetery.

## PRICE
Founded in 1879 and named after William Price, an early Mormon bishop, Price quickly became a coal-mining and railroad center, attracting immigrants from many countries. This diverse heritage is celebrated during Price's annual events.

Coal mining continues to be important. Uranium and natural gas are also mined, and there is some farming in the area. The seat of Carbon County, Price has almost 10,000 inhabitants. The town, which has an excellent museum, is a good base for exploring the area.

### Information
The Castle Country Travel Council (☎ 637 3009, 1 (800) 842 0789) in the museum at 155 E Main St, is open from 9 am to 5 pm, Monday to Friday. The chamber of commerce (☎ 637 2788, 637 8182) is at 185 E Main St. The Manti-La Sal National Forest Price Ranger Station (☎ 637 2817) is in the Creekview Shopping Center at 599 W Price River Drive, 84501. The BLM (☎ 637 4584), 900 N 700 East, is open from 7:45 am to 4:30 pm, Monday to Friday. The post office (☎ 637 1638) is at 95 S Carbon Ave. The library (☎ 637 0744) is at 159 E Main St. The hospital (☎ 637 4800) is west of town at 300 N Hospital Drive. The police (☎ 637 1344, or 911 in emergencies) are at 81 N 200 East.

### College of Eastern Utah Prehistoric Museum
The collection at this museum (☎ 637 5060), 155 E Main St, is a fine surprise. Several well-displayed dinosaur skeletons, plenty of superb Indian artifacts, a kids' area, local art and a good gift shop combine to make this a recommended stop. It's free but deserves a donation; the hours are 9 am to 6 pm, Monday to Saturday and noon to 5 pm on Sunday, from April to September; 10 am to 5 pm, Monday to Saturday the rest of the year.

### College of Eastern Utah
The main campus of this two-year community college (☎ 637 2120), 451 E 400

Dinosaur fossils at the College of Eastern Utah Prehistoric Museum (RR)

North, is between 400 and 600 North and 300 and 650 East. Apart from the off-campus prehistoric museum (above), the CEU has **Gallery East** – an art gallery in the Main Building with changing local and national shows from September to June. Various performing arts events take place throughout the year – call for information.

### Price Municipal Building
The building that houses city hall (☎ 637 5010), 185 E Main St, also contains a mural that is well worth seeing. Local artist Lynn Faucett was commissioned by the Depression-era WPA project to paint the indoor mural. The result was a four-foot-high, 200-foot-long mural illustrating local history – Faucett used old photos to accurately depict early pioneers in authentic settings. Entrance is free, and the museum is open from 8 am to 5 pm Monday to Friday. Faucett also painted a mural in the

UTAH

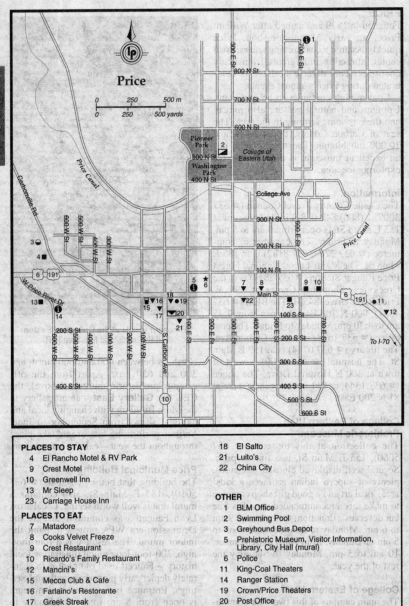

Price

## PLACES TO STAY
- 4   El Rancho Motel & RV Park
- 9   Crest Motel
- 10  Greenwell Inn
- 13  Mr Sleep
- 23  Carriage House Inn

## PLACES TO EAT
- 7   Matadore
- 8   Cooks Velvet Freeze
- 9   Crest Restaurant
- 10  Ricardo's Family Restaurant
- 12  Mancini's
- 15  Mecca Club & Cafe
- 16  Farlaino's Restorante
- 17  Greek Streak

- 18  El Salto
- 21  Luito's
- 22  China City

## OTHER
- 1   BLM Office
- 2   Swimming Pool
- 3   Greyhound Bus Depot
- 5   Prehistoric Museum, Visitor Information, Library, City Hall (mural)
- 6   Police
- 11  King-Coal Theaters
- 14  Ranger Station
- 19  Crown/Price Theaters
- 20  Post Office

Prehistoric Museum as well as work in several other cities and states.

## Historic Buildings

The Travel Council office has a brochure detailing nearby early-20th-century buildings that are listed on the National Register of Historic Sites – these are mainly on Carbon Ave and Main St between 300 N and 100 S, 100 W and 200 E.

## Activities

**Golf** the nine-hole Carbon Country Club Course (☎ 637 9949), four miles north of town. **Swim** daily, year-round, at the city pool (☎ 637 7946), 250 E 500 North. The surrounding Washington Park offers **tennis**, a playground and other facilities.

## Special Events

The Black Diamond PRCA Rodeo is held in mid to late June. Greek Days on the second weekend in July offers Greek food, music, dancing and tours of Utah's oldest Greek Orthodox Church. International Days & Carbon County Fair are held concurrently during the first week in August. They celebrate the county's multicultural background. There's a parade, rodeo, ethnic food stands and other events.

## Places to Stay – bottom end

Prices go up during special events and may drop a little from October to May. *El Rancho Motel & RV Park* (☎ 637 2424), 145 N Carbonville Rd, has a pool, coin laundry and RV sites with hookups. Fairly basic rooms are $24/30 for a single/double, or $35 with kitchenette. RV sites are $13. Cheap basic rooms, some with kitchenettes, are also available at the *Hi Way Motel* (☎ 637 0950), 685 N Carbonville Rd.

Somewhat nicer budget rooms can be had at the *Crest Motel* (☎ 637 1532), 625 E Main St, with 85 rooms and a restaurant (breakfast/lunch only) next door. Rates are about $26/32 and weekly discounts are offered. The *Greenwell Inn & Restaurant* (☎ 637 3520, fax 637 4858), 655 E Main St, is another good budget choice. The

nearly 100 rooms vary in size and range from $24/30 to $38/48, including continental breakfast. It has a coin laundry.

The *Carriage House Inn* (☎ 637 5660), 590 E Main St, has a pool and spa. Most rooms are pretty good for about $30/36; eight mini-suites with kitchenettes are $40/45. *Mr Sleep* (☎ 637 7000), 641 W Price River Drive, has a playground and over 90 fairly standard rooms for $32/36.

## Places to Stay – middle

*Days Inn* (☎ 637 8880, fax 637 7707), 838 Westwood Blvd, is the biggest and most comfortable hotel with 150 rooms, a pool, spa, sauna, restaurant, bar and meeting areas. Most rooms are $55/60; a few small suites go for up to about $90.

## Places to Eat

A locally popular place for breakfast is the *Crest Restaurant* (☎ 637 0843), 601 E Main St, which is open from 6 am to 3 pm. *Ricardo's Family Restaurant* (☎ 637 2020) in the Greenwell Inn offers inexpensive but good American and Mexican meals from 6 am to 9 pm. The *Golden Rock Cafe* (☎ 637 8880) in the Days Inn is a more upmarket American restaurant, open from 6 am to 10 pm.

Price offers more international dining choices than most towns in Utah. The *Greek Streak* (☎ 637 1930), 84 S Carbon Ave, is a little hole-in-the-wall place serving some of the best Greek snacks and pastries in Utah. It is open from 7 am to 8 pm, Monday to Saturday. For Mexican, you have the choice of *Luito's* (☎ 637 8224), 86 E 100 South, which is open daily for lunch and dinner, or *El Salto* (☎ 637 6545), 19 S Carbon Ave, which is closed on Sunday. *China City* (☎ 637 8211), 350 E Main St, serves steak, seafood and Chinese fare from 11 am to 10 pm daily.

The *Matadore* (☎ 637 9959), 355 E Main St, is locally popular for good steaks and 'Italian night' on Wednesdays. *Farlaino's Restorante* (☎ 637 9217), 87 W Main St, serves Italian dinners from 5:30 to 9 pm, Wednesday to Saturday; *Farlaino's Cafe* on the same premises is open for breakfast and lunch from 7 am to 2 pm, Monday to Saturday. *Mancini's* (☎ 637 3810), 1257 E Main St, serves steaks and Italian food from noon to 9 pm daily. *Cooks Velvet Freeze* (☎ 637 1954), 409 E Main St, has good ice cream desserts.

### Entertainment
Movies are screened at the *King-Coal Theaters* (☎ 637 1233), 1171 E Main St, or at the *Crown/Price Theaters* (☎ 637 1705), 30 E Main St.

For a beer, try *Mecca Club & Cafe* (☎ 637 9958), 75 W Main St, which is in the 1913 Mahleres-Siampenos Building and has been a bar (with many different names) since the building was constructed. (It serves meals, too.) Also try *Cork's Club* (☎ 637 9955), 63 W Main St; the *Arrow Club* (☎ 637 9803), 80 S Carbon Ave; the *El Rancho Lounge* (☎ 637 7809), 189 N Carbonville Rd; or the *C&W Office Lounge* (☎ 637 0940), 27 N 100 West.

### Getting There & Away
The Greyhound bus (☎ 637 3457) stops at the Phillips 66 Service Station, 277 N Carbonville Rd, and has one or two daily buses to Green River and Denver, Colorado, or to Provo and Salt Lake City.

### WELLINGTON
There's little reason to stop in this mining town of 1800 people, five miles southeast of Price, unless you want a meal or a place to stay. Pioneer Day (24 July) is celebrated with a rodeo and other events.

South of Wellington, a signed dirt road goes past the Desert Lake State Waterfowl Reserve (about 14 miles) and on to the Cleveland-Lloyd Dinosaur Quarry (about 22 miles) – see below.

Two miles east of Wellington, off Hwy 6/191, is the turnoff to the north along Soldier Creek Rd to the Nine Mile Canyon backroad, described in the chapter on northeastern Utah. Other remote dirt roads east of Wellington can be explored by prepared drivers with 4WD.

Hwy 6/191 continues 54 miles southeast of Wellington to intersect with I-70. Green River, four miles east of this intersection, is described in the chapter on southeastern Utah.

### Places to Stay & Eat
The *Mountain View RV Park* and the *National 9 Inn* (☎ 637 7980, fax 637 8929) are both at 50 S 700 East. The RV park charges $15 with hookups; there is a playground and RVers can use the hotel facilities. RV park facilities are limited from mid-November to mid-March – no water. The hotel has a pool and restaurant (open 6 am to 10 pm). Decent rooms are about $40 in summer or $30 in winter. There's also the small and basic *Pillow Talk Motel* (☎ 637 7706), 430 E Main St, with rooms in the $20s.

*Cowboy's Country Kitchen* (☎ 637 4223), off Hwy 6/91, is a locally popular country-style steak house and lounge bar with dancing on occasion. For a home-style breakfast, try the *J&J Cafe* (☎ 637 5431), 15 W Main St, which opens at 6 am in summer.

### HUNTINGTON & AROUND
This mining town, which was settled in 1878, has 2800 inhabitants. It is 20 miles south of Price on Hwy 10.

### Cleveland-Lloyd Dinosaur Quarry
This National Natural Landmark is operated by the BLM (☎ 637 4584 in Price). Over a dozen species of dinosaur were buried here 150 million years ago, and their fossilized bones are currently being excavated. A visitors center has information and a gift shop; behind this is a large hut built over the quarry itself. Within, you can see partially excavated dinosaurs and the tools used to uncover them. If the quarry building is closed, there's not much to see – certainly no dinosaur fossils lying around for the casual collector! There is a short nature walk and a driving tour through the stark high desert scenery.

The quarry and visitors center are open daily from 10 am to 5 pm, Memorial Day to Labor Day, and on weekends from Easter to Memorial Day – but phone the BLM to confirm this. The site is remote (I saw a North American badger crossing a road near the quarry) and accessible only by dirt roads – these are passable by car in dry weather but may be closed in wet or snowy conditions. Hwy 155 to the quarry leaves Hwy 10 almost three miles north of Huntington – there are signs. It is about 20 miles.

### Cedar Mountain Overlook
Six miles west of the quarry, a dirt road heads south for 20 miles, climbing 2000 feet through forest to the overlook. There are fine views, a short nature trail, interpretive geological markers, toilets and picnic areas. The road is closed by snow in winter and passable to cars only when dry. The BLM has maps and information.

### Desert Lake State Waterfowl Reserve
This small lake is a few miles northwest of the dinosaur quarry – look for signs along the road. It is managed by the Utah Department of Wildlife Resources (☎ 637 3310), 455 W Railroad Ave, Wellington. This is an unusual marsh and lake area in the desert – waterfowl and shorebirds pass through in spring and summer. During the summer, when the birds are breeding, access is limited – so call ahead.

### Huntington State Park
This park (☎ 687 2491), PO Box 1343, 84528, is two miles north of town. A lake offers fishing, boating, water-skiing and swimming. Ice skating, cross-country skiing and ice fishing are all possible winter activities. There are picnic areas and a campground with showers – these are turned off in winter to prevent freeze damage. Day use is $3, camping is $9.

### Huntington Canyon
Hwy 31 west of town leads up to the Skyline Drive and down to Fairview, 44 miles away (both described earlier in this chapter). The road parallels Huntington Creek for part of its length and provides access to Manti-La Sal National Forest campgrounds and fishing areas and, in winter, to snow-

mobiling and cross-country skiing. Look for beaver dams across the creek.

### Huntington Canyon Power Plant
This massive plant (☎ 381 2553) is nine miles west of town and can be seen from several miles away. Tours are sometimes given.

### Places to Stay & Eat
Campgrounds in Huntingdon Canyon with water, toilets but no showers are found at *Bear Creek* (eight miles), *Forks of Huntington* (18 miles) and *Old Folks Flat* (21 miles from Huntington). Sites are open from June to September and cost $6. Beyond are several highland lakes (for fishing and boating) as well as hiking trails. The ranger station in Price has complete details and maps of the area.

The *Village Inn Motel* (☎ 687 9888), 310 S Main St, has rooms, some with kitchenettes, in the low $30s. The *Lunch Box* (☎ 687 9906), 190 S Main St, and the *Canyon Rim Cafe* (☎ 687 9040), 505 N Main St, serve snacks and simple meals. *Jake's Place* (☎ 687 9080), north of town, serves steaks and other meals for lunch and dinner, Monday to Saturday.

### CASTLE DALE & AROUND
Eight miles south of Huntington, Castle Dale was settled in the 1880s. The town is the Emery County seat and has a population of about 2000. As with other towns in the area, mining has been the main industry and continues to be so, despite a disastrous fire that killed 27 miners in 1984. A block south of the museum outside the courthouse is the Wilberg Memorial, commemorating the miners.

The chamber of commerce (☎ 381 2547) is at 190 E Main St. The library (☎ 381 2554) is next door. A tiny medical center (☎ 381 2305) is at 90 W Main St.

### Joes Valley Reservoir
Paved Hwy 29 goes west from Hwy 10, two miles north of Castle Dale, through Orangeville and along Cottonwood Creek to Joes Valley Reservoir in the Manti-La

Sal National Forest, 22 miles away. (Ranger stations in Price and Ferron have information.) There are three monuments along the route with parking and historical markers. A small marina (☎ 381 2453) rents boats, and there is a store, restaurant and small lodge. Cross-country skiing is popular in winter when mule deer are often seen.

West of the reservoir, a dirt road (passable to cars in dry weather only) climbs about 15 miles to the Skyline Drive.

### San Rafael River & Swell
This geologically interesting area southeast of Castle Dale is remote and rarely visited – it used to be the hideout of outlaws. Much of it is BLM land – the office in Price has maps and information. You can explore by 4WD and camp almost anywhere – but be prepared for not seeing other people in the event of a breakdown.

The best road is a gravel one that leaves Hwy 10 one mile north of Castle Dale. After 13 miles, a signed turn to the south leads six miles to **Wedge Overlook**, which offers great views of the San Rafael River 1200 feet below and mountainous buttes in the distance. Returning from the overlook to the 'main' road, you can continue southeast on the Buckhorn Draw Rd for 30 miles or so to emerge at exit 129 on I-70, 30 miles west of Green River. The road crosses the San Rafael River on a suspension bridge – there is a campground here with toilets but no drinking water. The road is normally passable in ordinary cars except after heavy snow or rain.

The swell continues south of I-70 and into southeastern Utah – see Goblin Valley State Park in Southeastern Utah.

### Emery Museum of Natural History
This museum (also called the Emery County Museum) (☎ 381 5154) is in the City Hall complex (☎ 381 2115) at 64 E 100 North. There are plans to move it to (☎ 381 5252) 96 N 100 East. It is a small but interesting museum featuring a dinosaur skeleton, Indian artifacts, pioneer memorabilia, historical collections and local art. Hours are 9 am to 5 pm, Monday to Saturday from Memorial Day to Labor Day; call for other times.

### Special Events
Pioneer Day (24 July) features a parade, rodeo and other activities. The historical Castle Valley Pageant in early August is a reenactment of the pioneering history of the valley. Later in August is the Emery County Fair.

### Places to Stay & Eat
There are two small RV parks in town – hookups, no tents, no showers. *Esquire Estates* (☎ 381 2778), 270 W 380 North, is open year round, and *Olsen's Trailer Court* (☎ 381 2557), 715 N Center, is open June to October. There is plenty of camping around Castle Dale. At the Joes Valley Reservoir is *Joes Valley Campground*, with water but no showers, open from late May to mid-October. The fee is $6. About 10 miles before the reservoir, an unpaved road follows Cottonwood Creek to the north, reaching *Indian Creek Campground* in another 10 miles. The campground is operated by the USFS from June to September, has water but no showers, and costs $6.

The *Village Inn Motel* (☎ 381 2309), 375 E Main St, has a couple dozen rooms, some with kitchenettes, in the low $30s.

Places to eat include *Big Mama's Pizza & Deli* (☎ 381 5080), 340 E Main St, and the *K Bar K Cafe* (☎ 381 5474), 41 W Main St, both of which are closed on Sundays. There are a couple of fast-food outlets.

### FERRON
Settled in 1877, Ferron is the oldest town in this area. It is 11 miles south of Castle Dale and has 1800 inhabitants. The city hall (☎ 384 2350), 15 S State St, has information. The Manti-La Sal National Forest Ferron Ranger Station (☎ 384 2372, 384 2505) PO Box 310, 84523, is at 98 S State St.

### Things to See & Do
The **Presbyterian Church** was built in 1907 and is on the National Historic Register.

**Millsite State Park** (administered by

Huntington State Park) is four miles west of town and has a nine-hole **golf course** (☎ 384 2887) and a lake with boat launch facilities (day use $3) and camping.

**Ferron Canyon** is west of the state park and within the Manti-La Sal National Forest. A good dirt road passes several overlooks before reaching **Ferron Reservoir**, 28 miles away and the Skyline Drive, two miles beyond. The road is open from about June to September. At the reservoir is a USFS campground ($5), a boat launch area, and a lodge with cabins, a cafe and boat rentals. In winter, the canyon is a popular snowmobiling and cross-country skiing route.

**Special Events**

The Southern Utah Junior Livestock Show takes place in July. The city's main festival is Peach Days, which has been celebrated annually since 1906 in mid-September.

**Places to Stay & Eat**

The campground at *Millsite State Park* is open all year, has showers and charges $9.

*Castle Country Motel & Cafe* (☎ 384 2311), 45 S State, has a dozen modest rooms for about $30. The cafe serves breakfast, lunch and dinner. Or you might try the *Sunset Diner* (☎ 384 2477), 35 E Main St.

# Southwestern Utah

Locals call this part of the state 'Color Country', and colorful it certainly is. Almost every imaginable hue of red, from subtle pinks to vivid vermilions, seems to be represented in the wonderfully odd geological formations – and not only red but shades of orange, gray, yellow, brown and even blue can be seen. The shifting position and intensity of the sun, coupled with seasonal changes, make every vista a unique one. The landscape is mind-blowing and has to be seen to be believed.

An older nickname for the area is 'Dixie', because the warm climate reminded early settlers of the states in the southern USA – the settlers even grew cotton here. Indeed, much of the area is now part of the Dixie National Forest.

Relatively little is known of the Indians who lived in this part of Utah. The Anasazi people inhabited the area from about 1400 years ago, and their pictographs can be seen, but little remains in the way of ruins as found in other parts of the Southwest. Small groups of Paiute Indians were living in southwestern Utah when the first Europeans arrived – in this case, the Spanish

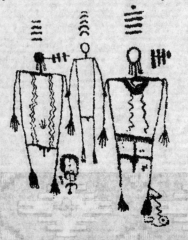

Dominguez-Escalante missionaries who quickly passed through in 1776. During the next 75 years, a few Anglos explored the area, but it was not until the Mormons arrived in 1851 that permanent White settlement occurred.

Mormon history tells of how the pioneers tried to befriend the Indians with gifts of food and clothing. Nevertheless, the Paiutes did not take kindly to Mormons turning large tracts of land into towns, ranches, farms and mines. The Indians lost their best hunting grounds and water supplies, thus disrupting their traditional way of life. Instead, they were encouraged to live like White people – not an easy or alluring option. Few Indians wished to change, and inevitably, there were several wars in the 1850s and 1860s. Only a small Indian Center in St George bears witness to today's Native American inhabitants of the area.

Settlement of this part of Utah continued the historical pattern set in central Utah in that two main Mormon pioneering routes can be identified. Interstate 15 now follows the main route used by Mormons to extend their influence into the southern part of the state. They were attracted by both iron mining and lower elevations in the area. Accordingly, Brigham Young sent out large groups of Mormon families to settle the region, extract much-needed iron and establish St George at a warm 2880-foot elevation. This town, which soon became Brigham Young's winter home, is now by far the largest city in the southern two-thirds of the state – though its population of only 35,000 attests to the low population density of the southern Utahan wilderness.

The second Mormon pioneering route was on the east side of the Markagunt Plateau, along what today is Hwy 89. Several early towns can be visited, and this route gives excellent access to forests, mountains, and Zion and Bryce Canyon National Parks on either side. Hwy 9 joins

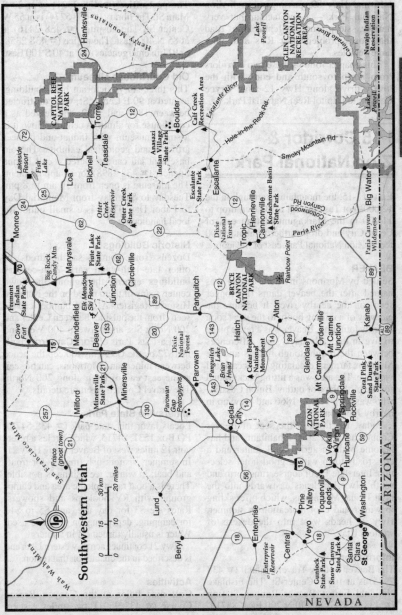

Southwestern Utah

I-15 and Hwy 89, passing through Zion National Park – a spectacular but very narrow, steep and switchbacking road that poses problems for RVs and other large vehicles.

This chapter follows these two corridors from north to south and ends with the lovely drive along Hwy 12 from Bryce Canyon to Capitol Reef National Park.

# I-15 Corridor & Zion National Park

East of I-15, the mountains start high in the 12,000-foot Tushars east of Beaver, drop to 11,000 in the Markagunt Plateau east of Cedar City and drop further to about 7000 feet in Zion National Park east of St George.

## BEAVER
Settled by Mormons in 1856, Beaver was named after the beaver dams (no longer seen) on the nearby river. It became the gateway of a mining boom to the west soon after its founding. Beaver was a tense place to live in the early days, with differences between the rough, tough miners and the Mormon farmers escalating to occasional violence. The area was a fitting background for the birthplace of outlaw Butch Cassidy, who was born here in 1866 and grew up in nearby Junction.

Today, the town is the seat of Beaver County, has over 2000 inhabitants and has become both an agricultural center and a crossroads town with a good hotel selection. Interstate 15, of course, runs north and south. Hwy 153 leads eastwards into the high Tushar Mountains, which offer skiing in winter and cool recreation in summer. Hwy 21 heads west into the deserts of western Utah.

## Information
The Beaver County Travel Council (☎ 438 2975) is at 105 E Center St. The Fishlake National Forest Beaver Ranger Station (☎ 438 2436) is at 190 N 200 East, 84713.

The post office (☎ 438 2321) is at 20 S Main St. The library (☎ 438 5274) is at 55 W Center St. The hospital (☎ 438 2416) is at 85 N 400 East. The police (☎ 438 2358, or 911 in emergencies) are at 40 S 100 East.

## Old Courthouse Museum
This three-story Victorian brick building, located at 90 E Center St, was constructed between 1877 and 1882, and served as a courthouse for almost a century. Now, it is a small museum with Indian and pioneer artifacts and geological exhibits. The old basement jail can be toured – call Donna Spencer (☎ 438 2898) for an appointment. The museum is open from 10 am to 8 pm, Tuesday to Saturday from Memorial Day to Labor Day. There is a small outlet for local handicrafts.

## Historic Buildings
Dozens (some sources say hundreds) of other late-19th- and early-20th-century buildings appear throughout the town center, many of them noted on the National Historic Register. A good number can be seen (from the outside) between Center and 200 North Sts, and between 400 West and 300 East Sts. Parts of **Fort Cameron**, built in 1872 by the US Army to keep the peace between miners and Mormons, can be seen at the east end of town along 200 North. The Travel Council has more details.

## Minersville State Park
Locals favor this state park (☎ 438 5472), PO Box 1531, 84713, which circles a reservoir 12 miles west of Beaver along Hwy 21. In summer, visitors fish (mainly for trout) and boat; in winter, ice fishing is possible. There is a boat ramp, picnic area and campground with RV hookups and showers. Rates are $3 for day use, and $5 to $11 for camping, depending on facilities used. Water is usually turned off in winter.

Hwy 21 continues across western Utah and is described in the chapter on that region.

## Activities
Golf nine holes at the Canyon Breeze Course (☎ 438 9601), two miles east on

UTAH

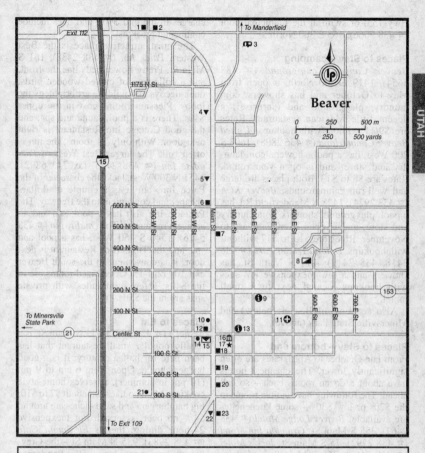

Exit 112

To Manderfield

Beaver

1175 N St

600 N St

500 N St

400 N St

300 N St

200 N St

100 N St

Center St

100 S St

200 S St

300 S St

To Minersville
State Park

To Exit 109

300 W St
200 W St
100 W St
Main St
100 E St
200 E St
300 E St
400 E St
500 E St
600 E St
700 E St

0   250   500 m
0   250   500 yards

**PLACES TO STAY**

1   Country Inn & Fuel Stop
2   Best Western Paradise Inn
3   Beaver KOA
6   Comfort Inn
7   Delano Motel & Trailer Park
12  Paice Mansfield Motel
18  Granada Inn Motel
19  Best Western Paice Inn
20  Jack's Motel
23  Beaver Lodge Motel

**PLACES TO EAT**

2   Garden of Eat'n, Paradise Club
    & Steak House
4   El Bambi Restaurant
5   Arshel's
19  Cottage Inn
22  Ponderosa

**OTHER**

4   Greyhound Bus Depot
8   Swimming Pool
9   Beaver Ranger Station
10  The Cinema
11  Hospital
13  Beaver County Travel Council
14  Library
15  Post Office
16  Old Courthouse Museum
17  Police
21  Western Dairyman's Coop

Hwy 153, or swim at the municipal pool (☎ 438 5066), 465 E 300 North.

## Places to Stay – camping

*Beaver Canyon Campground* (☎ 438 5654), 1419 E 200 North, is open from May to October and has showers, coin laundry, playground and (surprise!) a decent little Mexican restaurant. Rates are $9/11 without/with hookups. *United Beaver Camperland* (☎ 436 2808), 1603 S 200 West, has a pool, showers, coin laundry and store, and is open year round. Rates are $8 to $13. Both places are large and well-run campgrounds. *Beaver KOA* (☎ 438 2924), 1428 N Manderfield Rd, has a pool, playground, showers, coin laundry and store, and is open from February to November. Rates are $13 to $17 without/with hookups. *Delano Trailer Park* (☎ 438 2418, 438 2419), 480 N Main St, has showers and a few inexpensive RV sites with hookups located next to a small motel.

Also see East of Beaver (below) and Minersville State Park (above).

## Places to Stay – bottom end

From late October to April, rates are often significantly lower. The cheapest hotels have about a dozen rooms each – so call ahead. The following have simple rooms in the $20s or low $30s – some kitchenettes are available: *Beaver Lodge Motel* (☎ 438 2462), 355 S Main St; *Granada Inn Motel* (☎ 438 2292), 75 S Main St; *Jack's Motel* (☎ 438 5160), 265 S Main St; and *Paice Mansfield Motel* (☎ 438 2410), 10 W Center St.

## Places to Stay – middle

The 10-room *Delano Motel* (☎ 438 2418, 438 2419), 480 N Main St, has satisfactory rooms for about $30/34 for singles/doubles. The *Country Inn & Fuel Stop* (☎ 438 2484), 1450 N 300 West, may be noisy because of the adjacent gas station; it charges in the low $40s for a double. The more attractive and similarly priced *Sleepy Lagoon Motel* (☎ 438 5681), 882 S Main St, has a pool. *Comfort Inn* (☎ 438 2409), 645 N Main St,

charges in the mid $40s, and rates include continental breakfast.

The most attractive place is the Best Western *Paice Inn* (☎ 438 2438), 161 S Main St. Pretty flower beds line the front, and a collection of carved wooden birds, duck decoys and wildlife art brightens the lobby. Pleasant rooms cost in the upper $40s. There is a pool, sauna and spa, and the good Cottage Inn Restaurant is right next door. With only 24 rooms, the inn is often full. The larger Best Western *Paradise Inn* (☎ 438 2455, fax 743 6892), 1451 N 300 West, lacks the character of the Paice Inn, but it is a couple of dollars cheaper and convenient to the freeway. The Paradise Inn also has a pool, spa and an adjacent restaurant. The *Quality Inn* (☎ 438 5426), 1540 S 450 West, has a pool and spa, and the Timberline Restaurant is next door. It is convenient to the south Beaver exit 109 on I-15. Good-sized rooms are in the $40s; a few mini-suites with private spas are in the $50s.

## Places to Eat

*Arshel's* (☎ 438 2977), 711 N Main St, is a locally popular small restaurant that has been here for half a century; it is a good budget choice. Open from 6 am to 9 pm (10 pm in summer), it serves home-style cooking. Main courses run about $7 to $10; big hamburgers and sandwiches are around $4 – no beer is served. For inexpensive 24-hour dining, there's *El Bambi Cafe* (☎ 438 2983), 935 N Main St – the Greyhound bus stops here. The *Ponderosa* (☎ 438 2856), 330 S Main St, serves more upscale American fare.

The rustic *Maria's Cocina* (☎ 438 5654), 1419 E 200 North (in the Beaver Canyon Campground), serves as authentic a Mexican meal as you'll find in southern Utah – good and reasonably priced. It is open for dinner only (5 to 9 pm). A mile or two further up Beaver Canyon is the *Black Steer Steak House* (☎ 438 2442), which serves chicken and fish as well as steaks.

The town's hotel restaurants are generally good. Foremost among them is the *Cottage Inn* (☎ 435 5855), 171 S Main St (by the Paice Inn). The old-fashioned cottage interior, featuring antiques and a doll collection, is cozy. Meals are generally American fare, with most entrees under $12. Hours are 7 am to 10 pm. At the Paradise Inn, there's *Garden of Eat'n* (☎ 438 5464) and, a minute's walk away, the *Paradise Club & Steak House* (☎ 438 5476), 1425 N 400 West, which serves American fare and has occasional entertainment in the adjoining lounge. At the south end of town, there's the *Timberline Inn* (☎ 438 2474), 1542 S 450 West, next to the Quality Inn, which serves American cooking from 6 am to 10 pm.

### Entertainment
*The Cinema* (☎ 438 2331) is at 55 N Main St.

There is a summer theater season with productions in June and, especially, July at the Old Courthouse and the adjoining old Opera House – call the Travel Council for information. Horseracing takes place on occasional summer Saturdays.

A local invited me to the *Renegade Bar* – a private club – with beer, pool and cowboy music. I lost the pool game but had fun anyway. It's somewhere downtown, but I forgot to note the address and it's not in the phone book. You can probably find it – have fun!

### Things to Buy
Western Dairyman's Coop (☎ 438 2421), 330 W 300 South, gives tours of its cheese-making plant and sells factory-fresh cheeses and ice cream.

### Getting There & Away
The Greyhound bus (☎ 438 2229) stops at the El Bambi Cafe, 935 N Main St, several times a day southbound to St George and Las Vegas, Nevada; eastbound to Denver, Colorado, along I-70; or northbound to Salt Lake City.

### EAST OF BEAVER
Hwy 153 heads east into the Tushar Mountains, emerging at Junction, 40 miles away. The first half is paved, and the east side is graveled and passable to cars. The graveled road is closed by snow from about October to June.

Most of the land is part of the Fishlake National Forest (☎ 438 2436 in Beaver), which has small campgrounds at *Little Cottonwood* (six miles east of town) and *Mahogany Cove* (12 miles). Both have water and no showers, cost $6 and are open May to October. Several other campgrounds occur along unpaved side roads. There are several lakes and streams for fishing – the ranger station in Beaver has details. In October, fall colors make the drive especially pretty.

### Elk Meadows Ski & Summer Resort
Eighteen miles east of Beaver at 9200 feet above sea level (the road is paved and open up to here all winter), the resort (☎ 438 5433, 1 (800) 248 7669), PO Box 511, 84713, has 345 skiable acres. This is one of the smallest of Utah's alpine ski resorts, but it enjoys a reputation for good powder. The skiing season goes from Thanksgiving to early April, and three lifts and two tows service 30 runs between 10,400 and 9200 feet in elevation; 14% of the runs is for beginners and 62% for intermediate skiers. Adult lift tickets are $25 (9 am to 4 pm) or $18 for half a day. Children ski for $15 all day, and those over 65 ski free. There are ski rentals, a ski school (for skiers aged four to adult), a grocery/liquor/convenience store, places to eat and condos for rent.

During summer, the resort is a good base for fishing the nearby lakes, reservoirs and streams. Hiking, picnicking and mountain biking are also popular – there is a mountain bike shop offering rentals and guided trips. Horses are also available for rent or overnight pack trips. Naturalists will find plenty of mule deer, elk, yellow-bellied marmots and other wildlife to observe.

A popular fishing area is **Puffer Lake**, four miles east of Elk Meadows. There are boat rentals starting at around $55 a day, a fishing and grocery store, and very rustic cabins – bring your own bedding and kitchen utensils – starting around $35 a day.

## Southern Utah – Being Loved to Death?

The southern third of Utah, south of I-70, is a spectacular area containing five of the most famous national parks in the country, as well as numerous national monuments and state parks. So magnificent are the multihued canyons, cliffs, bridges, buttes, spires and other formations that no trip to the Southwest is complete without a visit to the region.

Unfortunately, massive increases in tourism during the 1980s and 1990s have meant that the most publicized areas are swamped by visitors, especially during the summer. National park lodges are booked up months in advance, and the main roads to and through the parks sometimes see traffic more like a city rush hour than a leisurely drive through stunning scenery.

Park authorities and wilderness watchdog groups are well aware of the dilemma, and they are scrambling to come up with management plans that will both protect parks and allow adequate access for millions of visitors. By the late 1990s, it is likely that private cars will be banned from some areas and that buses will transport travelers from parking areas outside the park boundaries to visitor centers inside. The restriction of motor vehicles is just one of several attempts at minimizing tourist impact.

Meanwhile, throngs of people continue to pour in to the area – and you are one of those people. If you want to avoid the worst of the crowds, yet still have a memorable visit, here are some suggestions.

The period between Memorial Day and Labor Day is the peak season – so avoid those months if possible. Many tourists try to do the 'Big Six' (Zion, Bryce Canyon, Capitol Reef, Canyonlands and Arches National Parks in southern Utah, plus Grand Canyon National Park in northern Arizona) in an exhausting 10-day or two-week tour – consider visiting just one or two of these parks for a longer period of time.

Hike or, better still, backpack away from the crowds – even during the height of tourist season in midsummer, camping permits for the backcountry in most but not all national parks are available on a day's notice even when drive-in campsites and park lodges have been filled to capacity for weeks.

Use your common sense: don't litter; stay on established trails (cutting trails causes erosion); be considerate of other visitors (loud music may not enhance everyone's experience – natural tranquility is a rare pleasure); never attempt to feed or touch wild animals; and drive carefully.

Consider visiting and spending time in some of the less well known state parks and national monuments, all of which have superb scenery. And remember the area's Indian and pioneering history by visiting museums, historic buildings and routes and ghost towns – sometimes you'll be the only one there. ■

*Elk Meadow Condos* are right at the base of the ski slopes. Most come with full kitchens and fireplace or wood stove. Winter rates for a studio sleeping two range from $80 to $110 (higher prices on weekends and holidays); a two-bedroom/one-bathroom condo sleeping six rents for $95 to $140; a three-bedroom/two-bathroom condo sleeping 10 costs $150 to $195; and homes sleeping 12 or more go for $275 to $375, plus tax. Stays of three midweek nights qualify for 10% to 20% discounts. Summer rates are $55 to $70 for a studio, $74 to $90 for a two-bed/one-bath, $105 to $120 for a three-bed/two-bath and $180 to $230 for a house.

### PAROWAN

Founded by Mormons on 13 January 1851, this is the oldest settlement in southern Utah. Today, this small town (population 1900) is the Iron County seat and the gateway to Brian Head Ski Resort and Cedar Breaks National Monument, south on Hwy 143. It offers cheaper lodging than the ski resort.

The city hall (☎ 477 3331), 5 S Main St, open from 9 am to 4 pm, Monday to Friday, has information and brochures about the area's historic heritage.

## Things to See

Historic buildings in town range from log cabins to a **rock church** built in the 1860s. Located behind city hall, the church now houses a small DUP museum (☎ 477 3549), open Monday, Wednesday and Friday during the summer or by appointment. Across the street to the south, the adobe **Jesse N Smith Home** was built in the 1850s and also can be toured – call the Parowan Hostess Committee (☎ 477 8728). Other historic buildings are found close by, as well as in **Paragonah**, four miles north.

The **Parowan Gap Petroglyphs**, an extensive range of chiseled symbols and pictures, line a gravel road 11 miles west of Parowan along 400 North. The area is on BLM land (information in Cedar City). Many hundreds of designs were made by Indians crossing the pass over a period of about 1000 years.

## Special Events

Cowboy Days & Poetry Gathering in March features anything from sheep shearing to mule races, as well as cowboy poetry readings. The Iron County Fair, which starts around Labor Day and continues for a week, features a rodeo, carnival, horse racing and many other events. Christmas in the Country is a candle-lit foot procession and Christmas lighting ceremony held Thanksgiving weekend. There are also historic home tours, a bazaar and entertainment.

## Places to Stay

**Camping** The *Pit Stop Campground* (☎ 477 9990), 492 N Main St, has showers and a fast-food restaurant. Rates are $12 with hookups, substantially less without. The Dixie National Forest (☎ 865 3200 in Cedar City) operates the small *Vermillion Castle* campground, six miles south along Hwy 143. The campground has water but no showers, and is open from mid-May to mid-November. Sites cost $5.

**Motels** Prices are highest in the summer, around Christmas and during winter weekends, and lowest in the spring after skiing season. The *Ace Motel* (☎ 477 3384), 82 N Main St, has eight modest rooms, some with kitchenettes, in the $30s. The *Crimson Hills Motel* (☎ 477 8662), 400 S Hwy 91 (follow 200 West to the south edge of town), has 17 rooms in the mid $30s. *Jedediah's Inn & Restaurant* (☎ 477 3326, fax 477 3473), 625 W 200 South, has 44 standard rooms in the $40s; a spa is available.

The nicest place is the alpine-style Best Western *Swiss Village Inn* (☎ 477 3391, fax 477 8642), 580 N Main St. It has a pool, spa and restaurant. Pleasant rooms cost around $60.

**B&Bs** *Grandma Bess' B&B* (☎ 477 8224), 291 W 200 South, has three nonsmoking rooms for $45. *Adam's Historic B&B* (☎ 477 8295), 94 N 100 East, has three nonsmoking rooms ranging from $60 to $120. The zip code for both is 84761.

## Places to Eat

The best restaurants are at Jedediah's Inn and the Swiss Village Inn (see above). Jedediah's is open from 8 am to 9 pm; the Swiss Village from 8 to 10:30 am and 6 to 9 pm. Also try *Parowan Cafe* (☎ 477 3593), 33 N Main St. It's a small family restaurant serving breakfast, lunch and dinner. *Pizza Barn* (☎ 477 8240) is at 595 W 200 South, and there are a few other fast-food places.

## Getting There & Away

The Greyhound bus (☎ 1 (800) 231 2222) stops on Main St – advance reservations for Salt Lake City, Las Vegas, Nevada, and Denver, Colorado, are required.

## BRIAN HEAD

At 9700 feet above sea level, Brian Head is Utah's highest town and has about 100 permanent residents and many more transient ones. Only 14 miles south of Parowan but almost 4000 feet higher, the town is reached on paved, but steep and winding,

Hwy 143. Brian Head Ski Resort is southern Utah's largest.

Southern Utah has few inhabitants, and Brian Head hasn't exactly been a booming resort. In fact, the ski resort was bankrupt from 1988 to 1992. New owners took over in 1992 and are implementing major changes, not the least of which is developing the area into a summer vacation center as well. This is an uncrowded place to visit in summer, and in winter, lift lines are not a problem.

### Information

Brian Head town offices (☎ 677 2029), PO Box 190068, 84719, or the chamber of commerce (☎ 677 2810), PO Box 325, 84719, has information. The medical clinic is at (☎ 677 2700).

Altitude sickness can be a real problem. Sleeping at Parowan (6000 feet) is one solution. If you feel altitude sick, a hasty descent will quickly provide relief (see the Health section in Facts for the Visitor).

### Winter Activities

Brian Head Ski Resort (☎ 677 2035) offers a great opportunity to **downhill ski** from Thanksgiving to early April. Six lifts service 55 runs between 9600 and 10,850 feet elevation. Of the 825 skiable acres, 38% are for beginners and 43% for intermediate skiers. Adult day passes (9 am to 4:30 pm) are $32 ; half day (from 12:30 pm) are $24. Children under 12 and seniors over 60 pay $20/16 for full/half day. Discounts are available for multi-day passes. Snowboards are allowed on most runs. Skis rent for $17 a day and snowboards for $25. There is night skiing on weekends. The resort offers child care and instruction in skiing and snowboarding.

Those who prefer **cross-country skiing** can rent equipment from Brian Head Cross Country & Mountain Bike (☎ 677 2012) in the Brian Head Hotel. The shop also offers guided tours and local information. **Snowmobile** rentals and tours are available from Crystal Mountain Recreation (☎ 677 2386). Groomed ski and snowmobile tracks lead to Cedar Breaks

National Monument and other areas; wilderness skiing is also possible.

### Summer Activities

The resort is very quiet in summer – year-round action is a recent occurrence at Brian Head. The deliciously cool climate (daytime highs in the 70°s F) attracts the lowlanders who are getting fed up with their summer basting. **Mountain biking** is good; rentals are available in the hotel and also at George's Ski & Mountain Bike Shop (☎ 677 2013) and Brian Head Boards & Bikes (☎ 677 3838).

From July to October, the road to 11,307-foot Brian Head Summit is open – go south two miles from town, then head east three miles on an unpaved road passable to cars. Great views! And Cedar Breaks National Monument is a short drive away.

### Places to Stay & Eat

There are no really cheap places, though you can find very nice one-bedroom condos fully equipped with kitchens starting around $50 in summer. There are also hotel rooms, but they're not any cheaper. Larger family units (three-bedroom condos) are available too. Reservations are accepted though hardly necessary – just show up.

In winter, places are more expensive – there are a few small units under $100, but most are over $100, and many of the larger units go for over $300 during the peak period (late December) and around $200 at other times. To economize, you need to bring your family or a group of friends and split a condo rental. New places are going up – your best bet is probably to call the following rental agencies to find something in your price range. (They'll find you cheap summer rentals too, if you prefer to reserve ahead.)

Accommodation Station
    (☎ 677 3333, 1 (800) 572 9705), PO Box 190128, 84719
Brian Head Condo Reservations
    (☎ 677 2045, 1 (800) 722 4742, 1 (800) 237 1410, fax 677 3926), PO Box 190217, 84719

Brian Head Reservation Center
   (☎ 677 2042, 1 (800) 845 9718, fax 677
   2827), PO Box 190055, 84719

Brian Head is a developing resort – the
restaurants are OK, but there aren't many
of them. The *Edge Restaurant* (☎ 677
3343) serves steaks and seafood and has
been around longer than most of the eateries in Brian Head. It's one of the better and
pricier places. To economize, look into the
Brian Head Mall, where you'll find a few
moderately priced choices.

## CEDAR BREAKS NATIONAL MONUMENT

This area has spectacular geological formations but is unusual because of its altitude
atop the Markagunt Plateau. Cars can reach
it only in summer (May to October) –
during winter, it is the province of snowmobilers and cross-country skiers.

From Brian Head south to Hwy 14 is
about 10 miles – half of this road is within
the national monument. West of the road,
erosion has formed a massive natural
amphitheater, three miles wide and over
2000 feet deep. Inside are fantastically
eroded formations – ridge after ridge of
spires and columns colored yellow, orange,
red, purple and brown by iron and manganese. East of the road lies the plateau,
carpeted with wildflowers from late June to
mid-August, peaking in late July.

Most visitors simply drive through,
stopping at the four scenic overlooks, each
about 10,400 feet above sea level, for stunning views of the amphitheater. There are
also two hiking trails, each two miles long.
The **Alpine Pond Trail** leads through a
conifer forest to a pond; the **Wasatch
Ramparts Trail** follows the southern
end of the amphitheater, passing ancient
bristlecone pines and giving good views.
Maps are available from the visitor center.

### Information

The visitor center, near the south entrance
of the monument, is open from 8 am to 6
pm from Memorial Day to Labor Day, and
8 am to 5 pm to early October. Facilities

include an exhibit, book and souvenir shop,
and rest rooms. Park rangers provide
information and lead scheduled walks,
talks and other programs. Admission to the
monument is $4 per car if you are using the
facilities in season; free out of season or if
you simply drive through. Golden Age,
Eagle and Access passports are accepted.

Further information is available from
Cedar Breaks National Monument (☎ 586
9451), PO Box 749, Cedar City, 84720.

### Places to Stay

Less than a mile from the visitor center is a
Park Service campground and picnic area.
The campground has water, toilets and fire
grills; it is open from June to September on
a first-come, first-served basis. The 30 sites
sometimes fill by mid-afternoon. Camping
fees are $7. Prepare for near freezing night
temperatures at this elevation.

### CEDAR CITY

Mormon settlers were sent south from
Parowan to found Cedar City in November
1851 – their purpose was to extract the
nearby iron ore. This venture largely
proved a failure (it was cheaper to import
iron by railroad from the east), and so the
people turned to ranching. After Zion
National Park was established in 1919,
tourism began to play an important role in
the economy.

Today, Cedar City hosts a Shakespearean
Festival that draws theatergoers from
within and beyond the state and several
other cultural events. Less than an hour's
drive from Zion, Cedar Breaks and Brian
Head, it is a natural stopping place for travelers. The town, southern Utah's second
largest (13,500 inhabitants), is 5800 feet
above sea level and has about 20 hotels to
choose from.

### Information

The chamber of commerce (☎ 586 4484),
286 N Main St, is open from 8 am to 5 pm,
Monday to Friday. In summer, hours
are extended to 7 pm, and 9 am to 1 pm
on Saturday. The Dixie National Forest
Cedar City Ranger Station (☎ 865 3200 or

UTAH

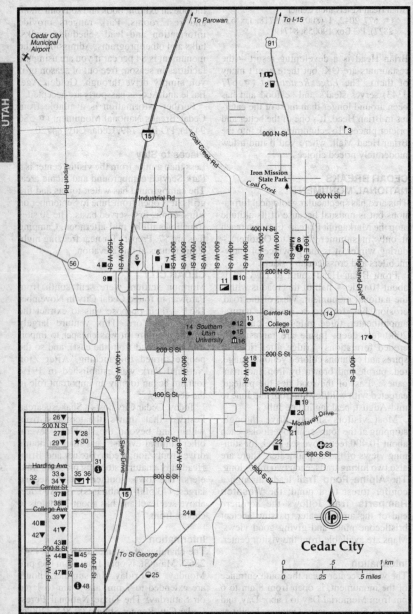

To Parowan

To I-15

91

Cedar City
Municipal
Airport

1
2

900 N St

3

Coal Creek Rd

15

Iron Mission
State Park

Coal Creek

600 N St

Airport Rd

Industrial Rd

400 N St

100 N St

Main St

100 E St

8
i

56

4
5
6
7

1550 W St

1400 W St

900 W St

800 W St

700 W St

600 W St

500 W St

400 W St

300 W St

200 W St

9

10

11

200 N St

Highland Drive

1400 W St

Southern
Utah
University

12

13

14

15

16

Center St

College
Ave

14

200 S St

17

400 E St

200 S St

800 W St

18

300 W St

200 S St

See inset map

400 S St

19

20

21

Monterey Drive

22

23

680 S St

600 S St

860 W St

680 S St

Sage Drive

31
i

15

800 W St

24

LP

25

To St George

**Cedar City**

0        .5        1 km
0    .25    .5 miles

26
200 N St
27
28
29
30

Harding Ave
32
33
34
35  36
Center St
37
38
College Ave
39
40
41
42
43
200 S St
44
45
46
47
48
i

100 W St

Main St

100 E St

**PLACES TO STAY**
1   KOA
4   Super 8 Motel
6   Comfort Inn
7   Abbey Inn
9   Holiday Inn
10  Paxman's Summer House B&B
18  Woodbury Guest House
19  Economy Motel
20  Daystop
22  Cedar Crest Motel
24  Cedar Village Motel & Condominiums
27  Best Western Town & Country Inn
37  Quality Inn
38  Best Western El Rey Inn
40  Theater B&B, Bard's Inn B&B
43  Super 7 Motel
44  Zion Inn

45  Rodeway Inn
46  Astro Budget Inn
47  Thrifty Motel

**PLACES TO EAT**
5   Sunshine Restaurant
7   Shoney's Restaurant
19  Bristlecone Restaurant
21  Hunan Restaurant
26  Sizzler Steak Seafood & Salad
27  Godfather's Pizza
28  China Garden
29  Escobar's
34  Kowloon Restaurant
39  Sullivan's Cafe, La Tajada Steak & Seafood House
41  Pizza Factory
42  Adriana's
46  Sugar Loaf Restaurant

**OTHER**
2   The Playhouse, Kittyhawk Tavern
3   Cedar Ridge Golf Course
8   Chamber of Commerce
11  Municipal Pool
12  Adams Memorial Theater
13  Randall Jones Theater
14  Centrum
15  Old Main
16  Braithwaite Fine Arts Gallery
17  Canyon Park
23  Medical Center
25  Greyhound Bus Depot
30  Police
31  Ranger Station
32  Library
33  Campus Theater
35  Post Office
36  Rock Church
48  BLM Office

865 3799 for a recorded message), PO Box 627, 84720, is at 82 N 100 East. The BLM has offices at 365 S Main St (☎ 586 2458) and 176 E DL Sargent Drive, at the north end of town (☎ 586 2401). These government offices are open 8 am to 4 pm Monday to Friday. The library (☎ 586 6661) is at 136 W Center. The local newspaper is the *Daily Spectrum*. The post office (☎ 586 6701) is at 10 N Main St. The medical center (☎ 586 6587) is at 595 S 75 East. The police (☎ 596 2955, or 911 in emergencies) are at 110 N Main St. Do your own or have someone wash your laundry at Raindance Laundromat (☎ 586 6964), 430 S Main St, which has about 40 coin-operated washers.

**Southern Utah University**
Founded in 1897, this four-year college (☎ 586 7700), 351 W Center, has over 3000 students. Visitors can see two early buildings, **Old Main**, built in 1898, and the old **Administration Building**, dating from 1904.

The **Braithwaite Fine Arts Gallery** (☎ 586 5432) is in the eastern part of the campus near Old Main. Both permanent and changing shows of local and national artists, past and present, are on display. Hours are 10 am to 7:30 pm Monday to Friday and 1 to 5 pm on weekends. Admission is free.

Near the gallery, the university **library** (☎ 586 7933) displays local Paiute Indian artifacts.

**Rock Church**
The Mormon Tabernacle, popularly called the Rock Church, was built in 1930 from locally quarried rock, which is red rather than the usual white of Mormon churches. Most of the indoor furnishings were hand-crafted by locals. Located at 75 E Center, the church is open for tours from 11 am to 5 pm Monday to Saturday in summer.

**Iron Mission State Park**
Exhibits at this park (☎ 586 9290), 595 N Main St, describe the Mormons' early mining attempts. More interesting are the scores of horse-drawn vehicles – stage-coaches, wagons, buggies, hearses, farm implements – that were used in the 19th century. Hours are 9 am to 5 pm (to 7 pm in summer), and admission is $1.50, $1 for children.

William Shakespeare (1564–1616)

## Activities

**Golf** nine holes at Cedar Ridge (☎ 586 2970), 200 E 900 North. **Swim** at the Municipal Pool (☎ 586 2869), 400 W Harding Ave. Play **tennis** at Canyon Park, 400 E Center, or at SUU.

## Special Events

**Utah Shakespearean Festival** The Shakespeare festival is the town's main annual event, for which it is famous throughout Utah and beyond. Held annually at SUU since 1962, the festival presents three of the Bard's plays plus three more by internationally famous playwrights. The productions are well done, but the many extras really make this an event for your calendar. There are free lectures discussing the plays, free 'Greenshows' with minstrels in Elizabethan dress juggling and playing period instruments, seminars on a variety of theatrical subjects ranging from acting to costume design, backstage visits and other entertainment.

Plays are performed on a rotating basis in the afternoons and evenings (except Sundays), so you could feasibly see all six plays in three days. Shakespeare's plays are performed in the roofless Adams Memorial Theater at the northeastern corner of the SUU campus. The theater is an excellent reproduction of the Globe Theater in London, where Shakespeare's plays were originally performed in the 16th century. The other plays are performed in the Randall Jones Theater across the street.

The season runs from late June to early September and reservations are recommended (☎ 586 7878), Cedar City, 84720. If you just show up, you may be able to buy a returned ticket at the Courtesy Booth (☎ 586 7790), near the Adams Theater. A few gallery tickets (the farthest back) go on sale on the day of the performance for the Shakespearean plays.

A number of other special events can be combined with the Shakespearean Festival. The Utah Summer Games are held in late June. The Midsummer Renaissance Fair (☎ 586 5943), held downtown for about four days in early July, is free and features magicians, games, Renaissance food and entertainment. A Gathering of the Clans (☎ 586 1994) celebrates the Scottish heritage of some local residents with events ranging from tossing the caber to highland dancing. This takes place in mid-July at the SUU Mountain Center, 11 miles east on Hwy 14. The American Folk Ballet (☎ 586 7872) has performances in the Centrum in the middle of the SUU campus in late July. The Iron County Fair, held in the twon of Parowan, 19 miles north, occurs in early September. A Summer Evening Concert Series (☎ 586 5483, 586 7756) features free performances by different musicians at various locations on Sunday evenings during the festival.

**Other Events** In addition to events that coincide with the Shakespearean Festival, the Paiute Powwow is held in early June, a Winterfest takes place in early December, and the SUU Theater Season (☎ 586 7878) offers five or six plays that are performed for week-long runs between October and May.

## Places to Stay – camping

*Cedar City KOA* (☎ 586 9872), 1121 N Main St, has showers, pool, playground, grocery store and coin laundry. Sites range from $13.50 to $18.50, and there are a few Kamping Kabins for $25 a double.

*Country Aire RV Park* (☎ 586 2550), 1700 N Main St, has similar facilities for $14 to $17. Also see Hwy 14 East of Cedar City (below).

## Places to Stay – bottom end
Summer rates can be 50% higher than the rest of the year because of the Shakespearean Festival, and there are no really cheap places. One of the best of the cheapest is the *Thrifty Motel* (☎ 586 9114, fax 586 4614), 344 S Main St, which has a pool and double rooms in the $40s in summer and around $30 at other times. Similarly priced places include the fairly basic *Economy Motel* (☎ 586 4461, fax 586 1336), 443 S Main St; the *Astro Budget Inn* (☎ 586 6557), 323 S Main St; and the *Cedar Crest Motel* (☎ 586 6534), 583 S Main St. These last two offer simple rooms, some with kitchenettes, and a pool.

The *Raycap Motel* (☎ 586 7435), 2555 N Main St, has a pool and spa; double rooms cost in the upper $40s in summer or $10 less otherwise. There's a popular diner next door. The *Super 7 Motel* (☎ 586 6566), 190 S Main St, has nice double rooms for about $50 in summer or $30 the rest of the year. The *Super 8 Motel* (☎ 586 8880), 145 N 1550 West, has standard rooms for $43.88/50.88 for singles/doubles in summer, $6 less at other times. The *Zion Inn* (☎ 586 9487), 222 S Main St, also has standard doubles in the $50s in summer and the $30s the rest of the year. The *Daystop* (in the Days Inn chain, ☎ 586 9471, fax 586 2688), 479 S Main St, offers similar rooms for about $60 in summer and includes continental breakfast.

## Places to Stay – middle
**B&Bs** Travelers preferring the B&B experience should book early, especially for the Shakespearean Festival. No smoking is allowed in these places.

*Paxman's Summer House B&B* (☎ 586 3755), 170 N 400 West, is a Victorian house with many period furnishings. Four rooms with a queen-size bed and private bath rent for $55 to $75. The *Willow Glen Inn* (☎ 586 3275) is two miles north of

town at 3308 N Bulldog Rd (take 400 West northbound and follow it around under I-15 on Coal Creek Rd, then Bulldog Rd). Four rooms are inside the house (shared baths), and a two-room family cottage with bath is also available. Rates are $50 to $80.

The *Theater B&B* (☎ 586 0404), 118 S 100 West, has three rooms for $50 each. The *Bard's Inn B&B* (☎ 586 6612), 150 S 100 West, has seven rooms for $60 to $75. The *Woodbury Guest House* (☎ 586 6696), 237 S 300 West, is a restored Victorian open in summer only. Four rooms with private bath are about $80; a suite with kitchenette costs about $100.

**Hotels** All the hotels in this section have a swimming pool and nicely kept, generally spacious rooms. The Best Western *Town & Country Inn* (☎ 586 9900, fax 586 1664), 189 N Main St, is by far the biggest place in town with 157 rooms – it's more like two hotels separated by 200 North. Despite the sprawl, it seems pretty well run. Facilities include two pools, two spas, a game room, coin laundry, National Car Rental, a steak house, a pizza parlor and half a dozen other restaurants within a block. Double rooms are $55 to $71, depending on the season, and there are a few more expensive suites.

The Best Western *El Rey Inn* (☎ 586 6518, fax 586 7257), 80 S Main St, has a spa, sauna and exercise room. Doubles vary from $42 to $58 for (a few) small rooms, $59 to $74 for larger rooms and up to about $100 for a few suites, some with private spa.

The *Abbey Inn* (☎ 586 9966, fax 586 6522), 940 W 200 North, looks nice and has a spa and coin laundry. Rooms come equipped with a microwave, and some have refrigerators. Doubles with two queen-size beds or one king-size are $60 to $75 in summer, $15 less at other times. A couple of suites with spas go for about $120. Continental breakfast is included.

The *Comfort Inn* (☎ 586 2082, fax 586 3193), 250 N 1100 West, has a spa and coin laundry. Big double rooms are in the $60s in summer, $40s at other times, and rates include continental breakfast. Even larger units, some with kitchenettes or spas, some with two bedrooms, cost about $20 more.

The *Quality Inn* (☎ 586 2433, fax 586 7257), 18 S Main St, has pleasant rooms, but all are up a flight of stairs – no elevator. Rates are in the $60s and $70s for a double in summer, $20 less otherwise, including continental breakfast.

The *Rodeway Inn* (☎ 586 9916), 281 S Main St, features a sauna, a whirlpool and an adjacent restaurant. Doubles are $57 to $70 in summer, $40 to $50 in winter. Some two-bedroom units are a few dollars more.

The *Cedar Village Motel & Condominiums* (☎ 586 9925), 840 S Main St, has one-, two- and three-bedroom units with kitchenettes from $50 to $100 in summer. There is a coin laundry and a lawn for picnics.

### Places to Stay – top end

The *Holiday Inn* (☎ 586 8888, fax 586 1010), 1575 W 200 North, has a pool, spa, sauna, a well-equipped exercise room and a coin laundry. There is a restaurant and bar with room service (7 am to 10 pm or 6 am to 11 pm in summer). Comfortable rooms run in the $80s in summer, in the $60s in winter.

### Places to Eat

With 30 or 40 places in town, you won't go hungry. Here's a selection.

*Ed & Deb's Cafe* (☎ 586 0627), 2555 N Main St, is a locally popular diner (next to the Ray Cap Motel) that serves inexpensive breakfast lunch and dinner – a short drive to the north side of Cedar City.

Downtown, the place to go for reasonably priced American-style meals is *Sullivan's Cafe* (☎ 586 6761), 86 S Main St. In business since 1946, the cafe is popular – hours are 6 am to 10 pm, but they say they'll rustle up breakfast anytime. The cafe has a large salad bar and also serves potatoes in a variety of ways. Upstairs, you'll find *La Tajada Steak & Seafood House*, which offers upmarket dining, cocktails, a salad bar and entrees in the $12 to $22 range. Hours here are 6 to 10 pm or from 5 pm for festival goers.

Another fine steak and seafood choice is *Milt's Stage Stop* (☎ 586 9344), five miles east of town along Hwy 14 in Cedar Canyon. The hours and food are similar to La Tajada, but the atmosphere is decidedly rustic and Western. It's been around for years and is popular – make a reservation before driving up there.

Famous among festival goers is *Adriana's* (formerly the Black Swan) (☎ 586 7673), 164 S 100 West. When it was the Black Swan, the servers wore old-fashioned costumes and the ambiance was, if not Shakespearean, an attempt at Olde Englande. Lunches ($6 to $8) included the 'Hamlet' (a ham 'n cheese in pastry invention); dinners ($7 to $25) ranged from pasta to Chateaubriand. The Olde Englande stuff predictably turned the Black Swan into something of a tourist trap, albeit an agreeable one. It'll be interesting to see what Adriana makes of it.

*Pancho & Lefty's* (☎ 586 7501), 2107 N Main St, is fairly fancy and open just for dinner; *Escobar's* (☎ 865 0155), 155 N Main St, is a cheap downtown place open all day. Both serve good Mexican food. Three Chinese restaurants seem acceptable if not outstanding. The longest established is the *China Garden* (☎ 586 6042), 170 N Main St. There are also the *Kowloon* (☎ 586 3419), 50 W Center, and the *Hunan* (☎ 586 8952), 501 S Main St. For pizza, try *Godfather's Pizza* next to the Best Western Town & Country Inn, or the *Pizza Factory* (☎ 586 9896), 124 S Main St.

The restaurants in or adjacent to the better hotels serve standard American fare for breakfast, lunch and dinner. The best of these is the *Bristlecone Restaurant* (☎ 586 8888) in the Holiday Inn, with lunches starting around $5 and some dinners going close to $20. Others include the *Sizzler Steak, Seafood & Salad* (☎ 586 0786) by the Best Western Town & Country Inn – it's not bad. *Shoney's* (☎ 586 8012), next to the Abbey Inn, is a standard family restaurant, as is the *Sugar Loaf* (☎ 586 6593), next to the Rodeway Inn.

Finally, the *Sunshine Restaurant* (☎ 586 6683), at I-15 exit 59 (west of downtown on 200 North to I-15), is open 24 hours and serves good road food.

### Entertainment

For 24-hour movie information, call 586 7469. Movies are shown downtown at the *Campus Theater* (☎ 586 6539), 33 N Main St, and on the outskirts at *Fiddler's Three Theaters* (☎ 586 5924), 170 E Fiddlers Canyon Rd.

*The Playhouse* (☎ 586 9010), 1027 N Main St, doesn't show plays (see Special Events for that) but does have pool tables and dancing some nights. Next door is the *Kittyhawk Tavern* (☎ 586 7659). Other bars to try are the *Circus Lounge* (☎ 586 9084), 150 N Main St, and the *Sportsmen's Lounge* (☎ 586 6552, 586 9036), 900 S Main St.

### Getting There & Away

**Air** Skywest Airlines (☎ 1 (800) 453 9417) flies to and from Salt Lake City four times a day. Flights to other cities are sometimes available. The airport is two miles northwest of downtown.

**Bus** Greyhound (☎ 586 9465), 1355 S Main St, runs two buses a day each way between Las Vegas, Nevada, and Salt Lake City. Another two go between Las Vegas, Nevada, and Denver, Colorado. The fare to Salt Lake City is about $30 with three-day advance purchase.

### Getting Around

National Car Rental is at the airport (☎ 586 7059) and at the Best Western Town & Country Inn (☎ 586 9900). Avis (☎ 1 (800) 331 1212) and Hertz (☎ 1 (800) 654 3131) also rent cars in Cedar City.

## AROUND CEDAR CITY

This paved scenic route leads 40 miles over the Markagunt Plateau ending in Long Valley Junction at Hwy 89. The road crests at about 10,000 feet, where there are splendid views of Zion National Park to the south. Much of the road is within the Dixie National Forest (Cedar City Ranger Station has maps and information), and there are campgrounds, hiking trails, fishing lakes and lodges. Distances given below are east of Cedar City.

*Cedar Canyon Campground* (12 miles) has about 20 sites at 8000 feet, open June to about October. There is water. Sites cost $5.

At 9200 feet **Navajo Lake** (26 miles) has a small marina with boat rentals, a lodge with cabins, a store, a small restaurant and *Spruce* and *Navajo Lake Campgrounds*, both on the lake with about 70 sites between them, and *Te-Ah Campground* with a further 40 sites about 1.5 miles away. These facilities are open Memorial Day to October – the campsites have water and are $7.

The **Duck Creek Area** (30 miles) has tiny Duck Lake and Aspen Mirror Lake, both good for trout fishing, as is Duck Creek. There is a small visitor center, open in summer, various hiking trails and *Duck Creek Campground* with 80 sites for $7. In **Duck Creek Village** (population 60, elevation 8000 feet), there are some small, rustic lodges. The area has been used for making various movies, of which *How the West Was Won* is perhaps the best known. This is a popular cross-country skiing and snowmobiling area in winter.

*Falcon's Nest Motel & Cabins* (☎ 682 2556, fax 682 2564) has a restaurant and rents rooms and cabins for $50 to $70 a double. *Pinewoods Resort* (☎ 682 2512, fax 682 2543) also has a restaurant as well as a spa, exercise equipment, mountain bike rental and spacious rooms with kitchenettes for about $80 a double. *Aspen Whispering Pines Lodge* (☎ 682 2378) has a spa, game room, and rooms with kitchenette and wood-burning stove for $80 and up. *Meadeau View B&B* (☎ 682 2495) offers rooms with breakfast for about $60 to $70 a double.

A couple of miles east of Duck Creek Village, a signed gravel road to the south leads about 10 miles to **Strawberry Point**, with superb vistas of the color country to the south.

## ST GEORGE

Less than an hour southwest of Cedar City along I-15, St George has a noticeably different climate because of its elevation at 2880 feet (3000 feet below Cedar City). Summers are hot, with frequent daytime highs over 100°F, and winters are mild.

Founded in 1861 as a cotton farming center, St George was named after a Mormon leader, George A Smith – no dragon-slaying stories here. Within a decade, the cotton-growing mission had failed for the same reason as the iron mission to the north – cheaper cotton became available from the east when the railroad arrived. Despite harsh conditions, the Mormons persevered, partly because of Brigham Young's insistence. In the 1870s, he spent the last few winters of his life here and ensured the building of the most impressive Mormon Temple and Tabernacle in southern Utah.

Today, the mild winter weather continues to promote prosperity in St George. It is southern Utah's largest city (35,000 inhabitants) and one of the region's fastest growing ones (only 7000 inhabitants in 1970). Despite the growth, it remains a fine Mormon town with wide streets, historic buildings and a spacious feel to it.

There are eight golf courses, and St George claims to have the best year-round golf in the state. With the golf and mild winter weather, and the proximity of cooler Zion National Park to the east and Pine Valley Mountains to the north for summer relief, St George relies on tourism as an economic mainstay.

You won't find much to do here unless you're an avid golfer or enjoy visiting pioneer buildings – but its excellent range of hotels makes St George a good base for visiting Zion and other nearby parks. The city is the seat of Washington County.

## Information

The chamber of commerce (☎ 628 1658), 87 E St George Blvd, is open from 9 am to 5 pm Monday to Friday, and from 9 am to 1 pm on Saturday. The county Travel & Convention Bureau (☎ 634 5747, 1 (800) 869 6635) is in the Dixie Center at 425 S 700 East. (The Dixie Center is used for concerts, conventions and other events). The Dixie National Forest Pine Valley Ranger Station (☎ 673 3431), PO Box 584, 84720, in the Federal Building at 196 E Tabernacle, is open 8 am to 5 pm Monday to Friday. The BLM (☎ 673 4654, 628 4491) is at 225 N Bluff. The library (☎ 634 5737) is at 50 S Main St. The local newspaper is the *Daily Spectrum*. The post office (☎ 673 3312) is at 180 N Main St. The medical center (☎ 634 4000) is at 544 S 400 East. The police (☎ 634 5001, or 911 in emergencies) are at 175 E 200 North.

## Historical Buildings

Brochures detailing some two dozen old buildings are available from the tourist information offices. The highlights are described below.

Utah's first **Mormon Temple** was built here between 1871 and 1877 – a magnificent building interesting both for its architecture and the difficult history of its construction. The Temple (like all Mormon temples) is open only to church members on official business, but a visitor center (☎ 673 5181), 440 S 300 East, open daily from 9 am to 9 pm (10 pm in summer), has audiovisual and other displays and hosts lectures about the temple's history and church beliefs in general.

The **Mormon Tabernacle**, on Tabernacle and Main St, was built between 1863 and 1876. The red-brick and white-spired building is open daily, and guided tours (☎ 628 4072) are offered from 11 am to 5 pm. The **Brigham Young Winter Home** (☎ 673 2517), 89 W 200 North, is where the Mormon leader spent his winters from 1873 until 1877. Many of the original furnishings remain. Hours are 9 am to 6 pm (8:30 pm in summer), and there are free guided tours. Across the street, lining the west side of 100 West between St George Blvd and 217 North, are several other pioneer homes, two of which house the Seven Wives Inn (at 217 N 100 West).

The **Old County Courthouse**, finished in the 1870s, now houses the chamber of

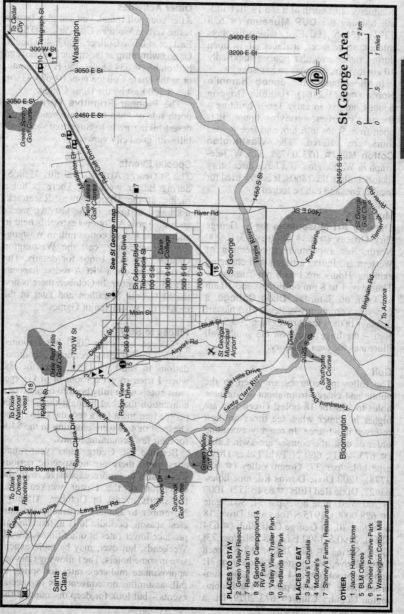

**St George Area**

0 2 km
0 1 miles

To Cedar City

Washington

300 W St
Telegraph St
3400 E St
3200 E St

3050 E St
3050 E St
2450 E St

Green Spring Golf Course

Middleton Dr
Red Cliff Drive

Twin Lakes Golf Course

1450 E St

River Rd

1400 E St

St George Golf Club

River Rd Drive
Fort Pierce
Tamarind
Brigham Rd

See St George map

Skyline Drive

St George Blvd
Tabernacle St
100 S St
300 S St
500 S St
700 S St

Dixie College

Virgin River

St George

15

To Arizona

Main St

Diagonal St
200 W St
700 W St

Dixie Red Hills Golf Course

Bluff St

Airport Rd

St George Municipal Airport

Dixie Drive

Ridge View Drive
Valley View Drive
1250 N St

Santa Clara Drive
Mathis Lane

To Dixie National Forest

18

Indian Hills Drive

Tonaquint Drive
Santa Clara River

Bloomington

2025 S St

Southgate Golf Course

Green Valley Golf Course

Sunbrook Dr

Sunbrook Golf Course

Lava Flow Rd

Dixie Downs Rd

To Dixie Downs Racetrack

W Canyon View Drive

2

Santa Clara

1

**PLACES TO STAY**
2   Green Valley Resort
7   Ramada Inn
8   St George Campground & RV Park
9   Valley View Trailer Park
10  Redlands RV Park

**PLACES TO EAT**
3   Paula's Cazuela
4   McGuire's
7   Shoney's Family Restaurant

**OTHER**
1   Jacob Hamblin Home
5   BLM Offices
6   Pioneer Primitive Mill
11  Washington Cotton Mill

commerce. Just north of it is a 1930s building housing the **DUP Museum** (☎ 628 7274), 135 N 100 East, which displays interesting pioneer artifacts; it is open during rather irregular hours (supposedly 10 am to 5 pm, Monday to Saturday).

In the suburbs, the **Jacob Hamblin Home** (☎ 673 2161), Hamblin Drive in Santa Clara, is an early 1860s building – the area's earliest surviving house. It is open from 9 am to 6 pm, and free guided tours are offered. The **Washington Cotton Mill** (☎ 673 0375), 375 W Telegraph in Washington, is a large three-story factory built in the 1860s. It is now used for local events and can be toured.

### Museums

The **City Art Museum** in the St George City Offices (☎ 634 5800), 175 E 200 North, has a permanent collection of Western art, Indian artifacts and changing exhibits. Hours are 1 to 5 pm Tuesday to Thursday, 1 to 8 pm on Friday, and 10 am to 4 pm on Saturday. **Dixie College**, a two-year community college, also has art displays in the Fine Arts Center, 200 S 700 East – the huge mural on the south wall illustrates the area's history.

### Golf

The following courses are open to the public and charge from about $6 for nine holes to $28 for 18 holes. Green fees are higher in winter when tee times are best reserved in advance. In roughly ascending order of cost, the courses are Twin Lakes (☎ 673 4441), 660 N Twin Lakes Drive, nine holes/par 27; Green Valley (☎ 628 3778), 1200 Dixie Downs Rd, nine holes/par 27; Dixie Red Hills (☎ 634 5852), 1000 N 700 West, nine holes/par 34; Southgate (☎ 628 0000), 1975 S Tonaquint Drive, 18 holes/par 70; St George Golf Club (☎ 634 5854), 2190 S 1400 East, 18 holes/par 73; Green Spring (☎ 673 7888), 588 N Green Spring Drive, Washington, 18 holes/par 71; and Sunbrook (☎ 634 5866), 2240 Sunbrook Drive, 18 holes/par 72. The Bloomington Country Club (☎ 673 2029) has a private course, 18 holes/par 72.

### Other Activities

After your golf round, you can play **tennis** at the Vernon Worthen City Park, 200 S 400 East, or at Dixie College, 700 E 400 South. Or go **swimming** at the municipal pool and hydrotube (☎ 634 5867), 250 E 700 South, or at the Dixie College pool (☎ 673 8386), 425 S 700 East by the Dixie Center.

The **Pioneer Primitive Park** on the north side of town has picnic benches and desert hiking trails to Sugarloaf – a small hill with good city views.

### Special Events

The St George Arts Festival fills Main St during Easter weekend. There is horse racing at the Dixie Downs Racetrack, northwest of town, in the last two weekends of April. A Cotton Festival is held in and around the old cotton mill in Washington in early May; call the Washington Chamber (☎ 628 1666) for details. The Dixie Round-up, a PRCA rodeo, happens in mid-September. In October, there is first the St George Marathon and later in the month, the World Senior Games.

### Places to Stay

St George has over 2000 hotel rooms, which is the biggest selection of accommodations in southern Utah. Nevertheless, when I tried to get a room in St George, most hotels were fully booked because of a convention that had brought thousands of people into town for a few days. Even the cheapest motels were charging in the $40s for their few remaining rooms.

Because St George has year-round attractions, there are no specific periods when rates are more expensive, with the exception of the Easter weekend and the sports events in October. Although November to January is usually the quietest season, periodic lulls in tourism can produce lower rates at other times as well. Weekends, however, may be more expensive in some hotels. The following rates are approximate midweek rates for spring to fall, assuming no conventions or special events – but look for deep discounts if the town is quiet.

Southern Utah Tourist Information & Services (☎ 628 7710, 1 (800) 765 7710, fax 628 3643), 135 N 900 East, Suite 2, is a reservation service that can book you into a wide range of hotels, though not the very cheapest.

### Places to Stay – camping

Camping, mainly in RVs, is popular here, and the following campgrounds offer almost 900 sites between them. All the following have toilets, showers and coin laundry. *McArthur's Temple View RV Resort* (☎ 673 6400), 975 S Main St, has pool, spa and recreation area; sites are $13 for tents, $19 with full hookups. *Settlers RV Park* (☎ 628 1624), 1333 E 100 South, has a pool, spa and games area; sites are $16 with hookups. *St George Campground & RV Park* (☎ 673 2970), 2100 E Middleton Drive, has a pool and charges from $12 to $16. *Valley View Trailer Park* (☎ 673 3367), 2300 E Middleton Drive, has RV sites only at $13 with hookups. *Redlands RV Park* (☎ 673 9700), 650 W Telegraph St, Washington, has a pool, spa, playground and grocery stores; sites are $14 to $19. Also see Around St George.

### Places to Stay – bottom end

The *Western Safari Motel* (☎ 673 5238), 310 W St George Blvd, is one of the cheapest with rooms in the lower $20s or about $30 with a kitchenette. The *Oasis Motel* (☎ 673 3551), 231 W St George Blvd, has a pool, coin laundry and modest rooms in the $20s. A few have kitchenettes. The *Red Mesa Motel* (☎ 673 3163), 247 E St George Blvd, is similar.

The *Dixie Palm Motel* (☎ 673 3531, fax 673 5352), 185 E St George Blvd, has well-kept rooms for about $30/35 for singles/doubles and pool privileges next door (at the Best Western Coral Hills). The *Motel 6* (☎ 628 7979), 205 N 1000 East, is by far the biggest budget hotel in town with over 100 rooms going for $30/36. It has a pool. The *Sands Motel* (☎ 673 3501), 581 E St George Blvd, has a pool and rooms in the low $30s. The *Desert Edge* (☎ 673 6137), 525 E St George Blvd, has a

pool, spa and fairly large if spartan rooms, many with kitchenettes. Rates are in the $30s. The *Southside Inn* (☎ 628 9000), 750 E St George Blvd, is similar but has no kitchenettes.

### Places to Stay – middle

**B&Bs** *Greene Gate Village* (☎ 628 6999, 1 (800) 350 6999), 62-78 W Tabernacle, is actually nine different early buildings, some dating from the 1870s. Most have been, literally, picked up and moved here from other parts of St George, then carefully restored and furnished with period pieces. The rooms vary, but all have modern private bathrooms, and some may have a fireplace, balcony or kitchenette, sitting room, hot tub or some combination thereof. Individual rooms start in the $50s, suites are $75 and up for two people; extra adults are $15 and children $10. Entire houses can be rented – one sleeps up to 20 people and has a $150 minimum charge. There are about 18 rooms and suites, a pool, spa, large grounds with picnic and barbecue areas and a library. A full breakfast is served. Smoking is not permitted.

The *Seven Wives Inn* (☎ 628 3737), 217 N 100 West, is made up of two houses. The first was built in 1873 and named after one of the owners' great-grandfathers, who had seven wives and hid in the attic room here after polygamy was outlawed in 1882. There are nine bedrooms here. Next door is an adobe house built in 1883 containing four more rooms. All the rooms have been given women's names (seven are the wives' names), and all have private bath and are individually and uniquely furnished with antiques. Most are fairly small (double occupancy only), and some have fireplaces or balconies. Rates are $55 to $100 including full breakfast. There is a pool, and each house has a living room with fireplace, books and games. The friendly owners can tell you about area history. No smoking allowed.

The above two places have been around since the 1970s, have good reputations and are often booked up – reservations are recommended. A couple of new small B&Bs

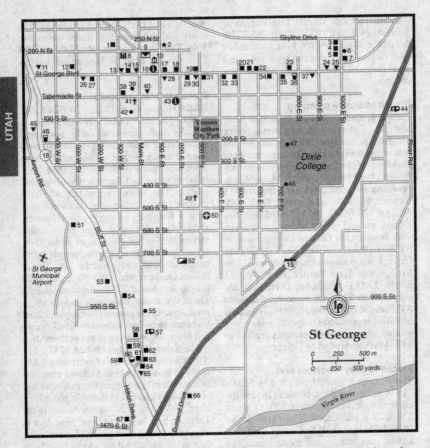

have opened recently – *Aunt Annie's Inn* (☎ 673 5504), 139 N 100 West, and *Morris Mulberry Inn* (☎ 673 7383), 194 S 300 East.

The zip code for all of these B&Bs is 84770.

**Hotels** *Sullivan's Rococo Inn* (☎ 628 3671), 511 S Airport Rd, is near the airport on the bluff overlooking St George from the west, a location that provides good city views. There is a pool, spa and steak house (dinner only). Rooms are quite large and feature refrigerators and either two queen-size beds or a king-size; they are a good deal for about $40 for a double – four

people can sleep in a room for that price. Also good is the *Chalet Motel* (☎ 628 6272), 644 E St George Blvd, which has a pool and decent double rooms in the $30s. Some have kitchenettes for about $40, and there are a few suites sleeping up to six for about $60. Another good choice for doubles at $40 or less is the *Sleep Inn* (☎ 673 7900), 1481 S Sunland Drive, which has a pool and spa.

The *Claridge Inn* (☎ 673 7222, fax 634 0773), 1187 S Bluff, has a pool and spa and is located a block away from a 24-hour restaurant. The rooms are pleasant and are all nonsmoking. They run in the low $40s

UTAH

**PLACES TO STAY**
1   Seven Wives Inn
3   Comfort Inn
4   Motel 6
5   Travelodge East
7   Thunderbird Inn
12  Western Safari Motel
14  Travelodge West
17  Best Western Coral
    Hills Motel
18  Dixie Palm Motel
19  Red Mesa Motel
20  Desert Edge
21  Coronada Family Inn
22  Sands Motel
23  Days Inn Four Seasons
27  Oasis Motel
29  Singletree Inn
31  Best Western Travel Inn
32  Sun Time Inn
33  Econo Lodge
34  Chalet Motel
35  Southside Inn,
    Regency Inn
38  Greene Gate Village
44  Settlers RV Park
51  Sullivan's Rococo Inn
53  Holiday Inn
54  Super 8 Motel

56  Ranch Inn
57  McArthur's Temple View
    RV Resort
58  Claridge Inn
59  Bluffs Motel
61  Budget 8 Motel
62  Days Inn South-Heritage
    Inn
63  Budget Inn
64  Comfort Suites
66  Sleep Inn
67  Hilton Inn

**PLACES TO EAT**
11  Baskin Robbins Ice Cream
13  Trafalga Restaurant
15  Ancestor Square
23  Shed Restaurant
24  Sil's Seafood Restaurant
25  Denny's Restaurant
26  Charlie's Malts &
    Ice Cream
28  Dick's Cafe
30  Andelin's Gable House
33  Rene's Restaurant
36  Blarney Stone Bar
37  Frostop
38  Judd's Store, Bentley
    Supper House
40  Ice Cream Parlour

45  Pancho & Lefty's
46  Chapter 11
51  Sullivan's Rococo
    Steak House
53  Palms Restaurant
62  Denny's Restaurant
65  JB's Restaurant
67  Tonaquint Restaurant

**OTHER**
2   City Offices (Police, City
    Art Museum)
6   The Movie Theater
8   Brigham Young Winter
    Home
9   Post Office
10  DUP Museum
16  Chamber of Commerce
39  Dixie Theater
41  Mormon Tabernacle
42  Library
43  Forest Ranger Station
47  Fine Arts Center
48  Dixie Center
49  Mormon Temple
50  Medical Center
52  Municipal Pool
55  The Cinemas
60  Greyhound Bus Depot

for a double, including continental breakfast. The *Super 8 Motel* (☎ 628 4251, fax 628 6534), 915 S Bluff, has a pool (closed in winter) and fairly good rooms for $39.88 to $46.88 for one to four people. The *Travelodge East* (☎ 673 4621, fax 628 1874), 175 N 1000 East, has a pool and satisfactory rooms for about $40/45 for singles/doubles and a couple of suites for $70. Also good is the *Sun Time Inn* (☎ 673 6181), 420 E St George Blvd, which has a pool, spa and pleasant nonsmoking rooms, some with kitchenettes, for $30 to $40 a single, $40 to $45 a double. A couple of mini-suites with king-size beds and in-room spa go for about $60.

Similar rates are available at the *Regency Inn* (☎ 673 6119), 770 E St George Blvd, which has decent rooms and a pool, spa and sauna. Another reasonable choice in the $40s is the *Budget Inn* (☎ 673 6661), 1221 S Main St, which has adults' and kids'

pools, spa and free continental breakfast. There's also the *Thunderbird Inn* (☎ 673 6123, fax 673 7030), 150 N 1000 East, with garden-like grounds, pool, spa and sauna. The *Comfort Inn* (☎ 628 4271), 999 E Skyline Drive, has a pool and nice spacious rooms for about $40/50 for singles/doubles. Others in this price range include the *Budget 8 Motel* (☎ 628 5234), 1230 S Main St, with a pool and spa; the *Coronada Family Inn* (☎ 628 4436), 559 E St George Blvd, with pool, spa, laundry and large rooms with kitchenettes; the *Travelodge West* (☎ 673 4666), 60 W St George Blvd, with pool, spa and sauna; and the *Days Inn South – Heritage Inn* (☎ 628 4481), 1165 S Bluff, with pool, spa, sauna and continental breakfast.

The friendly *Singletree Inn* (☎ 673 6161), 260 E St George Blvd, has a pool and spa and includes a continental breakfast. The *Econo Lodge* (☎ 673 4861, fax

628 4878), 460 E St George Blvd, has a pool, spa and sauna, and Rene's Restaurant is next door. They both charge in the $50s because they are close to the historic center – the rooms aren't much different than most hotels in the $40s above.

Nearby, nicer, larger rooms in the low $50s are available at the Best Western *Travel Inn* (☎ 673 3541, fax 673 5352), 316 E St George Blvd. A couple of two-bedroom units sleeping six go for about $60. It has a pool and spa. Also close to downtown is the larger Best Western *Coral Hills Motel* (☎ 673 4844, fax 673 5352), 125 E St George Blvd – the best hotel in the center. There are three pools (indoor, outdoor, kids'), spas, exercise room, game room, putting green and restaurants nearby. Spacious, comfortable rooms, some with balconies, are in the upper $50s for a double. Suites with spas cost $20 or $30 more.

There are also good accommodations away from the center of town. If you want to avoid the chains, *Bluffs Motel* (☎ 628 6699, fax 628 8270), 1140 S Bluff, is an attractive choice. It has adults' and kids' pools, spa and coin laundry. Pleasant rooms have queen- and king-size beds, some have kitchenettes and a couple of mini-suites have a spa. Rates are in the $50s for doubles and in the $70s for suites. The *Ranch Inn* (☎ 628 8000), 1040 S Main St, has a pool, spa, sauna and coin laundry. Some rooms have kitchenettes. Doubles are from the upper $40s to low $60s.

The *Days Inn Four Seasons* (☎ 673 6111, fax 673 0994), 747 E St George Blvd, bills itself as a convention center and has about 100 rooms in the $50s, and a few suites for twice that. Facilities include two pools, spa, tennis courts, the Shed Restaurant (dinner only) and free continental breakfast. The *Ramada Inn* (☎ 628 2828, fax 628 0505), 1440 E St George Blvd, has nice rooms in the upper $50s. There is a pool and spa, and continental breakfast is included.

### Places to Stay – top end
*Comfort Suites* (☎ 673 7000, fax 628 4340), 1239 S Main St, has 123 suites, each with a small kitchenette and sitting room.

There is a pool and spa. Rates are $50 to $90 for a double (highest rates at Easter, October and weekends), including continental breakfast. The *Hilton Inn* (☎ 628 0463, fax 628 1501), 1450 S Hilton Drive, has 100 rooms, among them the largest and most comfortable in St George. There is a pool, spa, sauna and tennis court. A golf course and health club (for a fee) are within short walking distance. The Tonaquint Restaurant and Bar are on the premises. Double rooms run $70 to $100.

The *Holiday Inn* (☎ 628 4235, fax 628 8157), 850 S Bluff, is the largest hotel in town with 164 comfortable rooms, some with refrigerators or balconies. Facilities include two pools, spa, exercise room, playground, tennis court, putting green, game room, coin laundry and business services. The Palms Restaurant and Bar are on the premises, and there is room service. Double rooms are $70 to $100.

*Green Valley Resort* (☎ 628 8060, fax 673 4084), 1515 W Canyon View Drive in Santa Clara, has 70 condos ranging from one to four bedrooms, each with kitchens. The resort has pools, spas, tennis and racquetball courts, and other sporting and exercise facilities. Condos rent for $120 to $210. Condos can also be rented from Holiday Resort Properties (☎ 673 6172, fax 628 6175), 141 Brigham Rd, Suite A, which is a reservation service for about 45 condos on the south side of town ranging in price from $60 to $180.

### Places to Eat
**Breakfast** St George slays monstrous breakfast appetites with all-you-can-eat breakfast wars. Several bland and similar-looking chain restaurants offer these gut-busting good mornings with prices around $4.50 – not bad if you're really hungry. They then stay open all day for reasonably priced lunch and dinner. Such establishments include: *Shoney's Family Restaurant* (☎ 628 8177), 1410 E St George Blvd; *Sil's Seafood Restaurant* (☎ 634 9910), 939 E St George Blvd; and *JB's* (☎ 628 9278), 1245 S Main St. Both *Denny's* 155 N 1000 East, or 1215 S Main St, are open 24 hours.

**American** For dining with some local atmosphere, the best-known place is *Dick's Cafe* (☎ 673 3841), 114 E St George Blvd. It has been here since 1935 under the motto 'Where the West Meets the Guest' – American dining amidst Western trappings. It is open from 6 am to 9:30 pm daily with mid-priced meals (around $5 for breakfast or lunch; $7 to $14 for dinner). There's both a coffee shop and a more old-fashioned diner area. A couple of blocks away is the *Trafalga Restaurant* (☎ 673 2933), 76 W St George Blvd, with slightly cheaper but good American meals. You'll also find all the usual fast-food spots in town – *Frostop* (☎ 673 2216), 858 E St George Blvd, is a little more old-fashioned in that it uses 'car hops' – people who deliver your burger to your car on a little tray that attaches to your car door. (This passes for American culture at some level...and it's disappearing quickly.) It is open from 11 am to 11 pm daily except Sunday.

*McGuire's* (☎ 628 4066), 531 N Bluff St, is a more upmarket restaurant, serving some Italian and continental dishes as well as American dinners from 5:30 to 10:30 pm. Most entrees cost between $10 and $20. *Andelin's Gable House* (☎ 673 6796), 290 E St George Blvd, is known for its fine five-course fixed-price dinners, homemade rolls and desserts as well as a conventional American menu. The ambiance here is Olde Worlde, with antiques everywhere and 'wenchresses' wearing 18th-century outfits. The place is very popular – partly because it's within walking distance of several good hotels. It is open from 11:30 am to 10 pm. Lunches (burgers, sandwiches, salads) are $5 to $8; dinners are $8 to $25. This is a no-smoking restaurant.

**Mexican** Try *Paula's Cazuela* (673 6568), 745 W Ridgeview Drive, which is closed on Sundays, and *Pancho & Lefty's* (☎ 628 4772), 100 S Bluff, open daily from 11:30 am to 10 pm.

**Ancestor Square** The northwest corner of Main St and St George Blvd has several decent restaurants as well as interesting shops. *Basila's Greek & Italian Cafe* (☎ 673 7671) has good food and is locally popular for business lunches, etc. It is open from Tuesday to Saturday for lunch (11 am to 2:30 pm, about $5 to $7) and dinner (5 to 9 pm, entrees from $8 to $18). *Libby Lorraine's* (☎ 673 0750) is open for breakfast, lunch and dinner, and serves great sandwiches for around $5, light pasta dishes for about $7 to $10, gourmet coffees, and beer and wine. It has some outdoor tables. There's also a *Pizza Factory* (☎ 628 1234), which has a salad bar, sandwiches and spaghetti as well as pizza. *JJ Hunan Chinese Restaurant* (☎ 628 7219) serves a huge variety of Chinese dishes from 11:30 am to 9:30 pm daily (8:30 pm on Sunday). Good Mexican food is dished up at *Los Hermanos* (☎ 628 5989), open from 11:30 am to 9:15 pm Monday to Saturday.

**Hotel Restaurants** For something different, make a reservation (required) at the *Bentley Supper House* (☎ 628 6999), in the Greene Gate Village B&B, where they serve old-fashioned home-cooked country dinners in a pioneer setting on Thursday, Friday and Saturday nights.

If you like steak or seafood, the best place in town is *Sullivan's Rococo Steak House* (☎ 628 3671) at the Rococo Inn. There are great city views from the dining room. Hours are 5 to 10 pm, and most dinners are in the $20s. The *Shed Restaurant* (☎ 673 7800) in the Days Inn Four Seasons, also has good steak, and a varied American menu of chicken and seafood at prices lower than the Rococo.

The *Palms Restaurant* (☎ 628 4235) at the Holiday Inn is an upmarket family restaurant open from 6 am to 10 pm. The *Tonaquint Restaurant* (☎ 628 0463) in the Hilton is also a good, mid-priced family restaurant; it's open from 7 am to 9:30 pm (closed from 2 to 5:30 pm). *Rene's Restaurant* (☎ 628 9300), offers 10% discounts to guests of the adjacent Econo Lodge. It is a quiet place, painted in pastels, very reasonably priced and popular with older or retired travelers.

**Ice Cream** The *Ice Cream Parlour* (☎ 634 9104), 94 E Tabernacle, is a modern ice-cream emporium serving snacks and ice cream desserts from 11 am to 10 pm, Monday to Thursday and to midnight on Friday and Saturday. This modern place is a popular hangout for local teens – compare it to the old-fashioned *Judd's Store* (☎ 628 2596), 62 W Tabernacle (part of the Greene Gate Village), which serves traditional shakes using ancient machines in a turn-of-the-century setting. Other good places for ice cream are *Baskin Robbins* (☎ 673 1950), 490 W St George Blvd, and *Charlie's Malts & Ice Cream* (☎ 628 6304), 287 W St George Blvd. Both are closed on Sunday.

### Entertainment
The *Southwest Symphony* (☎ 673 0700), 425 S 700 East (in the Dixie Center), performs a concert series from October to May. During the same season, Dixie College (☎ 673 4811) hosts a Celebrity Concert Series as well as plays and musicals at the *Fine Arts Center Theater* (☎ 628 3121), 225 S 700 East. Also call the Dixie Center (☎ 628 7003) for other cultural entertainment.

Movies are shown at *The Movie* (☎ 628 0669), 214 N 1000 East; *The Cinemas* (☎ 628 6113), 905 S Main St; *Dixie Theater* (☎ 673 2131), 35 N Main St; and *Gaiety Theater* (☎ 673 5151), 68 E Tabernacle.

The Mormon influence remains strong, and there is little in the way of bars and nightclubs. For a beer and a game of pool, try the modern and bare-looking *Blarney Stone Bar* (☎ 673 9191), 800 E St George Blvd, which has occasional live music on weekends. *Chapter 11* (☎ 673 0055), 195 S Bluff, is a private club.

### Getting There & Away
**Air** The airport is on a bluff overlooking downtown from the west – nice views. Skywest Airlines (☎ 1 (800) 453 9417) runs five flights a day to and from Salt Lake City, as well as flights to Las Vegas, Nevada, one flight to Page, Arizona, and sometimes to other destinations.

**Bus** Greyhound (☎ 673 2933) leaves from the McDonald's at 1235 S Bluff, with two buses (one around 1 am, the other late morning) to Salt Lake City, as well as buses to Denver, Colorado, and Las Vegas.

### Getting Around
Budget (☎ 673 6825, 1 (800) 527 0700), 116 W St George Blvd; Dollar (☎ 1 (800) 800 4000), 1175 S 150 East; and National (☎ 673 5098, 1 (800) 227 7378), all have booths at the airport. Local car rental agencies include A-1 (☎ 673 8811) and Bonnie & Clyde's (☎ 628 5722).

## AROUND ST GEORGE
Interstate 15 south of town soon swings southwest; after eight miles, it crosses the Arizona state line and, 30 miles further, the Nevada state line on its way to Las Vegas, about 120 miles southwest of St George. Joshua trees can be seen near the state line – an unusual species for Utah.

### Snow Canyon State Park
Snow? Ha! Not in this hot desert country. The park derived its name from early pioneers. The scenery is volcanic and well worth seeing – cinder cones and lava flows mixed in with the usual Southwestern sandstone cliffs and petroglyphs. The desert vegetation is interesting. There are hiking trails – a one-mile hike leads to lava caves, and longer hikes go to arches and canyons. Summers are searingly hot, so come prepared with plenty of water and sun protection – other seasons are more pleasant.

The *campground* has over 30 sites with water and showers; reservations (☎ 1 (800) 322 3770) are recommended during spring and fall weekends. Primitive camping (no facilities) is possible along the longer trails.

Fees are $3 for day use and $9/11 for camping without/with hookups. For more information, contact the park at 628 2255, PO Box 140, Santa Clara, 84738.

The park is nine miles north of St George on Hwy 18 and then left; the road continues through the park to Ivins, Santa Clara and back to St George. This 24-mile loop is a popular drive or bike ride.

## Veyo Area

Veyo is a tiny village 19 miles north of St George on Hwy 18. **Veyo Resort** is a swimming pool filled by naturally warmed spring water. It has been in use since the 1920s, thus making it a historical spot by Utahan standards. Note the nearby (extinct) volcano on the west side of Hwy 18, which provides the warmed waters. The resort (☎ 574 2744) has picnicking and a cafe and is open from April to Labor Day from 11 am to nightfall (or later). Swims are $3, or $2 for children. The resort is signed to the east of Hwy 18, 19 miles north of St George.

Ten miles southwest of Veyo, **Gunlock State Park** offers fishing and boating. There is no campground or development yet, so entrance is free – information is available from Snow Canyon.

Five miles north of Veyo, there is free camping at the BLM-owned **Baker Dam Reservoir**, which has no water for drinking but does offer decent fishing and boating. A few miles further north is the **Mountain Meadows Massacre Monument**, marking the site where Mormons killed about 120 non-Mormon pioneers in 1857 for reasons that are still unclear.

## Enterprise Area

This agricultural town of 1100 inhabitants is 19 miles north of Veyo and offers a couple of tiny motels. *Aspen Motel* (☎ 878 2325, 878 2413) at the west end of town, has four rooms, and the *Sleep E Motel* (☎ 878 2603) at the east end, next to a gas station, store and country cafe, has six rooms. Rooms are in the low $30s midweek, more on weekends.

Paved and then gravel roads lead 11 miles west to **Enterprise Reservoir** with fishing, boating and the USFS *Honey Comb Rocks Campground*, open from mid-May to November, with water but no showers. Sites cost $7. This campground is remote and uncrowded, especially midweek. The USFS also operates the free but waterless *Pine Park Campground*, about 10 miles west of the reservoir turnoff. This is a poor road, though cars can just make it in dry weather.

## Pine Valley Area

To reach the village of **Pine Valley**, exit Hwy 18 at Central, between Veyo and Enterprise, and head a few miles east. The village is 32 miles from St George, and its 6500-foot elevation gives some relief from the lowland heat. A fine white wood church, built in 1868, is the oldest continually operating Mormon church in Utah. It is open for tours.

The small *Pine Valley Lodge* (☎ 574 2544) offers 10 rustic rooms ranging from about $30 to $50 – higher rates on weekends. A few cheaper cabins sleep up to four – bring your own bedding. There are public coin showers and laundry, a store and a cafe. Nearby is the *Brandin' Iron Steak House* (☎ 574 2261), which serves dinners.

Half a mile to the east, you enter the Dixie National Forest (☎ 673 3431) and within three miles pass a cluster of four small campgrounds (with a total of about 70 sites) at 6800 feet. These are popular, especially during weekends in the May to October season. All campgrounds have water but no showers and cost $7. Arrive early or call 1 (800) 283 2267 for a reservation.

Several hikes and backpacking trips are possible from the campgrounds up into the Pine Valley Mountains – the ranger station in St George can provide maps and information about the trailheads as well as other campgrounds in the Dixie National Forest.

## Leeds Area

Leeds, a small town of 500, has a couple of places to eat and an RV park. It is off I-15 exit 22, 13 miles northeast of St George.

Over a thousand people lived in **Silver Reef** in the late 19th century, drawn to it by silver mining. Today, most of the buildings have disappeared, although a few dilapidated ruins remain. The Wells Fargo building has been restored and now houses a small museum and art gallery

(☎ 879 2254), open 9 am to 5 pm Monday to Saturday. Silver Reef is just over a mile northwest of Leeds by a signed, paved road.

South of Leeds is **Quail Creek State Park** (☎ 879 2378), PO Box 1943, 84770, four miles east of I-15 exit 16 towards Hurricane. The reservoir provides the usual fishing and boating, and there is a small campground with water but no showers for $8.

### Fort Pierce & Dinosaur Tracks

The ruins of Fort Pierce can be reached by heading east from River Rd on 1450 S and, after two miles, following signs along a dirt road for another six miles. From Fort Pierce, two more miles of dirt road lead to the dinosaur tracks, where there are interpretive signs. Cars can drive the road in good weather. There are also dinosaur tracks northeast of Washington, but you have to hike in the last few hundred yards – ask at the St George Chamber of Commerce for precise directions.

### HURRICANE

With 4000 inhabitants, this is a sizable and growing town. It attracts retirees, but travelers gravitate more toward St George, 15 miles away. Nevertheless, Hurricane hosts the **Washington County Fair** in August and offers a few places to stay for people on their way to or from Zion, 25 miles to the east. There is a Pioneer and Indian Museum on State St near Main St. The area is famous for its peaches.

A mile north of town, the Pah Tempe **hot springs** fill a series of dip pools and a swimming pool. Fees are $5, with discounts for children and seniors. There are places to stay and eat.

### Places to Stay

*Robert's Roost* (☎ 635 0126), 113 W 400 South, has 13 RV sites with showers and coin laundry. *Brentwood Utah RV Park* (☎ 635 2320), 150 N 3700 West (four miles west on Hwy 9), has 200 sites for $16 with hookups. Facilities include a restaurant, showers, pool, spa, golf course, tennis

courts, a play area and a water-slide park nearby. *Quail Lake RV Park* (☎ 635 9960), six miles west on Hwy 9, has a pool, spa and store. Sites are $11 with hookups. Two miles north in La Verkin is the *Zion RV Park* (☎ 635 4272), 44 W 500 North, with showers, pool and grocery store, and sites from $13 to $16.

*Park Villa Motel* (☎ 635 4010, fax 635 4025), 650 W State, has a pool and spa. Most rooms have kitchenettes and rent for about $40/50 for singles/doubles in summer, $10 less in winter. The Best Western *Weston's Lamplighter Motel* (☎ 635 4647, fax 635 0848), 280 W State, has a pool and spa. Rooms are in the $50s in summer, less in winter.

The *Pah Tempe Hot Springs B&B* (☎ 635 2879), 825 N 800 East, 84737, has a restaurant and access to the hot springs. Nine rooms range from about $55/65 for singles/doubles.

### Places to Eat

Next door to Weston's Lamplighter Motel is the *El Chaparral Restaurant* (☎ 635 4856), 270 W State, with a salad bar and American food served daily from 6 am to 10 pm. *Chumley's Cafe* (☎ 635 9825, 635 9831), 130 S Main St, which has local atmosphere, vegetarian cooking, interesting sandwiches, gourmet coffees and occasional live music, is open 8:30 am to 8:30 pm, Monday to Saturday, and 10 am to 2 pm on Sunday. There are a couple of fast-food places.

### TOQUERVILLE

This little town of 500, located seven miles north of Hurricane, is the heart of Dixie's wine country. The Mormons don't drink alcohol, but as far back as 1865, they built a winery in Toquerville and sold the product to non-Mormons. The winery has been restored and can be toured. Call the town hall (☎ 635 2826) for information about visiting this and other pioneer buildings.

*Your Inn Toquerville* (☎ 635 9964), 650 Springs Drive, 84774, is a B&B with five rooms, all with private bath, for about $60.

## GRAFTON GHOST TOWN & ROCKVILLE

Grafton has several buildings, including a church, a large two-storied house and general store, and others – all standing empty and mute save for the wind ghosting through them. The site has gained fame since it was the setting for the bicycle scene in *Butch Cassidy and the Sundance Kid*, starring Robert Redford (who owns Sundance Ski Resort in Utah).

Grafton is reached from Rockville, a few miles southwest of Springdale. From Hwy 9, turn south on 200 East (also called Bridge Lane – it crosses the river). The road is signed as a 'Scenic Byway' and reaches Grafton in four miles (turn right at a fork about half way). The last section is dirt, but it's passable to cars in good weather.

In Rockville, a couple of small B&Bs offer full breakfast. The *Handcart House* (☎ 772 3867), 244 W Main St, has three rooms with private baths and antique furniture. Rates are about $60 to $70 for two. The *Blue House* (☎ 772 3912), 125 E Main St, has four less expensive rooms. Neither B&B permits smoking. The zip code for both is 84763.

## SPRINGDALE

With a permanent population of 350, Springdale's main claims to fame are its position at the entrance to Zion National Park and its many hotels. Most of these are along Zion Park Blvd (lower address numbers are closest to the park entrance). There are nice mountain views from most parts of town.

### Things to See & Do

The **OC Tanner Amphitheater** (☎ 673 4811) has a variety of musical and theatrical events and a multimedia sound and light show about Zion – happenings occur nightly throughout the summer. The **Southern Utah Folklife Festival** is held here in September.

The new Zion Canyon Theater (☎ 772 2400) opened in 1995, just 200 feet from the entrance to Zion National Park in Springdale. The theater has a giant movie screen (82 feet wide and six stories high), and showings of *Zion Canyon – Treasures of the Gods* take place every hour from 9 am to 9 pm. The film starts with the prehistoric Anasazi dwellers of the area and continues with the history and legends of Zion. Admission is $7 for adults and $4.50 for children.

Both bicycles and inner tubes (for tubing down the Virgin River) are available for rent – just look for signs.

### Places to Stay – camping

*Zion Canyon Campground* (☎ 772 3237, fax 772 3844), 479 Zion Park Blvd (by the Virgin River), has a pizza parlor, store, playground and coin laundry. There are almost 200 sites for $13 to $16.50 with hookups and some camping cabins for about $40 and up. More camping sites are available in the national park.

### Places to Stay – middle

**Motels** Roughly April to October is the high season, with Memorial Day to Labor Day being very busy and hotels charging much more – an idea of summer/winter differences are given for some hotels below, but you can expect winter discounts in all of them. Reservations are recommended during the busy period, especially on weekends, though you can usually find somewhere to stay on most days if you don't arrive late in the day. St George is almost an hour away.

There are no cheap places to stay in the high season. One of the least expensive is the *El Rio Lodge* (☎ 772 3205), 995 Zion Park Blvd, with just 10 rooms in the lower $50s, or the $40s in winter. It has great views from the sun deck. The rustic-looking and popular *Pioneer Lodge* (☎ 772 3233), 838 Zion Park Blvd, has about 40 standard double rooms in the $50s and $60s during summer, $35 to $45 in winter. It has a restaurant, pool and spa. The *Terrace Brook Lodge* (☎ 772 3932), 990 Zion Park Blvd, has a pool and two dozen rooms in the $50s and $60s for a double in summer, in the $40s in winter. Some rooms have good views.

The pleasant *Bumbleberry Inn* (☎ 772 3224), 897 Zion Park Blvd, has a popular restaurant, large garden and pool, and 24 sizable rooms, some with mountain views, in the upper $50s for a double, some sleeping up to six people for around $75. The facilities at the *Zion Park Motel* (☎ 772 3251), 855 Zion Park Blvd, include a pool, playground, picnic area and coin laundry. Over 20 rooms rent in the $50s for a double; a couple of apartments (sleeping up to six) with kitchens rent for about $100.

The *Canyon Ranch Motel* (☎ 772 3357), 668 Zion Park Blvd, has a shaded lawn, pool and spa. Rooms are in cottages, most with good views. Doubles go for around $60, or $70 with a kitchenette. The Best Western *Driftwood Lodge* (☎ 772 3262, fax 772 3702), 1515 Zion Park Blvd, is quietly situated on the outskirts of town, two miles from the park entrance. The grounds are attractive and the views are good. Many rooms have balconies or porches and run in the $60s for a double including continental breakfast. There is a restaurant and bar (beer and wine only), room service, pool and spa.

*Flanigan's Inn* (☎ 772 3244, fax 772 3396), 428 Zion Park Blvd, just over a quarter of a mile from the park entrance, has a pool and picnic area in the nice grounds – good views. A restaurant, bar and convenience store are on the premises. Most doubles are in the upper $60s. The *Cliffrose Lodge* (☎ 772 3234, fax 772 3900), 281 Zion Park Blvd, the closest motel to the park, is set in five acres of trees and gardens bordered by the Virgin River. There is a pool, playground and coin laundry. All rooms are large, have good views and rent for about $70 and up; a few suites are well over $100.

**B&Bs** Built of local sandstone in the 1930s, quaint *Under the Eaves Guest House* (☎ 772 3457), 980 Zion Park Blvd, 84767, has two small, antique-filled rooms with shared bath and a larger suite with private bath. In the garden, a small cabin

built in the 1920s has two separate bedrooms, each with private bath. There is a spa. No smoking is allowed. Rates are $55 to $90 a double with full breakfast.

Half a mile from the park entrance, the *Harvest House* (☎ 772 3880), 29 Canyon View Drive, 84767, is a modern house (built 1989), with four spacious and light bedrooms, all with private bath. Two rooms have sun decks. There is a spa. No smoking is allowed. Rates range from $70 to $95 a double, including full breakfast and evening drinks.

The *Zion House* (☎ 772 3281), 801 Zion Park Blvd, 84767, has four large rooms, each with mountain views. Two share a bathroom, and one has a kitchenette. There is no smoking. Rates are $60 to $80 for two people.

**Places to Eat**

The most popular place in town is the *Bit & Spur Mexican Restaurant & Saloon* (☎ 772 3498), 1212 Zion Park Blvd, which serves dinner from 5 to 9:30 pm; the saloon stays open till midnight. The *Pioneer Family Restaurant* (☎ 772 3467), 828 Zion Park Blvd, next to the Pioneer Lodge, is also popular and serves home-style breakfast, lunch and dinner. The *Trail's End Restaurant* (☎ 772 3703), 805 Zion Park Blvd, serves American fare, including steak and seafood. *Electric Jim's Parkside Burgers* (☎ 772 3838), 198 Zion Park Blvd, cooks up decent fast food near the park entrance from 11 am to 10 pm in the summer. *Pizza & Noodle Company* (☎ 772 3815), 868 Zion Park Blvd, has cheap Italian food. *Pizza at the Park* (☎ 772 3462), 479 Zion Park Blvd, next to the campground, has pizza and other Italian food to eat in or take out – it's even open for breakfast in summer if you wake up craving a pepperoni pizza.

Several motels offer good restaurants. The *Bumbleberry Inn* serves home-style American food from 7 am to 9:30 pm in summer, 8 am to 8 pm in winter, closed Sunday. Here you'll find yummy bumble-berry pies and pancakes. Never heard of bumbleberries? You have now. The more upmarket *Driftwood Restaurant* at the Driftwood Lodge is open from 7 am to 10 pm and features local trout on the menu. *Flanigan's Inn Restaurant*, open from 7 am to 10 pm in summer, is the fanciest place in this casual town – great dining views. It features contemporary Western cooking.

## Getting There & Away

There is no public transport so you have to drive or cycle.

## ZION NATIONAL PARK

The white, pink and red rocks of Zion are so huge, overpowering and magnificent that they are at once a photographer's dream and despair. Few photos can do justice to the magnificent scenery found in this, the first national park established in Utah.

The highlight is Zion Canyon, a half-mile deep slash formed by the Virgin River cutting through the sandstone. Everyone wants to drive the narrow paved road at the bottom, straining their necks at colorful vistas of looming cliffs, domes and mountains with evocative names such as the Great White Throne or Mountain of the Sun. Other scenic drives are less crowded and just as magnificent. For those with the time and energy, day and overnight hikes can take you into spectacularly wild country.

## Orientation

Three roads enter the park. Hiking trails depart from all three roads, leading you further into the splendor.

At the southern end, the paved Zion-Mt Carmel Hwy (Hwy 9 between Mt Carmel Junction and Springdale) is the most popular route and leads past the entrance of Zion Canyon. This road has fine views, but it is also exceptionally steep, twisting and narrow for much of its length. A tunnel on the east side of Zion Canyon is so narrow that escorts must accompany vehicles over 7 feet 10 inches (2.4m) wide or 11 feet 4 inches (3.46m) tall (☎ 772 3256 in advance to arrange an escort; a $10 fee is charged). Bicycles are prohibited in the tunnel unless they are transported on a vehicle. The Zion Canyon Rd itself is an offshoot from Hwy 9, dead-ending about seven miles up the canyon. The main visitors center and campgrounds lie at the mouth of Zion Canyon, and lodging is nearby, either in the canyon or Springdale. The elevation in Zion Canyon is about 4000 feet and at the east entrance 5700 feet.

For the middle of the park, paved **Kolob Terrace Rd** leaves Hwy 9 at the village of Virgin (elevation 3550 feet), climbs north into the Kolob Plateau for about nine miles and then becomes gravel for two more miles to Lava Point (elevation 7890 feet), where there is a ranger station and primitive campground. This road is closed by snow from about November to May. The road continues out of the park to I-15 and Cedar City as a dirt road that becomes impassable after rain. This is the least used of the three roads into the park.

At the north end, the paved **Kolob Canyons Rd** leaves I-15 at exit 40 and extends five miles into the park. There is a visitors center at the beginning of the road, but no camping. The road, which is over 5000 feet above sea level, is open all year, and there are several scenic lookouts over the Finger Canyon formations.

There is so much to see in Zion that entire books have been written about it. The descriptions below are necessarily brief, but remember that free maps and information are available from the entrance stations and visitors centers. Likewise, you could read one of the hiking guidebooks.

## Information

The main visitors center (☎ 772 3256) is on Hwy 9 near the mouth of Zion Canyon, less than a mile from the south entrance near Springdale. Exhibits focus on the geology, wildlife, archaeology and history of the area. There is a store with books and maps. Park rangers answer questions about any aspect of the park and present a variety of programs, including Junior Ranger Programs for six- to 12-year-olds. These run from Memorial Day to Labor Day, last 2.5

UTAH

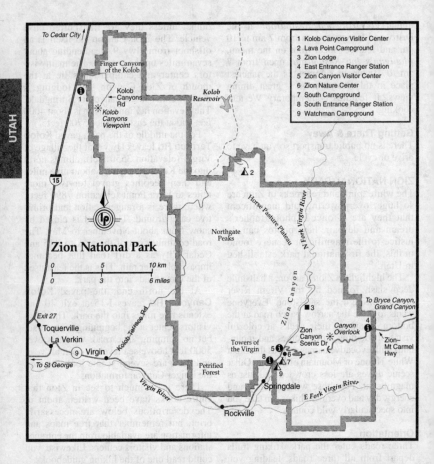

### Zion National Park

To Cedar City

Finger Canyons of the Kolob

Kolob Canyons Rd

Kolob Reservoir

Kolob Canyons Viewpoint

1 Kolob Canyons Visitor Center
2 Lava Point Campground
3 Zion Lodge
4 East Entrance Ranger Station
5 Zion Canyon Visitor Center
6 Zion Nature Center
7 South Campground
8 South Entrance Ranger Station
9 Watchman Campground

15

0    5    10 km
0    3    6 miles

Horse Pasture Plateau

Northgate Peaks

N Fork Virgin River

Zion Canyon

Kolob Terrace Rd

Exit 27

Toquerville

La Verkin

9 Virgin

To St George

To Bryce Canyon, Grand Canyon

Canyon Overlook

Zion Canyon Scenic Dr

Zion–Mt Carmel Hwy

Towers of the Virgin

Petrified Forest

Virgin River

Springdale

E Fork Virgin River

Rockville

hours, and are offered twice a day from Tuesday to Saturday at a charge of just $1. Parents can get a couple of hours to themselves! Other free programs (discussions, talks, demonstrations, hikes, etc) run from March to November both during the day and in the evenings. The center is open from 9 am to 5 pm daily, 8 am to 8 pm in summer.

The smaller Kolob Canyons Visitor Center (☎ 586 9548), at the beginning of Kolob Canyons Rd, is open from 8 am to 4:30 pm and also has park exhibits, information, and sells books and maps.

Entrance to the park is $2 per person (on foot, bicycle or motorbike) or $5 per private vehicle. Tickets are valid for seven days, and Golden Age, Eagle and Access passes are accepted. The south and east entrance stations (at either end of the Zion-Mt Carmel Hwy) and the visitors centers all provide free park maps and informative brochures for visitors.

In an emergency, call the visitors centers or 772 3322 or 911 24 hours a day.

Further information is available from the Superintendent, Zion National Park, Springdale, 84767.

## Climate & When to Go

From as early as March to as late as November, the campgrounds may fill, and in the Memorial Day to Labor Day high season they are often full by late morning, so plan on an early arrival if camping. Almost half of the park's annual visitors arrive in the Memorial Day to Labor Day period. Conversely, only about 7% of the annual visitors come in the December to February period.

Summer weather is hot (over 100°F is common), so be prepared with plenty of water and sun protection. Temperatures drop into the 60°s F at night, even in midsummer. The summers are generally dry with the exception of about six weeks from late July to early September, when the so-called 'monsoons' – short but heavy rainstorms – occur, transforming dry canyon walls into waterfalls.

Fall is my favorite season, with beautiful foliage colors peaking in September on the Kolob Plateau and October in the Zion Canyon. By October, daytime weather is pleasantly hot and nights are in the 40°s and 50°s F.

There is snow in winter, but the main roads are plowed and daytime temperatures usually rise above freezing even on the coldest days. Hikers climbing up from the roads will find colder and more wintry (snow and ice) conditions.

Spring weather is variable and hard to predict – rainstorms and hot, sunny spells are both likely. May is the peak of the wildflower blooms. Spring and early summer is also the peak of the bug season – bring insect repellent.

## Books & Maps

Many are available at the visitors centers and from good bookstores or libraries. They can also be ordered in advance from Zion Natural History Association (ZNHA), Springdale, 84767 (☎ 772 3264, or 1 (800) 635 3959 for credit card orders).

Hikers and backpackers can read *Exploring the Backcountry of Zion National Park – Off Trail Routes* by T Brereton & J Dunaway, or *Hiking in Zion National Park – The Trails* by B Lineback – both inexpensive and published by the ZNHA. *Utah's National Parks* by R Adkison (Wilderness Press, 1991, Berkeley, CA) covers all the main trails in Utah's national parks in detail.

Topographic maps with scales of one inch:one half mile are also available.

## Zion Canyon

From the visitors center, it is about a seven-mile drive to the north end of the canyon – almost every visitor does this drive at least once.

The narrow road follows the Virgin River, and you cannot stop just anywhere – nine parking areas line the way. Some of these simply allow you to get out of your car and take a photograph, but most are trailheads.

In order of increasing difficulty, the best trails accessible from the Zion Canyon road are outlined below. Which have the best views? All of them! There are signs at the trailheads.

You can stroll or roll along the 100-yard paved **Court of the Patriarchs Viewpoint Trail** or take an easy walk near the canyon's end along the paved and very popular **Gateway to the Narrows Trail**, about a mile long and fairly flat. (You can continue further along into the Narrows – a wet hike crossing the river as it flows through a narrow canyon – see Backpacking below.) The quarter-mile-long **Weeping Rock Trail** climbs 100 feet to a lovely area of moist hanging gardens. **Emerald Pools** can be reached by a mile-long paved trail or a shorter unpaved one climbing 200 feet to the lower pool; a shorter trail scrambles another 200 feet up to the upper pool. **Sandbench Trail** climbs almost 500 feet in two miles – great views but horses use this one too. **Hidden Canyon Trail** has a few long drop-offs and climbs 750 feet in just over a mile to a very narrow and shady canyon. **Angels Landing Trail** is 2.5 miles with a 1500-foot elevation gain. There are steep and exposed drop-offs, so don't go if you're afraid of heights, but the views looking back down are super. **Observation**

## The Price of Popularity

In the late 1970s, there were about a million annual visitors to Zion National Park – about the number for which the park facilities had been intended. The popularity of the park has grown tremendously since then, and now nearly 2.5 million visitors arrive annually, with more coming each year.

The pressure on the park is enormous, yet federal funding has not grown commensurately and the Park Service is struggling to cope with visitor problems. Problems? Hundreds of thousands of feet combine to erode the most popular trails, which must be paved. Exhaust fumes from many thousands of cars slowly pollute the area. Unthinking visitors feed wildlife, draw graffiti, dump litter, pick flowers, shit on the trails, make unnecessary noise or ignore trail markers.

Zion has to be seen to be believed, but you can see it without making an unnecessarily heavy impact. Don't drop trash (carry a resealable plastic bag for diapers, toilet paper, sanitary pads, sardine cans and other odorous objects). Don't disturb the wildlife – never feed or try to touch animals. Respect the beauty of the area in the same way that you would respect a museum, a home, a church, a school, a treasure . . . a national park is all of these and more.

Various solutions to the overcrowding problem have been discussed. The National Park Service is required to protect the parks for the enjoyment of the public, and this, the Park Service says, precludes the obvious solution of limiting the number of visitors. Now, vehicles over 21 feet long (6.4m) cannot park in some of the areas in Zion Canyon (though they can drive past). A shuttle tram service is available for those wishing to ride instead of drive. Future plans include providing large parking areas at the canyon mouth and making all visitors walk or ride shuttle buses within the canyon (this option has worked well in Yosemite National Park in California). Budget restrictions, however, may delay or limit the implementation of the plan, but be prepared for changes when going to Zion. ■

**Point Trail** is almost four miles long with a 2150-foot elevation gain; it's less exposed than Angels Landing and offers great views, too. (All distances are one-way.) There are some other day hikes, and extended overnight backpacking trips are also possible (see Backpacking below).

Note that all of these trails can be slippery with snow or ice in winter, or after heavy rain, so hike carefully in those conditions and ask park rangers for advice if you are not sure.

### Zion–Mt Carmel Hwy

The road east of Zion Canyon is somewhat of an engineering feat, with many switchbacks and a long tunnel giving access to vehicles (though check the Orientation section for vehicle restrictions). East of the tunnel, the geology changes into slickrock, with many carved and etched formations of which the mountainous **Checkerboard Mesa** is a memorable example. It's just

over 10 miles from the Zion Canyon turnoff to the east exit of the park, and there are several parking areas along the road. Only one has a marked trail (though other short walks are possible) – the half-mile-long **Canyon Overlook Trail**, which climbs over 100 feet and gives fine views into Zion Canyon, 1000 feet lower. The trailhead is just east of the one-mile-long tunnel (there is a second, much shorter, tunnel).

### Kolob Canyons Rd

This five-mile-long road penetrates the finger canyons area at the north end of the park. It is about a 40 mile drive from the main visitors center, out of the park along Hwys 9 and 17 to I-15, then north to exit 40. Perhaps visitors don't think it worth driving 40 miles just to see one more short scenic drive – whatever the reason, this road is much less busy than the above two, and this is one of its attractions. The other is the scenery, which is just as stupendous as in the south part of the park.

There are several parking areas. One gives access to the 2.7-mile-long **Taylor Creek Trail**, with a 450-foot elevation gain and the possibility of wet feet – the trail crosses the creek many times. A little further, the Lee Pass overlook gives access to the **La Verkin Creek Trail**, which drops 700 feet in 7.2 miles to the **Kolob Arch** – the biggest arch in the park and one of two vying for the title of 'biggest arch in the world' (the other is Landscape Arch in Arches National Park). Fit hikers can do the roundtrip (14.4 miles) to the arch in a day. This trail continues even further for extended backpacking trips. The last parking area has a picnic area and short trail at **Kolob Canyons Viewpoint**.

### Kolob Terrace Rd

This 11-mile road reaches Lava Point, at 7890 feet a cool relief from the Zion Canyon summer heat. This is the least driven road in the park, and it's as scenically rewarding as any of them. Three trails leave the road. The **Hop Valley Trail** is an alternate way of reaching Kolob Arch; it's about seven miles and an 1100-foot elevation drop along the watered Hop Valley – green fields amidst red cliffs. The **Wildcat Canyon Trail** is six miles long and begins along Kolob Terrace Rd, emerging at Lava Point. Beginning at Lava Point makes it more of a descent – either you need a car shuttle or you walk back the way you came. Also from Lava Point, the **West Rim Trail** goes about 14 miles to Zion Canyon – this is mainly a backpackers trail.

### Backpacking

You can backpack and wilderness camp along the over 100 miles of trails in Zion. Starting from Lee Pass on the Kolob Canyons Rd in the north, you could backpack along a number of connected trails emerging at the east entrance of the park. This entire traverse of the park is about 50 miles. A variety of shorter backpacking options are suggested in Adkison's book and by park rangers.

The most famous backpacking trip is through the **Narrows** – a 16-mile journey through canyons along the North Fork of the Virgin River. In places the canyon walls are only 20 feet apart and tower hundreds of feet above you. The hike requires wading and sometimes swimming the river many times. It is usually done from Chamberlain's Ranch (outside the park) to the Gateway of the Narrows Trail at the north end of Zion Canyon to allow hikers to move with the river current. The 16-mile trip takes about 12 hours, and camping for a night is recommended. This hike is limited to June to October, and may be closed from late July to early September because of flash flood danger. The few miles at the north end of Zion Canyon can get very crowded with hundreds of day hikers.

All backpackers need to obtain a free permit from either visitors center. The ranger will review your route with you. Normally, permits are issued the day before or the morning of the trip – there is rarely any problem with selecting a route, with the exception of the Narrows, for which you may need to wait a day or two. Camping is allowed in most places in the backcountry, but there are a few restricted areas. Rangers will warn you about restrictions and also give you current information about the availability of water. Unlike many desert parks, Zion has a number of springs and rivers flowing year-round. None of these sources is clean, and all water must be boiled or treated. Maximum group size is 12 people. Animals are not allowed.

Campfires are not allowed (except in the Narrows to allow wet and cold hikers to dry out and warm up), so you need to carry a camping stove or food that doesn't need to be cooked. Sun protection is essential – sun block, hat, dark glasses, long sleeves. Insect repellent is needed in spring and early summer. Backpacking supplies are limited in Springdale – stock up in St George.

Day hikes do not require a permit with the exception of people attempting the Narrows in one day.

Many backpacking trips require either retracing your footsteps or leaving a vehicle at either end of the trip. If you don't have two vehicles, ask at the main visitors center in Zion Canyon, which has a 'Ride Board' where you can connect with other backpackers. Also, Zion Lodge (☎ 772 3213) has a shuttle desk and will arrange a ride for you for a fee.

### Horseback Riding & Biking

Three-hour guided rides from the Zion Lodge up the Sand Bench Trail are offered daily from March to October by Bryce-Zion Trail Rides (☎ 772 3967, 679 8665 or call the lodge) for about $30 a person. Other trips can be arranged.

Bicycles are prohibited in the one-mile-long tunnel on the Zion-Mt Carmel Hwy (they can go through in a vehicle) and on all park trails. Biking on park roads is allowed but not very easy because of the steep grades, narrow roads and heavy traffic.

### Other Activities

Open-air **tram tours** run from Zion Lodge up and down the canyon several times a day in summer, offering narrated tours and photo stops. **Rock climbing** is permitted in most areas – contact the visitors center for information about routes and restrictions. Climbers should have their own gear as guides and equipment are not available. **Fishing** is poor but permitted with a Utah fishing license.

### Places to Stay & Eat

Between the south entrance and the main visitors center are two Park Service campgrounds, *Watchman* with 228 sites and *South* with 141 sites. Both offer water, barbecue grills, picnic tables, toilets but no showers and cost $7 a site. Watchman is open year-round, South from March to October, both on a first-come, first-served basis. Campgrounds usually fill up in the afternoons, so arrive early.

*Lava Point* has a free six-site campground – there's no water. Just outside the east entrance, free camping is permitted

near the Mt Carmel Restaurant. For campers who desire a hot shower, the Zion Canyon Campground in Springdale lets anyone shower for a small fee.

*Zion Lodge* (☎ 772 3213, reservations at 586 7686, fax 586 3157) is beautifully set in the middle of Zion Canyon. It offers about 80 comfortable motel rooms and 40 cabins – most have excellent views and private porches. Reservations should be made well in advance; summer dates are sometimes filled months ahead. Motel rooms sleep five and rent from about $70 a double to $85 for five. A few suites are $105 to $115 for two to four people. The cabins are $75 to $85 for one to four people.

The *Lodge Restaurant* is open from 6:30 to 9:30 am, 11:30 am to 2:30 pm, and 5:30 to 9 pm – dinner reservations are requested. There is also a *Snack Bar* open all day in summer. Otherwise, stay and eat in Springdale.

# Hwy 89 Corridor

Hwy 89 follows the Sevier River Valley at over 6000 feet above sea level. It retraces the route of Mormon pioneers as they moved south down the east side of the Markagunt Plateau.

## JUNCTION & AROUND

Tiny Junction (population 151) is the Piute County seat. The turn-of-the-century red-brick **County Courthouse** is the town's most interesting building and has a tourist information office. **Butch Cassidy** grew up around here, and his (unrestored and dilapidated) childhood home can be seen just off Hwy 89 in **Circleville**, two or three miles to the south. The Piute County Fair is held in Junction every August.

### Piute Lake State Park

This park, 7½ miles north of Junction, offers a boat launch area but no other development. It's popular for fishing and boating, and you can wilderness camp for free.

Bald eagle

## Otter Creek State Park

This park (☎ 624 3268), PO Box 43, Antimony, 84712, also offers a boat launch, and the trout fishing is reputedly good. The lake attracts many species of water birds, especially in spring and fall migrations, and raptors are often seen in winter – both golden and bald eagles have been recorded. A campground with hot showers is open all year; fees are $7 to $9. Day use is $3. The park is 15 miles east of Junction along Hwy 62 (which continues to Hwy 24 and Loa, 45 miles away; see the chapter on central Utah).

### Places to Stay & Eat

*Fat's Cafe & RV Park* (☎ 577 2672), 135 W Center St, has drinking water but no showers. Sites are $11 with hookups, $5 without. *Double W Campground* (☎ 577 2527), 85 S Hwy 89 in Circleville, has showers and coin laundry and charges from $7 to $14 for sites. The Fishlake National Forest operates the free *City Creek Campground*, which has drinking water. It is six miles northwest of town off Hwy 153. Opposite the Otter Creek park entrance is *Otter Creek Marina & Camp* (☎ 624 3292), which has showers, coin laundry and RV spaces for $11 with hookups, less without. Boats can be rented here, and there is a small restaurant.

The *Junction Motel* (☎ 577 2629), 300 S Main St, under a sign that reads 'A Li'l Bit Country', offers five rooms, some with

kitchenettes, from $18 and up. The *Country Motel* (☎ 577 2839), 30 W Main St in Circleville, has four rooms in the $20s. Next door is *Larry's Cafe*.

## PANGUITCH

Founded in 1864, this town of 1500 inhabitants is a center for the local ranching and lumbering communities and the Garfield County seat. Many early buildings remain. Panguitch is in the midst of a scenic region – Hwy 89 to the south, Hwy 143 to the west and Hwy 12 to the east have all been designated 'Scenic Byways'. The northern gateway to Bryce Canyon National Park (24 miles east), Panguitch is a popular stopping place for travelers. Zion is about 70 miles southwest. The elevation of 6666 feet makes for pleasant summer weather.

### Orientation & Information

Hwy 89 is the main drag through town and comes in along Main St from the north, then turns east at Center St. Main St south of Center St becomes Hwy 143 leading to Panguitch Lake.

The Garfield County Travel Council (☎ 676 2311), 55 S Main St, has regional travel information. There is also an information center (☎ 676 8131) at the park at 800 N Main St, open 9 am to 5 pm from May to October. The Dixie National Forest Powell Ranger Station (☎ 676 8815), PO Box 80, 84759, at 225 E Center, is open from 8 am to 4:30 pm Monday to Friday. The library (☎ 676 2431) is at 75 E Center. The local newspaper is the *Garfield County News*. The post office (☎ 676 8853) is at 65 N 100 West. The hospital (☎ 676 8811) is at 224 N 400 East. The police (☎ 676 8807, or 911 in emergencies) are at 45 S Main St.

### Things to See & Do

The **DUP Museum**, 100 E Center, is open on summer afternoons and at other times by appointment (curators' telephone numbers are posted on the door). Some of the **red-brick houses** in town date from the 1870s – ask at the information centers about historic buildings.

UTAH

Panguitch

0      200      400 m
0      200      400 yards

**PLACES TO STAY**
2   Horizon Motel
3   Marianna Inn
5   Hiett Lamplighter Inn
6   Color Country Motel
7   Bryce Way Motel
8   Hitch-n-Post Campground
9   Sands Motel
10  Nelson Motel
11  Canyon Lodge Motel
13  Blue Pine Motel
16  Cameron Motel
20  Tod's Travel Center
21  Purple Sage Motel
22  Best Western
     New Western Motel

**PLACES TO EAT**
4   Flying M Restaurant
7   Bryce Way Restaurant
15  Foy's Country Corner Cafe

**OTHER**
1   Information Center
12  Hospital
14  Post Office
17  Library & Panguitch Playhouse
18  DUP Museum
19  Powell Ranger Station
23  County & City Offices
     (Travel Council, Police)
24  Swimming Pool

**Swim** at the community pool (☎ 676 2259), 375 E 100 South.

### Special Events
There is horse racing the last weekend in June. Pioneer Day (24 July) is celebrated with a rodeo. The Garfield County Fair takes place in August.

### Places to Stay – camping
The *Big Fish KOA* (☎ 676 2225), 555 S Main St, has a pool, showers, playground, coin laundry and grocery store. It is open from April to October. Sites range from $13 to $19; four Kamping Kabins are $25 a

double. *Hitch-n-Post* (☎ 676 2436), 420 N Main St, has showers and a coin laundry. Tent sites are $9, RV sites with hookups are $13. *Sportsman's Paradise RV Park* (☎ 676 8348), 2153 N Hwy 89 (two miles north), has showers, coin laundry and store. Sites cost from $9 to $13.

*Red Canyon* (☎ 676 2690) is about 10 miles east of town on Hwy 12. It has showers, a playground, a grocery and an Indian souvenir store; it's open from March to October. Sites range from $9 to $13; camping cabins are $24 a double. Just to the east is the Dixie National Forest (☎ 676 8815) with its *Red Canyon* campground; no showers here and sites are $7 each. Contact the USFS for other sites in the area.

## Places to Stay – bottom end

Prices are highest from May to October. Many hotels charge $5 to $20 less in midwinter. Summer rates are given here. One of the best cheap places is *Bryce Way Motel* (☎ 676 2400, fax 676 8445), 429 N Main St, with 20 pleasant rooms, an indoor pool and a cafe. Rooms are about $32/40 for singles/doubles (one bed), $50 (two beds). Slightly cheaper basic rooms are available at *Nelson Motel* (☎ 676 8441), 308 N Main St. *Sands Motel* (☎ 676 8874, fax 676 8445), 390 N Main St, has a swimming pool and standard rooms in the upper $30s. Others with rooms in the $30s include the *Blue Pine Motel* (☎ 676 8197), 130 N Main St and the *Cameron Motel* (☎ 676 8840), 78 W Center, which has some rooms with kitchenettes.

## Places to Stay – middle

The *Color Country Motel* (☎ 676 2386, fax 676 8484), 526 N Main St, has a swimming pool and rooms with queen- and king-size beds for about $40/50 for singles/doubles. The similarly priced *Hiett Lamplighter Inn* (☎ 676 8362), 581 N Main St, has very clean rooms with no smoking allowed. The well-run and friendly *Horizon Motel* (☎ 676 2651, fax 676 8420), 730 N Main St, has pleasant rooms in the $40s for a single and the $50s for a double. A few two-bedroom suites cost about $70.

Others with fairly standard rooms in the $40s and $50s include the *Marianna Inn* (☎ 676 8844, fax 676 8340), 699 N Main St, which has a spa; the *Purple Sage Motel* (☎ 676 2659, fax 676 8533), 104 E Center; the *Canyon Lodge Motel* (☎ 676 8292), 210 N Main St; and *Tod's Travel Center* (☎ 676 8863), 445 E Center.

All the places above are small. By far the largest hotel is the Best Western *New Western Motel* (☎/fax 676 8876), 180 E Center, with 55 rooms. This is the most comfortable place in town and offers a pool, spa, exercise equipment and coin laundry. Standard double rooms with queen-size bed

are $50 to $60, with two beds $60 to $70. There are a few more expensive suites. Winter rates drop into the $30s.

Seven miles south, at the junction of Hwy 89 and Hwy 12, is the *Bryce Junction Inn* (☎ 676 2221, fax 676 2291). Standard rooms run in the $50s, and there is a restaurant nearby.

## Places to Eat

*Foy's Country Corner Cafe* (☎ 676 8851), 80 N Main St, is open from 6 am to 9:30 pm daily – it is a popular and reasonably priced, if rather bland, family restaurant. *Bryce Way Restaurant* (☎ 676 2400), 429 N Main St, is open from 6 am to 10 pm in summer and features all-you-can-eat buffets on some nights. The food is pretty good and inexpensive. The *Flying M Restaurant* (☎ 676 8008), Main St at 600 North, is a good choice for breakfast – it serves homemade pancakes, bread and rolls. Lunch and dinner are served as well.

## Entertainment

The *Panguitch Playhouse*, next to the library, often has melodrama on summer weekend nights. The *County Line Saloon* (☎ 676 8267), at 618 S Main St (almost opposite the KOA), is a small local bar.

## PANGUITCH LAKE

Hwy 143 goes south then west from Panguitch into the Dixie National Forest and the Markagunt Plateau. Panguitch Lake is reached after 15 miles and Cedar Breaks National Monument after 30 miles. The upper portion of the road may be closed in winter.

Panguitch Lake is a popular fishing spot in summer and ice fishing is possible in winter. Anglers claim the trout fishing is particularly good. The fall colors make this a beautiful drive in September and October.

### Places to Stay

The Dixie National Forest (☎ 865 3200 in Cedar City) runs the *Panguitch Lake South* and *Panguitch Lake North* campgrounds. The north area has a store, coin laundry and an RV dump station; sites cost $7 a night. The south has a boat ramp and is not suited to long RVs; sites here are $5 a night. A few miles northeast of the lake on Hwy 143 is the *White Bridge* USFS campground, with sites for $7. All have water but no showers and are open from May to October.

The *Panguitch Lake Resort* (☎ 676 2657), on the south shore, has a convenience store, boat rentals, restaurant, RV park with showers for $16 with hookups, and cabins renting from $60 to $80. Nearby, the *Panguitch Lake General Store & RV Park* (☎ 676 2464) also has RV hookups for $15, but no showers. *Lake View Resort* (☎/fax 676 2650) on the east shore has a store, boat rentals, RV sites with hookups for $13, and cabins for $50 to $60. All these are open during summer only.

The *Deer Trail Lodge* (☎ 676 2211), on the northwest corner of the lake, has tent sites for $8, RV sites with hookups for $16, a restaurant, and cabins for $50 to $100. *Beaver Dam Lodge* (☎ 676 8339, fax 676 8068) has a convenience store, boat rentals ($35 a day), restaurant and lounge, and rooms with two beds for $55, with four beds for $70. Both these are open year-round and offer lodging discounts in winter.

## HATCH

Hatch, with barely 100 year-round residents, is one of a handful of tiny Mormon towns along Hwy 89 (all described below) that provide services for people driving the 80 miles from Zion to Bryce Canyon National Parks. Hatch is at 7000 feet and so has pleasant summers. There is a Garfield County information booth on the south side of town, open in summer only. Hatch is 24 miles from Bryce.

The **Mammoth Creek Fish Hatchery** (☎ 735 4200) is located a mile south of town on Hwy 89, then three miles west (there's a sign). Trout and other fish are raised from eggs for release in the state's fishing areas – you can tour the facilities from about 8 am to 5 pm. The road, which continues west of the hatchery into the

Dixie National Forest, is a popular snow-mobiling route in winter.

No, Hatch wasn't named after the hatchery – it was named after the family who pioneered the area in the 1870s. For more about the area's history, drop by the small **DUP Museum** near the center of Hatch.

### Places to Stay & Eat

*Riverside Motel & Campground* (☎ 735 4223, fax 735 4220), on Hwy 89 one mile north of town, has riverside tent sites for $11 and RV sites with hookups for $14.50. There are hot showers, a playground, pool, convenience store, coin laundry, game room and a couple of camping cabins for $24. The motel has eight pleasant rooms for $35/45 a single/double, and there is a restaurant open from 7 am to 10 pm. The *Mountain Ridge Motel & RV Park* (☎ 735 4258), 106 S Main St, has showers and a coin laundry. Tent sites are $10; RVs with hookups are $13. The park is closed in winter. The motel has seven rooms for $36/40 for singles/doubles.

The *New Bryce Motel & Restaurant* (☎ 735 4265), 227 N Main St, has standard rooms in the $40s. The restaurant serves American food from 7 am to 10 pm. Cheaper rooms can be found at the *Galaxy Motel & Restaurant* (☎ 735 4327), 216 N Main St, which may be closed in winter. Other places to eat are *Escobar's* (☎ 735 4357), 138 N Main St, and the *Olde Towne Restaurant & Steak House* (☎ 735 4314), 244 S Main St.

### GLENDALE

Glendale (population 250) is 24 miles south of Hatch at an elevation of 5500 feet. It is the center of an apple growing region.

The *Glendale KOA* (☎ 648 2490), five miles north on Hwy 89, has showers, pool, playground, game rooms, horse rental, store and coin laundry. It is open from May to October and charges from $18.50 to $24. A few Kamping Kabins are $25 for two.

The historic *Smith Hotel* (☎/fax 648 2156), on Hwy 89 at the north end, was built in the 1920s and has been restored as a seven-room B&B. Rooms run about $40 to $65. *The Homeplace B&B* (☎ 648 2194), 200 S Main St, 84729, has three rooms in the $50s.

## ORDERVILLE & MT CARMEL JUNCTION

In 1875, the Mormons founded Orderville, almost five miles south of Glendale, as a commune or kibbutz-like venture called 'The United Order', which lasted about a decade. A small **DUP Museum** on Hwy 89 at the northeast end of town explains the story and is open on request. Information is available at the city offices (☎ 648 2534). There is a small medical center (☎ 648 2108), 425 E State. The Kane County Fair & Rodeo happens here in late August. There are several gift stores selling local rocks, gems, minerals and jewelry. About 450 people live here.

Four miles south of Orderville, Mt Carmel Junction is where Hwy 89 meets eastbound Hwy 9 going to Zion. About 130 people live in Mt Carmel Junction.

### Places to Stay & Eat

**Orderville** The *Tortoise & Hare Trailer Court* (☎ 648 2312), a mile north on Hwy 89, is open from April to October and has showers and a coin laundry. Sites are $9 for tents and $11 for RVs with hookups.

The *Starlite Motel* (☎ 648 2060) has over 50 rooms, some with kitchenettes. Rooms start in the $30s but can go to twice that in the high season. The *Orderville Motel* (☎ 648 2271) and the *Parkway Motel* (☎ 648 2380) both have seven rooms and may be a little cheaper. The *Hummingbird B&B* (☎ 648 2415), PO Box 25, 84758, has three rooms for $40 to $60.

Eat at *Marcella's Restaurant* (☎ 648 2063), next to the Starlite Motel, or the *JV Cafe* (☎ 648 2475). All the above places are along Hwy 89.

**Mt Carmel Junction** *East Zion Trailer Park* (☎ 648 2326), at the junction of Hwy 89 and Hwy 9, has no showers and charges $12 with hookups. *Mt Carmel Motel & Trailer Park* (☎ 648 2323) is on Hwy 89, 1.5 miles north of the junction, near the

separate community of Mt Carmel. It has showers, is open from March to November, and has cheap tent and RV sites. It also offers six basic rooms in the $20s.

The Best Western *Thunderbird Motel* (☎ 648 2203, fax 648 2239), on the southwestern corner of the junction of Hwy 89 and Hwy 9, is the best hotel between Panguitch and Zion. Facilities include a pool, spa, nine hole/par 34 golf course, coin laundry and the *Thunderbird Restaurant* (☎ 648 2262), open from 7 am to 10 pm in summer, shorter hours in winter. Rooms are in the $60s in summer, $40s in winter. Nearby, the *Golden Hills Motel* (☎ 648 2268) has decent rooms in the $30s for singles and the $40s for doubles, less in winter. The *Golden Hills Restaurant* (☎ 648 2602) is on the premises, serving breakfast, lunch and dinner.

The *Sugar Knoll Manor B&B* (☎ 648 2335) is on Hwy 89, 2.5 miles north of the junction.

## CORAL PINK SAND DUNES STATE PARK

Over half of this 3700-acre park is covered with shifting pink sand dunes. Roaring up and down the loose sand on off-road vehicles (ORVs) seems to be the main attraction here, although there is an area for hiking, a short nature trail and a visitors center. Day use is $3. A campground with showers and picnic areas is $9 (no water in winter). The park is reached via a 12-mile paved road heading east from Hwy 89. The signed turnoff is six miles southeast of Mt Carmel Junction or 13 miles north of Kanab. Dirt roads provide alternate access routes. More information is available from 874 2408, PO Box 95, Kanab, 84741.

A mile north of the park, a road heads east for a couple of miles to the free but waterless *Ponderosa Campground*, managed by the BLM.

## KANAB

The remote town of Kanab was permanently settled by Mormons in 1874, although a fort had been built here a decade earlier. Local historians say that for over

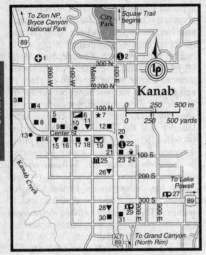

half a century, Kanab was further from a railway than any incorporated town in the USA. The Grand Canyon and Colorado River to the southeast, the mountains to the north and the deserts to the west helped maintain Kanab's inaccessibility until the advent of roads.

Kanab was 'discovered' in the 1930s by the film industry and almost 100 movies have been filmed here – actors like John Wayne, Clint Eastwood and dozens of others have made their appearance in Kanab.

The area is certainly spectacular, surrounded by the Vermillion Cliffs and a network of dirt roads on BLM land. Paved roads quickly lead to the area's famous national parks – Zion (40 miles), Bryce Canyon (80 miles), north rim of the Grand Canyon (80 miles) and Glen Canyon National Recreation Area (74 miles).

Because of its early isolation, the Kanab area was one of the most staunchly Mormon parts of Utah. Today, other churches have joined the LDS Church in Kanab, but some of the remote small communities on the Utah/Arizona border are said to be defiantly traditional Mormon, with polygamy quietly being practiced despite the church ruling against it.

Kanab has 3500 inhabitants and is the seat of Kane County. The elevation of 4925 feet means that the summers get hot, but not unbearably so, with highs normally in the 90°s F. Winter snows are usually brief. Ranching has been the traditional industry, but tourism is now a major part of Kanab's economy.

## Orientation & Information

Hwy 89 snakes through town and most motels lie along it. The highway enters from the east along 300 South, turns north on 100 East, west on Center St, and north again to leave town along 300 West. Hwy 89 heads south along 100 East toward the

Grand Canyon. The Arizona state line is three miles south.

The county Travel Information Center (☎ 644 5033), 41 S 100 East, is open from 9 am to 5 pm Monday to Friday in winter and 8 am to 6 pm Monday to Saturday, from March to October, plus Sundays from Memorial Day to Labor Day. The BLM (☎ 644 2672), 318 N 100 East, is open from 8 am to 4:30 pm, Monday to Friday. The library (☎ 644 2394) is at 13 S 100 East. The local weekly newspaper is the *Southern Utah News*. The post office (☎ 644 2760) is at 39 S Main St. The hospital (☎ 644 5811) is at 221 W 300 North. The police (☎ 644 5807, or 911 in emergencies) are in the city/county offices at 76 N Main St.

### Historical Buildings

The best known of these is **Heritage House** (☎ 644 2542), 100 South at Main St, built in the 1890s from local materials and open for free guided tours from 9 am to 5 pm, Monday to Saturday in summer. Both the house and the information center have brochures detailing a walking tour of 16 historic houses.

### Moqui Cave

Five miles north of town on Hwy 89, the cave (☎ 644 2987) houses a gift shop and collections of local Indian artifacts, fluorescent stones and fossils. It's open from 8:30 am to 7 pm in summer, 9 am to 6 pm in spring and fall, and closed on Sundays and in winter. Admission is $3.50, $3 for seniors, $2.50 for teenagers and $1.50 for six- to 12-year-olds.

### Lopeman's Frontier Movie Town

This attraction (☎ 644 5337), 297 W Center, is a movie set where 'gun fights' are staged. It also mounts Wild West displays, all from April to October. **Horse riding** and trail rides are available from here. Admission is $2.

### Backcountry Drives

There are many unpaved roads leading into the Vermillion Cliffs and White Cliffs in the area. Some roads are passable to ordinary cars, others require 4WD, and most are impassable after heavy rain. The BLM has good maps and information.

A popular drive is the **Johnson Canyon/Alton Amphitheater Backway**, which leaves Hwy 89 nine miles east of Kanab and heads north for 30 or 40 miles emerging at either Glendale or Alton. The first few miles are paved, and the remainder is gravel in fair condition. The road passes a Western movie set (on private land) and has good views of local geology.

### Activities

For a popular **hike** to the Vermillion Cliffs, 400 feet above the city, follow East north to the well-marked Squaw Trail. After one mile the trail leads to some great views.

You can **golf** at Coral Cliff (☎ 644 5005), 700 E Hwy 89, which has a nine hole/par 36 course. **Swim** at the city pool (☎ 644 5870), 44 N 100 West. Play **tennis** at the city park, 500 N 100 East.

### Special Events

The Fourth of July is the highlight of local events with fireworks, a parade, a concert, games and cookouts.

### Places to Stay – camping

*Hitch'n Post RV Park* (☎ 644 2681), 196 E 300 South, has showers and tent and RV sites for $8 to $13. *Coleman's Exxon & RV Park* (☎ 644 2922), 355 E 300 South, has showers and a coin laundry and RV sites (no tents) for about $8. *Crazy Horse Campark* (☎ 644 2782), 625 E 300 South, has showers, pool, playground and coin laundry. Sites range from $10 to $14.

### Places to Stay – bottom end

The May to October season sees high prices and high occupancy. Call ahead to get the best choice of rooms.

*Canyonlands International Hostel* (☎ 644 5554), 143 E 100 South, is one of the few dorm-style hostels in the Southwest and attracts international budget travelers. It's a private hostel, so you don't need a card. Bunk beds are about $10, and there are lockers for your possessions. There is a kitchen (with free coffee), reference library and travel info, coin laundry, TV lounge and yard.

The *Premium Motel* (☎ 644 2449), 99 S 100 East, has basic rooms in the $20s. Much nicer rooms in the $30s for a double with one bed or the $40s with two beds are available from *National 9 Aiken's Lodge* (☎ 644 2625), 79 W Center, or the *Treasure Trail Motel* (☎ 644 2687), 150 W Center, both of which have a pool. Others at these prices include the *Coral Sands Motel* (☎ 644 2616), 60 S 100 East, and the *Sun-n-Sand Motel* (☎ 644 5050), 347 S 100 East, which has both a pool and a spa.

Decent double rooms in the $40s are available at the small *Quail Park Lodge* (☎ 644 2639), 125 N 300 West; the *Budget Host K Motel* (☎/fax 644 2611), 330 S 100 East; and the *Brandon Motel* (☎ 644 2631), 223 W Center – all these are very clean and have a pool, and some rooms have kitchenettes.

### Places to Stay – middle
*Miss Sophie's* (☎ 644 5952), 30 N 200 West, 84741, is a B&B with four rooms with antique furnishings and private baths. The *Parry Lodge* (☎ 644 2601, fax 644 2605), 89 E Center St, has 89 rooms and has long been *the* place to stay in Kanab. Many of the actors who made films here stayed at Parry's, and there is plenty of movie memorabilia, as well as a coin laundry, a pool, old-fashioned entertainment (in summer) and a restaurant and bar. The place has some character and the rooms, despite being older, are well kept. Rates are in the $50s for a single or the $60s for a double.

There are three good modern motels. The *Four Seasons Motor Inn* (☎ 644 2635), 22 N 300 West, has both adults' and kids' pools, and a restaurant open from 7 am to 10 pm. Double rooms are around $60. The Best Western *Red Hills Motel* (☎ 644 2675, fax 644 5919), 125 W Center, has a pool, spa and large rooms,

some with refrigerators and/or balconies. Rooms are $65 to $80 in the summer. The *Shilo Inn* (☎ 644 2562, fax 644 5333), 296 W 100 North, is the biggest hotel in town with 119 spacious rooms, some with kitchenettes or refrigerators. There is a pool, spa and coin laundry, and continental breakfast is included in the rates, which range from $70 to $90 for a double in summer.

### Places to Eat
For cheap breakfast and lunch daily, except Sunday, there's *Paula's Gold Dust Cafe* (☎ 644 5938), 176 S 100 East. Also inexpensive, *Nedra's Too* (☎ 644 2030), 310 S 100 East, is a cozy place open for breakfast, lunch and dinner. (Nedra's Cafe is across the line in Fredonia, Arizona, so this is 'Nedra's Too'). The menu has some interesting Western specialties – deep-fried ice cream, Navajo tacos (taco fillings on top of fry bread), chimichangas and other Mexican food and standard American fare. *Houston's Trail's End Restaurant* (☎ 644 2488), 32 E Center, is a rustic, fun, Western-style place serving reasonably priced American and Mexican chow from 6 am to 10 pm, March to December.

*Chef's Palace* (☎ 644 5052), 153 W Center, is a slightly more upmarket family restaurant specializing in steak – there's a salad bar and good burgers for the kids. It is open from 6 am to 11 pm daily in summer, to 10 pm in winter. *Parry Lodge Restaurant* (in the hotel) serves good breakfast, lunch and dinner in a setting emphasizing the famous film stars who have dined here. The food is American. Parry Lodge Restaurant closes between meals, so call for hours.

### Entertainment
*Kanab Theater* (☎ 644 2334), 29 W Center, shows evenings movies. There are free concerts some evenings in the *gazebo* on Center St. The *Old Barn Theater* (☎ 644 2601), in the Parry Lodge at 89 E Center St, has old-fashioned melodramas on summer evenings.

# Bryce Canyon to Capitol Reef

Hwy 12 leaves Hwy 89 between Panguitch and Hatch and heads east through Bryce Canyon, past three state parks, and terminates at Torrey on Hwy 24, about four miles from Capitol Reef National Park. The 122-mile-long Hwy 12 is one of the most scenic roads in Utah.

## BRYCE CANYON NATIONAL PARK

The Grand Staircase, a series of steplike uplifted rock layers stretching north from the Grand Canyon, culminates in the Pink Cliffs formation at Bryce Canyon National Park. These cliffs were deposited as a 2000-foot-deep sediment in a huge prehistoric lake some 50 to 60 million years ago, slowly lifted up to over 7000 and 9000 feet above sea level, and then eroded into wondrous ranks of pinnacles and points, steeples and spires, cliffs and crevices, and the strangely named formations called hoodoos. The 'canyon' is actually an amphitheater eroded from the cliffs by the weather, rather than a real canyon formed by a river.

The similarity, yet variety, of the formations is strange at first sight. These odd hoodoos lined up one behind the other have been likened to military platoons – superficially made up of identical soldiers yet each one unique upon closer inspection. The pink-red color of the rock is also incredibly variable – a shaft of sunlight can suddenly transform the view from merely magnificent to almost other-worldly.

## Orientation

Scenic Hwy 12, the main paved road to the park, cuts across the northern portion. (There is no entrance fee for driving through this northern corner.) From Hwy 12 (14 miles east of Hwy 89), Hwy 63 heads south to the official park entrance, about three miles away. From here, a 20-mile dead-end drive continues along the rim of

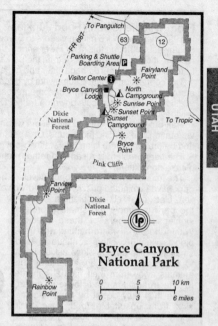

**Bryce Canyon National Park**

the 'canyon'. This rim drive climbs slowly past turnoffs to the visitors center (at almost 8000 feet), the lodge, campgrounds, scenic view points and trailheads, ending at Rainbow Point, 9105 feet above sea level. Trailers are allowed only as far as Sunset Campground, about three miles south of the entrance. Vehicles over 25 feet in length have some access restrictions in summer. Shuttle buses are available along this road.

## Information

The visitors center (☎ 834 5322) is the first main building along Hwy 63 after you officially enter the park. It is open from 8 am to 4:30 pm daily (except Christmas) and to 8 pm from Memorial Day to Labor Day. The center has exhibits about the park, audio-visual programs and a bookshop; rangers answer questions and (mainly during the summer) lead discussions, hikes, etc. There are free Junior Ranger Programs for six- to 12-year-olds.

UTAH

## From Wildlife to Junk Food Junkies

In 1993 there were 1.6 million visitors to Bryce Canyon, the smallest national park in the Southwest. Although this is far fewer annual visitors than some other parks in the region receive, it does, nevertheless, strain the park's limited resources. The main problems are traffic congestion, trail damage, litter and negative impact on wildlife.

The congestion is eased somewhat by rules limiting access by large vehicles and trailers, and more regulations will become necessary as visitation increases still further. In addition, a shuttle bus cuts down on traffic. Drivers should exercise extra caution when driving the busy park roads.

Trail problems are caused by visitors who try to take shortcuts and end up trampling vegetation and eroding the ground. One person does a little damage, others soon follow, and before long there is an ugly washed-out gully scarring the view.

The litter problem is a sad and rather pathetic one that could be solved by visitors – please don't litter.

The impact on wildlife has been severe – hunting, trapping and poisoning outside the park have eliminated grizzly bears and wolves and devastated populations of mountain lion, black bear, elk and bighorn sheep – the park is simply too small to protect significant numbers of these species. Within the park (where hunting and trapping is illegal), visitors continue to feed smaller wildlife despite signs asking them to refrain from doing so. This lures the animals away from their natural habitats to the roadsides and lookout areas, where they may be hit by cars, become sick from unsuitable food, lose their ability to find their own food in winter or become prey for predators. Feeding wildlife in the park is illegal – and subject to penalties. ∎

The entrance fee to the park is $3 per person (bicycle, motorbike, foot and noncommercial bus passengers) or $5 per private vehicle. Tickets are valid for seven days, and Golden Age, Eagle and Access passes are accepted. The entrance station and the visitors center provide free park maps and informative brochures.

Further information is available from the Superintendent, Bryce Canyon National Park, 84717.

### Climate & When to Go

The park is open year-round, with the five months of May to September seeing about 75% of the approximately 1.6 million annual visitors. Summer high temperatures at the 8000- to 9000-foot elevation of the rim may reach the 80°s F, but it's hotter below the rim, so carry water and sun protection when hiking. Summer nights can be chilly, with temperatures in the 40°s F. June is relatively dry, but in July and August the torrential late-summer storms descend – these are usually short-lived and transform the scenery in a matter of minutes.

Snows blanket the ground from about November to April, but most of the park's roads remain open. A few are unplowed and designated for cross-country skiing or snowshoeing. The main Rim Rd is occasionally closed after heavy snow, but only until the snow plows have done their job. January is the slowest month.

### Flaura & Fauna

Mule deer are frequently seen, especially early and late in the day. Drive carefully to avoid hitting them. Although other medium to large mammals are present, they are rarely seen. You will probably see plenty of chipmunks, ground squirrels and prairie dogs, however.

At least 164 bird species have been recorded in the park, especially in summer. My favorites are the ravens, which are often seen soaring close to the lookout areas – they are extremely agile and acrobatic for such big birds.

The visitors center has lists of animals and plants present in the park. Under *no* circumstances should you feed wildlife.

### Scenic Drives

Almost every visitor takes all or part of the Rim Rd drive, either by car or shuttle bus. The bus runs daily from May to September and departs every 30 minutes from 9 am to 5 pm, with extended hours at peak times. It begins from the parking area opposite Ruby's Inn outside the park and stops at the visitors center, campgrounds, lodge and major overlooks in the north part of the park. The cost is $4 per person, which includes entrance to the park and allows unlimited rides – you can get off anywhere and hop onto another bus later. Schedules are prominently posted and available at the park entrance or visitors center. This system began in 1994 and may well be expanded in future.

Near the visitors center, short side roads go to several popular view points overlooking the Bryce Amphitheater (these are visited by the bus). Further away from the visitors center, the Rim Rd passes half a dozen small parking areas and view points on its way to Rainbow Point – all are worth a look. The last few miles of the road to Rainbow Point have been closed for a road improvement project – they are scheduled to be reopened by the fall of 1995.

### Hiking

The views from the rim are superb, but a completely different perspective is gained by getting away from the traffic and taking a hike, either along the rim or, better still, below the rim. Remember that hikes below

the rim descend for quite a ways and the uphill return at over 8000 feet can be strenuous – leave enough time for it and carry extra water. Also bear in mind that most trails skirt steep drop-offs – if you suffer from fear of heights, these trails are not for you. During the July-August thunderstorm season, early morning departures are a good way to avoid the storms, which usually occur in the afternoons.

The easiest hike is along the **Rim Trail**, which is 5.5 miles long (one way) and skirts the Bryce Amphitheater. It passes several view points near the visitors center, so shorter sections can be done. The trail climbs about 550 feet from Fairyland Point to Bryce Point – there's more downhill the other way. The one mile section between the North Campground and Sunset Point is the most level and parts are paved and accessible to wheelchairs or strollers.

There are many trails descending below the rim. One of the most popular is three-quarters of a mile from Sunrise Point at 8000 feet down to the **Queen's Garden**, 320 feet below. (Sunrise Point is near the Nature Center, about a mile from the visitors center.) From here, you can either return the way you came or continue descending further, connecting with the **Navajo Trail** for a more strenuous hike. These trails tend to be fairly heavily used in summer and are among the few which may remain open even in winter.

One trail suitable even for those with a fear of heights is the one-mile-long **Whiteman Connecting Trail**, which leaves the Rim Rd about nine miles south of the visitors center. This trail follows an old dirt road that connects with the **Under-the-Rim Trail**; the descent is about 500 feet and you return the way you came.

One of the two most popular longer loop trails is the **Fairyland Trail**, which leaves from Fairyland Point north of the visitors center and includes three miles of the Rim Trail in the total eight miles of the loop – there is a 1000-foot elevation loss and gain. The other is the seven-mile-long **Peekaboo Trail**, which leaves from Bryce Point and involves an 850-foot elevation change.

UTAH

Both hikes go up and down more than the elevation change may suggest – allow half a day. The scenery is superb on both walks; the Peekaboo loop is also used by horses.

One of the most strenuous day hikes is the **Riggs Spring Loop Trail**, which leaves from Rainbow Point. It is almost nine miles long and involves almost 1700 feet of descent/ascent. This can be done in a day if you're fit, but many prefer to make it an overnight trip.

### Backpacking

Few visitors camp in the backcountry below the rim on any given night. This is not due to a lack of space – there are 10 designated campsites below the rim and most can accommodate up to six backpackers. So if you really want to get away from the crowds, shoulder a pack and get down below the rim for a night or two. It's free.

All backpackers must register at either the visitors center or (in summer) the Nature Center. Park rangers will issue you a free permit, tell you the few places where you'll find water, discuss your route with you and show you where camping is permitted. Note that campgrounds are primitive – no facilities at all. All water below the rim must be purified. You must be self-sufficient – hiking gear is not available for rent. No fires are allowed; eat cold food or carry a stove. Carry out *all* your trash.

From November to April, backcountry camping may be difficult because many trails are snow-covered and hard to find. One or two campsites should be accessible even then – the rangers will know.

The **Under-the-Rim Trail** is the longest in the park, at 22 miles from Bryce Point to Rainbow Point. You could add the Riggs Spring Loop to make your trip over 30 miles (one way), or you can use various connecting trails to make the trip as short as two miles roundtrip. The choice is yours. All backcountry campsites are along the Under-the-Rim and Riggs Spring Trails.

### Stargazing

Bryce Canyon is remote and doesn't suffer much from pollution. Visibility is usually over 100 miles year-round, and it can exceed 150 miles in the crisp, clear winters. Stargazing is superb, and astronomy evenings are presented by park rangers during the summer.

### Winter Activities

The one-mile road to Fairyland Point is not plowed in winter, and access is by snowshoe or cross-country skis. The Rim Trail and other areas may be reached this way too. Snowshoes can be borrowed from the visitors center. Snowmobiles are prohibited.

### Organized Tours

Canyon Trail Rides (☎ 679 8665), PO Box 58, Tropic, 84776, operates horse or mule tours into the backcountry. These last from two hours to all day. Bus tours along the park roads are available, starting at $8. The Bryce Canyon Lodge (see Places to Stay) also has information – the tours start there.

### Places to Stay & Eat

**Inside the Park** The Park Service operates *North Campground* near the visitors center and *Sunset Campground* two miles south. There are toilets, drinking water, picnic tables and barbecue grills. Sites are $7 a night and a few remain open year-round. During the summer, all of the over 200 sites are often full by noon or earlier. Between the two campgrounds is a *General Store* that offers basic food and camping supplies and coin-operated showers and laundry during the summer. (See Places to Stay & Eat – Outside the Park, below, for winter showers.)

The *Bryce Canyon Lodge* (☎ 834 5361), near the visitors center, is open from 15 April to 1 November. The attractive Western building dates from 1924 and has 110 rooms. There is a restaurant and bar (open from 6:30 am to 9:30 pm; dinner reservations requested), a coin laundry and occasional entertainment. Reservations (☎ 568 7686, fax 586 3157) are more or less essential, especially in summer when the lodge can be fully booked several months in advance.

Motel rooms with two queen-size beds, bath and private porch are $67.50 to $82.50

(plus tax) for two to five people. Suites are $100 a double. Cabins with two double beds, bath, fireplace and porch are $78.50 to $88.50 for two to four people.

**Outside the Park** The places below are motels and campgrounds within a few miles of the park entrance. Also see Tropic, Kodachrome Basin State Park, Panguitch and Hatch for places to stay within 25 miles of the park.

The Best Western *Ruby's Inn* (☎ 834 5341, fax 834 5265) is a huge, popular and unrelentingly 'Western' complex on Hwy 63, just over a mile north of the park entrance. It has a campground, hotel, restaurant, and store (food, beer, camping stuff, fishing stuff, funny stuff, souvenir stuff, Indian crafts, sundries). Facilities include a pool, spa, coin laundry and post office. Horse, bike and ski rentals are available.

The *Ruby's Inn Campground* has 200 sites ranging from $12 to $20 open from April to October – its coin showers and laundry stay open all year. The well-run *Ruby's Inn Motel* has over 300 large and surprisingly pleasant rooms. Rates are in the $80s for a double in summer (when reservations as far in advance as possible are advised) or in the $40s in winter. Family suites go for about $115. The *Ruby's Inn Restaurant & Steak House* is open from 6:30 am to 9:30 pm, and there is also a deli for making your own picnic. The motel offers 'chuck wagon' dinners (cowboy-style barbecue and entertainment) during the summer. Also during the summer there is Western entertainment including a rodeo most evenings (not Sunday) for a few dollars. Yiiii haaaa!

*Bryce Village Resort* (☎ 834 5351, fax 834 5256) is near the junction of Hwys 12 and 63, about three miles north of the park. It has an RV park, about 70 rooms, coin laundry, pool and a restaurant/bar at prices a little lower than Ruby's Inn, but the facilities are much more modest. However, the resort is more likely to have rooms available on short notice.

*Foster's Motel & Restaurant* (☎ 834 5227, fax 834 5304) is on Hwy 12 a couple of miles west of the junction with Hwy 63. It offers 40 simple but clean rooms in the $50s for a double in summer, less in winter. The restaurant isn't bad – it's open from 7 am to 10 pm from May to October but has limited winter hours. There's a store and service station here.

*Bryce Canyon Pines Motel* (☎ 834 5441, fax 834 5330) is on Hwy 12 about three miles west of Hwy 63. It has a pool, coin laundry, store, restaurant and campground. Rooms are in the $60s and $70s in summer, less in winter. Rooms are nice enough – some have fireplaces or kitchenettes. The restaurant is open from 6:30 am to 9:30 pm. It features Indian dancing and trail rides in summer. The campground is open from April to October and charges $8 to $13.

The Dixie National Forest borders much of Bryce Canyon National Park. Unpaved USFS Rd 087 heads south from Hwy 12 almost three miles west of Hwy 63. It reaches *King Creek Campground* after seven miles. This campground is open from June to September, has water but no showers and costs $7. The similar *Pine Lake* National Forest campground is reached by taking USFS Rd 16 to the north off Hwy 12 from opposite Hwy 63, and then USFS Rd 132. It's almost 20 miles from the park entrance. The ranger stations in Panguitch and Escalante have maps and information.

## TROPIC

This small town of about 400 inhabitants lies at 6300 feet on Hwy 12 about seven miles east of the junction with Hwy 63. Tropic can be seen from some Bryce Canyon lookouts – a six-mile trail leads from Sunset Point into the village.

Ebenezer Bryce, an early Bryce Canyon rancher for whom the park is named, lived in a wooden cabin that has been moved to the south end of town and now houses a small museum. A small information center is open in town during the summer.

### Places to Stay & Eat

*Bryce Pioneer Village* (☎ 679 8546, fax 679 8607) has about 30 rooms, some with kitchenettes, for about $60 in summer. There are also RV sites with hookups and showers open in summer. The restaurant hosts Western-style cookouts and outdoor 'cowboy breakfasts' in the summer. Some cabins are planned. *Doug's Place* (☎ 679 8632, 679 8633, fax 679 8605) has a motel with 28 standard rooms for about $65 a double, a restaurant open 7 am to 10 pm, a gas station and a grocery store. The *Bryce Valley Inn* (☎ 679 8811, fax 679 8846), with 63 clean modern rooms in the $60s for a double, is perhaps the best motel in town. There is a hot tub, coin laundry, store, deli and the *Hungry Coyote Restaurant*, which serves American and Mexican food from 6 am to 10 pm.

The *Bryce Point B&B* (☎ /fax 679 8629), PO Box 96, 84776, has five attractive and peaceful rooms with private shower in the $70s for a double. There is no smoking. *Francisco's B&B* (☎ 679 8721), PO Box 3, 84766, has three rooms (no smoking) with private baths in a log house on a small working farm. There is a spa. Rates are in the $60s for a double. The *Half House B&B* (☎ 679 8643), 320 Hwy 12, 84766, has three rooms.

The *Pizza Place* (☎ 679 8888) has eat-in, take-out or delivered pizzas.

## KODACHROME BASIN STATE PARK

Dozens of red, pink and white sandstone chimneys, and many other formations including the unusual double Grosvenor Arch make this one of the state's most colorful parks. There are hiking and mountain biking trails, and horses can be rented. You can also take guided tours by horse-drawn wagons. Further information is available from (☎ 679 8562), PO Box 238, Cannonville, 84718. The park campground has hot showers and 24 sites. It is open all year. Day use is $3; camping is $9. The elevation here is 5800 feet.

### Getting There & Away

The park is 14 miles south of Tropic by paved road. A sign in Cannonville, on Hwy 12 five miles south of Tropic, points the way to the park, which is a further nine

miles by paved road. Many of the sights within the park are accessible only by trails or dirt roads that may be impassable after heavy rain.

The **Cottonwood Canyon Rd** is a 'scenic backway' continuing about 40 miles south of the park emerging at Hwy 89 near Paria Canyon and Lake Powell (see the chapter on the Grand Canyon area in Arizona). This dirt road cuts about 50 miles off the drive between Bryce Canyon and Lake Powell and so is quite popular, and often dusty or washboarded. It is impassable after heavy rains.

## ESCALANTE & AROUND

The biggest settlement on Hwy 12, this town of 800 inhabitants lies halfway between Bryce Canyon and Capitol Reef National Parks. Many people speed through en route to one of the parks, but the Escalante area itself is also one of great beauty. The elevation here is over 5800 feet. To access many of the places in the Escalante area you'll need a good USFS, BLM or NPS map (see Information below). Also recommended is *Hiking the Escalante* by Rudi Lambrechtse (Wasatch Publishers, 1985).

Facilities for travelers are few, but adventurous travelers who have the time and necessary outdoor equipment will find the area has some of the least visited and most spectacular scenery in the country. Despite the remoteness, water sources are rarely clean and need to be chemically treated or boiled. Firewood is not always available and, when it is, campfires are often illegal, so you need to carry a stove. Biting insects are a problem in spring and early summer – combine long sleeves and pants with repellent. Help may be hard to find in the event of an accident in remote areas. Talk to the appropriate agency for information about remote drives and hikes.

### Information

The Interagency Information Center (☎ 826 5499), PO Box 246, 84726, is on Hwy 12 (Main St) at the west edge of Escalante; it's open 7 am to 6 pm daily from April to October and 8 am to 5 pm, Monday to Friday, at other times. The Dixie National Forest, BLM and National Park Service all are represented at this info center. Information, permits, brochures, maps and guidebooks are available here. There is also a city information booth near Main and Center Sts. Escalante Outfitters (☎ 826 4266), 310 W Main St, has information, arranges shuttles, and sells maps and outdoor gear. The post office (☎ 826 4314) is at 230 W Main St.

### Escalante State Park

This park is about two miles northwest of town along Hwy 12 and a paved access road. There are 1.75 miles of trails leading through a small 'forest' of petrified wood, a small lake with a boat ramp and opportunities for boating, windsurfing and fishing for trout and sunfish, and a 22-site campground with hot showers, open all year. Day use is $3; camping is $9. Information is available from PO Box 350, Escalante, 84726 (☎ 826 4466, 1 (800) 322 3770 for camping reservations).

### Calf Creek Recreation Area

This BLM-managed area is 15 miles east of Escalante on Hwy 12. It has a small campground and offers a scenic, popular and fairly easy hike to Calf Creek Falls, almost three miles away. A pool below the falls is good for swimming, and other more difficult hikes are possible. The campground, which has 13 sites and water but no showers, is open from March to October and costs $5.

### Smoky Mountain Rd

This dirt and gravel scenic backway crosses the rugged Kaiparowits Plateau between Escalante and Big Water (on Hwy 89 near the western end of Glen Canyon National Recreation Area). The 78-mile-long road is passable only in good weather. High clearance vehicles are recommended. There's little traffic – carry extra water. The southern section has good views of Lake Powell. Most of the road is on BLM land – the last few miles are in Glen Canyon.

### Hole-in-the-Rock Rd

Both the scenery and the history are wild along this scenic backway, which stretches about 60 miles southeast of Escalante.

Pioneering Mormons followed this route in 1879-1880 on their way to settle new lands in southeastern Utah. Little did they know that the precipitous walls of Glen Canyon of the Colorado River blocked their way. Over 200 pioneers literally blasted and hammered their way through the cliff, creating a route wide enough to lower their 80 wagons – a feat that is remembered and honored today by markers along the road. The final part of the descent cannot be seen – the Glen Canyon Dam flooded it along with countless other historical sites.

The dirt and gravel road leaves Hwy 12 about five miles east of Escalante and is passable to ordinary cars when dry. There are no camping or other facilities, although self-contained wilderness camping is possible. The BLM can tell you of side trails to arches and other scenic features. The main road stops short of the hole-in-the-rock, but hikers can continue through it down to Lake Powell, a scrambling descent that can be done in less than an hour. There are no taxis for the climb back up.

### North of Escalante

Most of the area north of the town is part of the Dixie National Forest – maps and information are available in Escalante. Various roads lead to campgrounds, fishing and hiking.

Posy Lake Rd goes north from Escalante and, after 13 miles, a right fork, USFS Rd 153, becomes Hell's Backbone Rd and the left fork, USFS Rd 154, goes two miles to *Posy Lake Campground* with 23 sites open in summer. There is water and a small lake (8700 feet) for fishing and boating; the fee is $5. Beyond Posy Lake, the road climbs up over the Aquarius Plateau at about 10,000 feet and emerges at Bicknell on Hwy 24, 25 miles away. Herds of pronghorn antelope roam the plateau and can often be seen in summer and fall – binoculars suggested. The road is mainly dirt, but it is passable to cars in dry weather and closed by snow in winter.

The Hell's Backbone Rd passes *Blue Spruce Campground* at 7800 feet, about five miles after the fork. Six sites with water cost $5 in summer. The rough road continues east and south for about another 20 miles, emerging on Hwy 132 near Boulder – cars can make it through in dry weather if driven carefully. Snow closes the road in winter. The road skirts the **Box-Death Hollow Wilderness** - a real wilderness area with no campgrounds or roads and only rudimentary trails.

These two roads give access to other, rougher roads, with trails and backpacking opportunities. Primitive camping is permitted.

### Hiking the Escalante Canyon

The town is near the headwaters of the Escalante River, which flows southeast to Lake Powell, nearly 90 miles away. You can hike the entire length, but you'll get wet – the 'trail' frequently crosses the river. Some canyoneers carry an inflatable air mattress to float gear across in the deepest sections. There are no campgrounds. The first third is BLM land, the rest is within Glen Canyon National Recreation Area.

Road access is from Hwy 12 at Escalante or from the Hwy 12 bridge midway between Escalante and Boulder. Trail access is from several trails heading east from Hole-in-the-Rock Rd, so you can do a day hike or a backpacking trip of as many nights as you want. The canyon scenery is quite marvelous, with sheer cliffs and soaring arches, waterfalls and pools and many side canyons where the chances of seeing anyone are slim indeed. You may, however, encounter Indian artifacts – it is illegal and immoral to disturb these.

For details, read Lambrechtse's book. The best seasons are spring and fall – summer sees high temperatures and flash flood danger. Get local info about current conditions before beginning any hike.

### Places to Stay & Eat

*Triple S RV Park* (☎ 826 4959), 495 W Main St, has showers, a coin laundry and 30 sites for $10 to $14; three camping cabins are about $22. Campsites at Escalante State Park are available for $9; at Calf Creek Recreation Area they're $5.

Four modest motels offer rooms in the $30s and $40s in summer, less in winter. In roughly increasing order of cost, they are the *Quiet Falls Motel* (☎ 826 4250), 75 S 100 West, which has some kitchenettes; the *Padre Motel* (☎ 826 4276), 20 E Main St; the *Moqui Motel* (☎ 826 4210), 480 W Main St, which has some kitchenettes and 10 RV sites with hookups and showers; and the *Circle D Motel* (☎ 826 4297), 475 W Main St, which is the biggest with 29 rooms and has a restaurant attached serving breakfast, lunch and dinner.

The new *Prospector Inn* (☎ 826 4653), 380 W Main St, has rooms in the $50s including a continental breakfast. It provides room service from the *Cowboy Blues Diner & Bakery* (☎ 826 4251), 530 W Main St.

Meals are also served at the *Golden Loop Cafe* (☎ 826 4433), 39 W Main St. There are a couple of fast-food places.

## BOULDER

This tiny village is about 25 miles northeast of Escalante on Hwy 12. The 32-mile drive from Boulder to Torrey is extremely scenic. At one point the road follows a knife-edge ridge with great views all-around for passengers – drivers had better keep their eyes on the road.

On the north side of Boulder is **Anasazi Indian Village State Park** (☎ 335 7308), an archaeological site that dates from 1050 to 1200 AD. A short trail leads through some of the excavated and restored ruins, and a museum has audio-visual programs and exhibits about the prehistory of the area. The site is small and provides intellectual rather than scenic stimulation – it's a worthwhile stop if you are interested in the pre-Colombian history of the Southwest. Hours are 8 am to 6 pm in summer, 9 am to 5 pm at other times. Admission is $1.50, $1 for seven- to 15-year-olds, or $6 per carload. There is a picnic area but no camping.

**Burr Trail** is a scenic backway that heads east from Boulder, crosses the Waterpocket Fold area of Capitol Reef National Park and reaches Bullfrog Marina on Lake Powell, about 70 miles from Boulder. It's paved as far as the Capitol Reef boundary and then becomes a spectacular dirt-road drive that you might do in a car after good weather, though high clearance or 4WD are sometimes necessary. Heavy rains or snow can make the road impassable.

### Places to Stay & Eat

About 20 to 25 miles north of Boulder, in the Dixie National Forest, the small *Oak Creek, Pleasant Creek* and *Singletree Campgrounds* all have water, no showers and $6 sites during summer. *Pole's Place* (☎ 335 7422), near the state park, has a cafe, groceries and 12 simple rooms for about $35 to $45. Nearby, the *Circle Cliff Motel* (☎ 355 7329, 355 7353) has three rooms. There's a fast-food place, too, and RV sites are available at a local store.

### LOA & FISH LAKE

The small town of Loa, 27 miles from Capitol Reef, was settled in the 1870s. Mormon missionaries named it after Mauna Loa in Hawaii. It has barely 500 inhabitants but is the Wayne County seat. This is ranching and farming country – you'll begin to see a lot of sheep as you enter the better irrigated lands of central Utah. The Fishlake National Forest Loa Ranger Station (☎ 836 2800, 836 2811), 138 S Main St, 84747, is open from 8:30 am to 4:30 pm, Monday to Friday.

About 20 miles northwest of Loa, **Fish Lake** is an attractive lake in the Fishlake National Forest. Unlike many of Utah's lakes, this is a natural one and not a reservoir. The elevation of 8800 feet makes it a cool summer destination. Prairie dog colonies are visible and, if you are lucky, you may catch sight of moose. The fall sees beautiful colors and excellent fishing (with a license). Trout fishing is especially good. In winter, the road up to the lake is usually open and provides access for cross-country skiing and snowmobiling.

The Fishlake Lodge Information Station (☎ 638 1033) has maps and information in summer.

### Places to Stay & Eat

**Loa** The *Road Creek Inn B&B* (☎ 836 2485, fax 836 2489), PO Box 310, 84747, at 90 S Main St in a restored 1912 general store, is the nicest hotel near Capitol Reef. The people are friendly, and dinners in their restaurant are home-cooked and good – especially the trout. (They'll tell you where to catch it yourself, too). They have a gym, spa, sauna and game room with billiards. Thirteen attractive rooms are $60 to $100, including breakfast.

There's also *Wayne Wonderland Motel* (☎ 836 9692), 42 N Main St, with 12 simple rooms in the $30s. *Gina's Place* (☎ 836 2873), 289 N Main St, has a small cafe that is locally popular for breakfast and serves lunch and dinner, too. The motel has some cheap and basic motel rooms and a small RV park with showers.

**Fish Lake** The USFS operates the *Doctor Creek, Mackinaw, Bowery* and *Frying Pan Campgrounds*, all with water but no showers or hookups; the fee is $6. These are open from May to October, and reservations can be made for some sites (☎ 1 (800) 283 2267). Bowery and Mackinaw both have boat ramps. *Piute Campground* is near the Johnson Valley Reservoir, a couple of miles north of the lake, and has free camping but no water. Free dispersed camping is allowed on roads and trails away from the lake.

The lodges offer marinas with boat rentals, fishing guides, stores selling food and fishing supplies, RV hookups and showers (in summer), restaurants and a variety of motel rooms and cabins.

The *Bowery Haven Resort* (☎ 638 1040 in season, 782 7378 off season), Fish Lake, 84701, is open from mid-May to October. It has rustic cabins (outside bathrooms) in the $20s and modern motel rooms or cabins in the $50s, each with kitchenettes (no utensils). Units sleep up to four.

The *Fish Lake Resorts* (☎ 638 1000),

Hwy 25, 84701, operates both the *Fish Lake Lodge* and *Lakeside Resort*. Rustic cabins start at around $30 and go up to almost $300 for large modern family cabins. They are open year round.

## CAPITOL REEF NATIONAL PARK

Just as Bryce Canyon isn't a canyon, Capitol Reef isn't a reef. The red-rock cliffs and ridges of the park were formidable barriers to early pioneers, who named them 'reefs'. Atop the red cliffs are whitish, domelike formations, reminiscent of the Capitol dome of the nation's capital – and hence the name.

As well as being interesting for its archaeology, history and desert wildlife, Capitol Reef is a textbook example of geology at work. For hundreds of millions of years, layer after layer of rock was deposited here. Then, some 65 million years ago, the earth's surface buckled up and folded, then became partly eroded to form what is today the 100-mile-long Waterpocket Fold, most of which lies within the park and provides extremely scenic views. Other park attractions are Indian petroglyphs, old Western pioneer buildings and fruit orchards, and great driving and hiking opportunities.

With over 375 sq miles, this is the second largest park in the state and receives about a million annual visitors – a much lower number than most of the other parks. Those venturing beyond the standard scenic drive will enjoy a relatively uncrowded visit.

### Orientation

Hwy 24 cuts through the northern section of this long, thin park – the Waterpocket Fold can be seen stretching off to the north and south. Unpaved roads that are partly outside the park itself lead north and south of the highway to give good looks at the geological formations. This is an isolated area – Hwy 24 wasn't built until the 1960s. The small village of Torrey, six miles west of the park on Hwy 12, provides the closest hotels to the park; other nearby towns, including Bicknell and Teasdale, provide more places to stay and eat.

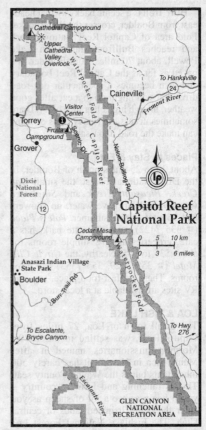

### Information

The visitors center (☎ 425 3791) is on Hwy 24 at the junction with the paved scenic drive. People driving through on Hwy 24 can cross the park without payment, but visitors taking the scenic drive pay $4 per vehicle or $2 per person from about April to October; Golden Age, Access and Eagle passes are accepted. Entrance is valid for a week.

The visitors center is open from 8 am to 7 pm from Memorial Day to Labor Day, and from 8 am to 4:30 pm otherwise (closed Christmas). Various ranger-led programs and activities are scheduled during the summer. Visitors will find books

UTAH

and maps for sale, exhibits, audiovisual presentations and information available throughout the year. Brochures describing the places below in some detail are also provided at the center. If you drive away from the main roads, carry extra water in case of breakdown. Further information is available from the Superintendent, Capitol Reef National Park, 84775.

Outside the park in the tiny town of Teasdale is the Dixie National Forest Teasdale Ranger Station (☎ 425 3702), PO Box 99, 84773, which is at 118 Main St.

### Climate & When to Go

The park is open year-round. Rainfall and humidity is low – annual rainfall averages just over seven inches of which over half falls between June and October. Summer thunderstorms make for ever-changing skies but also introduce the dangers of flash floods. At the visitors center (5400 feet), summer temperature highs are in the 90°s F, though they can reach over 100°F. Evenings usually cool into the 60°s F. Biting insects are the worst from mid-May to late June. Spring and fall are more pleasant months for hiking. The dry winter months see average highs in the 40°s F and lows around 20°F, although temperatures below 0°F are possible. Snowfall is light but may close some roads briefly.

### Fruita

At the junction of the Fremont River and Sulphur Creek, Fruita is the settlement established by Mormon pioneers in 1880. Today, the visitors center is here and nearby are several picturesque, rustic, turn-of-the-century buildings as well as a campground. A prominent formation, the Castle, rises just north of the visitors center.

Visitors like to stop by the well-tended Fruita orchards, which produce apricots, cherries, peaches, apples and pears. From mid-March to the end of April the orchards are a mass of flowers. The fruit is harvested from July to October and can be picked and eaten at no charge inside any unlocked orchard. During designated harvest days, fruit can be picked in quantity for a fee.

The Mormon pioneers weren't the first to arrive, of course. Fremont Indians lived here a thousand years ago – visitors can easily view their petroglyphs on a cliff just over a mile east of the visitors center along Hwy 24. Park rangers can suggest other places where Indian artifacts can be seen.

### Scenic Drive

Pick up brochures describing this drive and others at the visitors center. The scenic drive is part pavement and part gravel, but it's passable to all vehicles. This roughly 25-mile roundtrip south from the visitors center gives a look at the western side of the Waterpocket Fold. Several scenic view points, dirt side roads and trailheads invite further exploration.

### Notom-Bullfrog Rd

This dirt and gravel road follows the east side of the Waterpocket Fold and is accessible to ordinary vehicles in dry weather but may be impassable after heavy rains. The road heads south from Hwy 24 just outside the eastern park boundary and remains outside the park for the first 20 miles, then enters the park for about 17 miles. About 34 miles south of Hwy 24, it intersects the Burr Trail Rd – head west on the only road that climbs over the Waterpocket Fold (steep sections, great views) or head east to leave the park and head toward Lake Powell, almost 40 miles away. The road gives access to many trailheads.

### Cathedral Valley Rds

Two roads leave Hwy 24 a few miles east of the park boundary and head northwest to the Cathedral Valley area at the north end of the park – a scenic desert landscape of peaks and pinnacles. River Ford Rd is just over three miles east of the park and Caineville Rd is almost 11 miles east of the park. Both reach Cathedral Valley and so a roundtrip could be made without backtracking – about 80 miles in all. Caineville Rd is longer, but River Ford Rd involves fording the Fremont River. Both roads require high-clearance vehicles – you can manage without a 4WD in good weather.

## Hiking

The following is a varied selection of some of the most popular, easily reached and rewarding short hikes in the park. Getting away from the road gives rewarding and satisfying vistas. Some trails are very short and suitable for almost anyone. Just over two miles west of the visitors center on Hwy 24, a short unpaved but good road goes south to Panorama Point and the **Goosenecks Trail**. This 200-yard-long trail is almost flat and reaches an overlook with great views. From the same trailhead, the **Sunset Point Trail** goes a third of a mile to an equally scenic lookout – a favorite at sunset.

A few miles along the Scenic Drive, a good dirt road goes east to the Grand Wash parking area. The **Grand Wash Trail** continues east – it's a fairly flat and easy walk through the cliffs of the Waterpocket Fold, going through an impressive 'narrows' section before emerging at Hwy 24, 2.25 miles away. Either arrange a car shuttle or return the way you came. Much more strenuous hikes leave from the same trailhead. The 1.8-mile **Cassidy Arch Trail** climbs steeply to the west, switchbacking to the top of cliffs looking down upon the arch. (Butch Cassidy's outlaws supposedly had a hideout near here.) The **Frying Pan Trail** heads north from the arch trail and follows the high ridges back to Cohab Canyon and the Fruita Campground – about five miles.

At the end of the Scenic Drive, a good unpaved road dead-ends in the Capitol Gorge. From here, you have the choice of the **Capitol Gorge Trail** to the east or **Golden Throne Trail** to the west. The mile-long gorge trail is easy and leads enticingly into the Waterpocket Fold; petroglyphs are visible on the cliff walls. The two-mile-long Golden Throne trail climbs steeply to the cliff tops and gives fine views of the Golden Throne landmark.

## Backpacking

You can hike and camp almost at will in this desert wilderness, as long as you have a permit. This is available for free from the visitors center – rangers supply you with maps and information while registering you, so they'll know where you are in the event of an accident.

Backpacking trips usually involve taking poorly marked trails – often little piles of stones (cairns) are the only markers and the path is hard to see. You can camp almost anywhere as long as it's over 100 feet away from water and a half mile away from the main roads. Backpacking at Capitol Reef is a desert wilderness adventure – if you lack experience get full advice from park rangers and start with an easy trip. Get maps or use a guidebook – Adkison's *Utah's National Parks* details several good backpacking trips.

This dry desert environment is not conducive to quick recovery – the normal rules of no fires, no garbage and no cutting of vegetation are even more important here. Leave campsites as you found them. Don't bury garbage, as it decomposes very slowly and desert critters try to dig it up.

## Other Activities

In nearby Torrey, Hoodoo Rivers & Trails (☎ 425 3519), PO Box 98, 84775, runs horse and jeep expeditions from half a day to several nights.

## Places to Stay – camping

The *Fruita Campground* has 70 sites and is open all year on a first-come, first-served basis. Some sites can be driven to, others require a short walk (50 yards) from the parking area. At least walk-in sites are usually available if you arrive by early afternoon, even in summer. Water and grills are available but there are no showers, and the fee is $6.

Free primitive camping is possible at *Cathedral Campground* at the end of the River Ford Rd and at *Cedar Mesa Campground*, about 23 miles south along the Notom-Bullfrog Rd. Each has five sites, picnic tables, grills and pit toilets but no water. They are open year-round.

In Torrey, six miles west of the park on Hwy 12, there are a couple of campgrounds. *Thousand Lakes RV Resort*

(☎ 425 3500), a mile west of town on Hwy 24, has showers, coin laundry and grocery store. It's open April to October and sites are $8 (tent) to $14 (hookups).

The *Boulder Mountain Homestead RV Park* (☎ 425 3374), on Hwy 12 four miles south of Hwy 24, has RV sites with hookups for $14 but no laundry or showers. Also see the Chuckwagon Motel and Rim Rock Ranch, below.

The Fishlake National Forest *Sunglow Campground* is almost two miles east of Bicknell (six miles west of Torrey) amidst red-rock cliffs. Water is available but no showers. Seven sites are open from mid-May to October; the fee is $6.

### Places to Stay – bottom end
**Torrey** *Capitol Reef Inn & Cafe* (☎ 425 3271), 360 W Main St, has 10 rooms, one with kitchenette, in the $40s for a double. It sells local maps and guides. The cafe is open from 7 to 11 am and 5 to 9 pm. The whole operation closes down from November to March. *Chuckwagon Motel* (☎ 425 3288), 12 W Main St, has new rooms with two queen-size beds for about $50 a double in summer. Older rooms are cheaper, though the motel may close these down. The facility also runs a campground with showers and coin laundry, open from April to October, for $6 to $13.

*Rim Rock Ranch* (☎ 425 3843, fax 425 3855), 2523 E Hwy 24 (between Torrey and Capitol Reef) has a restaurant, pool and spa and charges about $50 a double for modest rooms. It also has a campground with showers and coin laundry – sites are $9 to $15. Horse rentals are available. In tiny Teasdale, three miles west of Torrey, are the *Cactus Hill Guest Ranch* (☎ 425 3578), 830 S 1000 East, and the *Cockscomb Inn B&B* (☎ 425 3511), PO Box 8, 84773, at 97 S State, both of which offer two nonsmoking rooms in the $50s.

**Bicknell** The *Aquarius Motel & Restaurant* (☎ 425 3835, fax 425 3771), 240 W Main St, has 27 standard rooms in the $30s

and a few with kitchenettes in the low $40s. The inexpensive restaurant is open from 6 am to 10 pm daily. The motel also runs a small and inexpensive *RV Campground* a few blocks away with hookups but no tents or showers.

The clean *Sunglow Motel & Restaurant* (☎ 425 3821), 63 E Main St, has 17 standard rooms for about $28/38 for singles/doubles. The inexpensive cafe is open from 6:30 am to 10 pm daily.

### Places to Stay – middle
**Torrey** *Skyridge B&B* (☎ 425 3222), 950 E Hwy 24, 84775, has a spa and five rooms for $65 to $95. The *Wonderland Inn & Restaurant* (☎ 425 3775, fax 425 3212), at the junction of Hwys 24 and 12, is on a little hill with pleasant views. The Inn has a coin laundry and rents bicycles. The restaurant is open from 6:30 am to 9 pm (shorter hours in winter). Good rooms are about $50/60 for singles/doubles in summer. The Best Western *Capitol Reef Resort* (☎ 425 3761, fax 425 3300), 2600 E Hwy 24 (about one mile west of the park border), has a pool, spa, and horse and bike rentals. Many rooms have good views. The restaurant is open from 7 am to 10 pm. Rates are in the $70s from June to September, in the $40s from mid-October to March, and in between at other times.

See Loa & Fish Lake above and Hanksville in the Southeastern Utah chapter for other lodging possibilities.

### Places to Eat
Torrey is your best bet for meals. Apart from the hotel restaurants, there's the *Sportsman's Bar & Grill* (☎ 425 3869), 288 W Main St, open from 7 am to 9 pm in summer, shorter hours in winter. It serves mid-priced American fare. *La Buena Vida Mexican Cafe* (☎ 425 3759), 599 W Main St, is a homey place serving lunch and dinner daily except Tuesday in the summer. They close in winter and may be closed at other times – call.

# Southeastern Utah

UTAH

'Canyonlands' is what Utahans call the southeastern corner of their state. And canyons there certainly are – sheer-walled and majestic, arid and desolate. They were formed by the Colorado River and many of its tributaries, most notably the Green and San Juan Rivers. Utah's largest and wildest national park, appropriately enough named Canyonlands, is found here, along with the exquisite Arches National Park and numerous other protected areas.

This is one of the most inhospitable yet beautiful terrains in the world. Not a great deal is known about the prehistoric Indians who lived here – their art and buildings can be seen throughout the area, but the reasons for their departure remain unclear.

The canyons proved to be formidable barriers to any kind of exploration or travel. Even the hardy Mormon pioneers settled this corner of the state well after other parts of Utah. Towns were tiny and distances were great until the discovery of uranium and the consequent post-WW II mining boom. Suddenly, dirt roads appeared everywhere (evidence of the search for radioactive pay dirt) and populations swelled. As more people moved here in the 1950s, word began to get out about the spectacular but unforgiving nature of this corner of the world. Slowly, tourists started drifting in to see these fantastic canyonlands.

It is ironic that the greatest canyon of them all has been destroyed. The Glen Canyon of the Colorado River was flooded by the Glen Canyon Dam (just across the state line in Arizona) and is now the artificial Lake Powell, which lies within the Glen Canyon National Recreation Area. The building of the dam and the subsequent flooding of Glen Canyon in the 1960s caused a great uproar. Many people fought to save and preserve the magnificent canyon and the many Indian ruins within it. These are now lost. Today, Lake Powell is a mecca for boaters and anglers and receives

millions of visitors every year – but there are still Southwestern desert rats who refuse to visit what they call 'Lake Foul'.

Author Edward Abbey, was one of the strongest protestors against the flooding of Glen Canyon. He wrote not so much for the preservation of the desert Southwest itself, but rather for its incalculable quality of untouched remoteness. It is another irony that in so unerringly evoking the stark beauty of life in the canyonlands in his books, he inadvertently attracted to the Southwest hundreds of thousands of people seeking that very remoteness.

Today, southeastern Utah is experiencing a tourist boom, which has had a negative impact in many areas and a positive one in others. The canyonlands are one of the most splendid areas in the Americas, and that splendor needs to be cared for. Travel lightly, slowly, thoughtfully, respectfully. You are only one of millions, but your voice and actions count. (See the aside 'Southern Utah – Being Loved to Death?' in the chapter on southwestern Utah.)

## GREEN RIVER

Green River, with almost 1000 inhabitants, is the only town of any size along I-70 between Salina, 108 miles to the west, and Grand Junction, Colorado, 95 miles to the east. It was settled in 1878 on a ford of the Green River and makes a good base for river running and for exploring the Maze District on the western side of Canyonlands National Park. The museum in town is worth a stop. Tourism and melon growing are the main industries.

### Orientation & Information

The I-70 business loop north of the freeway between exits 158 and 162 becomes Main St, the town's main drag. Almost everything lies along this street.

The visitors center (☎ 564 3526) is in the museum at 885 E Main St. It sells maps and

UTAH

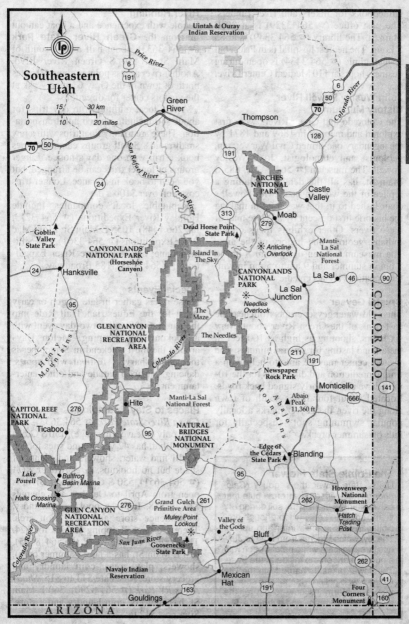

**Southeastern Utah**

0    15    30 km
0  10    20 miles

Price River

Green River

Thompson

Uintah & Ouray
Indian Reservation

Colorado River

Castle Valley

ARCHES
NATIONAL
PARK

Moab

Dead Horse Point
State Park

Anticline
Overlook

Manti-
La Sal
National
Forest

La Sal

Island In
The Sky

CANYONLANDS
NATIONAL PARK
(Horseshoe
Canyon)

CANYONLANDS
NATIONAL PARK

La Sal
Junction

Goblin
Valley
State Park

Hanksville

San Rafael River

Green River

Needles
Overlook

The
Maze

The Needles

GLEN CANYON
NATIONAL
RECREATION
AREA

Colorado River

Newspaper
Rock Park

Monticello

Abajo
Peak
11,360 ft

Henry Mountains

Hite

Manti-La Sal
National Forest

NATURAL
BRIDGES
NATIONAL
MONUMENT

Edge of
the Cedars
State Park

Blanding

CAPITOL REEF
NATIONAL
PARK

Ticaboo

Lake
Powell

Bullfrog
Basin Marina

Halls Crossing
Marina

GLEN CANYON
NATIONAL
RECREATION
AREA

Grand Gulch
Primitive Area

Muley Point
Lookout

Valley
of the Gods

Hovenweep
National
Monument

Hatch
Trading
Post

San Juan River

Goosenecks
State Park

Navajo Indian
Reservation

Mexican
Hat

Bluff

Gouldings

Four
Corners
Monument

ARIZONA

COLORADO

Abajo Mountains

guidebooks for hikers and river runners. The post office (☎ 564 3329) is at 20 E Main St. The library (☎ 564 3349) is at 85 S Long. The nearest hospital is in Price, but a small clinic (☎ 564 3434) is open during business hours at 110 Medical Center Drive.

### John Wesley Powell River History Museum

The Colorado and Green Rivers were first explored and mapped in 1869 and 1871 by the legendary one-armed Civil War veteran, geologist and ethnologist, John Wesley Powell. The museum (☎ 564 3427), 885 S Main St, has all the details, including a replica of the wooden boat, with Powell's chair lashed to it, that was used in making the historic first descent by a White man of these rivers. Other exhibits focus on the Indians, geology and history of the area. The museum is open daily from 8 am to 8 pm in summer and 9 am to 5 pm in winter; donations are accepted.

### Crystal Geyser

This cold-water geyser erupts from near the east bank of the Green River about every six hours, shooting as high as 100 feet in the air and lasting for several minutes. The visitors center may be able to help with a timing prediction and directions for the 10-mile drive along poorly signed back roads. Located about four miles south of town along the river, the geyser marks a locally popular swimming spot – especially for kids on summer break.

---

### The Edible State Flower

Utah's state flower, the sego lily (*Calochortus nuttallii*), grows from a bulb that can remain dormant in the soil during dry years, sprouting only when enough precipitation falls in the winter and spring. The lily, which blooms from May to July, has three delicate white petals, each with a purple mark on the inside at the base. The flower takes its name from the Ute Indians, who called it 'sago' and showed the early Mormons how to dig for the bulb, which is starchy and nutritious. ∎

---

### River Running

People with experience and a boat can put in from the **Green River State Park** (☎ 564 3633), about half a mile south of Main St at 150 S Green River Blvd. Another river access point is about 10 miles north of town in the Gray Canyon – ask at the visitors center for directions.

A few local outfitters run day trips for about $40 including lunch and transportation. These are mainly float trips with a few small rapids. Small groups can sometimes book a trip with one day's notice. Larger groups or longer trips can be arranged, but you need to book in advance. Longer trips cost well over $100 a day.

Reputable local companies include Holiday River Expeditions (☎ 564 3273, fax 266 1448), 1055 E Main St; Moki Mac River Expeditions (☎ 564 3361), 100 Silliman Lane; and Adventure River Expeditions (☎ 564 3648), 185 Broadway.

### Special Events

Horse riders gather in late March or early April for the Equestrian Trail Ride into the San Rafael Swell, a two-day event with a cookout and camping. Melon Days around the third weekend in September is the annual harvest festival with sports, dancing, music, a parade and other entertainment.

### Places to Stay – camping

*Green River State Park* (☎ 564 3633 – 8 to 9 am only or leave a message), 150 S Green River Blvd, has 42 year-round sites for $9. You'll find water, showers and plenty of shade but no hookups. *Green River KOA* (☎ 564 3651), 550 S Green River Blvd, is open from April to October and charges $12 to $18. It has a pool, coin laundry, convenience store and recreation area. There are three Kamping Kabins for $24. The *United Campground* (☎ 564 8195), 910 E Main St, has a pool (summer only), showers, play areas, coin laundry and grocery store. Rates are $11 to $15. *Shady Acres RV Park* (☎ 564 8290), 360 E Main St, has showers, coin laundry and a store. Sites cost $12 to $16.

## Places to Stay – bottom end

Summer rates are substantially higher than the rest of the year. One of the cheapest places is *Mancos Rose Motel* (☎ 564 9660), 20 W Main St, which has 14 simple rooms for $20 to $35 in summer but may close in winter. *Oasis Motel & Cafe* (☎ 564 8272), 118 W Main St, has 20 basic but OK rooms in the $20s and lower $30s in summer, $18 to $28 in winter. The similarly priced *Cottage Motel* (☎ 564 3441), 60 E Main St, has about 30 modest rooms.

The *Motel 6* (☎ 564 3436), 946 E Main St, is the largest hotel in town with over 100 budget rooms and a pool. Summer rates run about $34/40 for singles/doubles; winter rates are about $26/34. Others in this price range are the *National 9 Motel* (☎ 564 8237), 456 W Main St, which has a spa; the small *Robbers Roost Motel* (☎ 564 3452), 225 W Main St, which has a pool and spa; and the *Sleepy Hollow Motel* (☎ 564 8189), 94 E Main St.

## Places to Stay – middle

The *Bankurz Hatt B&B* (☎ 564 3382),

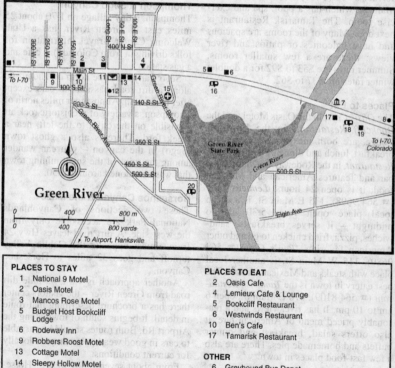

**Green River**

0    400    800 m
0    400    800 yards
↓ To Airport, Hanksville

**PLACES TO STAY**
1   National 9 Motel
2   Oasis Motel
3   Mancos Rose Motel
5   Budget Host Bookcliff Lodge
6   Rodeway Inn
9   Robbers Roost Motel
13  Cottage Motel
14  Sleepy Hollow Motel
16  Shady Acres RV Park
17  Best Western River Terrace Motel
18  United Campground
19  Motel 6
20  Green River KOA

**PLACES TO EAT**
2   Oasis Cafe
4   Lemieux Cafe & Lounge
5   Bookcliff Restaurant
6   Westwinds Restaurant
10  Ben's Cafe
17  Tamarisk Restaurant

**OTHER**
6   Greyhound Bus Depot
7   John Wesley Powell River History Museum & Information Center
8   Holiday River Expeditions
11  Post Office
12  Library
15  Clinic

214 Farrer St, 84525, has four rooms in a recently restored turn-of-the-century home. Rates are in the $60 to $80 range.

The *Budget Host Bookcliff Lodge* (☎ 564 3406), 395 E Main St, has almost 100 rooms, a pool, a restaurant open from 6 am to 10 pm (7 am to 9 pm in winter) and adequate rooms for about $60 in summer, $25 to $45 in winter. The *Rodeway Inn* (☎ 564 3421, fax 564 8162), 525 E Main St, has a restaurant. Rooms are nice enough and cost in the $50s in summer. The best hotel is the Best Western *River Terrace* (☎ 564 3401, fax 564 3403), 880 E Main St, which has a pool, spa and exercise room. The Tamarisk Restaurant is next door. Many of the rooms are spacious and have balconies or patios and river views; there are a few smaller rooms. Summer rates are $53 to $92 for a double; winter rates are $37 to $62.

### Places to Eat

The *Oasis Cafe*, in the Oasis Motel, and the *Bookcliff Restaurant*, in the Bookcliff Lodge, are both inexpensive places for breakfast, lunch and dinner. The *Westwinds Restaurant*, in the Rodeway Inn, has a salad bar and features American and Mexican food; it is open 24 hours. *Lemieux Cafe* (☎ 564 9698), 135 E Main St, is a cheap local place open from 5:30 am to midnight – it serves breakfasts, sandwiches, pizza, fried chicken to go and other American favorites. *Ben's Cafe* (☎ 564 9689), 115 W Main St, is another local place with steaks and Mexican dinners. The best eatery in town is the *Tamarisk Restaurant* (☎ 564 8109), 870 E Main St, open 6 am to 10 pm. It has river views and a reasonably priced menu of American fare; it also offers salad, breakfast and dinner buffets and homemade pies. There are also a few fast-food places in town.

### Entertainment

*Ray's Tavern* (☎ 564 8109), 25 S Broadway, has beer, a pool table and occasional live entertainment. It serves food as well. *Lemieux Lounge* (☎ 564 3653), next to the Lemieux Cafe, is another place for a drink.

### Getting There & Away

Greyhound (☎ 564 3421) has an office in the Rodeway Inn, 525 E Main St. There are three buses each morning to Grand Junction, Colorado, (one leaves in the middle of the night) and one or two each day to Salt Lake City or Las Vegas, Nevada. Amtrak (☎ 1 (800) 872 7245) stops in nearby Thompson (for passengers with reservations only) on its daily runs between Provo and Denver, Colorado. It's the only train station in use in southeastern Utah.

## AROUND GREEN RIVER
### Thompson & Sego Canyon

Thompson, a tiny village on I-70 about 25 miles east of Green River, has a Utah Welcome Center (travel information for folks driving in from Colorado), a cafe and a gas station.

Sego Canyon is due north of Thompson along a dirt road passable to cars except after heavy rain. Almost four miles north of Thompson, a variety of prehistoric rock art is visible on the cliffs to the left, near a creek ford. There is also a ghost town (Sego) in the canyon – you can wander among the ruins of the small mining town that was abandoned around 1950.

### Horseshoe Canyon & the Maze

These two sections of Canyonlands National Park are accessible only from the west side. A dirt road leaves Hwy 24 from almost opposite the Goblin Valley turnoff and goes 32 miles to Horseshoe Canyon.

Another approach is via a 45-mile dirt road from Green River – the visitors center there has a brochure describing that route in detail. It begins south of town along the Airport Rd. Both routes should be passable to cars in good weather but enquire locally for current conditions.

From about seven miles west of Horseshoe Canyon, a signed dirt road heads south for about 20 miles to Hans Flat Ranger Station, which is the entry point into the Maze. Beyond Hans Flat, 4WD is required. Further details of these areas are given in Canyonlands National Park, below.

## GOBLIN VALLEY STATE PARK

This park is about 46 miles southwest of Green River. To get there take Hwy 24 and turn right on a signed 12-mile-long dirt road, passable to cars. The park is near the southern end of the **San Rafael Swell** (see the chapter on central Utah), and various dirt roads continue beyond the park into the beautiful, rugged and relatively untraveled San Rafael area. The BLM in Price, the visitors center and state park in Green River, and the park itself have maps and information about these drives, for which high clearance is recommended and 4WD might be necessary. The BLM office in Hanksville also has maps and information, although these BLM lands are administered from Price.

The park itself is full of goblins – tortured and twisted rock formations that imaginative visitors have also described as ghosts, giant mushrooms and toadstools, chess pieces, spooks and assorted other weirdos. A couple of one- to two-mile trails wind their way through the eroded rocks. This would be a great place to spend Halloween with your kids. A campground provides 21 sites with barbecue grills, water and showers – it is open year round. Day use is $3; camping is $9.

The park headquarters are at the Green River State Park. Camping reservations can be made at 1 (800) 322 3770.

## HANKSVILLE

At the junction of Hwys 24 and 95, this small town of less than 500 inhabitants is a convenient stopping place on the way between the various natural attractions of the area.

The BLM (☎ 542 3461), 406 S 100 West, has maps and information about the lands surrounding Hanksville, especially the **Henry Mountains**. Hours are 7:45 am to noon and 12:45 to 4:30 pm, Monday to Friday.

### Places to Stay & Eat

*Red Rock Campground* (☎ 542 3235), 226 E 100 North, has 45 sites, showers and coin laundry and is open from late March to early November. Sites are $9 for a tent to $13 with hookups. The campground also has a restaurant. *Ekker's Campground* (☎ 542 3283), 110 S Center, has six RV sites with hookups (no showers) and is open all year.

Hotels in Hanksville are pretty basic but all charge $40 to $50 for a double in summer. *Whispering Sands Motel* (☎ 542 3238), 132 S Hwy 95 at the south edge of town, has 11 rooms each with two queen-size beds. Next door is *Stan's Burger Shak* – his burgers are better than his spelling.

The *Desert Inn* (☎ 542 3241), 197 E Hwy 24, is the biggest place with 20 modest rooms. *Fern's Place* (☎ 542 3251), 99 E 100 North, has eight rooms, some with kitchenettes, and looks OK. *Joy's B&B* (☎ 542 3252), PO Box 151, 84734, at 296 S Center, has three nonsmoking rooms.

## HENRY MOUNTAINS

This 11,000-foot-high range was the last to be named and explored in the lower 48 states. It is a remote and scenic area – like so many in southern Utah – but what makes it unique is the herd of bison that was introduced here in the 1940s. Now, some 200 animals freely roam the range – one of the last few wild bison herds in the country.

The bison usually graze high in the summer and drop down into the western flanks of the Henrys in winter. The BLM in Hanksville can tell you where the animals have been sighted recently. Pronghorn antelopes, mule deer and bighorn sheep are also seen in the Henrys. A good source book for the area is *Hiking & Exploring Utah's Henry Mountains and Robbers Roost* by M R Kelsey (Kelsey Publishing, 1990).

The BLM operates three small campgrounds in the area – all usually have water though it's a good idea to carry extra just in case. *Lonesome Beaver* is about 25 miles south of Hanksville along 100 East, which becomes the Sawmill Basin Rd. The elevation here is 8000 feet, and the area is open from May to October. There is water and a $4 fee. The free *McMillan Springs* campground is a further 10 miles in; it usually has water and is open from May to November. Both these campgrounds can also be reached from Hwy 95 via the Bull Mountain Scenic Backway, signed at about 20 miles south of Hanksville. At 6300 feet *Starr Springs* is open from April to November; the fee is $4. It is at the south end of the range, reached by a signed four-mile dirt road from Hwy 276, about 17 miles beyond the junction with Hwy 95.

Note that all these roads are poor, and high-clearance vehicles or 4WD are recommended – check with the BLM for current conditions.

The BLM also runs the free and waterless *Hog Spring* campground off Hwy 95 about 35 miles south of Hanksville.

Hwy 95 turns southeast and, about 45 miles from Hanksville, crosses Lake Powell near its north end at Hite (there's a bridge), then continues past magnificent scenery into Utah's far southeastern corner. About 25 miles south of Hanksville, Hwy 276 heads southwest and reaches Lake Powell at Bullfrog Basin, where Lake Powell can be crossed by car ferry. Both these places are within the Glen Canyon National Recreation Area, described later in this chapter and in the chapter on Arizona.

## ARCHES NATIONAL PARK

The arches and bridges found in the Southwest are all formed by erosion of sandstone – the difference between the two is that arches are carved by erosion from the weather and from rockfall, while the bridges begin by erosion from rivers. Sometimes it is difficult to tell which is which after a river has dried up or shifted.

Arches National Park boasts the greatest concentration of arches in the world (a good place to see bridges is at Natural Bridges National Monument, described later in this chapter). To qualify as an arch, a formation must be at least three feet across, and over 2000 have been found in the national park, including Landscape

Arch, which is over 100 feet high and over 300 feet across. This is probably one of the largest arches in the world, but it is eroded to the point where it is likely to collapse in the near geological future. That means any minute in the next few thousand years, so it probably won't happen when you're under it. Roads and hiking trails make many of the most spectacular arches accessible to everyone.

## Orientation & Information

The park is easily reached along paved Hwy 191, 20 miles southeast of I-70 and five miles northwest of Moab. From Hwy 191, a park road reaches the entrance station and visitors center almost immediately and continues nine miles to a 'Y' near Balanced Rock. From the 'Y', a 2.5-mile road to the right leads to the Windows Section, a good destination for those with little time. A 10-mile road to the left goes to Devils Garden. All these roads are paved and have numerous pullouts and trailheads for great views or scenic hikes to the arches. In addition, there are some dirt roads suitable for high-clearance or 4WD vehicles or mountain bikes.

The visitors center (☎ 259 8161) is open from 8 am to 6 pm from mid-April through

Delicate Arch is one of the most popular arches and is best viewed at sunset when the rock turns a vibrant red. (TW)

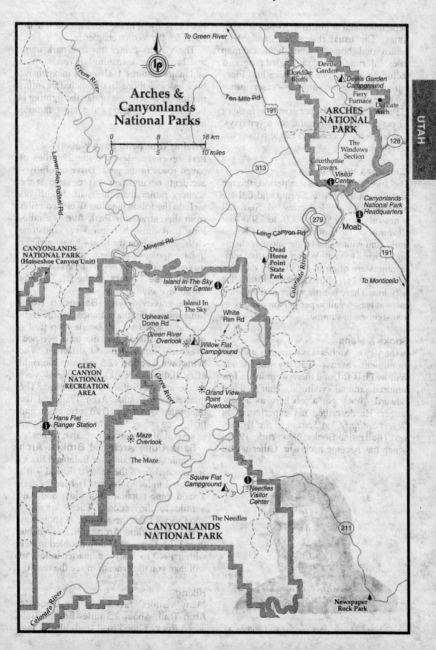

September and 8 am to 4:30 pm at other times. The usual things are available – audiovisual shows, exhibits, book and map sales, information and ranger-led programs including a daily two-hour hike into Fiery Furnace during the summer – reservations are necessary.

Park entrance is $4 per private vehicle or $2 per person; this is valid for seven days. Golden Age, Access and Eagle passes are accepted.

### Climate & When to Go

The summer is the busiest period, though highs often top 100°F. Spring and fall are more pleasant and less crowded. Snowfall is not very heavy at the 4000- to 5500-foot elevation of most of the park's roads and trails, and winter can be the most enchanting of times to visit. Winter nighttime temperatures are often in the 20°s F; daytime temperatures are above freezing. Rainfall is very low. There is little water in the park – carry at least a gallon per person per day as you sightsee in summer.

### Books & Maps

In the 1950s, Arches was a smaller national monument, access was by the sandy Willow Flats Rd, and there were just a few hundred annual visitors. That's when Edward Abbey got a job here as a park ranger. He described his experiences in *Desert Solitaire – A Season in the Wilderness* (Ballantine Books, New York, 1968), which has become a classic. Other useful books are listed in the Books section in the Facts for the Visitor chapter.

The visitors center has free park maps and brochures describing all roads, trails and major features. It also sells inexpensive booklets with more details, including information on which time of day the lighting is best for photographing the most famous arches.

### Driving Tour (with Easy Walks)

Park brochures describe the 22 miles of paved roads in the park. Drive carefully – accidents occur when drivers stare at the scenery rather than the road. Highlights include the following. Just over two miles from the entrance is **Park Ave** – a mile-long trail through impressive sandstone cliffs, emerging at the road – either arrange to have someone pick you up or return the way you came. Just north of Park Ave, the **Courthouse Towers** on the left form an impressive skyline.

The gravity-defying **Balanced Rock** (nine miles from the entrance) on the right can be reached by a 0.3-mile-loop trail – both the roadside and the trail perspectives are impressive and different. The **Windows Section** (2.5 miles to the right after Balanced Rock) has several very scenic arches visible from the road. The quarter-mile Double Arch Trail and the one-mile Windows Trail are easy and highly rewarding hikes to get you right up to several of the most impressive arches.

**Sand Dune Arch** and **Broken Arch** (8.5 miles straight on after Balanced Rock) are reached from the same trailhead – it's about 0.2 miles to the first (where there is a sand dune popular with kids) and half a mile to the second. There are very good views from these trails. A short way beyond is **Skyline Arch**, which is visible from I-70. This arch almost doubled in size with a 1940 rockfall – a quarter-mile trail will take you underneath to see the result.

### Hiking

Many visitors' favorite is the **Delicate Arch Trail**. About 2.5 miles beyond Balanced Rock, a good road leads almost two

Edward Abbey, park ranger and author

### The Desert's Delicate Skin

Travelers to deserts of the Southwest are often told to avoid stepping on the **cryptobiotic crust** – but what is this odd-sounding stuff? The crust is a unique combination of living organisms such as lichen, cyanobacteria, fungi and algae that forms a dark, powdery coating on the high deserts of the Colorado Plateau. It acts both as a protective covering and as a binding agent for tiny soil particles, retarding erosion, absorbing moisture and providing nutrients (especially nitrogen) for desert plants and the animals that rely on them. The cryptobiotic crust may not look like much, but it is the delicate and fragile basis of life in the desert.

In some ways, the crust is tough stuff – it survives the scorching summer sun, freezing winters, irregular downpours and windstorms. But it's not built to withstand a hiking boot: the force of a footprint crushes and kills the crust. Millions of visitors, billions of footprints – and the crust can suffer irreversible damage. Worse damage is caused by bicycle or vehicle tires; the crust breaks down in a continuous strip that makes the desert especially vulnerable to erosion. That's why you are told to stay on established roads and trails, and to step on the rock or in the sandy washes when traveling off the trail. ∎

miles right to **Wolfe Ranch**. (Here a log cabin built in 1908 by an early pioneer is quite well preserved – have a look to imagine how tough life must have been then.) Just east of the ranch, a bouncy suspension bridge crosses the Salt Wash – on the other side of the wash a short path leads to views of Ute Indian rock art. The bridge is also the beginning of the moderately difficult arch trail – it goes over slickrock (where it is marked by rock cairns), past pockets of vegetation and fine vistas, culminating in a wall-hugging narrow ledge to Delicate Arch itself – one of the most beautiful in the park and well worth the three-mile roundtrip hike. Expect some steep drop-offs on this trail, but no shade or water. Another (more distant) view of the arch is obtained by taking the road about a mile beyond the ranch, and hiking 0.4 mile to an overlook – again, steep sections.

About five miles north of Balanced Rock is **Fiery Furnace**. This maze of canyons offers the opportunity to hike off-trail (don't step on that cryptobiotic crust) and get thoroughly lost. Forget your water and you're buzzard-bait. Actually, because of the disorienting nature of the furnace and the damage done by so many people, the park requires you to go as part of a group (limited to 25). Space fills up fast and there could be a two-day waiting period. Sign up at the visitors center.

Nineteen miles from the visitors center, **Devils Garden** is at the end of the paved road. A variety of trails here allow you to hike from two to seven miles, roundtrip. The trail, which passes about 10 arches (including **Landscape Arch** – the biggest), is close to the park campground and therefore is very popular. The two-mile roundtrip to Landscape Arch (passing Tunnel Arch and Pine Tree Arch) is quite easy; beyond the trail gets more difficult but isn't bad for experienced hikers and offers  spectacular views of the La Sal Mountains.

### Driving & Hiking off the Main Road

There are three unpaved roads in the park. The Salt Valley Rd is suitable for cars most of the time (inclement weather may close the road). It leaves the main road just over a mile before the end and heads nine miles west to the very scenic **Klondike Bluffs**. This gives you a chance to get away from the densest crowds – though a good number of cars do make it out here! Fairly short hiking trails from here lead to the **Marching Men** and **Tower Arch**.

From Klondike Bluffs, a 10-mile dirt road leads back to the main park road at Balanced Rock. This requires 4WD and is best done from north to south (going the other way involves a steep and sandy climb that may be impassable).

From Balanced Rock, the Willow Flats Rd goes west (soon meeting the road described above). This used to be the way into the park (back when Abbey worked here) and is in fair shape for most vehicles to the park boundary (four miles). From there it requires high clearance or 4WD to reach Hwy 191, about another four miles. The distant views and solitude are the main attractions on this road – there are no important arches nearby. Before you go, ask rangers at the visitors center about road conditions.

### Backpacking

Free backpacking permits are required but are easy to obtain from rangers at the visitors center. However, backpacking here is not recommended for beginners. Rangers told me that few people backpack here because of the heat and scarcity of water – about a dozen backpacking permits are issued each day. Definitely a great way to escape – but talk to the rangers for the best suggestions. They'll help, not hinder, you – unless you aren't prepared. Backpackers must carry a gallon of water per day (minimum) and a stove. They also must camp at least a mile away from roads (limited areas) and refrain from camping right next to arches. They should never trample the cryptobiotic crust.

### Rock Climbing

Sites marked on USGS maps are off limits (ie, most of the famous arches), but rock climbing is permitted in much of the park.

---

### Park Etiquette

From a few thousand annual visitors in the 1960s to 100,000 in the 1980s to almost a million in the 1990s – the popularity of Arches National Park has only continued to soar. Regulations are enforced to help protect the desert from the onslaught of visitors. The Park Service has begun to survey park patrons to find out what measures would improve their visits – perhaps surprisingly, many people would like the park to limit the number of visitors at the major scenic points.

The best thing you can do is to stay on roads and trails – 4WD vehicles and mountain bikes can only be used on the paved and unpaved roads, not on hiking trails or off-road. ATVs and ORVs cannot be used anywhere in the park.

Hikers should stay on trails where they exist. When hiking in the backcountry, hike on the sandstone, slickrock or sandy washes. Avoid stepping on the desert vegetation, which is particularly vulnerable (see the preceding aside on the Desert's Delicate Skin). ■

---

Climbers should talk to a ranger (in the visitors center) for advice and a free permit.

### Places to Stay

The scenic *Devils Garden* campground is at the road's end about 20 miles north of the entrance. It has 52 sites, picnic tables, grills, water and toilets, but no showers. It's usually full by mid to late morning in the summer high season, so arrive early. All campers must register at the visitors center. From mid-March to mid-October the fee is $8; in winter water is turned off and camping is $5. Water can be obtained at the visitors center. There are lots more places to stay and eat in nearby Moab.

### DEAD HORSE POINT STATE PARK

This state park, although small, compares in dramatic scenery to the nearby Arches and Canyonlands National Parks and deserves the 22-mile side trip along paved Hwy 313 (which leaves Hwy 191 11 miles

View at dusk from Dead Horse Point State Park (RR)

northwest of Moab). The drive is a lovely one with the most exciting section near the end – the road crosses a narrow neck of land only 30 yards wide with 2000-foot cliffs all around.

The view from the point is simply fabulous – the Colorado River below has almost looped back on itself forming a splendid 'goose neck' opposite the point. A rough footpath follows the edge of the point, allowing views in all directions. Much of Canyonlands National Park can be seen to the southwest, immediately behind the goose neck.

There is a visitors center (☎ 259 2614) open from 8 am to 6 pm in summer and 9 am to 5 pm in winter. Slide shows, exhibits, information and a gift shop are here. Rangers lead walks and give talks in summer. A short nature trail is nearby.

The 21-site *Kayenta Campground* nearby has water but no showers. There are RV hookups in summer only. Reservations can be made (☎ 1 (800) 322 3770) or just show up early. Even in the busy summer, the campground usually has space until midday or early afternoon. Day use is $3; camping is $7.

## CANYONLANDS NATIONAL PARK

Covering over a third of a million acres, this is the largest and wildest national park in Utah – indeed, parts of it are as rugged as almost anywhere on the planet. Sheer-

walled and spectacular canyons provide great scenic beauty but also prevent you from getting around very easily. Take the primitive campgrounds at the Doll House and the Horsehoof Arch, for example. They are only five miles apart as the crow flies – but separated by the Cataract Canyon of the Colorado River. With a 4WD vehicle you'll cover 230 miles of (often very rough) road to get from one campground to the other! Not only canyons awe the visitor; there are arches, bridges, needles, spires, craters, mesas and buttes – just about every Southwestern geological formation you can imagine.

There's plenty of water, too, but it's usually 2000 inaccessible feet below you in the rivers. Only one campground in the park has drinking water in summer. Most areas are completely waterless – even visitors centers (they'll sell you bottled water). If you plan on anything more than a casual day trip to the main overlooks, load up several large containers of water – a gallon per person per day is considered minimal in summer.

The difficult terrain and lack of water make this the least developed and least visited of Southwestern national parks.

### Orientation

The canyons of the Colorado and Green Rivers divide the park into three completely separate and very different sections.

Imagine the canyons in a 'Y' shape. The long northeast-southwest arm of the 'Y' is the Colorado River and the northwest arm is the Green River. The most developed sector of the park is 'Island in the Sky' – the area enclosed by the two rivers at the top of the 'Y'. This is easily reached by paved Hwy 313, about a 30-mile drive from Moab. To the southeast of the Colorado is 'The Needles', easily reached by paved Hwy 211, about a 75-mile drive from Moab. To the west of the two rivers is the 'Maze' – about 130 miles from Moab and accessible by dirt roads. In addition, 'Horseshoe Canyon', an unconnected unit northwest of the Maze, is also reached by dirt roads. There are no bridges over the canyons within the park.

Island in the Sky and The Needles have visitors centers, developed campgrounds and paved roads leading to scenic overlooks and picnic areas. They also have dirt roads and hiking trails. The Maze and Horseshoe Canyon have only dirt roads (many accessible only to 4WD), hiking trails and primitive campgrounds – these areas have fewer visitors.

### Information

Information, maps and guidebooks for all park areas are available from: the headquarters in Moab (☎ 259 7164), 125 W 200 South, 84532, open 8 am to 4:30 pm, Monday to Friday; the Island in the Sky Visitor Center (☎ 259 4351), open 8 am to 5 pm daily; the Needles Visitor Center (☎ 259 4711), open 8 am to 6 pm daily; and the Hans Flat Ranger Station (☎ 259 2652, 259 6513) in the Glen Canyon National Recreation Area. The latter has information on the Maze and Horseshoe Canyon and is open from 8 am to 4:30 pm. During the summer, especially on weekends, interpretive activities are offered at the visitors centers. Winter hours may be shorter.

Entrance to the park is $4 per vehicle or $2 per person – this is valid for seven days and can be used to enter the different areas. Golden Age, Access and Eagle passes are accepted.

### When to Go & Climate

If you've read the earlier national park descriptions, you'll find the pattern familiar. Highest visitation is during the summer, which also sees average temperatures in the 90°s F (often over 100°F) and short but heavy thunderstorms in July and August. Biting insects are worst in late May and June. Spring and fall are the most pleasant seasons. Winter snows aren't very heavy but can close some roads. Best months overall are April and October – but don't tell anyone.

### Books & Maps

Apart from Adkison's *Utah's National Parks*, dedicated Canyonlands travelers will find the following useful: *Canyon Country Mountain Biking* by F A Barnes & T Kuehn (Canyon Country Publications, 1988); *Hiking, Biking and Exploring Canyonlands National Park and Vicinity* by M R Kelsey (Kelsey Publishing, 1992); and *River Guide to Canyonlands National Park* by M R Kelsey (Kelsey Publishing, 1991).

### Island in the Sky

This is the most easily reached and popular area in the park. The center of the area is a 6000-foot-high mesa – this is the 'Island in the Sky'. It is surrounded by a sandstone bench called the White Rim, 1200 feet below. From this rim, cliffs tumble a further 1000 feet to the rivers.

**Main Drive & Short Hikes** The visitors center is on the mesa top about two miles after the park boundary (pay entrance fees here). Paved roads continue to the edge of the 'island' with superb vistas of the White Rim, the rivers below and the national park stretching off into the distance. Most visitors take this paved road. From the visitors center, the road goes twelve miles south to Grand View Point; at about the halfway point of the drive, another paved road forks to the northwest and leads to Upheaval Dome, five miles away. Along these 17 miles of paved roads are several overlooks and trails – all well worth a stop. The best are described below.

## One Million Soles a Year

Canyonlands has traditionally been Utah's largest and wildest national park with the lowest visitation – this remains true although the number of annual visitors is fast approaching half a million (compared to about 50,000 visitors in 1980). Visitor services are not highly developed in this waterless and difficult landscape, which is just as well. It's easy to visit most national parks, and it's nice to know that some areas provide a minor challenge.

To minimize your impact, stay on trails and don't trample cryptobiotic crust (see The Desert's Delicate Skin aside in the section on Arches National Park for a discussion of cryptobiotic crust). All vehicle and bike use is limited to the paved and unpaved roads – neither can be used on hiking trails or off-road. ATVs and ORVs cannot be used anywhere in the park.

Because of heavy backcountry use, the park has set up a reservation system for backcountry campsites – you should reserve as far ahead as possible. The fees charged for these reservations are used to provide portable toilets and other maintenance. The reservation system is currently being overhauled, so call the park headquarters for current information. Make permit requests as far ahead as possible, but such requests must be postmarked no earlier than the second Monday in July of the calendar year prior to your visit. ■

The **Mesa Arch Nature Trail**, six miles south of the visitors center, has a brochure describing the vegetation. The easy half-mile loop trail passes Mesa Arch, which is on the very edge of the rim and makes a dramatic frame for the desert country below. The best light for photography is at dawn or in the afternoon.

At the picnic area almost a mile before the end of the road to Grand View Point, the **White Rim Overlook Trail** is an almost two-mile roundtrip, but it isn't difficult and gives some of the best views of the Colorado River over 2000 feet below. Another easy almost two-mile walk is the **Grand View Trail** at the road's end – many people say it has the best views in the park. Even if you are not up to hiking these trails, a stop at **Grand View Point Overlook** is a must.

Turning northwest six miles south of the visitors center leads to a picnic area and the **Upheaval Dome Trail**. An interpretive pamphlet describes the geology of this area. The trail is an easy half-mile roundtrip to the Upheaval Dome Overlook with fine views of a crater thought to have been the result of a meteor crashing into the planet. The trail continues a further half mile (but becomes a little more difficult) to Crater View Overlook.

**Green River Overlook** offers some of the best views of that river. The overlook is behind the Willow Flat Campground, reached by a short unpaved road at the beginning of the road to Upheaval Dome.

**Longer Trails & Backpacking** There are plenty of possibilities for half-day, all-day or overnight trips. These are strenuous because they involve the steep and often slippery descent down to the White Rim, and then the climb back out. About seven foot trails descend from the paved road down to the White Rim Rd – these form the basis of the longer hikes and backpacking trips. The trails have little or no shade or water, so you should be well prepared to deal with these hazards. The lack of water limits most backpacking trips to what you can carry.

In an attempt to cope with increasing numbers of backpackers and to ensure that backpackers do in fact find the solitude they expect in the backcountry, the park has instituted an elaborate reservation system for backpacking permits. For more information on making reservations, see the camping section below.

**White Rim Rd** Built by uranium prospectors after WW II, this 4WD road goes all the way around the Island in the Sky. It is about 100 miles long and is reached from the visitors center by the steeply descending Shafer Trail Rd. This circuit is a great favorite for 4WD trips, mountain bike trips and, to some extent, backpacking. The Park Service is trying to maintain the wilderness quality by limiting the number of vehicles using the road.

There are 10 primitive campgrounds along the trail, each with two campsites limited to either two or three vehicles and 10 or 15 people. None have water. Reservations are required and should be made as far in advance as possible (but not earlier than the second Monday in July of the year preceding your trip) by writing or calling the park headquarters for an application, a map and details of the campgrounds. A $25 fee per vehicular reservation ($10 for backpackers) is charged. A single reservation can consist of several consecutive days in different sites for a group of people traveling together.

There are occasional cancellations and no-shows – call the park about the chance of doing this very popular drive on short notice.

Park rangers regularly patrol the route to assist people whose vehicles break down or who have other problems. They also check for permits.

### The Needles

Paved roads make this spikily scenic area almost as popular as Island in the Sky. It is named after the mind-boggling landscape of striped white and orange spires, which really has to be seen to be believed. There are plenty of arches as well, many hidden in the backcountry and accessible only by hiking trails or 4WD roads. Also found in the backcountry are Anasazi Indian ruins and petroglyphs, many of which are difficult to reach.

Note that Newspaper Rock State Park, described later, is on Hwy 211 about 18 miles before the national park – these two are usually combined into one visit.

**Main Drive & Short Hikes** The visitors center is 2.5 miles beyond the park bound-

ary – pay your entrance fee (unless you already have a pass from another area) and obtain maps here.

From the visitors center, the paved road continues for almost seven miles to **Big Spring Canyon Overlook**; various stopping places, trails and paved and unpaved side roads line the way. A few hundred yards beyond the visitors center is the quarter-mile, easy loop **Roadside Ruin Trail** – a pamphlet describing the trailside vegetation and the ruins (which were Anasazi granaries) is available.

Half a mile beyond the Roadside Ruin Trail, a left turn leads past rangers' housing and continues, unpaved, to the **Cave Spring Trail**, 1.5 miles from the main road. This easy 0.6-mile loop trail crosses sandy areas and slickrock, descends two ladders, and passes thick vegetation in wet areas, Fremont Indian artwork and the remains of an old cowboy camp. A pamphlet describes these various facets of the walk.

Almost three miles beyond the visitors center, a side road to the left goes to a pump house with water year-round. A little further is Squaw Flat Campground, again to the left. About five miles from the visitors center is the **Pothole Point Trail** – an easy 0.6-mile loop with nice views. A pamphlet describes the geology and biology of the potholes along the trail. Just before the road ends, the **Slickrock Trail** offers a fairly easy 2.4-mile loop, with a 0.6-mile spur – fine views. At road's end, the **Big Spring Canyon Overlook** also has great views and is the beginning of a longer trail.

**Day Hikes** Good day hikes abound. Three of the best (scenic and only moderately difficult) are suggested here. They are not for the total novice, however. The trails often cross slickrock, where the trail is marked by rock cairns – keep your eyes peeled or you can get lost. Shoes or boots with good rubber soles for traction are recommended – sneakers don't offer as much traction. There is little shade and rarely any water (which, if found, must always be purified). Carry a gallon of water per person per day, use sun protection and bring insect repellent in the mid-May through June buggy months. June, July and August are very hot, with temperatures averaging in the 90°s F. Spring and fall are the best hiking seasons. January, the coldest month, has average highs around 40°F and lows in the teens.

From Squaw Flat Campground, climb up the **Squaw Canyon Trail** for fine views of the Needles. Return via the **Big Spring Canyon Trail** (roundtrip of 7.5 miles), or the less used **Lost Canyon Trail** (roundtrip nine miles). A still longer hike is from the Big Spring Canyon Overlook along the **Confluence Overlook Trail**, which leads 5.5 miles to a point overlooking where the Green and Colorado Rivers meet – you can see the gray-green waters of the one mixing slowly with the reddish main flow of the other. Head back the way you came.

## Horseshoe Canyon & the Maze

These two remote, western sectors of Canyonlands National Park can be reached only from Green River or Hwy 24 via dirt roads, which are usually accessible by cars as far as the rim of Horseshoe Canyon and the Hans Flat Ranger Station. Access routes to the sites are described above in Orientation.

**Horseshoe Canyon** The exceptional rock art here is considered some of the best in the USA. It was left by prehistoric Indians over thousands of years. The life-size figures are magnificent. Please don't disturb them in any way – even touching them with fingers deposits body oils that damage the millennia-old art. (Damaging the art is a criminal offense.)

A signed turn from the 'main' dirt road indicates the way. At a cattle guard near the canyon's edge, a very steep and narrow 4WD road goes almost to the canyon bottom in about a mile – this should be scouted first and attempted only by experienced 4WD drivers, preferably with a short-wheelbase vehicle. All vehicles must stop at a barrier, 1.5 miles before the rock art. The hike in runs along a fairly flat trail.

No camping is allowed in the canyon, but you can camp on the rim (BLM land). Carry water.

**The Maze** The only access to this remote jumble of colorful canyons is via 4WD tracks or hiking trails east of the Hans Flat Ranger Station. This is one of the wildest areas in the Southwest. The roads are very poor and can be closed by heavy rain or snow – call the ranger station for current conditions. Short-wheelbase, high-clearance 4WD is the best choice for vehicles. Hiking trails cut miles from the vehicle routes. Water can sometimes be obtained and must be boiled. It is highly recommended to call the ranger station before beginning any trip.

There are two main areas to visit. The **Maze Overlook** is reached on foot by a combination of 4WD roads and the North Trail – this is a 13-mile hike from the trailhead, 2.5 miles southeast of the ranger station. Drivers go via the Flint Trail – about six miles longer. From the overlook, an extremely steep foot trail descends into the maze where you can hike around and maybe find water. A topographical map and wilderness hiking skills are essential. There are two campgrounds reachable by 4WD road – permits are necessary.

The **Land of the Standing Rocks** is reached by jeep trails south of the Flint Trail. This area has five campgrounds accessible by 4WD, and there are other hiking possibilities.

Currently, backcountry campground permits are free, although a fee system similar to the one in the other park areas may be implemented in the future.

## River Running & Rock Climbing

Guided river trips are available from Green River for the river of that name and from Moab for the Colorado River. All outfitters in these towns take care of the logistics and obtain the necessary permits. A limited number of permits are available to members of the public who have the appropriate skills, experience and boating equipment. Write to the park headquarters as far in advance as possible for applications and information.

The trip from Green River down to the confluence with the Colorado is a scenic one with relatively easy rapids. The same is true of the Colorado above the confluence. Almost immediately below the confluence, however, the Colorado goes through the wild white water of Cataract Canyon – navigable by experienced or guided boaters only. Beyond this canyon, the river eases off as it approaches Lake Powell in the Glen Canyon National Recreation Area. A useful book is *River Guide to Canyonlands National Park* by M R Kelsey (Kelsey Publishing, 1991).

Climbing is permitted in most parts of the park. A climbing permit is required and is free.

### Places to Stay

There are only two developed campgrounds in the park, both easily reached by paved roads. Park rangers give talks in the evenings during the high season. Six or seven miles beyond the visitors center, *Willow Flat Campground* in Island in the Sky has 12 sites open all year. There is no water – you must haul it in from Moab. Camping is free.

*Squaw Flat Campground* in The Needles is just over three miles beyond the visitors center. Water is available at the 26 sites from April to September, and there is a $6 fee. It is free in winter. Both these campgrounds may fill by early afternoon, so arrive early to ensure a place.

There are primitive waterless campgrounds in the backcountry – these are for backpackers, mountain bikers and those traveling in 4WD vehicles. The Needles is the park's best backpacking area because a network of hiking trails allows you to reach some primitive campgrounds without long stretches on 4WD roads (see above section for suggestions and precautions). 4WD vehicles will have a hard time negotiating the infamous Elephant Hill, a couple of miles west of Squaw Flats – this is for experienced 4WD drivers only. Other roads are less difficult. Mountain bikers cannot

use hiking trails and may find the 4WD roads a little too rough for comfort – though not impassable. There are six primitive campgrounds, none with water. All can be reached by 4WD. Four can be reached by hiking trails with only minimal sections on the roads.

Anyone wishing to camp in the backcountry must obtain a site-specifc permit. Backpackers pay $10 per trip, and 4WD groups pay $25 per vehicle. To obtain a permit, you must contact the park headquarters and make a site reservation for each night you plan to spend in the backcountry. The number of visitors at each backcountry site is restricted, and many sites book up early. Rangers are happy to help prospective visitors plan an itinerary, but they recommend that you reserve at least six weeks prior to your arrival and preferably up to six months in advance. The busiest seasons are March through May and October. Even though permits can be difficult to obtain during those times, it's always worth asking if you happen to arrive without one.

It may be possible to wilderness camp for free if you are at least 300 feet away from any water source or archaeological site and out of sight of any road or trail. Enquire at the visitors center about this.

Just over a mile after crossing the park boundary on Hwy 211, a short signed road leads out of the park to *Needles Outpost* (☎ 259 2032, 259 8545). Open from mid-March to October, it has a campground with hookups and showers for $10 and up. Gas, food, maps, information, jeep tours and rentals are also available. If you aren't camping, Moab has a good selection of places to stay and eat.

### MOAB

Moab stands for Mormons, ores, actors and bicyclists – which sums up the town's history. Mormons set up a mission here in 1855, but Indians drove them away. In the late 1870s, Mormon farmers returned and weathered repeated attempts by Indians to oust them. Moab became the center of a ranching and farming region, and many of today's roads and tracks in the area follow the hoof prints of early cattle roundups.

Oil prospectors became interested in the area's mineral wealth in the 1920s. The big strike didn't come until the 1950s, however, when valuable uranium ores were discovered and the population tripled in three years. The uranium boom was successful for a few years, and a handful of people made their fortunes. Miners wove a network of 4WD roads, which now are used by tourists. They also left scars on the landscape including radioactive tailings ponds. (Tailings are the waste product of mineral extraction processes – only a fraction of 1% of ores is usable product in most cases.) Some mining, especially of salt and potash, still goes on.

The influx of prospectors put Moab on the map, and word began to spread of the grand scenery in southeastern Utah. Actors arrived and movies were filmed including some John Wayne Westerns and Indiana Jones footage – but the most memorable footage seems to be the TV commercials for cars that were helicoptered to the tops of nearby mesas. (I never did trust those TV commercials.)

The mineral boom is now bust, and although films are still shot here, tourism has been the economic mainstay of recent years. Vacationers swell the population greatly outside of winter. Mountain bikers and 4WD vehicle drivers and have discovered the miners' roads and begun using them. Mountain bikers have found that slickrock surfaces provide challenging and very scenic rides in the area.

Moab, with almost 5000 permanent residents, is the seat of Grand County and the largest town in southeastern Utah. It is a semirural yet trendy town with chic restaurants and art galleries, about 60 hotels ranging from tiny B&Bs to motels with over 100 rooms, and about 50 companies offering river running, biking, backpacking and 4WD tours and rentals. Despite, or perhaps because of, the large numbers of services, tourists swamp the place from spring to fall, and reservations are advised.

Much of the populace is delighted to profit from the influx of tourists. Others decry what Western writer Page Stegner calls 'an infestation of mountain-bike blight'. Like it or not, Moab is bursting at the seams – a Grand County councilmember writes 'tens of thousands of bikers, hikers, jeepers, spring-breakers, lycra-clad yuppies, foreign tourists and other refugees from the urban world are following the encouragement of the guidebook authors . . . It ain't pretty.'

## Orientation & Information

Hwy 191 becomes Main St, the main drag through town.

The multi-agency Moab visitors center, corner of Main and Center Sts, is open for walk-in visitors from 8 am to 9 pm in summer and 8 am to 5 pm in winter. The staff can answer almost any question you might have about the area's national parks, national forests, BLM areas, state parks and county and city information.

For information ahead of time, contact the Grand County Travel Council (☎ 259 8825, 1 (800) 635 6622, fax 259 4386), 210 N 100 West, PO Box 550, 84532; the National Park Service (☎ 259 7164), or the Manti-La Sal National Forest Moab Ranger Station (☎ 259 7155), both at 125 W 200 South, 84532, open from 8 am to 4:30 pm, Monday to Friday; the BLM at 82 E Dogwood (☎ 259 6111) or 885 S Sand Flats Rd (☎ 259 8193).

The post office (☎ 259 7427) is at 50 E 100 North. The library (☎ 259 5421) is at 25 S 100 East. Recycle your carload of cold drink cans and bottles at the Community Recycling Center, 100 E Sand Flats Rd. The hospital (☎ 259 7191) is at 719 W 400 North. The police (☎ 259 8938, or 911 in emergencies) are at 121 E Center.

## Dan O'Laurie Museum

The diverse collection at this museum (☎ 259 7985), 118 E Center, includes informative exhibits on everything from local archaeology to uranium, as well as local fine art. It is also the starting point of a self-guided walking tour of Moab's historic buildings – two dozen of them are within

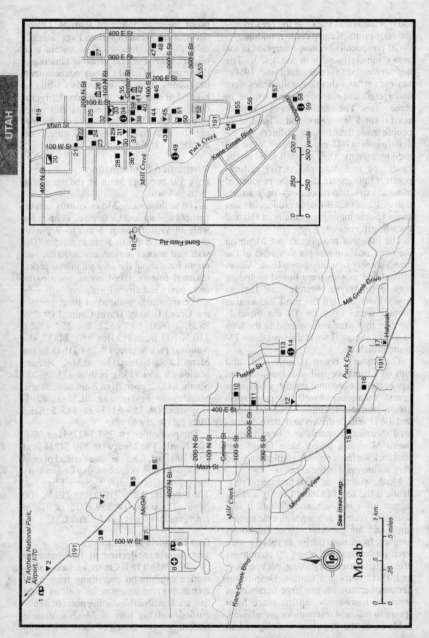

Moab

three blocks of the museum and are described in a free brochure. Hours are 1 to 5 pm and 7 to 9 pm Friday and Saturday year round and Monday to Thursday from April to October; 3 to 5 pm and 7 to 9 pm Monday to Thursday from November to March. Admission is free.

### Hollywood Stuntmen's Hall of Fame
A tribute to the fearless folks behind the serious action scenes in films, this museum (☎ 259 6100), 111 E 100 North, has movie clips, photos and equipment used for stunts. There's a gift shop. It is open daily, but hours vary. Admission is $3, $2 for seniors and students and $1 for three- to 11-year-olds.

### Arches Vineyards
Oenologists can visit Utah's only winery (☎ 259 5397), 2182 S Hwy 191, three miles south of town. Local grapes are used. Tasting room hours are 11 am to 7 pm,

Monday to Friday, 11 am to 9 pm on Saturday and 2 to 6 pm on Sunday.

### Hole 'n the Rock
This 5000-sq-foot home carved out of solid sandstone (☎ 686 2250), 15 miles south on Hwy 191, can be toured any time between 9 am and 5 pm; admission is $2 or $1 for six- to 12-year-olds. There is a picnic area and gift shop.

### Scenic Drives
Scenic drives ranging from easy paved roads to rugged and barely passable 4WD tracks are found all around Moab. Again, the Travel Council has free informative brochures. Most drives are in BLM or Park Service land, and officials emphasize that there are many hundreds of miles of 4WD roads of all levels of difficulty and challenge – driving off established roads or vehicle trails is damaging to the land and usually illegal. Please don't do it.

Useful books include the *Canyon Country Off-Road Vehicle Trails Series* by F A Barnes or J Bickers. This series of four books plus four accompanying maps covers the Moab area and the national parks. Also useful is Barnes' *Canyon Country Highway Touring* for descriptions of roads passable to cars. Some of the best drives are outlined below.

The paved roads to the nearby parks and south to Monticello all have beautiful views. Other scenic paved roads include the **Colorado River Byway** (Hwy 128) northeast of Moab, following the Colorado River to Cisco, 44 miles away just off I-70. Highlights are views of the Fisher Towers and Castle Rock (seen on TV commercials and movies), the 1916 Dewey Bridge (one of the first to cross the Colorado – you can only walk over it now), and sights of rafts running the rapids of the Colorado River. About 15 miles along Hwy 128, **La Sal Rd** heads south into the Manti-La Sal National Forest, climbing high via switchbacks (large RVs not recommended) into the forest and giving good views of canyon country below. The road emerges on Hwy 191, eight miles south of Moab. This is a 60-mile loop from Moab, paved almost all the way but snowed-in during winter.

The **Potash Scenic Byway** (Hwy 279) is named for the potash extraction plant near the end of it. Near the beginning of the road (which leaves Hwy 191 to the left about three miles north of Moab), a radioactive tailings pond is visible. Despite this, it's worth the drive because there are signed pullouts, side roads and short walks leading to Indian ruins and petroglyphs and dinosaur tracks. Also, the Corona Arch trailhead is about 10 miles along the road – a 1.5-mile foot trail leads to this and another arch. Near the end of the drive, about 14 miles from Hwy 191, Jug Handle Arch is on the right. This unusual arch is only three feet wide – but 15 times as high. Shortly beyond, you reach the potash plant – the road continues as a 4WD track into the Island in the Sky section of Canyonlands National Park or Dead Horse Point State Park.

The BLM's **Canyon Rims Recreation Area** lies to the east of Canyonlands National Park – many people think it's just as scenic. The area is reached by turning right off Hwy 191, 32 miles south of Moab. The paved Needles Overlook Rd goes about 22 miles to a great view of the national park. About two-thirds of the way along this road, the gravel Anticline Overlook Rd stretches 17 miles north to a promontory with great views of the Colorado River. The road is passable to cars. The two roads combined make a good day trip, and there is camping in the area.

The Canyon Rims Recreation Area is also reached via Kane Creek Blvd heading west from Moab. This soon becomes a gravel road following Kane Creek Canyon. About 10 miles out of Moab, you must ford the creek, which may be impossible after heavy rains or spring snowmelt. If passable, the road continues in good enough shape for ordinary cars driven with care, but eventually 4WD vehicles will be needed. Visitors to both the Anticline Overlook and the Needles Overlook can see this jeep road winding along the canyon below. The road eventually exits at Hwy 211, a few miles east of The Needles area of Canyonlands National Park. This total drive is about 60 or 70 very scenic miles, and there are several side roads to explore – the BLM has maps and information.

Renting a 4WD vehicle costs about $80 a day from Farabee 4x4 Adventures, Slickrock Jeep Rentals, Thrifty Car Rental, and Canyonlands 4x4 Rentals & Guided Tours. One-day guided tours are about $50 to $90 per person, depending on the difficulty and distance. Half-day and multi-day tours are also available. 4WD tour operators include Lin Ottinger Tours (Moab's oldest tour outfit, in operation since 1960), Adrift Adventures, North American River Expeditions & Canyon Tours, and Tag-a-Long Expeditions (see below for addresses and phone numbers).

### River Running

This is the third of the big triad of adventurous activities (along with biking and 4WD)

River running

that are big in Moab. The Colorado River northeast of Moab is easily accessible by Hwy 128, and so this is a favorite for day trips, with some flat sections and some Class II to III rapids. Overnight trips offering greater excitement run through the Westwater Canyon of the Colorado (near the Colorado state line) and through the Cataract Canyon of the Colorado (in and beyond Canyonlands National Park). Trips on the Green River are available as well. You can paddle a canoe or raft, float on a raft or go by jet boat. Rafting season is April to September, jet-boat season goes longer. The highest water is usually in May and June.

You can either do it yourself or go on a tour. Most rafting tours cost about $35 or $40 for a day, more for jet boats. Overnight tours of three to five days are about $400 to $800 per person. Children accompanying parents usually get discounts. Tours combining river trips with 4WD or mountain biking are available. Do-it-yourselfers can rent canoes, inflatable kayaks or rafts – rates are about $20 to $40 a day for canoes and kayaks; about $60 to $100 a day for rafts (all come with life jackets and paddles). Permits are required well in advance for national park rivers, but you can run the rivers outside the parks with no problems.

One-day trips are often available at a day's notice and half-day trips are an option. Overnight trips should be booked well in advance. Write to the companies for their brochures.

Rentals, shuttle or pick-up services, and half- or one-day trips are available from Red River Canoe Company, River Runner Sports, Tag-a-Long Expeditions, Tex's Riverways and Western River Expeditions.

One-day and multi-day river trips are available from the following companies: Sheri Griffith Expeditions is very experienced and has a variety of trips ranging from mainstream (pardon the pun) to tours for women only. Other experienced and recommended companies are World Wide River Expeditions, Adrift Adventures, Western River Expeditions, Tag-a-Long Expeditions, Navtec Expeditions, and North American River Expeditions & Canyon Tours.

One-day and half-day trips are offered by Canyon Voyages and the Moab Rafting Company – Wildwater. The latter also conducts overnight trips on the San Juan River (see also Bluff).

## Mountain Biking

There are dozens of mountain-bike routes in the area, the most famous of which is the **Slickrock Trail** – a 10-mile loop on BLM land beginning from the end of Sand Flats Rd about three miles east of town. This is a challenging trip with great views – not recommended for novices.

The BLM and Travel Council have brochures describing other trips. Whichever one you select, please stay on the trails – the cryptobiotic crusts are being heavily impacted by riders leaving the trails. Also read *Canyon Country Mountain Biking* by F A Barnes and T Kuehne or *Mountain Biking in Canyon Rims Recreation Area* by P & B Utesch, both from Canyon Country Publications.

Mountain bike rentals and tours are available from Kaibab Mountain Bike Tours & Cyclery, Nichols Expeditions, Rim Tours and Western Spirit Cycling.

## Other Activities

Those interested in **horse riding** can rent sturdy beasts for about $10 an hour or $60 a day including lunch. Breakfast and sunset rides with cookouts cost about $30. Overnight trips are also available. Call Cowboy Trails, Sunset Trail Rides or the Pack Creek Ranch for information. **Golf** at the 18-hole/par 72 Moab Golf Course (☎ 259 6488), 2705 S East Bench Rd. **Swim** at the municipal pool (☎ 259 8226), 181 W 400 North. Play **tennis** at Grand County Middle School Public Courts, 217 E Center St.

## Tour & Rental Companies

Global Expeditions rents backpacking, climbing, skiing and camping gear. Canyonlands Llamas operates one- to four-day treks with llamas to carry gear. Canyonlands Field Institute is a nonprofit organization that organizes educational or cultural expeditions and seminars, and hiking or river-running trips.

Scenic flights are available at the airport. Many local people, visitors and most National Park Service officials disapprove of them because the noise from the low-flying aircraft (and helicopters) ruins the quiet and scenic outdoor experience. In places like the Grand Canyon, aircraft noise is heard more often than not during busy summer periods. Although this is not yet the case in the Moab area, scenic flights may begin to pose a serious problem. All forms of aircraft are inappropriate vehicles for touring wilderness areas. Some aircraft drop low enough to endanger hikers, climbers and other visitors (this is not just what I read in local newspapers – it actually happened to me).

The companies mentioned above (and listed below) seem to have decent reputations and have been around for a few years (or decades). New companies open every year.

Adrift Adventures
    378 N Main St; PO Box 577, 84532 (☎ 259 8594, 1 (800) 874 4483)
Canyon Voyages River Tours
    352 N Main St; PO Box 416, 84532 (☎ 259 6007, 1 (800) 488 5884, fax 259 5659)

Canyonlands Field Institute
    1320 S Hwy 191; PO Box 68, 84532 (☎ 259 7750)
Canyonlands 4x4 Rentals & Guided Tours
    550 N Main St; PO Box 1234, 84532 (☎ 259 4567, fax 259 7067)
Canyonlands Llamas
    CVSR 2104, 84532 (☎ 259 5739)
Cowboy Trails
    2231 S Hwy 191; PO Box 104, 84532 (☎ 259 8053, fax 259 2226)
Farabee 4x4 Adventures
    234 N Main St; PO Box 664, 84532 (☎ 259 7494)
Global Expeditions
    3071 S Hwy 191; PO Box 1131, 84532 (☎ 259 6604, fax 259 8069)
Kaibab Mountain Bike Tours & Cyclery
    391 S Main St; PO Box 339, 84532 (☎ 259 7423, 1 (800) 451 1133, fax 259 6135)
Lin Ottinger Tours
    600 N Main St, 84532 (☎ 259 7312)
The Moab Rafting Company – Wildwater
    PO Box 801, 84532 (☎ 259 7238, 1 (800) 746 6622)
Navtec Expeditions
    321 N Main St, 84532 (☎ 259 7983, 1 (800) 833 1278, fax 259 5823)
Nichols Expeditions
    497 N Main St, 84532 (☎ 259 7882, 1 (800) 635 1792, fax 259 2312)
North American River Expeditions & Canyon Tours
    543 N Main St, 84532 (☎ 259 5865, 1 (800) 342 5938, fax 259 2296)
Pack Creek Ranch
    See Places to Stay – top end
Red River Canoe Company
    497 N Main St; CVSR Box 2812, 84532 (☎ 259 2298)
Rim Tours
    94 W 100 North, 84532 (☎ 259 5223, 1 (800) 626 7335)
River Runner Sports
    401 N Main St; PO Box 416, 84532 (☎ 259 4121)
Sheri Griffith Expeditions
    2231 S Hwy 191; PO Box 1324, 84532 (☎ 259 8229, 1 (800) 332 2439, fax 259 2226)
Slickrock Jeep Rentals
    284 N Main St, 84532 (☎ 259 5678)
Sunset Trail Rides
    nine miles south on Hwy 191; PO Box 222, 84532 (☎ 259 4362, fax 259 2523)
Tag-a-Long Expeditions
    425 N Main St, 84532 (☎ 259 8946, 1 (800) 453 3292)

Tex's Riverways
>    691 N 500 West; PO Box 67, 84532 (☎ 259
>    5101)

Thrifty Car Rental
>    711 N Main St, 84532 (☎ 259 7317, fax 259
>    4524)

Western River Expeditions
>    1371 N Hwy 191, 84532 (☎ 259 7019, fax
>    259 6121)

Western Spirit Cycling
>    38 S 100 West; PO Box 411, 84532 (☎ 259
>    8732, 1 (800) 845 2453, fax 259 2736)

World Wide River Expeditions
>    625 N Riversands, 84532 (☎ 259 7515, 566
>    2662)

## Special Events

Many of these celebrate the outdoor activities for which Moab is famous. Dates vary from year to year – call the Travel Council. There is a half marathon in late March and a Jeep Safari around Easter Weekend. During June, usually the second weekend, Butch Cassidy Days hosts a PRCA rodeo. Another rodeo and various horsy/agricultural/arty/outdoor events occur during the Grand County Fair in early August. October sees the Moab Gem & Mineral Show and, just before Halloween, the Fat Tire Bike Festival with tours, workshops, lessons, competitions and plenty of musical entertainment.

## Places to Stay

Whether camping or staying indoors, you have a wide variety of choices in or near Moab. Camping is possible at both public and private sites. If you're seeking a room, you might try either of two reservation services. Moab Central Reservations (☎ 259 5125, 1 (800) 748 4386), 92 E Center, PO Box 1150, 84532, makes reservations for most of the places in town and will also make tour reservations. Another place to try is Arches Reservation Central (☎ 259 4737, 1 (800) 775 4737), 76 S Main St, 84532. The high season in Moab is a long one – from mid-March to the end of October prices rise and reservations are recommended. (High-season rates are given below, but rates during holiday weekends or special events may be higher.)

## Places to Stay – camping

*Canyonlands Campark* (☎ /fax 259 6846), 555 S Main St, has almost 200 sites, many with tree shade, and is open all year. It has a pool, playground, showers and coin laundry. Rates are $11.50 (tents) to $18.50 (full hookups). *Slickrock Campground* (☎ 259 7660, fax 259 9402), 1301½ N Hwy 191 (two miles north of downtown), also has almost 200 tree-shaded sites year-round. Facilities include a pool, spa, recreation area, playground, showers, coin laundry, groceries and a cafe open from March to October. Rates are $13.50 to $18.50. Camping cabins are $26 for two people, $32 for four. Both these places will allow non-guests to use the showers for $4. *Moab Valley RV & Campark* (☎ 259 4469), 1773 N Hwy 191, has showers, coin laundry and a convenience store. It has about 100 sites and is located a couple of miles south of the Arches National Park turnoff. Rates are $12 to $16 from March to October.

*Up the Creek Campground* (☎ 259 2213), 210 E 300 South, has 18 tent-only sites with showers. Rates are $7 a person from April to October. *Holiday Haven RV Park* (☎ 259 5834), 400 N 500 West, has about 80 RV sites for $14 to $18. There are showers, a pool and coin laundry. Both places charge $3 for showers for non-guests.

*Moab KOA* (☎ 259 6682), 3225 S Hwy 191 (four miles south of town), has a pool, miniature golf, playground, showers, coin laundry and groceries. It is open from mid-February to mid-November and charges $15 to $20. *Edge of the Desert* (☎ 259 7813), 1251 S Millcreek Drive, near the Slickrock Trail, has showers and tent or RV sites starting at $10.

There are Manti-La Sal National Forest campgrounds about 25 miles east of Moab in the La Sal Mountains, reached by gravel roads off La Sal Rd. Coming from Hwy 191, the free *Oowah Lake Campground* is first – it's open from June to October but has no water. About 15 miles along La Sal Rd, a five-mile gravel road goes to *Warner Campground*, open from May to September; it has water and charges a $5 fee.

The BLM operates the *Big Bend, Hal Canyon* and *Oak Grove Campgrounds* along Hwy 128 next to the Colorado River. Big Bend is about 10 miles from Moab, has about 70 sites, pit toilets, no water, picnic tables and grills and charges $5. The others are much smaller with similar facilities. In the Canyon Rims Recreation Area, *Windwhistle Campground* is five miles west of Hwy 191 on the Needles Overlook Rd and *Hatch Point Campground* is 25 miles west and north along the Anticline Overlook Rd. Both have water, pit toilets and charge $5 from April to October.

### Places to Stay – bottom end

The friendly *Lazy Lizard International Hostel* (☎ 259 6057), 1213 S Hwy 191, has five dorms sleeping six people for $7 per person and five basic rooms at $20 plus tax for a double. Facilities include a hot tub, coin laundry and a TV/video room, and guests have kitchen privileges. The showers cost $2 for non-guests. The family-run, old-fashioned *Hotel Off Center* (☎ 259 4244, 1 (800) 237 4685, fax 259 4220), 96 E Center, has a dorm for $10 per person and nine rooms (each different) for $35 to $50, or $10 less in winter. Bathrooms are down the hall. No smoking allowed.

The *Virginian Motel* (☎ 259 5951), 70 E 200 South, is a good deal by Moab standards. It charges in the $40s for a clean double room with a kitchenette. Another good budget choice in the $40s is the *Inca Inn Motel* (☎ 259 7261) 570 N Main St, with small but tidy rooms and a pool. Other basic economy places include the *Silver Sage Inn* (☎ 259 4420), 840 S Main St, and the *Prospector Lodge* (☎ 259 5145), 186 N 100 West.

### Places to Stay – middle

**B&Bs** There seems to be a couple of new B&Bs every year in Moab. Almost all of them have no-smoking policies. One of the best is actually in Castle Valley, 20 miles northeast of Moab. The *Castle Valley Inn* (☎ 259 6012), 424 Amber Lane, CVSR Box 2602, Moab, 84532, has six rooms and two cottages with excellent views of mountains such as sheer Castle Rock. All rooms have private baths, and the cottages have kitchenettes. The owners are well traveled and friendly. Amenities include a hot tub, pleasant gardens, a living room with fireplace and good lunches and dinners available with advance notice. They may close in winter. Rates are $75 to $125 for a double.

In Moab itself, the *Canyon Country B&B* (☎ 259 5262), 590 N 500 West, 84532, is in a quiet residential area. It has a spa and a large backyard with games area, and it rents bicycles. There are five rooms, two with shared bath, renting from $60 to $100 for a double. No children under six allowed. Another good choice is the *Sunflower Hill B&B* (☎ 259 2974), 185 N 300 East. Parts of the house date from the 1800s, and there is a spa. It has eight rooms ranging from a small single to two-bedroom suites for $64 to $90 a double. The *Desert Chalet* (☎ 259 5793), 1275 E San Juan Drive, is a large log house with a hot tub and big storage area (for bikes, etc). Guests have use of kitchen and laundry facilities as well as games, books, a slide projector, etc. The five rooms with shared bathrooms cost about $35/65 for singles/doubles. *Sandi's B&B* (☎ 259 6359), 450 S Walker, is a homey place with a nice garden. Four rooms go for $40 to $80. The reservation agencies listed above can find other B&Bs.

**Hotels** There are several decent places with rooms in the $50 to $60 range, including the following. The friendly and helpful *Bowen Motel* (☎ 259 7132), 169 N Main St, has a pool and large clean rooms with two queen-size beds or smaller, cheaper ones with one bed. The *Days Inn* (☎ 259 4468, fax 259 4018), 426 N Main St, has a pool and includes continental breakfast in the rates. The *Red Rock Motel* (☎ 259 5431), 51 N 100 West, has a spa, complimentary coffee and rooms with refrigerators. The *Red Stone Inn* (☎ 259 3500, fax 259 2717), 535 S Main St, has a spa, coin laundry and some kitchenettes; with 50 rooms, it is easily the biggest place listed so far. The *Colorado River Lodge* (☎ 259 6122), 512 N Main St, is a decent place but closed in winter. The old *Sunset Motel* (☎ 259 5191), 41 W 100 North, has been renovated and features a pool. It has some more expensive suites with kitchens. The *Cottage Inn Motel* (☎ / fax 259 5738), 488 N Main St, has four rooms in a private no-smoking home. The *Kokopelli Lodge* (☎ 259 7615), 72 South 100 East, has eight rooms and a garden for barbecues. The price includes continental breakfast.

The *Apache Motel* (☎ 259 5727, fax 259 8989), 166 S 400 East, has a pool and standard rooms well off the highway for about $60. The *Moab Travelodge* (☎ 259 6171, fax 259 6144), 550 S Main St, has a pool and 56 fairly large rooms for about $70. The *Super 8 Motel* (☎ 259 8868, fax 8968), 889 N Main St, is by far Moab's largest motel with 146 sizable, pleasant rooms, a pool, spa and coin laundry. Rates are $73.88 for a single or double in midsummer, and it also has some more expensive suites. Others in the $60s and $70s include *JR's Inn* (☎ 259 8000, fax 259 6980), 1075 S Hwy 191, with 10 large rooms, some with king-size beds. It runs a decent restaurant. The *Rustic Inn* (☎ 259 6177, fax 259 2642), 120 E 100 South, has a pool and includes a continental breakfast.

**Condos & Apartments** The *Ron-Tez Guest Condos* (☎ 259 7599, 259 7273), 450 E 200 South, has eight two-bedroom apartments with kitchen for $60. *Cottonwood Condos* (☎ 259 8897), 338 E 100 South, has six one-bedroom apartments with kitchen for $50 to $60. Nichols Lane Accommodations (☎ 259 5047), 543 Nichols Lane, has four apartments with one or two bedrooms and kitchen, coin laundry, and barbecue area for $50 to $60. The reservation services listed above will find you other condo and house rentals in the middle and top-end price ranges.

**Places to Stay – top end**
The *Landmark Motel* (☎ 259 6147, fax 259 5556), 168 N Main St, has a pool, kids' pool, spa and coin laundry. Its 36 large double rooms are in the $70s; a few mini-

suites cost about $90. The *Comfort Suites* (☎ 259 5252, fax 259 7110), 800 S Main St, is an all-suite hotel. Units have a kitchenette, pleasant living area and queen- or king-size beds. There is a pool, spa, exercise room and coin laundry. Suites are $80 to $100 for a double in summer, $55 to $80 in winter. The *Ramada Inn* (☎ 259 7141, 1 (800) 228 2828), 182 S Main St, has a pool, spa and good restaurant next door. Rooms are spacious and some have balconies. Rates are about $90 in summer, half that in winter. The *Moab Valley Inn* (☎ 259 4419, fax 259 4332), 711 S Main St, has similar rates but smaller standard rooms. It includes a continental breakfast and has a pool and spa.

Best Western has two of the better hotels in town. Its *Greenwell Motel* (☎ 259 6151, fax 259 4397), 105 S Main St, has 72 nice rooms in spacious grounds that separate the rooms from highway noise. There is a pool. The restaurant is open from 7 am to 9:30 pm (closed 2 to 5 pm). Rooms cost $80 to $90 from mid-May to mid-October, in the $40s from mid-November to mid-March. The Best Western *Canyonlands Inn* (☎ 259 2300, fax 259 2301), 16 S Main St, is also in the heart of town, but it's reasonably quiet. It has a pool, spa, coin laundry and exercise room, and includes continental breakfast in the rates. Rooms have refrigerators and go for $90 to $110 from April to October – there are a few suites.

The *Pack Creek Ranch* (☎ 259 5505, fax 259 8879), PO Box 1270, 84532, is about 15 miles southeast of Moab – take La Sal Rd and, at the T junction shortly after leaving Hwy 191, go right almost six miles. The 300-acre ranch is scenically located at over 6000 feet in the La Sal Mountains. There are about 10 rustic but comfortable cabins, some with two or three bedrooms, all with bathrooms and kitchens, some with fireplaces. Facilities include a pool, spa, sauna, playground, picnic areas, reading room, coin laundry and restaurant. Summer rates are $125 per person including plentiful and tasty meals, less in winter when the restaurant may close. The restaurant is open to the public by reservation. There are hiking trails (cross-country skiing in winter). The owners know southeastern Utah extremely well and arrange horse-packing and river-running trips.

### Places to Eat

With so many tourists, it's hardly surprising that Moab has a good selection of restaurants.

For breakfasts, the following open at 6 am and stay open throughout the day. All are fairly inexpensive. *JR's Restaurant* (☎ 259 8352), 1075 S Hwy 191, seems to be popular with locals, perhaps because it's away from the central tourist traffic. *Honest Ozzie's* (☎ 259 8442), 60 N 100 West, features good vegetarian cooking and has outdoor garden dining in season. The *Grand Ice Cream Parlour* (☎ 259 5853), 189 S Main St, also has an outdoor patio and serves full breakfasts and burger or sandwich lunches. From 5 to 10 pm, it becomes *Vic's Barbecue Ribs*. The *Golden Stake* (☎ 259 7000), 540 S Main St, offers inexpensive family dining all day. The huge *Dos Amigos Mexican Cantina* (☎ 259 7903), 56 E 300 South, serves inexpensive breakfast, lunch and dinner – the outdoor patio seats 100 and there's more room inside. *Cattleman's* (☎ 259 6585), 1991 S Hwy 191 in the truck plaza, is open 24 hours and serves breakfast any time.

For more upscale day-long family dining, there's *Arches* (☎ 259 7141), 196 S Main St (next to the Ramada Inn), which has a mainly American menu, and the *Creekside* (☎ 259 6151), 105 S Main St (next to the Best Western Greenwell Motel), which offers both American and Mexican food.

For good and reasonably priced lunches and dinners, try the popular *Rio Colorado Restaurant & Bar* (☎ 259 6666), 2 S 100 West. It has an interesting Southwestern menu with items like Kaibab kebabs and Southwestern catfish as well as sandwiches and salads. Most items are under $10. *La Hacienda* (☎ 259 6319), 574 N Main St, has inexpensive Mexican and gringo food.

Classier dining spots include the *Center Cafe* (☎ 259 4295), 92 E Center, which opens at 6 pm. The food is fresh, well pre-pared and varied. There is a selection of excellent coffees and a decent wine list. Entrees are in the $11 to $18 range. The *Sundowner* (☎ 259 5201), 1393 N Hwy 191, is a local favorite, open nightly at 5 pm. It serves German, Italian and Southwestern meals plus good steaks in the $8 to $18 range and also has cheaper soups, sandwiches, burgers and a salad bar. A newer place is the *Slickrock Cafe*, 5 N Main St, which serves excellent food in a relaxed and stylish Moab ambiance.

Two of the very best and most historically interesting restaurants in town are *Mi Vida* (☎ 259 7146), 900 N Hwy 191, and *Grand Old Ranch House* (☎ 259 5753), 1266 N Hwy 191. Mi Vida is in the hilltop house of (now dead) billionaire Charlie Steen, who made a fortune from his discovery of uranium in 1950. You can dine outside and enjoy the views. Open from 11 am to 2 pm and 5 to 10:30 pm, it specializes in mesquite-broiled steak and seafood. Most dinner entrees are in the $10 to $20 range; lunches are inexpensive. Built in 1896, Grand Old Ranch House is decorated with period photos and antiques. Open from 5 to 10:30 pm, it offers American and German fare that is also in the $10 to $20 range.

The *Poplar Place Pub & Eatery* (☎ 259 6018), 11 E 100 North, is in an 1886 building that has been completely renovated following a 1989 fire. It's a popular watering hole and serves decent pizza, sandwiches, soups and salads. Another popular bar is *Eddie McStiff's* (☎ 259 2337), 57 S Main St, which runs a microbrewery making six kinds of beer and offers a selection of inexpensive meals. Finally, you can round off the day with a Western cook-out at the *Bar M Chuckwagon* (☎ 259 2276), 541 S 541 E South Mulberry Lane. It serves a meaty fixed-price cowboy dinner at 7:30 pm followed by a Western music show – reservations are suggested; dinners cost about $15. It is open daily except Sunday from April to September.

### Entertainment

Bars around town include the lively and popular *Woody's Tavern* (☎ 259 9981), 221

S Main St. The *Club Rio* in the Rio Colorado Restaurant is a private club that lets in folks passing through for a $5 temporary membership. They have rock & roll and blues bands playing on weekends and local bands or karaoke midweek. The locally popular *Sportsman's Lounge* (☎ 259 9972), next to the Cattleman's Restaurant, also has live music (mainly country & western) and dancing on weekends. The *Outlaw Saloon*, 44 W 200 North, has pool tables and weekend music and dancing.

A free *Canyonlands Slide Show* is presented nightly in summer at the Moab Rock Shop (☎ 259 7312), 137 N Main St.

*The Canyon's Edge* is a multimedia presentation showcasing the geology, native people and natural history of the Colorado Plateau, narrated by famed Western writer Terry Tempest Williams. It is produced by the Canyonlands Field Institute (☎ 259 7750 for info) and screened at 8 pm from Monday to Saturday, mid-April to mid-October, at the Hollywood Stuntmen's Hall of Fame, 111 E 100 North.

*Canyonlands by Night* is a two-hour guided boat trip on the Colorado at sunset, with a sound and light show played on the cliff and canyon walls during the return. Call 259 5261 for reservations. Trips depart from 1861 N Hwy 191 (by the river bridge) at sunset nightly during the summer and cost $18, or 50% off for children under 18.

### Things to Buy

For many of the books mentioned above, try the National Park Headquarters or one of the bookstores in town. My favorite is Back of Beyond Books (☎ 259 5154), 83 N Main St. B Osborne's Books & Magazines (☎ 259 2665), 50 S Main St, is also good. To purchase a book in advance, you can have it shipped from Back of Beyond or get a mail-order catalog from Canyonlands Marketing Coop (☎ 259 8431), PO Box 698, 84532.

Lin Ottinger's Moab Rock Shop (☎ 259 7312), 137 N Main St, has everything for the rock hound – fossils, semiprecious stones, minerals, geodes, etc, as well as local jewelry.

Lema Indian Trading Company has good selections of Indian arts and crafts at 60 N Main St (☎ 259 5055) and 860 S Main St (☎ 259 5942).

There are many tourist-oriented gift shops and art galleries along Main St – some are tacky, others are quite good and sell local artists' work. The Shop (☎ 259 8623), 33 N Main St, and Kokopelli (☎ 259 6066), 90 E Center, are two places featuring local art.

### Getting There & Away

Alpine Air (☎ 373 1508, 1 (800) 748 4899) flies between Salt Lake City and Moab once or twice on most days and between Grand Junction, Colorado, and Moab once a day. The fare is about $150 roundtrip from Salt Lake City with advance purchase. Alpine Air connects with Delta for long-distance destinations. Tag-a-Long Expeditions is Alpine Air's agent in Moab (see Tour & Rental Companies above).

There are no bus or train services to Moab.

## NEWSPAPER ROCK PARK

Formerly a state park and now administered by the BLM, this park showcases a large sandstone rock covered with over 300 petroglyphs chipped out by different Indian groups during a 3000-year period. Designs represent relatively recent mounted figures and much older pictures of animals and abstract art.

There is a small, free campground with eight sites, pit toilets and grills, but no water. It is open year-round about 12 miles along Hwy 211 en route to The Needles.

## MONTICELLO

Pronounced 'Montisello', this town is over 7000 feet in the foothills of the Abajo Mountains, and so is greener and cooler than most towns in the region. Settled in 1888, it became a ranching area, and then oil and uranium were discovered. Ranching, mining and tourism are all important. Monticello has 2000 inhabitants and is the

UTAH

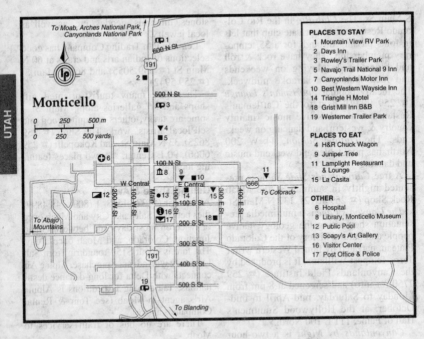

Monticello

To Moab, Arches National Park,
Canyonlands National Park

600 N St

191

500 N St

100 N St

W Central

E Central

To Colorado

100 S St

200 S St

300 S St

400 S St

500 S St

To Colorado

191

To Blanding

To Abajo
Mountains

0   250   500 m
0   250   500 yards

Main St
100 W St
200 W St
100 E St
400 E St
666

**PLACES TO STAY**
1   Mountain View RV Park
2   Days Inn
3   Rowley's Trailer Park
7   Navajo Trail National 9 Inn
9   Canyonlands Motor Inn
10  Best Western Wayside Inn
14  Triangle H Motel
18  Grist Mill Inn B&B
19  Westerner Trailer Park

**PLACES TO EAT**
4   H&R Chuck Wagon
11  Juniper Tree
13  Lamplight Restaurant
     & Lounge
15  La Casita

**OTHER**
6   Hospital
8   Library, Monticello Museum
12  Public Pool
13  Soapy's Art Gallery
16  Visitor Center
17  Post Office & Police

San Juan County seat – the highest county
seat in Utah.

### Orientation & Information
Hwy 191 (Main St) is the main drag through
town and runs north-south. Central St
becomes Hwy 666, which runs east into
Colorado.

The visitors center (☎ 587 3235, 1 (800)
574 4386, fax 587 2425), 117 S Main St, PO
Box 490, 84535, is open from 9 am to 5 pm,
Monday to Friday in winter. From mid-April
to October it is also open on weekends and
may have longer hours. The center has
extensive information about Monticello, San
Juan County and all the national parks,
national forests, BLM and state areas of
southeastern Utah. It also has a good bookstore. The library (☎ 587 2281) is at 80 N
Main St. The post office (☎ 587 2294) is at
197 S Main St. The hospital (☎ 587 2116) is
at 364 W 100 North. The police (☎ 587
2273, or 911 in emergencies) are at 197 S
Main St.

### Things to See & Do
The **Monticello Museum**, in the basement
of the library, has Anasazi and pioneering
items of local interest.

The **Abajo Mountains** rise to 11,360
feet in the Manti-La Sal National Forest
just west of town. There are camping,
hiking, backpacking, cross-country skiing
and snowmobiling opportunities – ask at
the visitors center for details.

Jeep tours are available from the KOA
campground.

The nine-hole/par 35 **golf course** (☎ 587
2468) is at 549 S Main St.

### Special Events
Pioneer Days around 24 July is a locally
popular event. The San Juan County Fair &
Rodeo is held in mid-August.

### Places to Stay
**Camping** *Mountain View RV Park* (☎ 587
2974), 632 N Main St, is open from May to
October. It has showers, coin laundry and

tent and RV sites from $8 to $12. Similar facilities are available at *Westerner Trailer Park* (☎ 587 2762), 516 S Main St, open from April to November, and *Rowley's Trailer Park* (☎ 587 2355), 480 N Main St.

The *Monticello KOA* (☎ 587 2884), six miles east on Hwy 666, is on a ranch with farm animals (including buffalo) and vintage farm implements. Open from May to September, it has a pool, spa, showers, playground, coin laundry, game room and convenience store. It runs jeep tours and presents slide shows of the area. Sites are $13 to $17.50.

*Dalton Springs* and *Buckboard* are two Manti-La Sal National Forest campgrounds accessible by paved roads about six miles west of town. Both are open from mid-May to October, have water and cost $5 a night.

Also see Newspaper Rock Park and Moab, above.

**Motels** Summer rates (given below) are a few dollars higher than winter rates. Higher rates will prevail during Pioneer Days, the County Fair and other sporadic events.

The friendly *Navajo Trail National 9 Inn* (☎ 587 2251), 248 N Main St, has rooms in the upper $30s in summer and in the $20s in winter. The very clean and tidy *Triangle H Motel* (☎ 587 2274, fax 587 2274), 164 E Central, has double rooms in the $40s in summer and in the $20s in winter. The similarly priced *Canyonlands Motor Inn* (☎ 587 2266, fax 587 2883), 197 N Main St, has a pool and spa.

The *Days Inn* (☎ 587 2458, fax 587 2191), 549 N Main St, is Monticello's largest motel (43 rooms). It has a pool and hot tub, and includes a continental breakfast in its rates – in the $60s for a double in summer. The Best Western *Wayside Inn* (☎ 587 2261), 197 E Central, also has a pool and spa and charges in the $60s for a double and in the $80s for a suite in summer. Both these are about $20 less in winter.

The *Grist Mill Inn B&B* (☎ 587 2597), 164 S 300 East, has six large rooms with antique brass beds and a private bath for about $50/60 for a single/double. Amenities include a spa, a reading room, sitting

room with fireplace, TV room and outdoor deck. It also has a three-bedroom cottage.

**Places to Eat**
The *H&R Chuck Wagon* (☎ 587 2531), 296 N Main St, is open from 6 am to 9 pm. They serve inexpensive and tasty American food – but I hope you don't get the same kind of service I did. The waitress got my 'orneriest waitress in the Southwest award' while I was researching this book. And all I did was ask for salsa.

For Mexican/American lunch and dinner, try *La Casita* (☎ 587 2959), 280 E Central. For dinner, two more-upscale places are the *Juniper Tree* (☎ 587 2870), 133 E Central, and the *Lamplight Restaurant and Lounge* (☎ 587 2170), 655 E Central. Both feature good steaks and a salad bar.

There are also a few fast-food and pizza places.

**Things to Buy**
Soapy's Art Gallery (☎ 587 3021), 81 S Main St, showcases local artists' work, which ranges from trite and touristy to attractive and artistic.

**BLANDING**
Settled relatively late, in 1905, Blanding is now an agricultural center and the biggest town in San Juan County, with 3800 inhabitants. It has an excellent museum and Indian ruins. The elevation is a pleasant 6000 feet.

**Information**
You can get visitor information at the museum at Edge of the Cedars State Park. The library (☎ 678 2335) is at 25 W 300 North. The post office (☎ 678 2627) is at 90 N Main St. The police (☎ 678 2334, or 911 in emergencies) are at 50 W 100 South.

**Edge of the Cedars State Park**
Well worth a stop, this park (☎ 678 2238), 660 W 400 North, has a short self-guided trail through Anasazi ceremonial and living quarters built between 700 and 1220 AD. The ruins were excavated in the early 1970s, and an informative brochure about

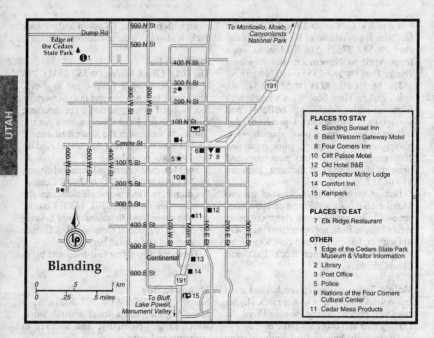

**Blanding**

To Monticello, Moab,
Canyonlands
National Park

**PLACES TO STAY**
4    Blanding Sunset Inn
6    Best Western Gateway Motel
8    Four Corners Inn
10   Cliff Palace Motel
12   Old Hotel B&B
13   Prospector Motor Lodge
14   Comfort Inn
15   Kampark

**PLACES TO EAT**
7    Elk Ridge Restaurant

**OTHER**
1    Edge of the Cedars State Park
     Museum & Visitor Information
2    Library
3    Post Office
5    Police
9    Nations of the Four Corners
     Cultural Center
11   Cedar Mesa Products

To Bluff,
Lake Powell,
Monument Valley

them is available at the **museum**, which
has good exhibits about this prehistoric
Indian culture. Audiovisual shows, talks
and demonstrations are often given, and
there is a small art gallery. Hours are 9 am
to 5 pm (to 6 pm mid-May to mid-September), and admission is $1.50 or $1 for children. It is closed on New Year's Day,
Martin Luther King Jr Day, Presidents'
Day, Thanksgiving and Christmas.

### Trail of the Ancients
The helpful staff at the museum at Edge of
the Cedars State Park has information
about this very scenic drive that begins in
Blanding and heads west to Natural Bridges
National Monument, south to Mexican Hat
and east to Bluff and Hovenweep National
Monument. Brochures describing other
sites along this route are available, and there
are road signs pointing them out. Unfortunately, many of the Anasazi ruins in the area
have been badly damaged by vandals and

pot hunters. The best preserved ones are at
Edge of the Cedars and Hovenweep. If you
want to see some of the others, seek advice
from the experts at the museum.

### Nations of the Four Corners Cultural Center
On 200 South at 600 West, the center has a
self-guided trail passing a Ute encamp-
ment, a Navajo hogan, a log cabin and pioneering farm implements, representing the
different cultures that have lived here. Just
to the north is the **White Mesa Institute**
(☎ 678 2220), 639 W 100 South, 84511. It
provides a variety of educational programs
about the lands and cultures of the area.
Both are affiliated with the College of
Eastern Utah (☎ 678 2201).

### Recapture Reservoir
Four miles north of town, the reservoir has
no developed facilities, but locals like to
boat, swim, water-ski and fish for trout.

Examples of Anasazi petroglyphs, Edge of Cedars State Park (RR)

## Special Events
The rodeo, ethnic folk fair and other activities leading up to the Fourth of July make this Blanding's most important annual holiday.

## Places to Stay
*Kampark* (☎ 678 2770), 861 S Main St, is open all year and has showers and a coin laundry. Rates are $10 to $14.

The Manti-La Sal National Forest operates the *Devil's Canyon Campground*, nine miles north along Hwy 191, and the *Nizhoni Campground*, 14 miles north along Mountain Rd (the northern continuation of 100 East). Devil's Canyon is open from mid-May to October, Nizhoni from June to September. Both have water, no showers, pit toilets and picnic facilities. Each costs $6.

Winter (November to March) rates are well below the average summer rates given here. Rates around the Fourth of July and weekends are likely to be higher. *Blanding Sunset Inn* (☎ 678 3323, fax 678 2379), 88 W Center, has a spa and modest rooms in the $30s for a double. The *Cliff Palace Motel* (☎ 678 2264), 132 S Main St, has doubles in the high $30s. The *Prospector Motor Lodge* (☎ 678 3231), 591 S Main St, has better rooms in the $40s.

The turn-of-the-century *Old Hotel B&B* (☎ 678 2388), 118 E 300 South, has eight pleasantly old-fashioned rooms with private bath for $44/56 for singles/doubles.

No smoking is permitted. It is open from April to October.

The *Four Corners Inn* (☎ 678 3257), 131 E Center, has nice large rooms for about $50 a double. The Best Western *Gateway Motel* (☎ 678 2278, fax 678 2240), 88 E Center, has a pool and charges in the $50s for a double. The *Comfort Inn* (☎ 678 3271, fax 678 3219), 711 S Main St, has a pool, spa, exercise rooms, game room and a coin laundry. Spacious and comfortable rooms, some with kitchenettes, are in the $60s and $70s including continental breakfast.

## Places to Eat
The best place to eat is the *Elk Ridge Restaurant* (☎ 678 3390), 120 E Center, with inexpensive American fare served from 6 am to 10 pm daily. There are four or five sandwich/burger/pizza type places as well.

## Entertainment
Melodramas are presented many nights of the summer somewhere in town. Recent shows have included *Heroes, Heroines and Harmony* – a rootin', tootin' Western review, featuring the mail-order sheriff of Robber's Roost . . . you get the picture. Cheer the hero, boo the villain and have fun for about $4 (less for kids). Shows in the past have been held at the *Edge of the Cedars State Park* and at *Cedar Mesa Products*, 333 S Main St. Ask around for present locations.

## Things to Buy
Cedar Mesa Products (☎ 678 2241), 333 S Main St, has Ute and Navajo hand-painted pottery – you can go in the workshop to watch. There's also other Indian arts and crafts and tourist junk.

Blue Mountain Trading Post (☎ 678 2218) is on Hwy 191 at the south end of town and has the best selection of Indian arts and crafts in town.

## NATURAL BRIDGES NATIONAL MONUMENT
This compact area, 40 miles west of Blanding, became a national monument in 1908 – the first National Park Service land in Utah. Three natural bridges, all visible

from a road and approachable by short hikes, are the highlight here. The three represent a natural aging process – there is a young, middle-aged and old bridge. My favorite is the oldest – the Owachomo Bridge – which spans 180 feet and rises over 100 feet above ground, but is only nine feet thick. This thin arch looks beautifully delicate.

## Orientation & Information

Hwy 275 branches off Hwy 95 and leads six miles to the visitors center, which is open 8 am to 6 pm in summer and to 4:30 pm the rest of the year. Audiovisuals, other exhibits, information, maps, books, toilets and water are available here at no charge. Ask about free ranger-led programs in summer. When the visitors center is closed, drinking water is available from a pump at the end of the parking area (to the right as you face the visitors center). There are no toilets or water beyond this point.

Beyond the visitors center, the paved one-way Bridge View Drive provides a nine-mile loop with views of the bridges. Trailers are prohibited (leave them at the visitors center).

Entrance to the monument is $3 per car or $1 per hiker or biker – this is valid for seven days. Golden Age, Access and Eagle passes are accepted.

Information is available from the Superintendent, Natural Bridges National Monument (☎ 259 5174), PO Box 1, Lake Powell, 84533.

Food, gas, and hotels are not available – Blanding or Mexican Hat (both about 40 miles away) provide the closest services.

## Bridge View Drive

This nine-mile loop has about 16 pullouts where you can park for photos – don't stop on the narrow road. From the three larger parking areas, trails lead to the bridges. One overlook gives views of the Anasazi Horsecollar Ruin.

You can mountain bike this drive but may not use any trails.

## Hiking

The following foot trails are given in the order they occur along the Bridge View Drive. The **Sipapu Bridge Trail** is 0.6 miles long (one-way) and involves stairs and ladders and a 500-foot descent. This bridge is the largest in the park. The **Horsecollar Ruin Trail** is an easy quarter-mile walk (one-way). If you are tempted to scramble to the ruins themselves, please don't climb on them. One misstep can destroy 1000 years of history – these are fragile places. The **Kachina Bridge Trail** is three-quarters of a mile (one-way) and has some steep stretches in the 400-foot descent. This bridge is the youngest. The **Owachomo Bridge Trail** is just a quarter mile and fairly easy, with a 180-foot descent. All of the trails are very rewarding.

In addition, hikers can take loop trails that join any two or all three of the bridges. Seeing all three bridges this way amounts to a hike of over eight miles, partly along steep and unmaintained trails, which puts it beyond the abilities of inexperienced walkers. Pick up a map at the visitors center. Don't hike off the trails – doing so damages the cryptobiotic soil crusts (see The Desert's Delicate Skin aside in the section on Arches National Park).

Trails are open all year, but the steeper sections may be closed after heavy rains or snow. During the summer, carry at least a gallon of water per person per day and use sun protection. No water is available anywhere on the drive or trails. Carry a plastic bag for all litter. Use the toilets in the visitors center or campground.

## Places to Stay

A small campground (13 sites) almost half a mile past the visitors center is open year-round. There are pit toilets, grills and picnic benches, but no water (you can get water at the visitors center). Camping is free. The campground fills on summer afternoons, after which you are allowed to camp in the pullouts along Hwy 275 leading to the park – no facilities. No camping is allowed beyond the official campground, along the Bridge View Drive or in the backcountry.

## HWY 261 – THE MOKI DUGWAY BACKWAY

Magnificently scenic Hwy 261 leaves Hwy 95 two miles east of the Natural Bridges turnoff and heads south to Hwy 163, about 33 miles away. It passes a number of interesting features, including the Moki Dugway, described here.

### Grand Gulch Primitive Area

About four miles south of Hwy 95 is the Kane Gulch Ranger Station, open from March to November – hours are irregular. This BLM station services the Grand Gulch Primitive Area to the west. Information about this area should be obtained from the visitors center in Monticello.

This area follows the wild Grand Gulch Canyon as it twists its way down to the San Juan River. It is wild and difficult country, with primitive trails and no developed camping. Despite this, the area is quite popular with adventurers seeking remote and beautiful wilderness.

There are hundreds of Anasazi ruins throughout the area – many have been vandalized by pot hunters. Prehistoric Indian sites (indeed, all Indian sites) are protected by law. Native Americans believe many of the sites to be of intrinsic religious significance, and archaeologists base their understanding of the peopling of the Americas on these early dwellings and ceremonial centers. Backcountry travelers should respect the spiritual and historical value of these places.

Unfortunately, people still try to search for and remove artifacts or damage ruins – this is illegal and, recently, the authorities have begun to crack down severely on those who damage Native American sites. Please report damage of archaeological sites to a park ranger.

### Moki Dugway

Less than 30 miles south of Hwy 95 the world falls away. This remains the most memorable driving experience of my first trip to the Southwest, over 20 years ago. The Moki Dugway is a (still unpaved) three-mile section of road that hairpins

down for over 1000 feet. From the top, the views of southern Utah and northern Arizona are among the best in the country. At the top of the Moki Dugway, an unpaved side road to the west leads about five miles to the **Muley Point Overlook**, which gives equally stunning – some say better – views.

### Valley of the Gods

Just below the Moki Dugway, a dirt road to the east heads into the Valley of the Gods. This is a spectacular 16-mile drive through stunning monoliths of sandstone. In good weather, you can do it in a car if you drive carefully. The Valley of the Gods road emerges at Hwy 163 about eight miles northeast of Mexican Hat.

### Goosenecks State Park

Near the southern end of Hwy 261, a four-mile paved road heads west to this state park. Here there are memorable views of the San Juan River, 1100 feet below, meandering in a series of massive curves over six miles as the river flows, but only 1.5 miles as the crow flies. It's a worthwhile side trip.

There are pit toilets and a few picnic tables – you can camp for free. There is no water.

### MEXICAN HAT & MONUMENT VALLEY

The settlement of Mexican Hat has about 40 inhabitants, most of whom work in the handful of hotels, restaurants and trading posts in town. The town was named after a distinctively sombrero-shaped rock that can be seen from Hwy 163 about three miles to the northeast. The whole area around here is scenically and geologically wonderful. The town lies on the north banks of the San Juan River. South of the river is the edge of the Navajo Indian Reservation – the largest in the country.

### Monument Valley

Southwest of Mexican Hat, Hwy 163 enters the Navajo Indian Reservation and Monument Valley. This is one of the most scenic drives in the Southwest, with sand dunes rolling up to a clear blue sky punctuated by

Despite being the background of countless Westerns and car commercials, the towering formations in Monument Valley are still breathtaking. (RR)

sheer red buttes and colossal mesas – you've probably seen the landscape in a TV commercial or a Hollywood Western. Half- and full-day tours of Monument Valley are available for about $30/50.

### Goulding's Trading Post

Opened in 1924, Goulding's Trading Post is two miles west of Hwy 163 just before you cross from Utah into Arizona. The original trading post remains, now converted into an interesting museum of Indian artifacts and movie memorabilia. There is also a modern gift shop selling high-quality Indian crafts, convenience store, and gas station.

Opposite the turnoff to Goulding's, a road heads southeast into Arizona and the Navajo-owned and operated Monument Valley Tribal Park – tours, camping and scenic drives are all available. See the Arizona section for more details.

### Places to Stay & Eat

As usual in this part of the world, rates are much higher from about April to October. *Valle's Trading Post & RV Park* (☎ 683

2226) has showers, coin laundry, and tent and RV sites for about $10 to $12.

*Burches Trading Post* (☎ 683 2221) has showers, coin laundry and RV sites with hookups for about $15. It also runs the *Valley of the Gods Inn* with modest double rooms for about $60. The reasonable cafe and lounge are open all day and serve regional food.

The cheapest motel is *Canyonlands Motel* (☎ 683 2230) with basic doubles for about $40. The *Mexican Hat Lodge* (☎ 683 2222) has doubles in the mid $50s, with the *El Sombrero Restaurant* on the premises. Both these places have only about 10 rooms each.

The *San Juan Inn & Trading Post* (☎ 683 2220, fax 683 2210) is the biggest place with over 30 standard rooms going for about $60 a double. The popular cafe is open from 6 am to 10 pm, serves Navajo, American and Mexican food, and has a lounge.

*Goulding's Lodge* (☎ 727 3231, fax 727 3344) with a pool, restaurant (open to the public from 7 am to 9:30 pm; may close in winter) and coin laundry is located at Goulding's Trading Post. All of the 62 rooms have balconies and outstanding views; rates are about $110 a double from mid-April to mid-October. A mile beyond the lodge is *Monument Valley Campground* (☎ 727 3235) with showers, coin laundry and convenience store. Over 100 sites range from $9 for tents to $20 for full hookups. It is open from mid-March to October. The campground lies in a valley which cuts down on the winds that often blow but also eliminates the views.

## GLEN CANYON NATIONAL RECREATION AREA

The massive Glen Canyon Dam flooded Glen Canyon in the 1960s, forming Lake Powell, most of which lies in Utah. The lake is GCNRA's foremost attraction. However, Glen Canyon dam itself, the main GCNRA Visitor Center, the largest and most developed marina (Wahweap), the biggest town on the lake (Page) and the main boating concessionaire are all in Arizona, so the entire GCNRA is described under the Arizona section.

## BLUFF

The 'Hole-in-the-Rock' pioneers (see Escalante & Around in the chapter on southwestern Utah) finished their arduous journey here, and established San Juan County's first non-Indian settlement in 1880. Some early pioneers' houses are still in use. About 250 people live here now.

The town is surrounded by red-rock scenery, of which the Navajo Twin sandstone pedestals are the most prominent. Driving west of town is spectacular. There are many **Anasazi ruins** hidden away in cliffs and canyons – tours are available or you can look for them yourself. The most famous are at Hovenweep. The best information about other ruins is available at the the museum at Edge of the Cedars State Park, 25 miles north in Blanding.

Bluff, on the north banks of the San Juan River, is near an ideal starting point for running that river. Across the river is the **Navajo Indian Reservation**.

## Information

Official tourist information is available at Blanding and Monticello. Informal visitor information is available from most Bluff businesses. There is a small public library behind the post office on the main road (Hwy 191/163). A brochure or newspaper available at most of Bluff's businesses describes the earliest local buildings. Look for signs around town.

## River Running

Most trips begin at the Sand Island Recreation Area (see below). Boaters must obtain permits from the BLM (☎ 587 2141, 587 2201), PO Box 7, Monticello, 84535 – arrange this as far ahead as possible. A book of specific local interest is *San Juan Canyons: A River Runner's Guide* by D Baars & G Stevenson (Canon Publishers, 1986). Most years around June, a low-key event called the 'Goosenecks Classic' involves a (long) one-day canoe and kayak descent of the river from Bluff to Clay Hills Crossing, over 80 miles away.

Wild River Expeditions (☎ 672 2244, 1 (800) 422 7654, fax 672 2365), PO Box 118, Bluff, 84512, has been guiding river trips for almost four decades. Their motto is 'Educational Adventure with an Emphasis on Pleasure', which sums them up well – trips are fun and you learn about geology, archaeology, Indian history and wildlife. White water is minimal to moderate. They run tours ranging from one-day adventures (about $75) to one week Bluff to Lake Powell river trips with plenty of side explorations (about $900) – six people minimum usually applies.

## Organized Tours

Recapture Lodge (see Places to Stay & Eat) arranges day and overnight hiking, packing or jeep trips into the local canyons to view ruins and search for wildlife (the owners are naturalists). Day trips start around $40 (hiking) or $60 (jeep) with a four-person minimum.

## Places to Stay & Eat

*Sand Island Recreation Area*, 2.5 miles

west on the San Juan River, has pit toilets and six free camping sites with grills and tables but no water. You can see petroglyphs half a mile away. Just follow the signs.

Arriving in town along Hwy 163/191 from the southwest, you pass the following (in order): Mokee Motel, Dairy Cafe, Turquoise Restaurant, Kokopelli Inn, Recapture Lodge, Wild Rivers Expeditions, and the post office. The road then turns north and passes the turnoff to the Sunbonnet Cafe, the Cow Canyon Trading Post & Restaurant, the Twin Rocks Trading Post and the Bluff B&B.

*Turquoise Restaurant & RV Park* (☎ 672 2219) has 12 RV sites with hookups for about $10 (no showers or tent sites). The restaurant serves a small menu of Navajo and American food from 7 am to 9 pm and 8 am to 8 pm on Sunday.

The cheapest place to stay is the *Mokee Motel* (☎ 672 2217) with seven simple rooms. The clean *Kokopelli Inn* (☎ 672 2322, fax 672 2385) has 26 standard rooms for about $40 for a double in summer. It also runs a grocery store next door.

The *Recapture Lodge* (☎ 672 2281), PO Box 309, Bluff, 84512, has a pool, spa, grounds with picnic and play areas, coin laundry, bicycle rental, local tours and slide shows. There are 28 rooms in the $30s and $40s for a double (depending on room size and number of beds) and some group accommodations in the 1890 Pioneer House behind the lodge.

The *Bluff B&B* (☎ 672 2220), PO Box 158, 84512, has two rooms with good views and private baths for $75 a double. Smoking is not allowed. The new *Calabre B&B* (☎ 672 2252), PO Box 85, 84512, has three cheaper rooms.

The Sunbonnet Cafe (☎ 672 2201) is in a historic house and is open 9 am to 9:30 pm, Monday to Saturday. The Dairy Cafe is next to the gas station and caters to highway traffic. The Cow Canyon Trading Post & Restaurant (☎ 672 2208) serves homemade dinners from Thursday to Monday in the eccentric-looking building; the trading post is open daily and sells Indian arts & crafts.

## HOVENWEEP NATIONAL MONUMENT

Hovenweep, meaning 'deserted valley' in the Ute language, is a fairly remote place straddling the Utah/Colorado state line. Six sets of Anasazi (prehistoric Pueblo Indian) ruins are found here – this was once home to a large population before droughts forced them out in the late 1200s.

Established in 1923, Hovenweep soon built up a reputation for being in the middle of nowhere. Rangers told stories of visitors who arrived after spending many hours lost on the poorly signed and roughly surfaced dirt roads leading to the monument. Some visitors were so disheartened by their trip that their first question was not 'What is there to see here?' but 'Where am I and how the hell do I get back to civilization?!' These days, the scenery is certainly desolate – grayer and grimmer than the red-rock country to the west – but there are signs to the monument.

### Information

The ranger station stays open from 8 am to 5 pm daily. Rangers answer questions and sell maps and booklets.

The monument is administered by the Mesa Verde National Park (☎ (303) 529 4461), CO 81330, which has further information.

### Hiking

Three easy to moderate loop hiking trails (each under a mile) leave from near the Ranger Station and pass a number of buildings in the Square Tower area. The trails give both distant and close-up views of the ruins – please stay on the trails and don't climb on the ruins. They are ancient, fragile and easily damaged. It is illegal to move or disturb anything within any prehistoric ruin or within the monument. Brochures describe each site in detail, as well as the plant life along the trails.

The Square Tower Ruins are the best preserved and most impressive. The five other sets of ruins are isolated and difficult to reach – several miles of rough hiking is usually involved. Ask the rangers for directions and advice.

## Places to Stay

The campground, about a mile from the ranger station, is open year round on a first-come, first-served basis. The 31 sites rarely fill except sometimes in summer. There are toilets and picnic facilities. Water is available from April to October only, when there is a $5 fee. Biting insects can be a problem in early summer – bring repellent.

The nearest hotels are over 40 miles away in Blanding and Bluff (or Cortez, Colorado). Limited food and supplies are available in Aneth, 20 miles south, or Hatch Trading Post, 16 miles west.

## Getting There & Away

Most maps still show the roads to Hovenweep as unpaved. In the 1990s both access routes (east of Bluff through Aneth and north, or east of Hwy 191 between Bluff and Blanding, through Hatch Trading Post) are now either paved or may have short gravel stretches suitable to all cars.

UTAH

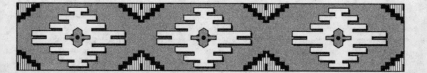

# Facts about Arizona

It's called the Grand Canyon State, and certainly the Grand Canyon is the one thing that schoolchildren from Nova Scotia to New Zealand will mention if quizzed about Arizona. But there's much more than canyons in this state, as visitors quickly discover. Deserts, mountains, forests and rivers provide a range of scenic attractions and outdoor activities. This variety is particularly enjoyed by Arizonans themselves. most of whom live in the hot desert cities of Phoenix and Tucson and in summer enjoy the cool mountains, forests and artificial lakes. Out-of-state visitors, on the other hand, are attracted more to the essentially Southwestern elements of the region, such as the spectacular canyons and mesas, the fascinating deserts and, of course, the Native Americans.

Arizona has the third largest Indian population of the 50 states (after California and Oklahoma) and the two largest Indian reservations in the country (the Navajo and the Tohono O'odham). About 26% of the state is reservation land. Many tribes have retained much of their cultures, languages and traditions, all of which differ from tribe to tribe. Some of their ancient dances and ceremonies are open to the public, but many are not. However, all visitors can experience the Indian cultures in the villages, trading posts and crafts stores that dot the reservations.

Oraibi village on the Hopi Reservation, built in the 12th century, is one of only two places in the country that has been continuously occupied for over 800 years. Visitors can also learn about the ancestors of today's tribes through the fascinating ancient ruins that have been preserved throughout the state.

The southern reaches of the state have close ties to Mexico. Tucson has a wonderful selection of Mexican restaurants that are as good as those in Mexico itself! The Spanish heritage can be discovered in the

## Arizona Trivia

**Statehood:**
  14 February 1912 (48th state)
**Area:**
  114,006 sq miles (sixth largest state)
**Highest Point:**
  Humphrey's Peak (12,663 feet)
**Lowest Point:**
  Colorado River near Mexican border (70 feet)
**Population (1993):**
  3,936,142 (23rd most populous state)
**Nickname:**
  Grand Canyon State (also Copper State)
**State Capital:** Phoenix
**State Motto:** God enriches.
**State Bird:** Cactus wren
**State Mammal:** Ringtail cat
**State Tree:** Blue paloverde
**State Flower:**
  Blossom of saguaro cactus
**State Reptile:**
  Arizona ridge-nosed rattlesnake
**State Fossil:** Petrified wood
**State Gem:** Turquoise
**State Neckware:** Bola tie
**Percentage of population over five years who speak a language other than English at home:** 20.8% (sixth in USA)
**Per capita spending on mental health programs (1987 figures):**
  $19.76 (lowest in USA)
**Suicide rate per 100,000 (1988):**
  19.5 (third highest in USA)

centuries-old missions of southern Arizona established by Padre Kino and in the historic barrios of Tucson where Spanish is as commonly heard as English.

Visitors interested in natural history can spot many species in Arizona found nowhere else in the USA. Southeastern Arizona is the undisputed hummingbird capital of the country, and many other rarities fly in from Mexico, including two species of tropical trogons. The tall, majestic saguaro and organ pipe cacti are found only in parts of southern Arizona and in Mexico. These cacti provide nests and shelter for many desert birds and animals. Arizona is one of three states where the wild pigs called javelinas and the raccoon-like coatis are regularly glimpsed in the wild. The country's only poisonous lizard, the gila monster, lives here, too.

## Recent History

At the end of the Mexican War in 1848, the land north of the Gila River was claimed by the USA and incorporated into the New Mexico Territory, which then included Arizona. The USA soon realized that the best route from the Mississippi River to the burgeoning territory of California lay south of the Gila River, through the Mexican town of Tucson. US diplomat James Gadsden arranged for the USA to purchase the land between the present international border and the Gila River from Mexico. In 1854, the USA annexed the territory, and Americans began to cross the area en route to California. Some travelers noted the potential mineral and agricultural wealth of the region and made the area their home, beginning the copper mining and cattle ranching industries that became mainstays of Arizona's economy.

Many of the settlers were from southern states, and when the American Civil War broke out in 1861, Arizona declared itself a Confederate state. This resulted in the westernmost battle of the Civil War, when a small Confederate force was defeated by Union troops at Picacho Peak in 1862. The Confederate forces killed three Union soldiers before retreating to Tucson and dis-

Employing guerrilla tactics, Geronimo, the great Apache leader, fought off US troops.

persing, aware that they would soon be greatly outnumbered. When Arizona became a separate territory the following year, Tucson was the largest town, but Prescott was chosen as the territorial capital because Tucson was perceived as a bastion of Confederate loyalty. From 1867 to 1877, however, Tucson held the position of territorial capital, after which it was returned to Prescott and finally moved to the Anglo-founded town of Phoenix in 1889, where it has remained. Historians and Hispanics alike attribute this to the anti-Hispanic sentiment then prevalent in US politics.

Meanwhile, the US Army was fighting the Indian wars, protecting settlers and wresting the land from the Indians who had little use for European concepts of land ownership. In 1864 the Navajo were forced to march from their land to the high plains of eastern New Mexico in the infamous 'Long Walk'. For another generation, a small number of Apache warriors under the leadership of Cochise and Geronimo fought far greater numbers of US settlers and soldiers using guerrilla tactics. Finally,

ARIZONA

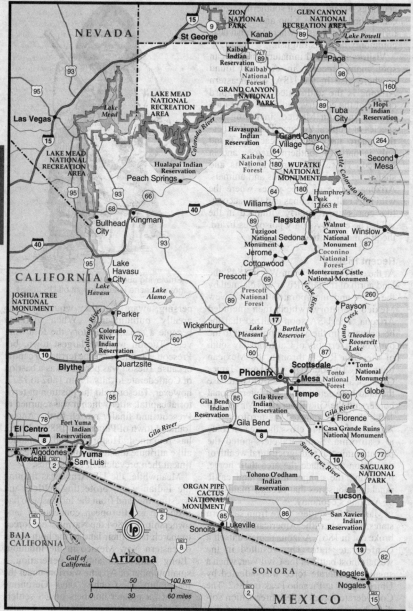

the ever-growing numbers of Americans overwhelmed the dwindling Indian forces, and Geronimo surrendered in 1886, marking the end of the Indian wars.

The railroad had arrived a few years earlier, and people from the East Coast started arriving in larger numbers. Mining towns grew up almost overnight, and they were wild and dangerous places. As the memory of the Indian wars faded and the number of Anglos increased, the territory began to petition for statehood. The federal government in Washington, DC, didn't take these petitions very seriously; Arizona's reputation as a wild and lawless territory of desert led politicians to suspect that statehood would prove a constant financial drain on the federal coffers. This opinion began to change after President Theodore Roosevelt visited Arizona in 1903 and supported the damming of the territory's rivers. The first dam, the Theodore Roosevelt Dam on the Salt River, was finished in 1911, providing year-round water for irrigation and drinking. This finally paved the way to statehood, and Arizona became the 48th state on 14 February 1912.

Over the next few decades, more dams were built and copper mining flourished. Some mines prospered, while other went bust and their accompanying towns dwindled to ghost towns. Irrigation increased crop yields, and cotton and cattle were important products. Tourists also started arriving, especially in the winter, and resorts and guest ranches for the wealthy began to appear in the Phoenix area in the '20s and '30s. Growth was steady but slow until WW II, when the population swelled with an influx of military personnel training for war in the deserts of Africa and other hot regions.

After the war, air conditioning was introduced, and many veterans who had trained in Arizona decided to return and settle in what appeared to be a land of new opportunity. Growth was phenomenal, and the small towns of Phoenix and Tucson quickly grew into the important cities they are today, with all the accompanying big-city problems of air pollution and urban crime. The warm climate has also attracted large

## Kickin' Down Route 66

Fenders! Huge, unwieldy, voluptuous fenders, pulling back the hot desert air just outside Tucumcari, New Mexico. It's 1949, and the occupants of this fat Hudson (looking like something out of a sci-fi serial from the '40s) have pointed it west, down Route 66 to the orange groves of Southern California. Maybe it's Kerouac's Sal Paradise on his endless ramble to find America.

That's the quintessential image that innumerable would-be bohemians have of the country's possibilities. Few highways have entered American history and folklore in the way that Route 66 has. In 1926 the road linking Chicago with Los Angeles became officially designated US Route 66 for its entire 2448-mile length. During the Depression, Route 66 was the main thoroughfare to California for migrant families escaping the dust bowl of the Midwest, some only to be turned back by state immigration at the California/Arizona border. This trip was immortalized in John Steinbeck's *The Grapes of Wrath*, which won the 1940 Pulitzer Prize. In 1938, Route 66 became the first cross-country highway to be completely paved.

After WW II, Americans began buying automobiles in earnest and sought to weld themselves to their vehicles on driving vacations. Along the way Route 66 became the most popular drive of all.

By the end of the 1950s, the growing love affair with the automobile was overwhelming the system of narrow roads linking the country's towns. Construction of the interstate highway system began, crossing the country with fast, limited-access, two-lane highways that bypassed town centers. Most of the parts of Route 66 that ran through northern Arizona and New Mexico were replaced by I-40. By 1984, the modern, efficient, soulless I-40 finally supplanted the last bit of Route 66, and the USA suddenly became a whole lot wider and the possiblities no longer so infinite. Williams was the last town on Route 66 to be bypassed by the freeway.

Many sections of old Route 66 fell into disuse and disrepair, but some sections, such as Bill Williams Ave or Santa Fe Ave in Flagstaff, have been revived for nostalgic and historic reasons. The longest remaining sections of Route 66 are in western Arizona between Seligman and Kingman and between Kingman and Topock.

Today, Route 66 inspires a strange blend of patriotism, nostalgia and melancholy in most Americans. Emblematic of the enduring restless nature of the country, it has become America's Silk Road – exotic.

So exotic, in fact, that the road was the basis for the 1960s *Route 66* TV series and has appeared in infinite films, including *Bagdad Café*, released in 1988. (Bagdad is in California, near Siberia.) In 1946, a song by Bobby Troup reached the airwaves and by the 1990s more than 20 musicians had recorded '(Get Your Kicks on) Route 66', including Perry Como, Bob Dylan, Buckwheat Zydeco, Asleep at the Wheel, Depeche Mode and – the most famous of all – Nat King Cole. ∎

numbers of retirees, some of whom spend winters in Arizona and summers in their northern home states. These 'snow birds' are an important part of the socio-economic fabric of the state.

Problems related to the scarce water resources remain among the foremost issues in Arizona. Dam after dam has been built, and every drop of water has a designated use, but there is not enough for the still-growing state. The simple solution, of course, would be to stop further building and development, but things don't work that way, especially in the USA where big money talks. And so growth continues, and the state desperately searches for water for its burgeoning desert cities.

The most recent water effort is the Central Arizona Project (CAP), which channels water hundreds of miles from the Colorado River to the Phoenix and Tucson areas. When CAP water arrived in Tucson households in 1994, residents shunned it, complaining that it looked bad and tasted worse and that the mineral content of the water was ruining their plumbing. In 1995, use of CAP water was temporarily put on hold, and legal steps commenced to reduce wasteful water use by residents. Paradoxically, the state has the world's highest water fountain and hundreds of golf courses sucking up moisture. The debate over water allocation and use will be among the most important issues the state faces as it moves into the 21st century.

### Economy
Similarly to other Southwestern states, much of Arizona's economy has been directly linked to the scarcity of water and projects to divert water to agricultural areas and population centers. Where farmers and ranchers can tap water reserves, crops such as citrus fruits, hay, cotton, sorghum and cotton thrive, and cattle and dairy products are major farm products. In the less arid central and northern areas, extensive forests, owned primarily by the US government, produce large lumber yields.

Deemed the Copper State (and also the Grand Canyon State), Arizona has bene-

fited heavily from huge copper reserves first noted by miners passing through the area on their way to the 1849 Gold Rush in California. The state has been the USA's largest producer of the mineral since 1907.

In addition to growing high-tech industries such as electronics and aerospace, the state's national and state parks lure millions of visitors each year, as do the Native American reservations, notably the Tohono O'odham near Tucson and the Hopi and Navajo, which extend across most of the northeast corner of the state.

The economies of the reservations, while linked to the state's general economy, have taken a different course than the rest of the state because of the complex history of Indian and US government relations. The Navajo have herded sheep for many generations, eating the meat and weaving the wool into rugs, which in turn constitute a major 'export'. Taking their cue from the Navajo, Anglo ranchers also began to raise sheep, and the Navajo adopted the main Anglo ranch animal – cattle. Limited agriculture on the Navajo and Hopi lands produces corn, squash and peaches. Both tribes have many artisans who produce jewelry, pottery and other arts & crafts. The reservation economies rely on the steady flow of tourist dollars despite some residents who resent the constant influx of visitors.

### Information
**Telephone** The Phoenix metropolitan area and surrounding Maricopa County uses the 602 area code. The rest of Arizona uses the 520 area code, which was implemented on 19 March 1995.

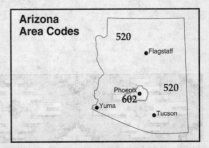

**ARIZONA**

**Driving Laws** You must be at least 18 years old, or at least 16 with parental consent, to obtain a driver's license. Drivers and front-seat passengers are required to wear a safety belt. Children under age four must use child restraints. You must be over 16 to obtain a motorcycle license. Motorcycle helmets are required for the rider and the passenger if under 18. The blood-alcohol concentration over which you are legally considered drunk while driving is 0.10%.

**Drinking Laws** You must be 21 to buy a drink in a store, bar or restaurant. Beer, wine and spirits are sold in grocery stores from 6 am to midnight except Sunday, when sales begin at 10 am. Restaurants must have licenses to serve alcohol; some licenses are limited to beer and wine. The sale of alcohol stops at 1 am and bars close at 2 am. Alcohol is prohibited on most Indian reservations.

**Time** Arizona is the only western state that does not observe daylight-saving time. From late spring to early fall, therefore, Arizona is on Pacific standard time (eight hours behind Greenwich Mean Time), and during the rest of the year the state is on Mountain Standard Time (seven hours behind GMT). The exception is the Navajo Reservation, which, in keeping with those parts of the reservation in Utah and New Mexico, observes daylight-saving time and is on mountain standard time year round.

**Gambling** The gambling laws in the state of Arizona are complicated. Casino gambling is illegal, but you can buy lottery tickets, bet on horse and dog races, and take part in bingo games organized by local church groups. Indian reservations have their own laws, and increasing numbers of tribes have been opening casinos in the past few years. Arizonan state leaders are not happy with this and threaten to take the tribes to federal court if necessary. The feds, however, seem to be leaning in favor of allowing the Indians to do what they want on the reservations, as long as they keep within federal laws. To avoid law suits, the tribes and the state recently agreed to permit casinos under a 10-year 'compact' in which gamblers could compete with machines or each other, but not against a dealer. Hence, games like blackjack (21) are not allowed, but poker, video keno, bingo and slot machines are. Profits are used to improve the reservations by investing in such programs such as education and health.

Currently, 14 casinos operate on reservations throughout the state, attracting mainly non-Indian gamblers. They draw good-size crowds who don't have the time or money to make it to Las Vegas. Only one casino, the Apache Gold Casino on the San Carlos Apache Indian Reservation, serves alcohol. More casinos are likely to open in the future. What happens at the end of the 10-year compact is anybody's guess.

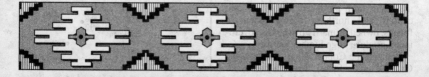

# Phoenix

With over a million inhabitants, Phoenix is the largest city in the Southwest and the eighth largest in the USA. It was surrounded by other towns before WW II, but rapid growth in the latter half of the 20th century has linked these into one huge, still-growing metropolitan area of over 2,300,000 people. Major towns adjoining Phoenix include Tempe (pronounced TEMpee, with 142,000 inhabitants), Scottsdale (population 130,000), Mesa (population 290,000), Sun City (population 54,000), Glendale (population 150,000), Chandler (population 90,000), and over a dozen other communities. Together, they cover well over 1000 sq miles, an area which is locally called 'The Valley of the Sun' or just 'the valley'. Sunny it certainly is; with over 300 days of sunshine a year, it's searingly hot in summer and pleasantly warm in winter.

The climate attracts winter visitors (locally called 'snow birds') who leave their colder northern states to spend several months soaking up the rays. Fall, winter and spring are the main cultural and tourist seasons, when places charge the highest prices. Visitors arriving during summer vacation periods will find the lowest prices in the hotels and resorts, but also temperatures above 100°F for weeks on end, commonly reaching well over 110°F in midsummer. Clothing is appropriately casual – you can wear shorts almost anywhere in summer.

## HISTORY

As early as 300 BC, the dry desert soil began yielding crops for the Hohokam people, who spent centuries developing a complex system of irrigation canals, only to mysteriously abandon them around 1450 AD. Remnants of the canals can be seen in the Pueblo Grande Museum.

Later, small groups of Pima and Maricopa Indians eked out an existence along the Gila and Salt Rivers, but there were no more permanent settlements until the mid-1860s when the US Army built Fort McDowell northeast of Phoenix. This prompted former soldier and prospector Jack Swilling to reopen Hohokam canals to produce crops for the garrison and led to the establishment of a town in 1870. Darrel Duppa, a British settler, suggested that the town had risen from the ashes of the Hohokam culture like the fabled phoenix, and the name stuck. Meanwhile, Charles Trumbull Hayden established a ferry crossing and trading post on the Salt River, southeast of Phoenix. Duppa, again plutting his knowledge of the classics to work, commented that the location reminded him of the Vale of Tempe near Mount Olympus in Greece, and, once again, his suggestion stuck.

Phoenix began to establish itself as an agricultural and transportation center. The railway arrived from the Pacific in 1887, and by the time Phoenix became the territorial capital in 1889, it had about 3000 inhabitants. Settlers built many Victorian houses during the 1890s that today stand as Phoenix's oldest historical buildings. Tempe, too, was growing, and in 1886 the Arizona Normal School was established here, later to become Arizona State University (ASU). Other villages began to grow; Mesa was founded by Mormon settlers in 1878, and Scottsdale followed a decade later, named after army chaplain Winfield Scott, one of its first settlers.

The lack of water remained a major stumbling block to further growth until 1911, when construction workers finished building the Roosevelt Dam on the Salt River, the first of many large dams to be built in the state. The stage was set for growth, and grow Phoenix did.

In 1926, Phoenix's railway link became transcontinental, enabling people from the east to pour into the state in increasing numbers. Many came for recreation – to

ARIZONA

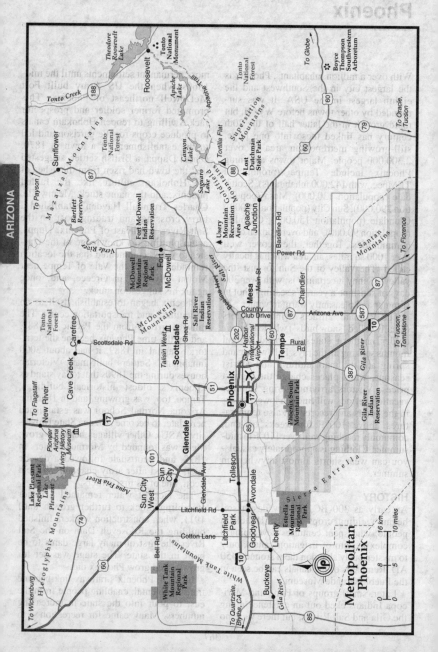

To Payson

Theodore Roosevelt Lake

Tonto National Monument

Roosevelt

188

Tonto Creek

Apache Lake

Apache Trail

Apache Trail

Sunflower

87

Tonto National Forest

Canyon Lake

Tortilla Flat

Saguaro Lake

Lost Dutchman State Park

Superstition Mountains

Mazatzal Mountains

Bartlett Reservoir

Fort McDowell Indian Reservation

Usery Mountain Recreation Area

Goldfield Mountains

88

To Globe

Tonto National Forest

60

Boyce Thompson Southwestern Arboretum

To Oracle, Tucson

79

60

Apache Junction

Baseline Rd

Power Rd

Santan Mountains

To Florence

60

Verde River

McDowell Mountain Regional Park

Fort McDowell

McDowell Mountains

Salt River Indian Reservation

Beeline Hwy

Mesa

Main St

Chandler

Arizona Ave

87

587

10

To Tucson, Tombstone

Gila River

Santan Mountains

To Flagstaff

Tonto National Forest

Carefree

Cave Creek

Scottsdale Rd

Talisin West

Shea Rd

Scottsdale

Salt River

202

Country Club Drive

60

Sky Harbor International Airport

Tempe

Rural Rd

387

Gila River

Gila River Indian Reservation

New River

17

51

Phoenix

17

85

Phoenix South Mountain Park

Glendale

101

Sun City West

Sun City

Glendale Ave

Tolleson

Avondale

Sierra Estrella

Estrella Mountain Regional Park

Liberty

Pioneer Arizona Living History Museum

Lake Pleasant Regional Park

Lake Pleasant

Agua Fria River

Hieroglyphic Mountains

74

To Wickenburg

White Tank Mountains

White Tank Mountain Regional Park

Litchfield Rd

Litchfield Park

Cotton Lane

Goodyear

Bell Rd

60

Buckeye

Gila River

10

85

To Quartzsite, Blythe, CA

**Metropolitan Phoenix**

16 km.

10 miles

0     8     16

0     5     10

stay in dude ranches and be cowboys for a few weeks, or to relax at the luxurious Arizona Biltmore resort, opened in 1929 and still one of the finest in the West. Others came for their health; the dry desert air was said to cure various respiratory ailments. Many of these visitors stayed, including Dwight and Maie Heard, who arrived in 1895 to cure Dwight's lung complaints. He became a leading businessman and editor, and with his wife founded Phoenix's most interesting museum, the Heard.

The combination of recreation and culture has been the valley's main attraction ever since. Today's visitors come to golf, ride, swim and shop or simply relax. Many spend a day or two visiting the area's several fine museums, and during their stay, take in a world premiere at the theater or watch a championship basketball game, in the evening dining in one of the many casual restaurants that serve some of Arizona's most acclaimed meals. Relaxed sophistication is a hallmark of Phoenix, where a cowboy hat and jeans are rarely out of place and where ties are seldom required.

The early history of the area is not immediately evident to most visitors, who see a sprawling modern city. The two major causes of this pervasive modernity are the advent of air conditioning after WW II and the authorization of the Central Arizona Project in 1968, which allowed the diversion of Colorado River water to Phoenix. Between WW II and today, the valley's population has grown fivefold; in the 1980s over 100,000 new residents arrived each year, making this the country's fastest growing area. Modern buildings have replaced most but not all of the old ones. The valley's economy continues to be, as always, driven by politics, the surrounding agriculture, transportation and tourism, but the recent growth has brought industry and manufacturing, especially of electrical and computer components, to the economic foreground.

## ORIENTATION

At about 1100 feet above sea level, the valley is ringed by mountains that range from 2500 feet in elevation to over 7000. Because Phoenix grew to engulf many small towns, the city has several historical centers, of which Phoenix, Scottsdale, Tempe and Mesa are the most interesting. Most of of this chapter is devoted to these towns.

Phoenix is the largest town and houses the state capitol, the oldest buildings and several important museums. Southeast of Phoenix lies Tempe, home of ASU and an active student population. East of Tempe, Mesa is the second largest town in the valley and is home to several museums and Arizona's main Mormon Temple. Scottsdale, northeast of Phoenix and Tempe, is known for both its Western downtown area, now full of galleries, boutiques and crafts stores, and its many upscale resorts.

Other towns, including Chandler to the southeast and Glendale and Peoria to the northwest, are thriving residential and manufacturing communities off the travelers' normal circuit. Sun City and Sun City West, in the northwest of the valley, are among the largest retirement communities in the country, with little industry or tourism but numerous quiet streets and golf courses for the dynamic older residents. Paradise Valley, nestled between the arms of Phoenix and Scottsdale, is the valley's most exclusive residential neighborhood, and Apache Junction, at the far east end of metropolitan Phoenix, is the gateway to the wild Superstition Mountains and the Apache Trail leading into east-central Arizona.

Because the valley's roads run north-south or east-west, to get from one point to another you often have to take two sides of a triangle; this, combined with large distances and slow traffic, can make getting around a challenge. Grand Ave (Hwy 60), which heads diagonally northwest from Phoenix through Glendale and Peoria to Sun City, is an exception that is helpful to residents but of limited use to the traveler. Allow extra time for driving and be prepared to be patient if you use the bus.

Central Ave, running north-south in Phoenix, divides west addresses from east addresses; west of Central Ave, avenues are north-south bound, while east of Central

Ave streets run north-south. Washington St, running west-east in Phoenix, divides north addresses from south addresses; thus 4100 N 16th St would be 16 blocks east of Central Ave and 41 blocks north of Washington St (this is only an approximation – blocks don't always correspond exactly to 100-address increments). This numbering system continues into Scottsdale and Glendale.

Tempe and Mesa each have their own numbering systems, which means you can drive from Phoenix's 4800 E Southern Ave to Tempe's 2800 W Southern Ave just by crossing the city limits. In Tempe, Mill Ave, running north-south, divides west addresses from east addresses, while the east-west flowing Salt River divides north from south addresses. In Mesa, north-south Center St divides west from east, and west-east Main St divides north from south. Other valley towns have similar systems.

To the east, Mesa's Main St becomes the Apache Trail in Apache Junction heading northeast along Hwy 88 into the Tonto National Forest and past the Roosevelt Dam. This unpaved and dramatic road is popular with Phoenicians and is described in the East-Central Arizona chapter.

Major freeways leaving Phoenix include I-17 North (Black Canyon Hwy; this has many motels along it), I-10 West (the Papago Freeway), I-10 South (the Maricopa Freeway) and Hwy 60 East (the Superstition Freeway).

## INFORMATION
### Visitors Centers
The Valley of the Sun Convention & Visitors Bureau (☎ 254 6500, 252 5588, fax 253 4415), One Arizona Center, 400 E Van Buren St, Suite 600, 85004-2290, is open Monday to Friday from 8 am to 5 pm, and also has branches at the airport and at the Hyatt Regency Hotel. This is the valley's most complete source of tourist information; ask for the free *Official Visitors Guide*.

Individual towns each offer their own services. The Scottsdale Chamber of Commerce (☎ 945 8481), 7343 E Scottsdale Mall, is open Monday to Friday 8:30 am to

5 pm, Saturday 10 am to 5 pm and Sunday 11 am to 5 pm. The Tempe Convention and Visitors Bureau (☎ 894 8158), 51 W 3rd St, Suite 105, and the Tempe Chamber of Commerce (☎ 967 7891), 60 E 5th St, Suite 3, are open Monday to Friday from 8:30 am to 5 pm, and the Mesa Chamber of Commerce (☎ 969 1307), 120 N Center St, is open Monday to Friday from 8 am to 5 pm. Other valley towns have chambers of commerce; call the main visitors bureau for details.

State-wide information is available at the Arizona Office of Tourism (☎ 542 8687, fax 542 4068), 1100 W Washington St, 85007, and the Arizona State Parks Department (☎ 542 4174), at 1300 W Washington St. The Arizona Game & Fish Department (☎ 942 3000) is at 2222 W Greenway Rd. The Tonto National Forest Headquarters (☎ 225 5200) is at 2324 E McDowell Rd, PO Box 5348, 85010. The nearest ranger station (☎ 379 6446) is at 26 N MacDonald St, Mesa, 85201. The BLM has an office at 2015 W Deer Valley Rd (☎ 780 8090) and at 3707 N 7th St (☎ 650 0200); these are open Monday to Friday from about 8 am to 5 pm. The Office of Environmental Programs (☎ 256 5669) can tell you the location of the nearest drop-off recycling center.

### Money
Foreign exchange is available at the airport or some bank branches; call the following for addresses and hours of the nearest branch: Bank of America (☎ 594 2891), Bank One (☎ 221 2900), First Interstate Bank (☎ 528 6000) or Norwest Bank (☎ 263 7226).

### Post & Telecommunications
The main post office (☎ 225 3158) is at 4949 E Van Buren St, and the main downtown post office (☎ 407 2028) is at 522 N Central Ave; for postal information call 407 2049 or 231 0892.

Metropolitan Phoenix uses the (602) **area code** before all phone numbers; the rest of Arizona uses (520). Telephone numbers in this chapter all take the (602) area code.

## Books & Periodicals

The main library (☎ 262 4636) is at 12 E McDowell Rd, and there are many others throughout the city. The local newspapers are the morning *Arizona Republic* and afternoon *Phoenix Gazette*. Good bookstores include the independent Houle Books (☎ 991 6607) in the Borgata Center, the huge Barnes & Noble (☎ 678 0088) in the Metrocenter, and, if you're after used books, Bookman's (☎ 835 0505), 1056 S Country Club Drive in Mesa.

## Medical Services

The Samaritan Health Service (☎ 230 2273) operates four valley hospitals and provides 24-hour doctor referral, but there are also many other hospitals and clinics; in Phoenix, try The Good Samaritan (☎ 239 2000) at 1111 E McDowell Rd or the Maryvale Samaritan in West Phoenix (☎ 848 5000), 5102 W Cambell Ave.

In Tempe, there's Tempe St Lukes (☎ 968 9411) at 1500 S Mill Ave. In Mesa, try the Desert Samaritan Mesa (☎ 835 3000), 1400 S Dobson St; Mesa General (☎ 969 9111), 515 N Mesa Drive; Mesa Lutheran (☎ 834 1211), 525 W Brown Rd; and Valley Lutheran (☎ 981 2000), 6644 E Baywood Ave.

Scottsdale has the Scottsdale Memorial Hospital (☎ 481 4000), 7400 E Osborn Rd, the Scottsdale Memorial Hospital North (☎ 860 3000), 10450 N 92nd St; and the Mayo Clinic (☎ 301 8000), 13400 E Shea Blvd.

## Emergency

The Phoenix police (☎ 262 7626, or 911 in emergencies) are at 620 W Washington St.

## Dangers & Annoyances

Phoenix is no more dangerous than any other large city in the USA or Europe. You are unlikely to run into gang or drug-related activities in the main tourist areas, but use the same precautions as you would in any major city.

## CENTRAL PHOENIX

### Heard Museum

One of the best museums to learn about Southwest Indian tribes' history, life, arts and culture, the Heard Museum emphasizes quality rather than quantity. Certainly, there are thousands of exhibits, but these are well displayed in a relatively small space, making a visit here much more relaxing than the torturous schleps of many major museums. The kachina-doll room is outstanding, as are the audiovisual displays, occasional live demonstrations and the superb gift shop. If you are at all interested in Native American history and culture, this museum should be at the top of your list.

The museum (☎ 252 8840), 22 E Monte Vista Rd, is open Monday to Saturday from 10 am to 5 pm (staying open to 9 pm on Wednesday) and Sunday from noon to 5 pm. Admission is $5; those over 65 pay $4, while 13- to 18-year-olds pay $3, four- to 12-year-olds pay $2 and Native Americans are admitted for free. You can take a free guided tour or rent a 45-minute audio-tape tour for $2.

### Phoenix Art Museum

Galleries show works from around the world produced between the 14th and 20th centuries; don't miss the collection of clothing from the last two centuries, and be sure to check out the many fine changing exhibitions.

The art museum (☎ 257 1880 or 257 1222 for a 24-hour recorded message) is at 1625 N Central Ave, and hours are the same as at the Heard (the two are proximate and make a good combination outing). Take a guided tour at 2 pm Tuesday through Sunday or at 6 pm on Wednesday (summer hours vary), or sit in on the half-hour talks given twice a day. Admission is $4, or $3 for those over 65 and $1.50 for children over five and full-time students. Admission is free to all on Wednesday from 5 to 9 pm.

### Arizona State Capitol Museum

The old capitol building was replaced with a new one that now houses the state's

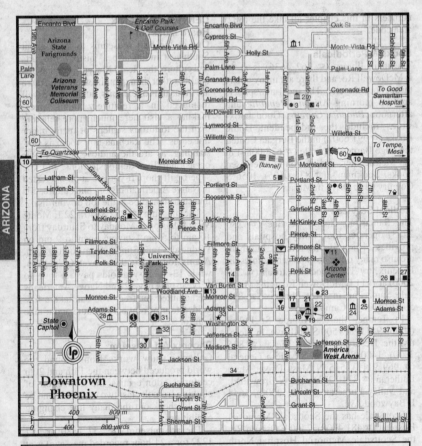

political offices. The old one is a museum of Arizona history displaying documents and exhibits from late-territorial and early-state days. The capitol (☎ 542 4675), 1700 W Washington St, is open Monday to Friday from 8 am to 5 pm. Guided tours are offered at 10 am and 2 pm. Admission is free.

### Arizona Mining & Mineral Museum
Apart from the rock and mining-history exhibits, the museum has a Rose Mofford room displaying memorabilia of the state's first woman governor. This free museum (☎ 255 3791), 1502 W Washington St, is open Monday to Friday from 8 am to 5 pm and Saturday from 1 to 5 pm.

### Arizona Hall of Fame
This free museum (☎ 255 2110), housed in the 1908 Carnegie Library building at 1101 W Washington St, presents changing exhibits on people who have contributed to Arizona's history in memorable and not-so-memorable ways. Hours are 8 am to 5 pm Monday to Friday.

### Heritage Square
Eight late-19th- and early-20th-century houses are preserved in Heritage Square (☎ 262 5029), the block southeast of 6th and Monroe St. This is about as historical as it gets in Phoenix. Try to ignore the surrounding skyscrapers and imagine thudding hooves and squeaking stagecoach wheels creating clouds of dust outside the buildings.

The square is open Tuesday to Saturday from 10 am to 4 pm and Sunday from noon to 4 pm, but it has shorter summer hours. Admission is free, but to tour the 1895 two-story restored **Rosson House**, the most splendid in the square, you'll have to pay a fee. Tours are offered every 30 minutes from 10 am to 3:30 pm Wednesday to Saturday and noon to 3:30 pm on Sunday; shorter hours are in effect in August. Costs are $3, or $2 for people over 62 years old, and $1 for six- to 13-year-olds. Also in the square, the **Arizona Doll & Toy Museum** (☎ 253 9337) offers free admission; other buildings contain places to eat and arts & crafts shops.

### Phoenix Museum of History
Displays here range from 2000-year-old archaeological artifacts to an exhibit about the sinking of the USS Arizona at Pearl Harbor in 1941. The museum (☎ 253 2734) recently moved to new quarters at 614 E Adams St on Heritage Square. Currently, the museum is free and open Wednesday through Sunday from 11 am to 4 pm; call for updates about the move.

### Arizona Science Center
With a large number of interactive exhibits, this museum (☎ 256 9388), 147 E Adams St, encourages the visitor to explore bubbles, weather, physics, biology and more. The museum is open Monday to Saturday from 9 am to 5 pm, Sundays and holidays from noon to 5 pm, and is closed New Year's Day, Thanksgiving and Christmas Day. Admission is $4.50, discounted to $3.50 for people over 65 and four-to 12-year-olds. Formerly the Arizona Museum of Science & Technology, the museum is scheduled to move to a new building at 600 E Washington St near the new Museum of History sometime in the near future.

### OUTER PHOENIX
### Desert Botanical Garden
This 145-acre garden in Papago Park exhibits thousands of species of arid-land plants from Arizona and around the world. The flowering season of March to May is the busiest and most colorful time to visit, but any month will provide you with insights into how plants survive in the desert. The garden (☎ 941 1225), 1201 N Galvin Parkway, has a gift shop and a cafe, and offers occasional tours and events; it is open daily May through September from 7 am to sunset, in other months from 8 am to sunset, and is closed Christmas Day. Admission is $6, or $5 for those over 60 and $1 for five- to 12-year-olds.

The surrounding **Papago Park** has picnic areas, jogging, biking and equestrian trails, a city golf course and a children's fishing pond, and also houses the Phoenix Zoo.

## Especially for Kids

Places like the zoo, the wildlife park, the Museum of Science & Technology, the Hall of Flame and Rawhide will interest the whole family, but the following are especially for kids.

Art exhibits and hands-on art workshops are aimed at elementary school children at the **Arizona Museum for Youth** (☎ 644 2467), 35 N Robson St in Mesa. Exhibitions and workshops change every few months, so call ahead for details. During the summer, the museum is open Tuesday to Friday from 9 am to 5 pm, Saturday from 10 am to 5 pm and Sunday from 1 to 5 pm; during the rest of the year, it's open Tuesday to Friday and also Sunday from 1 to 5 pm, and Saturday from 10 am to 5 pm. Admission is $2 for ages three and up. Preregistration for workshops is suggested.

Kids crawl, climb, swing and slide on the giant indoor jungle gym at the **Discovery Zone**, at 13615 N 35th Ave (☎ 993 2805), and 12651 N 48th St, Phoenix (☎ 494 7733), or 1352 W Southern Ave in Mesa (☎ 834 6776). Hours are 10 am to 9 pm, and admission is $3 for one- and two-year-olds and $5 for three- to 12-year-olds. Parents and older siblings get in for free – some of the old folks in there have just as much fun crawling around after their three-year-olds as the kids do. Wear socks and leave your shoes at the door.

Cool off in summer at **Waterworld** (☎ 581 1947), 4243 W Pinnacle Peak Rd in Phoenix; **Big Surf** (☎ 947 7873), 1500 N McClintock Drive in Tempe; and **Golfland/Sunsplash** (☎ 834 8318), 155 W Hampton Ave in Mesa. All offer acres of swimming pools, water slides and wave-making machines; Golfland also has tube floats, bumper boats, miniature golf and go-carts. They are open weekdays and weekend evenings from Memorial Day to Labor Day, and admission is about $12.50 or $10.25 for four- to 11-year-olds.

Local 'Family Fun Parks' offering miniature golf, video games, batting cages, bumper boats, go-carts, volleyball and other activities year round include **Crackerjax** (☎ 998 2800), 16001 N Scottsdale Rd, open Monday to Friday from noon to midnight, Saturday from 10 am to midnight, and Sunday from 10 am to 10 pm; **Fiddlesticks** (☎ 961 0800), 1155 W Elliot Rd in Tempe, open Sunday to Thursday from 9 am to 11 pm and Friday and Saturday from 9 am to 1 am; and **Outer Limits** (☎ 951 6060), 8800 E Indian Bend Rd in Scottsdale, open Sunday to Thursday from 10 am to 10 pm, and Friday and Saturday from 10 to midnight. ■

### Phoenix Zoo

The zoo (☎ 273 1341, 273 7771), 455 N Galvin Parkway, houses a wide variety of animals, including some rare ones, in several distinct and natural-looking environments. There is a children's petting zoo, walk-in aviary and food facilities. The zoo is open May to Labor Day from 7 am to 4 pm and during the rest of the year from 9 am to 5 pm; it is closed on Christmas. Admission is $6, or $5 for those over 60 and $3 for four- to 12-year-olds. Narrated safari train tours cost $1.50.

### Hall of Flame

Opposite Papago Park at 6101 E Van Buren St, the Hall of Flame (☎ 275 3473) exhibits over 100 fire-fighting machines from 1725 onwards, as well as related paraphernalia. The hall is open Monday to Saturday from 9 am to 5 pm, Sunday from noon to 5 pm, and is closed New Year's Day, Thanksgiving and Christmas. Admission is $5, discounted to $4 for those over 62 and to $2 for six- to 17-year-olds. Tours are given at 2 pm daily.

### Pueblo Grande Museum

Pueblo Grande is a Hohokam village that has been partially excavated and then reburied for its protection. Parts of the excavation remain exposed for the visitor, and a nice little on-site museum (☎ 495 0900, 495 0901), 4619 E Washington St, explains what is known of the canal-building Hohokam culture. Admission is 50¢ for those over five years old, and hours are 9 am to 4:45 pm Monday to Saturday, and 1 to 4:45 pm on Sunday; the museum is closed on major holidays.

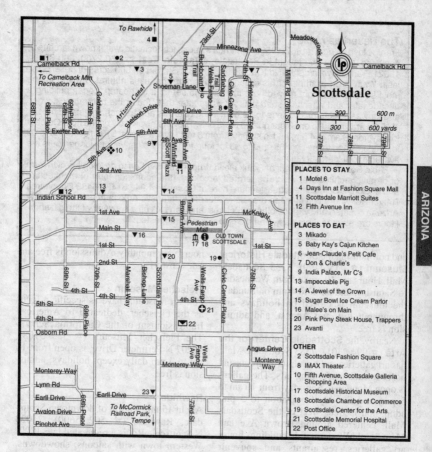

**PLACES TO STAY**
1 Motel 6
4 Days Inn at Fashion Square Mall
11 Scottsdale Marriott Suites
12 Fifth Avenue Inn

**PLACES TO EAT**
3 Mikado
5 Baby Kay's Cajun Kitchen
6 Jean-Claude's Petit Cafe
7 Don & Charlie's
9 India Palace, Mr C's
13 Impeccable Pig
14 A Jewel of the Crown
15 Sugar Bowl Ice Cream Parlor
16 Malee's on Main
20 Pink Pony Steak House, Trappers
23 Avanti

**OTHER**
2 Scottsdale Fashion Square
8 IMAX Theater
10 Fifth Avenue, Scottsdale Galleria Shopping Area
17 Scottsdale Historical Museum
18 Scottsdale Chamber of Commerce
19 Scottsdale Center for the Arts
21 Scottsdale Memorial Hospital
22 Post Office

## Mystery Castle

This 18-room fantasy was built between 1927 and 1945 by the reclusive Boyce Luther Gulley for his daughter, Mary Lou, who now gives tours of the oddly furnished property. Mystery Castle (☎ 268 1581), 800 E Mineral Rd, is open October to June, Tuesday to Sunday from 11 am to 4 pm; admission is $3, discounted to $2 for those over and to $1 for five- to 14-year-olds.

## Plotkin Judaica Museum

This Jewish heritage museum (☎ 264 4428), 3310 N 10th Ave, exhibits artifacts from America, Israel and the Middle East. It is open Tuesday to Thursday from 10 am to 3 pm, and Sunday from noon to 3 pm; the museum is closed on holidays, and admission is free.

## SCOTTSDALE
### Old Town

Half a dozen blocks near the chamber of commerce constitute 'Old Town', with some early-20th-century buildings and some more recent buildings styled to look like those of the Old West. One of the oldest is the 'Little Red School House', built in 1909

## The Desert as Muse

Frank Lloyd Wright (1867-1959), America's most iconoclastic well-known architect, designed, lived in and taught in Scottsdale at **Taliesin West** (☎ 860 2700, 860 8810), 12621 Frank Lloyd Wright Blvd (Cactus Rd at 108th St). Set on 600 acres of desert, Taliesin West is an example of his organic architecture that uses natural forms to shape most structures. Wright moved here in 1927 and set up a tent camp, began building a decade later and wasn't finished until 20 years after that. Today, the natural rock, wood and canvas structures continue to be both living quarters and a teaching establishment.

Visits are limited to one-hour guided tours only. They are given daily on the hour October to May from 9 am to 4 pm, and in summer from 8 to 11 am, and cost $10, discounted to $8 for students and those over 65, and to $3 for four- to 12-year-olds. Various longer tours are available; call for reservations.

Paolo Soleri was a student of Frank Lloyd Wright who went on to develop his own form of organic architecture, which he termed 'arcology' (the combined form of architecture and ecology). Soleri's headquarters are here at **Cosanti** (☎ 948 6145), 6433 Doubletree Ranch Rd, where you can see a scale model of his futuristic Arcosanti (see the Central Arizona chapter) and various other structures, and can pick up a souvenir at the gift shop. Hours are 9 am to 5 pm daily, and a $1 donation is suggested. ■

and now housing the **Scottsdale Historical Museum** (☎ 945 4499), 7333 Scottsdale Mall. Hours are 10 am to 5 pm Wednesday to Saturday, and noon to 4 pm on Sunday; the museum is closed on holidays and throughout July and August, and admission is free.

Nearby, the **Scottsdale Center for the Arts** (☎ 994 2301), 7383 Scottsdale Mall, has art galleries and a sculpture garden, and hosts various performing arts. The gallery is open Monday to Saturday from 10 am to 5 pm, and Sunday from noon to 5 pm; admission is free. West of the Scottsdale Mall, centered around Brown Ave and Main St, old Western-style buildings house art galleries, restaurants and souvenir shops. The chamber of commerce offers brochures describing this popular area.

### McCormick Railroad Park

If you're a train fan, don't miss the model steam trains at this park. You can ride the 5:12-scale trains, or just examine the smaller models. The park also has some full-size stock and a playground with a 1929 carousel, as well as two turn-of-the-century railroad depots now selling snacks and railroad memorabilia.

The Railroad Park (☎ 994 2312), 7301 E Indian Bend Rd, is open daily except Thanksgiving and Christmas Day, and hours vary monthly. Admission is free and rides cost $1.

### Fleischer Museum

Few art museums have as specific a focus as the Fleischer, dedicated to American Impressionism of the California School. The Fleischer Museum (☎ 585 3108), 17207 N Perimeter Drive, is open from 10 am to 4 pm daily except holidays; admission is free.

### Rawhide

About 15 miles north of downtown Scottsdale, Rawhide (☎ 502 5600), 23023 N Scottsdale Rd, is a re-created late-1800s Western town with saloons, showdowns, stagecoaches and all that stuff. Popular with tourists and fun for kids, it's open from 5 to 10 pm daily year round; October to May it is also open on Friday, Saturday and Sunday from 11 am to 10 pm. Hours may be extended for various holidays and festivals. Admission is $2, discounted to $1 for three- to 12-year-olds. Many re-enactments are free, but attractions such as the stagecoach, burro or train rides, the Indian village (with dance performances) and the children's petting zoo, charge an extra $2 to $3. A steak house is open from 5 pm (Rawhide admission is refunded if you chow down here).

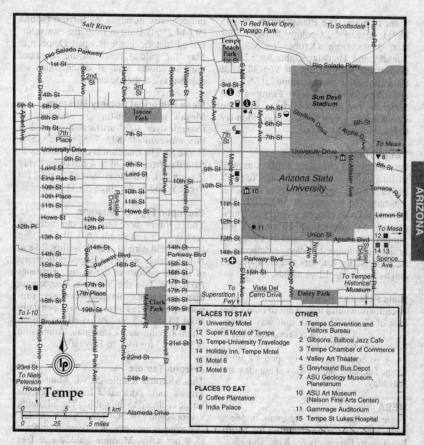

**PLACES TO STAY**
9  University Motel
12 Super 8 Motel of Tempe
13 Tempe-University Travelodge
14 Holiday Inn, Tempe Motel
16 Motel 6
17 Motel 6

**PLACES TO EAT**
6  Coffee Plantation
8  India Palace

**OTHER**
1  Tempe Convention and Visitors Bureau
2  Gibsons, Balboa Jazz Cafe
3  Tempe Chamber of Commerce
4  Valley Art Theater
5  Greyhound Bus Depot
7  ASU Geology Museum, Planetarium
10 ASU Art Museum (Nelson Fine Arts Center)
11 Gammage Auditorium
15 Tempe St Lukes Hospital

ARIZONA

## TEMPE

### Arizona State University

With over 43,000 students, this is the largest college in the Southwest and has several sites of interest, as well as sporting and cultural events year round. General information (☎ 965 9011) and a 24-hour recorded calendar of campus events (☎ 965 2278) will help orient you.

The **ASU Art Museum** (☎ 965 2787), headquartered in the architecturally acclaimed Nelson Fine Arts Center at 10th St and Mill Ave, showcases a varied collection of European and American art along with changing exhibits; the museum is open Wednesday to Saturday from 10 am to 5 pm, Sunday from 1 to 5 pm and Tuesday from 10 am to 9 pm. For more art and an experimental gallery exhibiting the work of emerging artists, visit the Matthews Center branch of the museum, on campus about a quarter mile northeast of the Nelson Center. Hours at the Matthews Center are from 10 am to 5 pm Tuesday to Saturday. Admission is free to both centers.

The interesting and free **ASU Geology Museum** (☎ 965 7065), about 250 yards west of McAllister and University Drive, exhibiting dinosaur bones, rocks, minerals and gems, is open Monday to Friday from

9 am to noon. The **Planetarium** (☎ 965 6891), next to the Geology Museum, has star shows from October to May on Tuesday and Thursday nights for $2. The **Gammage Auditorium** (☎ 965 3434) at the southwest corner of campus at Mill Ave and Apache Blvd was Frank Lloyd Wright's last major building; tour the inside between October and May, Monday to Friday from 1 to 4 pm.

### Tempe Historical Museum

Permanent and changing displays as well as interactive exhibits showcase Tempe's prehistory and modern history at this small museum. The museum (☎ 350 5100), 809 E Southern Ave, is open Monday to Thursday and Saturdays from 10 am to 5 pm, Sunday from to 5 pm, and is closed on Fridays and major holidays. Admission is $2.50, or $2 for students and those over 65 and $1 for six- to 12-year-olds.

### Niels Petersen House

Architecture buffs may want to take a free tour of this 1892 house that was remodeled in the 1930s and retains elements of both periods. The house (☎ 350 5151), 1414 W Southern Ave, is open 10 am to 2 pm, Tuesday, Wednesday, Thursday and Saturday.

### MESA

There are quite a few museums in Mesa, including the **Arizona Museum for Youth**, listed under Especially for Kids, above.

### Mesa Southwest Museum

Animated dinosaurs, dioramas of ancient Indians, an eight-cell territorial jail, gold panning near the Dutchman's Mine and changing art shows are just a few of the many displays and interactive exhibits at this museum with a Southwestern theme. The museum (☎ 644 2230), 53 N MacDonald St, is open Tuesday to Saturday from 10 am to 5 pm and Sunday from 1 to 5 pm, and is closed Mondays and most holidays. Admission is $4, or $3.50 for students and those over 55, and $2 for three- to 12-year-olds.

Two blocks away at 160 N Center St, the museum also manages the **Sirrine House** (☎ 644 2760). Built in 1896, the now refurbished historic home is open October to May for guided tours during weekend museum hours and at other times on request; ask at the museum.

### Mesa Historical Society Museum

Mesa's pioneer history is remembered through over 4000 artifacts displayed at this museum (☎ 835 7358) at 2345 N Horne St. The museum is open Monday to Saturday from 10 am to 4 pm (hours vary in summer), and admission is $3, or $2 for over 65s and $1 for three- to 11-year-olds.

### Champlin Fighter Museum

The fighters here are of the airborne variety – this museum (☎ 830 4540), in Falcon Field Airport at E McKellips Rd and N 48th St, has one of the largest collections of fighter aircraft in the world. Airplanes from WW I to the Vietnam War are on display, and are explained in extensive supporting exhibits. The museum is open daily from 10 am to 5 pm, and is closed Easter, Thanksgiving and Christmas. Admission is $6, or $3 for five- to 14-year-olds.

### Arizona Temple

This Mormon temple, 525 E Main St, is Mesa's most noticeable building, but the inside is closed to the public. The adjoining visitors center (☎ 964 7164) and surrounding grounds are open, at no cost, from 9 am to 9 pm daily. Mormon guides give free tours of the grounds and visitor center that explain the basic beliefs of the church.

### SUBURBAN PHOENIX
### Pioneer Arizona Living History Museum

About 25 authentic territorial buildings (carefully brought here from elsewhere) form a complete village inhabited by guides/interpreters in period dress at the Living History Museum. Daily performances in a turn-of-the-century opera house and various other reenactments present historically accurate depictions of pioneering life. The museum (☎ 993 0212) is almost 30

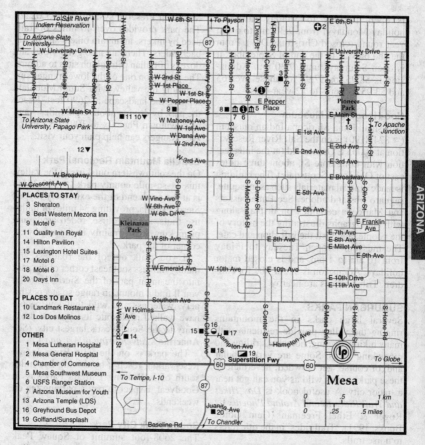

PLACES TO STAY
3 Sheraton
8 Best Western Mezona Inn
9 Motel 6
11 Quality Inn Royal
14 Hilton Pavilion
15 Lexington Hotel Suites
17 Motel 6
18 Motel 6
20 Days Inn

PLACES TO EAT
10 Landmark Restaurant
12 Los Dos Molinos

OTHER
1 Mesa Lutheran Hospital
2 Mesa General Hospital
4 Chamber of Commerce
5 Mesa Southwest Museum
6 USFS Ranger Station
7 Arizona Museum for Youth
13 Arizona Temple (LDS)
16 Greyhound Bus Depot
19 Golfland/Sunsplash

miles north of downtown Phoenix along I-17; take exit 225 to 3901 W Pioneer Rd (a good stop en route to Flagstaff). The museum is open Wednesday to Sunday from 9 am to 5 pm, and is closed June to September and Christmas Day. Admission is $5.75, or $4 for four- to 12-year-olds.

### Wildlife World Zoo
This zoo specializes in rare and exotic species ranging from white tigers to black jaguars. Attractions include a walk-in aviary filled with tropical birds, a lory (parrot) feeding area, a petting zoo and an aquarium with seahorses, piranhas and

electric eels. The zoo (☎ 935 9453), 16501 W Northern Ave (about 20 miles northwest of downtown Phoenix), is open from 9 am to 5 pm, and admission is $6.75, or $4 for three- to 12-year-olds.

### Out of Africa
See big cats from Africa and other continents, pet a lion cub or watch keepers swim with big cats at this wildlife park. The park presents a variety of continuous shows. Out of Africa (☎ 837 7779, 837 7677), 2 S Fort McDowell Rd (off Hwy 87 near the Fort McDowell Indian Reservation, almost 30 miles northeast of downtown Phoenix)

is open Tuesday to Sunday (also on holiday Mondays) from 9:30 am to 5 pm year round (closed Christmas Day). From the end of May to the end of September, it is open Saturdays until 9:30 pm. Admission is $8.95, or $7.95 for those over 65 and $3.95 for four- to 12-year-olds.

### Hoo-Hoogam Ki Museum
This small Pima-Maricopa Indian museum (☎ 874 8190) is on the Salt River Reservation at 10005 E Osborn Rd (at the intersection with Longmore St, about three miles east of Old Town Scottsdale). The building is made of local materials such as mesquite, saguaro ribs and adobe. See Pima baskets and Maricopa ceramics on display along with photographs illustrating the history of the people, and visit the gift shop and cafe. The museum is open Tuesday to Friday from 10 am to 4 pm, and is closed major holidays. Admission is $1, or 50¢ for children. Tribal offices are nearby.

### SUBURBAN PARKS
Several large parks in the mountains ringing the valley provide residents with many hiking, cycling, horseback riding and picnicking areas. Some are very popular and, of course, get crowded; nevertheless, these parks are as wild as you can get near a major city. A useful book is *Day Hikes and Trail Rides In and Around Phoenix* by Roger & Ethel Freeman (Gem Guide Books, 1991). 'Trail rides' in the title refers to horse trails.

To begin getting away from city crowds, the Tonto National Forest is the best immediate bet. Outdoors, people must beware of dehydration and sunburn in summer; be sure to carry water and sun protection.

The following are some of the most important parks, going from south to north. Unless otherwise noted, expect the parks to close at night with no camping allowed. For more information of campgrounds, see Places to Stay.

### Phoenix South Mountain Park
Covering 25 sq miles, this is the largest city park in the USA, and is part of the Phoenix Mountain Preserve system (☎ 495 0222). The park provides over 40 miles of trails used by hikers, mountain bikers and horseback riders. There are also good views and dozens of Indian petroglyph sites to admire. The park is on one of the lower ranges surrounding the valley, with South Mountain topping the landscape at 2690 feet. Reach the park by driving about eight miles south of downtown Phoenix to 10919 S Central Ave. Rangers can help plan your visit.

### Estrella Mountain Regional Park
On the southwestern outskirts of the valley, this 31-sq-mile county park (☎ 932 3811) is at the north end of the extremely rugged Sierra Estrella, providing 34 miles of multiuse trails, a golf course, rodeo arena and picnicking areas, mainly in the northwest corner of the park.

If you walk out of the roadless and mainly trailless southeast corner of the park into the main part of the Sierra Estrella, you'll find a mountain range so steep, slippery, waterless and wild that few people have walked it, despite its apparent proximity to the Southwest's largest city. (See Annerino's *Adventuring in Arizona*.)

The park is on the Gila River Indian Reservation; reach it by driving five miles south of I-10 along Estrella Parkway in Goodyear. Expect to pay a parking fee on weekends.

### Squaw Peak City Park
The 2608-foot summit of Squaw Peak affords one of Phoenix's most popular hikes (no bikes or horses are allowed), so much so that parking is very hard to find on weekends outside of summer; get there early in the morning to avoid problems. The parking lots are along Squaw Peak Drive, north of Lincoln Drive between 22nd and 22th Sts. For information, call 495 0222.

### McDowell Mountain Regional Park
Hiking, biking, horseback riding and camping are all permitted in this 33-sq-mile county park (☎ 471 0173). Access is along Fountain Hills Blvd from Shea Blvd

east of Scottsdale. Of the miles of trails, none reaches 4034-foot Mt McDowell standing west of the park.

### White Tank Mountain Regional Park
This 41-sq-mile park (☎ 935 2505) is the largest in Maricopa County and offers good hiking, mountain biking, horseback riding and camping. Of the many trails, one leads to the 4018-foot summit of White Tank Mountain and another goes to a waterfall (which is sometimes dry). A $2 per vehicle day use fee is collected during weekends from fall to spring. To get to the park from Phoenix, drive 10 miles northwest on Grand Ave, then head 15 miles west on Olive Ave to the park.

### Lake Pleasant Regional Park
The Lake Pleasant Reservoir is still being formed by the new Waddell Dam on the Agua Fria River. The county park (☎ 780 9875) offers boating, fishing and camping and is expanding; there are plans to open a visitor center in 1998 and a hotel in 1999. Currently, admission is $4 per vehicle, $2 per boat or motorcycle, and $1 to drive to the scenic overlook. Once you've paid the admission price, primitive camping is free. To get to the park, drive about 27 miles north of downtown Phoenix on I-17 to Hwy 74, then continue about 12 miles west.

### ACTIVITIES
#### Golf, Tennis & Swimming
Serious **golf** players probably already know that the valley, despite its desert location, is a major golfing center with about 100 greens that range from 'pitch and putt' to PGA championship courses. Information about these and other courses is available from the Arizona Golf Association (☎ 944 3035), 7226 N 16th St, Phoenix, 85020. Golf Xpress (☎ 278 8580, 1 (800) 878 8580), 3147 N 31st Ave, Phoenix, 85017, will suggest and arrange tee times at many of the better courses up to 60 days in advance and will rent and deliver golf clubs to your hotel. Many of the resorts offer fine courses and package golfing or tennis vacations (see the introduction to Places to Stay).

Phoenix Parks and Recreation (☎ 262 6861 for general information) runs dozens of city parks with several golf courses, tennis centers, swimming pools and other recreational programs.

You can do all three activities at city-run **Encanto Park** (☎ 261 8991), at N 15th Ave and Encanto Blvd, a couple of miles north of downtown Phoenix. Here, a nine-hole (☎ 262 6870) and an 18-hole golf course (☎ 253 3963), a swimming pool, tennis, racquetball and basketball courts, lakes with ducks and rowboat rentals, and picnic areas attract entire families.

Try other 18-hole city-run golf courses at Papago Park (☎ 275 8428); Maryvale (☎ 846 4022), 5902 W Indian School Rd; and Cave Creek (☎ 866 8076), 15202 N 19th Ave. City courses generally offer relatively inexpensive golfing.

City-run tennis centers where courts can be reserved for about $2 an hour include City Center Courts (☎ 256 4120), 121 E Adams St; Mountain View (☎ 788 6088), 1104 E Grovers Ave; Phoenix Tennis Center (☎ 249 3712), 6330 N 21st Ave; and Cave Creek Sports Complex (☎ 261 8011), 9833 N 25th Ave.

The city operates 27 swimming pools (call 258 7946 for general pool information). Also see Especially for Kids, above.

#### Shooting & Archery
The **Ben Avery Shooting Range** (☎ 582 8313), northwest of I-17 on Hwy 74, provides practice facilities for a variety of firearms as well as archery, and has a campground (see Places to Stay). The **Usery Mountain Recreation Area** (☎ 984 0032), on Ellsworth Rd about five miles north of Hwy 60 in Mesa, offers extensive archery facilities and a 70-site campground.

#### Horseback Riding
As if to emphasize the valley's Western roots, almost 40 horse rental and riding outfits are listed in the Phoenix yellow pages. Short rides, often combined with a country breakfast or barbecue cookout, are popular activities, and overnight packing trips can be arranged.

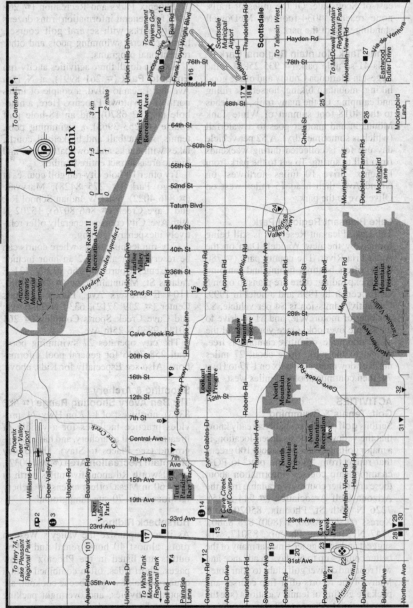

Phoenix

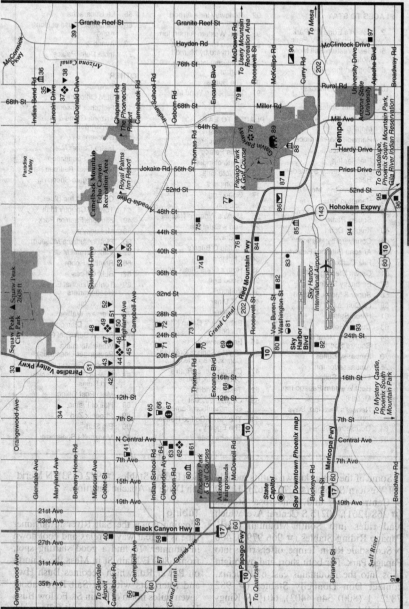

Some of the better known outfits include All Western Stables (☎ 276 5862), 10220 S Central Ave, and Ponderosa Stables (☎ 268 1261), 10215 S Central Ave, which lead rides into South Mountain Park. Papago Riding Stables (☎ 966 9793), 400 N Scottsdale Rd in Tempe, offers rides into Papago Park. For both short and overnight trips into the mountains east of Phoenix, contact Don Donnelly Stables (☎ 982 7822, 1 (800) 346 4403), 6010 S Kings Ranch Rd, Apache Junction, and Supersti-

tion Riding Stables (☎ 982 6353), N Meridian Drive in Apache Junction.

### Tubing

Floating down the Salt River in an inner tube is a great way to relax and cool down in summer. To find a good starting spot, from 6800 E Main St in Mesa, head north on Power Rd, which becomes Bush Hwy and intersects with the Salt River about seven miles north of Main St. Follow Bush Hwy for a few miles east as it follows the river; the road reaches Saguaro Lake after about 10 miles.

Along the Bush Hwy, Salt River Recreation (☎ 984 3305, 984 1857, fax 984 0875) and Saguaro Lake Ranch Resort (☎ 380 1239) will give you information, rent tubes and provide van shuttles to several good places to start for short or all-day floats. Costs start at about $8 per person for shuttle and tube, but are less if you bring you own tube. (Rafts can also be rented.) Bring sun block, shoes suitable to protect your feet from the bottom, and rent an extra tube for your cooler full of cold drinks (don't bring glass). Tubing season is mid-April through September, and weekends draw crowds of people bent on cooling off and partying on.

### Hot-Air Ballooning
Dozens of companies offer hot-air balloon flights over the valley. Flights usually lift off in the calm morning air, drift for about an hour and finish with a traditional champagne brunch; costs are in the low $100s per person, and most companies can arrange flights on a day's notice, but flights may be canceled in windy weather and in summer. Some experienced outfits include A Aerozona Adventures (☎ 991 4260), Naturally High (☎ 496 8134) and Unicorn Balloon Company (☎ 991 3666), but many others are just as good.

### ORGANIZED TOURS
Several companies offer tours in and around Phoenix. Gray Line (☎ 495 9100, 1 (800) 732 0327) runs three-hour narrated **city bus tours** for $27 a person, and Vaughan's Southwest (☎ 971 1381) offers four-hour tours for a few dollars more. Both these and other companies do longer tours such as a 14-hour tour to the Grand Canyon for $79 (for people with really limited time!); children under 12 get discounts.

Wagonmasters (☎ 423 1449 or 501 3239 mobile phone) gives **horse-drawn carriage tours** leaving from Main and Brown Sts in Old Town Scottsdale. Carriages hold six people and tours start at $20 for a 15-minute ride.

Many companies offer **4WD tours** into the surrounding desert that last anywhere from four hours to all day, and stress various themes: ghost towns, cookouts, Indian petroglyphs and ruins, natural history, sunset tours and target shooting. Costs start around $50 a person. Some reputable companies include Arizona Desert Jeep Tours (☎ 947 7852), 835 E Brown in Scottsdale; Arrowhead Desert Tours (☎ 942 3361, fax 993 3304), 841 E Paradise Lane, Phoenix; Arizona Bound Tours (☎ 994 0580), 5638 E Thomas Rd, Phoenix; and Wild West Jeep Tours (☎ 941 8355), 7127 E Becker Lane in Scottsdale.

Short **rafting tours** are offered by Desert Voyagers (☎ 998 7238, 1 (800) 222 7238). Short and longer trips, some combined with jeep or horseback excursions, are offered by Cimarron River Co (☎ 994 1199).

### SPECIAL EVENTS
Something is happening just about all the time from October to May in Phoenix, but few events occur during the searing summer. The chambers of commerce are knowledgeable about all the scheduled events and provide free calendars. Some of the most important include the following.

One of the biggest parades in the Southwest precedes the Fiesta Bowl college football game on New Year's Day at the ASU Sun Devil Stadium. Late January and early February sees Western events in Scottsdale, such as a horse-drawn parade, a rodeo, Pony Express reenactments and an All-Arabian Horse Show. Performers dress in Renaissance garb, joust and host many other medieval events on weekends from late February through early April during the Renaissance Festival (☎ 463 2700), held on Hwy 60, nine miles southeast of Apache Junction. Admission is $11 or $5 for four- to 12-year-olds.

The Heard Museum hosts the Guild Indian Fair and Market during the first weekend in March, which has been held annually since 1958. View Indian dancers, eat Native American food and browse and buy top-quality arts & crafts; admission is $5, or $3 for children.

ARIZONA

In mid-March, watch the Phoenix Rodeo of Rodeos, held at the Veterans Memorial Coliseum, 1826 W McDowell Rd. The costumed Yaqui Indian Easter Ceremonies are held Friday afternoons during Lent and from Wednesday to Easter Sunday of Holy Week. The events occur in the main plaza of the village of Guadalupe at the south end of Tempe (call 883 2838 for information).

The Arizona State Fair takes place in the last two weeks of October. Simultaneously and continuing into mid-November, the Cowboy Artists of America exhibition is on display at the Phoenix Art Museum. The Thunderbird Hot-Air Balloon Classic lifts off from Glendale Airport in early November, and dance, song and arts & crafts are featured at Pueblo Grande's Annual Indian Market during the second weekend in December.

## PLACES TO STAY

From very basic motels to ritzy resorts, the valley's hundreds of accommodations share one thing in common – prices drop in summer. From January to April, rates can be over twice as expensive as from Memorial Day to Labor Day in the top-end places, although at the cheapest ones the seasonal price difference is not so vast. The price drop presents a real bargain for summer vacationers, who, despite low prices, can rely on finding air conditioning in every hotel. High-season rates are listed below.

Reservation services for places in the mid to top price ranges (at no extra charge) include the Arizona Reservation Bureau (☎ 1 (800) 666 1316), 10315 Alden Spring Rd, Oro Valley, 85737, and Room Rez International (☎ 252 8846), 202 N Central Ave, No 200, Phoenix, 85004.

There are scores of B&Bs in the valley, most of which prefer advance reservations. The Arizona Association of B&B Inns (☎ 277 0775), 3101 N Central Ave, Suite 560, Phoenix, 85712, can provide a statewide list of their members. Many B&Bs can be reserved through the Mi Casa Su Casa B&B reservation service (☎ 990 0682, 1 (800) 456 0682), PO Box 950, Tempe, 85280, and some can be reserved

through B&B in Arizona (☎ 995 2831, 1 (800) 266 7829), PO Box 8628, Scottsdale, 85252. Expect mid-range to top-end rates at most of these places.

The most elegant and expensive places to stay are the resorts, of which Phoenix has more than its share. These aren't just places to stay – they are places to spend an entire vacation. Sure, the staff will arrange a day trip to the Grand Canyon for you, but when you are spending hundreds of dollars a day for the resort facilities, it makes no sense just to sleep there.

The pricey resorts generally offer attractively landscaped grounds suitable for strolling or jogging, spacious rooms or suites (including presidential suites priced well over a $1000 a night) and extensive indoor and outdoor public areas. Expect a helpful staff, and a variety of dining possibilities and room service, bars and entertainment, as well as several swimming pools, whirlpools, saunas, a fully equipped exercise/health center with instructors and trainers, and (at extra cost) massage, beauty treatments, tennis, racquetball and golf. Most can provide baby-sitting and some have children's clubs, again at extra cost. Gift and sundries shops should be on the premises along with a hairdresser, and various other attractions may include anything from bicycle hire to basketball courts, video rental to volleyball and horseback riding to hot-air ballooning. Resorts also tend, inhospitably, to nickel-and-dime guests to death with very expensive local phone calls or $3 in-room coffee machines.

With most resorts having several hundred units running at full occupancy in winter, this is big business, and there are several dozen resorts and resort wanna-bes in the valley. This tradition started in Phoenix, but now Scottsdale is clearly the resort center of Arizona, if not the Southwest. Some of the major resorts and their main claims to fame are listed here, and you can expect them to have most of the features mentioned above. If you plan on vacationing in a valley resort, I suggest you contact the establishment for complete details or talk to a travel agent.

## PLACES TO STAY – CAMPING

Boaters can camp at the free USFS *Bagley Flat Campground*, open year round on Saguaro Lake (see Tubing, above), but there is no drinking water (treat the lake water) and access is by boat only. About 20 miles north of Scottsdale, via Carefree and the unpaved Seven Creeks Rd (USFS Forest Rd 24), the *Seven Creeks Campground* with 23 sites, and the *CCC Campground* with 10 sites, are open year round, lack drinking water and are free; the elevation here is about 3500 feet.

The wildest camping is found east of the valley. The Tonto National Forest (see Information) runs *Tortilla Flat Campground* 18 miles northeast of Apache Junction along Hwy 88, offering 77 sites October through April for $8, with water but no showers or hookups. *Lost Dutchman State Park* (☎ 982 4485), 6109 N Apache Trail, 85219, five miles northeast of Apache Junction along Hwy 88, offers nature trails and picnic sites ($3 day use per vehicle) nestled under the Superstition Mountains and 35 campsites for $8, with water but no showers or hookups.

You can camp at several of the suburban parks and recreation areas (see Suburban Parks above for more information about these); *Lake Pleasant Regional Park* offers primitive camping for the $4 park admission fee, and *McDowell Mountain Regional Park* has about 100 campsites, some with water and electric hookups for $12, as well as showers. The campground closes from Memorial Day through September. The year-round campground at *White Tank Mountain Regional Park* offers 40 sites for $8, and provides showers but no hookups. both near shooting and archery ranges (see Shooting & Archery above for more information about these two), the *Ben Avery Shooting Range* has a campground with showers and 100 sites priced at $8, or $12 with hookups, and the *Usery Mountain Recreation Area* has a 70-site campground providing sites with hookups priced at $12; this campground is closed in summer.

For those 55 or older, the *Paradise RV Resort* (☎ 977 0344, 1 (800) 847 2280),

10950 W Union Hills Drive, in the retirement community of Sun City, features 950 RV sites with hookups for $25, as well as a pool, spa, sauna, exercise room, tennis courts and putting green.

Even larger adult-only RV parks (they should call them RV cities) are found in Mesa. All have extensive recreation facilities. *Trailer Village* (☎ 832 1770, 830 4878), 3020 E Main St, has almost 1700 sites priced at about $20. The *Mesa Regal RV Resort* (☎ 830 2821), 4700 E Main St, has about 1800 sites priced at $25, as does the *Valle del Oro RV Resort* (☎ 984 1146), 1452 S Ellsworth St. The *View Point RV and Golf Resort* (☎ 373 8700), 8700 E University Drive, offers over 1300 sites priced at $28, as well as the most extensive recreational activities of any RV park in the valley.

Two north Phoenix RV campgrounds with over 200 sites each are near I-17 at exit 215: *Desert's Edge RV Park* (☎ 869 7021), 22623 N Black Canyon Hwy, with RV sites for adults only; and *North Phoenix RV Park* (☎ 869 8189), 2550 W Louise Drive, which allows families and tenting as well. Both charge $15 to $19 depending on services used, and both have showers, a pool, a spa, a recreation area and coin laundry.

Other family-oriented RV parks include the 360-acre *West World of Scottsdale* (☎ 483 8800), 16601 N Pima Rd, offering 500 sites for $15, horseback riding, hiking, cookouts and outdoor recreation activities but no swimming pool. About a mile south of I-10 exit 124, 20 miles west of Phoenix, the *Phoenix West KOA* (☎ 853 0537), 1440 N Citrus Rd in Goodyear, has almost 300 sites for $19.50 with hookups, as well as many tent sites, a pool, spa, playground and other activities.

About 100 more RV parks, many for adults only, are listed in the Phoenix yellow pages.

## PLACES TO STAY – BOTTOM END
### Phoenix
Central Phoenix has the region's best selection of cheap places to stay. Many young budget travelers head over to the friendly

*Metcalf House Hostel* (☎ 254 9803), 1026 N 9th St. The hostel won't take telephone reservations but usually has space in the dorms, priced at $13 per person (less for HI/AYH members). Kitchen and laundry facilities are available.

The *YMCA* (☎ 253 6181), 350 N 1st Ave, rents single rooms with shared showers for $20 a night or $75 a week, and doubles for not much more. It is usually full and does not take reservations – show up around 9 am for the best chance at a room. The guests are mainly men, but women are welcome to stay in rooms on the women's floor, and use the gym and other fitness facilities.

Most of the cheapest motels are along Van Buren St. The downtown area is OK, but as you head east, the neighborhood deteriorates into boarded-up buildings, used-car lots and street walkers' turf (police patrols periodically scout the area). I wouldn't walk downtown along E Van Buren St with luggage at night looking for a cheap motel, though driving seems safe. The neighborhood improves around 24th St, and to get there from downtown you'd need a car anyway.

For decent cheap lodging downtown, try the *Budget Lodge Motel* (☎ 254 7247), 402 W Van Buren St, or the *Budget Inn Motel* (☎ 257 8331), 424 W Van Buren St, offering double rooms priced in the low $30s in the high season. Other adequate, inexpensive places nearby are the *Travel Inn 9 Motel* (☎ 254 6521), 201 N 7th Ave, and the *Las Palmas Inn* (☎ 256 9161), 765 NW Grand Ave. Further northwest, the slightly pricier *Desert Sun Motel* (☎ 258 8971), 1325 NW Grand Ave, has a 24-hour restaurant. Heading east, you could also try the *Economy Inn* (☎ 254 0181), 804 E Van Buren St, and the *American Lodge* (☎ 252 6823), 965 E Van Buren St.

East Van Buren St improves again close to the north side of the airport, where you'll find a bunch of budget places about four miles from the terminal. You'll find adequate rooms for around $30 at the *Flamingo Inn* (☎ 275 6211), 2501 E Van Buren St, the *Deserama Motel* (☎ 273 7477), 2853 E Van Buren St, *Wards Motor Inn* (☎ 273 1601), 3037 E Van Buren St, the clean and often full *Desert Rose Motor Hotel* (☎ 275 4421), 3424 E Van Buren St, the *Parkview Inn* (☎ 273 7303), 3547 E Van Buren St, and the *Phoenix Sunrise Motel* (☎ 275 7661), 3644 E Van Buren St. Most of these have a pool. The *Quality Inn – Airport* (☎ 273 7121, fax 231 0973), 3541 E Van Buren St, has more expensive larger-than-average rooms and a coffee shop on the premises. This is the best hotel along the cheap Van Buren strip.

The several Motel 6s in Phoenix are all large and have pools. These are at 2323 E Van Buren St (☎ 267 7511, fax 231 8701), offering rooms for $30/36 singles/doubles; 214 S 24th St (☎ 244 1155, fax 231 0043) for $31/37; 5315 E Van Buren St (☎ 267 8555), fax 231 9115) for $32/38; 4130 N Black Canyon Hwy (☎ 277 5501, fax 274 9724) for $33/39; 2548 W Indian School Rd (☎ 248 8881, fax 230 2371) for $36/42; 8152 N Black Canyon Hwy (☎ 995 7592, fax 995 9592) for $38/44; 2330 W Bell Rd (☎ 993 2353, fax 548 3461) for $39/45; 2735 W Sweetwater Rd (☎ 942 5030, fax 548 3483) for $39/45; and 1530 N 52nd Drive (☎ 272 0220, fax 278 4210) for $39/45.

Standard rooms start in the $50s during the high season but drop into the $30s in midsummer at the following hotels with pools. *Nendel's Valu Inn* (☎ 275 3691), 3307 E Van Buren St, has nice rooms and an airport shuttle. The *Super 8 Motel – Central* (☎ 248 8880, fax 241 0234), 4021 N 27th Ave, also has airport transportation and includes a continental breakfast in its rates. Two *Travelers Inns* have good rooms at 8130 N Black Canyon Hwy (☎ 995 8451, fax 995 8496) and at 5102 W Latham St (☎ 233 1988, fax 278 4598).

The *Ambassador Inn* (☎ 840 7500), 1 (800) 624 6759, fax 840 5078), 4717 E Thomas Rd, is a good value, providing a kitchenette with its rooms, an adjacent restaurant and a free airport shuttle from 7 am to 10 pm, as well as a spa and exercise area. The *Days Inn* (☎ 244 8244, fax 244 8240), 3333 E Van Buren St, has a restaurant, bar and whirlpool.

## Tempe, Mesa & Scottsdale

Heading east into Tempe and Mesa, some basic motels with rooms priced in the $30s and $40s include the *Tempe Motel* (☎ 894 0909), 947 E Apache Blvd, and the *Whispering Wind Motel* (☎ 967 9935), 1814 E Apache Blvd, east of the intersection with McClintock Drive; several more places line the blocks between here and Price Drive. About half a mile further, Apache Blvd becomes Main St in Mesa, where several cheap places line the half mile between the *Del Rio Motel* (☎ 833 3273), 2200 W Main St, and the *Roadrunner Motel* (☎ 834 8040), 2066 W Main St. Almost all have a pool.

The Motel 6 chain offers reasonably reliable budget accommodation and pools; try those in Mesa at 336 W Hampton (☎ 844 8899, fax 969 6749), offering rooms for $30/36; 630 W Main St (☎ 969 8111, fax 655 0747) for $33/39; and 1511 S Country Club (☎ 834 0066, fax 969 6313) for $38/44. Tempe's Motel 6s are at 513 W Broadway (☎ 967 8696, fax 929 0814) offering rooms for $35/41; 1612 N Scottsdale Rd/Rural Rd (☎ 945 9506, fax 970 4763) for $35/41; and 1720 S Priest Drive (☎ 968 4401, fax 929 0810) for $37/43.

Conveniently near ASU in Tempe, the *University Motel* (☎ 966 7221), 902 S Mill Ave, has rooms starting in the $50s, as does *Tempe-University Travelodge* (☎ 968 7871, fax 968 3991), 1005 E Apache Blvd.

Scottsdale, the resort capital of the valley, has very few budget places to stay as you pay extra bucks for the swanky location. One of the least expensive is the Motel 6 at 6848 E Camelback Rd (☎ 946 2280, fax 949 7583) offering rooms for $43/49.

## PLACES TO STAY – MIDDLE

These hotels offer rooms in the $60 to $100 range during the high season. The places listed here are nice, but not superluxurious; a $90 room in February can go for $40 in July, and is probably worth somewhere in between.

### Phoenix

The following above-average hotels in the $60 to $80 range all have a pool. The *Best*

*Western Airport Inn* (☎ 273 7251, fax 273 7180), 2425 S 24th St, is about a mile from the terminal and has a free shuttle, as well as a spa, sauna, restaurant and bar, making this a convenient and comfortable airport stop. The *Rodeway Inn – Airport West* (☎ 273 1211, fax 225 9170), 1202 S 24th, is cheaper and closer to the airport, providing a restaurant and bar and airport transportation.

North of downtown Phoenix, the *La Quinta Inn – Coliseum* (☎ 258 6271, fax 340 9255), 2725 N Black Canyon Hwy, has spacious rooms and includes continental breakfast in its rates. Further north, the *Knights Court* (☎ 242 8011, fax 242 8011), 5050 N Black Canyon Hwy, has a spa and decent rooms. The *Comfort Inn – Turf Paradise* (☎ 866 2089, fax 789 7669), 1711 W Bell Rd, provides a spa and continental breakfasts for guests, as does the *Best Western Bell Motel* (☎ 993 8300, fax 863 2163), 17211 N Black Canyon Hwy. The *Hampton Inn* (☎ 864 6233, fax 995 7503), 8101 N Black Canyon Hwy, also provides a spa and continental breakfast with its spotless, spacious rooms priced in the upper $70s. You'll find slightly cheaper decent rooms at the *Premier Inn* (☎ 943 2371, fax 943 5847), 10402 N Black Canyon Hwy.

West of downtown Phoenix, the *Fairfield Inn* (☎ /fax 269 1919), 1241 N 53rd Ave, is a good value in this price range, offering nice rooms priced in the $60s and complimentary continental breakfast.

For rooms in the $80 to $100 range, the following are all reasonable choices. Right downtown, the *San Carlos Hotel* (☎ 253 4121, 1 (800) 528 5446, fax 253 4121 ext 209), 202 N Central Ave, is the most fun. Built in 1927, it was downtown's swankest hotel for decades, and although recently refurbished and comfortable, the hotel retains many of its early fixtures and atmosphere. The rooms aren't huge, but there are more expensive suites if you need to spread out, and facilities include an exercise room, restaurant and bar. The *Los Olivos Executive Hotel* (☎ 258 6911, fax 257 0776), 202 E McDowell Rd, is smaller and more intimate than many business-oriented hotels;

ARIZONA

its 48 rooms, most with king-size beds and in-room coffeemakers, cost about $80, and 15 suites with kitchenettes cost $20 more. Continental breakfast is included in the prices, and the hotel has tennis courts, a spa and a coffee shop open for breakfast and lunch on weekdays only.

North of downtown, the *Quality Hotel* (☎ 248 0222, fax 265 6331), 3600 N 2nd Ave, offers large rooms, two pools and a spa, a restaurant, bar and international coffee shop, and free airport transportation. Much further north, the recently renovated *Ramada Inn Metrocenter* (☎ 866 7000, fax 942 7512), 12027 N 28th Ave, has nice rooms, a spa, restaurant and lounge. Nearby, the *Royal Suites* (☎ 942 1000, 1 (800) 647 5786, fax 993 2965), 10421 N 33rd Ave, offers mini-suites with kitchenettes.

At the south end of Phoenix, the *Quality Inn – South Mountain* (☎ 893 3900, fax 496 0815), 5121 E La Puente Ave, has good-size rooms and a spa, as well as a restaurant open for breakfast and dinner.

The *Lexington Hotel & City Square Sports Club* (☎ 279 9811, fax 631 9358), 100 W Clarendon Ave, charges in the low $100s for standard hotel rooms. The top-end prices aren't for the rooms, but for the sports club amenities (available at no extra charge) that include large locker rooms, aerobics and well-equipped machine workout rooms with trainers, a dozen racquetball courts, a basketball court, spa, sauna and steam room. There's also a restaurant open from 6:30 am to 10 pm, a busy sports bar and nightclub, and free airport transportation. Prices drop on weekends – I've even seen ads for $29 rooms during midsummer weekends.

## Tempe

Prices for comfortable standard rooms at the pleasant *Comfort Inn* (☎ 820 7500, fax 730 6626), 5300 S Priest Drive, are in the $60s and $70s and include use of the spa, a continental breakfast and free airport transportation. Close to ASU, the *Super 8 Motel of Tempe* (☎ 967 8891, fax 968 7868), 1020 E Apache Blvd, has a spa, sauna and better-than-average Super 8 rooms.

Rates at *Country Suites* (☎ 345 8585, fax 345 7461), 1660 W Elliot Rd, range from $75 to $95 for rooms with limited to full kitchen facilities (some with sitting rooms) and include continental breakfast, morning newspaper and airport transportation; there is a spa. The *InnSuites Hotel* (☎ 897 7900, 1 (800) 841 4242, fax 491 1008), 1651 W Baseline Rd, has pleasant rooms of various sizes priced from $80 to $105; basic rooms include kitchenettes, and some have sitting rooms. Continental breakfast, evening cocktail hour and airport transportation are included. With two tennis courts and an exercise room, you can get a workout while the kids are on the playground, or relax in the spa.

Opposite ASU, the *Holiday Inn* (☎ 968 3451, fax 968 6262), 915 E Apache Blvd, has spacious rooms with coffeemakers, many with balconies, for about $100. Amenities include a restaurant, open from 6 am to 10 pm (with room service), a lounge, airport transportation, a spa and an exercise room.

## Mesa

The *Best Western Mesa Inn* (☎ /fax 964 8000), 1625 E Main St, charges about $70 for standard rooms and has a spa and free coffee in the lobby, while the *Best Western Mezona Inn* (☎ 834 9233, fax 844 7920), 250 W Main St, offers rooms for about $80 and has a restaurant open from 6 am to 10 pm. Similar prices include a continental breakfast at the two *Days Inns*, one at 333 W Juanita Ave (☎ /fax 844 8900), and the other at 5531 E Main St (☎ 981 8111, fax 396 8027).

For decent rooms priced in the $80s, try the *Hampton Inn* (☎ 926 3000, fax 926 4892), 1563 S Gilbert Rd; rates include continental breakfast and there is a spa. The *Quality Inn Royal* (☎ /fax 833 1231, 1 (800) 333 5501), 951 W Main St, offers comfortable rooms with balconies or patios for around $90 and a few with kitchenettes for about $100; prices include continental breakfast, and the hotel has a spa, sauna, exercise room and restaurant with bar. *Lexington Hotel Suites* (☎ 964 2897, fax 833 0536), 1410 S Country Club Drive, offers 120 units, ranging from studios to suites with two bedrooms and sitting room, all with limited to full kitchen facilities. Rates range from $60 to $140, depending on the room, and include continental breakfast; the hotel has a spa and coffee shop.

## Scottsdale

The *Fifth Avenue Inn* (☎ 994 9461, fax 947 1695), 6935 5th Ave, has comfortable rooms priced about $80 double, and fashionable shopping is within walking distance. The *Days Inn at Fashion Square Mall* (☎ 947 5411, 1 (800) 325 2525, fax 946 1324), 4710 N Scottsdale Rd, offers standard rooms priced from $80 to $120 in winter, as well as a tennis court, putting lawn and spa; continental breakfast is included. The *Fairfield Inn by Marriott* (☎ 483 0042, fax 483 3715), 13440 N Scottsdale Rd, offers a spa and nice rooms for about $100.

## PLACES TO STAY – TOP END

As many top-end hotels cater to business travelers on an expense account, discounts can often be arranged for empty rooms on weekends. Many rooms are half price in summer.

## Phoenix

Two huge downtown convention-center hotels have all the expected amenities such as health club, restaurants, room service, concierge and shopping. Recently a Sheraton and before that a Hilton, the *Holiday Inn Crowne Plaza* (☎ 257 1525, fax 253 9755), 111 N Central Ave, has given its 534-room property a much-needed refurbishment, and it looks pretty spiffy now. Rooms range from $120 to $160 a double. The best place downtown is the 24-story *Hyatt Regency* (☎ 252 1234, 1 (800) 233 1234, fax 254 9472), 122 N 2nd St, offering over 700 rooms, many with balconies, for $175 to $225 a double; some suites go for as much as $700 a night. This is the city's biggest hotel, and the revolving rooftop restaurant (the Compass) has great views and excellent Southwestern food.

On the north edge of downtown, the smaller *Best Western Executive Park Hotel* (☎ 252 2100, fax 340 1989), 1100 N Central Ave, offers about 100 rooms that are as nice as the more expensive places downtown but costing only $120 a double, with 8th-floor view suites going for $150. The hotel has a restaurant, bar, spa, sauna and exercise room.

The most comfortable hotel close to the airport is the *Doubletree Suites* (☎ 225 0500, 1 (800) 800 3098, fax 225 0957), 320 N 44th St, with 242 two-room suites, all with a kitchenette, as well as a restaurant, bar, spa, sauna, fitness center, tennis court and free airport transportation. Rates are in the mid to high $100s, depending on the room, and include a full breakfast.

Other comfortable airport hotels include the *Airport Hilton* (☎ 894 1600, fax 921 7844), 2435 S 47th St, a popular business hotel with over 300 rooms, most with balconies. Rates range from $130 to $250. The most spacious and comfortable units are on the 4th-floor 'luxury level'. Facilities include a restaurant, bar spa, exercise room, massage (for an extra fee) and free airport transportation. Nearby, the *Airport Courtyard by Marriott* (☎ 966 4300, fax 966 0198), 2621 S 47th St, offers good rooms for about $125 and a few slightly more expensive mini-suites, all with free in-room coffee. A restaurant (open for breakfast and dinner only), bar, spa, exercise room and free airport transportation are available.

More *Courtyards by Marriott* with similar facilities and prices are at 2101 E Camelback Rd (☎ 955 5200, fax 955 1101), and at 9631 N Black Canyon Hwy (☎ 944 7373, fax 944 0079).

*Fountain Suites* (☎ /fax 375 1777), 2577 W Greenway Rd, offers two-room suites (with a bedroom, living room and refrigerator, but no kitchen) priced in the low $100s. Amenities include a restaurant with room service, bar with entertainment, spa, sauna and exercise room, and racquetball, tennis and volleyball courts.

*Embassy Suites* has three locations, all of which offer two-room suites with small kitchenettes. Each hotel has a spa, restaurant and bar and includes a full breakfast and an evening drinks hour in its rates. The cheapest is at 3210 NW Grand Ave (☎ 279 3211, fax 230 2145), with a sauna and units priced in the low $100s. Rooms are about $150 at 1515 N 44th St (☎ /fax 244 8800), and the hotel provides free airport transportation. The hotel at 2333 E Thomas Rd (☎ 957 1910, fax 955 2861) is slightly cheaper and has an exercise room and airport transportation. The *Hilton Suites* (☎ 222 1111, fax 265 4841), 10 E Thomas Rd, offers similar amenities (but no free airport transportation), and has more luxurious suites priced in the upper $100s. The fanciest looking suite hotel is the *Crown Sterling Suites* (☎ 955 3992, fax 955 6479), 2630 E Camelback Rd, which includes breakfast and evening drinks in its room rates in the high $100s.

The ritziest hotel in Phoenix is, of course, the elegant *Ritz-Carlton* (☎ 468 0700, fax 468 0793), 2401 E Camelback Rd, offering attractive rooms in the $160 to $220 range and suites for well over $300. Amenities include expensive but excellent restaurants, 24-hour room service, a bar with light entertainment, a fitness center with trainers and massage therapists, a spa, a sauna and a tennis court. Traditionally elegant, The Grill is one of the best American grills in Arizona.

Much of the design for the city's first luxury resort, the *Arizona Biltmore* (☎ 955 6600, 1 (800) 950 0086, fax 954 2571), 24th St and E Missouri Ave, was influenced by Frank Lloyd Wright. This beautiful and historically interesting resort, (opened in 1929) underwent various renovations in the early 1990s; its modern facilities include two golf courses and the very good Orangerie restaurant, with an innovative international menu. Standard rooms cost $360 in the high season ($120 in midsummer), while suites start at $750, and go as high as $2800 for the Presidential Suite.

The Hilton runs three Phoenix resorts. The *Pointe Hilton Resort at Squaw Peak* (☎ 997 2626, fax 997 2391), 7677 N 16th St, offers nine acres of pools, including water slides and a 'river' tubing area, as well as a popular kids' program. The *Pointe Hilton Resort at Tapatio Cliffs* (☎ 866 7500, fax 993 0276), 11111 N 7th St, and the *Pointe Hilton Resort on South Mountain* (☎ 438 9000, fax 431 6535), 7777 S Pointe Parkway, both have full facilities including excellent (but expensive) golf courses; rooms start around $200 in the high season. All three have good restaurants, but the chain's best is the spectacularly located Etienne's Different Pointe of View, serving continental food atop Tapatio Cliffs.

For a taste of resort living at 'budget' prices, try the *Royal Palms Inn* (☎ 840 3610, 1 (800) 672 6011, fax 840 0233), 5200 E Camelback Rd. This is one of the few resorts offering rooms priced under $200, and the golf courses and tennis courts are available at no extra charge.

## Tempe

The *Embassy Suites Hotel* (☎ 897 7444, fax 897 6112), 4400 S Rural Rd, has rooms similar to those at the Embassy Suites in Phoenix for about $150, and has a spa, sauna, exercise room, restaurant and free airport transportation.

The *Ramada Hotel – Sky Harbor* (☎ 967 6600, fax 829 9427), 1600 S 52nd St, offers free airport transportation, a spa, and a restaurant and bar with room service from 6 am to 10 pm. Rooms priced from $120 to $150 double have coffeemakers, and some have balconies.

Tempe's best hotel, *The Buttes* (☎ 225 9000, 1 (800) 843 1986, fax 438 8622), 2000 Westcourt Way, is a cross between a comfortable business hotel and a resort. Attractively set on top of a small desert mountain, it offers a beautifully landscaped pool, water slide, spas, sauna, exercise room, tennis courts and golf privileges, as well as the elegant Market Cafe (open from 6 am to 10 pm), the Top of the Rock restaurant (open from 5 to 19 pm), a bar, entertainment, 24-hour room service and airport transportation. The resort has rates in the low $200s but offers some slightly more expensive luxury rooms and a few very expensive suites.

## Mesa

The Sheraton and the Hilton chains present Mesa's best top-end hotels, both with almost 300 good-size rooms priced from $100 to $175. Both hotels have a spa, exercise room, restaurant and bar, and some more expensive suites. The *Sheraton* (☎ 898 8300, fax 964 9279) is at 200 N Centennial Way (off Sirrine St), and the *Hilton Pavilion* (☎ 833 5555, fax 649 1886) is at 1011 W Holmes Ave.

## Scottsdale

The *Best Western Papago Inn* (☎ 947 7335, fax 994 0692), 7017 E McDowell Rd, has coffeemakers in its pleasant rooms priced in the low $100s, and has a sauna, exercise room and a restaurant. The *Courtyard by Marriott* (☎ 860 4000, fax 860 4308) at 13444 E Shea Blvd is similar to those in Phoenix (see above). Conveniently near Old Town, *Marriott Suites* (☎ 945 1550, fax 945 2005), 7325 E 3rd Ave, offers two-room suites with refrigerators and coffeemakers, many with balconies, for $180, and facilities include a fitness room, spa and sauna, restaurant and bar.

The *Hilton Scottsdale Resort & Villas* (☎ 948 7750, fax 948 2232), 6333 N Scottsdale Rd, is a large hotel with some resort qualities, offering rooms for around $150, and one- or two-bedroom villas, some with fireplace and private spa, for $300. Amenities include spas, a sauna, a children's pool, tennis courts and exercise equipment complete with trainers. The restaurant provides room service from 6:30 am to 10 pm, and the bar provides a dance floor and entertainment.

*Marriott's Camelback Inn* (☎ 948 1700, 1 (800) 242 2635, fax 483 3424), 5402 E Lincoln Drive, opened in 1936, and, with many dedicated customers, is considered a world-class resort. Highlights are 36 holes of excellent golf, a full-service spa and health club, and the highly rated Chaparral restaurant, serving pricey continental food; but everything else you might expect is here as well. Even more expensive is the opulent and modern *Phoenician* (☎ 941 8200, 1 (800) 888 8234, fax 947 4311),

6000 E Camelback Rd, another world-class super-deluxe resort with the usual amenities, as well as some less usual activities such as archery, badminton and croquet. The resort's top-rated Mary Elaine's restaurant serves contemporary continental cuisine, while the Terrace Dining Room serves fine Italian fare.

Yet another world-class resort, the *Scottsdale Princess* (☎ 585 4848, fax 585 0086), 7575 E Princess Drive, is the home of the annual PGA Phoenix Open; with 450 beautifully landscaped acres, this is one of the valley's largest full-scale resorts. The resort's La Hacienda restaurant serves the valley's most sophisticated and pricey Mexican food, and the Marquesa is simply the best Spanish (Catalan) restaurant in Arizona. Rooms start at $300, suites at around $500. An even larger property, the *Hyatt Regency Scottsdale* (☎ 991 3388, fax 483 5550, 7500 E Doubletree Ranch Rd, is popular with families. Play in the dozens of fountains and waterfalls, 11 pools, artificial beach, water slide, or playground on the 640-acre Gainey Ranch property while the kids take part a program just for them. The resort's well-reviewed Golden Swan restaurant serves varied American fare.

## PLACES TO EAT

Phoenix has the biggest selection of restaurants in the Southwest. From fast food to ultra-fancy, it's all here. Serious foodies (I don't pretend to be one) will find several world-class kitchens that will lighten their wallets, if nothing else. A useful little book is *100 Best Restaurants in Arizona* by the serendipitously named Harry & Trudy Plate (Kelton Publishing). This book is updated annually and, despite its name, squeezes about 150 restaurants into its covers; sly digs make the reviews fun. About two-thirds of these places are in the valley, and some of the very best are in the resorts listed above – you don't have to stay at the resort to eat at the restaurants. Many resorts serve classy Sunday brunches that require reservations. In fact, reservations are recommended at all the fancier eateries.

Several free publications available from

the chambers of commerce, visitors bureau or newsstands around the valley have extensive restaurant listings. Here is a varied selection of some of the best, including good lower-priced places that are often overlooked in food roundups. Note that all addresses are in Phoenix, unless otherwise indicated.

## Breakfast

While the diners and coffee houses are often good choices, die-hard egg fans can have their breakfast omeletted, creped, Benedicted, scrambled, spiced or otherwise smashed at one of three The *Eggerys* at 5109 N 44th St (☎ 840 5734); 4326 E Cactus Rd (☎ 953 2342); and 50 E Camelback Rd (☎ 263 8554), or at the four related the *Good Egg*s at 2957 W Bell Rd (☎ 993 2797); 906 E Camelback Rd (☎ 274 5393); 13802 N Scottsdale Rd (☎ 483 1090); 6149 N Scottsdale Rd (☎ 991 5416), the last two in Scottsdale. All are open daily from 6:30 am to 2:30 pm and do serve other brunch stuff in a bright and cheerful environment.

Open wide at *Chompie's* (☎ 971 8010), 3202 E Greenway Rd, serving giant blintzes, bagels and huge puffy omelettes for breakfast and the kind of sandwiches you can't get your mouth around for lunch. This is a genuine New York kosher deli with a wide variety of fresh bagels, bialys, knishes, sweet pastries and mouth-watering treats, all made on the premises. Hours are about 6 am to 9 pm, and there's always a line for takeout. This relative newcomer to the valley has been so popular that the owners opened a new location at 9301 E Shea Blvd in Scottsdale (☎ 860 0475).

## Coffee Houses

Dozens of coffee houses dot the valley, many providing entertainment in the evenings. The *Coffee Plantation* (☎ 829 7878), 680 S Mill Ave in Tempe, is a good 24-hour espresso and cappuccino place popular with ASU students; it also serves light meals and a selection of tasty pastries, and provides various entertainment in the evening. Other Coffee Plantations have since opened in several of the valley's

shopping malls, including in the Biltmore Fashion Park, Borgata, Fashion Square and Metrocenter.

For a good selection of coffees, light meals and imported beers and wines, try the *Orbit Coffee House & Cafe* (☎ 265 2354), in the Uptown Plaza at Camelback Rd and Central Ave, providing nightly entertainment in a smoke-free environment. Wednesday is poetry night, and jazz, blues and acoustic are played on other nights; hours are 7 am to 11 pm Monday to Thursday, 7 am to midnight on Friday, 8 am to midnight on Saturday and 8 am to 11 pm on Sunday.

Downtown, *The Art of Coffee* (☎ 254 1566), in the old San Carlos Hotel at 200 N Central Ave, is open Monday to Wednesday from 7 am to 7 pm, and stays open to midnight during the rest of the week, when there is often evening entertainment. *The News* (☎ 852 0982), 5053 N 44th St, features a newsstand with arty publications to read along with your java. Hours here are 7 am to 7 pm Monday to Friday, and 7 am to 3 pm on Saturday.

## Diners

The *5 & Diner* (☎ 264 5220), 5220 N 16th St, is a lot of fun, with inexpensive 24-hour food and friendly service in a very '50s setting. The diner's success has led to the opening of a second location at 9069 E Indian Bend Rd in Scottsdale (☎ 949 1957). If you like this kind of atmosphere, you'll enjoy the ever-popular *Ed Debevic's* (☎ 956 2760), 2102 E Highland Ave, which calls itself 'Short Orders Deluxe', makes great burgers and shakes, and also has a salad bar. Bring change for Elvis on the jukebox. The diner is open from 11 am to 10 pm daily.

## Steak Houses

*Ruth's Chris Steak House*, 2201 E Camelback Rd (☎ 957 9600) and 7001 N Scottsdale Rd (☎ 991 5988), both part of a nationwide chain known for superb steak, serve huge steaks priced in the low $20s and slathered with melted butter; if you want vegetables or potatoes, you'll have to pay extra. Seafood and other meat dishes are also very good. Both are open from 5 to 10 pm daily, and the Phoenix location is also open Monday to Friday from 11:30 am to 3 pm.

Phoenix is a major baseball spring-training center, drawing the sports fans who crowd into *Don & Charlie's* (☎ 990 0900), 7501 E Camelback Rd in Scottsdale. Here, baseball memorabilia covers the walls and the food is meaty, with barbecue priced in the low teens and steaks heading up to over $20. Hours are 5 to 10 pm daily. Ball players, coaches, scouts, sportswriters and assorted hangers-on favor the *Pink Pony Steak House* (☎ 945 6697, 949 8677), 3831 N Scottsdale Rd in Scottsdale, offering ballpark-size servings Monday to Friday from 10 am to 10 pm, and on weekends from 4 to 10 pm.

Basketball fans heading for the America West Arena try to eat at *Majerle's Sports Grill* (☎ 253 9004), 24 N 2nd St, which is super-crowded on game nights. It's owned by the Phoenix Suns' dazzling three-point shooter, Dan Majerle, and has a fun menu (for Suns fans, anyway).

### Seafood

The Californian *Fish Market* (☎ 277 3474), 1720 E Camelback Rd, offers a rustic, net-hung ground floor and a more elegant and pricier *Top of the Market* upstairs. The menu selection is almost as wide as the sea, and prices are equally varied, ranging from about $8 for your basic fish and chips to over $30 for lobster. Hours are 11 am to 9:30 pm downstairs or 5 to 9:30 pm at the top.

The selection is also wide and the surroundings more upscale at *Steamers* (☎ 956 3631), 2576 E Camelback Rd, which is open from 11 am to 10 pm daily (staying open to 11 pm on Friday and Saturday). It also offers a few selections beyond the fish fare. Other recommended seafood places that also offer a few meat dishes are the *Rusty Pelican* at 9801 N Black Canyon Hwy (☎ 944 9646) and 1606 W Baseline Rd in Tempe (☎ 345 0972), and *Trappers* (☎ 990 9256), 3815 N Scottsdale Rd in Scottsdale. All of these are open from 5 to

9:30 or 10 pm, and the Rusty Pelicans also serve lunch Monday to Friday.

### Soul Food & Cajun

*Mrs White's Golden Rule Cafe* (☎ 262 9256), 808 E Jefferson St, is a hole-in-the-wall with hanging hand-lettered menus, but greasy spoon it ain't – the food is cheap, well-prepared and tasty. The Golden Rule is to remember what you ate when you pay at the register at the end of your meal. Hours are usually 9 am to 6 pm Monday to Friday. *Bev's Kitchen* (☎ 252 1455), 7 W Monroe St, and the newer *Bev's Kitchen South* (☎ 243 2788), 4621 S Central Ave, offers a more standard environment and great Southern cooking for a slightly higher price. Try the catfish and cabbage.

The Muslim-run *Unique Foods & Services* (☎ 257 0701), 1153 E Jefferson St, serves barbecued ribs and hot links, fried catfish and plenty of good greens and beans. The restaurant is open daily from 10:30 am to 7 pm except Friday and Saturday, when it stays open until midnight and features live jazz in a smoke and alcohol-free environment.

For the valley's best Cajun catfish and crawfish, try *Baby Kay's Cajun Kitchen* in the Town & Country Mall (☎ 955 0011) and 7216 E Shoeman Lane in Scottsdale (☎ 990 9080). Both are small, unpretentious places locally famed for delicious 'dirty rice', a mixture of rice with sausage, onions, peppers and seasonings. The Phoenix location serves lunch Monday to Saturday from 11 am to 3 pm, and both are open Monday to Saturday from 5 to 10 pm for dinner. Dinner entrees are in the $8 to $15 range.

### Southwestern

After enjoying great success in Tucson favorite, the owners of *Cafe Terra Cotta* opened a second location in Scottsdale (☎ 948 8100), 6166 N Scottsdale Rd at the Borgata Mall. The cafe is open from 11 am to 10 pm daily, and stays open to 11 pm on Friday and Saturday. The moderately priced menu is pretty innovative, even wild-sounding at times, but there are also a

ARIZONA

few fairly straightforward choices for the less adventurous. Be sure to leave room for one of the heavenly desserts.

The classiest Southwestern restaurant is *Vincent Guerithault on Camelback* (☎ 224 0225), 3930 E Camelback Rd, serving food with the famous chef's French touch; with dinner entrees priced around $20, the restaurant is not too outrageously expensive, considering the haute cuisine. The restaurant is open Monday to Friday from 11:30 am to 2:30 pm, and Monday to Saturday from and 6 to 10:30 pm. It may open for Sunday dinner in the high season.

Another expensively priced but well-recommended Southwestern restaurant is the *8700 at the Citadel* (☎ 994 8700), 8700 Pinnacle Peak Rd in Scottsdale, open from 6 to 10 pm daily. If you're a jazz fan, try the similarly priced *Timothy's* (☎ 277 7634), 6335 N 16th St, open from 6 pm to 1 pm and providing live jazz for no additional cover.

For somewhat cheaper Southwestern fare, visit *Sam's Cafe* (☎ 252 3545), downtown in the Arizona Center at N 3rd and Van Buren Sts. Sam's is open daily from 11 am to 10 pm, staying open to midnight on Friday and Saturday. Cheaper still but also good, the *Coyote Grill* (☎ 404 8966), 3202 E Greenway Rd, is open from 11 am to 10 pm daily and has a free buffet during happy hour Monday to Friday from 4 to 6:30 pm.

### Other American Cuisine

One of Mesa's best restaurants, the *Landmark* (☎ 962 4652), 809 W Main St in Mesa, has been serving good American food for over two decades. Built as a Mormon church in the early 1900s, the restaurant is decorated with turn-of-the-century antiques and photos, and has a huge salad bar; the home-style traditional American dinner entrees priced in the $10 to $14 range (including salad bar) draw crowds of knowing locals. It is open Monday to Friday from 11:30 am to 2 pm, Monday to Saturday from 4 to 9 pm and noon to 7 pm on Sunday.

*Christopher's Bistro*, next to Christopher's French Restaurant (see below),

serves sophisticated American food to an upscale yuppie clientele from 11 am to 10 pm daily; hours vary during summer. Dinner entrees cost around $20.

You can't help but feel intrigued by a name like that of the *Impeccable Pig* (☎ 941 1141), 7042 E Indian School Rd in Scottsdale. Just as interesting as its name, the restaurant, in an antique shop, features a chalkboard menu listing a changing selection of American and continental repasts priced in the upper teens for dinner (early-bird diners get a discount before 6:30 pm) Hours are 11 am to 3 pm Monday to Saturday and 5 to 9 pm from Tuesday to Saturday.

Scottsdale shoppers like to stop at the pink and white *Sugar Bowl Ice Cream Parlor* (☎ 946 0051), 4005 N Scottsdale Rd, which serves light meals but specializes in the cold stuff; it is open from 11 am to 11 pm daily.

If all this is just too fancy, frugal feeders can try the cafeteria-style *Furr's* at 8114 N Black Canyon Hwy (☎ 995 1588) and 1834 W Main St in Mesa (☎ 962 9107), serving a wide range of dinners for about $6; both are open from 11 am to 8 pm daily.

### French

*Christopher's* (☎ 957 3214), 2398 E Camelback Rd, is the work of the noted American chef Christopher Gross and competes with L'Auberge de Sedona for title of the best, most innovative (and expensive) French restaurant in Arizona. A-la-carte dinner entrees are about $30, while the prix-fixe six- or seven-course dinner, with appropriate wines, is close to $150 when you include tax and tip (that's for one person). The service in this small, intimate restaurant is excellent and unrushed, allowing you to spend hours over the gastronomic experience. Don't forget to make a reservation and men should wear a jacket (the one with the elbow patches might not quite do it). Hours are 6 to 10 pm daily, though the restaurant is closed two or more days in summer.

If innovation isn't high on your list when eating French food, you'll find *Voltaire*

(☎ 948 1005), 8340 E McDonald Drive in Scottsdale, perfect for traditional French dishes at much more reasonable prices. The atmosphere is elegant, the service attentive, and most entrees are priced in the high teens; it is open Tuesday to Saturday from 5:30 to 11 pm, and is closed on Sunday and Monday and from June to September. Another good and unpretentious French place with similarly priced food is *Jean-Claude's Petit Cafe* (☎ 947 5288), 7340 E Shoeman Lane in Scottsdale. This one is open Monday to Friday from 11:30 am to 2:30 pm and 6 to 10 pm, and Saturday from 6 to 10 pm.

### Italian

For top-notch Italian food in a sophisticated setting, dine at *Avanti*, 2728 E Thomas Rd (☎ 956 0900) and 3102 N Scottsdale Rd in Scottsdale (☎ 949 8333). The fancier entrees are in the $20s, though simple pasta dishes cost half that. Hours are 5:30 to 11 pm daily and, in Phoenix only, from 11:30 am to 3 pm Monday to Friday.

For great Italian food at half the price of the Avanti, try the busy and often crowded *Chianti* (☎ 957 9840), 3943 E Camelback Rd, which is open Monday to Friday from 11:30 am to 10 pm and weekends from 5 to 10 pm. Somewhere between these two choices lies *Christo's* (☎ 264 1784), 6327 N 7th St, a contemporary place serving excellent Italian food and some Mediterranean-influenced dishes from 11:30 am to 2:30 pm, Monday to Friday, and from 5:30 to 10 pm, Monday to Saturday.

Homemade pasta (you can watch it being made in the open kitchen) is the highlight at *Maria's When in Naples* (☎ 991 6887), 7000 E Shea Blvd in Scottsdale. Maria's serves pasta dishes for about $10 or $12, as well as other more expensive entrees. Hours are 11:30 am to 2:30 pm Monday to Friday and 5 to 10 pm daily.

Families with small children enjoy the kids' menu and the wide selection of pizza and pasta dishes (most well under $10) at *Tuchetti* (☎ 957 0222), 2135 E Camelback Rd close to the Town & Country Mall. The decor is Italy a la Disney, and hours are

from 11 am to 10 pm Monday to Thursday, from 11 am to 11 pm on Friday, noon to 11 pm on Saturday and 4:30 to 9 pm on Sunday.

### German

*Bavarian Point* (☎ 830 0999), 4815 E Main St in the Main St Plaza, is arguably the best and most authentic German restaurant in Arizona. Huge, tasty dinners run from $10 to $20; don't skip the delicious desserts. Hours are 11 am to 10 pm daily.

### Greek

Another 'best in Arizona' is *Greekfest* (☎ 265 2990), 1940 E Camelback Rd. Both food and ambiance are delightful, and the prices, in the teens for most dinner entrees, are reasonable. It is open for lunch Monday to Saturday from 11 am to 2:30 pm, and dinner starts at 5 pm daily and ends at 9 pm on Sunday, 11 pm on Friday and Saturday, and 10 pm the rest of the week.

### Mexican

*El Bravo* (☎ 943 9753), 8338 N 7th St, serves good combination plates for just $5 and offers a choice of inexpensive a la carte Sonoran dishes. (The piñatas that decorate the dining area are for sale, too.) This simple and genuine family restaurant has received great reviews but remains uncrowded because of its non-central location; it is open Monday to Thursday from 10 am to 8 pm and Friday and Saturday from 10 am to 9 pm. Another cheap local favorite, the basic-looking *La Cucaracha* (☎ 274 8312) at 998 E Indian School Rd has been serving genuine Sonoran food for over 50 years. Go for the food, not the surroundings. It is open Monday to Saturday from 11 am to 9 pm.

A downtown favorite, the large, modern *Matador* (☎ 254 7563), 125 E Adams St, is open from 7 am to 11 pm, so you can get a Mexican breakfast and a hangover-curing menudo. Choices include a few non-Mexican items as well, and lines are often out the door with office workers grabbing breakfast or lunch, but these usually move pretty quickly.

*Carlos O'Brien's* (☎ 274 5883), 1133 E Northern Ave, sells what is unkindly called 'gringo Mexican food'. The large and tasty portions provide good food value, and the huge restaurant has plenty of room and is popular with families. Hours are 11 am to 11 pm.

If you want great south-of-the-border food, try *Los Dos Molinos* at 8646 S Central Ave (☎ 243 9113) or at 260 S Alma School Rd in Mesa (☎ 243 9113). The food is New Mexican influenced, so it's hotter than Sonoran cuisine and delicious if you like chiles. The friendly family-run restaurant has family members working the stove and tables; ask them to hold the hot sauce if you're not a hot-chile fan. The restaurant is open Tuesday to Sunday from 11 am to 8:30 pm.

### Cuban

If you like Cuban food as much as I do, visit the *Havana Cafe* (☎ 952 1991), 4225 E Camelback Rd. The food is excellent and the prices, mostly in the $10 to $13 range for dinner entrees, are not too outrageous. The cafe is open from 11:30 am to 10 pm, and is closed Sunday except in the high season.

### Japanese

Three Japanese restaurants compete for reviewers' praise, and each has its adherents. One has been called the best in Arizona, while another is supposedly the best in the valley, and a third is the happening spot right now. All are good and serve both cooked dishes and sushi, so just visit the most convenient one. The three are *Mikado* (☎ 481 9777), 7111 E Camelback Rd in Scottsdale, open daily at 5 pm, closing Sunday to Thursday at 10 pm, and Friday and Saturday at 11 pm; *Shogun* (☎ 953 3264), 12615 N Tatum Blvd, open Tuesday to Saturday from 11 am to 2:30 pm and 5 to 10 pm, and Sunday and Monday from 5 to 9 pm; and *Yamakasa* (☎ 860 5605), 9301 E Shea Blvd in Scottsdale. The Yamakasa is closed on Wednesday. Most meals in these places are priced in the teens.

### Indian

Most Indian restaurants offer all-you-can-eat lunch buffets for about $5 that will fill you up but won't necessarily delight your palate. A la carte dinners, while somewhat pricier ($7 to $20), are freshly prepared and are also a good value unless you're very hungry and penurious.

The best is probably *A Jewel of the Crown* (☎ 840 2412), 4141 N Scottsdale Rd in Scottsdale, open from 11:30 am to 2 pm and 5 to 10 pm. Other locally popular places with similar hours are *Taste of India* at 1609 E Bell Rd (☎ 788 3190) and 3160 E Camelback Rd (☎ 955 7704). Also good is the *India Delhi Palace* (☎ 244 8181), 5050 E McDowell Rd, and three locations of *India Palace*, at 16842 N 7th St (☎ 942 4224); 933 E University Drive in Tempe (☎ 921 2200); and 4228 N Scottsdale Rd in Scottsdale (☎ 970 3300).

### Chinese

There are scores of Chinese restaurants. A local favorite is the bustling *Gourmet House of Hong Kong* (☎ 253 4859), 1438 E McDowell Rd. The menu is very long and the prices low, the food very good and the surroundings not particularly noteworthy. It is open daily from 11 am to 10 pm, staying open to 11 pm on Friday and Saturday. If you want opulent surroundings with your Peking duck, *Mr C's* (☎ 941 4460), 4302 N Scottsdale Rd in Scottsdale, will take care of you. The food is classic and pricey Canton; many say it's the best in town. Mr C's is open daily from 11 am to 2:30 pm and 5 to 10 pm, staying open to 11 pm on Friday and Saturday.

### Thai

The three moderately priced *Pink Peppers* offer locally popular and contemporary Thai cuisine: 245 E Bell (☎ 548 1333); 2003 N Scottsdale Rd in Scottsdale (☎ 945 9300); and 1941 W Guadalupe Rd in Mesa (☎ 839 9009), open Monday to Friday from 11 am to 2:30 pm and Monday to Thursday 4:30 to 10 pm, staying open to 11 pm on Friday, and 4:30 to 11 pm on Saturday and 4:30 to 10 pm on Sunday. Prices are very moderate. Slightly pricier is the very well recommended *Malee's on Main* (☎ 947 6042), 7131 E Main St in Scottsdale, open from 11:30 am to 2:30 pm and 5 to 9:30 pm daily.

## Eclectic

Eclectic, adventurous, risky, creative, international and transcontinental have all been used to describe *RoxSand* (☎ 381 0444), 2594 E Camelback Rd, in the Biltmore Fashion Park. The menu roams from Jamaican jerked rabbit to African pheasant to Japanese scallops (these entrees go for around $20) as well as some cheaper and less adventurous options (such as a $10 pizza). This is a good place to eat a complete meal or just drop in for a super dessert. Hours are 11 am to 10 pm Monday to Saturday, and Sunday hours vary.

## ENTERTAINMENT

For what's going on, read the free alternative weekly *New Times*, published every Thursday and available at numerous boxes and other outlets around the city. The daily papers also have entertainment information, especially in the Friday and Sunday editions of *The Arizona Republic* and the Saturday edition of the *Phoenix Gazette*. Look for the several other alternative papers that may also have information.

## Cinema

There are dozens of cinema multiplexes throughout the valley showing the year's best and worst movies. Call All Movies (☎ 813 2121) for times, prices and locations. The best selection is at the locally owned Harkins Theaters chain, but there are some alternatives, including the *Valley Art Theater* (☎ 829 6666 or 6668), 509 S Mill Ave in Tempe, with regular Saturday midnight showings of *The Rocky Horror Picture Show* and a variety of foreign and alternatives flicks throughout the week, and the *IMAX Theater* (☎ 945 4629) in Scottsdale, one block east of Scottsdale Rd on Civic Center Blvd, showing documentary-type movies designed for the eight-times-larger-than-normal screen.

## Nightlife

Many of the following spots are very busy on Friday and Saturday nights, but usually provide entertainment five to seven nights a week at a varying cover charge. For more ideas, see Coffee Houses under Places to Eat.

The entertainment scene in Tempe, home of ASU, is aimed at students. Mill Ave between 3rd and 6th Sts is the off-campus nightlife center with a number of bars and clubs. There are plenty of cops hanging around at closing time, and their attitude is generally friendly. Places come and go; currently *Gibsons* (☎ 829 7047, 967 1234), 410 S Mill Ave, is a popular joint where decent live rock bands play, and the *Balboa Jazz Cafe* (☎ 966 1300), 404 S Mill Ave, has good live jazz as well as rock bands.

In downtown Phoenix, the Arizona Center provides a number of options aimed at the younger post-work crowd. If you can't make up your mind, the $5 cover at *Phoenix Live!* (☎ 252 2112) allows you to circulate between four options. *Little Ditty's* has two pianos going full tilt and everyone singing along to old favorites. Can't remember the words? No worries. People hold up song boards with the 'lyrics' in huge letters, so everyone has fun. Next door, the *American Sports Bar* has dozens of coin-operated machines ranging from basketball to Foosball. Beyond that is *Puzzles*, a DJ-driven nightclub playing mainly modern and alternative rock for dancing; it also has a restaurant. If none of these appeal, spend $2 to get into *Cheyenne Trading Co* (☎ 253 6225), and dance to recorded country & western and top-40 music (lessons are given most nights). If dancing is not your thing, you can just listen to background music in one of the bars/eateries at no cover.

Go west for the best in country & western. *Mr Lucky's* (☎ 246 0686), 3660 NW Grand Ave, has live country & western and dancing on the ground floor, light rock and dancing in the basement, and a corral outside with bull riding competitions on weekends (with real bulls, not the mechanical kind), when there is a $5 cover. Almost

ARIZONA

every patron is dressed in Western wear (I think I was the only man there without a cowboy hat). It's a short ride to *Toolies Country* (☎ 272 3100), 4231 W Thomas Rd, booking some of the best country & western bands in the valley. *Denim & Diamonds* (☎ 225 0182), 3905 E Thomas Rd, has a DJ and dance floor with free country & western dance lessons several times a week. More upscale country & western places are found in some of the resorts, including *Rustlers Rooste* (☎ 431 6474) at the Pointe Hilton on South Mountain and the *Red River Opry* (☎ 829 6779), at Mill Ave and Washington St in Tempe, hosting various country performances, musical reviews and big-name acts in a theater setting.

Jazz lovers can listen to KJZZ FM (91.5) on the radio or call the jazz hotline (☎ 254 4545) for a schedule of top performances. Also see *Timothy's* and *Unique Foods & Services* under Places to Eat.

For good blues, stop by the popular and crowded *Char's Has the Blues* (☎ 230 0205), 4631 N 7th Ave. *Warsaw Wallies* (☎ 955 0881), 2547 E Indian School Rd, is a small place but had an exceptional blues band on my recent visit, when the cover was just $1.50. Good blues is also the staple of the *Rhythm Room* (☎ 265 4842), 1019 E Indian School Rd. *Coyote Springs Brewing Company & Cafe* (☎ 468 0403), 4883 N 20th St, is a microbrewery serving good handcrafted beers and hosting fine local R&B bands. For a variety of alternative rock, the *Mason Jar* (☎ 956 6271), 2303 E Indian School Rd, is a good choice, with three to five bands attracting a young crowd of people dressed in black nightly.

### Performing Arts

The following are the most highly acclaimed places to hear and see performing arts, but not much goes on here during the summer.

The *Herberger Theater Center* (☎ 252 8497, 678 2222), 222 E Monroe St, has two stages that host productions by the Arizona Theater Company (☎ 256 6995), Ballet Arizona (☎ 381 0184), the Actors Theater of Phoenix (☎ 256 6995) and occasionally others.

The *Helen K Mason Center for the Performing Arts* (☎ 258 8128), 333 E Portland St, is the home of the Black Theater Troupe and also hosts other African-American performers.

*Symphony Hall* (☎ 262 7272), 225 E Adams St, is the home of the Arizona Opera (☎ 266 7464) and the Phoenix Symphony Orchestra (☎ 264 6363).

The *Gammage Auditorium* (☎ 965 3434), on the ASU Campus at Mill Ave and Apache Blvd, is the university's main center for performing arts.

### Spectator Sports

Phoenix has some of the nation's top professional teams, but getting tickets for the best games is not always easy as they sell out early. Call as far in advance as possible or, if nothing is available, look in the yellow pages under Ticket Sales or in newspaper classifieds for tickets (they're often overpriced).

The Phoenix Suns (☎ 379 7867) play national championship-level **basketball** at the spiffy new America West Arena (☎ 379 7800), 201 E Jefferson St, from fall to spring. In summer, the arena is home of the Arizona Sandsharks (☎ 514 5425) **soccer** team and the Arizona Rattlers (☎ 514 8383) **arena football** team.

The Arizona Cardinals (☎ 379 0102) play professional **football** (fall to spring) at ASU Sun Devil Stadium in Tempe, the site of the 1996 Super Bowl, the nation's most prestigious football game. ASU student teams (such as the Sun Devils, ☎ 965 2381) also use the stadium.

Phoenix is in the process of starting a major-league **baseball** franchise that should be playing by the late 1990s. Meanwhile, several major-league teams carry out their spring training in the valley, providing a chance to watch the best players for low prices. Call the visitors bureau for the several teams, sites and schedules.

The Phoenix Roadrunners (☎ 340 0001) play **ice hockey** (fall to spring) at the Arizona Veterans Memorial Coliseum, in the State Fairgrounds at 1826 W McDowell Rd.

**Golf** professionals compete for a seven-figure purse at the PGA Phoenix Open, held every January at the Tournament Players Club (☎ 585 4334, ext 237 for tee times), 17020 N Hayden Rd in Scottsdale.

You can watch **horseracing** at Turf Paradise (☎ 942 1101), 19th Ave and Bell, from October to May, and **greyhounds** race year round at Phoenix Greyhound Park (☎ 273 7181), 3801 E Washington St. **Car racing** happens at Phoenix International Raceway (☎ 252 3833 or 2227 for tickets), 7602 S 115 Ave, Avondale.

## THINGS TO BUY

The question is not so much what to buy (you can buy just about anything) but where to go. The bottom line is that the valley has several notable shopping malls. Scottsdale is the art gallery capital of Arizona. The Heard Museum has the best bookshop about Native Americans and the most reliable, excellent and high-priced selection of Native American arts & crafts.

You may not be a fan of shopping malls, but the air conditioning does give them a certain allure when the mercury climbs in summer. Shopping malls include the Metrocenter at I-17 exit 208 and Peoria Ave, the largest enclosed mall in Arizona, which has four department stores, standard shopping and many attractions for kids. The Park Central Mall, at Central Ave and Osborn Rd, is the city's oldest (but still reasonably fashionable) shopping center.

For more upscale shopping, visit the Scottsdale Fashion Square at Camelback and Scottsdale Rds in Scottsdale, or the tonier Biltmore Fashion Park at Camelback Rd and 24th St in Phoenix; both provide a good selection of cheap to expensive restaurants and the Biltmore is home to some of the valley's best eateries. Near the Biltmore, the Town & Country shopping center also has several decent restaurants.

Perhaps the fanciest selection of boutiques and galleries is at the Borgata, 6166 N Scottsdale Rd in Scottsdale, a mall designed to look like a medieval town. Also very trendy are the Fifth Avenue Shops surrounding 6940 E 5th St in Scottsdale. You'll find many galleries, tourist-oriented shops

and the Scottsdale Galleria (at the intersection of 5th Ave and Scottsdale Rd) along Main St in nearby downtown Scottsdale.

The outdoor Arizona Center is revitalizing downtown at 3rd and Van Buren Sts, with several popular bars, restaurants and a small selection of interesting shops.

If you need camping or outdoor gear, REI (☎ 967 5494), 1405 W Southern Ave in Tempe, has one of the largest selections in the Southwest and does mail-order as well.

## GETTING THERE & AWAY
### Air

Phoenix's Sky Harbor International Airport (☎ 273 3300 for the main switchboard or 392 0310 for airport information) is three miles southeast of downtown. By far the largest airport in the Southwest, its three terminals (illogically called Terminal 2, 3 and 4) contain all the standard features of any major airport. Each terminal has a pricey parking lot, but to save money, you can leave your car at the Park 'n Ride lot northwest of 24th St and Sky Harbor Blvd, near the west entrance of the airport. A frequent free shuttle connects the terminals and Park 'n Ride.

Valley Metro (☎ 253 5000) has two bus lines serving the airport. The Red Line operates every 15 to 30 minutes Monday to Friday from 4 am to 9:45 pm, driving to Tempe and Mesa along Apache Blvd and Main St, or west into downtown and then into north Phoenix. Bus No 13 operates every 30 to 60 minutes from 5:15 am to 8:30 pm from Monday to Friday and until 7:45 pm on Saturday, taking a westerly route along Buckeye Rd. Fares are $1 and transfers are available. Super Shuttle (☎ 244 9000), Airport Direct (☎ 266 1322) and Tempest Shuttle (☎ 548 3399) have vans providing airport-to-your-door service at any time. Fares are somewhat lower than taxis, which add a $1 airport surcharge in addition to their metered rates.

### Bus

Greyhound (☎ 1 (800) 231 2222) has a main terminal (☎ 271 7425) at 525 E Washington St and suburban bus stations in

Tempe (☎ 967 4030), 502 S College Ave; in Mesa (☎ 834 3360), 1423 S Country Club Drive; and at Glendale, Buckeye, Chandler, Tolleson and Youngstown. Phoenix is at the center of a fairly extensive bus network throughout and beyond the state. White Mountain Passenger Lines (☎ 275 4245), 319 S 24th St, sends daily buses to Payson and Show Low, and the Arizona Shuttle Service (☎ 1 (800) 888 2749) has many vans a day linking Phoenix Airport with Tucson. Other local bus companies linking Phoenix Airport with Arizona towns beyond the valley are listed under those towns.

### Train

Amtrak (☎ 1 (800) 872 7245) trains stop at the Union Station (☎ 253 0121), 401 W Harrison St, on the south side of downtown Phoenix. Three night trains a week go to Yuma and Los Angeles, California, and three morning trains a week go to Tucson, east through New Mexico and on to Miami, Florida. Amtrak provides a daily bus connection to Flagstaff.

### Car Rental

All the main companies have airport offices, and many have offices in other parts of the valley or will deliver your car. It is best to reserve a car in advance for the best rates.

### GETTING AROUND

### Bus

Valley Metro (☎ 253 5000) operates buses all over the valley from Monday to Friday and on a limited basis on Saturday. Some routes are limited-stop Express Services, and most routes stop operating in the early evening. Fares are $1 or $3 for an all-day pass, or $28 for a monthly pass. Express Services cost $1.50 per trip, or $42 for a monthly pass. People over 65 or between six and 18 years old ride for half fare. (You may have to show picture ID if the driver questions your age.) Exact fare is required or you can buy 50¢ tokens from the Main Downtown Bus Terminal at 1st St and Washington St. Free transfers are available.

As of May 1995, Valley Metro became the first city in the country to allow riders to use their credit cards to pay the fare. About 130,000 people board Valley Metro every day, and officials say that during the first two days of the credit card system, a total of 78 passengers used their Visas or Master-Cards. Transit officials throughout the country are watching the new Phoenix system carefully.

The DASH bus system runs from downtown out to the State Capitol, leaving every six to 12 minutes from 6:30 am to 6 pm Monday to Friday. The flat fare for this route only is 25¢, and frequent downtown riders and groups can buy 250 DASH tokens for $25.

### Taxi

There are several 24-hour cab services, but with a $2 drop fee and fares of well over $1 per mile, you can rack up a pricey ride in the large valley area. Car rental is a better bet for most longer rides. Some of the main cab companies are Ace Taxi (☎ 254 1999), which claims to have the lowest rates but isn't licensed to pick you up at the airport; AAA Cab (☎ 253 8294 in Phoenix, 437 4000 in Scottsdale/Tempe, 968 8294 in Mesa/Chandler); Checker Cab (☎ 257 1818); and Yellow Cab (☎ 252 5262).

### Bicycle

The following are a few of several bike rental shops: Adventure Bicycle Co (☎ 649 3374), 1110 W Southern Ave in Mesa; Airpark Bicycle Center (☎ 596 6633), 15001 N Hayden Rd, and Wheels 'n Gear (☎ 945 2881), 7607 E McDowell Rd, both in Scottsdale; and Tempe Bicycles (☎ 966 6896), 330 W University Drive in Tempe.

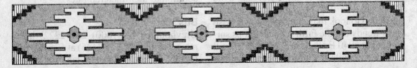

# Grand Canyon & Lake Powell

The slogan on the Arizona license plate says it all: 'Grand Canyon State'. The Grand Canyon of the Colorado River is Arizona's most famous sight – indeed, it is arguably the best known natural attraction in the entire country. This grandest of all canyons has been declared a UN World Heritage Site to be protected for all people.

At 277 miles long, roughly 10 miles wide and a mile deep, the canyon sounds big. But there is more than its sheer size that makes the sight so tremendous. It is also the incredible spectacle of differently colored rock strata, the many buttes and peaks within the canyon itself, and the meandering rims that give access to fantastic views which amaze the visitor. Staring from the many rim overlooks gives a great impression of the grandeur, but walking down into the canyon on a short hike or a multi-day backpacking trip gives a better sense of the variety in the landscape, wildlife and climate.

Although the rims are only 10 miles apart as the crow flies, it is a 215-mile, five-hour drive on narrow roads from the visitors center on the South Rim to the visitors center on the North Rim. Thus the Grand Canyon National Park is essentially two separate areas that are treated separately in this chapter. I begin by describing the South Rim, and continue with the countryside and small towns to the immediate south and east of the park. Then comes the remote and little visited area to the north of the park, known as the Arizona Strip, which contains the North Rim of Grand Canyon National Park the major sight of the area. Finally comes Page and the Glen Canyon Dam area, which is on the Colorado River just outside the northeastern corner of the park.

## History

Scattered throughout the canyon are signs of ancient Native American inhabitants.

The oldest artifacts are little twig figures of animals made by hunters and gatherers about 4000 years ago – a few of these can be seen in the Tusayan Museum in Grand Canyon Village. More common are the hundreds of stone ruins built by the Anasazi before their unexplained departure during the 12th century.

Cerbat people began living at the western end of the canyon around 1300 AD and are the ancestors of the present-day Hualapai and Havasupai tribes. Despite various attempts to dislodge them, these two tribes continue to live in (what are now) reservations on the southwestern rim of the canyon. These reservations abut the Grand Canyon National Park, but you can't enter them from the park – you need to drive south then west (see the reservations' sections in this chapter for details about visiting).

The earliest European visitors to the canyon were Spaniards who looked into the depths of the canyon in 1540. The canyon was hard to reach and involved crossing large areas with little water. Since there didn't appear to be any mineral wealth, and the general opinion was that the place was magnificent but valueless, European visits were few for over three centuries.

The first serious exploration was in 1869, when John Wesley Powell, a one-armed veteran of the Civil War, led an expedition along the Colorado River. Using simple wooden boats, they ran the entire length of the Grand and other canyons – a remarkable achievement. Powell led a similar expedition in 1871-72. These resulted in detailed scientific observations and his book, *The Exploration of the Colorado River of the West and its Tributaries*, reprinted by Penguin Books in 1989.

Although Powell's were the first expeditions to run the canyon, there are records of a prospector, James White, who claimed to have run the river on a log raft in 1867 while escaping from Ute Indians who had

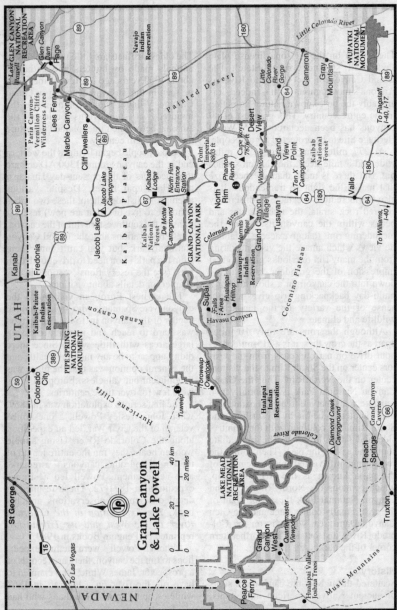

**Grand Canyon & Lake Powell**

killed one of his partners. The truth of this account is still open to debate.

During the late 1800s, Mormons began to settle the remote Arizona Strip and prospectors and miners ventured into the canyon in search of mineral wealth but found little. One miner, John Hance, arrived in 1883 and decided that catering to tourists would be more profitable than mining. He became one of the most colorful and well-known guides into the canyon, famous for his tall tales. Some simple lodges were built for the few tourists who made it to the South Rim by stagecoach or horseback. Then, in 1901, the railroad arrived and tourism began to be big business. The Fred Harvey Company started building lodges and providing tourist services – this company remains the park's main concessionaire today. President Theodore Roosevelt visited the canyon in 1903 and said 'You cannot improve on it'. He set out to protect the canyon, first as a national monument in 1908 and later as a park in 1919. The park has expanded since and its current size is 1892 sq miles.

## Geology

The oldest rocks, near the bottom of the inner canyon, are 1.7 billion years old – a good chunk of time even when compared to the age of the planet (4.6 billion years). However, the layers making up most of the canyon walls were laid during the Paleozoic Era, about 250 to 570 million years ago. These strata of the Grand Canyon were in place well before the Americas began drifting apart from the Old World roughly 200 million years ago. The result of sedimentary deposits from the oceans that once covered this land, these layers are clearly visible to even the most casual of observers. Many different marine fossils have been found in the canyon walls.

Some 60 or 70 million years ago, at about the same time that the Rocky Mountains were being formed, the uplift of the Colorado Plateau emerged. For millions of years after this uplift, rivers flowed north from the north side of the plateau and south from the south side. The Grand Canyon

itself began to form when a shifting of the San Andreas Fault created the Gulf of California about 5.5 million years ago. South flowing rivers combined into what is now the lower Colorado River along the Arizona-California boundary and emptied into this new sea. The headwaters of the river eroded northward into the Grand Wash Cliffs (near the present Arizona-Nevada boundary) and when the river broke through this barrier, it connected with the upper Colorado river system. This then changed its course from northward into Utah to southward to the Gulf of California and the combined rivers continued to erode the developing Grand Canyon.

Volcanic eruptions a mere 1.2 million years ago sent lava flows into the Grand Canyon, slowing the river and the erosion process. But by that time, most of the canyon had already been formed and what we see today has not substantially changed in the last million years.

Today's visitor can leave Flagstaff, drive past lava fields that are less than a thousand years old and, within a couple of hours, be walking down a trail that leads to schist formations which are almost two billion years old. The trip is physically demanding, but even more challenging is the mental struggle to comprehend the awesome geological and temporal significance of the canyon.

## Climate & When to Go

On average, South Rim temperatures are 20°F cooler than the bottom of the canyon. This means you could wake up to frost on the ground in April and be basking in the 80°s F by afternoon if you hike down into the inner gorge. The peak season ranges from about April to November, and the park is busiest from Memorial Day to Labor Day.

At the South Rim, from Memorial Day to Labor Day, expect highs in the 80°s F and lows around 50°F. June is the driest month of the year but summer thunderstorms make July and August the wettest months. Weather is cooler and changeable in the fall and you can expect snow and freezing overnight temperatures by November.

## The Most Popular National Park

The Grand Canyon National Park is by far the most heavily visited of all the national parks in the Southwest. During the early 1990s, about 4.5 million visitors arrived annually and five million are predicted by the middle of the decade, resulting in a great impact and strain on many aspects of the park.

It's easy to forget that much of the canyon is essentially a desert. Visitors require water for drinking and washing, but the only available water has to be piped in from a spring on the north wall of the canyon. A quick look over the rim will convince you that this was not the easiest pipe-laying project! When a storm broke the pipe in 1995, all water had to be trucked in.

During the busy summer season, hotels and campgrounds are booked up months in advance and parking lots are often filled to capacity – visitors have to wait just to park. This just adds to the air quality problems caused by the heavy traffic on the Rim Drive.

Some people drop litter, others attempt to feed wildlife (sometimes getting themselves bitten in the process). Animals become used to human food and seek it out. Recently 15 deer had to be shot because they were starving to death: their stomachs were so clogged with several pounds of indigestible food wrappers and plastic bags, they couldn't feed any more.

Other problems come from outside the park. Air pollution has seriously reduced visibility in the canyon in recent years. Smog, from as far west as Los Angeles, and sulfur emissions from the Navajo Generating Station near Glen Canyon Dam in the east are blown in. The flow and characteristics of the Colorado River have been changed and continue to change because of the Glen Canyon Dam. Half of the species of fish in the river before the dam was built are now extinct. Tourist flights over the national park create noise that is hard to get away from. And there is constant pressure to develop further.

The picture, however, is not a hopeless one. Essentially, the problem has resulted from a lot of poorly planned development over a short period of time. Part of the solution, therefore, is to plan carefully and to think ahead. Another part is to find ways of reducing the impact of existing operations, be they power plants or park visitors.

To some extent, this is being done. Perhaps the most successful, or at least best known, recent change was the signing, in 1991, of an agreement to reduce sulfur emissions of the

January is the coldest month with average overnight lows in the teens and daytime highs around 40°F. Winter weather can be beautifully clear but be prepared for occasional storms that can cause havoc.

Freezing overnight temperatures are still frequent in April when snowfall is possible and the weather is very changeable. In common with much of the Southwest, March and April are often very windy.

In the inner canyon, the weather is much drier with about eight inches of rain annually, about half that of the South Rim. Summer temperatures go above 100°F almost every day and often exceed 110°F in midsummer, which can be potentially lethal for unprepared hikers. July to September are generally the wettest months, though some rain is recorded even in the driest month of June. Strong hot winds often blow in summer. Even in midwinter, freezing overnight temperatures are rare,

with average lows in the upper 30°s F and highs in the upper 50°s F.

Although the South Rim is open all year, the majority of visitors come in the three months between Memorial Day and Labor Day. Avoid that time if at all possible – it is very crowded indeed.

On the North Rim, overnight temperatures drop below freezing as late as May and as early as October. The hottest month, July, sees average highs in the upper 70°s F and lows in the mid 40°s F. The North Rim is wetter than the South Rim although June is still the driest month. Summer thunderstorms occur from July into early September. Winter snowfall is heaviest from late December to early March, when overnight temperatures normally fall into the teens and sometimes below 10°F. However, since visitors services are closed on the North Rim from October to mid-May (although the park is still open and intrepid travelers may

Navajo Generating Station by 90% before the end of the century. But there are many other signs of progress in combating park deterioration: recycling projects; free shuttle buses to cut down on car traffic and exhaust; some management of the Glen Canyon Dam and air traffic; the requirement for river runners to carry portable toilets to be emptied away from the river at the end of the trip; encouragement of low impact camping techniques; and much more.

Many of these issues are addressed in a special exhibit called *Grand Canyon: Geography of Hope*, which opened at the main visitors center in 1995.

The problems are being tackled, but further work is clearly essential. One idea being discussed is the development of greater facilities in Tusayan, just outside the south entrance. This might relieve some of the immediate pressure on Grand Canyon Village, but it might also create a new destination in its own right, thus increasing overall visitation to the park. Another is the construction of a huge parking lot in Tusayan and transporting visitors by shuttle buses. A third is to create a reservation system for all visitors, not just those who are staying overnight. All of these ideas create their own problems, but at least there is serious and thoughtful discussion of management options.

Whether you spend two hours or two months visiting the Grand Canyon, you have the choice of being part of the problem or part of the solution. What can you do? The most immediately obvious thing is not to litter or feed the wildlife. Place recyclables into the appropriate containers. Consider bringing water jugs into the park with you and, if staying overnight, take short showers and follow the water conservation suggestions posted in hotel bathrooms. Use low impact hiking and camping techniques – don't cause erosion by cutting switchbacks, don't pick flowers or remove artifacts, don't risk wildfires and burn scarce wood in campfires. Visit the *Grand Canyon: Geography of Hope* exhibit and attend some ranger-led talks, walks and other activities to learn more about the canyon. Take part in volunteer projects (see Organized Activities below). Join an organization such as the GCA (see Books & Maps) or the excellent and worthwhile Grand Canyon Trust (☎ 774 7488), RR 4, PO Box 718, Flagstaff, 86001. The Grand Canyon Trust is a nonprofit organization dedicated to conserving the natural and cultural resources of the Colorado Plateau. ■

ARIZONA

ski in anyway), most visitors won't have to contend with such cold temperatures.

## Dangers & Annoyances

Each year, a few people fall to their deaths in the Grand Canyon. When visiting the rim of the canyon, stay inside guardrails and on trails. When hiking below the rim, use hiking shoes or boots rather than tennis shoes or sandals. Only a few trails below the rim are maintained; use extra caution when hiking on unmaintained trails.

In 1994, 457 search and rescue missions were served in the park, mostly for hikers. An average of 250 hikers a year on the most popular below-the-rim trails require ranger assistance to get out safely. The main problems are too much sun and too little water. Use a sun hat and sunblock and carry at least a gallon of water per person per day in summer. Hikers can (and do) run out of water and die. Even if it turns out

you don't need it, carrying extra water may save someone else's life. Before attempting long hikes, speak with backcountry rangers about where you can replenish your water bottles (see Hiking & Backpacking in both the North Rim and the South Rim sections).

Feeding wildlife is detrimental to the animals and illegal. It is also dangerous.

### Storm Watch
Severe storms in February and early March of 1995 washed away parts of hiking trails and broke the main water supply to the park, resulting in the closure of the park's most popular rim-to-rim trail (Bright Angel and North Kaibab) and cancellation of backpacking permits for five weeks. Toilet and washing facilities in park hotels, campgrounds and restaurants were severely disrupted, resulting in some temporary closures. ■

Every year visitors are bitten or otherwise injured by wild animals. Observe them from a distance.

With so many visitors, crime is a growing problem. Lock cars and hotel rooms. Do not leave valuable objects like cameras in view inside your car.

# South of the Colorado River

The Colorado River has always been a major barrier for travelers in this region. If state boundaries had been made on purely sensible geographical divisions, the river would have divided Arizona and Utah. This didn't happen.

## GRAND CANYON NATIONAL PARK – SOUTH RIM

The elevation of the South Rim ranges from 7000 to over 7400 feet, which is lower than the North Rim. More and better transportation facilities also make it more accessible. Therefore 90% of park visitors go to the South Rim. The foremost attraction is the rim itself, which is paralleled by a 33-mile scenic drive with several parking areas, scenic views and trailheads. Most visitors make part of this drive or walk some of the nine miles of trails along the rim. The other attraction is Grand Canyon Village, with historic turn-of-the-century hotels and modern amenities of all kinds. You can get away from all this on numerous hiking trails into the canyon, described below. If you really want to get away from the topside traffic, you can hike down to the canyon bottom and stay at Phantom Ranch or at one of the park's several campgrounds. Other activities include mule rides and river running, but all require advance planning.

## Orientation

Hwy 64 north from Williams reaches the Grand Canyon at Grand Canyon Village from due south – about a 60 mile drive. At

View from the South Rim of the Grand Canyon (NF)

the village, Hwy 64 turns east and becomes the Rim Drive. After exiting the national park, Hwy 64 continues east through the Kaibab National Forest and Navajo Indian Reservation to Cameron, a tiny community at the junction of Hwy 64 and Hwy 89. It is 53 miles from Grand Canyon Village to Cameron, and a further 51 miles south on Hwy 89 to Flagstaff. Hwy 64 is paved for its entire length. I prefer to enter the park from the east, particularly in the morning with the sun behind me. This gives easier access to the Rim Drive pullouts, which are almost all on the north side of the road.

## Information

**Visitors Centers** The main visitors center is in Grand Canyon Village about six miles north of the South Entrance Station. Here, there are a small museum, audio-visual presentations, an excellent bookstore and large bulletin boards with information about lodging, weather, tours, talks and a host of other things. If you can't find the information you need on the bulletin boards, rangers are available to assist you –

but they are usually swamped by visitors, so check the posted information first. Hours are 8 am to 6 pm year round, but may be extended in peak season. The South Rim is open year round.

A smaller visitors center is found at Desert View, near the east entrance of the park, about 25 miles east of Grand Canyon Village. Hours here vary according to season and demand.

Other visitors centers include ranger stations near the Grand Canyon Railway depot, Indian Gardens below the South Rim, the River ranger station, Phantom Ranch at the canyon bottom and Cottonwood campground below the North Rim.

Telephoning the park (☎ 638 7888) gets you through to an automated system that directs your call to the appropriate office. Like many people, I dislike these impersonal systems but, given the high volume of calls, it is the only practical way of answering everyone's questions and I've found that the system does work pretty efficiently. By following the simple instructions you can get recorded information on just about everything from weather conditions to applying for a river running permit. You can leave your name and address to receive written information or one of the free publications mentioned below. You can also get through to a live ranger during business hours.

Pets are not allowed in most parts of the park and nowhere below the rim. Where they are allowed they must be leashed. Kennels are available if necessary. Leaving pets at home, when practical, is encouraged.

**Fees & Permits** Entrance to the park is $10 per private vehicle or $4 for bicycles and bus/train passengers. The entrance ticket is valid for seven days and can be used at any entrance point, including the North Rim. A $15 annual pass is available and Golden Access, Age and Eagle Passes are honored.

For backcountry camping, permits are required from the Backcountry Reservation Office (BRO, see Hiking & Backpacking), and the NPS considers backpacking

without a permit a serious offense – those found without a permit are fined.

Permits are also required from the BRO for arranging your own private river-running trip and bringing your own horse into the park. See the River Running entry, and the Mule entry under Organized Tours.

**Books & Maps** The Grand Canyon Association (GCA) (☎ 638 2481, fax 638 2484) PO Box 399, Grand Canyon, 86023, has an excellent selection of about 300 books, maps, trail guides and videos related to the Grand Canyon. They have stores in the main visitors center, Yavapai Observation Station, Kolb Studio and Tusayan Museum. They will also send you a catalog and provide books by mail order. Members of the public are welcome to join the association and receive discounts on items for sale as well as discounts for classes offered by the Grand Canyon Field Insititute (see Organized Activities, below). Profits benefit the national park.

**Media** A park map and a seasonal newspaper, *The Guide*, are available at no charge to all visitors. *The Guide* is the best up-to-date source of park information available upon arrival. If you plan on spending any time in the park, get one. French, German and Japanese versions are available. Also very useful is the free annual publication *Grand Canyon Trip Planner*. You can receive information in advance from the Superintendent, Grand Canyon National Park, PO Box 129, 86023.

**Service Centers** The most developed visitors services of any national park in the Southwest are at Grand Canyon Village. However, prices here are substantially higher and lines longer than in Flagstaff, so think ahead.

Services available include hotels, restaurants, campgrounds, coin-operated laundry and showers, gift shops, pet kennels, churches and transportation services. Car towing and mechanics (☎ 638 2631) are available from 8 am to 5 pm and for 24-hour emergency service. A gas station is open from 6 am to 9:30 pm from mid-May to Labor Day and 7 am to 8 pm thereafter. A medical clinic (☎ 638 2551, 638 2469) is open 8 am to 5:30 pm, Monday to Friday and 9 am to noon on Saturday. Twenty-four-hour emergency care is available (☎ 911). The clinic's pharmacy (☎ 638 2460) is open 8:30 am to 12:30 pm and 1:30 to 5:30 pm, Monday to Friday.

A shopping center contains the following. A bank (foreign exchange available) is open from 10 am to 3 pm, Monday to Friday and 4 to 6 pm on Friday. A 24-hour ATM accepts American Express, Bank One, Plus, Star, Master Teller and Arizona Interchange Network cards. A post office is open 9 am to 4:30 pm, Monday to Friday and 11 am to 1 pm on Saturday. Stamp machines in the lobby are accessible from 5 am to 10 pm daily. A general store sells food, clothing and camping supplies and rents camping equipment from 9 am to 8 pm daily (opens earlier in summer).

Recycling bins are found in many areas where there are trash containers. Visitors are urged to place cans and plastic or glass bottles in the designated bins.

Near the east entrance, the Desert View Service Center has a visitors center, general store, gas station (closed in winter), campground (closed in winter), cafeteria and the Watchtower, which is the highest point on the South Rim.

## Museums & Historical Buildings
In addition to the exhibits at the visitors centers, check out the following.

**Yavapai Observation Station** At Yavapai Point, at the northeast end of Grand Canyon Village, this station has a geology museum and spectacular views all the way down to Phantom Ranch at the canyon bottom. There is a book shop and ranger-led activities. Hours are 8 am to 5 pm, or to 8 pm in summer.

**Kolb Studio** In Grand Canyon Village, this was a photography studio opened in 1904 and run by Emery Kolb until his death in 1976. Throughout the year, a variety of

changing exhibits display photographs or other items related to the canyon. The studio also has a bookstore and a gallery.

Several other nearby historic buildings date from the same period, including the El Tovar Hotel and the gift shops of Hopi House and Verkamps Curios.

**Tusayan Museum** Off the East Rim Drive, 23 miles east of Grand Canyon Village, this museum has exhibits and talks about the Anasazi. This is where ancient twig figures of animals can be seen. Nearby, the small Tusayan Ruin can be visited; guided walks are offered several times a day in summer and less frequently in the off-peak season. Hours are 8 am to 6 pm in summer and 9 am to 5 pm otherwise. Admission is free.

**Watchtower** At Desert View near the east entrance, you can climb the stairs of the Watchtower, the highest point on the South Rim built in 1932. Inside, the walls are decorated with reproductions of ancient petroglyphs as well as contemporary Native American artwork. There is a 25¢ admission to the tower and coin-operated telescopes are available.

## Over the Edge
This is a commercial presentation in the community building (☎ 638 2229) near the lodges in Grand Canyon Village. Great slides, along with narration, depict the canyon's history and geology, and are presented every half hour from 9 am to 9 pm. (In winter hours are shorter.) Tickets are $4, or $2 for eight- to 15-year-olds and discount coupons are available at gift shops.

## Organized Activities
Call the park's information service (☎ 638 7888) or ask at a visitors center about free ranger-led activities. These occur year round, though with much greater frequency in summer. Programs include free-ranging 'Coffee on the Rim' discussions in the mornings, half-hour talks throughout the day at Yavapai Observation Station, a variety of evening talks at the outdoor

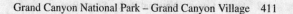

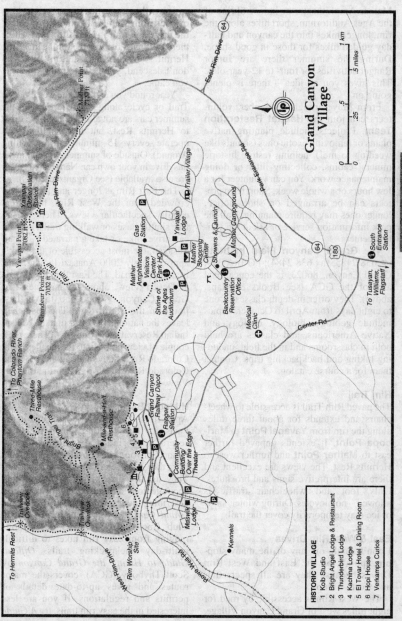

**Grand Canyon Village**

Mather Point 7130 ft

Yavapai Observation Station

Yavapai Point 7082 ft

Grandeur Point 7032 ft

East Rim Drive

East Rim Drive

Rim Trail

Trailer Village

Yavapai Lodge

Gas Station

Mather Amphitheater

Shrine of the Ages Auditorium

Visitors Center

Park HQ

Mather Shopping Center

Showers & Laundry

Mather Campground

Backcountry Reservation Office

Park Entrance Rd

Medical Clinic

Center Rd

South Entrance Station

To Tusayan, Williams, Flagstaff

64

180

64

To Colorado River, Phantom Ranch

Three-Mile Resthouse

Mile-and-a-Half Resthouse

Bright Angel Trail

Trailview Overlook

Trailview Overlook

Grand Canyon Railway Depot

Rapper Station

Community Building Over the Edge Theater

Maswik Lodge

Kennels

Rim Worship Site

Rowe Well Rd

West Rim Drive

To Hermits Rest

ARIZONA

**HISTORIC VILLAGE**
1 Kolb Studio
2 Bright Angel Lodge & Restaurant
3 Thunderbird Lodge
4 Kachina Lodge
5 El Tovar Hotel & Dining Room
6 Hopi House
7 Verkamps Curios

Mather Amphitheater or indoor Shrine of the Ages Auditorium, short hikes along the rim, longer hikes into the canyon and half-day guided hikes for those in good shape. During the summer there are Junior Ranger activities for four- to 12-year-olds. This gives you an idea – there is plenty going on.

From May through September, volunteers can join the **Habitat Restoration Team**. Projects include planting native plants or removing exotic ones (sounds like weeding to me!), helping restore historic miners' cabins, collecting litter or doing maintenance work. You can volunteer for a few hours or a whole week. Short term projects can be arranged on short notice; longer ones may require planning. Call the park information service or ask at the visitors centers.

The **Grand Canyon Field Institute** (☎ 638 2485, fax 638 2484), PO Box 399, Grand Canyon, 86023, is the educational arm of the GCA (see Books & Maps, above). They offer in-depth classes of one to eight days from April to October. Topics include geology, biology, ecology and Native Americans, and classes are held both in classrooms and in the field, including hiking and backpacking trips. Contact them for a course catalog.

### Rim Trail

The paved Rim Trail is accessible to wheelchairs and extends for about three miles along the rim from **Yavapai Point** to **Maricopa Point**. It extends unpaved further east to **Mather Point** and further west to Hermits Rest. The views are excellent and there are interpretive signs and brochures. Only foot and wheelchair traffic is allowed – no bicycles. During winter, snow or ice may temporarily cover the trail.

### East & West Rim Drives

I don't single out any of the many stopping points on the East and West Rim Drives because they are all spectacular and worth a stop.

The West Rim is accessible by road for eight miles west of Grand Canyon Village,

and by the unpaved Rim Trail which extends from Maricopa Point. At the end of the drive and trail is **Hermits Rest** where there is a snack bar and the trailhead for the Hermit Trail down into the canyon; if you don't descend, you have to return the way you came.

Year round you can hike the western Rim Trail or cycle along the road. During the summer cars are not allowed along the drive to Hermits Rest, but free shuttle buses operate every 15 minutes (see Getting Around). Outside of summer, you can make this drive in your own car. Narrated bus tours are also available (see Organized Tours).

The East Rim is longer and a little less crowded than the West Rim, but offers equally spectacular views. There are no free shuttle buses or walking trails, but you can drive, bike or take a narrated bus tour. Tusayan, the most accessible of the park's approximately 2000 Anasazi Indian ruins, is along this road. The East Rim Drive ends at Desert View, about 25 miles east of Grand Canyon Village and the highest point on the South Rim. The road then leaves the national park through the Navajo Indian Reservation to Cameron. There are a couple of view points into the smaller Little Colorado River canyon along the way. The Colorado River itself turns north at Desert View.

### Hiking & Backpacking

Apart from the general books listed in the Facts for the Visitor chapter, there are several trail guides specifically for the Grand Canyon. Most of these are available from the GCA (see Books & Maps, above). They usually give plenty of background about geology and other matters as well as describing the trails themselves. *Hiking the Grand Canyon* by John Annerino (Sierra Club Books, 1993), gives descriptions ranging from easy rim hikes to difficult multi-day backpacking trails. *Official Guide to Hiking the Grand Canyon* by Scott Thybony (GCA), covers the major routes and gives up-to-date details of permits and regulations. If you are less interested in the easy rim trails, try *A Guide to Hiking the Inner Canyon* by Scott Thybony (GCA, 1994). For hiking in the remotest areas of the north part of the park, there are *Grand Canyon Loop Hikes I & II* by George Steck (Chockstone Press, 1994), or *Grand Canyon Treks I, II & III* by J Harvey Butchart (La Siesta Press, 1970, 1975, 1984). *Grand Canyon Geology Along Bright Angel Trail* by Dave Thayer (GCA, 1986), will guide you through the geological features of that part of the canyon.

The easiest hikes are along the Rim Trail and these give rewarding views. Other hikes descend into the canyon. When meeting a mule train, hikers should stand quietly on the upper side of the trail until the animals have passed. Mule riders have the right of way.

Two important things must be borne in mind when attempting any hike into the canyon. The first is that it is easy to stride on down the trail for a few hours, but the uphill return during the heat of the day when you are tired can be very demanding. Allow two hours to return uphill for every hour of hiking downhill. The second is that the temperatures inside the gorge are much hotter than at the rim and that water is scarcely available. Carry plenty of water and protection from the sun. In summer, temperatures can exceed 110°F in the inner gorge.

The two most popular below-the-rim trails are the Bright Angel Trail and the South Kaibab Trail. These are the only maintained trails and are also used by mule riders. Both these trails are suitable for either day hikes or, with a permit and advance reservation, overnight backpacking trips. No permit is necessary for a day trip. Both trails are steep and strenuous. Nevertheless, they are considered the easiest rim-to-river trails in the canyon and even a short descent along part of these trails will completely alter your perspective – I recommend either or both.

**Bright Angel Trail** The trail leaves from the Rim Trail a few yards west of Bright Angel Lodge in Grand Canyon Village. From the trailhead at about 6900 feet, the trail drops to Indian Gardens 4.6 miles

away at about 3800 feet. Here, there is a ranger station, campground, restrooms and water. From Indian Gardens, an almost flat trail goes 1.5 miles to Plateau Point, with exceptional views into the inner gorge. The 12.2 mile roundtrip from the rim to Plateau Point is a strenuous all-day hike. Shorter hikes are, of course, possible – just walk down from the rim as far as you want. There are resthouses after 1.5 miles (1130 - foot elevation drop) and 3 miles (2110-foot elevation drop). The 1.5 mile resthouse has restrooms; both have water in summer.

From Indian Gardens, the Bright Angel Trail continues down to the Colorado River (2450 feet), which is crossed by a suspension bridge – the only bridge within the park. The Bright Angel campground is a short way north of the bridge and 9.5 miles from the South Rim. A few hundred yards beyond is Phantom Ranch. Water, food, accommodations and a ranger station are all here.

**South Kaibab Trail** This trail leaves the South Rim from near Yaki Point, about 4.5 miles east of Grand Canyon Village. From the trailhead at 7260 feet it's over 4800 feet down to the river and Bright Angel campground and the distance is only 6.7 miles. Clearly, South Kaibab is a much steeper trail than Bright Angel. It follows a ridge with glorious views. The first 1.5 miles drop 1300 feet to Cedar Ridge and this makes a good short half-day hike.

From the Bright Angel campground on the north side of the river, the **North Kaibab Trail** climbs to the North Rim at 8200 feet in 14 miles (see Grand Canyon National Park – North Rim later in this chapter). This allows a rim-to-rim crossing of the canyon. Extremely fit hikers can descend from the South Rim to the river and return or make a rim-to-rim crossing in one long day (the record for running rim-to-rim is now under four hours) but the NPS discourages such endeavors. Certainly during the summer the extreme temperatures make such attempts very dangerous for inexperienced hikers.

Although the unmaintained trails are

trickier than the maintained Bright Angel and Kaibab Trails, most are certainly not beyond the limits of any hiker with some experience. The least difficult are the **Hermit Trail**, which leaves from Hermits Rest at the end of the West Rim Drive, and the **Grandview Trail**, which leaves from Grandview Point of the East Rim Drive, 12 miles east of Grand Canyon Village. Both of these offer popular day hikes as well as backcountry camping possibilities.

Altogether, it is beyond the scope of this book to give details of the unmaintained trails and backcountry campgrounds in the canyon – contact the Backcountry Reservation Office for further information.

**Backpacking Permits** Rim-to-river and rim-to-rim hikes are best done as overnight backpacking trips. Permits are necessary and are available at no cost from the Backcountry Reservation Office (BRO) (☎ 638 7875) from 1 to 5 pm, Monday to Friday, or the park information service (☎ 638 7888), PO Box 129, Grand Canyon, 86023. Alternatively, hikers can stay at the Phantom Ranch Lodge (see Places to Stay) for which no permit is required.

The number of permits issued is limited by the number of campsites available. Indian Gardens (15 sites) and Bright Angel (31 sites) are among the most popular campgrounds in the park and are often booked months in advance, year round. Spring and fall are especially popular, before it heats up in summer. Several other smaller, less-developed campgrounds are available on unmaintained trails below the rim. Call or write the BRO for a complete listing and backcountry trip planner.

Reservations can be made in person at the BRO (open daily from 8 am to 5 pm or from 7 am in summer) or by mail. Phone reservations are not accepted. To obtain a permit, a complete night by night itinerary of your desired campgrounds must be submitted. Applications are accepted for the current month and the next four (eg, applications postmarked in January can be made for trips beginning as late as 31 May; trips beginning in June should be applied for in

February). There is no charge for using backcountry campgrounds. Permits must be picked up from the BRO the day before your hike or on the first day by 9 am at the latest, otherwise the permit will be given to someone else.

If you arrive at the Grand Canyon without a backcountry permit, don't give up. Head over to the BRO and get on the waiting list for cancellations. If you have a few days and are flexible with your itinerary you can often get a permit. You have a better chance of getting a permit on short notice if you are prepared to hike unmaintained trails to less developed campgrounds (ask the BRO ranger for advice) or if you avoid the peak season.

Although it may be tempting to try backpacking without a permit, remember that backcountry rangers do patrol the trails and check permits on a regular and frequent basis and so you are quite likely to get caught and fined. Backpacking without a permit is considered a serious offense by the NPS.

### River Running

You can run the Colorado River with a tour or arrange your own private trip. But before you throw a rubber raft into the back of a pickup and head up to the Colorado River, make sure you have serious river-running experience and a permit.

Obtaining a permit is straightforward but time consuming. Call or write the national park for an application, mail it in and wait about eight years. Then throw your raft into your pickup . . .

Most readers will go with a commercial tour and those who manage to get a private permit don't need information from me. (Sorry, no refunds if you bought this book expecting to find info about how to get a private Grand Canyon river running permit in eight days instead of eight years.)

Currently, well over 20,000 visitors a year run the river, almost all with commercial trips. These can be most simply divided into motorized and non-motorized. The motorized trips are usually in huge inflatable boats that go twice as fast as the oar boats but you have to put up with the roar of the engine. Non-motorized trips are slow but the only roar you'll hear is the roar of the rapids, mingled with gurgled screams. Whichever way you go, expect to get very wet during the day and spend nights camping on riverside beaches. This is not as primitive as it sounds – professional river guides are legendary for their combination of white-water abilities, gastronomy and information. David Lavender's *River Runners of the Grand Canyon* (University of Arizona Press, 1985) won't tell you how to run the river but will provide an entertaining history of the canyon's river runners.

Most trips run the river from Lees Ferry to Diamond Creek (in the Hualapai Indian Reservation), dropping over 2000 feet in almost 300 miles and running scores of rapids. Passengers have the option of getting on or off at Phantom Ranch, on the main rim-to-rim trail (the South and North Kaibab Trails) almost halfway into the entire river trip. Combining these options, you can take anything from a three- or four-day motorized trip of part of the canyon to a three-week non-motorized trip of the entire canyon.

Non-motorized trips are varied. Many are oar trips, where the captain controls the boat with large oars and the passengers hang on. Some are paddle trips, where the passengers paddle in response to the captain's commands. All these are generally in inflatable rafts but a couple of companies do paddle trips in wooden dories, reminiscent of those used by John Wesley Powell in 1869. In addition, experienced kayakers can join commercial trips – the gear goes in the rafts.

Commercial trips aren't cheap – expect to pay up to $200 per person per day. Family discounts can be arranged, but small children are not allowed – minimum age requirements vary from trip to trip. The following companies are authorized to run the Colorado through the national park. Their trips fill up several months (even a year) in advance, so contact them early for information.

Aramark-Wilderness River Adventures
Motor and oar trips. PO Box 717, Page, 86040 (☎ 645 3296, 1 (800) 992 8022)

Arizona Raft Adventures, Inc
Motor, oar, paddle and kayak trips. 4050-F East Huntington Drive, Flagstaff, · 86004 (☎ 526 8200, 1 (800) 786 7238)

Arizona River Runners, Inc
Mainly motorized, some oar trips. PO Box 47788, Phoenix, 85068-7788 (☎ 867 4866, 1 (800) 477 7238)

Canyon Explorations, Inc
Oar, paddle and kayak trips. PO Box 310, Flagstaff, 86002 (☎ 774 4559, 1 (800) 654 0723, fax 774 4655)

Canyoneers, Inc
Motor, oar and kayak trips. PO Box 2997, Flagstaff, 86003 (☎ 526 0924, 1 (800) 525 0924)

Colorado River & Trail Expeditions, Inc
Motor, oar, paddle and kayak trips. PO Box 57574, Salt Lake City, UT 84157-0575 (☎ (801) 261 1789, 1 (800) 253 7328)

Diamond River Adventures, Inc
Motor and oar trips. PO Box 1316, Page, 86040 (☎ 645 8866, 1 (800) 343 3121)

Expeditions, Inc
Oar, paddle and kayak trips. 625 N Beaver, Flagstaff, 86001 (☎ 779 3769, 774 8176)

Grand Canyon Dories
Oar, dory and kayak trips. PO Box 216, Altaville, CA 95221 (☎ (209) 736 0805)

Grand Canyon Expeditions Co
Motor, oar, dory and kayak trips. PO Box O, Kanab, UT 84741 (☎ (801) 644 2691, 1 (800) 544 2691)

Hatch River Expeditions, Inc
Motor and kayak trips. PO Box 1200, Vernal, UT 84078 (☎ (801) 789 3813, 1 (800) 433 8966)

Mark Sleight Expeditions, Inc
Motor, oar and kayak trips. PO Box 40, St George, UT 84771-0040 (☎ (801) 673 1200)

Moki Mac River Expeditions, Inc
Motor, oar and kayak trips. PO Box 21242, Salt Lake City, UT 84121 (☎ (801) 268 6667, 1 (800) 284 7280)

OARS, Inc
Oar, paddle and kayak trips. PO Box 67, Angels Camp, CA 95222 (☎ (209) 736 4677, 1 (800) 346 6277)

Outdoors Unlimited
Oar, paddle and kayak trips. 6900 Townsend Winona Rd, Flagstaff, 86004 (☎ 526 4546, 1 (800) 637 7238)

ARIZONA

## Grand Canyon Overflights

The idea of flying over the Grand Canyon at low altitude appeals to some people. However, passengers may want to consider that there have been many complaints about aircraft noise in the park and concerns about flight safety.

It is very difficult to get away from aircraft noise anywhere in the park for more than a few minutes. The NPS recently estimated that visitors have to put up with aircraft noise during 75% of daylight hours. The natural quiet of the Grand Canyon is part of its magnificence and the current levels of aircraft noise are not acceptable in a national park.

While recent efforts to limit air pollution have met with some success, stopping noise pollution has been a losing battle. Regulations are supposed to keep aircraft above 14,500 feet in 44% of the park and above the rim in the remaining area, but increased numbers of flights have led to violation of these laws.

Safety is another concern. In February 1995, eight people were killed in a small tourplane crash two miles north of the Grand Canyon Airport. Associated Press reports listed this as the 11th fatal air crash near Grand Canyon National Park in less than nine years. A total of 80 people died in these crashes, while fewer than 20 survived. ∎

Tour West, Inc
    Motor and oar trips. PO Box 333, Orem, UT 84059 (☎ (801) 225 0755, 1 (800) 453 9107)
Western River Expeditions, Inc
    Motor and oar trips. 7258 Racquet Club Drive, Salt Lake City, UT 84121 (☎ (801) 942 6669, 1 (800) 453 7450)

In addition, see Hualapai River Runners in the Hualapai Indian Reservation below.

### Cycling

Bicycles are allowed only on paved roads. Mountain biking on unpaved roads or on trails is not permitted – you will need to go outside the park in the Kaibab National Forest for that. In fact, no wheeled vehicles of any kind are permitted on the trails (except for wheelchairs and baby strollers on the paved Rim Trail).

The story is told of a river runner who pushed a dolly loaded with 10 cases of beer down the Bright Angel Trail to his rafting group. He received a ticket for using a wheeled vehicle on the trail and also had to push the loaded dolly all the way back to the South Rim.

### Fishing

There is good trout fishing in the Colorado River and several of its tributaries. Licenses and tackle can be purchased at the general store in Grand Canyon Village.

Licenses are not available for purchase on the national park's North Rim – the nearest area to get a permit is Marble Canyon, where there are also guides.

### Cross-Country Skiing

The higher North Rim area offers more snow for better cross-country skiing (see also the Jacob Lake section) than the South Rim area. However, you can ski in the South Rim area in the Kaibab National Forest at the Grand View Ski Area when snow conditions permit. There are 18 miles of easy- to medium-difficulty groomed and signed skiing trails near the east entrance of the park. The plowed parking area and access to the trails is on East Rim Drive 10.1 miles north of the junction of Hwys 64 and 180, two miles east of Grand View Point.

About a half mile into the access trail is an information kiosk that describes routes and distances; the longest trail is 7.5 miles. One trail has a canyon-view overlook, but all trails stay in the national forest and do not go to the South Rim of the national park.

Skiers are free to tour the national forest regardless of trails, and there are no restrictions on camping, unless you enter the park.

### Organized Tours

Within the park, most tours are run by the Fred Harvey Company (☎ 638 2631,

Many rafting trips through the Grand Canyon depart from Lee's Ferry near Page. (MM)

A mule team on the South Kaibab Trail at the South Rim of Grand Canyon National Park (TW)

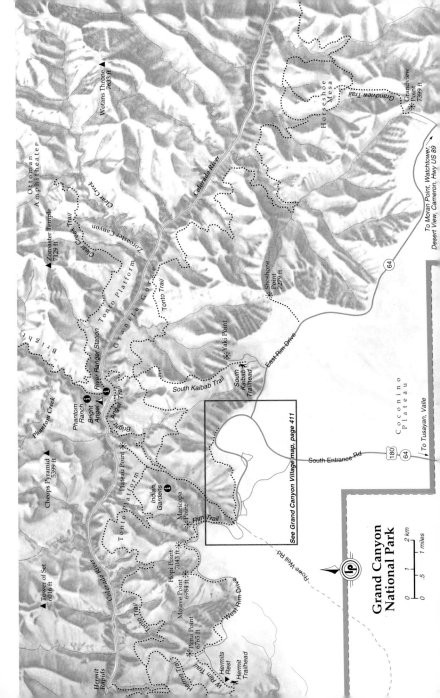

**Grand Canyon National Park**

See Grand Canyon Village map, page 411

To Moran Point, Watchtower, Desert View, Cameron, Hwy US 89

To Tusayan, Valle

Grandview Point 7399 ft

Horseshoe Mesa

Grandview Trail

64

Shoshone Point 7279 ft

East Rim Drive

Coconino Plateau

Colorado River

South Entrance Rd

180

64

Rowe Well Rd

Yaki Point

South Kaibab Trail

South Kaibab Trailhead

Wotans Throne 7633 ft

Ottoman Amphitheater

Zoroaster Temple 7129 ft

Clear Creek Trail

Clear Creek

Zoroaster Canyon

Granite Gorge

Tonto Platform

Tonto Trail

River Ranger Station

Bright Angel

Phantom Ranch

Bright Angel Trail

Brahma

Phantom Creek

Cheops Pyramid 5399 ft

Plateau Point

Tonto Platform

Indian Gardens

Maricopa Point

Rim Trail

Tower of Set 6016 ft

Colorado River

Tonto Trail

Hopi Point 7043 ft

Mojave Point 6980 ft

Pima Point 6765 ft

Hermit Rapids

Hermit Trail

W Rim Trail

West Rim Drive

Hermits Rest

Hermit Trailhead

0   .5   1 miles
0   1   2 km

Kayaking down Hermit Rapids in the Grand Canyon (MM)

A view downstream from Anasazi granaries at Nankoweap Canyon, Grand Canyon (MM)

Quartermaster Viewpoint of the Grand Canyon from the Hualapai Indian Reservation (RR)

A view from the South Rim of the Grand Canyon (TW)

Mule team climbing the South Kaibab Trail, on the Grand Canyon's South Rim (TW)

638 2401, fax 638 9247), PO Box 699, Grand Canyon, 86023. Their transportation desks are in the main visitors center and at the El Tovar, Bright Angel, Maswik and Yavapai Lodges. Some buses are wheelchair accessible by prior arrangement. Reservations are advised in summer but, even then, there are usually enough buses that you can get on a tour the next day. Tax (currently about 6%) and guide tips are not included in these prices.

**Bus** Narrated bus tours leave from the lodges mentioned above. A two-hour West Rim tour leaves in the morning, afternoon and evening (for sunset) and costs $11. A four-hour East Rim tour leaves every morning and afternoon for $17. A ticket for both tours (which can be taken on the same or on separate days) costs $20. Six- to 15-year-olds ride for half price.

All-day tours (10 to 13 hours, departing daily with a four adult minimum) visit the

Sinagua Ruins around Flagstaff or to visit the Navajo Reservation and Monument Valley with Navajo guides. These cost $80 including lunch; children under 12 pay $50.

**Train** A combined bus/train tour leaves every morning (that the train runs) for Williams, 50 miles to the south, returning on the historic Grand Canyon Railway (☎ 635 4000, 1 (800) 843 8724, fax 773 1610). Trains leave Williams Train Depot for the log depot near the El Tovar Hotel in Grand Canyon Village at 9:30 am daily from March 15 through October and on winter weekends. This costs $40, or $20 for children under 13, and includes the one-way train ticket. See Williams for more details.

**Mule** A one-day trip to Plateau Point inside the canyon is offered daily. It takes about seven hours roundtrip of which six hours are spent in the saddle. The cost is $102 including lunch.

Overnight trips to Phantom Ranch at the canyon bottom are offered daily. These take 5.5 hours down and 4.5 hours back up and cost $250 including meals and dormitory accommodations. During winter only, three-day/two-night trips to Phantom Ranch cost $350. There are discounts for a second person or larger group.

Reservations are suggested, although you can get on a waiting list if you don't have a reservation. During winter, trips can often be arranged with a day's notice; during the summer the waiting list is much longer and a wait of several days or even weeks may be necessary.

These trips are strenuous – they are supposedly easier than walking but I find them harder work than hiking! Riders must be in good physical shape and be able to mount and dismount without assistance, weigh under 200 pounds (including clothing and camera), be at least four feet, seven inches in height, be fluent in English (so they can understand instructions) and cannot be pregnant.

Horse and mule rides are also available from the town of Tusayan (see below). You can ride your own horse into the park, but a permit is required from the Backcountry Reservation Office (see Hiking & Backpacking).

**Raft** An all-day bus and boat tour includes an East Rim tour and drive to Glen Canyon Dam, a smooth water float trip to Lees Ferry, and a return trip by bus. About four hours are spent on the river and no white water is involved. The trip runs daily from late March to early November and costs $80 or $50 for children under 12, including picnic lunch.

**Special Events**
The Grand Canyon Chamber Music Festival (☎ 638 9215), PO Box 1332, Grand Canyon, 86023, has been presented at Grand Canyon Village in September for over a decade.

**Places to Stay**
Reservations for all the places listed below are essential in summer and a good idea in winter. Cancellations provide a lucky few with last minute rooms. Call to check. If you can't find accommodations in the national park, see Tusayan (four miles south of the South Entrance Station), Valle (31 miles south) and Cameron (53 miles east). Also see Williams (about 60 miles) and Flagstaff (about 80 miles) in the Central Arizona chapter.

**Camping** Campers should be prepared for freezing winter nights. Free backcountry camping is available by reservation only (see Hiking & Backpacking, above).

In Grand Canyon Village, *Mather Campground* has 320 sites (no hookups) for $10. Make reservations up to eight weeks in advance with MISTIX (☎ (619) 452 8787, 1 (800) 365 2267), PO Box 85705, San Diego, CA 92138-5705, from March through November. Otherwise it's first-come, first-served. Even in summer, a few sites may be available in the mornings. Nearby, the Fred Harvey *Trailer Village* (☎ 638 2401), has 84 RV sites with hookups for $17 year round. Coin showers and laundry are available near the Backcountry Reservation Office.

The *Desert View Campground* near the east entrance has 50 campsites on a first-come, first-served basis from April to October. They are often full by lunchtime so arrive early. There is water but no showers or RV hookups and fees are $10.

**Lodges** About 1000 rooms are available on the South Rim in a variety of lodges all run by the Fred Harvey Grand Canyon National Park Lodges (☎ 638 2401, 638 2631, fax 638 9247), PO Box 699, 86023. In Grand Canyon Village, there are four lodges on the canyon rim – canyon view rooms command higher prices. Two lodges, Maswik and Yavapai, are away from the rim, while Phantom Ranch is at the bottom of the canyon near the Colorado River. Prices are the same for single or double occupancy; add $7 to $11 per extra person.

On the rim, the most famous and expensive is the 1905 *El Tovar Hotel*, a rustic lodge with high standards of comfort and the best dining in the area. About 10 suites are $182 to $271 and several have private balconies with canyon views. There are 78 small to mid-sized rooms from $111 to $166. The rustic 1935 *Bright Angel Lodge & Cabins* has 30 simple lodge rooms, some with shared bath, from $53. There are 42 cabins, all with bath, a few with fireplaces and some with canyon views, for $61 to $111. The canyon view/fireplace cabins are often booked up a year or more in advance. Between these two places are the modern *Kachina Lodge* with 49 rooms and *Thunderbird Lodge* with 55 rooms, all comfortable motel style units with private bath, some with canyon views. Rates are $96 to $106.

A short walk away from the rim, the *Maswik Lodge* has almost 300 rooms with private bath ranging from rustic cabins for $48 to motel-style units, some with balconies, for $69 to $103. Near the visitors center, the *Yavapai Lodge* has about 350 reasonably-sized motel rooms, all with private bath and some with forest views. Rates are $79 to $89. The Yavapai Lodge and the Maswik cabins are closed in winter.

*Phantom Ranch* has cabins sleeping four to 10 people and segregated dorms sleeping 10 people in bunk beds. Most cabins are reserved for the overnight mule tours but hikers may make reservations as well. There are separate shower facilities. Rates are $21 per person and bedding, soap and towels are provided. Meals are available in the dining hall by advance reservation only. Breakfast is $11.50, box lunch is $5.50 and dinner varies from $16.25 (stew) to $26.50 (steak). Meals are plentiful to feed hungry hikers. Snacks, limited supplies, beer and wine are also sold. Postcards bought and mailed here are stamped 'Mailed by Mule from the bottom of the Canyon'.

## Places to Eat

By far the best place for quality food in an elegant setting is the *El Tovar* where dinner reservations are recommended, especially in summer. They are open from 6:30 am to 2 pm and 5 to 10 pm. Continental dinner entrees are in the $15 to $25 range and smoking is not permitted.

More moderate prices and an American menu are available at the *Bright Angel Dining Room* which is open from 6:30 am to 10 pm. Next door to the Bright Angel Lodge, the *Arizona Steakhouse* serves steaks and seafood from 5 to 10 pm from March through December. Canyonside snacks and sandwiches are sold from 11 am to 9 pm at the *Bright Angel Fountain* near the Bright Angel trailhead from March to October. Self-service dining is available at the *Maswik Cafeteria* from 6 am to 10 pm and at the *Yavapai Cafeteria and Grill* from 6 am to midnight from March through December. *Babbitt's Deli* in the shopping center opposite the visitors center has a dining area or carry out from 8 am to 7 pm. At the end of the West Rim Drive, *Hermits Rest Snack Bar* is open from 9 am to 5 pm, or 8 am to 6:30 pm in summer. *Desert View Cafeteria* near the east entrance is open from 9 am to 5 pm or 8 am to 6 pm in summer.

## Entertainment

The El Tovar has a piano bar, while there's a lounge bar with live entertainment from Wednesday to Sunday at the Bright Angel Lodge. The Maswik Lodge has a sports bar.

## Getting There & Away

The majority of people drive or arrive on a bus tour.

**Air** The Grand Canyon Airport is at the south end of Tusayan. Flights to and from Las Vegas operate several times a day with Air Nevada (☎ 1 (800) 634 6377), Air Vegas (☎ 1 (800) 255 7474), Las Vegas Airlines (☎ (702) 647 3056, 1 (800) 634 6851) and Scenic Airlines (☎ (702) 739 1900, 1 (800) 634 6801). Scenic Airlines also has one or

ARIZONA

two flights a day from Phoenix, and TWA Express (☎ (213) 484 2244, 1 (800) 221 2000) has a daily flight from Los Angeles.

Many of these flights include an over-flight of the Grand Canyon. In addition, tours in airplanes and helicopters starting from and returning to the Grand Canyon Airport are available from about $50 for the shortest flights.

There are shuttles from the airport to Grand Canyon Village (see Van below).

**Bus** See Flagstaff for the Nava-Hopi Bus Company, which is the only regularly scheduled bus service into the park.

**Train** See Organized Tours, above, and Williams for the Grand Canyon Railway.

**Van** Grand Canyon Transportation and Tours (☎ 638 2023, 1 (800) 378 2023), has shuttle services that require a five passen-ger minimum. Costs are $20 to Williams, $25 to Flagstaff, $67 to Phoenix and $74 to Las Vegas, Nevada. They also offer shuttles from Grand Canyon Village to Tusayan and the airport for $5. You can charter a van for your own tour for $32.50 per hour.

Tusayan-Grand Canyon Shuttle (☎ 638 0821) leaves the airport in Tusayan at 15 minutes past every hour from 8:15 am to 5:15 pm and returns to Tusayan from Grand Canyon Village at 40 minutes past every hour from 8:40 am to 5:40 pm. Addi-tional buses run in summer. The fare is $5 and discounted group and multiple-use tickets are available.

### Getting Around
**Free Shuttle Buses** Free shuttles operate along two routes in summer only. One goes around Grand Canyon Village, stopping at lodges, campgrounds, the visitors center, Yavapai Observation Station and other points. Bus stops are clearly marked. Buses leave every 15 minutes from 6 am to 10 pm and take 50 minutes for the entire loop.

The village loop bus connects with the West Rim shuttle at the Bright Angel trail-head (called the West Rim Interchange Stop). The West Rim shuttle operates

every 15 minutes from 7:30 am to 7 pm, stops at eight scenic points along its route and takes 90 minutes roundtrip. When the shuttle is running, private cars are not allowed along the West Rim Drive. The shuttle buses are not wheelchair accessible and visitors with wheelchair needs can obtain a permit from the visitors center to drive along the West Rim.

**Other Shuttles** Ask at any of the trans-portation desks for other shuttle services. Morning shuttles to the South Kaibab trail-head cost $3. South to North shuttles around the rim are available from May to October (when the North Rim is open) and cost $60 one-way or $100 roundtrip. Other services are available on request.

## TUSAYAN
Eight miles south of Grand Canyon Village and a couple of miles south of the south entrance, the sprawling community of Tusayan offers several motels, restaurants, souvenir shops and the Grand Canyon Airport all strung along Hwy 64.

### Information
A visitors information booth is in the IMAX Theater lobby. The Kaibab National Forest Tusayan Ranger Station (☎ 638 2443), PO Box 3088, 86023, is at the north end of town and open from 8 am to 5 pm, Monday to Friday. The post office is oppo-site the IMAX Theater.

### IMAX Theater
Using a film format three times larger than normal 70mm movie frames, a screen up to eight times the size of conventional cinema screens and a 14-speaker stereo surround system, the IMAX Theater presents *Grand Canyon – The Hidden Secrets*. This 34-minute movie plunges you into the history and geology of the canyon through the eyes of ancient Indians, John Wesley Powell, and a soaring eagle. The effects are quite splendid and are a cheaper, safer and quieter way of getting an aerial perspective than taking a flight. The IMAX Theater (☎ 638 2468, fax 638 2807) is on Hwy 64,

a couple of miles south of the park entrance. Shows are at 30 minutes past the hour from 8:30 am to 8:30 pm March through October and from 10:30 am to 6:30 pm the rest of the year. Admission is $7 or $4 for four- to 11-year-olds.

### Horseback Riding

Apache Stables (☎ 638 2891, 638 2424), at the Moqui Lodge a half mile south of the park entrance, has a variety of horseback rides available in both the national forest and national park. Costs are $20 to $55 for one to four hours. Children as young as six can ride on the shorter trips.

### Other Activities

The Kaibab National Forest provides many opportunities for ourdoor fun. Mountain biking on dirt roads and trails (not allowed in the Grand Canyon) is permitted throughout the national forest. Groomed cross-country skiing areas are found two miles east of Grandview Point along the East Rim Drive of the Grand Canyon. Hiking, backpacking and camping can be practiced without the crowds of, or the need of a backcountry permit from, the NPS Backcountry Reservation Office.

### Places to Stay

**Camping** In the Kaibab National Forest, free dispersed camping is allowed as long as you are at least a quarter of a mile from paved highways. USFS Forest Roads provide access but many are closed in winter. USFS Forest Road 686 heading west from Hwy 64, almost a mile south of the Ten X turnoff, is often open year round.

The USFS operates the *Ten X Campground* about three miles south of Tusayan. It is open from May through September and has 70 sites for $10 on a first-come, first-served basis. There is water but no showers or RV hookups. A large group site (25 to 100 people for $25 to $55) is available by reservation only (☎ 638 2443).

*Grand Canyon Camper Village* (☎ 638 2887) is at the north end of Tusayan, 1.5 miles south of the park entrance. About 300 sites are available year round ranging from $15 for tents to $22 for full hookups. There are showers and a playground. This place often has a tent site when everywhere else is full.

**Hotels** As with the Grand Canyon, reservations are recommended, especially in summer. Winter rates (November to March) are $20 to $30 lower. All are along Hwy 64.

The cheapest is *Seven Mile Lodge* (☎ 638 2291) with motel rooms for about $80. Better is the *Moqui Lodge* (☎ 638 2424, fax 638 2895) with 140 rooms at $85/90 for singles/doubles including breakfast. It is closed from December to mid-March (subject to change). There is a desk for the Apache Stables (see above) and a decent restaurant and bar with Mexican and American food open from 6:30 to 10 am and 6 to 10 pm. Live country & western music is presented on weekends. The *Red Feather Lodge* (☎ 638 2414, 1 (800) 538 2345, fax 638 9216) has about 100 nice rooms for $110 in summer and as low as $50 in winter.

The Best Western *Grand Canyon Squire Inn* (☎ 638 2681, 1 (800) 622 6966, fax 638 2782) has 250 spacious rooms, most for $125, and a few suites for $195. There is a pool, spa, sauna, tennis court, exercise room, coin laundry, gift shop and (at extra charge) a fun center with bowling, billiards and other games. A good restaurant, an inexpensive coffee shop (open 6:30 am to 10 pm) and a bar are on the premises. The *Quality Inn* (☎ 638 2673, fax 638 9537), has 176 pleasant rooms for $128. There is a pool, spa, restaurant (open 6 am to 10 pm) and bar.

### Places to Eat

The hotel restaurants offer the best food, but there is also a pizza place, Denny's and a McDonald's. A steakhouse is open for dinner only.

### Getting There & Away

**Air** There are several flights a day to and from the Grand Canyon Airport in Tusayan (see the Getting There & Away section for Grand Canyon National Park – South Rim, above).

**Car Rental** Budget (☎ 638 9360, 1 (800) 527 0700) and Dollar (☎ 638 2625) have cars available at the airport. Rates are cheaper at Flagstaff or Phoenix.

## VALLE

About 25 miles south of the south entrance of Grand Canyon National Park, Valle is the intersection of Hwy 64 to Williams and Hwy 180 to Flagstaff. There is no town here, just a few places to stay and eat and a gas station.

*Flintstones Bedrock City* (☎ 635 2600) has 68 sites for $12 for tents and $16 for hookups. There are coin showers and laundry, a snack bar and a Flintstones recreation area complete with concretosaurs. The campground is open from mid-March through October.

The *Grand Canyon Inn & Motel* (☎ 635 9203) has several sections with motel rooms ranging from $60 to $85 a double. There is a restaurant and gift shop.

## HUALAPAI INDIAN RESERVATION

This reservation borders many miles of the Colorado River northeast of Kingman. It contains the only road to the river within the Grand Canyon area. Back in the 1800s, when the area was being invaded by miners, the Hualapai fought hard to retain control of their lands. Today, most of the tribe works in ranching, logging or tourism. Although no roads directly connect the South Rim and the reservation, it offers visitors a good opportunity to see some of the Grand Canyon area accompanied by guides from the tribe that originally inhabited the region.

### Information & Orientation

The tribal headquarters (☎ 769 2216) is at Peach Springs, a small community about 50 miles northeast of Kingman on Route 66. Information and permits can be obtained from PO Box 179, Peach Springs, 86434.

Entrance into the reservation for sightseeing, picnicking and hiking is $3 per day, per person (free for children under 13). No firearms are allowed on the reservation. Camping is available for $7 per night.

Fishing costs $8 per day, with a catch limit of eight fish.

From Peach Springs, 22-mile, unpaved Diamond Creek Rd heads north to the Colorado River. Three miles west of Peach Springs on Route 66 is unpaved Buck and Doe Rd, which leads about 50 miles to Grand Canyon West, which can also be reached by alternative routes from Kingman (see Getting There & Away, below).

### Things to See & Do

**Peach Springs** There's not much in Peach Springs apart from the tribal powwow held in late August.

With the appropriate permit, you can drive the scenic Diamond Creek Rd to the Colorado River – 2WD cars can usually make it except after heavy rains.

Hualapai River Running (☎ 769 2210, 769 2219, 1 (800) 622 4409), PO Box 246, Peach Springs, 86434, offers one- and two-day river trips along the lower reaches of the Colorado River from May to October. They use motorized rafts and Hualapai Indian guides. Rates are $175/275 per person for one/two days from Peach Springs; a discount is offered to groups of 10 or more. They'll also arrange hotel and pickup from Kingman on request. Children must be at least eight years old.

**Grand Canyon West** This area has an airstrip and tribal office where permits, bathroom facilities and soft drinks are available. A $3 permit (kids under 13 are free) allows you to drive three miles to the **Quartermaster Viewpoint** which has a parking area and good views of the lower Grand Canyon, but no facilities. A five-minute hike on a rough trail brings you to a small bluff with better views. You won't see many people – it's a far cry from the masses thronging the (admittedly more spectacular) South Rim of the national park.

The Hualapai tribe also operates a guided bus tour out to the canyon rim. This goes to a different area, reachable only with the tour. It costs $15 per person (kids under five free) and includes a barbecue lunch on the rim and plenty of local lore and information as presented by the Hualapai guide – an interesting trip.

### Places to Stay & Eat

There are no hotels in Peach Springs or on the Hualapai Reservation – most people visit Grand Canyon West on day trips from Las Vegas, Nevada or Kingman. The nearest off-reservation motels are the inexpensive *Frontier Motel* (☎ 769 2238) in Truxton, 10 miles west of Peach Springs or the *Grand Canyon Caverns Motel* (☎ 422 3223) about nine miles east of Peach Springs. Kingman offers the best choice of accommodations in the region.

There are simple cafes in Peach Springs, Truxton and Grand Canyon Caverns – they usually close very early.

The Hualapai tribe operates basic campgrounds near the end of Diamond Creek Rd by the Colorado River. Bring everything you'll need.

### Getting There & Away

Direct access from Kingman is northwest on Hwy 93 to the paved Pearce Ferry Rd, which heads northeast to Lake Mead (see Lake Mead National Recreation Area for a full description). About 30 miles along the road is the dirt Diamond Bar Rd, heading 21 miles to Grand Canyon West. A slightly shorter route to Peach Springs is north of Kingman on Stockton Hill Rd, which is paved for about 15 miles and then becomes a good, flat dirt road for about 30 miles to the paved Pearce Ferry Rd. Turn right onto it and proceed for 7.3 miles to the Diamond Bar Rd.

### HAVASUPAI INDIAN RESERVATION

This reservation is centered on Havasu Canyon, a southern tributary of the Colorado River. It is the traditional home of the peaceful and energetic Havasupai Indians, who now offer Grand Canyon visitors a unique look at the canyon and river. Tribal headquarters is in Supai – the only village within the Grand Canyon – which has been there for centuries. The first European visitor was the Spanish priest, Francisco Garcés, in 1776. Just as in the old days,

Supai can be accessed only by a steep eight-mile-long trail from the canyon rim. Below Supai, the trail leads past some of the prettiest waterfalls within the Grand Canyon.

Word has recently gotten out about this beautiful area. Although no roads directly connect Grand Canyon National Park's South Rim with the reservation, there are hundreds of daily visitors during the peak summer months. Nevertheless, it is much more tranquil than the South Rim.

### Information

Information is available from Havasupai Tourist Enterprise (☎ 448 2121), Supai, 86435. All visitors pay an entry fee of $12; $8 in winter (November to March). The Supai Post Office distributes its mail by pack animals – postcards mailed from there have a special post mark to prove it.

### Things to See & Do

The eight-mile hike down to Supai is attractive, but the most memorable sections are along the four or five miles of trail below the town. Here, there are four major waterfalls and many minor ones.

Just over a mile beyond Supai is Navajo Falls, the first of the four big falls. Next comes the 100-foot-high Havasu Falls, with a sparkling blue pool popular for swimming. Beyond this is a campground, and the trail then passes 200-foot-high **Mooney Falls**, the largest in the canyon. The falls were named after a miner who died in a terrifying climbing accident in 1880; although Mooney was roped, he was unable to extricate himself and hung there for many hours until the rope finally broke and he was killed. A very steep trail (chains provide welcome handholds) leads to the pool at the bottom, another popular swimming spot. Finally, two miles further on, is Beaver Falls. From there, it is a further four miles down to the Colorado River (almost seven miles below the campground).

### Special Events

There are tribal dances held around Memorial Day and a Peach Festival in August. Call Havasupai Tourist Enterprise for exact dates.

ARIZONA

## Places to Stay & Eat

In Supai is the *Havasupai Lodge* (☎ 448 2111) with 24 comfortable rooms, all with canyon views, two double beds, air conditioning and private showers. There are no TVs or telephones – a plus for travelers wishing to get away from that stuff! Reservations are essential and should be made well in advance in the summer – credit cards are not accepted. Rates range from $75 to $96 for one to four people (about $30 less in winter).

Two miles below Supai is the *Havasupai Campground* with 400 tent sites, pit toilets and plenty of water. Fires are not permitted so bring a camp stove to cook. Camping fees are $9 per person and a reservation (with Havasupai Tourist Enterprise) is a good idea in summer. Don't leave gear unattended at the campground – thefts have occurred. There is no camping elsewhere in Havasu Canyon or down at the Colorado River.

Meals and snacks are served at the *Village Cafe* (☎ 448 2981) near the lodge, and there is a small tribal museum adjoining. A general store sells food and camping fuel and there is a picnic area in the village.

## Things to Buy

The Havasupai are noted for basketmaking and beadwork. Their crafts are sold in the lodge's souvenir shop.

## Getting There & Away

Seven miles east of Peach Springs on Route 66 is a signed turnoff to Hualapai Hilltop on the Havasu Canyon rim in the Havasupai Reservation. The 62-mile road is paved but has no gas stations or other services.

At Hualapai Hilltop is an unguarded parking area – try and arrive with as little stuff as possible and lock what you aren't taking to Supai in the trunk. Don't leave valuables. From the hilltop, a steep trail drops eight miles to Supai and a further two miles to the campground. If you call Havasupai Tourist Enterprise two months in advance, they can arrange for you to be met by horses or mules. Roundtrip fees per animal are $80 from hilltop to Supai, $100

from hilltop to campground, or $40 from Supai to campground. Credit cards are not accepted; horses must be reserved by sending a check or money order for half the fee two months in advance. Deposits are refunded for cancellations made three weeks in advance. You can bring your own horse for a $15 trail fee – you supply feed. Mountain or trail bikes are not allowed. Most visitors walk. Recently, a helicopter service became available from the hilltop to Supai – call the Havasupai Tourist Enterprise for details.

## CAMERON

On Hwy 89 just north of the intersection with Hwy 64, Cameron is a tiny community on the western end of the Navajo Indian Reservation. The reservation is described in the Northeastern Arizona chapter, but Cameron is included here because it is on the main route from the South Rim to the North Rim of the Grand Canyon.

About 10 miles west of Cameron on the way to the Grand Canyon is the **Little Colorado River Gorge Navajo Tribal Park** with a scenic overlook – it's worth a stop.

The modern *Cameron Trading Post Motel* (☎ 679 2231, 1 (800) 338 7385, fax 679 2350) adjoins an 80-year-old trading post. About 70 attractive motel rooms, some with balconies, are $70 or $80 in summer and as low as $20 in winter. Suites are $175 to $250. There is a restaurant but no alcohol is served (it's prohibited on the reservation). Other facilities here include a cafeteria, gas station, post office, visitor information center, RV park ($14 for hookups but no showers) and several Native American crafts shops and stalls. Cheaper rooms are available at the *Gray Mountain Trading Post Motel* (☎ 679 2214) about eight miles south of Cameron on Hwy 89.

# The Arizona Strip

Traditionally and geographically, this area north of the Grand Canyon has closer ties with Mormon Utah than Arizona. It is a long way from here to Salt Lake City, though, and the area attracted some of the most old-fashioned members of the Mormon religion. The Arizona Strip is wild, large, poorly roaded and, even until the present, remains the last holdout of the 19th-century practice of polygamy. This has not been condoned by the Mormon Church for over a century, but the Arizona Strip is remote enough that old ideas die hard, particularly around the tiny community of Colorado City on the Utah border. The places described below, however, are on the few routes available to travelers from the South Rim of the Grand Canyon to the North Rim and beyond, into Utah. Don't be expecting to meet polygamists at every turn.

## MARBLE CANYON & LEES FERRY AREA

Hwy 89 splits a few miles before crossing the Colorado River, with Hwy 89 heading northeast to Page and then swinging west to Kanab, Utah, and Alt Hwy 89 taking a shorter route to Kanab through the Arizona Strip. Alt Hwy 89 crosses the Navajo Bridge over the Colorado at Marble Canyon. This is the only road bridge into the Arizona Strip from the south and the only one on the Colorado River between Glen Canyon Dam and Hoover Dam in Nevada. Almost immediately after the bridge, a side road to the right leads six miles to Lees Ferry, historically the only crossing point of the river for many miles and today the major put-in for river runners making the exciting descent through the Grand Canyon.

Lees Ferry is named after John D Lee, who established a ranch and primitive raft ferry here in 1872. Later, Lee was executed for his part in the Mountain Meadows Massacre (see the Veyo Area in Southwestern Utah). The ferry operated until the Navajo Bridge was opened in 1929 (a new bridge is under construction here). Some of the historic buildings near Lees Ferry can still be seen. Lees Ferry is at the southern edge of Glen Canyon National Recreation Area. The boundary of Grand Canyon National Park is less than a mile southwest of Lees Ferry at the mouth of the spectacular Paria River Canyon.

## Paria Canyon-Vermilion Cliffs Wilderness Area

**Paria Canyon** Experienced canyoneers enjoy the Paria Canyon because of the amazing Buckskin Gulch arm – miles of slot canyons so deep and narrow that the sun almost never shines directly into them. Hiking Buckskin Gulch-Paria Canyon requires four to six days. Trailheads along the same route can be found along dirt roads off Hwy 89 in Utah, about 30 miles west of Page, and the exit point is at Lees Ferry.

The best time to do this adventurous hike is spring or fall. Winter is too cold and summer downpours create deadly flash floods. Near the trailhead is a BLM Ranger Station (no phone) that is sometimes open from March to November. When closed, it posts weather information and flash-flood warnings. The area is managed by the BLM in Kanab (see Southwestern Utah) although most of the canyon is actually in Arizona. They have detailed information – also read Annerino's *Adventuring in Arizona*.

A car shuttle between the trailhead and the exit point can be arranged by the Marble Canyon Lodge or Cliff Dwellers Lodge (see Places to Stay & Eat).

**Vermilion Cliffs** These spectacular cliffs stretch out along the north side of Alt Hwy 89 for most of the way from Marble Canyon to Jacob Lake.

## Places to Stay & Eat

*Lees Ferry Campground* is at Lees Ferry in the GCNRA (☎ 355 2234 for the local ranger) and has 54 sites for $8 with water and a boat ramp but no showers or RV hookups. There are public coin showers at the Marble Canyon Lodge.

Summer rates are given below – they drop in winter. *Marble Canyon Lodge* (☎ 355 2225, 1 (800) 726 1789, fax 355 2227) is on Alt Hwy 89 half a mile west of Navajo Bridge. About 60 rooms are $60 for a double and there are a few condos

ARIZONA

sleeping eight for up to $125. A restaurant is open from 6 am to 9 pm and there is a coin laundry, store and bar.

*Lees Ferry Lodge* (☎ 355 2231, 355 2230) is on Alt Hwy 89 three miles west of Navajo Bridge (not at Lees Ferry). There are about 10 rooms at $45 a double, a restaurant and bar, and a fishing tackle shop and guide service next door.

*Cliff Dwellers Lodge* (☎ 355 2228, 1 (800) 433 2543, fax 355 2229) is under the Vermilion Cliffs, nine miles west of the Navajo Bridge. Twenty modern motel rooms rent for $57 to $67 a double in summer. There is a restaurant and bar, and a store.

## JACOB LAKE AREA

Alt Hwy 89 intersects with Hwy 67 at the small community of Jacob Lake, 41 miles west of Marble Canyon. Hwy 67 heads south to the North Rim of Grand Canyon National Park, 44 miles away, but snow closes the road from late October to early May. Jacob Lake's high elevation (7921 feet) explains the long snow season. Alt Hwy 89 remains open all year, but winter travelers should carry chains or have 4WD.

A USFS visitors center (☎ 643 7298) in Jacob Lake, on Alt Hwy 89 near the intersection, has information, displays and interpretive programs on the Kaibab National Forest. The district headquarters are in Fredonia.

### North Rim Nordic Center

In winter, the Kaibab Lodge, on Hwy 67 about 25 miles south of Jacob Lake, becomes a cross-country skiing center run by Canyoneers, Inc (☎ 526 0924, 1 (800) 525 0924), PO Box 2997, Flagstaff, 86003. A specially equipped 'snow van' transports skiers from Jacob Lake to the lodge from late December to mid-March (depending on snow). Well-reviewed locally and nationally, the center maintains about 25 miles of groomed skiing trails, plus plenty of ungroomed trails, and you can rent skis if necessary.

Rustic but comfortable accommodations are available in yurt dorms and private duplex cabins. Reservations for the cabin packages, which include the snow van from Jacob Lake, good meals and use of trails, should be made about six months in advance. Prices start in the $300s for three-days and two-nights. Longer accommodations packages, transportation in the snow van for trips to the South Rim of the Grand Canyon, extended ski tours, and lessons are also available.

### Places to Stay & Eat

Free dispersed camping in the Kaibab National Forest is permitted as long as you are over a quarter of a mile from the paved highway – several unpaved forest roads give access.

Near the USFS visitors center, the USFS-run *Jacob Lake Campground* (☎ 643 7395) is on Alt Hwy 89. Over 50 sites are $10 on a first-come, first-served basis. Two group sites (minimum $50 for 50 people) can be reserved. There is water but no showers or hookups. *Demotte Park Campground* is about 25 miles south on Hwy 67 and has 22 similar $10 sites. Both campgrounds are open from mid-May through October.

*Jacob Lake RV Park* (☎ 643 7804), on Hwy 67 about a mile south of Alt Hwy 89, has over 100 sites from $10 (tents) to $19 (hookups) open from May through October. There is water but no showers. Space is nearly always available.

*Jacob Lake Inn* (☎ 643 7232) has motel rooms and cabins for about $70 in summer, or $50 in winter. There is a restaurant and store that are open erratically in winter. The *Kaibab Lodge* (☎ 638 2389) is open in summer with rooms with private bath in duplex cabins from $65 for a single to $95 for rooms that sleep five. The lodge provides a base and accommodations for cross-country skiers in the winter. In summer, the main lodge serves a breakfast buffet open to guests and non-guests from 6 to 9 am and dinner from 6 to 9:30 pm.

## GRAND CANYON NATIONAL PARK – NORTH RIM

The differences between the North and South Rims of the Grand Canyon are elevation and accessibility. The North Rim is over 8000 feet above sea level, with some points going over 8800 feet. Winters are colder, the climate is wetter, and the spruce-fir forest above the rim is much thicker than the forests of the South Rim. Winter snows close the roads to car traffic into the area from late October to mid-May. There is only one road in so visitors must backtrack over 60 miles after their visit.

Since it's such a long drive from any major city or airport, only 10% of Grand Canyon visitors come to the North Rim. But the views here are just as spectacular – perhaps even more so than at the South Rim. North Rim visitors are drawn more by the lack of huge crowds and the desire for a more peaceful, if more spartan, experience of the canyon's majesty than by superior scenery.

### Orientation & Information

It is 44 miles on Hwy 67 from Alt Hwy 89 to the Grand Lodge, near the main visitors' services. Almost 30 miles of paved roads lead to various other overlooks to the east. In winter, the North Rim is considered open for backcountry day use only – those wishing to stay overnight then will be backcountry camping and will require a permit. You can enter the park when the services are closed. Depending on snow conditions, the road may be open in spring and fall and you can ski in (without prior arrangements

with the North Rim Nordic Center a three-day proposition from Jacob Lake) when the road is closed.

The visitors center (☎ 638 7864) is in the Grand Lodge (the North Rim's only hotel) and is open from 8 am to 6 pm from about mid-May through October. The usual NPS activities and information are available in summer.

The park headquarters are at the South Rim. See that section for general information, entrance fees and backcountry permits. The park's automated telephone system (☎ 638 7888) has both South and North Rim information.

Services available at the North Rim (in season) are lodging, camping, a restaurant, gas station, post office, bookshop, general store, coin laundry and showers, medical clinic and tours.

### North Rim Drives

The drive on Hwy 67 through the Kaibab Plateau to the Grand Lodge takes you through thick forest. There are excellent canyon views from the lodge, but to reach other overlooks you need to drive north from the lodge almost three miles and take the signed turn to the east to **Point Imperial** and **Cape Royal**. It is nine miles to Point Imperial, which is, at a lofty 8803 feet, the highest overlook in the entire park and has stunning views.

View from the North Rim (KH)

Backtrack about four miles from Point Imperial and then drive 15 miles south to Cape Royal where there are more great views and some short hiking trails.

With 4WD and high clearance, you can take unpaved roads to several other outlooks along the North Rim. These roads may be closed by bad weather or other factors – information is available from any ranger or the park information line. Many of these roads require leaving the park, driving through USFS or BLM lands, then reentering the park.

One of the most spectacular of these remote overlooks is the **Toroweap Overlook** at **Tuweep** far to the west of the main park facilities. An unpaved road, usually passable to cars, leaves Hwy 389 from nine miles west of Fredonia and heads 55 miles to the Tuweep Ranger Station, which is staffed year round. An alternative route is a 90-mile dirt road from St George, Utah. It is five more miles from Tuweep to the Toroweap Overlook where there is primitive camping but no water or other facilities – you must be totally self-sufficient.

### Hiking & Backpacking

In summer, the forests of the North Rim offer more backpacking potential than the South Rim, but there are fewer inner canyon hikes. The most popular quick hike is the paved half-mile trail from the Grand Lodge south to **Bright Angel Point** which offers great views at sunset. The 1.5 mile **Transept Trail** goes north from the lodge through forest to the North Rim Campground, where there are rim views.

Two trailheads, including the North Kaibab trailhead, are at a parking lot two miles north of the lodge. The **Ken Patrick Trail** travels through rolling forested country northeast to Point Imperial, about 10 miles away. This trail is often overgrown and requires route-finding skills. About a mile along this trail, a fork to the right (east) becomes the Uncle Jim Trail, a fairly rugged five-mile loop offering fine views from the rim.

A rugged, rarely-used (and therefore crowd-free) inner-canyon hike follows the Old Bright Angel Trail, from the Ken Patrick Trail, through the Roaring Springs Canyon to hook up with the North Kaibab Trail. Before embarking on this hike, consult with a North Rim ranger.

The **North Kaibab Trail** plunges down to Phantom Ranch at the Colorado River, 5,750 feet below and 14 miles away. This is the only maintained rim-to-river trail from the North Rim and it connects with trails to the South Rim. The first 4.7 miles are the steepest, dropping well over 3000 feet to **Roaring Springs** – a popular all-day hike and mule ride destination. Cottonwood campground is about two miles further and 4000 feet below the rim. Here, there are 14 backcountry campsites (available only by free permit), water and a ranger station. A little over a mile below the campground a short side trail leads to pretty **Ribbon Falls**. Phantom Lodge and the Bright Angel campground are seven miles below Cottonwood (see the South Rim section).

**Backcountry Permits** In the winter, the trails of the North Rim are regarded as backcountry use areas, as snow can accumulate to five feet. Though the USFS campground (see below) is closed, it is still open for backcountry use. However, there are only two ways to get to the campground – either hike from the South Rim up to the North Rim via the North Kaibab Trail (a trip only for the truly Nordic) or cross-country ski 52 miles from Jacob Lake, a route which takes three days.

Permits for Cottonwood campground and any other backcountry campground must be applied for as far in advance as possible from the BRO on the South Rim (see that section for full details). If you are beginning your hike from the North Rim, you can pick up your permit from the ranger station about 1.5 miles north of the Grand Lodge. This is also where to go to get on the waiting list if you don't have a permit – though your chances of getting a Cottonwood or Bright Angel campground permit are slim, at best. The ranger station can advise you of other, much more remote, backcountry campgrounds, most of which require a long drive on dirt roads followed by a hike.

## Fishing

The Colorado River, and several of its tributaries, provide good trout fishing. Licenses and tackle can be purchased in the South Rim at the general store in Grand Canyon Village. However, licenses are not available for purchase on the national park's North Rim – the nearest area to get a permit is Marble Canyon, where there are also fishing guides available.

## Cross-Country Skiing

Experienced and self-sufficient winter campers can ski to the North Rim – backcountry camping permits are necessary. Otherwise, if you just want to ski, see the North Rim Nordic Center, in the Jacob Lake section above.

## Organized Tours

**Bus** TW Recreational Services (see Places to Stay & Eat) offers daily three-hour narrated tours to Point Imperial and Cape Royal for $20 or $10 for four- to 12-year-olds.

**Mule** Trail Rides (☎ 638 2292 in season, (801) 679 8665 otherwise), PO Box 58, Tropic, UT 84776, offers rides for $10 for an hour (minimum age six), $30 for half day (minimum age eight) and $70 for an all-day tour into the Grand Canyon including lunch (minimum age 12). Advance reservations are recommended or stop by their desk in the Grand Lodge to see what is available. Mule rides are not available to the Colorado River (see Mule Tours in the South Rim section for more information).

## Places to Stay & Eat

Free backcountry camping is available year round. Permits must be obtained from the BRO (see Hiking & Backpacking).

The *North Rim Campground*, 1.5 miles north of the Grand Lodge, has 83 sites for $10 each. There is water, a store, snack bar and coin-operated showers and laundry, but no hookups. Reservations (☎ (619) 452 8787, 1 (800) 283 2267) can be made up to eight weeks in advance and are highly recommended. All other campgrounds are undeveloped and require a backcountry permit.

The *Grand Lodge* (☎ 638 2611 in season) is operated by TW Recreational Services (☎ (801) 586 7686, fax (801) 586 3157), PO Box 400, Cedar City, UT 84721. The lodge is usually full and reservations should be made as far in advance as possible. There are about 200 units: both motel rooms and a variety of rustic cabins sleeping up to five people. All have private bath; a few cabins have canyon views. Rates vary from $55 to $85 for a double and $70 to $100 for five people.

The lodge has a cafeteria, a restaurant and bar. Dining hours are 6:30 am to 10 pm. Reservations for breakfast and dinner in the attractive restaurant are advised.

## Getting There & Away

There is no public transport. A North to South Rim shuttle (☎ 638 2820) runs daily for $60 one-way or $100 roundtrip.

## FREDONIA

From Jacob Lake (7921 feet), Alt Hwy 89 drops 3250 feet in 30 miles to Fredonia, which is much hotter at 4671 feet. Founded by Mormons in 1885, Fredonia now has over 1200 inhabitants and is the biggest town in the Arizona Strip where logging and ranching are the main industries. The larger Kanab, seven miles north in Utah, has much better developed tourist facilities, but Fredonia has information about the Kaibab National Forest.

## Information

The chamber of commerce (☎ 643 7241), is at 130 N Main St. The Kaibab National Forest District Headquarters (☎ 643 7395), 430 S Main St, PO Box 248, 86022, is open from 8 am to 5 pm, Monday to Friday, and in summer from 8 am to 4 pm on Saturdays. The library (☎ 643 7137) is at 130 N Main St. The post office (☎ 643 7122) is at 85 N Main St. The police (☎ 643 7108, or 911 in emergencies) are at 116 N Main St.

## Pipe Spring National Monument

Ancient Indians and Mormon pioneers knew about this permanent spring in the arid Arizona Strip. Ranching began here in 1863 and a fort named **Winsor Castle** was built in 1870 to protect the ranchers from Indian attacks. In 1923, the 40-acre ranch was bought by the NPS as a historical monument to cowboy life on the Western frontier.

Today, visitors can relive late-19th-century cowboy life by touring the well-preserved ranch buildings and fort, examining historic exhibits and watching historically accurate reenactments by rangers in period costume. At various times of year cattle are rounded up and branded, and there are demonstrations of other aspects of frontier life.

A visitors center (☎ 643 7105) is open from 8 am to 4 pm daily except New Year's Day, Thanksgiving and Christmas. There is a bookshop and snack bar. Admission is $2 for adults and Golden Access, Age and Eagle passes are honored. The monument is 14 miles west of Fredonia on Hwy 389. Further information can be obtained from the Superintendent, HC65, Box 5, Fredonia, 86022.

### Places to Stay & Eat

Three small motels provide basic rooms in the $30s and may close in winter. *Blue Sage Motel & RV* (☎ 643 7125), 330 S Main St, has a few RV hookups. Opposite is the *Ship Rock Motel* (☎ 643 7355), 337 S Main St. The *Grand Canyon Motel* is open intermittently at 175 S Main St.

*Nedra's Cafe* (☎ 643 7591), 165 N Main St, serves Mexican and American food, Navajo tacos and breakfast anytime between 6 am and 10 pm, Monday to Saturday. Two miles north of town just before the state line, *Travelers Inn Restaurant & Lounge* (☎ 643 7402), 2631 N Alt Hwy 89 serves American fare for lunch and dinner but is closed on Sunday.

### AROUND FREDONIA
### Kaibab-Paiute Indian Reservation

This reservation completely surrounds the Pipe Spring National Monument. Fewer than 200 Paiutes live here. Some of their baskets may be seen at Pipe Spring. The tribally operated *Heart Canyon RV Campground* (☎ 643 7245) provides 45 tent sites for $8 and RV hookups for $12. Showers cost $2 and there is a laundry. The campground is a half mile east of Pipe Spring. This desolate camping area is rarely full.

### Kanab Canyon

Marked on most maps as Kanab Creek, this is actually the largest canyon leading to the Colorado River's north side. In places, Kanab Canyon is 3500 feet deep and it effectively splits the relatively developed eastern part of the Arizona Strip from the remote western part. From Fredonia, Kanab Canyon goes south for 60 miles to the Grand Canyon. Adventurous canyoneers enjoy hiking this route, which is described in Annerino's *Adventuring in Arizona*. Permits are required in some stretches. Drivers of high clearance vehicles can drive through the Kaibab National Forest to Hack Canyon and Jumpup Canyon, two popular entry points into the lower part of Kanab Canyon.

### The Northwest Corner

This is the most remote part of the state. Much of it is BLM land managed by offices in Kanab, Utah and St George, Utah. There are a few ranches and mines, as well as wilderness areas with absolutely no development. They are reachable by a network of dirt roads. To explore this area, you need a reliable high clearance vehicle and plenty of water and food. If you break down, you might not see another car for days. Consult with the BLM before you go.

# Lake Powell Area

The next major canyon system on the Colorado River northeast of the Grand Canyon was Glen Canyon. Called 'The Canyon That No One Knew', it was, in the 1950s, the heart of the largest roadless area in the continental USA. A few old-time river runners and canyoneers tell of a canyon that rivaled the Grand Canyon for scenic grandeur and Anasazi sites, but most people hadn't even heard of this remote wilderness area when work began on the Glen Canyon Dam in 1956. Conservationists fought hard against the construction of the dam, realizing that not only would the beautiful canyon be destroyed, but the character of the Southwest would also change dramatically. Seven years later, the dam was finished, and Glen Canyon began filling up to become the second largest artificial reservoir in the country, helping fuel the uncurbed population growth of the desert.

## PAGE
This was high desert before dam construction caused the mushrooming of a new town to house workers. At the height of construction, 7500 people lived here but the population dropped considerably after work was finished. Over the last decade, the popularity of newly-formed Lake Powell as a boaters' resort area has caused Page's population to return to former peak levels.

Page is a modern little town with no special attraction apart from its location. It is now the largest town in the huge area of Arizona north of I-40 and is a regional center for southeastern Utah as well. Tourists value Page not only as a convenient stopping place between the two states but also for the recreation opportunities afforded by Lake Powell (seven miles from the town center). The tourism industry is experiencing a boom and hotel rooms are pricey and booked-up in summer.

## Information
The chamber of commerce (☎ 645 2741, fax 645 3181), in the Page Plaza at 106 S Lake Powell Blvd, PO Box 727, 86040, is open from 8 am to 7 pm, Monday to Saturday and 10 am to 6 pm on Sunday from mid-May to mid-October. Hours are 8:30 am to 5 pm, Monday to Friday from December through February. At other times, hours are 8 am to 6 pm, Monday to Saturday.

The library (☎ 645 2231) is at 697 Vista Ave. The post office (☎ 645 2571) is at 615 Elm St. The hospital (☎ 645 2424) is at Vista Ave and N Navajo Drive. The police (☎ 645 2461 or 911 in emergencies) are at 547 Vista Ave.

## Things to See & Do
The small **Powell Museum** (☎ 645 9496), 6 N Lake Powell Blvd, has exhibits pertaining to Colorado River explorer John Wesley Powell, as well as regional information. Hours are 8 am to 6:30 pm from Monday to Saturday and 10 am to 6:30 pm on Sunday during summer, with shorter hours in spring and fall; it's closed in winter. A donation is appreciated.

Stop by the **Big Lake Trading Post** (☎ 645 2404), just over a mile south on Hwy 89, to see their small museum of Native American artifacts.

The **Page Golf Course** (☎ 645 2715), on Hwy 89 west of town, has nine holes. A **swimming pool** is open to the public year round at the high school (☎ 645 4124, 645 8801), 434 S Lake Powell Blvd.

## Organized Tours
The chamber of commerce will make tour reservations. Tours available include half or full day boat tours to Rainbow Bridge National Monument ($56/72), Wahweap Bay boat cruises ($9 to $43), half day float trips from Lees Ferry ($39) and a variety of Jeep tours. The International Hostel puts together budget tours with the 'European backpacker' in mind. Or you can directly contact Duck Tours (☎ 353 4281) and Lake Powell Jeep Tours (☎ 645 5501) for land tours, Wilderness River Adventures (☎ 645 3279, 1 (800) 528 6154) for float trips or Wahweap Marina (see below) for lake trips.

## Places to Stay
From May to October, high summer rates apply and reservations are recommended. In winter, some hotels (especially the more expensive ones) halve their rates. Tourism has hit Page quickly and new motels and one- and two-room B&B accommodations are scrambling to catch up. Rooms are

ARIZONA

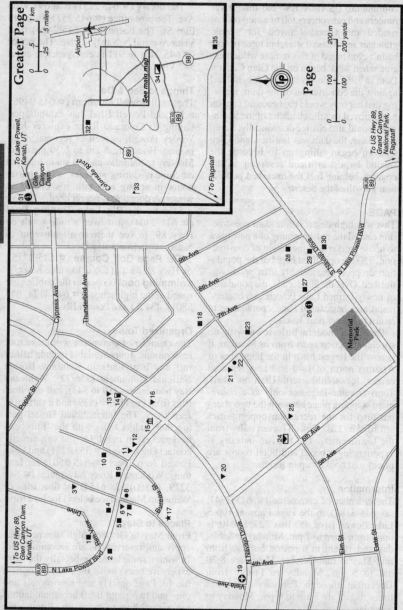

| PLACES TO STAY | | | |
|---|---|---|---|
| 1 | Inn at Lake Powell | 11 | Canyon Bowl Bistro |
| 2 | Holiday Inn | 12 | Bubba's Texas BBQ |
| 4 | Best Western at Lake Powell | 13 | Bella Napoli |
| 5 | Best Western Weston Inn | 16 | Strombolli's |
| 7 | Navajo Trail Motel II | 20 | Zapata's |
| 9 | Page Boy Motel | 21 | Starlite |
| 10 | Navajo Trail Motel I | 25 | Dos Amigos |
| 18 | Super 8 Motel | | |
| 23 | Empire House | **OTHER** | |
| 27 | Econo Lodge | 8 | Library |
| 28 | Lake Powell International Hostel, | 14 | Windy Mesa Bar |
|    | International Pension | 15 | Powell Museum |
| 29 | Bashful Bob's Motel | 17 | Police |
| 30 | Holiday Inn Express | 19 | Hospital |
| 32 | Courtyard by Marriott | 22 | Mesa Theater |
| 35 | Page/Lake Powell Campground & | 24 | Post Office |
|    | Trailer Motel | 26 | Chamber of Commerce, Page Plaza |
| | | 31 | Carl Hayden Visitor Center |
| **PLACES TO EAT** | | | (Glen Canyon Dam) |
| 3 | Ken's Old West | 33 | Golf Course |
| 6 | Glen Canyon Steak House | 34 | High School (Swimming Pool) |

**ARIZONA**

generally clean and modern – no Route 66 motels or creaky Victorian hotels in Page. Note that there are campgrounds and a motel at Wahweap Marina, five miles away (see Glen Canyon National Recreation Area below).

In the past few years, dozens of people have opened one or two rooms in their homes to provide simple B&B accommodations. Places open and close every year. The chamber of commerce can send you a listing – there are currently 26 names on it.

### Places to Stay – camping
*Page/Lake Powell Campground & Trailer Motel* (☎ 645 3374), 949 S Hwy 98, has over 70 sites, mainly for RVs with hookups ($18) and a few for tents ($15). There are showers, a pool, a spa and a coin laundry. Trailer motel rooms are about $60 a double.

### Places to Stay – bottom end
*Lake Powell International Hostel* (☎ 645 3898, 1 (800) 545 5405), 141 8th Ave, PO Box 1077, 86040, charges $12 to $15 per person in dorms (up to six people) or about

$40 for private double rooms in the *International Pension* next door. All have bathrooms. There is a laundry, kitchen privileges, free coffee and free shuttles to the airport and Lake Powell. In summer, call about a week ahead and they'll hold a bed for you. You don't have to have an HI/AYH card.

The cheapest motels, which have rooms starting in the $40s in summer, include *Bashful Bob's Motel* (☎ 645 3919), 750 S Navajo Drive, and the *Page Boy Motel* (☎ 645 2416), 150 N Lake Powell Blvd, which also has a small pool. Slightly more expensive rooms are available in the *Navajo Trail Motel I* (☎ 645 9508), 800 Bureau St and *Navajo Trail Motel II* (☎ 645 9510), 640 Vista Ave.

### Places to Stay – middle
*Empire House* (☎ 645 2406, 1 (800) 551 9005, fax 645 2647), 107 S Lake Powell Blvd, has 70 nice motel rooms for about $70 as well as a pool, restaurant (6 am to 9 pm) and bar. The *Lake Powell Motel* (☎ 645 2477, 1 (800) 528 6154) has 24 reasonable rooms from $70 to $80 about four miles north of the Glen Canyon Dam at the

junction of Hwy 89 and Wahweap Marina Rd. The motel sits on a hill with nice views and is away from road noise. They are closed from November through March.

The *Super 8 Motel* (☎ 645 2858), 75 S 7th Ave, has 40 standard rooms at $79.88 (half price in winter). The *Econo Lodge* (☎ 645 2488), 121 S Lake Powell Blvd, has over 60 units, including some large, family-size rooms with three queen-sized beds and mini-suites with refrigerators for $70 to $95. They have a swimming pool.

### Places to Stay – top end

The *Inn at Lake Powell* (☎ 645 2466, 1 (800) 826 2718), 716 Rim View Drive, has over 100 rooms, some with balconies and distant lake views, for $70 to $95. There is a pool, spa, restaurant (6 am to 10 pm in a separate building) and bar.

The *Best Western Weston Inn* (☎ 645 2451, 1 (800) 637 9183, fax 645 9552), 207 N Lake Powell Blvd, has 100 rooms, some with balconies, for around $80 to $90 for a double. There is a pool, a restaurant next door and free airport shuttle. Opposite is the newer *Best Western at Lake Powell* (☎ 645 5988, fax 645 2578), 208 N Lake Powell Blvd, with 132 spacious rooms for $80 to $100 and some mini-suites for up to $135. There is a pool, spa and breakfast bar (extra charge). Newer still, the *Courtyard by Marriott* (☎ 645 5000, fax 645 5004), 600 Country Club Drive, offers 150 large and attractive rooms for about $110 with coffeemakers in each room. There is a pool, spa, exercise area, restaurant (6 am to 11 pm) and bar.

The *Holiday Inn* (☎ 645 2466, fax 645 2523), 287 N Lake Powell Blvd, has 130 rooms in the $80 to $100 range in summer. The hotel features a nice pool area, coin laundry, restaurant (6 am to 10 pm), room service and bar. A *Holiday Inn Express* (☎ 645 9000) is at 749 S Navajo Drive opposite Bashful Bob's Motel.

### Places to Eat

For breakfast, your best bet is the family restaurant in one of the hotels (see above), which serve mainly American food.

*Strombolli's* (☎ 645 2605), 711 N Navajo Drive, serves pizza and other Italian specialties and is popular because of its large outdoor deck. More upscale Italian dining in a more intimate atmosphere is found at *Bella Napoli* (☎ 645 2706), 810 N Navajo Drive. This is considered by many to be the best restaurant in Page and is open from 5 to 9 pm daily in summer, closed on Sundays in fall and spring and closed entirely from mid-November through February. Dinners are in the $8 to $17 range, and there is a patio.

Page's Disneyesque attempt at a Wild West steakhouse is *Ken's Old West* (☎ 645 5160), 718 Vista Ave, open from 4 to 11 pm with meaty meals priced from $13 along with cheaper alternatives. *Canyon Bowl Bistro* (☎ 645 2682), 24 N Lake Powell Blvd, serves vaguely Southwestern lunches and dinners, and breakfast in summer. Both these places have entertainment. *Bubba's Texas BBQ* (☎ 645 9624) is next door to the Canyon Bowl. *Glen Canyon Steak House* (☎ 645 3363), 201 N Lake Powell Blvd, serves American food from 6 am to 10 pm.

Average Mexican food is served from 11 am to 10 pm (9 pm on Sundays) at *Zapata's* (☎ 645 9006), 615 N Navajo Drive, and the plastic-looking *Dos Amigos* (☎ 645 3036), 608 Elm St. Eat Chinese at *Starlite* (☎ 645 3620), 46 S Lake Powell Blvd.

### Entertainment

Movies are shown at the *Mesa Theater* (☎ 645 9565), 42 S Lake Powell Blvd.

*Ken's Old West* features live and recorded country & western music and dancing nightly except Sunday in the summer and a few times a week during other seasons. *Canyon Bowl Bistro* has eclectic entertainment – a bowling alley, a stand-up comedy club and occasional live music. *Windy Mesa Bar* (☎ 645 2186), 800 N Navajo Drive, occasionally has live music on weekends. Several other lounge bars advertise live music, usually of the background variety.

### Getting There & Away

**Air** At the Page Airport, Skywest-Delta

Connection (☎ 1 (800) 453 9417) has one to three flights a day to and from Phoenix.

**Bus** There are no bus lines. The International Hostel runs a shuttle to Flagstaff's Downtowner International Hostel for $15 per person.

### Getting Around
Budget (☎ 645 3977, 1 (800) 527 0700) rents cars at the Page Airport. Rates are expensive and you can save money by renting in Flagstaff or Phoenix and driving.

### GLEN CANYON NATIONAL RECREATION AREA
When the Glen Canyon Dam was finished in 1963, the Colorado River and its tributaries (especially the San Juan River) began backing up for 186 miles. It took until 1980 to fill the artificial Lake Powell, flooding the canyon to a depth of 568 feet at the dam and creating almost 2000 miles of shoreline. The 1933-sq-mile Glen Canyon National Recreation Area (GCNRA) was established in 1972, primarily emphasizing activities on the lake. In addition, many square miles of remote backcountry can be explored on foot or by a few roads north of the confluence of the Colorado and San Juan Rivers.

### Climate & When to Go
The area is open year round. The water-level elevation of 3700 feet makes the GCNRA cooler than Lake Mead and other downstream recreation areas but summer temperatures can still rise over 100°F on some days. Average summer maximum temperatures are in the 90°s F with water temperatures ranging from 70°F to 80°F from June to September. Overnight temperatures drop between 20°F and 30°F making sleeping bearable but chilly. The humidity is low year round and there is little rainfall. Summer is the most popular season with the highest rates for boat rentals and motel rooms.

Spring can be very windy and cold water temperatures preclude swimming or water-skiing without a wet suit – in May the water averages a brisk 64°F. Fall water temperatures average 69°F in October; the lowest average is 46°F in February.

Hikers and backpackers will find April to June and September to October to be the most pleasant months. In winter, overnight temperatures often fall into the 20°s F but rise into the 40°s F during the day in December and January, the coldest months.

Water levels fluctuate depending on season and water use. The highest levels are in late spring and early summer, when you can boat just a little further into some of the side canyons.

### Information
The Carl Hayden Visitor Center (☎ 608 6404, 608 6405) is at the dam, two miles north of Page (the only town close to the GCNRA). Hours are 7 am to 7 pm from Memorial Day to Labor Day and 8 am to 5 pm at other times. Most of the GCNRA is in Utah but it is treated as a whole here. Entrance to the area is free and up-to-date information is available in the free newspaper *Glen Canyon Visitor's Guide* available on arrival.

Five miles north of the visitors center is Wahweap Marina, the largest marina on Lake Powell. It offers complete visitors services. Four more marinas are scattered along the shores of Lake Powell in Utah. There is an NPS ranger station at every marina. Details of services available in each marina are described under individual marina headings below.

Further information is available from the Superintendent (☎ 608 6200), GCNRA, PO Box 1507, Page, 86040.

**Books & Maps** The *Boater's Guide to Lake Powell* by Michael R Kelsey (Kelsey Publishing, 1989), is for boaters interested in doing side hikes from the shore, and has plenty of other background as well. It includes information about shore camping for people using small boats. *Houseboating on Lake Powell: First Class Adventure* by Bob Hirsch (1988), is a locally available booklet geared to the houseboating experience. *Lake Powell and its 96 Canyons: Boating and Exploring Map* by Stan Jones

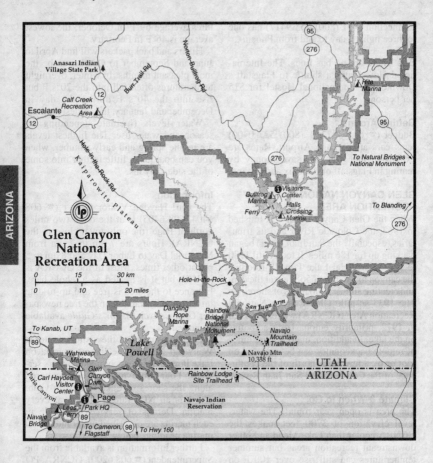

Glen Canyon
National
Recreation Area

(Sun Country Publishing, Page, 1985) is an annotated map with plenty of other useful information.

**Dangers & Annoyances** Several people drown every year in boating, swimming or diving accidents, many of which are alcohol related. Lake Powell has no lifeguards, but the lake is patrolled by park rangers. Children under 12 are required by law to wear life jackets when on a boat, while everyone in a boat, regardless of age, is required to have a preserver immediately accessible (not stowed). Use common sense.

### Glen Canyon Dam

Right next to the Carl Hayden Visitor Center, the dam can be visited on self-guided tours, or free guided tours lasting 60 to 90 minutes given every hour on the half hour, from when the center opens until an hour before it closes. Tours take you along the top and then deep inside the dam in elevators that drop to near the bottom. The dam is 710 feet high and required over 5 million cubic yards of concrete to build.

### Wahweap Marina

Only seven miles from Page, Wahweap

Marina & Lodge (☎ 645 2433), PO Box 1597, Page, 86040, offers complete services – boat tours and rentals, boat and car service and fuel, laundry, showers and supply store (prices are cheaper in Page). Call the marina directly for information and reservations less than seven days in advance or call Aramark (see Water Sports below) for reservations, which are recommended in summer.

*Wahweap Campground* has about 180 sites without hookups on a first-come, first-served basis open from April through October. Sites are $8.50. Next door *Wahweap RV Park* has 123 year-round sites with hookups for $20.50, or $13.50 from November through March (when tenting is permitted). There are showers and a playground.

*Wahweap Lodge* has 350 comfortable rooms with balconies or patios for $110 to $130 from April through October (about 35% less in winter). Many have lake views. Suites are $190. There are two pools and a spa. The lodge has room service, a moderately priced coffee shop and a good restaurant. Hours are 6 am to 10 pm (7 am to 9 pm in winter). A bar has live entertainment ranging from Native American dancing to piano music. Sunset dinner cruises on a paddlewheeler are $43.

### Bullfrog Marina

Bullfrog Resort & Marina (☎ (801) 684 2233), PO Box 4055, Lake Powell, UT 84533, is 96 miles upstream from the dam and the lake's second largest marina. It is on Lake Powell's north shore and the nearest town is tiny Hanksville, 72 miles north.

There is a GCNRA visitors center (open 8 am to 5 pm daily, 7 am to 7 pm in summer), a medical clinic (summer only), post office, ranger station, laundry, showers, boat rentals, fuel and services, auto fuel and services and an expensive supply store. Services and advance reservations (which should be made more than one week in advance) at the campground and Defiance House Lodge are provided by Aramark (see Water Sports below).

*Bullfrog RV Park and Campground* has a similar season and rates to Wahweap. Free primitive camping (no water) is permitted at several places along the shore – ask at the ranger station for recommendations.

*Defiance House Lodge* has 48 comfortable rooms for $100 to $120 in summer, less in winter. Housekeeping trailers, with three bedrooms, two bathrooms, fully-supplied kitchen and electricity (but no phone or TV) range from $115 a double to $160 for six people in summer, less in winter. The lodge has a restaurant open for breakfast, lunch and dinner year round and a fast-food place open during the summer. There is also a bar.

### Halls Crossing Marina

Halls Crossing Marina (☎ (801) 684 2261), PO Box 5101, Lake Powell, UT 84533, is on the south shore of the lake opposite Bullfrog. The nearest town is Blanding, 75 miles to the east. Services include a ranger station, boat rentals, fuel and service, auto fuel and service, laundry, showers, supply store and an air strip. Services are provided by Aramark.

The ranger station can suggest where you can camp for free along the shore. An RV park and campground offers the same season and prices as at Wahweap. Housekeeping trailers are available (see Bullfrog Marina for details). There is no restaurant.

### Hite Marina

Hite Marina (☎ (801) 684 2278), PO Box 501, Lake Powell, UT 84533, is 139 miles upriver from the dam and is the most northerly marina. Hanksville, 45 miles northeast, is the nearest little town. Services at Hite include a ranger station, boat rental, fuel and service, auto fuel and service, and supply shop.

The marina has a free primitive campground (no water) and housekeeping trailers (see Bullfrog Marina for details).

### Dangling Rope Marina

This marina is about 40 miles upriver from the dam and can be reached only by boat. This is the closest marina to Rainbow Bridge

National Monument (see below). Services include a ranger station, boat fuel and services and supply store.

## Fishing

You can fish year round. Spring and fall are considered the best times although summer isn't bad. Bass, crappie and walleye are the main catches on the lake. Licenses are needed and are available from any marina. Rent boats from Aramark (see Water Sports).

## Water Sports

The public can launch boats from NPS launch ramps at the marinas. Boats ranging from 16-foot runabouts to 50-foot houseboats sleeping 12 are available for rental from Aramark, but the marinas aren't geared to renting kayaks or dinghies so bring one if you want one.

Water-skiing, scuba diving, sailing and swimming are summer activities. Average water temperatures of 62°F in November and 64°F in May are too chilly except for the most dedicated enthusiasts with wet or dry suits.

Aramark (☎ 278 8888, 1 (800) 528 6154, fax 331 5258), PO Box 56909, Phoenix, 85079 rents boats. A 16-foot skiff seating six with a 25-hp motor is $63 a day or $290 a week in summer. These are suitable for exploring and fishing. Larger boats with larger engines for towing water-skiers cost three or four times as much.

Water 'toys' include jet skis for about $175 a day or $1050 a week in summer, or water skis and other equipment packages for $19 a day or $90 a week.

## Houseboating

Houseboating is popular – hundreds of houseboats are available for rent and there are more every year. Despite the number of boats, the large size of the lake still allows houseboaters to get away from others. Houseboats can sleep from six to 12 people, but accommodations are tight so make sure you are good friends with your fellow shipmates.

Houseboats on Lake Powell are provided by Aramark (see Water Sports, above),

which also provides other boats, tours and lodging in marinas – these can be combined into a variety of packages.

Summer rates range from $700 to $2000 for three days or $1250 to $3500 for a week in boats sleeping from six to 12 people. (Note that 12-berth boats are available for $1200/$2000 for three/seven days and the higher rates reflect more luxurious boats.) Two-day rentals are available outside of summer. Spring and fall discounts of 25% and winter discounts of 40% are available but dates vary. Winter is usually from November through March. Summer begins in mid to late May and ends between late September and mid-October.

All houseboats have tiny to mid-sized refrigerators, simple cooking facilities, toilet and shower, gas barbecue grill and 150-quart ice chests.

Larger boats may have some of the following: electric generator (allowing air conditioning, microwave, toaster, coffeemaker, TV, VCR and radio), canopies and swim slides and ladders. Luxury boats have all these features upgraded and with extra space. Boats are booked up well in advance in summer.

## Organized Tours

Aramark offers seven tours ranging from a one-hour ride on a steam-powered paddlewheel riverboat ($9) to a seven-hour tour to Rainbow Bridge ($72). There are discounts for three- to 11-year-olds.

All tours leave from Wahweap Marina. Rainbow Bridge tours also leave from Bullfrog and Halls Crossing Marinas.

## Getting Around

For those who need to cross the lake at its north end, the Lake Powell Ferry provides a link between Bullfrog and Halls Crossing Marinas year round. The crossing takes 20 minutes and costs $2 for foot and bicycle passengers, $5 for motorbikes and $10 to $50 for cars to extra-long trailers (including passengers). The ferry makes six roundtrips daily in summer and four in winter. You can usually get on the next departure.

## RAINBOW BRIDGE NATIONAL MONUMENT

On the south shore of Lake Powell, Rainbow Bridge is the largest natural bridge in the world and a site of religious importance to the Navajo. No camping or climbing on the bridge is permitted, but visitors can come by boat, horse or on foot. Primitive camping is allowed outside the monument, less than a mile from the bridge. Most people visit the bridge by boat tour and then hike a short trail. Rainbow Trails & Tours (☎ 672 2397) in Shonto on the Navajo Reservation offers horseback trips to the monument. See Shonto in the Northeastern Arizona chapter for details.

Very few people arrive on foot. However, hikers leave from the Rainbow Lodge Trailhead in Arizona (the lodge is abandoned) or Navajo Mountain Trailhead in Utah and walk about 14 miles to the monument. The trailheads are reached by dirt roads and the trails themselves are not maintained. This is for experienced backpackers only; backpackers should carry water and be self-sufficient. Both trailheads are on the Navajo Reservation and a tribal permit should be obtained from the Navajo Nation Recreational Resources Department (☎ 871 6647), PO Box 308, Window Rock, 86515. Further information is available from the Navajo Nation and the GCNRA.

ARIZONA

# Western Arizona

Western Arizona is not only the hottest part of the state, it is often the hottest area in the nation. The low-lying towns along the Colorado River – Bullhead City, Lake Havasu City and Yuma – boast average maximum daily temperatures of over 100°F from June to September, and temperatures in excess of 110°F are not unusual. The balmy weather during the rest of the year attracts thousands of winter visitors and many of them end up staying. Western Arizona has one of the fastest growing populations in the USA, with Yuma experiencing a 10% population increase between 1990 and 1992. Bullhead City grew by 12.9%, Kingman by 13.4% and Lake Havasu City by 15.2% in the same two-year span.

After the Colorado River leaves the Grand Canyon, it turns south and forms the western boundary of Arizona. A number of dams form huge artificial lakes that attract holidaymakers seeking to escape the intense summer heat – water skiing and jet skiing, sailing and boating, fishing, scuba diving and plain old swimming are all popular activities. In addition, travelers can enjoy the wild scenery and visit dams, wildlife refuges, ghost towns, casinos and, perhaps the most incongruous of sights in the desert Southwest, London Bridge.

In the northwestern corner of the state, the massive Hoover Dam forms Lake Mead and the smaller Davis Dam forms Lake Mohave, both of which are major attractions lying within the Lake Mead National Recreation Area. The far shores of the Colorado River and the two lakes lie in the state of Nevada, which provides plenty of gambling opportunities for Arizonans and other visitors. The Nevada town of Laughlin, joined by a short bridge across the Colorado to Bullhead City in Arizona, provides the closest casinos to Phoenix and Tucson.

In the center of Arizona's western border is Lake Havasu, formed by the Parker Dam.

Lake Havasu City, with the popular tourist destination of London Bridge, is on the lake's eastern shore. The western shores lie in the state of California. Yuma, the third-largest metropolitan area in Arizona, is in the extreme southwestern corner of the state. Southwest of Yuma, the Colorado River is bordered by the USA's huge southern neighbor, Mexico.

# Grand Canyon to I-40

This area is bounded by the Colorado River and Lake Mead to the north and west, the small town of Seligman to the east and Parker to the south. Most of the area falls into Mohave County, named after the Mohave Indians who used to live in the area and who now have reservations along the lower Colorado River. Other important Indian tribes include the Hualapai and Havasupai, both of whom have reservations bordering the southwestern reaches of Grand Canyon National Park and provide tourist services to the canyon (see the Grand Canyon chapter).

The area is generally desert interspersed with several north-south mountain ranges that created a barrier to east-west exploration. The highest are the Hualapai Mountains. Pine-clad Hualapai Peak reaches 8417 feet. The more modest Cerbat Mountains and Black Mountains are rich in minerals. Below these, the Colorado River drops from 1221 feet at Lake Mead to only 482 feet at Lake Havasu City.

Northwestern Arizona was virtually unknown to Europeans until the mid-19th century. In 1857, Edward Beale, using camel caravans, surveyed a wagon route across northern Arizona near what is now Kingman. Twelve years later, John Wesley Powell made the first boat descent of the Grand Canyon, emerging at what is now

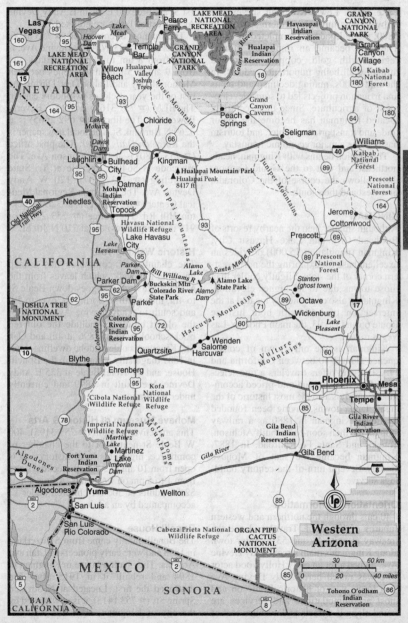

**Western
Arizona**

| 0 | | 30 | 60 km |

| 0 | | 20 | 40 miles |

Lake Mead. Lewis Kingman surveyed a railway route through northern Arizona in 1880; the railroad was completed in 1883. The area became an important mining region, with gold, copper, silver and turquoise all being important products. In the mid-1900s, mining declined and dams and irrigation projects led to some development of agriculture. Since then, centrally located Kingman has become the major trade and transportation center, and tourism has become a major economic mainstay.

This section begins with Kingman, heads northeast and east to the Grand Canyon, then follows the course of the Colorado, first west and then south.

## KINGMAN

Although smaller than the nearby resorts of Bullhead City and Lake Havasu City, Kingman (population 15,000) provides an excellent base for exploring the northwestern corner of the state. Slightly cooler than those towns due to its higher elevation, Kingman is also conveniently located at the intersection of I-40 with both historic Route 66 and US 93, the main Phoenix-Las Vegas route.

Kingman is the only town of consequence along I-40 between California and Flagstaff, and offers travelers a fine selection of inexpensive and mid-priced accommodations. It is also the most historic of the area's larger towns, having been founded by Lewis Kingman in 1880 as a railway stop on the then soon-to-be-built Atchison, Topeka and Santa Fe Railroad. In 1887, Kingman became the seat of Mohave County. Several turn-of-the-century buildings survive.

### Orientation & Information

I-40 cuts through the northern and western suburbs of Kingman. Travelers leave the freeway at exits 48 and 53 to enter town along Kingman's main street, Andy Devine Ave, named after an early Hollywood actor who was raised here. Andy Devine Ave also forms part of historic Route 66 and most accommodations and services are found along it. Streets and avenues east of

1st St are prefixed E (as in E Andy Devine Ave); west of 1st St are prefixed W.

The chamber of commerce (☎ 753 6106, fax 753 1049), 333 W Andy Devine Ave, is open from 8 am to 7 pm weekdays and from 9 am to 5 pm on weekends between Memorial Day and Labor Day. During the rest of the year it closes two hours earlier. The BLM (☎ 757 3161) is at 2475 Beverly Power Ave. The library (☎ 692 2665) is at 3269 N Burbank St. The local newspaper is the *Kingman Daily Miner*. The post office (☎ 753 2480) is at 1901 Johnson Ave. The zip code is 86402. Recycle at Tri-State Recycling (☎ 753 2267), 120 W Andy Devine Ave. The Kingman Regional Medical Center (☎ 757 2101) is at 3269 Stockton Hill Rd. The police (☎ 753 2191, or 911 in emergencies) are at 310 N 4th St.

### Historic Walking Tour

The chamber of commerce has a map detailing this walk, which leaves from the Mohave Museum and goes down Beale St to 4th, then north to Spring St, over to 5th and south to Andy Devine Ave. Some of the oldest buildings include the old red brick school, built in 1896 at 4th and Oak Sts; Kingman's oldest adobe dwelling, built in 1887 diagonally across from the Bonelli House; and the Hotel Beale at 325 E Andy Devine Ave, built in 1899 and currently under restoration.

### Mohave Museum of History & Arts

This attractive museum (☎ 753 3195), 400 W Beale St next door to the chamber of commerce, highlights local history and is open from 10 am to 5 pm on weekdays and from 1 to 5 pm on weekends. Admission is $2 for adults or 50c for children under 13 accompanied by an adult.

### Bonelli House

The Bonelli family came from Switzerland in 1858 and were early pioneers in Utah and Arizona. They built a house in Kingman in 1894 and rebuilt it in 1915 after fire destroyed the first. Located at N 5th and Spring Sts (☎ 753 1413), it is now owned by the city of Kingman, is on the National

Register of Historic Places, and is open to the public as an excellent example of early Anglo architecture in Arizona. Opening hours are from 1 to 5 pm, Thursday to Monday. There's no admission charge, but donations are greatly appreciated.

### White Cliffs

This historic site has tracks made by wagons in the late 1800s – there's not much else to see but history buffs like to glimpse a part of the past here. Head north on 1st St to White Cliff Rd.

### Hualapai Mountain Park

This park (☎ 757 3859) surrounds 8417-foot Hualapai Peak and offers a popular summer getaway for local residents. The park is 14 miles southeast of Kingman (take Hualapai Mountain Rd from Andy Devine Ave) and features picnicking, camping, cabins, wildlife observation, six miles of maintained trails and 10 miles of undeveloped trails.

Near the park is the Hualapai Mountain Lodge Resort (see Places to Stay – middle).

### Activities

Kingman Municipal Golf Course (☎ 753 6593), 1001 E Gates Ave, has nine holes. Valle Vista Golf Course (☎ 757 8744), 16 miles north of town on Route 66 (mile marker 71) has 18 holes.

Centennial Park, just north of I-40 between Burbank and Harrison Sts, offers miniature golf (☎ 757 5566, 757 5561), a swimming pool (☎ 757 7910) and tennis courts.

### Special Events

As part of the Route 66 Fun Run, a car rally along Route 66 between Seligman and Topock held during the last weekend in April, there is a car show in Kingman, followed by dancing in the evening. The Arts Festival during Mother's Day weekend in May includes metal workers and woodcarvers as well as the more usual types of artists. In September, the Mohave County Fair is held during the second weekend and Andy Devine Days, which include a

parade, rodeo, gem show and other events, during the last weekend. There are plenty of other minor events – call the Kingman Chamber of Commerce for a more complete schedule.

### Places to Stay – camping

At *Hualapai Mountain Park*, over 70 campsites are available, most with picnic tables and grills, for $6. There are 11 RV sites with hookups for $12. Water and toilets are available.

There are also 16 rustic cabins, all with beds, kitchens and hot and cold showers. Most cabins have a fireplace or wood-burning stove. Visitors must bring their own bedding, cooking utensils and towels. Most cabins sleep two to four people and rent for $25 (no heat), $30 (stove), or $40 (fireplace). One cabin sleeps six and has a stove ($45) and another sleeps 10 and has a fireplace ($55). Weekly discounts are seven nights for the price of five.

Campsites are on a first come, first served basis. Cabins should be reserved at the Mohave County Parks Department in Kingman (☎ 757 0915), 3675 E Andy Devine Ave, PO Box 7000, 86402, which is open from 8 am to 5 pm, Monday to Friday. Credit cards are accepted. Cabins are very popular in summer – book well in advance. Both cabins and campsites are open in winter, though snow may necessitate 4WD or chains at times.

The BLM runs the *Wild Cow Campground*, six miles by steep dirt road south of Hualapai Mountain Park. The campground is open from May to October, has no water and is free.

The *KOA* (☎ 757 4397), 3820 N Roosevelt, has mainly RV sites, although there is a small tenting area. Rates are from $15 to $19 for two people, with an extra $1 for sewage hookup and $3 for electric hookup. A swimming pool, game room, coin laundry, convenience store and miniature golf are available.

The *Quality Star RV Park* (☎ 753 2277), 3131 McDonald Ave, offers sites from $10 to $16 depending on whether you use the hookups. There is a coin laundry and spa.

ARIZONA

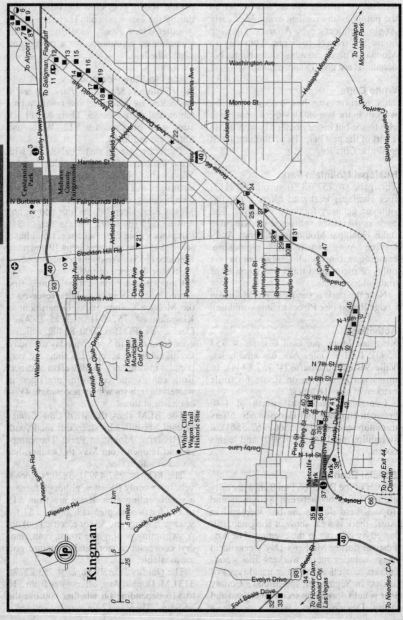

ARIZONA

| PLACES TO STAY | | 31 | El Trovatore Motel | | 34 | House of Chan |
|---|---|---|---|---|---|---|
| 4 | Super 8 | 32 | Holiday House Motel, | | 41 | 4th Street Social Club |
| 5 | Motel 6 | | Uptown Motel | | 47 | JR's |
| 7 | Sunny Inn, | 33 | Frontier Motel | | | |
| | Silver Queen | 35 | Rodeway Inn | | **OTHER** | |
| 9 | Motel 6 | 36 | Motel 6 | | 1 | Kingman Regional |
| 11 | Quality Star RV Park | 43 | Star Motel | | | Medical Center |
| 12 | Days Inn | 44 | Arcadia Lodge | | 2 | Public Library |
| 13 | Lido Motel | 45 | Ramblin' Rose Motel | | 3 | BLM Office |
| 14 | Days Inn | 46 | Brandin' Iron Motel | | 6 | Greyhound Bus Depot |
| 15 | Holiday Inn | 47 | Quality Inn | | | (behind McDonald's) |
| 16 | Mohave Inn | | | | 22 | Police Station |
| 17 | Route 66 Motel | **PLACES TO EAT** | | | 24 | Smokehouse Bar |
| 18 | Best Western A | 8 | Denny's | | 26 | Post Office |
| | Wayfarer's Inn | 10 | Golden Corral Family | | 37 | Chamber of Commerce, |
| 19 | Best Western King's Inn | | Steak House | | | Mohave Museum |
| 20 | High Desert Inn | 21 | La Poblanita | | 38 | Tri-State Recycling |
| 25 | Kingman Motel, Orchard | 23 | Silver Spoon Family | | 39 | Hotel Beale, Nighthawk |
| | Inn Motel | | Restaurant | | | Bar |
| 29 | Imperial Motel | 27 | Dam Bar & Steak House | | 40 | Bonelli House |
| 30 | Hilltop Motel | 28 | City Cafe | | 42 | Amtrak Railway Station |

## Places to Stay – bottom end

Plenty of cheap hotels can be found along Andy Devine Ave and W Beale St, with which W Andy Devine Ave merges west of the chamber of commerce. Prices may rise during holiday or special events weekends; reservations then and during most summer weekends aren't a bad idea for the best choice of rooms. Winter rates are several dollars lower than summer rates – summer rates are given below.

The cheapest places have basic double rooms for about $25 or less and include the *Arcadia Lodge* (☎ 753 1925), 909 E Andy Devine Ave; the *Brandin' Iron Motel*, (☎ 753 2374), 1403 E Andy Devine Ave; *Frontier Motel* (☎ 753 6171), 1250 W Beale St; the *Lido Motel* (☎ 753 4515), 3133 E Andy Devine Ave; the *Kingman Motel* (☎ 753 6413), 2021 E Andy Devine Ave; the *Mohave Inn* (☎ 753 9555), 3016 E Andy Devine Ave; the *Orchard Inn* (☎ 753 5511), 1967 E Andy Devine Ave; the *Route 66 Motel* (☎ 753 5586), 2939 E Andy Devine Ave; the *Star Motel* (☎ 753 2410), 617 E Andy Devine Ave; and the *Uptown Motel* (☎ 753 2773), 1239 W Beale St. Of these, the Mohave is a good choice; the Arcadia, Lido, Orchard and Route 66 advertise a swimming pool.

For doubles in the upper $20s or low $30s (more on weekends) the *Sunny Inn* (☎ 757 1188), 3275 E Andy Devine Ave, is a good choice with large rooms and a small spa and swimming pool. Next door, the *Silver Queen* (☎ 757 4315), 3285 E Andy Devine Ave, is a little cheaper, lacks the pool and spa, but is also good. Other reasonable hotels with pools and rooms around $30 are (in roughly descending order of price) the attractive and recommended *Hilltop Motel* (☎ 753 2198), 1901 E Andy Devine Ave; the newly-remodeled *El Trovatore Motel* (☎ 753 6918), 1440 E Andy Devine Ave; the well-run *Ramblin' Rose Motel* (☎ 753 5541), 1001 E Andy Devine Ave; the *Imperial Motel* (☎ 753 2176), 1911 E Andy Devine Ave, which offers long-term discounts; and the *Holiday House Motel* (☎ 753 2153), 1225 W Beale St.

The *High Desert Inn* (☎ 753 2935), 2803 E Andy Devine Ave, charges about $25/30 for singles/doubles. There are three *Motel 6*s, all with a pool. The ones at 3270 E Andy Devine Ave (☎ 757 7121) and 3351 E Andy Devine Ave (☎ 757 7151) are both $28/32 for singles/doubles; the one at 424 W Beale St (☎ 753 9222) costs about $5 more.

## Places to Stay – middle

The *Super 8 Motel* (☎ 757 4808), 3401 E Andy Devine Ave, lacks a pool but has nice enough single/double rooms for around $37/40, including continental breakfast. The following hotels have a pool: the *Rodeway Inn* (☎ 753 5521), 411 W Beale St, has a coffeeshop and charges about $30/40; the *Kingman Travelodge* (☎ 757 7878), 3421 E Andy Devine Ave, has nicer rooms for $36/42; There are two *Days Inns* – both have a spa and some rooms with microwave and fridge – at 3023 E Andy Devine Ave (☎ 753 7500), which charges from $35/45 (up to $15 more during summer weekends), and at 3381 E Andy Devine Ave (☎ 757 7337), which charges $39/45; the *Holiday Inn* (☎ 753 6262), 3100 E Andy Devine Ave, has large rooms from $44/49, less during the low season.

The *Quality Inn* (☎ 753 4747), 1400 E Andy Devine Ave, has a sauna, spa and exercise area and a decent adjoining restaurant. Rooms cost about $50/60, continental breakfast included. The similarly priced *Best Western King's Inn* (☎ 753 6101), 2930 E Andy Devine Ave, has a spa, sauna and free in-room coffee. The *Best Western A Wayfarer's Inn* (☎ 753 6271), 2815 E Andy Devine Ave, has a spa and all rooms include a microwave and fridge. Rates are $55/60 with king-sized beds or a little less with double beds.

Near Hualapai Mountain Park is the *Hualapai Mountain Lodge Resort* (☎ 757 3545), with rooms from $50 to $90 and a restaurant.

## Places to Eat

The *Silver Spoon Family Restaurant* (☎ 753 4030), 2011 E Andy Devine Ave, is a popular local place. It was called Nick's for many years and locals still sometimes call it that. Breakfasts cost from $2.50 to $5 and dinners are in the $5 to $7 range – a good value. The Silver Spoon is open from 5 am to 10 pm.

*JR's* (☎ 753 1066), at 1410 E Andy Devine Ave next to the Quality Inn, is one of the best restaurants in town and has been

known for years as La Posada (locals still call it that). Breakfasts cost $4 to $6 and dinner entrees, mostly Italian and Mexican American dishes, are in the $7 to $15 range. They are open from 9 am to 10 pm. Another well-recommended and similarly priced choice is the *House of Chan* (☎ 753 3232), 960 W Beale St. Service is good and prime rib, steak and seafood are featured in addition to Chinese food. They are open from 11 am to 10 pm and are closed on Sundays.

Other possibilities include the locally popular greasy spoon, the *City Cafe* (753 3550), 1929 E Andy Devine Ave. The venerable *4th Street Social Club* (☎ 753 7877), 401 E Andy Devine Ave, considers itself Kingman's gourmet restaurant. *La Poblanita* (☎ 753 5087), 1921 Club Ave, is one of the better Mexican restaurants with meals in the $5 to $9 range. Hours are 11 to 10 pm and they are closed on Mondays. The *Dam Bar & Steak House* (☎ 753 3523), 1960 E Andy Devine Ave, specializes in big steaks ($10 to $20, most around $13) in a sawdust-on-the-floor atmosphere. They're open from 4 to 10 pm. Cheaper steaks are served at the *Golden Corral Family Steak House* (☎ 753 1505), 3157 Stockton Hill Rd, open form 11 am to 10 pm. For 24-hour food service, head east to *Denny's* (☎ 757 2028), 3255 E Andy Devine Ave, or the *Flying J Truck Plaza* (☎ 757 7300), 3300 E Andy Devine Ave.

## Entertainment

The *Smokehouse Bar* on Andy Devine Ave almost opposite the Silver Spoon Restaurant, has music and dancing on weekends and sometimes midweek in summer. The *Nighthawk Bar* (☎ 753-2297) is your basic drinking establishment, but interestingly set next to the lobby of the historic Hotel Beale St, 325 E Andy Devine Ave. *The Movies* (☎ 757 7985), 4055 Stockton Hill Rd, is the local cinema.

## Getting There & Away

**Air** Kingman Airport (☎ 757 2134), is about six miles northeast of town, just off Route 66. America West (☎ 1 (800) 235

9292) flies between Kingman and Phoenix three or four times a day.

**Bus** The Greyhound Bus Terminal (☎ 757 8400), 3264 E Andy Devine Ave, is behind the McDonalds Restaurant. They have four departures a day to Phoenix (at 5 and 11:45 am, and at 6:55 and 11:45 pm; four hours, $40), four to Las Vegas, Nevada (two hours), two to Flagstaff (three hours) and Albuquerque, New Mexico (11 hours), and two to Los Angeles, California (eight hours).

**Train** Amtrak (☎ 1 (800) 872 7245) has a daily train west to Los Angeles, California, and east to Flagstaff, Albuquerque, New Mexico, and Kansas City, Missouri. Trains leave late at night or very early in the morning and the station is on Andy Devine Ave between 4th and 5th Sts.

## CHLORIDE
Founded in 1862 by silver miners, Chloride is the oldest mining town in Arizona and home to the oldest continuously operating post office in the state (since 1871). It makes a good day trip from Kingman.

In the late 1800s, some 5000 people lived here, working dozens of mines, of which the Tennessee Schuylkill Mine was one of the most famous. At its closure in 1948, it had operated for over 60 years and locals claim that it produced well over $100 million worth of gold, silver, lead and zinc (at today's prices).

Today, about 300 people live here and tourism is the economic mainstay. There are several interesting antique and art stores, old buildings and occasional melodramas, usually held on the first and third Saturdays of summer months. A dirt road (look for the sign) goes 1.3 miles southeast of town to huge murals painted by artist Roy Purcell on a rocky hillside.

Contact the chamber of commerce (☎ 565 2202), PO Box 268, 86431, or the Tennessee Saloon (☎ 565 2225). Tennessee Ave is the main street through town – continue on it to see the murals.

Locals dress in turn-of-the-century garb on Old Miners Day, the last Saturday in June. A parade and old-time music and dancing are featured – but watch out for gunfights and showdowns!

There is a small RV park but no hotels. The locally famous Sheps General Store rents rooms, which are usually full with long-term clients. There are three homey cafes and a couple of Western saloons.

The easiest way to get to Chloride is to head northwest from Kingman on Hwy 93 for about 19 miles to mile marker 53; turn right and drive 3.5 paved miles into town on Tennessee Ave. More adventurous travelers can take dirt roads past two of the area's ghost towns. Head northwest on Hwy 93 and near mile marker 62, take the dirt road to your right. After 0.8 miles turn left and then, after half a mile, turn right and continue for two miles to the old mining town of **Cerbat**, which was briefly the Mohave County seat in the 1870s. Today, you can see is the ruined headframe of an old mine and some decrepit cabins and foundations. Most any car can handle the dirt roads already mentioned; those beyond require 4WD, bicycles or foot for exploration.

Return two miles to where you made the last right turn and turn right on a good dirt road. After 3.2 miles you intersect with a paved road from Hwy 93 heading for the massive scar of the (now idle) Duvall copper mine to your right. Nearby is the ghost town of **Mineral Park**, which was briefly the county seat before Kingman. Little remains to be seen now except for the old cemetery on private mine property. Five miles further along, the dirt road brings you into Chloride on 2nd Ave, which soon intersects with Tennessee Ave.

## GRAND CANYON CAVERNS
These caverns, 12 miles east of Peach Springs or 23 miles west of Seligman on Route 66, are 210 feet underground. Tourists visited them as early as the 1920s, when entrance was gained by being lowered on a rope. Today, an elevator takes people below ground, where a three-quarter-mile trail winds by the geological formations.

The *Grand Canyon Caverns and Motel* (☎ 422 3223), PO Box 180, Peach Springs 86434, is open year round. Entrance and a 45-minute guided tour costs $7.50 for adults and $4.75 for four- to 12-year-olds. Hours are from 7 am to 6 pm in summer and from 10 am to 5 in winter. The motel charges about $34/42 in summer and half that in winter. There is a restaurant. Note that in winter the motel desk is open only from 8 am to 6 pm and the restaurant from 9:30 am to 5 pm. The caverns are a mile behind the motel.

## SELIGMAN

This small town of about 850 inhabitants dates from 1886 when it became a railway town. Today, it is of interest as one end of the longest remaining stretch of historic Route 66, the approximately 90 miles between Kingman and Seligman (compared to 70 miles along I-40).

The visitors center (☎ 422 3352), 217 E Route 66, provides information. There is a Route 66 memorabilia store along the main street, Chino Ave.

Campers can stay at the *KOA* (☎ 422 3358) at the east end of town or at the slightly cheaper *Northern Arizona Campground* (☎ 422 3549) at the west end.

There are half a dozen cheap and basic motels, mainly along Chino Ave and dating from the heyday of Route 66. These include, in alphabetical order, the *Bil Mar Den Motel* (☎ 422 3470), the *Canyon Shadows Motel* (☎ 422 3255), the *Deluxe Motel* (☎ 422 3244), the *Navajo Motel* (☎ 422 3204), the *Romney Motel* (☎ 422 3294) and the *Supai Motel* (☎ 422 3663).

The *Copper Cart Restaurant* (☎ 422 3241) and the *Ranchside Kitchen* (☎ 422 3618), both on Chino Ave, serve breakfast, lunch and dinner.

## LAKE MEAD NATIONAL RECREATION AREA

The extreme heat and aridity of the far northwestern corner of Arizona made this one of the least hospitable areas of the USA, attracting prospectors and miners but few others. Then, between 1931 and 1936,

the Hoover Dam (at that time the world's largest) was built. It backed up the Colorado River, flooding canyons, archaeological sites, wilderness areas and communities and producing Lake Mead, one of the world's largest artificial lakes. In 1953, the smaller Davis Dam was completed, forming Lake Mohave. The purposes of the dams were flood control, irrigation, hydroelectricity and the supply of water to the burgeoning population of the Southwest and southern California.

At the time of the building of the dams, some people decried the flooding as a destructive waste of archaeological, historical, natural and scenic resources. Today, these lie largely forgotten and the two lakes, surrounded by wild desert scenery, attract millions of annual visitors, ranging from curious day-trippers looking at the dams to vacationing families spending a week or more boating on the lakes. Barely an hours' drive from Las Vegas, the recreation area certainly doesn't suffer from a shortage of potential visitors.

### Orientation

Hwy 93, which connects Kingman with Las Vegas, is the major access road to the area. This highway crosses the Hoover Dam (where the road is very narrow – expect delays) and passes the main visitor center and park headquarters. Another important access road is Hwy 68, which runs from Kingman to Bullhead City, near the Davis Dam. Both dams straddle the Arizona/Nevada state line, as does most of the recreation area. Many minor paved and dirt roads access a number of lodges, marinas, camping areas, boating areas and wilderness areas around the lakes.

The 2337-sq-mile Lake Mead National Recreation Area encompasses both 110-mile-long Lake Mead and 67-mile-long Lake Mohave, about 700 miles of shoreline, and many square miles of desert around the lakes, in both Arizona and Nevada. In addition, the remote Shivwits Plateau area in Utah, reachable only by long dirt roads from the Arizona Strip north of the Grand Canyon, offers a largely unwatered, high desert wilderness area administered by Lake Mead National Recreation Area.

Motels, developed campgrounds, restaurants, marinas, grocery stores and gas stations are available in three lakeside areas in Arizona and six in Nevada. There are also a number of undeveloped backcountry campgrounds and boat launch areas.

### Information

The Alan Bible Visitor Center (☎ (702) 293 8906) is in Nevada, five miles west of the Hoover Dam. It is open from 8:30 am to 5 pm (4:30 pm in winter) daily except Thanksgiving, Christmas and New Year's Day. The center provides maps, books and information and has an exhibit room and theater showing films and slide shows. There is a desert botanical garden outside.

The Katherine Landing Visitor Center (☎ 754 3272), also providing maps, books and information, is in Arizona, three miles north of Davis Dam. Opening hours are from 8 am to 4 pm. Information is also available from eight ranger stations throughout the area. Advance information is available from the Superintendent, Lake Mead National Recreation Area, 601 Nevada Hwy, Boulder City, NV 89005 (☎ (702) 293 8907).

Each year, several people die in boating, swimming or diving accidents, many of which are alcohol related. Take care. In any emergency, contact a ranger or call the 24-hour emergency number (☎ (702) 293 8932).

The area is open year round but summer temperatures rise over 100°F almost every day. This is the time for water activities. Winter high temperatures are in the 50°s and 60°s – this is the best time for hiking and backpacking. Long hikes are not recommended in summer, when heat prostration is a real problem. The National Weather Service forecast can be heard by calling (702) 736 3854.

### Hoover Dam & Davis Dam

At 726 feet high, the Hoover Dam remains one of the tallest in the world. There is an exhibit room, and guided tours (☎ (702)

293 8387, 293 8321) are available at frequent intervals throughout the day between 8 am and 5:45 pm from Memorial Day to Labor Day, and between 9 am and 3:15 pm the rest of the year. Tours descend into the dam by elevator, last 40 minutes, cost $1 (free for kids under 16) and are quite popular – lines can be very long. Parking is limited to several lots along Hwy 93 and free shuttle buses take visitors to the dam.

The 200-foot-high Davis Dam, at the south end of Lake Mohave, can be visited on a free self-guided tour from 7:30 am to 3:30 pm daily.

### Fishing

The lakes are said to have some of the best sport fishing in the country. Striped bass (some in excess of 50 pounds) are one attraction; rainbow trout, largemouth bass, channel catfish, black crappie and bluegill are also likely catches. November to February is the best time for trout and crappie; March to May is OK for trout, crappie, catfish and bass; June to August is best for catfish, bass and bluegill; September to mid-October continues to be OK for bass and, as the water cools, for crappie. There is no season – fish any time with a license, available at the boating marinas (which also have fishing supplies and charters). Those in possession of a state fishing license (Arizona or Nevada) can fish from the appropriate shore. Boat anglers need a state license with a special-use stamp from the other state.

### Boating

Free public boat launch areas are available at the resort marinas mentioned above and elsewhere in the recreation area. Parking near the boat launches is available, but limited to seven days.

Because of the large number of powerboats and the huge area of the lakes, small vessels such as canoes and rafts are not encouraged, except through the Black Canyon of the Colorado River, just below the Hoover Dam. Here, the water flows at a controlled three to five mph and the 11-mile trip to Willow Beach Marina or the further 13 miles to Eldorado Canyon are popular trips – backcountry camping is possible. Canoe launching is free but by permit only. Call (702) 293 8356 from 8 am to 5 pm, Monday to Thursday, for permit applications, maps and information. Call at least two weeks in advance for weekend launching dates; only 30 canoe launches are allowed per day.

**Boat Tours** Lake Mead Cruises (☎ (702) 293 6180) have four to six narrated cruises a day from Lake Mead Resort Marina to Hoover Dam – a 90-minute excursion. The boat is an air-conditioned, three-decked Mississippi paddle wheeler. Departures are at 11:30 am and 1:30 pm year round, plus 3:30 and 5:30 pm from April to October. Fares are $12/5 for adults/children under 12; also available are breakfast buffet cruises at 9 am ($16.50/8), dinner cruises at 5:30 pm, April to October ($23/10.50) and dinner/dance cruises at 7:30 pm ($32.50, adults only).

The more adventurous can do a raft tour from below the Hoover Dam, down the Black Canyon of the Colorado River to Willow Beach Resort. The motorized rafts hold up to 45 passengers and the tour costs $65 for adults, $35 for children under 12 and free for kids under five. Lunch is included and a bus returns you to your starting point at Black Canyon Raft Tours (☎ (702) 293 3776), Expedition Depot, 1297 Nevada Highway, Boulder City, NV 89005. Departures are from February to November. During the summer months, desert bighorn sheep may be sighted, especially in the early hours of the day.

**Boat Rentals** Fishing, ski, patio and houseboats are all available, as well as jet skis. Seven Crown Resorts (☎ 1 (800) 752 9669), PO Box 16247, Irvine, CA 92713, operates the Lake Mohave Resort near Katherine Landing on Lake Mohave; the Temple Bar Resort on the southeast arm of Lake Mead; the Lake Mead Resort, near Boulder Beach by the Hoover Dam, Nevada; and the Echo Bay Resort and Overton Beach Marina on the north arm of Lake Mead in Nevada. All of these resorts have small boat rentals ranging from $60 per day for fishing boats to $225 a day for ski boats or jet skis (hourly and weekly rates are also available).

The Lake Mohave Resort and Overton Beach have houseboats that sleep from six to 10 people and include kitchen, shower, ice box and air conditioner. Rates for the high season (15 June to 15 September) range from $850 to $1150 for three days/ two nights or $1450 to $1750 for seven days/six nights. During the rest of the year, rates are from $200 to $400 less. Add taxes of 5% in Arizona or 7% in Nevada. Houseboats use about five gallons of gas per hour of boating – it takes the best part of a day to get from Overton Beach to Temple Bar.

Forever Resorts (1 (800) 255 5561, (702) 565 7340; fax (702) 293 4934), also has houseboat rentals at *Callville Bay Marina* (☎ (702) 565 7340), Box 100 HCR-30, Las Vegas, NV 89124-9410, on the north side of Lake Mead, Nevada; and *Cottonwood Cove Marina*, PO Box 1000, Cottonwood Cove, NV 89046, on the west side of Lake Mohave, Nevada. Their boats sleep 10 and high-season rates are $1700 for three or four nights and $2795 for seven nights. Rates for the low season (November to April) are $700 and $1000; the rest of the year is cheaper ($1200 and $1825). Taxes and fuel are extra. Three-night trips begin on Friday, four-night trips on Monday and seven-day trips on Friday, Saturday or Sunday.

Two things to consider when renting a boat are to bring binoculars (helps to read buoy numbers) and that a boat sleeping 10 will be very cramped for 10 adults. Make sure you are very good friends! All the above places are authorized concessionaires of the National Park Service. In addition to boat rentals, they provide a grocery store, gas station and fishing bait, tackle and license facilities.

### Places to Stay & Eat
Kingman and Bullhead City in Arizona, and Las Vegas, Boulder City and Laughlin in Nevada all have accommodations.

RV campers can stay at the *Temple Bar Resort* and *Lake Mohave Resort* for $18 daily or $350 monthly (including hookups). *Cottonwood Cove* charges $20 a night with hookups. The *National Park Service* (☎ 767 3401 at Temple Bar; 754 3272 at Katherine Landing) operates campgrounds for tenters for $6. There are also campgrounds on the Nevada side.

Seven Crown Resorts and Forever Resorts (see Boat Rental above for the telephone number) operate motels and restaurants at several of their resorts. The *Temple Bar Resort* (☎ 767 3211) is 47 miles by paved road east of the Hoover Dam. Rates range from $43 to $95 for fishing cabins, double rooms and kitchen suites sleeping four. The *Lake Mohave Resort* (☎ 754 3245) at Katherine Landing charges $60 to $83 for doubles or kitchen suites sleeping three. Seven Crown Resorts also have similarly priced motels at the *Lake Mead Resort* and the *Echo Bay Resort*. Forever Resorts' *Cottonwood Cove Motel* (☎ (702) 297 1464) on the Nevada shores charges $80 to $85 for doubles from mid-March to October and holidays, and $55 to $58 the rest of the year.

## BULLHEAD CITY & LAUGHLIN

Bullhead City (population 25,000), or 'Bull' as some locals call it, is 34 miles west of Kingman at the south end of Lake Mohave. It was established in the 1940s for the builders of Davis Dam and is now a popular vacation destination for tourists wishing to visit Lake Mohave or cross the bridge over the Colorado River to Laughlin, Nevada, which has the closest casinos. Laughlin is named after Don Laughlin, who opened a bar and eight-room motel here in 1966. By 1983, Laughlin had five casinos and about 400 hotel rooms. Today, there are about 10 casinos in Laughlin, complete with hotels (for a combined total of over 10,000 rooms!), restaurants, shopping areas and nightclubs – a modern American growth story.

## Orientation & Information

Hwy 95 is the main thoroughfare and runs north-south, parallel to the Colorado River – many places to stay and eat are found along or just off this strip. At the north end of town, a short bridge across the Colorado joins Bullhead City to Laughlin, Nevada.

The Bullhead Area Chamber of Commerce (☎ 754 4121), 1251 Hwy 95, is open Monday to Friday from 8 am to 4 pm between April and October and from 9 am to 5 pm the rest of the year. Saturday hours are from 9 am to 3 pm. The post office (☎ 754 3717) is at 990 Hwy 95 or (☎ 758 5711) 1882 Lakeside Drive. Bullhead Community Hospital (☎ 763 2273) is at 2735 Silver Creek Road. The police (☎ 763 1999, or 911 in emergencies) are in the Bullhead City Complex, 1255 Marina Blvd.

The Laughlin Chamber of Commerce (☎ (702) 298 2214), 1725 Casino Drive, is almost opposite the huge Hilton Flamingo Casino.

## Things to See & Do

The **Colorado River Museum** (☎ 754 3399), 355 Hwy 95, features local area history. Its hours are from 10 am to 3 pm, Wednesday to Sunday, and admission is free.

The nearby Davis Dam and Lake Mohave Resort & Marina at Katherine Landing can be visited (see Lake Mead National Recreation Area).

In Laughlin, **gambling** is a big attraction. Also in Laughlin, Blue River Safaris (☎ (702) 298 0910) and Laughlin River Tours (☎ (702) 298 1047) have **river cruises**, depending on water levels. Blue River Safaris also has bus tours to local areas of interest.

Chaparral Country Club (☎ 758 6330), 1260 E Mohave Drive, off Hwy 95 at the south end of town, has a nine-hole **golf** course. Nearby, the Chaparral Health Club (☎ 763 2582), 1290 E Mohave Drive, features racquetball and a gym. A few miles further south is the Desert Lakes Golf Course (☎ 768 1000), 5701 Desert Lakes Drive, with 18 holes. Over in Laughlin, the Emerald River Golf Course (☎ (702) 298 0061), 1155 S Casino Drive, also has 18 holes.

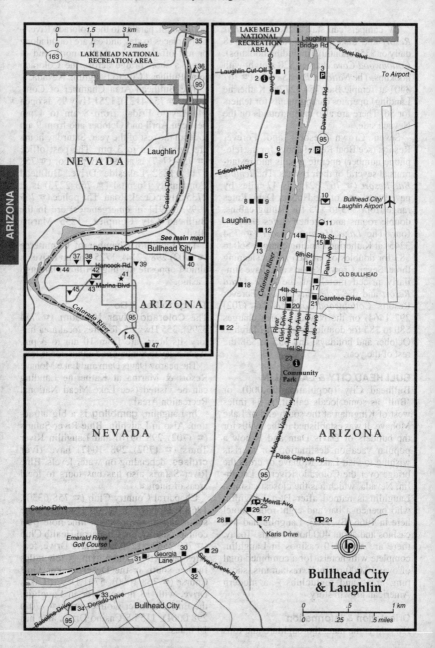

Bullhead City & Laughlin

| PLACES TO STAY | | |
|---|---|---|
| 1 | Don Laughlin's Crystal Palace, Riverside Resort Hotel & Casino | |
| 4 | Flamingo Hilton Laughlin | |
| 5 | Edgewater Hotel & Casino | |
| 8 | Ramada Express Hotel & Casino | |
| 9 | Colorado Belle Hotel & Casino | |
| 12 | Pioneer Hotel & Gambling Hall | |
| 13 | Golden Nugget | |
| 14 | River Queen Resort | |
| 15 | Palms Motel | |
| 16 | Desert Rancho Motel, Arizona Clearwater Hotel | |
| 17 | Nevada Club Inn, Super 8 Motel | |
| 18 | Gold River Resort & Casino | |
| 19 | Bullhead River Lodge | |
| 20 | Colorado River Resort | |
| 21 | Highland Motel, Travelodge | |

| 22 | Harrah's Laughlin Casino & Hotel |
|---|---|
| 24 | River City RV Park |
| 25 | Bullhead RV Park |
| 26 | Motel 6 |
| 27 | Arizona Bluffs, Days Inn |
| 28 | El Rio Motel & Trailer Park |
| 29 | Silver Creek Inn |
| 30 | Riverfront Motel, Econo Lodge |
| 31 | Shangri La |
| 32 | Best Western Grand Vista Hotel |
| 34 | La Plaza Inn |
| 36 | Davis Camp |
| 40 | Silver Creek RV Park |
| 47 | Sunshine Motel |

| PLACES TO EAT | |
|---|---|
| 13 | El Encanto Restaurant |
| 29 | Gerard's Restaurant |
| 33 | El Palacio, China Szechuan |
| 37 | Vito's Pizza & Restaurant |

| 38 | Casa Garcia |
|---|---|
| 39 | China Panda |
| 43 | Casa Garcia |
| 45 | Iguanas |

| OTHER | |
|---|---|
| 1 | Riverside Cinemas 1-2-3 |
| 2 | Laughlin Chamber of Commerce |
| 3 | Parking for Colorado River Ferries |
| 6 | Laughlin River Tours |
| 7 | Parking for Colorado River Ferries |
| 10 | Post Office |
| 11 | Greyhound Bus Depot |
| 23 | Bullhead Area Chamber of Commerce |
| 35 | Davis Dam |
| 41 | Bullhead City Complex, Police Station |
| 42 | Post Office |
| 44 | Movie House |
| 46 | Chapparal Country Club |

**ARIZONA**

## Places to Stay – camping

RVs can park overnight in the casino parking lots. There are no hookups, but restaurants and gambling are right on your doorstep. There are several RV parks in Bullhead City; most prefer long-term visitors. Try the *Bullhead RV Park* (☎ 763 8353), 1610 Hwy 95, $15 per night; the *Fiesta Resort* (☎ 758 7671), 3190 Hwy 95, $21; the *River City RV Park* (☎ 754 2121), $14 per night, 2225 Merrill Ave; or the *Silver Creek RV Park* (☎ 763 2444), 1515 Gold Rush Drive, $16.58 per night. There are also more RV parks near Hwy 95 south of Bullhead City.

Both tent and RV sites are available at *Davis Camp*, run by Mohave County Parks (☎ 586 3977), on Hwy 95 almost a mile north of the Laughlin Bridge. Rates are $8 for tents, $15 for RVs with hookups. RV and tent camping is also found at Katherine Landing (see above, Lake Mead National Recreation Area).

## Places to Stay – bottom end

Probably the cheapest place is the *Palms Motel* (☎ 754 2644), 115 Palm Ave, with basic doubles starting as low as $18 midweek, or $110 for a week. Rooms at the *La Plaza Inn* (☎ 763 8080), 1978 Hwy 95, are quite nice and start at $22 midweek, $29 weekends, and $120 per week. The *Motel 6* (☎ 763 1002), 1616 Hwy 95, has a pool and charges $26 for singles or doubles midweek, and $30/36 on weekends. The *Highland Motel* (☎ 754 2224), 464 Lee Ave, has doubles for $130 per week or $40 a day.

The *Riverfront Motel* (☎ 763 3869), 1715 Hwy 95, has kitchenettes in some rooms and charges $30 midweek or $165 per week for a double. The *Sunshine Motel* (☎ 758 3300), 3138 Hwy 95, is similarly priced. The *Desert Rancho Motel* (☎ 754 2578), 1041 Hwy 95, has a pool and charges $30 midweek and $40 on weekends. Other places to try in this price range are the *Arizona Clearwater Hotel* (☎ 754 2201), 1081 Hwy 95; the *Bullhead River Lodge* (☎ 754 2250), 455 Moser Ave; or the *El Rio Motel & Trailer Park* (☎ 763 4385), 1641 Hwy 95.

For a few dollars more, try the *Colorado River Resort* (☎ 754 4101), 434 River Glen Drive; the *Shangri La* (☎ 758 1117), 1767 Georgia Lane; or the *Arizona Bluffs* (☎ 763 3839), 2220 Karis Drive.

## Places to Stay – middle

**Casinos** Room rates at casinos vary greatly, but most casinos offer a good deal for accommodations and expect to make their money on gambling. The weekend travel sections of major newspapers in Arizona and California sometimes advertise special midweek rates – I stayed in a very comfortable double room at the Ramada Express for $8 using one of these special rates! Don't expect to get rates as low as this, but do expect to get nice double rooms in the high teens or low 20s if you go midweek – just show up at a reasonable hour. Weekend rates jump drastically to $50 or more.

All the casinos in Laughlin are along Casino Drive:

Colorado Belle Hotel & Casino
  (☎ (702) 298 4000, 1 (800) 458 9500)
Don Laughlin's Crystal Palace and the Riverside
  Resort Hotel & Casino
  (☎ (702) 298 2535, (520) 763 7070,
  1 (800) 227 3849)
Edgewater Hotel & Casino
  (☎ (702) 298 2453, 1 (800) 647 7483)
Flamingo Hilton Laughlin
  (☎ (702) 298 5111, 1 (800) 352 6464)
Gold River Resort & Casino
  (☎ (702) 298 2242, 1 (800) 835 7903)
Golden Nugget
  (☎ (702) 298 7111, 1 (800) 950 7700)
Harrah's Laughlin Casino & Hotel
  (☎ (702) 298 4600, 1 (800) 447 8700)
Pioneer Hotel & Gambling Hall
  (☎ (702) 298 2442, (520) 758 5557,
  1 (800) 634 3469)
Ramada Express Hotel & Casino
  (☎ (702) 298 4200, (520) 763 2010,
  1 (800) 272 6232)

**Motels & Hotels** The *Econo Lodge* (☎ 758 8080), 1717 Hwy 95, has nice rooms for $32 midweek and $38/44 for singles/doubles on weekends. More expensive rooms (up to $60) with balconies and river views as well as suites (up to $90) are also available. Continental breakfast is included and some rooms have microwaves and fridges. There is also a pool and coin laundry. The *Days Inn* (☎ 758 1711), 2200 Karis Drive, charges $38 midweek, about

$50 on weekends, and has a few pricier suites. They also have a pool, spa and coin laundry. The *Nevada Club Inn* (☎ 754 3128), 336 Lee Ave, has a pool, spa and tennis court. Double rooms cost from $37 to $42. The *River Queen Resort* (☎ 754 3214), 125 Long Ave, also has rooms in this price range, some with kitchenettes, as well as a pool and the El Encanto restaurant.

The *Travelodge* (☎ 754 3000), 2360 4th St, has attractive rooms for $35 to $45 single and $45 to $55 double midweek. Singles/doubles cost $55 to $65 on weekends, including continental breakfast. Weekly discounts are available. Rooms have refrigerators, some have microwaves, and there is a pool and spa. The *Super 8 Motel* (☎ 754 4651), 338 Lee Ave, has a pool and coin laundry. Rooms are about $38/44 for singles/doubles midweek, more on weekends.

The *Silver Creek Inn* (☎ 763 8400), 1670 Hwy 95, has spacious rooms with refrigerators for $44 midweek or $54 on weekends; there is a pool and Gerard's Restaurant. The *Holiday Inn* (☎ 754 4700), 839 Landon Drive, which has a pool, spa, exercise rooms and restaurant, offers single/double rooms well off the highway for $45/50. The *Best Western Grand Vista Hotel* (☎ 763 3300), 1817 Arcadia Plaza, has a pool and spa. Rates are $50 to $60 midweek, $60 to $90 on weekends, and weekly discounts are available. There is also the Lake Mohave Resort at Katherine Landing (see Lake Mead National Recreation Area above).

## Places to Eat

The casino restaurants in Laughlin have 24-hour service and cheap buffet meals, but lines can be long.

In Bullhead City, *Gerard's* (☎ 763 8400), at 1670 Hwy 95 in the Silver Creek Inn, is popular for breakfast and lunch. It is open from 7 am to 1:45 pm and closed Monday. Meals are in the $7 range. *El Encanto* (☎ 754 5100), at 125 Long Ave in the River Queen Resort, is good for Mexican and American food. They are open from 11 am to 10 pm. Meals are in the $7 range. Other decent Mexican restaurants include *Iguanas* (☎ 763 9109), 2247 Clearwater Drive; *El Palacio* (☎ 763 2494), 1884 Hwy 95; and two locations of *Casa Garcia* (☎ 758 8400), 1999 Riviera Blvd, and (☎ 758 8777), 967 Hancock Rd. For Italian food, try *Vito's Pizza & Restaurant* (☎ 758 4040), 805 Hancock Rd, and for Chinese, try the *China Szechuan* (☎ 763 2610), 1890 Hwy 95, or the *China Panda* (☎ 763 8899), 2164 Hwy 95.

### Entertainment

The Laughlin casinos often have nightclub shows. Catch films at the *Movie House* (☎ 758 6360), 590 Hancock Rd, Bullhead City, or at *Riverside Cinemas 1-2-3* (☎ (702) 298 2535) next to Laughlin's Riverside Casino.

### Getting There & Away

**Air** The airport (☎ 754 3020) is at 600 Hwy 95. It is currently expanding and services and carriers change frequently. America West (1 (800) 247 5692) operates several flights a day to and from Phoenix. Arizona Airways (1 (800) 274 0662) has flights on most days to and from Tucson.

**Bus** KT Services & Greyhound Bus (☎ 754 4655), 1010 Hwy 95, has four buses a day to Kingman and on to Flagstaff, Phoenix or Albuquerque, New Mexico. There are also buses to Las Vegas, Nevada and Los Angeles, California.

### Getting Around

Free ferry boats cross the Colorado River from several points in Bullhead City between the Laughlin Bridge and the Bullhead Area Chamber of Commerce. They go to the Laughlin casinos. Service is available 24 hours a day and there are parking lots on the Bullhead City side.

### OATMAN

This gold-mining town in the rugged Black Mountains southwest of Kingman was founded about 1906. Two million ounces of gold were extracted before the last mine closed in 1942 and the population of several thousand plummeted to a few hundred. Today, visitors come to see the old buildings, browse the gift shops (which sell area artifacts and mineral specimens), enjoy the weekend shenanigans undertaken on weekends by the locals (gunfights at high noon and Western dancing at night) and feed the wild burros (descendants of burros freed by the miners after the boom went bust).

Route 66 is the main and only street of any size through town. The chamber of commerce (☎ 768 3719) and the post office are both on Main St.

The *Oatman Hotel* (☎ 768 4408) was rebuilt in 1920 after the first one burnt down. The two-story adobe structure is on the National Register of Historic Places and the simple rooms are pretty much unchanged since Hollywood legends Clarke Gable and Carole Lombard honeymooned here in the 1930s. Rooms cost $35 and the shared bathroom is down the hall. Non-guests can go upstairs to see the Gable-Lombard room, or grab a bite alongside the grizzled miners in the *Saloon & Restaurant* downstairs (the bar is wallpapered with $1 bills). The *Z-Inn* (☎ 768 4603) is a small motel offering rooms with private baths for about $35, including breakfast. Other places to eat include *Cactus Joe's Cantina* (☎ 768-3242), which serves Indian fry bread and burgers, and the *Mission Inn Coffee Shop* (☎ 768-5973).

Either come on a tour (from nearby Bullhead City) or drive yourself the 30 miles from Kingman along paved Route 66. Parts of the road are very steep and winding – vehicles over 40 feet long are prohibited.

### HAVASU NATIONAL WILDLIFE REFUGE

This is one of a string of wildlife refuges and other protected areas along the lower Colorado River. Habitats include marshes, sand dunes, desert and the river itself. Popular activities include bird-watching and, in the northern reaches, boating through the 16-mile-long Topock Gorge.

Osprey

Over-wintering birds – geese, ducks and cranes – are all found here in profusion. After the migrants' departure, herons and egrets are found nesting in large numbers. Many other species are found, especially shore and marsh birds. Bald eagles and ospreys are often sighted in winter. Desert bighorn sheep are sometimes seen and the elusive bobcat is present, along with common desert mammals such as coyotes, rabbits and pack rats.

### Information & Orientation

The refuge headquarters (☎ (619) 326 3853), 1406 Bailey Ave, Suite B, PO Box 3009, Needles, CA 92363, is open from 8 am to 4 pm, Monday to Friday. Limited funds/staff may cause the office to be closed at times. They have maps, bird lists and information.

The section of the reserve north of I-40 is the Topock Marsh. South of I-40, the Colorado flows through Topock Gorge. The southern boundary of the reserve abuts the northern boundary of Lake Havasu State Park, about three miles north of London Bridge.

### Boating

A day of canoeing or floating through Topock Gorge usually begins at either *Golden Shores Marina* (☎ 768-2325), in Arizona, or *Park Moabi Campground* (☎ (619) 326 4777), in Needles, California. Both places are just north of where I-40 crosses the Colorado River and Park Moabi has boat rentals. Allow about seven hours for the float through the gorge. You can

also paddle north into the marsh area. Power boaters should beware of submerged sandbars and other obstacles.

The Jerkwater Canoe Company (☎ 768 7753), PO Box 800, Topock 86436, offers canoe rentals and guided day trips through the gorge, as well as a variety of overnight excursions along the river. Jet boat tours from Lake Havasu City are operated by Bluewater Charters.

### Places to Stay

There is no camping allowed in Topock Gorge. Camping is permitted on the Arizona side of the river south of the gorge everywhere except Mesquite Bay. Tent and RV camping is available at *Five Mile Landing* (☎ 768 2350) on the Arizona side of Topock Marsh, approximately six miles north of I-40 on Hwy 95, for $7 and $14.50 respectively.

### LAKE HAVASU CITY

The Parker Dam, finished in 1938, created 46-mile-long Lake Havasu. Until 1963, there was no town along the lake. Developer Robert McCullouch planned Lake Havasu City as a center for water sports and light industry/business. The city received a huge infusion of publicity when McCullouch bought London Bridge for $2,460,000, disassembled it into 10,276 granite slabs, and reassembled it at Lake Havasu City. The bridge, originally opened in London, England, in 1831, was rededicated in 1971 and has become the focus of the city's English Village – a complex of restaurants, hotels and shops built in English style.

The bridge move was a huge success, and today Lake Havasu City is host to millions of visitors coming not just to see the strange sight of London Bridge in the desert, or to walk or drive across it, but also to enjoy water sports, boat tours, shopping, golf and tennis. I've read a local claim that Lake Havasu City attracts more tourists than anywhere in Arizona except the Grand Canyon! The population of the city is now over 30,000, and it is one of the fastest-growing communities in the Southwest.

London Bridge, Lake Havasu City (RR)

## Orientation

Hwy 95, the main drag through town, runs north-south. McCullouch Blvd is the main east to west street, and goes over London Bridge. Note that you can't turn from Hwy 95 onto McCullouch Blvd – you have to turn a block before or after and reach McCullouch via Lake Havasu Ave.

## Information

The chamber of commerce (☎ 855 4115, 1 (800) 242 8278), 1930 Mesquite Ave, is open from 9 am to 5 pm, Monday to Friday. A visitor information center at the English Village is open daily, 10 am to 4 pm. The parking lot at the English Village costs $2 per day. The library (☎ 453 0718) is at 1787 McCullouch Blvd. The post office (☎ 855 2361) is at 1750 McCullouch Blvd. The zip code is 86403. The Havisu Samaritan Regional Hospital (☎ 855 8185) is at 101 Civic Center Lane. The police (☎ 885 4884, 911 in emergencies) are at 296 London Bridge Rd.

## Activities

**Boating** Departing from the English Village, one-hour narrated day and sunset boat tours cost about $12 – call Dixie Belle (☎ 855 0888, 453 6776) or Miss Havasupai

(☎ 855 7979) across the bridge at the Island Fashion Mall. Also here is Adler Marine (☎ 855 1555), which offers tours and rentals on a sailboat. Bluewater Charters (☎ 855 7171) in the English Village has jet boat tours at 9 am daily; they cover 60 miles in three hours. Fares are $20, $11 for children, free for kids under six. A cheap, quick cruise can be taken on the Colorado River Express ferry operated by the Chemehuevi Indian Tribe. They leave from English Village at 9 am, noon and 5:30 pm daily, heading for the Havasu Landing Resort operated by the tribe on their reservation across the lake in California. Ferry return times are 30 minutes later. Fares are $2 each way; kids under 12 pay $1.

Fishing, water-skiing or sightseeing boats can be rented from Lake Havasu Marina (☎ 855 2159), 1100 McCullouch Blvd; Resort Boat Rentals (☎ 453 9613), in the English Village; or the Havasu Landing Resort (☎ (619) 858 4593), across the lake in California. Boat rentals vary from about $40 a day for a four-person fishing boat to as much as $300 a day for a decked ski boat. Jet skis and parasailing are available from the Water Sports Center at the Nautical Inn (☎ 855 2141, ext 429, or 453 6212).

ARIZONA

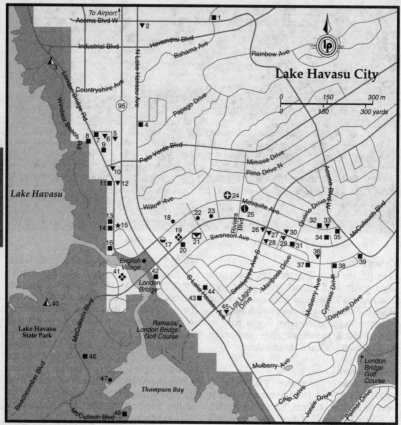

**Lake Havasu City**

**Other Activities** Licenses, gear and information for **fishing** are available from the boat rental places and Bob Lee's Tackle Shop in the True Value Hardware Store (☎ 855 6744), 40 Capri Blvd.

The Nautical Inn (see Places to Stay below) has an 18-hole **golf** course (☎ 855 2131), **tennis** courts and other amenities. The London Bridge Golf Course (☎ 855 2719), 2400 Club House Drive off the south end of Acoma Ave, has two 18-hole courses. The London Bridge Resort Golf Course (☎ 855 4777), 1477 Queens Bay, has nine holes.

Outback Off-Road Adventures (☎ 680

6151), 2169 Swanson Ave, offers **4WD desert tours** for $65 half day, $130 full day with lunch. Groups of four or more and children get discounts.

Rent **bicycles** at Havasu Wheels (☎ 855 3119), 1665 Mesquite Ave.

Across the bridge, London Bridge Racquet & Fitness Center (☎ 855 6274), 1425 McCullouch Blvd, in the Island Fashion Mall, has tennis and racquetball courts, a pool, gym and other amenities.

**Special Events**
The chamber of commerce has information on dozens of annual events. The most

**ARIZONA**

important are given here. The dedication of London Bridge on 10 October, 1971 is celebrated annually during London Bridge Days, held during the week before 10 October. Concerts and dancing, sporting events and contests, art shows and a parade are featured. The World Jet Ski Finals are held at the Nautical Inn in late October. The Lake Havasu Classic Outboard World Championships, an annual tradition going back about 30 years, are held during the fourth weekend in November at the Nautical Inn. Aficionados of Dixieland Jazz flock to the Annual Dixieland Festival held in mid-January. Non-stop jazz is played at the Ramada Resort at the English Village – an all-concert ticket is about $40.

### Places to Stay

The winter season sees the lowest prices. Hotel costs rise in summer, which in Lake Havasu City stretches from March to November! Reservations are a good idea for summer weekends and holidays, when prices rise still further.

### Places to Stay – camping

Lake Havasu State Park has two campgrounds. The *Windsor Beach Campground* (☎ 855 2784), two miles north on London Bridge Rd, and *Cattail Cove* (☎ 855 1223), 15 miles south on Hwy 95, both offer showers, boat launch and tent camping for $9 per day. Cattail Cove also has 40 RV sites with hookups.

The *Crazy Horse Campground* (☎ 855 4033), 1534 Beachcomber Blvd, has about 300 RV sites with full hookups for $22 and tenting sites for half that. Showers, laundry room and a grocery store are available. The huge *Islander RV Resort* (☎ 680 2000), 751 Beachcomber Blvd, offers about 500 sites with full hookups for $24. There are two pools, a spa, boat launch, grocery store, showers, a laundromat and a clubhouse in the resort. The *Sandpoint Marina* (☎ 855 0459), 15 miles south on Hwy 95 near Cattail Cove, has many RV sites with hookups for $20 and a few cheaper tent sites. There are showers, a laundromat, grocery store, play area and boat rentals available.

There are more camping areas near Parker Dam and Parker (described below) and also on the California side of Lake Havasu.

## Places to Stay – bottom end

The cheapest places, with doubles around $25 midweek in winter but into the $30s in summer, or over $40 during holiday weekends (weekly discounts are often available) include the following: the *E-Z 8 Motel* (☎ 855 4023), 41 Acoma Blvd, with pool, spa and coin laundry; the *Havasu Motel* (☎ 855 2311), 2035 Acoma Blvd; the *Lakeview Motel* (☎ 855 3605), 440 London Bridge Rd; the *Shakespeare Inn* (☎ 855 4157), 2190 McCullouch Blvd, with a pool; and the *Windsor Inn* (☎ 855 4135), 451 London Bridge Rd, with a pool and spa. All the above have kitchenettes. The cheapest of all (starting at $20/25) is the basic *Highlander Motel* (☎ 764 3013 or 2664), 3350 London Bridge Rd, north of town.

## Places to Stay – middle

The *Super 8 Motel* (☎ 855 8844), 305 London Bridge Rd, has a pool and spa and summer weekday rates around $39/41 for singles/doubles, more on weekends and less in winter. Other places charging in the $40s for a summer weekday double include the *Bridgeview Motel* (☎ 855 5559), 101 London Bridge Rd, which has a pool; the *El Aztec Motel/Apartments* (☎ 453 7172), 2078 Swanson Ave, which has a pool and rooms with kitchenettes and BBQ areas; and the *Sandman Inn* (☎ 855 7841), 1700 McCullouch Blvd, with pool, laundry room, and some (more expensive) suites or better rooms with kitchenettes.

The *Havasu Travelodge* (☎ 680 9202), 480 London Bridge Rd, has a spa and exercise room and charges about $45/50 for single/doubles midweek or $50/60 on weekends. Continental breakfast is included. The similarly priced *Pioneer Hotel* (☎ 855 1111), 271 Lake Havasu Ave, has a pool, spa, laundry room, as well as a nightclub with dancing. The *Best Western Lake Place Inn* (☎ 855 2146), 31 Wings Loop, has a pool and restaurant and charges about $50/60 for spacious singles/doubles. The *Howard Johnson Lodge & Suites* (☎ 453 4656), 335 London Bridge Rd, has a pool, spa, coin laundry and rooms for about $45/55 in summer and larger rooms with kitchenettes or suites for around $75. Some rooms have balconies and lake views. Continental breakfast is included.

For suites with kitchens, try the *Hidden Palms All-Suite Inn* (☎ 855 7144), 2100 Swanson Ave, or the *Sands Resort Hotel* (☎ 855 1388), 2040 Mesquite Ave. One-bedroom suites begin around $50 in winter, rather more in summer, and long-term discounts are available. The Sands Resort has more expensive two-bedroom suites as well. There is also the *Pecos II Condominiums* (☎ 855 7444), 465 N Lake Havasu Ave, which charges $350 per week for two-bedroom, two-bathroom condos and the *Xanadu Condo Resort* (☎ 855 8300), 276 S Lake Havasu Ave. All these places have swimming pools.

Other mid-priced hotels include the *Acoma Inn* (☎ 855 2084), 89 N Acoma Blvd, which has rooms for $55, $88 on holiday weekends, and a pool and spa, as does the *Blue Danube Inn* (☎ 855 5566), 2176 Birch Square, which charges $45, $110 in peak season. They also offer more expensive rooms with kitchenettes. The *Tamarisk Inn* (☎ 764 3033), 3101 London Bridge Rd, is about four miles north of town and offers a pool, shuffleboard, Ping Pong, putting and horseshoes – many of the rooms ($45, $58 on holiday weekends) are rented on a time-share basis.

## Places to Stay – top end

The *Holiday Inn* (☎ 855 4071), 245 London Bridge Rd, has rooms starting at around $50, but they are better than most for this price. Many rooms come with a refrigerator and a balcony. The hotel offers a pool and spa, bar and restaurant, and entertainment (music with dancing) most nights. There is also a coin laundry.

The *Island Inn Hotel* (☎ 680 0606, fax 680 4218), 1300 McCullouch Ave, is one of the newer hotels and has a pool, spa, restaurant, bar and many rooms with balconies and lake views for $65 to $85.

The *Nautical Inn* (☎ 855 2141, 1 (800) 892 2141), 1000 McCullouch Blvd, was the first of Lake Havasu's resort hotels and has a reputation for water sports – fishing, boating, water skiing, jet skiing and para-sailing are available. The inn also has a pool, spa, golf and tennis, restaurant and bar, and a coin laundry. Large rooms sleep up to four people and start about $90 ($120 on weekends). Some suites are available for about $150. Reservations are recommended.

The *Ramada London Bridge Resort* (☎ 855 0888, 1 (800) 624 7939), 1477 Queens Bay Rd, as its name implies, is built in 'Olde Worlde' style. No, the Tudors never made it out here, but mock facades try to make you imagine they did. The hotel has three pools, a spa, exercise room, golf, tennis, three restaurants, shops and views of London Bridge. Rooms are big enough but their olde worlde windowes are small. Doubles with a view of town begin at $70, $80 with view of the bridge – more on weekends.

## Places to Eat

A good area for a variety of restaurants is on or near the half-mile of McCullouch Blvd between Smoketree Ave and Acoma Blvd.

*Shugrues* (☎ 453 1400), 1425 McCullouch Blvd, is considered by many to be not only the best restaurant in town, but the best in all northwestern Arizona. They advertise American cuisine, which translates into several dozen entrees featuring fresh seafood, steak and chicken. Dinner entrees include soup or salad and range from about $10 to over $30, most in the mid-teens. Cheaper lunches are served. Many tables have some sort of a bridge view, though there are very few tables actually next to the window. Shugrues is open from 11 am to 10 pm.

Less well known is *Versailles* (☎ 855 4800), 357 S Lake Havasu Ave, with French and Italian cuisine, both quite good. The French menu is more expensive (most entrees in the mid-teens) but the budget-conscious will find a pleasing selection of pasta dishes around $10. The restaurant is open for dinner only (5 to 10 pm).

Other good restaurants are found in the better hotels – the *Captain's Table* (☎ 855 2141) at the Nautical Inn, the *King's Retreat* (☎ 855 0888) at the London Bridge Resort and the *Bridge Room* (☎ 855 4071) at the Holiday Inn all serve breakfast, lunch and dinner at somewhat more economical prices than Shugrues. Another choice for mid-priced but good American dinners is *Krystal's* (☎ 453 2999), 460 El Camino Way.

For Mexican food, *Casa de Miguel* (☎ 453 1550), 1550 S Palo Verde Blvd, is a popular spot, especially with younger eaters who stay on for beer and dancing in the adjoining Hussongs Night Club (see below, Entertainment). The restaurant is open from 11 am to 10 pm. Other Mexican places with bars include *El Rio Cantina & Grill* (☎ 680 0088), 2131 McCullouch Blvd (with nightly karaoke and a sports bar) and *Chili Charlies* (☎ 453 5055), 790 N Lake Havasu Ave, No 25 (with pool tables and video games). If you prefer a chimichanga without the bar scene, head over to *Taco Hacienda* (☎ 855 8932), 2200 Mesquite Ave. This locally popular place has been in town for two decades – eons by Lake Havasu City standards. It's open from 11 am to 9 pm.

Italian food lovers can try *Nicolino's Restaurant* (☎ 855 3484), 86 S Smoketree Ave, with a variety of entrees; it's closed on Sundays. There's also a *Nicolino's Bakery & Deli* (☎ 680 6009), 67 Mulberry Ave, which opens daily at 6 am for all your picnic needs. *Petrossi's Pizza* (☎ 855 9468), 344 London Bridge Rd, has good pizzas with fresh homemade crusts – and they deliver.

For other European menus try one of the following: the *Allee Cafe* (☎ 680 1011), 1530 El Camino Way, has a European-trained cook and specializes in German, French and Italian cuisine. They are open from 3 to 10 pm and are closed Mondays. Entrees are in the $11 range. Breakfast, lunch and dinner can be had at the *Cafe Mocha Tree* (☎ 453 6444), 2126 McCullouch Blvd, which features lighter fare such as crepes, quiches, Belgian waffles, pastries and sandwiches. The Mocha Tree is open form 7 am to 3 pm and opens again for dinner at 5, closing at 10 pm. German food is on the menu at the *Shakespeare Inn*

ARIZONA

*Restaurant* (☎ 855 1262), 2190 McCullouch Blvd.

Good Chinese food is served at *New Peking* (☎ 855 4441), 2010 McCullouch Blvd. Nearby is the reasonably priced *Jerry's Restaurant* (☎ 855 2013), 1990 McCullouch Blvd, which serves breakfast 24 hours a day. The budget-conscious will find inexpensive breakfast, lunch and dinner at *J B's* (☎ 453 8484), 1210 McCullouch Blvd, in the Basha's Supermarket Shopping Plaza. They are open from 6 am to 11 pm.

### Entertainment
Several of the hotels and restaurants mentioned above have lively nightlife. *Hussongs*, adjoining Casa de Miguel, is one of the most popular dance spots for the college-age crowd. Slightly more sedate dancing is found in the *Reflections Lounge* at the Holiday Inn and the *Captain's Cove* at the Nautical Inn.

Catch a movie at *The Cinema* (☎ 855 3111), 2130 McCullouch Blvd, or the *London Bridge Theater* (☎ 453 5454), in the English Village. Dinner plays are performed by the *Drury Lane Repertory Players* (☎ 453 5605, 855 0888) at the London Bridge Resort. Call the chamber of commerce for other performing arts information.

### Getting There & Away
**Air** Lake Havasu City Airport (☎ 764 3330), 5600 N Hwy 95, is about seven miles north of town. America West (☎ 1 (800) 235 9292, 1 (800) 247 5692) has several flights a day to and from Phoenix. Flight schedules and commercial carriers change frequently.

**Bus** KT Bus departures leave from the EZ Stop Food Mart (☎ 453 6633), 54 N Lake Havasu Ave, at the Texaco Gas Station. There are daily departures for Phoenix ($26 one way) at 4:40 pm and to Las Vegas at 12:20 pm.

### PARKER
After almost 40 years of being a post office for the surrounding Colorado River Indian Reservation, Parker was founded in 1908 as a railroad town (there are no passenger trains today). The town became the base for the building of the Parker Dam and since then, it has thrived, albeit on a smaller scale than Lake Havasu and Bullhead Cities, on agriculture and tourism. Visitors come for water sports in the summer and for fishing and desert exploration in the mild winter. The area between Parker and the Parker Dam, known as the Parker Strip, has dozens of campsites, boat launch areas and marinas.

Parker is the La Paz County seat and has a population of about 3000.

### Information
The chamber of commerce (☎ 669 2174), 1217 California Ave, is open from 9 am to 5 pm, Monday to Friday. The library (☎ 669 2622) is at 1001 Navajo Ave. The post office (☎ 669 8179) is at Joshua Ave and 14th St. The hospital (☎ 669 9201) is at 1200 Mohave Rd. The police (☎ 669 2264, 911 in emergencies) are at 1314 11th St.

### Colorado River Indian Tribes Museum
Members of four tribes live on the Colorado River Indian Reservation – Mohave, Chemehuevi, Navajo and Hopi. Their culture, past and present, is preserved in the museum (☎ 662 4717 or 669 9211, ext 335) at Mohave Rd and 2nd Ave, southwest of town. Reservation inhabitants are very active in agriculture and some of them make crafts and jewelry that are sold at the museum. Its hours are from 9 am to 5 pm, Monday to Friday.

Adjacent to the museum is the Reservation Administrative Center, where you can get tribal fishing and hunting permits and information about camping and hiking.

### Parker Dam
This dam is 15 miles north of Parker and 19 miles south of Lake Havasu City. Completed in 1938, its closure formed 45-mile-long Lake Havasu. The dam looks small, but about 70% of its structural height is buried beneath the original riverbed, thus making it the world's deepest dam. The

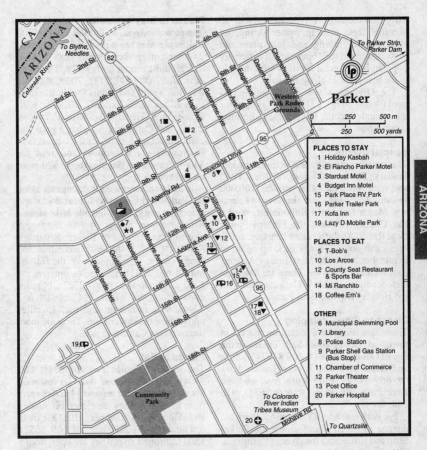

Parker

PLACES TO STAY
1  Holiday Kasbah
2  El Rancho Parker Motel
3  Stardust Motel
4  Budget Inn Motel
15  Park Place RV Park
16  Parker Trailer Park
17  Kofa Inn
19  Lazy D Mobile Park

PLACES TO EAT
5  T-Bob's
10  Los Arcos
12  County Seat Restaurant
     & Sports Bar
14  Mi Ranchito
18  Coffee Ern's

OTHER
6  Municipal Swimming Pool
7  Library
8  Police Station
9  Parker Shell Gas Station
     (Bus Stop)
11  Chamber of Commerce
12  Parker Theater
13  Post Office
20  Parker Hospital

ARIZONA

dam can be visited on a self-guided tour from 8 am to 5 pm daily – there is an orientation area with information and exhibits.

### La Paz County Park
Eight miles north of Parker, this park (☎ 667 2069) has a tennis court, horseshoe pits, playground, beach, boat ramp, swimming and tent and RV camping. Camping rates are $7 to $10. Opposite is the Emerald Canyon Golf Course (☎ 667 3366) with 18 holes.

### Buckskin Mountain State Park
Located 11 miles north of Parker, Buckskin Mountain State Park (☎ 667 3231) offers tent and RV camping, boat ramp, beach, swimming, picnicking, a playground, recreation room, laundry and grocery store. Some cabanas with electric and water hookups are also available for $20. Call ahead for reservations. About a mile north is the Buckskin Mountain River Island Unit (☎ 667 3386), with more camping spaces in a scenic desert setting. Rates range from $3 for day use to $12 for camping.

### Activities
Many people bring their own boats, and launching areas abound along the Parker

Strip. Launching is free or subject to nominal fees. Fishing, water skiing, jet skiing, inner tubing and just plain old messing around with boats are all extremely popular. Some rental services are available at the many places along the strip.

The Olympic-sized, public municipal pool (☎ 669 5678), 1317 9th St, is used for an annual Special Olympics swimming competition.

### Special Events

The year begins with SCORE 400 in late January. This is a 400-mile, off-road, 4WD and motorbike race that attracts 100,000 visitors. There are water ski races in February. March features a Balloonfest, the La Paz County Fair and the Enduro Power Boat Races. As the weather heats up, activities calm down. Things pick up again in September, with the Miss Indian Arizona pageant and a powwow. There are rodeos in October and December. The year ends with the Holiday Lighted Boat Parade.

### Places to Stay – camping

There are three RV camping parks in town – all charge about $12. These are the Lazy D Mobile Park (☎ 669 8797), 15th St and Reata Ave; the Parker Trailer Park (☎ 669 5487), 1509 Kofa Ave; and the Park Place RV Park (☎ 669 2675), 916 16th St.

For both tent and RV camping, there are dozens of other places along the Parker Strip and just across the river in California. The chamber of commerce lists over 40 nearby campgrounds and RV parks, including the state and county parks described above. Call them for the complete listing.

### Places to Stay – bottom end

The Budget Inn Motel (☎ 669 2566), 912 Agency Rd, has basic singles for $26 and larger family units with kitchenettes are available for $200 a week. The El Rancho Parker Motel (☎ 669 2231), 709 California Ave, has a pool, complimentary coffee, and rates beginning around $30.

### Places to Stay – middle

The pleasant Kofa Inn (☎ 669 2101), 1700 California Ave, has a pool and an adjacent 24-hour coffee shop. Rates start at $34, though most rooms go for $38. The Stardust Motel (☎ 669 2278), 700 California Ave, has a pool and rooms for similar rates as well as more expensive rooms with kitchenettes. The Holiday Kasbah (☎ 669 2133), 604 California Ave, has a pool and complimentary continental breakfast. Rooms have refrigerators and rent for $40/45 for singles/doubles (up to $20 more on weekends).

In addition, there are several motels along the Parker Strip, most with boat docks and launching areas. These include Mike Mack's Arizona Shores Resort (☎ 667 2685), 5.5 miles upriver (north) of Parker; Branson's Resort (☎ 667 3346), with recreation and fitness center, 7.5 miles upriver; the Harbor Inn (☎ 667 2931), 13.5 miles upriver; the Casa del Rio Resort (☎ 667 2727), 14 miles upriver; and the Winner's Circle (☎ 667 3244), with restaurant and bar, 15 miles upriver near the Parker Dam. There are more places on the California side.

### Places to Eat

The locally popular Los Arcos (☎ 669 9904), 1200 California Ave, serves good Mexican lunches for around $4 and dinners from $5 to $12. They are closed on Sunday and Monday. A cheaper little Mexican restaurant is Mi Ranchito (☎ 669 8652), 1500 California Ave. They are open from 8 am to 9 pm daily except Tuesday. Coffee Ern's (☎ 669 8145), 1720 California Ave, is a decent 24-hour family restaurant. Other reasonable choices for daily breakfast, lunch and dinner are T-Bob's (☎ 669 9396), 1000 Hopi Ave, and the County Seat Restaurant & Sports Bar (☎ 669 9474), 1005 Arizona Ave. There are plenty of fast-food and other places both in Parker and along the strip.

### Entertainment

The Parker Theater (☎ 669 2211) is at 1007 Arizona Ave.

## Getting There & Away

Though there is a small airport and railway station, there are no scheduled air or train services.

KT Bus departures stop at Parker Shell Gas Station (☎ 669 8181), 1100 California Ave, at 5:30 pm for Phoenix and 11:30 am for Las Vegas.

## QUARTZSITE

Quartzsite has about 2000 permanent residents, but during the winter hundreds of thousands of visitors arrive. The attraction is gems and minerals. Several thousand dealers are on hand during the early January to mid-February gem and mineral shows that attract about a million visitors who buy, sell, trade and admire. These folks can't quite all squeeze into the town's three tiny motels and so, as the chamber of commerce puts it, the desert around Quartzsite turns into a sea of aluminum. Thousands upon thousands of RVs stretch out as far as the eye can see – a strange sight, indeed.

The chamber of commerce (☎ 927 5600) is on Hwy 95, a few hundred yards north of I-10. Note that you can't get off I-10 where it crosses Hwy 95 – you have to exit a mile before or after at exits 17 or 19.

Obviously, the January/February Gem & Mineral Shows (there are as many as eight separate events) are the main thing to do. During this time there are also rodeos, balloon rides, stagecoach rides, cookouts, dances and other Western events. All winter long (October to March) there are less important, but still popular, shows and flea markets. During the prostrating heat of summer the population dwindles to a tiny fraction of the January crowds – almost an estival ghost town!

Near the center of town is a curious monument consisting of a medium-sized stone pyramid topped by a small metal camel. The plaque explains that the memorial is to Haiji Ali, a Syrian camel driver who came here in 1856 to help with the army's experiments in using camels in the Southwestern deserts. These trials failed and Ali, who

Hi Jolly monument at Quartzsite (RR)

had become known as Hi Jolly, became a prospector and died here around 1902.

The Hi Jolly monument is Quartzsite's most loved landmark. Hi Jolly 'Daze', with a parade and other festivities, occurs the weekend before Thanksgiving to welcome back winter visitors. Quartzsite is a friendly place and the gem shows have thrived annually since the first one in 1967.

There are petroglyphs, ghost towns, ruins, wildlife and desert scenery around Quartzsite – much of it along dirt roads or trails reachable by 4WD, horseback or on foot. If you have spare time, ask at the chamber of commerce for exploring ideas. Also read below for nearby places that can easily be visited with an ordinary car.

The three tiny motels have, at last count, 26 rooms between them, so almost everyone stays in one of the scores of RV camps surrounding town. Most have hookups for RVs and charge accordingly (up to $20 a night at the most expensive places). The further you park from the center, the cheaper it becomes.

The BLM (☎ 726 6300 in Yuma) runs the *La Posa Long Term Visitor Area* at the south end of town on Hwy 95. Here, for a $50 fee, you can camp (tent or RV) for as long as you want between 15 September and 15 April. The permit also allows you to use other BLM sites in the Yuma area. The rest of the year you can camp free but can stay in the same place for only 14 days. Facilities include toilets, water (no showers), and dump stations. South of La Posa at mile marker 99, and north of town at mile marker 112, are areas where you can camp for free at any time, but there are no services.

Most people rustle up their own vittles on their camp stoves or RV kitchens, but you'll find plenty of fast-food places and small restaurants on the I-10 business loop between exits 17 and 19.

The nearest place for a better selection of motels and restaurants is Blythe, in California about 21 miles west along I-10, where there are over a dozen motels of varying prices. (Drivers heading for California should gas up in Arizona – gas prices are about 10c per gallon more expensive in California). Parker is 35 miles north and Salome is 35 miles east along I-10 and Hwy 60.

## SALOME

This is one of numerous little mining towns founded in the area around the turn of the century. Some of these became ghost towns, others continue a precarious existence. Salome gained a mild notoriety in the 1920s through the antics of Dick Wick Hall, a local wit who published the *Salome Sun* broadsheet and ran the 'Laughing Gas Station' on the rutted road joining Wickenberg with Los Angeles. His broadsheet (no longer published) ran 'extravagant tales of the desert adaptations of species' such as the story of his 'seven year old frog that never learned to swim, because he didn't want to.' There's not much to do in Salome, but it's a place to stop if you don't feel like the next 55 miles to Wickenberg.

Call or write the McMullen Valley Chamber of Commerce (☎ 859 3846), PO Box 477, 85348 for information.

There are a couple of RV Parks, including the *Desert Gem* (☎ 859 3373), which charges $10 per night, and the *Arizona Sunset* (☎ 859 3995), which charges $12.

There are also four motels, of which the best are *Sheffler's Motel* (☎ 859 3801) and the *International Inn* (☎ 859 3452). Both have restaurants and Sheffler's has a pool. Rates are in the $25 to $40 range depending on the room. Cheaper (and very basic) places include the *Westward Motel* (☎ 859 3316) and *Circle N Motel* (☎ 859 3396).

## ALAMO LAKE STATE PARK

Alamo Lake was formed in 1968 by a flood-control dam on the Bill Williams River. The lake has good fishing – good enough to attract an estimated 50,000 annual visitors, most of whom come in the spring and fall. Winter sees many migrating waterfowl on the lake and summer is hot enough to discourage heavy visitation.

Information is available from Alamo Lake State Park (☎ 669 2088), PO Box 38, Wenden, 85357. A small store sells supplies and rents boats (12- to 16-footers; sample rates are $28 to $48 for six hours). There are picnic and boat launch facilities. Day use costs $3. Camping is $6 for tents, a little more for RVs with hookups. There are showers.

From Wenden (five miles east of Salome or 50 miles west of Wickenberg) a paved road runs 34 miles north to the lake.

# The Lower Colorado

This section traces the lower Colorado River south of I-10 to where it enters Mexico, a corner of the state that contains some of the West's wildest areas where, for whatever reason, very large things come in twos. Two huge military testing grounds with restricted entry cover most of the region. These are proving grounds and bombing and gunnery ranges – the borders are very clearly marked so you won't blunder into a firefight by accident. There are also two extremely rugged and remote national wildlife refuges protecting desert flora and fauna. (One of these, the Cabeza Prieta NWR, was established over half a century ago, but is now being threatened by Marine Corps training flights which are harming the wildlife.) Two other national wildlife refuges protect riparian habitats stretching along the Colorado River.

The parched land is crossed by two east-west interstate highways barreling through as straight as they can. Along the northern boundary runs I-10, linking Florida with Los Angeles, California. Toward to the south, I-8 links Arizona to San Diego, California. In this bombed and beautiful southern region is Yuma, Arizona's rapidly growing third-largest city.

## KOFA NATIONAL WILDLIFE REFUGE

This is one of the wildest of the wildlife refuges. Three rugged mountain ranges, the Kofa, the Castle Dome and the Tank Mountains, meet together in a splendid tangle. A few dirt roads penetrate the area; otherwise, visitor facilities are nonexistent. The refuge covers just over 1000 sq miles, of which more than two-thirds are designated wilderness with no vehicular access. Bighorn sheep roam the area, but are hard to spot.

Most visitors drive in from the west side on Hwy 95. The entrance to Palm Canyon is about 29 miles south of Quartzsite, or 51 miles northeast of Yuma. A 7.2-mile dirt road (usually passable to all vehicles) leads to a parking area from where a steep, rocky, half-mile trail climbs to views of Palm Canyon – a sheer-walled crack to the north within which a stand of California palms (*Washingtonia filifera*) can be seen. Botanists claim that this is the only place in Arizona where these palms grow naturally. Best views are around midday – at other times the palms are in deep shadow. There are several other access points and poor dirt roads through the refuge. Off-road driving is prohibited.

Get information from Kofa NWR (☎ 783 7861), 356 W 1st St, PO Box 6290, Yuma,

85366-6290. Hunting is allowed in season with appropriate licenses. Camping is allowed any time, anywhere (except within a quarter-mile of water holes), with a 14-day limit.

## CIBOLA NATIONAL WILDLIFE REFUGE

Another of the string of refuges along the Colorado River, Cibola NWR is an important over-wintering site for Canada Geese and other waterfowl – a good place to watch for migrants in the spring and fall. Some 237 species have been recorded, including the endangered Yuma clapper rail.

Information is available from Cibola NWR (☎ (602) 857 3253), PO Box AP, Blythe, CA 92226. Hunting and fishing, with licenses and in the appropriate seasons, is permitted. Camping is not.

Refuge headquarters on the Arizona side is reached only by a 21-mile dirt road leaving from the west side of the service center in the Flying J truck plaza in Ehrenberg. It is easier to cross to California on I-10, take the Neighbors Blvd exit (about eight miles into California), follow it south for 13 miles to a sign for the Cibola NWR, cross over the Colorado River (back to Arizona) on the Cibola Farmers Bridge, and proceed four miles to the refuge headquarters. Its hours are from 8 am to 4:30 pm, Monday to Friday. During winter, the Canada Geese Drive auto tour road is open daily from 10 am to 3 pm. It leaves from the headquarters.

## IMPERIAL NATIONAL WILDLIFE REFUGE

Named after the little Imperial Dam on the Colorado River, this is the southernmost of the string of refuges and other protected areas on the lower Colorado. Birding for migrants is good in spring and fall and over-wintering waterfowl are numerous. The small Martinez Lake at the south end has some water skiing and boating activity.

Refuge headquarters (☎ 783 3371), PO Box 72217, Martinez Lake, 85365, is on the north side of Martinez Lake. There is no camping, though there are sites just outside the refuge. Hunting is permitted with licenses in season.

There are two resorts just outside of the refuge. The main one is the *Martinez Lake Resort* (☎ 783 0253, 783 9589) and there is also *Fisher's Landing* (☎ 783 6513, 783 5357). Both offer boating, RV camping, a grocery store and lounge. In addition, Martinez Lake has a boat rental, motel and restaurant. Fisher's Landing has tent camping. Rooms at the motel start around $50 and sleep up to four; RV sites are about $22 at Martinez Lake and less at Fisher's Landing.

Get there by driving east and north from Yuma on Hwy 95 for 22 miles, then take Martinez Lake Rd to the left. After 10 miles the road forks – right to the Martinez Lake Resort and left to Fisher's Landing. Refuge headquarters is about four miles north of the fork.

## YUMA

This town of 60,000 inhabitants is Arizona's third-largest metropolitan area, and one of the sunniest and driest. Weather records indicate that 93% of daylight hours during the year are sunny and rainfall averages about three inches annually. The low elevation (138 feet above sea level at the lowest point) ensures hot weather. In winter, temperatures in the 70°s F attract tens of thousands of winter visitors, many of whom spend the entire winter in trailer parks in and around the city. Triple-digit temperatures are expected almost daily from June to September, but the low humidity makes it bearable and there are plenty of swimming pools, air-conditioned sites of interest and water sports on the Colorado River for visitors to enjoy. The proximity of towns in Mexico is an added attraction.

Yuma was built where the Colorado River narrows, making it the easiest place to cross the river for hundreds of miles. This was known to the local Quechan, Cocopah and Mohave Indians, collectively known as the Yumas. Early Spanish explorers and later American adventurers soon discovered Yuma Crossing, as it became known. Some 30,000 people were estimated to have

crossed the Colorado here after the California Gold Rush of 1849. Steamships made it up to here from the Gulf of Mexico along the Colorado, making Yuma Crossing an important river port.

The town was founded in 1854, after the area was purchased from Mexico by the USA, and was first known as Colorado City, then Arizona City – these terms were somewhat misleading when you consider that the 'city' population was only 85 in 1860, though it grew to over 1100 by 1870. In 1873, Arizona City was renamed Yuma. Three years later, Arizona's Territorial Prison was opened here – a notorious hellhole that operated for 33 years until a new prison was built in Florence. The old jail can be visited and is a major local historical attraction.

Various 20th-century dam projects have changed the course of the river so that today's Yuma Crossing site is very different than what it was in the 1800s. Nevertheless, Yuma still remains an important transportation center, with both the railway and I-8 crossing the Colorado at this point. Today, agriculture (with easy distribution to the Californian metropolises) is the major economic mainstay, closely followed by tourism and the economic input of the local military bases. Yuma International Airport shares parts of its facilities with the Marine Corps. There is also a growing amount of industry in the area. The town is the Yuma County seat.

### Orientation & Information

Interstate 8 approaches Yuma from the east, turns and runs north just outside of town, crosses the Colorado (which defines Yuma's northern boundary), then shoots west to San Diego. Exit 1 off I-8 (one mile from the Californian state line) is the best exit for downtown. Exit 2 takes you to 16th St (also known as Hwy 95), which crosses 4th Ave (also called Hwy 80 or Bus 8) – these are the main hotel/restaurant drags. Exit 3 is best for the airport.

The chamber of commerce (☎ 782 2567), 377 S Main St, is open from 9 am to 5 pm on weekdays and from 10 am to 3 pm on Saturdays and Sundays. There is also a visitors center (☎ 783 0071, fax 783 1897), 488 S Maiden Lane, open from 9 am to 5 pm, Monday to Friday. The Kofa NWR headquarters (☎ 783 7861), is at 356 W 1st St. The BLM (☎ 726 6300), is at 3150 Windsor Ave and has information about their long-term and inexpensive camping areas in southwestern Arizona.

The library (☎ 782 1871) is at 350 3rd St, and is open from 9 am to 9 pm Monday to Thursday and to 5 pm on Friday and Saturday. The aptly named local newspaper is the *Yuma Daily Sun*. The post office (☎ 783 2124) is at 2222 4th Ave with a branch at 370 S Main St (☎ 782 4131). You can recycle items at AA Yuma Recycling Center (☎ 783 7381), 620 E 20th St (cardboard, aluminum, plastic bottles). The Yuma Regional Medical Center (☎ 344 2000) is at 2400 Ave A. The police (☎ 782 3236, 911 in emergencies) are at 1500 1st Ave.

### Yuma Territorial Prison
Between 1876 and its closure in 1909, the prison housed over 3000 men and 29 women – Arizona's most feared criminals. Many of the buildings still exist, notably the guard tower and the rock-wall cells fronted by gloomy iron-grille doors – these give an idea of what life here was like. Despite the grim conditions, this was considered a model prison at the time. The jail is complemented by a small but interesting museum of period artifacts – the whole is slightly gruesome, mildly historical, definitely off-beat and suitable for the whole family!

Outside, there is a picnic area and the unfinished **Yuma Crossing Park** which will have interpretive displays of local history from the time of the Spanish explorers to the 20th century. This leads along the river to the US Army Quartermaster Depot. The whole area (prison, park and depot) may eventually be incorporated into one visitor site.

The prison (☎ 783 4771) is reached from Giss Parkway just west of the underpass below I-8. Hours are 8 am to 5 pm daily,

except Christmas Day. Admission is $3, $2 for 12- to 17-year-olds, free for kids under 12.

### US Army Quartermaster Depot
The supply buildings of the US Army predate the prison by a decade or more. Some parts still exist, others have been restored, and there is a museum and guided tours of what was once the hub of southwestern Arizona. Tour guides dressed in period clothing interpret the era in a variety of demonstrations.

The depot (☎ 329 0404), 180 1st St, is open from 10 am to 5 pm daily except Christmas. Admission is $2, $1 for ages six to 15.

### Century House Museum
Sponsored by the Arizona Historical Society, this museum (☎ 782 1841), 240 S Madison Ave, is in one of the oldest houses in the southwestern corner of the state. There are exhibits of local historical interest and a garden full of exotic plants and birds. A good cafe and gift shop adjoin the house. It is open from 10 am to 4 pm from Tuesday to Saturday. Admission is free.

### Yuma Art Center
Located in the old railway depot at 281 Gila St, the Yuma Art Center (☎ 783 2314) houses changing shows of mainly Arizonan artists. Its hours are from 10 am to 5 pm, Tuesday to Saturday, and from 1 to 5 pm on Sunday. Admission is $1.

### Quechan Museum at Fort Yuma
Across the river on Indian Hill Rd (off Picacho Rd), Fort Yuma was built in the 1850s. The building now houses a small museum (☎ 572 0661) operated by the Quechan tribe. A variety of photographs and historical artifacts can be seen. The tribal offices are nearby. Museum hours are from 7 am to noon and from 1 to 4 pm, Monday to Friday. Admission is $1 for those over 12.

### Sahati Camel Farm
See and learn about camels, Asian water buffalo, desert foxes, Arabian horses,

Red fox

Watusi cattle and desert antelopes at this farm (☎ 627 2553), 15672 S Ave 1E, which offers guided tours ($3) of their breeding facilities (by appointment only. Take Ave B south to County 16th St and turn left.

### Peanut Patch
This peanut farm with gift shop (☎ 726 6292, 1 (800) 872 7688), 4322 E County 13th St, sells all kinds of peanut products. During the October-to-December harvest season, tours of the fields and shelling plant are available for free and last about a half hour. Hours are from 9 am to 6 pm daily from October to April. If agriculture interests you, ask the chamber of commerce for suggestions about visiting local citrus and date farms.

### McElhaney Cattle Company Museum
This museum (☎ 785 3384), 36 miles east of Yuma, displays 19th-century wagons and early antique cars. Take exit 30 off I-8, head north to Welton Elementary School, turn right on Los Angeles Ave (old Hwy 80) and look for museum signs. Its hours are from 8 am to 4 pm, Monday to Friday, and admission is free.

### Visiting Mexico
The small town of Algodones is eight miles west of Yuma on I-8, then two miles south to the border. The town has dozens of dentists and several drug stores, and visitors come for dental work and prescriptions at cheaper-than-US prices. There are also several restaurants and crafts stores.

The city of San Luis is 23 miles south of Yuma on Hwy 95 and, with 150,000 inhabitants, is the largest city on the Arizona-Sonora border. It offers hotels, restaurants and plenty of shopping opportunities.

### Activities
There are several golf courses and tennis courts. The Mesa del Sol Golf & Tennis Club (☎ 342 1283), 10583 Camino del Sol, is off exit 12 from I-8. It has seven tennis courts and the Arnold Palmer 18-hole championship golf course, for which advance reservations are recommended. The 18-hole courses at Desert Hills (☎ 344 4653), 1245 W Desert Hills Drive; and Arroyo Dunes (☎ 726 8350), 32nd St & Ave A, are both next to the Yuma Convention Center (☎ 344 3800) and are the closest to downtown. There are nine tennis courts here, too. The chamber of commerce can suggest others.

You can cool off in one of the three municipal swimming pools (☎ 343 8686 for hours and charges). Carver pool is at 5th Ave and 13th St; Kennedy pool is at 24th St Kennedy Ave; and Marcus pool is at 5th St and 5th Ave.

The Greyhound Park (☎ 726 4655), 4000 4th Ave, has greyhound racing from Wednesday to Sunday in the evenings and also afternoons on Saturdays and Sundays. They also have horse racing. The season runs from November to April. Admission is free; the air-conditioned club house charges $2.

### Organized Tours
Yuma River Tours (☎ 783 4400), 1920 Arizona Ave, has jet boat tours to Imperial NWR, Imperial Dam and historic sites (petroglyphs, mining camps, etc). Tour guides provide a chatty explanation of local history and Indian lore. Tours are $32/49 for a half/full day and include lunch. Sunset cruises ($22 with dinner) and custom charters are also available. Children ages three

to 12 go for half price. All tours leave from Fisher's Landing (see Imperial National Wildlife Refuge). They also run jeep tours from Yuma that cost $45 per person for four hours or $75 for six hours, including lunch. One-day jeep and canoe trips are $45. Tours run almost daily in the winter, less frequently in the hot months.

The Yuma Railway (☎ 783 3456) leaves from the north end of Pacific Ave near the river at Levee Rd. This vintage train (a 1941 Whitcombe diesel engine pulling a 1922 Pullman coach) makes two-hour runs along the Arizona-Sonora border. Departures are at 10 am and 1 pm on Fridays, Saturdays and Sundays from January to March, and less often from October to December and April to May (though the 10 am Saturday run leaves all season). On some Saturdays they have family picnic lunches or steak dinner runs – call for dates. Make reservations for meal runs 48 hours in advance. Adult fares are $9/12/16 for regular/luncheon/dinner runs. Fares for children under 16 are $5/7/9. Kids under four are free on regular runs. (These rates are expected to rise soon.)

The chamber of commerce has information about (and sometimes organizes and escorts) local tours during the winter.

### Special Events
The cooler winter months see the most noteworthy events. The annual Silver Spur Rodeo during the first weekend in February has been held for over half a century and features Yuma's biggest parade, arts & crafts shows and various other events along with the rodeo. Yuma Crossing Days, during the last weekend in February, celebrates the town's history. The Yuma County Fair is held at the beginning of April. During much of the year there are monthly Main Street Block Parties with free street entertainment for the whole family.

### Places to Stay
Winter rates (usually January to April) can be up to $30 higher than summer rates, especially on weekends. In addition, the opening days of dove-hunting season (30 August to 3 September) sees hotels booked well in advance and the highest prices of the year. Rates vary substantially according to demand and those given below are an approximate guide only.

### Places to Stay – camping
There are scores, if not hundreds, of campsites, but most are geared to RVs on a long-term basis during the winter. Most of these campsites have age restrictions (ie, no children). People planning on a long RV stay are advised to call the chamber of commerce for lists of campsites.

The BLM operates a number of sites on the California side of the Imperial Dam. These range from the Imperial Dam Long Term Visitors Area ($50 for unlimited use from 15 September to 15 April; $10 for one week, basic water facilities included, to the Squaw Lake Campground ($5 per night, showers, boat launch). These areas are reached by taking 1st St east and north out of Yuma and across the river into California, then driving north for 24 miles on Hwy S-24. Alternately, take Hwy 95 east and north of Yuma for 18 miles, then turn left on the Imperial Valley Dam Rd to the dam, where the river can be crossed to the California side.

### Places to Stay – bottom
Many bottom-end hotels charge middle prices in winter and dove-hunting season. The two *Motel 6* franchises (☎ 782 9521), 1445 16th St, and (☎ 782 6561), 1640 Arizona Ave, are among the cheapest. Both have swimming pools (as do most Yuma motels) and charge about $25/31 for singles/doubles in the summer, $40/46 in winter.

Most of the cheapest places are downtown. The basic *El Cortez Motel* (☎ 783 4456), 124 1st Ave, charges only $20 a room, gives weekly discounts, is usually full and rarely raises its prices. The *Desert Sands Motel* (☎ 782 3846), 97 W 1st St, is an old, rundown basic downtown motel. The *Bow & Arrow Motel* (☎ 782 9019), 1215 4th Ave, starts around $25 and has

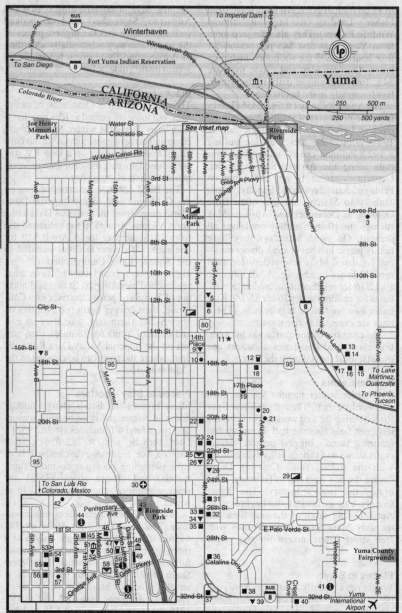

| PLACES TO STAY | | 54 | Best Western Coronado Motor Hotel | 10 | Plaza Theaters |
|---|---|---|---|---|---|

**ARIZONA**

only modest winter increases. They are often full with guests paying by the week ($120) in winter. The *Yuma Inn* (☎ 782 4592), 260 4th Ave, charges about $25 for a summer double, $35 and up in winter. The *Pike's Motel* (☎ 783 3391), 200 4th Ave, is about $35/50 in summer/winter. The *Corcovado Motel* (☎ 344 2988), 2607 4th Ave, starts around $20 in summer and $31 in winter. The *El Rancho Motel* (☎ 783 4481), 2201 4th Ave, is popular and charges $24 a double in summer and about $30 and up in winter. Some rooms have kitchenettes.

Other possibilities include the *Caravan Oasis Motel* (☎ 342 1292), 10574 Fortuna Rd (take exit 12 off I-10), with $22/28 singles/doubles in summer, $31/44 in winter. The *Interstate 8 Inn* (☎ 726 6110), 2730 4th Ave, costs about the same.

**Places to Stay – middle**
Some of the better places are good deals in the summer. *Yuma Cabaña Motel* (☎ 783 8311), 2151 4th Ave, charges $25/30 for singles/doubles in summer but $35/40 in winter and more in dove season. It also has some kitchenettes. The *Regalodge* (☎ 782 4571), 344 S 4th Ave, is one of the better downtown motels and has refrigerators in

the rooms and some kitchenettes. Summer rates start at $30/35 for singles/doubles, going up to $35/40 in winter and more in dove season. The *Hacienda Motel* (☎ 782 4316), 2150 4th Ave, charges about $25 for a summer double and about $45 in winter. The *Royal Motor Inn* (☎ 344 0550), 2941 4th Ave, offers a spa along with the usual pool, and charges about $35 for a double in summer, about $50 in winter.

The *Desert Grove Resort Hotel* (☎ 344 1921, 726 1400), 3500 4th Ave, has a spa, rooms with kitchenettes and charges $35 for doubles in summer, $60 in winter. The *Travelodge* (☎ 782 3831), 2050 4th Ave, charges $32 for a room with one bed in summer (single or double occupancy), $45 in winter, including a continental breakfast. The pleasant *Torch Lite Lodge* (☎ 344 1600), 2501 4th Ave, charges only $27 for a double in summer, around $40 in winter. The *Airporter Stardust Inn* (☎ 726 4721, fax 344 0452), 711 E 32nd St, is the closest to the airport, has a free airport shuttle, a spa and fitness center, restaurant and bar, and good rooms (some with kitchenettes) for about $40 in summer, from $55 to $70 in winter. The *Holiday Inn Express* (☎ 344 1420, fax 341 0158), 3181 4th Ave, has a spa and complimentary breakfast and an evening cocktail hour. Most rooms have a refrigerator. Rates are about $45 and up in summer, between $60 and $80 in winter.

## Places to Stay – top end

The line between the best middle hotels and top end ones is a hazy one at best. The Best Western chain seems to have the town wrapped up at this level, but there are a few other choices. Here's my selection.

The *Best Western Coronado Motor Hotel* (☎ 783 4453, fax 782 7847), 233 4th Ave, is the most attractive hotel close to downtown. It features a spa, gift shop and complimentary continental breakfast. Rooms have microwave and refrigerator; some have a private spa. Some units have two bedrooms and there are several suites. Summer rates start at $35/40 for singles/doubles, winter rates are $55/70, and the larger units go to $80 for a double, up to $110 for a suite sleeping six.

The *Best Western Chilton Inn* (☎ 344 1050, fax 344 4877), 300 E 32nd St, is close to the airport and provides an airport limo. There is a 24-hour restaurant and room service, spa, adults' and children's pools, and a fitness center. Continental breakfast with the morning newspaper is included in the rates, which range from $55 to $95 for one or two people.

The *Best Western Innsuites Hotel Yuma* (☎ 783 8341, fax 783 1349), 1450 Castle Dome Ave, has a spa, two tennis courts, exercise room, playground and snack bar. Rates include continental breakfast, morning newspaper and evening cocktails. The large and attractive rooms have microwaves and refrigerators; the larger suites have spas. Rates run from about $60 to $80 in summer, $70 to $100 in winter.

The *La Fuente Inn* (☎ 329 1814, 1 (800) 841 1814, fax 343 2671), 1513 E 16th St, is a modern Spanish colonial style building surrounding a landscaped garden and pool. There is a spa and exercise room. Rooms are mainly one- or two-room suites, many including microwaves and refrigerators. Rates, which include continental breakfast and evening cocktail hour, run from $50 to

$70 in the summer and from $60 to $90 in winter.

*Park Inn International* (☎ 726 4830, 1 (800) 437 7275, fax 341 1152), 2600 4th Ave, has a spa and offers free airport shuttle service. All units are two-room suites with refrigerators and microwaves. Rates, including continental breakfast and evening cocktails, are about $70 in summer and $100 in winter for doubles.

The *Shilo Inn* (☎ 782 9511, 1 (800) 222 2244, fax 783 1538), 1550 Castle Dome Ave, is the fanciest place in town. Amenities include an exercise room, spa, sauna and steam bath, and the pool is said to be the town's largest. There is a good restaurant and lounge, and room service. A shuttle will take you to the airport. Some rooms have kitchenettes, others feature a balcony or open onto the courtyard. All have refrigerators. Rates range from $80 to $110.

## Places to Eat

Restaurants can be pretty dead midweek in summer but bustling during the busy winter season. *Lute's Casino* (☎ 782 2192), 221 Main St, is a locally popular hamburger joint. It has a bar, pool room, dominoes and pinball. Kids are welcome. It's open daily from 10 am to 7 pm (6 pm on Sunday). *Chester's Chuck Wagon* (☎ 782 4152), 2256 4th Ave, is a simple place offering American food 24 hours a day and an all-you-can-eat pancake breakfast. *Denny's* (☎ 782 2202), 1435 E 16th St, also offers 24-hour family dining.

For breakfast and lunch, *The Garden Cafe* (☎ 783 1491), 250 Madison Ave, is locally popular. They serve good coffees, pancakes, sandwiches, salads and desserts in an indoor/outdoor setting. Tuesday to Friday hours are from 9 am to 2:30 pm, from 8 am to 2:30 pm on Saturdays and Sundays. *Brownie's Restaurant* (☎ 783 7911), 1145 4th Ave, also looks good for breakfast and other meals. For lunches and dinners, try *The Crossing* (☎ 726 5551), 2690 4th Ave, which specializes in prime rib, catfish and ribs and also has Italian dishes. Hours are from 11 am to 9 pm daily, and to 10 pm on Fridays and Saturdays. Dinner entrees are in the $7 to $15 range. One of the best places in town for steak and fresh seafood is the *Hungry Hunter* (☎ 782 3637), 2355 4th Ave, which is open from Monday to Friday from 11:30 am to 2:30 pm, and daily from 5 to 10 pm. Most dinner entrees range from about $10 to $20.

With its close ties to Mexico, Yuma has no lack of Mexican restaurants. I like *Chretin's* (☎ 782 1291), 485 15th St, a homey and locally popular place tucked away inconspicuously on a residential street. They are open from 11 am to 11 pm, Monday to Saturday. *Pappagallo's* (☎ 343 9451), 1401 Ave B, is also out of the way and features weekday lunch specials for less than $5. Another good choice is the *El Charro Cafe* (☎ 783 9790), 601 W 8th St, open from 11 am to 9 pm, Tuesday to Sunday.

For Chinese food, the *Mandarin Palace* (☎ 344 2805), 350 E 32nd St, is both elegant and excellent. Hours are from 11 am to 10 pm daily, and to 11 pm on Fridays and Saturdays. Dinner entrees are a very reasonable (for the quality) $7 to $14.

### Entertainment

Professional baseball teams do their spring training in sunny Yuma. These include the Japanese Yakult Swallows and the San Diego Padres. They play at the 7000-seat Desert Sun Stadium, south of town off Avenue A. Call 317-3394 for a schedule (most games are in March).

Take your choice of movies on the six screens of the *Plaza Theaters* (☎ 782 9292), 1560 4th Ave. The chamber of commerce will provide dates of performances by the local chamber orchestra, community theater and ballet company.

For pool, dominoes and pinball during the day, see Lute's Casino under Places to Eat. Next door is *Red's Bird Cage Saloon* (☎ 783 1050), 231 Main St, for pool, darts and drinking after Lute's closes. They sometimes have live entertainment. Other bars include *Johnny's Sports Bar & Grill* (☎ 783 9367), 432 E 16th St, which is locally popular for country & western dancing, has big-screen sports events, and may have a cover charge on weekends. For a wilder time, roar over to *PJJ's Place* (726 9946), 2852 E Hwy 95 (16th St east of I-8), with pool, darts, bikers, dancing and DJs playing LOUD rock.

For other entertainment ideas, check the Thursday and Friday editions of the *Yuma Daily Sun*.

### Getting There & Away

**Air** The airport (south of 32nd St) is served by Skywest Airlines (☎ 1 (800) 453 9417) with about six flights a day to and from Phoenix and Los Angeles, California. America West Express (☎ 1 (800) 235 9292) has four to six flights a day to and from Phoenix. Avis, Budget, Hertz and National all have rental car offices at the airport.

**Bus** The Greyhound Bus Terminal (☎ 783 4403), 170 E 17 Place, is open from 7 am to 6 pm and from 9 to 10 pm daily. They have three buses a day to Phoenix; Tucson; Lordsburg, New Mexico; and El Paso, Texas. There are departures in the late morning, late evening and the middle of the night. Approximate travel times are four hours to Phoenix, six to Tucson and 14 to El Paso. The usual fare to Tucson is $45/65 one way/roundtrip – but three-, seven- and 14-day advance purchase earns a 20% to 50% discount. There are also three buses a day running to San Diego, California.

The Yuma Bus Company (same terminal) has 9 am and 5 pm departures to San Luis on the Mexican border. Fares are $6/10 one way/roundtrip and a third bus is sometimes added.

**Train** The Amtrak station is at 291 Gila St. No tickets are sold here, but trains will stop for passengers who have made advance reservations at (☎ 1 (800) 872 7245). Trains pass through Yuma on Monday, Wednesday and Friday in the dark, early hours of the morning heading for Los Angeles, California, or El Paso, Texas, and beyond.

## AROUND YUMA
### Algodones Sand Dunes
These rolling and completely barren dunes have been featured in several movies. They can be admired from the rest stop off I-8, 17 miles west of Yuma in California. You can't get to the dunes from the stop, however. Instead, leave I-8 at the Grey's Well exit and take the frontage road. This goes near remains of the old plank road by which cars and carriages crossed the sand dunes from 1915 to 1926.

### Cabeza Prieta National Wildlife Refuge
This, the driest, wildest and most remote desert area in the Southwest, is 45 miles southeast of Yuma. The NWR headquarters (☎ 387 6483) are on the eastern side of the refuge in on Hwy 85 near Ajo. The address is 1611 N 2nd Ave, Ajo, 85321, and you'll need a permit to visit the area.

The Cabeza Prieta NWR was set aside in 1939 as desert bighorn sheep habitat and you may be lucky enough to catch sight of some. This is 135 sq miles of wilderness, with no facilities and only the most rudimentary of dirt roads. The main track is called 'El Camino del Diablo' (the Devil's Highway) and has been used for centuries. It emerges at Wellton on I-8 about 30 miles east of Yuma and 110 miles from Ajo. It takes about two days to drive it today. Many people have died of thirst, and heat prostration along this route. It is a real desert experience.

You'll need a 4WD vehicle (preferably two vehicles, because it can be days between vehicles if yours breaks down). The north and west boundaries of the wildlife refuge are bounded by bombing and gunnery ranges and entrance is occasionally prohibited when the military are carrying out war games.

When you get your permit you'll also receve a bunch of safety tips and other information. If you want to read more, see Annerino's *Adventuring in Arizona* for a detailed description of the Camino del Diablo, both as a drive and as one of the toughest and most dangerous hikes in the country. Also see Bowden's *Blue Desert*.

# Central Arizona

North of greater Phoenix's Valley of the Sun, there is nowhere to go but up. During the summer, droves of southern Arizonans head north to camp, fish and find cool relief among the pines and high deserts of the Colorado Plateau. During the winter, many of the same folks make the trip in search of snow and skiing. This is not to say the area is just the province of canny locals – on the contrary, Central Arizona, with the important town of Flagstaff, is the gateway to the Southwest's most famous destination – the Grand Canyon (described in its own chapter).

Apart from the outdoor activities in central Arizona's national forests, visitors will find many sights of historical and cultural interest. Several national monuments are sprinkled throughout the area, established to protect impressive Indian ruins. Old mining towns either lie forgotten or flourish with a new lease on life as artists' communities. Prescott, the first territorial capital, preserves many buildings from its Wild West days. Sedona, a modern town amid splendid red-rock scenery, draws tourists seeking comfort and relaxation as well as New Agers looking for spiritual and psychic insights at the area's many vortexes. And Flagstaff, home of Northern Arizona University, provides museums, cultural events, nightlife and a laid-back atmosphere fueled by students, skiers and visitors from all over the world.

From Phoenix, you can drive north to Flagstaff in under three hours along I-17, or you can take several days wandering through the intriguing small towns that dot the countryside along and around Hwy 89 southwest of Flagstaff. This latter route is described below.

## WICKENBURG

Just an hour northwest of Phoenix, Wickenburg (elevation 2100 feet) is only 1000 feet higher than the Valley of the Sun,

perched just below the Colorado Plateau. Fall, winter and spring are the best times to visit to avoid the heat.

In the 1860s, prospector Henry Wickenburg found gold in the area and by 1866 Wickenburg had become a thriving community surrounded by gold mines. Today much of the Old West heritage can still be seen in the small town's historic center and in the ghost towns in the area. In addition, Wickenburg has become a dude ranch center, with several ranches offering cowboy-style vacations. Even if you're just passing through, it merits a stop to see the Western buildings and the museum.

### Orientation & Information

Wickenburg Way (Hwy 60), the main drag through town, runs east-west, intersecting in the middle of town with northbound Tegner St (Hwy 93).

The chamber of commerce (☎ 684 5479), 216 N Frontier St, is open from 9 am to 5 pm Monday to Friday and from 10 am to 3 pm on Saturday. The library (☎ 684 2665) is at 164 E Apache St. The post office (☎ 684 2138) is at 55 W Yavapai St. The hospital (☎ 684 5421) is at 520 Rose Lane. The police (☎ 684 5411, or 911 in emergencies) are at 155 N Tegner St.

### Historic Buildings

The downtown blocks between the railway line and the Hassayampa River contain about 20 buildings constructed between the 1860s and the 1920s – many are on the National Register. The chamber of commerce has a free brochure describing them in detail. The 1863 home of the Trinidad family is said to be the oldest house in Arizona and now houses the **Golden Nugget Art Gallery**. Locals like to point out the 19th-century 'jail' – outlaws were chained to a tree at the north corner of Wickenburg Way and Tegner St. Other historic buildings are marked with copper plaques.

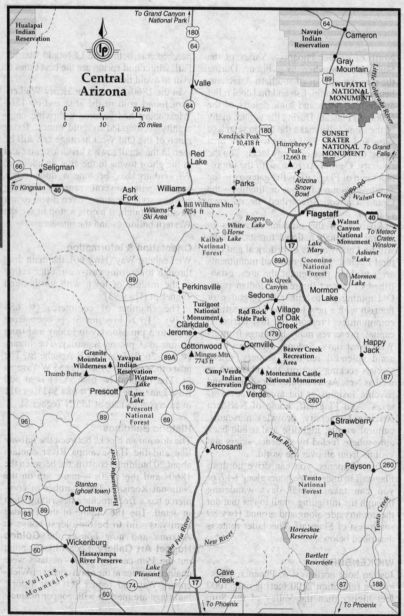

Central Arizona

ARIZONA

### Desert Caballeros Western Museum

This museum (☎ 684 2272), 21 N Frontier St, features a fine collection of canvases and bronzes by famous Western artists such as Frederic Remington, George Catlin and Charles M Russell. Displays include historical dioramas and Indian artifacts, and the museum offers changing shows and a gift shop. Hours are from 10 am to 4 pm daily except Sundays, when it's open from 1 to 4 pm, and the museum is closed on major holidays. Admission is $4, or $1 for six- to 16-year-olds.

### Hassayampa River Preserve

This preserve, operated by The Nature Conservancy, protects one of the few riparian habitats remaining in Arizona (over 90% have been destroyed). A visitors center (☎ 684 2772) provides information, trail guides and a bookshop. Guided walks are offered on occasion, or you can hike the two miles of trails yourself. Preserve hours are from 6 am to noon, mid-May to mid-September and from 8 am to 5 pm the rest of the year. The preserve is closed on Monday and Tuesday, and a $5 donation to the Nature Conservancy is suggested for nonmembers. The preserve is on the west side of Hwy 60, about three miles south of town.

### Mines & Ghost Towns

The most famous mine is **Vulture Mine**, where Henry Wickenburg found gold nuggets lying on the ground in 1863. The mine continued to operate until WW II, which explains why the accompanying ghost town of **Vulture City** is better preserved than most. For information, call 377 0803; admission is $5, or $4 for six- to 12-year-olds. Rent a gold pan for another $4 – you might strike it rich! Hours here are 8 am to 4 pm daily except Tuesday and Wednesday, when the area is closed. The mine is 12 miles south along Vulture Mine Rd, which is three miles west of downtown.

The ghost town of **Stanton** also dates from the 1860s. Several buildings remain in fair condition and are all on private property owned by the Lost Dutchman Mining Association (☎ 427 9908). The association grants permission to look around upon request. To get there, drive 18 miles north on Hwy 89 and then seven miles east on a signed, unpaved road.

**Robson's Mining World** (☎ 685 2609), PO Box M2, 85358, is a commercial venture about 30 miles west of town on the west side of Hwy 71 and north of mile marker 89. Over two dozen early buildings have been restored, and there is a huge collection of early mining equipment, a restaurant (offering lunch daily and dinner by reservation) and a B&B. Hours are from 10 am to 4 pm weekdays and from 8 am to 6 pm weekends, but they may be shortened or the area may be closed from June to September. Admission is $4, and children ages 10 and under are free.

### Golf

The 18 holes at Rancho de los Caballeros (☎ 684 2704), two miles south on Vulture Mine Rd, have been rated one of Arizona's 10 best courses by *Golf Digest*. Wickenburg Country Club (☎ 684 2011), Country Club Drive, has nine holes.

### Organized Tours

Wickenburg Desert Tours (☎ 684 0438, 1 (800) 596 5337), 295 E Wickenburg Way (next to the Best Western hotel), offers two- to three-hour local jeep tours for $40 to $65 per person (kids under 12 pay half fare). The jeeps carry up to eight and leave four times a day.

### Special Events

Wickenburg celebrates its Western heritage during the town's Gold Rush Days, held the second Friday to Sunday in February since the 1940s. Rodeo action, parades, gold panning and shootouts headline the events. Late fall is busy, with the Bluegrass Festival drawing big crowds on the second weekend in November and the Square Dance Festival on the third weekend. The first weekend in December sees the Cowboy Christmas Poets' Gathering.

**ARIZONA**

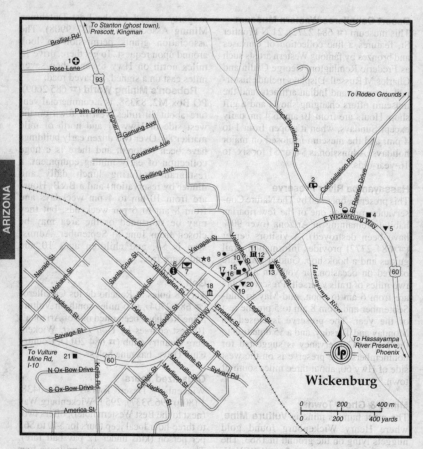

To Stanton (ghost town),
Prescott, Kingman

Brailiar Rd

Rose Lane

93

Palm Drive

To Rodeo Grounds

Genung Ave

Cavaness Ave

Swilling Ave

Constellation Rd

Jack Burden Rd

E Rodeo Drive

Yavapai St

E Wickenburg Way

Navaho St

Mohave St

Santa Cruz St

Washington St

Vulture St

Valentine St

Kerkes St

Tegner St

Hassayampa River

Jackson St

Yavapai St

Adams St

Apache St

Wickenburg Way

Frontier St

Madison St

Savage St

Jefferson St

Adams St

Mesquite St

Sylvan Rd

To Vulture
Mine Rd,
I-10

60

21

N Ox-Bow Drive

S Ox-Bow Drive

Center St

Kellis Rd

Madison St

Jackson St

America St

To Hassayampa
River Preserve,
Phoenix

60

**Wickenburg**

0    200    400 m
0    200    400 yards

## Places to Stay

Rates tend to drop during the hot summer months, and a few ranches close altogether. Call to confirm prices. Most hotels are located along Wickenburg Way.

## Places to Stay – camping

*Horspitality RV Park* (☎ 684 2519), two miles southeast of downtown on Hwy 60, has hookups, showers and horse stables. Rates are $15 per vehicle, and you should call for a reservation in winter. Similar facilities, plus a pool, are found at the adult-only *Desert Cypress Trailer Ranch* (☎ 684 2153), 610 Jack Burden Rd.

Self-contained campers can stay opposite the rodeo grounds for $2 per night, but water is not available.

## Places to Stay – bottom end

The better inexpensive places, with rooms in the low $30s, include the *Mecca Motel* (☎ 684 2753), 162 E Wickenburg Way, and the *La Siesta Motel* (☎ 684 2826), 486 E Wickenburg Way, which has a pool and cafe attached. Other basic cheapies include the *Wagon Wheel Motel* (☎ 684 2531), 573 W Wickenburg Way; the *Capri Motel* (☎ 684 7232), 521-A W Wickenburg Way; and the *Peak Motel* (☎ 684 2702),

1623 W Wickenburg Way. The small *Circle JR Motel* (☎ 684 2661), 741 W Wickenburg Way, has rooms in the upper $30s, and the smaller *Westerner Motel* (☎ 684 2493), 680 W Wickenburg Way, charges in the $40s; both have pools.

### Places to Stay – middle

The *Americinn* (☎ 684 5461), 850 E Wickenburg Way, has a pool, spa and restaurant with a bar that is open from 7 am to 1:30 pm daily and from 5 to 8:30 pm Monday to Saturday. Some of its 30 rooms have balconies and cost about $50. The *Best Western Rancho Grande* (☎ 684 5445, fax 684 7380), 293 E Wickenburg Way, has a pool, spa and tennis court. Many of the 80 rooms are priced in the upper $50s; some more expensive units have kitchenettes.

### Places to Stay – top end

The *Flying E Ranch* (☎ 684 2690, fax 684 5304), PO Box EEE, 85358, is a 21,000-acre working cattle ranch four miles west of town with a long-standing

reputation as a well-run, comfortable and friendly place. The 16 rooms, each with private bath and refrigerator, start at $120/180 for singles/doubles and go up to $150/250. Take advantage of family rates and eat and play till you drop; costs include all meals and use of the pool, spa, sauna, exercise room, shuffleboard, horseshoes, tennis and Ping-Pong. Or try horseback riding (with instruction) for an added fee. Many of the hearty meals are cookouts and are served family style (no alcohol is served, but you're welcome to bring your own). The ranch is open from 1 November to 30 May and requires a two-night minimum stay.

The smaller *Kay El Bar Ranch* (☎ 684 7593), PO Box 2480, 85358, has eight rooms with private bath in a historic adobe ranch house two miles north of town on Hwy 93. Enjoy the excellent food, lounge by the pool, or play board games and read in the casual atmosphere of the large common area. Rates are about $130/230 for singles/doubles and include meals and horseback riding; family rates are available. The ranch is open from mid-October to 30 April and requires a two- to four-night minimum stay.

*Rancho de los Caballeros* (☎ 684 5484, fax 684 2267), 1551 S Vulture Mine Rd, 85390, is famous for its golf course. Enjoy the pool, four tennis courts and nature walks, or try horseback riding, mountain biking or trap shooting while the kids are busy with the children's program. Twenty adobe houses contain over 70 spacious rooms with baths and patios. Rates are $145 to $200 single and $255 to $375 double, depending on rooms and season. High season is February to mid-May and low season is October to January. Rates include meals; golf, horses and shooting cost extra.

The *Wickenburg Inn Tennis and Guest Ranch* (☎ 684 7811, 1 (800) 942 5362, fax 684 2981), PO Box P, 85358, is eight miles north on Hwy 89, and is the only ranch open year round. The 11 tennis courts and horseback riding facilities are both top class, and instruction is available. Enroll the kids in a children's program and enjoy arts & crafts activities and nature hikes, or lounge by the pool and spa. There are six rooms in the lodge and 41 casitas of three different types and prices. Rates during the January to April high season range from $280 to $390 a double, and include all meals, tennis and two daily horseback rides. Family rates are available and prices drop substantially out of season.

## Places to Eat

Wickenburg has many restaurants; for a start try the following. The *Gold Nugget* (☎ 684 2858), 222 E Wickenburg Way, is open from 6 am to 10 pm daily and has a 'Gay '90s' Western atmosphere – 1890s, that is. American meals here are moderately priced and good. *La Casa Alegre* (☎ 684 0206), 512 E Wickenburg Way, has cheap breakfast and lunch specials, and is open from 7 am to 9 pm daily. *Rancho 7 Restaurant* (☎ 684 2492), 111 E Wickenburg Way, has been locally popular for 60 years, featuring home-style American and Mexican cooking from 11 am to 9 pm daily. You can play darts, pool and shuffleboard in the adjoining bar. *Charley's Steak House* (☎ 684 2413), 1101 W Wickenburg Way, the town's best steak house, is open from 5 to 10 pm daily except Monday. The *Swiss Chalet* (☎ 684 5775), 169 E Wickenburg Way, is arguably the town's best restaurant, offering continental dining from 5:30 to 10 pm, Tuesday to Sunday. Most entrees are priced in the teens and the restaurant is closed in September.

*Sangini's Pizza* (☎ 684 7828), 107 E Wickenburg Way, is open for lunch Monday to Friday, and open for dinner daily. They deliver. Try *Anita's Cocina* (☎ 684 5777), 57 N Valentine St, for Mexican food served daily from 11 am to 9 pm. Eat Chinese at the *Sizzling Wok* (☎ 684 3977), 621 W Wickenburg Way, open from 11 am to 2:30 pm and from 4:30 to 9:30 pm daily. *The Chaparral* (☎ 684 3252), 45 N Tegner St, serves homemade ice cream, pastries and snacks from 6 am to 7 pm daily.

## Entertainment

The *Saguaro Theater* (☎ 684 7189), 176 E Wickenburg Way, screens movies. The *Rancher Bar* (☎ 684 5957), W Wickenburg Way by Los Altos Drive, has live country & western music and dancing on weekends. The *Rancho 7 Restaurant* has a popular bar.

## Things to Buy

Art and antiques are big sellers in Wickenburg, and the chamber of commerce has a list of the several art galleries and antique shops downtown. The Gold Nugget Art Gallery (☎ 684 5849), behind the restaurant in the historic Trinidad House, and the Wickenburg Gallery (☎ 684 7047), 67 N Tegner St, are among the best. For a real whiff of the Old West, mosey into Ben's Saddlery (☎ 684 2683), 183 N Tegner St; even if you aren't in the market for a saddle, it's the most memorable shop in town.

## Getting There & Away

**Bus** Greyhound (☎ 684 2601), 412 E Wickenburg Way (in the Star-C Convenience Store) has three night buses to Phoenix, a morning and an evening bus to Kingman and Las Vegas, and a morning bus to Los Angeles. Wickenburg Express (☎ 684 6059) has a van to Phoenix Airport.

**Car** From Phoenix, Hwy 60 is the most direct route to Wickenburg, but going north on I-17 and then west on Hwy 74 is only marginally longer and much more scenic. Northwest of town, Hwy 93 leads to Wickenburg from Kingman. This route is also called the Joshua Tree Parkway for the many stands of those plants lining the highway.

## PRESCOTT

Founded in 1864 by gold prospectors, Prescott soon became Arizona's first territorial capital. The political decision was handed down by President Abraham Lincoln as the US Civil War was drawing to a close. He preferred the progressive small mining town to the more established, conservative Tucson, considered to have Confederate leanings. At this time, the various Indian ruins in the area were thought to be Aztec, and Prescott was named after William Prescott who had written a history of Mexico.

Although the gold has long since played out, vestiges of early territorial life remain in Prescott's many early buildings, including the first Governor's Mansion. Prescott's historic character and the cool elevation of 5346 feet attract many of Phoenix's two million residents seeking to escape the heat of summer, as it's only a two-hour drive. The town, almost surrounded by the Prescott National Forest, offers many outdoor recreation opportunities, and the tiny neighboring Yavapai Indian Reservation provides legal gambling. Two colleges, a small artists' community and galleries add to the town's bohemian air. Today, many of Prescott's almost 30,000 residents are involved to some degree in the tourist industry or in government, and the old territorial capital is now the Yavapai County seat.

### Orientation & Information

Hwy 89 runs generally southwest to northeast through town, becoming the north-south Montezuma St, and then bending east sharply on the east-west Gurley St. The main center of town is around the square formed by the intersection of Montezuma, Gurley, Sheldon and Pleasant Sts.

The chamber of commerce (☎ 445 2000, 1 (800) 266 7534, fax 445 0068), 117 W Goodwin St, is open from 9 am to 5 pm, Monday to Saturday, and from 10 am to 4 pm on Sunday. The Prescott National Forest Bradshaw Ranger Station (☎ 445 7253), 2230 E Hwy 69, 86301, is open from 8 am to 4:30 pm Monday to Friday, and Saturday from April to September. The Forest Supervisor's Office (☎ 771 4700) is at 344 S Cortez St, 86303. The library (☎ 445 8110) is at 215 E Goodwin St. The local newspaper is the *Prescott Courier*. The main post office (☎ 778 1890) is at 442 Miller Valley Rd; the downtown branch is in the Federal Building at Goodwin and Cortez Sts. Recycle at Recycle Prescott Inc (☎ 445 9108), 745 N 6th St. The hospital

(☎ 445 2700) is at 1003 Willow Creek Rd. The police (☎ 778 1444, or 911 in emergencies) are at 222 S Marina St.

### Historic Buildings

Montezuma St west of the Courthouse Plaza was once the infamous 'Whiskey Row' where cowboys and miners would enjoy a drink and then wander over to the next saloon until they had had a drink at each of the Row's 40 drinking establishments. (They must have poured small shots in those days!) Despite a devastating 1900 fire that destroyed 25 saloons, five hotels and Prescott's then-thriving red-light district, many early buildings remain and many were rebuilt immediately after, so you can still have a drink in an early saloon on colorful Whiskey Row. The County Courthouse, in the center of the Plaza, dates from 1918.

Buildings east and south of the plaza escaped the 1900 fire and date from the late

Rancher monument in Prescott (RR)

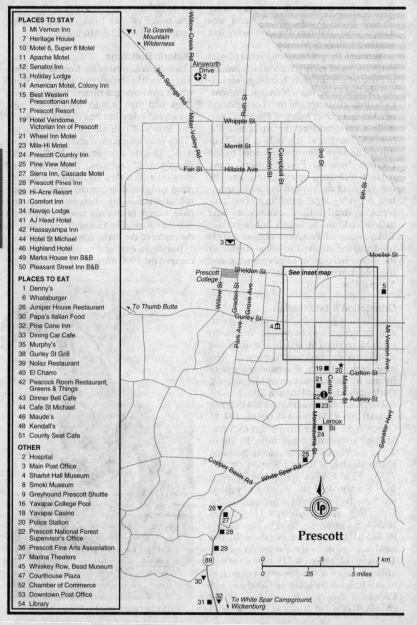

**PLACES TO STAY**

5 Mt Vernon Inn
7 Heritage House
10 Motel 6, Super 8 Motel
11 Apache Motel
12 Senator Inn
13 Holiday Lodge
14 American Motel, Colony Inn
15 Best Western
   Prescottonian Motel
17 Prescott Resort
19 Hotel Vendome,
   Victorian Inn of Prescott
21 Wheel Inn Motel
23 Mile-Hi Motel
25 Prescott Country Inn
26 Pine View Motel
27 Sierra Inn, Cascade Motel
28 Prescott Pines Inn
29 Hi-Acre Resort
31 Comfort Inn
34 Navajo Lodge
41 AJ Head Hotel
42 Hassayampa Inn
44 Hotel St Michael
46 Highland Hotel
49 Marks House Inn B&B
50 Pleasant Street Inn B&B

**PLACES TO EAT**

1 Denny's
9 Whataburger
26 Juniper House Restaurant
30 Papa's Italian Food
32 Pine Cone Inn
33 Dining Car Cafe
35 Murphy's
38 Gurley St Grill
39 Nolaz Restaurant
40 El Charro
42 Peacock Room Restaurant,
   Greens & Things
43 Dinner Bell Cafe
44 Cafe St Michael
46 Maude's
48 Kendall's
51 County Seat Cafe

**OTHER**

2 Hospital
3 Main Post Office
4 Sharlot Hall Museum
8 Smoki Museum
9 Greyhound Prescott Shuttle
16 Yavapai College Pool
18 Yavapai Casino
20 Police Station
22 Prescott National Forest
   Supervisor's Office
36 Prescott Fine Arts Association
37 Marina Theaters
45 Whiskey Row, Bead Museum
47 Courthouse Plaza
52 Chamber of Commerce
53 Downtown Post Office
54 Library

To Granite
Mountain
Wilderness

Ainsworth
Drive

Willow Creek Rd
Iron Springs Rd
Miller Valley Rd
Ruth St
Campbell St
Lincoln St
3rd St
4th St

Whipple St
Merritt St
Hillside Ave
Fair St

See inset map

Prescott
College

Sheldon St
Willow St
Grader St
Grove Ave
Park Ave

To Thumb Butte

Gurley St

Moeller St

Mt Vernon Ave
Senator Hwy

Carlton St
Cortez St
Aubrey St
Marina St
Leroux St
Montezuma St

Copper Basin Rd

White Spar Rd

**Prescott**

0          .5          1 km
0       .25       .5 miles

To White Spar Campground,
Wickenburg

To Granite
Mountain
Wilderness

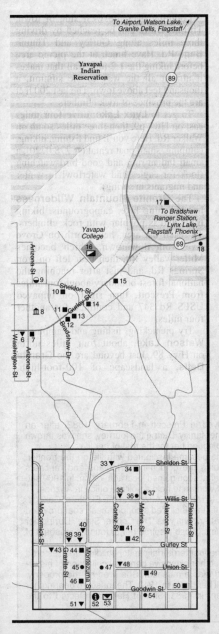

1800s. Some were built by settlers from the East Coast who, using wood from the surrounding forests, built Victorian houses in a New England style, markedly different from the adobe Southwestern buildings found in old towns like Tucson and Santa Fe. The chamber of commerce sells an informative map and brochure for $1 describing 35 buildings and five statues to be seen on a walking tour of downtown – it's well worth a buck.

## Phippen Museum of Western Art

Six miles north of town, the Phippen Museum (☎ 778 1385), 4701 N Hwy 89, named after the cowboy artist George Phippen and displaying a number of his works, has a good collection of Western paintings, bronzes and photographs. March to December, hours are 10 am to 4 pm daily, except Sunday, when hours are 1 to 4 pm, and Tuesday, when the museum is closed. In January and February hours are 1 to 4 pm daily except Tuesday. Admission is $2 for adults, $1 for children and students.

## The Bead Museum

Old and new beads from all over the world are on display at this unique museum Monday to Saturday from 9:30 am to 4:30 pm. Admission to the museum (☎ 445 2431), 140 S Montezuma St, is free and there is a bead shop.

## Smoki Museum

Built like an Indian Pueblo, this museum (☎ 445 1230), 147 N Arizona St, displays Southwestern Indian artifacts dating from pre-historical times to the present. The 'Smokis' were a group of Prescott residents who formed a 'tribe' in the 1920s and performed replicas of Indian dances and ceremonials. Objections from genuine Indian tribes led to the end of the dances in the 1990s, but the items used in the dances can be seen at the museum. Hours from 1 May to 30 September are 10 am to 4 pm and 1 to 4 pm on Sundays; the museum is closed Wednesday. In October, hours are 10 am to 4 pm, Friday to Sunday. Group tours are given by appointment, year round. Admission is a $2 donation for adults.

### Sharlot Hall Museum

This is Prescott's most interesting and important museum. Covering two city blocks, the museum (☎ 445 3122), 415 W Gurley St, invites visitors to stroll by the two-story log building that was the first governor's mansion. You can also view Fort Misery, one of the territory's first log cabins, as well as many other buildings from the 1860s and '70s. The Museum Center, housing offices, workshops and archives, displays historical artifacts and old photographs. Hours are from 10 am to 5 pm Monday to Saturday and 1 to 5 pm on Sunday. Winter hours (October to April) are 10 am to 4 pm, Tuesday to Saturday and from 1 to 5 pm on Sunday. Admission is a suggested $2 donation per adult.

### Prescott National Forest

The Bradshaw Ranger Station can suggest many hikes, climbs, picnic areas, campgrounds and fishing holes in the Prescott National Forest. Local lakes are stocked with trout, bluegill, bass and catfish. Nearby popular areas are Thumb Butte, Lynx Lake and the Granite Mountain Wilderness.

Looming over the west side of town, **Thumb Butte** can be reached by driving three miles along Gurley and Thumb Butte Rd. Have lunch at the picnic area before hiking the 1.2-mile trail that makes it almost all the way to the summit, a thousand feet above town. The last 200 feet are the province of rock climbers.

To get to **Lynx Lake**, drive four miles east on Hwy 69, then three miles south on Walker Rd. Here you'll find fishing, hiking, camping, small boat rental (☎ 778 0720), a small Indian ruin and good bird-watching (look for eagles and waterfowl in winter and migrants in spring).

The **Granite Mountain Wilderness** has a fishing lake, campgrounds, hiking trails and is popular with rock climbers. To reach the area, head north on Grove Ave from downtown, which becomes Miller Valley Rd, then bear left on Iron Springs Rd, and just after reaching the national forest boundary about four miles from Prescott, turn right on unpaved USFS Rd 347 and continue for another four miles.

Try picnicking, fishing and camping at **Watson Lake**, about four miles north on Hwy 89. Just beyond are the **Granite Dells**, a landscape of 100-foot-high,

---

### Sharlot Hall

Twelve-year-old Sharlot Mabrith Hall arrived in Prescott in February, 1882, after an arduous horseback trip from Kansas with her family. During the journey, she was thrown by her horse, receiving a back injury that plagued her for the rest of her life.

While helping run her family's ranch, she became fascinated with life on the frontier. Largely self-schooled, she began describing the gold miners, Indians and ranchers around her in a series of stories and poems that soon gained local admiration. In 1909 she was appointed Territorial Historian, the first woman to hold a political office in Arizona.

In 1924 she traveled to Washington, DC, to represent Arizona in the Electoral College. She caused a stir in the capital with her outfit that included a copper mesh coat provided by a local mine. There was no mistaking that Arizona was 'The Copper State'. During her visit to the east, she toured several museums; these inspired her to found a museum of Arizona history.

On her return to Prescott, Hall leased the first territorial capitol building and restored the governor's mansion. In 1928, she moved her extensive personal collection of historical artifacts into the mansion and opened it as a museum. She lived on the property, expanding and adding to the collection until her death in 1943. The museum bearing her name has continued to flourish since then. In 1981, Sharlot Hall was elected to the Arizona Women's Hall of Fame. ■

rounded red-rock outcrops that you can hike through or rock climb on.

## Activities

Play **golf** at the two 18-hole courses offered at Antelope Hills (☎ 776 7888, 1 (800) 972 6818), eight miles north of Prescott on Hwy 89. The old north course is one of Arizona's better public courses. There are also 18 holes at Prescott Country Club (☎ 772 8984), 14 miles east of town on Hwy 69.

On a hot day, go **swimming** at Yavapai College Pool (☎ 776 2175), 1100 E Sheldon St. For information about **mountain biking** or to rent mountain bikes, visit the Bikesmith (☎ 445 0280), 723-A N Montezuma St. Buy or rent **camping** and **climbing** equipment at Basecamp (☎ 445 8310), 142 N Cortez St, or Granite Mountain Outfitters (☎ 776 4949), 320 W Gurley St.

If you're interested in **gambling**, the Yavapai Indian tribe runs a casino on its tiny reservation northeast of town. The casino, on Hwy 69 a mile northeast of town, is open 24 hours and offers mainly slots, bingo and video keno.

## Special Events

The chamber of commerce has a calendar listing hundreds of events. The most important are the Western Art and Arts & Crafts festivals held simultaneously over Memorial Day weekend. Territorial Days, on the second weekend in June, features free 19th-century entertainment, tours of the Victorian houses and general old-fashioned fun. Frontier Days, during the week leading up to the Fourth of July, has the world's oldest rodeo and other celebrations, and the Bluegrass Festival on the third weekend in July is held in an outdoor auditorium backed by the Granite Dells. The Faire on the Square provides arts, crafts and entertainment during Labor Day weekend.

## Places to Stay

Approximate midweek summer rates are given below; winter rates (from November to March) are substantially lower. Summer weekends may be as much as $20 higher,

and weekend reservations are a good idea, especially for Frontier Days, when prices go up the most.

### Places to Stay – camping

*Point of Rocks RV Park* (☎ 445 9018), 3025 N Hwy 89 (four miles north of town in the Granite Dells) has 100 RV-only sites for $15.25 with hookups. Nearby, *Watson Lake Park* (☎ 778 4338) has showers and cheaper RV and tents sites. *Willow Lake RV Park* (☎ 445 6311) has RV sites with hookups for $17.50 and tent sites for $13 (less in winter) as well as a pool, showers, playground and coin laundry. To get there, drive four miles north on Hwy 69, then head west on Willow Lake Rd and follow signs for about four miles.

The USFS (☎ 445 7253) operates many campgrounds. *White Spar*, 2.5 miles south of town on Hwy 89, has 62 sites with picnic tables, grills, toilets, water but no showers, and is open all year for $6 a night. Similar fees and facilities are available at *Lynx Lake* (see the Prescott National Forest above) from April to early November, and *Hilltop*, near Lynx Lake, from mid-May through September.

Free USFS campsites with pit toilets but no water are available at *Granite Basin* in the Granite Mountain Wilderness (see above) year round. Try the similar facilities at *Indian Creek*, six miles south on Hwy 89 and one mile left on USFS Rd 97, open from mid-May through September, and at *Lower Wolf Creek*, seven miles south on Senator Hwy and 1.25 miles right on USFS Rd 97, open from mid-May to mid-November.

### Places to Stay – bottom end

The cheapest place is Whiskey Row's old *Highland Hotel* (☎ 445 9059), 154 S Montezuma St, which charges about $19/23 for basic singles/doubles with bathrooms down the hall. With large weekly discounts available, the Highland is often full with long-term residents. The popular *Hotel St Michael* (☎ 776 1999, 1 (800) 678 3757), 205 W Gurley St, is another Whiskey Row hotel rebuilt in 1900. It has nice, though old, rooms with bath for $38/42 and some pricier suites. The old *AJ Head Hotel* (☎ 778 1776), 129 N Cortez St, offers basic rooms with shared bathrooms in the $20 price range and rooms with private bathrooms for up to twice that; ask about long-stay discounts. The restaurant and bar has entertainment some evenings.

It's hard to find a motel room under $40 in the summer. The cheapest motel is the basic *Navajo Lodge* (☎ 445 7007), 115 E Sheldon St, with rooms starting in the $30s and long-stay discounts available. Some possibilities around $40 include the *American Motel* (☎ 778 0787); the *Colony Inn* (☎ 445 7057), which has a pool; the *Apache Motel* (☎ 445 1422); the *Holiday Lodge* (☎ 445 0420); the *Senator Inn* (☎ 445 1440), with a pool; and the *Heritage House* (☎ 445 9091), all on E Gurley St. The *Mile-Hi Motel* (☎ 445 2050), 409 S Montezuma St; the *Motel 6* (☎ 776 0160, fax 445 4188), 1111 E Sheldon St, which has a pool and coin laundry; the *Pine View Motel* (☎ 445 4660), 500 Copper Basin Rd; and the *Wheel Inn Motel* (☎ 778 7346), 333 S Montezuma St, are also in the $40 price range.

## Places to Stay – middle
**Hotels** South of town along a quiet wooded road, the *Comfort Inn* (☎ 778 5770), 1290 White Spar Rd, has a spa, rooms starting in the $50s and some pricier mini-suites with kitchenettes. Several restaurants are nearby. Other hotels in this area that may be marginally cheaper are the *Sierra Inn* (☎ 445 1250), 809 White Spar Rd, which provides a pool and complimentary in-room coffee, and the small *Cascade Motel* (☎ 445 1232), 805 White Spar Rd, which offers kitchenettes. The *Hi-Acre Resort* (☎ 445 0588), 1001 White Spar Rd, has rooms starting in the $40s and cabins with kitchenettes for $60 to $90 depending on size.

The *Super 8 Motel* (☎ 776 1282, fax 778 6736), 1105 E Sheldon St, has a small pool and charges $46.88/52.88 for singles/doubles. The *Best Western Prescottonian Motel* (☎ 445 3096, fax 778 2976), 1317 E Gurley St, has a small pool, spa and restaurant and bar that is open from 6 am to

11 pm. Large rooms with coffeemakers are in the $50s for singles and the $60s for doubles; suites are also available.

The historic *Hotel Vendome* (☎ 776 0900), 230 S Cortez St, has charm dating to 1917. There are 25 rooms in the $60s, all with modern private bath, and four suites for about $100, including continental breakfast. The lobby with a cozy wooden bar is an attractive place for a drink. The equally historic *Hassayampa Inn* (☎ /fax 778 9434), 122 E Gurley St, was one of Arizona's most elegant hotels when it opened in 1927. Carefully restored in 1985, the hotel has a vintage hand-operated elevator, many of its original furnishings and hand-painted wall decorations. The 67 rooms vary (standard, choice, suite, suite with spa) and run $90 to $110 for a double room and $135 to $160 for a suite; prices include full breakfast and an evening cocktail. The lovely dining room is open from 7 am to 2 pm and from 5 to 9 pm.

**B&Bs** Several old houses have been attractively restored as B&Bs, and it's hard to choose the nicest. None allow smoking indoors.

The *Marks House Inn* (☎ 778 4632), 203 E Union St, 86303, is an 1894, two-story, turreted and colonnaded Queen Anne house. The four double rooms range from $75 to $120 (the $120 is for the Queen Anne suite, with a sitting room in the turret), and prices include full breakfast and afternoon tea. The similarly priced *Pleasant Street Inn* (☎ 445 4774), 142 S Pleasant St, 86303, in a 1906 Victorian restored in 1991, offers two rooms and two suites, one with a fireplace.

The *Victorian Inn of Prescott* (☎ 778 2642), 246 S Cortez St, 86303, is an 1893 Victorian house with three rooms priced in the $90s and a suite for $135 a double, each with private bath. The *Mt Vernon Inn* (☎ 778 0886), 204 N Mt Vernon Ave, Prescott, is a turreted 1900 Victorian house set in a tree-filled garden. Four rooms, each with private bath and queen bed, go for $80 double; the price includes breakfast and afternoon refreshments. In addition, three cottages with kitchens are $90 to $110 double (without breakfast).

At the edge of town, the *Prescott Country Inn* (☎ 445 7991), 503 S Montezuma St, has 12 cottages, each different but all with baths and kitchenettes. Rates are $90 to $150, depending on the cottage, and prices include continental breakfast.

Out of the town center, the very popular *Prescott Pines Inn* (☎ 445 7270, fax 778 3665), 901 White Spar Rd, 86303, is centered on a 1902 country Victorian house surrounded by four guesthouses that contain a total of 13 rooms, one of which sleeps up to eight, three of which have gas fireplaces and eight of which have kitchens or kitchenettes. Most rooms are priced at $55 to $85 a double, $10 more on weekends. The full breakfast is optional and costs an extra $5, but you can also have just coffee for free. Reservations are recommended – rooms are sometimes booked a year in advance.

Five miles east of town, the *Lynx Creek Farm B&B* (☎ 778 9573), PO Box 4301, 86302, is set in orchards and surrounded by a small farm. Six large rooms, some with outdoor hot tubs and decks, others with wood-burning stoves, and all with king-size beds and private bathrooms, are $85 to $110 double. Suites with kitchenettes are $105 to $130 double, including breakfast, and multi-night discounts are available.

### Places to Stay – top end

The *Prescott Resort* (☎ 776 1666, 1 (800) 967 4637, fax 776 8544), 1500 Hwy 69, sits high on a hill overlooking Prescott from the east. The resort has a casino (machines only), an indoor pool, a whirlpool, two tennis courts, racquetball, full exercise facilities, massage, a restaurant and room service, a bar with entertainment and dancing and a barber/beauty shop. Large rooms with balconies, coffeemakers and refrigerators are $140 double, and one-bedroom suites are $170; prices are discounted 20% during the winter.

### Places to Eat

To start of the day, try one of the several popular and reasonably priced places near the plaza. *Greens & Things* (☎ 445 3234), 106 E Gurley St, is a well-liked breakfast and lunch spot serving a wide variety of breakfasts from 7 am. *Maude's* (☎ 778 3080), 146 S Montezuma St, is a clean favorite in the middle of Whiskey Row, open 7 am to 3 pm weekdays, 8 am to 3 pm on Saturday and 8 am to 1 pm on Sunday. A few doors away, the *Café St Michael*, under the Hotel St Michael, is also a happening place. The *Dinner Bell Cafe* (☎ 445 9888), 321 W Gurley St, is an inexpensive, down-home diner open from 6 am to 1:50 pm daily except Sunday, when it's open 7 to 11:45 am, and Wednesday, when it's closed. It might be cheap and plain, but the food is good. Another diner, this one more upscale, is the *Dining Car Cafe* (☎ 778 5488), 100 E Sheldon St, which is open for breakfast and lunch and has an outdoor patio.

If you are staying out along the White Spar Rd, a good choice is the *Pine Cone Inn* (☎ 445 2970), 1245 White Spar Rd, which opens at 7 am for breakfast and serves delicious American lunches and dinners; Prescottians drive out from town for a change of pace and to enjoy the frequent live music and dancing. Dinner entrees are in the $8 to $16 range but look for an all-you-can-eat fish-fry on Fridays for just $6. In the same area, *Papa's Italian Food* (☎ 776 4480), 1124 White Spar Rd, serves lunch and dinner, and the inexpensive family *Juniper House* (☎ 445 3250), 810 White Spar Rd, serves American breakfasts, lunches and dinners and has a cocktail lounge.

Back in town, the following are all good for lunch or dinner. The *Gurley St Grill* (☎ 445 3388), 230 W Gurley St, has burgers, sandwiches, pastas and grill or seafood dinners at moderate prices. Another fine joint is *Kendall's* (Famous Burgers & Ice Cream) (☎ 778 3658), 113 S Cortez St, a 1950s-style place that does not believe in small portions. The upscale *County Seat Cafe* (☎ 778 9570), 214

S Montezuma St, is a small smoke-free place with a small menu tending toward meat and pasta, but the food is fresh and good and there is a nice wine list. The restaurant is open from 11:30 am to 2:30 pm and from 5:30 to 9:30 pm, Tuesday to Saturday, to 10 pm on Friday and Saturday and 5 to 9 pm on Sunday. Dinner entrees are in the teens, and reservations are recommended. For Mexican food, try *El Charro* (☎ 445 7130), 120 N Montezuma St, open daily from 11 am to 8 pm, to 8:30 pm on Friday and Saturday.

Enjoy authentic Cajun and Creole cooking at *Nolaz* (☎ 445 3765), 216 W Gurley St, open from 11 am to 2 pm and from 5 to 9 pm Monday to Saturday (the name is an acronym for New Orleans, Louisiana and Arizona). Sample the good beer selection and listen to live jazz or blues in the lounge on weekends. Most dinner entrees are priced in the teens. *Murphy's* (☎ 445 4044), 201 N Cortez St, one of Prescott's best, was a general store in the 1890s. Much of the old charm remains, and the American food is good and fairly priced in the $11 to $18 range. Try a beer from the excellent selection. Hours here are 11 am to 3 pm and 4:30 to 10 pm. The *Peacock Room* (☎ 778 9434), in the Hassayampa Inn, serving a wide range of breakfasts, lunches and dinners, is another highly recommended dining spot. It's open from 6:30 am to 2 pm and 5 to 9 pm daily.

West of town, the *Prescott Mining Co* (☎ 445 1991), 155 Plaza Drive (two miles west on Gurley St to the Plaza Shopping Center) is one of Prescott's best, serving fantastic prime rib and fresh seafood in a rustic atmosphere; dine amid old mining equipment with Butte Creek tumbling by. Hours are 11 am to 3 pm Monday to Saturday and 4 to 9:30 pm weekdays, to 10:30 on weekends. Dinner entrees are in the $10 to $19 range.

Finally, for a 2 am snack, try the 24-hour *Whataburger* (☎ 778 0450), 715 E Gurley St, or *Denny's* (778 1230), 1316 Iron Springs Rd, two miles northwest of town via Grove Ave and Miller Valley Rd.

## Entertainment

See movies at the *Marina Theaters* (☎ 445 1010), 205 N Marina St, or the *Plaza West Cinemas* (☎ 778 0207), 1509 W Gurley St, or wander down Whiskey Row for a selection of bars and saloons, some of which have live music and dancing.

The *Prescott Fine Arts Association* (☎ 445 3286), 208 N Marina St, presents music and drama. Also check Prescott College's *Elks Theater* (☎ 445 3557), 113 E Gurley St, and the *Yavapai College Performance Hall* (☎ 776 2015), 1100 E Sheldon St, for a schedule of performances.

## Things to Buy

There are many antique stores and art galleries in town. Brochures detailing many of these are available at the chamber of commerce and at the stores themselves. Several antique stores line Cortez St north of Gurley St. Also stop by the Prescott Fine Arts Association Gallery (☎ 778 7888), 208 N Marina St, for a selection of works for sale by regional artists or to view the changing art shows. Hours are 11 am to 4 pm, Wednesday to Saturday, and noon to 4 pm on Sunday.

## Getting There & Away

**Air** Prescott Municipal Airport is nine miles north on Hwy 89. America West Express (☎ 445 7701, 1 (800) 235 9292) has three or four flights a day to and from Phoenix, and two or three flights a day to and from Kingman.

**Bus** The Greyhound Prescott Shuttle (☎ 445 5470, 778 7978), 820 E Sheldon St, has a 10 am bus to Camp Verde for $10; there you can connect with north or southbound Greyhound services along I-17. Shuttle U (☎ 772 6114, 1 (800) 304 6114), runs five vans a day between Prescott and Phoenix Airport for $29 one way and $50 roundtrip.

## Getting Around

**Car Rental** Hertz (☎ 776 1399, 1 (800) 654 3131) has an office at the airport. Other rental agencies in Prescott include

Enterprise (☎ 778 6506, 1 (800) 325 8007), which will deliver your car to the airport or anywhere in Prescott, Budget (☎ 778 3806), York Motors (☎ 445 4970), 209 N Montezuma, and Lamb Chevrolet (☎ 778 5262).

**Taxi** Prescott City Cab (☎ 445 1551) and Reliable Taxi (☎ 772 6618, 1 (800) 206 5987) have 24-hour service. Ace City Cab (☎ 445 1616, 445 5510), at the Greyhound office, operates from 6 am to 2 am daily.

## JEROME
Named after New Yorker Eugene Jerome, who invested $200,000 in the local United Verde Mine in 1882 (a chunk of money in those days), Jerome is the most celebrated of Arizona's old mining towns. Rich in copper, gold and silver, the area was mined by Indians before the arrival of Europeans. Jerome grew to 15,000 inhabitants by the 1920s, but the stock market crash and resulting depression shut down many of the mines. The last closed in 1953, and with only a few dozen residents, Jerome looked as if it would become another ghost town.

In the late 1960s, Jerome's spectacular location and empty houses were discovered by hippies, artists and retirees, and slowly Jerome became what it is today, a collection of late 19th- and early 20th-century buildings housing art galleries, souvenir shops, restaurants, saloons and a few B&Bs, all precariously perched on a steep hillside. The setting is quite extraordinary – the entire town looks to be about to slide off the mountainside. Indeed, many buildings did just that; the famous 'sliding jail' can be seen today 225 feet below its original location.

Most of the buildings lining Main St and the streets just to the north and south date from between 1895 and the 1920s, and all of Jerome is part of a National Historic District. The chamber of commerce has a historic map showing each building's location, and you can view Jerome's historic homes on tours given during the third weekend of May for $6.

The town, elevated a pleasant mile above

sea level, has about 400 permanent residents and, on a busy summer day, has many more tourists than locals.

### Orientation & Information
Hwy 89A loops and winds its way over the steep hills leading to and from Jerome, between Prescott and Clarkdale. The chamber of commerce (☎ 634 2900), Drawer K, 86331, is in Blue Heron Gifts at 116 Main St. The library (☎ 639 0574) is at 111 Jerome Ave. The post office (☎634 8241) is at 120 Main St. The police (☎ 634 8992, or 911 in emergencies) are in the Town Hall on Main St.

### Things to See
The **Mine Museum** (☎ 634 5477), 200 Main St, is run by the Jerome Historical Society (☎ 634 7349) and displays old photos, documents, tools and other memorabilia to explain Jerome's history. Hours are 9 am to 4:30 pm and admission is 50¢ for people 13 and over. The museum is housed in the 1898 Fashion Saloon.

A mile beyond the north (upper) end of Main St is the **Gold King Mine Museum** (☎ 634 0053), a miniature ghost town with frequent demonstrations of antique mining equipment, a walk-in mine, a gift shop and (don't ask me why) a children's petting zoo. Hours are 9 am to 5 pm; admission is $3 and $2 for six- to 12-year-olds.

The **Jerome State Historic Park** (☎ 634 5381), two miles beyond Jerome off Hwy 89A en route to Cottonwood, is in and around the 1916 mansion of colorful mining mogul 'Rawhide' Jimmy Douglas. Of Jerome's museums, this gives the most thorough understanding of the town's mining history. View models, exhibits and a video presentation inside the mansion and old mining equipment outside. There is a picnic area with great views. Admission is $2, or $1 for 12- to 17-year-olds, and hours are 8 am to 5 pm daily except Christmas.

### Places to Stay
**Camping** The Prescott National Forest surrounds Jerome, and ranger stations in Prescott and Camp Verde have information.

ARIZONA

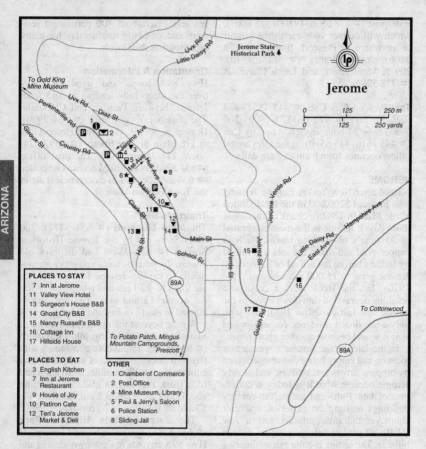

**Jerome**

To Gold King
Mine Museum

To Potato Patch, Mingus
Mountain Campgrounds,
Prescott

To Cottonwood

**PLACES TO STAY**
7   Inn at Jerome
11  Valley View Hotel
13  Surgeon's House B&B
14  Ghost City B&B
15  Nancy Russell's B&B
16  Cottage Inn
17  Hillside House

**PLACES TO EAT**
3   English Kitchen
7   Inn at Jerome
    Restaurant
9   House of Joy
10  Flatiron Cafe
12  Teri's Jerome
    Market & Deli

**OTHER**
1   Chamber of Commerce
2   Post Office
4   Mine Museum, Library
5   Paul & Jerry's Saloon
6   Police Station
8   Sliding Jail

The *Potato Patch* campground, 6.5 miles along Hwy 89A toward Prescott, has 14 sites open from April through November. Nearby, turn left along USFS Rd 104 and drive for three miles to *Mingus Mountain*, a campground with 27 sites open from May through November. Both campgrounds are free and have pit toilets and picnic tables but no drinking water.

**Hotels** Don't expect luxury, as accommodations tend toward the historic rather than the deluxe. The nearest motels are in Cottonwood, nine miles away.

The *Inn at Jerome* (☎ 634 5094), 309

Main St, has six clean Victorian rooms with shared baths and one room with a private bath; prices are in the $40s for a double, but expect to pay more on weekends. There is a restaurant/bar downstairs.

**B&Bs** Aside from this, it's B&Bs. One of the biggest is the *Ghost City B&B* (☎ 634 4678), 541 Main St, PO Box 382, 86331. This 1898 building has a veranda with great views and six rooms sharing three bathrooms for $65 to $85 a double, with prices including breakfast and afternoon tea. The *Surgeon's House B&B* (☎ 639 1452, 1 (800) 639 1452), 101 Hill St, PO Box 998,

86331, built in 1917 at the top of the town, has two rooms sharing a bath for $65/85 single/double. A suite with private bath and balcony and a guesthouse with private bath and kitchenette are each $100 double. To relax, soak in the hot tub or make an appointment for a massage.

The *Cottage Inn* (☎ 634 0701), 747 East Ave, PO Box 823, 86331, and the *Hillside House* (☎ 634 5667), 687 Main St, PO Box 305, 86331, are in historic buildings near downtown and both have two rooms sharing one bathroom, each offered for around $70 double. The well-known *Nancy Russell's B&B* (☎ 634 3270), 120 Juarez St, PO Box 313, 86331, has just been bought by the Wheelers (Anna and Jack, not Tony and Maureen) who have renovated the one room with private bath. They're haven't decided on a new name, but have decided on a price ($89).

Private houses offering B&B accommodations can be contacted through *Mi Casa Su Casa* (☎ (602) 990 0682, 1 (800) 456 0682), PO Box 950, Tempe, 85281. Jerome's accommodations are currently experiencing a boom, so call the chamber of commerce for the latest information about new B&Bs and the new Valley View Hotel, which will double the number of rooms in Jerome when (if?) it opens in 1996.

### Places to Eat

The *English Kitchen* (☎ 634 2132), 119 Jerome Ave, has been serving meals since 1899 – the owners say it is the oldest restaurant in Arizona. Munch breakfasts, burgers, salads and sandwiches inside or on the outside deck from 8 am to 3:30 pm, Tuesday to Sunday. The *Flatiron Cafe* (☎ 634 2733), 416 Main St, has a great selection of coffee and baked goods, and also serves light snacks. *Teri's Jerome Market & Deli* (☎ 639 2218), 515 Main St, makes a good salad or a sandwich that you can eat indoors, or in the summer on sidewalk tables.

For dinner, eat at the restaurant in the *Inn at Jerome*, which serves inexpensive American food from 7 am to 7 pm daily, and to 9 pm on Friday and Saturday. The best and most expensive restaurant in the Jerome-Cottonwood area is the small (seven tables) but colorful *House of Joy* (☎ 634 5339), 416 Hull Ave, which is housed in a former bordello and retains a raffish decor. Open for Saturday and Sunday dinner only, reservations are essential and must be made several weeks in advance. The restaurant has a small continental menu offering good desserts, and does not take credit cards.

### Entertainment

A good place to get drinks is *Paul & Jerry's Saloon* (☎ 634 2603), 206 Main St, originally called the Senate Saloon when it first opened in 1899.

### Things to Buy

A stroll along Main St will take you past plenty of art galleries, antique shops and souvenir stands. Serious gallery shoppers shouldn't miss the Old Mingus Art Center, about a mile from 'downtown' along Hwy 89A to Cottonwood. Here, there are a number of high quality artists' studios and galleries, the best known of which is the huge 20,000-sq-foot Anderson-Mandette Art Studio (☎ 634 3438). Other noteworthy galleries showcasing many local artists are the Raku Gallery (☎ 639 0239), 250 Hull Ave, displaying ceramics among other art, the Aurum (☎ 634 3330), 369 Main St, showcasing jewelry, and the Copper Shop (☎ 634 7754), 140 Main St, where you can get a copper souvenir.

### Getting There & Away

There is no public transport. If you're driving Hwy 89A from Prescott to Cottonwood, it's impossible to avoid Jerome as the road winds steeply through town. With so many tourists stopping, the town is somewhat of a bottleneck; allow the better part of an hour just to drive the last 14 miles from Prescott to Jerome and the next four miles out of Jerome toward Cottonwood. The map shows the one-way system through town. Vehicles pulling trailers over 20 feet are not recommended.

## COTTONWOOD

Nine miles east of Jerome, Cottonwood is a good base for exploring various interesting sites in the area and offers modern motels. Named after the trees growing alongside the Verde River, which flows north of town, Cottonwood was first settled in the 1870s. Despite its age, it is essentially a modern town, and with some 6000 inhabitants it is the main trade center for the area. The elevation is a warm 3300 feet.

### Orientation & Information

Hwy 89A is the main thoroughfare, and Main St, several blocks north of Hwy 89A, is the heart of 'Old Town'. Bordering Cottonwood to the northwest is the smaller town of Clarkdale, and a couple of miles east is the neighboring village of Cornville. All three towns are described below.

The chamber of commerce (☎ 634 7593), 1010 S Main St, is open from 9 am to 5 pm. The library (☎ 634 7559) at 100 S 6th St opens at 9 am and closes Monday and Friday at 5:30 pm, Tuesday to Thursday at 7:30 pm and Saturday at 5 pm. The post office (☎ 634 9526) is at 700 E Mingus Ave. The hospital (☎ 634 2251) is at 202 S Willard St. The police (☎ 634 4246, or 911 in emergencies) are at 816 N Main St.

### Clemenceau Heritage Museum

One of Arizona's newest museums, the Clemenceau (☎ 634 2868), 1 N Willard St, in a wing of a 1924 school building, illustrates local history and has a model railroad exhibit. It's open from 9 am to noon on Wednesday and from 11 am to 3 pm Friday to Sunday; admission is free.

### Tuzigoot National Monument

This monument (☎ 634 5564) protects the ruins of a Sinaguan pueblo dating from 1125 to 1425 AD. The pueblo's two stories and over 100 rooms once housed about 200 people; now the remains are memorable for their location on a small ridge affording fine views of the Verde River Valley. Don't miss the visitor center's exhibit of Sinaguan artifacts. Hours are 8 am to 7 pm from Memorial Day to Labor Day and 8 am to 5 pm the rest of the year. Admission is $2 for adults; Golden Access, Age and Eagle Passes are honored. The ruin is two miles north of Cottonwood – look for signs from Hwy 89A or from town follow N 10th St north through Dead Horse State Park and continue on a bit farther.

### Dead Horse Ranch State Park

This small area at the north edge of town offers picnicking, fishing, nature trails, a playground and camping. Day use costs $3.

### Verde Canyon Railroad

Restored locomotives provide four-hour guided roundtrips into the countryside north of Cottonwood Pass, traveling through roadless areas containing Indian ruins and wildlife. Departing from 300 N Broadway in Clarkdale (the northern continuation of Cottonwood's N Main St), the railroad (☎ 639 0010, 1 (800) 293 7245), has year-round departures Wednesday to Sunday, from June through August at 10 am and at 11 am the rest of the year. Moonlight rides are available near the full moon. First-class tickets for adults cost $53, and regular ones are $35, or $31 for those over 65. Kids under 12 pay $20. Reservations are required.

### Places to Stay

Rates drop slightly outside of the summer high season, and motels are full for the Verde Valley Fair and Rodeo during the third or fourth weekend in late April.

### Places to Stay – camping

The *Dead Horse Ranch State Park* (☎ 634 5283) at the north end of town has showers and 45 basic sites for $8, as well as some with partial hookups for $11. *Rio Verde RV Park* (☎ 634 5990), 3420 Hwy 89A, has showers, a coin laundry and over 60 sites costing $9 for tents or $17 for those with hookups. The similar *Turquoise Triangle RV Park* (☎ 634 5294), 2501 E Hwy 89A, has $14 tent sites or $16 sites with hookups. *Camelot RV Park* (☎ 634 3011), 651 N Main St, offers 50 RV-only sites for

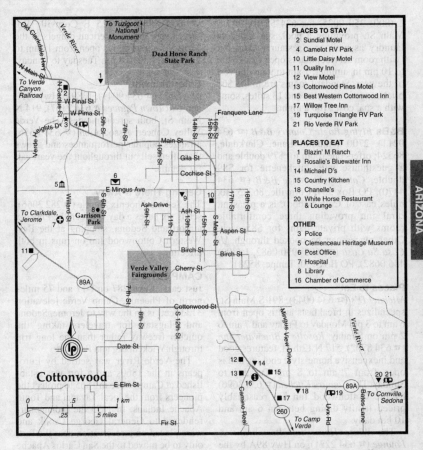

**PLACES TO STAY**
2   Sundial Motel
4   Camelot RV Park
10   Little Daisy Motel
11   Quality Inn
12   View Motel
13   Cottonwood Pines Motel
15   Best Western Cottonwood Inn
17   Willow Tree Inn
19   Turquoise Triangle RV Park
21   Rio Verde RV Park

**PLACES TO EAT**
1   Blazin' M Ranch
9   Rosalie's Bluewater Inn
14   Michael D's
15   Country Kitchen
15   Chanelle's
20   White Horse Restaurant
     & Lounge

**OTHER**
3   Police
5   Clemenceau Heritage Museum
6   Post Office
7   Hospital
8   Library
16   Chamber of Commerce

$15 with hookups. All of these campgrounds are open year round.

### Places to Stay – bottom end

There are no very cheap places in and around Cottonwood. If this is a concern, try Flagstaff. The least expensive in the area, with rooms starting in the mid-$30s, is the *Sundial Motel* (☎ 634 8031), 1034 N Main St, but the 24 rooms are often filled with guests staying the week. In the upper $30s and lower $40s are the *Little Daisy Motel* (☎ 634 7865), 34 S Main St, with 20 rooms, and the *View Motel* (☎ 634 7581), 818 S Main St, which has 34 rooms, a pool, spa

and hilltop location. All of these offer some rooms with kitchenettes. Also in this price range is the eight-room *Cottonwood Pines Motel* (☎ 634 9975), 920 S Camino Real.

### Places to Stay – middle

**Motels** The *Willow Tree Inn* (☎ 634 3678), 1089 S Hwy 260, has 30 standard rooms in the $40 range. The *Quality Inn* (☎ 634 4207, fax 634 5764), 301 W Hwy 89A, has a pool, spa and restaurant open for lunch and dinner. Prices for good-size rooms are in the $60s in summer, dropping to the $40s in winter. The nicest motel is the *Best Western Cottonwood Inn* (☎ 634 5575,

1 (800) 350 0025, fax 634 5576), 993 S Main St, providing a pool, spa and coin laundry as well as a restaurant and bar (with room service) that is open from 6 am to 10 pm in summer, 7 am to 9 pm the rest of the year. Standard rooms are in the $60 price range in summer, and 13 suites, some with a spa, cost $100 a night.

**B&Bs** *Flying Eagle Country B&B* (☎ 634 0211), 2700 Windmill Lane, Clarkdale, 86324, offers one room for $79 double and a guesthouse with kitchenette for $89 double. *Country Elegance B&B* (☎ 634 4470), PO Box 564, Cornville, 86325 (six miles east of Cottonwood), is a pleasant, rural inn providing three comfortable rooms with private baths for $85 each. Other places can be booked through *Mi Casa Su Casa* (☎ (602) 990 0682, 1 (800) 456 0682), PO Box 950, Tempe, 85281.

### Places to Eat

*Michael D's* (☎ 634 0043), 891 S Main St, specializes in breakfasts and is open from 6 am to 3 pm Monday to Friday and 7 am to 2 pm on Sunday. *Rosalie's Bluewater Inn* (☎ 634 8702), 517 N 12th St, features good and inexpensive home-style cooking and is open from 7 am to 8 pm Tuesday to Sunday. The *Country Kitchen* (☎ 634 3696) by the Cottonwood Inn has reasonably priced family dining between 6 am and 10 pm daily.

The *White Horse Inn Restaurant & Lounge* (☎ 634 2271), on Hwy 89A by the Verde River, serves decent American lunches and dinners; hours are from 11 am to 2 pm and 5 pm to midnight daily except Sunday, when hours are noon to 9 pm. *Blazin' M Ranch* (☎ 634 0334), next to the entrance of Dead Horse Ranch State Park, has chuckwagon suppers with cowboy entertainment for about $13. The doors open at 5:30 with seating at 7 for dinner. *Chanelle's* (☎ 634 0505), 2181 E Hwy 89A, has a great rustic Western atmosphere and good American and continental food. Hours are 11 am to 2 pm and 5 to 9 pm; dinner entrees are priced in the low teens.

Out in Cornville, the *Manzanita Inn*

(☎ 634 8851), 11425 E Cornville Rd, serves very good American dinners in the $7 to $15 range and is open from 11 am to 2 pm and 4:30 to 8 pm Tuesday to Sunday.

### Entertainment

*Movieola* (☎ 634 9041), 1389 E Hwy 89A, and *Old Town Palace* (☎ 634 7167), 914 N Main St, both screen movies. The Verde Valley Concert Association (☎ 634 0636) arranges popular performances and shows that often sell out throughout the year; call for details.

### Getting There & Away

The Sedona-Phoenix Shuttle (☎ 282 2066), sends six buses a day between the Phoenix airport and Sedona, stopping at the Best Western Cottonwood Inn on runs in both directions.

### CAMP VERDE

Just east of exit 287 on I-17 and 75 miles north of Phoenix, Camp Verde (elevation 3133 feet) is on the way to Jerome, Sedona and Flagstaff for travelers taking the quicker freeway rather than the long trip through Wickenburg and Prescott.

The Verde River was settled by Europeans in the 1860s and a fort was established at Camp Verde in 1865 to protect the pioneers from the local Yavapai and Tonto Apache Indians. In 1873 the Indians surrendered to General George Crook and were placed on a reservation near the fort, only to be moved to the San Carlos Apache Reservation in 1875. In the early 1900s the Yavapai started drifting back, and now have a few very small reservations in the Camp Verde and Prescott areas.

Meanwhile, Camp Verde prospered and is now a town of about 6000 that provides services to the ranching and agricultural communities of the Verde River basin. There are several nearby sights of interest to the traveler.

### Orientation & Information

The chamber of commerce (☎ 567 9294) is at 435 Main St. The Prescott National Forest Verde Ranger Station (☎ 567 4121),

PO Box 670, 86322-0670, is on Hwy 260 southeast of town, just past the Verde River. The post office (☎ 567 3175) is on Hwy 260 just west of town. The closest hospital is Marcus J Lawrence Memorial (☎ 634-2251) at 202 S Willard Rd in Cottonwood. The police are reached at 567 6621 or 911 in emergencies.

### Fort Verde State Historic Park

Only four buildings remain of the original 18 composing Fort Verde when it was decommissioned in 1891. These have been restored, and together with the original parade grounds and some foundations, serve to give the visitor an idea of what life was like here over a century ago. Visit the museum (☎ 567 3275) and pick up self-guided tour brochures describing the area. Staff in period costumes give interpretive demonstrations on Saturdays during the winter. Fort Verde Day, on the second Saturday of October, has a full schedule of historical reenactments and other events.

Fort Verde is open from 8 am to 5 pm daily except Christmas Day, and admission is $2 for adults or $1 for 12- to 17-year-olds.

### River Running

The Verde River can be canoed, kayaked or rafted. The section from Clarkdale to Camp Verde is fairly flat, but the river becomes much wilder south of Camp Verde, and to run this section you should be experienced. High water from January to April is the best time to try the descent from Camp Verde to the Horseshoe Reservoir, 60 miles south. The Verde Ranger Station has maps and information. River Otter Canoe Co (☎ 567 4116), 458 S 1st St, provides information and equipment, rents canoes from $35 a day and provides shuttles to anywhere in the Verde Valley for $30 and up. Verde River Boat Rides (☎ 567 4087), 537 S Yaqui Circle, also rents boats.

### Horseback Riding

Blazing Trails (☎ 567 6611), at the Best Western Cliff Castle Lodge, offers semi-private guided rides for groups or individuals, ranging from one to two hours in length to overnight pack trips. The shorter rides cross Beaver Creek and continue to Montezuma Castle, while longer rides follow a trail up over Pine Mountain. Arrange to eat a chuckwagon breakfast, lunch or dinner on the trail and listen to Arizona cowboy stories told by the experienced owner and his wrangler.

### Places to Stay

**Camping** The *Yavapai-Apache RV Park* (☎ 567 3109), near I-17 exit 289, has showers and charges $7 for tent sites and $10 for RV sites with hookups. The Coconino National Forest maintains both the *Clear Creek* campground, six miles southeast of Camp Verde on USFS Rd 9, open from April through October, and the *Beaver Creek* campground, three miles southeast of I-17 exit 298 along USFS Rd 618, open from April through September. Both campgrounds are small, have water but no showers and charge $5 per night.

**Motels** Rooms at the *Fort Verde Motel* (☎ 567 3486), 628 S Main St, all have two double beds and cost $36 a double. The *Super 8 Motel* (☎ 567 2622), 1550 Hwy 260, has a pool and spa and charges summer rates of $46.88/54.88 for singles/doubles with queen-size beds. The *Best Western Cliff Castle Lodge* (☎ 567 6611, fax 567 9455), half a mile east of I-17 exit 289, has a pool and spa, as well as a restaurant open from 7 am to 9 pm. Rooms are priced in the $70s in the summer and in the $50s in winter. The lodge has a few suites in the $100 to $150 range.

### Places to Eat

You won't find anything approaching haute cuisine in Camp Verde, but you won't find haute prices either. A down-home, locally popular little place is the *Verde Cafe* (☎ 567 6521) at 368 Main St, serving daily breakfast, lunch and dinner Monday to Thursday from 6 am to 3 pm and Friday to Sunday from 6 am to 8 pm. Slightly more upscale family restaurants include *Bo's Valley View Restaurant* (☎ 567 3592), 102 Arnold at Main St, open from 6 am to 9 pm daily, and the *Branding Iron Restaurant* (☎ 567 3136), open 5 am to 3 pm, in the Fort Verde Shopping Plaza. All three serve American food. For Chinese, *Ming House* (☎ 567 9488), 288 S Main St, is open daily from 11 am to 9 pm and has a lunch buffet. The restaurant in the Cliff Castle Lodge is also a good choice (see above).

### Getting There & Away
Greyhound (☎ 567 6663, 1 (800) 231 2222) stops at 583 W Middle Verde Rd four times a day on its way to Phoenix and three times on the way to Flagstaff. There are connections to and from Prescott.

The Sedona-Phoenix Shuttle (☎ 282 2066) stops at the Camp Verde Chevron Gas Station, 1851 Hwy 260, en route to the Phoenix airport or to Sedona; there are six buses going each way each day.

### AROUND CAMP VERDE
### Montezuma Castle
### National Monument
Like nearby Tuzigoot, Montezuma Castle contains Sinaguan ruins built between the 12th and 14th centuries and then abandoned. The name refers to their splendid castle-like location high on a cliff; early explorers thought the five-story-high ruins were Aztec and hence dubbed them Montezuma. A museum (☎ 567 3322) has exhibits explaining

Montezuma Castle

the archaeology of this well-preserved ruin, which can be seen from a self-guiding, wheelchair-accessible trail. Entrance into the ruins themselves is prohibited.

Montezuma's Well is a separate site 11 miles northeast of the castle, but is also administered as part of the monument. The well is a natural limestone sinkhole, 470 feet across and surrounded by the remnants of Sinaguan and Hohokam dwellings. Water from the sinkhole was used for irrigation by the Indians as it is today.

Both areas have picnic sites and are open from 8 am to 5 pm, or to 7 pm from Memorial Day to Labor Day. Admission to the Castle is $2 for adults, and the Well is free; Golden Age, Access and Eagle Passes are honored. Despite its small size, Montezuma Castle receives nearly a million visitors annually due to its convenient location close to the freeway.

### Coconino National Forest
East of Camp Verde, the Coconino National Forest provides wild and rugged country for outdoor backpacking, fishing, hunting and camping adventures. Several wilderness areas are completely undeveloped and provide real backcountry challenges, including canyoneering.

Further information is available from the Beaver Creek Ranger Station (☎ 567 4501), HC 64, Box 240, Rimrock, 86335, or the Forest Supervisor in Flagstaff. The ranger station is near Beaver Creek Campground (see Places to Stay above).

### Arcosanti
Twenty-five miles south of Camp Verde and two miles east of I-17 exit 262, an unpaved road leads to this architectural experiment in urban living. Designed by architect Paolo Soleri, Arcosanti will be home to 5000 people who want to live in a futuristic, aesthetic, relaxing and environmentally sound development.

The space-age project is still under construction, but it's worth a look if you're in the area. Tours leave hourly from 10 am to 4 pm and cost $5, or you can look around the visitor center freely between 9 am and

5 pm. There is a cafe and gift shop, as well as accommodations with room prices ranging from $15 for a basic room with shared bath, to $50 for a suite. Weeklong and month-long seminars on various aspects of the project are also offered. For information contact Arcosanti (☎ 632 7135), HC 74, PO Box 4136, Mayer, 86333.

## SEDONA

Sedona, seated among splendid crimson sandstone formations at the south end of lovely Oak Creek Canyon, has one of the prettiest locations in Arizona. The year-round waters of Oak Creek attracted ancient Indian farmers as well as late-19th-century European settlers. Among the early settlers were the Schneblys, who established a rough road to Flagstaff through Oak Creek Canyon in 1901. When a post office was established in 1902, the village was named after Sedona Schnebly, one of the few women so honored by a Western town.

For decades, Sedona was a quiet farming community sending produce up from its balmy elevation of 4400 feet to Flagstaff, 2500 feet higher and 28 miles away over a twisting scenic road. In the 1940s and '50s, Hollywood began using Sedona as a major motion-picture location, but it wasn't until the 1960s and '70s that the beauty of Sedona's surroundings started attracting retirees, artists and tourists in large numbers and the town experienced much growth. Around 1980, New Agers (seekers of metaphysical and psychic enlightenment) began finding vortexes, or points where the earth's energy is focused, and these have attracted thousands more visitors.

Sedona was not incorporated as a town until 1988, and rapid, poorly controlled growth took the area somewhat by surprise. The malls and strips look out of place among the red-rock scenery, although now the town is making some effort to blend in with its surroundings. The McDonald's of Sedona does not boast the famous 'Golden Arches'; instead, pastel green arcs are

---

### In Search of the New Age

Sedona is the foremost New Age center in the Southwest and one of the most important anywhere. The term 'New Age' loosely refers to a trend toward seeking alternative explanations or interpretations of what constitutes health, religion, the psyche and enlightenment. Drawing upon new and old factual and mystical traditions from around the world, 'New Agers' often seek to transform themselves psychologically and spiritually in the hopes that such personal efforts will eventually transform the world at large. The New Age Information Center (see Information) offers lectures, seminars, psychic readings, massage healings and vortex information. You can't miss the New Age stores in town – most of them have the word 'crystal' in their names. They distribute free maps showing the vortex sites and selling books, crystals and other New Age paraphernalia.

The Healing Center of Arizona (☎ 282 7710), 25 Wilson Canyon Rd, 86336, offers anything from an hour in a sauna to several days of holistic healing. Spend the night in the guest rooms for $70 a double or the communal sleeping domes for about $20 per person (depending on the number of people), and partake of reasonably priced vegetarian meals and as much acupressure, massage, yoga, nutrition counseling, herbology, tai chi, meditation and psychic channeling as you need. The Healing Center offers seminars, vortex tours, ceremonials and local information and strives to run an environmentally friendly establishment.

'New Agers' (for want of a better description) are generally gentle folk, but some have been criticized for performing rituals such as chantings or offerings in scenic areas. Chanting in a public scenic area can be as irritating as a loud radio, revving motorcycle or droning aircraft, and leaving offerings of crystals or food is tantamount to littering. If you want to participate in such public rituals, please keep your vocal interactions with the planet to a peacefully personal level, pick up your offerings when you're through, and leave nothing but your love, energy and blessings. ■

ARIZONA

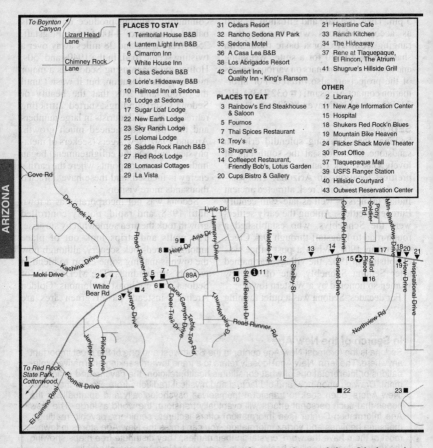

**PLACES TO STAY**
1  Territorial House B&B
4  Lantern Light Inn B&B
6  Cimarron Inn
7  White House Inn
8  Casa Sedona B&B
9  Lorie's Hideaway B&B
10  Railroad Inn at Sedona
16  Lodge at Sedona
17  Sugar Loaf Lodge
22  New Earth Lodge
23  Sky Ranch Lodge
25  Lolomai Lodge
26  Saddle Rock Ranch B&B
27  Red Rock Lodge
28  Lomacasi Cottages
29  La Vista

31  Cedars Resort
32  Rancho Sedona RV Park
35  Sedona Motel
36  A Casa Lea B&B
38  Los Abrigados Resort
42  Comfort Inn,
    Quality Inn - King's Ransom

**PLACES TO EAT**
3  Rainbow's End Steakhouse
    & Saloon
5  Fournos
7  Thai Spices Restaurant
12  Troy's
13  Shugrue's
14  Coffeepot Restaurant,
    Friendly Bob's, Lotus Garden
20  Cups Bistro & Gallery

21  Heartline Cafe
33  Ranch Kitchen
34  The Hideaway
37  Rene at Tlaquepaque,
    El Rincon, The Atrium
41  Shugrue's Hillside Grill

**OTHER**
2  Library
11  New Age Information Center
15  Hospital
18  Shukers Red Rock'n Blues
19  Mountain Bike Heaven
24  Flicker Shack Movie Theater
30  Post Office
37  Tlaquepaque Mall
39  USFS Ranger Station
40  Hillside Courtyard
43  Outwest Reservation Center

painted on a pink stuccoed wall. Despite the random development, there are relatively few fast-food joints and the tourist development has tended toward the high end. The town is home to several fine resorts, some of Arizona's best restaurants, fine art galleries and boutiques, but there are no cheap motels.

Sedona has about 15,000 residents and receives five to six million visitors a year. Despite the bustle, it is relatively easy to get away from the crowds and enjoy the beautiful scenery on a 4WD tour, bike ride or hike. There's not much to do in town

apart from eat, sleep and shop. It's the environs that make Sedona an attractive, if pricey destination.

### Orientation & Information

Hwy 89A is the main drag through town and runs roughly west-east, turning north at the east end where it heads to Flagstaff. It intersects with Hwy 179 from the south in the middle of town; this point is known as the 'Y'. Hwy 89A northeast of the 'Y' is 'uptown', where many of the tourist-oriented places are, and it continues north into Oak Creek Canyon. West Sedona,

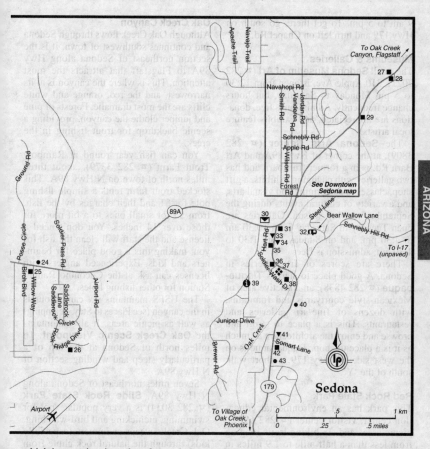

which is experiencing a lot of growth these days, is along Hwy 89A west of the 'Y'. South of the 'Y', Hwy 179 leads in seven miles to the Village of Oak Creek, a Sedona 'suburb' with a number of places to stay, and continues for eight more miles to I-17.

The chamber of commerce (☎ 282 7722), Forest Rd and Hwy 89A, is open from 9 am to 5 pm daily except Sunday, when it closes at 3 pm. The Coconino National Forest Ranger Station (☎ 282 4119) is at 250 Brewer Rd, 86339. The New Age Information Center (☎ 282 1949), 2445 W Hwy 89A (in the Village

West Plaza), is open from 9 am to 5 pm daily and may have evening seminars as well. The library (☎ 282 7714) is at the end of White Bear Rd. The post office (☎ 282 3511) is on Hwy 89A at Hwy 179. The hospital (☎ 282 1285) is at 75 Kallof Place. The police (☎ 282 3100, or 911 in emergencies) are at 431 Forest Rd.

## Chapel of the Holy Cross

Spectacularly located between red-rock towers three miles south of town, this chapel (☎ 282 4069) is open daily for non-denominational meditation or prayer from

9 am to 5 pm. To get there, go south on Hwy 179 and turn left on Chapel Rd.

## Museums & Galleries

The small **Sedona Museum of Art** (☎ 282 7021), 310 Apple Ave, is open from 12:30 to 5 pm Monday to Saturday, but hours change frequently. Admission is free, donations are appreciated, and exhibits feature local artists.

The **Sedona Arts Center** (☎ 282 3809), at the corner of Hwy 89A and Art Barn Rd, is in a former fruit barn and has two galleries with changing exhibits, a gift shop, classes in performing and visual arts, and a variety of cultural events during the September to May season. Galleries are open Tuesday to Saturday from 10:30 am to 4:30 pm, and on Sunday from 1:30 to 4:30 pm; admission is free.

There are scores of art galleries in Sedona. A good place to start is **Tlaquepaque** (☎ 282 4838), an attractive area of Mexican-style courtyards and fountains, with dozens of fine-art galleries and restaurants. This is a place to stroll and browse and enjoy the architecture as much as it is a place to shop. Tlaquepaque is on the west side of Hwy 179, a short walk south of the 'Y'.

## Red Rock State Park

This park has an environmental education center, visitor center (☎ 282 6907), picnic areas and six hiking trails ranging from less than a half mile to 1.9 miles in length. The 286-acre park protects riparian habitat and provides good birding and pleasant walking amid gorgeous scenery; you can fish in Oak Creek, but swimming and wading are not allowed. Ranger-led activities include nature walks, bird walks and full-moon hikes during the warmer months. The park is open from 8 am to 5 pm, or to 6 pm in summer, and the visitor center is open from 9 am to 5 pm. Admission is $5 per private vehicle or $1 for pedestrians. The park is 5.5 miles west of the 'Y' along Hwy 89A, then three miles left on Lower Red Rock Loop Rd.

## Oak Creek Canyon

Although Oak Creek flows through Sedona and continues southwest of town, it is the section northeast of Sedona along Hwy 89A to Flagstaff that attracts the most attention. This is where the canyon is at its narrowest, and the red, orange and white cliffs are the most dramatic. Forests of pine and juniper clothe the canyon, providing a scenic backdrop for trout fishing in the creek.

You can fish year round at Rainbow Trout Farm (☎ 282 3379), about three miles north of town on N Hwy 89A. This stocked trout farm rents a simple fishing pole for $1 and then charges by the fish, from $3 for small ones to a bit more for those over 14 inches. You don't need a license and the staff will clean the fish for you, making this a good place for beginners and kids. Experienced anglers with licenses can ask at the Coconino Ranger Station for other fishing holes.

The USFS maintains six campgrounds in the canyon (see Places to Stay – camping) as well as picnic areas. It also maintains the **Oak Creek Scenic Viewpoint**, 16 miles north of Sedona at the top of a particularly steep and winding section of N Hwy 89A.

Seven miles northeast of Sedona along N Hwy 89A, **Slide Rock State Park** (☎ 282 3034) is a very popular spot for swimming, picnicking and bird-watching. Oak Creek sweeps swimmers (especially kids) through the natural rock chute from which the park derives its name. Hours here are 8 am to 6 pm, and admission is $5 per car. Another popular swimming hole is **Grasshopper Point**, just over two miles north of town on the right side of N Hwy 89A.

## Hiking & Mountain Biking

There are easy scenic trails in Red Rock State Park and more difficult ones in the Coconino National Forest (surrounding Sedona on all sides). These provide a variety of hikes for all abilities.

Hiking is possible year round, and although some higher trails may be closed

## Canyoneering

At its simplest, canyoneering is visiting canyons under your own power. A canyoneer's adventures can vary from a pleasant day hike to a multi-day walking excursion stretching the length of a canyon. Longer trips may involve rock climbing with ropes, swimming across pools and down waterfalls, and camping; many experienced canyoneers bring inflatable mattresses to float their backpacks on as well as to sleep on. Some canyon areas designated as 'wilderness' are very remote, as no development is allowed. Canyoneers must reach the edges of these areas by dirt roads and then continue on foot over poor or barely existent trails to canyon bottoms.

Arizona, the Grand Canyon State, along with its northern neighbor, Utah, provides some of the best canyoneering anywhere. The first canyoneers in the huge gashes of the Colorado Plateau were ancient Indians, and Anasazi and Sinagua cliff-dwelling ruins and artifacts mark their passage. Adventurers and explorers in the 19th and 20th centuries sought to unravel the many secrets of the canyons. The most famous was John Wesley Powell, the one-armed geologist who led the first boat descent of the Colorado River.

Today, the Grand Canyon is the most popular place for canyoneering, with thousands of hikers descending from the rim every year. Many other canyons, however, are more difficult to access and provide uncrowded and equally scenic challenges. One of the most remote and lovely areas is the rarely visited **Sycamore Canyon Wilderness**, about 16 miles due west of the heavily traveled Oak Creek Canyon. It takes three days to hike, scramble and wade the canyon's 25-mile length; Coconino National Forest rangers in Sedona or Flagstaff can provide information. In the same forest, the Wet Beaver Creek Wilderness (east of Camp Verde) provides an even more challenging three-day canyoneering adventure; you'll need to swim through over 20 ponds, so be sure to bring a flotation device.

Then there are the slot canyons, hundreds of feet deep and only a few feet wide. These must be negotiated during dry months, because summer monsoon rains can cause deadly flash floods that may raise the height of the river by many feet in mere minutes. Always check with the appropriate rangers for weather and safety information. The **Paria Canyon**, a tributary of the Colorado River on the Arizona-Utah border, includes the amazing Buckskin Gulch, a stretch of canyon 12 miles long, hundreds of feet deep and only 15 feet wide for most of its length.

Adventures in these and other canyons are described in Annerino's *Adventuring in Arizona*. One of the greatest canyoneering challenges, however, is to get topo maps and set out on your own to explore side canyons of the better known areas, or to find new canyons that aren't described in guidebooks. ∎

---

in winter, they may be ideal in the heat of summer. Be sure to carry plenty of water on summer hikes, as you will need four quarts per person per day to avoid dehydration. The USFS ranger station sells good hiking maps and has up-to-date information; also see Things to Buy for bookstores carrying hiking guides to the area.

There is also a hiking group in Sedona. Ask at the chamber of commerce about where and when they meet.

Ask about mountain biking in the area at Mountain Bike Heaven (☎ 282 1312), 449 W Hwy 89A, or Sedona Sports (☎ 282 1317), 242 N Hwy 89A; both stores offer bicycle rental, repair and sales.

### Golf

Play nine holes in the small Village of Oak Creek (south of town on Hwy 179) at the Canyon Mesa Country Club (☎ 284 0036, 284 2176), 500 Jacks Canyon Rd (see Places to Stay). There is also Oak Creek Country Club (☎ 284 1660), 690 Bell Rock Blvd, with 18 holes, and the 18-hole Sedona Golf Resort (☎ 284 9355), 7256 Hwy 179.

### Scenic Drives

Aside from the scenic drives around Oak Creek Canyon and the Chapel of the Holy Cross (see above), the following drives give good views. The short drive up paved

**Airport Rd** is one good option, especially at sunset. **Dry Creek Rd**, at the west end of town, leads to scenic Boynton Canyon, where you can hike as well. View the photogenic Cathedral Rock along the roads of Lower and Upper **Red Rock Loop** (which you can take without having to enter the park), but be prepared for a short unpaved section. A rougher unpaved road (4WD not essential in good weather) is the scenic 12-mile **Schnebly Hill Rd**, which turns off Hwy 179 near Oak Creek and ends up at exit 320 of I-17. This road is closed in winter.

## Organized Tours

City Tours (☎ 282 5400, 282 6826) depart on the hour from the Sedona Trolley Uptown Bus Stop and the chamber of commerce. Narrated tours that last 45 minutes and cover Tlaquepaque and the Chapel of the Holy Cross leave at 10 am and noon, 2 and 4 pm; tours to West Sedona and Boynton Canyon leave at 11 am and 1, 3 and 5 pm. Tours are $6 each, or pay $9 for both; kids 12 and under pay $2. Other tour possibilities include horseback riding, hot-air ballooning and bicycling. Aircraft tours are also available, but the noise makes them a less attractive alternative.

Many companies offer 4WD 'Jeep Tours' of Sedona's backcountry and surrounding areas. These run from two hours to all day at costs ranging from $25 to $130 per person. Choose tours to see or photograph scenery, experience energy vortexes, look at archaeological sites or visit the Grand Canyon or Hopi Indian Reservation. The following list gives information about several specialty tour companies.

Crossing Worlds – Native/Nature Journeys
    Ruins, reservations. PO Box 314, 86339
    (☎ 204 1946)
Dorian Tours
    Vortexes, Indian reservations,
    Grand Canyon. PO Box 3151, 86340
    (☎ 282 4562, 1 (800) 728 4562)
Earth Wisdom Tours
    Vortexes, Indian lore. 293 N Hwy 89A,
    86339 (☎ 282 4714,
    1 (800) 482 4714)

Kachina Stables
    One-hour to six-day horseback rides. Lower
    Red Rock Loop Rd, PO Box 3616, 86340
    (☎ 282 7252, 1 (800) 723 3538)
Kiva Serenity Tours
    Ruins, geology, natural history. 135 Kiva
    Drive, 86340 (☎ 282 5696)
Northern Light Balloon Expeditions
    Daily sunrise flights. PO Box 1695, 86339
    (☎ 282 2274)
Pink Jeep Tours
    Backcountry scenery. 204 N Hwy 89A,
    86339 (☎ 282 5000, 1 (800) 873 3662)
Red Rock Balloon Adventures
    Daily morning flights. PO Box 2759, 86336
    (☎ 284 0040, 1 (800) 258 3754)
Roadrunner Tours
    Backcountry scenery and history. Outwest
    Reservation Center, 841 Hwy 179, 86336
    (☎ 282 4696)
Sedona Adventures
    Vortexes, sunsets, scenery and hikes.
    273 N Hwy 89A, PO Box 1476, 86339
    (☎ 282 3500)
Sedona Red Rock Jeep Tours
    Backcountry scenery, vortexes. 270 N Hwy
    89A, PO Box 10305, 86339 (☎ 282 6826,
    1 (800) 848 7728, fax 282 3281)
Time Expeditions
    Ruins, geology, vortexes. 276 N Hwy 89A,
    86339 (☎ 282 2137)

## Special Events

The chamber of commerce has information about the many events throughout the year; most are oriented toward the arts. The annual all-day Jazz on the Rocks (☎ 282 1985), PO Box 889, 86339, celebrating its 15th year in 1996, features big-name musicians on the last Saturday in September. The concert usually sells out, so buy tickets ahead of time. Other noteworthy events are the Festival of the Arts (☎ 774 7750) during the first week in August, the Mexican-style fiesta (☎ 282 4838) over the first weekend in October and the lighting of the luminarias at Tlaquepaque during the second weekend in December. Both Tlaquepaque and the neighboring Los Abrigados Resort are fantastically lit up over the Christmas period.

## Places to Stay

Sedona is a popular weekend getaway, and

many places raise their rates on Friday and Saturday; reservations are a good idea (especially for the Jazz Festival the last weekend in September). Due to the romantic views, a good number of hotels don't have TVs in the rooms, so you'll have to enjoy the scenery, not the soap operas.

Sedona has a growing number of B&Bs, several of which are popular for their comfortable and attractive rooms and 1st-class service; however, prices tend toward the high side. Several are out along Oak Creek Canyon or in the village of Oak Creek, seven miles south of town along Hwy 179.

There is a short low season from December through February when prices drop by 20% or so. *Outwest Reservation Center* (☎ 282 5112, 1 (800) 688 9378, fax 282 0522), 841 Hwy 179, 86336, will make lodging reservations and arrange any kind of tour package you want. *Sedona Central Reservations* (☎ 282 1518, 1 (800) 445 4128) offers similar services. Peak-season rates are given below.

### Places to Stay – camping

The USFS (☎ 282 4119) runs the following campgrounds in Oak Creek Canyon along N Hwy 89A. *Manzanita*, six miles from town, offers 19 sites; *Banjo Bill*, eight miles from town, has eight sites; *Bootlegger*, 8.5 miles from town, provides 10 sites; *Cave Springs*, 11.5 miles down the road, has 78 sites; and *Pine Flat*, 12.5 miles from town offers 58 sites. Sites cost $10, and none of the campgrounds have hookups or showers. Bootlegger has no drinking water, and RVs and trailers are allowed only at Cave Springs and Pine Flat. The official season is May through September, but some campgrounds may open for a couple of months longer. Most sites are on a first-come, first-served basis and campgrounds are often full on Friday morning for the weekend. Reservations (☎ 1 (800) 280 2267) can be made at a few sites in Cave Springs only.

If you're camping with a large group, try one of the three USFS group sites at *Chavez Crossing*, just over two miles south of town on Hwy 179. These sites, open year round and lacking showers and hookups,

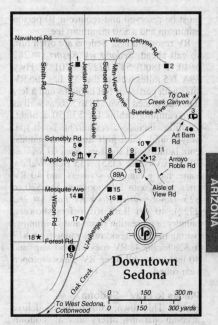

**Downtown Sedona**

To Oak Creek Canyon

To West Sedona, Cottonwood

| 0 | 150 | 300 m |
| 0 | 150 | 300 yards |

**PLACES TO STAY**
1  A Touch of Sedona B&B
2  Healing Center of Arizona
3  Hawkeye Red Rock RV Park
8  Rose Tree Inn
9  Matterhorn Motor Lodge
11 Best Western Arroyo Roble Hotel
13 Canyon Portal Motel
14 Star Motel
15 The Orchards of L'Auberge
16 L'Auberge de Sedona

**PLACES TO EAT**
7  Sedona Swiss Restaurant & Bakery
10 Hitching Post
12 Rosebuds

**OTHER**
4  Sedona Arts Center
5  Library
6  Sedona Museum of Art
12 Sinagua Plaza
17 Sedona Sports
18 Police Station
19 Chamber of Commerce

must be reserved and require a 10-person minimum and a $30 minimum fee.

RV resorts in/near Sedona are often full, so call ahead. *Sedona RV Resort* (☎ 282 6640, 1 (800) 547 8727), 6701 W Hwy 89A, 6.5 miles west of the 'Y', has 196 RV sites with partial or full hookups and a few tent sites priced from $18 to $26, as well as four camping cabins for $38.50 a night. Facilities include a restaurant, pool, spa, playground, mini-golf and other games, coin laundry and showers. *Rancho Sedona RV Park* (☎ 282 7255), 135 Bear Wallow Lane, has a laundry, showers and 40 RV sites, most with full hookups, for $20 to $25. *Hawkeye Red Rock RV Park* (☎ 282 2222), 40 Art Barn Rd, offers showers, laundry, a recreation room and swimming/fishing in Oak Creek; rates range from $17 to $28 for the 48 RV sites with hookups and 40 tent sites. All three RV parks are open year round.

### Places to Stay – Sedona

**Hotels** This town, known for its deluxe accommodations, offers no real 'bottom-end' places compared to other towns in Arizona. The following are $50 to $70 for a double, which is considered cheap during Sedona's lengthy high season.

The *Cimarron Inn* (☎ 282 9166), 2991 W Hwy 89A, with a pool and spa, has 76 rooms all with refrigerators and many with balconies or patios. Nonsmoking rooms are available if you pay a refundable $100 deposit (the hotel staff checks that you didn't sneak a cigarette!). The *Lolomai Lodge* (☎ 282 2835, fax 282 0535), 50 Willow Way, has a spa and 12 quiet rooms with kitchenettes. Gaze at beautiful views from the *Sedona Motel* (☎ 282 7187), on Hwy 179 near 89A, which has 16 standard rooms and is often full. The *Sugar Loaf Lodge* (☎ 282 9451), 1870 W Hwy 89A, also offers 16 standard rooms. The *White House Inn* (☎ 282 6680), 2986 W Hwy 89A, has 22 motel rooms, some with kitchenettes.

The *Railroad Inn at Sedona* (☎ 282 1533, 1 (800) 858 7245, fax 282 2033), 2545 W Hwy 89A, has a pool, restaurant and 66 rooms in the upper $60s and offers a choice of a king or two double beds, as well as packages with the Verde Valley Railroad (see Cottonwood). *La Vista* (☎ 282 7301), 500 N Hwy 89A, and *Star Motel* (☎ 282 3641), 295 Jordan Rd, have 23 jointly managed units (☎ 1 (800) 896 7301) with rooms starting at $59; much more expensive units with kitchenettes and suites are also available. *Cedars Resort* (☎ 282 7010), Hwy 89A at Hwy 179, has 39 nonsmoking motel rooms, some with balconies, and a pool and spa.

The *Red Rock Lodge* (☎ 282 3591), 901 N Hwy 89A, offers a few regular rooms priced in the $50s and some rooms with fireplaces and/or spas priced in the $80s. A more expensive cottage and bungalow is also available. The *Sky Ranch Lodge* (☎ 282 6400, fax 282 7682) on Airport Rd is a good value by Sedona standards; its 94 rooms, pool and spa are in a nicely landscaped setting above town. Standard rooms are in the $55 to $70 range, and larger units with kitchenettes, fireplaces and good views go for up to $95. The *Desert Quail Inn* (☎ 284 1433, fax 284 0487), 6626 Hwy 179 (seven miles south of town) has 21 above average rooms with refrigerators and in-room coffee in the $60s. The *Healing Center of Arizona* offers New Age accommodations – see the New Age aside for details.

The 20 standard rooms at the *Matterhorn Motor Lodge* (☎ 282 7176), 230 Apple Ave, have balconies or patios overlooking uptown Sedona and Oak Creek. Rates are in the $80s, and there is a pool (closed in the winter) and a spa. The *Canyon Portal Motel* (☎ 282 7125, 1 (800) 542 8484), 280 N Hwy 89A, has a pool and 30 rooms, some with fireplaces, others with balconies or patios and many with views priced in the $70 to $80 range. Try one of the eight cottages with kitchens and fireplaces at the *New Earth Lodge* (☎ 282 2644), 665 Sunset Drive, for accommodations priced in the $80s and $90s – call about New Age seminars held here as well. On a quiet street with a garden, the *Rose Tree Inn* (☎ 282 2065), 376 Cedar St, has just four pleasant rooms, three with kitchenettes, as well as a spa; high-season rates are close to $100. The similarly priced *Lomacasi Cottages* (☎ 282 7912), 880 N Hwy 89A, offers rustic cabins with kitchens and swimming in Oak Creek.

Two pools, two spas, tennis courts, nearby golf privileges and complimentary champagne make the *Bell Rock Inn* (☎ 282 4161, 1 (800) 881 7625), 6246 Hwy 179 (six miles south of town), one of the nicest places in the area. Half of the nearly 100 rooms are mini-suites with fireplaces, and the red-rock views and pleasant pastel decor lend a Southwestern flavor. A restaurant and lounge provides weekend entertainment, and room rates are in the $80 to $120 range.

A few of the better motel chains are scattered on Hwys 89A and 179. The *Quality Inn – King's Ransom* (☎ 282 7151, fax 282 5208), 771 Hwy 179, has a pool, spa, restaurant and lounge and offers 65 rooms, some with balconies or patios, priced in the $80 to $120 range. Next door, the *Comfort Inn* (☎ 282 3132), 725 Hwy 179, has a pool and spa and 53 rooms in the $85 to $105 range; prices include a continental breakfast. Most of the 53 rooms at the *Best Western Arroyo Roble Hotel* (☎/fax 282 4001), 400 N Hwy 89A, have balconies or patios with good views for $95 to $125, and king-size or two queen-size beds. Enjoy the two pools, spa, sauna, tennis court and exercise room. Villas with two bedrooms, two bathrooms, fireplace and kitchen are in the $200 price range.

**B&Bs** *A Touch of Sedona B&B* (☎ 282 6462), 595 Jordan Rd, 86336, in a residential area just north of uptown, offers five modern, individually decorated rooms with private baths for $85 to $135. The new pueblo-style *A Casa Lea B&B* (☎ 282 2833, 1 (800) 385 7883), 95 Portal Lane, 86336, just south of the Y, features a spa, kiva fireplaces and patios with views. Prices for eleven rooms range from $120 to $220.

In West Sedona, *Casa Sedona* (☎ 282 2938, 1 (800) 525 3756, fax 282 2259), 55 Hozoni Drive, 86336, is a large Southwest-

ern-style inn with 16 attractive, unique rooms featuring private whirlpool tubs, fireplaces, refrigerators and access to terraces with great red-rock views. There is a TV room but no TVs in the guest rooms, and smoking is not permitted. Full breakfast and refreshments during the day are included in the rates, which go from $95 to $150. The *Lodge at Sedona* (☎ 204 1942, 1 (800) 619 4467), 125 Kallof Place, 86336, has 13 nonsmoking rooms (two are suites) in a sprawling house set in 2.5 acres with lawn games and picnic areas. All rooms have private bathrooms and lack TVs, but some have fireplaces or balconies; prices range from $95 to $195 a double. Be sure to try the gourmet breakfasts.

Relax on the patio, splash in the pool or soak in the hot tub at the hilltop *Saddle Rock Ranch B&B* (☎ 282 7640), 255 Rock Ridge Drive, PO Box 10095, 86336. The 1926 ranch has been the setting for several Western movies and has a fantastic view. Three spacious and romantic guest rooms, each with private bath and fireplace, range from $110 to $130 a double and are often booked months ahead; a two-night minimum stay is requested. Smoking and small children are not permitted. The rural *Territorial House B&B* (☎ 204 2737), 65 Piki Drive, 86336, offers three rooms and a suite decorated in old Arizona Territorial style for $90 to $130. All have private baths and there is a spa.

A number of small B&Bs with just two or three rooms, all with private baths, are listed below. The *Kennedy House B&B* (☎ 282 1624), 2075 Upper Red Rock Loop Rd, HC30, PO Box 785K, has rooms for $75 to $85. *Moestly Wood B&B* (☎ 204 1461), 2085 Upper Red Rock Loop Rd, 86336, with rooms priced at $85, sells handcrafted wood products and has great views of Cathedral Rock, as does the nearby *Cathedral Rock Lodge* (☎ 282 7608), 61 Los Amigos Lane, Star Route 2, PO Box 856, 86336, with rooms in the $70 to $100 range. *Lantern Light Inn* (☎ 282 3419), 3085 W Hwy 89A, 86336, charges $75 to $110 a night. *Lorie's Hideaway B&B* (☎ 282 1944, 1 (800) 201 1944, fax

204 2442), 2900 Hopi Drive, 86336, charges $75 to $125, and *Casa de Abuelita B&B* (☎ 282 6241, 1 (800) 854 8152, fax 282 5636), 41 Arrow Drive, PO Box 10685, 86339, offers rooms for $100 to $150.

**Resorts** Sedona is known for several very upscale resorts. *Los Abrigados* (☎ 282 1777, 1 (800) 521 3131, fax 282 2614), 160 Portal Lane, 86336, is built in a Mexican style in keeping with its neighbor, Tlaquepaque. This is the place to stay if you want to be in the heart of Sedona and like to shop, exercise and enjoy spacious, comfortable suites. Prices for the 172 units range from $210 for a standard suite to $395 for a two-bedroom, two-bathroom suite with a kitchenette. Some suites have fireplaces, balconies or private patio spas. If you really want to impress someone, spring for the 'Historic Stone House', at a cool $1500 a night. The exercise facilities include a pool, saunas, whirlpools, three tennis courts, volleyball courts, aerobics instruction, Nautilus and other equipment, weight rooms, massage and fitness instructors. Check the kids into the children's program and take a stroll along the footpaths by Oak Creek, which flows through the resort, or have a family picnic in the barbecue area. The resort has three restaurants, and a bar with nighttime entertainment.

The *Enchantment Resort* (☎ 282 2900, 1 (800) 826 4180, fax 282 9249), 525 Boynton Canyon Rd, 86336, is the most spectacularly located of the resorts, tucked in a canyon northwest of Sedona. All the rooms have private balconies and great views; trails take you high above or far into the canyon. You'll get plenty of exercise with four pools, a dozen tennis courts (lessons are available), a croquet field and a fitness center, and can recover with a relaxing massage, sauna or soak in the spa. A children's program provides activities for the kids, and there is a wonderfully innovative restaurant and bar. High-season rates are from about $200 for a large room to $575 for a two-bedroom, three-bathroom casita with kitchen, living room, deck with grill, and several balconies.

*L'Auberge de Sedona* (☎ 282 1661, 1 (800) 272 6777, fax 282 2885), 301 L'Auberge Lane, 86339, is a 'Country French Inn' next to Oak Creek in uptown Sedona. Although there is a pool and spa, the emphasis is on relaxation and eating fancy French food (and I mean fancy French – this is one of the few places in Arizona where a jacket is required for men). The highlight is the 34 romantic one- and two-bedroom cottages scattered in the gardens and along the creek. With fireplaces and no TVs, the cabins run from $270 to $385 in the high season, while spacious rooms in the attractive lodge overlooking the cottages are $160 to $230. *The Orchards of L'Auberge*, under the same management but up the hill on Hwy 89A, overlooks the L'Auberge complex and affords the best views. Rooms here are more American style and run $125 to $165; most have private balconies and some have fireplaces.

*Poco Diablo Resort* (☎ 282 7333, 1 (800) 528 4275, fax 282 2090), PO Box 1709, 86336, located two miles south of town on Hwy 179, has a nine-hole 'pitch and putt' golf course, as well as two pools, four tennis courts, spas, and a restaurant and bar. The nearly 100 large rooms provide scenic views and include refrigerators, wet bars and coffee for $135 to $185 in the high season; a few suites cost $250 to $350. Some rooms have fireplaces and whirlpools, while others have private balconies.

### Places to Stay – Oak Creek Canyon

**Hotels & Cabins** *Don Hoel's Cabins* (☎ 282 3560, 1 (800) 292 4635), 9440 N Hwy 89A (10 miles north of Sedona) has 20 modern, rustic cabins with kitchens priced around $70. *Slide Rock Lodge* (☎ 282 3531), six miles north of town, has 20 motel rooms, as well as barbecue grills and picnic tables, and offers free coffee and pastry in the morning. Couch potatoes beware – there are no TVs in the rooms, which cost about $80. Next to the lodge and with similar facilities, the *Canyon Wren* (☎ 282 6900, 437 9736) has one small and three larger cabins with fireplaces, fully equipped kitchens and whirlpool tubs, priced at $125 or $135 a double. Smoking is not allowed. The *Forest House Resort* (☎ 282 2999), 10 miles north of town, has cottages with kitchens and fireplaces priced in the low $100s. *Oak Creek Terrace Resort* (☎ 282 3562, 1 (800) 224 2229), 4.5 miles north of town, has 17 rooms and cabins, some with kitchenettes and fireplaces, ranging from $80 to $150.

**B&Bs** The *Briar Patch Inn* (☎ 282 2342, fax 282 2399), HC 30, Box 1002, three miles north of town on Hwy 89A, has 15 rustic cabins, some with kitchenettes and/ or fireplaces, attractively located on eight wooded acres right next to Oak Creek, making it convenient for swimming and fishing. Most cabins are for two, a few hold four people; rates are $155 to $215 for a double. There are no TVs but frequent classical music performances accompany breakfast, and a variety of workshops and seminars keeps guests entertained. A two-night minimum stay is requested.

The *Garland's Oak Creek Lodge* (☎ 282 3343), PO Box 152, 86336, eight miles north of town on Hwy 89A, is more than just a B&B; prices for the 15 cabins include afternoon tea and full dinner. The 17-acre grounds feature an orchard, tennis court, volleyball net and croquet field. Rates are $150 to $170 a double, and the place is closed in winter. Both Oak Creek Canyon places are very popular; book as far ahead as possible.

**Resorts** The *Junipine Resort* (☎ 282 3375, 1 (800) 742 7463, fax 282 7402), 8351 N Hwy 89A, 86336, eight miles north of Sedona, provides easy access to hiking, swimming and fishing in Oak Creek. The 50 one- and two-bedroom townhouses (they call them 'creek houses'), all with kitchens, living/dining rooms, fireplaces and decks and some with lofts, range from $180 to $250. Try the excellent restaurant if you're not in the mood to cook. There is a spa.

With over 150 townhouses, *Canyon Mesa Country Club* (☎ 284 1740), 500 Jacks Canyon Rd, in the Village of Oak

Creek, offers quite exceptional views and reasonable prices. Forty-four one- and two-bedroom casitas and 109 spacious two-bedroom, two-bathroom townhouses with fireplaces and decks rent for $80 to $120 a night. These individually owned properties all have fully equipped kitchens and rent for a minimum of two nights. Apart from the challenging golf course, the club has tennis courts, a pool and a spa.

### Places to Stay – Village of Oak Creek

Canyon Circle Drive is just off Bell Rock Blvd, which intersects with Hwy 179 on the west, about seven miles south of Sedona. The road fronts the Coconino National Forest, providing easy access to the forest from nearby B&Bs. Two of Arizona's most luxurious are found in this area.

The *Graham B&B Inn* (☎ 284 1425, 1 (800) 228 1425, fax 284 0767), 150 Canyon Circle Drive, 86351, has six very comfortable and attractive rooms. The owners claim that the Sedona Suite, priced at $209 a double, is the largest and most luxurious B&B suite in Arizona. It features a large Jacuzzi bathtub as well as twin showers, a living room with fireplace, a private patio with a fine view and, of course, a king-size bed. The other rooms, ranging in price from $119 to $179, all have private balconies, and some have whirlpool bathtubs and/or fireplaces. Sip complimentary beverages in the library or by the swimming pool. A two-night minimum stay is suggested.

Almost next door is the equally splendid *Canyon Villa B&B* (☎ 284 1226, 1 (800) 453 1166, fax 284 2114), 125 Canyon Circle Drive, 86351. The Mediterranean-style villa has 11 uniquely decorated rooms, some with Southwestern decor, with prices ranging from $105 to $175. Most rooms have balconies or patios, and many have whirlpool bathtubs and fireplaces. Enjoy the superb views from the pool while partaking of afternoon and evening refreshments.

The modern *Cozy Cactus B&B* (☎ 284 0082, 1 (800) 788 2082), 80 Canyon Circle

Drive, 86351, offers five rooms with private bath and scenic views for $95 a double; two kitchens are available for guest use, and full breakfast and afternoon drinks are provided.

The *Greyfire Farm B&B* (☎ 284 2340), 1240 Jacks Canyon Rd, 86336, surrounded by woods and near the national forest, offers four rooms with private baths for $70 to $90. The road is off Hwy 179 to the east, seven miles south of Sedona.

## Places to Eat

Sedona has plenty of upscale restaurants, but also a good selection of budget places serving decent food. Even the pricier places are a reasonable value, providing high-quality, innovative dishes and agreeable surroundings. In fact, some visitors consider the cuisine to be as much of an attraction as the scenery. Reputable chefs are drawn to the town, rewarded both by the lovely setting and by an appreciative and (sometimes) discerning audience of food-loving travelers. Reservations are a good idea.

For breakfast, the *Coffeepot Restaurant* (☎ 282 6626), 2050 W Hwy 89A, has been the place to go for decades. It's always busy and service can be slow, but meals are inexpensive and the selection is huge – they offer more types of omelettes than most restaurants have menu items (they claim 101, but I didn't count). Opening at 6 am, the Coffeepot serves breakfast all day, and burgers, sandwiches and Mexican food round out the lunch and dinner menus. Enjoy your food on the outdoor patio, or stare at the five-foot screen in the sports lounge if you can't bear to stay in Sedona without seeing how the Suns are doing. Almost next door, *Friendly Bob's* (☎ 282 1826), 2070 W Hwy 89A, is the place to go if you're in a hurry; it's open from 5:30 am to 2 pm daily except Sunday, when it opens at 7 am. Bob's inexpensive breakfasts and sandwiches are served a tad more quickly than those at the crowded Coffeepot. Listen to live and recorded jazz while you sip gourmet coffee and lunch on low-priced organic and vegetarian cuisine at *Cups Bistro & Gallery* (☎ 282 2531), 1670 W Hwy 89A, open from 8 am to 4 pm daily,

possibly later in summer. Try the brunch on Sunday.

A couple of popular and reasonably priced American family restaurants are conveniently located uptown; the *Hitching Post* (☎ 282 7761), 269 N Hwy 89A, is open from 7 am to 8:30 pm; and the *Ranch Kitchen* (☎ 282 0057), at the 'Y', is open from 6 am to 8 pm. Locals say the best American family restaurant is the slightly more expensive *Shugrue's* (☎ 282 2943), 2250 W Hwy 89A, offering dinner entrees in the low teens or lighter fare in the adjoining coffee shop for less. Hours here are 8 am to 3 pm and 5 to 9 pm except Friday and Saturday, when it stays open to 10 pm, and Monday, when it does not open until 11 am. Shugrue's has been around for years and recently opened *Shugrue's Hillside Grill* (☎ 282 5300), 671 Hwy 179, affording panoramic red-rock views and both indoor and outdoor dining, as well as jazz entertainment on weekends. The seafood and meat menu is somewhat more adventurous and pricier than its simpler counterpart. Hours are 11:30 am to 3:30 pm and 5:30 to 9:30 pm.

Shoppers at Tlaquepaque have plenty of restaurants to choose from. *El Rincon* (☎ 282 4648) serves very good Sonoran Mexican food from 11 am to 9 pm Tuesday to Saturday and noon to 5 pm on Sunday. Prices are a little higher than most Mexican places, but are still moderate. *The Atrium* (☎ 282 5060) has recently reopened, and critics say that the fresh and innovative bistro cuisine is an affordable bargain. *Rene at Tlaquepaque* (☎ 282 9225), long considered one of Sedona's best, is a non-smoking restaurant with upscale continental cuisine (lamb is a specialty) and plenty of art on the walls. Lunch is served from 11:30 am to 4:30 pm. Dinner is served from 5:30 to 8:30 pm, with entrees in the teens and $20s.

The *Heartline Cafe* (☎ 282 0785), 1610 W Hwy 89A, serves imaginative and tasty Southwestern cuisine. It's a pretty place filled with flowers and has a patio for summer dining. Dinners, priced in the mid-teens, are a good value, and lunches, most under $10, are very good, too. Hours are 11 am to 3 pm Monday to Saturday and 5 to 9 or 10 pm daily. Another very attractive restaurant with good food is *Troy's* (☎ 282 3532), 2370 W Hwy 89A (in the Park Sedona Plaza), offering an American and continental menu with dinner entrees priced in the teens. Hours are 11:30 am to 2 pm for lunch and 5 to 9 pm for dinner.

For Italian dining, the *Hideaway* (☎ 282 4204), 251 Hwy 179 (in the Country Square Plaza), serves $8 to $15 dinners on a patio overlooking Oak Creek from 11 am to 3 pm Monday to Saturday and 5 to 9 or 10 pm daily. The more expensive *Pietro's* (☎ 282 2525), 2445 W Hwy 89A, considered by many to have Sedona's best Italian food, is open from 5 to 9 pm daily. For Greek food, a good choice is the small and casual *Fournos* (☎ 282 3331), 3000 W Hwy 89A. Open for dinner daily, it specializes in seafood but also serves Sunday brunch; reservations are recommended.

If you're dying for Swiss chocolates and other yummy chocolate things, get your fix at the *Sedona Swiss Restaurant & Bakery* (☎ 282 7959), 350 Jordan Rd. Before sampling the delectable desserts, pastries and gourmet coffees, go for a 1st-class Swiss-French meal in the pretty dining room next to the bakery. The inexpensive buffet lunch draws crowds, but it quiets down for dinner when entrees are in the teens or low $20s. Hours are 7 am to 9:30 pm Monday to Saturday.

*Thai Spices* (☎ 282 0599), 2986 W Hwy 89A, serves good, spicy and inexpensive authentic Thai food, including a wonderful coconut soup. The restaurant is open from 12 to 3 pm Monday to Friday and 5 to 9 pm daily. The best Chinese restaurants are the *Lotus Garden* (☎ 282 3118, 282 3256), 164H Coffee Pot Drive (in the Basha's Center), and *Mandarin House* (☎ 284 9088), 6486 Hwy 179 (at Castle Rock Plaza in the Village of Oak Creek). Both places are open from 11 am to 9 pm daily, and to 10 pm on Friday and Saturday.

Also in the Village of Oak Creek, try *Irene's* (☎ 284 2240), in the Castle Rock Plaza, serving home-style breakfast, lunch

and dinners at moderate prices. The *Mexicali Rose* (☎ 284 4693), offering Mexican lunches and dinners, is also in the Castle Rock Plaza. Nearby, the *Wild Toucan Restaurant and Cantina* (☎ 284 1604), 6376 Hwy 179, open from 7 am, serves large portions of Mexican and American food inside or out on the patio and has a kids' menu. Entrees start at around $9. The restaurant at the *Bell Rock Inn* is open from 7 am to 9 pm and is quite good.

Of course, you're here to drop your jaw for the views as well as the vittles. So which restaurant has the most spectacular views in Sedona? Tough question. Certainly, *Rosebuds* (☎ 282 3022), 320 N Hwy 89A (in the Sinagua Plaza), is designed to be a contender – the huge windows provide a memorable panorama. Serving mainly standard steak and seafood dinners in the $10 to $18 range, Rosebuds is open 11 am to 9:30 pm daily, and to 10 pm on Friday and Saturday.

For even better views, dine to a magnificent sunset out of town at the Enchantment Resort, where the *Yavapai Dining Room* (☎ 282 2900) serves superb food in a superb setting (do make a reservation). The Southwestern cuisine has all sorts of interesting twists, not the least of which is the rattlesnake chili, made with two parts beef to one part rattler, and doused with plenty of seasoning. If that's way too wild for you, chicken breast sauteed in piñon nuts is a tamer Southwestern choice. Seafood, meat and pasta dinner entrees range from $15 to $25, a fair value for the food and a bargain considering the location. The restaurant also puts on a good champagne Sunday brunch – again, make reservations. Hours are 11:30 am to 2 pm and 6 to 9:30 pm daily.

All Sedona's resorts have good restaurants. The most famous is *L'Auberge de Sedona* (☎ 282 1667) in the resort of the same name. It's beautiful, elegant, romantic and very French; the high prices, small portions and formal dining are irresistible to many visitors and reservations are required. The best value is the prix-fixe dinner menu that is changed daily and runs at about $50 for six courses. Otherwise, dinner entrees are around $30 and include

French delicacies such as frog legs, pheasant, veal and snails.

The highly regarded *Steak and Sticks* restaurant (formerly the *Canyon Rose*) (☎ 204 7849) at Los Abrigados Resort has recently undergone a radical remodeling – they reopened in mid-1995 with a unique dining room, even by Sedona standards. Out in Oak Creek Canyon's Junipine Resort, *La Rotisserie* (☎ 282 7406) serves Southwestern meals with a light French touch (the chef is the owner of the acclaimed Chez Marc French bistro in Flagstaff). Prices are in the teens for dinners, and you can dine out on the deck during the summer.

Finally, if you are fed up with all this fancy stuff and just want a huge steak and country & western music, head over to *Rainbow's End Steakhouse & Saloon* (☎ 282 1593), 3235 W Hwy 89A, where you can stomp to live country & western bands on weekends.

### Entertainment

Read the weekly *Sedona News*, published on Friday, for local events. Apart from the saloon at *Rainbow's End* (see above), nightlife is fairly quiet, with mainly lounge entertainment at the resorts. *Shukers Red Rock'n Blues* (☎ 282 1655), 1730 W Hwy 89A, is a nightclub with live music, pool and dancing. Check the *Sedona Arts Center* (see under Art, above) for cultural events, and *The Book Loft* (☎ 282 5173), 175 Hwy 179, for poetry readings. The old-fashioned *Flicker Shack* (☎ 282 3777), in the shopping plaza 1.5 miles west on Hwy 89A, shows movies.

### Things to Buy

Despite its size, Sedona is a prime shopping destination. The uptown area along Hwy 89A is the place to get souvenirs. Good bookshops here include Native & Nature (☎ 282 7870), 124 N Hwy 89A, stocking a selection of books about the Southwest, and the Happy Wanderer (☎ 282 4690), 320 N Hwy 89A, in the Sinagua Plaza, with an excellent selection of travel books. Also in this plaza is South-

west Gourmet Gallery (☎ 282 2682), which offers more varieties of hot sauces, salsas, chile products and other culinary treats than you ever thought existed. Sedona Kid Company (☎ 282 3571), 333 N Hwy 89A, is the place to go for the kids on your list. The Book Loft (☎ 282 5173), 175 Hwy 179, has new and used books.

Tlaquepaque (☎ 282 4838) has high-quality art galleries that are also high priced, but they can give you a good place to start for comparison shopping. Almost opposite is the Crystal Castle (☎ 282 5910), one of several stores selling New Age books and gifts. Continuing south along Hwy 179, Garlands's Navajo Rugs (☎ 282 4070), in the complex at the junction of Hwy 179 and Schnebly Hill Rd, has thousands of rugs to choose from as well as other Indian crafts. In the same complex is Sedona Pottery (☎ 282 1192), selling interesting ceramics. The Hozho Center (☎ 282 4070), 431 Hwy 179, and the Hillside Courtyard (☎ 282 4500), 671 Hwy 179, both have several good art galleries. The Village of Oak Creek has Oak Creek Factory Outlets (☎ 284 2150), 6657 Hwy 179, with about 30 outlets providing many name brands at cut prices.

### Getting There & Away

**Air** Air Sedona, also known as Scenic Airlines (☎ 282 7935, 1 (800) 535 4448) has three flights a day to and from Phoenix for $59 one-way with a three-day advance purchase, or $79 any time. The airport sits spectacularly atop a mesa.

**Bus** The Sedona-Phoenix Shuttle (☎ 282 2066) leaves Phoenix Airport every two hours between 10 am and 8 pm and returns from Sedona every two hours from 6 am to 4 pm. The fare is $30 one way or $55 roundtrip.

### Getting Around

**Car Rental** Budget Rent A Car (☎ 282 4602, 1 (800) 527 0700) and Avis (☎ 282 2227, 1 (800) 831 2847) are at the airport. Also try Enterprise (☎ 634 0049, 1 (800) 325 8007), 1423 W Hwy 89A, and

Sedona Rent A Car (☎ 282 2897), 2730 W Hwy 89A.

Sedona Jeep Rentals (☎ 282 2227, 1 (800) 879 5337) at the Sedona Airport offers full- and half-day rentals and has a booklet suggesting self-guided tours.

**Taxi** Call Bob's Sedona Taxi and Tours (☎ 282 1234) to get around the area.

## FLAGSTAFF

Flagstaff was first settled by a flock of sheep, which arrived in the spring of 1876 accompanied by Thomas Forsyth McMillan, who settled down and built a cabin. On the Fourth of July of that year, a pine tree was stripped of its branches and a US flag hung from it to celebrate the country's centennial, hence the town's name. The arrival of the railroad in 1882 really put Flagstaff on the map. Cattle and sheep ranching became economic mainstays, and the surrounding forests formed the basis of a small logging industry.

By the turn of the century, Flagstaff was becoming an important town. The famous Lowell Observatory was founded in 1894, the still-functioning Hotel Weatherford was built in 1897 and the school that later became Northern Arizona University (NAU) was established in 1899. In the early 1900s, the Riordan Mansion and several other historic buildings were erected. Although Flagstaff didn't have the mineral resources of other parts of the state, the pleasant climate attracted settlers.

Today, ranching, forestry and the railroad have been supplanted by tourism, Flagstaff's major industry. During the summer, the city's 6900-foot elevation attracts lowland Arizonans escaping the heat as well as travelers from all over the world. From Flagstaff, it is less than a two-hour drive to the Grand Canyon, and other attractions are even closer, such as the impressive Sinagua Indian ruins, the splendid (though inactive) volcano at Sunset Crater National Monument, beautiful Oak Creek Canyon and the 12,663-foot Humphrey's Peak, Arizona's highest mountain. The Navajo and Hopi Indian

Reservations are longer day trips. In winter, the nearby Arizona Snowbowl Ski Area provides convenient skiing.

Although 'Flag', as locals call it, is a great base for trips into the surrounding area, it is also a destination in its own right, with museums, a historical downtown, cultural attractions and, thanks to NAU students and tourists looking for evening excitement, northern Arizona's best nightlife. Attracting international budget travelers, Flag is the Katmandu or Cuzco of Arizona.

With about 50,000 inhabitants, Flagstaff is Arizona's fourth largest urban area, and the largest between Phoenix and Salt Lake City. It is the seat of Coconino (pronounced 'cossoneeno') County which, at 18,608 sq miles, is the second largest county in the USA (San Bernardino County in California is the largest).

## Orientation

Flagstaff is a major crossroads at the intersection of I-17 and I-40. Its main drag, Route 66 (also called Santa Fe Ave and marked both ways on maps), runs north of and roughly parallel to I-40, passing through the old town and by the visitors center; at the edge of town it becomes the main motel strip.

## Information

The visitors center (☎ 774 9541, 1 (800) 842 7293), 1 E Route 66, is in the historic Amtrak railway station. The center is staffed from 8:30 am to 5 pm, Monday to Friday, but the station is open from 6:15 am to 11:25 pm daily, and stands with free maps, events listings and accommodations brochures are available during those hours.

The Coconino National Forest Peaks Ranger Station (☎ 526 0866), 5075 N Hwy 89, 86004, has information about the forests north of Flagstaff, and is open from 7:30 am to 4:30 pm Monday to Friday as well as summer Saturdays. The Mormon Lake Ranger Station (☎ 527 3650), 4825 S Lake Mary Rd, 86001, provides information about the Coconino National Forest south of Flagstaff. Their office is open from 7:30 am to 4:30 pm Monday to Friday.

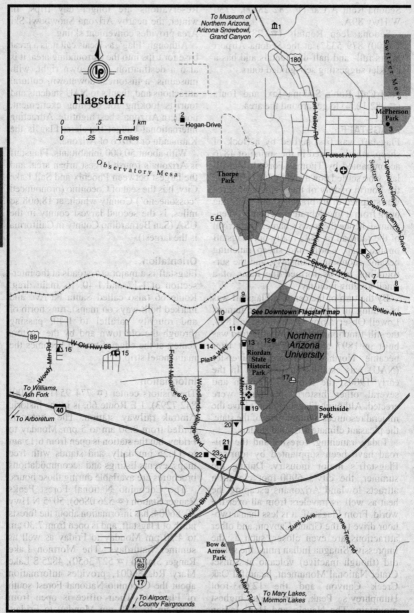

**Flagstaff**

To Museum of
Northern Arizona,
Arizona Snowbowl,
Grand Canyon

Hogan Drive

Observatory Mesa

Thorpe
Park

Fort Valley Rd

180

Switzer Mesa

McPherson
Park

Forest Ave

Turquoise Drive

Switzer Canyon Drive

Switzer Canyon

Santa Fe Ave

Butler Ave

See Downtown Flagstaff map

Northern
Arizona
University

Riordan
State
Historic
Park

Plaza Way

Milton Rd

Southside
Park

W Old Hwy 66

Forest Meadows St

Woodland Village Blvd

Woody Mtn Rd

To Williams,
Ash Fork

To Arboretum

89

40

Beulah Blvd

Zuni Drive

Lone Tree Rd

Lake Mary Rd

Bow &
Arrow
Park

ALT
89

17

To Airport,
County Fairgrounds

To Mary Lakes,
Mormon Lakes

0      .5      1 km
0    .25    .5 miles

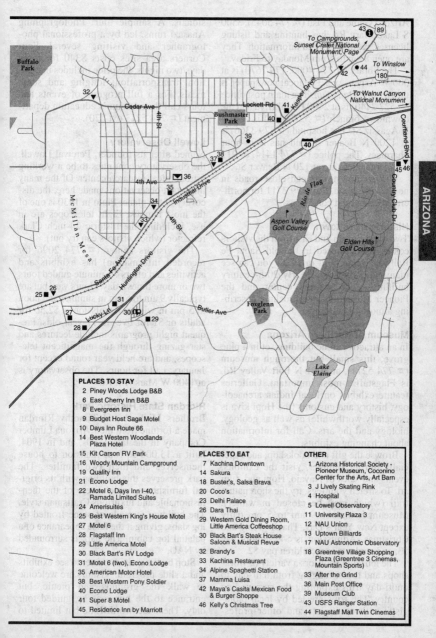

Buffalo Park

To Campgrounds, Sunset Crater National Monument, Page

To Winslow

To Walnut Canyon National Monument

Cedar Ave

Lockett Rd

Bushmaster Park

4th St

4th Ave

Industrial Drive

4th St

McMillan Mesa

Santa Fe Ave

Huntington Drive

Lucky Ln

Butler Ave

Mars Hill Rd

Leupp Drive

Rio de Flag

Aspen Valley Golf Course

Elden Hills Golf Course

Foxglenn Park

Lake Elaine

Courtland Blvd

Country Club Dr

ARIZONA

**PLACES TO STAY**
2 Piney Woods Lodge B&B
6 East Cherry Inn B&B
8 Evergreen Inn
9 Budget Host Saga Motel
10 Days Inn Route 66
14 Best Western Woodlands Plaza Hotel
15 Kit Carson RV Park
16 Woody Mountain Campground
19 Quality Inn
21 Econo Lodge
22 Motel 6, Days Inn I-40, Ramada Limited Suites
24 Amerisuites
25 Best Western King's House Motel
27 Motel 6
28 Flagstaff Inn
29 Little America Motel
30 Black Bart's RV Lodge
31 Motel 6 (two), Econo Lodge
35 American Motor Hotel
38 Best Western Pony Soldier
40 Econo Lodge
41 Super 8 Motel
45 Residence Inn by Marriott

**PLACES TO EAT**
7 Kachina Downtown
14 Sakura
18 Buster's, Salsa Brava
20 Coco's
23 Delhi Palace
26 Dara Thai
29 Western Gold Dining Room, Little America Coffeeshop
30 Black Bart's Steak House Saloon & Musical Revue
32 Brandy's
33 Kachina Restaurant
34 Alpine Spaghetti Station
37 Mamma Luisa
42 Maya's Casita Mexican Food & Burger Shoppe
46 Kelly's Christmas Tree

**OTHER**
1 Arizona Historical Society - Pioneer Museum, Coconino Center for the Arts, Art Barn
3 J Lively Skating Rink
4 Hospital
5 Lowell Observatory
11 University Plaza 3
12 NAU Union
13 Uptown Billiards
17 NAU Astronomic Observatory
18 Greentree Village Shopping Plaza (Greentree 3 Cinemas, Mountain Sports)
33 After the Grind
36 Main Post Office
39 Museum Club
43 USFS Ranger Station
44 Flagstaff Mall Twin Cinemas

Arizona Game and Fish (☎ 774 5045), 3500 S Lake Mary Rd, has hunting and fishing licenses, regulations and information. They are open 8 am to 5 pm Monday to Friday.

The library (☎ 774 4000, 779 7670) is at 300 W Aspen Ave. The local newspaper is the *Arizona Daily Sun*. The main post office (☎ 527 2440) is at 2400 Postal Blvd and the downtown branch (☎ 527 2440) is at 104 N Agassiz St. The hospital (☎ 779 3366) is at 1200 N Beaver St and has a 24-hour pharmacy. The police (☎ 774 1414, or 911 in emergencies) are at 120 N Beaver St.

Winter snowstorms can close roads in northern Arizona. Call 779 2711 for northern Arizona road conditions.

### Historic Downtown

Two blocks north and east from the visitors center, itself housed in the old Santa Fe Railway Depot built in 1926, you can see many late-19th- and early-20th-century buildings. The visitors center and the Pioneer Museum have a brochure describing almost 40 buildings.

### Museum of Northern Arizona

In an attractive stone building set in a pine grove, this small but thorough museum (☎ 774 5211), at 3001 N Fort Valley Rd, is Flagstaff's most important. Galleries feature exhibits on local Indian archaeology, history and customs (the Hopi kiva is especially worthwhile) as well as geology, biology and the arts. Call for information about changing exhibits.

Browse the gift and bookshop, and especially during summer, visit the exhibits, events and sales of Navajo, Hopi and Zuni art. To stretch your legs, try the short nature trail (which may be closed in winter). Museum hours are 9 am to 5 pm daily except New Year's Day, Thanksgiving and Christmas. Admission is $4, seniors pay $3, and students and children pay $2.

The museum sponsors a variety of workshops and tours, ranging from half-day to multi-day trips exploring the surrounding country. The trips are led by local biologists, anthropologists and other professionals. A sample tour: Photographing Anasazi ruins, led by a professional photographer and visiting several Four Corners area sites costs $340 for three days/two nights; the price includes instruction, transportation, lodging and some meals. For a full program of events and tours call the museum's education department (☎ 774 5213 ext 220).

### Lowell Observatory

Named after its founder, Percival Lowell, the observatory continues to be a working astronomical research center. Of the many important observations made here, the discovery of the planet Pluto in 1930 is one of the most famous. Eight telescopes are in use, including the historic 24-inch Clark refractor (which visitors can try out).

The visitors center (☎ 774 2096 for recorded information) has exhibits and activities and offers 75-minute guided tours two or more times a day. Hours vary but are typically 9 am to 5 pm in summer and noon to 5 pm in winter. Admission is $2.50 for adults or $1 for five- to 17-year-olds. Frequent night programs include lectures and star gazing through the magnificent telescopes, and are held year round except for January; call for hours. The observatory is at 1400 W Mars Hill Rd.

### Riordan State Historic Park

Brothers Michael and Timothy Riordan made a fortune from their Arizona Lumber Company in the late 1800s, and in 1904, built a 13,000-sq-foot mansion to house themselves and their two families. The park preserves this building with its original furnishings, which were of the then-fashionable and luxurious Craftsman style. The building is made of stone fronted by log slabs, giving it the false appearance of a palatial log cabin. The park is surrounded by NAU.

Stop by the visitors center to see exhibits and a slide program. Visitors are welcome to walk the grounds and picnic, but entrance to the house is by guided tour only. These are worthwhile but limited to

20 people and reservations (☎ 779 4395) are recommended. Park hours are 8 am to 5 pm from mid-May to mid-September and 12:30 to 5 pm the rest of the year; the park is closed Christmas Eve and Christmas Day. Tours leave hourly from 9 to 11 am and 2 to 4 pm in summer and from 1 to 4 pm the rest of the year. For a spooky tour, reserve space well in advance for an evening preceding Halloween. Admission is $3 or $2 for 12- to 17-year-olds. The park is at 1300 Riordan Ranch St.

## Arizona Historical Society – Pioneer Museum

Housed in the old 1908 county hospital, the Pioneer Museum (☎ 774 6272), 2340 N Fort Valley Rd, preserves Flagstaff's early history in photographs and memorabilia that ranges from vintage farm equipment to early medical instruments. Take a look at the old barn and root cellar on the premises, or participate in one of the various special events highlighting the area's past. Hours are 9 am to 5 pm Monday to Saturday; the museum is closed New Year's Day, Easter, Thanksgiving and Christmas. Admission is free but donations are welcomed.

## Coconino Center for the Arts

Located next to the Pioneer Museum, the Center for the Arts (☎ 779 6921), 2300 N Fort Valley Rd, exhibits works by local artists and presents a variety of performances and programs throughout the year. The center's scope is wide and, at times, whimsical, with exhibits and performances ranging from Celtic folk music and Native American storytellers to an artistic miniature golf course. There's always something going on. A gift shop features local fine art.

## Art Barn

Almost next to but not attached to the Center for the Arts, the Art Barn (☎ 774 0822), 2320 N Fort Valley Rd, has been displaying and selling local and Reservation artists' work for three decades. The selection is varied and good and you are welcome to simply browse the ever-changing exhibits. Hours are 9 am to 5 pm daily.

## Northern Arizona University

On the NAU campus, visit the three art galleries, two with changing local exhibits and one with a permanent collection, in the **Old Main Building** (☎ 523 3471), 10 Knowles Drive. Admission is free; call for hours.

The **NAU Astronomic Observatory** (☎ 523 7170), on San Francisco St just south of University Drive, has public viewing sessions on clear Fridays year round and on Thursdays in summer at 7:30 pm.

## The Arboretum

The Arboretum (☎ 774 1441), S Woody Mountain Rd, has 200 acres of grounds and greenhouses dedicated to horticultural research and display. At 7150 feet on the southwest side of Flagstaff, this is the highest research arboretum in the country. Locals come to discover what to grow in their back yards, and plant-loving visitors can learn about alpine flora. Hours are 10 am to 3 pm Monday to Friday and also on Saturday in summer, when plant displays are at their best. Guided tours are given at 11 am and 1 pm and admission is free. S Woody Mountain Rd is 2.5 miles west of the visitor center on Route 66; the arboretum is about four miles south.

## Activities

In addition to **hiking** on Humphrey's Peak and **skiing** (see Around Flagstaff), the mountains and forests around Flagstaff offer scores of hiking and **mountain biking** trails – far too many to describe here. A useful resource is *Flagstaff Hikes and Mountain Bike Rides* by Richard & Sherry Mangum (Flagstaff: Hexagon Press, 1992). The USFS ranger stations have maps and advice and bookshops have trail guides.

Sports stores that have maps, books, gear or rental equipment include Peace Surplus (☎ 779 4521), 14 W Route 66, Mountain Sports (☎ 779 5156, 1 (800) 286 5156), 1800 S Milton Rd, Absolute Bikes (☎ 779 5969), 18 N San Francisco St, and Cosmic Cycles Mountain Bike Rental (☎ 779 1092), 113 S San Francisco St. These are all good information sources.

ARIZONA

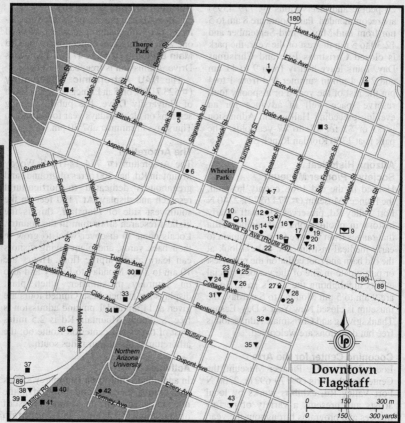

Downtown
Flagstaff

Flagstaff Mountain Guides (☎ 526 4655), PO Box 2383, 86003, offers guided nature hikes, and beginning to advanced **rock climbing**, winter climbing and back-country skiing trips.

Hitchin' Post Stables (☎ 774 1719, 774 7131), 4.5 miles down S Lake Mary Rd, has day-long **horseback riding** trips to Walnut Canyon and other destinations on request; Flying Hart Barn (☎ 526 2788), 8400 N Hwy 89, offers guided rides in the San Francisco Mountains. Both places offer horse-drawn sleigh rides in winter.

J Lively Rink (☎ 774 1051), 1850 N Turquoise Drive, has **ice skating** in winter

and **roller skating** in summer. Rentals and lessons are available. You can **golf** 18 holes at Elden Hills (☎ 527 7997), 2380 N Oakmont Drive.

### Organized Tours

The Gray Line subsidiary, Nava-Hopi Tours (☎ 774 5003, 1 (800) 892 8687, fax 774 7715), 114 W Route 66, has narrated bus tours of most of the nearby sites of interest, including the Grand Canyon, Indian reservations and several others. Tours last seven to 11½ hours and cost $34 to $74 depending on time and distance. Five- to 15-year-olds travel at half price, and motel pickup

ARIZONA

**PLACES TO STAY**
2   San Francisco St B&B
3   Inn at 410 B&B
4   Birch Tree Inn B&B
5   Dierker House B&B
8   Monte Vista Hotel
10  Townhouse Motel
13  Weatherford Hotel
25  Motel du Beau HI/AYH
27  Downtowner International Hostel
30  Family Inn
33  Highland Country Inn
34  Starlite Motel
37  Knights Inn Suites
39  Rodeway Inn
40  Embassy Suites
41  Comfort Inn, Arizonan Motel

**PLACES TO EAT**
1   Chez Marc Bistro
8   Monte Vista Coffeeshop
13  Charly's Restaurant & Pub
14  Alpine Pizza
16  Pasto
17  Kathy's
21  Lola J's, Cafe Express
23  Beaver Street Brewery
24  Cottage Place
26  Macy's, La Bellavia
28  Main St Bar & Grill
31  Ni-Marco's Pizza
35  Hassib's
38  Brix Grill & Wine Bar
39  Fiddlers
43  El Charro

**OTHER**
6   Library
7   Police
9   Downtown Post Office
11  Nava-Hopi Tours (bus)
12  Orpheum Theater
15  Peace Surplus
18  Flagstaff Brewing Company, Monsoon's
19  McGaugh's Newstand
20  Absolute Bikes
22  Visitors Center in Amtrak Station
29  The Depot
32  Cosmic Cycles
36  Greyhound Bus Depot
42  NAU Old Main Building

is included; national park admission and meals are extra. During the busy summer, the company also runs city trolley tours. Tours can be booked through travel agents.

Also see the Museum of Northern Arizona above for specialty tour possibilities.

**Special Events**

Flagstaff is busy throughout the summer with many ongoing events, often held simultaneously. The visitors center has details. Events include the Flagstaff Festival of the Arts, held from early July to mid-August and hosting plays, operas, concerts, films and other performances, many on the NAU campus. From late June to early August, in the Coconino Center for the Arts there is a Festival of Native American Arts with performances and art exhibits. The Museum of Northern Arizona hosts Indian arts exhibits throughout the summer with particular weekends highlighting the work of specific tribes, including the Zuni (in late May), the Hopi (usually the Fourth of July weekend) and Navajo (usually the last weekend of July and/or first weekend in August). The Festival in the Pines, held in early August, has great selections of arts & crafts and food booths, as well as strolling performers. A rodeo and an Indian powwow are held in June, and the Coconino County Fair is held over Labor Day. Things quiet down during the rest of the year. The Flagstaff Winter Festival over Presidents Day weekend is also a big highlight, with sled dog races, snowmen contests and winter survival workshops among other events.

**Places to Stay**

Flagstaff provides the best cheap and moderate lodging in this region, offering many motels and hotels as well as some youth hostels. There are no expensive destination resorts as in Sedona. Obviously, summer is the high season and hotel prices rise accordingly. In addition, weekends attract many of the two million sweltering inhabitants of the Valley of the Sun (2½ hours away by freeway) pushing room prices to a premium – a room costing $20 in April can be $50 or more on an August weekend. Avoid summer weekends if possible, or if you're up for dealing with the crowds, be sure to make reservations or arrive by early afternoon to have a reasonable hotel selection. At other times of year, you can easily get very cheap rooms. If you want to stay at a B&B, be aware that all the ones listed here are nonsmoking.

## Places to Stay – camping
Campgrounds can fill up in summer, so be sure to make reservations where possible. *Motel du Beau – International Hostel* (☎ 774 6731), 19 W Phoenix Ave, allows limited tent camping for $6 per person; the price includes free breakfast and hostel showers. *Fort Tuthill County Park* (☎ 774 3464), half a mile west of exit 337 on I-17 and three miles south of Flag, has 100 sites for $8, and 10 sites with hookups for $12. There are showers but facilities are basic. The campground is open from May to September; at other times you can make reservations at 774 5130 for a $5 reservation fee.

The Coconino National Forest operates the following campgrounds. Unless otherwise noted, all have drinking water but no showers or hookups, allow both tents and RVs, charge $7 and are open May to September. They may fill on summer weekends, so arrive early.

*Lake View*, about 16 miles along USFS Rd 3 by Lower Lake Mary offers 30 sites and has a boat ramp. *Pine Grove*, with 46 sites, is a few miles further and south of Lower Lake Mary, and charges an $8 fee. *Ashurst* has 23 sites and *Forked Pine* has 33 sites; both are on Ashurst Lake and have boat ramps. *Dairy Springs* with 27 sites and *Double Springs* with 16 sites are both on the west side of Mormon Lake near the Mormon Lake Lodge (see Cross-Country Skiing in the Around Flagstaff section) and are near a laundry. They are also near the *Lake Mary's Country Store & Trailer Park* (☎ 774 1742), with a grocery store and an RV park offering 40 sites with hookups for around $13 (this is often booked full months in ahead). Dairy Springs has three group sites (with a 20-person minimum and a $35 fee for the first night) that must be reserved by calling 1 (800) 280 2267). There are more campgrounds deeper into the Coconino National

Forest, and free dispersed camping is allowed off dirt forest roads.

The *Woody Mountain Campground* (☎ 774 7727), 2727 W Route 66, offers 149 sites, some with full hookups, for $14 to $19, as well as a pool, playground and coin laundry. It is open from April (sometimes earlier) to 1 November. Nearby, the *Kit Carson RV Park* (☎ 774 6993), 2101 W Route 66, has 200 RV sites amid ponderosa pines available year round, with full hookups costing $19 or less. *Black Bart's RV Lodge* (☎ 774 1912), 2760 Butler Ave (next door to the restaurant) provides hot showers and 175 sites with full hookups for $18; tenting costs $10.

*Flagstaff KOA* (☎ 526 9926), 5803 N Hwy 89, has 200 sites, most with full RV hookups, ranging in price from $16 to $22 depending on the season and facilities needed. Two Kamping Kabins are available for $28, and there is a playground, coin laundry and showers. The *Big Tree Campground* (☎ 526 2583), 6500 N Hwy 89, has 50 RV sites with hookups starting at $23 in the high season and tents for about $15, depending on the number of people at your site. A swap meet is held here Friday to Sunday during the summer. *Greer's* (☎ 526 4677), 7101 N Hwy 89, has 60 RV sites with full hookups for $15, but lacks showers; sites are available from April through October, and children and tents are not permitted. *J & H RV Park* (☎ 526 1829), 7901 N Hwy 89, has 55 RV sites with full hookups for $19.50, and does not allow tents; it's open April through October.

## Places to Stay – bottom end
There are plenty of cheap and basic motels along Route 66, especially along the three-mile stretch east of downtown and around the intersection with Butler Ave southwest of downtown. Route 66 parallels the railway and the cheap places don't have soundproof rooms. Almost anytime from September to May you can cruise along here and find 15 or 20 motels advertising rooms for under $20, and some as cheap as $14 a double. In summer, though, these

same cheap places double their rates, and raise them even more during a busy weekend. At these times you need to arrive in town by early afternoon to snag a cheapish basic room. I don't list all the most basic cheapies here – during summer they are over-priced and during the rest of the year you'll have no trouble in finding one. Check the room before you pay though – some are a lot worse than others.

Flagstaff is something of an international budget travelers' center – many of these travelers stay downtown in the interesting older hotels that double as youth hostels. These are all great places to meet travelers and get local travel information.

The *Weatherford Hotel* (☎ 774 2731), 23 N Leroux St, dates back to 1897 and was then northern Arizona's finest hotel. Now it functions mainly as an HI/AYH hostel with $10 dorm beds for members, and a slightly higher price for nonmembers; however, there are a few private rooms for $25 a double. Beds come with kitchen privileges, and the popular Charly's Restaurant & Pub is downstairs. The independent *Downtowner International Hostel* (☎ 774 8461), 19 S San Francisco St, charges $8 to $12 per person in various-size rooms (including some doubles), and offers pickup from the Greyhound station or airport. The *Motel du Beau – International Hostel* (☎ 774 6731), 19 W Phoenix Ave, dates from 1929 and charges $30 for double rooms or $11 for dorm beds; prices include a free breakfast as well as kitchen privileges, and a few bikes are available for guest use.

Several scenes of *Casablanca* were filmed at the 1927 *Monte Vista Hotel* (☎ 779 6971, 1 (800) 545 3068, fax 779 2904), 100 N San Francisco St, a popular place with many of the almost 50 rooms named after the film stars who slept in them. Rooms are comfortable and old-fashioned but far from luxurious. The cheapest, lacking a private bathroom, are priced in the $20s, rooms with a bathroom are around $50, and you'll pay a little more for one of the several suites. Check out the popular blues bar downstairs – I overdid it

there one night but only had to drive the elevator to get to my room.

There are four *Motel 6*s, all with pools and over 100 rooms each; summer doubles are in the upper $30s or low $40s. They are, in increasing order of cost, at 2440 E Lucky Lane (☎ 774 8756, fax 774 2067); 2500 E Lucky Lane (☎ 779 6184, fax 774 2249); 2010 E Butler Ave (☎ 774 1801, fax 774 1987); and 2745 S Woodlands Village Blvd (☎ 779 3757, fax 774 2137).

Of the many cheap motels, some of the better ones that start in the $30s or $40s for a double in summer ($20s or less during the rest of the year) include the following: the *Arizonan Motel* (☎ 774 7171), 910 S Milton Rd, the *Starlite Motel* (☎ 774 7301), 500 S Milton Rd, the *Family Inn* (☎ 774 8820), 121 S Milton Rd, the *Townhouse Motel* (☎ 774 5081), 122 E Route 66, the *Evergreen Inn* (☎ 774 7356), 1008 E Route 66, and the *Americana Motor Hotel* (☎ 526 2200), 2650 E Route 66.

Two above-average budget hotels with pools and summertime rates starting in the upper $40s are the *Budget Host Saga Motel* (☎ 779 3631), 820 W Route 66 and the *Highland Country Inn* (☎ 774 5041), 223 S Milton Rd.

## Places to Stay – middle

**Hotels** Many of the standard chain motels are priced in the middle range. The *Super 8 Motel* (☎ 526 0818, fax 526 8786), 3725 Kasper Drive, has doubles priced in the $50s. The *Flagstaff Inn* (☎ 774 1821, fax 774 7662), 2285 E Butler Ave, is similarly priced and has a pool, sauna and spa.

Of the many hotels with rooms with summertime rates in the $60s and $70s, one of the nicer places is the *Best Western Pony Soldier* (☎ 526 2388, 1 (800) 356 4143, fax 527 8329), 3030 E Route 66, with attractive rooms, indoor pool and spa, restaurant and lounge, and complimentary continental breakfast. Unfortunately, it is close to the railway, which may bother light sleepers. Away from the railway is the *Comfort Inn* (☎ 774 7326, fax 774 7328), 914 S Milton Rd, which also has pleasant rooms and free continental breakfast and a pool open in summer. *Knights Inn Suites* (☎ 774 4581, 1 (800) 654 4667,·602 W Route 66, has spacious rooms (they're not really suites) and a swimming pool.

Average motels with standard rooms in the $60 to $80 price range during summer include the *Best Western King's House Motel* (☎ 774 7186, fax 774 7189), 1560 E Route 66, which has a pool and free continental breakfast; *Days Inn Route 66* (☎ 774 5221, fax 774 4977), 1000 W Route 66, with a pool and a coffee shop; *Days Inn I-40* (☎ 779 1575, fax 779 0044), 2735 S Woodlands Village Blvd, with a spa; and the *Rodeway Inn* (☎ 774 5038), 913 S Milton Rd, with a pool and spa. There are three *Econo Lodges* at 2480 E Lucky Lane (☎ 774 7701, fax 774 7855), with a pool, spa, playground and continental breakfast; 3601 E Lockett Rd (☎ 527 1477, fax 527 0228), with a spa; and 2355 S Beulah Blvd (☎ 774 2225) with a spa and summer pool.

**B&Bs** Cheaper options near downtown include the *Dierker House B&B* (☎ 774 3249), 423 W Cherry Ave, 86001, a 1914 antique-filled Craftsman house with three rooms sharing a bath. Rates start at $45 and include complimentary afternoon tea and cookies or wine. The *Birch Tree Inn* (☎ 774 1042), 824 W Birch Ave, 86001, is a 1917 house with a wraparound veranda and a game room with billiards. Five bedrooms, three with private bath, range from $65 to $85, including afternoon tea and snacks. The *East Cherry Inn* (☎ 774 1153), 427 E Cherry Ave, 86001, has a two-bedroom suite that sleeps four, with a kitchen, bath, and deck for $95. The *San Francisco St B&B* (☎ 779 2257), 622 N San Francisco St, 86001, has rooms with and without bath for $60 to $80.

On the outskirts of town, *Piney Woods Lodge* (☎ 774 8859, 1 (800) 774 8859), 2800 W Hogan Drive, 86001, set in five acres of pine forest, offers rooms for $60. Five miles northeast of town (call for directions) *Starlit Farm B&B* (☎ 1 (800) 484 7389 code 5759), 8455 Koch Field Rd, 86004, has a hot tub and two large rooms available for $65 or $75. Children under 14

and alcohol are not allowed. The Christian *Arizona Mountain Inn* (☎ 774 8959), 685 Lake Mary Rd, 86001, offers three B&B rooms with private bath for $65. The 13 acres surrounding the inn have 15 cottages with bath, kitchen and fireplace or stove, ranging from one-bedroom A-frames to five-bedroom cabins. These run from $65 to $135. There are various outdoor activities.

### Places to Stay – top end
**Hotels** Of several hotels charging about $100 for a double in summer, the *Little America Motel* (☎ 779 2741, 1 (800) 352 4386, fax 779 7983), 2515 E Butler Ave, is one of the better ones. The spacious rooms have balconies, and there is a swimming pool and spa, as well as a 24-hour coffee shop, a good restaurant and lounge providing occasional entertainment and acres of lawns and pine trees.

Rather closer to downtown, the *Best Western Woodlands Plaza Hotel* (☎ 773 8888, 1 (800) 972 8886, fax 773 0597), 1175 W Route 66, is one of the best of the usually reliable Best Western chain. The ambiance is trans-Pacific, with a Japanese restaurant and Southwestern coffee shop, severely square chandeliers and tightly clipped plants in the lobby, and contemporary desert colors in the guest rooms. Facilities include a pool, spa, sauna, steamroom and exercise equipment. Large and attractive rooms are priced at $90 to $110 in summer and suites go for $130. Room service is available and the restaurants are both very good.

The recently refurbished *Quality Inn* (☎ 774 8771, fax 773 9382), 2000 S Milton Rd, is a comfortable choice, offering most of the large, modern Southwestern-style rooms for under $100 (prices drop to the $50s in the low season). The hotel has a pool and provides complimentary coffee and rolls for breakfast. A 24-hour restaurant is next door.

*Embassy Suites* (☎ 774 4333, 774 0216), 706 S Milton Rd, has units with two rooms (bedroom and living room) and a kitchenette with a small microwave, refrigerator, coffeemaker and wetbar for $120 a double;

prices include breakfast and an evening cocktail hour. Larger suites are available. A spa and a pool are open in the summer. Similar suite facilities are available at the *Residence Inn by Marriott* (☎ 526 5555, fax 527 0328), 3440 N Country Club Drive. Slightly cheaper mini-suites with bedrooms and living rooms separated by a half wall are available at *Ramada Limited Suites* (☎ 773 1111), 2755 Woodlands Village Blvd, and *Amerisuites* (☎ 774 8042, fax 774 5524), 2455 S Beulah Blvd.

**B&Bs** The most upscale B&B is the *Inn at 410* (☎ 774 0088, 1 (800) 774 2008), 410 N Leroux St, 86001, an elegant and fully renovated 1907 house with eight spacious rooms, each with private bath, coffeemaker and refrigerator, and some with a fireplace or whirlpool bath. This popular place raised its rates by 50% from 1994 to 1995, and rates are now $90 to $135 a double.

*Comfi Cottages* (☎ 774 0731), reservations at 1612 N Aztec, 86001, offers a new B&B concept with its fine cottages, each with a kitchen stocked with your choice of breakfast items – you make your own whenever you feel like it. All cottages are about half a mile from downtown, with four around Beaver and Columbus Sts and one at 710 W Birch Ave. Two cottages have fireplaces, four have washers and dryers, and all have yards or gardens with barbecue grills and bicycles available for use. Rents are $90 to $110 for the smaller cottages, $200 for the large one.

## Places to Eat

Tourists in summer, skiers in winter, and NAU students year round add impetus to both the eating and entertainment scenes in Flag. Diners should note that City Ordinance 1722 passed in 1993 prohibits smoking in all restaurant dining areas.

**Breakfast** For breakfasts (not to mention great coffees and light meals throughout the day), there are plenty of good choices in or near downtown. *Macy's* (☎ 774 2243), 14 S Beaver St, a long-time favorite coffee shop, also serves good pastries and light

meals. Students, outdoorsy types and coffee lovers crowd this place, which is open from 6 am to 8 pm daily and to 10 pm from Thursday to Saturday. Expect lines in the mornings – it's just a couple of blocks north of NAU. Neighboring *La Bellavia* (☎ 774 8301), 18 S Beaver St, is equally casual, has just as much caffeine in its espressos and cappuccinos (though there are often breakfast lines here as well), and also serves quiches, pancakes, sandwiches, etc. It is open from 6:30 am to 2:30 pm daily.

In the heart of downtown, *Cafe Express* (☎ 774 0541), 16 N San Francisco St, has something for almost everyone except dedicated carnivores, including various coffees, vegetarian and natural-food meals and salads, juices, beer and wine and pastries, which you can consume on the outdoor deck. It is open from 7 am to 10 pm, and closes at 11 pm on Friday and Saturday. Opposite, *Kathy's* (☎ 774 1951), 7 N San Francisco St, is a small friendly place with good solid breakfasts, open from 6:30 am to 3 pm. The *Monte Vista Coffee Shop* (☎ 774 8211), in the historic hotel at 104 N San Francisco St, is another good choice, open from 6:30 am to 6 pm.

*Brandy's* (☎ 779 2187), 1500 E Cedar Ave, an offshoot of the popular La Bellavia, is out of the way in the Cedar Hills Shopping Center north of town. Try the great pastries and desserts without the crowds, and view local artists' work on the walls. It is open from 6:30 am to 3 pm daily, closing at 9 pm from Thursday to Sunday.

In the *NAU Union* in the middle of campus you'll find students grabbing fast food and dining in the deli and the Italian and American restaurants. If these don't suit your taste, ask around about the other dining areas around campus.

**American** Near the south end of NAU, *Coco's* (☎ 774 8886), 350 W Forest Meadow Rd, is a wholesome family-style restaurant that draws in students with its $3 breakfast specials. Later on during the day, try the straightforward meat and fish dishes for low to moderate prices. Hours here are 6:30 am to 10 pm, or 11 pm on

Friday and Saturday. *Buster's* (☎ 774 5155), 1800 S Milton Rd (in the Greentree Village Shopping Plaza), has one of Flag's best fresh seafood selections, including an oyster bar, as well as steaks and prime rib. While most dinner entrees are in the teens, you can eat cheaper 'sunset dinners' between 6:30 and 8:30 pm, when it's less crowded. It is open from 11:30 am to 10 pm daily, and to 11 pm on Friday and Saturday.

*Fiddlers* (☎ 774 6689), 702 S Milton Rd, is another good all-around American restaurant with a varied dinner menu in the $10 to $18 range, offering some low-priced daily specials. Hours are from 11:30 am to 10 pm. The similarly priced *Western Gold Dining Room* (☎ 779 2741), in the Little America Hotel at 2515 E Butler Ave, has a buffet at lunchtime and one of the best American dinner menus in town. Hours are 11 am to 2 pm, Monday to Friday, 5 to 10 pm daily and 9 am to 2 pm for Sunday brunch.

*Kelly's Christmas Tree* (☎ 526 0776), 5200 E Cortland Blvd (in the Continental Shopping Plaza), has Christmas trees outside and an elegant turn-of-the-century holiday air inside – don't ask me why. Chicken 'n dumplings and homemade pastries are house specialties and the rest of the menu is nicely varied. Most dinner entrees cost $10 to $15, and hours are 11:30 am to 3 pm Monday to Saturday and 5 to 9 pm daily.

For big old-fashioned steaks and beans in rustic 'singing cowboy' surroundings, head over to *Black Bart's Steak House Saloon & Musical Revue* (☎ 779 3142), 2760 E Butler Ave, open 5 to 10 pm daily or to 11 pm on Friday and Saturday. For equally good steaks in a Western atmosphere without the singing hoopla, *Horseman Lodge Restaurant* (☎ 526 2655), 8500 N Hwy 89 (three miles north of town) is a fine choice and is locally popular.

*Brix Grill & Wine Bar* (☎ 779 5117), 801 S Milton Rd, definitely stretches the definition of American food – the restaurant calls it 'Traditional Southwestern-Tinged Fusion Cuisine', which should warn you

that this will be a dining adventure, but not an unpleasant one. The menu changes daily so that the food is always fresh and delicious and there is something for everybody among the interestingly prepared vegetarian, meat and seafood dinners. The service is among the friendliest of any restaurant I've eaten at, and most dinner entrees are a very reasonable $9 to $14. Hours are 11 am to 3 pm and 5 to 10 pm daily.

The following restaurants are open 24 hours a day. The *Little America Coffeeshop* (☎ 779 2741), 2515 E Butler Ave (in the top-end hotel of the same name) is perhaps the most upscale bet for food at 4 am. Other places to try for midnight munchies include *Mary's Cafe* (☎ 526 0008), 7135 N Hwy 89; *Denny's* at 2122 S Milton Rd (☎ 779 1371) and 2306 Lucky Lane (☎ 774 3413); *Perkins Family Restaurant* (☎ 773 1380), 1900 S Milton Rd; the *Crown Restaurant* (☎ 526 1826), in the Hojo Inn at 3300 E Route 66; and *Jack-in-the-Box* fast food (☎ 774 1723), 505 S Milton Rd.

**Mexican** The authenticity of Mexican food declines as you head north of the border – *Maya's Casita Mexican Food & Burger Shoppe* (☎ 526 0809), 4217 N Hwy 89, was recently voted Flagstaff's best burger place. Still, the Mexican food is tasty and cheap, and the place is open from 9 am to 9 pm daily.

Of the dozen or so other Mexican places, *Salsa Brava* (☎ 774 1083), 1800 S Milton Rd, with Guadalajaran rather than Sonoran food, is a good choice. Hours are 11 am to 9 pm, Monday to Thursday, to 11 pm on Friday, 8 am to 10 pm on Saturday and 8 am to 9 pm on Sunday. Another good choice, closer to Sonoran cuisine, is *Kachina Downtown* (☎ 779 1944), 522 E Route 66, open from 11 am to 9 pm. There is another branch at 2220 E Route 66 (☎ 556 0363), which has Mexican breakfasts as well, and is open from 7 am to 9 pm but closed Tuesday and Wednesday.

For cheaper Mexican food, *El Charro* (☎ 779 0552), 409 S San Francisco St, is open 11 am to 9 pm and may have mariachis playing on weekends. Tiny *Lola J's*

(☎ 773 9236), 10 N San Francisco St, serves cheap Mexican lunches from 10:30 am to 5 pm Tuesday to Friday and 8 am to 3 pm on Saturday.

**Italian** *Mamma Luisa* (☎ 526 6809), in the Kachina Square Shopping Center at 2710 E N Steves Blvd, is traditionally Flag's best Italian restaurant. Open for dinner only, from 5 to 10 pm, Mama Luisa serves a wide range of Italian food for $8 to $14 in an appropriate cozy, red-checked-tablecloth setting. *Pasto* (☎ 779 1937), 19 E Aspen St, has a courtyard and is vying with Mama Luisa for 'best Italian' honors. This popular little place is open from 11 am to 10 pm weekdays, 11 am to 11 pm on Friday and Saturday, and 5 to 10 pm on Sunday.

*Alpine Pizza* (☎ 779 4109), 7 N Leroux St, serves more than just pizza, has a pool table and is popular with young people. Hours are 11 am to 11 pm or to midnight on Friday and Saturday, and you can have food delivered. *Ni-Marco's Pizza* (☎ 779 2691), 101 S Beaver St, is open 11 am to 9 pm and is also popular with the student crowd. *Alpine Spaghetti Station* (☎ 779 4138), 2400 E Route 66, is a more family-oriented version of the downtown Alpine Pizza. It's open from 11 am to 10 pm Monday to Saturday and 4:30 to 10 pm on Sunday, and they also deliver.

**Asian** The recommended *Sakura* (☎ 773 9118), in the Woodlands Plaza Hotel at 1175 W Route 66, has fresh seafood served either as sushi or grilled right in front of you. Steak and other food is also available and most entrees are in the teens. Hours are 11:30 am to 2 pm and 5 to 10 pm. At the other end of both price range and the Asian continent is *Hassib's* (☎ 774 1037), 211 S San Francisco St, which serves inexpensive Lebanese and Middle Eastern food from 11 am to 7:30 pm. In between in price, *Dara Thai* (☎ 774 8390, 774 0047), 1580 E Route 66, serves very good Thai food at reasonable prices, and is open from 11 am to 10 pm Monday to Saturday and 4 to 10 pm on Sunday.

For an inexpensive curry or other Indian food, try the *Delhi Palace* (☎ 556 0019), 2700 S Woodlands Village Blvd, offering inexpensive all-you-can-eat lunch buffets as well as better food at dinnertime. Hours are 11:30 am to 2:30 pm and 5 to 10 pm. There are also several Chinese restaurants that are generally satisfactory, if unremarkable.

**European** No roundup of Flag's restaurants is complete without the *Chez Marc Bistro* (☎ 774 1343), 503 N Humphreys St, and the *Cottage Place* (☎ 774 8431), 126 W Cottage Ave, universally considered Flagstaff's finest (though the Brix Grill & Wine Bar is becoming a contender).

Both places offer intimate dining. Chez Marc is classic French, complete with a French-born chef and a romantic country-French atmosphere in a lace-curtained 1911 house. Dinner entrees are mainly in the high teens and there is a reasonable list of French wines. There is a patio open in summer, and hours are 11:30 am to 3 pm and 5:30 to 9:30 pm. The Cottage Place has a similar ambiance with its several small and pretty rooms in an early 20th-century house, but it has a more varied continental menu with entrees ranging in price from the low teens to the low $20s. The inviting, delicious appetizers pose a minor dilemma in that the entrees already include both soup and salad; it's best to come hungry. Hours are 5 to 9:30 pm, and the restaurant is closed on Monday.

**Pub Grub** Several bars near NAU serve decent food at reasonable prices, are popular with students (and professors) and often have entertainment later on, when food service can deteriorate. *Main Street Bar & Grill* (☎ 774 1519), 14 S San Francisco St, serves burgers, pastas, sandwiches, soups, salads and more from 11 am onwards. The recently opened *Beaver Street Brewery* (☎ 779 0079), 11 S Beaver St, is very popular for its microbrewery (five handmade ales are usually on tap) and well-prepared gourmet pizzas as well as other food. It opens at 11:30 am and has a beer garden in the summer. *Charly's* (☎ 779 1919), 23 N Leroux St, on the ground floor of the historic Weatherford Hotel, offers soups, salads and sandwiches for $4 to $7 as well as a small selection of steak, chicken and pasta dinners in the $10 to $14 range. You can listen to live music in an adjoining room. Hours are 11 am to 3 pm and 5:30 to 10 pm, Monday to Saturday, and 9 am to 3 pm on Sunday.

### Entertainment

For a relatively small town, Flagstaff has plenty going on. During the summer there are many cultural performances (see Special Events) and skiers, students and passers-through seem to fuel a lively nightlife year round. Read the Sundial (the Friday entertainment supplement to Flag's *Arizona Daily Sun*) and the free monthly *The Guide* to find out what's happening.

You can catch a movie at *Flagstaff Mall Twin Cinemas* (☎ 526 4555), 4650 N Hwy 89; *Flag-East* (☎ 774 6992), 2009 N 4th St; *Greentree 3* (☎ 779 3202), 1800 S Milton Rd; *Orpheum* (☎ 774 7823), 15 E Aspen Ave; or the *University Plaza 3* (☎ 774 4433), 1300 S Plaza Way.

Flagstaff has plenty of bars, especially downtown, where you can relax to live music (usually for a $3 to $5 cover on weekends but often for free during the week). Wander around a few blocks and make your choice. *Charly's* and *Main St Bar & Grill* (see Places to Eat) have varied live music, ranging from bluegrass to blues, folk to fusion. The *Monte Vista Lounge* (☎ 774 2403), in the Monte Vista Hotel at 100 N San Francisco St, has good blues. The *Beaver Street Brewery* has occasional acts and the *Flagstaff Brewing Co* (☎ 773 1442) 16 E Route 66, also has handmade beers and attracts a hairier crowd. Next door, *Monsoon's* (☎ 774 7929), 22 E Hwy 86, has rock & roll performances, as does *After the Grind* (☎ 779 1790), 2229 E Spruce Ave. *The Depot* (☎ 773 9550), 26 S San Francisco St, is a new dance club.

More sedate live music can be heard on weekends at the *Little America Lounge* (☎ 779 2741), 2515 E Butler Ave. For a livelier time, try the far-from-sedate

Navajo silverwork fills shops in towns along the reservation border.

country & western music, both live and recorded, at the *Museum Club* (☎ 526 9434), 3404 E Route 66. This popular barn-like place dates from the 1920s and '30s, and used to house a taxidermy museum, which may account for its local nickname, 'The Zoo'. In the 1960s and '70s, big name acts played here, but now mainly local bands perform. For pure spectacle, The Zoo, with its open and friendly cowboy spirit and spacious dance floor (which the locals unsuccessfully try to hide with their huge Stetsons) is not to be missed. Check out the entrance, which is made from a single, forked trunk of a large ponderosa pine.

*Uptown Billiards* (☎ 773 0551), 1300 S Milton Rd, has plenty of pool tables and a good beer selection in a nonsmoking environment.

### Things to Buy

For books about the Southwest and newspapers and magazines from all over, stop by McGaugh's Newstand, 24 N San Francisco St, open from 7:30 am to 9 pm Monday to Saturday and 8 am to 6 pm on Sundays. See Activities for stores that sell and rent outdoor equipment.

There are several galleries and crafts stores in the downtown area. Serious shoppers should stop by the Art Barn, Coconino Center for the Arts and the Museum of Northern Arizona to examine a selection of reliable arts & crafts, and then comparison shop downtown.

## Getting There & Away

**Air** America West Express (☎ 1 (800) 235 9292) has several flights a day to and from Phoenix. Sky Harbor airport is five miles south of town on 24th St.

**Bus** Greyhound (☎ 774 4573, 1 (800) 231 2222), 399 S Malpais Lane, sends buses between Flagstaff and Albuquerque, New Mexico (stopping in towns along I-40) four times a day; to Las Vegas, Nevada (via Kingman and Bullhead City) every evening; to Los Angeles, California (via Kingman) twice a day; and to Phoenix five times a day.

Nava-Hopi Tours (☎ 774 5003, 1 (800) 892 8687), 114 W Route 66, has buses at 8 and 10:15 am and 3:45 pm to the Grand Canyon for $12.50 one-way, plus a $4 national park entrance fee. There are three return trips each day, and less frequent services may be offered in winter. Nava-Hopi also has buses to Phoenix stopping at Phoenix Airport.

There are no buses north to Page and Utah (unless you take the Greyhound via Las Vegas); however, the Downtowner International Hostel runs a shuttle to the hostel in Page for $15 per person.

**Train** Amtrak (☎ 774 8679, 1 (800) 872 7245), 1 E Hwy 66, operates daily with its *Southwest Chief* service between Chicago, Illinois, and Los Angeles, California. Trains depart in the evening for Los Angeles (via Kingman) and in the morning for Chicago (via Winslow, Gallup and Albuquerque).

## Getting Around

**Bus** Pine Country Transit (☎ 779 6624, 779 6635 between 8 am and 5 pm Monday to Friday) has four local routes running Monday to Friday between about 6 am and 6 pm. There is limited service on Saturday and no service on Sundays and major holidays. The visitors center has schedules, and all four routes stop at the bus stop on Beaver St between Aspen and Birch Aves, a couple of blocks north of the visitors center.

**Car Rental** Flagstaff has offices of the following car rental agencies:

| | |
|---|---|
| AAA Discount Agency | ☎ 774 7394 |
| | ☎ 526 4239, |
| | 1 (800) 321 1972 |
| Avis | ☎ 774 8421, |
| | 1 (800) 831 2847 |
| Budget | ☎ 779 0306, |
| | 1 (800) 527 0700 |
| Enterprise | ☎ 779 0494, |
| | 1 (800) 325 8007 |
| Hertz | ☎ 774 4452, |
| | 1 (800) 654 3131 |
| National | ☎ 779 1975, |
| | 1 (800) 227 7368 |
| Sears | ☎ 774 1879, |
| | 1 (800) 527 0770 |
| Ugly Duckling | ☎ 774 1931, |
| | 1 (800) 843 3825 |

**Taxi** In town, taxi service is provided by A Friendly Cab (☎ 774 4444), Alpine Taxi (☎ 526 4123) and Arizona Taxi & Tours (☎ 779 1111).

## AROUND FLAGSTAFF

The places described here are within an hour's drive of Flagstaff. Also see Sedona for the Oak Creek Canyon, and the chapters on the Grand Canyon and Northeastern Arizona for longer day trips if your time is limited.

### Sunset Crater National Monument

Combine your trip to Sunset Crater with a side trip to neighboring Wupatki National Monument for an excellent day-long excursion from Flagstaff covering about 80 miles roundtrip. Sunset Crater is reached by taking Hwy 89 north about 12 miles and then heading east on paved Hwy 545 (also known as the Sunset Crater/Wupatki Loop Rd). This leads through the monument and continues to and through Wupatki National Monument, rejoining Hwy 89 about 35 miles beyond.

Sunset Crater (elevation 8029 feet) was formed in 1064-65 AD by volcanic eruptions that covered large areas with lava and much larger areas still with ash. The devastation must have greatly frightened the

Wupatki National Monument – Wukoki ruin  (RR)

local people, who moved away after the main eruptions, returning a few decades later to find the soil had been made more fertile by the volcanic ash. Minor eruptions continued for over 200 years but no activity is predicted for the near future. Today, the Loop Rd goes through the Bonito Lava Flow and skirts the Kana-a Lava Flow. Overlooks and a mile-long interpretive trail allow visitors to get a good look at volcanic features, although walking on the unstable cinders of the crater itself is not allowed.

Almost two miles from Hwy 89 along the Loop Rd (before you reach the monument proper) unpaved and rough USFS Rd 545A climbs steeply for five miles north to 8916-foot-high O'Leary Peak. You can make it most of the way in good weather in a car if you drive carefully, though high clearance is good to have. From near the top of this road, check out the views to the south and east down onto the lava flows and Sunset Crater. Back on the Loop Rd, you'll find a Coconino National Forest campground shortly after the USFS Rd 545A turnoff. The monument entrance is less

than a mile beyond, and the visitors center is just past the entrance.

**Information** The visitors center (☎ 556 7042) houses a seismograph and other exhibits pertaining to volcanology and the region. Rangers give interpretive programs in summer, when the center is open from 8 am to 5 pm. A $4 fee per vehicle, or a $2 individual fee gets you into both the Sunset Crater National Monument and the Wupatki National Monument (see below), which manages Sunset Crater. A mile beyond the center is the Lava Flow Nature Trail, where you can pick up an interpretive trail brochure on your way to take the one-mile hike across a lava field.

No food or accommodations are available in the monument, but just west of the monument, the *Coconino National Forest Bonito Campground* has 44 sites for RVs and tents. The $8 sites have drinking water but no showers or hookups, and are available from April through September. Sites fill up on summer weekends, so come early.

## Wupatki National Monument

This monument is off Hwy 89 about 30 miles north of Flagstaff, or can be reached by continuing along the Loop Rd from Sunset Crater. Wupatki has many Anasazi and Sinagua Indian pueblos that are different from most others in the area in that they are free-standing rather than built into a cliff or cave. The pueblos have a distinct southern influence, indicating strong trading links with people from what is now southern Arizona and Mexico.

The pueblos seen today date mainly from the 1100s and early 1200s, although the area was inhabited from the 7th century. By about 1225, in common with other Southwestern settlements, the people abandoned the area for reasons not yet understood. Today's Hopi Indians are descended from the ancient inhabitants of Wupatki; the Hopi call their ancestors the Hisatsinom. Of the hundreds of sites in the park, five pueblos are easily visited, and a sixth requires an overnight backpacking trip. The names of the pueblos are in the Hopi language.

**Information** The narrow Loop Rd passes the visitors center and continues on past pullouts or short side roads that lead to the pueblos. Other pullouts along Loop Rd offer scenic views.

At the visitors center (☎ 556 7040), about 15 miles beyond Sunset Crater, there is a museum with exhibits interpreting the lives of the area's ancient inhabitants as well as other exhibits of local interest, including a history of Navajo settlement in the area. The center's shop sells books and gifts, but no food. During the summer, rangers give talks and may lead walks into the ruins. Hours are 8 am to 5 pm (to 6 pm in summer) and the center is closed on Christmas Day. Further information is available from the superintendent (☎ 556 7152), 2717 N Steves Blvd, Suite 3, Flagstaff, 86004. (This office also supervises the Sunset Crater and Walnut Canyon national monuments).

There are no overnight facilities in the monument and the fee ($4 per car or $2 per individuals on bikes or buses) paid at Sunset Crater National Monument permits you to visit Wupatki as well. Golden Age, Access and Eagle Passes are honored.

**The Pueblos** The largest of the pueblos, **Wupatki Pueblo** (tall house) is reached by a very short trail from the visitors center. Interpretive trail brochures are available for self-guided tours – the ball court found here is an example of the influence of more southerly cultures. From the Loop Rd just before reaching the visitors center, a 2.5-mile side road leads to **Wukoki Ruin** (meaning 'wide house').

About nine miles beyond the visitors center (five miles from Hwy 89) there is a pullout with a short trail to **Citadel Ruin**, which stands on top of a small hill, and the smaller nearby **Nalahiku Ruin** (meaning 'house outside the village'). Shortly after this pullout is a short road to the appropriately named **Lomaki Pueblo** (pretty house). This well-preserved ruin is reached by a quarter-mile trail that passes other smaller ruins as it winds through Box Canyon. There are views of the San Francisco Mountains in the background.

**Crack-in-the-Rock Ruin** can be visited only on a ranger-led, 16-mile roundtrip, weekend backpacking tour; the trails pass petroglyphs and other ruins en route. Trips are offered during weekends in April and October and cost $25, and you must supply all equipment, food and water. Each trip is limited to 25 participants and these are chosen by a lottery system – you need to apply two months in advance to be included in the lottery. For further information about this trip, call the visitors center or write to Wupatki National Monument, Attention CIR Reservations, HC33, PO Box 444A, Flagstaff, 89004.

## Schultz Pass Rd

This unpaved USFS road skirts the south flanks of the San Francisco Mountains and provides a longer but more scenic alternative to Hwy 89 during the summer. The road leaves Flagstaff from N Fort Valley Rd shortly past the Museum of Northern Arizona. Take Elden Lookout Rd to your

### Grand Falls of the Little Colorado

The Grand Falls give an insight into Southwestern hydrography. The Little Colorado River is a minor tributary of the Colorado, and like many Arizonan rivers, it is nearly dry for much of the year. During spring runoff, however, the river swells and the Grand Falls come into being. The 185-foot drop is impressive, with muddy brown spray giving the falls their local nickname of 'Chocolate Falls'. The best time for viewing is March and April, although earlier in the year can be good if there has been enough winter precipitation. Occasional summer storms will also fill the falls.

The falls are on the Navajo Reservation. Drive 14 miles east of Flagstaff along I-40 to the Winona exit, then backtrack northwest about two miles to the Leupp Rd. Head northeast on Leupp Rd for 13 miles to the signed turn for Grand Falls. An unpaved road, passable for cars, leads 10 miles to the river and a quarter-mile trail goes to a falls overlook. At this time the Navajo tribe allows free access to the falls, where there are basic picnic facilities. ■

right, and in less than a mile you'll see the Schultz Pass Rd (also called USFS Rd 420). Although unpaved, the road is passable to cars in the summer.

A drive down Schultz Pass Rd gives views of the San Francisco Mountains and access to the Kachina Peaks Wilderness Area, so named because of the religious significance of the mountains to the Hopi people. The road emerges at Hwy 89 about a mile south of the turn for the Sunset Crater/Wupatki Loop Rd.

### Humphrey's Peak

Arizona's highest mountain, the 12,663-foot Humphrey's Peak in the San Francisco Mountains, is a fairly straightforward though strenuous hike in summer and a snowy ascent for experienced outdoorspeople in winter. To get there in summer, drive up to the Arizona Snowbowl (see Downhill Skiing) and continue to the last parking lot near the Agassiz chair lift at 9500 feet. From the lift, a sign points the way. Note that this trail may be closed by the USFS. An alternative start is a signed trail that leaves from the lower parking lot. The trails join in less than a mile.

The trail starts through forest, and eventually comes out above timberline where it is windy and cold, so hike prepared. The last mile of the trail is over crumbly and loose volcanic rock, so you'll need decent boots. The alpine tundra is very delicate, so it is essential that you stay on the trails;

no camping or fires are allowed here. The elevation, steepness and loose footing make for a breathless ascent, but the views make the work worthwhile. The total distance is 4.5 miles one way; allow six to eight hours roundtrip if you are in average shape.

### Walnut Canyon National Monument

The Sinagua ruins at Walnut Canyon are not as immediately impressive as those at other nearby sites, but their spectacular setting makes this a worthwhile visit. The ruins are set in shallow caves in the near-vertical walls of a small limestone butte set like an island in the middle of the heavily pine-forested canyon.

The mile-long **Island Trail** steeply descends 185 feet (there are over 200 stairs) and then encircles the 'island', passing 25 cliff-dwelling rooms; many more can be seen in the distance. Before setting out on the Island Trail, consider that the 7000-foot elevation and the 185-foot steep climb out at the end of the trail could prove taxing for those with heart or other health problems.

A shorter, wheelchair-accessible **Rim Trail** affords views of the ruins from a distance.

A visitors center (☎ 526 3367) is near the beginning of both trails and has a museum, bookshop and overlook. Rangers give talks during the summer; the museum is open from 8 am to 5 pm daily and from 7 am to

6 pm in summer; it's closed on Christmas. The Island Trail closes one hour before the visitors center. Admission is $4 per vehicle or $2 for bus passengers and bicyclists, and Golden Age, Access and Eagle passes are honored. You can eat at the picnic area, but no food or overnight facilities are available.

To get to the monument, drive seven miles east of Flagstaff on I-40, take exit 204, then continue south for three miles. The monument is administered by the Wupatki superintendent.

## Meteor Crater

This crater was once thought to be the remains of an ancient volcano, but scientists now agree that it was caused by a huge meteor crashing into our planet almost 50,000 years ago. The resulting crater, 570 feet deep and almost a mile across, was formed in the seconds after impact – it must have been one heck of a crash!

The cratered site was used as a training ground for some of the Apollo astronauts. Visit the on-site museum to see exhibits about meteors and space missions and to browse in the gift shop. Although you can't descend into the crater, you can walk the 3.5-mile Rim Trail.

The whole area is privately owned and operated, and is open from 6 am to 6 pm mid-May to mid-September, and from 8 am to 5 pm the rest of the year. Admission is $7, $6 for seniors, $4 for students with ID, $2 for 13- to 17-year-olds and $1 for six- to 12-year-olds. The crater is five miles south of exit 233 on I-40. For more information call the Meteor Crater site (☎ 289 2362) or the Flagstaff office (☎ 774 8350).

A coffee shop and picnic area are on the premises, and the *Meteor Crater RV Park* (☎ 289 4002) has 72 RV sites with hookups and showers, a coin laundry and a playground for $15.50 (tents are not permitted).

## Lakes Southeast of Flagstaff

The Mormon Lake Ranger Station (see Information under Flagstaff) is the place to stop for information about the lakes and forests southeast of Flagstaff. Lakes are stretched out along paved S Lake Mary Rd (also called USFS Rd 3), beginning with **Upper Lake Mary**, eight miles southeast of Flagstaff, and continuing with **Lower Lake Mary** and **Mormon Lakes** about 25 miles away. Paved USFS Rd 82E leaves USFS Rd 3 between Lower Lake Mary and Mormon Lake and heads east four miles to Ashurst Lake. Other lakes can be reached by dirt roads.

The lakes vary greatly in size depending on local rainfall and water use (the Mary Lakes are formed by a dam on Walnut Creek). Upper Lake Mary usually has the most water and water-skiing is possible here. Fishing and boating are seasonal activities on the other lakes; call the ranger for current conditions.

Paved USFS Rd 3 continues south past Mormon Lake to the tiny community of Happy Jack (about 15 miles away), where the Long Valley Ranger Station (☎ 354 2216), HC 31, PO Box 68, Happy Jack, 86024, provides information about the southern part of the Coconino National Forest. About 20 miles further, USFS Rd 3 reaches Hwy 87, which goes to Payson.

## Skiing

**Downhill** Skiing at the Arizona Snowbowl (☎ 779 1951) is not world class, but it's pretty good, has been here over half a century and is popular with Arizonans. The elevation goes from 9200 to 11,500 feet, but only one chair lift makes this ascent and this run for experienced skiers only. Three much shorter lifts offer intermediate and beginner skiing, and there are over 30 runs and two day lodges. The first is Hart Prairie, which offers lessons, ski rental and food. A quarter mile beyond is the Agassiz Lodge, catering to experienced skiers only; no lessons or rentals are available, but food is. The season begins sometime in December and ends sometime in April, depending on snow conditions.

All-day (9 am to 4 pm) lift passes cost $30, or $16 for eight- to 12-year-olds and $10 for people over 65. Half-day (noon to 4 pm) passes are $18 on weekdays, $23 on weekends, or $11 for kids. Call about

The possibilities for cross-country skiing are many in national forests around Flagstaff. (BW)

special offers; recently you could buy two adult day passes for the price of one every Tuesday. The ski school has options ranging from beginners' two-hour group lessons, ski rental and an all-day pass for $46, to three-hour private lessons costing $80/110/140 for one/two/three people. Snowboard rental with a two-hour lesson and an all-day pass is $60. Children's lessons are also offered.

During the summer, the longest lift (climbing to 11,500 feet) runs for sightseeing from 10 am to 4 pm. The trip takes almost half an hour, provides fine views and costs $9 for adults, $5 for seniors and kids ages six to 12. Kids under six are free.

To get to the Arizona Snowbowl, drive about seven miles northwest of Flagstaff along N Fort Valley Rd (Hwy 180), then another seven miles north on Snowbowl Rd. Sometimes the road from Hwy 180 to the Snowbowl requires chains or 4WD, but ski buses will pick you up from the Hwy 180 turnoff for $4 roundtrip, though a fare

increase is planned. The nearest accommodations are at this turnoff.

**Cross-Country** The Flagstaff Nordic Center (☎ 774 6216), about 15 miles northwest of Flagstaff on Hwy 180, offers nearly 30 miles of groomed trails, skiing lessons, rentals and food. Trail passes cost about $8, and a little less for kids. If you continue past the Nordic Center, you'll find plenty of USFS cross-country skiing pullouts along Hwy 180, where you can park and ski for free (no facilities or rentals are provided). The season varies depending on snowfall, but generally is not very long. Call the USFS to check conditions before you go.

To get to Mormon Lake Ski Center (☎ 354 2240), head southeast of Flagstaff for 20 miles along S Lake Mary Rd and then take USFS Rd 90 for another eight miles to the center. A day pass for the almost 20 miles of groomed trails costs $5, and the center offers both ski rentals and lessons, as well as snowmobile rentals. The small Mormon Lake Lodge (☎ 774 0462, 354 2227) has a restaurant and a few rooms. During the summer, the lodge has cookouts, cowboy dinner theater and horseback rides.

## WILLIAMS

Both the town and the mountain overlooking it were named after mountain man Bill Williams, who passed through the area several times before his death in 1849. The first White settlers arrived in 1874, and Williams soon developed a reputation as a lawless town, having been ravaged by disastrous fires several times. In 1901, when a railway to the Grand Canyon opened, Williams proclaimed itself 'the Gateway to the Grand Canyon' and began developing the tourist industry, which is now the mainstay of the town's economy.

Eventually, roads became a cheaper way to visit the park, and the railway closed in 1969, only to return in 1989 as a popular historic steam train. Williams, 30 miles west of Flagstaff and 60 miles south of the Grand Canyon by good road, is the nearest town to the canyon with inexpensive lodging. The elevation is a cool 6770 feet.

### Orientation & Information

The Business Loop of I-40 between exit 165 and exit 161 goes through downtown on Railroad Ave (westbound) and the parallel Bill Williams Ave (eastbound), the old Route 66.

The visitors center (☎ 635 4061, fax 635 1417), 200 W Railroad Ave, is open from 8 am to 6 pm daily; pick up a walking tour brochure here if the turn-of-the-century buildings downtown spark your interest. The Kaibab National Forest has two ranger stations – Chalender (☎ 635 2676), 501 W Bill Williams Ave, and Williams (☎ 635 2633), behind the Best Western hotel west of town. The supervisor's office (☎ 635 8200) is at 800 S 6th St. The library (☎ 635 2263) is at 113 S 1st St. The post office (☎ 635 4572) is at 114 S 1st St. The police (☎ 635 4461, or 911 in emergencies) are at 113 S 1st St.

### Grand Canyon Deer Farm

This deer farm (☎ 635 4073, 1 (800) 926 3337), near I-40 exit 171 eight miles east of town, is a petting and feeding zoo with several deer species, llamas, peacocks and other animals. Fawning season (May to July) is a nice time to go with kids. Hours are 8 am to dusk, June through August; 9 am to dusk, March through May and September and October; and (weather permitting) 10 am to 5 pm, November through February. It is closed on Thanksgiving and Christmas. Admission is $4.75 or $3.50 for seniors and $2.50 for three- to 13-year-olds.

### Grand Canyon Railway

This restored steam railway takes 2¼ hours to reach the Grand Canyon. En route, characters in period costume offer historical and regional narration, while others stroll around playing a banjo and answering questions. Often, the train is held up by train robbers, but the sheriff usually takes care of them.

Roundtrips allow about 3½ hours at the canyon. Trains leave at 9:30 am daily from 15 March through October and on winter weekends, but schedules are expanding. A small museum, gift shop, breakfast area and cowboy performances at the Williams Train Depot (just north of the visitors center) make it worth getting there early. The train returns to Williams at 5:30 pm.

The fare was $3.95 when the railway opened in 1901. Today, most passengers travel coach class ($49 roundtrip, $19 for two- to 16-year-olds) with snacks and drinks available. Club Class (more room plus a bar) is $12 extra, and 1st class is $40 extra and allows access to the open-air back platform. National park admission is $4 extra. It's a short walk from the Grand Canyon train depot to the rim, but narrated bus tours of various lengths are also offered as are overnight packages with accommodations at either Williams or the Grand Canyon. Contact the railway (☎ 635 4000, 1 (800) 843 8724, fax 773 1610) for more information or reservations.

ARIZONA

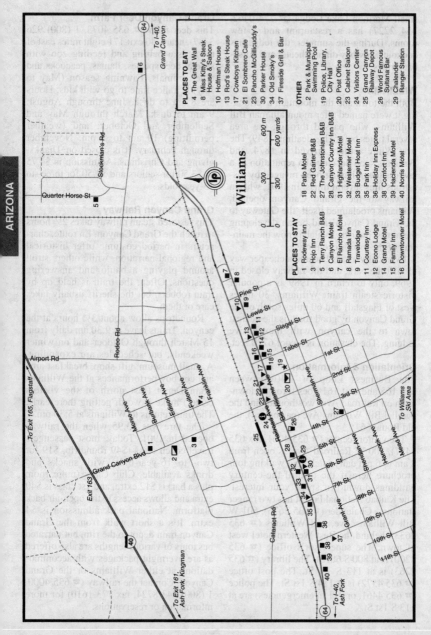

Williams

To I-40,
Grand Canyon

Stockman's Rd

Quarter Horse St

To Exit 165, Flagstaff

Airport Rd

Rodeo Rd

To Exit 163

Grand Canyon Blvd

To Exit 161
Ash Fork, Kingman

To I-40,
Ash Fork

To Williams
Ski Area

Pine St
Lewis St
Slagel St
Taber St
1st St
2nd St
3rd St
4th St
5th St
6th St
7th St
8th St
9th St
10th St
11th St

Morse Ave
Burbank Ave
Edison Ave
Fullton Ave
Franklin Ave
Railroad Ave
Bill Williams Ave
Sherman Ave
Sheridan Ave
Hancock Ave
Mesa Ave
Grant Ave
Cottaract Ave

0    300    600 m
0    300    600 yards

**PLACES TO EAT**

4　The Great Wall
8　Miss Kitty's Steak
　　House & Saloon
10　Hoffman House
13　Rod's Steak House
17　Cowboys Kitchen
21　El Sombrero Cafe
23　Pancho McGillicuddy's
30　Parker House
34　Old Smoky's
37　Fireside Grill & Bar

**OTHER**

2　Park & Municipal
　　Swimming Pool
19　Police, Library,
　　City Hall
20　Post Office
23　Cabinet Saloon
24　Visitors Center
25　Grand Canyon
　　Railway Depot
26　World Famous
　　Sultana Bar
29　Chalender
　　Ranger Station

**PLACES TO STAY**

1　Rodeway Inn
3　Hojo Inn
5　Terry Ranch B&B
6　Canyon Motel
7　El Rancho Motel
8　Ramada Inn
9　Travelodge
11　Courtesy Inn
12　Econo Lodge
14　Grand Motel
15　Family Inn
16　Downtowner Motel
18　Patio Motel
22　Red Garter B&B
27　The Johnstonian B&B
28　Canyon Country Inn B&B
31　Highlander Motel
32　Westerner Motel
33　Budget Host Inn
35　Park Inn
36　Holiday Inn Express
38　Comfort Inn
39　Hacienda Motel
40　Norris Motel

## Skiing

Williams Ski Area (☎ 635 9330), four miles south of town along 4th St, has a poma lift that climbs from 7500 to 8150 feet and serves three runs for beginner, intermediate and advanced skiers, as well as a few side trails. A short rope tow pulls beginners up the easiest slope. The lodge serves food and has a ski school and a downhill and cross-country ski and snowboard rental shop. The area is open from about mid-December until early April from 9:30 am to 4:30 pm daily except Wednesday and Christmas. Full-day lift tickets are $20 on weekends and $15 midweek. Those over 60 pay $15, and people 12 and under pay $12. For beginners using the rope tow only, prices are 25% less.

Try cross-country skiing in the Kaibab National Forest. Maintained trails are found at Spring Valley, six miles north of the Parks exit 178 on I-40 via USFS Rd 141. Stop by the forest ranger stations for information about undeveloped cross-country skiing areas, as well as snowshoeing, inner-tubing and sledding.

## Other Activities

Play **golf** at the Elephant Rocks Golf Course (☎ 635 4936), a mile west of town near I-40 exit 161, with nine holes, or play **tennis** on the courts on S 10th St. Go **swimming** at the municipal pool on Grand Canyon Blvd. Ask at the forest ranger station or visitors center about **hiking** and see the following descriptions of camping areas under Places to Stay for **fishing** possibilities.

## Special Events

Bill Williams Rendezvous Days over Memorial Day weekend features 'mountain man' events, such as shooting demonstrations using powder muskets, as well as stage entertainment, a carnival, arts & crafts stalls, balloon rides, a parade and more. Apart from the usual fireworks display, the Fourth of July is celebrated with a carnival and barbecue. The first weekend in August the town celebrates the Cowpuncher's Reunion &

Old-Time Rodeo, and another rodeo is scheduled over Labor Day weekend.

## Places to Stay

Rates from mid-May to mid-September can be over twice those charged in winter. Reservations are advised in summer unless you arrive by early afternoon; Reservations of the West (☎ 635 5351, 1 (800) 943 3310, fax 635 5334) is a free reservation service for lodging and excursions out of Williams and the Four Corners area.

## Places to Stay – camping

Near Cataract Lake, north of I-40 exit 161, *Cataract Lake County Park* (☎ 774 5139) offers 35 sites for $5 and access to the lake. *Red Lake Campground & Hostel* (☎ 635 4753, 635 9122), on Hwy 64 eight miles north of I-40 exit 165, has 30 year-round sites. Tenting costs $10, RVs with hookups cost $16 ($2 less from October to April) and there are coin showers, laundry and a grocery store. Summer reservations are recommended.

The *Circle Pines KOA* (☎ 635 4545, 1 (800) 732 0537), 1000 Circle Pines Rd (half a mile north of I-40 exit 167), has 165 year-round sites ranging in price from $17 for tents to $20 for RVs with full hookups, and six Kamping Kabins available for $27. There are hot showers, a coin laundry, an indoor pool and spa, and a playground. Similar facilities and prices are found at the *Grand Canyon KOA* (☎ 635 2307), on Hwy 64, five miles north of I-40 exit 165, with 100 sites open from March through October.

The Kaibab National Forest operates the following campgrounds. All are open on a first-come, first-served basis from about May to October, with drinking water but no showers or RV hookups, and all offer fishing and boating (for those using paddles or small engines – call for limits) but no swimming. *Cataract Lake* is about a mile north of I-40 exit 161 (follow signs) and has 18 sites for $6. *Kaibab Lake*, almost two miles north on Hwy 64 from I-40 exit 165, has 60 sites for $10. Forest rangers give talks in summer, when the campground often fills early. To get to *Dogtown*, with 60 sites at $8, drive four miles south on 4th St (becoming USFS Rd 173), then nearly three miles east on USFS Rd 140 and another mile on USFS Rd 132. To get to *White Horse Lake*, with 85 sites for $10, drive nine miles south on 4th St, then left about eight miles southeast on USFS Rd 110, and left three more miles on USFS Rd 109.

## Places to Stay – bottom end

*Red Lake Campground & Hostel* (see above) has hostel beds and family units for $15 per person during the high season, or $12 from October through March. The *Canyon Motel* (☎ 635 9371), on Rodeo Rd just off old Route 66 at the east end of town, has a Santa Fe railroad carriage converted into a youth hostel, where 20 sleeper berths cost $18 per person with showers, kitchen facilities and a pool. Motel rooms are $55/60 for singles/doubles in summer. Early reservations are recommended at both hostels.

In Williams itself, you'll see a number of motels offering rooms for about $20 in winter, but in summer the same places charge in the $40s and fill up early. The most reliable of these include the 12-room *Highlander Motel* (☎ 635 2541), 533 W Bill Williams Ave; the *Budget Host Inn* (☎ 635 4415, 1 (800) 745 4415), 620 W Bill Williams Ave, with 26 rooms; and the 24-room *Courtesy Inn* (☎ 635 2619, 1 (800) 235 7029, fax 635 2610), 344 E Bill Williams Ave, which serves coffee and donuts for breakfast.

Other basic motels in the bottom-end price range, all along Bill Williams Ave, include the *Downtowner Motel* (☎ 635 4041), *Family Inn* (☎ 635 2562), *Grand Motel* (☎ 635 4601), *Hacienda Motel* (☎ 635 2051), *Patio Motel* (☎ 635 4791), and the *Westerner Motel* (☎ 635 4312, 1 (800) 385 8608, fax 635 9313).

## Places to Stay – middle

The following have decent rooms priced in the $50s and $60s in summer and reduced to under $30 in winter. The *El Rancho Motel* (☎ 635 2552, 1 (800) 228 2370, fax 635 4173), 617 E Bill Williams Ave, has 25 rooms and a pool in summer. The *Norris Motel* (☎ 635 2202, 1 (800) 341 8000, fax 635 2202), 1001 W Bill Williams Ave, has a spa and all of its 33 rooms have refrigerators. Both of these hotels are reasonable value for Williams, have free coffee in the lobby and both advertise 'British hospitality' (kippers and warm beer available at odd hours of the day?!). Standard rooms are also available at the 20-room *Rodeway Inn* (☎ 635 9127), 750 N Grand Canyon Blvd, and the 42-room *Econo Lodge* (☎ 635 4085), 302 E Bill Williams Ave.

During summer, standard rooms in the $70s and $80s are available at the *Comfort Inn* (☎ 635 4045, fax 635 9060), 911 W Bill Williams Ave, which has an indoor pool, spa and coin laundry. The *Days Inn* (☎ 635 4051, fax 635 4411), 2488 W Bill Williams Ave, has the same facilities, and each has over 70 rooms. The similar *Hojo Inn* (☎ 635 2541, fax 635 9565), 511 N Grand Canyon Blvd, charges a little more. The *Super 8 Motel* (☎ 635 4700), 2001 E Bill Williams Ave, charges $70.88 for doubles and lacks a pool. The *Travelodge* (☎ 635 2651, 1 (800) 578 7878), 430 E Bill Williams Ave, is also in this price range, but has an outdoor pool and an indoor spa. The *Park Inn* (☎ 635 4464, 1 (800) 733 4814, fax 635 4814), 710 W Bill Williams Ave, lacks a pool, but prices include a continental breakfast. It has some extra-large family rooms with refrigerators at a higher cost.

## Places to Stay – top end

**Hotels** The *Holiday Inn Express* (☎ 635 9000, fax 635 2300), 831 W Bill Williams Ave, has nicer than average rooms priced in the $90s, including a free breakfast bar, and it also has an indoor pool and spa. The *Ramada Inn* (☎ 635 4431, 1 (800) 462 9381, fax 635 2292), 642 E Bill Williams Ave, is very popular and its 96 attractive rooms are often full. The big draw here is the steak house (see Places to Eat), which has entertainment. There is also a regular restaurant without music, and an outdoor pool and spa. Rooms cost around $100 in summer. The similarly priced *Best Western*

*Inn of Williams* (☎ 635 4400, 1 (800) 635 4445, fax 635 4488), 2600 W Bill Williams Ave, sits among pine trees a mile west of town. Rooms are large and attractive, and some mini-suites are available.

Two hotels under construction will probably be in the upper-middle or top-end price ranges. The *Fray Marcos Hotel* (☎ 1 (800) 843 8724) in the Williams Grand Canyon Railway depot has just been restored and will be managed by the railway; it was scheduled to open in late July 1995. Doubles range from $89 to $119 – call them for rail tour package details. The *Fairfield Inn by Marriott* (☎ 635 9888) is being built by I-40 exit 163 and will be Williams' largest hotel, with over 100 rooms as well as a pool and exercise facilities. It will be opening in late 96.

Eight miles east of Williams near I-40 exit 171, the *Quality Inn Mountain Ranch & Resort* (☎ 635 2693, fax 635 4188), has two tennis courts (closed in winter), an outdoor pool and spa, outdoor games area and a restaurant, and offers horseback rides at extra cost. Most rooms have views of the forest or mountains and run in the $90s in summer.

**B&Bs** The *Canyon Country Inn B&B* (☎ 635 2349), 442 W Bill Williams Ave, 86046, has 13 rooms, pleasantly decorated with local arts & crafts. Summer rates are in the $75 to $95 range for a double with private bath. The *Johnstonian B&B* (☎ 635 2178), 321 W Sheridan Ave, 86046, was built in 1900 and has four rooms and a guest house priced from $65 to $110; some rooms share baths. Neither place allows smoking.

The smoke and alcohol-free *Terry Ranch B&B* (☎ 635 4171), 701 Quarter Horse St, 86046-9520, has four rooms with turn-of-the-century furnishings and private baths for $105 a double. Downtown, the *Red Garter B&B* (☎ 635 1484), 137 W Railroad Ave, 86046, has a variety of rooms with private baths in a restored 1890s bordello.

**Places to Eat**
Opening hours given below may be short-ened in winter. For home-style breakfasts, try *Old Smoky's* (☎ 635 2091), 624 W Bill Williams Ave, which is open from 6 am to 1:30 pm and advertises 14 kinds of home-made breads as well as pancakes and cinnamon rolls. Simple family restaurants serving reasonably priced American food all day include the *Hoffman House* (☎ 635 9955), 425 E Bill Williams Ave, open 6 am to 10 pm; *Cowboys Kitchen* (☎ 635 2708), 117 E Bill Williams Ave, open 5 am to 10 pm; *Parker House* (☎ 635 4590), 525 W Bill Williams Ave, open 6 am to 9:30 pm; and *Denny's* (☎ 635 2052), 2550 W Bill Williams, open 24 hours a day.

*Pancho McGillicuddy's* (☎ 635 4150), 141 W Railroad Ave, is a 'Mexican cantina' popular with tourists that also serves gringo food and has a patio outside its nicely restored 100-year-old building. Hours are 3 to 10 pm, and the restaurant often has live entertainment. For Mexican and New Mexican food without the frills, try *El Sombrero Cafe* (☎ 635 2209, 635 9284), 126 E Railroad Ave. For Chinese food, there's *The Great Wall* (☎ 635 2045), 412 N Grand Canyon Blvd, open from 11 am to 9 pm Monday to Friday and 4 to 9 pm on Saturday. For Italian, the best is the *Fireside Grill & Bar* (☎ 635 4130), 106 S 9th St, open from 11:30 am to 1 am.

At the Ramada Inn, *Miss Kitty's Steak House & Saloon* (☎ 635 9161) features live western or country & western bands most nights in the summer and on weekends in winter, and strives to make the atmosphere as Western as possible. Hours are 6 am to 2 pm (sorry, no singing cowboys at breakfast) and 5 to 10 pm. For a steak without the hoopla, *Rod's Steak House* (☎ 635 2671), 301 E Bill Williams Ave, has been here for half a century and is the best place in town. Apart from good steaks priced in the teens, there are cheaper chicken and fish dinners and a kid's menu. Hours are 11:30 am to 9:30 pm.

**Entertainment**
Apart from the restaurants mentioned above, many of the 'old town' bars may have live music on weekends. Check out

ARIZONA

the *World Famous Sultana Bar* (☎ 635 2021), 301 W Bill Williams Ave, in a 1912 building with a checkered history. Then stop by the *Cabinet Saloon* (☎ 635 4150), on the southeast corner of Railroad Ave and Grand Canyon Blvd and housed in one of the town's oldest buildings. Constructed of stone in 1895, the building survived several fires that burnt down other buildings in this block. This was once known as 'Saloon Row' with many bars, brothels and opium dens along here. If only walls could talk . . .

### Getting There & Away

**Bus** Greyhound (☎ 1 (800) 231 2222) has a morning eastbound bus and an afternoon westbound bus traveling on I-40, both of which drive through downtown Williams. There is no bus station – call Greyhound to make a reservation and find out where they'll pick you up. Nava-Hopi Tours (see Organized Tours in the Flagstaff section) stop at the Grand Canyon Railway depot on the way to and from the Grand Canyon (tickets are $9) and Flagstaff (tickets are $7).

**Train** Amtrak does not stop here so the only service is the Grand Canyon Railway (see the preceding paragraph).

**Car** Apart from the obvious main highways, drivers enjoy the scenic Perkinsville Rd. This leaves town south along 4th St and heads through forests and river valleys to Jerome, almost 50 miles away. Only the first half is paved but ordinary cars can negotiate the unpaved section except after heavy rain or snow. See Annerino's *Adventuring in Arizona* for a detailed description.

## ASH FORK

The countryside becomes flatter and grassier west of Williams. The small town of Ash Fork, 20 miles west along I-40, is home to about 1000 people and is a cattle ranching center. If you pull off the freeway and drive through town, you'll see big piles of stone slabs. These are Kaibab slate, a resource that caused Ash Fork to dub itself 'The Flagstone Capital of America'. Hwy 89 south from Ash Fork reaches Prescott in 52 miles.

### Orientation & Information

Ash Fork is north of I-40 between exits 144 and 146. The main streets are Lewis Ave (old Route 66, one way westbound) and Park Ave (one way eastbound). There is a tourist office (open intermittently) and a post office at Park and 5th Sts.

### Places to Stay & Eat

The *KOA – Ash Fork* (☎ 637 2521), near exit 144, has 75 tent and RV sites from $12.50 to $16.50, year round. Facilities include a pool, showers, playground and recreation area, but not all are open in winter. *Hillside RV Park* (☎ 637 2300) is cheaper, especially for tenters.

The cheap and basic motels aren't up to much. There's the *Ashfork Inn* (☎ 637 2514) on Lewis near exit 144; the *Copperstate Motel* (☎ 637 2335), 101 E Lewis; *Hi Line Motel* (☎ 637 2766), 124 E Lewis Ave; and the *Stagecoach Motel* (☎ 637 2551), 823 Park Ave.

The *Bull Pen Restaurant* (☎ 637 2330), on Park near exit 146, draws interstate traffic 24 hours a day.

# Northeastern Arizona

Some of Arizona's most beautiful and photogenic landscapes lie in the northeastern corner of the state. Between the fabulous buttes of Monument Valley on the Utah state border and the fossilized logs of the Petrified Forest National Park at the southern edge of the area, lie lands that are locked into ancient history. Here is the Navajo National Monument, with ancient and deserted pueblos, and Canyon de Chelly with equally ancient pueblos adjacent to contemporary farms. Here are mesas topped by some of the oldest continuously inhabited villages on the continent. Traditional and modernized Navajo hogans dot the landscape and Hopi kivas nestle into it. (Hogans are octagonal, usually earth-covered homes made of wood and earth with the door facing east.) Native Americans have always inhabited this land, which is known today as the Navajo and Hopi Indian Reservations.

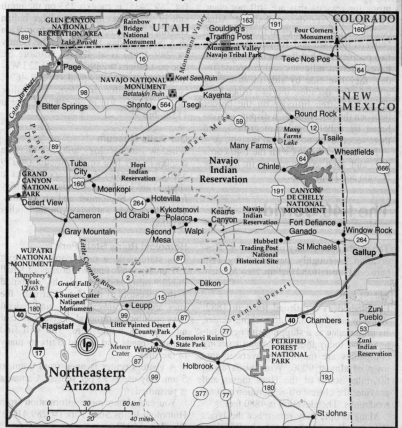

Tribal laws take precedence over state laws, although both tribes accept federal laws and are fiercely proud and patriotic citizens. The Navajo Indian Reservation is the biggest in the USA and spills over into its neighboring states of Utah, Colorado and New Mexico. It completely surrounds the Hopi Indian Reservation. It's the biggest reservation partly because its harsh landscape didn't seem to offer much when reservations were doled out.

The Navajo and Hopi are recent neighbors. The Hopi are the descendants of the Sinagua people who left their more westerly pueblos in the 12th and early 13th centuries for reasons that are still not clear. The Navajos are descendants of Athapaskan Indians who arrived from the north between the 14th and 16th centuries. The two peoples speak different languages and have different religions and customs. Today, they live side by side in an uneasy alliance. For decades, the two tribes have disagreed, often bitterly, on the border between the reservations, a dispute exacerbated by tribal population growth, and there seems to be no solution in sight.

This chapter begins with the I-40 corridor, and then continues north into the Navajo and Hopi lands.

# The I-40 Corridor

The southern boundary of the Navajo Reservation is roughly paralleled by I-40 between Flagstaff and Gallup, New Mexico.

## WINSLOW
Established as a railroad town in 1882, Winslow soon became a ranching center. Its importance as a shipping site never faltered and today the railroad and trucking companies are major employers in this town of almost 9000. Winslow is about 60 miles south of the Hopi mesas and provides the closest off-reservation accommodations. The elevation is 4880 feet.

Many people may remember the lyrics 'I'm standing on the corner in Winslow, Arizona, such a fine sight to see' from the '70s song Take It Easy made popular by the Eagles (but written by Jackson Browne). The famous corner is downtown on old Route 66 at Kinsley Ave and 2nd St and is in the heart of the oldest part of Winslow.

## Orientation & Information
Old Route 66 is the main drag through town and runs west-east parallel to and south of I-40 between exits 252 and 255. 2nd St is one-way eastbound and 3rd St is one-way westbound.

The chamber of commerce (☎ 289 2434, fax 289 2435) is by exit 253 on the north side of town, next to a rather large Indian carving by Peter Toth. Hours are from 9 am to 5 pm, Monday to Friday. The library (☎ 289 4982) is at 420 W Gilmore St. The post office (☎ 289 2131) is at 223 Williamson Ave. The hospital (☎ 289 4691) is at 1501 Williamson Ave. The police (☎ 289 2431, or 911 in emergencies) are at 115 E 2nd St.

## Old Trails Museum
Winslow's archaeology and history is on display in this free small museum (☎ 289 5861), 212 Kinsley Ave. Hours (subject to change) are 1 to 5 pm, Tuesday to Saturday from May to September and on Tuesday, Thursday and Saturday during other months.

## Homolovi Ruins State Park
This state park, a mile north from exit 257 on Hwy 87, features dozens of small Pueblo ruins and petroglyphs attributed to the ancestors of the Hopi. Currently the sites are under investigation, and federal laws prohibit the removal or disturbance of any artifacts found here. You will find unpaved roads and signed trails to many of the sites.

A visitors center is open from 8 am to 5 pm. Day use is $3 per vehicle. Camping is permitted.

You can obtain more information from Homolovi Ruins State Park (☎ 289 4106), Winslow, 86047.

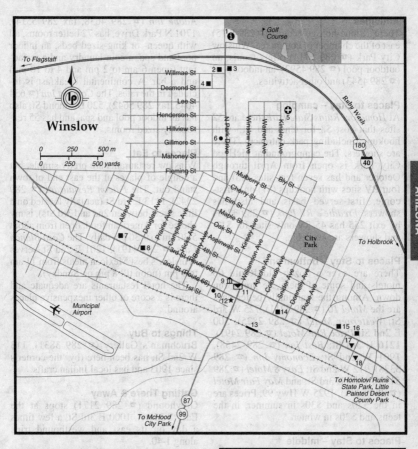

Winslow

To Flagstaff

Golf Course

Willmae St
Desmond St
Leo St
Henderson St
Hillview St
Gillmore St
Mahoney St
Fleming St

N Park Drive
Winslow Ave
Warren Ave
Kinsley Ave

Ruby Wash

180
40

Mulberry St
Cherry St
Elm St
Maple St
Oak St
Aspinwall St

Bly St

To Holbrook

City Park

Alfred Ave
Douglas Ave
Prairie Ave
Campbell Ave
Hicks Ave
Berry Ave
4th St
3rd St (Route 66)
2nd St (Route 66)
1st St

Williamson Ave
Apache Ave
Colorado Ave
Seldon Ave
Donnelly Ave
Pope Ave

To Homolovi Ruins
State Park, Little
Painted Desert
County Park

Municipal
Airport

87
99

To McHood
City Park

0    250    500 m
0    250    500 yards

ARIZONA

## McHood City Park

The Clear Creek Reservoir offers fishing, boating, swimming and picnic and camping facilities. Day use is $3 per vehicle.

Head south on Williamson Ave as it becomes Hwy 87 for about one mile, then turn left on Hwy 99 and continue for four miles to reach the park. For more information call the park ranger station (☎ 289 3082) or the city parks office (☎ 289 5714).

## Little Painted Desert County Park

This park is 15 miles north from exit 257 on Hwy 87, and offers picnic facilities and colorful views.

**PLACES TO STAY**
2   Best Western Adobe Inn
3   Econo Lodge
4   Comfort Inn
7   Economy Inn
8   Motel 10
14  Westerner Motel
15  Easy 8 Motel
16  Price Rite Motel

**PLACES TO EAT**
17  Falcon Restaurant
18  Casa Blanca Cafe

**OTHER**
1   Chamber of Commerce
5   Hospital
6   Library
9   Old Trails Museum
10  Bruchman's Gallery
11  Post Office
12  Police
13  Amtrak Station
15  Greyhound Bus Stop

## Activities

There's a nine-hole golf course (☎ 289 4915) east of the chamber of commerce. Winslow City Park (☎ 289 5714) offers tennis, an outdoor pool (☎ 289 4592), an indoor pool (☎ 289 4543) and other activities.

## Places to Stay – camping

At *Homolovi Ruins State Park* there are 52 sites that cost $8 for tents and $13 with hookups (including park entrance). There are showers. The campground at McHood City Park is open from April through October and has seven tent sites ($6) and four RV sites with hookups ($7) on a first-come, first-served basis and also has showers. *Freddie's RV Park* (☎ 289 3201) by exit 255 has 45 RV-only sites for $13, and showers are available.

## Places to Stay – bottom end

There are over a dozen old Route 66 motels and some of them are pretty run down. Among the marginally better ones are the *Motel 10* (☎ 289 3211), 725 W 3rd St; *Westerner Motel* (☎ 289 2825), 500 E 2nd St; *Price Rite Motel* (☎ 289 2491), 1216 E 3rd St; *Best Inn* (☎ 289 2458), 1901 W 2nd St; *Economy Inn* (☎ 289 3328), 912 W 2nd St; *Easy 8 Motel* (☎ 289 5130), 1000 E 3rd St; and *May Fair Motel* (☎ 289 5445), 1925 W Hwy 99. Prices are in the $20s and $30s in summer, in the teens and $20s in winter.

## Places to Stay – middle

Several chain motels provide the best lodging with summer prices substantially lower than in Flagstaff, 60 miles away. Expect off-season discounts of $10 to $15. Posted summer prices for the following hotels are $50 to $60 for a double.

The *Econo Lodge* (☎ 289 4687, fax 289 9377), 1706 N Park Drive, has 73 standard rooms. There is a pool, coin laundry and free coffee. The *Super 8 Motel* (☎ /fax 289 4606), 1916 W 3rd St, has 46 rooms. The *Best Western Town House* (☎ 289 4611), 1914 W 3rd St, has 68 larger rooms, a pool, coin laundry, a restaurant open for breakfast and dinner and a bar. The *Best Western*

*Adobe Inn* (☎ 289 4638, fax 289 5514), 1701 N Park Drive, has 72 better rooms, all with queen- or king-sized beds, an indoor pool and spa, a coin laundry and a restaurant (open 6 am to 2 pm and 4 to 10 pm) and a bar. A continental breakfast is included in the rates. The *Comfort Inn* (☎ 634 4045, fax 289 5642), 520 Desmond St, also has an indoor pool and spa, and has 55 reasonably sized rooms.

## Places to Eat

Winslow restaurants are pretty simple, but a couple of places at the east end of town stand out. The *Falcon Restaurant* (☎ 289 2342), 1113 E 3rd St (actually located on a little street between 2nd and 3rd Sts), is my choice for American food, open from about 5:30 am to 9:30 pm daily. The *Casa Blanca Cafe* (☎ 289 4191), 1201 E 2nd St, serves Winslow's best Mexican meals from 11 am to 9 pm (noon till 8 pm on Sunday).

The hotel restaurants are adequate and there is a score of other inexpensive places around.

## Things to Buy

Bruchman's Gallery (☎ 289 3831), 113 W 2nd St, has been here (by 'the corner') since 1903 and has local Indian crafts.

## Getting There & Away

Greyhound (☎ 289 2171) stops at the Easy 8 Motel, 1000 E 3rd St, a few times a day on its east and westbound trips along I-40.

Amtrak (☎ 1 (800) 872 7245) has a morning eastbound train and an evening westbound train. There is no ticket office – call Amtrak for information.

## HOLBROOK

Named after a railroad engineer, Holbrook was established in 1881 when the railroad reached this point. It soon became an important ranching center and the Navajo County seat. The proximity of the Petrified Forest National Park has added tourism to the town's economic profile. The elevation is 5080 feet and about 6000 people live here.

## Not Quite Federal Express

The Hashknife Posse, named after the area's biggest early cattle company, has an official contract with the US Post Office to carry mail from Holbrook to Scottsdale via pony express. They don't have daily or even weekly service. In fact, delivery is only once a year, usually in late January or early February, and the arrival in Scottsdale is an important part of that city's Western week. The ride takes three days. Letters with normal postage marked 'Via Pony Express' in the lower left will receive special postmarks and be delivered by the Hashknife Posse if left at the Holbrook post office during the first two weeks in January. Or put your stamped and marked letter in another envelope and send it to The Postmaster, Pony Express Ride, Holbrook, 86025. After letters reach Scottsdale, they continue via normal mail. This tradition dates back to 1959. ■

### Orientation & Information

The chamber of commerce (☎ 524 6558, 1 (800) 524 2459) is in the county courthouse at 100 E Arizona St. The library (☎ 524 3732) is at 451 1st Ave. The post office (☎ 524 3311) is at 216 E Hopi Drive. Recycle at F&M Recycling (☎ 524 2351), 111 SW Central Ave. The police (☎ 524 3991, or 911 in emergencies) are at 100 E Buffalo St.

### Things to See & Do

The **Navajo County Museum** is operated by the chamber of commerce in the 1898 county courthouse, 100 E Arizona St. See the old city jail and learn about the area's history, which was pretty wild in the 19th century and rivals Tombstone's for sheer bloodiness. Visitors can obtain an invitation to a public hanging or stop by the Bucket of Blood Saloon. The museum is free and worth a look. Hours are 8 am to 5 pm, Monday to Friday. In summer, hours are extended to 8 pm and the museum is open from 8 am to 5 pm on Saturday. The chamber has a brochure describing the courthouse and other historic buildings nearby.

Indian Country Tours (☎ 524 2979, 1 (800) 524 4350, fax 524 6086), 611 W Hopi Drive, PO Box 388, 86025, operates local **van tours** to the Petrified Forest,

Indian reservations and other sites of interest. Full-day tours range from $55 to $75 per person, and half-price for six- to 12-year-olds. Half-day and overnight tours are also available.

You can play **golf** at the Hidden Cove Golf Course (☎ 524 3097), two miles north of I-40 exit 283. There is a **swimming pool** (☎ 524 3331) and **tennis courts** in the park at 507 7th St.

### Special Events

The annual city festival is Old West Days in early June. The Navajo County Fair and Rodeo takes place in late August or early September.

### Places to Stay – camping

The *Holbrook KOA* (☎ 524 6689), 102 Hermosa Drive, is northwest of I-40 between exits 286 and 289. Open from mid-May to mid-September, they have cowboy cookouts and entertainment, a pool, a recreation room, mini-golf and a playground. There are showers and a coin laundry. Rates are $16 to $21, with a small discount from mid-September to mid-May when the pool is closed. Summer reservations are suggested. *Cholla Lake County Park* (☎ 524 6161), 10 miles west of Holbrook (take I-40 exit 277 and follow signs

ARIZONA

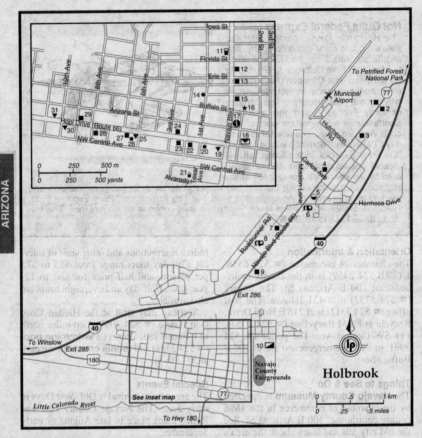

Holbrook

to the south and east) has 15 $7 tent sites and five $10 RV sites with partial hookups. There are showers. Day use costs $3 and a boat launch and fishing are available. The *OK RV Park* (☎ 524 3226), 1576 Roadrunner Rd, has tent and RV sites for $18 and showers.

**Places to Stay – bottom end**

The *International Youth Hostel* in the old Arizona Rancho Motor Lodge, 58 Tovar Ave, was going through restoration at press time, so may or may not be open. Call the chamber of commerce to find out its status and rates.

There are several basic motels along old Route 66 (Hopi Drive east from I-40 exit 285) advertising rates in the teens for a double in the low season rising to the low $20s in summer. Hopi Drive parallels the railway tracks. Other cheapies are found along Navajo Blvd. They include *Brad's Motel* (☎ 524 6929), 301 W Hopi Drive, and the *Sun & Sand Motel* (☎ 524 2186), 902 W Hopi Drive, which has a pool, as does the *Budget Inn* (☎ 524 6263), 602 Navajo Blvd. The *Western Holiday Motel* (☎ 524 6216, fax 524 1521), 720 Navajo Blvd, has a pool and a restaurant and a bar, which sometimes offers weekend entertainment. Other low-budget digs include the *Royal Motel* (☎ 524 6490), 310 W Hopi Drive, *Holbrook Inn* (☎ 524 3809), 235 W Hopi Drive, and the *Moen Kopi Motel* (☎ 524 6848), 464 Navajo Blvd.

Devotees of historic Route 66 schlockabilia won't want to miss the *Wigwam Motel* (☎ 524 3048), 811 W Hopi Drive. This motel court has a village of concrete wigwams doubling as rooms, each with restored 1950s-era furniture. Quite a sight! Rates start around $30 and they may close in winter. The *Motel 6* (☎ 524 6101, fax 524 1806), 2514 Navajo Blvd, has a pool and 126 rooms for $30/36 for

singles/doubles. This is Holbrook's biggest motel.

**Places to Stay – middle**
The *Rainbow Inn* (☎ 524 2654, 1 (800) 551 1923), 2211 Navajo Blvd, is a standard clean motel and the only one in this category that isn't part of a chain. Double rooms are about $40 for one queen-sized bed or a little more for two beds. All rooms have refrigerators.

The remaining chain hotels all have a pool. The *Super 8 Motel* (☎ 524 2871, fax 524 3514), 1989 Navajo Blvd, has a spa, coin laundry and doubles starting at $48.88. The *Econo Lodge* (☎ 524 1448), 2596 Navajo Blvd, has a restaurant and standard rooms for $45 to $55 a double. The *Days Inn* (☎ 524 6949, fax 524 6665), 2601 Navajo Blvd, has a spa and comfortable modern rooms in the high $50s, including continental breakfast. The *Best Western Adobe Inn* (☎ 524 3948, fax 524 3612), 615 W Hopi Drive, has rooms in the $50s with continental breakfast.

The *Best Western Arizonian Inn* (☎ 524 2611, fax 524 2253), 2508 Navajo Blvd, has pleasant rooms in the $60s and adjoins the 24-hour Denny's restaurant. The *Comfort Inn* (☎ 524 6131, fax 524 2281), 2602 Navajo Blvd, also has a 24-hour restaurant and includes free continental breakfast. Rooms, some of which have microwaves and refrigerators, are in the $50s and $60s. The *Holiday Inn Express* (☎ 524 1466, fax 524 1788), 1308 Navajo Blvd, has a spa and rooms for about $60 including continental breakfast. Holbrook's newest is the *Ramada Limited* (☎ 524 2566, fax 524 6427), 2608 Navajo Blvd, with a spa and rooms in the $60s.

**Places to Eat**
There are plenty of cheap and not especially noteworthy places to eat, mostly serving American food. The *Plainsman* (☎ 524 3345), 1001 W Hopi Drive, serves inexpensive breakfast, lunch and dinner. The basic-looking and cheaper *Cholla Restaurant* (☎ 524 3529), 1120 W Hopi Drive, seems locally popular and open

**ARIZONA**

from 5 am to 9 pm. *Romo's Cafe* (☎ 524 2153), 121 W Hopi Drive, is a hole-in-the-wall Mexican restaurant. The restaurants at the Best Western Arizonian Inn and the Comfort Inn are open 24 hours.

The best place in town is the *Butterfield Stage Co Steak House* (☎ 524 3447), 609 W Hopi Drive, which is open from 4 to 10 pm daily. The steaks are in the teens and there is a salad bar and seafood.

### Entertainment

The *Roxy Theater* (☎ 524 2060), 153 W Hopi Drive, shows movies. Local Indians perform Social Dances outside the county courthouse at 7 pm from Monday to Friday during summer. These are free and photography is allowed. The *Holiday Cocktail Lounge* in the Western Holiday Motel (☎ 524 6697), 720 Navajo Blvd, and *Young's Corral* (☎ 524 1875), 865 Navajo Blvd, may have live music and dancing on weekends.

### Getting There & Away

The Greyhound bus (☎ 524 3832) stops at 2106 Navajo Blvd several times a day heading east and west along I-40. Amtrak comes through but does not stop.

### PETRIFIED FOREST NATIONAL PARK

On my first visit many years ago, I had the naive impression that some of the trees here would still be standing in little glades, eerily frozen in time. Parents traveling with small kids might avoid major disappointment by explaining that the 'forest' is actually a bunch of horizontal fossilized logs, some broken up, scattered around over a large area. Nevertheless, they are impressive, some greater than six feet in diameter and at least one spanning a ravine, forming a fossilized bridge.

The trees are conifers that date from the Triassic (225 million years ago) and were contemporary with the dinosaurs (some fossils of which are seen in the visitors centers). Washed by floods into this area, logs were buried by mud and then volcanic ash, and later became fossilized by the action of mineral-laden water that left

colorful deposits around the wood cells. Slowly, these deposits turned into stone. Much more recently, the area was uplifted, and then erosion exposed the logs.

Before 1906, when parts of the forest were designated a national monument, thousands of tons of petrified wood was taken by souvenir seekers, builders and entrepreneurs. Since then, the area has been protected and now encompasses 146 sq miles. No collecting of any kind is allowed (it is punishable by fines and imprisonment), but souvenirs of similar wood collected outside the park can be easily bought from many stores in the area, particularly in Holbrook and at the south entrance to the park.

Apart from the petrified logs, visitors can see a few small ancient Indian ruins (including one building made entirely from blocks of fossilized wood), many petroglyphs and the picturesque scenery of the Painted Desert – some 67 sq miles of picturesque lands that change colors as the sun plays tricks with the minerals in the earth. The original 1906 monument was the southern part of the present park, and the greatest concentration of petrified wood is found here. The northern section gives outstanding views of the Painted Desert. Remnants of past Indian habitations are found in the central and southern sections.

### Orientation & Information

The park straddles I-40 at exit 311, 25 miles east of Holbrook. From this exit, a 28-mile paved park road goes briefly north and then heads south, over the freeway, to emerge at Hwy 180, 18 miles southeast of Holbrook. Unless you want to make the complete loop, it is more convenient to begin at the north end if you are driving west and the south end if you are driving east. There is no other advantage to either direction.

The Painted Desert Visitor Center near the north entrance and the Rainbow Forest Museum near the south entrance both have exhibits about the park, bookshops and rangers with information. At Painted

Desert, there is a 17-minute film describing how the logs were fossilized, and at Rainbow Forest there are dinosaur skeletons. Between these two places, the park road passes over 20 pullouts with interpretive signs and some short trails.

The park is open from 8 am to 5 pm in winter, and hours may be extended in late spring and fall. From Memorial Day to Labor Day, hours are 6 am to 7 pm if staff is available. Entrance is $5 per vehicle or $3 per bus passenger or bike rider. Golden Age, Access and Eagle passes are accepted. Visitors receive a (free) park map showing pullouts and parking spots along the road. Further information is available from the Superintendent (☎ 524 6228), Petrified Forest National Park, 86028.

### Hiking & Backpacking

Apart from some short trails at some of the lookouts, there are no trails into the park. Hikers can walk cross-country, but should speak with a ranger first to discuss their plans as there are no maintained or labeled trails. Backpackers can hike into the backcountry and camp after obtaining a free permit from a ranger. There are no camping facilities or water away from the road, so hikers and backpackers need to carry all water. Campsites must be at least a half mile from paved roads and no fires, firearms, pets or collecting are allowed. Backcountry hiking and camping are permitted only in designated wilderness areas in the southeast corner and the northern parts of the park. Almost half the park is off-limits to backcountry travel.

### Places to Stay & Eat

Apart from backcountry camping, there are no overnight accommodations in the park. Snacks are available at the Rainbow Forest Museum and meals at the Painted Desert Visitor Center. There are a couple of picnic areas. In the town of Chambers, 22 miles east of the park, the *Best Western Chieftain Inn* (☎ 688 2754) has 52 standard rooms, a pool open from June through September, and a restaurant open from 6 am to 9:30 pm. Rates are in the $60s for a double.

# Navajo Indian Reservation

The Navajo Indian Reservation, or the Navajo Nation as the Navajos themselves prefer to call it, covers about 25,000 sq miles. It's the largest reservation in the USA, and the Navajo tribe is the largest – about one in seven Native Americans in the USA is a Navajo. The reservation is mainly in northwestern Arizona, but also includes parts of neighboring Utah and New Mexico. About 75% is high desert and the remainder is high forest. The scenery is, in places, some of the most spectacular in North America, particularly in Monument Valley. Equally impressive are the beautiful ruins amid splendid settings in the Canyon de Chelly and Navajo National Monuments. After some background on the Navajo, this section will describe the highlights of the reservation beginning with the tribal capital of Window Rock in the east and then move west and north.

### History

In the 14th and 15th centuries, many bands of Athapaskan-speaking people migrated from the plains of Canada into the Southwest. The reasons for this migration aren't known, but by 1500 they had established themselves in the Southwest; these people were the ancestors of both the Navajo and the Apache Indians. In those days, they were a wandering people, hunting and gathering for food and occasionally raiding neighboring tribes. Influenced by the more sedentary and agricultural Pueblo tribes, the Navajo eventually began farming and making arts & crafts, but they never built any large stone villages such as the Anasazi or Pueblo Indians did.

Contact with the Spaniards in the 16th, 17th and 18th centuries was surprisingly limited, considering the Spaniards' involvement with the Pueblo and Hopi peoples. The best-documented Navajo-Spanish interaction was the massacre of over 100

## The Navajo Language

The Navajo, or Dineh (the People), belong to the Athapascan language family, a group of languages that also includes Apache. Other tribes speaking Athapaskan languages live in Alaska, northwest Canada, and coastal Oregon and California. The distribution of these tribes is considered evidence of migration patterns across the continent.

Some Navajo, especially the elders, speak only the Navajo language, but most speak both Navajo and English. All members of the tribe have a deep respect for the Navajo language whether they are fluent or not. During WW II, the Navajo Code Talkers spoke a code based on Navajo for US military radio transmissions. The code was never broken. The Code Talkers are now famous for their wartime contribution. Since 1942 the US government has been working with experts in Indian languages to develop a popular alphabet to encourage the writing of Navajo.

Navajo and English have very different sentence structures. Whereas normal word order in English is subject-verb-object, Navajo is subject-object-verb. The possessive pronouns of Navajo are always prefixed to the noun: for instance, shimá (my mother), nimá (your mother), bimá (his mother). But the stem -má has no independent form and never occurs just on its own.

The structure of the Navajo verb has similar characteristics to English but is more complex. The subject of the sentence is always incorporated in the verb. Similarly, affixes are added to verbs to show person, time and mood. Ideas conveyed in English by auxiliaries such as will, did, have, might and so on are expressed by different forms of the verb itself, as they are in most European languages other than English.

Another difference between the two languages is that English prepositions are postpositions in Navajo. For example, the phrase 'with my elder sister' translates as 'my elder sister, with her'.

Indians say 'ai eeeeee' when they are pulling your leg and they get afraid that you might know that they are pulling your leg and be offended by it, and then they chicken out and make sure you know that they are pulling your leg so you can laugh too. For myself I never chicken out . . . ai eeeeee. – *Eagle/Walking Turtle*

---

Indians at Canyon de Chelly in 1805 in response to years of Navajo raids.

When the Anglos arrived in the 19th century, they tended to follow the better known routes in New Mexico and southern Arizona. By the middle of the 1800s, the US Army was defeating tribes, including the Navajo, along the Western frontier and 'buying' the land from the Indians in exchange for peace. (This may have made sense to the Anglos, but it didn't to the Indians, who didn't value the European concept of land ownership.) Once their land had been purchased, the surviving tribes were often relocated onto distant reservations.

Canyon de Chelly, site of the massacre by the Spanish in 1805, also became the place where the US Army defeated the Navajo. During the winter of 1863-64, US Cavalry troops, led by Colonel Kit Carson destroyed fields and property, killed anyone they found, and drove the Indians up into the canyon until starvation forced their surrender. Thousands of Indians were rounded up and forced to march to Fort Sumner in the plains of eastern New Mexico (see Fort Sumner in the Southeastern New Mexico section) in an episode that has gone down in tribal history as 'The Long Walk'.

Hundreds of Navajo died on the march or on the inhospitable new reservation. Despite this, the Navajo were one of the luckier tribes. A treaty in 1868 gave the Navajo a reservation of about 5500 sq miles in the heart of the lands on which they had lived for about half a millennium. The 8000 or so inhabitants of Fort Sumner along with about another 8000 scattered Navajos were allowed to settle on this new reservation. This grew over the years to its present size, and today over half of the approximately

170,000 members of the Navajo Nation live on the reservation.

## Information

The best information about the reservation is found at Window Rock (see below). Other good information sources are the *Navajo Times* newspaper and KTNN radio station. This broadcasts out of Window Rock at 660 AM and has mainly Navajo language programming in the morning and English in the afternoon and evening. The music varies between country & western and traditional and recent Navajo music, much of which involves drums and song or flutes.

**Money** Banking facilities on the reservation are available only at Window Rock and Tuba City. These banks lack 24-hour ATMs. Think ahead about your banking needs. Credit cards are accepted at most hotels and trading posts.

**Time** Note that the Navajo Reservation does observe daylight-saving time and so, during the summer, the reservation is one hour ahead of Arizona on the same time as Utah and New Mexico.

**Photography** Photography is permitted almost anywhere there's tourism. Taking photographs of people, however, is not appropriate unless you ask for and receive permission from the individual involved. A tip is expected. (During major public festivals, discreet photography of performers is acceptable.)

**Restrictions** Alcohol and drugs are strictly prohibited throughout the reservation. The few hotels and restaurants in Navajoland provide clean accommodations and decent food, but no alcoholic beverages. The law of the land is as follows: It is a violation of Federal, State and Navajo Tribal laws to disturb, destroy, injure, deface or remove any natural feature or prehistoric object.

**Dangers & Annoyances** Be very careful of farm animals on the roads as you are driving through reservation land. Because most of the land is not fenced, animals will roam onto the highways. Hitting one can do as much damage to you as to the animal.

Be careful, as well, of the occasional drunk driver. Even though the sale and use of alcohol is prohibited on the reservation, there are problems of drinking and drunk driving.

The phone system on the reservation, while usually dependable, occasionally goes dead for short or sometimes long periods. This is more likely to occur in remote locations and during severe weather.

## Special Events

Summer and fall are the big tribal fair seasons in Navajoland. The following are the major events to which the general public is welcome. The world's biggest Indian event is the Annual Navajo Nation Fair, held over Labor Day weekend (Thursday through Sunday) in Window Rock. The fair has been taking place since 1946. Most visitors stay in Gallup, New Mexico and travel to Window Rock for the inter-tribal powwow, Indian rodeo, traditional song and dance displays and competitions, a barbecue with Navajo food and many other events. Also, there is a Fourth of July powwow and rodeo held in Window Rock.

See Shiprock in the Northwestern New Mexico chapter for information on the oldest and most traditional fair, held in late September or early October. Similar events on a smaller scale are held during the Western Navajo Fair in Tuba City, Central Navajo Fair in Chinle, the Southwestern Navajo Fair in Dilkon as well as the Eastern Navajo Fair in Crownpoint, New Mexico. These usually take place between July and October. The Navajoland Tourism Department has the exact dates of these and other smaller rodeos and powwows that are held in many of the smaller towns on the reservation.

Private dances and sings (gatherings where singing is the main activity) are organized by individual families for particular religious or ceremonial occasions or for medicinal purposes. These could happen at any time of the year but are not advertised as they aren't tourist attractions. However, if you happen upon one and want to watch, you might be allowed to do so if you act respectfully.

## Accommodations

The few motels on the reservation are found at Window Rock, Chinle (by the Canyon de Chelly National Monument), Kayenta, Tuba City, Cameron (see the Grand Canyon chapter), Goulding's Trading Post (see Southeastern Utah), and near the Four Corners Monument (see below). These are often full in summer when reservations are a good idea. Most are expensive (averaging $60 to $110 for fairly standard motel rooms); Tuba City is the only place with cheap accommodations.

Off-reservation towns offering conveniently close accommodations are Gallup and Farmington in New Mexico, Holbrook, Winslow, Flagstaff and Page in Arizona and Goulding's Trading Post, Mexican Hat, Bluff and Blanding in Utah.

Tribally operated public campgrounds are found at Monument Valley Tribal Park, the Navajo National Monument, Chinle, Tsaile and Window Rock. RV facilities are very limited.

Coyote Pass Hospitality (☎ 724 3383, 674 9655), PO Box 91, Tsaile, 86558, is run by Willie Tsosie, Jr. He can arrange stays with local families or in a traditional hogan in the Tsaile and Canyon de Chelly area. Accommodations are rustic (a sleeping bag is a good idea) and bathroom facilities are primitive (most hogans lack plumbing). Rates are about $80 including a Navajo breakfast; add $10 per extra person. Additional meals for longer stays can be arranged.

## Things to Buy

The large Anglo towns on the perimeter of the reservation (Farmington and Gallup, New Mexico, and Flagstaff) have galleries and pawn shops where Navajo weavings, silverwork and jewelry, and other arts can be purchased. On the reservation itself, you can purchase such items from trading posts, gift shops or museums, but it's likely that you will encounter Navajos offering their wares at tourist stops and in parking lots. Sometimes they will approach you, but more often they spread their items on blankets on the ground and small tables, or even across the hood or tailgate of a truck. Then they wait for you to come to them.

Buying items at 'official' stores is no guarantee of their quality; high- and low-quality wares appear on trading-post shelves just as they do at roadside stalls. When you buy direct, you may find that you pay less and have more luck negotiating the price down, and the sellers may still make more from the transaction than if they had sold their wares to a trading post. In addition, you may even be able to talk directly to the artisan.

## Getting There & Away

The Navajo Transit System (☎ 729 5449, 729 5457) provides the only public transportation on the reservation using modern buses. From Gallup, New Mexico (which can be reached by Greyhound Bus or Amtrak), Navajo Transit System has buses to Window Rock and Fort Defiance four times a day on weekdays and three times on Saturdays. There is no Sunday service.

In Window Rock you can connect with an afternoon bus (weekdays only) to Tuba City along Hwy 264 (with stops at Ganado, Keams Canyon (on the Hopi Reservation), the Hopi Cultural Center and several other small towns and villages. The bus returns from Tuba City early every morning. The fare is about $14 for the four-hour journey. Another afternoon bus goes to Kayenta via Wheatfields, Tsaile, Chinle and other small villages. The bus returns early every weekday morning from Kayenta and costs about $12 for the four-hour trip. An evening bus goes to Crownpoint, New Mexico, taking about two hours. It also returns early every weekday morning.

## WINDOW ROCK

The tribal capital is at Window Rock, a small town of about 3500 people almost on the New Mexican border at the intersection of Hwy 264 and Hwy 12. The town is named after a natural arch at the north end of town (there is a picnic site here). Below the arch are the Navajo Nation Council Chambers (☎ 871 6417), which contain colorful murals and can be toured.

## Information
Information about the whole reservation is available from Navajoland Tourism Department (☎ 871 6436, 871 7371, fax 871 7381), PO Box 663, 86515. Their office is on the western outskirts of town on Hwy 264 in the Economic Development Building.

Backpacking and other backcountry use anywhere on the reservation requires a permit from the Navajo Parks & Recreation Department (☎ 871 6647, fax 871 6637), PO Box 9000, 86515. The office is next to the Zoological and Botanical Park on the east side of Window Rock. (Note that campgrounds mentioned in this chapter are not considered 'backcountry' and don't require a tribal permit beyond the camping fee.) Hunting (very limited), fishing and boating require tribal (not state) licenses obtainable from Navajo Fish & Wildlife (☎ 871 6451, 871 6452, fax 871 7040), PO Box 1480, 86515.

## Navajo Tribal Museum
Indian history and arts & crafts are highlighted at this museum (☎ 871 6673, 871 6675) next to the Navajo Nation Inn in the middle of town. Hours are 8 am to 5 pm, Monday to Friday in winter and 8 am to 6 pm, Monday to Saturday, from April to October. This is the headquarters of the Navajo Arts and Crafts Enterprise (NACE), which runs a jewelry and crafts store here (☎ 871 4090). The NACE was established in 1941 and is wholly Navajo operated. It guarantees the authenticity and quality of its products.

## Navajo Nation Zoological & Botanical Park
At the east end of town on Hwy 264, this park (☎ 871 6573) shows native wildlife

and Navajo architecture. Hours are 8 am to 5 pm daily except New Year's Day and Christmas. Admission is free.

## St Michael's Mission Museum
Housed in an 1898 Franciscan Mission, three miles west of Window Rock just off Hwy 264, this museum (☎ 871 4171) describes the missionary work of the Franciscans in Navajoland. Hours are 8 am to 5 pm, Monday to Friday and 9 am to 5 pm on weekends from Memorial Day to Labor Day. Call for an appointment at other times.

## Places to Stay & Eat
There are no developed campgrounds here. However, you can camp at *Tse Bonito Tribal Park* next to the Zoological & Botanical Park or at the *Summit Campground* nine miles west of Window Rock on Hwy 264. There are picnic tables but no water. A $2 per person fee is charged.

The *Navajo Nation Inn* (☎ 871 4108, 1 (800) 662 6189, fax 871 5466), 48 W Hwy 264, is in the middle of town. There are 56 pleasant rooms decorated in modern Southwestern style. Rates range from $55 to $70 for a single and $5 for each extra person. A swimming pool is open in summer and there is a reasonably priced restaurant open from 6:30 am to 9 pm daily that serves Navajo and American food.

## HUBBELL TRADING POST NATIONAL HISTORIC SITE
John Lorenzo Hubbell established this trading post in 1878 and worked here until his death in 1930. He was widely respected by Indians and non-Indians alike for his honesty and passion for excellence. Today, his trading post is operated by the National Park Service and looks much as it would have at the turn of the century. Indian artists still trade here, Navajo women often give weaving demonstrations and men may demonstrate silversmithing. Tours of Hubbell's house (with a fantastic collection of early Navajo rugs and period furniture) are given several times a day. The trading post continues to sell local crafts, specializing in top-quality Navajo weavings worth

## Navajo Weaving

The Navajo are the best known tribe for the art of rug weaving. A Navajo rug requires many months of labor and can involve several family members. Children tend the sheep, and various people participate in shearing, washing, carding, spinning or dyeing the wool before it even touches the loom. All is done by hand. The loom is a simple upright wood frame, and the designs and colors used are passed down from generation to generation, usually to the women. Legend has it that Spider Woman taught the women how to weave. You can watch weavers at work at some museums and trading posts; the Hubbell Trading Post near Ganado is a good place for this.

Traditional Navajo rugs are woven on looms hung from the ceiling. (RR)

Navajo weavings were originally heavy blankets used in winter. When Anglos became interested in the work as a folk craft, they found that the origin of the rug could be recognized by the various designs and colors used in the rug. For instance, a Ganado Red was a rug with a red background coming from the settlement of Ganado. Rugs with geometrical designs in earth colors bordered by black were from the Two Grey Hills region from the eastern part of Navajo lands. And the Shiprock area was known for Yei rugs, depicting supernatural beings revered by the Navajo. Several other regional styles can easily be detected with a little experience.

Today, weavers from any part of the reservation can produce designs that were once specific to a particular area. While traditionally the designs have been geometric, some weavers today use figurative designs. Such rugs are technically as valuable as the traditional ones.

**Tips on Buying a Rug** Whether used as a floor covering or displayed on a wall, a good quality rug can last a lifetime. Given the cost of purchasing a good quality rug, buying one is not for the average souvenir seeker. It can take months of research, or can be bought on a whim if you see one you really love. If you're a more cautious shopper, visit museums, trading posts and crafts stores in Indian country. Talk to weavers, exhibitors and traders to learn about the various designs. Don't just look at the rugs – feel them. A good rug will be very tightly woven and even in width. Prices of rugs vary from the low hundreds to thousands of dollars. This reflects the size of the rug, the weeks of work involved, the skill of the weaver and whether the yarn is store-bought or hand-spun.

Be aware that cheap imitation rugs are available. These may look nice, but they aren't handmade by Navajos. Some are mass-produced in Mexico using Navajo designs. The staff at a reputable store can show you the difference. ■

thousands of dollars. If you can't quite scrape the money together, you can buy a postcard or a candy bar instead!

The site is 30 miles west of Window Rock, about a mile west of the village of Ganado just off Hwy 264. Hours are 8 am to 6 pm from June through September, 8 am to 5 pm otherwise, and closed Thanks-giving, Christmas and New Year's Day. Admission is free.

There are no places to stay, but there are a couple of small restaurants in the village of Ganado (although they close on Sundays). Further information is available from the Superintendent (☎ 755 3475), PO Box 150, Ganado, 86505.

## CANYON DE CHELLY NATIONAL MONUMENT

Pronounced 'd'SHAY', this many-fingered canyon is the site of several beautiful Anasazi ruins and is also important in the history of the Navajo. Ancient Basket-maker people inhabited the canyon almost 2000 years ago and left some pit dwellings dated to about 350 AD. These inhabitants evolved into the Pueblo people who built large cliff dwellings in the canyon walls between 1100 and 1300 AD. Droughts and other unknown conditions forced the Anasazi to leave the canyon after 1300 AD and it is supposed that they became the ancestors of some of today's Pueblo or Hopi Indians.

The Navajo began farming the canyon bottom around 1700 and used the canyon as a stronghold and retreat for their raids of other nearby Indian groups and Spanish settlers. In 1805, the Spaniards retaliated and killed over 100 Navajos in what is now called Massacre Cave in the Canyon del Muerto (Death Canyon). The Spaniards claimed that the dead were almost all warriors but the Navajo say that it was mostly women and children. In 1864, the US Army drove thousands of Navajo into the canyon and starved them until they surrendered over the winter, then relocated them in eastern New Mexico after 'The Long Walk'. Four years later, the Navajo were allowed to return. Today, many families have hogans and farms on the canyon bottom. Most of the families live on the canyon rims in winter, and move to the canyon bottom in the spring and summer. The whole canyon is private Navajo property administered by the National Park Service. Please don't enter hogans unless with a guide and don't photograph people

Traditional Navajo silverwork utilizes turquoise and sometimes coral.

without their permission. A tip is expected if permission is given.

The mouth of the canyon opens at its west end near the village of Chinle. Here, the canyon walls are only a few feet high but soon become higher until they top out at about a 1000 feet in the depths of the canyon. Two main arms divide early on in the canyon and several side canyons connect with them. A paved road follows the furthest south and furthest north rims of the canyon complex, affording excellent views into the splendid scenery of the canyon and distant views of the Anasazi ruins in the canyon walls. Most of the bottom of the canyon is off-limits to visitors unless they enter with a guide. The exception is a trail to the White House Ruin.

### Information

A visitors center is on the south side near the mouth of the canyon just east of the village of Chinle. There are signs – you won't get lost. The visitors center has exhibits about the canyon, a book shop, and information about guides and tours. They also sell inexpensive booklets with descriptions of the sights on the South and North Rim Drives. The center is open from 8 am to 6 pm daily, extended to 7 pm from May through September. Admission to the monument is free as long as you stick to the visitors center, paved rim roads and White House Ruin trail. Further information is available from the Superintendent (☎ 674 5500), PO Box 588, Chinle, 86503.

### White House Ruin Trail

The trailhead is about six miles east of the visitors center on the South Rim Drive, and the steep trail is about 1.25 miles one-way. Don't forget to carry water. The ruin which dates back to about 1040 to 1284 AD is one of the largest in the monument.

### Rim Drives

Both drives are about 21 miles long and afford numerous overlooks. Lock your car and don't leave valuables in sight when taking the short walks at each scenic point. The South Rim Drive ends at the

ARIZONA

## Anasazi Settlement in the Southwest

| Anasazi Period | Chronology |
|---|---|
| Hunter-Gatherer | 5500 BC |
| I Basketmaker | 1 AD-450AD |
| II Modified Basketmaker | 450-750 |
| III Developmental Pueblo | around 750 to 1100 |
| IV Classic Pueblo | around 1100 to 1300 |

The earliest period of Anasazi settlement, the so-called Modified Basketmaker phase that extended to about 750 AD, found the Anasazi dispersed across the mesa tops in small clusters of permanent pithouse dwellings – semi-subterranean structures with posts supporting low-profile roofs. The windowless design provided protection from the elements, yet entry via the roof opening over the firepit poses some humorous speculation.

During the Developmental Pueblo Period, up to 1100 AD, the Anasazi built surface houses with simple shared walls – like row-house apartments – that formed small hamlets surrounded by fields of maize, beans and squash. Again, like the pithouse, shelter was accomplished with a minimum of material and effort, but with improved egress.

The following Classic Pueblo phase, to 1300 AD, saw the Mesa Verde Anasazi elaborate on the earlier structures, using masonry building materials. Their efforts housed a peak population of perhaps several thousand in pueblo villages, the precursors to cities. Greater clusters of people created opportunities for united accomplishments and perhaps a rudimentary division of labor, social organization, political control and even organized raids on neighboring villages. During this period the Anasazi developed subsurface roundrooms, or kivas – for decades thought to be ceremonial by archaeologists but more recently seen to have more basic uses. At this time they also developed hydraulic schemes to irrigate crops and provide water for villages.

There is mounting evidence of regular communication between Mesa Verdeans and Chaco Canyon peoples in northwestern New Mexico during this period. Some researchers suggest that the political, economic and social influences extended from even farther afield in Mesoamerica (present-day Mexico and Central America).

The Mesa Verdeans suddenly moved to the alcoves of the cliff faces around 1200 AD, inhabiting the cliff dwellings for less than a century before disappearing in accord with a regional demographic collapse that is the greatest unexplained event of the Anasazi era. Death, disease, invasion, internal warfare, resource depletion and climatic change are among the hardships that the Anasazi may have faced. Tree-ring chronologies have proved that a widespread drought lasted from 1276 to 1299 AD, yet this explanation fails to account for the earlier population decline at Chaco Canyon or for Mesa Verde's survival of earlier droughts. Population movements did occur and it is probable that many Anasazi migrated south to the Pueblos of present-day New Mexico and Arizona.

Although archaeologists adopted the Navajo term Anasazi during the 1930s to refer to these early inhabitants of the American Southwest, they have often mistaken it to mean 'ancient people'. Instead, and much to the chagrin of modern Pueblo peoples of Anasazi heritage, it literally means 'enemy ancestors' in the Navajo tongue. ■

Canyon de Chelly contains many sites sacred to the Navajo. (KH)

spectacular Spider Rock Overlook, with views down onto the 800-foot-high sheer-walled tower atop of which lives Spider Woman. The Navajos say that she carries off children who don't listen to their parents! This is a dead-end drive so you'll have to return the way you came.

The North Rim Drive ends at the Massacre Cave overlook. However, you can continue on the paved road to Tsaile, about 13 miles further east, from which Hwy 12 will take you to Window Rock or into the northern reaches of the reservation.

### Organized Tours

Ask at the visitors center information desk about all tours. Guides belong to the Tsegi Guide Association and are usually local Navajos who know the area well and who can liven up your tour with witty commentary. (*Tsegi* is Navajo for 'canyon'.)

**Foot** Free half-day hikes into the mouth of the canyon are led by park rangers during the summer. You need to register in advance. For more difficult hikes or to visit more remote areas, you can hire a guide for $10 an hour (three hours minimum, 15 people per guide maximum). Make sure to take along insect repellant if you go during spring or summer; the wash attracts hoards of mosquitoes in some places. Overnight hikes with camping in the canyon can be arranged.

**Horse** Justin Tso's Horseback Tours (☎ 674 5678), PO Box 881, Chinle, 86503, is near the visitors center and has horses available year round. Twin Trails Horseback Tours (☎ 674 8425), PO Box 1706, Window Rock, 86515, is on the north rim, about nine miles from the visitors center. They have horses available from 15 May to 15 October. Guided trips of two hours to several days can be arranged. Expect to pay about $50 for a six-hour ride.

**4WD** There are no roads into the canyon, only rough tracks, so you need 4WD. If you have your own vehicle you can hire a guide to go with you for $10 an hour (one guide can accompany up to five vehicles). Heavy rain may make the roads impassable.

Otherwise, you can take a Thunderbird Tour from the lodge next to the visitors center. They don't bother with little 4WD vehicles. Instead, they use heavy-duty army-style 6WD vehicles that can get through streams that would stop a 4WD. Some Navajo refer to these tours as the 'shake 'n' bake' tours. Half-day tours leave at 9 am and 2 pm and cost $32 ($23 for children under 12). They leave year round. Full-day tours are $52 for everyone and include a picnic lunch. These are only available from April to October. Visitors who are environmentally conscious should be aware that the use of such vehicles causes erosion.

ARIZONA

## Places to Stay

The *Cottonwood Campground* is near the visitors center and has about 90 sites on a first-come, first-served basis and a group site that can be reserved through the visitors center (☎ 674 5500). There is some water but no hookups or showers. Camping is free and popular, so get there early in summer. During the summer, rangers may present talks. From November to March, water may be shut off. *Spider Rock RV Park & Camping Too* (☎ 674 8261, 1 (800) 817 2702) is 10 miles east of the visitors center along South Rim Drive. The remote campground, under Navajo management, is surrounded by pinon and juniper trees and is a pleasant get-away from the activity of the visitors center. Sites cost between $6 and $12. There is no water or electricity, but the owner has bottled water and lanterns available. The Navajo Chapter House in Chinle has showers available for a fee.

The attractive *Thunderbird Lodge* (☎ 674 5841, fax 674 5844), PO Box 548, 86503, is near the visitors center. Comfortable rooms vary in size; some are in the old lodge (which dates from the late 1800s) but all have private baths and air-conditioning. Rates are in the $80s for a double; there are discounts from November to February. A few suites are $150. An inexpensive cafeteria offers tasty American and Navajo food from 6:30 am to 9 pm, with shorter winter hours.

A half mile west of the visitors center is the modern *Holiday Inn* (☎ 674 5000, 1 (800) 465 4329, fax 674 8264), Garcia Trading Post, 86503. They have a pool and the area's most upscale restaurant (though still not very fancy) open from 6:30 am to 10 pm. Over 100 rooms are available with rates in the low $100s from July through October.

In Chinle, just east of Hwy 191 and three miles west of the visitors center, is the *Best Western Canyon de Chelly Inn* (☎ 674 5875, 1 (800) 327 0354, fax 674 3715), PO Box 295, 86503, with 100 pleasant motel rooms for about $100 from May to October. They have a pool and dining room open from 6:30 am to 9 pm, or 10 pm in summer.

## Places to Eat

The culinary options in Chinle are limited. In addition to the hotel restaurants, there are a few fast-food restaurants and *Basha's*, the only supermarket for at least 50 miles.

## Things to Buy

The Navajo Arts & Crafts Enterprise (see Window Rock above) has a store in Chinle (☎ 674 5338) at the intersection of Hwy 191 and Hwy 7. The gift shop at the Thunderbird Lodge also sells a good range of crafts and T-shirts. The walls of the Thunderbird cafeteria are often covered in high-quality Navajo rugs and paintings, which are for sale.

## TSAILE

A small town at the northeast end of Canyon de Chelly, Tsaile (pronounced say-LEE) is the home of the Navajo Community College. On campus, the modern six-story glass building housing the **Ned A Hatathlie Museum** (☎ 724 3311) has its entrance facing east, just like in a traditional hogan. The museum has exhibits about Indian history, culture and arts & crafts and a gift shop selling a variety of arts & crafts. Hours are 8:30 am to 4:30 pm, Monday to Friday.

South of the college and two miles off Hwy 12 is the small (two sites) *Tsaile Lake Campground*, accessible by dirt road. RVs aren't recommended and there is no drinking water or facilities. Ten miles south of Tsaile on Hwy 12 is the larger and more attractive *Wheatfields Lake Campground* with nice lake views. There are pit toilets but no water. RV and tent sites are available for $2 per person. A nearby store sells food and fishing permits.

## FOUR CORNERS MONUMENT

Make a fool of yourself as you put a foot into Arizona, another into New Mexico, a hand into Utah and another into Colorado. Wiggle your butt for the camera. Everyone does! The site is marked with a slab and state flags and surrounded by booths selling Indian souvenirs. It's the only place in the USA where four states come together at one point. Hours are 7:30 am to

Navajo Community College in Tsaile (RR)

7:30 pm, extended to 8:30 pm in summer, and admission is $1 per car (50¢ for bikes and motorbikes).

About six miles to the southwest is the village of Teec Nos Pos with the small *Navajo Trails Motel* (☎ 674 3618).

## KAYENTA

This sizable town of about 5000 people was established in 1908 by Richard Wetherill as a trading post, but since the late 1960s has developed a strong coal mining industry predominantly on Black Mesa. Needless to say, controversies surrounding the mine have evolved over the years.

It provides convenient tourist services for visitors to nearby Monument Valley and Navajo National Monument. Vehicle tours to Monument Valley are provided by Crawley's Tour (☎ 697 3463/3724), PO Box 187, 86033, and Golden Sands (☎ 697 3684), PO Box 458, 86033. The visitors center (☎ 697 3527) can help with questions about the town.

### Special Events

The Fourth of July Indian Rodeo attracts a lot of people to this town over the Fourth of July weekend (usually Friday through Sunday). Besides the rodeo, there are horse races, food stalls, Navajo dances and sings and powwows. On weekends, Kayenta hosts a big flea market.

### Places to Stay & Eat

The *Wetherill Inn* (☎ 697 3231/3232, fax 697 3233) is 1.5 miles north of Hwy 160 on Hwy 163. About 50 standard motel rooms are about $80 from April to October, about $50 in winter.

The *Holiday Inn* (☎ 697 3221, 1 (800) 465 4329, fax 697 3349) at the junction of Hwy 160 and Hwy 163, is the reservation's largest hotel with 160 rooms and a few suites. Rates are about $110 for a double from July to October, dropping to about $80 in midwinter. There is a pool, a kid's pool, and a decent restaurant open from 6 am to 10 pm. They serve American food and Navajo tacos.

Other places to eat include the *Golden Sands Cafe*, serving American food near the Wetherill Inn, and the *Amigo Cafe* (☎ 697 8448) on Hwy 163 a short way north of the intersection with Hwy 160, which serves the best Mexican food on the reservation. Both are open for breakfast, lunch and dinner. There's also a *Basha's*

**The High Cost of Coal**
From satellite photos taken 567 miles over the Navajo and Hopi Indian Reservations, Peabody Mine to the west of Kayenta looks like a black head. The fact that it appears at all is testimony to its size and to the size of the controversies surrounding the mine at Black Mesa. One of the main issues that arises is the use of ground water. Coal mines use exhorbitant amounts of water to transport the coal to smelters, depleting a vast supply of rainwater that has accumulated over the centuries.

Take into account that this land is desert and water is a precious resource for the Navajo and Hopi. Without the water, their ability to raise livestock and grow crops – the basis of their lifestyle – is threatened. Historically, treaties about tribal land have only defined the land, not the water under the surface. Bureaucracy takes over and the Indians find themselves fighting not only the federal bureaucracy, but also each other over disputed borders and use of land and resources. The issue is further complicated by the fact that Peabody is one of the major employers on the reservation. ■

supermarket where you can pick up some food for that long drive ahead.

About 10 miles west on Hwy 160 at the village of Tsegi is the *Anasazi Inn* (☎ 697 3793) with motel rooms for about $80 in summer, less in winter. They have a dining room.

## MONUMENT VALLEY NAVAJO TRIBAL PARK

The first time I saw the magnificent mesas and buttes of Monument Valley, shivers ran up and down my spine. The views are simply stupendous and I still get a thrill every time I drive up or down Hwy 163 and see the buttes perched on the horizon. Some people may have a feeling of déjà vu here: this is the landscape seen in famous Westerns like the classic 1938 production of *Stagecoach*, directed by John Ford, or *How the West Was Won*.

Great views of Monument Valley are had from Hwy 163 but to really get up close you need to visit the Monument Valley Navajo Tribal Park (☎ (801) 727 3353/3287). Although most of the park is in Arizona, the area code is for Utah. The park is 24 miles north of Kayenta near the state line. A four mile paved road leads to a small visitors center with information, a few exhibits and crafts sales.

From the visitors center, a rough unpaved loop road covers 17 miles of stunning valley views. You can drive it in your own vehicle (ordinary cars can just get by) or take

a tour. Self-driven visitors pay $2.50 ($1 for seniors, free for kids under six). Several tour companies have booths next to the visitors center and offer two- to three-hour trips for about $15 a person. Tours leave frequently in summer but may be infrequent or nonexistent in midwinter. The road is open from 7 am to 7 pm, May through September, and 8 am to 5 pm the rest of the year; it's closed New Year's Day and Christmas. Bad weather may also close the road.

### Places to Stay

The tribally operated *Mitten View Campground* has coin-operated hot showers but no RV hookups. There are about 100 sites for $10 each and these may fill up in summer. They are available on a first-come, first-served basis and reservations are accepted only for groups in summer. The showers may be closed in winter, when the sites can be very cold and windy (it snowed when I was there).

There are camping and motel facilities just across the state line at Goulding's Trading Post in Utah (see the Southeastern Utah chapter).

## NAVAJO NATIONAL MONUMENT

This monument protects three Anasazi ruins. The small and fragile Inscription House ruin has been closed for almost 30 years, but the larger Betatakin and Keet Seel ruins are open to public visitation and are both exceptionally well preserved, extensive and impressive. They are well worth a visit but are not very easy to get to. Thus part of their charm comes from your sense of achievement when they are reached. They can be visited only in summer.

## Information

The visitors center (☎ 672 2366) is nine miles north of Hwy 160 along paved Hwy 564. There are audiovisual shows and a small museum of Anasazi artifacts. Information, a small but excellent gift shop, ranger-led programs, camping and picnicking are available.

Hours are 8 am to 5 pm daily (extended in summer if there is enough staff) and closed on major holidays. Admission to the monument is free.

Information is also available from the Superintendent, HC-71, Box 3, Tonalea 86044-9704.

## Betatakin Ruin

This ruin is visible from the Sandal Trail, an easy one mile loop from the visitors center. The view is a distant one and binoculars are recommended. Trail signs point out local plants along the way. This trail is open year round.

During the summer, you can make the five-mile (roundtrip) hike to the ruin, accompanied by a ranger. (The ruin is not open to visitation without a ranger.) These hikes are offered most days at 11 am from about May to October, and there may be two departures (9 am and noon) in mid-summer. Tours may be offered in other months if there is enough demand.

You have to register for the hike at the visitors center. The tours are free and limited to 25 people so register as early as possible. The elevation (7300 feet at the visitors center, 6600 at Betatakin) means that the hike can be strenuous, especially on a hot summer's day when you should carry plenty of water and sun protection, including a hat. Allow five to six hours for the roundtrip.

Visiting the ruin without a ranger is prohibited.

Keet Seel ruin (RR)

## Keet Seel Ruin

This is a more challenging trip, but the ruin is worth the trip if you are up to it. It's one of the largest and best preserved in the Southwest and can be reached by foot or horseback only. Keet Seel is eight miles (one-way) from the visitors center. The hike involves a steep 1000-foot descent into a canyon then a 400-foot gentle climb. The trail is often loose and sandy and may involve wading through a shallow stream bed. Although the 16-mile roundtrip can be done in a day, most visitors prefer to backpack in and stay at the primitive campsite below the ruin. There is no drinking water (although there is water that you can purify). At the ruin is a small ranger residence where visitors need to register. The ruin may be visited only with a ranger and visitation is limited to 20 people a day and five people at a time, so you may need to wait. The last visit is at 3:30 pm. To enter the ruin requires using a very long ladder that is not for people afraid of heights.

Keet Seel is open daily from Memorial Day weekend to Labor Day. The twenty daily permits are often taken ahead of time, and you should call or write up to two months in advance to reserve a permit. This must be picked up at the visitors center by 9 am on the day you begin your hike. A map and precise directions are available at the visitors center. The permit is free and allows you to cross Navajo land en route to the ruin, but hiking away from the main trail is not allowed. No fires are allowed so bring a stove or cold food.

Local Navajos may be able to provide horses for the trip. Inquire at the visitors center. Costs are about $50 a horse.

### Places to Stay

The campground at the visitors center is open from May through September and has 30 sites with water, but no showers or RV hookups. Camping is free on a first-come, first-served basis. A couple of large group sites are available by reservation. During other months, the campground remains open but the water is turned off. If the campground is full, there is a small overflow campground with no water.

### SHONTO

This small Navajo village west of the monument has a store and offers horseback trips to Rainbow Bridge National Monument. (See Glen Canyon National Recreation Area for more information about Rainbow Bridge.)

Contact Rainbow Trails & Tours (☎ 672 2397), PO Box 7218, Shonto, 86054.

### TUBA CITY

A mile north of the intersection of Hwy 160 and Hwy 264, Tuba City, with over 7000 inhabitants was originally a Mormon town settled in 1875 and is now the major town in the western half of the Navajo Reservation. It was named after a Hopi chief.

The **Tuba Trading Post** dates back to the 1880s and sells authentic Indian arts & crafts as well as food. A motel and restaurant are next door. The trading post is a mile north of Hwy 160. **Dinosaur tracks** can be seen five miles west along Hwy 160 on the north side of the road. Look for a small sign and a few Navajo crafts stalls at the turnoff.

### Places to Stay & Eat

The *Grey Hills Inn* (☎ 283 6271), PO Box 160, 86045, is in the Grey Hills High School. To get there, go a half mile east along Hwy 160 from the intersection with Hwy 264, then turn left (north) at the pedestrian overpass. During the summer only, students operate a simple motel/youth hostel and reservations are accepted. Rooms are in the $30s and dorm beds are $11 with an AYH card. A temporary AYH membership is $3. Bathrooms are shared.

The former Tuba Motel & Trading Post has expanded into an 80-room *Quality Inn* (☎ 283 4545/4546, fax 283 4144). Rooms are in the $80s for a double from May to October, less at other times. A restaurant is on the premises. Next door is *Pancho's Family Restaurant* (☎ 283 5260) serving Mexican and American food.

At the intersection of Hwy 160 and Hwy 264, truckers stop at the *Truck Stop Cafe* (☎ 283 4975). You can eat Chinese at the *Han Yen Chinese Restaurant*.

# Hopi Indian Reservation

The Hopi are the oldest, most traditional and most religious tribe in Arizona, if not the entire continent. Their earliest villages were contemporary with the cliff dwellings of the Anasazi. Unlike the Anasazi, however, who abandoned their villages around 1300 AD for largely unknown reasons, the Hopi have continuously inhabited three mesas in the high deserts of northeastern Arizona for centuries. Old Oraibi, for example, has been continuously inhabited since 1150 AD and vies with Acoma Pueblo in New Mexico for the title of oldest continuously inhabited town in North America. It is thought that the ancestors of some of today's Hopi were the Anasazi who mysteriously abandoned their cliff dwellings 700 years ago.

The Hopi are a deeply religious and agricultural people. They are also private people and would just as soon be left alone to celebrate their cycle of life on the mesa tops. Because of their isolated location, they have received less outside influence than most other tribes.

When the Spaniards arrived, they mainly stuck to the Rio Grande valley and rarely struck out into the high deserts were the Hopi lived. Spanish explorers Pedro de Tovar and García López de Cárdenas, members of Coronado's expedition, were the first Europeans to visit the Hopi mesas in 1540, and Hopi guides led Cárdenas to see the Grand Canyon. In 1592, a Spanish mission was established at Awatovi and the zealous friars attempted to close down kivas and stop the religious dance cycle that is an integral part of the Hopi way of life. Because of this, the Hopi joined the Pueblo Revolt of 1680, drove out Spanish missionaries and destroyed the church. When the Spaniards returned to New Mexico in 1692, their attempts at reviving this mission failed and the entire area is now uninhabited and in ruins. Although unsuccessful in establishing their religion among the Hopi, the Europeans were, unfortunately, successful importers of disease: Smallpox wiped out 70% of the tribe in the 1800s.

Meanwhile, the Hopi were forced to deal with raids by Navajo and other groups. When the Navajo were rounded up for the 'Long Walk', the Hopi, perceived as peaceful and less of a threat to US expansion, were left on their mesa tops. After the Navajo were allowed to return from their forced exile, they came back to the lands surrounding the Hopi mesas. Historically, the Hopi have distrusted the Navajo, and it is ironic, therefore, that the Hopi Reservation is completely surrounded by the Navajo Reservation.

Today, about 11,000 Hopi live on the 2410-sq-mile reservation, of which over 1400 sq miles are partitioned lands used by the Navajo. A century-old legal conflict between the two tribes about the boundaries of the reservations is still going on and there seems to be no end in sight.

## Orientation

The reservation is crossed by Hwy 264, which goes past the three mesas that form the heart of the reservation. These are pragmatically named, from east to west, First Mesa, Second Mesa and Third Mesa and villages on the reservation will likewise be described from east to west. In addition, paved Hwys 6, 87 and 2 enter the reservation from the south, giving access from the I-40 corridor. Travel on paved highways is freely allowed but you can't drive or hike off the main highways without a permit.

## Information

A tribal government coordinates activities among the 12 main Hopi villages and between the tribe and the outside world. Information is available from the tribe's Office of Public Relations (☎ 734 2441, ext 100, 101 or 190, and 734 6648), PO Box 123, Kykotsmovi, 86039. Tribal offices are open from 8 am to 5 pm, Monday to Friday. Each village has its own leader, who often plays an important role in the religious practices of the village. Rules about visiting villages vary from village to village and you should contact each village (telephone numbers given below) to learn about their particular rules. These rules can change at any time.

Outside each village and in prominent places on the highways are signs informing visitors about the villages' individual policies. All villages very strictly prohibit any form of recording, be it camera, video, audio tape or sketching. Students of anthropology and related disciplines require tribal permits as well and these are not issued without very careful scrutiny. As a general rule, the Hopi are not interested in having their culture dissected by outsiders. Alcohol and drug use is prohibited throughout the reservation. Visitors are allowed to attend some ceremonial dances but many are closed to the public.

## A Hopi Cultural Glossary

**Angaktsina** – the long-haired kachina who is beautiful and sings with beauty. Anga is hair.

**Hasookata** – he steals from the people and traps them into gambling with him for their lives, which they always lose.

**Hopi** – the sounds of the word Hopi imply a gamut of positive character traits and qualities, such as moral uprightness, unobtrusive behavior, poised disposition, nonagressive conduct and modesty. One connotation from its core meaning of 'good in every way' has led to the popular interpretation of Hopi as meaning the 'peaceful ones'.

**kachina** – (pronounced katsina) one of the most important aspects of the Hopi culture. The spiritual ties related to this figure bind the people together. When the human dancer dons the mask of the spirit, he becomes, in essence, the spirit. All the good things the spirit can do, the impersonator can do as well. The spirit kachinas are not worshipped: they are personal friends. See the following aside on Kachinas for more details.

**kiva** – Hopi term for the underground spiritual celebration chamber.

**Kookyangwwuuti** – (Spider Woman) With divine powers, wisdom and an all-encompassing knowledge, she is always ready to intervene, assist, counsel, guide and save.

**Kooyemsi** – the Hopi version of a Zuni kachina. The popular name is 'Mudhead'. He may carry a drum (pusukinta).

**Kwikwilyaqa** – translates literally as 'Striped Nose'. This kachina is never seen in a line dance. He always behaves in a clownish manner.

**Kwingyaw** – the 'Chief of Cold'. Kwingyawmongwi is the one responsible for cold weather, winds and snowstorms.

**Maasaw** – the owner and keeper of the underworld, he is thought of as the one who will save the world from wickedness.

**Masmana** – the demon girl, who has supernatural powers that allow her to come back to life. She is a sexually attractive seductress of men. She is evil.

As with the rest of Arizona (and different from the surrounding Navajo Reservation), the Hopi Reservation does not observe daylight-saving time in summer.

There are no banks on the reservation. Credit cards are occasionally accepted but cash is preferred for most transactions.

Keam's Canyon and Second Mesa have the only two motels on the reservation.

### Special Events

There are scores of ceremonial dances throughout the year but most were closed in 1992 to the non-Indian public. There are two reasons for this. The first is that the religious nature of the dances was being threatened by visitors, and the second was that the remote mesa top locations did not have the infrastructure (bathrooms, water, food, emergency services and space) to deal with scores of visitors.

The attendance of non-Indian visitors at dances is determined by each individual village. The Kachina Dances, which are held frequently from January to July, are mostly closed to the non-Indian public, as are the famous Snake or Flute Dances held in August. Social Dances and Butterfly Dances, held from late August through November, are often open to public viewing.

**mötöplalwa** – a dart game that was a game for boys only but is no longer practiced. Members of some women's societies practice a similar game during fall spiritual ceremonies.

**Neyangmakiwa** – the Mixed Hunt. A rabbit hunt participated in by unmarried girls, men and boys, this event provides an opportunity for amusement and courtship.

**Oraibi** – Pronounced 'orayvi', this is the Third Mesa village, which may be the oldest continuously inhabited settlement in the USA.

**pik'ami** – a delicious cornmeal dish that requires a lot of work to prepare. Contents include wheat sprouts (ngaakuy-vani) and often a sweetener, and are cooked in corn husks.

**piki** – (pronounced piiki) a very nutritional bread that is eaten at special occasions, such as weddings or ceremonial events.

**Pöqangwhoya & Palöngawhoya** – the little demigod brothers that live at Poqangwwawarpi, north of old Oraibi. They are the grandchildren of Spider Woman, and since they live with her, reference is frequently made to the trio. Today, the brothers have the difficult task of keeping a gigantic water serpent in check to prevent it from destroying the planet with floods and earthquakes.

**powaqa** – witch (of either sex) or witchcraft, black magic.

**shinny** – a Hopi stickball game formerly played after the Powamuy ceremony in February.

**Sikyaqöqlö** – this Hopi kachina comes during the Powamuy ceremony in February. His mask is painted yellow, hence his name, 'Yellow Qöqlö'.

**somiviki** – a Hopi food for special occasions, made from blue cornmeal and sweetened with sprouted wheat (ngaakuyvani).

**sosotukwpi** – a guessing game formerly played among the Hopi at the beginning of this century. It was not uncommon for participants to play all through the night.

**Tiikuywuuti** – ugly, terrifying and powerful, this female is said to be the owner of all the game animals. She grinds corn at night and is related to Maasaw.

**totolospi** – a popular board game similar to checkers.

All dances are very important to the Hopi people, who attend them in large numbers.

The dances are part of the Hopi ceremonial cycle and are performed in order to create harmony with nature. Particularly important aspects of this are to ensure rainfall for the benefit of all living things. The dances are expressions of prayer that require a traditional and responsible performance. The precise dates of performances are not known until one or two weeks in advance. Village officials can tell you about dance dates close to when they happen and advise you if they will be open to the public.

The best bet for tourists is to try and see a Social Dance or Butterfly Dance in the fall. These normally occur on weekends and go intermittently from dawn to dusk. There is information in Facts for the Visitor on visiting pueblos.

### Things to Buy

Apart from Kachinas, the Hopi are traditionally known for fine pottery, basketware and, more recently, jewelry and paintings. These crafts can be purchased from individuals or from stores on the reservation at prices below what you'd pay off the reservation. Hopi religious paraphernalia,

## Kachinas

Kachinas are several hundred sacred spirits that live in the San Francisco Mountains north of Flagstaff. At prescribed intervals during the year they come to the Hopi Reservation and dance in a precise and ritualized fashion. These dances maintain harmony among all living things and are especially important for rainfall and fertility.

The Hopi men who carefully and respectfully perform these dances prepare for the events over many days. They are important figures in the religion of the tribe, and it can be said that the dancers are the kachinas that they represent. This is why the dances have such a sacred significance to the Hopi and why the tribe is reluctant to trivialize their importance by turning a religious ceremonial into a tourist spectacle. The masks and costumes used by each kachina are often spectacular.

One of the biggest kachina dances is the Powamuya, or 'Bean Dance', held in February. During this time, young Hopi girls are presented with kachina dolls that incorporate the girls into the religious cycle of the tribe. The dolls are traditionally carved from the eroded root of a cottonwood tree, a tree that is an indicator of moisture. Recently, these dolls have become popular collectors' items and Hopi craftsmen are producing them for the general public as an art form. Not all kachinas are carved for the tourist trade: some are considered too sacred. Other tribes, notably the Navajo, have copied kachina dolls from the Hopi.

Kachina doll

In March 1992, the well-known comic book publisher, Marvel Comics, issued an *NFL Superpro* comic book in which there was a story about kachinas trying to violently capture a Hopi ice-skating champion who was not living a traditional lifestyle. The Hopi people considered this an inaccurate and blasphemous portrayal of the sacred nature of the kachina's role in Hopi life. It was also the last straw in many years of inappropriate actions regarding Hopi religious practices, and almost all kachina dances are now closed to public viewing. ■

however, is not offered for sale. Reputable stores include Keams Canyon Arts & Crafts (☎ 738 2295) in Keams Canyon, Hopi Arts and Crafts Guild & Coop (☎ 734 2463) and Shalake's Gallery (☎ 734 2384) both next to the Cultural Center on Second Mesa, and the Monongya Gallery (☎ 734 2344) near Old Oraibi.

## KEAMS CANYON

This easternmost village houses federal government offices and officials, a small hospital, a crafts store and several churches. It is not a traditional Hopi village.

*Keams Canyon Motel* (☎ 738 2297) has basic rooms in the $30s. Nearby is a free campground with no water or facilities.

There is a simple restaurant here serving American and Hopi food from 7 am daily.

## FIRST MESA

This mesa is about 15 miles west of Keams Canyon. **Polacca** is a non-traditional village at the bottom of the mesa. A steep road climbs to the mesa top but large RVs and trailers won't make it; leave them in Polacca. The first village on the mesa is **Hano**, inhabited by Tewa-speaking Pueblo Indians who arrived in 1696 after fleeing from the Spaniards. They have been integrated into the Hopi tribe. Hano runs into the Hopi village of **Sichomovi** (you can't tell the difference), which is an 'overflow' of Walpi. Tourist information and guides are available here at Ponsli Hall (☎ 737 2262). Note that the mesa is occasionally closed to visitors during Kachina Dances, so call ahead if you really want to visit.

At the very end of First Mesa is the tiny village (six permanent families) of **Walpi**. This was built in the 1400s and is in a spectacular setting on a finger-mesa jutting out into space. It is the most dramatic of the Hopi villages. The mesa is so narrow at this point that you can't drive in; cars must be left in a parking area near the entrance to the village. There is a tourist office (☎ 737 2670) that has information about First Mesa and also provides guides for walks into Walpi. You aren't allowed to walk in without a guide. Guides are usually available from about 9:30 am to 4 pm and their services are free, although a tip is in order if you enjoy their tour.

There are several artisans living on First Mesa who sell pots, Kachina dolls and other crafts. Ask your tour guide about them, or watch for a sign in the window of a house. I bought a lovely Crow Mother Kachina carved by Burke Silas, Jr, up here – it's one of my favorite things.

## SECOND MESA

This is about 10 miles west of First Mesa. The **Hopi Cultural Center** (☎ 734 6650) is here with a small museum about the Hopi. Admission is $3 ($1 for children 12 and under) and hours are 8 am to 5 pm, Monday to Friday, and 9 am to 4 pm on summer weekends. Next door is the *Hopi Cultural Center Motel & Restaurant* (☎ 734 2401), PO Box 67, Second Mesa, 86043. About 30 modern nonsmoking motel rooms cost in the $60s a double. They are often fully booked in summer so call as far in advance as you can. The restaurant serves both American food and some Hopi dishes like lamb stew, but they don't serve beer or alcohol. On the other side of the museum is a free camping area with no facilities. Crafts stores are also nearby.

Also on Second Mesa are three Hopi villages that often have dances, a few of which may be open to public viewing. Call the villages between 8 am and 5 pm from Monday to Friday for information or ask at the Hopi Cultural Center. **Shungopavi** (☎ 734 2262) is the oldest village on the mesa and is famous for its Snake Dances, where dancers carry live rattlesnakes in their mouths. These are religious events, not circus acts, and tourists have been banned since 1984. Kachina dances held here are generally off-limits too, but Social and Butterfly Dances may be open to public viewing. The other villages are **Mishongnovi** (☎ 737 2520) and **Sipaulovi** (☎ 734 2570) both of which may have some dances open to the public.

## THIRD MESA

About 10 miles west of Second Mesa, this area includes both villages on the mesa and others to the west of it. The first you'll come to is **Kykotsmovi** (☎ 734 2474), founded in the late 19th century and now the tribal capital.

On top of the mesa is **Old Oraibi**, which has been continuously occupied since about 1150 AD. Oraibi is a couple of miles west of Kykotsmovi. The roads are unpaved and dusty so residents ask you to park next to crafts shops near the village entrance and visit on foot, to avoid unnecessarily stirring up clouds of dust.

Many of the residents left in 1906, after a disagreement led to a 'pushing contest'.

ARIZONA

The disagreement was over educational philosophies and school funding. One faction wanted US-funded schools for their children while the other preferred a more traditional approach. The traditionalists lost and left to establish the new town of **Hotevilla** (☎ 734 2420) and, soon after,

**Bacavi** (☎ 734 2404). Despite the relative newness of Hotevilla and Bacavi, their inhabitants remain old-fashioned and carry out yearly dance ceremonials that other villages have abandoned.

**Moenkopi** (☎ 283 6684) is a Hopi village off the reservation near Tuba City.

# East-Central Arizona

East of Phoenix, between the high desert of northeastern Arizona and the low Sonoran Desert of southeastern Arizona, lies not desert, but mainly mountainous and forested land. Two geographic features stand out in this area: the Mogollon Rim, between 1000 and 2000 feet high, which separates the Colorado Plateau from the lower deserts of Arizona; and the forested lands below the rim, composed of national forests and the Fort Apache, San Carlos and Tonto Apache Indian Reservations.

Whether national forests or Apache lands, east central Arizona is a highland area that offers cool respite for the citizens of Phoenix and Tucson. These cities' inhabitants form the backbone of tourism in the area. Travelers from outside of the Southwest, most of whom have forests at home, tend to focus more on what is, to

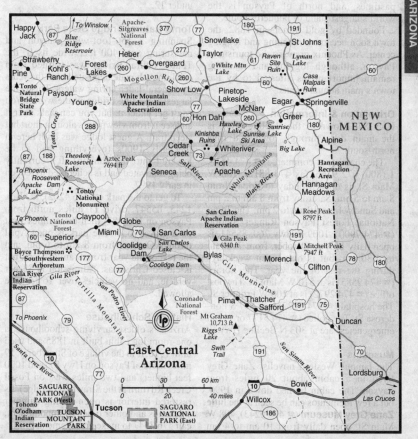

East-Central Arizona

them, exotic desert areas surrounding east central Arizona. Perhaps instead they should come here to meet Arizonans and avoid the out-of-state tourist hordes.

## PAYSON AREA

Only 80 miles northeast of Phoenix, Payson's pleasant altitude of 5000 feet and surrounding Tonto National Forest lure Valley of the Sun residents seeking to escape the summer heat. The main thing to do is enjoy the countryside and mild climate; hiking, fishing and hunting in the forests surrounding Payson are all popular pastimes, and north of Payson is the world's largest stand of ponderosa pine.

Founded by gold miners in 1882, the town soon became a ranching and logging center. As Phoenix grew, so did tourism in Payson, although logging and ranching remain important, as attested to by the town's main annual events.

### Orientation & Information

Hwy 87, known as the Beeline Hwy, is the main drag through town and runs north-south.

The chamber of commerce (☎ 474 4515, 1 (800) 672 9766, fax 474 8812), 100 W Main St, is open Monday to Friday from 8 am to 5 pm, Saturday from 8 am to 2 pm and Sunday from 10 am to 2 pm. The Tonto National Forest Payson Ranger Station (☎ 474 7900), 1009 E Hwy 260, 85541, is open daily May to October, from 7:45 am to 4:30 pm, but is only open weekdays during the rest of the year. The library (☎ 474 2585) is at 510 W Main St. The post office (☎ 474 2972) is at 100 W Frontier St. The hospital (☎ 474 3222) is at 807 S Ponderosa St. The police (☎ 474 5177 or 911 in emergencies) are at 303 N Beeline Hwy.

### Museums

The famous Western novelist Zane Grey lived in a cabin about 20 miles from Payson. The cabin burned down in 1990, but a few mementos can be seen at the little **Zane Grey Museum** (☎ 474 6243), 408 W Main St, open daily from 10 am to 4 pm

except Wednesday. The **Museum of the Forest** (☎ 474 3483), 1001 W Main St, explores the history of Native Americans, mining, cattle and lumber in the area; it is wheelchair accessible and open Wednesday to Sunday from noon to 4 pm; admission is $1.

### Payson Zoo

You can view over 50 animals, many of which have 'starred' in movies, at the small Payson Zoo (☎ 474 5435), seven miles east of town along Hwy 260. Hours are 10 am to 4 pm and admission is $4 or $1 for kids under 12.

### Tonto Natural Bridge State Park

Spanning a 150-foot-wide canyon and measuring over 400 feet wide itself, the Tonto Natural Bridge was formed from calcium carbonate deposited over the years by mineral-laden spring waters. This is the largest travertine bridge in the world. You can't get under it, but you can walk over it and see it from viewpoints along a short but steep trail. A guest lodge was built here in the early 1900s (everything had to be lowered into the canyon). It's currently being renovated and is scheduled to reopen in early 1997.

To get to the park (☎ 476 4202), PO Box 1245, 85547, drive 11 miles north from Payson on Hwy 87, then three miles west on a gravel road. The park is open April through October from 8 am to 6 pm, and the rest of the year from 9 am to 5 pm, but is closed Christmas. Admission is $3 per vehicle, and no vehicles over 16 feet are allowed.

### Historic Schoolhouse

Arizona's oldest surviving schoolhouse, a one-room log cabin built in 1885 and used until 1916, is in the village of Strawberry, 19 miles north of Payson on Hwy 87 (and 1000 feet higher) and two miles west on Fossil Creek Rd (turn at the Strawberry Lodge). Its restored interior is open during summer weekends and other times by appointment; call 476 3547 to make arrangements.

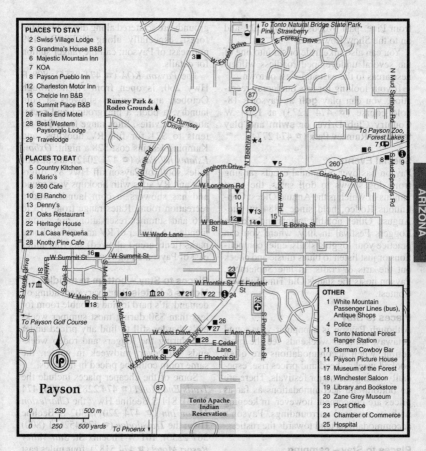

**PLACES TO STAY**
2 Swiss Village Lodge
3 Grandma's House B&B
6 Majestic Mountain Inn
7 KOA
8 Payson Pueblo Inn
12 Charleston Motor Inn
15 Chelcie Inn B&B
16 Summit Place B&B
26 Trails End Motel
28 Best Western Paysonglo Lodge
29 Travelodge

**PLACES TO EAT**
5 Country Kitchen
9 Mario's
8 260 Cafe
10 El Rancho
13 Denny's
21 Oaks Restaurant
22 Heritage House
27 La Casa Pequeña
28 Knotty Pine Cafe

**OTHER**
1 White Mountain Passenger Lines (bus), Antique Shops
4 Police
9 Tonto National Forest Ranger Station
13 German Cowboy Bar
14 Payson Picture House
17 Museum of the Forest
18 Winchester Saloon
19 Library and Bookstore
20 Zane Grey Museum
23 Post Office
24 Chamber of Commerce
25 Hospital

**Payson**

0   250   500 m
0   250   500 yards
To Phoenix

## Activities

The chamber of commerce and USFS ranger stations can advise you about outdoor activities in the Payson area.

There are many rivers and lakes suitable for **fishing**, but only Woods Canyon Lake east of Christopher Creek has a boat rentals and a bait shop. If you're really into fish, learn about the life of a trout at the Tonto Fish Hatchery (☎ 478 4200), about five miles north of Kohl's Ranch (see Places to Stay); it's open from 8 am to 4 pm daily.

Although there are many trails in the forest surrounding Payson for **hiking** and **mountain biking**, the best known is the 51-mile-long Highline Trail following the base of the Mogollon Rim from Pine to Christopher Creek. This and other trails are also suitable for **horseback riding**; you can rent horses and get information at the OK Corral (☎ 476 4303) in Pine and at Kohl's Ranch (☎ 478 4211).

Forest roads give access for hunters and anglers but are usually closed by snow in winter, when they are used for **cross-country skiing**. The best known road is the General Crook Trail (USFS Rd 300), which follows the top of the Mogollon Rim from Pine, past Woods Canyon Lake and on to the Show Low area.

You can also hike, ride or ski into one of the several undeveloped roadless wilderness areas to the east and west of town.

If your looking for less outdoorsy recreation, you can play **golf** at Payson's 18-hole course (☎ 474 2273) at 1504 W Country Club Drive, or **swim** and play **tennis** at Rumsey Park (☎ 474 2774).

### Special Events
Payson has over 50 annual events ranging from dog shows to doll sales, the most famous of which is the Annual Oldest Continuous Rodeo, held since 1884 in mid-August. Other notable events include the Loggers Festival in July, where you can practice your logging skills, enter competitions or just listen to blues music and check out the arts & crafts. In late September, Payson hosts the state's Old Time Fiddlers Contest.

### Places to Stay
Although Payson is a popular year-round getaway, summer weekends see the most action, when accommodations are often booked weeks ahead and prices rise, especially during the major festivals. There are no bottom-end accommodations as far as prices are concerned; however, in keeping with its forested surroundings, Payson's accommodations tend towards the rustic.

### Places to Stay – camping
Free dispersed camping is allowed almost anywhere in the national forest, as long as you are a quarter mile from a paved road.

Several developed USFS campsites sit along Hwy 260 east of Payson. *Ponderosa* is 15 miles east, *Tonto Creek* is 17 miles east on Hwy 260 and then a short drive north on USFS Rd 289, and *Christopher Creek* is 21 miles east and a short way south on USFS Rd 159. These are open from May to September, have water but no showers or RV hookups, and charge $7 or $8 a night on a first-come, first-served basis. Tonto Creek remains open in winter with no water or fee. Other primitive camp-

grounds are scattered along dirt roads in the forest, especially along USFS Rd 199 northeast of Payson; call the ranger station for details.

The *Payson KOA* (☎ 474 8555), 808 E Hwy 260, is open from April through October, and provides showers, a coin laundry, a pool, a playground and recreational activities. Sites range from $16 for tents to $21 for full RV hookups, and Kamping Kabins cost $28 a night. *Oxbow Estates RV Park* (☎ 474 2042), about four miles south of Payson off Hwy 87, offers tent and RV sites with hookups year round and has showers, a coin laundry and a recreation room. Rates range from $13 to $16 and summer reservations are recommended. A cluster of RV and mobile home parks (tents aren't allowed) sits four miles east of Payson along Hwy 260.

### Places to Stay – bottom to middle
**Motels & Hotels** Rates vary depending on demand; it's hard to find a double room for less than $50 during most summer weekends, harder still to find any priced under $75 during the loggers and rodeo weekends. However, midweek in winter, the same room could be priced in the $30s.

Some of the cheaper places include the *Trails End Motel* (☎ 474 2283, 1 (800) 474 2283), 811 S Beeline Hwy; the *Charleston Motor Inn* (☎ 474 2201), 302 S Beeline Hwy; the *Travelodge* (☎ 474 4526, 1 (800) 367 2250), 101 W Phoenix St; *Star Valley Resort Motel* (☎ 474 5182), four miles east of town on Hwy 260; *Ye Olde Country Inn* (☎ 478 4426), 13 miles east of town on Hwy 260; and, north of Payson in Strawberry, the *Windmill Corner Inn* (☎ 476 3064), on Hwy 87 and *Strawberry Lodge* (☎ 476 3333). The friendly Strawberry Lodge offers some of the cheapest rooms in the area (ranging from $42 a double on the ground floor to $52 for a room upstairs with a balcony and fireplace), but you need to reserve weeks in advance for summer weekends by sending a check. Rooms lack TVs and telephones.

Nicer places include the *Payson Pueblo Inn* (☎ 474 5241), 809 E Hwy 260, offering standard rooms for around $60 in summer and some suites with private spa for about $100. The *Majestic Mountain Inn* (☎ 474 0185), 602 E Hwy 260, also has pricier suites with whirlpools, and rooms have refrigerators and coffeemakers. Most of the rooms at the *Swiss Village Lodge* (☎ 474 3241), 801 N Beeline Hwy, have identical balconies or patios, and some have kitchenettes (without utensils) and/or fireplaces; prices range from $59 to $99. The lodge has a pool and an adjacent restaurant and bar.

**B&Bs** The best known B&B is the *Chelcie Inn* (☎ 474 6525), 208 E Bonita St, PO Box 0722, 85547. In a 1915 ranch house with a long porch, it offers five nonsmoking rooms, each with private bath, for about $60; the price includes a full breakfast.

Smaller B&Bs, often with just one room, can be reserved through Mi Casa Su Casa Reservation Service (☎ 990 0682, 1 (800) 456 0682). Some small places to try include *Grandma's House* (☎ 472 6362), 305 W Forest Drive, 85547; and *Summit Place* (☎ 474 6752), 716 W Summit St, 85547.

**Cabins** You can fish from your front porch at the rustic *Christopher Creek Lodge* (☎ 478 4300), 22 miles east of Payson on Hwy 260. Motel rooms are priced in the $40s, and cottages sleeping two to five are in the $60 to $100 range. Cottages have fireplaces and equipped kitchens, but beds have no linens – bring a sleeping bag or whatever. Nearby *Grey Hackle Lodge* (☎ 478 4392) offers 10 cabins with fireplaces and kitchens (without utensils) priced from about $50 to $100 depending on the size of the cabin. Also at Christopher Creek are *Creekside Mountain Cabins* (☎ 478 4557) and, two miles beyond on Colcord Rd, *Mountain Meadow Cabins* (☎ 478 4415) both with comparable prices.

**Places to Stay – top end**
The best hotel in town is the *Best Western Paysonglo Lodge* (☎ 474 2382, fax 474 1937), 1005 S Beeline Hwy, which caters to and is popular with retired people. Prices for rooms that vary from standard to mini-

suites with fireplaces range from $90 to $110 during summer weekends and include a continental breakfast. The pool and spa are open in summer only, and a family restaurant is next door.

*Kohl's Ranch Resort* (☎ 478 4211), 17 miles east of town on Hwy 260, offers motel rooms and rustic cabins, some with two bedrooms and fireplaces, priced from $70 to almost $200 depending on the unit and the season. Near Tonto Creek, the ranch offers fishing, horseback riding and cookouts, and has a restaurant, bar, sauna and pool.

**Places to Eat**
The unpretentious *260 Cafe* (☎ 474 1933), 803 E Hwy 260, is a good place for early risers, serving home cooking from 5 am to 9 pm. Other decent places with American family dining include the *Knotty Pine Cafe* (☎ 474 4602), 1001 S Beeline Hwy, and the *Country Kitchen* (☎ 474 1332), 210 E Hwy 260. *Denny's* (☎ 474 4717), 317 S Beeline Hwy, is open 24 hours.

For good Italian food, try *Mario's* (☎ 474 5429), 600 E Hwy 260, open from 11 am to 9 pm daily, and to 10 pm on Friday and Saturday. For Mexican food, dine at *El Rancho* (☎ 474 3111), 200 S Beeline Hwy, or the slightly more upscale *La Casa Pequeña* (☎ 474 6329), 911 S Beeline Hwy, which has a lounge and live music during the weekends.

The *Heritage House* (☎ 474 5501), 202 W Main St, is a tea room serving fancy sandwiches, soups and salads on a pleasant patio. The *Oaks Restaurant* (☎ 474 1929), 302 W Main St, serves excellent steaks and seafood in a pleasant atmosphere, and is open Tuesday to Sunday from 11 am to 2 pm and 5 to 8 pm daily. On Friday and Saturday the Oaks stays open to 9 pm.

**Entertainment**
See a movie at the *Payson Picture House* (☎ 474 3918) in the Payson Plaza at Bonita and Mariposa Sts.

Various bars and lounges provide drinks and live entertainment on weekends. The *Winchester Saloon* (☎ 474 4510), 615

W Main St, is a Western-style bar. The *German Cowboy Bar*, 310 S Beeline Hwy, has live music and dancing on weekends as does *Pete's Place* (☎ 474 9963), four miles east of town on Hwy 260.

The Tonto Apache Tribe (☎ 474 2068, 474 5000) operates the *Mazatzal Casino* on Hwy 87 half a mile south of Payson.

### Things to Buy

Payson has a sprinkling of antique shops, especially around the 800 block of N Beeline Hwy. If you need a good book, the bookstore next to the public library has a good selection.

### Getting There & Away

White Mountain Passenger Lines (☎ 474 1822), 814 N Beeline Hwy, has buses to Phoenix (tickets cost $17.25) at 10:15 am and to Show Low (tickets cost $16) at 3:20 pm. There is no service on Sundays and major holidays.

## SCENIC HWY 260

Hwy 260 continues about 70 miles beyond Christopher Creek to Show Low. Although the towns along the route don't offer much themselves, they do serve as good bases for camping, hiking and fishing in the wild and scenic Tonto and Apache-Sitgreaves National Forests.

### Young

About 10 miles beyond Christopher Creek, dirt Hwy 288 heads south from Hwy 260 through the Tonto National Forest and past the historic village of Young as it winds its way to Lake Roosevelt. This is cattle country, and the small and remote ranching town of can only be reached by unpaved roads.

In the late 19th century, this area was the site of a bloody feud between farmers and sheep and cattle ranchers that left anywhere between 19 and 30 people dead (historians are not in agreement). Historical markers in the area document some of the details.

There's no real town as such. The main thing to do is stop in the unique *Antler Cafe* (☎ 462 3511) on Hwy 288 for a beer or burger and examine the eclectic collection of historical artifacts hanging from every wall and ceiling beam. The cafe will rent one of three rooms for about $30 or suggest other accommodations in the area, including the inexpensive *Valley View Cabins* (☎ 464 3422). The Antler Cafe hosts country dances on weekends.

Just off the highway (look for a sign), the Tonto National Forest Pleasant Valley Ranger Station (☎ 462 3311), PO Box 450, Young, 85554, can provide information about camping, hiking and fishing in the surrounding forest and wilderness areas. The ranger station is open Monday to Friday from 7:45 am to 4:30 pm, and on Saturday and Sunday from Memorial Day to Labor Day from 7:45 am to 2:30 pm. During the rest of the year it closes on weekends and for lunch.

### Forest Lakes

Back on Hwy 260, the tiny community of Forest Lakes sits about six miles east of the turnoff to Young. The General Crook Trail intersects with Hwy 260 near here, the only place along its length where you can get onto a paved road. The 7700-foot elevation provides a cool climate for fishing and hiking in the surrounding Apache-Sitgreaves National Forest (for information stop by the ranger station in Heber). During the winter, you can try the groomed cross-country ski trails at Forest Lakes Touring Center (☎ 535 4047), which also rents canoes in summer and may have cabins available for rent as well.

Otherwise, stay at the *Forest Lake Lodge* (☎ 868 5875), offering 20 motel rooms with microwaves and refrigerators for about $60 a double on summer weekends; prices include a continental breakfast. Almost a mile east of the lodge, the *Rustic Rim Hideaway* (☎ 535 9030) has A-frame cabins that sleep up to eight people, each with two bedrooms, a fully equipped kitchen, bathroom, patio and barbecue grill. Rates are about $100 for four people and $5 for each additional person, but rates go up during holidays, when minimum stay requirements may also apply.

## Heber-Overgaard

This town's main draw is the Apache-Sitgreaves Heber Ranger Station (☎ 535 4481), PO Box 968, Overgaard, 85933, at the east end of this small twin community about 15 miles east of Forest Lakes. The station is open from 8 am to 4:30 pm, Monday to Friday, plus Saturdays in summer, and provides details of the many remote campgrounds in the area, as well as information about good fishing spots near Forest Lakes. The most accessible campground is *Canyon Point*, just off Hwy 260 about two miles west of Forest Lakes; the campground offers showers and over 100 sites for $10, about half of which have partial hookups available for $12, and is open from early May through September. Other more primitive campgrounds are along the General Crook Trail and along several other dirt roads. They too are open in summer only.

From Heber you can take Hwy 277 to the small village of Snowflake (en route to Holbrook and northeastern Arizona) or continue east on Hwy 260 to Show Low.

## Snowflake & Taylor

Technically beyond Hwy 260, these towns are included because they offer a couple of places to stay just outside the Sitgreaves-Apache National Forest.

The *Best Western Whiting Motor Inn* (☎ 536 2600, fax 536 3250), on Hwy 77 halfway between Snowflake and Taylor, provides a sauna, spa, exercise room and continental breakfast; the rooms are priced in the $40s. Slightly cheaper rooms are available at the *Cedar Motel* (☎ 536 4606), 39 S Main St in Snowflake.

## SHOW LOW

Named after a card game played in 1876 in which the winner won a ranch by showing the lowest card (it was a deuce of clubs, which is the name of the main street), Show Low sits at 6400 feet on the Mogollon Rim at the intersection of five highways. This compact town is the gateway to the White Mountains, a region of forests and mountains popular with Arizonans; along with neighboring Pinetop-Lakeside, it's a center for Mogollon Rim activities such as hunting, fishing, camping and horseback riding in spring, summer and fall and skiing and snowmobiling in winter.

The area's population is said to triple in summer when lowlanders from Phoenix and Tucson drive up to escape the summer heat. The whole area is a major forest resort, but for out-of-state visitors there isn't as much of interest as in the more northerly and central parts of Arizona. After all, for desert-dwelling Arizonans, fishing in the cool pines is a welcome getaway, but for many other folks it's not much different from fishing in the woods near home.

### Orientation & Information

Hwy 60 to the southwest goes through the Salt River Canyon and provides spectacular descent/ascent en route to Globe. To the east Hwy 60 goes to Springerville and on into New Mexico. Hwy 77 north goes to Holbrook (see the Northeastern Arizona chapter), while Hwy 260 heads west to Payson or southeast to the twin communities of Pinetop-Lakeside and continues into the White Mountain Apache Indian Reservation.

The chamber of commerce (☎ 537 2326), 951 W Deuce of Clubs, is open weekdays from 9 am to 5 pm and on weekends from 10 am to 2 pm. The library (☎ 537 2447) is at 20 N 6th St. The post office (☎ 537 4588) is at 191 W Deuce of Clubs. The hospital (☎ 537 4375) is on Hwy 260 between Show Low and Pinetop-Lakeside. The police (☎ 537 5091 or 911 in emergencies) are at 541 E Deuce of Clubs.

### Things to See & Do

Three miles northwest of town, the **Fool Hollow Lake Recreation Area** (☎ 537 3680), has boat ramps, fishing, showers and a campground, and **Show Low Lake**, four miles south on Hwy 260, and a mile east on Show Low Lake Rd, has boat rentals (☎ 537 4126), fishing and camping.

The **scenic drive** along Hwy 60 between Globe and Show Low goes through

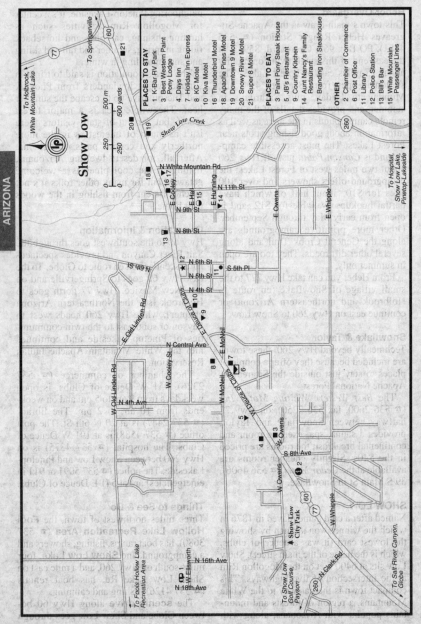

## Show Low

**PLACES TO STAY**

1  K-Bar RV Park
3  Best Western Paint
   Pony Lodge
4  Days Inn
7  Holiday Inn Express
8  KC Motel
10  Kiva Motel
16  Thunderbird Motel
18  Apache Pines Motel
19  Downtown 9 Motel
20  Snowy River Motel
21  Super 8 Motel

**PLACES TO EAT**

3  Paint Pony Steak House
5  JB's Restaurant
6  Country Kitchen
14  Aunt Nancy's Family
   Restaurant
17  Branding Iron Steakhouse

**OTHER**

2  Chamber of Commerce
6  Post Office
11  Library
12  Police Station
13  Bill's Bar
15  White Mountain
   Passenger Lines

the Salt River Canyon and is one of the most spectacular drives in eastern Arizona.

Play 18 holes of **golf** at Show Low Country Club (☎ 537 4564), Hwy 260 and Old Linden Rd (northwest of town), or Silver Creek Golf Club (☎ 537 2744) at White Mountain Lake, seven miles north on Hwy 77. You can play **tennis** at the courts at Show Low City Park.

### Places to Stay

Late May to September are the busiest months, but the area is busy year round and prices drop only a little in the off season. Rates may rise a few dollars during summer weekends and holidays.

**Camping** Undeveloped free dispersed camping is available in the Apache-Sitgreaves National Forest surrounding town. (The nearest ranger station is in Lakeside-Pinetop.) The USFS campground at Fool Hollow Lake offers showers, tent sites for $7 and RV sites with hookups for $13, while the one at Show Low Lake has sites for $7 and showers but no hookups.

*Venture In RV Resort* (☎ 537 4443), east of town on Hwy 260, is an adult RV park with 400 sites priced at $19, and has a spa and recreational activities. *K-Bar RV Park* (☎ 537 2886), 300 N 18th Ave, rents 93 RV sites for $17 and is often full in summer, so call ahead.

**Motels & Hotels** Most hotels are along Deuce of Clubs and range in price from about $30 to $70 per night.

Basic but adequate rooms for about $30 a double are available along E Deuce of Clubs at the *Snowy River Motel* (☎ 537 2926); the *Downtown 9 Motel* (☎ 537 4334) which has a restaurant and bar; the *Apache Pines Motel* (☎ 537 4328); and the *Thunderbird Motel* (☎ 537 4391).

Nice rooms with refrigerators and coffeemakers in the low $40s, a sauna and spa make the *Kiva Motel* (☎ 537 4542, fax 537 1024), 261 E Deuce of Clubs, a good choice, but call ahead as there are only 20 rooms. The *KC Motel* (☎ 537 4433, 1 (800) 531 7152), 60 W Deuce of Clubs,

also has nice rooms in the upper $40s or lower $50s.

The *Super 8 Motel* (☎ 537 7694, fax 537 1373), 1941 E Deuce of Clubs, offers standard rooms priced in the $40s. The *Days Inn* (☎ 537 4356, 1 (800) 329 7466, fax 537 8692), 480 W Deuce of Clubs, provides a pool and over 100 very standard rooms for a pricey $60 or so. JB's Restaurant is conveniently in the same complex and provides room service. Nicer rooms in the $60s are available at Show Low's newest hotel, the *Holiday Inn Express* (☎ 537 5115, fax 537 2929), 151 W Deuce of Clubs. This has a spa, pool and includes a continental breakfast in its rates, which will probably go up once the hotel has established itself. The *Best Western Paint Pony Lodge* (☎ 537 5773, fax 537 5766), on W Deuce of Clubs at Owens St, has nice rooms priced in the $70s, and the next-door Paint Pony Steak House provides room service.

### Places to Eat

Food in Show Low definitely tends towards American. For standard family dining from 6 am to 10 pm, try *JB's Restaurant* (☎ 537 1156), 480 W Deuce of Clubs, or the *Country Kitchen* (☎ 537 4774), 201 E Deuce of Clubs. The homier *Aunt Nancy's Family Restaurant* (☎ 537 4839), in a large house at 21 N 9th St, serves food Monday to Saturday from 7 am to 7:30 pm, and Sunday to 2 pm.

For steak and Western food, dine at the *Paint Pony Steak House* (☎ 537 5773), 581 W Deuce of Clubs, open from 11 am to 2 pm and 5 to 10 pm, or the *Branding Iron Steakhouse* (☎ 537 5151), 1231 E Deuce of Clubs, open similar hours.

There are also a couple of Mexican, Chinese, pizza and fast food places, but none are outstanding.

### Entertainment

The lounge bars at both steak houses may have entertainment and dancing on weekends, but for a wilder and rowdier time, dance to the live music at *Bill's Bar* (☎ 537 2031), 800 E Deuce of Clubs.

ARIZONA

## Getting There & Away

White Mountain Passenger Lines (☎ 537 4539) has an 8 am bus to Phoenix via Snowflake, Heber-Overgaard, Forest Lakes, Christopher Creek, Payson, Mesa, Tempe and Sky Harbor Airport. Buses don't run on Sundays or major holidays, and the fare is $32 one-way. The bus leaves from Phoenix at 1 pm to return to Show Low at 5:30 pm.

## PINETOP-LAKESIDE

Southeast of Show Low along Hwy 260, Pinetop and Lakeside (averaging an elevation of 7000 feet) were originally separate towns, but have now combined services and extend for several miles along the highway with many motels, cabins and stores. This is the biggest resort in the White Mountains, indeed in eastern Arizona.

## Orientation & Information

Northwest-southeast Hwy 260, known as White Mountain Blvd in town, winds its way between three public lakes as it heads east to Springerville.

The Pinetop-Lakeside Chamber of Commerce (☎ 367 4290), 592 E White Mountain Blvd, opens in the summer at 8:30 am Monday to Friday, closing at 4:30 pm Monday to Wednesday, 5 pm Thursday, and 8 pm on Friday. Saturday hours are 9 am to 1 pm, and Sunday hours are 9 am to noon; winter hours are shortened. The Apache-Sitgreaves Lakeside Ranger Station (☎ 368 5111), 2022 W White Mountain Blvd, RR3, Box B-50, 85929, is open Monday to Friday from 8 am to 4:30 pm, and summer Saturdays from 8 am to noon.

The Arizona Department of Game & Fish (☎ 367 4281, 367 4342), 2878 E White Mountain Blvd, provides fishing and hunting information and permits (as do several outfitters along White Mountain Blvd).

The library (☎ 368 6688) is at 1595 W Johnson Lane. The Pinetop Post Office (☎ 367 4756) is at 712 E White Mountain Blvd and the Lakeside Post Office (☎ 368 6686) is at 1815 W Jackson Lane. The nearest hospital is in Show Low. The police

(☎ 368 8802 or 911 in emergencies) are at 1360 Niels Hansen Lane.

Show Low has the nearest bus terminal.

## Fishing & Boating

The chamber of commerce has a brochure describing over 60 White Mountain lakes and streams suitable for fishing, and the USFS ranger station and Department of Game & Fish (see above) are also excellent sources of information. Stillwater Adventures (☎ 367 0516), PO Box 3, Lakeside, 85929, will take you on a guided fishing trip. Right in town, Rainbow Lake, Woodland Lake and Scotts Reservoir all offer fishing and boating, and Rainbow Lake has boat rentals. Also in town, the private Fred's Lake offers license-free fishing; you pay for your catch by the pound. Fred's will provide fishing tackle and will even cook your fish for you.

## Other Activities

Pinetop-Lakeside is a base for **cross-country skiing** and **hiking** as well as other activities in the White Mountains. Thirty miles east of town on Hwy 260, the Sunrise Ski Area (☎ 735 7669) has **downhill skiing**, but Pinetop-Lakeside is a good place to pick up any last-minute gear. Skiers Edge Mountain Outfitters (☎ 367 6200), next to the chamber of commerce, rents and sells skiing, fishing and camping gear, and there are several other outfitters and outdoor stores. Action Ski Rental (☎ 367 3373), 713 E White Mountain Blvd, rents skis in winter and mountain bikes in summer.

Porter Mountain Stables (☎ 368 5306), Pinetop Lakes Stables (☎ 369 1000) and White Mountain Stables (☎ 333 5857) all offer **horseback riding** in the area.

Play **golf** and **tennis** at the Pinetop Lakes Golf & Country Club (☎ 369 4531/2 or 369 4184), a mile east of Hwy 260 at the south end of Pinetop-Lakeside. Call the chamber of commerce to find out about other private courses.

## Special Events

Celebrate the West with gunfighters, chili

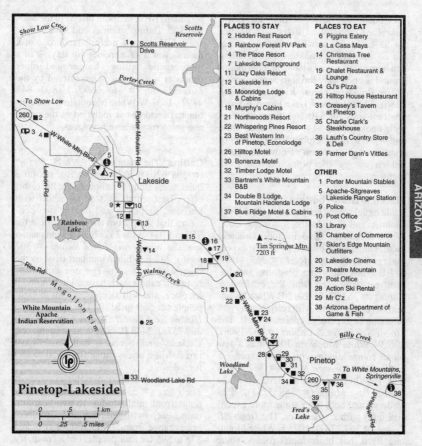

**PLACES TO STAY**

2 Hidden Rest Resort
3 Rainbow Forest RV Park
4 The Place Resort
7 Lakeside Campground
11 Lazy Oaks Resort
12 Lakeside Inn
15 Moonridge Lodge & Cabins
18 Murphy's Cabins
21 Northwoods Resort
22 Whispering Pines Resort
23 Best Western Inn of Pinetop, Econolodge
26 Hilltop Motel
30 Bonanza Motel
32 Timber Lodge Motel
33 Bartram's White Mountain B&B
34 Double B Lodge, Mountain Hacienda Lodge
37 Blue Ridge Motel & Cabins

**PLACES TO EAT**

6 Piggins Eatery
8 La Casa Maya
14 Christmas Tree Restaurant
19 Chalet Restaurant & Lounge
24 GJ's Pizza
26 Hilltop House Restaurant
31 Creasey's Tavern at Pinetop
35 Charlie Clark's Steakhouse
36 Lauth's Country Store & Deli
39 Farmer Dunn's Vittles

**OTHER**

1 Porter Mountain Stables
5 Apache-Sitgreaves Lakeside Ranger Station
9 Police
10 Post Office
13 Library
16 Chamber of Commerce
17 Skier's Edge Mountain Outfitters
20 Lakeside Cinema
25 Theatre Mountain
27 Post Office
28 Action Ski Rental
29 Mr C'z
38 Arizona Department of Game & Fish

**ARIZONA**

cook-offs, arts & crafts, horseshoe competitions, and entertainment during Mountain Frontier Days in late June. The White Mountain Native American Art Festival & Indian Market in late July brings together many of the region's best Native American artists for shows, sales and demonstrations. The Bluegrass Music Festival in mid-August is a popular event for bluegrass music fans. The year's largest event is the Fall Festival held in late September with many fun events for the whole family.

### Places to Stay

Slightly higher and more rural than Show

Low, Pinetop-Lakeside has a wide variety of motel rooms, cabins, condos and rustic accommodations set in the forest. The location brings higher prices, which during summer weekends can rise to what the market will bear and be double what they are off season. Two- or three-day minimum stays may apply at many places during summer. Frank Smith & Associates (☎ 369 4000) assists with resort rentals.

### Places to Stay – camping

Pick up a USFS map to find several roads heading northeast into the forest where free dispersed camping is allowed.

Opposite the ranger station, the USFS *Lakeside Campground* offers over 80 sites for $8 each, and provides drinking water but no showers or hookups. A boat ramp and boat rental are available, and the campground is open May through September.

The *Rainbow Forest RV Park* (☎ 368 5286), 3720 Rainbow Lake Drive, offers a few tent sites for $10 and many RV sites with hookups for $14, and is open from mid-April to mid-October. The chamber of commerce can tell you of other RV parks hidden among the pines off the main highway.

### Places to Stay – bottom end

Basic motel rooms are priced in the $40s in summer and include the following along White Mountain Blvd in approximately increasing order of price. Don't expect luxury! The *Hilltop Motel* (☎ 367 4451), 577 E White Mountain Blvd, has an adjacent restaurant. The *Blue Ridge Motel & Cabins* (☎ 367 0758), 2012 E White Mountain Blvd, has rooms with refrigerators and offers more expensive cabins as well. The *Moonridge Lodge & Cabins* (☎ 367 1906), 596 W White Mountain Blvd, has a few motel rooms along with more expensive cabins. The *Bonanza Motel* (☎ 367 4440), 850 E White Mountain Blvd, and the *Bear's Paw Motel* (☎ 368 5231), 4229 Vallery Lane both offer some more expensive units with kitchenettes. The *Double B Lodge* (☎ 367 2747), 1075 E White Mountain Blvd, has basic motel rooms, some with kitchenettes, as well as some duplex cabins priced in the $50s and $60s. Opposite, the *Timber Lodge Motel* (☎ 367 4463), 1078 E White Mountain Blvd, offers rooms priced in the $40s and $50s, as does the nearby *Mountain Hacienda Lodge* (☎ 367 4146, fax 367 0291), 1023 E White Mountain Blvd.

### Places to Stay – middle

**Motels & Hotels** Standard modern motel rooms at the *Econo Lodge* (☎ 367 3636, fax 367 1543), 458 E White Mountain Blvd, and at the *Best Western Inn of Pinetop* (☎ 367 6667, fax 367 6672), 404 E White

Mountain Blvd, are both priced in the $80s and $90s during summer and have indoor spas. Unless you prefer standard motel rooms, you'll save money by staying in a more rustic setting. Larger and nicer rooms at similar prices are offered by the *Lakeside Inn* (☎ 368 6600, 1 (800) 843 4792), 1637 W White Mountain Blvd; continental breakfast is included in the price, and some rooms have fireplaces.

**Cabins** The small *Lazy Oaks Resort* (☎ 368 6203), 1075 Larson Rd, sits on a quiet street along Rainbow Lake; the resort offers boat rentals as well as cabins with kitchens, fireplaces and one or two bedrooms that sleep from two to 10 people for $50 to $100. With 35 cabins, a sauna and a spa, the *Whispering Pines Resort* (☎ 367 4386), 237 E White Mountain Blvd, is the biggest cabin resort. The one- and two-bedroom cabins each have a kitchen and a fireplace, and will sleep from two to eight people for $60 to $120. The cabins at the *Hidden Rest Resort* (☎ 368 6336, 1 (800) 260 7378), 3448 Hwy 260, have fireplaces, kitchens and porches, and some have private spas; prices range from $50 to $80 for a double.

The two dozen comfortable cottages at *The Place* (☎ 368 6777), 3179 Hwy 260, range from small studios to two-bedroom units, each with kitchen and fireplace; prices range from $60 to $80 for two, and $75 to $95 for four people. For a group, try either the three-bed, two-bath or a five-bed, three-bath cottage. The *Northwoods Resort* (☎ 367 2966), 165 E White Mountain Blvd, charges similar prices, offering 10 pleasant one- to three-bedroom cabins, each with fireplace and kitchen. For the most historic cabins in the area, try *Murphy's Cabins* (☎ 367 2332), 325 E White Mountain Blvd, which, despite recent renovation, are also some of the most rustic. Most come with kitchens and fireplaces and rates are in the $50 to $70 range. There are comparably priced cabins at the Blue Ridge Motel & Cabins and Moonridge Lodge & Cabins (see above).

**B&Bs** *Bartram's White Mountain B&B* (☎ 367 1408, 1 (800) 257 0211), 1916 W Woodland Lake Rd, Route 1, Box 1014, 85929, offers three attractive nonsmoking rooms with private bath for $75 a double, and one large room sleeping up to four for $95.

The *Coldstream B&B* (☎ 369 0115), PO Box 2988, 85935, at the southeast end of Pinetop (call for directions) rents five rooms, three with private bath, for $105 double, and provides a hot tub, pool table, bicycles and afternoon tea as well as full breakfast. Other B&Bs can be arranged through reservation services.

### Places to Stay – top end

Eight luxurious cottages and houses nestle in 76 acres of forest and lakes at the new *Sierra Springs Ranch* (☎ 369 3900, 1 (800) 247 7590), HC 62, Box 32100, 85935, southeast of town. Call for reservations and directions. Rates for the cottages, all nonsmoking with fireplaces, kitchens and laundry facilities, start at $150 a double and include breakfast. For large groups, two houses accommodate 10 and 13 people respectively. Enjoy the two private fishing ponds, tennis court, exercise room, game room, sauna and barbecue areas.

### Places to Eat

For breakfasts and meals throughout the day, try the *Hilltop House Restaurant* (☎ 367 4617), 579 E White Mountain Blvd; *Piggins Eatery* (☎ 368 5348), 2251 W White Mountain Blvd; or one of the fast food joints. *Farmer Dunn's Vittles* (☎ 367 3866), next to Fred's Lake, serves home-style breakfasts, lunches and dinners, and will cook the trout you just caught in the lake.

For Mexican food, your best bet is *La Casa Maya* (☎ 368 6444), 1825 W White Mountain Blvd, and for pizza try *GJ's Pizza* (☎ 367 3312), 436 E White Mountain Blvd. Get picnic items or sit down for breakfast or lunch at *Lauth's Country Store & Deli* (☎ 367 2161), 1753 E White Mountain Blvd.

As in Show Low, the best places serve American food. The following four are all open for dinner and serve meals in the $8 to $20 range. *Charlie Clark's* (☎ 367 4900), at the corner of E White Mountain Blvd and Penrod Lane, has been a favorite steak house for decades. The *Christmas Tree Restaurant* (☎ 367 3107), 455 Woodland Rd, serves great American food amid a rustic Christmas decor; the varied menu is not limited to steak and seafood, offering chicken 'n' dumplings as the house specialty. It closes on Tuesdays (and Mondays in winter) and you can dine outside in summer. *Creasey's Tavern at Pinetop* (☎ 367 1908), 984 E White Mountain Blvd, is a somewhat more adventurous place with game on the menu; it also offers a Sunday brunch. The *Chalet Restaurant & Lounge* (☎ 367 1514), 348 E White Mountain Blvd, offers steaks and seafood and the biggest salad bar in town; it is open daily in summer, but is closed on Sunday and Monday the rest of the year.

### Entertainment

The *Lakeside Cinema* (☎ 367 8866, 367 8867), 20 E White Mountain Blvd, shows movies year round. *Theater Mountain* (☎ 368 8888), 537 S Woodland Rd, puts on plays and musicals in summer – boo the villain. *Mr C'z* (☎ 367 6221), 814 E White Mountain Blvd, has a variety of pretty decent live music on weekends.

### WHITE MOUNTAIN APACHE INDIAN RESERVATION

Lying between the Mogollon Rim and the Salt and Black Rivers, this reservation, known to US government officials as the Fort Apache Indian Reservation, houses the White Mountain Apache tribe. To confuse you further, it is a separate entity from the San Carlos Apache Indian Reservation, which is south of the Salt River and described later in this chapter.

Like the Navajo, with whom they share linguistic similarities, the Apache were relatively late arrivals in the Southwest, arriving in the 14th century from the plains of Canada. They were a hunting people and, as such, very mobile. Living in temporary shelters and moving often, they frequently raided other Indian tribes and, later, Europeans. Of the many different Apache groups living in the Southwest, the White Mountain Apache were willing to work with US expansion more than most, and many of the US Army's famous Apache scouts were secured from this group.

The White Mountain Apache were fairly isolated until the 1950s, when the tribal leaders decided to take advantage of modern lifestyles and embarked on long-term development planning. Accordingly, they built roads and dams, and created some of the Southwest's best fishing lakes. Later they built a ski resort and, most recently, a casino, both of which have attracted tourists. The **Hon Dah Casino** (☎ 369 0299), just a couple of miles south of Pinetop-Lakeside and three miles east of McNary, is at the junction of Hwy 260 and Hwy 73. Hon Dah, which means 'welcome' in the Apache language, welcomes gamblers 24 hours a day with card games and slot machines. The complex includes a store and an RV park.

For those seeking outdoor recreation, the over 2500 sq miles of forest offers some of the greatest outdoor recreation in the state, including hiking, cross-country and downhill skiing, fishing, camping and boating. Because it's under tribal jurisdiction, you don't need state licenses for fishing, boating or hunting, but you do need relatively inexpensive tribal permits for most activities, including camping, hiking, cross-country skiing and snowmobiling.

### Whiteriver

About 20 miles south of Pinetop-Lakeside tucked in a river valley, Whiteriver (population 3800) is the tribal capital and main information source; inquire at the Tribal Office (☎ 338 4346, fax 338 4778), PO Box 700, Whiteriver, 85941, in the middle of town on the main road, Hwy 73.

Obtain permits and information from various outfitters and lakes in the area or from the Tribal Game & Fish Department (☎ 338 4385/4386), PO Box 220, 85941,

open Monday to Friday from 8 am to 5 pm and summer Saturdays from 8 am to 3 pm. The office is next to the White Mountain Apache Shopping Center, at the south end of town on Hwy 73. Here, you'll find a supermarket, bank, post office, restaurant and the simple *White Mountain Apache Motel* (☎ 338 4927), offering 20 standard rooms priced in the $40s and a restaurant.

### Fort Apache

Built as a US Army post in 1870, the fort remains in much better condition than most structures of that period. The two dozen or so remaining buildings of the fort give the visitor a sense of what army life was like on the Western frontier a century ago. The fort was closed in 1922, whereupon it became an Indian boarding school, which contributed to its preservation. Stop by the **Apache Cultural Center** (☎ 338 4625), open Monday to Friday from 8 am to 5 pm (with extended summer hours) to learn about the history of the fort and the soldiers and scouts stationed there. There may be a small admission fee.

To get to the fort, drive three miles south of Whiteriver on Hwy 73, then follow the sign leading a mile east.

### Kinishba Ruins

Of various ruins on the reservation, the Kinishba Ruins are the only ones open to the public. Built by Native Americans in the 13th and 14th centuries, the buildings are not in very good condition and you can view them only from the outside. To visit the ruins, drive about five miles south of Whiteriver on Hwy 73, then head west a couple of miles along a signed dirt road. Check with the tribe about current admission policies; you may need a permit.

### McNary

The small town of McNary, on the north side of the reservation, was founded in 1916 as a logging center. There's not much to see here, but you can pick up a fishing permit at the grocery store.

## Hawley Lake

This lake is one of the two most developed fishing areas on the reservation (see Sunrise Park Resort for the other). You can rent boats from the marina (☎ 335 7511/7871) from mid-May to mid-October, and can pick up fishing permits at the store. Other facilities include a gas station, and a campground that offers tent sites for $6 and RV sites with hookups for $16, as well as showers and laundry. There are also the *Hawley Lake Cabins* (☎ 335 7511), which rent for $60 to $80 a double. During the winter, you can go ice fishing if the weather is OK; the road is plowed and usually open, although the store and cabins may not be. This is a good place to start asking around about the many more isolated and less developed fishing holes in the area.

## Sunrise Park Resort

This area offers excellent fishing, well-developed skiing in winter, and the most comfortable hotel on the reservation. The entire enterprise is run by the White River Apache Indian Tribe.

**Winter Activities** Spreading across three peaks, the highest stretching to 11,000 feet, the **Sunrise Ski Area** (☎ 735 7669, 735 7600) has runs that drop 1800 feet to the lower of two base areas. The approximately 60 runs are serviced by seven chair and four tow lifts, and are evenly divided among beginner, intermediate and advanced levels. Snowboarders are welcome. Adult all-day (9:30 am to 4 pm) lift tickets cost $29; kids under 13 pay $16, seniors over 62 pay $10, and those over 70 ski free. Adult half-day passes cost $23; kids pay $11. Try night skiing on Friday and Saturday until 9 pm for $15 for adults or $10 for kids. Services include ski and snowboard rental, child care, children's programs and a ski school (☎ 735 7518).

Two miles from the alpine ski area, the **Sunrise Sports Center** (☎ 735 7335) offers $6 passes for six miles of groomed cross-country trails, $6 snowshoeing passes, snowmobile tours, ice fishing, cross-country skiing lessons and ski, snowshoe and sled tube rentals. The Sports Center is open from 7 am to 5 pm every day except Tuesday.

**Summer Activities** At 9100 feet, **Sunrise Lake** has some of the best trout fishing in the area, and other lakes are close by. The Sunrise Sports Center has boat rentals and fishing gear as well as bike rentals, and can make arrangements for horseback riding. Sunrise began as a fishing and skiing area, but mountain biking, horseback riding, sailing and other activities are becoming more popular.

**Places to Stay** Next to the Sunrise Sports Center is a year-round RV Park offering sites with electrical hookups for $7 and tent camping in summer. Sites are booked through the Sports Center.

The *Sunrise Park Hotel* (☎ 735 7669, 1 (800) 554 6835, fax 735 7315) is near the lake and a couple of miles from the ski area. Free shuttle buses run frequently in winter, and the restaurant, swimming pool, spa, sauna and bar – with winter weekend entertainment – keep guests relaxed and happy. (Yes, it has a bar. This is one of the few Indian reservations where responsible alcohol use is permitted.) Rates start in the $50s for a standard double, but expect to pay a little more for a mountain view; $70 for a deluxe room; or $190 for a suite with a kitchenette and whirlpool. During the high season (winter weekends and mid-December through the first week in January) room prices jump to between $90 and $110, and suites to $280. The hotel offers a variety of special packages to tie in with resort activities; call for details.

## GREER

Halfway between Sunrise and Springerville on Hwy 260, Hwy 373 turns south into the town of Greer. Founded in 1879, Greer (elevation 8500 feet) has a permanent population of 94 residents, most of whom are involved in tourism.

In summer Greer provides a cool getaway with convenient fishing and shady hikes, and in winter an excellent base for skiing, with the Sunrise Park Resort just

15 miles away and cross-country skiing, if conditions permit, outside your door. (It doesn't always snow, even at this elevation.) Lee Valley Outfitters (☎ 735 7454) leads horseback riding trips in summer, and the Greer Lodge (☎ 735 7515) arranges romantic horse-drawn sleigh rides when winter conditions permit, as does Greer Cabin Keepers (☎ 735 7617). The small Circle B Market (☎ 735 7540) has food, fishing information, maps and cross-country ski rentals.

## Places to Stay & Eat

**Camping** The USFS has two campgrounds on Hwy 373. *Benny Creek* offers 30 sites for $6 with no drinking water; and *Rolfe C Hoyer* offers 100 sites for $10, and has drinking water, lake access and a boat ramp, but no showers or RV hookups. Both are open mid-May to mid-September.

**Motels & Hotels** Most of the places are pretty rustic, and two night minimum stays are usually required. For basic motel rooms in the $40s, try the *Tripp Inn* (☎ 735 7540). The *Molly Butler Lodge* (☎ 735 7226) opened in 1910 and claims to be the oldest lodge in Arizona; it offers rooms for around $45 a double, cabins for $60 to $70, and the best restaurant in Greer.

Surrounded by forest and with a deck overlooking the town of Greer, the *Peaks Resort Hotel* (☎ 735 7777, fax 735 7204), PO Box 132, 85927, is the fanciest place in town. Rooms with two queen beds cost $89 double (you pay $15 more for each additional person), the honeymoon suite costs $149, and larger suites sleeping four to six people cost $149, or $159 with a loft. The resort does not allow smoking, and the restaurant is open for breakfast, lunch and dinner.

**Cabins** *Greer Cabin Keepers* (☎ 735 7617) a half mile north of town on Hwy 373 rents units ranging from a cabin with kitchen for $55 a double to a four-bedroom, three-bathroom cabin with spa and laundry for $200 for six people.

The *Big 10 Resort* (☎ 735 7578) offers quaint rustic cabins with fireplaces starting around $75.

Also try the *Greer Mountain Resort* (☎ 735 7560), at the north end of Greer, with a restaurant open for breakfast and lunch from 7 am to 3 pm, and housekeeping cottages priced from $50 to $85 a double; the *Rivers Edge Resort* (☎ 735 7477), with fishing outside of your door and one- and two-bedroom cabins with kitchenettes for $55 and $65 a double; *Greer Point Trails End Cabins* (☎ 735 7513) with one-, two-, and three-bedroom cabins with kitchens for $60 to $100 for two people. See the Greer Lodge and the Snowy Mountain Inn below.

**B&Bs** At the far south end of Greer, the attractive *Red Setter Inn B&B* (☎ 735 7441), PO Box 133, 85927, is one of the newest and most modern (though rustic-looking) places in town. Rooms with a private bath and possibly a fireplace, spa, deck or patio cost around $120 a double, including full breakfast and light lunch. Smoking is not allowed.

The *Greer Lodge* (☎ 735 7216, 735 7217), PO Box 244, 85927, offers nine B&B rooms for $120 a double and eight cabins for $75 to $95 a double; children are not allowed.

The *Snowy Mountain Inn* (☎ 735 7576), PO Box 337, 85927, off Hwy 373 amid the trees, offers four rooms with private baths for $69 a double as well as seven log cabins with fireplaces and lofts that sleep four for $110. The restaurant serves gourmet continental cuisine in a high-ceiling dining room decorated with artifacts from around the world.

The *White Mountain Lodge B&B* (☎ 735 7568, fax 735 7498), PO Box 143, 85927, is in an 1892 farmhouse with rooms, some with shared baths, priced from $50 to $70 and cabins from $65 to $100.

This list isn't exhaustive so check around for others.

## SPRINGERVILLE & EAGAR

Founded as a small trading post in 1879, Springerville, with a population of 2000, has become an important ranching center along with its adjacent town, Eagar (population 4000). Along the Little Colorado River and surrounded by hills, the two towns sitting at a comfortable 7000 feet draw tourists to the cool climate. The area has the added attraction of being close to two archaeological sites that are currently under excavation.

## Orientation & Information
In the Round Valley, Hwy 60 becomes Main St in Springerville, and Alt Hwy 180 is S Mountain Rd in Springerville and becomes Main St in Eagar.

Springerville, although smaller, offers more information than neighboring Eagar. The Round Valley Chamber of Commerce (☎ 333 2123), 148 E Main St, Springerville, is open Monday to Saturday from 9 am to 5 pm (though the staff told me that funding problems might cut hours back). The Apache-Sitgreaves National Forest Supervisors Office (☎ 333 4301), 309 S Mountain Rd (Alt Hwy 180), PO Box 640, Springerville 85938, is open Monday to Friday from 7:30 am to 4:30 pm. A short way north on Hwy 180, the Springerville USFS Ranger Station (☎ 333 4372), PO Box 640, is open the same hours. The library (☎ 333 4694) is at 367 N Main St in Eagar. The post office (☎ 333 4962) is at 5 Main St in Springerville or visit the Eagar Post Office (☎ 333 4764), at 113 W Central Ave. The hospital (☎ 333 4368) is at 118 S Mountain Rd. The police (☎ 333 4000 or 911 in emergencies) are next to the chamber of commerce.

## Casa Malpais Ruin
At Casa Malpais Ruin, a Great Kiva, underground burial chambers, a plaza, numerous buildings, two stairways and many rock art panels were built by the Mogollon people in the mid-13th century and then mysteriously abandoned in the late 14th century. The site lies two miles northeast of Springerville and can be visited only on guided tours led by researchers; these leave several times a day from the **Casa Malpais Archaeology Center**.

The center (☎ 333 5375), 318 Main St, PO Box 390, Springerville, 85938, has a very small museum, a short video about the site, and an excellent bookstore on archaeology and Southwest Indians. Winter hours are 10 am to 4 pm, Wednesday to Sunday, and guided tours to the ruins are

### Archaeology in Action
The Mogollon people did not leave us with quite as many ruins as some of the other cultures living in the early part of the present millennium, but two that did survive are currently being excavated in the Springerville area. If you have ever wondered what archaeologists do for a living, you can watch them work on these sites.

If you really want to get involved, ask about the project's participatory research programs, but beware; research is very painstaking. The archaeologist uses brushes and hand trowels to slowly and gingerly loosen the centuries of debris that have covered the sites. Each object found, be it an entire pot or just a tiny shard or scrap of wood, must be carefully labeled and recorded. Archaeologists must know exactly where one piece was found in relation to the next in order to build up an accurate record of the history of the site. A helper who just brings in a pot and says 'Look what I found!' is not much help at all; archaeologists must know exactly where it was found and what was underneath, over and next to it. The work requires care and attention, but can be very rewarding. ■

offered at 11 am and 1:30 pm. In summer, the center is open from 9 am to 5 pm and tours are offered at 9 and 11 am and 2:30 pm. Tours are weather dependent, last about 90 minutes, and involve a half-mile walk with some climbing. Entrance fees are $3, or $2 for those over 55 or between 12 and 18 years old. Groups can make reservations for tours at other times. Call about their participatory archaeological research program.

### Raven Site Ruin

Built and occupied between 1100 and 1450 AD, this Mogollon pueblo shows Anasazi influence. Over 800 rooms have been identified at this site, located one mile down an unpaved road west of Hwy 191, about 12 miles north of Springerville or 16 miles south of St Johns.

The **White Mountain Archaeological Center** (☎ 333 5857), HC 30, Box 30, St Johns, 85936, 12 miles north of Springerville off Hwy 191, has a museum and gift shop open daily from 10 am to 5 pm, and organizes guided tours of the site that leave hourly from 10 am to 4 pm (except noon) from May through mid-October, and less often in winter. Tours cost $3.50, or $2.50 for those between the ages of 12 and 17 and over 60.

During summer, guided hikes lasting half a day (three hours) cover two miles and cost $18, or $15 for nine- to 17-year-olds. Full-day guided hikes that include lunch are $48 or $40 for nine- to 17-year-olds. Lunch at 12:30 pm and dinner at 6 pm are available at the center by reservation.

If you're a real archaeology fan, try one of the summer archaeological programs that last from a day (8:30 am to 5 pm, including orientation lecture, lunch, lab and field work) to overnight programs that also include all meals and bunkhouse accommodations. Rates are $59 for a day and $83 for overnight, or $37 and $61 for nine- to 17-year-olds. Six-day programs begin on Monday, and there are no programs on Sunday. Reservations are needed for all programs, and RV accommodations can also be arranged on request.

### Cushman Art Museum

If you've ever wanted to wander around a small but high-quality collection of European art from the Renaissance to the early 20th century without being surrounded by hordes of other museum goers, this may be the place. The private Renee Cushman collection was willed to the Mormon Church which displays it at the Springerville Church on request. The church is two blocks north of Main St on Aldrice Burk Rd; look for the sign. At the church, a poster on the door gives the phone number of the current curator – call for an appointment. The chamber of commerce usually will give out the curator's telephone number as well.

### Fishing

Three miles west of Eagar on Hwy 260 and then about 20 miles south on mainly paved Hwy 261, **Big Lake** offers excellent fishing at about 9100 feet in the Apache-Sitgreaves National Forest. There are several other lakes accessible from this road, several USFS-operated campgrounds open during summer (most with drinking water, but no showers or RV hookups and in the $6 to $10 range) and a marina with boat ramp and boat rentals. The season is about May through September. Call or visit the ranger station in Springerville for more details.

Fishing permits and supplies are available at Western Drug (☎ 333 4321), 105 E Main St, Springerville, and Bear Mountain Sports Center (☎ 333 2789), 446 S Mountain Rd, Springerville.

### Other Activities

The Springerville-Eagar area makes a good base for outdoor pursuits such as hiking and mountain biking in summer and skiing during the winter in the surrounding mountains and forests. Ask at the ranger station for details on trails and places to go. You can rent skis and mountain bikes at Mountain Cyclery & Ski (☎ 337 5750), 50 W Central Ave, Eagar, or around the corner at the Sweat Shop (☎ 333 2950), 74 N Main St, Eagar.

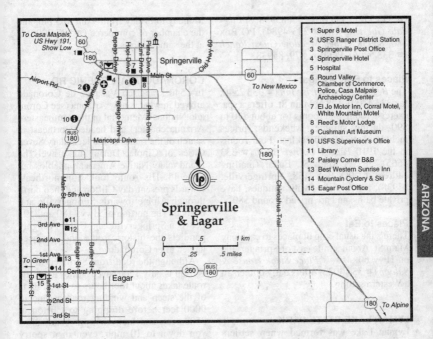

1  Super 8 Motel
2  USFS Ranger District Station
3  Springerville Post Office
4  Springerville Hotel
5  Hospital
6  Round Valley
   Chamber of Commerce,
   Police, Casa Malpais
   Archaeology Center
7  El Jo Motor Inn, Corral Motel,
   White Mountain Motel
8  Reed's Motor Lodge
9  Cushman Art Museum
10 USFS Supervisor's Office
11 Library
12 Paisley Corner B&B
13 Best Western Sunrise Inn
14 Mountain Cyclery & Ski
15 Eagar Post Office

**Springerville & Eagar**

ARIZONA

## Special Events

Rodeos and related events are held over Memorial Day weekend and the Fourth of July. The biggest event of the year is Valle Redondo Days, held on Friday and Saturday of Labor Day weekend in a historic part of town. Watch various late-19th-century demonstrations, including blacksmithing, old-time fiddling, needlepoint, entertainment and a whole lot more. Many locals dress up in period clothes for the events.

## Places to Stay – camping

The USFS offices can tell you about campgrounds in the Apache-Sitgreaves National Forest (some of the closest are at Greer and Big Lake, see above). *Casa Malpais Campground & RV Park* (☎ 333 4632), 1.5 miles northwest of town on Hwy 60, offers RV sites with hookups for $16 and a few tent sites for $10, as well as showers and a recreation area.

## Places to Stay – Springerville

Local workers often fill the cheaper motels and pay by the week. Rooms for about $30 a single are available at the *White Mountain Motel* (☎ 333 5482), 333 E Main St; *Reed's Motor Lodge* (☎ 333 4323), 514 E Main St, which has a spa; and the *Corral Motel* (☎ 333 2264), 433 E Main St.

Rooms start in the upper $30s at the *El Jo Motor Inn* (☎ 333 4314, 1 (800) 638 6114), 425 E Main St, which has a restaurant and lounge. The pleasant-looking *Springerville Inn* (☎ 333 4365), 242 E Main St, also has a restaurant and lounge and rooms starting in the $40s. The *Super 8 Motel* (☎ 333 2655, fax 333 5149), 123 W Main St, has standard rooms for $39.88/41.88 for singles/doubles.

The following guest ranches offer rustic getaways with horseback riding and other rural activities (call or write for details): *South Fork Guest Ranch* (☎ 333 4455), PO Box 627, 85938; *Coyote Creek Cattle Co*

(☎ 333 5521), PO Box 277, 85938; *Sprucedale Guest Ranch* (☎ 333 4984), PO Box 880, 85938; *Aspen Meadow Guest Ranch* (☎ 333 5206), PO Box 879, 85938.

### Places to Stay – Eagar
The *Best Western Sunrise Inn* (☎ 333 2540, fax 333 4700), 128 N Main St, offers a spa, exercise room, and rooms for about $70 to $90 during summer weekends; prices include continental breakfast. Four rooms in the 1910 *Paisley Corner B&B* (☎ 333 4665), 287 N Main St, Eagar (mailing address is PO Box 458, Springerville, 85938), are furnished with antiques, have private baths, and are priced around $80.

### Places to Eat
There's the usual crop of places to eat along Main St. About a mile east of Springerville on Hwy 60, *Mike's Place Steak House & Saloon* (☎ 333 4022) offers daily dinners in a Western setting.

### LYMAN LAKE STATE PARK
Lyman Lake was formed when settlers dammed the Little Colorado River in 1915, bringing fine fishing, boating and watersports to the area, where even at 6000 feet summer temperatures are often in the 90°s F. You can rent a boat at the small marina, or bring your own and use the boat ramp. Rangers offer special programs in summer, including tours of nearby petroglyphs and ruins, and a small herd of buffalo lives in the park. Day use costs $3.

The park (☎ 337 4441), off Hwy 191 about 12 miles south of St Johns, offers tent camping for $8 and partial RV hookups for $11, and provides showers. In St Johns (population 350), the moderately priced *Whiting Motor Inn* (☎ 337 2990, 1 (800) 800 8000), 75 E Commercial, and the cheaper looking *Trail Riders Inn* (☎ 337 4422), 125 E Commercial, are the only accommodations.

If you venture into town, you can learn about the area's history in the Apache County Museum (☎ 337 4737), a little west of downtown at 180 W Cleveland. It's open Monday to Friday from 9 am to 5 pm, and the chamber of commerce (☎ 337 2000) is at the same address.

### CORONADO TRAIL SCENIC RD
In 1540 Francisco Vásquez de Coronado arrived in what is now Arizona (see Coronado National Memorial in the Southeastern Arizona chapter) and headed northeast in search of the riches of the legendary Seven Cities of Cibola. During his travels he found many Native American pueblos but no gold. His route took him northeast towards present-day Clifton and then north through Alpine towards Springerville and beyond. The portion of Hwys 180 and 191 between Springerville and Clifton roughly parallels the historic route and has been named after Coronado.

Although the road from Springerville to Clifton is only 120 (paved) miles long, the route takes about four hours to drive. Parts of the steep and winding road ascend to 9000 feet before dropping to Clifton at 3500 feet, and many hairpin bends slow you down to 10 mph, even in a sporty sedan. There are scenic views and lookout points where you can occasionally pull over, but trailers over 20 feet long are not recommended. The fall colors, peaking in September and October, are among the most spectacular in the state, especially those of the aspen-covered Escudilla Mountain near Alpine. Many unpaved side roads can get you into pristine forest for hiking, camping, fishing, hunting and cross-country skiing, but winter snows sometimes close the road south of Alpine. The Apache-Sitgreaves Ranger Stations in Clifton, Alpine or Springerville have detailed local information.

### ALPINE
At 8050 feet, Alpine is one of the highest towns in Arizona. Early settlers proudly named the town after the Swiss Alps, but although the forested surroundings and rolling mountains are beautiful, the resemblance requires a stretch of the imagina-

tion. About 600 people live here, although you can hardly tell as there's not much of a town center. Alpine is an excellent base for outdoor activities in the surrounding Apache-Sitgreaves National Forest.

## Orientation & Information

The town is loosely scattered around the junction of Hwy 180 and Hwy 191 (formerly Hwy 666), and 'downtown' is along Hwy 180 shortly east of the junction. The chamber of commerce (☎ 339 4330), PO Box 410, 85920, is on Hwy 180. The Apache-Sitgreaves Alpine Ranger Station (☎ 339 4384), PO Box 469, 85920, is near the junction, and is open Monday to Friday from 8 am to 4:30 pm. The library (☎ 339 4925) and post office (☎ 339 4697) are both on Hwy 180.

## Escudilla Mountain Wilderness

A well-maintained, three-mile hiking trail climbs to a fire lookout at 10,877 feet on Escudilla Mountain, affording the best and highest views in the area. To get to the trailhead, take Hwy 180 six miles north of Alpine, then turn right on USFS Rd 56 for five miles, passing Terry Flat. The unpaved road is passable to cars in good weather.

## Hannagan Recreation Area

At over 9000 feet and about 20 miles south of Alpine along Hwy 191, the Hannagan Recreation Area is the highest part of the Coronado Trail, and offers plenty of summertime mountain biking and hiking, as well as some of the best cross-country skiing and snowmobiling in the state. You can fish in a small nearby lake, and can camp in one of the many campgrounds near the area. Stop at the ranger station to pick up more information.

## Activities

If you're into mountain biking, pick up a mountain bike trails map at the USFS ranger station. For horseback riding, rent a steed from Judd's Ranch (☎ 339 4326), on Hwy 180. You can play 18 holes of golf at the Alpine Country Club (☎ 339 4944),

three miles east and then south on County Rd 2122, when it's not snow-covered.

## Places to Stay

**Camping** There are plenty of USFS campgrounds in the area, and free dispersed camping is allowed throughout much of the forest, for example in the Terry Flat area in the Escudilla Mountain Wilderness. The closest developed USFS campsites are at *Alpine Divide*, four miles north of town on Hwy 180, offering 12 sites for $5 from mid-May to mid-September. The campground has water but no showers or RV hookups, and may remain open in winter with no fee (call the ranger station to check). *Luna Lake*, six miles east on Hwy 180, offers 50 similar sites for $6, and one large group site that can be reserved in advance. Fishing and boat rental are nearby, and the campground is closed in winter. There are more USFS campgrounds further afield.

*Alpine Village RV Park* (☎ 339 1841), on Hwy 180 near the junction, has showers and tent and RV sites with hookups. Tent sites are $5 and shower privileges are an extra $3 per person. An RV site with full hookups is $15. Nearby, *Meadow View RV Park* (☎ 339 1850) only has RV sites at $11 for full hookups.

**Hotels, Cabins & B&Bs** Standard rooms go for around $30 and those with kitchenettes go for $40 or more at the *Mountain Hi Lodge* (☎ 339 4311), the *Sportsman Motel* (☎ 339 4576), and *Alpine Cabins* (☎ 339 4378), all near downtown on Hwy 180. *Coronado Trail Cabins* (☎ 339 4772) offers similar prices and is south of town on Hwy 191.

The *Tal-Wi-Wi Lodge B&B* (☎ 339 4319), PO Box 169, 85920, four miles north on of town on Hwy 180, offers 20 rooms ranging from standard motel rooms to rooms with hot tubs and fireplaces for anywhere from $40 to $90; prices include continental breakfast, and the B&B's restaurant serves breakfast, lunch and dinner. *Hannagan Meadow Lodge* (☎ 339 4370), about 20 miles south of town along

Hwy 191, provides cabins with kitchens starting around $60 and a restaurant (which may close in winter).

### Places to Eat

Aside from the restaurants at the Tal-Wi-Wi Lodge B&B and the Hannagan Meadow Lodge (see above), you can eat at *Sportsman's Steak House* (☎ 339 4451) and *M&J's Corral* (☎ 339 4378); both are on Hwy 180 in Alpine's 'downtown', and serve Western-style breakfasts, lunches and dinners.

### Things to Buy

If you're using Alpine as a base for adventures in the surrounding mountains and forest, you may need to pick up some supplies. Alpine Market (☎ 339 4914), on Hwy 180, and the Tackle Shop (☎ 339 4338), on Hwy 191, have fishing and outdoor supplies and rent cross-country skis. Alpine Hardware & Building Supply (☎ 339 4711) on Hwy 180 also has outdoor equipment and supplies.

### Getting There & Away

There are no gas stations along the 90 miles of Hwy 191 between Alpine and Clifton, so plan accordingly.

## CLIFTON & MORENCI

Miners searching for gold arrived in the 1860s, but soon discovered that the area's copper deposits were a better source of mineral wealth. By 1873, prospectors founded the town of Clifton, which soon became a major mining center and the Greenlee County seat.

A huge underground copper mine operated in neighboring Morenci from the 1870s until the 1930s and was later turned into an open-pit mine that slowly engulfed the town. In the 1960s, Phelps Dodge Morenci Inc buried the old town and built a modern, company-owned town at the present site. Above Morenci, an overlook from Hwy 191 gives dizzying views of the biggest producer of copper in the country – an open-pit mine two miles in length with 200-ton trucks with tires nine feet in diam-

eter crawling like insects at the bottom. Free mine tours are offered Monday to Friday at 8:30 am and 1 pm and last about three hours; call Phelps Dodge (☎ 865 4521 ext 435) for an appointment.

Today, most of the miners live either in Morenci, four miles above Clifton, or an hour's drive away in Safford. Although Clifton remains the county seat, it has a deserted feel to it and the once splendid buildings lining historical Chase St are boarded up and in a state of disrepair. Most sights of interest lie along Hwy 191 and historic Chase St at the north end of town. For a history lesson, stop by the **Greenlee Historical Museum** (☎ 865 3115/3307) at 315 Chase St in Clifton between 2 and 4:30 pm on Tuesday, Thursday or Saturday, or call to make an appointment.

Simple accommodations are available for about $40 at the *Rode Inn Motel* (☎ 865 4536), 186 S Coronado Blvd (or Hwy 191 at the south end of Clifton) and at the *Morenci Motel* (☎ 865 4111) on the main street in Morenci.

For information about the area, visit the USFS ranger station (☎ 687 1301), HC 1, Box 733, Duncan, 85534, 10 miles southeast of Clifton at Hwy 191 and Hwy 75.

## SAFFORD

Founded in 1874 near the confluence of the Gila and San Simon Rivers, Safford (elevation 2900 feet) soon grew into an important agricultural center for farmers along the Gila River Valley. Many of the early settlers were Mormons, who later founded the neighboring town of Pima and settled in the small towns throughout the valley. Over 60% of Graham County's irrigated 55 sq miles grow cotton (one of Arizona's 'Four Cs', along with copper, cattle and citrus), and local tourism, such as it is, places second to agriculture in the local economy.

With a population of about 7500, Safford is the Graham County seat. There's not much to see in town itself, though several motels make this the most convenient gateway for the Coronado Trail to the northeast, the San Carlos Apache Indian Reservation to the northwest and the

Swift Trail up lofty Mt Graham to the southwest.

## Orientation & Information

Safford is mostly spread out along east-west Hwy 70, also called Thatcher Blvd and 5th St in the town center. Hwy 191 breaks from Hwy 70 on 1st Ave in Safford, and continues south to I-10 and Douglas, near the Mexican border.

The chamber of commerce (☎ 428 2511), 1111 Thatcher Blvd (Hwy 70), is open Monday to Saturday from 8 am to 5 pm, and has a display of local industries (cotton, copper and the controversial new astronomy observatory on Mt Graham) as well as information about the fast-developing tourist industry. The Coronado National Forest Ranger Station (☎ 428 4150), PO Box 709, 85548, is on the 3rd floor of the post office. The BLM (☎ 428 4040), is at 711 14th Ave, 85546.

The library (☎ 428 1531) is at 808 7th Ave. The post office (☎ 428 0220) is at 504 5th Ave and Thatcher Blvd. The hospital (☎ 348 8000) is at 1600 S 20th Ave. The police (☎ 428 6884 or 911 in emergencies) are at the corner of 11th Ave and 7th St.

ARIZONA

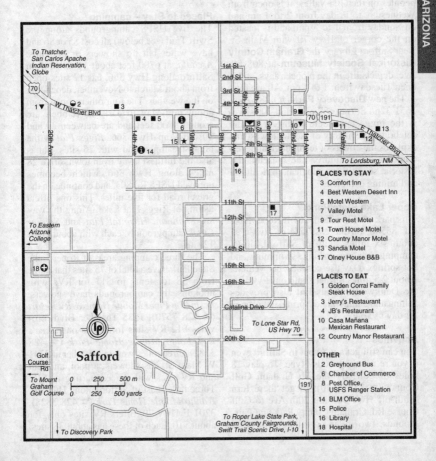

**Safford**

To Thatcher,
San Carlos Apache
Indian Reservation,
Globe

To Eastern
Arizona
College

To Mount
Graham
Golf Course

Golf
Course
Rd

0    250    500 m
0    250    500 yards

To Lone Star Rd,
US Hwy 70

To Lordsburg, NM

To Roper Lake State Park,
Graham County Fairgrounds,
Swift Trail Scenic Drive, I-10

To Discovery Park

**PLACES TO STAY**
3  Comfort Inn
4  Best Western Desert Inn
5  Motel Western
7  Valley Motel
9  Tour Rest Motel
11 Town House Motel
12 Country Manor Motel
13 Sandia Motel
17 Olney House B&B

**PLACES TO EAT**
1  Golden Corral Family
   Steak House
3  Jerry's Restaurant
4  JB's Restaurant
10 Casa Mañana
   Mexican Restaurant
12 Country Manor Restaurant

**OTHER**
2  Greyhound Bus
6  Chamber of Commerce
8  Post Office,
   USFS Ranger Station
14 BLM Office
15 Police
16 Library
18 Hospital

## Museums

The Safford area has three small local museums. At Eastern Arizona College, three miles west in Thatcher, the **Museum of Anthropology** (☎ 428 8310), displays artifacts of Native American culture, archaeology and anthropology; the collection is available to students and researchers during the school year (September to May) Monday to Friday from 9 am to noon and 1 to 4 pm. Six miles further west in the village of Pima, the **Eastern Arizona Museum** (☎ 485 2269), has exhibits describing the influences of various peoples on the Gila Valley; it is open from Wednesday to Friday from 2 to 4 pm and on Sunday from 1 to 5 pm, and is located on the corner of Hwy 70 with Main St. Near Safford Library, the **Graham County Historical Society Museum** at 808 8th Ave, depicts life in the pioneer days, and is open Tuesday from 1 to 4 pm. All are free.

The new **Discovery Park** (☎ 428 6260), 1651 32nd St (near 32nd St and 20th Ave) is the biggest museum in the area, and celebrates the history of the Southwest and explores the effects of technological developments on its future. The museum has historic, scientific, ecological, agricultural and mining exhibits.

## Roper Lake State Park

This park (☎ 428 6780), 101 E Roper Lake Rd, 85546, on the east side of Hwy 191 about six miles south of Safford, offers camping, boating, fishing, swimming and hot springs. Day use costs $3 per vehicle. About 2.5 miles further south on Hwy 191, the Dankworth Ponds Init also provides fishing and a mineral hot spring, but is open for day use only.

## Activities

You can still get a workout in Safford even if you're not the woodsy type. To play 18 holes of golf, try the Mt Graham Golf Course (☎ 348 3140); to get there turn south off Hwy 70 onto 20th Ave to Golf Course Rd. Graham County Park and Fairgrounds, two miles out along Hwy 191,

offers tennis, racquetball and skating along with other activities. If you're in the mood for swimming, take a splash in the pool (open summer only) in the park behind the chamber of commerce.

## Special Events

The most notable local events are Pioneer Days in late July, celebrating the early Mormon settlement of the area, the PRCA Rodeo in August and the Graham County Fair in October. There are other events throughout the year – call the chamber of commerce for details.

## Places to Stay – camping

The five USFS campgrounds along the Swift Trail (see below) all cost $5 or $6 and have water but no showers or hookups. *Arcadia*, at 6700 feet about 11 miles from Safford along Hwy 366, has 17 sites open from about March to November, depending on the weather. The four others, open from about mid-May to early November, are around 9000 feet and are between 20 and 30 miles up Hwy 366. *Riggs Flat* is the biggest campground with 26 sites, but is also the furthest away from town; drive 28 miles along Hwy 366, which becomes unpaved USFS Rd 803, and continue on the gravel road for five miles. This one offers fishing at Riggs Flat Lake. Along the way are *Shannon*, *Hospital Flat* and *Soldier Creek* campgrounds, each with about 10 or 12 sites.

The three camping areas at Roper Lake State Park have a total of 75 sites that range from $8 for tents to $11 for RVs with hookups; the campgrounds have showers. *Lexington Pines Mobile Home & RV Resort* (☎ 428 7570), 1535 Thatcher Blvd, provides $12 RV sites for adults only. *Lee's Red Lamp Mobile Home Park* (☎ 428 3382), three miles west in Thatcher at 3341 W Main St, has showers, a pool, and tent and RV sites with prices starting at $10. Three miles east of Safford along Hwy 70, *Ivanho Mobile Home Park* (☎ 428 3828), 3201 E Hwy 70, offers RV sites only for about $10. Each of these has about 35 sites.

## Places to Stay – bottom end

For double rooms priced around $30, try the *Motel Western* (☎ 428 7850), 1215 W Thatcher Blvd; or the *Town House Motel* (☎ 428 3474), 225 E Thatcher Blvd. Each has a pool. Other cheap places include the *Tour Rest Motel* (☎ 428 3881), 110 W Thatcher Blvd; the *Valley Motel* (☎ 428 2713), 1050 W Thatcher Blvd; and the *Pioneer Lodge* (☎ 428 0733), 2919 W Hwy 70 in Thatcher. The cheap and basic-looking *Pima Motel* (☎ 485 2484), 191 W Center St, is on Hwy 70 in Pima and is the last motel for 70 miles.

Rooms start in the $30s in the *Country Manor Motel* (☎ 428 3200, 1 (800) 555 3664), 420 E Thatcher Blvd, which has a pool and a 24-hour restaurant. Rooms start around $40 in The *Sandia Motel* (☎ 428 5000, 1 (800) 578 2151), 520 E Thatcher Blvd. It has a pool and spa and a 24-hour restaurant across the street.

## Places to Stay – middle

Room rates are about $60 a double and include a continental breakfast at the *Comfort Inn* (☎ 428 5851, fax 428 4968), 1578 W Thatcher Blvd. The *Best Western Desert Inn* (☎ 428 0521, fax 428 7653), 1391 W Thatcher Blvd, has double rooms in the $60 to $80 range. Both hotels have a pool and are next door to a restaurant.

*Olney House B&B* (☎ 428 5118), 1104 Central Ave, 85546, has a spa and charges $70 for a double room with bath.

## Places to Eat

Standard American fare is offered at the *Country Manor Restaurant* (☎ 428 2451), open 24 hours; *Jerry's Restaurant* (☎ 428 5613), next door to the Comfort Inn; and *JB's* (☎ 348 0083), next to the Best Western Desert Inn. For cheap steaks, stop by the *Golden Corral Family Steak House* (☎ 428 4744), at the corner of W Hwy 70 and 20th Ave.

The best Mexican place is *Casa Mañana* (☎ 428 3170), 502 1st Ave, open Monday to Thursday from 11 am to 9 pm and Friday and Saturday from 11 am to 10 pm. It has been here for 45 years.

## Getting There & Away

The Greyhound bus (☎ 428 2150) stops at 1850 W Thatcher Blvd. Buses leave three times a day for Phoenix or Lordsburg, New Mexico, and beyond.

## AROUND SAFFORD
## Hot Springs

There are natural hot springs in the Safford area, but few have been very developed. Ask at the BLM office in town for directions to lesser known ones. There is a small spa at Kachina Springs (☎ 426 7212), near Roper Lake State Park.

## Swift Trail Scenic Drive

Hwy 366, popularly known as the Swift Trail, is a paved road up the Pinaleno Mountains almost to the top of 10,713-foot

ARIZONA

## Development on Mt Graham

Mt Graham is one of the 'sky islands' of southeastern Arizona, separated from other summits in the area by lowlands. Because plants and animals living near the top of the mountain have been isolated from similar species living on other nearby ranges, some have evolved into different species or sub-species; this makes these high peaks a living natural laboratory for the study of evolution.

However, because Mt Graham is the highest mountain in the area and is a long way from city lights and other sky pollutants, it has been chosen as the site of a major telescope observatory that is currently under construction. The project threatens the habitat of the Mt Graham red squirrel, among other 'sky island' species, and is therefore embroiled in controversy. Mt Graham is also a sacred site for some Apache Indian groups, which adds to the conflict. A small exhibit in the Safford Chamber of Commerce describes the astronomy project in glowing terms as a source of more employment and tourism for the area. ■

Mountain lion

ARIZONA

**Mt Graham**, which is the highest peak south of the White Mountains and provides the highest base to top elevation change of any peak in the state. The road begins from Hwy 191 almost eight miles south of Safford and climbs 34 miles to the summit. This is part of the Coronado National Forest; stop by the Safford ranger station for detailed information.

The road passes through a succession of ecological life zones beginning with desert (it's in the transition between the Sonoran and Chihuahuan Deserts) and climbing into dense, mainly coniferous, forests of the Canadian and Hudsonian zones. These are the haunts of squirrel, wild turkeys, deer, bear, mountain lion and many other species. There are several USFS campgrounds and picnic areas along the way and access to good hiking, fishing and hunting. The top section, which is gravel, is closed by snow in winter.

The Columbine Visitor Station, over 20 miles along the Swift Trail, offers maps and information and is open daily from 9 am to 6 pm from Memorial Day to Labor Day. The winding road is not recommended for extra-long RVs or trailers, and the top gravel section is closed by snow in winter.

## SAN CARLOS APACHE INDIAN RESERVATION

About 2900 sq miles of lakes, rivers, forests and desert belong to the San Carlos Apache Tribe, whose members number over 8000 on the reservation, 3000 of whom live in the tribal capital of San Carlos on Hwy 70. Cattle ranching forms the backbone of the economy, but some logging, mining and tourism also bring in revenue. Most tourists come for outdoor recreation, although there is also a casino. There are no motels, but you can camp at various campgrounds, including those at San Carlos Lake and Seneca.

A maze of unpaved roads penetrates the reservation, leading to scores of little lakes and river fishing areas as well as primitive camping areas. You'll need a high clearance pickup or 4WD vehicle for many of them; contact the San Carlos Recreation and Wildlife Department for a detailed map and information.

Trout fishing on the Black River is especially good, and big game hunting is permitted in season. Local guides can help you find rich hunting grounds for a high fee.

The Apache Gold Casino, on the north side of Hwy 70 at the western edge of the reservation, offers 24-hour gambling and a restaurant and lounge. This is the only casino in the state that serves beer and wine.

### Information

To camp, hike, fish, hunt and drive off the main highways, you'll need a permit from the San Carlos Recreation and Wildlife Department (☎ 475 2343), PO Box 97, 85550. The office occupies a big building on Hwy 70 in San Carlos – you can't miss it. Permits and information are also available at the Exxon station (☎ 426 2640) and the Circle K store on Hwy 70 in Globe, just outside the reservation. Arizona state permits are not valid on reservation land.

For more information, contact the San Carlos Tribal Offices (☎ 475 2361, fax 475 2567), PO Box 0, 85550.

## San Carlos Lake

Formed by the Coolidge Dam on the Gila River, this is the largest lake wholly in Arizona; when full, it covers 30 sq miles and has 158 miles of shoreline. The lake has excellent fishing, and recently bore the state's record-winning catfish (65 lbs) and crappie (4 lbs 10 ozs). Largemouth bass are also abundant. Near Coolidge Dam (10 miles south of San Carlos) there is a marina and a convenience store, as well as a campground with RV hookups, water and tent spaces but no showers. Fees are $5 a person.

## Seneca

There is a small lake and campground here, just off Hwy 60 about 33 miles northeast of Globe. Camping is $5 a person but there are no drinking water nor RV hookups.

## Special Events

Sunrise Ceremonies featuring traditional dances in honor of young girls' coming of age are held during the summer. Some of these dances may be open to the public; call the tribal office for dates and details. The tribal rodeo and fair, held in San Carlos over Veterans' Day weekend (closest weekend to 11 November), also features traditional dancing. A spring roundup rodeo is held in April, and other rodeos and dances may be held throughout the year.

## GLOBE

The discovery of a globe-shaped boulder formed of almost pure silver sparked a short-lived silver boom in here in the 1870s, which was followed by the development of a long-lasting copper mining industry. Globe (population 6000, elevation 3500) became the Gila County seat, a distinction it retains even though most of the copper mining has moved to the nearby towns of Miami and Superior. Globe offers the best accommodations in the area and provides a pleasant rural alternative to Phoenix (80 miles west) for its various attractions.

## Orientation & Information

Hwy 60, the main thoroughfare, is called Ash St, then Willow St and finally Broad St as it snakes through town from east to west.

The Globe-Miami Chamber of Commerce (☎ 425 4495, 1 (800) 804 5623), 1360 N Broad St, is open Monday to Friday from 8 am to 5 pm, and may also open during winter weekends. The Tonto National Forest Ranger Station (☎ 425 7189) is on Six Shooter Canyon Rd at the south end of town. The library (☎ 425 6111) is at 339 S Broad St. The post office (☎ 425 2381) is at 101 S Hill St. The hospital (☎ 425 3261) is south of the Hwy 60 and Hwy 88 intersection between Globe and Miami. The police (☎ 425 5752 or 911 in emergencies) are at 175 N Pine St.

## Historic Downtown

Many turn-of-the century buildings still line Broad St south of Hackney Ave, making the downtown area a pleasant place to walk that isn't as touristy as some old centers. The chamber of commerce has a walking tour brochure describing over 20 buildings.

## Gila County Historical Museum

Find out about the area's history in this museum (☎ 425 7385) behind the chamber of commerce. The building the museum is housed in used to be the home of a mine rescue training station, so the museum is heavy in mining artifacts. Hours are 10 am to 4 pm, Monday to Friday, plus Saturday in winter.

## Cobre Valley Center for the Arts

The turn-of-the-century Gila County Courthouse houses this arts center (☎ 425 0884), 101 N Broad St. A variety of local artists' works are on display Monday to Saturday from 9 am to 5 pm, and Sunday from noon to 5 pm.

## Besh-Ba-Gowah Archaeological Park

A small pueblo built by the Salado culture in the 1200s and abandoned by the early 1400s is the principal sight here, although

ARIZONA

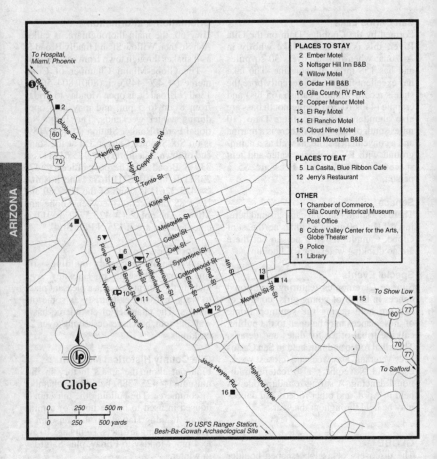

**PLACES TO STAY**
2 Ember Motel
3 Noftsger Hill Inn B&B
4 Willow Motel
6 Cedar Hill B&B
10 Gila County RV Park
12 Copper Manor Motel
13 El Rey Motel
14 El Rancho Motel
15 Cloud Nine Motel
16 Pinal Mountain B&B

**PLACES TO EAT**
5 La Casita, Blue Ribbon Cafe
12 Jerry's Restaurant

**OTHER**
1 Chamber of Commerce,
   Gila County Historical Museum
7 Post Office
8 Cobre Valley Center for the Arts,
   Globe Theater
9 Police
11 Library

To Hospital,
Miami, Phoenix

To Show Low

To Safford

To USFS Ranger Station,
Besh-Ba-Gowah Archaeological Site

Globe

0    250    500 m
0    250    500 yards

there are some signs of earlier Hohokam occupation. Contact the park office (☎ 425 0320), 150 N Pine St, 85501, about guided tours or walk around by yourself. Visit the museum's fine collection of Salado pottery and ethnobotanical garden between 9 am and 5 pm daily; admission is $2 for those over 12 years old.

### Activities
Cobre Valley Country Club (☎ 473 2542), off Hwy 88 just north of Hwy 60, offers a nine-hole golf course and tennis and raquetball courts.

Far Flung Adventures (☎ 425 7272, 1 (800) 359 2627), PO Box 2804, 85501, offers one- to five-day Salt River rafting trips. High water is February to June.

### Special Events
Of the yearly events, the most interesting are the Historic Homes Tour held over a weekend in mid-February, the Old Time Fiddlers Contest in late July, the Gila County Fair in mid-September and Apache Days, exhibiting tribal arts and traditional dancing, on the third or fourth Saturday in October.

## Places to Stay – camping
For free dispersed camping and some small developed campgrounds, drive south of Globe along Six Shooter Canyon Rd past the USFS ranger station (which can provide a map), where the road becomes USFS RD 122. The *Gila County RV Park* (☎ 425 4653), 300 S Pine St, offers sites with full hookups for $15.

## Places to Stay – bottom end
Basic double rooms with one bed in the upper $20s are available at the *Willow Motel* (☎ 425 9491), 792 N Willow St; *Belle Aire Motel* (☎ 425 4406), 1600 N Broad St; and the *El Rancho Motel* (☎ 425 5757, fax 425 8402), 1300 E Ash St. The *El Rey Motel* (☎ 425 4427), 1201 E Ash St, charges $23/35 for singles/doubles and offers RV parking (but no hookups) for $3 a night. The *Ember Motel* (☎ 425 5736, 1 (800) 253 1123), 1105 N Broad St, charges $25/32 for singles/doubles and has a pool. Rooms with two beds cost a bit more.

## Places to Stay – middle
**Motels** The *Copper Manor Motel* (☎ 425 7124, 1 (800) 421 7124, fax 425 5266), 637 E Ash St, has standard rooms, some with refrigerators, that rent for about $50 and budget rooms across the street priced in the low $30s; there is a pool and a 24-hour restaurant next door.

*Cloud Nine Motel* (☎ and fax 425 5741, 1 (800) 265 8399), 1699 E Ash St, rents comfortable rooms, some with spas and refrigerators, priced from $55 to $80 a double, and has a pool. The *Best Western Copper Hills Inn* (☎ 425 7151, fax 425 2504), on Hwy 60 a short way east of the intersection with Hwy 88, has a pool, restaurant and bar and rooms with refrigerators in the $55 to $70 range.

**B&Bs** The *Pinal Mountain B&B* (☎ 425 2562), 360 Jess Hayes Rd, PO Box 1593, 85502, offers two nonsmoking rooms with private bath for $75. Housed in a renovated school dating from 1907, the *Noftsger Hill Inn* (☎ 425 2260), 425 North St, has smaller rooms with shared bath as well as more expensive rooms with private bath and king-size beds; prices range from $45 to $65. *Cedar Hill B&B* (☎ 425 7530), 175 E Cedar St, charges $50.

## Places to Eat
In the old center of town, *La Casita* (☎ 425 8462), 470 N Broad St, and the *Blue Ribbon Cafe* (☎ 425 4423), 474 N Broad St, are both good, inexpensive choices. La Casita serves Mexican lunches and dinners, and the old-fashioned Blue Ribbon serves home cooking Monday to Friday from 6:30 am to 9 pm, Saturday from 7:30 am to 9 pm, and Sunday from 7:30 am to 8 pm. *Jerry's Restaurant* (☎ 425 5282), 699 E Ash St, serves standard American fare 24 hours a day.

## Entertainment
Catch a movie at the *Globe Theater* (☎ 425 5581), 141 N Broad St, or stop by one of the old bars along Broad St for to sip a beer in aged surroundings.

## Getting There & Away
Greyhound (☎ 425 2301) runs three buses a day to Phoenix (tickets are $15) and three to Safford (tickets cost $11) and beyond, and stops behind the Burger King on the south side of Hwy 60, 1.6 miles west of the chamber of commerce.

## AROUND GLOBE
Hwy 60 west of Globe passes staggering mountains of mine tailings from copper mines north of the highway; these continue for several miles through the small towns of Claypool and Miami. From here, the road winds through the Devil's Canyon section of the Pinal Mountains, affording vistas of jagged ridges. Twenty-five miles west of Globe, the mining town of **Superior** has a couple of cheap motels, the *El Portal* (☎ 689 2886) and *Apache Tear Village RV Park & Motel* (☎ 689 5800). Visit the chamber of commerce (☎ 689 2441), 151 Main St, for information about the area.

You can stop by the outstanding **Boyce Thompson Southwestern Arboretum**

ARIZONA

(☎ 689 2811), about three miles west of Superior, for a quiet garden walk. Stop at the visitor center to pick up information about the trails that wind through the 35 acres of arid-land plants. The arboretum is open daily from 8 am to 5 pm, except on Christmas, and is well worth a visit. Admission is $4, or $2 for five- to 12-year-olds.

## THE APACHE TRAIL

The Apache Trail (Hwy 88) heads northwest from Globe past the Tonto National Monument to Theodore Roosevelt Lake and Dam before heading southwest to Apache Junction, 45 miles away. The 22-mile section west of the Roosevelt Dam is steep, winding, narrow and unpaved, and is not recommended for trailers or large RVs. Heading west from the dam puts you on the outside of the road during the steepest climb; nervous drivers prefer the 'security' of traveling this from west to east in order to hug the cliff wall rather than the drop-off. This is certainly one of the most spectacular drives in the area. Once you're back on paved highway, the trail will take you past the small community of Tortilla Flat and the ghost town of Goldfield before reaching Apache Junction and the greater Phoenix area.

### Tonto National Monument

About 28 miles northwest of Globe along the well-paved section of the Apache Trail, the Tonto National Monument protects a highlight of the area: a two-story Salado pueblo built in a cave, that, like most other pueblos, was mysteriously abandoned in the early 1400s.

From the visitors center (☎ 467 2241) a paved half-mile footpath climbs gently to the ruins, affording good views of the saguaro cactus-studded hillsides in the foreground and the Theodore Roosevelt Lake in the distance. The visitors center has a museum and water, but does not offer food or camping facilities.

If you call or write ahead, you can arrange to join a free ranger-led, three-hour hike to an upper ruin along an unpaved footpath. Further information is available from the Superintendent, Tonto National Monument, HC 02, Box 4602, Roosevelt, 85545. The monument is open from 8 am to 5 pm daily, 6 pm in summer, but the trail closes an hour earlier. Admission is $4 per private vehicle or $2 per bicyclist or bus passenger and Golden Eagle, Age and Access passes are honored.

### Theodore Roosevelt Lake & Dam

Built of bricks on the Salt River in 1911, this is the earliest of the large dams flooding the Southwest and, at 280 feet, is the world's highest masonry dam. Sweating at a hot 2100-foot elevation, the lake attracts water-sport enthusiasts year round, and swimming, water-skiing and boating are popular activities from spring to fall. The fishing is great throughout the year, and bass and crappie are two favored catches.

A marina and the Tonto Basin Ranger Station (☎ 467 3200), PO Box 649, Roosevelt, 85545, are about 1.5 miles east of the dam, just off Hwy 88, and are open

Saguaro cactus

Monday to Friday from 7:45 to 4:30 pm. The Roosevelt Lake Marina (☎ 467 2245) has groceries fishing and camping supplies, a snack bar, a boat ramp and boat rentals that range from fishing boats for $45 a day to ski boats for $250 a day. You can also rent jet skis and water-skiing gear.

**Places to Stay** There are several USFS campgrounds in the area. *Windy Hill Campground*, with 348 campsites, is the largest in the USFS system, and has showers, drinking water and boat ramps but no RV hookups. Rates are $8 to $18 depending on the site. To get to the campground, drive about six miles east of the dam on Hwy 88, then head north on USFS Rd 82 for two miles to the lake. Ask at the ranger station about smaller campgrounds in the area.

### Apache Lake

This long and narrow lake is west of Roosevelt Lake, and is reached via the unpaved steep portion of the Apache Trail. About 12 miles west of Roosevelt Dam, the Apache Lake Marina (☎ 467 2511) offers a boat ramp and rentals, tent and RV camping with hookups, and a small lodge with standard motel rooms priced in the $40s and rooms with kitchenettes priced in the $60s.

### Tortilla Flat

The Wild West look makes this little village a popular stop for drivers on the Apache Trail. You can pick up food and souvenirs, or spend the night in the campground, which offers sites without drinking water for $8. Tortilla Flat is 27 miles west of the dam or 17 miles east of Apache Junction. A couple of miles further west, the Canyon Lake Marina (☎ 986 5546) has a boat ramp and boat rentals and a primitive campground with sites priced at $10.

### Goldfield Ghost Town

Three or four miles before you get to Apache Junction, you'll come across Goldfield Ghost Town. This ghost town has been renovated enough that you can take tours; try your hand at gold panning, eat at the Western steak house or examine the old artifacts in the mining museum. Hours are 10 am to 6 pm and admission is $4, or $2 for six-to 12-year-olds.

### Superstition Wilderness

Supposedly home to the fabled Lost Dutchman Mine, this rugged area is full of hiking trails and mining stories. It is a designated wilderness, so no development or vehicles are allowed. You can hike in on foot and camp anywhere, but hike prepared – there's some remote and difficult terrain in here. The Superstition Wilderness lies east of Apache Junction and south of the Apache Trail and is part of the Tonto National Forest. Ranger stations in Roosevelt or Mesa have maps and information.

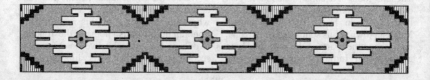

# Southeastern Arizona

When isolated groups of Spanish explorers straggled through in the 1530s, this region of desert, mountain ranges and grasslands was inhabited by the Tohono O'odham (called the Papago until 1986) and the closely related Pima Indians, who were perhaps the descendants of the Hohokam people, whose culture disappeared around 1400 AD. The Apache Indians, who arrived later on, lived in the far southeast of present-day Arizona.

The first big Spanish expedition was in 1540, led by Francisco Vásquez de Coronado, who entered the area near present-day Sierra Vista on his way north in search of the 'Seven Cities of Cíbola'. His descriptions are the earliest we have of the region, which were then largely ignored by the Spanish for well over a century until the Jesuit priest Padre Eusebio Francisco Kino arrived in arrived the late 1600s and spent two decades establishing missions primarily among the Pima people. One of the churches he founded, San Xavier del Bac south of Tucson, is still in use today. It is the finest example of Spanish colonial architecture in Arizona, rivaling the missions of New Mexico for architectural beauty and historic interest. Kino is also credited with introducing cattle into the area.

With the missions came immigrants – Spanish settlers from the Mexican colonies. They lived in an uneasy truce with the Indians until 1751, when the Pimas rebelled against the unwanted new arrivals and killed or forced out many settlers and missionaries. The Spanish authorities sent in soldiers to control the Indians and protect the settlers, building several walled forts, or *presidios*. One of these became Tucson, today Arizona's second largest city. After Mexico won its independence from Spain in 1821, Tucson became a Mexican town. Thus southeastern Arizona, more than other parts of the state, had both a traditional Indian culture and a rich Hispanic heritage that predated the arrival of the Anglos.

The Gadsden Purchase of 1853 turned southeastern Arizona, on paper at least, from Mexican into US territory. Anglos began to arrive, homesteading the grasslands in the southeastern corner and finding that it made good ranching country. But they failed to realize that the Apaches, who inhabited the desert grasslands and mountains of the far southeastern corner of Arizona, didn't much care about the Gadsden Purchase – after all, from their point of view, it was Apache country and not Mexican in the first place. Tensions arising from this difference erupted in conflicts between Indians and Americans. Although such conflicts marked the US expansion from the east throughout most of the 1800s, the ones in Apache territory were particularly fierce. Led by Cochise and Geronimo, warriors whose names are now legendary, Apaches became the last holdouts in the so-called Indian Wars, which lasted until the 1886 surrender of Geronimo.

Today, the Apaches live on reservations in east-central Arizona and in New Mexico, and what used to be their territory is now cattle ranching and mining country, where rolling vistas of ranchlands are studded with small but steep mountain ranges, the 'sky islands' of southeastern Arizona. The most dramatic are the Chiricahuas, protected in a national monument of the same name. The early ranchers and miners begot some of the classic tales of the Wild West, and now tourists flock to small towns like Tombstone and Bisbee, which retain much of their Old Western look.

West of these ranchlands lies the Sonoran desert, home of the majestic saguaro cacti, which are a symbol of this region. The Sonoran desert is also home to the Tohono O'odham Indians, who live on Arizona's second largest Indian reservation west of

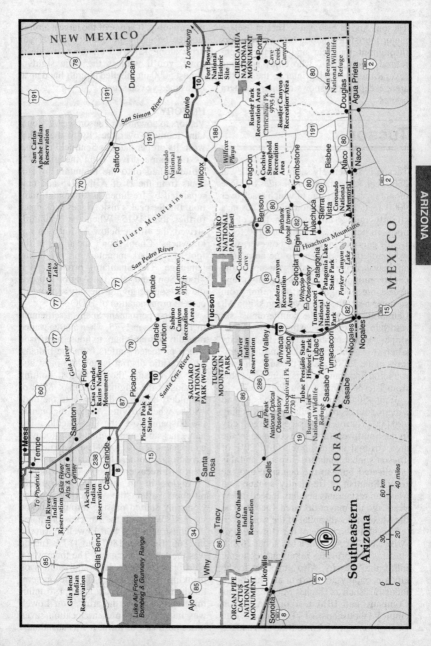

ARIZONA

Tucson. And in between is Tucson itself, a major tourist destination both for travelers throughout the year and for the often-retired 'snow birds' who enjoy spending several months each winter in the Tucson area, escaping the snows of their northern homes.

# Tucson

Tucson is attractively set in a flat valley at 2500 feet, surrounded on all sides by close mountain ranges, some of which reach over 9000 feet. The elevation gives Tucson a slightly milder climate than that of its northern neighbor, Phoenix (at 1100 feet). It still gets hot in summer, however, with weeks of 100°F days being the norm. But an hour's drive can take you up to the cooler mountains which are high and accessible enough to afford relief from summer heat. In winter, you can ski on Mt Lemmon, which is the southernmost ski resort in the country. After a day on the slopes, you can drop down to the city where pleasant winter daytime temperatures in the 70°s F are not unusual. The surrounding Sonoran desert is more accessible from Tucson than it is from Phoenix.

With 450,000 inhabitants in the city and a metropolitan area population approaching 700,000, Tucson is the second largest city in the Southwest (at least as defined by the area covered in this book). Over 20% of Tucson's inhabitants are Hispanic, and this is reflected both in the language and the food. Spanish is frequently spoken and Mexican restaurants abound. Indeed, a few years ago the mayor declared Tucson to be the Mexican food capital of the world.

Tucson is the home of the University of Arizona (U of A), which has about 36,000 students and provides important economic influx into the city. Also important to the city's economy are tourism and high-tech industries such as Hughes Missile Systems Company and IBM Corporation, which employ thousands of Tucsonans. The Davis-Monthan Air Force Base also adds to the economy. It is one of the largest aircraft storage bases in the country and, if you drive along Kolb Rd on the east side of town, you'll witness the eerie sight of almost 5000 mothballed aircraft lined up as far as the eye can see.

## HISTORY

Visitors to downtown Tucson see 'A Mountain' looming over the city to the southwest. Its proper name is Sentinel Peak, but its nickname drives from the giant 'A' whitewashed onto the mountain by students from the U of A in 1915 and now repainted by freshmen as an annual tradition. But the peak's history goes back much further than 1915. When the Spaniards arrived, the village below A Mountain was known as 'Chook Son', meaning 'at the foot of the dark mountain' in the Indian language. The Spaniards pronounced it 'Took Son' and later the Anglos dropped the 'k' sound, giving the city's name its current pronunciation of 'TOO-son'.

The first permanent Spanish settlement in Tucson was in 1775, when a large walled presidio was built here to house a garrison which protected settlers from the Indians. The presidio district is now the most historic in Tucson, though almost nothing remains of the original buildings. Most of the oldest buildings date back to the mid-1800s, when arriving Anglos nicknamed the Hispanic fort 'the Old Pueblo'. The name has stuck and is often heard today as a nickname for Tucson. 'The Old Pueblo is expecting another 112° day' announce weather forecasters cheerily on the radio.

Anglos began to arrive in greater numbers after the Butterfield Stage Company started passing through Tucson in 1857. War with the Apaches prompted the construction of Fort Lowell in Tucson in 1866. Between 1867 and 1877, Tucson was the territorial capital. The town was a wild place in those days, and soldiers on drinking sprees added to the general mayhem. In 1873, in an attempt to minimize carousing by the army, Fort Lowell was moved to its present location seven miles northeast of town. It was abandoned

### Metropolitan Tucson

To Florence
79
77
Oracle
Oracle Junction
1
To Phoenix
10
2
Tangerine Rd
Catalina State Park
Mt Lemmon ▲ 9157 ft
3
Summerhaven
Santa Catalina Mountains
Coronado National Forest
Twin Peaks Rd
Casa Grande Hwy
Santa Cruz River
Tucson National Golf Course
77
Pusch Ridge Wilderness
Sabino Canyon
Bear Canyon
Cortaro Farms Rd
Kolb Rd
5
6
Ina Rd
4
Silverbell Rd
Rillito River
Skyline Dr
Oracle Rd
8
9
7
Sunrise Dr
10
Sabino Canyon Recreation Area
11
SAGUARO NATIONAL PARK (West)
12
Tucson Mountains
15
17
13
Kinney Rd
Gates Pass Rd
16
Sentinel Peak 2897 ft
See Tucson map
Grant Rd
Campbell Ave
Alvernon Way
Swan Rd
Catalina Hwy
Tanque Verde Rd
Broadway Blvd
18
86
San Joaquin Rd
Camino de Oeste
14
Golf Links Rd
19
Escalante Rd
Fred Enke Golf Course
Benson Hwy
23
Kolb Rd
Houghton Rd
SAGUARO NATIONAL PARK (East)
Aja Hwy
Valencia Rd
Pascua Yaqui Indian Reservation
20
21
22
Tucson International Airport
24
Valencia Rd
Old Spanish Trail
Pantano Wash
26
Coronado National Forest
Rincon Mountains
San Xavier Indian Reservation
19
BUS 19
25
To Nogales
Mission Rd
Nogales Hwy
10
To Benson
27

0   8   12 km
0   4   8 miles

1  Biosphere 2
2  Breakers
3  Mt Lemmon Ski Area
4  Fun City
5  Tohono Chul Park
6  Westward Look Resort
7  Westin La Paloma Resort & Country Club
8  Anthony's in the Catalinas
9  De Grazia's Gallery in the Sun, Papagayo
10 Loews Ventana Canyon Resort
11 Molino Basin Campground
12 Casa Tierra B&B
13 Arizona-Sonora Desert Museum
14 Justin's Water World & RV Park
15 Gilbert Ray Campground
16 Old Tucson Studios
17 International Wildlife Museum
18 Suncatcher B&B
19 Davis-Monthan Air Force Base
20 Casino of the Sun
21 Mission San Xavier del Bac
22 Desert Diamond Casino
23 Pima Air & Space Museum
24 Voyager RV Resort
25 Cactus County RV Resort
26 Colossal Cave
27 R W Webb Winery

**ARIZONA**

in 1891, and there is a museum and a small historic district on the site today. Meanwhile, in 1880 the railroad had arrived and Tucson, already Arizona's largest city, continued growing. The university opened in 1891, and an air of sophistication and coming-of-age descended on the wild city. Despite being the largest city in the territory, it was first denied the position of political capital in favor of Prescott and, then in 1889, by Phoenix, which was less than half Tucson's size. There were various reasons for this, not least the fact that Phoenix was a predominantly Anglo city while Tucson thrived on its Hispanic roots.

It was not until the 1920s that Phoenix finally eclipsed Tucson in size. Tucson grew a little more slowly until WW II brought an influx of young men to train at the Davis-Monthan Air Force Base. After WW II, many of these trainees came back to Tucson and this, along with the widespread development of air conditioning, ensured Tucson's rapid growth in the latter half of the 20th century.

## ORIENTATION

Tucson lies mainly to the north and east of I-10, linking Phoenix with southern New Mexico and Texas, at its intersection with

I-19, which continues to the Mexican border with Nogales. Downtown Tucson and the main historic districts are east of I-10 exit 258 at Congress St, which becomes Broadway Blvd east of I-10.

Congress St/Broadway Blvd is a major west-east thoroughfare. Most west-east thoroughfares are called streets, while most north-south thoroughfares are called avenues. Stone Ave, at its intersection with Congress St, forms the zero point for Tucson addresses. Streets are designated west and east and avenues north and south from this point.

Downtown Tucson is quite compact and best visited on foot, although you have to battle the heat from May to September. Away from downtown, major thoroughfares are at one-mile intervals, with minor streets (mainly residential) filling in the spaces in a checker-board arrangement.

About a mile northeast of downtown is the U of A campus, with some worthwhile museums, and just over a mile south of downtown is the sq mile of South Tucson. This is a separate town inhabited mainly by the Hispanic population with few tourist sites, but it does have some cheap and funky restaurants with tasty Mexican food. The rest of the city is mainly an urban sprawl of shopping malls and residential areas interspersed with golf courses and parks. The main section of the city, between Campbell Ave and Kolb Rd, is known as midtown.

The south end of town is the industrial area where you'll find Tucson International Airport, the Davis-Monthan Air Force Base and industrial parks. You'll go past this to visit San Xavier del Bac, Arizona's most impressive Spanish colonial site.

The north end of town is the Catalina Foothills, bounded by the steep and rugged Santa Catalina Mountains and home to the pricier residential districts, resorts and country clubs. Northwest of town, the city oozes around the western edge of the Catalinas into the I-10 corridor to Phoenix. This is where most of the current development is taking place.

East and west of town are wilderness areas, parts of which are protected by the east and west units of Saguaro National Park. Until late 1994 this was a national monument; it's now the country's newest national park.

## INFORMATION
### Visitors Centers

The Convention and Visitors Bureau (☎ 624 1817, 1 (800) 638 8350), downtown at 130 S Scott Ave, is open from 8 am to 5 pm Monday to Friday and 9 am to 4 pm on weekends. It is closed on major holidays and may also close on weekends in summer. Ask for their detailed and free *Official Visitors Guide*. The Coronado National Forest Supervisor's Office (☎ 670 4552), in the Federal Building at 300 W Congress, 85701, is open from 8 am to 4:30 pm Monday to Friday. The Santa Catalina Ranger Station (☎ 749 8700), 5700 N Sabino Canyon Rd, 85715, in the visitors center at the entrance to Sabino Canyon, is open similar hours and is also open from 8:30 am to 4:30 pm on weekends. The BLM Tucson Office (☎ 722 4289) is at 12661 E Broadway Blvd and the Arizona Department of Game & Fish (☎ 628 5376) is at 555 N Greasewood Rd (south of Speedway Blvd over two miles west of I-10).

### Money

Currency exchange is quite limited; Bank One of Arizona (☎ 792 2000, 792 5906), 2 E Congress St, exchanges major currencies.

### Post

The main post office (☎ 620 5174, 620 5157) is at 1501 S Cherrybell Strav. (Strav is short for Stravenue, one of Tucson's few diagonal street/avenues!) It has a 24-hour lobby with stamp machines and window service for express mail. The downtown branch (☎ 622 8454) is at 141 S 6th Ave, and there are 14 other branches.

### Foreign Embassies

The Mexican Consulate (☎ 882 5595) is at 553 S Stone Ave.

**Books & Periodicals**

The main library (☎ 791 4393, 791 4010) is at 101 N Stone Ave. Hours are 10 am to 9 pm Monday to Wednesday, 9 am to 6 pm on Thursday, 10 am to 5 pm on Friday, 9 am to 5 pm on Saturday and 1 to 5 pm on Sunday. The U of A libraries (☎ 621 6441) have extensive and excellent collections, including a superb map room, open to the general public.

The local newspapers are the morning *Arizona Daily Star*, the afternoon *Tucson Citizen* and the free *Tucson Weekly*, published on Thursdays. The *Citizen* leans to the right, and the *Star* is less conservative. The best source of entertainment, arts and current events news is the *Weekly*. Two glossy but quite informative local magazines are the monthly *Tucson Lifestyle* and the quarterly *Tucson Guide*.

**Medical Services**

Pima County Medical Society (☎ 795 7985) provides doctor referrals during business hours. Ask A Nurse (☎ 544 2000) provides medical information and doctor referrals 24 hours a day. There are six major hospitals and many smaller health care facilities. The police (☎ 791 4452, or 911 in emergencies) are at 270 S Stone Ave.

**Recycling**

Recycle at Recycle America (☎ 622 4731), 945 S Freeway St, or call the Recycling Info-Line (☎ 791 5000) from 9 am to 5 pm Monday to Friday.

**Dangers & Annoyances**

People visiting the major tourist sites are unlikely to run into major crime problems except for theft. (See Dangers & Annoyances in the Facts for the Visitor chapter.)

Visitors often remark on the river bridges that cross nothing but sand. In the monsoon season of late summer and during the rains of late winter and early spring, these rivers flow in earnest, sometimes in raging floods. Because heavy rains are infrequent, Tucson's road drainage system becomes overwhelmed for a few hours several times a year. Roads that are liable to flood have warning signs. Flood waters occur infrequently and last for only a few hours, but when they do happen unsuspecting drivers could get trapped or swept away.

**DOWNTOWN TUCSON**

**Historic Buildings**

The Convention and Visitors Bureau has a brochure detailing a downtown walking tour with over 40 sites. Some of the more noteworthy ones are mentioned here.

Many of the most interesting and colorful historic buildings are in the **Presidio Historic District**, especially in the few blocks between Franklin and Alameda Sts and Main and Court Aves. This district merits a leisurely stroll. **La Casa Cordova**, 175 N Meyer Ave, at the north end of the Tucson Museum of Art (see below) is believed to be the oldest house, dating from 1848, and can be visited during the same hours as the museum. Just north of La Casa Cordova is the **Romero House**, dating from 1868 and now part of the Tucson Museum of Art School. Opposite, buildings dating from 1862 to 1875 feature saguaro-rib ceilings and now house the approximately 10 recommended arts and crafts galleries of **Old Town Artisans** (☎ 623 6024), 186 N Meyer Ave.

The **Fish House**, 120 N Main Ave, built in 1868 for political representative Edward Nye Fish, and the roughly contemporary **Stevens House**, 150 N Main Ave, home of Hiram Sanford Stevens, formed the heart of Tucson's social scene during the 1870s and '80s. They now house the **El Presidio Art Gallery** (☎ 884 7379) and the famous Janos restaurant, respectively. Other restaurants in historic buildings include Tucson's oldest Mexican restaurant, **El Charro Cafe**, 311 N Court Ave, in a 1900 stone house (most of the earlier houses were of adobe), and the **Cushing St Bar & Grill**, several long blocks to the south at 343 S Meyer Ave, housed in an 1880s store and displaying many old photographs.

Cushing St is the north end of the **Barrio Historico** district, which was an important

ARIZONA

The Rillito River for most of the year is dry – as it is here in June...

...but during heavy winter storms, it becomes a torrent. (both photos: RR)

business district in the late 1800s. Many of the old buildings around here continue to house businesses. **El Tiradito** is a quirky and crumbling little shrine south of El Minuto Cafe on Cushing St on the west side of Main Ave. The story behind the shrine is one of passion and murder. Apparently a young herder was caught making love with his mother-in-law and was shot dead by his father-in-law at this spot, where he was buried. Pious locals burned candles here because it was unconsecrated ground. The practice continues today, with candle-burners praying for their own wishes to be granted. If a candle burns throughout the night, your wish will be granted!

Between the Presidio and Barrio Historico districts is the modern Tucson

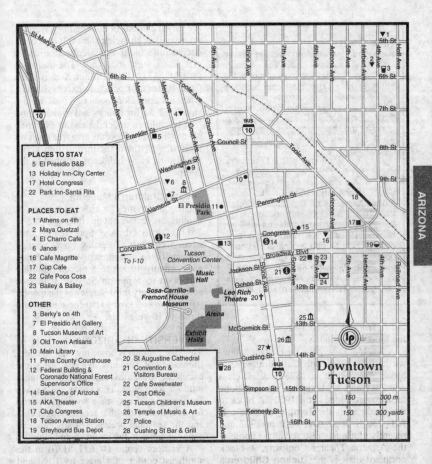

PLACES TO STAY
5 El Presidio B&B
13 Holiday Inn-City Center
17 Hotel Congress
22 Park Inn-Santa Rita

PLACES TO EAT
1 Athens on 4th
2 Maya Quetzal
4 El Charro Cafe
6 Janos
16 Cafe Magritte
17 Cup Cafe
22 Cafe Poca Cosa
23 Bailey & Bailey

OTHER
3 Berky's on 4th
7 El Presidio Art Gallery
8 Tucson Museum of Art
9 Old Town Artisans
10 Main Library
11 Pima County Courthouse
12 Federal Building & Coronado National Forest Supervisor's Office
14 Bank One of Arizona
15 AKA Theater
17 Club Congress
18 Tucson Amtrak Station
19 Greyhound Bus Depot
20 St Augustine Cathedral
21 Convention & Visitors Bureau
22 Cafe Sweetwater
24 Post Office
25 Tucson Children's Museum
26 Temple of Music & Art
27 Police
28 Cushing St Bar & Grill

Convention Center (TCC) complex. Only one house survived the construction of the TCC. At the northwest end is hidden the **Sosa-Carrillo-Fremont House Museum** (☎ 622 0956), 151 S Granada Ave. Built in the 1850s by the Sosa family, it was then bought by the Carrillo family and rented briefly by John H Fremont, Arizona's fifth governor. The restored house is now an 1880s period museum open from 10 am to 4 pm Wednesday to Saturday; admission is free. It is operated by the Arizona Historical Society, which offers guided walking tours (☎ 622 0956 to register) of historic

Tucson at 10 am on Saturdays from October to April. The cost is $4.

In addition to the oldest buildings, the downtown area has several notable newer buildings from the early 20th century. The **Pima County Courthouse**, at 115 N Church Ave, is a colorful blend of Spanish and Southwestern architecture with an impressive mosaic-tile dome. **El Presidio Park**, on the west side of the courthouse, covers what was the southern half of the original Presidio and also houses a Vietnam Veterans Memorial, as well as a sprinkling of homeless people who hang

### Kids' Stuff

Highlights for children include water sports in summer and the Tucson Childrens Museum, open year round, for younger kids. The Flandrau Science Center shows are aimed at older kids and teenagers. The Reid Park Zoo and the Arizona-Sonora Desert Museum are good for the entire family, as is the Pima Air & Space Museum, if your kids are plane nuts.

Also fun for kids is the Discovery Zone (☎ 748 9190), 6238 E Broadway Blvd, where kids (and adults) can crawl, climb, swing and slide on the giant indoor jungle-gym. The Zone is open from 10 am to 8 pm daily and till 9 pm on Friday and Saturday. Admission is $6 for two- to 12-year-olds. Two places that offer miniature golf, go-carts, bumper boats, batting cages and other fun stuff are Funtasticks (☎ 888 4653), 221 E Wetmore, and Golf 'N Stuff (☎ 885 3569), 6503 E Tanque Verde Rd. ■

out in front of the courthouse and nearby the modern city hall.

A few blocks south is the elegant, white-washed St Augustine Cathedral, 192 S Stone Ave, begun in 1896. Stained-glass windows and a Mexican-style sandstone façade were added in the 1920s. A block to the southeast is the Temple of Music & Art, 330 S Scott Ave, built in 1927 and recently gloriously restored as the home of the Arizona Theater Company. A block northeast of it is the Tucson Children's Museum (see below), 200 S 6th Ave, housed in a 1901 library designed by the noted Southwestern architect Henry Trost, who also designed several other turn-of-the-century buildings in Tucson. Two which still stand are the Steinfeld House, 300 N Main Ave, and the Owl's Club Mansion, 378 N Main Ave.

### Tucson Museum of Art

My first visit here was a pleasant surprise. The museum houses a small collection of pre-Columbian artifacts from South America. Apart from the Inca pots, there are varied exhibits of 20th-century Western art as well as changing shows. It also has a decent little multi-media collection and a gift shop with local art. The museum (☎ 624 2333), 140 N Main Ave, is open from 10 am to 4 pm daily except Sunday, when it's open from noon to 4 pm. Admission is $2, $1 for seniors and students, and free to children under 12 and to everyone all-day Tuesday. Docents give free tours on request. Ask them for information about the historic early buildings attached to the complex.

### Tucson Children's Museum

Hands-on activities for kids and permanent exhibits are featured at this museum (☎ 884 7511), 200 S 6th Ave. Special programs occur frequently. Weekday hours change seasonally, so call ahead. Weekend hours are normally 10 am to 5 pm on Saturday and noon to 5 pm on Sunday, with free admission every third Sunday of the month. Admission is $3, or $1.50 for seniors and three- to 16-year-olds.

### UNIVERSITY OF ARIZONA

This fine campus is home not only to many thousands of students, but also to some excellent museums and several notable outdoor sculptures. This is not just a place for young students, it's a worthwhile stop for everyone. Note that recent budget cuts and the seasonal presence of students can cause changes in the hours given below.

A visitors center (☎ 621 5130) at the southeast corner of University Blvd and Cherry Ave is open from 8 am to 5 pm Monday to Friday. Campus tours are offered during the school year. Old Main on University Blvd near the middle of the campus is the original university. The Student Union, just northeast of Old Main, has an information desk (☎ 621 7755) and various restaurants, art displays, a campus bookstore and the Gallagher movie theater. Note that University Blvd, east of Old Main, becomes a grassy pedestrian walkway called the University Mall.

Parking can be a little problematic near campus when school is in session; if the

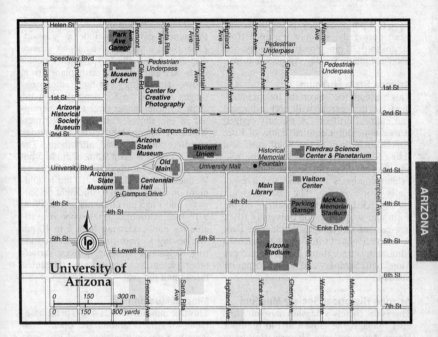

Map legend (as labeled): Helen St, Speedway Blvd, Euclid Ave, Tyndall Ave, Park Ave, Fremont Ave, Santa Rita Ave, Mountain Ave, Highland Ave, Vine Ave, Cherry Ave, Warren Ave, 1st St, 2nd St, 3rd St, 4th St, 5th St, 6th St, 7th St, Campbell Ave, Martin Ave, E Lowell St, E Speedway Blvd; Park Ave Garage, Pedestrian Underpass, Museum of Art, Olive Rd, Center for Creative Photography, Pedestrian Underpass, Arizona Historical Society Museum, N Campus Drive, Arizona State Museum, Old Main, Student Union, Historical Memorial Fountain, University Mall, Flandrau Science Center & Planetarium, Arizona State Museum, Centennial Hall, S Campus Drive, Main Library, Visitors Center, Parking Garage, McKale Memorial Stadium, Enke Drive, Arizona Stadium, University of Arizona, 0 150 300 m, 0 150 300 yards

**ARIZONA**

U of A Wildcats are playing a home game, it's downright frustrating. There are large parking garages at the northeast corner of Park Ave and E Speedway Blvd and at Cherry Ave and E 4th St. These charge a few dollars but are always full when a game is being played. Call the U of A Parking & Transportation Department (☎ 621 3550) for details.

Other useful campus numbers are the general operator (☎ 621 2211), athletic events ticket information (☎ 621 2411), cultural events ticket office at Centennial Hall (☎ 621 3341), theater arts ticket office (☎ 621 1162) and a concert hotline (☎ 621 1111).

### Center for Creative Photography

This has one of the world's best collections of works by American photographers, as well as some European and other artists. Most of Ansel Adams and Edward Weston's work is stored in the archives. Serious photography buffs need to think ahead, however, because most of the many thousands of photographs are not on display. You can call for an appointment to view the works of one or two particular photographers, which are archived. There is a small public display of some images by various famous photographers and changing exhibits throughout the year. The center (☎ 621 7968), 1030 N Olive Ave, is open from 11 am to 5 pm Monday to Friday and noon to 5 pm on Sunday during the school year (September to mid-May); in the summer it's open from 11 am to 5 pm Wednesday to Friday. Admission is free.

### University of Arizona Museum of Art

This museum (☎ 621 7567), across the street from the photography center, displays changing shows of mainly student works. These exhibits range widely in quality but are always intriguing. There are also fine permanent collections of European art and a variety of sculptures. Hours are 9 am to 5 pm Monday to Friday and noon to 4 pm on Sunday during the school year; during the summer it's open from 10 am to 3:30 pm Monday to Friday, and noon to 4 pm on Sunday. Admission is free.

## Arizona State Museum

This museum focuses on the Indian inhabitants of the region, with archaeological and cultural artifacts. A recently opened permanent exhibit entitled 'Paths of Life: American Indians of the Southwest' is a state-of-the-art representation of the past and present lives of several tribes; this exhibit continues to expand and is especially worth seeing. The state museum (☎ 621 6302) is in two buildings on the north and south sides of University Blvd, just east of the campus entrance at Park Ave. The 'Paths of Life' is in the north hall; admission is free. Hours are 10 am to 5 pm Monday to Saturday and noon to 5 pm on Sunday.

## Arizona Historical Society Museum

This is the society's flagship museum; they also manage the Sosa-Carrillo-Fremont House Museum (see Historic Buildings above) and the Fort Lowell Museum (see Beyond Downtown below). The museum (☎ 628 5774) is just outside the campus boundary at 949 E 2nd St. The collection is a comprehensive trip through Tucson's history as a Spanish colonial, Mexican, territorial and state city. Anything from colonial silverware to vintage automobiles can be seen in this wide-ranging selection of historical artifacts. Changing exhibits keep bringing locals back. Southwestern history buffs should not miss this museum. The society has a research library here that is open to the public. The museum's opening hours are 10 am to 4 pm daily except Sunday when it's open from noon to 4 pm. It's free but donations are appreciated.

## Flandrau Science Center & Planetarium

At the northeast corner of Cherry Ave and University Mall, the Flandrau (☎ 621 7827) has a permanent collection and many changing shows ranging from traditional astronomy to Pink Floyd laser light shows. Permanent exhibits include a 'walk-in' meteor and a variety of hands-on science displays. Admission to the science center costs $2, and admission to planetarium shows (including exhibits admission) ranges from $3 to $5, depending on the show. Children under three are not permitted in the shows. Call for show times, which are usually Wednesday to Saturday evenings and weekend afternoons. The science center is open from 10 am to 5 pm Monday and Tuesday, 10 am to 9 pm on Wednesday and Thursday, 10 am to midnight on Friday, 1 pm to midnight on Saturday and 1 to 5 pm on Sunday. In addition, a 16-inch astronomical telescope is available for public viewing from 8 to 10 pm Wednesday to Saturday, weather permitting. Telescope viewing is free. Various other scientific events are scheduled throughout the year.

## Mineral Museum

This free museum (☎ 621 4227) in the basement of the Flandrau is open from 9 am to 5 pm on weekdays, and 1 to 5 pm on weekends. Minerals, meteorites and gemstones from all over the world are exhibited, with an emphasis on local stones.

## Campus Sculptures

Beginning with *The Flute Player* commissioned in 1979 and now standing in front of the main library, the U of A has steadily acquired an eclectic collection of about a dozen sculptures scattered throughout the campus. The most controversial? The huge *Curving Arcades (Homage to Bernini)* at the main eastern entrance at University Mall and N Campbell Ave. My favorite? The whimsical *25 Scientists* in front of the new chemistry and biology building on University Mall, just west of the main library. Ask at the visitors center or the Museum of Art about the others.

## BEYOND DOWNTOWN
## Tucson Botanical Gardens

These quiet and pleasant gardens (☎ 326 9255, 326 9686), 2150 N Alvernon Way, cover five acres and focus on native dry-land plants. There is also a small tropical greenhouse, a herb garden and other plant attractions. Various workshops and events are offered throughout the year. Hours are from 8:30 to 4:30 pm daily, except in summer when hours are from 7:30 am to 4:30 pm. A gift shop is open from 9 am to 4 pm Monday to Saturday and noon to 4 pm on Sunday. Admission is $3, $2 for those over 62 and free for those under 12.

### Reid Park Zoo

This small but excellent zoo (☎ 791 4022), in Reid Park north of 22nd St at Lake Shore Lane, provides a good look at animals from all over the world, including some less usual ones such as giant anteaters and pygmy hippos. All the standard favorites are here, and the compact size of the zoo makes it a great excursion for children because they don't get overwhelmed and tired out. The small size means fewer animals, but the cages are still of a reasonable size. There is a gift shop and fast-food restaurant. Hours are from 9 am to 4 pm daily except Christmas. Admission is $3.50, $2.50 for those over 62, and 75¢ for five- to 14-year-olds accompanied by an adult.

Outside the zoo, the surrounding Reid Park provides picnic areas, playgrounds and a duck pond with paddle boat rentals in summer – definitely a kids' fun day out.

### Fort Lowell Museum

The army set up camp here in 1873 after moving from downtown Tucson. After Geronimo surrendered, Fort Lowell's important role in the Indian Wars faded, and the army shut it down in 1891. Only weathered ruins remain today, but the museum is housed in reconstructed officers' quarters with furnishings and exhibits of the fort's heydays. The museum (☎ 885 3832) is in Fort Lowell Park off the 2900 block of N Craycroft Rd. There is a playground and picnic areas. Across Craycroft Rd, a short way north of the fort, Fort Lowell Rd heads west past several early

houses in the small Fort Lowell historical district.

### Pima Air & Space Museum

Housing over 200 aircraft, which represent a history of aviation, this museum (☎ 574 9658), 6000 E Valencia Rd, sits on the south side of the Davis-Monthan Air Force Base. It's a must-see for aircraft buffs. The museum also operates the Titan Missile Museum (see Green Valley in the South of Tucson section below). The Pima Museum is open from 9 am to 5 pm daily except Christmas. There is no admission after 4 pm. Admission is $5, $4 for those over 62 or with military ID, and $3 for 10- to 17-year-olds.

Across the street, note the approximately 5000 mothballed aircraft at Davis-Monthan. The best way to see them is to drive north on Kolb Rd and west on Escalante Rd. Free tours of the base are given at 9 am on Monday and Wednesday only and require an advance reservation (☎ 750 3204).

### Tohono Chul Park

This small desert oasis, surrounded by encroaching development, is a good place to see desert flora and fauna in a natural setting. There are demonstration and ethnobotanical gardens, an exhibit room with changing shows, gift shops, plant sales and a tea room. A variety of docent-led tours are offered. The park (☎ 575 8468), 7366 N Paseo del Norte near Ina Rd, is open from 7 am to dusk daily; the other attractions have shorter hours. Admission is a suggested $2 donation.

## ACTIVITIES

### Hiking & Backpacking

Tucson is ringed by mountains. The Rincons to the east and the Tucson Mountains to the west are easily explored from Saguaro National Park (see Around Tucson below). The Santa Ritas, topped by 9453-foot Mt Wrightson, are visible in the distance, to the south.

The Santa Catalina Mountains, topped by 9157-foot Mt Lemmon, form Tucson's northern boundary and prevent the city from expanding further north. The Santa Catalinas, which lie within the Colorado National Forest, are the best loved and most visited of Tucson's mountain ranges. There are several trailheads on the north side of town, including the Mt Kimball Trailhead at the far north end of Alvernon Way, which leads steeply up Finger Rock Canyon past Finger Rock – an obvious point on the northern skyline from many parts of Tucson. (Note that Alvernon Way in midtown Tucson stops at Fort Lowell Rd. You have to take Campbell Ave north to Skyline Drive and then head east to pick up Alvernon Way again to reach this trailhead.) Other trailheads are found in Sabino Canyon and Catalina State Park (see below).

Take extra precautions when hiking around Tucson in summer, when dehydration can be a potentially lethal problem. You should carry water with you at all times and drink a gallon of water per day. Sunburn can be debilitating, so protect yourself. And watch out for those spiny plants. It's worth carrying tweezers and a comb to help remove cactus spines from your skin.

Backpackers should contact a USFS ranger station about suitable places to camp and where to leave their cars.

**Books** Useful books for hiking specifically in the Tucson area are *Tucson Hiking Guide* by Betty Leavengood (Pruett Publishing, 1991), *Trail Guide to the Santa Catalina Mountains* by Eber Glendening & Pete Cowgill (3rd ed, Rainbow Expeditions, 1987) and *Hiking Guide to the Santa Rita Mountains of Arizona* by Bob & Dotty Martin (Pruett Publishing, 1986). The Summit Hut (☎ 325 1554), 5045 E Speedway Blvd, is an excellent source of hiking books, maps and equipment.

**Sabino Canyon** This is the most popular and accessible part of the Santa Catalinas. There is a visitors center which includes a USFS ranger station (☎ 749 8700) open weekdays from 8 am to 4:30 pm and

weekends from 8:30 am to 4:30 pm. Maps, hiking guides and information is available here, and there is a short nature trail nearby. The visitors center is at the entrance of the canyon at 5900 N Sabino Canyon Rd, where there is also a large parking lot.

Roads continue beyond the visitors center into the canyon but only shuttle buses (☎ 749 2861 for recorded information) are allowed to drive on these. The Sabino Canyon Rd goes a scenic 3.8 miles up the canyon, crossing the river several times. Narrated shuttle bus tours spend 45 minutes doing the roundtrip and stop at nine points along the way. Tours leave every half hour from 9 am to 4:30 pm, and ticket holders can get on and off at any point whenever they feel like it. There are several riverside spots and picnic places on the way. At the top is a trailhead for hikers wanting to go high into the Santa Catalinas. Fares are $5, or $2 for three- to 12-year-olds. In addition, full-moon shuttle tours are given by reservation on the nights around a full moon. Call 749 2327 for dates and reservation information.

Another road goes 2.5 miles to the Bear Canyon Trailhead. A shuttle bus (no narration or stops) takes hikers there every hour from 9 am to 4 pm. The fare is $3, or $1.25 for three- to 12-year-olds. From the trailhead a 2.3-mile (one-way) hike leads to Seven Falls, a scenic and popular spot for picnics and swimming, but there aren't any facilities. From there, the trail continues up as high as you want to go.

Bicycles are allowed on the roads only before 9 am and after 5 pm and not at all on Wednesday and Sunday. Hikers can walk along the roads at any time from dawn to dusk. You don't have to take a shuttle to get to a trailhead; starting from the visitors center, there's plenty of hiking possibilities. The Phoneline Trail, skirting Sabino Canyon high on its southeastern side, is a popular alternative to taking the road.

Several picnic areas with grills, tables and bathrooms are in the area. Camping is not allowed within those areas. Backpackers can hike into the Santa Catalinas and wilderness camp almost anywhere that's over a quarter mile away from a road or trailhead.

**Catalina State Park** This park is in the western foothills of the Santa Catalinas and is popular for hiking, picnicking, bird-watching and camping. You'll find both short nature trails and trailheads for long-distance hiking and backpacking. Horseback riding is permitted and one trail is specifically developed for horses. The Equestrian Center has boarding for horses. Natural swimming holes occur along some of the trails and make good day-hike destinations. Ask the ranger for directions. (See Places to Stay for information on the campground.) For more information call Catalina State Park (☎ 628 5798), PO Box 36986, 85740. The park is about 15 miles north of downtown along Oracle Rd (Hwy 77).

**Mt Lemmon** You can spend a couple of days hiking up to the summit of Mt Lemmon along some of the many trails in the Santa Catalinas, or you can head east on Tanque Verde Rd, pick up the Catalina Hwy and drive to the top in an hour. This is a favorite getaway for Tucsonans wishing to escape the summer heat. Along the way are four USFS campgrounds and several pullouts with great views. The road is narrow and winding, however, and requires some concentration. Several hiking trails intersect with the highway. Near the top of the drive is the Palisades Ranger Station (no phone) with information about the area, or call the Sabino Canyon Ranger Station (☎ 749 8700).

At the top is the small village of **Summerhaven** where there are cabins to rent, a B&B, some restaurants, a picnic area and a ski area (see below). During the summer you can take scenic rides on the chair lift from 10:30 am to 5 pm on weekdays and 10 am to 5:30 pm. Costs are $5 or $2 for three- to 12-year-olds.

**Bird-Watching**
Southeastern Arizona is a mecca for bird watchers, who come from all over the USA

Trogon

to see birds found nowhere else in the country. Many of these are species flying from Mexico. The most notable are the 16 species of hummingbirds, eight of which are uncommon or rare. While the months between April to September see the most species, there's always a few around at any time. By comparison, most eastern states have only one hummingbird species and most western states have half a dozen or so. Sightings of trogons are highly prized. Both birds are very colorful, with green heads and wings, red bellies and white tails. The eared trogon is very rare and sure to excite any birder and the elegant trogon is less rare but still uncommon. The latter has a yellow bill and a white band on its chest. Ramsey Canyon near Sierra Vista (see below) is one of the most celebrated spots for hummers and trogons. In addition, the various species of common desert birds such as roadrunners, gila woodpeckers, elf owls and cactus wrens

Roadrunner

attract out-of-state birders wanting to add to their life lists.

The best resource for bird watchers is the Tucson Audubon Society, 300 E University Blvd, 85705. They have an excellent nature shop (☎ 629 0510) with a fine selection of bird guides and related materials. Hours are 10 am to 4 pm Monday to Saturday and to 6 pm on Thursday. A research library is also available. The nature shop has information about monthly meetings and slide shows held from September to May, as well as a variety of field trips, many of them free. The society has published an essential handbook for birders: *Finding Birds in Southeastern Arizona* by William A Davis and Stephen M Russell (1995). The book is $16.95 plus $3 shipping if you want to order one from the nature shop. There is a bird-sightings and information hot line (☎ 798 1005) that is updated weekly.

### Skiing

Mt Lemmon Ski Area (☎ 576 1400, 576 1321) is the most southerly ski area in the USA. One chair services 16 runs between 9150 and 8200 feet. These are mainly for intermediate and experienced skiers. There is also a rope tow for beginners. Rentals, lessons and food are available. Depending on the weather, the slopes are open from mid-December to early April. Lift tickets are $26, or $10 for children under 13.

### Hot-Air Ballooning

Several companies offer hot-air balloon flights over the desert and foothills. Flights usually take place in the calm morning air, last about an hour and finish with a traditional champagne breakfast. Flights may be canceled in windy weather and in summer because of the extreme heat. Most companies can arrange flights on a day's notice. Experienced companies include Balloon America (☎ 299 7744), which charges from $100 to $195 a person, and A Southern Arizona Balloon Excursion (☎ 624 3599, 1 (800) 524 3599) which charges $125 a person.

### Horseback Riding

Several stables offer excursions by the hour, half day or longer. Summer trips tend to be short breakfast or sunset rides because of the heat. Desert cookouts can be arranged. One of the most reputable companies is Pusch Ridge Stables (☎ 825 1664), 13700 N Oracle Rd, which also offers overnight pack trips. At the other end of town is Pantano Stables (☎ 751 4235), 4450 S Houghton Rd. Several others advertise locally.

### Golf

There are so many courses in Tucson and so many people who come to golf them that an entire book could be written about it. The following is only a sampling of the facilities available. Tucson Parks & Recreation (☎ 791 4336 for golf information and tee reservations) manages five municipal 18-hole golf courses: Randolph North, par 72, at 600 S Alvernon Way is the most reputable and the longest; Randolph South, par 70, is popular with beginners; El Rio, par 70, at 1400 W Speedway Blvd, has been around since its country club days in the 1930s; Silverbell, par 72, 3600 N Silverbell Rd, borders the Santa Cruz River; Fred Enke, par 72, 8251 E Irvington Rd, is a limited-turf desert course – lots of cacti to hit the balls over. All five charge between $15 and $17.

Dorado Golf Course (☎ 885 6751) 6601 E Speedway Blvd, par 62, charges $10 for nine holes and $14 for 18 holes.

There are many more expensive golf courses at various resorts and clubs in Tucson. Some that come recommended are Starr Pass Golf Club (☎ 622 6060), 3645 W Starr Pass Blvd, 18 holes, par 72; Tucson National Golf & Conference Resort (☎ 575 7540), 2727 W Club Drive, 27 holes, par 73; and Westin La Paloma Resort & Country Club (☎ 299 1500) 3800 E Sunrise Drive, 27 holes, par 72. The Tucson Country Club (☎ 298 6769) is tempting, but its private. The *Tucson Guide* quarterly magazine (☎ 322 0895), Box 42195, 85733, regularly reviews the many local courses and will send you their latest review for the cost of mailing. The Convention and Visitors Bureau can also provide a list. Tee Time Arrangers (☎ 296 4800, 1 (800) 742 9939, fax 886 1067), 6286 E Grant Rd, 85712, arranges golfing vacations.

### Tennis

Most high schools and the U of A have tennis courts open to the public after school hours. Municipal public tennis centers can be found at Fort Lowell Park (☎ 791 2584), 2900 N Craycroft Rd; Alvina Himmel Park (☎ 791 3276), 1000 N Tucson Blvd; and Randolph Park (☎ 791 4896), 100 S Alvernon Way.

### Water Sports

Tucson Parks & Recreation (☎ 791 4873) manages about two dozen swimming pools throughout the city. Many hotels have their own pool.

During the summer, water parks offer something a little more exciting than swimming laps. Breakers (☎ 682 2530), 8555 W Tangerine Rd (1.5 miles east of I-10 exit 242, 16 miles north of downtown), has a huge wave pool with four-foot waves for surfing. Hours are 9 am to dusk and admission is $9.95, or $7.95 for children under 13. Fun City (☎ 579 7388) is on the west side of I-10 exit 248 at 6901 N Casa Grande Hwy. They have long, twisting

waterslide tubes, as well as go-carts and miniature golf. Hours are 4 to 10 pm Monday to Friday, and 11 am to 10 pm on weekends. Admission is $6.95 for four- to 59-year-olds and free to everyone else. Justin's Water World & RV Park (☎ 883 8340), 3551 S San Joaquin Rd (eight miles west of I-19 exit 99 along Ajo Way, then two miles north), has many swimming pools, toddlers' paddling pools, water slides galore, a tubing area and an 'Atlantis – the lost continent' attraction. Hours are 10 am to 5 pm Friday to Sunday and holidays. Admission is $8.50 for six- to 60-year-olds.

### ORGANIZED TOURS

Gray Line (☎ 622 8811) offers standard coach and van tours of the city and its surroundings as well as excursions all over the state. Tours of Tucson and southeastern Arizona are offered by Tucson Tour Company (☎ 297 2911) and Off the Beaten Track Tours (☎ 529 6090). Trail Dust Jeep Tours (☎ 747 0323) takes you into the desert in open jeeps. The Center for Desert Archaeology (☎ 881 2244) has tours led by archaeologists to sites in downtown Tucson and the surrounding desert. Old Pueblo Tours (☎ 575 1175) specializes in historical tours of Tucson. Note that some tours don't operate in the summer heat.

### SPECIAL EVENTS

Hundreds of events happen year round, of course. The following is a selection of some of the most notable and important. The Convention and Visitors Bureau has a complete listing of events and can give exact dates.

The Southern Arizona Square and Round Dance & Clogging Festival attracts thousands of dancers, who gather at the Tucson Convention Center in late January.

In the first half of February, the Tucson Gem and Mineral Show attracts exhibitors and visitors for what is said to be the largest show of its kind in the world. The Fiesta de los Vaqueros, held from the last Thursday to Sunday of February, features the world's largest non-motorized parade followed by a rodeo and other cowboy events – even the city's schools are closed for the last two days of what is locally called 'Rodeo Week'.

The Tohono O'odham tribe hosts many Southwestern Indian tribes for several days of dances, singing, food and other entertainment during the Wa:k Pow Wow, held at the San Xavier del Bac Mission in early March.

See Deer Dances on the tiny Pascua Yaqui Indian Reservation on the Saturday before Palm Sunday (one week before Easter) and the Saturday before Easter Sunday. The reservation is almost five miles west of I-19 exit 95 along Valencia Rd, then a mile south along Camino de Oeste.

In April, the Tucson International Mariachi Conference and the Waila Festival (Tohono O'odham music) celebrate ethnic music. The Pima County Fair, with carnival rides galore and many other events, takes place in April at the county fairgrounds. Also in April and repeated in December is the 4th Avenue Street Fair, celebrated with hundreds of arts & crafts booths and free street entertainment.

Tucson's Hispanic heritage is celebrated during Cinco de Mayo at Kennedy Park on or close to 5 May with parades, dances, music, arts & crafts booths and Mexican food. Things slow down somewhat during the hot summer months, although a June blues festival at Mt Lemmon brings out music lovers enjoying the cool pines and tunes. Mexican Independence Day is celebrated at Kennedy Park in mid-September.

October sees Tucson Meet Yourself, with the cities many different ethnic groups presenting food and crafts at their booths. In mid- to late October the Fiesta de los Chiles celebrates this most Southwestern of all agricultural products at Tucson Botanical Gardens. Another 4th Avenue Street Fair kicks off the December holiday season and many of the Christmas celebrations have a strong Hispanic flavor.

## PLACES TO STAY

As with Phoenix, January through April is the high season in Tucson, when rooms are at a premium. During major events like the Tucson Open, the Gem and Mineral Show and the Fiesta de los Vaqueros prices can rise above their already high winter rates. Prices drop substantially in the low season, from May to September, when some places, especially the pricier resorts, charge less than half of their high-season rates. Because of this seasonal variation, the prices given for the following can only be used as a rough guide. Hotels will charge what the market will bear (and Tucson has many visitors), but it's always worth asking for a discount for AAA members, seniors, family rates, students, business-rate, military, multi-night, or just plain not being able to afford the quoted price.

## PLACES TO STAY – CAMPING

The USFS (☎ 749 8700) operates four simple campgrounds on the Catalina Hwy going up to Mt Lemmon. About 12 miles from the Tanque Verde Rd turnoff is *Molino Basin*. Open from mid-October to mid-April, the campground is at an elevation of 4500 feet and has 50 free sites but no water. A few miles further is *General Hitchcock* at 6000 feet, open year round with 13 free sites but no water. About eight miles further is *Rose Canyon* at 7000 feet with a trout-fishing lake and drinking water, but no showers or RV hookups. The 74 sites are open from mid-April till mid-October and cost $7. *Spencer Canyon* is four miles further at 8000 feet with 77 sites and the same fees and dates as Rose Canyon.

The campground at *Catalina State Park* has 48 campsites that fill up on a first-come, first-served basis. Fees are $8 or $13 with electrical hookups and water and showers are available. A group campground (minimum of 20 people) can be reserved. For more information call Catalina State Park (☎ 628 5798), PO Box 36986, 85740. The park is about 15 miles north of downtown along Oracle Rd (Hwy 77).

Southeast of Tucson and a short way east of Colossal Cave you'll find a small, free campground with no water that's open year round. The campground gate is closed from 6 pm to 8 am and there is a one-night limit.

*Gilbert Ray Campground* (☎ 883 4200) is on Kinney Rd a couple of miles east of the Arizona-Sonora Desert Museum. There are almost 200 sites open year round, drinking water but no showers and electrical hookups. Sites are $6 or $9 with hookups.

*Justin's RV Park* (☎ 883 8340) is next to Justin's Water World (see Water Sports above) and has 150 sites with hookups for $12. Children are allowed to stay from May to September only (when the Water World is open).

Two huge RV resorts, each with over 1000 sites, provide many entertainment and recreational facilities for adults. They are *Voyager RV Resort* (☎ 574 5000, 1 (800) 424 9191), 8701 S Kolb Rd, near I-10 exit 270, which charges $27, and *Rincon Country West* (☎ 294 5608), 4555 S Mission Rd, a short way west of I-19 exit 99, which charges $21. Similar facilities are found at the 460-site *Rincon Country East* (☎ 885 7851), E Escalante Rd.

If you have kids, there's the 260-site *Cactus Country RV Resort* (☎ 574 3000, 1 (800) 777 8799, fax 574 9004), 10195 S Houghton Rd, a half mile north of I-10 exit 275. There are various recreational facilities and sites are $19.50 with hookups. There are also five tent sites for $12.50. Another family choice is *Prince of Tucson* (☎ 887 3501, 1 (800) 955 3501), 3501 N Freeway St, near I-10 exit 254. They have recreational facilities and over 200 sites for $17.50. Tent camping is only allowed in the summer.

There are many more smaller RV resorts, but the above should get you started. Note that weekly and monthly discounts are available at most RV resorts and that winter reservations are recommended.

## PLACES TO STAY – BOTTOM END

Young budget travelers like to stay at *Hotel Congress* (☎ 622 8848, 1 (800) 722 8848), 311 E Congress St, right downtown. The best alternative music club as well as a bar and a cafe are downstairs. The hotel dates back to the 1920s and has some charm. There are dormitory rooms for HI/AYH

members at $12 a person. Students under 26 who aren't HI/AYH members can also stay here. Private rooms with showers are in the $30s and $40s for a double depending on the number of beds.

Outside of downtown, cheap motel rooms start in the $30s in the winter. However, they can be hard to find because they are often booked up by long-term clients who pay by the week. In the summer, single rooms can be found from about $20.

There are two main areas for cheap and basic motels, mainly independent 'Mom 'n Pop' types, with a few pricier chain-owned places thrown in. The cheapest area is on the south side of South Tucson around the intersection of 6th Ave with I-10 exit 261, and southeast from here along Benson Hwy as far as Alvernon Way. The other area is north of downtown along Stone Ave, between Speedway Blvd and Drachman St, then along Drachman St west of Stone Ave to Oracle Rd, then north of Oracle to Miracle Mile and west again on Miracle Mile. This isn't the most salubrious of neighborhoods, but it isn't especially dangerous either.

At I-10 exit 261 the hotels are the very cheapest: *Budget Inn* (☎ 884 1470), 3033 S 6th Ave, *San Diego's Franciscan Motel* (☎ 792 0712), 3031 S 6th Ave, *El Camino Motel* (☎ 624 3619), 297 E Benson Hwy, and the *Sun-Ray Motel* (☎ 622 9737), 220 E Benson Hwy. For a few dollars more, the *Lazy 8 Motel* (☎ 622 3336), 314 E Benson Hwy, has a pool and restaurant. *Econo Lodge* (☎ 623 5881) is in the same cluster as Budget Inn at 3020 S 6th Ave and has a pool, a restaurant and a spa. In summer they charge a reasonable $27/33 for singles/doubles but charge about $50 in winter and can get overpriced during the February Gem and Mineral Show when their official rates go up into the $70s.

East of exit 261 along Benson Hwy there are about 20 motels. Some cheap but adequate ones are the *Western Motel* (☎ 746 9892), 3218 E Benson Hwy (one of the cheapest), the *Redwood Lodge* (☎ 294 3802), 3315 E Benson Hwy, *El Pais Motel*

ARIZONA

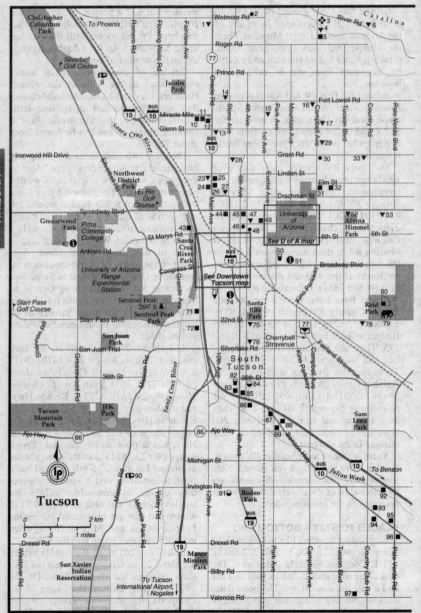

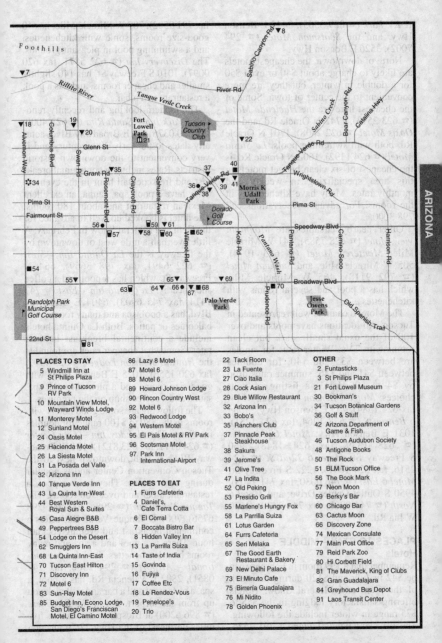

ARIZONA

**PLACES TO STAY**

5  Windmill Inn at St Philips Plaza
9  Prince of Tucson RV Park
10  Mountain View Motel, Wayward Winds Lodge
11  Monterey Motel
12  Sunland Motel
24  Oasis Motel
25  Hacienda Motel
26  La Siesta Motel
31  La Posada del Valle
32  Arizona Inn
40  Tanque Verde Inn
43  La Quinta Inn-West
44  Best Western Royal Sun & Suites
45  Casa Alegre B&B
49  Peppertrees B&B
54  Lodge on the Desert
62  Smugglers Inn
68  La Quinta Inn-East
71  Tucson East Hilton
71  Discovery Inn
72  Motel 6
83  Sun-Ray Motel
85  Budget Inn, Econo Lodge, San Diego's Franciscan Motel, El Camino Motel
86  Lazy 8 Motel
87  Motel 6
88  Motel 6
89  Howard Johnson Lodge
90  Rincon Country West
92  Motel 6
93  Redwood Lodge
94  Western Motel
95  El Pais Motel & RV Park
96  Scotsman Motel
97  Park Inn International-Airport

**PLACES TO EAT**

1  Furrs Cafeteria
4  Daniel's, Cafe Terra Cotta
6  El Corral
7  Boccata Bistro Bar
8  Hidden Valley Inn
13  La Parrilla Suiza
14  Taste of India
15  Govinda
16  Fujiya
17  Coffee Etc
18  Le Rendez-Vous
19  Penelope's
20  Trio
22  Tack Room
23  La Fuente
27  Ciao Italia
28  Cock Asian
29  Blue Willow Restaurant
32  Arizona Inn
33  Bobo's
36  Ranchers Club
37  Pinnacle Peak Steakhouse
38  Sakura
39  Jerome's
41  Olive Tree
47  La Indita
52  Old Peking
53  Presidio Grill
55  Marlene's Hungry Fox
58  La Parrilla Suiza
59  Lotus Garden
64  Furrs Cafeteria
65  Seri Melaka
67  The Good Earth Restaurant & Bakery
69  New Delhi Palace
73  El Minuto Cafe
75  Birrería Guadalajara
76  Mi Nidito
78  Golden Phoenix

**OTHER**

2  Funtasticks
3  St Philips Plaza
21  Fort Lowell Museum
30  Bookman's
34  Tucson Botanical Gardens
36  Golf & Stuff
42  Arizona Department of Game & Fish
48  Tucson Audubon Society
48  Antigone Books
50  The Rock
51  BLM Tucson Office
56  The Book Mark
57  Neon Moon
59  Berky's Bar
60  Chicago Bar
63  Cactus Moon
74  Discovery Zone
74  Mexican Consulate
77  Main Post Office
79  Reid Park Zoo
80  Hi Corbett Field
81  The Maverick, King of Clubs
82  Gran Guadalajara
84  Greyhound Bus Depot
91  Laos Transit Center

& *RV Park* (☎ 889 3305), 3445 E Benson Hwy, and the *Scotsman Motel* (☎ 294 7002), 3526 E Benson Hwy.

North of downtown, the cheapest motels are likely to charge about $40 or even $50 for a double in winter, but they are more convenient to the center of town. Some of the cheapest here are the *Hacienda Motel* (☎ 623 2513), 1742 N Oracle Rd, and the *Oasis Motel* (☎ 622 2808), 1701 N Oracle Rd, both with swimming pools. *La Siesta Motel* (☎ 624 1192), 1602 N Oracle Rd, is the cheapest of six clean budget motels in this area specializing in weekly and monthly rates. Many have kitchenettes in the rooms. For advance reservations call 798 3000.

Other nearby cheapies are *Mountain View Motel* (☎ 628 7585), 741 W Miracle Mile, *Monterey Motel* (☎ 623 1974), 505 W Miracle Mile, and *Sunland Motel* (☎ 792 9118), 465 W Miracle Mile, which has a pool and several rooms with kitchenettes.

The Motel 6 chain is well represented in Tucson. All locations have pools and over 100 of the usual small, stark but clean rooms with TVs. Winter rates for singles are between $35 and $40, for doubles between $41 and $46; summer rates drop by $4 to $9. Here's a listing of your choices: *Motel 6 Benson N* (☎ 622 4614, fax 624 1584), 755 E Benson Hwy; *Motel 6 Benson S* (☎ 628 1264, fax 624 1731), 1031 E Benson Hwy; *Motel 6 Congress* (☎ 628 1339, fax 624 1848), 960 S Freeway St; *Motel 6 22nd St* (☎ 624 2516, fax 624 1697), 1222 S Freeway St; *Motel 6 East* (☎ 746 0030, fax 741 7403), 4950 S Outlet Center Drive; and *Motel 6 North* (☎ 744 9300, fax 744 2439), 4630 W Ina Rd.

## PLACES TO STAY – MIDDLE
### Hotels

Remember that a $99 room in February can be $42 in July and $120 during the week of the Gem and Mineral Show. Hotels offering satisfactory lodging in the $55 to $75 range in winter include the following. The *Wayward Winds Lodge* (☎ 791 7526, fax 791 9502), 707 W Miracle Mile, has 40 good-size rooms, some with kitchenettes, and a swimming pool in pleasant grounds. The *Discovery Inn* (☎ 622 5871, fax 620 0097), 1010 S Freeway St, has 140 slightly smaller and cheaper rooms, and has a pool, a restaurant and a bar.

The modern-looking and recently renovated *Park Inn – Santa Rita* (☎ 622 4000, fax 620 0376), 88 E Broadway Blvd, actually dates to the early 20th century and is very convenient to the downtown historic districts. Rates include a continental breakfast and free cocktail hour in the evening. They have a pool, spa, sauna, an excellent Mexican restaurant and about 180 rooms. The hotel is booked up well in advance for the Gem and Mineral Show in February. A little over half a mile west of downtown by the freeway is the *La Quinta Inn – West* (☎ 622 6491, fax 798 3669), 664 N Freeway St, which has a pool and a coffee shop nearby. *La Quinta Inn – East* (☎ 747 1414, fax 745 6903), 6404 E Broadway Blvd, has a pool, spa and many rooms with balconies or patios. Both La Quinta hotels include a continental breakfast in their rates. Somewhat cheaper rates are found at the *Howard Johnson Lodge* (☎ 623 7792, fax 620 1556), 1025 E Benson Hwy, with good-size rooms and a pleasant pool, spa, sauna and a coffee shop on the premises.

The following are some good hotels with rooms in the $80 to $100 range for doubles in winter. The *Holiday Inn – City Center* (☎ 624 8711, fax 623 8121), 181 W Broadway Blvd, is right downtown next to the Tucson Convention Center and is popular during conventions. They have a pool, a restaurant, a bar and over 300 rooms. The *Tanque Verde Inn* (☎ 298 2300, fax 298 6756), 7007 E Tanque Verde Rd, offers a continental breakfast and evening cocktail hour. There is a pool and a spa and many rooms have kitchenettes. *Park Inn International – Airport* (☎ 294 2500, fax 741 0851), 2802 E Valencia Rd, has a pool, a spa, a restaurant and a bar and will pick you up from the airport. *Inn at the Biosphere* (☎ 896 6200) at Biosphere 2, which is five miles northeast of the Hwy 77/79 junction (see Biosphere 2 under Around Tucson), has rooms in the $80s, or in the $50s in summer. They have a pool, tennis courts and an exercise room. Tickets to Biosphere 2 are $10 if purchased at reception.

### B&Bs

The most practical way to obtain a description of facilities and prices of B&Bs and to make reservations is through one of the agencies listed here. Half a dozen of the nicest places are reserved through Premier B&Bs of Tucson (☎ 628 1800), 3661 N Campbell Ave, Suite 237, 85719. A wider range, both in Tucson and southeastern Arizona, are represented by Old Pueblo Homestays (☎ /fax 790 2399, 1 (800) 333 9776), PO Box 13603, 85732. Also refer to the three organizations listed in the Phoenix chapter. They also represent Tucson area B&Bs.

*Casa Tierra* (☎ 578 3058), 11155 W Calle Pima, 85743, is just west of the western section of Saguaro National Monument. Take Kinney Rd to Mile Wide Rd then turn left at the second mailbox. Sound remote? It is – a modern-day adobe surrounded by desert. Rates are between $70 and $85 including breakfast. They close for the summer. *Casa Alegre* (☎ 628 1800, fax 792 1880), 316 E Speedway Blvd, 85705, is a peaceful 1915 house decorated with historical memorabilia that is convenient to U of A and downtown. Rooms range from $65 to $80 and there is a pool. *El Presidio* (☎ 623 6151), 297 N Main Ave, 85701, has suites within an adobe home and guesthouses with private entrances off a courtyard. Bathrobes and fruit are some of the features offered at this garden oasis in the heart of the city. Rooms cost from $85 to $120. They close in summer and don't take credit cards.

### PLACES TO STAY – TOP END
### Hotels

The following hotels cost in the low $100s during the winter. The *Smugglers Inn* (☎ 296 3292, fax 722 3713), 6350 E Speedway Blvd, has attractive gardens and spacious rooms with a balcony or a patio. Facilititis include a pool, spa, tennis, putting green, restaurant and bar. Room service, weekend entertainment and pickup from the airport are available.

The *Tucson East Hilton* (☎ 721 5600, fax 721 5696), 7600 E Broadway Blvd, has a pool, spa, restaurant, bar, room service and a 7th-floor 'Summit Level' with extra services such as complimentary breakfast, a cocktail hour and newspapers.

The *Best Western Royal Sun & Suites* (☎ 622 8871, fax 623 2267), 1015 N Stone Ave, is one of the most comfortable Best Westerns. They have a pool, spa, sauna, exercise room, restaurant and bar. Room service and weekend entertainment is offered. The rooms are a good size, and the slightly more expensive suites have whirlpool tubs. The hotel is situated in a nondescript commercial area but is only a bit more than a mile to downtown.

An excellent new hotel is the *Windmill Inn at St Philips Plaza* (☎ 577 0007, fax 577 0045), 4250 N Campbell Ave, in one of the more upscale shopping plazas. The attractive rooms are decorated in Southwestern style and have microwaves and refrigerators. Newspapers, coffee and pastries are delivered to your room every morning. There is a pool, spa and a lending library of paperback bestsellers.

The *Lodge on the Desert* (☎ 325 3366, 1 (800) 456 5634, fax 327 5834), 306 N Alvernon Way, has 40 rooms in a 1936 lodge that is a small oasis in the heart of midtown. The adobe architecture is attractive, the lawns and gardens give the place a spacious feel, and the rooms are attractively furnished. There is a good restaurant, a pool and a free continental breakfast.

The grand dame of Tucson hotels is the sedate and lovely *Arizona Inn* (☎ 325 1541, 1 (800) 933 1093, fax 881 5830), 2200 E Elm St, built in 1929. The grounds are attractively landscaped and the public areas are elegant and traditional. A pool, tennis court and croquet are available. The rooms, decorated in Southwestern style, are spacious though the bathrooms are not very large (people spent less time in them in 1929, perhaps). Many of the rooms have

ARIZONA

patios or fireplaces. The restaurant is good enough to attract the local citizenry, and you can order room service. The service is friendly and unpretentious, yet professional. Expect to pay around $150 in the winter.

### B&Bs

*Peppertrees B&B* (☎ 622 7167), 724 E University Blvd, 85719, is a quick walk away from U of A. Large guest rooms in the 1905 house cost $70 in the summer and $88 in the winter, and the guesthouses, equipped with TVs, phones, laundry facilities and full kitchen, cost $120 in the summer and $160 in the winter. Gourmet breakfasts and an afternoon tea are included in the price. *La Posada del Valle* (☎ 795 3840), 1640 N Campbell Rd, 85719, is also close to U of A and has a beautiful courtyard. It features five rooms with private entrances and bathrooms. Three rooms cost $90, the more luxurious costs $115 and a cottage goes for $125. Rates include breakfast and an afternoon tea.

Take Broadway all the way east to the Saguaro National Park and look for the signs before the fork in the road to get to the luxurious and remote *Suncatcher B&B* (☎ 885 0883, fax 290 8821), 105 N Avenida Javelina, 85748. This B&B has four rooms all individually decorated to resemble some of the world's most exclusive hotels. Summer rates for the two-night minimum range from $170 to $213 and, in the winter, from $298 to $351. These quotes include tax, breakfast, maid service, an open bar, hors d'oeuvres, endless details and a friendly host. They also have a pool and spa. Reservations should be made months in advance. (For information on reservation services see the entry on B&Bs in Places to Stay – middle.)

### Resorts & Ranches

Although Phoenix and Scottsdale are undeniably the resort capitals of the Southwest, Tucson does have a growing number of fine resorts that rival the Valley of the Sun for beauty, comfort and diversity of facilities. Rates for guest ranches include meals and

riding but not the 15% gratuity tax they throw at you.

*Lazy K Bar Guest Ranch* (☎ 744 3050, 1 (800) 321 7018, fax 744 7623), 8401 N Scenic Drive, 85743, offers horseback riding twice a day on desert and mountain trails. Tennis, mountain biking and hayrides are some of the other activities. The style is very much family-oriented with plenty of activities for children and large sit-down dinners with all the guests. The ranch has 23 rooms in adobe buildings, all with air conditioning and private baths. Rates from mid-December to January and from February to May are $140 to $170 for a single and $230 to $260 for a double; suites cost $140 a person. From October to mid-December a single costs $125 to $155 and a double costs $200 to $230; suites cost $125 a person. Summer rates drop by about $20. Rates for a third person (ie, a child) range from $25 to $80.

*White Stallion Ranch* (☎ 297 0252, 1 (800) 782 5546, fax 744 2786), 9251 W Twin Peaks Rd, 85743, is a quiet, peaceful family-style ranch where you can brush down your own horse before a ride, let the children roam free in a petting zoo, relax on a patio and listen to the birds or take a challenging hike through the desert mountain wilderness. The ranch is only open from October to April. Rates from October to mid-December are $125 a single and $200 to $260 a double. From mid-December to April a single costs $141 and a double from $220 to $318. If you stay more than seven days, the rates are lower. They don't take credit cards.

Fifteen miles east of Tucson, *Tanque Verde Guest Ranch* (☎ 296 6275, 1 (800) 234 3833, fax 721 9426), 14301 E Speedway Blvd, 85748, sits in the Rincon Mountains, offering plenty of opportunities for hiking, riding and nature walks. For more 'resort-style' activities there are two pools, tennis courts, a spa and basketball courts. This is one of the more famous ranches in the area, with well-decorated 'casitas', attentive service, great food and beautiful surroundings. In the low season, from May to October, rates are $190 to $225 a single and $225 to $290 a double. High-season rates are $245 to $285 a single and $280 to $395 a double.

*Loew's Ventana Canyon Resort* (☎ 299 2020, 1 (800) 234 5117, fax 299 6832), 7000 N Resort Drive, 85715, is in a spectacular setting surrounded by the golf course. The atmosphere is a bit pretentious and holds all the standards for a resort – shopping arcade, impeccable rooms, elegant dining, golf and entertainment. Room rates are based on the view, not occupancy. From mid-January to late June rooms cost from $295 to $325, from July to September they are $115 to $145 and from September to January rates jump to $215 to $295.

*Westward Look Resort* (☎ 297 1151, 1 (800) 722 2500, fax 297 9023), 245 E Ina Rd, 85704, was originally a dude ranch and retains much of its original intimate style. There is a top-notch restaurant and the rooms have views of either the mountains or the city. Rates range from $90 to $150 depending on the view and season. Swimming pools, tennis courts, a golf course and spas keep guests occupied.

## PLACES TO EAT

Tucson has a well-deserved reputation for Mexican food and if you like it, you'll never be at a loss for a place to eat. If you don't like Mexican food, you'll still find a varied assortment of excellent American and international restaurants, as well as Southwestern cuisine.

### Breakfast Cafes

The popular and busy *Coffee Etc* (☎ 881 8070), 2830 N Campbell Ave, serves breakfast 24 hours a day, as well as burgers, sandwiches, soups, salads, light meals and, of course, a variety of coffees.

For home-style breakfast, the friendly *Marlene's Hungry Fox* (☎ 326 2835), 4637 E Broadway Blvd, is a good choice favored by locals, some of whom have been eating breakfast here for years. They feature 'double yolk eggs' and are open from 6 am to 2 pm on weekdays and 6:30 am to 2 pm on weekends. Another friendly and funky local place that has good breakfasts and

lunches at low prices is *Bobo's* (☎ 326 6163), 2938 E Grant Rd, near what Tucsonans call 'the airplane corner' (you'll know what they mean when you go there). Pancakes are stuffed with fruit or, if you're feeling adventurous, get the UFO, which is a pancake made with spinach and melted cheese. It is open from 5 am to 2:30 pm.

*The Good Earth Restaurant & Bakery* (☎ 745 6600), 6366 E Broadway Blvd, is an attractive, well-lit restaurant serving baked goods and breakfast all day, as well as an excellent variety of reasonably priced light meals ranging from vegetarian walnut and mushroom casserole to beef stroganoff. Hours are from 7 am to 10 pm Monday to Thursday, to 11 pm on Friday and Saturday, and from 9 am to 10 pm on Sunday.

Many people think that the *Blue Willow Restaurant* (☎ 795 8736), 2616 E Campbell Ave, serves the best breakfast in town, and they serve it just about any time. Their soups, salads and sandwiches are really good and an excellent value. The place is popular, so there's sometimes a wait during which you can browse their card and poster shop. They open for breakfast at 7 am (8 am on weekends) and close at 11 pm (midnight on Friday and Saturday). They have an attractive patio.

Good downtown spots for breakfasts include *Bailey & Bailey* (☎ 792 2623), 135 S 6th, which is open from 7 am to 7 pm Monday to Saturday, and is a popular spot for a light meal before a night out on the town. The *Cup Cafe* (☎ 798 1618), 311 E Congress St, is in the same building as the Hotel Congress and Club Congress, all recommended spots for people searching for something more eclectic and artistic. The breakfasts are good, as are their light meals. Hours are from 8 am to 1 am, or to 3 pm on Friday and Saturday.

For breakfast in the desert, head to the *Tohono Chul Tea Room* (☎ 797 1711), 7366 N Paseo del Norte, where you can dine on a pleasant patio or indoors from 8 am to 5 pm daily. The varied menu features Mexican and American food, and they serve an English-style high tea from 2:30 to 4:30 pm.

ARIZONA

If you want your eggs Benedict served in the most elegant of surroundings, the dining room at *Arizona Inn* (☎ 325 1541), 2200 E Elm St (see Places to Stay above), is open to the public. Breakfast hours are 7 am to 10:30 am.

## Buffets

Cafeteria-style places are great places for people watching their pennies. Mexican food is always reasonably priced, and many of the Indian and some of the Chinese restaurants have all-you-can-eat lunchtime buffets during the week for about $4.95. For people with large appetites and little money, *Furrs Cafeterias* are a good deal. There's one at 5910 E Broadway Blvd (☎ 747 7881) and another at 4329 N Oracle Rd (☎ 293 8550). They have all-you-can-eat buffets with a good variety of food and unlimited trips to the buffet counter for about $5 on weekdays and $6 on weekends. Drinks cost extra. Hours are from 11 am to 8 pm and to 8:30 pm on Friday and Saturday.

## Mexican

There must be over 100 Mexican restaurants in Tucson. It would be a worthwhile culinary adventure would be to spend a few months eating at every one! Some people say they don't like Mexican food because it's too 'hot', but there are many dishes which are spiced very mildly or not at all. Most tacos and tostadas can be made without any peppers. If you don't like spicy food, stay away from the salsa that appears at your table along with chips and the menu at most Mexican restaurants. The salsa is often one of the hottest things in the restaurant. Ask your server to recommend non-spicy dishes.

With so many Mexican places to choose from, it's hard to narrow them down to a manageable list, but here are some of my favorites. The least expensive restaurants are generally in or near South Tucson. For Mexican fast food, *Birrería Guadalajara* (☎ 624 8020), 304 E 22nd St, is very tasty and beats the heck out of any American fast food. The menu here is in Spanish, but the

servers will translate for you. Hours are from 9:30 am to 9:30 pm daily, or till about midnight on Friday and Saturday. For sit-down dining, there are half a dozen good places along S 4th Ave between 22nd St and I-10, any one of which provides satisfactory food. *Mi Nidito* (☎ 622 5081), 1813 S 4th Ave, frequently gets good reviews and there's often a wait; they don't take reservations. Hours are from 11 am to 10 pm Wednesday and Thursday, to 2 pm on Friday and Saturday, and they closed on Monday and Tuesday.

There are several good choices downtown. One of the cheapest and most interesting is *La Indita* (☎ 792 0523), 622 N 4th Ave. Apart from the excellent Mexican food, this is one of the few places where you can also try Tohono O'odham Indian dishes. Hours are from 11 am to 9 pm Monday to Friday, 6 to 9 pm on Saturday and 9 am to 9 pm on Sunday. There is another *La Indita* (☎ 886 9191) at 8578 E Broadway Blvd, with similar food but no alcohol.

Mexican food in more upscale environments costs a few dollars more but has some innovative twists and is still an excellent value. Recommended downtown places include the excellent *Cafe Poca Cosa* (☎ 622 6400), 88 E Broadway Blvd, in the Park Inn-Santa Rita, open from 11 am to 9 pm Monday to Thursday and to 10 pm on Friday and Saturday. Late-night downtown dining is available at *El Minuto Cafe* (☎ 882 4145), just south of downtown at 354 S Main Ave, open from 11 am to 11 pm daily and to 2 am on Friday and Saturday. The oldest place in town is *El Charro Cafe* (☎ 622 1922), 311 N Court Ave, which they say has been in the same family since 1922 and is very popular with tourists and locals alike. Hours change seasonally and they open for breakfast sometimes.

Away from downtown, *Papagayo* (☎ 577 6055), 4717 E Sunrise Drive, has good food and is popular with Foothills residents. It also makes a convenient choice after a day in Sabino Canyon. They are open from 11 am to 9 pm, till 10 pm on Friday and Saturday. *La Parrilla Suiza* (☎ 747 4838), 5602 E Speedway Blvd, serves grilled Mexico City-style food. Hours are from 11 am to 10 pm Monday to Thursday, to 11 pm on Friday and Saturday, and 1 to 10 pm on Sunday. There is another location (☎ 624 4300) at 2720 N Oracle Rd. *El Saguarito* (☎ 297 1264), 7216 N Oracle Rd, is open from 7 am to 9 pm Monday to Saturday and serves health- and heart-conscious food using canola oil rather than the traditional lard. *La Fuente* (☎ 623 8659), 1749 N Oracle Rd, often has strolling mariachis in the evening to give that extra Mexican ambiance. They are open from 11:30 am to 10 pm daily and till 11 pm on Friday and Saturday.

### Guatemalan

*Maya Quetzal* (☎ 622 8207), 429 N 4th Ave, is a small friendly place that has been very well received locally and serves delicious dishes at pequeño prices. They have a little outdoor patio and are open from 11 am to 9 pm, till 10 pm Friday and Saturday and are closed on Wednesday.

### Asian

*Cock Asian* (☎ 623 7765), 2226½ N Stone Ave, has great Vietnamese-Chinese food, which many locals claim is the best in town and is a good value. Hours are 11 am to 9:30 pm Monday to Saturday. The *Lotus Garden* (☎ 298 3351), 5975 E Speedway Blvd, is one of Tucson's favorites. They serve mainly traditional Cantonese dishes from 11:30 am to 11 pm, or till midnight on Friday and Saturday. If you prefer spicier Mandarin food, *Old Peking* (☎ 795 9811), 2522 E Speedway Blvd, is a good choice. They are open from 11:30 am to 9:30 pm, till 10:15 pm on Friday and Saturday. For good dim sum, served weekends only, try the *Golden Phoenix* (☎ 327 8008), 2854 E 22nd St. Hours are 11 am to 9:30 pm. *Seri Melaka* (☎ 747 7811), 6133 E Broadway Blvd, serves reasonably priced Malaysian food and some Chinese dishes. They are open daily for lunch and dinner.

For Japanese dining, *Fujiya* (☎ 795 7121), 1800 E Fort Lowell Rd, is open for lunch and dinner Tuesday to Saturday and has good food at lower prices than most

Japanese restaurants. Sushi and other Japanese food is served at *Sakura* (☎ 298 7777), 6534 E Tanque Verde Rd, open daily from 11 am to 2 pm and 5 to 10 pm, till 11 pm on Friday and Saturday.

For buffet-style vegetarian and vegan Indian food, the inexpensive, Hare Krishna-run *Govinda* (☎ 792 0360), 711 E Blacklidge Drive, off 1st Ave, is recommended. Lunch is from 11:30 am to 2:30 pm Wednesday to Saturday, and dinner is from 5 to 9 pm Tuesday to Saturday. The atmosphere is meditative and no alcohol is served. Other good Indian restaurants, serving meat and alcohol, include *Taste of India* (☎ 292 1738), 150 W Fort Lowell Rd, and *New Delhi Palace* (☎ 296 8585), 6751 E Broadway Blvd, both of which are open from 11:30 am to 2:30 pm and 5 to 9 pm.

### Italian

If expense is not a concern, elegant *Daniel's* (☎ 742 3200), 4310 N Campbell Ave in St Philips Plaza, is one of the best in town. They specialize in Tuscan-style meals, and most dinner entrees are in the $20s except for several less-expensive pasta selections. Hours are from 5 to 9 pm daily. The more casual *Boccata Bistro Bar* (☎ 577 9309), 5605 E River Rd, is a little less expensive and serves northern Italian food with a few French-influenced dishes. This is a local favorite and is nearly always packed. Hours are from 5:50 to 9 pm, and to 10 pm on Friday and Saturday. Less expensive still is *Ciao Italia* (☎ 884 0000), 1535 N Stone Ave, with a good variety served from 11:30 am to 2 pm and 5 to 9 pm from Monday to Friday and 5 to 9 pm on Saturday.

### French

*Le Rendez-Vous* (☎ 323 7373), 3844 E Fort Lowell Rd, looks like a little Southwestern house in a parking lot and has a refreshingly unpompous atmosphere, but the food is recommended and a bit cheaper than most French restaurants of this caliber. Hours are from 11:30 am to 2 pm Tuesday to Friday and 6 to 10 pm Tuesday to Sunday.

*Penelope's* (☎ 325 5080), 3071 N Swan Rd, is a lovely restaurant with a strong local following. Excellent six-course dinners are prix fixe at $29 or $41 with appropriately selected wines; cheaper lunches are also served. Hours are from 11:30 am to 2 pm Tuesday to Friday and 5:30 to 9:30 pm Tuesday to Sunday.

### Greek

I like *Athens on 4th Ave* (☎ 624 6886), 500 N 4th Ave, simply because the food is delicious and the prices reasonable. It's a small place and a reservation is a good idea if you don't want to wait. Hours are from 11:30 am to 2:30 pm and 5 to 10 pm Monday to Friday and 5 to 10 pm Saturday. A little more upscale and very good is the *Olive Tree* (☎ 298 1845), 7000 E Tanque Verde Rd. They are open from 11:30 am to 9 pm Monday to Thursday, to 10 pm Friday and Saturday and 5 to 9 pm Sunday.

### Worldly & Eclectic Cuisine

*Trio* (☎ 325 3333), 2990 N Swan Rd, is one of the latest additions to the Tucson restaurant scene and serves Southeast Asian, Latin American and European dishes – hence the name. Most dinner entrees are in the teens. Lunch is from 11:30 am to 2:30 pm, dinner from 5 to 9 pm, to 10 pm on Friday and Saturday, and a late-night menu is offered from 10 pm to midnight. They are closed Sunday.

Downtown, the little *Cafe Magritte* (☎ 884 8004), 254 E Congress St, has a small but varied menu with Southwestern and Middle Eastern influences. The food is good, the service friendly, the clientele arty and the prices quite low,. They have sidewalk dining, too. Hours are from 11 am to 11 pm, till midnight on Friday and Saturday. They are closed on Monday.

At the more pricey end of the market, *Anthony's in the Catalinas* (☎ 299 1771), 6440 N Campbell Ave, has excellent food and a genteel ambiance. There's a nice little garden patio for pre-dinner drinks and a huge picture window overlooking the lights of Tucson in the distance. Hours are from 11:30 am to 2:30 pm and 5 to 10 pm Monday to Saturday and 5 to 10 pm on Sunday.

### Southwestern

*Cafe Terra Cotta* (☎ 577 8100), 4310 N Campbell Ave, in St Philips Plaza, is the best Southwestern restaurant in Tucson. The food is as good as any of the other places at prices that are definitely more moderate. The menu is pretty innovative, even wild-sounding at times, but there are also a few fairly straightforward choices. The appetizers sound so appetizing that many people order two of them and forgo an entree, supposedly to leave room for one of the divine desserts. There is a pleasant patio and appropriate Southwestern decor. Hours are from 11 am to 9:30 pm and till 10:30 on Friday and Saturday.

Another moderately priced restaurant with a delicious and eclectic Southwestern menu but a decidedly un-Southwestern ambiance is the *Presidio Grill* (☎ 327 4667), 3352 E Speedway Blvd. They are open 11 am to 10 pm, till midnight on Friday and Saturday. Sunday brunch begins at 8 am.

Many locals will argue that *Janos* (☎ 884 9426), 150 Main Ave, is by far the best Southwestern restaurant, set in the 1855 Stevens House, complete with saguaro-rib ceilings. The food is great and the building is fun to see, but I found that the service wasn't very helpful. Most dinner entrees are in the $20s and some creep over $30, though they do offer summer sampler specials for about $13. Hours are from 5:30 to about 10 pm Tuesday to Saturday.

Tucson's most celebrated restaurant is the *Tack Room* (☎ 722 2800), 2800 N Sabino Canyon Rd. This is one of only six restaurants in the West to receive top billing from both Mobil and AAA. Dinner entrees average around $30. The food is American with a Southwestern twist, but it's not as adventurous as the restaurants listed above. Hours are 5 to 10 pm, closed on Monday in the summer.

### Steak & Seafood

There are plenty of steak houses that serve what Southwestern food used to be until the good chefs like Janos Wilder (of Janos listed above) came along and reinvented the concept. For those on a budget, *El Corral* (☎ 299 6092), 2201 E River Rd, is a good choice. Service is a little amateurish but aims to please. Prime rib is the specialty of the house and a great deal at $7 to $9. They have kids' cheeseburgers for $1.75. Hours are 5 to 10 pm daily.

The same owners run the *Pinnacle Peak Steakhouse* (☎ 296 0911), 6541E Tanque Verde Rd, where the atmosphere is Wild Western and fun, if slightly touristy. Wooden sidewalks pass dance halls and saloons as you swagger into the dining room. The sign outside warns 'Stop! No Ties Allowed' and if you've got one on, you can donate it to the rafter decorations. The food is inexpensive and good. Hours are 5 to 10 pm daily.

The *Hidden Valley Inn* (☎ 299 4941), 4825 N Sabino Canyon Rd, is unique. It has that Old Wild West look to bring in the crowds and reasonable priced steaks, but inside is a museum of thousands of tiny woodcarvings set in Western dioramas. The carvings are the life work of Jean Le Roy, with new pieces by his son-in-law, Rudy Castilla. Hours are from 11:30 am to 3 pm and 5 to 10 pm daily.

The most upscale steak house is the *Ranchers Club* (☎ 321 7621), in the Hotel Park Tucson at 5151 E Grant Rd. You can pay over $30 for a steak grilled to perfection weighing a pound and a half, that will feed two. Hours are from 11:30 am to 2 pm and 5:30 to 10 pm Monday to Friday and 5:30 to 10 pm on Saturday.

If you're hankering for seafood, try *Jerome's* (☎ 721 0311), 6958 E Tanque Verde Rd. The emphasis is on Cajun-style grilled seafood and it's probably the best in town. Most entrees are in the mid-teens. Hours are from 11:30 am to 2 pm Monday to Friday and 5 to 10 pm daily. Sunday brunch is served from 11 am to 2 pm.

## ENTERTAINMENT

Read the free alternative *Tucson Weekly*, published every Thursday and available throughout the city, for updates on local happenings. The daily papers also have entertainment information every day, especially in the Friday 'Starlight' section of the *Arizona Daily Star* and the Thursday 'Calendar' section of the *Tucson Citizen*.

### Cinema

There are a dozen or more cinema multiplexes showing the year's best and worst movies. A few of them have decent movies screening every day for as low as $1.50. Check the dailies for details. Theaters frequently screening more artistic, alternative and foreign movies include *The Loft* (☎ 795 7777), 3233 E Speedway Blvd; *The Screening Room* (☎ 622 2262), 127 E Congress St; and *The Gallagher* (☎ 621 3102) at the student union on the U of A campus.

### Nightlife

Tucson's Hispanic and Western heritages and the U of A have all influenced the city's nightlife. So every week you get a good variety of mariachi, country & western, cowboy, blues, rock, jazz and alternative music. In addition, the local Indian tribes occasionally provide days or evenings of dancing and music.

For mariachi and other Mexican music, restaurants like *La Fuente* (☎ 623 8659), 1749 N Oracle Rd, or *Gran Guadalajara* (☎ 620 1321), 2527 S 4th Ave, are good places to start. This is dinner music, admittedly, but if you like what you hear, your server or the locals can direct you to lesser known places.

There are plenty of fun boot-scooting country & western bars. *Wild Wild West* (☎ 744 7744), 4385 W Ina Rd, advertises 'An Acre of Dancin' & Romancin' which refers to a racetrack dance floor which is the biggest in Tucson (perhaps the Southwest) and attracts serious country music dancers, cowboys, students and tourists alike. They have DJs, occasional live bands, inexpensive all-you-can-eat buffets almost every night, shops selling Western gear and bouncers on horseback (I'm not kidding – except they call them 'security men'). It's quite a scene.

If the Wild Wild West is too wild for you, try *The Maverick, King of Clubs* (☎ 748 0456), 4702 E 22nd St. This friendly place is smaller and has live music most nights, and the crowd is a little more country. The *Cactus Moon* (☎ 748 0049), 5470 E Broadway Blvd, is loud, brash and the place to see and be seen if you're into the two-stepping scene. While all three places offer free dance lessons (call them for hours), the Cactus Moon is where you'll fit in if you're dressed in the latest Western wear and already know how to dance.

*Club Congress* (☎ 622 8848), 311 E Congress St, stands out as the best alternative music place, with plenty of dancing room when necessary, though a few live acts are more of the listening variety. DJs take over early in the week. Check out the listings in *Tucson Weekly* to find out what's going on from Thursday to Sunday. Another good live music venue is *The Rock* (☎ 629 9211), 136 N Park, with a good variety of bands ranging from pop rock to blues to reggae. *Cushing St Bar & Grill* (☎ 622 7984), 343 S Meyer Ave (on the corner of Cushing St), has mainly jazz and blues attracting college students. The *Chicago Bar* (☎ 748 8169), 5954 E Speedway Blvd, presents blues, rock and reggae bands, and is popular with students. *Cafe Sweetwater* (☎ 622 6464), 340 E 6th St, has a small but lively bar attached to its restaurant and features modern and Latin jazz, with occasional blues bands.

*Berky's Bar* (☎ 296 1981), 5769 E Speedway Blvd, attracts an older crowd and often has decent live bands, mainly blues, and dancing with no cover charge. *Berky's on 4th* (☎ 622 0376), 424 N 4th Ave, is an offshoot and offers a similar atmosphere. The *Neon Moon* (☎ 881 7500), 5150 E Speedway Blvd, is a pretty good blues venue. Catch bluesman Sam Taylor for a taste of Tucson's local talent. Taylor also hosts a blues and R&B hour at 5 pm on Saturdays on KXCI, 91.3 FM, Tucson's Community Radio Station. The Tucson Blues Club hotline (☎ 570 7955) has information about events.

More upscale venues for live music are the resorts. Try the bars at the *Westward Look Resort* (☎ 297 1151), 245 E Ina Rd; the *Sheraton – El Conquistador* (☎ 544 5000), 10000 N Oracle Rd; *Loew's Ventana Canyon* (☎ 299 2020), 7000 N Resort Drive; and *Westin La Paloma* (☎ 742 6000), 3800 E Sunrise Drive.

The Tucson Jazz Society operates a jazz events hotline (☎ 743 3399).

## Performing Arts

There are several places to hear and see performing arts. The following are the most highly acclaimed. During the summer, not much happens at these places.

The renovated 1920s *Temple of Music & Art* (☎ 884 4875), 330 S Scott Ave, is the home of the Arizona Theater Company (☎ 884 8210 or 622 2823 for the box office), which produces shows from October to May. The *Tucson Convention Center* (☎ 791 4101 or 791 4266 for the box office), 260 S Church St, plays host to many events including performances by Ballet Arizona (☎ 882 5022), December to May; Arizona Opera Company (☎ 293 4336), October to March; Tucson Symphony Orchestra (☎ 882 8585), November to March; and the Southern Arizona Light Opera Company (☎ 323 7888, 884 1212). The U of A *Centennial Hall* (☎ 621 3364, or 621 3341 for the box office), 1020 E University Blvd, hosts a variety of excellent international acts throughout the academic year.

Tucson has a lively theater scene, with several local companies, some offering year-round performances of alternative and avant-garde productions. One of the best is the *AKA Theater* (☎ 623 7852), 125 E Congress St. See the newspapers above for other current offerings.

Although cultural performances dwindle in summer, you can catch plenty of fun and free events at *Downtown Saturday Night*, held along Congress St and Broadway Blvd between Stone and 4th Aves the first and third Saturday of every month from about 7 am to 10 pm. Galleries stay open late and there are plenty of free street performances.

It's sponsored by the Tucson Arts District (☎ 624 9977). A variety of free music performances take place in the spring and the summer in some of the city parks. Call the parks outdoor entertainment department (☎ 791 4079) for details.

### Spectator Sports

Phoenix has most of the top professional sports teams in Arizona, although the minor-league Tucson Toros (☎ 325 2621) play baseball at Hi Corbett Field in Reid Park from April to October. The Colorado Rockies have their spring training here every March. Inexpensive tickets for the ball game are easy enough to obtain. It's exactly the opposite for college sports – the U of A Wildcats have top ranked teams. Tickets for the U of A men's basketball team are some of the hardest to get when the October to February season gets underway. Football tickets are also in demand.

The Northern Telecom Open Golf Tournament (☎ 624 4653, 1 (800) 882 7660) has over a million dollars worth of prize money. It's held at the Tucson National Golf Course in mid-January. In March the Ping/Welch's LPGA Golf Tournament with women competing for almost half a million dollars in prizes is held at the Randolph North municipal golf course.

Greyhounds race year round at Tucson Greyhound Park (☎ 884 7576), 2601 S 3rd Ave. Stock-car races take place at Tucson Raceway (☎ 762 9200), 12500 S Houghton Rd (southwest of town on I-10 to the Houghton Rd exit). Horseracing recently began at the new Rillito Race Track during winter. Call the Convention and Visitors Bureau for the most recent information.

### THINGS TO BUY

Southwestern arts & crafts are of the most interest to travelers. Small but exquisite pieces of jewelry can easily be carried and bulky items can be shipped.

Some of the best arts & crafts stores are in the Presidio historic district (see Downtown Tucson for recommended stores).

Another good place for quality arts & crafts is St Philips Plaza at the southeast corner of River Rd and Campbell Ave. Prices are high but so is the quality. Particularly good stores here are the Obsidian Gallery (☎ 577 3598), Bahti Indian Arts (☎ 577 0290) and the Turquoise Door (☎ 299 7787). Another Turquoise Door is at 5675 N Swan Rd (☎ 299 7551). Further north is De Grazia's Gallery in the Sun (☎ 299 9191), 6300 N Swan Rd, which is the former home, present resting place and gallery of famous local artist Ted De Grazia, whose simple depictions of Southwestern people and life can be found on calendars, postcards and prints. You can view some of his originals in the adjoining museum (admission is free) and purchase reproductions.

For fun shopping and browsing, you can't beat 4th Ave between University Blvd and Congress St. Here you'll find books and beads, antiques and African art, jewelry and junk, clothes and collectibles, and all sorts of treasures. Then head west along Congress St for the Arts District.

Several large, enclosed shopping malls are in Tucson. Three of the most noteworthy are Tucson's oldest major mall, El Con Mall (☎ 795 9958), 3601 E Broadway Blvd; the Tucson Mall (☎ 293 7330), 4500 N Oracle, which is the city's largest, and Park Mall (☎ 748 1222), 5870 E Broadway Blvd. Call the malls for information about their free shuttle service to and from the major hotels and resorts.

For bookstores, the following stand out. The Haunted Bookshop (☎ 297 4843), 7211 N Northern Rd (a block west of Oracle and Ina, next to Tohono Chul Park) has a great selection on most subjects, and has an underground play area to keep small kids occupied while you browse. The Book Mark (☎ 881 6350), 5001 E Speedway Blvd, has the biggest selection of new books in town while the two Bookman's at 1930 E Grant Rd (☎ 325 5767) and 3733 W Ina Rd (☎ 579 0303) have the largest selection of used books, tapes and CDs in Arizona. Antigone Books (☎ 792 3715), 600 N 4th Ave, has books by and about women and nonsexist books for kids.

ARIZONA

## GETTING THERE & AWAY
### Air
Tucson International Airport (☎ 573 8000) is about nine miles south of downtown. It has a few direct flights into a limited number of cities in Mexico. Flights to other countries involve connections at larger airports. Therefore, international airport facilities in Tucson are limited; there are immigration and customs facilities, but no international currency desks. Passengers arriving from abroad should either buy US dollars before they leave, which is recommended, or exchange currency at the first major airport they arrive in. Most of the major carriers have direct flights to and from Tucson and many large US cities.

The terminal has a pricey parking lot, or you can save at the Park 'n Save lot at Tucson Blvd and Corona, near the main entrance. A frequent and free shuttle connects the Park 'n Save with the terminal.

Sun Tran (☎ 792 9222) has buses during the day to the Laos Transit Center at Irvington St and Liberty Ave, about halfway between the airport and downtown. This is bus No 25. From here you have to connect to another bus. The fare is 75¢ and a transfer is free. Bus No 11 leaves from the airport and goes north through town along Alvernon Way. You can connect with many east-west routes from this line. Timetables and bus maps are available at the airport.

A more convenient option is using Arizona Stagecoach (☎ 889 1000, 881 4111), which has door-to-door, 24-hour van service to anywhere in the metropolitan Tucson area. The fare varies from $9 to over $20, depending on the location. The fare usually works out to be roughly half of what a taxi would cost.

### Bus
Greyhound (☎ 1 (800) 231 2222) has a terminal (☎ 792 3475) at 2 S 4th Ave. There are several buses a day that run east along I-10 to New Mexico, and northwest along I-10 to Phoenix, connecting to the rest of Arizona and California. Greyhound also connects with Citizen Auto Stage Vans

to Nogales every hour from 7 am to 7 pm for $6.50, with stops at towns along I-19.

Another company using the Greyhound bus terminal is Bridgewater Transport (☎ 628 8909) with buses for Douglas ($19), via Sierra Vista ($14) and Bisbee ($17), leaving at 7 am and at 1 and 6 pm. Fares are 50% less for children under 12. Greyhound sells tickets connecting to this service.

Arizona Shuttle Service (☎ 795 6771, 1 (800) 888 2749) has hourly vans leaving Tucson International Airport for Phoenix Airport from 4 am to 8 pm. They also have pickup locations in midtown, but not downtown. The fare is $19.

### Train
Amtrak (☎ 1 (800) 872 7245) has trains to the Tucson Station (☎ 623 4442), 400 E Toole Ave, on the east side of downtown. Three night trains a week go to Phoenix, Yuma and Los Angeles, California, and three morning trains a week go east through New Mexico and on to Miami, Florida.

## GETTING AROUND
### Bus
Sun Tran (☎ 792 9222) has buses all over the metro Tucson area from early morning into the evening every day, but there are no night buses. Fares are 75¢ with a free transfer. A monthly pass for unlimited rides costs $22 for a calendar month. Discounted fares and passes are available for students under 18 (with ID) and seniors and disabled riders (who will need to obtain a special ID from Sun Tran). Passes and timetables are available at dozens of outlets around town; call Sun Tran for the nearest one. There are many park and ride lots around town and some buses have bike racks. Major transit centers are the Laos Transit Center at Irvington St and Liberty Ave to the south; the Ronstadt-Downtown Center at Congress St and 6th Ave; and the Tohono Tadai Center at Stone Ave and Wetmore Rd to the north.

The Sun Tran Trolley is an old fashioned-looking trolley (it is air conditioned) linking U of A (it leaves from Old Main) with the 4th Ave shopping area, Congress St and the Arts District, the Ronstadt-Downtown Center and historical downtown. Trolleys run two or three times an hour from about 10 am to 6:30 pm Monday to Friday, less frequently on Saturday and not on Sunday. Trolleys run until 11 pm on the nights of Downtown Saturday Night or when the U of A has a home game. Trolley fare is 25¢.

### Car Rental

All the main companies have offices in the airport and many have offices in other parts of the valley or will deliver your car. It is best to reserve a car in advance for the best rates.

### Taxi

There are plenty of cabs operating 24 hours. A fare from the airport to downtown is around $15. Cab rates can vary somewhat, so call several companies to ask for the best deal. Companies include Yellow Cab (☎ 624 6611), Allstate Cab (☎ 798 1111), City Cab (☎ 792 2028) and Checker Cab (☎ 623 1133).

### Bicycle

Bargain Basement Bikes (☎ 624 9673), 428 N Fremont Ave; the Bike Shack (☎ 624 3663), 940 E University Blvd; Full Cycle (☎ 327 3232), 3232 E Speedway Blvd, all rent bikes. Rates are about $20 a day. Helmets are required for cyclists under 18.

## AROUND TUCSON
### Mission San Xavier del Bac

Founded by the Jesuit Padre Kino in 1700, this is Arizona's oldest European building which is still in use. Most of it was destroyed in the Pima Indian uprising of 1751, but it was rebuilt by Franciscans in the late 1700s and today looks very much like it did 200 years ago. Much of it has been restored, and work continues on the frescoes inside. A visit to San Xavier is a highlight of many people's trip to Tucson.

Catholic masses are held daily. The church itself (☎ 294 2624) is open daily from 8 am to 6 pm, and the church museum

Detail of the Mission San Xavier del Bac. (RR)

and gift shop is open from 9 am to 5 pm. Admission is free and donations are accepted. Photography is permitted when religious ceremonies are not taking place.

Nicknamed 'the white dove of the desert', its dazzling white walls are a splendid site as you drive south on I-19. Get there by taking I-19 exit 92, about nine miles south of downtown Tucson, and heading west on San Xavier Rd for nearly a mile. The mission is on the San Xavier Indian Reservation (part of the Tohono O'odham tribe), and the plaza on the south side of the mission parking lot has several stores selling Indian jewelry, arts & crafts and snacks.

Especially colorful religious ceremonies are held on the Friday after Easter, the Fiesta of San Xavier in early December and Christmas. Call the mission for details.

### Arizona-Sonora Desert Museum

The ASDM is a living museum representing the flora and fauna of the Arizona-Sonora Desert and, as such, is more like a

Bighorn sheep

zoo than a museum. It is one of the best of its kind in the country. Just about any local desert animal you could think of is displayed, often in quite natural-looking settings. The grounds are thick with desert plants too, many of which are labeled. You'll see scorpions and saguaros, coatis and coyotes, bighorn sheep and rattlesnakes, golden eagles and tiny hummingbirds. It's all here.

Docents are on hand to answer question about the live animals and to show other exhibits throughout the day – you might get a chance to pet a snake! There are two walk-through aviaries, one dedicated solely to hummingbirds; a geological exhibit featuring an underground cave (kids love that one); an underground exhibit with windows into ponds containing beavers, otters and ducks (yes, these are found along the riparian corridors of the desert); and much more. It's one of the best things to see in the Tucson area and a great way to learn about the natural history of the desert.

Allow a minimum of two hours (a half day is better) and come prepared for outdoor walking. Strollers and wheelchairs are available. There is a gift shop, art gallery, restaurant and cafe.

The drive out to the ASDM, 2021 N Kinney Rd, is about 15 miles west along Speedway Blvd, which goes over the very scenic Gates Pass. The narrow and winding Gates Pass Rd is unsuitable for trailers and RVs, which should take the longer route west along Ajo Way – follow the signs. A visit to the ASDM can be combined with a visit to the Old Tucson Studios, the International Wildlife Museum or Saguaro National Park (West) to make a full-day outing.

The ASDM (☎ 883 2702) is open from 8:30 am to 5 pm daily, or from 7:30 am to 6 pm in summer, and admission is $8.95 for those over 12 and $1.75 for six- to 12-year-olds.

### Old Tucson Studios

This film set was used in hundreds of Western movie productions from 1939 to the 1995. Visitors were treated to shootouts, stagecoach rides and Wild West events galore, and it was Tucson's most popular tourist destination until most of it burnt down in May 1995. Nobody was hurt, but the famous site is now closed. The owners vow to rebuild, and it may be open for business again in 1996. But it's going to be hard to replace those personally autographed John Wayne posters. Call 883 0100 for an update. Old Tucson is on Kinney Rd a few miles southeast of the ADSM (see above for directions).

### International Wildlife Museum

Housed in an odd castle-like building at 4800 W Gates Pass Rd (between Speedway Blvd and Gates Pass), this museum (☎ 624 4024) is a taxidermist's delight. Hundreds of animals from all over the world have been killed and expertly mounted. There are various hands-on exhibits and hourly movies about wildlife, but no live animals. Hours are from 9 am to 5 pm daily, and admission costs $5, $3.75 for students and those over 62, and $1.50 for six- to 12-year-olds.

### Biosphere 2

This place is unique. It is a three-acre glassed dome built to be completely sealed off from Biosphere 1, ie, the biosphere you

The controversial Biosphere 2 is a completely enclosed biosphere. (RR)

are living in. Inside the dome are seven different micro-habitats, ranging from tropical forest to ocean environment, designed to be completely self-sustaining. In 1991, eight bionauts entered Biosphere 2 for a two-year tour of duty during which they would be physically cut off from the outside world. Although this experiment could be used as a prototype for future space stations, it was a privately funded endeavor.

The bionauts emerged two years later, all thinner but otherwise in pretty fair shape for having been cut off from its atmosphere for two years. The experiment was much criticized, however, because the dome leaked gases, and it was opened a few times to allow a bionaut to emerge for medical treatment and to allow supplies to be taken in. Carbon dioxide rose to unhealthy levels inside. There were also the accompanying petty wranglings that happen when entrepreneurs, scientists, businesspeople and glory-seekers come together.

Now, bionauts enter only on short missions of a few weeks or a few months. The public has always been welcome to tour around the outside on a three-quarter mile paved trail, but you can't go inside – after all, it's cut off from Biosphere 1. Outside, there are greenhouses containing examples of the plants and animals inhabiting Biosphere 2, and guided tours of these and other facilities and exhibits are given. There is a

restaurant, gift shop and hotel (see Places to Stay above).

Biosphere 2 (☎ 896 6200) is five miles northeast of the junction of Hwy 77 and Hwy 79 and about 30 miles north of Tucson. It is open daily from 8 am to 6 pm (but hours have changed frequently in the past so it's a good idea to call first), and guided tours are offered every hour. Admission is $12.95 or $10.95 for those over 62 and $6 for 12- to 17-year-olds. If you are staying at the hotel you can get tickets for $10. Discounts are often given – look for coupons in Tucson newspapers or ask at the Convention & Visitors Bureau whether they have any discount coupons.

### Colossal Cave

This dry limestone cave is six stories under the ground and was a legendary outlaw hideout. It's called a dry cave because there is no dripping water and the geological formations are no longer growing. A half-mile trail takes you through several different chambers with many geological formations. Parts of the cave are still unexplored. Entrance includes a guided tour that lasts about 45 minutes. The temperature inside is a pleasant 72°F year round.

Colossal Cave (☎ 647 7275) is open daily from 9 am to 5 pm from mid-September to mid-March and from 8 am to 6 pm the rest of the year. It stays open one hour later on Sundays and holidays. Tours leave at least every half hour and every

10 minutes when it's busy. Admission is $6.50, or $5 for 11- to 16-year-olds and $3.50 for six- to 10-year-olds. The cave is eight miles north of I-10 exit 279, about 25 miles southeast of Tucson. Alternatively, head southeast on Old Spanish Trail and follow the signs.

### R W Webb Winery

This is Arizona's biggest winery. You can take a tour and enjoy a local wine-tasting for $1. Hours are 10 am to 5 pm Monday to Saturday and noon to 5 pm on Sunday. The winery (☎ 762 5777) is about a mile east of I-10 exit 279 (and about 20 miles southeast of downtown) along East Benson Hwy.

### Gambling

The Casino of the Sun (☎ 883 1700, 1 (800) 344 9435) is on the Pascua Yaqui Indian Reservation at 7406 S Camino de Oeste. Take exit 95 on I-19 and go west on Valencia Rd for almost five miles and then south on S Camino de Oeste, following the signs. The Desert Diamond Casino (☎ 294 7777, 889 7354) is on the San Xavier Indian Reservation at 7350 S Nogales Hwy. From I-19 exit 95, head east on Valencia Rd for 1.5 miles, then south on Nogales Hwy for 1.5 miles. The casinos are open 24 hours a day and feature slots, keno, bingo and poker games.

### SAGUARO NATIONAL PARK

Designated a national monument in 1933, this became the Southwest's newest national park in 1994. There are two sections, Saguaro East and Saguaro West, which are about 30 miles apart and separated by Tucson. Not many cities in the USA can claim to have a national park on their doorstep!

Neither section has drive-in campgrounds or lodges, and only Saguaro East allows overnight backpacking, so, for the most part, Saguaro National Park is visited as a day trip from Tucson. As the park's name implies, its main purpose is to preserve large stands of the giant saguaro cactus and associated habitat.

### Flora & Fauna

Young saguaro seedlings are vulnerable to intense sun and frost so they often grow in the shade of palo verde or mesquite trees, which act as 'nurse trees'. Saguaros begin growing slowly, taking about 15 years to grow to a foot in height and about 50 years to reach seven feet. They are almost a hundred years old before they begin to take on their typical many-armed appearance.

Most of the saguaros in the park are old ones. This is because the area is the northeastern corner of the saguaros' range and more prone to killer frosts. In addition, ranching was allowed in some parts of the park as late as 1979 and the cattle trampled the saguaro seedlings and compacted the ground, causing the nurse trees to die. Now ranching has stopped, but occasional frosts, and even vandalism and theft continue to create problems for the young plants. Nevertheless, there are some signs of recovery and stands of young saguaro are being monitored by park authorities.

Saguaros are only part of the landscape. Various birds make nests in holes in these giant cacti. Gila woodpeckers and flickers (a kind of woodpecker) excavate holes in the plants. The holes form hard scar tissue on the inside of the plant that protects the nest and the cactus. In subsequent years, owls, cactus wrens, kestrels and other birds may use these nests, which are often 20°F cooler than the outside. On the ground are many other kinds of cacti and a variety of vegetation which is home to javelinas, desert tortoises, gila monsters, jackrabbits, coyotes, kangaroo rats, rattlesnakes, roadrunners, tarantulas and many other animals.

Good times to visit the park are from late April, when the saguaros begin blossoming with lovely white flowers – Arizona's state flower. By June and July, the flowers give way to ripe red fruit which has been traditionally picked by desert Indians. They use them both for food (as fruit and jam) and to make saguaro wine.

### Saguaro East

Also called the Rincon Mountain District, this is the larger and older section of the

Woodpecker

park and encompasses both the desert and mountain country of the Rincon Mountains and their western slopes. The saguaro grows only up to about 4000 feet and then the scenery gives way first to oak woodland, then pine and finally, at elevations of over 7000 feet, to mixed conifer forest.

**Information** The park is open from 7 am to sunset in summer and till 5 pm in winter. The visitors center (☎ 733 5153) at the park entrance is open from 8 am to 5 pm and is the only place with drinking water. It has a bookstore, information, an audiovisual display and exhibits. Ranger-led programs are offered, especially in the cooler months. The park is 15 miles east of downtown along Old Spanish Trail. Admission is $4 per private vehicle or $2 for walkers, cyclists or bus passengers. Golden Age, Access and Eagle Passes are honored.

**Cactus Forest Drive** This paved, one-way, eight-mile loop road gives access to a couple of picnic areas (no water), some nature trails of varying lengths and good

views of the saguaro forest. The road is accessible to all vehicles, including bicycles. In addition, a 2.5-mile trail off the drive is suitable for mountain bikes only.

**Hiking & Backpacking** There are almost 130 miles of trails in Saguaro East. The easiest is the quarter-mile wheelchair-accessible Desert Ecology Nature Trail, which leaves from the north end of Cactus Forest Drive. Progressively longer trails strike off into the park, including the Tanque Verde Ridge Trail, which climbs fairly steeply from the south end of Cactus Forest Drive up into the Rincon Mountains, where the highest elevation is Mica Mountain at 8666 feet. There are six designated backcountry camping areas, most of which lack water. Campers must have permits, which are available at the visitors center at no charge up to two months ahead of your chosen date. They must be picked up by noon of the day you start your hike to give enough time to reach the first camping area. Horses are permitted on trails.

**Saguaro West**
Also called the Tucson Mountain District, this is just north of the Arizona-Sonora Desert Museum, and a drive through the area can be combined with a visit to the ASDM. Saguaro West is much lower than Saguaro East, with the highest point being 4687-foot Wasson Peak.

**Information** The visitors center (☎ 733 5158) on Kinney Rd, two miles northwest of the ASDM, is open from 8 am to 5 pm daily with similar facilities to Saguaro East. The two paved roads through the park (Kinney Rd and Picture Rocks Rd) are open 24 hours a day. Unpaved loop roads and hiking trailheads close at sunset, however. Admission to this part of the park is free. The visitors center has a free map of the park.

**Bajada Loop Drive** The unpaved, six-mile Bajada Loop Drive begins 1.5 miles west of the visitors center and can normally be negotiated by ordinary vehicles. Apart

ARIZONA

Petroglyphs

from the fine views of cactus forests, there are several picnic areas and trailheads.

**Hiking** Short, paved nature trails are found near the visitors center. Longer trails climb several miles into the Tucson Mountains and give access to Indian petroglyphs as well as fine views. The King Canyon Trailhead is just outside the park boundary almost opposite the ASDM. This trailhead is open till 10 pm. Although night hiking is permitted, camping is not. The nearest campground is the Gilbert Ray Campground (see Places to Stay) in Tucson Mountain County Park, about four miles southeast of the park.

# Between Tucson & Phoenix

Most people barrel through from city to city along I-10 in a couple of hours. It is not a particularly attractive ride except for the view of Picacho Peak at almost the halfway point. There are several worthwhile side trips however, for travelers with a little time.

## PICACHO PEAK STATE PARK

Picacho Peak (3374 feet) is an obvious landmark on the west side of I-10 exit 219 about 40 miles north of Tucson. The westernmost 'battle' of the American Civil War was fought here, with the Confederate forces killing two or three Union soldiers. The Confederates then retreated to Tucson and dispersed, knowing that their forces would soon be greatly outnumbered.

The state park provides camping, picnicking and two steep hiking trails to the summit of the peak. Fixed ropes and ladders are used to aid hikers, but no technical climbing is involved. It's about two miles and 1500 feet up to the top.

The campground (☎ 466 3183) has about 100 sites open year round. Rates are $8 for tents, $13 for hookups. There is drinking water and showers. Sites are available on a first-come, first-served basis. The 1800-foot elevation makes this a hot stop in summer.

A short way outside the state park, in the community of Picacho, is the *Picacho Peak Resort* (☎ 466 7841). It has a pool, recreation area and about 200 sites, most with full hookups ($20). Tent camping is $9. There are discounts from mid-April to mid-October.

## CASA GRANDE AREA
### Casa Grande

The small town of Casa Grande is a few miles northwest of the I-10 interchange with I-8, on Hwy 238. Though it was founded in 1878, little remains of that era and it is essentially a modern town. The ruins of Casa Grande (described below) are about 30 miles away and have nothing to do with the town apart from the name.

From I-10 exit 194, Florence Blvd goes west into Casa Grande, passing a visitors center on the left and reaching the small **Heritage Hall Historical Museum** (☎ 836 2223), 110 W Florence Blvd, four miles west of the freeway. The museum is open from 1 to 5 pm daily 15 September to 1 June. It's closed on Mondays, holidays and all summer.

Today, Casa Grande is known for its two huge factory outlet shopping malls that sell brand name products at discounted prices. At I-10 exit 194 is the Casa Grande Mercado & Factory Stores, and at exit 198 is the Tanger Outlet Center.

There are annual Indian dances and a powwow during **O'odham Tash**, held in mid-February. Information is available from the O'odham Tash office (☎ 836 4723, fax 426 1731).

### Places to Stay & Eat
The *Sunland Motel* (☎ 836 5000) near exit 198 has basic rooms in the $20s. There are a couple of other cheap places on Florence Blvd west of the museum. The *Motel 6* (☎ 836 3323, fax 421 3094) is at exit 200 and charges $33/39 for singles/doubles in winter, less in summer. The *Best Western Casa Grande Suites* (☎ 836 1600, fax 836 7242) is just over a mile west of exit 194 along Florence Blvd. Rooms are about $70 in winter or $50 in summer, and there is a pool. There are plenty of chain restaurants along Florence Blvd and at the interstate exits.

### Casa Grande Ruins National Monument
Once a major Hohokam Indian village covering about one sq mile, this site was abandoned around 1350 AD and little remains today except for one ruin, the Casa Grande (big house).

The Casa Grande is quite imposing. About 30 or 40 feet high, it is built of mud walls several feet thick. The mud was made from caliche, the rock-hard soil of the area that is the bane of the modern gardener. A huge amount of work went into constructing the building, which is the most unusual Hohokam structure standing today. Rain and human intrusion have caused some damage, but the general structure of the building remains clear. To prevent further erosion, Casa Grande has been capped by a large metal awning built in the 1930s, an effective, if incongruous, preservation tool. You cannot enter the building itself. From the outside it's still impressive, though, and you should also check the girders of the modern roof protecting the ruin. I found a pair of owls nesting there.

The site, about 20 miles north of I-10 exit 212 or 14 miles east of I-10 exit 185, has a visitors center (☎ 723 3172) with an excellent small museum explaining the history of the Hohokam in general and this ruin in particular. There are picnic tables, drinking water and a bookshop, but no overnight facilities. The ruins are open daily except Christmas, from 7 am to 6 pm. Admission is $4 per vehicle or $2 per bike or bus passenger. Golden Age, Access and Eagle Passes are honored.

### Florence
Founded in 1866, this is one of Arizona's earliest Anglo towns. Arizona's second governor, Richard C McCormick, named it after his sister. Today, this small town is the Pinal County Seat and the home of the Arizona State Prison, which replaced Yuma's notorious prison in 1909. About 8000 people live here (including the prisoners) and the elevation is a toasty 1493 feet.

Few travelers stay overnight, because of the proximity to Phoenix, but there is a motel and Florence would make a good base for seeing Casa Grande, just 10 miles west. There are several historical buildings; the most interesting is the 1878 adobe brick courthouse (with assorted later additions) in the **McFarland Historical State Park** (☎ 868 5216), Main St at Ruggles Ave, which has various exhibits about Florence's past. This is open from 8 am to 5 pm Thursday to Monday and admission is $2, or $1 for teenagers and younger folk. Also visit the free **Pinal County Historical Museum** (☎ 868 4382), 715 S Main St, which has a surprisingly varied collection of a little bit of everything to do with the area. The museum is open till 4 pm on most Wednesday to Sunday afternoons.

The visitors center (☎ 868 4331), 912 N Pinal St, 85232, is open from 9 am to noon and from 1 to 4 pm Monday to Friday, with shorter hours in summer. It has a brochure describing some of the historic buildings.

The *Blue Mist Motel* (☎ 868 5875), at the junction of Hwys 287 and 79, has about 20 simple rooms in the $30s and $40s. Some rooms have a kitchenette and there is a pool. There are several little restaurants along Hwy 287 as you head west towards the Casa Grande Ruins.

### Gila River Arts & Crafts Center

The name doesn't sound particularly interesting, but this is an above-average stop on the freeway. The name comes not from the river, but from the Gila River Indian Reservation, Arizona's earliest reservation, established in 1859 for the Pima and Maricopa Indian tribes. It was relatively good acreage until the early 20th century, when dams caused the river to run almost dry, ruining the Indians' agricultural livelihood.

After years of poverty and neglect, the Indians have finally been able to start taking some advantage of the growth of Phoenix by building this center. Although it's only a half mile from exit 175 off I-10, it's different from the average freeway stop. They have a museum (☎ 963 3981) about the Pima and Maricopa tribes, and a gift shop selling arts & crafts from most Southwestern tribes. Part of the museum is outside, with a park containing a variety of Southwest Indian dwellings. A restaurant serves mainly American food along with a few Indian items. Although the tribal office (☎ 562 3311, fax 562 3422) is in Sacaton several miles to the east, the center can provide information. There is a grocery store and a basic RV park (☎ 315 3205) next door which has showers and charges $13 with hookups, less without.

# West of Tucson

Hwy 86 heads west of Tucson toward some of the driest parts of the Sonoran Desert. Much of the land is part of the Tohono O'odham Indian Reservation, the second-largest in the country, although there is little here for the curious traveler. Highlights of a trip out west are the Kitt Peak Observatory and the Organ Pipe Cactus National Monument.

Much of the area is particularly well described in Bowden's *Blue Desert* (U of A Press, 1986).

### BUENOS AIRES NATIONAL WILDLIFE REFUGE LOOP

From Robles Junction, on Hwy 86 about 20 miles west of Tucson, Hwy 286 goes south to the 175-sq-mile Buenos Aires NWR. This was formerly ranchland and became a refuge operated by the US Fish & Wildlife Service in 1985. There are about 200 miles of dirt roads in the area, which is good for grassland birding. There is an ongoing project to reintroduce masked bobwhites, a small, quail-like bird that became extinct in Arizona around the turn of the century. The refuge is open daily during daylight hours, and guided tours are occasionally offered. Information is available from Buenos Aires NWR (☎ 823 4251), PO Box 109, Sasabe, 85633. The office is open from 7 am to 3:30 pm Monday to Friday.

At the south end of the NWR is the border village of **Sasabe**. Here is the *Rancho de la Osa Guest Ranch* (☎ 823 4257, 1 (800) 872 6240, fax 823 4238), PO Box 1, Sasabe, 86633. The ranch is in a 100-year-old Spanish hacienda, and horseback riding, bird- and wildlife-watching and walking are the main activities. Advance reservations and a two-night minimum are usually required. Rates are approximately $100 per person with Western-style meals and riding, less if you don't ride, more during holiday periods. Summers are hot (elevation 3500 feet) and rates are lower. Guest rooms are rustic but comfortable, with fireplaces or wood-burning stoves and bathrooms. There is a pool and spa. This ranch makes a nice desert getaway.

A few miles east of the NWR is the small village of **Arivaca** with several buildings dating from the 1880s. There is a cafe but no motel. From Arivaca, you can return to Tucson via the paved road to Arivaca

Junction and then I-19, the quickest way, or take the unpaved **Ruby Road** to Nogales. This is a scenic route with plenty of border history. The road is passable to ordinary cars in dry weather but should be avoided in rain; it passes through the Coronado National Forest (see Nogales) where you can camp almost anywhere. There are some small lakes along the way which attract wildlife.

The Buenos Aires NWR and Ruby Road make an interesting trip which few people make, so you'll get away from the crowds. Birders will want to have Davis and Russell's *Finding Birds in Southeastern Arizona* (Tucson Audubon Society, 1995) and drivers/historians will find useful information in Annerino's *Adventuring in Arizona* (Sierra Club, 1991).

## TOHONO O'ODHAM INDIAN RESERVATION

This large desert and mountain reservation of almost 4500 sq miles is home to the Tohono O'odham, traditionally an agricultural people. They still practice farming and, since the Spaniards introduced cattle, ranching as well. Maize, beans and cotton are important crops and naturally growing saguaro fruit is harvested for jams and a kind of wine. Mesquite beans are also an important part of the diet and various other naturally occurring plants are harvested. Small branches of the reservation are around the Mission San Xavier del Bac (see Tucson) and just north of Gila Bend, but the majority of the land is in the deserts beginning about 25 miles west of Tucson.

As you drive west out of Tucson, you'll see a humpbacked mountain that stands out above all the others. This is Baboquivari Peak, at 7730 feet the highest in this area and sacred to the tribe. To the north of it is Kitt Peak (6875 feet), home of the observatory described below. The tribal capital is Sells, almost 60 miles west of Tucson on Hwy 86.

The Tohono O'odham have little interest in tourism. Their only tourist facility is the Desert Diamond Casino on the San Xavier section of the reservation (see Tucson). The Indians are known for their fine basket work, which can be purchased from a couple of shops in Sells, the gift shop at Kitt Peak and the Gu-Achi Trading Post at Quijotoa, on Hwy 86, 23 miles west of Sells.

The main event is the annual Tohono O'odham All-Indian Tribal Fair & Rodeo, which attracts Indians from many tribes and is open to the general public. The rodeo is the main attraction, but there are also some dances and the chance to eat Indian food and buy basket work. The date varies from year to year and it has reportedly been held in October, and January to March. For information, call the Tucson Visitor Center or the Tribal Office (☎ 383 2221, fax 383 2417), Sells, 85634. Other events are held at the San Xavier Mission and the O'odham Tash Indian Celebration in Casa Grande in February.

Sells has a couple of places to eat and some stores but no accommodations. Dirt roads leading off the main highway are often in poor shape and a permit may be required to travel on them. Contact the tribe for details .

## KITT PEAK NATIONAL OPTICAL OBSERVATORY

Both Baboquivari and Kitt Peaks are visible from Tucson, and, if you look very carefully, you can just make out the white telescope domes on top of Kitt Peak, even though it is a 55-mile drive (or about 40 miles as the crow flies). This attests both to the clarity of the desert air and the size of the telescopes.

This is the largest observatory in the world and includes 22 telescopes, one of which is a solar telescope used for studying the sun via a series of mirrors. The largest telescope has a diameter of four meters and is housed in a 19-story-high dome.

There is a visitors center (☎ 318 8726, 318 8200) with a museum, gift shop and information, but no food, though there are picnicking areas if you bring your own. Guided tours lasting about an hour and visiting two or three telescopes leave daily at

11 am, 1 and 2:30 pm and also at 9:30 am on Saturdays. (You don't get to look through the telescopes.) Self-guided tours are also possible. The observatory is open from 9 am to 3:45 pm daily except Thanksgiving, Christmas Eve and Day and New Year's Day. Admission is $2 including the tour. The almost-6900-foot elevation can mean snow in winter, and the steep road up the mountain may occasionally be closed.

A few times a year, the observatory offers a night visit with public viewing. This is very popular and should be booked well in advance. Call for details.

## ORGAN PIPE CACTUS NATIONAL MONUMENT

The organ pipe is a species of giant columnar cactus. It differs from the saguaro in that it branches from its base – both species are present in the monument, so you can compare them. Organ pipe cacti are common in Mexico, but this national monument is one of the few places in the USA where they are commonly seen. The third species of columnar cactus found here (and nowhere else in the USA) is the senita, which, like the organ pipe, branches from the bottom but has fewer pleats in its branches, which are topped by the hairy white tufts that give the senita its nickname of 'old man's beard'.

This is prime and mainly undisturbed Sonoran Desert habitat. Not only do three types of large columnar cacti grow here, but an excellent variety of other desert flora and fauna also thrive. In spring, in years which have the right combination of winter rains and temperatures, the monument can be carpeted with annual wild flowers, with March and April being the best time for this. Cacti flower at different times, particularly from late April to early July, although some species can flower in March or as late as October.

There are many animals present, but the heat and aridity of the desert force them to use survival strategies make them hard to see. The best survival strategy is to hide out in a hole or burrow during the day, which means that early morning or evening are

Organ pipe cactus (WB)

the best times to look for wildlife. Walking around the desert by full moon or flashlight is also a good way to catch things on the prowl, but wear boots and watch where you step, because rattlesnakes will be out and about, particularly in late spring and summer.

The monument offers six hiking trails ranging from a 200-yard paved nature trail to strenuous climbs of over four miles. Cross-country hiking is also possible, but have a topographical map and compass and know how to use them – a mistake out here is deadly if you get lost and run out of water. There are also two scenic loop drives of 21 and 53 miles which are steep, winding and unpaved; they start near the visitors center. They are passable to cars except after heavy rain, but motor homes and trailers are not recommended. Other roads are passable only to 4WD vehicles.

Carry extra water in your car in case of a breakdown. There are several picnic sites along the way, but no water.

## Information

The visitors center (☎ 387 6849), Route 1, Box 100, Ajo, 85321, is 22 miles south of the Hwy 86 junction at Why. It's open from 8 am to 5 pm daily and has drinking water, a bookstore, small museum, slide show and information. Ranger-led programs take place from about October to April. Admission to the monument is $4 per vehicle or $2 per bike or bus passenger. Golden Eagle, Age and Access Passes are honored. There is no charge to drive through the monument on the main road, Hwy 85, from Why to Lukeville.

Winter is the most pleasant time to visit. Summer temperatures soar above 100°F most days from June to August, although nights are pleasant with lows typically 30°F lower than daytime highs. The summer monsoons of July to September are the wettest months, although the rains tend to be of the brief, torrential variety and rarely stop anyone for more than an hour or two. Winter temperatures are pleasant, with January, the coolest month, experiencing average highs of 67°F and lows of 38°F.

## Places to Stay

Over 200 sites are available at the campground by the visitors center. There is drinking water but no showers or RV hookups. Sites cost $8, are on a first-come, first-served basis, and are often full by noon during the winter months. Free backcountry camping (no water) is allowed by permit only, which you can obtain at the visitors center.

Outside of the monument, Lukeville (see below) has the nearest accommodations. There are basic RV sites at Why, 22 miles north, and a variety of accommodations at Ajo, 32 miles north (see below).

## LUKEVILLE & SONOITA (MEXÌCO)

Lukeville is a small border town five miles south of the Organ Pipe Visitor Center. You can stay at the small *Gringo Pass Motel &*

*RV Park* (☎ 254 9284) with rooms in the $40s and $50s, RV sites with hookups for $14 and tent sites for $9. There are showers, a pool and a recreation room. A coffee shop is nearby.

A couple of miles south, across the border in Mexico, Sonoita offers several decent restaurants, gift shops and a few motels. Another 60 miles brings you to the small Mexican seaside resort of Puerto Peñasco (Rocky Point) on the Sea of Cortez, offering hotels, restaurants, swimming and scuba diving. It is a four hour drive from Tucson and is the nearest beach to that city.

A tourist card and Mexican car insurance are needed to enter Mexico beyond Sonoita. These are available at the border which is open from 8 am to midnight.

## AJO

Prospectors roamed the area in the late 1800s, and in 1911 industrial copper mining began. Ajo became a major mining town and a mile-wide open-pit mine can be seen just south of town. Dropping copper prices finally closed the mine in 1985 and Ajo became hard hit with unemployment. Some of the miners left and housing costs dropped, attracting retirees and reviving the town. The town plaza, built in Spanish-colonial style and flanked by two architecturally similar white churches, is very attractive and has several pleasant restaurants and shops.

## Information

The chamber of commerce (☎ 387 7742), on the main highway near the plaza, is open from 8:30 am to 4:30 pm daily in winter and from Monday to Friday in summer.

## Things to See & Do

The **Ajo Historical Society Museum** (☎ 387 7105) is in an attractive church near the copper mine, south of town. Hours are from 1 to 4 pm daily except mid-July to mid-August. The **Ajo Country Club** (☎ 387 5011) is seven miles northeast of town and has a nine-hole golf course.

**ARIZONA**

The **Windowpane Observatory** (☎1 (800) 727 4367), PO Box 842, 85321, has a 17.5-inch telescope and other equipment available for public astronomical viewing by reservation. Viewing starts at $25 an hour and astronomers are on hand to give instruction and explain what you see.

A few miles west of Ajo is one of the most rugged areas in the country, the **Cabeza Prieta National Wildlife Refuge**, a stretch of barren desert traversed only by dirt roads. See the Western Arizona chapter for details.

### Places to Stay

The *Shadow Ridge RV Resort* (☎ 387 5055), 431 N 2nd Ave (Hwy 85), and *Belle Acres RV Park* (☎ 387 6907), 2050 N Hwy 85, are both just off the main highway north of town and offer sites with hookups in the mid-teens.

The little *Marine Resort Motel & RV Park* (☎ 387 7626), 1966 N Hwy 85, has 20 large, clean motel rooms with refrigerators and coffeemakers for about $40 to $60 in winter, less in summer. RV hookups are available. The smaller *La Siesta Motel* (☎ 387 6569), 2561 N Hwy 85, has 11 simple rooms in the $30s.

The 1925 *Guest House Inn B&B* (☎ 387 6133), 3 Guest House Rd, 85321, has four comfortable rooms decorated in a Southwestern motif and with private baths for $69 a double. The *Mine Manager's House Inn B&B* (☎ 387 6505, 1 (800) 266 7829, fax 387 6508), 1 Greenway Drive, 85321, is in one of Ajo's earliest houses built in 1919 on a hill with fine views. Five rooms and suites, all with private bath, range from $65 to $100 double.

### GILA BEND

About 40 miles north of Ajo and 60 miles west of Casa Grande, Gila Bend is a minor agricultural center, dependent on what's left of the Gila River after upstream damming. Cotton is an important crop. For centuries this has been an agricultural area. It's an I-8 travelers' stop with inexpensive lodging, but there's little to do. The main drag is Pima St.

### Information

The visitors center (☎ 683 2002) is on Pima St near the west exit of the town (exit 115) and has a nice little museum. Hours are from 8 am to 4 pm daily, but they may close on summer weekends. Ask them about the status of the 1000-year-old Hohokam ruins (the Gatlin site) at the east end of town. Excavation of the ruin is planned.

### Places to Stay & Eat

Several cheap and basic motels offer rooms starting in the low $20s. All have pools. These include the *Yucca Motel* (☎ 683 2211), 836 E Pima St; the *Payless Inn* (☎ 683 2294), 515 E Pima St; *El Coronado Motel* (☎ 683 2281), 212 W Pima St; and, cheapest of all, *Desert Rest* next door to El Coronado. The *American Western Inn* (☎ 683 2248), 1046 E Pima St, has a restaurant and lounge and rooms for a few dollars more.

The *Super 8 Motel* (☎ 683 6311, fax 683 2120) at exit 119 has nicer rooms for $42.88/46.88 for singles/doubles. There's a restaurant next door. The Best Western *Space Age Lodge* (☎ /fax 683 2273), 1046 E Pima St, has rooms in the $60s and $70s in winter, a little less in summer. They have a spa and a 24-hour restaurant.

# South of Tucson

I-19 due south of Tucson heads to Nogales, on the Mexican border 62 miles away. The freeway exits and speed limits are all in kilometers along here, as a courtesy to Mexican drivers and to prepare US drivers for the metric change in Mexico. While most people barrel along I-10 bent on reaching either Mexico or Tucson in an hour, there is a lot to see along this route, which follows the Santa Cruz River Valley and has been a historical trading route since pre-Hispanic times. The most interesting site is San Xavier del Bac, just south of Tucson and described under that city. If you continue further south you'll find the following sites.

## GREEN VALLEY & AROUND

Green Valley is a retirement community of about 15,000 people at I-19 exits 69, 65 and 63. (These are exits at kilometer intervals, so they come up pretty quickly.) The chamber of commerce (☎ 625 7575) is just west of exit 63 and is open from 9 am to 5 pm Monday to Friday. They have information about nearby golf courses. A huge open-pit copper mine can be seen west of the freeway along here.

### Titan Missile Museum

During the Cold War, the USA had dozens of Intercontinental Ballistic Missiles armed with nuclear warheads and ready to fly within a few seconds of receiving a launch order. Fortunately, that order never came. With the SALT II treaty, all the missiles and their underground launch sites were destroyed except for this one, which has been kept as a national historic landmark. The nuclear warhead was removed but the rest remains as it was during the tense 1960s and '70s, when the push of a button could have started a cataclysmic nuclear war.

The public can tour the entire complex. The museum (☎ 791 2929, 625 7736) is west of I-19 exit 69. Guided tours (reservations recommended) leave hourly from 9 am to 4 pm daily except Christmas, November to April. From May to October the museum is closed on Mondays and Tuesdays. Tours involve stair climbing, but wheelchair-accessible tours can be arranged. Admission is $5, or $4 for those over 62 or with military ID, and $3 for 10- to 17-year-olds.

### Madera Canyon Recreation Area

This canyon gives access to hiking trails into the Santa Ritas, including a trail up the biggest peak, Mt Wrightson, in the Coronado National Forest (the ranger station is in Nogales). The riparian habitat in the canyon attracts an unusually large variety and number of birds, and this is one of the most popular places for birding in southeastern Arizona. Parking may be difficult to find, especially on weekends, when an early arrival is essential. Madera Canyon

is about 12 miles east of I-19 exit 63 and there are signs. Day use is $5 per vehicle. The elevation is a pleasant pine-shaded 5200 feet.

The USFS runs the 13 sites at *Bog Springs Campground* on a first-come, first-served basis. There is water but no showers or hookups. The fee is $5. There is also a USFS-run picnic area.

*Santa Rita Lodge* (☎ 625 8746), HC 70, Box 5444, Sahuarita, 85629, has about a dozen large rooms and cabins which are popular with birders and usually booked in advance. There are cooking facilities but no food. Rates start in the $60s.

### Whipple Observatory

A new paved road leads up to the observatory from I-19 exit 56. The multi-mirror telescope atop Mt Hopkins at 8500 feet is one of the largest in the world. It can be visited only by a tour which lasts most of the day and costs $7, or $2.50 for six- to 12-year-olds. Tours are offered on Monday, Wednesday and Friday and are by reservation only (☎ 670 5707).

Two miles below the observatory, a visitors center shows a film and has exhibits about the telescope. This is free and open from 9 am to 4:30 pm Monday to Friday and sometimes on weekends. The observatory may closed in winter.

### Places to Stay

The *Green Valley RV Resort* (☎ 222 2969), 19001 S Richfield Ave, west of I-19 exit 69, has RV sites with full hookups for $27. There is a pool and recreation area.

The *Quality Inn* (☎ 625 2250), 111 S La Canada, west of I-19 exit 65, has a restaurant, bar, pool and spa and pleasant rooms around $100 a double in winter, less in summer.

### Getting There & Away

Greyhound/Citizen Auto Stage vans connect Tucson and Nogales along I-19 hourly between 7 am and 7 pm, stopping at Green Valley on the way. Call the Greyhound stations in Tucson (☎ 792 3475) and Nogales (☎ 287 5628) for information.

ARIZONA

## TUBAC

There was a Pima Indian village here before the Spaniards arrived. In 1752, they built a presidio, which fell into disuse when the garrison moved to Tucson in 1776. Soldiers returned a few years later, but Indians forced the settlers out again in the 1830s. After the Gadsden Purchase, Americans revived mining operations here which ceased after the Civil War. Tubac became a sleepy farming community. After an art school opened in 1948, Tubac began its transformation into a major artists' community. The village has the best selection of arts & crafts shops outside of Tucson and Phoenix.

### Information

Tubac is east of I-19 between exits 40 and 34. It's a small village and is easily accessible by walking. The chamber of commerce (☎ 398 2704) answers questions during the week. The Tubac Center for the Arts (☎ 398 2371) is near the entrance of town at Plaza Rd and Calle Baca and has local art exhibits and information. They are open from 10 am to 4:30 pm Tuesday to Saturday, and from 1 to 4:30 pm on Sunday.

Most of the approximately 80 galleries, art studios and crafts stores in town have a map showing the location of the shopping district and shops, most of which are open from 10 am to 5 pm daily, year round.

### Tubac Presidio State Historic Park & Museum

The presidio now lies in ruins, but you can see the 1885 school house and other historical buildings nearby. The exhibits in the museum (☎ 398 2252) tell about the history of Tubac. Hours are from 8 am to 5 pm daily except Christmas, and admission is $2, or $1 for 12- to 17-year-olds. The park is at the east end of Tubac and has picnicking facilities.

### Tumacacori National Historical Park

Three miles south of Tubac at I-19 exit 29 are the well-preserved ruins of the Tumacacori Franciscan Church, built in 1800 but never completed. Although abandoned in the late 1800s, the church was protected as a national monument in 1908. It gives the visitor an idea of the Spanish history of the area. There is a visitors center (☎ 398 2341) with a museum and gift shop. Mexican and Indian artists demonstrate their techniques on weekends. There are picnicking facilities but no food or accommodations. Hours are from am to 5 pm daily except Thanksgiving and Christmas. Admission is $2 per person over 17 and Golden Age, Access and Eagle Passes are honored.

Two other Spanish missions are being excavated about 15 miles south of Tumacacori. Ask at the visitors center to see whether they are open yet.

### Special Events

The Tubac Arts & Crafts festival is held every February and lasts over a week. A mass is said in the Tumacacori Church on Christmas Eve, and a couple of times a year besides. Call the Tumacacori visitors center for information. An Indian arts & crafts fair is held in Tumacacori in early December.

### Places to Stay & Eat

*Tubac Trailer Tether* (☎ 398 2111) in the center of town has overnight RV parking with hookups for $14.

*Country Inn B&B* (☎ 398 3178), at Plaza Rd and Burruel St in downtown Tubac, PO Box 1540, 85646, has four large rooms with private baths for $65 to $80 double. Two rooms have kitchenettes and all rooms open onto a porch and garden. On the outskirts of Tubac, *Secret Garden Inn B&B* (☎ 398 9371), PO Box 1561, 85646, has two rooms surrounded by gardens. Rates are $75 a double. Both B&Bs are non-smoking.

The *Tubac Golf Resort* (☎ 398 2211, 1 (800) 848 7893, fax 398 9261) is near exit 40 on the east side. Apart from the 18-hole golf course, there is a tennis court, pool, spa and a good restaurant and bar. Rooms are all spacious and some have fireplaces, living rooms or kitchenettes attached. Winter rates are $85 to $145, depending on the size of the room. Summer rates are $60 to $100. On the other side of the freeway is the *Burro Inn* (☎ 398 2281) with suites and kitchenettes for about $100.

Eat at the *Tubac Country Market Place* (☎ 398 9532), 410 E Frontage Rd, between the golf resort and Tubac village. They have great views and decent breakfasts and lunches, as well as a fixed-menu gourmet dinner by reservation only. There are several other eateries.

### Getting There & Away
Greyhound/Citizen Auto Stage vans connect Tucson and Nogales along I-19 hourly between 7 am and 7 pm, stopping at Tubac on the way. Call the Greyhound stations in Tucson (☎ 792 3475) and Nogales (☎ 287 5628) for information.

### NOGALES & AROUND
Nogales, Arizona, and Nogales, Sonora, are separated only by the USA/Mexico border. You can easily walk from one into the other. The twin towns (locally called *Ambos Nogales* or 'Both Nogales') were founded in 1880, although the area had been much visited by Indians and Spanish missionaries before then as they wandered up and down the Santa Cruz River Valley.

Nogales, Arizona, is the Santa Cruz County seat and has about 20,000 inhabitants. The elevation here is 3865 feet. Many visitors come to shop for Mexican goods just across the border. Nogales is Arizona's most important gateway into Mexico. For Mexico, it is the major port of entry for the agricultural produce Mexico sells to the USA and Canada. It's a busy place with about 200,000 inhabitants.

### Information
The chamber of commerce (☎ 287 3685) is in Kino Park at the north entrance to town; follow signs for Arizona Information. They also have information about the Mexican side. Hours are from 8 am to 5 pm Monday to Friday. The Mexican Consulate (☎ 287 2521), 480 Grand Ave, is open from 8:30 am to 3 pm from Monday to Friday and from 9 am to 2 pm on Saturday. Call

287 3609 for US Immigration. The Coronado National Forest Ranger Station (☎ 281 2296), 2252 N Grand Ave, 85621, a couple of miles north of town on Hwy 89, is open from 8 am to 4:30 pm Monday to Friday. The library (☎ 287 3343) is at 748 Grand Ave, and the post office (☎ 287 9246) is at 300 N Morley Ave. The hospital (☎ 287 2771) is at 1171 W Target Range Rd.

### Pimeria Alta Historical Society Museum
This historical museum (☎ 287 4621) is housed in the old town hall (built in 1914) at 136 Grand Ave and gives a good introduction to the area. Hours are 10 am to 5 pm Tuesday to Friday, and 10 am to 4 pm on Saturday; admission is free.

### Visiting Mexico
Most visitors go to shop for a few hours and maybe have a meal in Nogales, Sonora (Mexico). You can park on the US side (there are plenty of lots for about $4 a day) and walk over into the Nogales, Sonora, shopping district. US dollars and credit cards are accepted and prices are good, but the quality varies so shop around. Bargaining is certainly possible. All kinds of Mexican goods are available – pottery, stoneware, silver, tin, glass, weavings, leather, basketry and wood carvings.

You can bring almost anything you buy back into the USA duty free as long as it's worth a total of less than $400 and doesn't include more than a quart of booze or 200 cigarettes. Many handicrafts are exempt from the $400 limit. Fresh food is prohibited, as are fireworks, which are illegal in the state of Arizona. (Fourth of July fireworks displays are arranged by special license, and the general public is not allowed to possess or set off fireworks.) Importing weapons and drugs is also illegal, of course. For further information, ask for the brochure *Before You Go* from the US Customs Service (☎ (202) 566 8195), 1301 Constitution Ave, Washington, DC 20299.

From Nogales, buses and trains continue further into Mexico. The bus terminal is

ARIZONA

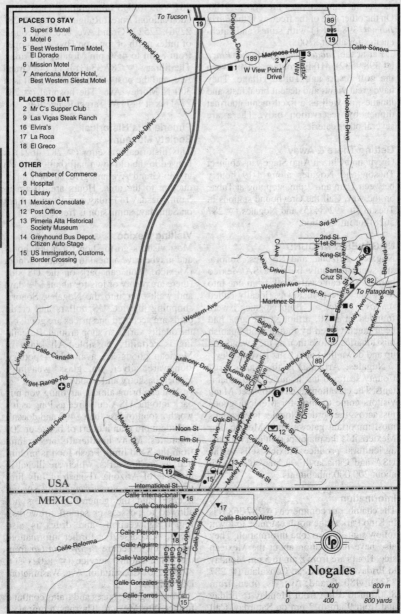

PLACES TO STAY
1   Super 8 Motel
3   Motel 6
5   Best Western Time Motel,
    El Dorado
6   Mission Motel
7   Americana Motor Hotel,
    Best Western Siesta Motel

PLACES TO EAT
2   Mr C's Supper Club
9   Las Vigas Steak Ranch
16  Elvira's
17  La Roca
18  El Greco

OTHER
4   Chamber of Commerce
8   Hospital
10  Library
11  Mexican Consulate
12  Post Office
13  Pimeria Alta Historical
    Society Museum
14  Greyhound Bus Depot,
    Citizen Auto Stage
15  US Immigration, Customs,
    Border Crossing

To Tucson

Nogales

0        400       800 m
0        400       800 yards

USA
MEXICO

## Crossing the Border

You can freely walk across the border into Mexico at any of the border towns for shopping or a meal. Returning from Mexico into the USA, however, is another matter. You need to carry a passport to show the US immigration authorities when you want to walk back. US citizens on a day trip don't need passports if they carry their birth certificate (if they were born in the USA) or naturalization certificate. Although a US drivers license has been sufficient in the past, there have been recent problems with this, too. US resident aliens need to carry their resident alien card when returning to the USA.

If you want to enter Mexico for more than a border day trip, you need a passport and a Mexican tourist card, which will be checked a few miles inside the country. The tourist card is available for free at the border upon production of a passport. US citizens can obtain a tourist card with a birth certificate, but a passport is a more convenient and quickly recognized document and enables you to change money, etc. Mexican tourist cards are valid for up to 180 days, but normally much less is given. Ask for as many days as you'll need. A few nationalities require a Mexican visa; recently, these included some African and Asian nationals, Israelis and Finns, but the situation changes so, if in doubt, check with the Mexican consul in your home country or in Tucson and Nogales. Be warned that even the Mexican consul might not be aware of the latest changes.

Traveling by Mexican public transport is a little more adventurous than the equivalent in the USA. However, it's also much more far reaching, and you can get almost anywhere on a bus at reasonable cost. If you prefer to bring your own car, you should get Mexican car insurance because US car insurance is not normally valid in Mexico. Car insurance can easily be bought at one of many places at the border. Rates are expensive at about $10 a day, but if you buy insurance by the week or month, rates drop substantially. Remember: Mexico's legal system is Napoleonic, that is, you are guilty until proven innocent, and so you are likely to be arrested and held after a car accident until you can either prove your innocence or can show Mexican car insurance covering the accident.

Nogales is the main USA/Mexico border crossing and is also the safest. Along the southeastern Arizona border, drug smuggling and international car theft are frequent occurrences, and, west of Nogales, illegal immigration is a concern. Immigration and customs officials are working to control these problems. Not all officials are honest, however. Both Mexican and US officers have broken the law in the recent past. US border officials have been involved in drug smuggling, theft and sexual abuse in recent years. This is a recognized problem that the USA is trying to solve, but travelers should be aware that a small percentage of officials on both sides of the border are corrupt. The best defense is to make sure that your documents are in scrupulous order, to travel by day and to not allow officials to intimidate you for any reason. ■

about three miles south of the border (take a taxi) and there are frequent departures. There is a daily train south to Guadalajara and Mexico City. Information is available near the border.

For border crossing information, see the aside Crossing the Border, above.

### Winery

Arizona Vineyards (☎ 287 7972), 1830 Hwy 82, is open from 10 am to 5 pm daily, offering tours and tastings of their colorfully named 'Arizona Dust' and 'Coyote Red' wines.

### Places to Stay

**Camping** *Mi Casa RV Park* (☎ 281 1150), 2901 N Grand Ave, is about three miles north of town on Hwy 89. RV sites are $15.40 with hookups, and there are showers and a few cheap tent sites. The USFS-operated *Upper/Lower White Rock* campgrounds are on Peña Blanca Lake, nine miles west of I-19 exit 12 north of Nogales. There are 15 sites with water but no showers or hookups, available year round on a first-come, first-served basis. Sites are $5 and there is fishing and boating. Also see below under Patagonia.

**Hotels & Motels** November to April or May, when the snowbirds are in Arizona, is the high season, for which rates are given below. In summer and early fall, prices drop 10% or 20%.

The *Mission Motel* (☎ 287 2472), 820 N Grand Ave, is the cheapest with rooms in the $20s and a Spanish-speaking staff. All these following motels have pools. The *Motel 6* (☎ 281 2951, fax 281 9592), 141 W Mariposa Rd, east of I-19 exit 4, has singles/doubles for $33/39. There are two Best Westerns, both with a spa and small but clean rooms in the $40s. The *Best Western Time Motel* (☎ 287 4627, fax 287 6949), 921 N Grand Ave, is usually a few dollars cheaper than the *Best Western Siesta Motel* (☎ 287 4671, fax 287 9616), 673 N Grand Ave, which includes a continental breakfast in its rates. The *Super 8 Motel* (☎ 281 2242, fax 281 2242 x 400), 543 W Mariposa Rd, on the east side of I-19 exit 4, has a spa and restaurant open from 6 am to 9 pm and a bar. Rooms are in the $40s. The *El Dorado* (☎ 287 4611), 945 N Grand Ave, also has rooms in the $40s. The *Americana Motor Hotel* (☎ 287 7211, fax 287 5188), 639 N Grand Ave, has large rooms, a restaurant open from 6:30 am to 10 pm, a bar with poolside service, room service and double rooms from $55 to $70.

North of Nogales at I-19 exit 17 is the *Rio Rico Resort* (☎ 281 1901, fax 281 7132), situated on a hilltop with a view. It features a pool, spa, sauna, golf course, tennis courts, exercise room and horseback riding. Outdoor barbecues and weekend entertainment are also provided. Most rooms have a private patio or balcony and are in the low $100s in winter. More expensive suites are available.

There are plenty of places to stay across the border in Mexico, but their prices aren't much lower than on the US side, especially when they see a gringo face. The further you get from the border, the more likely you are to find budget accommodation at non-US prices.

**Places to Eat**

Most restaurants on the Arizona side are along Grand Ave. There is the usual unremarkable assortment of fast-food places, Denny's, pizza parlors and Mexican-American restaurants, none particularly outstanding. The best restaurant in Nogales is *Mr C's Supper Club* (☎ 281 9000), 282 W View Point Drive, off Mariposa Rd (east of I-19 exit 4). Reserve ahead for a window seat with a view. Guaymas shrimp is the house specialty, and American steak and seafood is served from 11:30 am to midnight with dinner entrees mainly in the teens. Another good choice is *Las Vigas Steak Ranch* (☎ 287 6641), 180 W Loma St, which serves Mexican meals and steaks at half the price of Mr C's in a rustic atmosphere. Hours are from 10 am to 10 pm Tuesday to Sunday.

Diners on the Mexican side have a reasonable choice of Mexican restaurants at US prices, but even in the USA, Mexican restaurants always offer tasty meals at tempting prices. Good choices are *Elvira's*, Calle Obregon 1, with meals under $10 and a free margarita thrown in; the similar *El Greco*, Calle Obregon 152; and the slightly pricier *La Roca*, Calle Elias 91. These clean places have Mexican atmosphere designed with the American visitor in mind. Cheaper places can be found away from the border.

### Getting There & Away

The Greyhound/Citizen Auto Stage (☎ 287 5628), 35 N Terrace Ave, has buses about once an hour during the day and early evening to Tucson ($6.50) with stops at the towns along I-19.

## PATAGONIA & SONOITA

Travelers visiting Nogales often return to Tucson via Hwy 82 through Sonoita to make a loop. It's also a well-traveled route to destinations such as Sierra Vista, Tombstone and Bisbee. Apart from being cattle country, this is also grape country, and there are several wineries in the area. Patagonia and Sonoita are both very small towns; call 394 0060 for tourist information on Patagonia.

**Patagonia Lake State Park**

A dam across Sonoita Creek forms this 2.5-mile-long lake, about 15 miles northeast of Nogales. The elevation is 3750 feet, and the park remains open year round for camping, picnicking, walking, birdwatching, fishing, boating (including water skiing) and swimming. A marina provides boat rentals (no motor boats) and supplies. The campground has showers and hookups and over 100 sites available on a first-come, first-served basis. These can fill up in summer. Rates are $5 for day use, $10 for camping and $15 with hookups. Information is available from Patagonia Lake State Park (☎ 287 6965), PO Box 274, Patagonia, 85624. The main gate is closed from 10 pm to 5 am.

**Patagonia-Sonoita Creek Preserve**

This is managed by the Nature Conservancy, which is in the process of building a visitors center that should open by the end of 1995. Sonoita Creek is the home of four endangered species of fish, and the riparian habitat on the preserve attracts a good variety of birds, including rarities from Mexico, and this in turn attracts some 30,000 visitors a year. In order to let the preserve 'rest' from the user pressure, it is closed on Mondays and Tuesdays. On other days, hours are from 7:30 am to 3:30 pm, and short guided tours are given at 9 am on Saturday mornings, by reservation.

The preserve is reached by going west on N 3rd Ave in Patagonia, then south on Pennsylvania Ave. The preserve is across a small creek which you have to drive or wade across. Entrance is free for Nature Conservancy members and nonmembers are asked to make a donation. There are no camping or picnicking facilities. Beware of insects in spring and summers (chiggers are bad!) and wear long pants and insect repellent. Further information is available from the preserve (☎ 394 2400), PO Box 815, Patagonia, 85624.

**Special Events**

The Sonoita Quarter Horse Show is the oldest in the country and runs in early June. Sonoita is home of the Santa Cruz County Fair & Rodeo Grounds (☎ 455 5553) with a rodeo over Labor Day weekend. The county fair held the third weekend in September.

**Places to Stay & Eat**

The *Stage Stop Inn* (☎ 394 2211), 303 W McKeown St in Patagonia, is a modern motel with a Western facade. Rooms are in the $50s and $60s, and there is a pool, restaurant and saloon bar. Some rooms have kitchenettes.

The *Circle Z Ranch* (☎ 287 2091, fax 394 2010), PO Box 194, Patagonia, 85624, is a few miles southwest of Patagonia on Sonoita Creek. From November to mid-May they offer horseback-riding vacations with a three-night minimum. Accommodations are in comfortable rooms and all meals are provided. Rates are about $400 for three days and nights, including riding.

This area boasts a few remarkable restaurants. In Sonoita, *Er Pastaro* (☎ 455 5821), 3084 E Hwy 82 (just east of Hwy 83) is one of Arizona's best Italian restaurants, owned and operated by a celebrated Italian chef and his friendly wife who got fed up with big-city restaurants.

Now they have this little rural place with great food at very reasonable prices. They are open only from 4 to 9 pm Wednesday to Sunday and close completely in the summer. No credit cards are accepted.

Nearby is *The Steak Out* (☎ 455 5205), Hwy 82 at Hwy 83, serving steaks as well as chicken and fish from noon to 10 pm daily. They have a bar with live entertainment on weekends.

In tiny Elgin, about 10 miles east of Sonoita, is *Karen's Wine Country Cafe* (☎ 455 5282), which serves a limited menu of gourmet meals made with the freshest of ingredients, much of which they grow themselves. It has received rave reviews. Call ahead to check their limited hours, recently 10 am to 4 pm from Thursday to Sunday and 5 to 8 pm on Friday and Saturday. Prices are reasonable, and no credit cards are accepted.

# Southeastern Corner

Whereas the I-19 corridor south of Tucson has Spanish history, the area to the east of it tends to have more Anglo history. This is the land of American cowboys, Indians, miners, outlaws, gunslingers and Western lore. Today, the cattle ranches are still there, but the mining operations have mainly closed down. Two towns, Tombstone and Bisbee, have capitalized upon their Western heritage and have turned tourism into a major industry. There are also some very scenic areas here, notably the Huachuca Mountains south of the modern town of Sierra Vista and the Chiricahua Mountains in the extreme southeast corner.

## BENSON

This small rural town, 45 miles west of Tucson on I-10, grew around a railway stop in the 1880s. Today it is a quiet travelers' stop with some simple places to eat and a few motels.

## Information

The main drag is 4th St, running west-east between exits 303 and 306 on I-10. Ocotillo St is the main north-south street, leaving I-10 at exit 304. The chamber of commerce (☎ 586 2842), 363 W 4th St, is open from 9 am to 4 pm Monday to Friday and sometimes on Saturdays. The hospital (☎ 586 2261) is at 450 S Ocotillo Ave. The police (☎ 586 2211, or 911 in emergencies) are at 360 S Gila St.

## San Pedro Valley Arts & Historical Museum

This small local museum (☎ 586 3070), 242 S San Pedro St (off 4th St), is open 10 am to 4 pm Tuesday to Saturday, and from 10 am to 2 pm in summer. It's closed altogether in August. Admission is free.

## Kartchner Caverns State Park

This spectacular limestone cave is 2.5 miles long and was completely undamaged and unexplored upon its discovery. It is a moist cave and the geological features within are still growing. Hikers stumbled across it in 1974, but the location of this spectacular cave was kept secret until 1988, when it became a state park and its protection could be assured. Since then, over $10 million has been spent in preparing the cave for visitation beginning in 1995, but it was still not ready at press time. The State Parks Director said that about another $10 million would allow the cave to be open by 1997, but funding is hard to get and it may be the year 2000 before you'll get in. Camping and other facilities are being built. The park is 10 miles south of Benson on Hwy 90.

For current information call the park (☎ 586 7257) or Arizona State Parks headquarters in Phoenix (☎ (602) 542 4174).

## Places to Stay & Eat

*Red Barn Campground* (☎ 586 2035) and *Chief Four Feathers KOA* (☎ 586 3977) are both on Ocotillo Ave, north of I-10 exit 304. Both have showers, hookups, tenting and recreational facilities, and the KOA has a pool. Rates are $12 to $18.

The *Benson Motel* (☎ 586 3346), 185 W 4th St, and the *Sahara Motel* (☎ 586 3611), 1150 S Hwy 80, a few miles south of Benson, both offer cheap motel rooms. At exit 304 is the *Best Western Quail Hollow Inn* (☎ 586 3646), with a pool and spa and decent rooms in the $40s. Across the street, the *Berryhill Family Restaurant* (☎ 586 7758) is open 24 hours.

There are plenty of fast-food and chain restaurants, especially along 4th St. If you want more Western character, try the *Horseshoe Cafe* (☎ 586 3303), 154 E 4th St, serving American food from 6 am to 9 pm daily, till 10 pm on Friday and Saturday. It's been a favorite ranchers' hangout since the 1940s and can show you life before the Big Mac.

## Getting There & Away

The Greyhound Bus (☎ 586 3141) stops at 248 E 4th St on its runs along I-10.

## AROUND BENSON
### Amerind Foundation

This excellent museum and archaeology research center (☎ 586 3666) is in Dragoon, 15 miles east of Benson. The exhibits of American Indian archaeology, history and culture cover many tribes from Alaska to South America, with a special focus on Southwestern Indians. An art gallery features Indian and Western artists of the last century. Hours are from 10 am to 4 pm daily September to May, closed on Monday and Tuesday in summer. Admission is $3 or $2 for those over 60 and 12- to 18-year-olds. This is a worthwhile freeway stop. Take I-10 exit 318 and head southeast; there are signs.

### San Pedro & Southwestern Railroad

This is a new train ride on a historic track between Benson and the ghost town of Charleston, 27 miles south of Benson, between Tombstone and Sierra Vista. The track goes along the San Pedro River Valley and does not follow a paved road, so you get to see countryside that you otherwise would have missed. The service began in 1995 and there are plans to expand it further, perhaps all the way to Douglas. The train leaves the Benson station on Country Club Drive (off Hwy 80 south of town) at 1:30 pm on Friday, Saturday and Sunday and 9 am on Saturday and Sunday from late September to the end of May. This schedule is subject to change. The 54-mile roundtrip takes about 3.5 hours and costs $24 or $21 for those over 65 and $15 for two- to 12-year-olds. Call the railroad (☎ 586 2266) for reservations.

### SIERRA VISTA

Sierra Vista (elevation 4600 feet) was founded in the 1950s as a service center for Fort Huachuca (see below) and is essentially a modern town of 35,000 inhabitants. It makes a good center from which to visit southeast Arizona's attractions.

### Information

The chamber of commerce (☎ 458 6940, 1 (800) 288 3861), 77 S Calle Portal, is open 8 am to 5 pm Monday to Friday, and from 9 am to 1 pm on Saturday. The Coronado National Forest Sierra Vista Ranger Station (☎ 378 0311) is seven miles south at 5990 Hwy 92, Hereford, 85615. The library (☎ 458 4225) is at 2950 E Tacoma St. The local newspaper is the *Daily Herald Dispatch*. The post office (☎ 458 2540) is at 2300 E Fry Blvd. The hospital (☎ 458 4641, 458 2300) is at 300 El Camino Real. The police (☎ 458 3311, or 911 in emergencies) are at 2400 E Tacoma St.

### Fort Huachuca Military Reservation

Founded in 1877 as a US Army camp during the wars with the Apaches, Fort Huachuca has had a colorful history. In 1913 it was a training ground for the famous Buffalo Soldiers, made up entirely of African-American fighting men. It played important roles in training soldiers for all of the country's major wars. Today, the 115-sq-mile fort is important for information-gathering, testing new communications and other electronic technology that performs well in the dry desert air. It is one of the largest employers in Arizona. So this old fort looks like it will continue to be important well into the 21st century.

You can visit several buildings that date from the 1880s. The Fort Huachuca Museum (☎ 533 5736, 533 3638) has displays explaining the history of the fort. Hours are from 9 am to 4 pm weekdays and 1 to 4 pm on weekends. There is no admission fee, but you need to register yourself and your car at the main gate of the fort at the west end of Fry Blvd. The guard will give you directions to the museum, which is about three miles west of the main gate.

### Activities

The City Park (☎ 458 6742), 3025 E Fry Blvd, has a pool and other outdoor recreation. The Pueblo del Sol Golf Course (☎ 378 6444), 2770 S Saint Andrews Drive, has 18 holes.

### Places to Stay

**Bottom End** The cheapest is the basic-looking *Blue Horizon Motel* (☎ 458 7820),

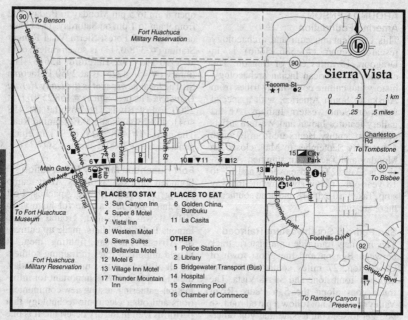

**PLACES TO STAY**
3 Sun Canyon Inn
4 Super 8 Motel
7 Vista Inn
8 Western Motel
9 Sierra Suites
10 Bellavista Motel
12 Motel 6
13 Village Inn Motel
17 Thunder Mountain Inn

**PLACES TO EAT**
6 Golden China, Bunbuku
11 La Casita

**OTHER**
1 Police Station
2 Library
5 Bridgewater Transport (Bus)
14 Hospital
15 Swimming Pool
16 Chamber of Commerce

5150 E Hwy 90. The *Motel 6* (☎ 459 5035, fax 458 4046), 1551 E Fry Blvd, has 100 rooms for $26/32 for singles/doubles. They have a pool. Similar rates are found at the *Western Motel* (☎ 458 4303), 43 W Fry Blvd. Other places with rooms in the $30s and low $40s, all with swimming pools, include the clean *Bellavista Motel* (☎ 458 6737, fax 458 5264), 1101 E Fry Blvd, which has some rooms with kitchenettes; the *Vista Inn* (☎ 458 6711), 201 W Fry Blvd, which offers a free continental breakfast; and the *Village Inn Motel* (☎ 458 4315), 2440 E Fry Blvd, which has a 24 hour restaurant on the premises. The *Super 8 Motel* (☎ 459 5380), 100 Fab Ave, charges $40.88/45.88 and offers free coffee and pastries for breakfast.

**Middle** The *Sun Canyon Inn* (☎ 459 0610, fax 458 5178), 260 N Garden Ave, has rooms in the $50s, most with microwaves and refrigerators. The inn also offers golf packages, a spa, a continental breakfast and a lounge with occasional entertainment. *Thunder Mountain Inn* (☎ 458 7900), 1631 S Hwy 92, has a spa, coffee shop and Baxter's Restaurant & Lounge with room service. *Sierra Suites* (☎ 459 4221, fax 459 8449), 391 E Fry Blvd, has large rooms with a refrigerator and microwave for about $50 and a few two-room suites for $70. There is a spa, and continental breakfast and evening cocktail are included in the rates.

The *Ramada Inn* (☎ 459 5900, fax 458 1347), 2047 S Hwy 92, has a spa, lounge, restaurant with room service and good-size rooms with coffeemakers. Rates are in the $60s including continental breakfast and there are a few suites in the low $100s.

**Places to Eat**
There are plenty of restaurants to choose from along Fry Blvd. I couldn't find anything outstanding, but two places that have

been recommended as being popular with off-duty base personnel are the *Golden China* (☎ 458 8588), 325 W Fry Blvd, which is open daily for inexpensive buffet lunches and fancier dinners from the varied menu, and *Bunbuku* (☎ 459 6993), 297 W Fry Blvd, for Japanese lunches and dinners. Decent Mexican food is served at *La Casita* (☎ 458 2376), 465 E Fry Blvd, from 11 am to 9 pm Monday to Thursday and to 10 pm on Friday and Saturday. For American steak and seafood, the best place is seven miles south at *The Mesquite Tree* (☎ 378 2758), 6398 S Hwy 92, which is open Tuesday to Sunday from 11 am to 2:30 pm and 5 to 9 pm (to 8 pm on Sunday).

### Getting There & Away
America West Express (☎ 459 8575, 1 (800) 235 9292) has several flights a day between Phoenix and Fort Huachuca Airport. Bridgewater Transport (☎ 458 3471), 28 Fab Ave, has two or three buses a day for Tucson, Bisbee and Douglas.

### Getting Around
Rent cars from Enterprise (☎ 458 2424, 1 (800) 325 8007), Ugly Duckling (☎ 459 5242, (1 (800) 843 3825), Practical Rent-a-Car (☎ 458 4441) and Rent-a-Ride (☎ 459 1296), all in Sierra Vista.

Call-A-Cab (☎ 458 5867) has 24 hour taxi service.

### AROUND SIERRA VISTA
### Ramsey Canyon Preserve
At an elevation of about 5500 feet in the Huachuca Mountains south of Sierra Vista, this Nature Conservancy-owned preserve is famous throughout the birding world as one of the best places in the USA to see hummingbirds. The highest numbers are seen from April to September (April, May and August especially), but there are always a few species year round. Trogons and other rarities from Mexico are also seen in the wooded riparian habitat in the canyon. Also protected is the Ramsey Canyon leopard frog, found nowhere else in the world. Visitors are quite likely to see deer, and sightings of coatis, ring-tailed

Hummingbird

cats, javelinas and even mountain lion and black bear are reported regularly.

Entrance to the preserve is limited by the small size of the parking lot, at the end of a very narrow and winding road that doesn't offer much parking either. There's no room for RVs or trailers. During the busy months you should make reservations for parking spaces at the preserve (☎ 378 2785), 27 Ramsey Canyon Rd, Hereford, 85615. Reservations are essential during summer weekends. At other times, parking is on a first-come, first-served basis, so arrive early.

The preserve is open from 8 am to 5 pm daily and a $5 donation is requested for non-Nature-Conservancy members. At the parking lot there is a visitors center with a gift and book shop, and many hummingbird feeders are hung on the grounds to attract the birds. From the parking lot, two trails lead up into the canyon. The 0.7-mile nature loop is quite easy, and the longer Hamburg Trail climbs high into the Huachucas. You have to register at the visitors center to use the trails.

There are 10 one- and two-bedroom housekeeping cabins available for rent that enable you to stay on the preserve overnight. These are often booked a year ahead for the peak summer season, and reservations are needed at any time. Rates start at $65 for the one-bedroom and $75 for the two-bedroom cabins and go up $10 for every extra person.

ARIZONA

Ring-tailed cat

If the cabins are full or you prefer to have more amenities, you can stay at the *Ramsey Canyon Inn B&B* (☎ 378 3010), 31 Ramsey Canyon Rd, Hereford, 85615, which is right next door to the preserve. They have two housekeeping cottages with full kitchens for $95 to $115 (no breakfast) and six bedrooms with private bathroom for $90 to $105 (gourmet breakfast included). The B&B attracts just as many humming-birds as the preserve cabins next door – the birds aren't fussy about who hangs up the feeders!

Both these places may require minimum two- or three-night stays in the busy season. If they are full, Sierra Vista is just 10 miles away.

### Coronado National Memorial

US history, as taught in US schools, tends to begin with the pilgrims and slowly moves west from there. The historically verifiable earlier incursions of Spain into the Southwest during the 16th century are generally ignored. The Coronado National Memorial fills in some of those gaps between Indian prehistory and Anglo history. Francisco Vasquez de Coronado, accompanied by hundreds of Spanish soldiers and Mexican Indians, passed through here in 1540 on his way from Mexico City to search for gold in the Seven Cities of Cibola. This was the first major European expedition into the Southwest, and Coronado is credited with introducing horses to the Indians.

The memorial is at the southern end of the Huachuca Mountains on the Mexican border, 20 miles south of Sierra Vista on Hwy 92. The visitors center (☎ 366 5515, 458 9333) is open from 8 am to 5 pm daily except Thanksgiving and Christmas and has exhibits explaining Coronado's expedition as well as the area's wildlife. The memorial itself is open during daylight hours and admission is free. The road from Sierra Vista to the visitors center is paved. West from the visitors center (at 5300 feet), an unpaved road climbs over the 6575-foot-high Montezuma Pass offering great views. A 3.3 mile hiking trail also links these two points. From the pass, a 0.7-mile trail climbs to Coronado Peak (6864 feet) with great views into Mexico and to Baboquivari Peak, 80 miles west, if the weather is clear. West of the pass, an unpaved road goes through the Coronado National Forest emerging at Nogales, about 50 miles away. This road is passable to cars except after rain. A detailed description of the drive is given in Annerino's *Adventuring in Arizona*.

There is no camping in the memorial, but you can camp for free almost anywhere in the Coronado National Forest to the west. *Lakeview* is a developed USFS campground at **Parker Canyon Lake**, which can be reached by driving west from the memorial or south from Sonoita on Hwy 83; both roads are unpaved. At the lake is a marina (☎ 455 5847) with boat rentals and fishing supplies. A five-mile hiking trail encircles the lake. There are 65 camping sites with water but no hookups for $8, available on a first-come, first-served basis. Day use is $5.

### San Pedro Riparian National Conservation Area

About 95% of Arizona's riparian habitat has disappeared, victim to poor grazing practices, logging for firewood, dropping water tables and development. Loss of this habitat has endangered many species' existence, and about 10% of the over 500 species on the Endangered Species List are found along the San Pedro River. Clearly, this is valuable habitat. Almost 400 species of birds, over 80 species of mammals and about 47 species of reptiles and amphibians have been recorded along the 40-mile stretch of the San Pedro within the conservation area. This is the healthiest riparian

ecosystem in the Southwest and is part of the Nature Conservancy's 'Last Great Places' Program. The San Pedro is also the longest remaining undammed river in Arizona, and developers and ranchers have their eye on it. Whether the San Pedro remains conserved or becomes exploited is still undecided.

The conservation is currently managed by the BLM (☎ 458 3559), 1763 Paseo San Luis, Sierra Vista, which can give information. The area is accessed from several roads that cross the river east of Sierra Vista. Hwy 82 crosses the river at **Fairbank**, a ghost town that now houses the area's headquarters and visitors center, open from 7:45 am to 4:15 pm Monday to Friday. Hwy 90 crosses the river at San Pedro House, a 1930s ranch that now houses an information center and bookshop run by the Friends of the San Pedro River (☎ 459 2555). It's open daily from 9:30 am to 4:30 pm. Camping is allowed by permit, which costs $2 per day and is available at the centers above or at self-pay stations at parking areas wherever a road crosses the river.

### TOMBSTONE

Despite being told by friends that all he would find out here would be his own tombstone, prospector Ed Schieffelin braved the dangers of Apache attack and struck it rich. The year was 1877, and a rip-roaring, brawling silver-mining town appeared here very quickly. In 1881, 110 saloon licenses were sold, and there were 14 dance halls for the entertainment of the get-rich-quick miners. By then the population was 10,000 and Tombstone became the Cochise County seat. Also in 1881 the famous shootout at the OK Corral happened, during which the Earp brothers and Doc Holliday gunned down three members of the Clanton cowboy gang. This was one of dozens of gunfights in Tombstone, but it has caught people's imagination like no other and is now perhaps the most famous shootout in history.

Tombstone was typical of the Southwestern mining towns of the period. Saloons,

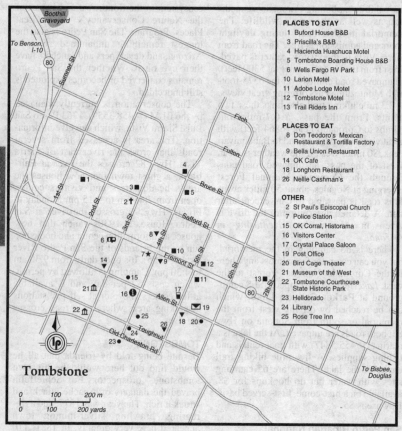

Boothill
Graveyard

To Benson,
I-10

**Tombstone**

| 0 | 100 | 200 m |
| 0 | 100 | 200 yards |

To Bisbee,
Douglas

**PLACES TO STAY**
1   Buford House B&B
3   Priscilla's B&B
4   Hacienda Huachuca Motel
5   Tombstone Boarding House B&B
6   Wells Fargo RV Park
10  Larion Motel
11  Adobe Lodge Motel
12  Tombstone Motel
13  Trail Riders Inn

**PLACES TO EAT**
8   Don Teodoro's Mexican
    Restaurant & Tortilla Factory
9   Bella Union Restaurant
14  OK Cafe
18  Longhorn Restaurant
26  Nellie Cashman's

**OTHER**
2   St Paul's Episcopal Church
7   Police Station
15  OK Corral, Historama
16  Visitors Center
17  Crystal Palace Saloon
19  Post Office
20  Bird Cage Theater
21  Museum of the West
22  Tombstone Courthouse
    State Historic Park
23  Helldorado
24  Library
25  Rose Tree Inn

gambling halls and bordellos made up a good portion of the buildings, but there were, as always, a sprinkling of sober citizens writing newspapers, running businesses and opening banks. The silver-mining boom was a short-lived one, however, and declining sliver prices and floods in the mines closed down the last operation in the early 1900s. Most other boomtowns in this situation became ghost towns, but Tombstone, nicknamed the 'Town Too Tough to Die', continued to be a commercial center and the Cochise County seat until the seat moved to Bisbee in 1929.

After WW II, the growing population of Arizona gave Tombstone a new lease on life and the old county courthouse opened as a museum in the 1950s. Tombstone became a National Historic Landmark in 1962 and now attracts large crowds of tourists who browse the town's old Western buildings, most of which are now gift shops. Reenactments of gunfights and other late 1800s events provide entertainment.

## Information

The visitors center (☎ 457 3929) at the corner of 4th and Allen Sts, the Office of

Tourism (☎ 457 2211) at 5th and Allen Sts (behind the Crystal Palace Saloon), and the chamber of commerce (☎ 457 9317) all provide tourist information, which gives you an idea of how dependent on tourism Tombstone is. The library (☎ 457 3612) is at 4th St and Toughnut. The post office (☎ 457 3479) is at 516 E Allen St. The police (☎ 457 2244 or 911 in emergencies) are by the City Hall at 315 E Fremont St.

### Shootouts & the OK Corral

A prime tourist attraction is the shootouts reenacted by various acting troupes in town. The most professional are the Wild Bunch, who perform the events leading to the shootout at the OK Corral at 2 pm on the first and third Sunday of the month. It happens at the corral itself (see map), admission is $3 and they often sell out, so buy a ticket early.

On other Sundays, the Tombstone Vigilantes perform the shootout and donations are accepted. The rest of the week, the OK Corral (☎ 457 3456) is open from 8:30 am to 5 pm, admission is $1.50 and you can see models of the gunfighters and other Western exhibits. The most interesting among them is C S Fly's photography studio. Next door is the **Historama** with 30-minute presentations of Tombstone's history using animated figures, movies and narration. These cost $1.50 and are shown on the hour between 9 am and 4 pm.

The OK Corral is on Allen St between 3rd and 4th Sts.

Shootouts are also performed at the Helldorado stage at 2 pm on other days of the week (small admission fee) and can occur spontaneously at other times especially during the various special events during the year.

### Tombstone Courthouse
### State Historic Park

Built in 1882, abandoned in 1931, and rehabilitated in the 1950s, the courthouse displays thousands of artifacts telling of the town's history. The courthouse (☎ 457 3311) at 3rd St and Toughnut, is open daily

from 8 am to 5 pm. Admission is $2 or $1 for 12- to 17-year-olds.

### Museum of the West

A varied collection of Western memorabilia is displayed at this museum (☎ 457 9219), 109 S 3rd St. Admission is $2 or $1 for seven- to 14-year-olds, and hours are from 9:30 am to 5 pm daily.

### Rose Tree Inn

Antique 1880s furniture and the world's largest rose tree are displayed in this period house (☎ 457 3326) at 4th St and Toughnut. Hours are 9 am to 5 pm and admission is $1.50, free for under-14-year-olds accompanied by an adult.

### Bird Cage Theater

Named after 14 bed-sized draped cages suspended from the ceiling, used by prostitutes to entertain their clients, the Bird Cage Theater (☎ 457 3421), 517 E Allen St, was also a gambling den, dance hall and saloon during the 1880s. This was the wildest place in the West in those days, and you can see it for $3.50, or $1.75 for teenagers and $1 for eight- to 12-year-olds. Hours are from 8 am to 6 pm daily.

### Boothill Graveyard

One of the few places you can see for free in this tourist town (though you have to enter through a gift shop!), this cemetery has the graves of many of Tombstone's early desperadoes. Some of the headstones make interesting reading. It's off Hwy 80 just north of town and is open from 7:30 am to 6 pm.

### Special Events

Tombstone's events revolve around weekends of Western fun with shootouts (of course!) and stagecoach rides, chili cookoffs, fiddling contests, mock hangings and melodramas. The biggest event is Helldorado Days over the third weekend in October. Other events are Territorial Days (first weekend in March), Wyatt Earp Days (Memorial Day weekend), Rendezvous of the Gunfighters (Labor Day weekend) and other smaller events.

## Places to Stay – camping
*Tombstone KOA* (☎ 457 3829), one mile north on Hwy 80, has a pool, playground, showers, laundry and tent and RV sites from $17 to $21. Kamping Kabins are $27. *Wells Fargo RV Park* (☎ 457 3966), at 3rd and Fremont Sts, charges $17.50 for full hookups and has a few cheaper tent sites. Both places get full from October to March, when reservations are advised.

## Places to Stay – bottom end
The cheapest place is the *Hacienda Huachuca Motel* (☎ 457 2201), 320 Bruce St, which provides refrigerators, coffeemakers in the rooms and a pool, and boasts that John Wayne once spent the night. It looks like the building has received little attention since he was here, but the beds are clean enough. Rates start at $25. They have larger rooms with kitchenettes for $39. The *Trail Riders Inn* (☎ 457 3573, 1 (800) 574 0417), 13 N 7th St, has rooms starting in the $30s, as does the *Larion Motel* (☎ 457 2272), 410 E Fremont St.

## Places to Stay – middle
**Motels** The *Adobe Lodge Motel* (☎ 457 2241), 505 E Fremont St, has satisfactory rooms in the $40s. Across the street, the *Tombstone Motel* (☎ 457 3478), 502 E Fremont St, charges a few dollars more for similar rooms. The most comfortable motel is on Hwy 80 a mile north of downtown at the *Best Western Lookout Lodge* (☎ 457 2223, fax 457 3870), which has a pool, nice views and good-size rooms in the $60s including continental breakfast.

**B&Bs** The 1880 *Buford House* (☎ 457 3969), 113 E Safford St, 85638, has five antique-filled rooms, three with sinks but shared bathrooms, two with private bathrooms, and one with a fireplace for $65 to $95. No smoking is allowed inside. *Priscilla's B&B* (☎ 457 3844), 101 N 3rd St, PO Box 700, 85638, a Victorian house dating from 1904, has three rooms with a

sink and shared bathroom. Rates are $40/55 for single/double occupancy. *Tombstone Boarding House B&B* (☎ 457 3716), 108 N 4th St, PO Box 905, 85638, is a restored 1880s adobe home. Five bedrooms with private baths rent for $60 to $80.

## Places to Eat
*Nellie Cashman's* (☎ 457 2212), 5th St and Toughnut, dates from 1882 when it was opened by Nellie, a tough Irishwoman who stood no nonsense but helped out many a miner down on his luck. This is a no-alcohol establishment, and serves excellent meals from 7 am to 9 pm daily. Huge hamburger plates are around $5 and steaks are in the $11 to $16 range. Chicken, pork, fish and spaghetti are also served in the quietly charming dining room. For something a little wilder, the popular *Longhorn Restaurant* (☎ 457 3405), 5th and Allen Sts, serves American and Mexican breakfast, lunch and dinner.

For the most authentic Mexican food, *Don Teodoro's Mexican Restaurant & Tortilla Factory* (☎ 457 3647), 15 N 4th St, is a hole-in-the-wall kind of place with homemade lunches and dinners every day. For buffalo burgers and other American delights, the *OK Cafe*, 220 E Allen St, serves them up fast at breakfast and lunch. The fanciest-looking place is the *Bella Union Restaurant* (☎ 457 3656), 401 E Fremont St, which has a lovely old wooden bar as well as decent steaks and other American favorites. They are open from 6 am to 9 pm.

## Entertainment
Several bars along Allen St have old Wild Western ambiance. The best kept of these is the *Crystal Palace Saloon*, at 5th and Allen Sts, which dates from 1879. There's not much else to do in the evening but go on a pub crawl – or perhaps that should be a saloon stagger.

## BISBEE
Bisbee is just 24 miles south of Tombstone. Both towns were founded in the late 1870s as mining towns, and both places shared a

similar wild early history. The difference between the two lies in what was mined. Tombstone had silver, which fizzled out in the 1890s, while Bisbee had copper, which became Arizona's most important industry. Accordingly, when Tombstone faltered, Bisbee grew and by 1910 had 25,000 inhabitants and was the biggest city between El Paso, Texas, and San Francisco, California. In 1929, the Cochise County seat moved from Tombstone to Bisbee, and it has remained here ever since.

Many elegant Victorian brick buildings were constructed here, reminiscent of the East Coast and reasonably suited to the cooler 5300-elevation of Bisbee. The town was built in a narrow canyon, and soon there was no room for more construction. Today, many of the buildings in town date from the heyday of the early-20th century, and Bisbee has more of a Victorian feel to it than any town in Arizona. Copper mining declined after WW II and the mine closed in 1975, when the ore finally ran out. By then, eight billion pounds of copper worth $11 million had been produced, which was less than some other mines. Paradoxically, the mines here produced more gold and silver than any other mine in Arizona, but Bisbee is still thought of as an old copper-mining town.

Bisbee's pleasant climate and old-fashioned ambiance attracted artists and the artistically inclined, and now the town is an intriguing mix of aging miners and gallery owners, ex-hippies and artists. It has more of an upscale air than Tombstone. Where Tombstone thrives on gunfight reenactments, Bisbee offers mine tours, which are more relevant and realistic. The population is about 7000.

### Orientation & Information

The steep canyon walls encompassing Old Bisbee make the layout rather contorted, but you'll get used to it once you accept the fact that Bisbee isn't set up on the typical Western checkerboard formation. East of Old Bisbee is the Lavender Pit Copper Mine followed by Lowell and the suburb of Warren, about three miles southeast of

Bisbee. Warren also has many Victorian homes and has the hospital and several places to stay.

The chamber of commerce (☎ 432 5421), 7 Main St, is open from 9 am to 5 pm on weekdays and from 10 am to 3 pm on weekends. It is very helpful in trying to reserve you space on a mine tour or calling a B&B to see if they have room. The library (☎ 432 4232) and the post office (☎ 432 2052) are both at 6 Main St. The Copper Queen Hospital (☎ 432 5383) is at Bisbee Rd and Cole Ave in Warren. The police can be reached at 432 2261, or 911 in emergencies.

### Bisbee Mining & Historical Museum

Housed in the 1897 office building of the Phelps Dodge Copper Mining Co, the museum (☎ 432 7071), at Copper Queen Plaza, has a fine display depicting the first 40 years of Bisbee's history, along with exhibits about mining, and has a research library about the copper mining industry. Many of the buildings described are still standing. Hours are from 10 am to 4 pm daily except Christmas and New Year's Day; admission is $3 for 18- to 64-year-olds, $2.50 for seniors; kids are free.

### Tours

On the other side of Hwy 80 from the downtown exit is the (no longer working) **Queen Mine** (☎ 432 2071) which can be visited in underground mine cars guided by retired miners. Reservations are suggested. Tours last a little over an hour and leave at 9 and 10:30 am, noon, 2 and 3:30 pm daily. Participants wear hard hats and go deep into the mine, which is a chilly 47°F so bring warm clothes. Costs are $8 or $3.50 for seven- to 11-year-olds and $2 for three- to six-year-olds. They also offer guided van tours of the **Surface Mines & Historic District** at 10:30 am, noon, 2 and 3:30 pm for $7 per person over age two and **Historic District Walking Tours** at 10:30 am and 2 pm for the same price.

You can do your own walking tour by picking up a detailed brochure at the chamber of commerce. The giant Lavender

ARIZONA

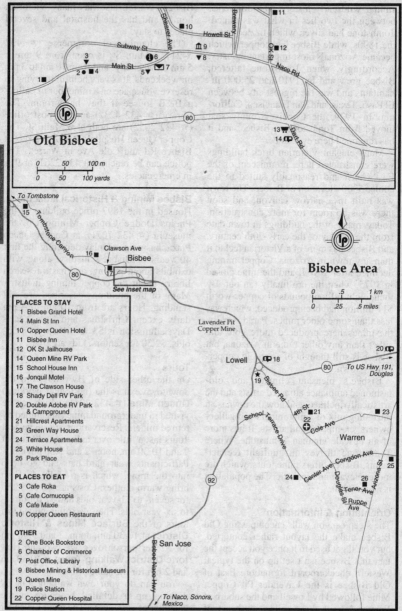

**Old Bisbee**

0    50    100 m
0    50    100 yards

To Tombstone

Tombstone Canyon

Clawson Ave

Bisbee

See inset map

**Bisbee Area**

0    .5    1 km
0    .25    .5 miles

Lavender Pit
Copper Mine

Lowell

To US Hwy 191,
Douglas

Bisbee Rd

Warren

4th St

Cole Ave

School Terrace Drive

Center Ave

Congdon Ave

Douglas

Tener Ave

Ruppe Ave

San Jose

Bisbee Naco Hwy

To Naco, Sonora,
Mexico

**PLACES TO STAY**
1   Bisbee Grand Hotel
4   Main St Inn
10  Copper Queen Hotel
11  Bisbee Inn
12  OK St Jailhouse
14  Queen Mine RV Park
15  School House Inn
16  Jonquil Motel
17  The Clawson House
18  Shady Dell RV Park
20  Double Adobe RV Park
    & Campground
21  Hillcrest Apartments
23  Green Way House
24  Terrace Apartments
25  White House
26  Park Place

**PLACES TO EAT**
3   Cafe Roka
5   Cafe Cornucopia
8   Cafe Maxie
10  Copper Queen Restaurant

**OTHER**
2   One Book Bookstore
6   Chamber of Commerce
7   Post Office, Library
9   Bisbee Mining & Historical Museum
13  Queen Mine
19  Police Station
22  Copper Queen Hospital

Pit Copper Mine, over a mile across, can be seen from Hwy 80 a short way southeast of town.

### Visiting Mexico

Naco is a quiet border town 11 miles south of Bisbee. It doesn't have the tourist shopping bustle of Nogales or Agua Prieta, but you can get buses here further into Mexico. Customs is open from 8:30 am to 4:30 pm, although the border is open 24 hours.

### Special Events

Art fairs and other events take place regularly. The biggest events are the Vuelta de Bisbee multistage bicycle race held in spring, a poetry festival in August, a couple of arts & crafts shows in September and a gem and mineral show in October.

### Places to Stay

Bisbee, at 5300 feet, is a year-round destination, hot but not baking in summer, cold but not frozen in winter. Therefore there are no high or low seasons. Most accommodations are B&Bs in older houses or historic hotels. As yet, there are no modern chain motels, which is a welcome relief.

Bisbee is not an Econo Lodge sort of place.

**Camping** *Queen Mine RV Park* (☎ 432 5006) next to the Queen Mine has 25 RV sites with hookups for $12. *Turquoise Valley Golf & RV Park* (☎ 432 3091) is five miles south along Hwy 92 and has 45 RV sites with hookups for $14. You can play nine holes here. Reservations are recommended for both places. The *Shady Dell RV Park* (☎ 432 7305), 1 Douglas Rd behind a gas station at the traffic circle east of town in Lowell, has showers and 16 sites for tents ($5) and RVs with hookups ($12). *Double Adobe RV Park & Campground* (☎ 364 4000), 4.5 miles southeast along Hwy 80 then 4.5 miles east of Double Adobe Rd, is in a bird sanctuary with hiking trails. Tent camping is $8, RVs with hookups are $12. There are showers. Reservations are recommended in winter.

**Hotels & Motels** The *Jonquil Motel* (☎ 432 7371), 317 Tombstone Canyon, is affordable at $30 to $40 and is near Old Bisbee. One-bedroom units with kitchenettes at *Hillcrest Apartments* (☎ 432 3598), 1 Hillcrest Drive, and *Terrace Apartments* (☎ 432 2017), 310 Center Ave, rent for around $40 a night.

Bisbee's three luxury hotels are all in the center of the historic area. The *Bisbee Grand Hotel* (☎ 432 5900, 1 (800) 421 1909), 61 Main St, is of the red-velvet and stuffed-peacock school of 'elegance', if you're into that sort of thing. Rooms are in the $60 to $80 range, suites around $100; breakfast is included. The *Copper Queen Hotel* (☎ 432 2216, 1 (800) 247 5829), 11 Howell St, has an outdoor swimming pool, a saloon that hearkens back to mining days, and an award-winning dining room. Rates are $65 to $95. Once a boarding house for miners, the *Main Street Inn* (☎ 432 5237), 26 Main St, is a bit more upscale now, with Southwestern decor and rates in the $50 to $75 range; the inn's one suite goes for about $100.

**B&Bs** A number of beautiful older homes offer classy accommodations in and around Bisbee. Many are outside of historic Bisbee, but the most affordable, *Bisbee Inn* (☎ 432 5131), 45 OK St, is also quite central. Rates are $29 for a single and $39 to $45 for a double, breakfast included.

Also in Old Bisbee is *The OK Street Jailhouse* (☎ 432 7435, 1 (800) 821 0678), 9 OK St. Built in 1904, this county jail was part of the prison system until 1915. Now it rents as one two-floor apartment complete with a kitchen, living room, bedroom and a Jacuzzi tub. Rates are $100 for the first night, $75 for the second. The *Clawson House* (☎ 432 5237, 1 (800) 467 5237), 116 Clawson Ave, was built in 1895 for one of the managers of the Lavender Pit Copper Mine; its three bedrooms go for $55 to $75 a night.

Outside of the center, the more moderately priced B&Bs ($40 to $70, including breakfast) are *Park Place* (☎ 432 3054, 1 (800) 388 4388), 200 East Vista in

Warren, and *The School House Inn* (☎ 432-2996, 1 (800) 537 4333), 818 Tombstone Canyon, where the nine guest rooms follow school-house themes such as the Principal's Office and the Writing Room.

For a bit more money, *The Greenway House* (☎ 432 7170, 1 (800) 253 3325), 401 Cole Ave, pampers their guests with wine, flowers, bubble bath and the like. Their eight suites, all with private bath and kitchenette, cost from $75 to $125 per night. The two suites at *The White House* (☎ 432 7215), 800 Congdon Ave, have Jacuzzi tubs; rates are $100 a night.

### Places to Eat
The elegant old *Copper Queen Hotel* (☎ 432 2216), on Howell St, has a restaurant open to the public from 7 am to 2:30 pm and from 5:30 to 9 pm. They serve good American food. *Cafe Cornucopia* (☎ 432 3364), 14 Main St, serves sandwiches and a tasty variety of blended juices and smoothies from 6:30 am to 4 pm daily except Saturday. *Cafe Maxie* (☎ 432 7063) in Queen Center Plaza, serves soups and sandwiches and has Bisbee's only salad and fruit bar. Hours are from 7:30 am to 8 pm Monday to Thursday, to 9 pm on Friday and Saturday and from 8:30 am to 6 pm on Sunday. The best restaurant is *Cafe Roka* (☎ 432 5153), 35 Main St, which serves excellent and innovative dinners from 5:30 to 9 pm, closed Sunday and Monday. There are also several other decent places to eat downtown.

### Things to Buy
The best stores are in the center of Old Bisbee, and many exhibit and sell the work of local artists. The quality is mixed, but the discerning eye may discover an as-yet-undiscovered artist here. It's worth a browse if you are looking for Western art, jewelry or crafts.

The oddest and most famous store is the One Book Bookstore (☎ 432 5512), 30 Main St. Here, Walter Swan sold the one book he wrote about his boyhood in early-20th century Arizona. He couldn't find a publisher or distributor, so he self-published

the book and opened up a store to sell it and nothing else. It was a success. Walter got onto TV and into the newspapers, and then self-published four more titles that he sold in the Other Book Bookstore, partitioned off from the One Book Bookstore. Walter passed away recently, but his family keeps the place going.

### Getting There & Away
Bridgewater Transport has two buses a day to Tucson (via Sierra Vista) and Douglas. Buy tickets at One World Travel (☎ 432 5359), 7 OK St.

## DOUGLAS & AROUND
James Douglas of the Phelps Dodge Co founded this town on the Mexican border in 1901 and built a copper smelter here. Although this ceased production in 1987, Douglas, along with its sister city of Agua Prieta in Mexico, has become a ranching and manufacturing center. The downtown area looks pre-WW II without the hoopla of Bisbee or Tombstone. The population is about 15,000, but another 80,000 people live across the border in Agua Prieta. Many Mexicans work in Douglas. The elevation here is 4000 feet.

### Information
The chamber of commerce (☎ 364 2477), 1125 Pan American Ave, is open from 9 am to 5 pm Monday to Friday. The Coronado National Forest Douglas Ranger Station (☎ 364 3468, 364 3231), Leslie Canyon Rd, RR1, Box 228-R, 85607, is open from 7:30 am to 4:30 pm Monday to Friday. The library (☎ 364 3851) is at 625 10th St. The post office (☎ 364 3631) is at 601 10th St. The hospital (☎ 364 7931) is four miles west of Douglas. The police (☎ 364 8422, or 911 in emergencies) are at 300 14th St.

### Gadsden Hotel
Established in 1907, the hotel (see Places to Stay, below) is now a National Historic Site. The lobby is one of the most opulent turn-of-the-century public areas to be seen in Arizona. A white Italian marble staircase

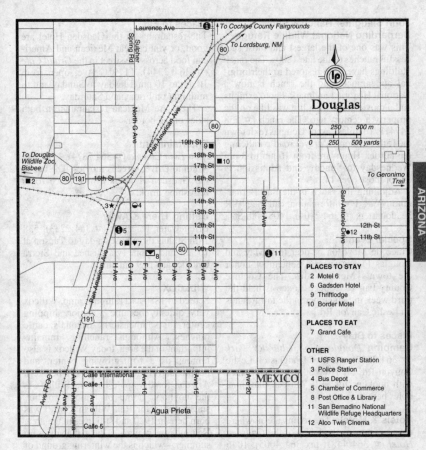

**PLACES TO STAY**
2    Motel 6
6    Gadsden Hotel
9    Thriftlodge
10   Border Motel

**PLACES TO EAT**
7    Grand Cafe

**OTHER**
1    USFS Ranger Station
3    Police Station
4    Bus Depot
5    Chamber of Commerce
8    Post Office & Library
11   San Bernadino National
     Wildlife Refuge Headquarters
12   Alco Twin Cinema

and marble pillars with gold-leaf decorations, a superb 42-foot Tiffany stained-glass mural and vaulted stained-glass skylights combine into an elegant surprise. It's well worth a visit even if you aren't staying here.

### Douglas Wildlife Zoo

This zoo's motto is 'Saving Our World's Wildlife through Propagation'. There is a small but varied collection of exotic animals, some of which you can feed. The zoo (☎ 364 2515) is 2.5 miles west on Hwy 80, then 1.5 miles north on Plantation Rd. Hours are from 10 am to 5 pm (closed

major holidays), and admission is $3 or $2 for three- to 12-year-olds.

### Visiting Mexico

Agua Prieta is a large border town and you can enter from Arizona on foot. It is much more leisurely and relaxed than Nogales and has a selection of gift shops and restaurants in a pleasant setting. From the international border, walk south six blocks to Calle 6 and turn left for two blocks to the church and plaza, which are pleasant.

Agua Prieta hotels are few in number and not especially cheap. Buses go from here to the rest of Mexico.

## John Slaughter Ranch & San Bernardino National Wildlife Refuge

This was one of the largest and most successful ranches of the late 1800s. The ranch buildings have been restored to their original appearance, and the ranch is now a National Historic Landmark. Photo exhibits and a movie show what life was like on the property a century ago. The ranch (☎ 558 2474) is 16 miles east of Douglas (exit town on 15th St) along a gravel road paralleling the border. Hours are from 10 am to 3 pm Wednesday to Sunday, and admission is $4 for those over 14.

Adjoining the ranch is the San Bernardino NWR. For information, call the NWR headquarters (☎ 364 2104), 1408 10th St.

## Special Events

Cinco de Mayo on or near to 5 May and Douglas Fiestas in mid September honor the town's Mexican ties. The Cochise County Fair & College Rodeo is held the third week in September in the fairgrounds on Leslie Canyon Rd.

## Places to Stay

**Camping** *Douglas Golf Club RV Park* (☎ 364 3722), north of Douglas on Leslie Canyon Rd, off Hwy 80, has 28 RV sites with hookups for $12. You can play nine holes here.

**Hotels & Motels** The rooms are nowhere near as fancy as the lobby of the *Gadsden Hotel* (☎ 364 4481, fax 364 4005), 1046 G Ave, but they are comfortable enough and the price is right. There are 160 rooms and suites ranging from $32 to $115; most are under $51. The rooms contain an eclectic grouping of styles and amenities, but just sitting in the lobby makes this a great value.

Other places include the *Motel 6* (☎ 364 2457, fax 364 9332), 111 16th St, with a pool and rooms at $27/33 for singles/doubles, the more basic *Border Motel* (☎ 364 8491), 1725 A Ave, for $21/26, and the *Thriftlodge* (☎ 364 8434, fax 364 5687), 1030 19th St, with a pool and rooms for $33/39.

## Places to Eat

The restaurants in the Gadsden Hotel are good, or you can eat Mexican and American food across the street in the *Grand Cafe* (☎ 364 2344), 1119 G Ave, open from 10 am to 10 pm Tuesday to Sunday and to midnight on Friday and Saturday.

There are Mexican restaurants on both sides of the border.

## Entertainment

*Alco Twin Cinema* (☎ 364 7874), 1111 San Antonio Drive, screens movies. The bar in the Gadsden Hotel is a nice place for a refreshing drink.

## Getting There & Away

Bridgewater Transport (☎ 364 2233), 538 14th St, has three buses a day to Tucson at 10 am and 4 pm (via Bisbee and Sierra Grande) and at 9 pm direct.

## WILLCOX

Settled in 1880 as a railroad camp, Willcox very quickly became a major shipping center for southeastern Arizona's cattle ranches. Although ranching remains important in the area, today Willcox is also famous as a fruit-growing center, and people drive from all over southeastern Arizona for the apple harvest. Willcox is the boyhood home of famous cowboy singer and actor Rex Williams, who was born here in 1920 and still lives in the area. Nearby is a playa – a lake that dries in summer – which is the wintering ground of thousands of sandhill cranes, a spectacular sight for bird watchers.

## Information

The chamber of commerce (☎ 384 2272, 1 (800) 200 2272), 1500 N Circle I Rd, northeast of I-10 exit 340, is open from 9 am to 5 pm daily except Sunday, when its hours are from noon to 5 pm. There is a small museum of local history and Indian lore here; admission is free. The library (☎ 384 4271) is at 450 W Maley St. The post office (☎ 384 2689) is at 200 S Curtis Ave. The hospital (☎ 384 3541) is at 901 W Rex Allen Drive. You can contact the

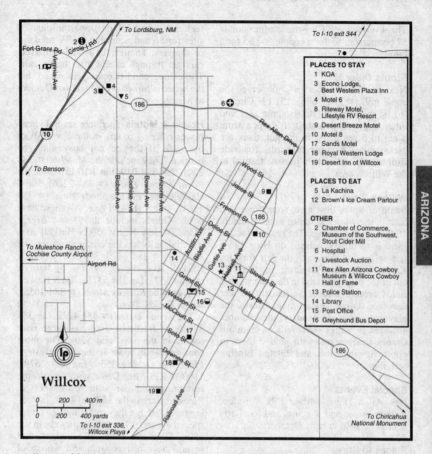

**Willcox**

```
0    200    400 m
0    200    400 yards
```

To I-10 exit 336,
Willcox Playa

**PLACES TO STAY**
1  KOA
3  Econo Lodge,
   Best Western Plaza Inn
4  Motel 6
8  Riteway Motel,
   Lifestyle RV Resort
9  Desert Breeze Motel
10 Motel 8
17 Sands Motel
18 Royal Western Lodge
19 Desert Inn of Willcox

**PLACES TO EAT**
5  La Kachina
12 Brown's Ice Cream Parlour

**OTHER**
2  Chamber of Commerce,
   Museum of the Southwest,
   Stout Cider Mill
6  Hospital
7  Livestock Auction
11 Rex Allen Arizona Cowboy
   Museum & Willcox Cowboy
   Hall of Fame
13 Police Station
14 Library
15 Post Office
16 Greyhound Bus Depot

police (☎ 384 4673, or 911 in emergencies) at 151 W Maley St.

### Museum of the Southwest

Inside the chamber of commerce (see Information, above), this small museum houses military artifacts, remnants of town history and, oddly, information about the area's ostriches. Apparently there are a lot of ostrich farms around Willcox, and every part of the large bird is put to use: the feathers, the bones, the hide and, of course, the meat! The museum is open from 9 am to 5 pm Monday to Saturday and from 1 to 4 pm on Sunday.

### Rex Allen Arizona Cowboy Museum & Willcox Cowboy Hall of Fame

This museum (☎ 384 4583), 155 N Railroad Ave, is in an 1890s adobe building and presents the life of Rex Allen; opposite the museum is a large bronze statue of the star. Exhibits also interpret the lives of pioneers. The whole block where the museum is situated is one of Willcox's most historic areas with a real Old West appearance. The Willcox Commercial Store at the corner northeast of the museum dates to 1881 and is the oldest continuously operating store in Arizona. The museum is open from 10 am to 4 pm daily except New Year's Day,

Thanksgiving and Christmas; admission is $2 per person, $3 for a couple and $5 for a family.

## Stouts Cider Mill

Next to the chamber of commerce, the apple mill (☎ 384 3696), 1510 N Circle I Rd, is famous for HUGE apple pies and other apple-related stuff. It's open from 9 am to 6 pm daily. In the fall, there are pick-your-own apple orchards, roadside fruit stands and often a harvest festival in the Willcox area.

## Willcox Playa

South of town, this huge, sometimes dry, lake is the winter home of approximately 10,000 sandhill cranes. The best way to see them is to drive southeast on Hwy 186 a few miles and then take the left fork for Kansas Settlement. At dawn, the birds fly out of the playa and land in the corn stubble fields around Kansas Settlement, where they feed during the day, flying back to the playa at sunset. In January, the chamber arranges a 'wings over Willcox Sandhill Cranes Celebration' with guided tours to good viewing sites and related birding activities.

## Special Events

Rex Allen Days, with a PRCA rodeo, country music and dancing, and local arts & crafts is held in early October.

## Places to Stay

**Camping** At *KOA* (☎ 384 3212), west of I-10 exit 340, tent sites are $10 and RV sites with full hookups are $16; amenities include a swimming pool, showers and a recreation area. *Lifestyle RV Resort* (☎ 384 3303), 622 N Haskell Ave, has a pool, spa, recreation area and RV sites with hookups for $15. Tents are allowed.

*Cochise Stronghold* is a USFS-run campground (Douglas Ranger District) in the Dragoon Mountains within Coronado National Forest, about 30 miles southwest of Willcox. The great Apache leader Cochise spent time in this beautiful canyon. The campground is at about 5000 feet, has good hiking opportunities, 20 sites for $6 and water but no RV hookups or showers. Though the road is unpaved, cars get through except after heavy rain. The campground is open year round, but the water is turned off from about October to March.

**Hotels & Motels** There are several cheap places offering rooms in the low $30s or the $20s if they're not busy and you bargain. They include the *Motel 6* (☎ 384 2201, fax 384 0194) at I-10 exit 340, the *Royal Western Lodge* (☎ 384 2266), 590 S Haskell Ave, and the *Sands Motel* (☎ 384 3501), 400 S Haskell Ave. All these have pools. Others include the *Desert Breeze Motel* (☎ 384 4636), 556 N Haskell Ave, which usually has the cheapest rooms, the *Motel 8* (☎ 384 3270, 384 3391), 331 N Haskell Ave, the *Desert Inn of Willcox* (☎ 384 3577, fax 384 5371), 704 S Haskell Ave, and the *Riteway Motel* (☎ 384 4655), 660 N Haskell Ave.

The *Econo Lodge* (☎ 384 4222, fax 384 3785), at I-10 exit 340, has large bare rooms in the $40s and $50s. The most comfortable in town is the *Best Western Plaza Inn* (☎ 384 3556, fax 384 2679), 1100 W Rex Allen Drive, with a pool, spa, restaurant and bar with room service. Rates here are in the $50 and $60s, including breakfast, but they sometimes go up for special events. A few mini-suites are in the $80s. All rooms have coffeemakers, and several have refrigerators and whirlpool baths as well.

Near Pearce, 20 miles south of Willcox, is the *Grapevine Canyon Ranch* (☎ 826 3185, 1 (800) 245 9202, fax 826 3636), PO Box 302, Pearce, 85625. This is a working cattle ranch offering horseback rides and cattle roundups. The staff here emphasizes personal attention and small riding groups, so the rides are varied depending on skill level. There is a pool, spa and recreation room. Rates are about $200 a day including meals and riding. No children under 12 are allowed. There are 12 rooms and a two-night minimum stay is required, or four nights when they are busy.

## Places to Eat

There are plenty of restaurants, none outstanding. The one in the Best Western is probably the best. *La Kachina* (☎ 384 2175), 905 W Rex Allen Drive, and *Brown's Ice Cream Parlour* (☎ 384 2057), 135 E Maley St, both serve ostrich meat, if you're seeking a new culinary experience.

## Getting There & Away

Greyhound (☎ 384 2183) buses stop at 144 S Haskell Ave several times a day on its runs down I-10.

## AROUND WILLCOX
### Muleshoe Ranch

This is cooperatively managed by the Nature Conservancy, BLM and USFS. It is a good place for birding and wildlife observation. The ranch is about 30 miles northwest of Willcox (leave town via Airport Rd) in the foothills of the rugged Galiuro Mountains, which forms the watershed of seven permanently flowing streams – an important ecosystem. At the ranch headquarters (☎ 586 7072), RR 1, Box 1542, Willcox, 85643, is a visitors center, nature trail, cabins for rent by reservation and a camping area ($6, cold showers, no RV hookups). Primitive backcountry camping is allowed by permit and there are hiking and horse trails. Call about road conditions – it's an unpaved road.

### Dos Cabezas

This village of a few tumbledown houses and trailers is 15 miles southeast of Willcox. There's an interesting one-man museum of local artifacts collected by Orville Mickens. You'll see his house on the left side as you drive towards the Chiricahuas and a sign will indicate if the collection is open or not. Call 384 3481 in advance.

## CHIRICAHUA MOUNTAINS & NATIONAL MONUMENT

The strangely eroded volcanic rocks of the Chiricahua Mountains are unlike any other in Arizona. Geologists aren't sure exactly how these ranks of hundreds of standing pinnacles and balanced rocks were formed, but clearly they are the result of millions of years of erosion by the weather. This is one of the smaller and more remote NPS areas in the Southwest, but it can be reached easily enough by paved road and the scenery alone makes it a worthwhile trip.

The monument itself is small and encompasses the wildest and weirdest of the geological formations. It is surrounded to the north, east and south by the Coronado National Forest (see Douglas, Sierra Vista and Safford for the nearest USFS offices), which has interesting rock formations as well as camping and nature study.

There's a lot more here than just weird geology, however. The remoteness of the area makes it attractive to wildlife. The Chiricahuas were the last place in the USA where a jaguar was sighted, way back in 1912, but even today there is a good chance of seeing deer, coatis and javelinas. Mountain lions, bobcats and bears are sighted many times a year on the hiking trails within the monument. The Chiricahuas are the nearest high mountains to the Mexican mountain ranges and several Mexican bird species are found here, including the Mexican chickadee and elegant trogon (although the latter is found east of the monument itself, in the Cave Creek Canyon in the National Forest near Portal). The highest peak is 9795-foot Chiricahua Peak, just south of the monument in the national forest.

Apart from geology and wildlife, there is history and architecture in the form of the turn-of-the-century Faraway Ranch, built in the early part of the century and now restored and open to visitation on tours led by monument rangers.

## Climate & When to Go

March to May are by far the busiest months, due in part to the pleasant spring climate. By June, daytime highs average around 90°F and visitation drops substantially. July through early September are the wettest months, with frequent summer storms. In August of 1993, a record-setting four inches of rain fell in six hours, although usually that is almost the entire month's rainfall. Beware of flash floods after summer storms. Visitation picks up again after the summer rains, and then drops during the winter. Freezing overnight temperatures are normal from late November through February and the trails, though open year round, may be snow-covered.

## Orientation & Information

The monument is almost 40 miles southwest of Willcox by paved road and there is no gas along this route. From the south it is 70 miles by paved road from Douglas. Access to the monument from the east is limited to a dirt road to Cave Creek Canyon. This road is passable to ordinary vehicles in good weather and is closed by snow in winter. From the north, the unpaved Apache Pass Rd is normally open all year to all vehicles except after bad weather. Both of these dirt roads have some rough stretches and may be problematic for large RVs and vehicles with trailers, so inquire locally.

The monument is open 24 hours a day. The visitors center (☎ 824 3560) is open from 8 am to 5 pm daily (except Christmas) and has a slide show about the Chiricahuas, a small exhibit area and a bookstore. Ranger-led programs are offered from March to October but may be curtailed in midsummer. The monument offers no gas, food or lodging (except camping). Admission is $4 per private vehicle or $2 per bicycle, foot or bus passenger and Golden Age, Access, Eagle Passes are honored. Further information is available from the Superintendent, Chiricahua National Monument, Dos Cabeza Route, Box 6500, Willcox, 85643.

## Scenic Drive

The Bonita Canyon Scenic Drive is a paved eight-mile road climbing from the entrance gate (at a little over 5000 feet) to Massai Point at 6870 feet. The visitors center is two miles along this road from the entrance station. There are several scenic pullouts and trailheads along this road. The views from Massai Point are the most spectacular, so it's worth going all the way.

## Faraway Ranch

Begun in 1888, the ranch was built during a 30 year period. Originally a pioneer's cattle ranch, it became one of Arizona's earliest guest ranches in the 1920s. The ranch is near the monument entrance and a short hiking trail leads to it and on to a cabin dating from the same period. To go inside the ranch, you need to go on a ranger-led tour which is free and offered several times a day during the busy season, less often in other months. Call the visitors center for a schedule.

## Hiking

Numerous hiking trails wind through the monument. These range from easy flat loops of 0.2 miles to strenuous climbs of over seven miles. None are accessible to wheelchairs. A park map showing the scenic drive and trails is available for free upon arrival. A detailed hiking guide with descriptions of all the trails is available for 25¢. Generally, the short, flat trails west of the visitors center and campground are the easiest and are good for birding and wildlife observations. The trails east of the visitors center lead into rugged mountain country with the most spectacular geology.

A hikers shuttle bus leaves daily from the visitors center and camping area at either 7:45 am or 8:30 am or both times if there is demand. It goes up to Massai Point and is free. This is not a sightseeing bus. It drops hikers off at the top and allows them to return to the visitors center and campground by hiking downhill.

## Places to Stay

No wilderness camping is permitted, so hikers must use the trails for day use only. There is a campground with 24 sites about 0.2 miles north of the visitors center. There is water but no hookups or showers and the sites are too small for large RVs and trailers. During the busy months, the campground is full by noon and may be full earlier on weekends. Sites are available on a first-come, first-served basis and cost $7.

If the campground is full, there are numerous campgrounds in the Coronado

National Forest south of the monument. Rangers will give you a map (there's one outside the visitors center if the center is closed) showing where the campgrounds are. These usually have space available.

### Beyond the Monument

The Chiricahua Mountains extend north, east and south of the monument and are on Coronado National Forest land. Pinery Canyon Rd (closed in winter) is an attractive and wild drive southeast of the monument entrance station through the national forest emerging on paved highways at Portal, where food and gas are available. From Portal, the paved road continues east into New Mexico. A gravel road, open all year, goes north to I-10.

There are several USFS campgrounds along the Pinery Canyon Rd. On the east side of the Chiricahuas, near Portal, is Cave Creek Canyon, which is one of the best places in the USA to see or hear both the elegant and the much rarer eared trogon, as well as the Mexican chickadee, all birds normally found in the mountains of Mexico. The elegant trogon nests here from April to June and is occasionally sighted in winter. The eared trogon has been heard or seen only in the fall.

Also near Portal is the American Museum of Natural History Southwestern Field Station (☎ 558 2396), which has a bird list for the area. Cabins here are usually filled with researchers but are sometimes available for rent. Nature study programs are occasionally offered.

The dirt Rucker Canyon Rd, further south, also enters the national forest and has several campgrounds along it.

North of the monument is the **Fort Bowie National Historic Site**, where there is a ranger station (☎ 847 2500) and small interpretive exhibit. Only the ruined foundations of the 1862 fort are still standing. It can be reached by taking the unpaved Apache Pass (5115 feet) road to Bowie. A mile or two north of the pass (which can become impassable to ordinary cars after heavy rains), there is a parking lot from which you hike 1.5 miles to the historic site. (Carry water and sun protection in summer, and watch for rattlesnakes and flash floods.) There is no vehicular access. The ranger station is open from 8 am to 5 pm; admission is free.

ARIZONA

# New Mexico

# Facts about New Mexico

New Mexico is as much a cultural experience as a place to visit. The tri-culturalism of the state, with its strong Indian, Hispanic and Anglo heritage and influences, is often remarked upon. The USA prides itself on its multicultural diversity, so what's the big deal about New Mexico's three cultures? The state's tri-culturalism is simply older and more apparently seamless than in the rest of the country, and many visitors glide almost effortlessly from one to another.

Some of the country's most inspiring ancient Indian sites are found in the northwestern corner of the state. Here, the Chaco Culture National Historical Park is my favorite of all the many southwestern archaeological sites. It is more than just a ruin: It has a sense of timelessness and spirituality which is almost palpable. Not far away is the living mesa-top town of Acoma Pueblo, which has been continuously inhabited for about eight centuries. Other pueblos are also centuries old and provide insight into life here before the continent received its name of America.

Thousands of years before advanced Indian cultures were building massive stone buildings and towns, nomadic hunters and gatherers were wandering through the area tracking woolly mammoths and giant sloths and were themselves being tracked by saber-toothed tigers. The continent's oldest known Indian sites have been discovered in eastern New Mexico: Folsom, where the remains of Folsom man, dating back 10,800 years, were uncovered; and near Clovis, where items from Clovis culture date back 11,000 years.

New Mexico's European history, by comparison, is very recent. Nevertheless, the late-16th- and early-17th-century Spanish buildings are the oldest non-Indian structures in the country, predating the arrival of the Pilgrims in New England. The old center of Santa Fe is as historic a place as any in the country and attracts and charms throngs of visitors.

The natural beauty of the state comprises many unique features, not the least of which is the luminescent quality of the light. This has attracted many artists during the 20th century, the best known of whom is Georgia O'Keeffe, whose canvases superbly capture the vivid colors of the landscape and sky. The south part of New Mexico has the huge and empty dunes of the White Sands National Monument as well as one of the most impressive and accessible natural cave systems in the world at Carlsbad Caverns National Park.

With such a combination of culture, light and landscape, it is no wonder that New Mexico hosts travelers from all over the world – and beyond! The area has had among the highest number of UFO sightings anywhere (there's even a museum dedicated to them in Roswell) – maybe the next wave of tourists will be from a different galaxy!

## Recent History

The territory of New Mexico included Arizona and some of Colorado when the USA annexed the land from Mexico in 1848. When the territories of Colorado and Arizona were proclaimed in 1861 and 1863, respectively, New Mexico's present borders were defined.

During the American Civil War, the Confederate forces tried to control New Mexico in an effort to keep access to the ports of California, but they were defeated by the Union in the second of two major battles in

## New Mexico Trivia

**Statehood:**
    6 January 1912 (47th state)
**Area:**
    121,598 sq miles (5th largest state)
**Highest Point:**
    Wheeler Peak, 13,161 feet
**Lowest Point:**
    Red Bluff Reservoir (southeast Utah), 2817 feet
**Population (1993):**
    1,616,483 (36th most populous state)
**Percentage over the age of five speaking a language other than English at home:**
    35.5% (highest in USA)
**Nickname:** Land of Enchantment
**State Capital:** Santa Fe
**State Motto:** It grows as it goes.
**State Bird:** Roadrunner
**State Mammal:** Black bear
**State Tree:** Piñon
**State Flower:**
    Soaptree yucca flower (only commercially viable state flower)
**State Gem:** Turquoise

Baked yucca fruit tastes like sweet potato.

1862. After the Civil War came the Indian Wars, particularly against the Navajos and Apaches in western New Mexico and eastern Arizona (see Arizona). Despite the wars with the Indians, settlers in the form of cowboys and miners began to arrive in large numbers in the 1870s. Cattle drives from Texas up the Pecos River Valley into the high plains of eastern New Mexico were some of the largest ever known, with tens of thousands of head of cattle moving across the land. The miners ventured even further west, especially into the mountains around Silver City.

The arrival of the railroads in the late 1870s opened the state to a period of economic boom, with settlers arriving and cattle and ores being shipped to the east where there was a ready market for them. Fortunes were made and lives were lost in the lawless days of the Wild West. Most famous among the many violent incidents was the Lincoln County War, which pitted rival ranch factions against one another from 1878 to 1881. A major player in this incident was Billy the Kid, perhaps the West's most famous outlaw even though he was gunned down at the early age of 21. The violence and lack of law and order dissuaded the federal government from granting statehood to the territory of New Mexico. A second factor was an unfounded distrust of the Hispanic population by the Anglo powers in Washington, DC.

This distrust was partially dispelled by the Hispanic soldiers from New Mexico who fought with distinction in the Spanish-American war of 1898. The lawlessness of the late 19th century was brought under control and, by the early 20th century, New Mexico was ready for statehood. After a drawn-out process, New Mexico became the 47th state on 6 January 1912.

As with most of the Southwest, the lack of water greatly limited the state's growth. The construction of the Elephant Butte Dam on the Rio Grande in 1916 began to relieve this. The 1920s were an important decade for New Mexicans. Pueblo Indians gained legal control over their lands after white squatters tried to take them over, and

NEW MEXICO

NEW MEXICO

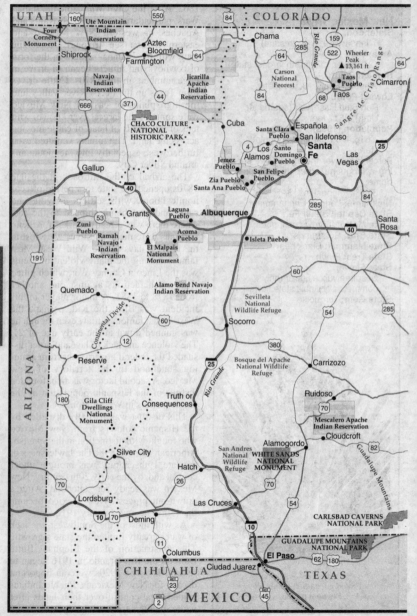

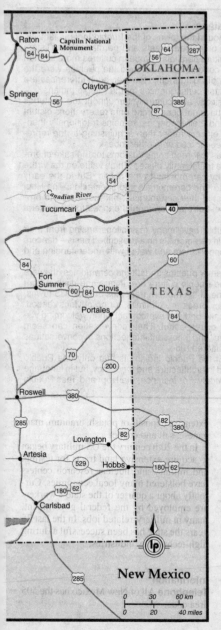

Raton
Capulin National Monument
64  84
Springer
56
Clayton
56
OKLAHOMA
64  287
56
87  385
54
Canadian River
Tucumcari
40
84
60
Fort Sumner
60  84  Clovis
TEXAS
Portales
84
70
200
Roswell
380
285
Lovington
82  380
Artesia
529  Hobbs
82
180  62
180  62
Carlsbad
New Mexico
285

0    30    60 km
0    20    40 miles

all Indians won US citizenship (although it was not until 1947 that they were allowed to vote). The 1920s also saw the arrival of many artists to the fledgling artist colonies in the Santa Fe and Taos areas.

The Great Depression of the 1930s hit New Mexico hard, although various WPA projects served to alleviate the misery somewhat. WW II revived the state's economy and initiated perhaps the most important project of the war. The Manhattan Project at Los Alamos saw the secret development and testing of the nuclear bomb, which was finally deployed against Japan in 1945 and quickly led to an end to the war. Los Alamos remains an important military research and development center, as does the White Sands Missile Range.

The second half of the 20th century has seen great population growth in New Mexico and throughout the Southwest. This created pressure on the oldest inhabitants of the state, the Indians and the Hispanic inhabitants who had farmed the land for generations. In 1970, the Taos Pueblo Indians contested the USFS use of their sacred Blue Lake and surrounding region in the Carson National Forest, and Congress set aside the contested area for sole use of the tribe. Disagreements over the land and resource rights continue today, usually taking the form of lengthy legal wranglings.

## Economy

Although the Spanish established missions and haciendas during their first two centuries in New Mexico, agricultural growth was not extensive due to the aridity of the region and Indian opposition to being forced to work Spanish farms. However, in the 18th century, the development of farming, mining and ranching expanded. Not long after Mexico won its independence from Spain, the Santa Fe Trail opened trade with the USA to the east. Despite opposition from Indian tribes, ranchers and farmers slowly took over the state's extensive grasslands, and in 1879 the Santa Fe Railroad arrived, fueling the growth of the cattle industry during the next decade. Ranching continues

NEW MEXICO

## Breaking Stereotypes of Pueblo Indians

People of European heritage have always found the towns of the Pueblo Indians familiar, at least upon first impression. Seeing the organized streets and permanent, multistory buildings, they have inferred that Pueblo culture parallels European cultures more so than do other Indian cultures. In fact, Spanish conquistadors believed the pueblos were the fabled 'Seven Cities of Gold' and set about pillaging them. However, such inferences are misguided and one-sided, and have had harsh consequences for the Pueblo Indians.

The Pueblo villages have survived physically and culturally throughout the centuries despite barrages of intrusions. Inhabitants have not been forced onto reservations distant and disparate from their original homes, and their leadership remains traditionally theocratic: The religious leaders choose tribal officers rather than acquiescing to the representative system of government that has been forced onto other tribes.

But intrusions have forced Pueblo peoples to forego some customs for the sake of preserving others. The Hopi, for example, have traditionally placed a high value on the virtue of hospitality, which led them to open many ceremonies to the public. But in the early 1990s, excessive tourism threatened to turn the ceremonials into spectacles. The Hopi could have profited from the tourist interest in their ceremonials, but they opted to preserve their religious integrity by closing most of their ceremonial dances to the general public.

The ceremonies that are open to the public have many restrictions arising from their spiritual nature. Tribal members participate in ceremonials on a prescribed basis – dancers are carefully chosen, and the observers support them and watch with understanding and appreciation.

When non-Indian visitors are allowed to enter pueblos and attend ceremonies, they are often surprised to find that the pueblos and Pueblo culture are unique and distinct from Anglo culture. The pueblos have few or none of the modern trappings of other US towns, such as cars, phones and neon signs. Many areas are off-limits, for no obvious reason. Pueblo Indians rarely offer a hearty handshake or direct eye-contact when welcoming visitors, because eye-contact is considered disrespectful. Their conversation can seem muted or limited, but quiet listening is valued, and incessant interjections in conversations such as 'Uh huh' and 'Oh, really?' are considered rude.

Another assumption visitors make about the Pueblo Indians is that only one Pueblo culture exists. The Pueblo groups are united in architecture and theocracy, but in language and dialect, religion and ritual, they differ widely. For instance, the Hopi and Taos Pueblo

to be important to the state's economy today despite extensive overgrazing.

The scarcity of water that had impeded farming efforts and population growth was greatly alleviated by the Elephant Butte Dam on the Rio Grande. Today major crops include hay, sorghum, onions, potatoes, piñon nuts, chile peppers and pinto beans. However, population growth and agricultural expansion in both New Mexico and Colorado have called into question whether the state will have enough water to support more fast growth.

In addition to agriculture, mining has also played a considerable role in the state's economy. New Mexico has tapped into

extensive deposits of potash, uranium, manganese, salt and copper.

In the 20th century the US military began to acquire extensive land tracts for testing, and military and nuclear research centers have bolstered many local economies. Currently about a quarter of the state's workers are employed by the federal government, many in military-related jobs. In the last 25 years the state has been successful at luring high-technology industries.

## Information

**Telephone** All of New Mexico has the 505 area code.

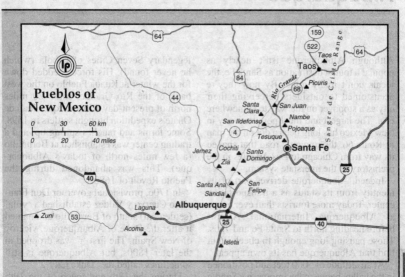

**Pueblos of New Mexico**

0        30        60 km
0      20      40 miles

Indians are both Pueblo tribes living in ancient towns, but their languages and customs are as different as the Serbs' and the Croats' (although, thankfully, the Indians' differences are not expressed with violence). The same differences apply to the many pueblos in the Four Corners Area, where several languages and dialects are spoken and customs distinct. These disparities arose not only from the distances between the pueblos but also from the assimilation of various tribes into many of them, sometimes centuries ago.

Being prepared to encounter and respect these differences will help non-Indian visitors to focus on each pueblo's unique traditions. It's also important to remember that each pueblo has its own rules pertaining to acceptable behavior, particularly in the realm of photography, sketching and other forms of recording sights and sounds. ■

**Time** New Mexico is on Mountain Time, which is one hour later than the West Coast two hours earlier than the East Coast, and seven hours behind Greenwich Mean Time.

**Driving Laws** You must be at least 16 years old, or at least 15 with parental consent, to obtain a drivers license. Drivers and front-seat passengers are required to wear a safety belt. Children under age 11 must use child restraints. You must be over 16 to obtain a motorcycle license. Motorcycle helmets are required for rider and passenger if under 18. The blood alcohol concentration over which you are legally considered drunk while driving is 0.10. It is illegal to have an open container of alcohol in your car while driving.

**Drinking Laws** You must be 21 to buy a drink in a store, bar or restaurant. Beer, wine and spirits are sold in grocery stores and liquor stores from 6 am to midnight, except Sunday, when sales begin at noon. Restaurants must have licenses to serve alcohol; some licenses are limited to beer and wine. Sales of alcohol stop at 1 am and bars close at 2 am except on Sundays when bars are open from noon until midnight. Alcohol is prohibited on Indian reservations.

# Albuquerque

Although Albuquerque isn't nearly as popular a tourist destination as Santa Fe, the locals don't really mind. By now they're accustomed to outsiders perceiving their city as a stopover on the way to somewhere else. The largest and most populous city in New Mexico has long been a dot on the map of Route 66, the romantic road that snaked its way from Chicago to Los Angeles in the prehistory of the interstate system.

Indeed, Albuquerque derives part of its identity from its status as a transportation center. Today more tourists than ever arrive at Albuquerque International Airport before heading north to Santa Fe and Taos. Those pausing long enough to check it out find that Albuquerque has its own appeal.

At an altitude of 5000 feet and positioned in the valley between the impressive Sandia Mountains to the east and the Rio Grande to the west, Albuquerque exists in a comfortable life zone. Cottonwood trees shade city streets, and the weather is friendly. Winter brings snow to the mountains sufficient for skiers' needs but not enough to make for driving hazards in the valley, and while summer days can reach 100°F, the nights are always forgiving and cool.

Native, Hispanic and Anglo Americans today make up the bulk of the city's 400,000 residents. The story of Albuquerque rests in the coexistence of these three cultures as evidenced in the regional art, architecture and food.

## HISTORY
The Anasazi were the area's first permanent occupants, probably arriving in the sixth century. They planted corn, beans and squash, and constructed dwellings of adobe and brick along the banks of the Rio Grande. These ancestors of the Pueblo Indians ultimately abandoned the region around 1300.

In 1540 the Spanish explorer Francisco Coronado arrived in search of riches in the legendary Seven Cities of Cibola (which he never found). His forces bedded down for the winter at Kuaua Pueblo on the west bank of the Rio Grande, some 20 miles north of present-day Albuquerque. Juan de Oñate's expedition brought settlers in 1598. Some farms and ranches sprung up, and a trading center was established at Bernalillo (a few miles north of today's Albuquerque). This was abandoned during the Pueblo Revolt of 1680.

In 1706, provisional governor Don Francisco Cuervo y Valdez established a 'villa' (settlement) south of Bernalillo and named it after the Duke of Alburquerque, viceroy of New Spain. The first 'r' was dropped in the later 1800s, but Albuquerque is still sometimes called the 'Duke City'.

During the 18th and much of the 19th centuries, the villa was a dusty trading center along the trail linking Mexico with Santa Fe. Close-knit families of Spanish descent accounted for most of the population. They lived around the central plaza today called Old Town.

Albuquerque changed with the arrival of the railroad in 1880. The station, constructed about two miles east of the plaza, gave rise to a new town reminiscent of the

East Coast in design and attitude, and many businesses relocated there. Outsiders arrived in numbers enough to change the ethnic makeup of the area. By the time it was incorporated as a town in 1885, Albuquerque had become predominantly Anglo.

Growth continued in the 20th century. Route 66, the easiest way to travel east to west through New Mexico, brought a steady stream of traffic right through the middle of town. During the 1930s, motels, restaurants and shops arose along Central Ave to service those motorists.

## ORIENTATION

Two interstate highways, I-25 (north-south) and I-40 (east-west), intersect in Albuquerque. An approximate grid surrounds that intersection, the major boundaries of which are Paseo del Norte Drive to the north, Central Ave to the south, Rio Grande Blvd to the west and Tramway Blvd to the east. Central Ave is the main street, passing through Old Town, downtown, and the university and state fairgrounds areas.

Street addresses often conclude with a directional designation, for example, Central Ave NE. The center is where

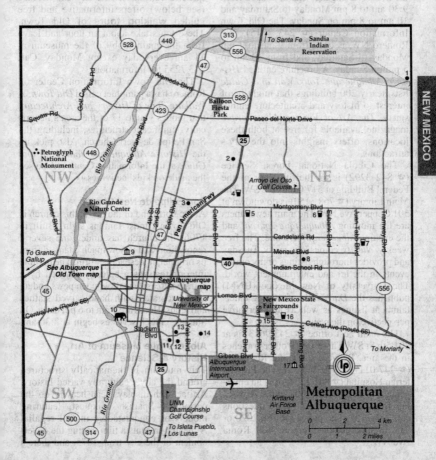

NEW MEXICO

Central crosses the railroad tracks, just east of downtown (see Albuquerque map). Any location north of Central and east of the tracks would have a NE designation. Any-place south of Central and west of the tracks is called SW.

## INFORMATION

The Albuquerque Convention & Visitors Bureau (☎ 243 3696), 121 Tijeras Ave NE, is open Monday to Friday from 8 am to 5 pm, and has information on Albuquerque and New Mexico. The airport branch, near the first-level baggage claim, is open from 9:30 am to 8 pm Monday to Saturday and 10 am to 8 pm on Sunday. The Old Town Information Center (☎ 243 3215), 303 Romero NW, is open from 9 am to 7 pm Monday to Saturday, and from 10 am to 5 pm on Sunday. A brochure entitled *Historic Albuquerque Tour Map and Guide* lists nearly 200 buildings that might be of interest to history and architecture enthu-siasts. *The Art of Visiting Albuquerque* magazine, available for free at both these locations, offers insights into the city's attractions.

The Cibola National Forest Service (☎ 842 3292) is on the 5th floor of the Federal Building at 517 Gold Ave SW. The Main Library (☎ 768 5150) is downtown at 501 Copper Ave NW. The main newspapers are the morning *Albuquerque Journal* and the evening *Albuquerque Tribune*. The free weekly *NuCity* comes out every Tuesday and provides thorough listings of upcoming events in the art and entertainment world. The University of New Mexico (UNM) publishes the *Daily Lobo*, featuring enter-tainment listings as well as an alternative perspective on the news.

The main post office (☎ 243 9613) is at 201 5th St SW. There are 19 other branches in the area. Recycle at Capital Recycling (☎ 247 0117), 2330 2nd SW. The Presby-terian Hospital (☎ 841 1234, or in an emer-gency 841 1111) is at 1100 Central Ave SE. For free answers to health-care questions call 224 7737. The police (☎ 768 2020 or 911 in emergencies) are at 400 Roma Ave NW.

## OLD TOWN AREA

From its founding in 1706 until the arrival of the railroad in 1880, Old Town was the spiritual, social and geographical center of Albuquerque. Many original period struc-tures still stand, making it the city's most popular tourist attraction. Built around a central plaza, Old Town is a four-block his-torical and architectural museum, with many art galleries and souvenir shops. The area is bounded by Central Ave, Rio Grande Blvd, Mountain Rd and 19th St.

From April to November, the Albuquer-que Museum of Art, History and Science (see below) offers informative and free guided **walking tours** of Old Town. These tours take about an hour and leave from the main lobby of the museum at 11 am every day except Monday. Call 243 7255 for information.

The Old Town Information Center on Romero has a pamphlet called *Old Town: A Walking Tour of History and Architecture* that guides you to 17 of the area's histori-cally significant structures, including the San Felipe de Neri Church. Also pick up the *Historic Albuquerque Tour Map and Guide* at the Information Center. (Also see the aside on kids' activities.)

### San Felipe de Neri Church

At the north end of the plaza, this church is Old Town's most famous sight. Built in 1706, the church has undergone several renovations and is now much changed from its original modest adobe form. The humble interior features a balcony reached by a spiral staircase, small wooden pews and an altar decorated with hand-carved statues and icons. Hours are 7 am to 6 pm daily. On Sunday, church services begin at 8:30 am.

### Albuquerque Museum of Art, History & Science

This museum is thematically structured around the city's culturally varied history. Artifact-rich displays lean heavily on the period of Spanish conquest, featuring models of conquistadors in full regalia. A theater presents a film tracing the devel-opment of the city from 1875, and there's also a gallery exhibiting works by New Mexican artists. The museum (☎ 242 4600), 2000 Mountain Rd NW, is open from 9 am to 5 pm Tuesday to Saturday, and admission is free. It is closed on holidays.

## New Mexico Museum of Natural History

This museum (☎ 841 8837), 1801 Mountain Rd NW, is just outside the Plaza area. The museum features an interactive walk through 4.6 billion years of Southwestern natural history, taking you back to the dinosaur age, down into an 'active' volcano, into New Mexico's Ice Age and then to the region's saltwater era. The *Evolator* (evolution elevator) transports visitors through 38 million years of New Mexico's geologic and evolutionary history, through the use of video technology, while the *Origins* exhibit traces the creation of the universe from the Big Bang to the present. Kids love the reconstructed dinosaurs displayed next to replicated skeletons, and the Natu-

ralist Center provides an opportunity for them to get their little hands on snakes, frogs and fossils. The museum is open 9 am to 5 pm, seven days a week. Admission is $4.20 for adults, $3.15 for seniors and students, and $1.05 for kids ages three to 11.

The **Dynamax Theater** within the museum, features huge-screen 3D 'movies' that give viewers the sensation of physical participation. Programs are shown hourly and last 40 minutes. Admission is $4.20 for adults, $3.15 for students and seniors, and $2 for kids.

## Rattlesnake Museum

This museum (☎ 242 6569), 202 San Felipe NW, claims the largest public collection of different species of rattlers in the world. Some 40 snakes are on exhibit at any one time. The focus is on education, and the curator Bob Myers stresses the importance of the rattlesnake to the ecosystem. Although the snakes are safely encased, anyone who views them receives a Certifi-

NEW MEXICO

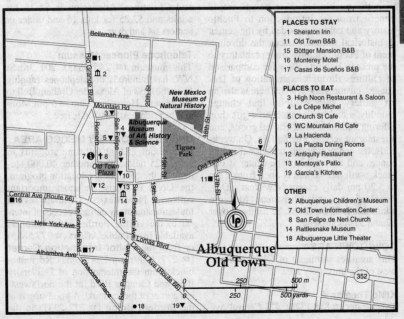

**PLACES TO STAY**
1  Sheraton Inn
11  Old Town B&B
15  Böttger Mansion B&B
16  Monterey Motel
17  Casas de Sueños B&B

**PLACES TO EAT**
3  High Noon Restaurant & Saloon
4  Le Crêpe Michel
5  Church St Cafe
6  WC Mountain Rd Cafe
9  La Hacienda
10  La Placita Dining Rooms
12  Antiquity Restaurant
13  Montoya's Patio
19  Garcia's Kitchen

**OTHER**
2  Albuquerque Children's Museum
7  Old Town Information Center
8  San Felipe de Neri Church
14  Rattlesnake Museum
18  Albuquerque Little Theater

New Mexico Museum of Natural History

Albuquerque Museum of Art, History & Science

Tiguex Park

Old Town Plaza

Bellamah Ave

Rio Grande Blvd

Mountain Rd

Romero

San Felipe

20th St

19th St

18th St

15th St

Old Town Rd

Central Ave (Route 66)

Rio Grande Blvd

New York Ave

San Pasquale Ave

Lomas Blvd

Alhambra Ave

Checoma Place

Central Ave (Route 66)

**Albuquerque Old Town**

352

0   250   500 m
0   250   500 yards

●18   19▼

Old Town is home to the world's largest
public collection of rattlesnakes.

cate of Bravery. The museum is open 10 am
to 7 pm daily and to 9 pm in summer.
Admission is $2. There is also a gift shop,
packed with reptilian curios.

### Indian Pueblo Cultural Center
Just north of old town above I-40, this
center (☎ 843 7270), 2401 12th St NW, is
owned and run by an association of New
Mexico's 19 pueblos. Anyone planning to
visit the pueblos in their travels would
benefit from the introduction to Pueblo
history and culture provided by the center.
A historical museum traces the development of Pueblo cultures from prehistory to
the present. Exhibits allow for comparison
of cultures through examination of languages, customs and crafts. There is also an
art gallery with exhibits that change
monthly, a children's museum, a gift shop
offering authentic hand-crafted goods, and
a restaurant serving Pueblo fare. On weekends, the center presents traditional Indian
dances and art exhibits. The center is one
block north of I-40 and is open from 9 am
to 5:30 pm daily except New Year's Day,
Thanksgiving and Christmas. Museum
admission is $3 for adults, $2 for those over
62 and $1 for students.

### DOWNTOWN AREA
This area lies southeast of Old Town and
west of the university area.

### KiMo Theater
This theater (☎ 848 1370), 423 Central Ave
NW, was built in 1927. The architect, Carl
Boller, created a kind of Pueblo Art Deco
in the KiMo using impressions gathered on
visits to Indian pueblos and reservations.
KiMo took its name from the Tiwa phrase
meaning 'king of its kind'.

Today, the city-owned KiMo is a community arts center, featuring all types of
entertainment. (See Performing Arts section under Entertainment below.) The
adornments inside, including steer-skull
light fixtures with glowing eyes, must be
seen to be believed. The theater may be
toured during performances, or between
9 am and 5 pm Monday to Friday.

### Rio Grande Zoological Park
This zoo (☎ 843 7413), 903 10th St SW, on
60 shady acres along the river is home to
more than 1300 animals from around the
world, including a rare snow leopard. There
is also a children's petting zoo. The zoo is
open from 9 am to 5 pm Monday to Friday
and 9 am to 6 pm on the weekends. It is
closed on New Year's Day, Thanksgiving
and Christmas. Admission is $4.25 for
adults and $2.25 for kids 15 and under or
seniors 64 and over.

### Telephone Pioneer Museum
This museum (☎ 245 5883), 201 3rd St
NW, has hundreds of telephones ranging
from the days of Alexander Graham Bell to
the present. Hours are 9 am to 5 pm Monday to Friday. Admission is free.

### UNIVERSITY OF NEW MEXICO AREA
With about 25,000 full-time students in
some 125 fields, plus another 40,000 students in the continuing education program,
the UNM is easily the most important
college in New Mexico. There are several
museums and many cultural events of interest to the visitor. Further information is
available from Public Affairs (☎ 277 5813)
or from the **Visitor Information Center**
(☎ 277 1989), on Las Lomas Rd half a
block from the intersection of University
Blvd and Campus Blvd (at the northwestern corner of the campus). A good stop is at
the **Student Union** (☎ 277 2331) in the

center of campus, where you can pick up a campus map, schmooze with students, get a bite to eat and examine current student art on display.

Campus Tours (☎ 277 5161) are available and last about 30 minutes. All museums are closed on legal holidays.

## Maxwell Museum of Anthropology

This UNM museum (☎ 277 4404), just off Redondo Drive near the Visitor Information Center, has a permanent 'People of the Southwest' exhibit tracing human history in the region through pottery. A fabricated dig, complete with tools, demonstrates the painstaking methods of archaeology. There are other changing exhibits as well, and the gift shop has a good selection of scholarly books. Hours are from 9 am to 4 pm on weekdays, 10 am to 4 pm on Saturday and 12 pm to 4 pm on Sunday. Donations are accepted.

## University Art Museum

This collection (☎ 277 4001) is in the Fine Arts building at Redondo Drive and Cornell Drive on the south side of campus. The smallish space is crammed with paintings, prints and sculptures from a permanent collection of 24,000 pieces, many of which highlight New Mexico's rich Hispanic tradition. The museum is renowned for its ample collection of photographs, and the interesting temporary exhibits change frequently. The museum is open from 9 am to 4 pm Tuesday to Friday, 5 to 8 pm Tuesday evenings, 1 to 4 pm Sunday, and during most weekend evening performances at adjoining Popejoy Hall.

Affiliated with the University Art Museum, the **Jonson Gallery** (☎ 277 4967), 1909 Las Lomas Rd, is the former home and studio of painter and longtime UNM professor Raymond Jonson. His modernist works, conspicuously devoid of Southwestern influence, are displayed during the summer months. During the rest of the year the gallery's changing exhibits include the works of his contemporaries. The gallery is open from 9 am to 4 pm Tuesday to Friday and from 5 to 8 pm Tuesday evenings.

## Other UNM Museums

The **Meteorite Museum** (☎ 277 2747) in Northrough Hall displays meteorites from around the world and answers the often-asked question 'Why do meteorites always land in deserted areas?' Hours are 9 am to noon and 1 to 4 pm Monday to Friday.

Next door in Castetter Hall, the **Biology Museum** (☎ 277 3411) is for biology buffs only. Although more research library than museum, this place nonetheless has a large collection of bio information on Southwestern plant and animal life. There are no regular hours, so call for an appointment.

The **Geology Museum** (☎ 277 4204), in the Earth and Planetary Sciences Building at 200 Yale Rd, is open from 8 am to 5 pm Monday to Friday except holidays.

## Spanish History Museum

South of UNM, this museum (☎ 268 9981), 2221 Lead Ave SE, is the creation of Elmer Martinez, who has spent a lifetime accumulating information and artifacts on the Spanish in the New World. The museum focuses on the Southwest, demonstrating the influence of Spanish settlers on New Mexico. Check out the wealth of information on coats of arms. Hours are from 10 am to 5 pm daily in summer and 1 to 5 pm the rest of the year. Admission is $1.

## Tamarind Institute

Highly regarded by lithographers, the Tamarind Institute (☎ 277 3901), 108 Cornell Drive SE, features modern lithographs, most of which are for sale. It's open weekdays from 9 am to 5 pm, and admission is free.

## Ernie Pyle Memorial Library

Once the home of the Pulitzer Prize-winning war correspondent, this branch of the city's public library pays tribute to the achievements of Ernie Pyle. Fondly remembered by veterans of WW II for his firsthand accounts of action in Europe and North Africa, Pyle was killed by enemy fire in the Pacific. The library (☎ 256 2065) is at 900 Girard Blvd SE. Hours are 12:30 to 9 pm Tuesday and Thursday, and 9 am to

**NEW MEXICO**

5:30 pm Wednesday, Friday and Saturday. Admission is free.

## OUTSIDE THE CITY
### Rio Grande Nature Center
The nature center (☎ 344 7240), 2901 Candelaria Rd NE, is a 270-acre reserve with gentle hiking trails winding through meadows and groves of trees. Raccoons, rodents and occasionally coyotes can be spotted. About 260 species of birds have been observed here.

The visitors center displays a range of insightful exhibits, has a glass-walled library overlooking a wetland home to turtles, ducks and beaver, and offers information on weekend educational programs. Admission is $1 or 50¢ for those under 17. Hours are 10 am to 5 pm daily except Thanksgiving and Christmas.

### Petroglyph National Monument
This monument (☎ 897 8814), 6900 Unser Blvd, is home to about 15,000 prehistoric rock etchings, most created around 1300 AD by Indians who hunted in the area. There is an ongoing battle between those who wish to preserve the petroglyphs

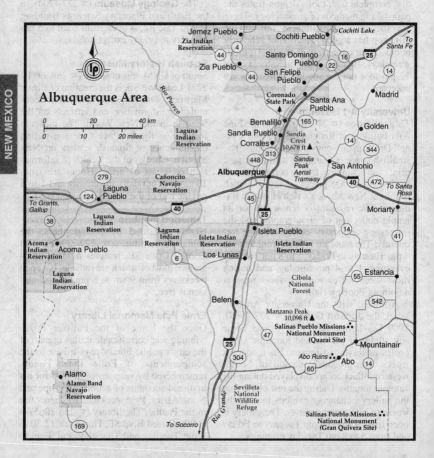

**Albuquerque Area**

0    20    40 km
0    10    20 miles

Jemez Pueblo
Zia Indian Reservation
Zia Pueblo
Cochiti Pueblo
Cochiti Lake
To Santa Fe
Santo Domingo Pueblo
San Felipe Pueblo
Coronado State Park
Santa Ana Pueblo
Madrid
Bernalillo
Golden
Sandia Pueblo
Sandia Crest 10,678 ft
Corrales
Sandia Peak Aerial Tramway
San Antonio
Albuquerque
To Santa Rosa
Cañoncito Navajo Reservation
Laguna Indian Reservation
Laguna Pueblo
To Grants, Gallup
Moriarty
Laguna Indian Reservation
Laguna Indian Reservation
Isleta Indian Reservation
Isleta Pueblo
Acoma Indian Reservation
Acoma Pueblo
Isleta Indian Reservation
Los Lunas
Estancia
Laguna Indian Reservation
Cibola National Forest
Belen
Manzano Peak 10,098 ft
Salinas Pueblo Missions National Monument (Quarai Site)
Mountainair
Abo Ruins
Abo
Alamo
Alamo Band Navajo Reservation
Sevilleta National Wildlife Refuge
Salinas Pueblo Missions National Monument (Gran Quivera Site)
To Socorro
Rio Puerco
Rio Grande

## Kids' Stuff

Albuquerque has a number of attractions that are great for kids. Although many of the attractions listed below are suitable for the adults and children, they are primarily aimed at kids.

The **Albuquerque Children's Museum** (☎ 842-5525), 800 Rio Grande Blvd NW, has programs and exhibits designed to give free reign to creativity and imagination. The museum's hands-on emphasis make the puppet theater, cartoon making and science experiments especially fun. Hours are 10 am to 5 pm Tuesday to Saturday and 12 to 5 pm on Sunday. Admission is $2 per person over two years old, and kids must be accompanied by an adult.

The **Explora Science Center** (☎ 842 6188), in the basement of the Galleria at 2nd St and Tijeras Ave, is an interactive museum geared toward teaching kids scientific principles. Thirty-five exhibits explore light, electricity, sound, motion, anatomy and more. Explora is open from 10 am to 5 pm Wednesday to Saturday and 12 pm to 5 pm on Sunday. Admission is $2 for adults and $1 for children ages four to 16.

Use **Cliff's Amusement Park** (☎ 881 9373), 4800 Osuna NE just off I-25, to reward your kids for being so patient and cooperative in the back seat. The park has about 25 rides, including a roller coaster, Ferris wheel and other traditional favorites. An unlimited ride pass costs $10. The park is open April to October.

At **Planet Fun** (☎ 294 1099), 2266 Wyoming NE, kids leave their shoes at the door and clamber on a giant jungle gym. The coolest feature is the 2000-sq-foot Laser Storm, where kids play 'laser tag' with beams of light. Planet Fun is open 10 am to 8 pm daily except Sunday, when it's open 11 am to 7 pm. Admission for two- to 12-year-olds is $5.50 on weekdays, $6.50 on weekends; parents get in free.

Adults might enjoy **The Beach** (☎ 345 6066), 3 Desert Surf Circle, just as much as the kids do. There are four water slides and a giant pool that creates five-foot swells for body surfers. If you're timid, tired or just a toddler, float down the Lazy River or in one of the kiddie pools. Splash all day for $10 April to Labor Day. ■

(the 'National' designation is a recent one) and those who want to further develop northwestern Albuquerque housing.

Four numbered trails of varying degrees of difficulty take you around the petroglyphs. The most challenging, Mesa Point Trail, climbs to the top of a lava flow and gives good views of the petroglyphs, the surroundings and the abutting housing developments.

The monument is open from 9 am to 6 pm in the summer and from 8 am to 5 pm in winter. Admission is $1 per car. There are picnic facilities, drinking water and bathrooms, but no camping.

### Sandia Peak Tramway

This 2.7-mile-long tramway (☎ 856 6419, 856 7325) is one of the world's longest, extending from the edge of the city to the top of Sandia Peak. It's a beautiful ride, especially at sunset. Starting in an Upper Sonoran desert realm of cholla cactus, the 18-minute ride soars through a variety of vegetational zones, passing above piñon pine, Rocky Mountain juniper and Douglas fir before reaching the Hudsonian-zone climate at the 10,300-foot summit. Here riders can enjoy an observation deck, a restaurant and trails for hikers and bikers. You can't bring your bike on the tram, but you can rent one at the top. Bikers wishing to ride trails on the other side of the mountain can take their bikes with them on the ski area chair lift during the summer. (See the section on skiing below.) The tram is also a convenient way for skiers to reach the Sandia Peak ski area. (For additional nearby hiking, see the hiking section.)

From I-40 East, take the Tramway Blvd exit, then go north nine miles on Tramway Blvd. From I-25 North, take the Tramway Rd exit, and head about five miles east. During the summer, trams run from 9 am to

10 pm. Hours are somewhat abbreviated in the winter. Roundtrips are $12.50 for adults and $9.50 for people between the ages of five and 12, or over 62.

### Elena Gallegos Picnic Area in Albert G Simms Park

This picnic area (☎ 291 6224, 823 4016) in the foothills of the Sandia Mountain is just off 1700 Tramway Blvd NE. The area offers a sq mile of wilderness with spectacular views of the city and mountains.

The eight-mile Pino Trail leads hikers to the crest. There are three shorter multiuse trails that bikers can enjoy. The large picnic area has with water. Hours are 7 am to 9 pm in the summer and 7 am to 7 pm in the winter. A $1 per car charge is collected during the week, and the fee goes up to $2 on Saturday and Sunday.

### National Atomic Museum

This museum (☎ 845 6670), Building 20358, Wyoming Blvd SE, is on the Kirtland Air Force Base. Depending on your perspective, the museum is either a tribute to good old scientific know-how, or a bizarre public relations center, extolling the virtues of nuclear technology. Outside you'll see a full range of atomic weaponry, including replicas of the innocuously named 'Little Boy' and 'Fat Man' – the bombs that destroyed Hiroshima and Nagasaki. Inside, a film theater shows *Ten Seconds That Shook the World*, an hourlong film about the development of the atomic bomb. There are many other related exhibits, including one oxymoronically named 'Nuclear Weapons Safety'. The museum is open from 9 am to 5 pm daily, and the film is shown four times a day – call for times. There is no charge, but you must stop and identify yourself at the guard house at the base entrance to be admitted. The museum is closed on New Year's Day, Easter, Thanksgiving and Christmas.

### Wineries

Spanish priests began making wine from local grapes by the mid-17th century. Flash floods and years of drought almost elimi-nated wine production by 1900, but in the past 20 years the area has seen a revival of the ancient art.

Several vineyards in or near Albuquerque offer tours and wine tasting:

Anderson Valley Vineyards
    4920 Rio Grande Blvd NE (☎ 344 7266)
Gruet Winery
    8400 Pan American NE (☎ 821 0055)
Las Nutrias Vineyard and Winery
    4627 Corrales Rd, Corrales (☎ 897 7863)
Sandia Shadows Vineyard
    11704 Coronado NE (☎ 856 1006)

## ACTIVITIES
### Skiing

The omnipresent Sandia Mountains provide a convenient outlet if you've got a skiing jones. You can leave downtown and be on the slopes at the Sandia Peak Ski Area (☎ 242 9133) in less than an hour. The tramway, four chair lifts and two surface lifts reach 26 downhill runs that are 35% beginner and 55% intermediate. The 200-acre area averages 180 inches of snow annually, but there's snowmaking on 30 acres, just in case. Full-day lift tickets are $30 for adults, and $21 for kids and seniors. Half-day tickets are $21 and $13. $40 buys both a convenient roundtrip on the Sandia Peak Tramway and full-day lift use. In summer, a chair lift ride is $6. Mountain bikers can hop on the chair lift in summer with their bikes for $6 (one-way, one time) or $10 (unlimited rides all day).

Cross-country trails atop the mountain are maintained by the Cibola National Forest and are reached by the Tramway or via Hwys 14 and 536 (east of town, take exit 175 north off I-40). This route, known as the **Sandia Crest National Scenic Byway**, passes several picnic areas and biking and hiking trails. Information is available from the Sandia Ranger Station (☎ 281 3304), 11776 Hwy 337, Tijeras, 87059, about a mile south of I-40. Hours are 8:30 am to 5 pm.

### Hiking

If you only have time for one hike while in town, **La Luz Trail** is the one to take. It is a beautiful seven-mile trail to the top of the Sandias, with spectacular views over Albuquerque, the West Mesa, and the mountain ranges beyond. The trail goes over varied landscape, taking you from high desert, past a small waterfall and into the pine forests of the peak. If you want, you can hike up and take the tram down, but then you'll need to get back to your car at the trailhead! To get to the trailhead, take I-25 north to the Tramway exit and head east. The first road on the left, USFS Rd 444, heads toward the Sandias, and La Luz starts at the end of the road. Follow the signs.

### Other Activities
**Golf** at the UNM Championship Course (☎ 277 4546), 3601 University Blvd SE, one of the finest in the Southwest. Other popular courses are Arroyo del Oso (☎ 888 8815), 7001 Osuna Rd NE, and Paradise Hills (☎ 898 7001), 10035 Country Club Ln NW. For more information about these and other courses, call the city's Golf Management Department (☎ 888 8115).

There are about 30 city parks equipped with **tennis** courts. For information, call the Albuquerque Parks and Services Department (☎ 243 4387), or look in the 'Reference Guide' pages of the telephone yellow pages for a complete listing.

About a dozen companies offer **hot-air balloon** rides for about $100 per person. The visitors bureau can give you a list, or look under 'Balloons – Hot Air' in the yellow pages.

### ORGANIZED TOURS
Several companies tour Albuquerque and outlying areas of interest. Gray Line (☎ 242 3880) has narrated bus tours of the city for $21 per person, of Acoma Pueblo for $29 and of Sandia Peak for $27, including the tram fee. Seniors and kids pay less, and there are a number of package deals available. The tours take three to four hours and include hotel pickup. An all-day roundtrip to Santa Fe costs $35 per person.

Rio Grande Super Tours (☎ 242 1325) offers similar excursions for about the same prices. For information on group charters and specialty tours, call the visitors bureau (☎ 243 3696).

### SPECIAL EVENTS
There are weekly events in the city or at nearby pueblos. For an exhaustive listing, check with the visitors bureau. Major annual events are described below.

### International Balloon Festival
This festival attracts almost a million spectators during nine days between the first and second weekends in October. Hundreds of hot-air balloon pilots show their skills in a variety of events and competitions. After sunset, hundreds of giant balloons are internally illuminated, giving them the appearance of giant Chinese lanterns hovering over the festival grounds. With so many spectators, parking and accommodations are a problem. Book hotels ahead of time, and call the visitors bureau for parking information and a schedule. For more specific information about the festival, call 821 1000.

### New Mexico State Fair
This fair is one of the country's finest. It begins the second week in September and runs for two weeks. Attractions include the daily PRCA rodeo, Native American dances, live music, thoroughbred horse racing, midway rides, livestock demonstrations and an unusually wide variety of food booths. Tickets to the fair are free Monday and Tuesday and cost $1 Wednesday to Friday and $2 on weekends. Events within require additional admission charges. Fairground entrances are on Central Ave NE and Lomas Blvd NE, between Louisiana and San Pedro Blvds. Call 265 1791 for more information.

### Founders Day
Held on the closest Saturday to April 23, Founders Day takes place around the Old Town Plaza. Replicated patron saints are on parade, and there's traditional New Mexican entertainment and food in this one-day celebration of Albuquerque's 1706 founding.

NEW MEXICO

Albuquerque

| 0 | 250 | 500 m |
| 0 | 250 | 500 yards |

To Barelas
Bridge

## Gathering of Nations Powwow

This powwow features dance competitions, displays of Native American arts & crafts and the 'Miss Indian World' contest. The powwow is held for two days in late April in The Pit, the UNM indoor sports arena.

## New Mexico Arts & Crafts Fair

Held in late June, this two-day fair features works by more than 200 New Mexican artists, with an emphasis on Hispanic and Native American works. Kids' art is also exhibited, and there's food and continuous entertainment.

## PLACES TO STAY

Albuquerque offers an abundance of lodging possibilities. The least expensive places are along Central Ave, the urban thoroughfare that passes Old Town, downtown, the UNM campus, the state fairgrounds, fine restaurants, sleazy dives and porno stores along the 12-mile stretch from the Rio Grande east to I-40 exit 167.

There are plenty of middle and top-end lodgings, although these are less centralized. Generally, hotel rates are lower in winter and higher in summer. (Summer rates are listed here.) They are higher still

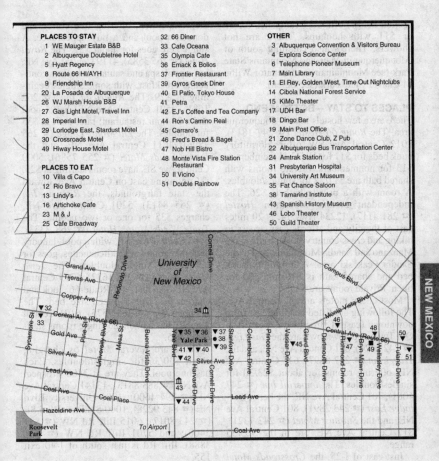

**PLACES TO STAY**
1  WE Mauger Estate B&B
2  Albuquerque Doubletree Hotel
5  Hyatt Regency
8  Route 66 HI/AYH
9  Friendship Inn
20  La Posada de Albuquerque
26  WJ Marsh House B&B
27  Gas Light Motel, Travel Inn
28  Imperial Inn
29  Lorlodge East, Stardust Motel
30  Crossroads Motel
49  Hiway House Motel

**PLACES TO EAT**
10  Villa di Capo
12  Rio Bravo
13  Lindy's
16  Artichoke Cafe
23  M & J
25  Cafe Broadway

32  66 Diner
33  Cafe Oceana
35  Olympia Cafe
36  Emack & Bolios
37  Frontier Restaurant
39  Gyros Greek Diner
40  El Patio, Tokyo House
41  Petra
42  EJ's Coffee and Tea Company
44  Ron's Camino Real
45  Carraro's
46  Fred's Bread & Bagel
47  Nob Hill Bistro
48  Monte Vista Fire Station Restaurant
50  Il Vicino
51  Double Rainbow

**OTHER**
3  Albuquerque Convention & Visitors Bureau
4  Explora Science Center
6  Telephone Pioneer Museum
7  Main Library
11  El Rey, Golden West, Time Out Nightclubs
14  Cibola National Forest Service
15  KiMo Theater
17  UDH Bar
18  Dingo Bar
19  Main Post Office
21  Zone Dance Club, Z Pub
22  Albuquerque Bus Transportation Center
24  Amtrak Station
31  Presbyterian Hospital
34  University Art Museum
35  Fat Chance Saloon
38  Tamarind Institute
43  Spanish History Museum
46  Lobo Theater
50  Guild Theater

NEW MEXICO

during the New Mexico State Fair and International Balloon Festival in September and October. During those times it's best to book a room well in advance, or you may be out of luck.

## PLACES TO STAY – CAMPING

*KOA Albuquerque Central* (☎ 296 2729), 12400 Skyline Rd NE, charges about $20/26 for sites without/with hookups. Kamping Kabins are $33 to $40. Officially there are 208 sites, but tenters often get in even if the sites are full. There's a pool, indoor spa, miniature golf course, coin laundry and convenience store on the premises. At the west end of town across the Rio Grande, the *Palisades RV Park* (☎ 831 5000), 9201 Central Ave NW, has 113 sites and charges $17/21 for sites without/with hookups. *Albuquerque West RV Park* (☎ 831 1912), 5739 Ouray Rd NW, also on the west side of the river, has a 100 sites, mainly for RVs, for $18 with hookups. Tent sites are $13. There is a pool, a playground, showers and coin laundry.

North of town in Bernalillo, *Coronado State Park* (☎ 867 5589) (see Bernalillo section below) offers 24 campsites for $7 or $11 with hookups. There are hot showers. There's also camping south of Albuquerque in Manzano Mountains State Park (see Mountainair) and Senator Willie M Chavez State Park (see Belen).

## PLACES TO STAY – BOTTOM END

There are a few hostels in the Albuquerque area. The *Route 66 Hostel* (☎ 247 1813), 1012 Central Ave SW, offers dormitory bunk beds for $11 for HI/AYH members or $13 for nonmembers. Private rooms with shared bath are $17/22 for singles/doubles. A room with a private bath is $26. The independent *Sandia Mountain Hostel* (☎ 281 4117), 12234 Hwy 14, is 20 miles east of the city and affords easy access to hiking and cross-country skiing trails in the Manzano and Sandia Mountains, and to the Sandia Peak ski area. A dormitory bunk bed and shared bath is $10, plus $2 for linen. Private rooms are $25.

Most cheap motels are on Central Ave. The following are listed heading east from downtown (east of Broadway). Nearest to Old Town and downtown are the *Gas Light* (☎ 242 6020), 601 Central Ave NE, and the *Travel Inn* (☎ 247 8897), 615 Central Ave NE, offering rooms for about $23/30 for singles/doubles. The *Imperial Inn* (☎ 247 4081), 701 Central Ave NE, the better *Lorlodge East* (☎ 243 2891), 801 Central Ave NE, and the *Stardust Motel* (☎ 243 1321), 817 Central Ave NE, are in the $25/35 range.

Just east of I-25, the *Crossroads Motel* (☎ 255 7586), 1001 Central Ave NE, is a bargain at $34 for one or two double beds. The rooms, some with king-size beds or kitchenettes, are among the cleanest and nicest you'll find on the strip. There is a pool and a sauna, and weekly rates are available.

Further east in the University/Nob Hill districts are the *Hiway House Motel* (☎ 268 3961), 3200 Central Ave SE, and the *Nob Hill Motel* (☎ 255 3172), 3712 Central Ave SE, with rates in the $25/35 range. Across the street, the *University Lodge* (☎ 266 7663), 3711 Central Ave NE, is a cut above

the competition, offering free coffee and donuts, a pool and a tidy appearance. A single here goes for about $22. The *Royal Hotel* (☎ 265 3585), 4119 Central Ave NE, has a pool, spa and sauna, and offers continental breakfast, with some singles beginning at $29. The *American Inn* (☎ 262 1681), 4501 Central Ave NE, has a pool and a 24-hour restaurant; rates start at $35 for doubles. The *Zia Motor Lodge* (☎ 265 2896), 4611 Central Ave NE, and the *Desert Sands Motel* (☎ 255 7586), 5000 Central Ave SE, have rooms starting at $25.

Continuing east on Central Ave, toward the state fairgrounds, the *Riteway Inn* (☎ 265 8413), 5201 Central Ave NE, charges $35 for one or two people. The *Trade Winds Motor Hotel* (☎ 268 3333), 5400 Central Ave SE, with a pool, laundry and some rooms with kitchenettes, goes for $25/29 for singles/doubles. The *Tewa Motor Lodge* (☎ 255 1632), 5715 Central Ave NE, has that 'old-Route-66' look and charges $22 for a queen-size bed. The *Economy Inn* (☎ 265 7575), 6101 Central Ave NE, has a pool and single rooms starting at $35.

There are several *Motel 6s* charging about $30/36 for singles/doubles. Each has one pool. They are at 3400 Prospect Ave NE (☎ 883 8813); 13141 Central Ave NE (☎ 294 4600); 1701 University Blvd NE (☎ 843 9228); 1000 Stadium Blvd SE (☎ 243 8017); 6015 Iliff Rd NW (☎ 831 3400); and 5701 Iliff Rd NW (☎ 831 8888). Iliff Rd is just south of I-40 exit 155.

The *Friendship Inn* (☎ 247 1501) is a six-story building at 717 Central Ave NW. It has a restaurant, bar and free shuttle service to and from the airport, bus and train station. Rooms at this chain hotel are in the $40s but often drop into the $30s when the inn isn't full.

## PLACES TO STAY – MIDDLE

Albuquerque's middle and top-end lodgings are clustered in various convenient locations. Many hotels offer weekend rates if you ask for them. Nearly all provide shuttle service to and from the airport.

## Hotels

**Old Town & Downtown** There are only a few mid-range places in this area. The *Traveler's Inn* (☎ 242 5228, fax 766 9218), 411 McKnight Ave NW (go north on 4th St), is a good deal with queen-size beds, a pool and whirlpool for $42/49. The *Monterey Motel* (☎ 243 3554), 2402 Central Ave SW, is a clean nonsmoker's motel with 15 rooms for a very reasonable $35 to $45. There's a coin laundry and a pool.

The *Rio Grande Inn* (☎ 843 9500, 1 (800) 959 4726, fax 843 9238), 1015 Rio Grande NW north of the Plaza just below I-40, is very convenient for Old Town. Pleasant rooms in this remodeled four-story hotel are in the $40 to $70 range, depending on room size and season. The hotel has a pool and a restaurant open from 6 am to 9 pm.

**Airport** All these hotels have a pool. The *Best Western Airport Inn* (☎ 242 7022, fax 243 0620), 2400 Yale Blvd SE, has a spa. Rates are in the $50s and include continental breakfast. Next door, the *Comfort Inn* (☎ 243 2244, fax 247 2925), 2300 Yale SE, has singles/doubles for $53/62 with breakfast included. The *La Quinta Inn – Airport* (☎ 243 5500, fax 247 8288), 2116 Yale Blvd SE, offers large, comfortable rooms and long-stay discounts. Rates are about $55/60 for singles/doubles including breakfast. The *Radisson Inn* (☎ 247 0512, fax 843 7148), 1901 University Blvd SE, is nicely landscaped and has a good restaurant and popular cantina. Weekend rates are a bargain at $59 for one or two people; rates are $79/89 Monday to Thursday.

The distinguishing feature of the *Courtyard by Marriott* (☎ 243 6600, fax 843 8740), 1920 Yale Blvd SE, is its central courtyard – a lush and comfortable place to lay about. There's also a mini-gym and a coffee shop and lounge just off the lobby. Some rooms have refrigerators. Rates are $79/89 for singles/doubles, and lower weekend rates are offered.

**Midtown** This area is north of UNM and downtown, from approximately the intersection of I-40 and I-25 northwards.

The *Super 8 Motel* (☎ /fax 888 4884) at 2500 University NE is affordable with queen-size beds for $39/49. The hotels below all have pools, and most have coin laundries. The *Clubhouse Inn* (☎ 345 0010, fax 344 3911), 1315 Menaul Blvd NE, includes a breakfast buffet in its rates, which are in the $60s, or in the $80s for a kitchen suite. Marriot's *Fairfield Inn* (☎ 889 4000), 1760 Menaul Blvd NE, has an exercise room and singles/doubles starting at $45/55. The *Rodeway Inn* (☎ 884 2480, fax 889 0576), 2108 Menaul Blvd NE, has singles/doubles starting at $45/55. The recently renovated *Le Baron Inn* (☎ 884 0250, fax 883 0594), 2120 Menaul Blvd NE, has rooms in the $50s. A couple of miles east, *La Quinta Inn – San Mateo* (☎ 884 3591, fax 881 3065), 2424 San Mateo Blvd NE (just north of I-40 exit 161), has pleasant rooms in the $55 to $65 range.

Further north, the *Budgetel Inn* (☎ 345 7500, fax 345 1616), 7439 Pan American Fwy NE (take exit 231 off I-40), charges $40 to $60 depending on the room's size. *La Quinta Inn – North* (☎ 821 9000, fax 821 2399), 5241 San Antonio NE, has attractive Southwestern rooms at $52/65; across I-25, the *Hampton Inn* (☎ 344 1555, fax 345 2216), 5101 Ellison NE, has singles/doubles for $54/59, including continental breakfast. The full-service *Amberly Suite Hotel* (☎ 823 1300, 1 (800) 333 9806, fax 823 2896), 7620 Pan American Freeway (north of I-25 exit 231), has one- and two-room suites, each with kitchenettes that include refrigerators and microwaves. There's a restaurant and a bar with live music. Rates range from $75 to $90 and include continental breakfast.

**East Side** Accommodations on Albuquerque's east side offer convenient access to the Sandia Peak Tramway and hiking trails.

The *Best Western American Motor Inn* (☎ 298 7426, fax 298 0212), 12999 Central Ave NE, with a pool, spa and restaurant, charges $52/62 for singles/doubles. *Comfort Inn – East* (☎ 294 1800, fax 293 1088),

NEW MEXICO

13031 Central Ave NE, offers free breakfasts and charges around $40/50. The *Days Inn* (☎ 294 3297, fax 293 3973), 13317 Central Ave NE, has an indoor pool/sauna facility and rooms from $45. The *Travelodge* (☎ 292 4878, 299 1822), 13139 Central Ave NE, has acceptable rooms in the $40s.

### B&Bs

The very helpful Albuquerque Bed & Breakfast Association (☎ 1 (800) 916 3322) can assist you in reserving a room at one of the area's many B&Bs.

The *Böttger Mansion* (☎ 243 3639), 110 San Felipe NW, 87104, is right in Old Town. Built in 1912, it retains its original early Anglo style. There's a comfortable living room, with grand piano and marble fireplace, and a verandah where breakfast is served. Three first-floor suites range from $99 to $109 and four newly remodeled second-floor rooms range from $79 to $99 for doubles. Ask about long-stay and group discounts.

Also convenient to Old Town, *Casas de Sueños* (☎ 247 4560, 1 (800) 242 8987), 310 Rio Grande Blvd SW, 87104, was built as an artists' colony in the 1930s, and consists of a dozen casitas in a lovely garden. All have private baths, some have kitchenettes and fireplaces, and there is a spa. Rates range from $85 to $245. Smoking and kids under 12 are not allowed at 'Houses of Dreams'.

*Old Town B&B* (☎ 764 9144), 707 17th St NW, 87104, two blocks from Old Town, has an upstairs room with a private bath and queen-size bed, and a larger, downstairs room with a king-size bed and a shared bath and spa. Rates are $60 to $75.

The *WJ Marsh House* (☎ 247 1001), 301 Edith Blvd SE, 87102, is an 1895 brick Queen Anne Victorian house. Six rooms share baths, and the separate Snyder Cottage has a private bath and kitchen and sleeps up to six people. Rates range from $50/60 to $100/110 for singles/doubles. Smoking is not allowed.

The 1897 *WE Mauger Estate* (☎ 242 8755), 701 Roma Ave NW, 87102, is

another restored Victorian convenient to Old Town and downtown. This one has eight no-smoking suites with private baths, some with kitchenettes. Singles range from $60 to $90, and doubles from $70 to $110.

The modern and fanciful *Sandcastle B&B* (☎ 256 9462), 327 Arizona SE, 87108, has four rooms with private bath in the $75 to $85 range. Smoking and children under 12 are not permitted.

In the rural village of Corrales, about 20 minutes north of downtown Albuquerque, you can stay at the *Nora Dixon Place* (☎ 898 3226), 312 Dixon Rd, Corrales, 87048. Rooms with private entrances look out on a courtyard with spectacular views of the Sandias, and the Bosque and Rio Grande is a five-minute walk. One room has an Indian-style fireplace, the other is a two-room suite, and both have a refrigerator and microwave. The $80 price includes a full breakfast. During slow times, you can rent a room by the week for $150.

### PLACES TO STAY – TOP END
### Hotels

**Old Town & Downtown** The *Sheraton Inn* (☎ 843 6300, 842 9863), 800 Rio Grande Blvd NW, is just a stroll away from Old Town. The Sheraton has a restaurant, lounge, coffee shop, shopping arcade, barber shop, beauty salon, indoor pool and exercise facilities. Attractive rooms with Southwestern furnishings range from $95 to $115, with weekend packages available.

Two modern, luxury downtown hotels are full-service establishments, featuring all the amenities. The 20-story *Hyatt Regency* (☎ 842 1234, fax 842 1184), 330 Tijeras NW, has rooms in the $125 to $150 range, as well as suites starting at $325. Inside you'll find a restaurant, lounge, lobby bar and an extensive art collection. Across from the civic plaza, a night at the *Albuquerque Doubletree Hotel* (☎ 247 3344, fax 247 7025), 201 Marquette Ave NW, is as low as $70 during the weekend. Weekday rates start at $94/104, and suites range from $150 to $500.

Verging on the historic, *La Posada de Albuquerque* (☎ 242 9090, fax 242 8664),

125 2nd St NW, was built in 1939 by Conrad Hilton, a Socorro area native. The lobby's tiled fountain, white stucco walls rising to a dark wooded mezzanine, and gaslight-style chandeliers all give La Posada the look of an Old World hacienda. Spacious Southwestern rooms with handmade furniture are in the $80 to $120 range, and suites go up to over $200. The hotel has weekend jazz in the lobby lounge and a popular restaurant.

**Midtown** The *Albuquerque Hilton* (☎ 884 2500, fax 889 9118), 1901 University Blvd NE, has 262 rooms starting at $90, and suites for $375 and up. Facilities include two tennis courts and two pools. The *Holiday Inn Midtown* (☎ 884 2511, fax 881 4806), 2020 Menaul Blvd NE, has a sauna, spa, exercise area, restaurant and coffee shop. Rooms start at about $100.

The *Residence Inn by Marriott* (☎ 881 2661, fax 884 5551), 3300 Prospect Ave NE, looks like an apartment complex and offers weekly rates. The hotel's 112 rooms (28 of which are two-bedroom suites) all have kitchenettes and start at $109. The hotel has a heated pool and sauna and offers complimentary drinks in the evenings. Further east, the *Albuquerque Marriott Hotel* (☎ 881 6800, fax 888 2982), 2101 Louisiana Blvd (I-40 exit 162), has all the usual amenities and is a good deal with large rooms for about $100.

Further north, the *Holiday Inn Pyramid Hotel* (☎ 821 3333, fax 828 0230), 5151 San Francisco Rd NE, is an architectural change of pace on the Southwestern scene. This modern, 10-story monument to the Aztecs is complete with indoor waterfalls and hanging gardens. One of Albuquerque's finest (and priciest) continental restaurants, The Gallery, is on the premises as well as a less expensive coffee shop. Room prices range from $100 to $140.

## PLACES TO EAT
### Budget
There are plenty of cheap, fast-food, all-you-can-eat and Mexican restaurants for the budget conscious, especially around the university. Mexican food is an especially great food value.

The *Frontier* (☎ 266 0550), 2400 Central Ave SE, is a 24-hour restaurant that attracts students by day and hungry revelers in the wee hours. Inexpensive breakfasts, burgers and burritos are always available in this barn-size Albuquerque favorite.

Grab a tray and stand in line (usually a long one) at *Furr's Cafeteria* (☎ 265 1022), 6100 Central Ave SE in the first block west of San Pedro Drive, for all the turkey, mashed potatoes and gravy you can eat for $5 at lunch weekdays, $6 at dinner and on weekends. Furr's is open 11 am to 8 pm daily and to 8:30 pm on Friday and Saturday. Furr's also operates eight other Albuquerque locations. Other all-you-can-eat places are listed at the beginning of each specialty, below.

Meet students at the *UNM Student Union*, which has an inexpensive cafeteria and other restaurants. The *66 Diner* (☎ 247 1421), 1405 Central Ave NE, is a former service station on old Route 66. It serves low-priced 'blue plate' specials, such as meat loaf or macaroni and cheese, and are known to have some of the best milk shakes in town. The diner is open from 9 am to 11 pm Monday to Thursday, 9 am to midnight on Friday and Saturday, and 8 am to 10 pm on Sunday.

Downtown, *Lindy's* (☎ 242 2582), 500 Central Ave SW, is a true-blue diner with daily specials, good hamburgers, great chilis and homemade pies all in the $2.50 to $5.75 range.

### Coffee Shops
There are several good ones in the UNM/ Nob Hill areas. *Fred's Bread and Bagel* (☎ 266 7323), 3009 Central Ave NE, is a hangout for students and Nob Hill workers who enjoy great coffee, juices, bagels, sandwich specials and reasonable prices. Open from 6:30 am to 8 pm or to 6 pm on Sunday, Fred's always has music and interesting faces.

*Emack & Bolios* (☎ 262 0103), 3001 Central NE across from UNM, is an ice cream chain that originated in Boston and has thankfully made its way to Albuquerque. The ice cream and frozen yogurt is fantastic, and it serves sandwiches, soups and pastries as well. It is open from 7 am to 11 pm Monday through Thursday, from 7 to midnight Friday and Saturday, and from 8 am to 11 pm on Sunday.

*Double Rainbow* (☎ 255 6633), 3416 Central in Nob Hill, is the place to go for delicious homemade soups, muffins, breads, desserts, ice cream, coffee and sandwiches. Bakers come every morning at 3 am to work on the day's pastries, and the blackberry pie is outstanding. Herbs are brought in fresh daily, and you can get unlimited refills on the gourmet coffee for $1.20. This is a casual place, where you order at the counter and servers bring your food to the table. Lines tend to go out the door in the late evening and for Saturday and Sunday brunch. In 1995 the owners opened a second location in the Northeast Heights (☎ 275 8311), 4501 Juan Tabo NE, so customers didn't have to traipse all the way across town when they get a craving for a Double Rainbow piece of cake! Hours are 6:30 am to midnight every day, and brunch is served Saturday and Sunday until 11:30 am.

*EJ's Coffee and Tea Company* (☎ 268 2233), 2201 Silver Ave SE, serves inexpensive soups, salads, sandwiches, bagels and stir-fries as well as various coffees and teas to go with the many desserts. During the week poetry readings, open-mike night and live music draw an eclectic crowd. Hours are 7 am to 11 pm Monday to Thursday, 7 am to midnight on Friday, 8 am to midnight on Saturday and 8 am to 9:30 pm on Sunday.

Near Old Town Plaza, *WC Mountain Rd Cafe* (☎ 243 9550), 1501 Mountain Rd NW, is a good breakfast spot with home-baked breads, muffins and variety of omelets and dairy-free dishes. The cafe is open for breakfast from 7 to 11 am Monday to Saturday and serves brunch from 9 am to 3 pm on Sunday. New Mexican-style lunches, including plenty of daily specials, are served from 11 am to 3 pm Monday to Saturday.

## Mexican & New Mexican

*Pancho's Mexican Buffet* (☎ 265 5634), 8601 Central Ave NE in the first block west of Wyoming Blvd, serves all-you-can-eat Mexican food for $5 from 11 am to 9 pm on weekdays. The *Adobe Rose* (☎ 255 7673), 6724 Central Ave SE across from the fairgrounds, has tostadas and enchiladas for about $1. Its one-pound fajita, served with eight flour tortillas for $10.99, can feed three people.

*Ron's Camino Real* (☎ 255 0973), 416 Yale Blvd SE, serves delicious New Mexican food in a funky adobe house. Ron's has a good selection of Mexican beer, and the tasty carne adovada is the most expensive item on the menu at only $6. Hours are 11 am to 10 pm Monday to Saturday. *Mac's La Sierra Coffee Shop* (☎ 836 1212), 6217 Central Ave NW across the Rio Grande and near Coors Rd, is a busy spot that's been catering to local families for 40 years. The home-style Mexican dishes are quite good, and the prices are low; dinners are about $6. Mac's opens at 5 am, closing at midnight Monday to Thursday, 3 am on Friday and Saturday, and 10 pm on Sunday. It runs about 10 drive-ins around town.

UNM students favor *El Patio* (☎ 268 4245), 142 Harvard Drive SE, for its tasty dishes and relaxed atmosphere. The menu includes specialties that you can enjoy on the patio while you listen to live guitar music. El Patio is open from 11 am to 9:30 pm daily except Sunday, when it opens at noon; entrees range from $4 to $7. *Garcia's Kitchen* (☎ 842 0273), 1736 Central Ave SW, is a friendly family restaurant that draws crowds of locals with its homemade specialties, carne adovada, fajitas and chili stew. The dinner specials for under $5 change daily, while other entrees range from $3 to $7. Breakfasts (menudo is optional) of ham and eggs are $4.

For $5 to $12 including a frosty beer from the ice bucket next to your table, you can get the best and most authentic Mexican food in town at *El Norteño* (☎ 255 2057), 4616 Zuni SE two blocks east of San Pedro Blvd. Leo and Martha Nuñez (both from Mexico) and their children run this family restaurant, focusing on fresh ingredients and traditional Mexican recipes. The pollo norteño (grilled chicken with onions, tomatoes, beans, homemade tortillas and Pico de Gallo salsa) is outstanding, as is the carne adobada, the chicken mole and the cabrito al horno (oven-roasted goat). For under $5.50, you can choose from 12 tacos and ten burritos. This is a simple place, a secret favorite with locals, and a real treat! Hours are 9 am to 10 pm daily.

*Sadie's* (☎ 345 5339), 6132 Fourth St NW near Montaño Rd, used to be in a tiny bowling alley, but the lines got to be so long that it moved into a massive place next door. Unfortunately, the atmosphere changed from a local dive to a crowded barn, but the food remains a local institution and a favorite with many. The portions are giant, and dinners run from $5 to $13. There is a big-screen TV in the bar, where you will likely have to wait munching on chips and salsa. Hours are 11 am to 10 pm Monday through Friday, noon to 10 pm on Saturday and noon to 9 pm on Sunday.

*Los Cuates* (☎ 255 5079), 4901 Lomas NE at Monroe St between San Mateo and Carlisle Blvds, serves up huge plates of Southwestern specialties for under $8, but come during lunch or for an early dinner if you want to avoid a wait. This place is not for tender palates, as the salsa and chili is full-strength, but the food is excellent and the locals keep coming! Hours are 11 am to 9 pm daily. If the tiny place is packed, the same owners run a second restaurant directly across the street (☎ 268 0974), 5016B Lomas NE.

*M & J* (☎ 242 4890), 403 2nd St SW, calls itself both a restaurant and a 'Sanitary Tortilla Factory'. Locals know it as a good lunch spot serving great Mexican food. You can buy a stack of fresh tortillas, too. It's open from 9 am to 4 pm Monday to Saturday.

In Old Town, *Montoya's Patio* (☎ 243 3357), 202 San Felipe NW, serves low-priced breakfasts, as well as burritos and fajitas. The outdoor patio makes for good summer sitting. It is open from 9 am to 5 pm daily, later in summer. Historic Casa Ruiz, home to one of Albuquerque's founding families for over 250 years, now houses the *Church St Cafe* (☎ 247 8522), 2111 Church St NW, a good place for breakfast. Strong coffee compliments huevos rancheros, omelets or any of the $3 breakfast specials. Sandwiches and New Mexican classics are the lunchtime fare. The cafe is open from 8 am to 4 pm daily.

Built in 1706 and restored in 1930, *La Placita Dining Rooms* (☎ 247 2204), 208 San Felipe NW on the southeast corner of the Old Town Plaza, claims to have one of the oldest dining rooms in the country. Popular with tourists, it escapes being a tourist-trap by serving tasty, good-size meals at reasonable prices. Weekday lunch specials are a good deal at around $5, and most dinner combo plates are under $10. The art on the walls is worth checking out. The restaurant is open from 11 am to 9 pm every day.

A block north on San Felipe, *La Hacienda* (☎ 243 3131), 302 San Felipe NW, is also a hit with out-of-towners. You go through a gift shop to reach the dining room, which serves New Mexican specialties as well as burgers and fries. Dinners are in the $8 to $14 range. Lunch is served from 11 am to 4 pm and dinner from 4 to 9 pm daily. The newer *La Hacienda Cantina* (☎ 243 3709), 1306 Rio Grande Blvd NW, is under the same management.

The *Rio Bravo* (☎ 242 6800), 515 Central Ave NW, one of the city's newest restaurants, offers an adventurous New Mexican menu and a variety of homemade beers. Dinners such as red trout dusted in blue cornmeal are priced around $15, or you can have an appetizer and beer. Either way, it's a good place for a quiet chat. Lunch is served from 11:30 to 5 pm Monday to Saturday, and dinner hours are 5 to 10 pm during the week and 5 to 11 pm on weekends.

### Italian
*Carraro's* (☎ 268 2300), 108 Vassar Drive SE, is a UNM favorite for its cheap pizza, pasta, entrees and casual atmosphere.

NEW MEXICO

Lunch specials change daily and cost about $3. It is open from 11 am to 11 pm daily and will deliver. The *Cafe Zurich* (☎ 265 2556), 3513 Central Ave NE in the first block west of Carlisle Blvd, sports a neon and checkerboard interior and serves espresso, Italian sodas and upscale appetizers – this is a good place for late-night desserts and is a popular meeting place. It is open from 10 am to midnight daily.

*Il Vicino* (☎ 266 7855), 3403 Central in Nob Hill, is a small and trendy bistro with sidewalk tables, reasonable prices and a good selection of tasty home-brewed beer. With a choice of interesting toppings like spinach, feta and fresh herbs, as well as the standard fare, you can create your own pizza masterpiece, which will be baked in a wood-burning oven. Order at the counter and they'll bring it to your table, or get it to go. Calzones and salads, as well as beer and wine, are available. Hours are 11:30 am to 11 pm Monday through Thursday, 11 am to midnight Saturday and Sunday, and 11 am to 10 pm on Sundays. This place opened in 1993, and they did so well that they opened a second location in Santa Fe.

A large, shaded patio area at *Villa di Capo* (☎ 242 2007), 722 Central Ave SW, make this Northern and Southern Italian restaurant a favorite lunching spot for Albuquerque's downtowners. There's a decent wine list, but the house red goes just as well with the full range of home-cooked specialties, including pasta, fish and veal. Most dinner entrees are under $10, and the service is quite good. It is open daily except Sunday from 11 am to 9 pm, to 10 pm on Friday and Saturday.

*Scalo* (☎ 255 8781), 3500 Central Ave SE in the first block west of Carlisle Blvd, mixes Northern Italian cuisine with casual elegance. This fashionable ristorante features adventurous seafood and meat dishes, as well as more traditional pasta specialties. Dine inside or in a candle-lit outdoor patio. Most entrees are in the $10 to $18 range. Lunch is served from 11:30 am to 2:30 pm weekdays, and dinner from 5 to 11 pm Monday to Saturday.

## Mediterranean
*Petra* (☎ 266 2477), 115 Harvard Drive SE, serves vegetarian, Arabic and other dishes. Dinner specials, like kifta (garlic-spiced ground beef and potatoes on a bed of pilaf rice) plus a Greek salad and soup are only $6. The restaurant has Turkish coffee and a patio. Hours are 11 am to 9 pm on weekdays and 1 pm to 9 pm on weekends.

*Gyros Greek Diner* (☎ 255 4401), 106 Cornell Drive SE, specializes in generously portioned Greek dishes for around $5. Hours are 11 am to 9 pm Monday to Thursday, 11 am to 10 pm Friday and Saturday, and noon to 9 pm Sunday. Around the corner the *Olympia Cafe* (☎ 266 5222), 2210 Central Ave SE, offers the same inexpensive Greek food with a bare minimum of atmosphere. It is open 10 am to 10 pm Monday to Saturday.

*Michelle's Old World Cafe* (☎ 884 7938), 6205 Montgomery Blvd at the corner of San Pedro Blvd, serves an interesting combination of Greek, Lebanese and German cuisine. Entrees such as chicken kebobs and weinerschnitzel with sauerkraut are in the $7 to $14 range. This unpretentious place is open for lunch Tuesday to Saturday and for dinner Tuesday to Sunday. A guitarist strums in the evenings.

## Asian
The *New Chinatown* (☎ 265 8859), 5001 Central Ave NE in the third block west of San Mateo Blvd, is an Albuquerque favorite for Chinese cuisine. Budget-conscious travelers will enjoy the all-you-can-eat lunch specials on weekdays, as well as the dim sum buffet on Sunday. There's live evening entertainment in the Polynesian Lounge Thursday to Saturday. Hours are 11 am to 9:30 pm weekdays and 11 am to 10:30 pm Friday and Saturday. The *Imperial Wok* (☎ 294 1555), 601 Juan Tabo NE Suite B-1 at the I-40 exit, is Albuquerque's best Chinese restaurant and has a pleasant atmosphere. Dinners range from $8 to $18. Hours are 11 am to 9:30 pm weekdays and 11 am to 10 pm weekends.

*Tokyo House* (☎ 266 8388), 138 Harvard Drive SE, offers inexpensive

Japanese cuisine. Sushi appetizers range from $1 to $4, and the tempura is $3.50 for vegetable and $6.50 for salmon. It is open for lunch from 11:30 am to 3 pm and for dinner from 4:30 to 9 pm Monday to Friday. Saturday hours are noon to 9 pm.

Open and airy, the *Vegetarian Gourmet* (☎ 883 8870), 6900 Montgomery Blvd NE one block east of Louisiana Blvd, serves delicious vegetarian Chinese cuisine, with entrees ranging from $5 to $8. Sauteed eggplant is one of 20 $4 weekday lunch specials. Hours are 11 am to 9:30 pm daily.

The nearby *India Kitchen* (☎ 884 2333), 6910 Montgomery Blvd NE, is locally favored for its spicy East Indian cuisine. Tandooris, curries, seafood and vegetarian dishes are custom-made to suit anyone's heat tolerance. Dinner prices range between $7 and $10, and the restaurant has imported beer and good desserts. It is open for dinner only from 5 to 9 pm Monday to Thursday and to 9:30 pm Friday and Saturday.

Nob Hill diners enjoy the flavors of North and South India at *Nirvana* (☎ 265 2172), 3523 Central Ave NE in the first block west of Carlisle Blvd. A decent all-you-can-eat lunch buffet is $5 from 11 am to 2:30 pm, Monday to Saturday. Dinners are served from 5:30 to 9 pm.

## French

The romantic *Le Crêpe Michel* (☎ 242 1251), 400 San Felipe NW, features a wide variety of crêpes and other traditional French dishes of beef, veal and fresh fish. The lunch menu selections average around $6, and dinner entrees are around $15. It is open from 11:30 to 2 pm and 6 to 9 pm Tuesday to Sunday.

*Le Marmiton* (☎ 821 6279), 5415 Academy NE just off Eubank Blvd, serves French cuisine in a graceful provincial atmosphere. Main courses (seafood is especially good) are in the $15 to $25 price range. The 'early bird' specials reduce prices Monday to Thursday from 5 to 6 pm. The restaurant is open from 5 to 9 pm Monday to Thursday, 5:30 to 9:30 pm Friday and Saturday, and 6 to 9 pm Sunday.

## Seafood

*Gulf Coast Eatery and Jazz Club* (☎ 293 2922), 5809 Juan Tabo NE just west of Eubank Blvd, has Cajun cooking. Weekday lunch specials like po' boys, gumbo or Cajun fish are about $6, while dinner entrees (try the barbecue shrimp New Orleans) average around $12. There's live Dixieland jazz on the weekends at this fun French Quarter-style restaurant. Hours are 11 am to 2 pm Tuesday to Friday and 5:30 to 10 pm Tuesday through Sunday.

The casual *Cafe Oceana* (☎ 247 2233), 1414 Central Ave SE, is the city's favorite oyster bar. The line between New Mexican and Cajun cooking sometimes gets crossed with interesting results in many of the fresh seafood specialties. The restaurant is open for dinner from 5 to 11 pm Monday to Thursday and 5 to 11:30 pm Friday and Saturday. Lunch hours are 11 am to 3 pm during the week.

With shingle roof and sea stone walls *Seagull Street* (☎ 821 0020), 5410 Academy NE just off San Mateo Blvd, looks like a Cape Cod restaurant. Most entrees, such as grilled halibut (for $13), are traditional, but there is a smattering of Southwestern flavor. Lunch hours are 11 am to 2:30 pm Monday to Friday. Dinner is served 5 to 10 pm or to 11 pm Friday and Saturday. Sunday hours are noon to 9 pm.

## Other Eateries

Albuquerque's first microbrewery, *Assets* (☎ 889 6400), 6910 Montgomery Blvd NE just east of Louisiana Blvd, serves a wide selection of handmade beer, as well as a full menu of pizza, seafood, steaks and pasta, and it has plenty of atmosphere indoors or out on the patio. Lunch hours are 11:30 am to 2:30 pm Monday to Friday; on Saturday it opens at noon. Dinners are served from 5 to 10 pm during the week and to 11 pm on the weekends.

The unpretentious service at the *Artichoke Cafe* (☎ 243 0200), 424 Central SE, belies the fact that the place has been voted an Albuquerque favorite for four years. The creative menu has full meals, salads and interesting appetizers. Dinners can reach

$20, but it's certainly possible to dine for much less. Salmon and lamb are among the specialties. The cafe is in an old brick building around a cozy patio, liberally decorated with works of local painters. Lunch hours are 11 am to 2 pm on weekdays, and dinner is served from 5:30 to 10 pm Tuesday to Saturday.

The *High Noon Restaurant & Saloon* (☎ 765 1455), 425 San Felipe, has a rough-hewn atmosphere in keeping with the 18th-century building that houses it. This is basically a steakhouse, but it also serves seafood and poultry. Hours are 11 am to 3 pm and 5 to 9 pm Monday to Thursday; on weekends it stays open to 10 pm. Sunday hours are 5 to 9 pm.

Intimate *Nob Hill Bistro* (☎ 255 5832), 3118 Central Ave SE, features elegant contemporary cuisine in the $15 to $20 range. Lunch is served Monday to Friday from 11:30 am to 2 pm, and dinner from 5:30 to 9 pm or to 10 pm on weekends (closed Sundays). Locals go to the *Monte Vista Fire Station* (☎ 255 2424), 3201 Central Ave NE, for crab cake appetizers and ambitious entrees with hints of Southwestern and European influences. Entrees run from $14 to $20. The Pueblo Revival building was home to Fire Engine Company 3 for nearly 40 years and still has the brass pole. Upstairs, the popular bar spills onto a balcony overlooking the nighttime scene on Nob Hill. Lunch hours are 11 am to 2:30 pm Monday to Friday. Dinner is served daily from 5 to 10 pm and 11 pm on weekends.

*Stephen's* (☎ 842 1773), 1311 Tijeras Ave NW at 14th St, offers superb Southwestern nouvelle cuisine in an elegant, comfortable atmosphere. The diverse menu features a broad range of entrees using lamb, fish and fowl as main ingredients, and good salads are available at lunchtime. It is voted one of the city's top restaurants. The restaurant is open for lunch from 11 am to 2 pm Monday to Friday and for dinner from 5:30 to 9:30 pm daily and to 10:30 pm on Friday and Saturday.

Tucked into an Old Town side street, the *Antiquity Restaurant* (☎ 247 3545), 112 Romero NW, serves continental cuisine in an elegant dining area from which patrons can observe the activity in the kitchen. Try the *salmon en papillote* with champagne for $16. Dinner is served from 5 to 9 pm nightly.

*Cafe Broadway* (☎ 842 9998), 606 Broadway SE at Iron St, is the only place in town for Spanish tapas, and they are delicious! And most of them are under $3. You can get a plate of sauteed shrimp with garlic or grilled chorizo for only $2.75. If you'd prefer a main course to a selection of tapas, their hamburger is one of the best in town, but fancier options include paella, grilled lamb chops and fresh fish. The restaurant is housed in a beautifully renovated home, and you can eat in the garden courtyard during nice weather. This is an excellent place for an upscale meal at a reasonable price. On Saturday night, there is a $6 cover for flamenco dancing, and there is free classical, Spanish and Arabic music on Wednesday and Thursday. Hours are from 11 am to 9 pm Monday through Saturday.

For great views, try the *High Finance* (☎ 243 9742) at the top of Sandia Peak – take the tramway there. The affordable lunch menu features soups and sandwiches, as well as Southwestern specialties. Dinners here can range from $14 for the basics to about $30 for steak and lobster tail. Reservations are requested, and diners receive a discount on the tram. Hours 11 am to 3 pm and 5 to 9 pm daily.

Hotel restaurants deserving special mention include the elegant, charming, candle-lit *Nicole's* (☎ 881 6800) in the Albuquerque Marriott. This features continental cuisine with a Southwestern influence, and the traditional decor and broad wine list go hand in hand. It is open from 11:30 am to 2 pm Monday to Friday and from 6 to 10 pm daily, to 11 pm Friday and Saturday nights.

Within the Albuquerque Hilton, *The Rancher's Club* (☎ 884 2500) uses piñon and other aromatic wood to cook meat, fish and poultry dishes. (Diners get their choice of wood.) The restaurant is open from

11 am to 2 pm and 5:30 to 10 pm, to 11 pm on Friday and Saturday.

## ENTERTAINMENT
### Cinemas

A complete listing of what's showing in Albuquerque's many cinemas can be found in the entertainment section of the daily newspapers.

The *Lobo Theater* (☎ 265 4759), 3013 Central Ave NE, screens new foreign or alternative American releases. It has midnight movies on Friday and Saturday. Another art house, the *Guild* (☎ 255 1848), is at 3405 Central Ave NE. On the UNM campus, the Southwest Film Center (☎ 277 5608) has several series running concurrently. This is where you'll see, for example, a Japanese, Gay and Lesbian or Truffaut Film Festival. Films show in the *SUB Theater*, in the basement of the Student Union Building.

### Nightlife

Albuquerque has a wide range of nightly diversions. For a comprehensive list of nightspots and a detailed calendar of events, pick up the free weekly *NuCity*. Entertainment sections of Thursday evening's *Albuquerque Tribune* and the Friday and Sunday *Albuquerque Journal* are helpful too. You must be 21 to enter most nightclubs.

Albuquerque's downtown has several live music clubs and lounges within a concentrated area. Some of them honor one another's cover-charge stamp, making bar hopping quite a bit cheaper. *El Rey* (☎ 243 7546), 624 Central Ave SW, attracts well-known national rock, blues, jazz and country acts, as well as local favorites, three nights a week. The cavernous former movie theater has two large dance floors and a lively crowd.

Next door, the *Golden West* (☎ 243 7546), 620 Central Ave SW, showcases local and regional bands, mostly alternative-tinged rock or folk. There's a good-size dance floor, a couple of pool tables and a different beer special every night. Cover charges at both clubs are $2 to $6.

The *Time Out* (☎ 764 8887), 618 Central Ave SW, is popular for its 'crazy drink and food specials' and a good selection of live music (for a cover charge). Rock, blues, reggae and acoustic jam nights keep the place jumping. The *UDH* (☎ 843 7078), 318 Central Ave SW, has request DJ music, lots of different beers on tap, no cover charge and a college-aged crowd whooping it up. The *Dingo Bar* (☎ 243 0663), 313 Gold Ave SW, pumps out blues and R&B music. Expect to pay about $3 for regional acts, and $10 for the big boys.

*Zone* (☎ 843 7330), 124 Central Ave SW, is a popular dance club that'll keep you waiting in line to get in. Frequent special events, such as dance contests and other giveaways, attract an energetic crowd. The cover charge is usually $5. *Z Pub*, a bar in the same building, has a happy hour, with complimentary buffet and good drink prices from 5 to 7 pm weeknights. After 8 pm, when it becomes something of a singles bar, you have to go through the Zone (and pay the cover) to get in.

*La Posada* (☎ 242-9090), in the lobby of the hotel at 125 2nd St NW, has a locally popular happy hour weeknights from 5 to 7 pm, with a buffet and piano bar. There's a jazz combo every Friday and Saturday night for a $3 cover charge.

The *Fat Chance Saloon* (☎ 265 7531), 2216 Central Ave SE, is popular with UNM students. Live folk, blues, reggae or world beat bands play Wednesday to Sunday; the cover varies, and there's a dance floor. *Señor Buckets* (☎ 881 3110), 4100 San Mateo Blvd NE, has local rock bands several nights a week.

The *Caravan East* (☎ 265 7877), 7605 Central Ave, features country & western bands and a giant dance floor. One thing to remember: They mean it when they say you're not allowed to bring your firearms in with you. Check them when you pay your $3 cover. They give free dance lessons (call for hours) and have a buffet and cheap drinks during the 5 to 7 pm happy hour. The *Midnight Rodeo* (☎ 888 0100), 4901 McLeod Rd NE, also has live country & western bands, a huge happy-hour buffet and a race-track dance floor that vies with Tucson's Wild Wild West for title of biggest dance floor in the West. Other country & western bars with nightly live bands include the *Cadillac Ranch* (☎ 298 2113), 9800 Montgomery Blvd NE, and the *Sundance Saloon* (☎ 296 6761), 12000 Candelaria NE, which has free dance lessons.

### Performing Arts

Two long-standing Albuquerque cultural institutions call the University of New Mexico's *Popejoy Hall* (☎ 277 3121) home. The Albuquerque Civic Light Opera (☎ 345 6577) stages five Broadway musical productions each year usually in March, June, July, September and December; the tickets start at $9. The New Mexico Ballet Company (☎ 292 4245), made up of local talent, often features reputable guest dancers in lead roles. The season runs from October to April, with ticket prices ranging from $5 to $25.

The New Mexico Symphony Orchestra (☎ 842 8565) features a variety of classical programs. Their rendition of Handel's *Messiah* is a Christmas favorite. The orchestra plays at various venues.

The *Albuquerque Little Theater* (☎ 242 4750), 224 San Pasquale Ave SW, is a long-standing, nonprofit community company staging about four shows a year from December to May. The intimate theater was built in 1936 as a Depression-era Works Progress Administration (WPA) project. New to the scene, the *Matchbox Theater* (☎ 265 8991) has been drawing rave reviews for its quality productions of eclectic, off-Broadway plays. Shows are performed from Friday to Sunday, and tickets are $5 and $7.

Something is always happening at the *KiMo Theater* (☎ 848 1370), 419 Central Ave NW. The venerable old building plays host to a broad range of cultural activities. *La Compania de Teatro de Albuquerque* (☎ 242 7929), a bilingual Hispanic theater group, does many shows on the road at area community centers but calls the KiMo home for four months of the year.

### Spectator Sports

True, there's no match for a big league **baseball** game, but the Albuquerque Dukes of the Pacific Coast League come pretty close. There are no players' strikes, and the Albuquerque Sports Stadium (☎ 243 1791), Stadium Blvd at University, is friendlier than its major league counterparts. The sunken playing field gives fans good views from the grassy picnic area overlooking the outfield. Ticket prices range from $2 to $6 – less than you'd pay for parking at major league games.

If you're interested in **horseracing**, the Downs at Albuquerque (☎ 266 5555) in the state fairgrounds has races every Wednesday, Friday, Saturday and Sunday from January until June. Post time is 1 pm, and admission is $2 to $6.

### THINGS TO BUY

There are plenty of galleries and trading posts around and near the Old Town Plaza. In addition, vendors spread out jewelry and crafts along the sidewalk. There's quite a selection to choose from at all price levels, from cheap tourist schlock to top-dollar artwork.

A few of the better Old Town shops include the Palms Trading Post (☎ 247 8504), 1504 Lomas NW, where knowledgeable salespeople help you sort through high-quality and fairly priced Native American crafts. Luz de Nambe (☎ 242 5699), 328 San Felipe NW and also at 3107 Eubank NE (☎ 293 0814), sells Nambeware (described in Santa Fe, Things to Buy). Mariposa Gallery (☎ 842 9097), 113 Romero NW, has high-quality contemporary crafts including jewelry, ceramics and wearable art. Chili Pepper Emporium (☎ 242 7538), 328 San Felipe NW, has everything for the chile lover – from salsas to statues of the state vegetable. Local foods and Southwestern-style kitchenware is also sold at PotPourri (☎ 243 4087), 303 Romero NW.

If you're in the market for just the right cowboy boots, head over to PT Crow Trading Company (☎ 256 1763), 114 Amherst SE. It's a small store but offers a great variety of all styles of new and used boots. You can even have a pair custom-made for you and shipped to you.

## GETTING THERE & AWAY
### Air
Albuquerque has the state's main airport, and various airlines fly here from cities around the USA. Mesa Airlines (☎ 1 (800) 637 2247) provides local service to and from Denver, Colorado Springs, Colorado; Santa Fe; Dallas, Texas (via Roswell); and Hobbs, Clovis, Carlsbad, Farmington, Las Cruces and Silver City.

The Albuquerque International Airport, five miles south of downtown, is served by the No 50 SunTrans bus weekdays from around 7 am to 6 pm and Saturdays from 8 am to 4 pm. There is no Sunday service. A taxi downtown takes 10 minutes and charges about $8. You can get to and from most hotels and some motels via free hotel shuttles.

### Bus
The Albuquerque Bus Transportation Center, 300 2nd St SW, is the home of Greyhound (☎ 243 4435, 1 (800) 231 2222) and several local carriers. Greyhound has four buses a day to Santa Fe at $10.50. It also has several daily buses west to Los Angeles, California, and south to El Paso and east to Dallas, Texas.

### Train
Amtrak's (☎ 1 (800) 872 7245) Southwest Chief makes two daily stops in Albuquerque. The eastbound train departs at 1:15 pm, and the westbound pulls out at 5:15 pm. Service to Santa Fe is by train to Lamy, connecting with a bus arriving in Santa Fe by 4:15 pm. The total fare is $36. The station is at 214 1st St SW.

## GETTING AROUND
### Bus
SunTrans (☎ 843 9200), Albuquerque's bus company, covers the city well enough, but its hours of operation aren't the most convenient. Buses stop running at around 6 pm, and only three lines run on Sunday.

Bus fare is 75¢, and free transfers are available upon request. Schedules are available from the visitors centers and city buildings.

### Taxi
Cabbies patrol the airport, train and bus stations and the major hotels. There are three cab companies with 24-hour service: Albuquerque Cab (☎ 883 4888), Checker Cab (☎ 243 7777) and Yellow Cab (☎ 247 8888).

### Car Rental
Most major agencies are at the airport.

### Bicycle
Rio Mountainsport (☎ 766 9970) rents mountain bikes for $12/20 per half/whole day, including lock and helmet. It also rents roller blades for $4/10 per hour/day. Maps and local information are available.

## NORTH OF ALBUQUERQUE
### Sandia Pueblo
This Indian pueblo, 13 miles north of Albuquerque, was established around 1300 AD but is perhaps best known for its modern offerings. **Sandia Indian Bingo** (☎ 897 2173), at the northwest side of exit 234 off I-25 at Tramway Rd, is a 24-hour, Las Vegas-style bingo parlor advertising a nightly million dollar jackpot. On the northeast side of exit 234, the **Bien Mur Indian Market Center** (☎ 821 5400) features authentic arts & crafts from pueblos around the state. Hours are 9 am to 5:30 pm Monday to Saturday and 11 am to 5 pm on Sunday.

The **Sandia Lakes Recreation Area** (☎ 897 3971), almost two miles west of exit 234, has three lakes well stocked with trout and bass for the angler not wanting to come away empty-handed. Full/half day permits are $8/4, and the area is open from sunrise to sunset. Nearby, **Sandia Trails** (☎ 898 6970) offers horse rides for $15 an hour – reservations are recommended.

Saint Anthony's Day (13 June) is celebrated with ceremonial dancing open to the public. Photography and sketching are prohibited. Other dances are held on 6 January and Christmas.

Take I-25 north to the Tramway exit, then head four miles north on Hwy 313 to the entrance. Further information is available from the Governor's Office (☎ 867 3317, fax 867 9235).

### Bernalillo

On the west bank of the Rio Grande, just north of Albuquerque in the town of Bernalillo, **Coronado State Park** (☎ 867 5589) has hiking trails and picnic areas that afford splendid views of the river and valley beyond, as well as of the Sandia Mountains. Camping is available, and day use is $3.

Within the state park is the **Coronado State Monument** (☎ 867 5351), the ruin of multitiered Kuaua Pueblo. Built by the ancient Anasazi, this is where Coronado decided to spend the winter in 1540. You can climb down into a restored kiva, decorated with a reproduction of the original wall paintings that are on display (along with other artifacts) in the visitors center.

From Albuquerque, take I-25 north to Bernalillo, then Hwy 44 west. Hours are from 9 am to 6 pm 1 May to 15 September, and 10 am to 6 pm at other times. Admission is $2 for those over 16 and is free to children and seniors.

The Bernalillo Wine Festival takes place every year on Labor Day weekend. This has grown into quite a festivity, featuring samples from all the New Mexican wineries, live music, excellent food and crafts booths. This outdoor event is a wonderful way to enjoy the Southwestern sun and relax on the grass. Although the festival can be very crowded, it's a lot of fun! There is an entrance fee of $6.

The *Prairie Star* (☎ 867 3327), 1000 Jemez Dam Rd, is considered by many to be the best restaurant in the Albuquerque area. It's also one of the most expensive, but the innovative and delicious Southwestern cuisine justifies the prices and the drive out there. It is open daily from 5 to 10 pm and to 11 pm on weekends. Sunday brunch is from 10:30 am to 2:30 pm. To get there,

take exit 242 off I-25, head two miles west on Hwy 44 and then go a half mile north.

The *Range Cafe and Bakery* (☎ 867 1700), 681 Camino del Pueblo, serves Southwestern food, burgers and simple continental food in the $6 to $13 range. This is a pleasant place, more like a private adobe home than a restaurant, and the food and service are very good. You can also get excellent baked goods and desserts to go. It can be very crowded and the lines long, especially on the weekends.

### San Felipe Pueblo

This conservative Keresan pueblo is best known for the ceremonial Green Corn Dance performed on 1 May. The daylong celebration coincides with the feast day of San Felipe. Photography, recording and sketching are strictly prohibited.

Other dances are held during the year but may be closed to the general public. In addition, the pueblo has a growing reputation for its intricate and beautiful beadwork. San Felipe is located off I-25 about 10 miles north of Bernalillo. Further information is available from the Governor's Office (☎ 867 3381).

### Santo Domingo Pueblo

Santo Domingo Pueblo and Indian Reservation is along I-25 about halfway between Albuquerque and Santa Fe. This is a historic place. Juan de Oñate stopped here in 1598 to establish a mission center for the whole area. Long ago destroyed by Rio Grande floods, the original mission was replaced in 1886 by the current church, which contains paintings and frescoes by local artists.

The church and plaza are the center of the pueblo, which is about six miles northwest from I-25 exit 259 along Hwy 22. Near this exit is a modern cultural center, with a small museum of historical artifacts, photographs, crafts and a gift shop. In the pueblo itself, some small shops sell both crafts and food. The best known shop is the funky Santo Domingo Trading Post, which is about three miles north of town and dates from the 1880s. It sells everything from junk souvenirs to high-quality crafts, as well as snacks and items of daily use.

Santo Domingo is known for its jewelry, especially the delicate *heishi* beads, which are carved from shells and turquoise and made into attractive necklaces. The local pottery, which employs traditional geometric designs, is also distinctive.

Santo Domingo is open to the public daily from about 8 am to an hour before sunset. The residents are more conservative and traditional compared to those of other pueblos. No photography, sketching or other kind of recording is allowed anywhere at any time.

The impressive annual Corn Dance, which is usually held on 4 August, but may be held the first weekend in August, involves hundreds of dancers and is open to public viewing. An arts & crafts market is held over Labor Day weekend.

Further information is available from the Office of the Governor (☎ 465 2214), Santo Domingo Pueblo, 87052.

## Cochiti Pueblo

Due north of Santo Domingo, this pueblo can be reached by continuing north on Hwy 22 for about 10 miles or by heading northwest on Hwy 16 from I-25 exit 264. The Cochiti Pueblo mission dates from 1628 and, although it has changed a great deal since then, parts of the original building are still visible. There are no shops or trading posts in the pueblo, but local crafts makers may post a sign on their houses to advertise work for sale.

Two crafts are especially distinctive. Cochiti is the main center for making the bass drums used in ceremonials. These are usually constructed of hollow sections of aspen log covered with leather and then painted. Also noteworthy are the storyteller ceramic figurines first made famous in the 1960s by Cochiti potter Helen Cordero. Other potters from various tribes have copied this work.

Photography, sketching and other recording are prohibited. The annual feast day is on 14 July, and the public may attend. Further information is available from the Office of the Governor (☎ 465 2244), Cochiti Pueblo, 87072.

## Cochiti Lake

This artificial lake, formed by a dam across the Rio Grande, provides water recreation on land leased by the federal government from Cochiti Pueblo. The lake is a few miles north of the pueblo and offers boat ramps, fishing and swimming.

At the dam, the village of Cochiti Lake has a small marina (☎ 465 2219), an 18-hole golf course (☎ 465 2239) and a recreation center (☎ 465 2282) with tennis and swimming.

The *Cochiti Lake Campground* is operated by the US Army Corps of Engineers (☎ 242 8302); it has water but no showers. RV sites with hookups cost $8, and tent sites are $6 from mid-April to mid-September. At other times there is free camping with no facilities. On the north end of the lake, the *Tetilla Site Campground* (☎ 242 8302) has similar fees plus cold showers and is open from early April through October. Reach it via a signed road off Hwy 16 about four miles from I-25.

## EAST OF ALBUQUERQUE
### Moriarty

This small town of 1500 people is 35 miles east of Albuquerque along I-40 and provides lodging for those not ready to face the city. Moriarty is a bean-growing center and the largest town in sparsely populated Torrance County. There is an annual bean festival in August. Most of the town is along Central Ave, paralleling I-40 to the south.

The *Sunset Motel* (☎ 832 4234), on Central Ave at the east end of town, has clean, standard rooms in the low $30s. The *Howard Johnson* (☎ 832 4457, fax 832 4965), 1316 Central Ave, has standard rooms in the $30s most of the year, though prices rise in summer and go well into the $50s during the balloon festival in Albuquerque. Cheaper basic places along the strip include the *Lariat Motel* (☎ 832 4351), the *Sands Motel* (☎ 832 4445), the *Siesta Motel* (☎ 832 4565) and the

## Turquoise Trail

East of Albuquerque, Hwy 14 parallels I-25 heading north, offering a scenic alternative for reaching Santa Fe. This 'trail' passes through three mining towns where silver, gold, turquoise and coal were once excavated. Today, many artists and craftspeople live in the former 'ghost towns', bringing new life to the historic sites.

The highway begins at Tijeras, at exit 175 off I-40. After 23 miles, the winding, narrow but paved highway passes through **Golden**, where gold was discovered in 1825 and, later, silver. The town's heyday was in the 1890s, when the population reached about 1500. Today, it's a nearly a ghost town with a general store and an old adobe church that provides a great photo opportunity.

About 12 miles further north sits **Madrid** (pronounced MAH-drid), a thriving coal-mining town from the late 1800s to the mid-1950s. Madrid went bust with the development of alternative energy sources. In 1974 the town was purchased lot by lot in just two weeks and has been experiencing a resurgence ever since. Artists and craftspeople now make up the bulk of the population, opening their studios to the public during the 'Christmas in Madrid' celebration held here in December. You can shop at any of the galleries and boutiques housed in the old storefronts along the rustic main street. During the summer, there's a series of classical, jazz and bluegrass concerts held outdoors at the old ballpark.

Remnants of the town's boom years are now part of the attraction. The **Old Coal Mine Museum** (☎ 473 0743) affords access to a mine shaft and all the old mining equipment. There are railroad relics on display as well, including Engine 769, an old steam locomotive. Admission to the museum is $3 for adults and $1 for kids.

In front of the museum, the Mine Shaft Tavern (☎ 437 0743) proudly features the longest stand-up bar in New Mexico. You see why it's needed when the tour buses drop off about 100 thirsty tourists for lunch. At other times it's kind of quiet in the 50-year-old bar. The restaurant serves generously portioned lunches and dinners, and the menu includes sandwiches, burgers and burritos for about $7. The Tavern also presents Saturday Evening Theater, a dinner buffet followed by a melodrama. There's live local music to listen and dance to on weekends. The Tavern opens at 11 am daily, an hour later on Sunday.

Another boom-to-bust town, **Cerrillos** is three miles further along. Built by the Santa Fe Railroad after gold was discovered in 1879, Cerrillos had 21 saloons, four hotels and a peak population of about 2500 miners. Today the shell of the old town is home to a couple of gift shops and occasionally attracts Hollywood directors wanting an authentic Old West atmosphere. The Casa Grande (☎ 438 3008), something of a mining museum, is also a petting zoo, gift shop and an information outlet. ∎

*Ponderosa Motel* (☎ 832 4403) in roughly ascending order of price. The best motel is the *Days Inn* (☎ 832 4451, fax 832 6464), near I-40 Exit 194 at the west end of town. Most rooms are in the $40s.

For food, try *El Comedor* (☎ 832 4442), *Mamma Rosa's* (☎ 832 4966) and the *Silver Fox* (☎ 832 9935); all are on Central Ave and serve Mexican, Italian and American food. No prizes for guessing which cuisine gets served where.

## SOUTH OF ALBUQUERQUE
### Isleta Pueblo
This pueblo is 16 miles south of Albuquerque, just south of exit 215 off I-25. It is best known for its church, **San Agustin Mission**

(☎ 869 3398), built in 1613 and in constant use since 1692. It is open daily from 9 am to 6 pm. Several shops on the plaza sell local pottery, and there is a bingo hall (☎ 869 2614) open from 5 to 10 pm. Saint Augustine's Day is celebrated with ceremonial dancing on 4 September, and there is also dancing on 28 August. For more information, contact the Governor's Office (☎ 869 3111, fax 869 4236).

### Los Lunas
This small town, located 25 miles south of Albuquerque along I-25, is the Valencia County seat. There is little of interest apart from a decent motel and restaurant. The *Comfort Inn* (☎ 865 5100, fax 866 0858),

1711 Main St SW, has spacious rooms in the $40s including continental breakfast and a spa. Half a mile to the east is the recommended *Luna Mansion Restaurant* (☎ 865 7333) in a restored 1881 adobe mansion. It specializes in prime rib, steak and seafood dinners, and is open from 5 to 10 pm; entrees run more than $20, but you can get cut-price 'early bird specials' before 7 pm.

### Belen

A further 13 miles south along I-25 brings you to Belen, the largest town in Valencia County. In addition to places to stay, there is a small museum at the Harvey House, 104 N 1st St by the railway tracks, featuring railway memorabilia; it is open from 12:30 to 3:30 pm, Tuesday to Saturday.

You can camp in the *Senator Willie M Chavez State Park* (☎ 864 3915), two miles east of town. There are 10 campsites for $7; six have hookups for an extra $4. The park has water but no showers. Trout are stocked in the river, and there is a playground. Day use is $3. The *Super 8 Motel* (☎ 864 8188, fax 864 0884), 428 S Main, has rooms in the $40s and a family restaurant next door.

### Mountainair

This village can be reached by continuing south past Estancia and then 12 miles back west. Or take the more attractive 54-mile winding scenic route along Hwy 337 and Hwy 55 south from Tijeras (I-40 exit 175, 15 miles east of Albuquerque). This route follows the western flanks of the Manzano Mountains. About 12 miles north of Mountainair, you pass **Manzano Mountains State Park** (☎ 847 2820), which has a small campground charging $7 or $11 for a few sites with hookups. There is drinking water but no showers, hiking trails in the pine-forested mountains, a picnic area and a playground. Day use is $3.

*El Rancho Motel* (☎ 847 2577), 901 Hwy 60, offers basic accommodations for $28 a

double. The historic *Shaffer Hotel* (☎ 847 2888), 103 E Main, has rooms with shared bath for $35 or a suite with private bath for $55. The hotel is designed and decorated by local folk artist Pop Shaffer. The *Pueblo Cafe* (☎ 847 2375), in the hotel, serves breakfast, lunch and dinner.

### Salinas Pueblo Missions National Monument

Three pueblos and their accompanying 17th-century Spanish missions were abandoned in the late 17th century and not resettled. The ruins of these remain in good shape and can be visited, but first stop by the monument headquarters in nearby Mountainair where there is information and a museum. (See Mountainair above for directions from Albuquerque.) Hours here and at all three sites are 9 am to 5 pm daily except New Year's Day and Christmas. Admission to all sites is free.

**Gran Quivira** This is the biggest of the three sites, where about 300 rooms and several kivas have been excavated. The ruins of two churches dating from 1630 and 1659 can also be visited. The visitor center shows movies about the site, and there is a museum and picnic area. Gran Quivara (☎ 847 2770) is 26 miles south of Mountainair along Hwy 55.

**Quarai** The 40-foot-high ruins of a 1630 church are the highlight here. The remains of the Tiwa-speaking Indian Pueblo have not been excavated. There is a small museum and picnic area. Quarai (☎ 847 2290) is eight miles north of Mountainair along Hwy 55.

**Abo** A 1620 ruined church, one of the oldest in the country, and the remains of a large Tompiro Pueblo can be seen here. There is a small visitor center and picnic area. Abo (☎ 847 2400) is nine miles west of Mountainair along Hwy 60.

NEW MEXICO

# Santa Fe & Taos

The last 30 years have brought extraordinary changes to the land and cultures of Santa Fe and Taos. In the 1970s most roads in Santa Fe were unpaved, and Taos had become a dusty mecca primarily for artists and hippies. But land development and an influx of tourism have altered the landscapes and histories of the region. And while tourism has prompted interest in preserving what is unique to the area, savvy marketing has trivialized the very term 'Southwestern'. In the last decade, Southwestern-style furniture, clothes and housewares have become a distinctive trend in the USA, with Bloomingdales in New York City devoting an entire advertising campaign to it. Chiles and salsas, staples of the Southwestern diet, have become favored foods of the '90s.

Today, Santa Fe and Taos rank as top tourist destinations in the USA. Santa Fe, especially, offers cosmopolitan conveniences and culinary delights, and movie stars and other wealthy Americans have built adobe mansions in the piñon- and cedar-spotted hills. Hispanic families who have lived in the river valleys for generations and Native Americans who have called them home for even longer all find themselves confronting waves of tourists and sometimes profiting from them.

Nevertheless, the national forests and deserts surrounding Santa Fe and Taos are still stunning, and the Native American reservations and missions foster an awareness of the connection between human history and the environment. The phenomenon of desert light, in part a factor of the high altitude, can only be appreciated through experience. The Chama and Rio Grande Rivers cut through dry hills, forming oases of green valleys, lined with cottonwood trees that turn brilliant yellow in the fall. The incredibly varying landscapes of red rocks, tubular rock formations, desert and high mountain lakes, and ponderosa-pine forests guarantee a spectacular drive no matter which direction you go. Take the time to explore the area beyond the cities. Wander into small Hispanic villages, and follow your nose down dirt roads and through canyons. Despite the tourism, which tends to surface in pockets around the area, plenty of places offer unexpected moments of awe.

In addition to simply wandering, you can head to a wide variety of sites and pursue a wealth of activities. You can hike the forests, ski at the world-renowned Taos Ski Valley, cross-country ski, camp, white-water raft, fly-fish, rock climb, mountain bike and swim within minutes of either Santa Fe or Taos, and numerous companies are eager to arrange guided tours or rent you equipment. The surrounding pueblos offer tours, and their feast days and festivals provide a window into historic and spiritual elements of Native American culture. The history of the area's peoples – Indians, Hispanic settlers, traders and mountain men – cannot be separated from the landscape. Any visit to Santa Fe and Taos can shed light on the connections between landscape and history, especially if you combine visits to museums, pueblos and ancient dwellings with outdoor activities.

Today restaurants and shopping are an integral part of Santa Fe and Taos, and sampling the local flavors and scouring shops and markets for local pottery and jewelry can be habit-forming. The abundance of artists in recent decades has supported numerous galleries showcasing contemporary works that rank among the nation's best. Indian art and cultural artifacts have become popular collectibles, and at Southeby's and Christie's in New York City, Native American blankets have been auctioned for as much as $500,000.

Regardless of budget, you can find plenty to do, whether you choose to camp

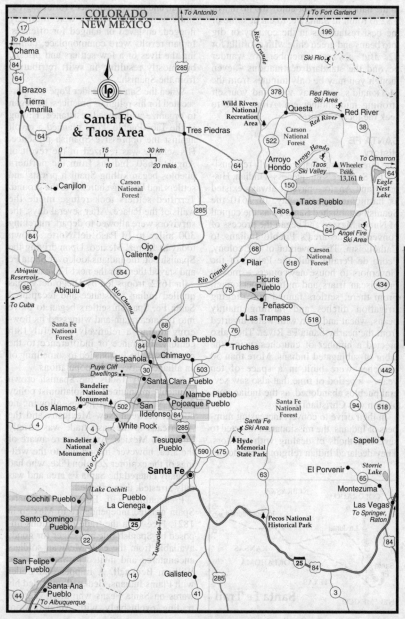

COLORADO
NEW MEXICO

To Antonito

To Fort Garland

17
To Dulce
Chama

84
64

Brazos
Tierra
Amarilla

64

Canjilon

**Santa Fe
& Taos Area**

0        15        30 km
0    10    20 miles

285

Carson
National
Forest

84

Ojo
Caliente

*Abiquiu
Reservoir*

96

To Cuba

Abiquiu

554

285

*Rio Chama*

Santa Fe
National
Forest

Puye Cliff
Dwellings

**Bandelier
National
Monument**

502

Los Alamos

4

4

**Bandelier
National
Monument**

White Rock

Cochiti Pueblo

*Lake Cochiti*

Santo Domingo
Pueblo

22

San Felipe
Pueblo

Santa Ana
Pueblo
44
To Albuquerque

196

*Rio Grande*

Ski Rio

378

Red River
Ski Area
Questa

**Wild Rivers
National
Recreation
Area**

522

38  Red River

*Red River*

Carson
National
Forest

Arroyo
Hondo

150

Taos
Ski Valley

▲ Wheeler
Peak
13,161 ft

To Cimarron

64

*Eagle
Nest
Lake*

Taos   Taos Pueblo

64   Angel Fire
Ski Area

68

Pilar

*Rio Grande*

Picuris
Pueblo

75

518

Carson
National
Forest

434

Peñasco

Las Trampas

518

Tres Piedras

64

Española
30

San Juan Pueblo

68
84

Chimayo

Santa Clara Pueblo

Nambe Pueblo

San
Ildefonso

Pojoaque Pueblo

84

76
Truchas

503

Tesuque
Pueblo

285

590   475

**Santa Fe**

Pueblo
La Cienega

*Turquoise Trail*

25

14

Galisteo

285

Santa Fe
Ski Area

Santa Fe
National
Forest

Hyde
Memorial
State Park

63

**Pecos National
Historical Park**

El Porvenir

*Storrie
Lake*

Montezuma

94   518

Sapello

65

Las Vegas
To Springer,
Raton

84

41

3

25

in the national forest or enjoy the luxury of a $290 room in Santa Fe, to eat at some of the best restaurants in the country or dig into beans and green chile with a tortilla for $2. But always remember to wander beyond the standard destinations – even though you may be only minutes from the McDonald's, you may well find yourself strolling into another era. Allow time to seek the local treasures.

## SANTA FE
### History

The three cultures that are largely responsible for Santa Fe's uniqueness – Indian, Hispanic and Anglo – haven't always existed as harmoniously as today. In 1610 the Spanish established Santa Fe as the capital of Nuevo Mexico and began the process of converting the area's Pueblo Indians to Catholicism. The governor of the colony, Pedro de Peralta, built the Palace of the Governors to house newcomers – mostly Franciscan friars and military personnel. From there, settlers fanned out, digging irrigation ditches and farming mainly beans, wheat and corn with water diverted from the nearby Santa Fe River. They also erected a number of churches, using the labor of subjugated Indians. More than 50 churches were built in a space of ten years – a period of time that also saw several pueblos abandoned, as the Indian population was Christianized.

In their drive to convert increasing numbers of Indians, the missionaries resorted to severe methods of dealing with resistors. They declared Indian religious ceremonies illegal, and the consequences for transgressions were harsh; leaders were routinely flogged, enslaved or hanged for offenses. Indian revolts were commonplace, claiming the lives of a few settlers and priests, but mostly resulting in swift retribution from the Spanish.

When the San Juan leader Popé was persecuted for his religious practices, he began to organize widespread resistance. Hiding in the Taos Pueblo, Popé planned a revolt against the oppressive Spanish presence. His scheme was realized in the revolt of August 1680. Indians from the northern pueblos began killing Spanish priests and settlers and burning churches to the ground. Terrified settlers took refuge inside the walls of the Palace. After several days, the survivors were allowed to depart, marching 300 miles to El Paso del Norte, known today as Juarez, Mexico. Upon driving the Spanish out, the Indians took over Santa Fe and stayed there for the next 12 years.

In 1692, troops led by Diego de Vargas quelled Indian resistance and recaptured Santa Fe. Spanish settlers began to move into the area again and witnessed its flowering during a relatively peaceful 18th century. Tolerance or indifference to the practices of the Indians led to something of an alliance between the populations.

In the early 1800s, the Spanish crown staunchly maintained an isolationist policy for its New World territories, allowing no contact between New Mexicans and the Americans to the east; trade was strictly limited to Mexico. Anglos were aware of the area, however, in part due to the writings of the explorer Zebulon Pike, who had illegally entered the Santa Fe area and was duly arrested, then expelled.

Preoccupied with European conflicts, Spain granted independence to Mexico in 1821. Free from the trade restrictions imposed by Spanish rule and eager for goods available from the east, Mexican soldiers encountered and invited to Santa Fe one William Becknell. A trapper and trader with Plains Indians, Becknell unloaded his wares on Santa Feans who after years of trading exclusively with Mexico were

Santa Fe Trail

looking for something new. After his initial visit, Becknell hurried back to Missouri, reloaded his wagons and returned, followed soon after by ever-increasing numbers of American traders and settlers over the 800-mile route that would become known as the Santa Fe Trail.

In 1846, during an imperialist period of westward expansion, the USA declared war on Mexico and sent General Stephen W Kearny to claim New Mexico. Mexico put up no resistance, and in 1848, the signing of the Treaty of Guadalupe Hidalgo made Texas, New Mexico, Arizona and California property of the United States.

The USA declared New Mexico a US territory in 1851, which brought in even more settlers from the east. Among them was Jean Baptiste Lamy, who eventually built some 40 churches including the St Francis Cathedral and the Loretto Chapel, and who also established a parochial school system during his tenure as Archbishop of Santa Fe. An even larger population boom occurred in 1879, when the railroad arrived, bringing passengers to the terminal in nearby Lamy. In 1912, New Mexico became the 47th state in the union, and Santa Fe changed from being a territorial to a state capital.

Santa Fe's reputation as an art mecca had early roots, with painters – intent upon capturing the ethereal essence of the area – arriving in the 1920s and quickly establishing the Santa Fe Art Colony. Central to that group was a quintet known as Los Cincos Pintores, or 'the Five Painters'. These post-impressionists, led by Will Shuster, were the first to take up residence along Canyon Rd, which remains the heart of the local art scene.

A scientific community descended on the area in 1943, establishing a lab at Los Alamos for developing the first atomic bomb. The community, 35 miles northwest of Santa Fe in the Jemez Mountains, was at first wholly secret and travel out of the area was prohibited. But with the completion of the mission and the end of WW II, restrictions on travel were relaxed enough to allow members of the intelligentsia living

there to take advantage of Santa Fe's offerings.

The birth and subsequent rise of the tourist industry has had a great impact on the city. By the 1950s, painters – long attracted to area for its land- and skyscapes – were able to locally exhibit and sell their works as galleries began appearing in town. The opening of Taos Ski Valley in 1956 added skiers to the list of newcomers. Interest in alternative lifestyles attracted others to the area during the '60s and '70s.

## Orientation

Cerrillos Rd, a six-mile strip of hotels and fast-food restaurants, runs southwest to northeast through town, ending where Paseo de Peralta joins it from the east. North of Paseo de Peralta, Cerrilos Rd becomes Galisteo. Paseo de Peralta circles the center of town to the east, composing the southern, eastern and northern borders of downtown Santa Fe. Running north-south, St Francis Drive intersects with Cerrillos Rd on the outskirts of the town center; north of Cerrillos Rd, it forms the western border of downtown and turns into Hwy 285, which heads toward Española, Taos and Los Alamos. The Plaza, the focal point of downtown Santa Fe, is often used as a base for giving directions. Alameda follows the canal through the center of town, intersecting with St Francis Drive west of downtown and with Paseo de Peralta east of downtown. Guadalupe St is the main north-south street through downtown, and most restaurants, galleries, museums and sites are either on or east of Guadalupe St.

## Information

The Santa Fe Convention and Visitors' Bureau (☎ 984 6760, 984 6760, 1 (800) 777 2489), 201 W Marcy St, and the New Mexico Department of Tourism (☎ 827 7400), in the Lamy Building at 491 Old Santa Fe Trail, are open Monday through Friday 8 am to 5 pm. The chamber of commerce (☎ 983 7317, fax 984 2205), at the north end of De Vargas Mall, is open

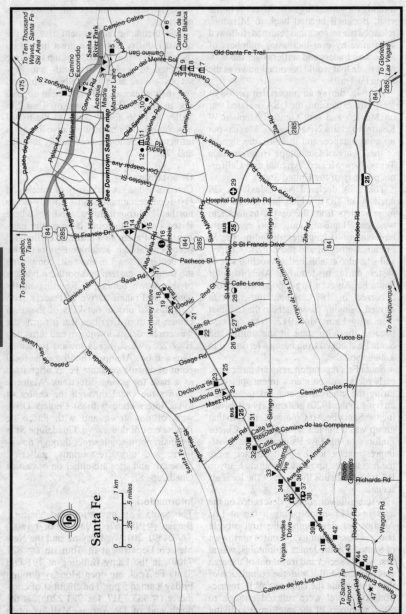

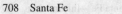

NEW MEXICO

Santa Fe

0    .25    .5 miles
0    .5    1 km

| PLACES TO STAY | | | |
|---|---|---|---|
| 1 | Alexander's Inn | 43 | Holiday Inn |
| 5 | Dunshees | 45 | La Quinta |
| 18 | Santa Fe HI/AYH | 46 | Comfort Inn |
| 19 | King's Rest Court | | |
| 22 | El Rey Inn | | PLACES TO EAT |
| 23 | Best Western Lamplighter Motel | 2 | Celebrations |
| | | 3 | Willy's |
| 30 | Motel 6 | 4 | El Farol |
| 31 | Park Inn Limited | 14 | Wild Oats Community Market |
| 32 | Quality Inn | | |
| 34 | Best Western High Mesa Inn | 15 | Furrs Cafeteria |
| | | 17 | Telecote Cafe |
| 35 | Trailer Ranch RV Park | 20 | Natural Cafe |
| 36 | Super 8 | 21 | Peking Palace |
| 37 | Stage Coach Motor Inn | 24 | Baja Tacos |
| 38 | Los Campos RV Park | 25 | Souper Salad |
| 39 | Hampton Inn | 26 | Wild Oats Community Market |
| 40 | Days Inn | | |
| 41 | Motel 6 | 27 | Carrows Restaurant |
| 42 | Luxury Inn | 33 | La Tosena |
| | | 44 | Kettle Restaurant |

| OTHER | |
|---|---|
| 6 | St John's College |
| 7 | Wheelwright Museum of the American Indian |
| 8 | Museum of International Folk Art |
| 9 | Museum of Indian Arts & Culture |
| 10 | School of American Research |
| 11 | Santa Fe Children's Museum |
| 12 | Center for Contemporary Arts |
| 13 | Walgreens |
| 16 | Santa Fe National Forest Supervisor |
| 28 | Greyhound Bus Depot |
| 29 | St Vincent Hospital |
| 47 | Police |

Monday through Friday, 8 am to 5 pm. The Santa Fe National Forest Supervisor's Office (☎ 988 6940), 1226 St Francis Drive, is open 7:30 am to 4:30 pm Monday to Friday and to 5 pm from Memorial Day to Labor Day. The main library (☎ 984 6780) is just off the Plaza at 145 Washington. The *New Mexican* and *Journal North* are Santa Fe's daily newspapers. The free weekly *Santa Fe Reporter* comes out every Wednesday and provides thorough listings of upcoming events in the art and entertainment world. Local and national news, as well as coffee and pastries, is available at two newsstand coffee bars: Galisteo News and Ticket Stand (☎ 984 1315), 201 Galisteo St, open from 7 am to 8 pm daily; and Downtown Subscription (☎ 983 3085), 376 Garcia St, open from 7:30 am to 7 pm Monday through Thursday, until 10 pm Friday, Saturday and Sunday, and until 5 pm on Sunday. Downtown Subscription has international newspapers.

The main post office (☎ 988 6351) is at 120 S Federal Place. St Vincent Hospital (☎ 983 3361 or 820 5250 in an emergency) is at 455 St Michael's Drive; it provides 24-hour emergency care as well as walk-in service. The police (☎ 473 5000 or 911 in emergencies) are at 2515 Camino Entrada. There is a district station next to the main library as well. The Santa Fe Council on International Relations (☎ 982 4931), located in room 281 at La Fonda Hotel, can arrange translators and interpreters, and provide special assistance for foreign travelers. A 24-hour pharmacy is open at Walgreens (☎ 982 4643 or 982 9811 for prescription service), 1096 S St Francis Drive.

### The Plaza

The Plaza dates back to the city's beginning in 1610, and from 1821 to 1880, it was the end of the Santa Fe Trial. Traders from as far away as Missouri drove in their wagons laden with goods. Today, Native Americans sell their jewelry and pottery along the wall of the Palace of the Governors, kids skateboard and play hacky-sack, and tourists weighed down with cameras and video cameras flock the square. You can buy T-shirts and howling coyotes carved from wood at many of the stores surrounding the square. In the summer the Plaza can be depressingly filled with tour groups, but even then the grass and shade of the trees make it a pleasant place to relax and people-watch!

## Museum of New Mexico

The Museum of New Mexico (☎ 827 6451, 24-hour hotline 827 6463) administers four museums in Santa Fe. A three-day pass to all four is $5.25, and a single museum ticket is $4.20. You can buy a single or multi-museum ticket at any of the four museums. Hours are 10 am to 5 pm everyday, closed on Mondays in January and February only.

The **Palace of the Governors** (☎ 827 6474), 100 Palace Ave, on the Plaza, is one of the oldest public buildings in the country. Built in 1610 by Spanish officials, it housed thousands of villagers when the Indians revolted in 1680 and was home to the territorial governors after 1846. Since 1909 the building has been a museum, with more than 17,000 historical objects reflecting Santa Fe's Indian, Spanish, Mexican and American heritage. There is an excellent bookshop in the museum, with access from the street if you don't want to see the museum.

The **Museum of Fine Arts** (☎ 827 4452), 107 Palace Ave, on the Plaza, shows works by contemporary regional artists, including 13 noteworthy paintings by Georgia O'Keeffe. Built in 1918, the architecture is an excellent example of the original Santa Fe-style adobe that has inundated the area.

The state opened the **Museum of Indian Arts & Culture** (☎ 827 6344), 710 Camino Lejo, in 1987 to display artifacts that have been unearthed by the Laboratory of Anthropology, which must confirm that any proposed building site in New Mexico is not historically significant. Since 1931 it has collected over 50,000 artifacts. Rotating exhibits explore the historical and contemporary lives of the Pueblo, Navajo and Apache cultures.

The **Museum of International Folk Art** (☎ 827 6350), 706 Camino Lejo, housing more than 100,000 objects from more than 100 countries, is arguably the best museum in Santa Fe. None of the exhibits are simply laid out in cases, the historical and cultural information is concise and thorough, and a festive feel permeates the rooms. The Hispanic Wing displays religious art, tin work, jewelry and textiles from northern New Mexico and throughout the Spanish Colonial Empire, dating from the 1600s to the present.

## Institute of American Indian Arts Museum

The National Collection of Contemporary Indian Art, with more than 8,000 pieces of basketry, paintings, pottery, sculpture, textiles and beadwork from different tribes, is on permanent display at this museum (☎ 827 6344), at 108 Cathedral Place. The museum encourages visitors to view the art as Native Americans do, and the hope is that you will take the time to think about the work quietly, rather than simply rush through the museum. This is the place not only to see the art but to try to understand its role in Native American culture. Hours are 10 am to 5 pm Monday through Saturday and noon to 5 pm on Sunday. Admission is $3.50.

## St Francis Cathedral

Jean Baptiste Lamy was sent to Santa Fe by the Pope with orders to tame the wild western outpost town through culture and religion. Convinced that the town needed a focal point for religious life, he began construction of this cathedral in 1869. Lamy's story has been immortalized in Willa Cather's *Death Comes for the Archbishop*. Inside the cathedral (☎ 982 5619), 213 Cathedral Place, is a small chapel, Capilla de Nuestra Señora la Conquistadora, Reina de la Paz, where the oldest Madonna statue in North America is housed. The statue was carved in Mexico and brought to Santa Fe in 1625, but when the Indians revolted in 1680, the villagers took it into exile with them. When Don Diego de Vargas retook the city from the Indians in 1692, he brought the statue back, and legend has it that its extraordinary powers are responsible for the reconquest of the city. Each June, she is carried through the streets of the city to Rosario Chapel in honor of De Vargas's reconquest of the Indians.

## Loretto Chapel

This gothic structure, modeled on St Chapelle in Paris, was built from 1873 to 1878 for the Sisters of Loretto, the first nuns to come to New Mexico. St Chapelle has a circular stone staircase, but when the Loretto Chapel was being constructed, no local stone masons were skilled enough to build one, and the young architect didn't know how to build one of wood. The nuns prayed for help and a mysterious traveling carpenter, whom the nuns believed afterward to be St Joseph, arrived. He built what is known as the Miraculous Staircase, a wooden spiral staircase with two complete 360-degree turns and no central or visible support. He left without asking for any money for his labors, and despite much research devoted to identifying him, his identity remains elusive. Today, the chapel (☎ 984 7971), 219 Old Santa Fe Trail, is open from 9 am to 5 pm daily (on Sunday it opens after services at 10:30). There is a $1 fee and a self-guided, recorded tour.

## Footsteps across New Mexico

Located inside the Inn at Loretto (211 Old Santa Fe Trail), Footsteps Across New Mexico (☎ 982 9297) is a theater and bookstore. In the theater a state-of-the-art audiovisual slide show involving nine projectors presents the geology, culture and history of New Mexico, beginning with the land before the arrival of Native Americans and ending in the present. The 30-minute presentation is shown continually from 9:30 am to 4:30 pm daily. The bookstore, which specializes in books on New Mexico and the Southwest, is a good resource for historical and cultural information. Admission is $3.50 for adults and $2.50 for children six to 16. (Entry to the bookstore is free.)

## San Miguel Mission

Original construction of this church (☎ 983 3974), 401 Old Santa Fe Trail, was started in 1625, and it served as a mission church for the Spanish settlers' Tlaxcalan Indian servants, who had been brought from Mexico. Though it is considered the oldest church in the United States, much of the original building was destroyed during the Pueblo Revolt of 1680, and it was rebuilt in 1710. New walls were added to the remaining walls, and in 1887 the current square tower was added. The interior was restored in 1955. The chapel and gift shop is open free of charge Monday through Saturday from 9 am to 4:30 pm and on Sunday from 1 to 5 pm. On Sunday, there is a 5 pm mass.

## Cross of the Martyrs

At the northeastern end of downtown, you can take a short walk up to the top of a hill and read plaques telling about the city's history along the way. It is an easy walk, and there are spectacular views of the city and the three mountain ranges – the Sangre de Cristos to the northeast, the Jemez to the west and the Sandias to the south. The cross at the top of the hill is a memorial to the more than 20 Franciscan priests who were killed during the Pueblo Revolt of 1680. The walk begins at Paseo de Peralta between Otero and Castillo Place.

## Canyon Rd

Though at one time Canyon Rd was a dusty street lined with artists' homes and studios, today most of the artists have fled to cheaper digs, and the private homes have been replaced with a flock of upscale galleries comparable to New York's Soho. There are about 100 galleries and a few restaurants on this small, adobe-lined street, and despite the commercialism and packs of tourists, it's worth a stroll. It is a one-way street that intersects Paseo de Peralta just south of the canal. There is very little parking space, so it's best to come on foot.

## State Capitol

Locally known as the Roundhouse, this is the center of New Mexico's government, in which the governor and legislators have their offices. It is designed after the state symbol, the Zia sign. There are free tours of the building, located on Old Santa Fe Trail at Paseo de Peralta, Monday through

## Santuario de Guadalupe

This adobe church, the oldest extant shrine to Our Lady of Guadalupe, the patroness of the poor in Mexico, was constructed between 1776 and 1796 near the end of the Camino Real, a 1500-mile trading route from Mexico that ended in Santa Fe. There have been several additions and renovations since. The oil-on-canvas Spanish-baroque *reredo* (alter painting) inside the chapel was painted in Mexico in 1783 by Jose de Alzibar, whose signature appears in the lower-left corner. For the trip to Santa Fe, the painting had to be taken apart and transported up the Camino Real in pieces on muleback. Look closely, and you can see the seams where the painting was put back together. Now there is mass once a month, and the church (☎ 988 2027), 100 S Guadalupe St, is used as a venue for performing arts. Hours are Monday through Saturday, 9 am to 4 pm, and noon to 4 pm on Sundays.

## Santa Fe Southern Railway

You can ride in the caboose of an old Santa Fe Southern Railway train (☎ 989 8600), 410 S Guadalupe St, to Lamy, 20 miles to the south, and back. It's a pretty trip through the desert hills, and since the car holds only 16 people, it is never too packed. Lunches are available, as are sunset trips. Though rates vary, expect to pay about $21 roundtrip for adults and less for children ages two to 16. Toddlers ride for free.

## Santa Fe Children's Museum

This museum (☎ 989 8359), 1050 Old Pecos Trail, features hands-on exhibits on science and art, among other things for children ages two to nine, but adults will enjoy it as well. Admission is $2.50 for adults and $1.50 for children under 12. Hours are 10 am to 5 pm Thursday through Saturday and noon to 5 pm on Sunday. Call for special events.

## School of American Research

A center for advanced studies in anthropology and archaeological research since 1907, the School of American Research (☎ 982 3584), 660 E Garcia St, has a comprehensive collection of textiles and Indian art. Tours are given by appointment only and cost $15.

## Santa Fe River Park

With 19 acres of grassy park and towering shade trees along the canal, this is a relaxing place to escape the Santa Fe crowds and summer heat. It's near the end of Canyon Rd and has security lighting.

## Wheelwright Museum of the American Indian

In 1937 Mary Cabot established this museum (☎ 982 4636), 704 Camino Lejo, with the intention of focusing on Navajo ceremonial art. It now includes contemporary Native American art and historical artifacts, but its strength continues to be Navajo exhibits. There is an extensive collection of sand-painting reproductions taken from Navajo healing ceremonies and notes, photographs and recordings from the ceremonies. It is open Monday through Saturday 10 am to 5 pm and on Sunday 1 to 5 pm. Admission is free.

## Ten Thousand Waves

This Japanese health spa (☎ 982 9304 or 988 1047), nestled in the hills 3.5 miles outside of town, offers private and public hot tubs, massages, watsu (massage in water), couple's massages, body treatments and facials. Everything about this place is relaxing and first-class, and even though you are close to town, it feels like you're alone up in the mountains. Kimonos, sandals and bathing suits are provided, and light food, mineral water and juices are for sale. The Waterfall Tub, with a private steam room and waterfall into a cold plunge, holds up to 12 people and costs $20 per person, per hour. The communal tub and sauna and women's tub are $12 for unlimited time. Massages and all-natural body treatments range from $30 for a half-hour massage to $90 for a 1½-hour East Indian Cleansing Treatment. Spa packages are available. Hours for different tubs and treatments vary. The last bath begins at 11 pm on Friday and Saturday, and at 9:30 pm Sunday through Thursday.

Three luxurious private rooms are available, each accommodating up to four. The Full Moon suite has a full kitchen, two of the rooms have fireplaces, and all have natural wood floors and futon beds. Rates range from $125 to $155 for single or double occupancy, and $10 for each additional person. To get there, take Hwy 475 toward the Santa Fe Ski Area.

### Santa Fe Opera

Regardless of whether you like opera, try to see one at the open-air auditorium in the hills north of town if you can at all manage it. Evening summer storms over Los Alamos add to the drama on the stage, but since not all seats provide cover from the weather, be sure to come prepared with warm clothing and rain apparel. The season runs from late June to the end of August. Tickets range from $20 to $110, with weekday seats among the cheapest. At the end of the August there are two apprentice concerts for $10. Backstage tours are available July through August, Monday through Saturday at 1 pm and cost $6. You can eat at the opera for $35 per person. Tickets go on sale in early May at the Eldorado Hotel, Galisteo News & Ticket Office or at the Opera Theater Box Office. Call 986 5900 for credit-card orders by phone. Tickets are sold at the box office until the first intermission. The opera grounds are located five miles north of Santa Fe, on Hwy 84/285.

### Activities

**Skiing** The **Santa Fe Ski Area** (☎ 982 4429) is a half hour from the Plaza up Hwy 475. The basin is 12,000 feet high, and there are 39 trails for all levels. (For more advanced skiing, see Taos Ski Valley.) From the top of the mountain, 80,000 sq miles of desert and mountains spread out before you. Lift tickets are $24/35 for a half/full day, and the season generally runs from roughly Thanksgiving through Easter. Shuttlejack (☎ 982 4311) provides shuttle service from Santa Fe to the ski basin for $10 roundtrip, but call three days in advance to confirm a seat. For a snow report call 983 9155. During the summer, the chair lift is open for $4 one-way and $6 roundtrip. You can then hike down through the basin.

There are numerous cross-country ski trails in the Jemez Mountains and the Santa Fe National Forest. The Santa Fe National Forest Supervisor's Office (☎ 988 6940) can provide a free packet of cross-country ski information. Cross-country skiers will want to locate the useful *Skiing in the Sun: Ski Touring in New Mexico's National Forests* by Jim Burns and Cheryl Lemanski (Los Alamos Ski Touring, 1985). A popular trek is the Aspen Vista Trail, which starts about two-thirds of the way up Hwy 475 near the scenic outlook sign.

**River Running** Busloads of people head up to the Taos Box for white-water river running, but there are also mellow floating trips throughout New Mexico. Three Santa Fe companies offering such excursions are Rocky Mountain Tours (☎ 984 1684), 1323 Paseo de Peralta; White-water Information and Reservations (☎ 983 6565, 1 (800) 338 6877), 100 E San Francisco; and Santa Fe Rafting Company (☎ 988 4914). Santa Fe Rafting Company offers, among other trips, a 4.5-hour Rio Grande Evening Dinner Float for $60, a full-day white-water trip to the Taos Box for $81 and a three-day trip down the Chama for $220. Stop at the tour desk at La Fonda Hotel for additional information.

**Hiking** Just walking around Santa Fe is quite strenuous because of the 7000-foot elevation. Spend a day or two here to acclimatize before rushing off into the mountains of the Carson National Forest, immediately to the east of Santa Fe. The heart of the national forest is the undeveloped Pecos Wilderness, with trails leading to several peaks over 12,000 feet. Nearly

NEW MEXICO

1000 miles of trails are suitable for short hikes and multi-day backpacks.

Weather changes rapidly in the mountains and summer storms are frequent, especially in the afternoons, so check weather reports and hike prepared. Permits are not required. The trails are usually closed by snow in winter, and the higher trails may be closed through May. These are then used by cross-country skiers.

Maps are available from the Santa Fe National Forest Supervisor's Office (☎ 988 6940). Local bookstores carry New Mexico hiking guides including the following locally useful ones: *Day Hikes in the Santa Fe Area* by the Santa Fe Group of the Sierra Club (3rd ed, 1990), and *One-Day Walks in the Pecos Wilderness* by Carl Overhage (Sunstone Press, Santa Fe, 1984). The Santa Fe Sierra Club (☎ 983 2703), 440 Cerrillos Rd, organizes hikes.

The most immediately accessible trailheads are northeast of Santa Fe along Hwy 475, which goes to the Santa Fe Ski Area. There are several campgrounds along the way (see Places to Stay). The first trailhead is the Chamiza Trail (Trail 183), on the north side of the road just a few hundred yards after entering the national forest. More trails leave from Hyde Memorial State Park and the ski area. All these trails climb steeply into the forest but start leveling after a mile or two. Short loops are possible – the four-mile Tesuque Creek Loop leaving from the north end of Hyde Memorial State Park is a good one (begin along Trail 182). These trails connect with the popular Winsor Trail (Trail 254), which gives access to a huge network of trails in the Pecos Wilderness.

Another good starting point is from the Holy Ghost and Iron Gate campgrounds north of the Pecos National Historical Park (see below). Trailheads at these campgrounds will lead you onto trails that you can hike for an hour or a week.

**Fishing** Local fish include bass, perch, Kokanee salmon and five species of trout. Lake fishing is possible at various pueblo lakes (see individual pueblos) and at Abiquiu Lake (75 miles northwest), as is fly fishing in streams and rivers throughout northern New Mexico. High Desert Angler (☎ 988 7688), 435 S Guadalupe St, rents and sells rods, reels, flies and other fishing gear, gives classes and provides guide services for the area. The staff can answer questions on fishing in the area and provide maps. A fishing license for nonresidents costs $9.25 for one day and $17 for five days. For regulations and licenses, you can either ask them or call the New Mexico Department of Game and Fish (☎ 827 7911).

**Other Activities** The Downs at Santa Fe (☎ 471 3311), about 15 minutes south on I-25, runs **horse races** from June through Labor Day. You have a choice of general admission seats, Turf Club seats (with access to a concession stand and cocktail service) and Jockey Club seats (with a full restaurant).

**Golf** at Cochiti Lake (☎ 465 2239), southwest of town, which has an 18-hole golf course open from 7:30 am to 6 pm. A round costs $19 on weekdays and $23 on weekends. A nine-hole round costs $13/15. Closer to town is the Santa Fe Country Club (☎ 471 0601) and Santa Fe Golf and Driving Range (☎ 474 4680).

Santa Fe maintains three public indoor **swimming** pools and one outdoor pool; specific times are set aside for lap swimming. Call 984 6758 for information. (See also Abiquiu Lake in the section on Abiquiu in Northwest New Mexico.) You can play **tennis** at 44 public courts in Santa Fe. Call the City Recreation Department (☎ 984 6864) for information. Deer, elk, squirrels, waterfowl, turkey and antelope are **hunted** in northern New Mexico. For regulations and licenses, call 827 7911.

**Organized Tours**
At least 20 companies offer bus tours of Santa Fe and northern New Mexico, and others organize guided trips to the pueblos, as well as biking, hiking, rafting and horseback riding trips. Gray Line (☎ 983 6565) offers a three-hour lecture tour of the city

for $15 per person. Private tours or a car and driver can also be arranged. Nambe Pueblo Tours (☎ 820 1340), 112 W San Francisco, run by members of the Nambe Pueblo north of town and specializing in Pueblo culture, have tours to Bandelier, Nambe Pueblo, Abiquiu, Taos and the Puye Cliff Dwellings, as well as special events. Aboot About Santa Fe Walks (☎ 983 3311), at the Eldorado Hotel, offers walking tours at 9:30 and 1:30 daily for $10. You can design your own guided tour through Pathways Customized Tours (☎ 982 5382), 161 F Calle Ojo Feliz, or Rocky Mountain Tours (☎ 984 1684, 1 (800) 231 7238), 1323 Paseo de Peralta.

### Special Events

**Indian Market** The Indian Market (☎ 983 5220) draws more crowds to Santa Fe than any other event. On the third weekend in August, more than 1,000 Indian artists from around the country show their works in booths on and around the Plaza. This is a judged show, and the quality of the work presented here is phenomenal. Collectors arrive in town as early as dawn on Saturday, and often the best items are gone by Saturday afternoon. It runs till 6 pm Saturday and Sunday. Downtown hotels as well as the motels on Cerrillos Rd are usually booked months in advance for Indian Market, so if you want to go, plan ahead.

**Santa Fe Fiesta** Every year on the weekend after Labor Day (the first weekend of September) the Santa Fe's Fiesta commemorates Don Diego de Vargas's reconquering of the city in 1692. A variety of religious and historical festivities are scheduled, and food booths are set up on the Plaza, where music plays from morning until past midnight. There is dancing in the streets, general raucous partying and a pet parade, but the highlight of the weekend is the **Burning of Zozobra** (☎ 988 7575) on Friday night at Fort Marcy Park. Old Man Gloom, a 40-foot-high papier-mâché doll dressed in black and white, is burned to symbolize the end of last year's problems. Up to 40,000 people gather in the ballfield

as the evening progresses, and when darkness falls, a firedancer touches Zozobra with a torch, it goes up in flames, and the crowd goes wild. The whole weekend is characterized by drunken revels. If you're claustrophobic, this is a fiesta to avoid!

**Other Events** Another far less crowded market is **Spanish Market** (☎ 983 4038) on the last weekend of July. Traditional and Hispanic crafts are sold at booths set up on and around the Plaza.

The **Rodeo of Santa Fe** (☎ 471 4300) is a four-day regional rodeo held on the second weekend of July. A rodeo parade marches through the downtown Plaza on Wednesday or Thursday morning, and competitions run through Sunday night.

### Places to Stay

When looking for accommodations in Santa Fe, remember that rates vary from week to week, so always ask if a hotel will lower its rates. One traveler arrived in town looking for a place, and the hotel quoted $440 for a double. By the end of a three-minute conversation, the rate had been reduced to $135! Generally, January and February is a slow time, and B&Bs as well as major hotels will lower their rates if you ask. During spring break, festivals and summer, finding accommodations of any kind can be a challenge. Cerrillos Rd, the five-mile main strip of motels and fast-food restaurants, is on the south end of town, and without a car it can be very inconvenient. However, rates closer to the Plaza and at the big hotels can be excruciatingly high.

Alternative Reservations (☎ 983 1290, 1 (800) 995 2272); Santa Fe Central Reservations (☎ 983 8200, 1 (800) 776 7669); and the Accommodations Hotline (☎ 986 0038, 1 (800) 338 6877) can help find short-term rooms within your budget. They are especially helpful during special events when finding any room at all is difficult.

### Places to Stay – camping

There are numerous camping sites in the Santa Fe National Forest. Stop at the Santa Fe National Forest Supervisor's Office

**NEW MEXICO**

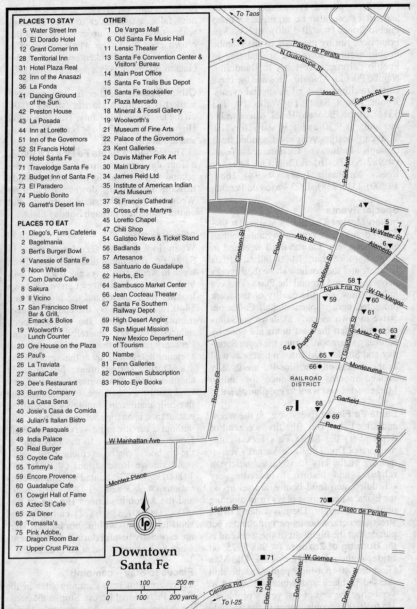

**PLACES TO STAY**
5  Water Street Inn
10 El Dorado Hotel
12 Grant Corner Inn
28 Territorial Inn
31 Hotel Plaza Real
32 Inn of the Anasazi
36 La Fonda
41 Dancing Ground of the Sun
42 Preston House
43 La Posada
44 Inn at Loretto
51 Inn of the Governors
52 St Francis Hotel
70 Hotel Santa Fe
71 Travelodge Santa Fe
72 Budget Inn of Santa Fe
73 El Paradero
74 Pueblo Bonito
76 Garrett's Desert Inn

**PLACES TO EAT**
1  Diego's, Furrs Cafeteria
2  Bagelmania
3  Bert's Burger Bowl
4  Vanessie of Santa Fe
6  Noon Whistle
7  Corn Dance Cafe
8  Sakura
9  Il Vicino
17 San Francisco Street Bar & Grill, Emack & Bolios
19 Woolworth's Lunch Counter
20 Ore House on the Plaza
25 Paul's
26 La Traviata
27 SantaCafe
29 Dee's Restaurant
33 Burrito Company
38 La Casa Sena
40 Josie's Casa de Comida
47 Julian's Italian Bistro
48 Cafe Pasquals
49 India Palace
50 Real Burger
53 Coyote Cafe
55 Tommy's
57 Encore Provence
60 Guadalupe Cafe
61 Cowgirl Hall of Fame
63 Aztec St Cafe
65 Zia Diner
68 Tomasita's
75 Pink Adobe, Dragon Room Bar
77 Upper Crust Pizza

**OTHER**
1  De Vargas Mall
6  Old Santa Fe Music Hall
11 Lensic Theater
13 Santa Fe Convention Center & Visitors' Bureau
14 Main Post Office
15 Santa Fe Trails Bus Depot
16 Santa Fe Bookseller
17 Plaza Mercado
18 Mineral & Fossil Gallery
19 Woolworth's
21 Museum of Fine Arts
22 Palace of the Governors
23 Kent Galleries
24 Davis Mather Folk Art
30 Main Library
34 James Reid Ltd
35 Institute of American Indian Arts Museum
37 St Francis Cathedral
39 Cross of the Martyrs
45 Loretto Chapel
47 Chili Shop
54 Galisteo News & Ticket Stand
56 Badlands
57 Artesanos
58 Santuario de Guadalupe
62 Herbs, Etc
64 Sambusco Market Center
66 Jean Cocteau Theater
67 Santa Fe Southern Railway Depot
69 High Desert Angler
78 San Miguel Mission
79 New Mexico Department of Tourism
80 Nambe
81 Fenn Galleries
82 Downtown Subscription
83 Photo Eye Books

**Downtown Santa Fe**

0       100      200 m
0       100      200 yards

To I-25

NEW MEXICO

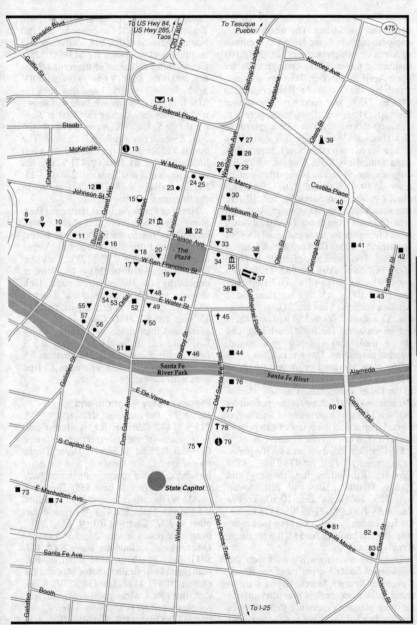

To US Hwy 84,
US Hwy 285,
Taos

To Tesugue
Pueblo

475

Rosario Blvd

Old Taos Hwy

Bishop's Lodge Rd

Kearney Ave

Griffin St

Magdalena

Clara St

Staab

S Federal Place

14

McKenzie

Chapelle

13

W Marcy

Washington Ave

39

27

28

29

26

12

Johnson St

Grant Ave

23

24 25

30

Castillo Place

15

Sheridan

Nusbaum St

40

8

9

10

Burro Alley

21

31

Lincoln

11

16

22

32

18

20

Palace Ave

33

Otero St

38

41

42

Cienega St

Faithway St

17

W San Francisco St

34

35

19

36

43

54 53

Otero St

47

Cathedral Place

55

52

49

45

57

56

50

51

44

46

Shelby St

Santa Fe River Park

Old Santa Fe Trail

76

Santa Fe River

Alameda

E De Vargas

80

Canyon Rd

Don Gaspar Ave

77

S Capitol St

78

75

79

E Manhattan Ave

73

74

State Capitol

81

Acequia Madre

Weber St

82

Garcia St

83

Old Pecos Trail

Santa Fe Ave

Booth

Galisteo

To I-25

NEW MEXICO

(☎ 988 6940), 1226 St Francis Drive, for maps and conditions. The nearest USFS campgrounds are along Hwy 475 northeast of Santa Fe, which becomes USFS Rd 101 inside the forest. These campgrounds are open April to October. They are administered by the Española Ranger Station (☎ 753 7331), and none have showers or hookups. However, if you're desperate to clean up thoroughly, consider a splurge at Ten Thousand Waves, which is along Hwy 475 closer to town (see above). Seven miles from Santa Fe is *Black Canyon*, which has 46 sites for $6 each. Some sites can be reserved (☎ 1 (800) 280 2267). *Big Tesuque*, 12 miles from Santa Fe, has 10 free tent sites with no drinking water. At the ski area 15 miles from Santa Fe, *Aspen Basin* has 14 free sites for tents and small RVs but no drinking water. Between Black Canyon and Big Tesuque campgrounds is *Hyde Memorial State Park* (☎ 983 7175) with about 90 sites, seven of which have hookups and half of which have three-sided wooden shelters. Sites are $11 with hookups, $7 with shelters and $6 without. There are no showers. The park has hiking and skiing trails and is open year round, weather permitting. Day use is $3.

The New Mexico Department of Game and Fish (☎ 827 7911) runs campgrounds in the Pecos Wilderness. The *New Mexico Recreation and Heritage Guide*, put out by the New Mexico Department of Tourism, is a good map for an overview of camping in the area. You can get one at their offices.

On Cerrillos Rd, there are two RV parks. *Los Campos RV Park* (☎ 473 1949), 3574 Cerrillos Rd, offers hot showers and laundry facilities; sites with full hookup cost $23, and tents are $10.50. *Trailer Ranch RV Park* (☎ 471 9970), 3471 Cerrillos Rd, basically just a parking lot on the strip, has full hookups for $18/108 for daily/weekly stays.

There are numerous RV parks on the outskirts of Santa Fe, but most are closed November through March. If you want to camp and have a car, however, they offer a far more pleasant experience than the ones on Cerrillos Rd. All have hot showers and

laundry facilities. Ten miles north of town, *Tesuque Pueblo RV Campground* has full hookups for $16/102/305, daily/weekly/monthly, and campsites for $13/$82/$250. Eleven miles southeast of town off I-25 at exit 290 is the *KOA* (☎ 466 1419), with RV hookups for $19 to $23 and tent sites for $16. It runs a convenience store and shows nightly movies. Also at exit 290 is *Rancheros de Santa Fe Camping Park* (☎ 466 3482), which has a convenience store. The cost is $15 for a tent site and $18 for a full hookup. *Piñon RV Park* (☎ 471 9288), ten miles south of Santa Fe at exit 276 off I-25, has full hookups for $17.50 and tent sites in the summer for $10.

North of Pecos National Historical Park along Hwy 63, there are three campgrounds in the Santa Fe National Forest administered by the Pecos/Las Vegas Ranger District (☎ 757 6121). They are open from April or May to October depending on the weather, and lack showers and RV hookups. *Field Tract* is about 12 miles north of the park and has 15 sites for $7. *Holy Ghost* is 16 miles north and then three more miles along USFS Rd 122. It has 24 campsites at $7. *Iron Gate* is about 15 miles north, then 4.5 miles on USFS Rd 223. There are 15 free sites with no water.

## Places to Stay – bottom end

*Santa Fe International Hostel* (☎ 988 1153), 1412 Cerrillos Rd, is almost one mile south of the intersection between Cerrillos Rd and St Francis Drive. Dorm rooms are $12 for members, $15 for non-members. Private rooms with shared bath are $30, with private bath $38. There are two *Motel 6s* in town, one at 3695 Cerrillos Rd (☎ 471 4140, fax 474 4370), and the other at 3007 Cerrillos Rd (☎ 473 1380). Both have rooms in the $35 to $50 range. Other options include the *Super 8* (☎ 471 8811, fax 471 3239), 3358 Cerrillos Rd, with Santa Fe-style doubles for $40, and *La Quinta* (☎ 471 1142, fax 438 7219), 4298 Cerrillos Rd, with good-size singles/doubles for $53/71. The *King's Rest Court* (☎ 983 8879), 1452 Cerrillos Rd, has rooms with one bed for $28 and two beds for $36, but it is a bit seedy. A better option is the *Stage Coach Motor Inn* (☎ 471 0707), 3360 Cerrillos Rd, with rooms for $35 to $50.

Closer to downtown and off the main strip, *Travelodge Santa Fe* (☎ 982 3551, 1 (800) 578 7878), 646 Cerrillos Rd, and the *Budget Inn of Santa Fe* (☎ 982 5952, fax 984 8879), 725 Cerrillos Rd, have doubles in the $40 to $70 range. Although they cost a bit more, you can walk to most restaurants and sites in the city.

### Places to Stay – middle

**Hotels** The recently built *Hampton Inn* (☎ 474 3900, fax 474 4440), 3625 Cerrillos Rd, has an indoor swimming pool, hot tub and exercise room, with rooms in the $50 to $75 range. At the *Best Western Lamplighter Motel* (☎ 471 8000, fax 471 1397), 2405 Cerrillos Rd, rooms with kitchens go for $72 to $95, and singles/doubles range from $52 to $75. The *Days Inn* (☎ 438 3822, fax 438 3795), 3650 Cerrillos Rd, with an indoor pool and spa, and the *Luxury Inn* (☎ 473 0567, fax 471 9139), 3752 Cerrillos Rd, offer complimentary breakfast with rooms in the $45 to $90 range. The *Park Inn Limited* (☎ 473 4281, 1 (800) 279 0894, fax 471 5646), 2900 Cerrillos Rd, is a nice place, with singles ranging from $39 to $75 and doubles for $45 to $85, depending on the month. The *Comfort Inn* (☎ 474 7330), 4312 Cerrillos Rd, a newly built hotel, is one of the few where the individual rooms are all in one building, with access from the hallway only. There is an indoor pool and hot tub, and rates range from $80 to $101. A big hotel with a restaurant, bar, indoor pool and two hot tubs is the *Best Western High Mesa Inn* (☎ 473 2800, fax 473 5128), 3347 Cerrillos Rd. Rates range from $79 to $115.

Conveniently located only a few blocks from the Plaza, *Garrett's Desert Inn* (☎ 982 1851, fax 989 1647), 311 Old Santa Fe Trail, has a Chinese restaurant and lounge, and nondescript singles, doubles and suites ranging from $69 to $105.

An interesting place on the Cerrillos Rd strip is the *El Rey Inn* (☎ 982 1931, fax 989 9249), 1862 Cerrillos Rd, situated on 3.5 grassy acres with a playground and picnic area, a pool, hot tub and complimentary continental breakfast. Southwest-style rooms and suites, some with fireplaces, patios and kitchenettes, range from $60 to $155.

The *Quality Inn* (☎ 471 1211, 438 9535), 3011 Cerrillos Rd, has about 100 modern rooms, many with private balconies or patios. Facilities include a pool, restaurant and bar, and airport transportation is provided on request. High-season rates are $90 for one or two people, dropping into the $50s in the low season. The *Holiday Inn* (☎ 473 4646, fax 473 2186), 4048 Cerrillos Rd, offers similar amenities, plus a sauna and spa. Rooms come with coffee makers and are priced in the low $100s.

**B&Bs** *Alexander's Inn* (☎ 983 1431), 529 E Palace Ave, 87501, is a turn-of-the-century Victorian house with five doubles, plus one casita and one cottage, in the $65 to $150 range. Though located in a quiet, tree-lined residential neighborhood with grassy grounds and lilac trees, both Canyon Rd and the Plaza are within easy walking distance. There is no attempt at Southwest style here, and no cutesy feel either. Breakfast is family style and includes fresh fruit, cereal and pastries.

Down the street from La Posada, just off of Palace Ave, is the *Preston House* (☎ 982 3465), 106 Faithway St, 87501. Built in 1886, this Queen Anne Victorian with a dark wood stair railing and leaded stained-glass windows is another place that avoids Southwest style. Rooms of various sizes – six in the main house, four in the two cottages in the backyard and five across the street – range from $90 to $145 and include a full hot breakfast.

*Grant Corner Inn* (☎ 983 6678) 122 Grant Ave, 87501, is a Cape Cod-style home with a picket fence and flower gardens two blocks from the Plaza. Rooms feature brass beds and quilts, and range from $70 to $130, with a big breakfast.

*Water Street Inn* (☎ 984 1193), 427 W Water St, 87501, is off of Guadalupe St a couple blocks from the El Dorado. The award-winning adobe restoration features a variety of rooms, some with fireplaces, four poster beds and patios. New Mexican wine and hot hors d'oeuvres are served nightly, and breakfast includes fruit, pastries and cereal.

The *Territorial Inn* (☎ 989 7737), 215 Washington Ave, 87501, is a territorial home centrally located one-and-a-half blocks from the Plaza. Complimentary wine and cheese are served in the early evening, and brandy and cookies are put out by the fire at bedtime. Continental breakfast is brought to your room or to seats by the fireplace or outside in the courtyard. Rooms vary in size, and some have private bath and a fireplace. They range from $90 to $160.

All five casitas at *Dancing Ground of the Sun* (☎ 986 9797, 1 (800) 645 5673, fax 986 8082), 711 Paseo de Peralta, 87501, feature fully equipped, Mexican-tiled kitchens. Most are spacious two-room suites, with a dining/living room where continental breakfast is provided. Some have fireplaces and/or a washer and dryer, and all are tastefully done in Southwest style. Rates range from $130 to $160.

*El Paradero* (☎ 988 1177), 220 W Manhattan Ave, 87501, is a mishmash of mission-, territorial- and Victorian-style architecture. Rooms vary in size and style, some with skylights, fireplaces, tiled floors, woven textiles and folk art. Doubles range from $60 to $130 and include a hot breakfast. A thick adobe wall encloses private courtyards, brick paths and 20 casitas at *Pueblo Bonito* (☎ 984 8001), 138 W Manhattan, 87501. All have fireplaces and rates include continental breakfast and afternoon tea. Rates range from $65 to $130.

*Dunshees* (☎ 982 0988), 986 Acequia Madre, 87501, is a one-unit guest house with a living room, two fireplaces, Mexican tile in the bath, a TV, VCR and stereo. The single or double rate is $115, $15 for each extra person. There is also a casita on the grounds, with a private kitchen, that is $120/750/2400, daily/weekly/monthly. This place is in a residential area of Santa Fe, off the north end of Canyon Rd, and it can be very difficult to find.

### Places to Stay – top end
Top-end accommodations are predominantly located in downtown, where you can park at the hotel and walk to most of the sites, museums, restaurants and galleries.

One block from the Plaza and directly across from the St Francis Cathedral is *La Fonda* (☎ 982 5511, 1 (800) 523 5002, fax 988 2952), 100 E San Francisco. A hotel has existed on the site since 1610, and the guest list includes Kit Carson, General and Mrs Ulysses S Grant, President and Mrs Rutherford B Hayes, and more recently, Errol Flynn, John Travolta, Shirley MacLaine and Ross Perot. The current hotel, built in 1920, is a huge adobe with stores, a courtyard restaurant and a cozy bar lounge with great local entertainment. The dark lobby of heavy vigas, overstuffed armchairs and Mexican tile is always bustling with activity. There is a tour service desk in the lobby that will help book rafting trips, Pueblo tours and other outings, and the staff can answer any questions about things to do in the area. Southwest-style rooms, some with fireplaces, range from $155 for a single to $500 for a suite. The hotel parking lot is a convenient, safe and inexpensive place to park even if you're not staying here. Rates are $1 for one hour to a maximum of $7.

The *Inn at Loretto* (☎ 988 5531, 1 (800) 727 5531, fax 984 7988)), 211 Old Santa Fe Trail, along the canal three blocks from the Plaza, is a sprawling adobe inspired by Taos Pueblo. It has an indoor pool, and rooms range from $90 to $200 for a single and $105 to $215 for a double. Rooms and suites at the *Inn of the Governors* (☎ 982 4333, 1 (800) 234 4534, fax 989 9149), 234 Don Gaspar Ave, range from $99 to $259. This is really no more than a glorified motel, and the rooms are rather small and nondescript. Inside, Mañana the Bar is a popular and cozy piano bar, and the restaurant serves breakfast, lunch and dinner either inside by the fire or outside in the shady courtyard. *St Francis Hotel* (☎ 983 5700, fax 989 7690), 210 Don Gaspar Ave, was built in 1924 on the spot of another hotel destroyed in a fire, and it was renovated in the 1980s. This is one of the few hotels that does not strive for Southwest style; it has a clean and elegant lobby, an afternoon tea, a courtyard restaurant and a busy bar. All 82 rooms have a refrigerator; doubles range from $70 to $180 and suites from $225 to $275.

*Hotel Santa Fe* (☎ 982 5700, 1 (800) 825 9876, fax 984 2211), 1501 Paseo de Peralta, which opened in 1981, is owned in part by the Picuris Pueblo. A sprawling adobe off Cerrillos Rd, this hotel is more low-key than most of the other upper-end accommodations. There is a cafe bar serving breakfast and lunch in the lobby, and though it is not open for dinner, a variety of restaurants are nearby. The rooms are spacious and tastefully done, some with terraces and fireplaces and all with refrigerators. Rates range from $69 to $150, and call for special ski-weekend discounts.

Perhaps the most elegant and coziest place in town is *Inn of the Anasazi* (☎ 988 3030, 1 (800) 688 8100, fax 988 3277), 113 Washington Ave, located a half block from the Plaza. Though it opened in 1991, it achieves an Old World feel with heavy wood, textiles, stone floors and leather furniture. Compared to most of the huge, busy hotels in town, the Inn of the Anasazi offers a quiet retreat. The rooms are gorgeous, with hand-carved furniture, wood floors and throw rugs. Known worldwide for its luxury and personal service, the rooms, the bar and restaurant, and the service is all first rate, and you pay for it! Prices for doubles and suites start at $199 in low season and at $230 during high season. At least stop in for a drink.

Right next to the Inn of the Anasazi is *Hotel Plaza Real* (☎ 983 5700, 1 (800) 279 7325), 125 Washington Ave. This territorial-style hotel is a light and cheerful place, with a brick courtyard and a street cafe. Most rooms have a fireplace and balcony, and continental breakfast is complimentary. Doubles range from $130 to $199, and one- or two-bedroom suites with a kitchen range from $295 to $500.

The *El Dorado Hotel* (☎ 988 4455, 1 (800) 955 4455, fax 982 0713), 309 W San Francisco St, is Santa Fe's largest hotel, with 218 rooms and suites, a huge bar and lobby, two restaurants, shops, a pool and a sauna. Stop in for some free hot hors d'oeuvres from 5:30 to 7 pm, Monday through Friday. There is no escaping the big city feel of this place, and its massive five-story structure is a sore point with locals. Rates range from $119 to $131.

*La Posada* (☎ 986 0000, 1 (800) 727 5276, fax 982 6850), 330 E Palace Ave, with six acres of grass and fruit trees only blocks from the Plaza, is reminiscent of an English country hotel with an outdoor pool, a Victorian-style bar and a peaceful patio in the grassy courtyard. It was built in 1882 by a German immigrant, Abraham Staab, and rumor has it that his wife, Julia Shuster Staab, resides permanently in room 256. Doubles and private *casitas* (adobe structures with private entrances, and in this case, hardwood floors and fireplaces) range from $89 to $297 in the low season and $110 to $400 in high season.

Eight miles north of Santa Fe in the hills around Tesuque is *Rancho Encantado* (☎ 982 3537, 1 (800) 722 939, fax 983 8269), a 168-acre resort offering tennis, horseback riding and swimming. The original lodge was built in 1932, and today you can stay in a beautifully decorated double or in a personal cottage with a private kitchen. Princess Caroline, Robert Redford and the Dalai Lama have stayed here, and though this is an expensive place, it is relaxed and casual. The hotel restaurant, *The Desert Rose* (☎ 982 3537), is open for breakfast, lunch and dinner. Doubles range from $110 to $235, and private casitas are $145 to $415, depending on the season.

Another rural option is the *Galisteo Inn* (☎ 466 4000), a beautiful, old ranch-style adobe, more like a private home than a hotel, surrounded by fields and lawn, 23 miles south of Santa Fe in the tiny town of Galisteo. There is an outdoor pool in the garden courtyard, a sauna and a cozy sitting room with a fireplace. Horseback riding trips with picnic lunches can be arranged. The small restaurant serves delicious dinners, with a focus on natural, organic cooking and creative dishes. It is open Wednesday through Sunday, 6 to 8:30 pm. Double occupancy rooms with a private bath range from $100 to $170, and there are two single rooms with a shared bath for $60 and $65. Rates include a buffet breakfast. To get there, take I-25 north to exit 285 south, and then take Hwy 41 to Galisteo.

## Places to Eat

**The Plaza** The number of restaurants within a three-block radius of the Plaza is staggering, and among them you'll find a meal to match every budget and most gastronomic desires. Despite the rising cost of real estate, Woolworth's has managed to survive right on the Plaza, and lunch at *Woolworth's Lunch Counter* (☎ 982 1062) is a bit of American nostalgia. It's open 9 am to 4:30 pm, and meals are under $5. Another convenient spot for a quick, cheap meal is the *Burrito Company* (☎ 982 4453), 111 Washington Ave, right next to the Plaza, where you can get hot dogs and New Mexican fare for under $5. It has great breakfast burritos. Hours are Monday through Saturday from 7 am to 7 pm, Sunday 11 to 5 pm.

In the Plaza Mercado on San Francisco St just west of the Plaza, the *San Francisco Street Bar and Grill* (☎ 982 2044), open 11 am to 11 pm, serves 'first-rate hamburgers and fries', according to the *New York Times*. It also has a broiled fish sandwich on a baguette, salads and grilled fare for under $10. The only drawback to this place is that it is in the basement, but it is a great place for lunch near the Plaza. Also in the Plaza Mercado, don't miss *Emack & Bolios* (☎ 989 1216) for ice cream and frozen yogurt. This place won awards in Boston for its ice cream, which is some of the best in the country!

*Real Burger* (☎ 988 3717), 227 Don Gaspar Ave, doesn't look like much, just a tiny adobe with a wooden counter, but it has

excellent sandwiches and hamburgers with chile seasoned fries for under $5. *Dee's Restaurant* (☎ 984 8396), 213 Washington Ave, is a fast-food place two blocks from the Plaza, open Monday through Friday from 6:30 am to 3 pm, and until 1:30 pm on Saturday and Sunday. *Josie's Casa de Comida* (☎ 983 5311), 225 E Marcy, open for lunch Monday through Friday 11 am to 3 pm, is a simple mom-and-pop place serving a limited menu of home-style New Mexican fare and famous fruit cobblers and pies for under $6. You can also get pints or gallons of chile and salsa, Southwestern casseroles and pies to go.

Go to *Upper Crust Pizza* (☎ 982 0000), 329 Old Santa Fe Trail, for unbeatable traditional or whole-wheat crust pizza, with interesting toppings like feta cheese and broccoli, Italian sandwiches and calzones. Eat on the front porch; they also deliver seven days a week from 11 am to 10 pm. Try *Il Vicino* (☎ 986 8700), 321 W San Francisco, for excellent wood-oven pizza.

*Cafe Pasquals* (☎ 983 9340), 121 Don Gaspar Ave, is famous for its breakfasts, which are served all day, but lunch is excellent as well. The menu, which incorporates fresh herbs, whole grains and high-quality meats, includes chorizo, salmon or free-range chicken burritos and pancakes with apple-smoked bacon. There is almost always a wait, but if you're willing to sit at the community table, it's not long and it is definitely worth it. Hours are 7 am to 3 pm, Monday through Saturday, Sunday 8 am to 2 pm and daily for dinner from 6 to 10 pm.

Excellent Indian food, including a $7 lunch buffet from 11:30 am to 2:30 pm daily and a wide selection of vegetarian dishes, can be found at *India Palace* (☎ 986 5859), 227 Don Gaspar Ave. It is open for dinner from 5:30 to 10 pm.

Choose from the list of 100 margaritas and watch the crowds from the 2nd-story balcony of the *Ore House on the Plaza* (☎ 983 8687), 50 Lincoln Ave. The menu features fresh seafood, prime beef, rack of lamb and New Mexican dishes. Hours are Monday through Saturday from 11:30 am to 10 pm and from noon on Sundays.

*Tommy's* (☎ 989 4407), 208 Galisteo St, a narrow, dimly lit pub with nightly live music, including Dixie, jazz, blues and a Sunday open mike, is a popular spot. The menu includes a marinated tuna melt, a reuben and a half-pound burger for under $6.50. This place is packed in the evenings, but the music and food are excellent. Hours are Monday through Saturday, 11 am to 1 am, Sunday noon to 11 pm.

*Paul's* (☎ 982 8738), 72 W Marcy, features imaginative dishes like stuffed pumpkin bread, and it won first place in a local restaurant cookoff for its baked salmon with pecan-herb crust. It is a small and whimsical place, with folk art on the walls and impeccable service, but expect to pay between $13 and $19 for a dinner entree. Hours are 11:30 am to 2 pm and 5:30 to 9 pm, Monday through Saturday.

For a quiet, romantic Italian meal, try *Julian's Italian Bistro* (☎ 988 2355), 221 Shelby St, a cozy, adobe restaurant serving excellent duck, pasta and veal in the $12 to $23 range. If you prefer Italian food in a more boisterous and crowded setting, *La Traviata* (☎ 984 1091), 95 W Marcy, is a cafe offering some of the best Italian food in town. There is often a line for a seat at the simple wood tables, so call for a reservation. It is a tiny place, with a European feel, and the portions are hearty but expensive. Hours are Monday through Friday, 8:30 to 11 am, 11:30 am to 2:30 pm, and 6 to 10 pm, Saturday and Sunday 6 to 10 pm.

Santa Fe boasts two world-famous restaurants, and though they are expensive, the menus are imaginative and the food is first-rate. *SantaCafe* (☎ 984 1781), 231 Washington Ave, has enjoyed well-deserved critical acclaim in *Condé Naste Traveler, Gourmet Magazine* and the *New York Times* for its eclectic blending of Asian and Southwestern cuisine. The menu changes seasonally, and expect to pay between $10 and $25 for an entree. The grilled filet mignon with roasted garlic/green chile mashed potatoes is huge and delicious, but then anything you order will be perfect! The decor is simple white-walled adobe and white tablecloths, and in warm weather you can eat in the brick courtyard. It's open for brunch Sunday 11:30 am to 2 pm, for lunch Monday through Friday, 11:30 am to 2 pm, and for dinner nightly starting at 6 pm.

Celebrities and out-of-towners head for the cowhide barstools at the *Coyote Cafe* (☎ 983 1615), 132 W Water St. The hype about this place has become almost comical, and though the food, at $10 to $25, doesn't always live up to its reputation, a trip to Santa Fe wouldn't be complete without at least seeing the place! The outdoor rooftop cantina in the summer, however, is an excellent spot to watch the street activity and enjoy fresh Southwestern cooking for half the price of the main restaurant. Call for hours, as they vary according to season.

The upscale *La Casa Sena* (☎ 988 9232), 125 E Palace Ave, is actually two restaurants right next to each other, one a formal, territorial-style adobe home serving creative continental cuisine with a Southwestern twist, and the other a casual cantina, where the wait staff sings Broadway hits and serves gourmet food. You can also eat in the courtyard. The restaurant is open 11:30 am to 3 pm and 5:30 to 10 pm every day, and the cantina is open from 5 pm to midnight. Shows run from 6 to 11 pm.

Another option for a high-end meal is *Anasazi* (☎ 988 3030), inside the Inn of the Anasazi. Though the food can be very good, it is inconsistent. The primary reason to come here it to enjoy the dramatic and cozy interior of heavy wood and hand-woven textiles. The New Mexican and Native American dishes, with an emphasis on fresh, local ingredients and creative combinations, are in the $10 to $25 range, but you can have something less expensive at the bar.

An excellent spot for a sunset drink is the *Belltower*, the rooftop bar at *La Fonda* (☎ 982 5511), 100 E San Francisco. It's the only spot in town where you get far enough above the rooftops to watch the desert sky.

**Guadalupe St** Guadalupe St runs roughly north/south along the western edge of downtown. Most of the establishments described below are either on or near Guadalupe, and all are within walking distance of the Plaza. At the southern end, *Tomasita's* (☎ 983 5721), 500 S Guadalupe St, is housed in a former rail-yard warehouse. It has become a loud and crowded tourist hangout, but the New Mexican food is good, and prices are in the $6 to $12 range. Hours are Monday to Saturday from 11 am to 10 pm.

The *Zia Diner* (☎ 988 7008), 326 S Guadalupe St, serves reasonably priced, upscale diner food like meatloaf and hot turkey sandwiches, as well as daily specials, Southwestern fare and homemade pies. The blue corn chicken enchiladas are fantastic. This is a popular local hang out, and it is always busy, but you're guaranteed a good meal at great value. Prices range from $5 to $12, and hours are Monday through Saturday 11:30 am to 10 pm, Sunday 5 to 10 pm. Across the street and one block north, the *Guadalupe Cafe* (☎ 982 9762), 313 S Guadalupe St, is another simple, unpretentious place serving excellent New Mexican fare for under $8. Locals rather than tourists generally cram this small place, and they don't take reservations. Hours are 7 am to 2 pm, Tuesday through Friday, 8 am to 2 pm Saturday and Sunday, and 5:30 to 9 pm Tuesday through Saturday.

The small and busy *Cowgirl Hall of Fame* (☎ 982 2565), 319 S Guadalupe St, has all-you-can-eat specials, including a honey fried chicken picnic for $9.95 and a fried catfish and barbecued chicken meal on Mondays for $5.95/7.95 lunch/dinner. The decor is relaxed Old West, and the menu focuses on hearty Texan specialties with a Cajun twist. This is a fun place, and the bar has live music nightly. Lunch is from 11 am to 4 pm, Monday through Friday and brunch is Saturday and Sunday 10 am to 4 pm. It's open for dinner Sunday through Thursday 4:30 to 10 pm, and on Friday and Saturday until midnight, with a limited menu until 2 am.

A popular hangout for the black-turtleneck crowd is the *Aztec St Cafe* (☎ 983 9464), 317 Aztec St, serving coffee drinks and pastries from 7:30 am to 11 pm, Monday through Saturday, and 8 am to 9 pm on Sunday.

Housed in a yellow adobe home on a residential street, *Encore Provence* (☎ 983 7470), 548 Agua Fria, offers superb French food in an elegant yet simple atmosphere. There is no attempt at Southwestern flavor, either in the decor or menu, and the service is excellent. The menu changes daily, but expect to pay $15 to $25 for an entree. It is open 6 to 9 pm daily and closed on Sunday.

Just north of the canal, you can escape the tourist crowds and enjoy a good sandwich for under $5 at the *Noon Whistle* (☎ 988 2636), 451 W Alameda. A block north is the light and airy *Corn Dance Cafe* (☎ 986 1662), 409 W Water St, which features Native American dishes from tribes across the country, such as buffalo chile in a jalapeño bread bowl, venison shanks, wild turkey with cornbread and a buffalo burger with grilled yams. The food is very good, the menu interesting, and the service relaxed. A dinner for two, with a bottle of wine, appetizers and dessert, will run about $90, but the appetizers are huge and you could get by spending far less than that.

*Vanessie of Santa Fe* (☎ 982 9966), 434 W San Francisco, is a massive place with a high beamed ceiling, 12-foot adobe doors and big fireplaces. The menu includes only the basics, like a whole rotisserie chicken for $10.95 and an 18-oz ribeye for $21.95, but don't come here unless you've worked up an appetite. Everything is a la carte, and everything is huge. The lounge is open from 4:30 pm to 2 am, and a piano bar gets going at about 9 pm, seven days a week. This is a popular, fun spot. Dinner is served 5:30 to 10:30 pm.

For excellent sushi and other Japanese dishes, try *Sakura* (☎ 983 5353), 321 W San Francisco, where you can dine in the grassy courtyard or in a private tatami room. It's open for lunch Tuesday through Friday from 11:30 to 2 pm, and for dinner Tuesday through Sunday 5:30 to 9 pm.

A great spot for a legendary burger is *Bert's Burger Bowl* (☎ 982 0215), 235 N

Guadalupe St. There are no tables inside, and only a few out, but get a green chile cheeseburger for $3 to go. *Bagelmania* (☎ 982 8900), 420 Catron St, behind Bert's Burger Bowl, is the only New York-style deli in Santa Fe; you can get bagels and lox, pastrami and other deli goodies from 7 am to 6 pm Monday through Saturday, and until 3 pm on Sunday.

At the north end of Guadalupe St in De Vargas Mall, *Diegos* (☎ 983 5101) is considered by many to be Santa Fe's best bargain, and judging from the crowds, the New Mexican fare is excellent. Hours are 11 am to 9 pm daily. Also in De Vargas Mall is *Furrs Cafeteria* (☎ 988 4431), open 11 am to 8 pm daily, with all-you-can-eat meals for under $6. There is a Furrs at 522 Cordova Rd as well.

**Canyon Rd** *El Farol* (☎ 983 9912), 808 Canyon Rd, with a great old bar, low ceilings, heavy beams and live music, including blues and Latin, at 9 pm nightly, is a local favorite. The restaurant specializes in a delicious variety of Spanish tapas, including grilled cactus, chorizo and mussels, for $5, and main dishes go for $11 to $23. It's worth stopping by for a drink if nothing else. The bar is open daily from 2 pm to 1:30 am, and the restaurant serves from 6 to 10 pm nightly.

*Celebrations* (☎ 989 8904), 613 Canyon Rd, offers a pleasant place to relax on the patio or inside by the fire. Big salads, burgers, interesting sandwiches and Southwestern dishes range from $5 to $9, and hearty breakfasts are $4 to $7. It's open seven days a week from 7:30 am to 2 pm and for dinner Wednesday through Saturday, 5:30 to 9 pm. *Willy's* (☎ 986 3833), 802 Canyon Rd, claims to be the 'Home of New Mexican White Trash Cookin', serving inexpensive dishes like green chile macaroni and cheese in a funky atmosphere. Hours are 11 am to 3 pm, Wednesday through Monday, and 6 pm to 9 pm, Friday and Saturday.

**Cerrillos Rd** There are two places on Cerrillos Rd that are especially noteworthy.

Well known for its emphasis on light, clean cooking with organic ingredients and vegetarian entrees, the *Natural Cafe* (☎ 983 1411), 1494 Cerrillos Rd, is a tidy and light cafe with an outdoor patio. Try the East Indian tempeh curry or the free-range Sichuan chicken. Lunch is in the $6 to $9 range, and dinner is $10 to $16. It is open for lunch Tuesday through Friday from 11:30 am to 2:30 pm, and for dinner Tuesday through Sunday from 5 to 9:30 pm. Also consider trying *Telecote Cafe* (☎ 982 1632), 1203 Cerrillos Rd. This bright, unpretentious breakfast spot is popular with the locals. Atole piñon hotcakes for $5.25 and a carne adovada burrito for $7.25, as well as the homemade bakery items, fresh fruit and standard fare, are excellent, and the portions are generous. Hours are 7 am to 2 pm; it's closed Sunday.

The *Kettle Restaurant* (☎ 473 5840), 4250 Cerrillos Rd, is open 24 hours with an all-you-can-eat salad bar for $4.80. A local chain, *Souper Salad* (☎ 473 1211), 2428 Cerrillos Rd, offers cafeteria-style soup, salad, breads, sandwiches and all-you-can-eat specials. Hours are Monday through Saturday from 11 am to 9 pm and Sunday noon to 8 pm; no credit cards accepted. Another place open 24 hours is *Carrows Restaurant* (☎ 471 7856), located at 1718 St Michael's Drive. *Peking Palace* (☎ 984 1212), 1710 Cerrillos Rd, has a $6.50 lunch buffet Monday through Friday, 11:30 am to 2 pm, and noon to 2 pm on weekends. *La Tosena* (☎ 471 5700), 3279 Cerrillos Rd, is open from 8 am to 10 pm, seven days a week, and offers basic meals for $3 to $12.

*Baja Tacos* (☎ 471 8762), 2621 Cerrillos Rd, is another popular hangout. It's no more than a drive-through, but lunch lines can be long.

**Other** The *Tesuque Market* (☎ 988 8848) in the trendy valley village of Tesuque, seven miles north of town, has great breakfasts and sandwiches, seven days a week from 7 am to 9 pm. You can also buy the Sunday *New York Times* here! The bar at *Rancho Encantado* (☎ 982 3537), nestled in the foothills to the north of town, offers a

**NEW MEXICO**

spectacular view to the west over the Rio Grande Valley. You can eat at the hotel's restaurant, *Cactus Rose* (☎ 982 3537), and enjoy the view from the huge windows, but it's expensive. Another rural dining option is *Rancho de Chimayo* (☎ 351 4444), where you can eat in the outdoor courtyard against the mountains (see the Chimayo section below). The drive out there is breathtaking, and the food is good.

The *Wild Oats Community Market* at St Francis Drive and Cordova Rd (☎ 983 5333) and at St Michael's and Llano (☎ 473 4943) sells all kinds of health foods, including organic produce, free range chicken and fresh bread. They also have a deli, with delicious sandwiches and gourmet takeout, a salad and juice bar and pastries. Hours are 8 am to 11 pm daily.

## Entertainment

Go to the ticket counter at *Galisteo News and Ticket Stand* (☎ 984 1316), 201 Galisteo, for information on what's playing in the area and to buy advance tickets. Check the free weekly *Santa Fe Reporter* for the calendar of weekly events.

**Cinemas** A complete listing of what's showing in Santa Fe's cinemas can be found in the entertainment section of the daily newspapers.

The *Lensic Theater* (☎ 982 0301), 211 W San Francisco St, was built in 1930 and remains as it looked then with minor renovations. It is one of the few traditional movie theaters in the country, with a huge screen, red velvet curtains and intricately painted walls and high ceiling. The Lensic plays modern releases, as well as old favorites like *Casablanca*, but regardless of the film, the theater's worth the trip.

The *Jean Cocteau Theater* (☎ 988 2711), 418 Montezuma, and the *Center for Contemporary Arts* (☎ 982 1338), 291 E Barcelona Rd, play foreign and alternative films.

**Nightlife** *El Farol* (☎ 983 9912), 808 Canyon Rd, the oldest bar in town; *Tommy's* (☎ 989 4407), 208 Galisteo St;

and the *Cowgirl Hall of Fame* (☎ 982 2565), 319 S Guadalupe St, are small but popular venues for nightly blues, jazz, folk, Latino and Dixie. There may be a $2 to $6 cover charge. The lounge at *La Fonda* (☎ 982 5511), 100 E San Francisco, has surprisingly good country and folk music, among other draws. The piano bar at *Vanessie of Santa Fe* (☎ 982 9966), 434 W San Francisco, is another busy spot. *La Casa Sena* (☎ 988 9232), 125 E Palace, features waiters and waitresses singing Broadway show tunes. It sounds cheesy, but it's a hopping place! The *Dragon Room Bar* (☎ 983 7712), 406 Old Santa Fe Trail, has live entertainment nightly. It's a dark, cozy place, with free popcorn and bar food. Hours are 5 to 11 pm nightly. Nationally and internationally known rock & roll, folk, and blues bands play at the nightclub *Badlands* (☎ 820 2985), 213 W Alameda.

*Legends, Saloon & Dance Hall* (☎ 473 2998), on Hwy 14, one mile south of I-25, has country music and free dance lessons.

**Performing Arts** Santa Fe enjoys an incredible variety of music programs, many of them recognized internationally. It is not only the quality of the performances but the variety of venues – cathedrals, chapels and outdoor theaters – that make them particularly interesting. The Orchestra of Santa Fe (☎ 988 4640), known for its unique programming of classical and contemporary music, plays February through May, September and October, offering Handel's *Messiah* in November. The Santa Fe Symphony (☎ 983 3530, 1 (800) 658 7974) has seven subscription concerts annually and seven special event performances. The symphony performs at *Sweeney Convention Center* at Marcy and Grant Sts. Chamber music performed by the Ensemble of Santa Fe (☎ 984 2501) in the *Loretto Chapel* and the *Santuario de Guadalupe* can be heard October through May.

The Santa Fe Chamber Music Festival (☎ 983 2075), which runs from the middle of July through the end of August, brings internationally renowned classical and jazz musicians to Santa Fe. Another seasonal event is the Desert Chorale (☎ 988 7505, 1 (800) 244 4011), with six eclectic programs from early July through mid-August. They also perform Christmas concerts at the *Santuario de Guadalupe*.

Poetry readings, dance concerts and other performances are presented at the *Center for Contemporary Arts* (☎ 982 1338), 291 E Barcelona. The Maria Benitez Spanish Dance Company (☎ 983 8477) performs flamenco and other Spanish dances from June through September. Santa Fe Community Theater, the state's oldest theater company, performs avant-garde and traditional theater and musical comedy year-round. Call 988 4262 for information. During July and August, the free Shakespeare in the Park program (☎ 982 2910) takes place every Friday, Saturday and Sunday at *St John's College*. There is seating for 350 and space for blankets, and food is available. The *Old Santa Fe Music Hall* (☎ 983 3311), 100 N Guadalupe St, has dinner theater consisting of an original off-Broadway Western musical. Tickets, which include dinner, run $28 to $35. Summerscene (☎ 438 8834), sponsored by the City of Santa Fe Arts Commission, features a series of free noon and evening concerts twice a week on the Plaza from June to August.

There are numerous other smaller companies performing a variety of shows. The Santa Fe Theater Alliance (☎ 984 8464) publishes a quarterly brochure that includes a schedule of upcoming performances, and you can pick one up at any major hotel or at the convention center at Marcy and Grant Sts.

## Things to Buy

You can spend weeks shopping in Santa Fe, and some people do just that. During the summer, the stores can be annoyingly crowded, but if you have the patience and the pocketbook, you'll find many beautiful things to buy. Native American jewelry, predominantly of silver and turquoise, basket work, pottery and textiles are for sale at about every other store, as well as along the Palace of the Governors and in

the Plaza. The quality and prices vary considerably from store to store, and though the choices can be overwhelming, it is worth shopping around before buying. If you browse in the nicest shops first, you'll learn what distinguishes the best quality items. Even shops with mediocre stock often have a few good-quality items, and if you know the difference between good and poor quality items, you'll save time and money. The *Wingspread Collectors Guide* provides specific information and maps for all the galleries in town; you can pick one up at most of the big hotels. Store hours vary according to the season, but generally stores are open from 9 am to 5 pm, Monday through Saturday.

*Coyote Cafe General Store* (☎ 982 2454), 132 W Water, stocks an incredible variety of Southwestern salsa, hot sauces, chiles, tortilla and sopaipilla mixes and other local food items, as well as cookbooks. Another place for Southwestern culinary delights is the *Chili Shop* (☎ 983 6080), 109 E Water. You can also get chile pepper ceramics, chile pepper placemats, chile pepper door handles . . . you get the idea! A unique metal alloy that contains no silver, lead or pewter but looks like silver was discovered in 1951 to the north of Santa Fe near Nambe. As durable as iron and able to retain heat and cold for hours, the alloy is ideal for cookware. Nambeware capitalizes on this idea. Each piece is individually sandcast in designs that have won national and international recognition, including being selected for the Museum of Modern Art's exhibition entitled *US Design at Its Best*. There are two *Nambe* foundry outlets in Santa Fe, one at 112 W San Francisco (☎ 988 3574) and the other at 924 Paseo de Peralta (☎ 988 5528).

If you're looking for Mexican-style tiles, go to *Artesanos* (☎ 983 5563), 222 Galisteo St, which has a wide variety of tile by the piece, as well as tile sinks, door knobs, bathroom objects and other Mexican folk art. For $2, you can get a catalog. You can also send *ristras* (wreaths of chile peppers) directly from the store. *James Reid Ltd* (☎ 988 1147), 114 E Palace Ave, has some beautiful handcrafted silver jewelry and an exceptional collection of belt buckles. *Kent Galleries* (☎ 988 1001), 130 Lincoln Ave, represents local craftsmen, featuring contemporary furniture, jewelry, woodwork and ceramics. All the work is of superior quality, and it is considered the best craft gallery in town.

You can buy what has become known as Santa Fe-style folk art, including brightly painted snakes, coyotes and rabbits, at the *Davis Mather Folk Art Gallery* (☎ 983 1660), 141 Lincoln. If you love rare and fine art books, don't miss the *Santa Fe Bookseller* (☎ 983 5278), 203 W San Francisco, a small place packed to the ceiling with books that encourages browsing by the hour. For photography books, including first editions and out of print books, go to *Photo Eye Books* (☎ 988 4955) 376 Garcia St. The *Mineral and Fossil Gallery* (☎ 984 1682, 1 (800) 762 9777), 127 San Francisco, has an excellent collection of, of course, minerals and fossils. For outdoor equipment and an excellent selection of local hiking guides, go to *Base Camp* (☎ 982 9707), 121 W San Francisco.

Any kind of herb you can think of, including Chinese and homeopathic remedies, can be found at *Herbs, Etc* (☎ 982 1265), 323 Aztec St. From June through April, on Tuesdays and Saturdays from 7 am to noon, the Farmers Market at Sambusco Market Center features local produce, fresh salsas and chile and baked goods. Also in the Sambusco Plaza is *The Winery* (☎ 982 9463), with a great selection of domestic and imported wine.

*Trader Jack's Flea Market*, next to the opera north of town, runs from Easter through Thanksgiving, Friday through Sunday from 8 am to 4 pm. There are hundreds of vendors selling everything from cast iron pots to Indonesian textiles to old hinges and doorknobs in the dusty parking lot. You never know what you'll find here, and it's a great place to poke around. Remember to bargain!

Perhaps more of a museum than a gallery is *Fenn Galleries* (☎ 982 4631), 1075 Paseo de Peralta, one of Santa Fe's best

known galleries. The outdoor garden features larger-than-life bronze sculptures, and the low-ceilinged adobe interior is filled with masterpieces. Even if you can't afford to buy anything here, it's worth a stop just to admire the work.

*Santa Fe Factory Stores* (☎ 474 4000), at the southern end of Cerrillos Rd, is an outdoor mall with discount shopping. Major chains, predominantly clothes and shoe stores, sell overstocked and last year's items at reduced rates. The adobe buildings and garden courtyard make this a pleasant place to stroll, and there is a delicious cafe, Cactus Zack's Cafe (☎ 473 0444), offering homemade soups, salads and sandwiches.

## Getting There & Away

**Air** Mesa Airlines (☎ 842 4414, 1 (800) 637 2247) flies daily from Albuquerque into the Santa Fe Municipal Airport (☎ 473 7243) for between $49 and $99 one-way. Transportation to local hotels can be arranged through Santa Fe Hotel Limo Service (☎ 1 (800) 927 3536).

**Bus** TNM&O (☎ 471 0008), St Michael's Drive and Calle Lorca, is a subsidiary of Greyhound. It runs four buses daily from Albuquerque to Santa Fe for $10.50. Shuttlejack (☎ 982 4311) has a shuttle service from Albuquerque International Airport for $20 each way. It stops at the Inn of the Loretto and El Dorado Hotel but will pick up at other hotels if you are staying there and give them notice 24 hours in advance.

**Train** Amtrak (1 (800) 872 7245) runs between Albuquerque and Lamy, 17 miles from Santa Fe. From there Amtrak puts you on a bus to Santa Fe. The trip takes just over two hours one-way and costs $36/72 one-way/roundtrip. The Lamy ticket office number is 988 4511.

## Getting Around

**Bus** Santa Fe Trails (☎ 984 6730), Santa Fe's public bus system, is the country's first completely natural gas bus system. The cost is 50¢. Weekly passes are available for $3, and a monthly pass costs $10. You can

NEW MEXICO

buy passes at Wild Oats Market (☎ 983 5333), 1090 St Francis Drive, and Galisteo.

**Taxi** Capital City Cab (☎ 438 0000) provides service throughout town.

**Car Rental** Most major agencies have offices in Santa Fe. If you are flying in, check at the airport. Major hotels can help arrange car rental from town.

**Parking** Because of the swarms of pedestrians, one-way streets and heavy traffic, driving in town can be frustrating. Your best bet is to park in one of the indoor parking lots and walk to the downtown sites, stores and restaurants. La Fonda Hotel has parking for $1 an hour, with a $7 maximum per day, and there is a parking lot at the corner of W San Francisco and Guadalupe Sts.

**Bicycle** Near the Plaza, Palace Bike Rentals (☎ 986 0455), 409 E Palace Ave, rents mountain bikes for $15/20/85, half day/daily/weekly; maps, water bottle, lock and helmet are included. Reservations are recommended. Santa Fe Schwinn (☎ 983 4473), 1611 St Michael's, rents bikes as well. City bike maps are available at the chamber of commerce (☎ 983 7317) in the De Vargas Mall.

## AROUND SANTA FE
### Shidoni Foundry
Located five miles north of Santa Fe on Bishop's Lodge Rd in Tesuque, the Shidoni Foundry (☎ 988 8001) is an eight-acre apple orchard devoted to bronze sculptures. Founded in 1971, it has since evolved into a world-renowned fine-art casting facility and showplace. There is a gallery hosting changing exhibits, as well as a year-round outdoor sculpture garden set on the lawn. Every Saturday, and periodically throughout the week, you can watch 2000° F molten bronze being poured into ceramic shell molds, one of the several steps in the complex lost-wax casting technique. The artists practice mold-making and sand-casting on the premises as well, and will explain the process and answer questions. There are daily demonstrations of glass blowing at *Tesuque Glass Works* (☎ 988 2165), located on the grounds.

### El Rancho de las Golondrinas
El Rancho de las Golondrinas (☎ 471 2261), a 200-acre ranch with 70 restored and original buildings in the town of La Cienega, is a living history museum that shows what life was like for Spanish settlers in the 18th and 19th centuries. There are festivals in the spring, summer and fall, when volunteers dressed in period costumes demonstrate traditional domestic and farming activities, such as making bread and soap and drying chile. To get there, take I-25 16 miles south of the Plaza to exit 276 and follow the signs. It is closed November through March and prices vary. Call for information on festivals and special events.

### Pecos National Historical Park
When the Spanish arrived, Pecos was one of the largest pueblos. Five stories high and with almost 700 rooms, Pecos was an important trading center between the Pueblo Indians of the Rio Grande and the Plains Indians to the east. The Spaniards completed a church there in 1625 that was destroyed in the Pueblo Revolt of the 1680s. Another mission was finished in 1717 and remains of this one make up the prominent attraction today. The pueblo itself declined until there were only 17 inhabitants who moved to Jemez Pueblo in 1838. The five-story-high buildings fell into ruins that today are only grassy mounds.

The visitors center (☎ 757 6414, 757 6032) is open daily from 8 am to 5 pm, till 6 pm in summer, and closed on Christmas. A museum and short film convey a sense of the history of the area. A 1.25-mile self-guided trail goes through the ruins. Admission is $4 per car or $2 per bus passenger or bicycle; Golden Age, Access and Eagle Passes are honored. Pecos is about 25 miles southeast of Santa Fe. Take I-25 to exit 299, and head east to Pecos for eight miles;

or take exit 307 from I-25 and head north for three miles.

There are no facilities in the park, but you can camp in the Santa Fe National Forest to the north along Hwy 63. (See Places to Stay – camping above.)

## SANTA FE TO ESPAÑOLA
### Tesuque Pueblo

Nine miles north of Santa Fe along Hwy 285/84 is the Tesuque Pueblo, whose members played a major role in the Pueblo Revolt of 1680. Offices are closed on 10 August to commemorate their first strike against the Spanish. Today, the reservation encompasses spectacular desert landscape, and there is a small plaza with a Catholic church. The pueblo runs a bingo hall and a campground and RV park at Camel Rock (see Places to Stay above). San Diego Feast Day is on 12 November and features dancing, but no food booths or vendors are allowed then. Photography may or may not be allowed. Call the governor's office (☎ 983 2667) for information.

### Pojoaque Pueblo

Although this pueblo's history predates the Spaniards, a smallpox epidemic in the late 19th century killed many inhabitants and forced the survivors to evacuate. No old buildings remain. The few survivors intermarried with other Pueblo people and Hispanics, and their descendants now number about 200. They live in 'new' Pojoaque, which dates from 1934.

The pueblo operates a visitor information center (including information about other parts of New Mexico) and a museum/gift shop with top quality crafts from several area pueblos.

The pueblo public buildings are 16 miles north of Santa Fe on the east side of Hwy 84/285 just south of the Hwy 502 intersection. The annual feast day is 12 December, which is celebrated with ceremonial dancing. A commercial fiesta is held in early August with food and crafts vendors, entertainment and hot-air balloon ascents. Information is available from the Office of the Governor (☎ 455 2278).

### San Ildefonso Pueblo

Eight miles west of Pojoaque along Hwy 502, the ancient pueblo of San Ildefonso is where the art of pottery making was revitalized in the 20th century. This was the home of Maria Martinez, who with her husband, Julian, created a distinctive black-on-black style that has become world-famous and is considered some of the best pottery ever produced. Her work, now valued at many tens of thousands of dollars, can be seen in museums including the Popovi Da Studio of Indian Arts (☎ 455 3332), which is run by her family who continues the tradition.

Several other exceptional potters work in the pueblo, and many different styles are produced, but black-on-black remains the hallmark of San Ildefonso. A pueblo museum (☎ 455 3549) is open on request. Several gift shops and trading posts sell the pueblo's pottery. A fishing lake is stocked during the summer, and visitors can purchase permits on site.

Admission to the pueblo is $3 per car. Camera permits are $5, or $15 for sketching and videotaping. No photography or sketching is allowed during ceremonial dances. Pueblo hours are 8 am to 5 pm daily, but the museums and stores are usually closed on weekends. Ceremonial dances take place on the annual 23 January feast day. Other ceremonies include Matachine Dances around Christmas as well as Easter dances and Corn Dances in June, August and September, which are usually open to the public. Obtain information from the Office of the Governor (☎ 455 3549, 455 2273).

### Nambe Pueblo

Thirty sq miles set in a valley of piñon and juniper is home to some 600 members of Nambe Pueblo. Inhabited since around 1300 AD, the pueblo now has less than two dozen of the precolonial structures. Set in the agricultural river valley west of Española, the pueblo does not offer tourists much of historical significance, and it really doesn't have a town center.

On Hwy 503, follow signs for the

NEW MEXICO

**Nambe Trading Post** (☎ 455 2513), where you can find Navajo rugs, painted gourds and other crafts. Surrounded by farmland and woods, it's a welcome change from the hectic pace of Santa Fe. **Nambe Falls Recreational Site**, located in the hills above the pueblo, has one of the few waterfalls in New Mexico, and you can camp along the river and hike through the canyon to the falls. Fishing and electric motor boating is also available at Nambe Reservoir, a desert lake surrounded by sand and cedar. There is a $6 fee for fishing and a $7 fee for boating.

St Francis of Assisi Feast Day, celebrated on 3 and 4 October, is open to the public, but no photography is allowed. On the Fourth of July, the pueblo celebrates with dances at the falls. You can arrange a variety of northern New Mexican tours through **Nambe Pueblo Tours** (☎ 820 1340), 112 W San Francisco St, on the upper level of the Plaza Mercado in Santa Fe, which offers a 'Traditional Pueblo Feast' that includes native dances, story-telling and native foods at Nambe Falls Recreation Site two evenings a week from May through September.

There is a $10 fee to sketch or use a video or movie camera, and a $5 fee to use still cameras. Call the Governor's Office (☎ 455 2036) for further information.

### Santa Clara Pueblo

The well-marked pueblo entrance is 1.3 miles southwest of Española on Hwy 30. The Santa Clara Tourism Office (☎ 753 7326, fax 753 8988)), in the main tribal building just north of the pueblo entrance, is open from 8 am to 8 pm in the summer and from 9 am to 4:30 pm in the winter. Admission to the pueblo is $3, a camera permit is $5 and a permit for video cameras is $15. Private tours of the pueblo, which take you to see artists at work on intricately carved pottery, can be arranged with five days' notice.

Situated at the entrance to Santa Clara Canyon on the Santa Clara Reservation, 5.7 miles from the junction with Hwy 30 southwest of Española, are the **Puye**

**Cliff Dwellings**, an excellent example of Anasazi architecture. Ancestors of today's Santa Clara Indians lived here until about 1500. The original carvings were cut into the Puye Cliffs on the Pajarito Plateau, and structures were later added on the mesas and below the cliffs. You can climb around in the 740 apartment-like rooms on the top and enjoy a spectacular view of the Rio Grande Valley. There is a $5 fee for a self-guided tour, or you can arrange for a private tour by calling 753 7326. It is open from 8 am to 5 pm but stays open a little longer during the summer.

The Santa Clara Canyon Recreation Area offers camping, fishing for $10 per day, and picnicking and sightseeing for $8 per vehicle. It is open from 1 April through 31 October, and is located 12 miles south-west of Española on Hwy 30. Santa Clara Feast Day, featuring the Harvest and Blue Corn Dance, is open to the public, but sketching and videotaping are not allowed. Photography may or may not be allowed – ask beforehand.

### ESPAÑOLA & AROUND

In some ways Española is the gateway to the real New Mexico, separating the tourist infested wonderland of Santa Fe from the reality of the rural state, and as late as 1993, residents in the area did not have official addresses. The Rio Grande, Rio Chama and Santa Cruz River converge near the city, and the surrounding area is farmland, much of which has been deeded to Hispanic land-grant families since the 1600s. Though the town itself doesn't offer much beyond a disproportionate number of hair salons, its central location and abundance of good budget restaurants make it a convenient place from which to explore northern New Mexico. Instead of Santa Fe's quaint plaza, adobe buildings and expensive restaurants only 24 miles away, Española is predominantly made up of trailer homes and a strip of motels and fast-food restaurants. There has been an increase in violent crime in the area, so be careful walking late at night and lock your valuables.

## Orientation & Information

Hwy 84/285 runs from Santa Fe through Española. It's the main north/south road, splitting north of town into Hwy 84 heading northwest toward Abiquiu and Hwy 285 heading north toward Ojo Caliente. Hwy 30 runs southwest toward Los Alamos. The police (☎ 753 5555 or 911 for emergencies) are at 408 Paseo de Oñate. The hospital (☎ 753 7111) is at 1010 Spruce; for an ambulance call 753 3114. The chamber of commerce (☎ 753 2831) is located in the Big Rock Shopping Center next to Walgreens; it is open from 9 am to 5 pm Monday through Friday. The Santa Fe National Forest Supervisor's Office (☎ 753 7331) is on the Los Alamos Hwy.

## San Juan Pueblo

Driving one mile north of Española on Hwy 68 and one mile west on Hwy 74 will take you to the *San Juan Pueblo* (☎ 852 4400). It's no more than a bend in the road, but with a compact main plaza and cottonwoods, it is more pristine than most of the pueblos in New Mexico. The pueblo was visited by Juan de Oñate in 1598, who named it San Gabriel and made it the short-lived first capital of New Mexico. The original Catholic mission, dedicated to St John the Baptist, survived until 1913 but was replaced by the adobe, New England-style building that faces the main plaza. Adjacent to the mission is the **Lady of Lourdes Chapel**, built in 1889. The kiva, shrines and some of the original pueblo houses are off-limits to visitors. There is a $10 fee for photography and video cameras.

Stop in at the *Tewa Restaurant*, open 9 am to 2:30 pm, which serves traditional Indian foods, including posole, bread pudding and red and green chile stews. The arts & crafts cooperative **Oke Oweenge** (☎ 852 2372), open Monday through Saturday from 9 am to 5 pm in the summer, and until 4:30 in the winter, has a good selection of traditional red pottery, seed jewelry, weaving and drums. San Juan Feast Day is celebrated 23 and 24 June with buffalo and Comanche dances from late morning until mid-afternoon, food booths and arts & crafts.

The tribe operates **San Juan Tribal Lakes**, open for fishing at $7 per day with an eight-fish limit. Local rangers sell tribal permits. Plans are underway to open a 20-space RV park and a tent camping area and to add river fishing. Call the San Juan Pueblo Business Office (☎ 852 4213) for more information. Both Nambe and Santa Clara Pueblos offer opportunities for fishing (see below). Also open to the public is **San Juan Pueblo Bingo** (☎ 753 3132), located three miles north of Española next to the Pueblo Shell station. Wednesday through Saturday the games begin at 7 pm and Sunday at 1 pm. The Video Games Room is open all day and night, seven days a week. The casino tends to be smoke-filled and rather depressing, so don't come expecting the excitement of an upscale casino.

## Ojo Caliente

Billed as America's oldest health resort, Ojo Caliente (☎ 583 2233, fax 583 2464) draws therapeutic mineral waters from five springs. The waters have traces of arsenic, iron, soda, lithium and sodium, each with unique healing powers. Massages, facials and herbal wraps are $30 to $50. There are rooms with shared baths available for $70/340 daily/weekly and cottages for $76/380. Rates include two visits daily to the tubs and a full breakfast. Nonguests pay $7 for a bath during the week and $9 on the weekend. Hours are 8 am to 8 pm Sunday through Thursday, and 8 am to 9 pm Friday and Saturday. You can hike in the surrounding hills, and though this place is nothing fancy, it's relaxing. There is an outdoor pool, and horses are available for riding.

## Places to Stay

Nambe Pueblo, southeast of Española along Hwy 503, runs *Nambe Falls Recreational Site*, where camping sites with hookups go for $15 per night or $8 without hookups. From the sites you can hike to one of the few waterfalls in the state. South of town on Hwy 84/285, the *Cottonwood RV Park* (☎ 753 6608) at Cottonwood Plaza has nothing to do with cottonwoods; it is basically a parking lot with hookups. It operates a small store with Fedex and packing services, open from 7 am to 7 pm. Rates are $15/17 for a full hookup in the winter/summer and $12/14 for a tent. Camping is also possible at Santa Clara Pueblo for $10 per vehicle. Ten miles east of Española outside Chimayo is **Santa Cruz Lake**, which has camping for $7 a site, with a shelter and a grill. Follow signs down a winding road off Hwy 503 to the desert lake.

Rooms in Española are generally less expensive than in nearby Santa Fe. As everywhere in New Mexico, rates vary both by the month and according to how busy an establishment is when you call. Always ask for a discount! A couple of small, basic places to stay on Riverside Drive are the eight-room *Arrow Motel* (☎ 753 4095) with doubles for $35 and *Travelers Motel* (☎ 753 2040), with doubles for $30. The *Comfort Inn* (☎ 753 2419), 247 S Riverside Drive, has an indoor pool, with rooms anywhere from $40 in January to $85 during the summer. Built in 1995, the *Days Inn* (☎ 747 1242), 292 S Riverside Drive, has rooms from $40 to $60 all year, and the *Super 8* (☎ 753 5374), 298 S Riverside Drive, is comparably priced.

The *Park Inn* (☎ 753 7291), 920 Riverside, has singles in the low forties and doubles for $47. On the Taos Hwy, heading north out of town is the Ranchero Motel (☎ 753 2740) with singles/doubles for $30/35.

The most upscale place in town is the newly constructed adobe *Inn at the Delta* (☎ 753 9466, fax 753 9466), 304 Paseo de Oñate. All the rooms are huge, with hot tubs in the bathroom, Mexican tile, a fireplace, high ceilings with vigas and locally carved Southwestern furniture. Rates range from $85 to $150 for a double, with $10 for each additional person, and include a hot buffet breakfast.

## Places to Eat

Run by the same family that runs the Inn at the Delta, *Anthony's at the Delta* (☎ 753 4111), 228 Oñate NW, is open Monday through Saturday from 5 to 9 pm. It is a two-story adobe with trees in the indoor courtyard, a garden patio, a cozy bar and local weavings and pottery on the walls. This is the fanciest place in town, specializing in steak and seafood; rates range from $12 for barbecued ribs to $24 for lobster. *Angelina's* (☎ 753 7291), 210 Paseo de Oneote, doesn't look like much from the outside, but it is a great place for simple New Mexican fare, serving some of the best sopaipillas in the area and delicious beans and green chile. Hours are 7:30 am to 9 pm daily, and prices are under $8. Whereas Angelina's is popular with locals, *El Paragua* (☎ 753 3211), a two-story adobe home on the corner of Hwy 285 and Hwy 76 draws the tourist crowd. It enjoys a reputation for authentic, home-cooked New Mexican food and is popular with visitors, but the food is nothing spectacular. The restaurant is open daily from 11 am to 9 pm.

## Getting There & Away

Española is 86 miles north of Albuquerque, 24 miles north of Santa Fe and 44 miles south of Taos. All the major car rental agencies are in Santa Fe and Albuquerque. Greyhound offers service from Albuquerque for $15/28 one-way/roundtrip and from Santa Fe for $5.25/10 roundtrip. Buses stop at Box Pack Mail at 1114 N Riverside Drive. Call 758 1144 or 1 (800) 231 2222 for a schedule. Unfortunately, once you get to Española there is no public transportation.

## ESPAÑOLA TO TAOS

Off Hwy 84/285 you can take either Hwy 68 (known as the Low Road) northeast toward Taos or Hwy 76 (the High Road), a route that goes east and then north. Another option is to turn east on Hwy 503 toward Nambe Pueblo and connect with Hwy 76 in Chimayo.

## High Road to Taos

Generally considered the scenic road to Taos, the High Road winds through a spectrum of landscapes including river valleys, 100-foot-high sandstone cliffs reminiscent of road runner cartoons and high mountain pine forests. There are numerous galleries and small villages along the way. Plan on spending at least an afternoon, but if you don't stop at all you can make it to Taos in 2½ hours. Either start the drive north of Santa Fe at Tesuque (town, not pueblo), taking Hwy 590 north to Hwy 503 and then east on Hwy 76, or go east on Hwy 503 from Pojoaque through Nambe and take Hwy 520 north to Hwy 76.

**Chimayo** If at all possible, make the drive to Chimayo during sunset – the light on the high desert hills is simply spectacular. Originally established by Spanish families with a land grant, Chimayo is famous for its **Santuario de Chimayo**, built in 1816. Legend has it that the dirt from the church has healing powers, and the back room stands as a shrine to its miracles, with canes, wheelchairs, crutches and other medical aids hanging from the wall. Kneel into a hole in the ground and smear dirt on the parts of your body that are ailing. As many as 30,000 people make an annual pilgrimage to the church every spring on Good Friday.

Even if you're not going to Taos, go to *Rancho de Chimayo* (☎ 351 4444 for the restaurant, 351 2222 for rooms) on Hwy 520 in Chimayo, an old ranch house backing up to the hills, to enjoy New Mexican food in the courtyard or by the fire in the winter. The ranch also has seven attractive rooms with private bath for $70 to $110 a night.

Another option for accommodations is *La Posada de Chimayo B&B* (☎ 351 4605), PO Box 463, 87522. It's at the end of a quiet dirt road – call for directions to this rustic retreat. There are two unpretentious suites each with a private bath and Indian-style fireplace, and four rooms with a private bath. Rates range from $85 to $115 for a double.

Stop in at the *Oviedo Gallery* (☎ 351 2280) on Hwy 76. The Oviedo family has been carving native woods since 1739, and today the gallery is housed on the family farm. Marco Oviedo, a donkey breeder with a PhD, was the first in the state to freeze donkey semen, and he conducts research on artificial insemination in donkeys when he's not working on his art. His carvings have consistently won awards at the Indian Market in Santa Fe. If you're interested in handloomed weaving, you're better off avoiding the tourist infested *Ortegas* (☎ 351 4215) and stopping instead at *Centinela Traditional Arts* (☎ 351 2180). Irvin Trujillo, a seventh-generation Rio Grande weaver, whose carpets are in collections at the Smithsonian in Washington, DC, and the Museum of Fine Arts in Santa Fe, works out of and runs this cooperative gallery of sixteen weavers. Naturally dyed blankets, vests and pillows are sold, and you can watch the artists weave on handlooms in the back.

The quaint-looking Chimayo has developed a reputation for drug and gang problems. Don't be fooled into thinking it's a safe rural village. Be careful walking around after dark, and always lock your car.

**Truchas** Continue up Hwy 76 to Truchas, where Robert Redford's *Milagro Beanfield War* was filmed. On a clear day you can see across the Rio Grande Valley to the Jemez Mountains, Los Alamos and the flat-topped Pedernal, and south to the Sandia Mountains by Albuquerque. The *Truchas Mountain Cafe* serves New Mexican food in a dining area with a spectacular view. Private rooms or casitas for $60 to $110 a night are available at the *Truchas Farmhouse* (☎ 689 2245), PO Box 410, 87578. Call for weekly rates.

**Las Trampas** Built in 1760 and considered one of the finest surviving 18th-century churches, the **Church of San Jose de Gracia** is worth a stop. The church is open from 9 am to 5 pm daily in June, July and August.

**Picuris Pueblo** Just past **Peñasco** village near the junction of Hwys 75 and 76 lies Picuris Pueblo (☎ 587 2957). Though the smallest of the pueblos, Picuris played a major role in the Pueblo Revolt of 1680, and when the Spanish retook control the Picuri fled their pueblo. In 1706 they returned, with only about 500 of the original 3,000 members, and today that population has fallen to 250. Few original mud and stone houses remain at Picuris, and those that do overlook the Pueblo Creek and house mostly elders of the tribe. Today, the Picuri are working to return the bison to all-Indian land, not for commercial use but for the animal's spiritual significance.

There is a $10 fee for sketching, a $5 fee to use still cameras and a $10 fee for movie or video cameras. During celebrations, photography may or may not be allowed. Permits can be purchased at the tribal office. Write or call Picuris Visitor Center (☎ 587 2957), PO Box 487, Peñasco, 87553, for further information.

Pottery, beadwork and weaving, as well as historical artifacts, are on display at the **Picuris Pueblo Museum**. There is no charge. Pick up a self-guided tour, explaining the significance of points of interest, from the tribal office. Fishing permits for Pu-Na and Tu-Tah Lakes can be bought for $4 from the Tribal Game and Fish Ranger.

The ceremonies celebrating San Lorenzo Feast Day, commence on the evening of 9 August, with mass at San Lorenzo Mission, native rituals and a procession along the shrine path through the northern part of the village. There are foot races and dances the following day. Be sure to ask at the tribal office exactly when photography is allowed, as it changes throughout the celebration. On the first weekend of July, there is an arts & crafts fair with food booths and a fishing derby to raise money for the restoration of San Lorenzo Church.

The *Hidden Valley Shop and Restaurant* overlooking Tu-Tah Lake is open for lunch and dinner seven days a week, with breakfast at 9 am on Sundays only. Primitive camping requires a $5 permit from the tribal office.

From Picuris Pueblo, follow Hwy 75 east and go north on Hwy 518 to connect with Hwy 68, the main road to Taos.

### Low Road to Taos

Hwy 68 out of Española turns into a winding, two-lane road, following the Rio Grande 37 miles to Taos. Though the High Road is pushed as the scenic route, this way is equally beautiful and will get you to Taos more quickly. Much of the road cuts through the river valley, with steep sides of rock to one side and the river on the other, and it's crowded with impatient drivers in both summer and winter. Rather than rushing up to Taos, give yourself time to explore. There are numerous spots to pull over and fish, fruit stands with ristras and local apples, and art galleries, as well as several wineries and cafes.

**Velarde** Fifteen miles north of Española is **Black Mesa Winery** (☎ 852 2820), 1502 Hwy 68 in Velarde, where you can stop and try the locally made wine. The winery also runs a B&B, with two rooms, each for $75 including a bottle of wine and a full, hot breakfast. The highway then cuts through the apple orchards of Velarde and into the Rio Grande Canyon.

Eight miles further down the road is *Embudo Station* (☎ 852 4707), a brewery and cafe that make a pleasant place to enjoy a freshly brewed beer under the cottonwoods along the Rio Grande, though the food leans toward the expensive side. The restaurant offers the standard New Mexican fare and sandwiches, and specializes in fresh smoked ham and trout. It is closed in the winter.

**Pilar** Seven miles further north (and 17 miles south of Taos), Pilar comprises no more than four buildings, but it's the regional center for summer white-water rafting. The **Plum Tree Gallery** (☎ 758 4675, 1 (800) 373 6028) features theme-oriented shows of sculpture and paintings. Rich Thibodeaux, who owns the gallery, grows all his own food and makes his own cheese and yogurt on his small organic farm and orchards. For $25 a person, he will take you for a day hike through the foothills on a goat walk, which literally means walking his goats through the government-owned land. The walk includes a complete lunch produced on his farm. The foothills are a great place for rock hounds, and Thibodeaux is an expert on the area.

Pilar is a peaceful, rural alternative to some of the more expensive Taos accommodations. Camping is possible at the *Orilla Verde National Recreation Site* (☎ 758 4060). To get there, take Hwy 567 west at the Pilar Yacht Club. The BLM runs four campgrounds with shelter, toilets and drinking water, and three are right on the Rio Grande. With great fishing and spectacular high desert/river valley landscape, this is a convenient and beautiful place to camp, but it tends to be busy in the summer. There is a $5 charge per site, per night.

The Greyhound bus will drop you off at the front step of the *Plum Tree Hostel* (☎ 758 0090), a friendly, relaxed place next door to the Pilar Yacht Club. Eva Behrens, the owner, runs Rio Grande Reservations and can help arrange rafting trips, horseback riding, and B&B accommodations in the area. There are two dorms with six beds in each, and they cost $8 during the summer and $9 in the winter. Private rooms are $27/39/50 for two/three/four members and $3 more for nonmembers. Also available are two dome houses by the orchards in the back of the hostel, which sleep one or two people in a loft bed. Though you have to walk to the main house for the bathroom, they're very quiet, private and only $16.50 a night for one ($19.50 for nonmembers) or $20/24 for two. Weekly and monthly rates are negotiable. The kitchen is available to all guests, and towels and linens are provided at no charge.

The *Pilar Yacht Club* (☎ 758 9072) sells burritos and pastries in the summer, as well as arranging river trips. *Sweetwater B&B* (☎ 758 9362), Box 3A, No 83, Hwy 570, 87531, has double beds with continental breakfast for $52 .

## TAOS
## History

The first permanent residents of the area were descendants of the Anasazi, or 'enemy ancestors', who arrived around 900 AD. The Taos Pueblo, a spectacular example of Indian architecture dating back to 1440, was a thriving community by the time conquistador Hernando de Alvarado came to the area in 1540. By 1598, Padre de Zamora had established the first mission, and in 1617 Frey Pedro de Miranda led the first flock of Spanish colonists to the area we now know as Taos, a Tewa phrase meaning 'place of the red willows'. After 100 years of Spanish rule and shaky tolerance between the Indians and the Spanish colonists, the pueblo people rebelled in the Great Pueblo Revolt of 1680. All the Spaniards in the area were either killed or forced to flee, and many ended up in what is now El Paso, Texas. The next influx of Spanish settlers began again in 1692, when Don Diego de Vargas arrived with orders to reconquer the Indians. After four years of violence, colonists came to live in areas around the pueblo and in Rancho de Taos and Taos Plaza.

French trappers came in 1739 to hunt in the rich beaver ponds of the surrounding area, and the second phase of Taos history began. The town soon became a trading center for British and American mountain men and Indians in surrounding pueblos. Its reputation spread, and traders from as far away as Missouri and Mexico came with wagon trains full of goods to trade at the famous Taos trade fairs. Kit Carson, the most prominent name in the westward expansion, first came to Taos in 1826 and continued to come sporadically between expeditions. In 1843 he married the 14-year-old daughter of a wealthy Taos family and settled in Taos as a permanent resident.

In 1847 Taos was involved in another uprising after the American conquest. Hispanics and members of the Taos Pueblo fought against American rule, and Governor Charles Bent died in the massacre that followed. Except for occasional disputes

Bull riding at the rodeo of the Inter-Tribal Ceremonial in Gallup (RR)

Well-preserved Old West building on Manzanares St, Socorro (RR)

A shop in Santa Fe's Burro Alley (AN)

Shops in Albuquerque's Old Town (RR)

Mural of Virgen de Guadalupe in Santa Fe (AN)

Mural on Guadalupe St in Santa Fe (AN)

A cemetery in Taos (RR)

A dwelling in Taos Pueblo (RR)

A view of the Sangre de Cristo mountains from Los Cordovas (RR)

Taos Pueblo and the Sangre de Cristos (RR)

John Lujan, a Taos Indian (GW)

during the Civil War and Indian skirmishes, Taos remained a relatively quiet outpost through the rest of the 19th century.

The third phase of Taos' history hinged on the arrival of Anglo artists and writers. In 1898, the painter Ernest Blumenschein and Bert Phillips were on a sketching expedition that took them 30 miles north of Taos, but a broken wagon wheel forced them to stay for an extended period in Taos. After returning for many summers, Blumenschein and his family took up permanent residence in 1919. In 1915 he was one of six artists to establish the Taos Society of

Artists, an organization that today still organizes shows of local artists, and he is recognized as the founding father of Taos' artists' colony. During the late 19th and early 20th centuries, Anglo artists thrived in Taos, attracted to the striking landscape and brilliant colors as well as the Indian history, spirit and lifestyle. Bert Harwood, Nicholai Fechin, Leon Gaspard and later DH Lawrence, Georgia O'Keeffe and Ansel Adams all contributed to Taos' reputation as a center for artists and writers.

In 1957, Ernie Blake transformed the tiny mining village of Twining, north of

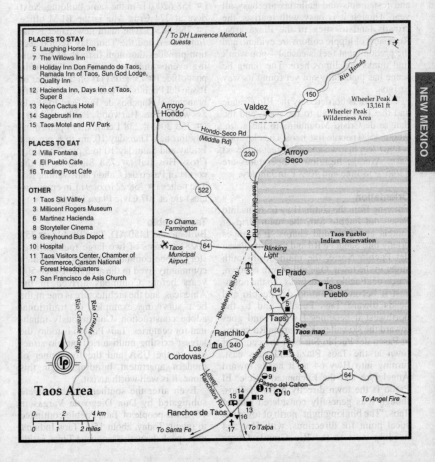

**PLACES TO STAY**
5 Laughing Horse Inn
7 The Willows Inn
8 Holiday Inn Don Fernando de Taos, Ramada Inn of Taos, Sun God Lodge, Quality Inn
12 Hacienda Inn, Days Inn of Taos, Super 8
13 Neon Cactus Hotel
14 Sagebrush Inn
15 Taos Motel and RV Park

**PLACES TO EAT**
2 Villa Fontana
4 El Pueblo Cafe
16 Trading Post Cafe

**OTHER**
1 Taos Ski Valley
3 Millicent Rogers Museum
6 Martinez Hacienda
8 Storyteller Cinema
9 Greyhound Bus Depot
10 Hospital
11 Taos Visitors Center, Chamber of Commerce, Carson National Forest Headquarters
17 San Francisco de Asis Church

To DH Lawrence Memorial, Questa

Rio Hondo

150

Wheeler Peak ▲
13,161 ft
Wheeler Peak
Wilderness Area

Arroyo Hondo

Valdez

Hondo-Seco Rd (Middle Rd)

230

Arroyo Seco

522

To Chama, Farmington

Taos Ski Valley Rd

Taos Pueblo Indian Reservation

Rio Grande Gorge

Rio Grande

Taos Municipal Airport

64

Blinking Light

3

El Prado

64

Taos Pueblo

Blueberry Hill Rd

See Taos map

Taos

Ranchito

6

240

Los Cordovas

Salazar

68

Kit Carson Rd

7

Lower Ranchitos Rd

8

9

Paseo del Cañon

64

To Angel Fire

14

15

11

12

10

13

16

17

To Talpa

Ranchos de Taos

To Santa Fe

**Taos Area**

0    2    4 km
0    1    2 miles

Taos, into a thriving ski resort. Thus began the fourth phase of Taos history. Despite Taos' current international reputation as an expert ski area, Taos Ski Valley is rather low key.

Today, visitors flock to Taos all year to enjoy the Carson National Forest, the plethora of art galleries and Taos Pueblo. Many of the historic adobe buildings are intact, and besides the Hwy 68 strip as you enter from the south, Taos has maintained a feeling of old Southwest. White-water rafting in the summer and skiing in the winter are the primary outdoor activities, and restaurants and galleries are busy all year. Though it is busy with tourists, the crowds tend to stick to the Plaza area. Remnants of hippie culture are evident, and the predominant feel is casual – you won't find minks and limos here. The Santa Fe scene has thankfully not yet found its way to Taos.

The town is bordered by the Rio Grande and the Taos Plateau to the west, and the Sangre de Cristo Mountains to the north. About 4500 people live here. The elevation is 6967 feet in town and 9207 feet at the ski base. Average high/low temperatures are 82/45°F in June and 40/9°F in January.

## Orientation

Entering from the south, Hwy 68 turns into Paseo del Pueblo Sur, the main strip of motels and fast-food chains. It changes briefly into Santa Fe Rd and then into Paseo del Pueblo Norte, the main north-south street in the town. One mile north of town, Paseo del Pueblo Norte forks. To the northeast it becomes Camino del Pueblo and heads toward Taos Pueblo; and to the northwest it becomes Hwy 64 and goes toward the ski valley. Kit Carson Rd begins at Paseo del Pueblo Sur near the center of town at the Taos Plaza and runs east, turning into Hwy 64 as it heads toward Angel Fire and the Enchanted Circle. El Prado is the town directly north of Taos, though it is generally considered part of Taos. 'The blinking light' north of town is a focal point for directions, with Hwy 64 heading west to the Rio Grande Gorge

Bridge, Hwy 150 heading northeast toward Arroyo Seco and the Taos Ski Valley, and Hwy 522 heading northwest toward Arroyo Hondo, and Red River and the Enchanted Circle.

## Information

Taos Visitors Center and Chamber of Commerce (☎ 758 3873, 1 (800) 732 8267), on the corner of Paseo del Pueblo Sur and Paseo del Cañon across the street from the Greyhound depot on the main strip, is open Monday through Sunday 9 am to 5 pm. The Carson National Forest Headquarters (☎ 758 6200) is in the same building. Next door at 224 Cruz Alta is the BLM office (☎ 758 8851). The main newspaper is the *Taos News*, and the Thursday Tempo section provides thorough listings of upcoming events and entertainment. The main post office (☎ 758 2081) is on the corner of Paseo del Pueblo Norte and Brooks St, with branches at Ranchos de Taos and El Prado as well. The Harwood Public Library (☎ 758 3063), 238 Ledoux, is open Monday through Thursday 10 am to 8 pm and Friday and Saturday 10 to 5 pm. The Holy Cross Hospital (☎ 758 8883) is on the corner of Paseo del Cañon and Weimar Rd. The police (☎ 758 2216 or 911 in emergencies) are at 107 Civic Plaza Drive.

## Taos Pueblo

Built around 1450 AD, Taos Pueblo (☎ 758 1028) consists of two large four- to five-story adobe communal houses. An Indian community lived in the area more than 500 years before Columbus arrived in the Americas, and the architecture is one of the best surviving examples of traditional adobe construction. Continuously inhabited for centuries, Taos Pueblo is today the largest existing multistoried pueblo structure in the USA and the forerunner of modern apartment buildings. For this alone, it is well worth a visit.

Even after the southern pueblos were subjugated by Don Diego de Vargas in 1692, the people of Taos Pueblo continued to revolt. Today, about 1500 Taos Indians, who speak the native language Tewa, reside

Taos Pueblo craft store (RR)

here. Sensing that Taos residents both welcome and resent tourists, visitors may be disconcerted and saddened to walk around the ancient complex with its various tourist shops. The pueblo is open to visitors from 8 am to 5 pm, but it is best to call to confirm times. In February, March and August the Taos Pueblo may be closed for sacred ceremonial dances. Visitors are charged $5 for parking though rates vary. Remember to ask permission to photograph, sketch or paint the pueblo. There is a $5 fee to use a still camera, a $10 fee for movie or video cameras, a $15 fee to sketch and a $35 if you want to paint. If you use residents as models, remember to tip them.

San Geronimo Day, 29 and 30 September, is celebrated with dancing and food. It is one of the largest and most spectacular Indian celebrations in New Mexico. Other special days are the Turtle Dance (1 January), the Deer or Buffalo Dance (6 January), Corn Dances (3 May, 13 June and 24 June), the powwow (in July), Santiago's Day (25 July), and the Deer Dance or Matachines (Christmas Day). Dances are open to the public, but cannot be photographed. Six kivas (ceremonial chambers) are closed to the public.

## Historical Homes

The homes of three influential figures in Taos history reflect three distinct elements of Taos history – the mountain man, the artist and the trader. It's well worth visiting at least one of these homes. Small and compact, they offer a great way to get a feel for Taos history. They are run by the same management (☎ 758 0505), and tickets for one or all can be purchased at any of the three museums – $4 for one museum, $6 for two and $8 for all three. There is no expiration limit on the tickets. The homes are open in the winter from 9 am to 5 pm and in the summer from 8 to 6 pm.

The **Kit Carson Home and Museum** (☎ 758 4741), located a block from the Plaza on Kit Carson Rd, houses such artifacts as Carson's rifles, telescope and walking cane. Kit Carson (1809 – 1868) was the Southwest's most famous mountain man, guide, trapper, soldier and scout, and his home and life serve as excellent introduction to Taos during the mid-19th century. Built in 1825 with 30-inch adobe walls and traditional territorial architecture, the 12 rooms are today furnished as they may have been during Carson's days, with exhibits on all periods of Taos history and mountain man lore. There is an excellent gift shop here, with a variety of books on outlaws, old-time trapping and farming, and traditional remedies. The shop also stocks local biking, skiing and hiking guides.

The **Blumenschein Home & Museum** (☎ 758 0330), 222 Ledoux St, dates back to 1797. In the 1920s it was the home of artist Ernest Blumenschein, his wife and daughter. It is today maintained much as it would have been when they lived here. Unusual European antiques, Spanish colonial furniture and original art fill the 11 rooms. Get the free guide to use as you walk through the home.

Resembling an adobe fortress, with no exterior windows and massive walls, the **Martinez Hacienda** (☎ 758 1000) on Ranchitos Rd two miles south of Taos served as a refuge for neighbors and valuable livestock during the Comanche and Apache raids of the late 18th century. Don Antonio Severino Martinez bought it in 1804 and enlarged it to accommodate his flourishing

NEW MEXICO

trade business. By his death in 1827 there were 21 rooms and two interior courtyards, and today the museum focuses on the life of a colonial family in New Mexico. There are daily craft demonstrations and an annual trade fair.

## Governor Bent Museum

When New Mexico became a US territory after the Mexican War in 1846, Charles Bent was named as the first governor. Hispanics and Indians did not appreciate being forced under US rule, and on 19 January 1847 they attacked the governor in his home. Bent's family was allowed to leave, but he was killed and scalped. Today, his home is a small museum with memorabilia from his early days as a trader along the Santa Fe Trail and his life as governor, and explanations of the historical circumstances that led to his death. The museum (☎ 758 2376), 117 Bent St, is open from 9 am to 5 pm in the summer, and 10 am to 5 pm in the winter. There is a $2 admission fee.

## Harwood Foundation Museum

The Harwood Foundation Museum (☎ 758 9826), 238 Ledoux St, housed in the historic adobe compound dating back to the mid-19th century, features paintings, drawings, prints, sculpture and photography by Taos artists. Founded in 1923, the museum has been run by the University of New Mexico since 1936, making it the second oldest museum in the state. Today, the Taos Public Library is on the first floor, but plans are in the works to move the library and expand the museum. Until this happens, much of the permanent collection, including 19th-century retablos (religious paintings on wood) and works by many of Taos' best known artists, are in storage. There is a $2 entrance fee.

## Fechin Institute

This museum (☎ 758 1710), 227 Paseo del Pueblo Norte, was home to Russian artist Nicolai Fechin, who emigrated to New York City in 1922 at age 42 and moved to Taos in 1926. His interest in art stemmed from working with his father, a woodcarver who built elaborate church alters. Today his paintings, drawings and sculpture are in museums and collections worldwide. Between 1927 and 1933, Fechin completely reconstructed the interior of his adobe home, adding his own distinctly Russian wood carvings. The Fechin House hosts exhibits of Asian art, as well as frequent chamber music events and art workshops. Unfortunately, until the heating system is renovated, the Fechin Institute is open May through October only, Wednesday to Sunday from 1 pm to 5 pm. Tours are available.

## San Francisco de Asis Church

Four miles south of the town of Taos is the San Francisco de Asis Church (☎ 758 2754), St Francis Plaza in Ranchos de Taos, open daily from 9 am to 4:30 pm, with mass on Saturday at 7 pm and on Sunday at 7 am, 9 am and 11:30 am. Built in the mid-1700s and opened in 1815, it has been memorialized in numerous Georgia O'Keeffe paintings. The light and shadows on its mud walls draw photo bugs and painters. The history of the church is summarized in a slide show. Ask at the church office. Today the church is used for ceremonies such as weddings and funerals.

## Millicent Rogers Museum

This museum (☎ 758 2462) on Millicent Rogers Museum Rd about four miles from the Plaza is predominantly filled with pottery, jewelry, baskets and textiles from the private collection of Millicent Rogers, a model and oil heiress who moved to Taos in 1947 and acquired one of the best collections of Indian and Spanish colonial art in the USA. Also displayed are contemporary and traditional Hispanic (both Spanish and Mexican) and Native American art forms and annual invitational shows of Hispanic and Native American artwork, as well as prehistoric and contemporary Pueblo pottery and paintings. A research library with more than 3000 books and pamphlets is open by appointment. The hours are 9 am to 5 pm daily, but call to

The San Francisco de Asis Church in
Ranchos de Taos is a popular subject for
photographers and painters. (RR)

confirm. Admission is $4 for adults, $3 for
students.

### Rio Grande Gorge Bridge

On Hwy 64 about 12 miles northwest of
Taos, this bridge is the second highest suspension bridge in the USA and is well worth
a stop. Built in 1965, the vertigo-inducing
steel bridge spans 500 feet across the gorge
and 650 feet above the river below. The
views west over the emptiness of the Taos
Plateau and down into the jagged walls of
the Rio Grande are awe inspiring.

### Earthships

Earthships (☎ 751 0462) are the brainchild
of architect Michael Reynolds, whose idea
was to develop a building method that
'eliminates stress from both the planet and

its inhabitants'. The Earthships are constructed of used automobile tires and cans
into which earth has been pounded. Buried
on three sides by earth, they are designed to
heat and cool themselves, make their own
electricity and catch their own water.
Sewage is decomposed naturally and
dwellers grow their own food. About 300
Earthships have been built around the
world, at an average of $75 per sq foot, and
the Taos Plateau is home to three prototype
communities for Earthship dwellers. Call
for information on tours.

### Enchanted Circle

This 84-mile loop around Wheeler Peak,
New Mexico's highest mountain at 13,161
feet, is a beautiful drive through the Carson
National Forest, with a few small towns
along the way. This is the way to the three
other ski resorts in the area: Angel Fire,
Red River and Ski Rio. There is a spectrum
of hiking trails, rivers and lakes along the
way, but you need to veer off the main road
to find them. You can buy a $1 guidebook
outlining everything you can see or do
along or near the Enchanted Circle from
the USFS at the Taos Visitors Center.
Storms arise quickly in both the summer
and winter, and parts of this drive are at
9000 feet. Be sure to check road conditions
before heading out (☎ 1 (800) 432 4269).

Take Hwy 522 north out of Taos through
the farming village of Arroyo Hondo to a
dirt road on the right that will lead to the
**D H Lawrence Memorial** (☎ 776 2245).
Mabel Dodge Luhan tried to give the ranch
to him in the 1920s, but he didn't want to
be indebted to her. His wife, Frieda, later
accepted it in exchange for the original
manuscript of *Sons and Lovers*. The Lawrences lived at the ranch for several years,
and when he died in Paris, Frieda brought
his ashes here. But she was so afraid that
Mabel would try to steal them that she had
them mixed into the cement of a small
shrine in the shape of a cabin. She was later
buried outside the memorial. Today, the
ranch is owned by the University of New
Mexico, which uses it for academic
research. There is no museum, but you can

come here to pay your respects to the Lawrences! Admission is free, and it's open 8 am to 5 pm.

Stop in at *Louie's Cafe* (☎ 586 0590) for the best greasy green chile cheeseburger in the area, and then just north of Questa, take a detour on Hwy 378 to the **Wild Rivers Recreation Area**. Flat, sagebrush-covered mesas surround the deepest part of the Rio Grande Gorge, and this is one of the most spectacular camping and hiking sites in the area. Though it can be busy in the summer, it is easy to get away from the crowds. La Junta and Big Arsenic Springs trails go into the gorge. There are other trails for all levels, including one which tracks through an extinct volcano. The small museum explains local geology, and staff offer interpretive hikes and evening campfire programs.

Take Hwy 378 back onto Hwy 522. Head south and at Questa take Hwy 38 east toward **Red River** and past the Enchanted Forest Cross Country Ski Area (see Red River section). The next stretch is completely barren high-mountain terrain until you get to **Eagle Nest Lake**, which is busy in the summer with boaters and anglers. Right on the lake, the *Moore Rest Inn* (☎ 377 6813) has 37 rooms, with doubles ranging from $50 to $100.

Continue west on Hwy 64 toward **Angel Fire** (see Angel Fire section) through the Carson National Forest, and back to Taos.

## Skiing

Founded by Ernie Blake, the **Taos Ski Valley** has been owned and operated by the Blake family for 39 years. Ernie Blake's vision of a skier's mountain preserving the alpine experience that he had enjoyed in the Swiss Alps still influences the feel of the town. This is a small, low-key, no-frills, ski valley. From the parking lot you can see all the hotels and restaurants, and the condominiums are tastefully nestled in the woods.

With all the ski and lodging packages available, it can be confusing to arrange your own trip. If you're interested in a ski trip, your best bet is to work through the Taos Valley Resort Association (☎ 776 2233, 1 (800) 776 1111, fax 776 8842), which can arrange complete packages, including roundtrip flight to Albuquerque and transfer to Taos, plus lodging, lifts and lessons. The association offers custom packages for all interests, as well as accommodations. In addition to Taos Ski Valley, good downhill skiing can be found at Red River, Angel Fire and Ski Rio (see Red River and Angel Fire sections).

Though skiing is the primary focus of Taos Ski Valley, it is trying to develop a summer clientele, and summer 1994 marked the first time that the lifts ran during summer months and hotels stayed open. Call the Taos Ski Valley for information on summer festivals and special events. If you are coming when the ski slopes are closed, be sure to call in advance to find out what areas are open, and plan on having a car or getting a ride. Shuttle service is sporadic and undependable.

**Information** With a peak elevation of 11,819 feet and a 2612-foot vertical drop, Taos offers some of the most challenging skiing in the USA. The 72 slopes (36 expert, 19 intermediate and 17 beginner) are serviced by 11 lifts. Snowboards are not allowed. The ski season runs from Thanksgiving through Easter, and rates both for lift tickets and ski packages vary significantly during the season.

Taos Super Saver rates are generally Thanksgiving to the week before Christmas, and the end of March to closing. A full-day lift ticket is $23, and a half day is $20. Prime Time skiing includes Christmas/New Year's, and generally all of February and March. Full-day lift tickets cost $37, and a half day is $22. The lifts are open 9 am to 4 pm. Half-day rates start at 12:30 pm.

Taos Ski Valley does not offer the amenities of a real town. There is no grocery store, and unless meals are included in a ski package, the restaurants tend to be pricey. You really are pretty isolated in the valley, and it is important to remember to bring any supplies or groceries from the town of

Taos. There isn't even a gas station anywhere in the vicinity! If you are staying in one of the hotels at the base, you don't need a car, but if you are staying in one of the lodges on the way from Taos, a car is critical because a shuttle for the two miles or so to the slopes averages $10 one-way.

Taos Ski Valley, Inc (☎ 776 2291, 1 (800) 776 1111) can answer all questions about the valley. The 24-hour number for snow conditions is 776 2916. There is a local sheriff (☎ 758 3361 or 911 in emergencies). Any other medical questions or problems should be directed to the Taos Ski Valley or to someone at the desk of any of the hotels.

To reach the valley, take Hwy 64 north out of Taos to the blinking light, and veer right on Hwy 150 toward Arroyo Seco. The whole trip is under 20 miles.

**Ernie Blake Ski School** The Ernie Blake Ski School (☎ 776 2291) boasts the best ski school in the country and offers an incredible variety of ski packages. If you're only interested in skiing, this is the way to go. The packages are coordinated with hotels in the valley but can also be arranged independently if you choose to camp in the area or stay anywhere beyond the ski valley.

The quintessential Taos ski-school experience is the traditional Learn to Ski Better Week, in which you can participate in a five- or six-day program that includes five days of ski lessons, accommodations and meals. They are offered all season, with reduced packages during Super Saver season. Other options include weekends of lessons for women by female instructors beginning 3 December; two-hour Mogul Mastery classes for $28, Sunday to Friday at 1:45 pm; a $50 beginners' program including ski rental, tickets and two lessons; ski guides who take 10 skiers into the high mountain ridges for two hours at a cost of $130; two-hour group lessons (seven students maximum) for $28; and private lessons at $65 an hour or $210 for a half day. Call the ski valley for more options.

**Other Activities**
Taos Outdoor Adventure (☎ 751 0721, 1 (800) 455 4453) enjoys a great reputation for organizing a wide variety of outdoor activities, including custom guided day hikes or cross-country skiing, with everything you need and lunch for $125; rafting trips for $40 to $90; rock climbing for $85 to $125; glider rides for $90; and fly-fishing for $225. The variety of outdoor activities in the Taos area is exhausting, and this company is helpful for either directing you where you want to go or organizing custom trips.

**River Running** The major attraction in the summer is white-water rafting in the Taos Box, the steep-sided cliffs that frame the Rio Grande. Busloads of rafters go up to Pilar from Santa Fe, and it can be a nightmare of sunburned and screaming tourists, but you can also enjoy quiet float trips away from the masses. There are several rafting companies offering day and overnight trips, so it helps to shop around. Be sure that you raft with a licensed company; there have been deaths due to inexperienced guides.

Some companies to try are Los Rios River Runners Inc (☎ 776 8854, 1 (800) 544 1181), a quarter mile east of the blinking light along Ski Valley Rd; Pilar Yacht Club & Cafe (☎ 758 9072) in Pilar; and Big River Raft Trips (☎ 758 9711), 231C S Pueblo Rd. If you're not interested in white-water or want to avoid any kind of group activity, the Pilar Yacht Club in Pilar rents one-person inflatable kayaks for $50, and they're a great way to relax down the river.

**Hiking** There is no shortage of nearby hiking trails, ranging from easy day hikes to overnight backcountry trips. Stop at the Carson National Forest Service for guides and maps. Before setting out on any kind of hike, be sure to check weather forecasts, let someone know where you're going and bring raingear. New Mexico is infamous for its volatile weather patterns, and the

NEW MEXICO

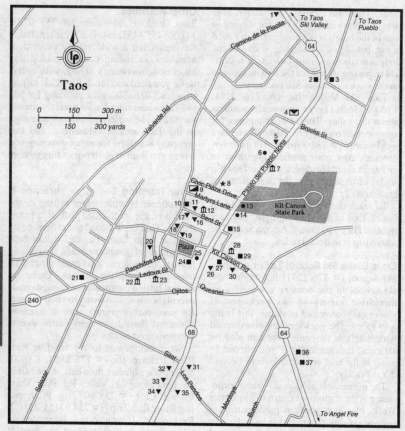

**Taos**

0    150    300 m
0    150    300 yards

Kit Carson
State Park

To Taos
Ski Valley

To Taos
Pueblo

northern mountain ranges can be dangerous in sudden rain- or snowstorms.

**Fishing** Los Rios Anglers (☎ 758 2798), 226 Paseo del Pueblo Norte, has guided fly-fishing trips. If you're a hard-core angler, and you know what you're doing, and you're willing to pay the $250 for a local guide, this is a fine place. But if you're just learning and are just as interested in enjoying the tranquility of the river as catching the big one, they can be a bit condescending.

**Horseback Riding** Shadow Mountain Ranch (☎ 758 7732), along Hwy 1, arranges rides through the alpine forest of the Sangre de Cristo Mountains, as well as specialty rides. The cost is $25 for one hour.

**Golf** The 18-hole golf course and driving range at Taos Country Club (☎ 758 7300), Hwy 570 W, is open from May to October.

**Swimming** The Don Fernando Pool (☎ 758 9171), 124 Civic Plaza Drive, is open all year to the public for $2.

**Ice Skating** There is skating on the pond in the Kit Carson State Park (☎ 758 8234) in the middle of town. Admission is $1, and skate rental is $1. It's open from 24 November through 28 February.

### Special Events

There are numerous athletic and cultural events all year, as well as workshops in the visual arts. For details on seasonal events, call 732 8267.

Major annual events include Taos Pueblo dances and celebrations (see section on Taos Pueblo), the Taos Film Festival in April and the Taos Mountain Balloon Rally (☎ 758 8321) in October. This last is a smaller version of the Albuquerque Balloon Fiesta, which tends to be overwhelmingly crowded. There are two mass ascensions of balloons, as well as parades, parties and community events. In Taos and Angel Fire, the Summer Chamber Music Festival draws crowds to outdoor concerts.

### Places to Stay

Taos offers a wide variety of accommodations, ranging from free camping in national forests to gourmet B&Bs in historic adobes. Driving in on Paseo del Pueblo Sur, you'll find standard motel chains. Winter skiing rates are the highest, dropping somewhat in summer and by up to $50 in the low seasons of spring and fall. Christmas and New Year's are peak periods

when many rooms are booked far ahead. Even during the low seasons, budget travelers will find no motels under $40. There are, however, two HI/AYHs in the nearby towns of Pilar and Arroyo Seco (see Pilar above and Places to Stay – bottom end, below).

In typical Taos style, prices are not always strictly adhered to, depending on how busy an establishment is. Be sure to call before assuming that the rates quoted below are accurate, and always ask if they are willing to go lower! Most places offer reduced weekly rates as well, and many have self-contained suites with a kitchen and hot tub. All rates listed are winter rates and do not include the 11% tax. The ski valley hotels generally offer only week-long packages, and these usually should be booked months in advance (see Taos Ski Valley section above).

The Taos Valley Resort Association (☎ 776 2233, 1 (800) 776 1111), PO Box 85, Taos Ski Valley, NM 87525, is an excellent general source for booking hotels, B&Bs, condominiums and private homes. If you let them know your budget and what you're looking for, they'll do the legwork and save you the hassle for no charge. They also arrange vacation packages that include car rental and airfare, as well as rafting, snowmobiling, horseback riding – whatever you're looking for – for less than you would pay if you worked it out on your own.

## Places to Stay – camping

The *New Mexican Recreation and Heritage Guide*, available at the chamber of commerce, is a map noting official camping sites, and the USFS also offers a free guide called *Recreation Sites in Southwestern National Forest*, which has detailed descriptions of USFS camping facilities. If you are planning on backcountry camping, be sure to stop in at the ranger station to check on conditions. Summer storms develop quickly, and winter weather can be treacherous and unpredictable. Campgrounds in and around Taos tend to be crowded in the summer.

There is no shortage of camping in the Carson National Forest. Most of these sites are under the jurisdiction of the USFS (☎ 758 6200) or the BLM (☎ 758 8851). The closest USFS campgrounds are east of Taos along Hwy 64. They are open spring to fall, depending on the weather, and have no showers. Vehicles must be under 16 feet. *Las Petacas*, four miles east, has nine free campsites with no water. Seven miles east of Taos, *Capulin* has 11 campsites with drinking water for $6. Just beyond is *La Sombra* with 13 similar sites. Some have a fee of $7 to $10. Generally, a fee indicates that drinking water is available.

The Carson National Forest Quest Ranger Station (☎ 586 0520) maintains three small campgrounds on the road to Taos Ski Valley. They are open from May to October, weather permitting. All lack drinking water and are free. *Lower Hondo*, 12 miles north of Taos and eight miles before Taos Ski Valley, has five sites. *Cuchillo de Medio* is two miles further and has three sites, and *Twining*, just before the ski area, has four sites.

The Wild Rivers Recreation Area, 14 miles north of Taos along Hwy 522 and then west on Hwy 378, offers some of the finest year-round camping and hiking in the area. Twenty campsites with drinking water but no showers or RV hookups are available for $7 a night, or you can camp in the backcountry. There is no river access. The BLM office (☎ 758 8851) is open from 1 May through 30 September. (See section

on the Enchanted Circle.) There's also camping at *New Buffalo* in Arroyo Hondo (see B&Bs).

The *Taos Motel and RV Park* (☎ 758 2524, 1 (800) 323 6009), 1799 Paseo del Pueblo Sur, has seven grassy camping sites for $12 and full RV hookups for $17 per vehicle. Weekly rates are $75 without hookups and $105 with. There is a $1.50 charge per person for more than two people. The *Taos Valley RV Park & Campground* (☎ 758 4469), Este Es Rd in Ranchos de Taos, has 92 sites open from April 15 until October. Tent sites cost $14, and RV sites with hookups are $19. Facilities include hot showers, a coin laundry and a playground.

## Places to Stay – bottom end

Taos' budget motels line the strip along Paseo del Pueblo Sur as you enter town from the south, and there are more along Kit Carson Rd. Some of the B&Bs offer rates equal to or less than the least expensive motel in the area, and offer a far more interesting experience!

Ten minutes north of Taos in the town of Arroyo Seco is *Abominable Snowmansion* (☎ 776 8298, fax 776 2107), which provides bunk-style lodging, as well as teepees and camping in the summer. Dorm beds are $15.50 in the summer, $22 in the winter, and private double rooms are $45 to $60 all year. Teepees cost $13 and camping is $8, including the use of showers and bathrooms. Linens are provided at no charge. Winter rates include a hearty ranch-style breakfast and summer rates include full use of the kitchen. There are six dorm rooms with private baths and a two-story lodge room with a circular fireplace. This is a clean, spacious hostel, popular with skiers and backpackers.

The *Taos Motel and RV Park* (☎ 758 1667, 1 (800) 323 6009), 1799 Paseo del Pueblo Sur, offers singles for $47, doubles for $49 with one bed or $52 for two beds. The *Super 8 Motel* (☎ 758 1088), 1347 S Santa Fe Rd, has singles/doubles for $47/52. The *Days Inn of Taos* (☎ 758 2203), 1333 Paseo del Pueblo Sur, offers rooms in the $55 to $70 range including continental breakfast. The *Hacienda Inn* (☎ 758 8610), 1321 Paseo del Pueblo Sur, has singles/doubles for $60/65. Singles at *El Pueblo Lodge* (☎ 758 8700, 1 (800) 433 9612, fax 758 7321), 412 Paseo del Pueblo Norte, are $48, and doubles are $63. Within walking distance of the Plaza is *El Monte Lodge* (☎ 758 8700, 1 (800) 828 8267, fax 758 1536), 317 Kit Carson Rd, offering singles for $65 and doubles for $75. Rooms have refrigerators, and there is access to a coin laundry. The *Koshari Inn* (☎ 758 7199), 910 E Kit Carson Rd, has rooms in the $45 to $70 range.

### Places to Stay – middle

**Hotels** *Ramada Inn of Taos* (☎ 758 2900, 1 (800) 659 8267 fax 758 1662), on the corner of Frontier Rd and Paseo del Pueblo Sur, has a pool and restaurant, with singles/doubles for $69/84. Suites with kitchen facilities are available for $100 at the *Sun God Lodge* (☎ 758 3162, 1 (800) 821 2437, fax 758 1716), 909 Paseo del Pueblo Sur, for $100, with singles/doubles in the $55 to $90 range. The Southwestern-style decor is well done, and some rooms have fireplaces. All rooms have a TV and telephone. The *Best Western Kachina Lodge* (☎ 758 2275, 1 (800) 748 2932, fax 758 9207), 413 Paseo del Pueblo Norte, a big complex with an outdoor pool, coffee shop, restaurant, entertainment, and conference facilities for up to 400, is walking distance from the Plaza. Rates are $65 for a single and $95 for a double. On Sunday mornings it has an all-you-can-eat breakfast for $7, and during the summer it hosts Indian dances on the weekends.

The *Sagebrush Inn* (☎ 758 2254, 1 (800) 428 3626, fax 758 5077), 1508 Paseo del Pueblo Sur, has a great long bar offering live music and country line dancing on the weekends. It's a huge 1929 mission-style building with giant wooden portals, an outdoor patio, tennis court and a swimming pool. Rates are in the $60 to $120 range, including a full breakfast. The *Holiday Inn Don Fernando de Taos* (☎ 758 4444, 1 (800) 759 2736, fax 758 0055), 1005

Paseo del Pueblo Sur, is the newest hotel in town and has a pool, tennis courts, a bar and restaurant. It offers a complimentary hors d'oeuvres buffet Monday through Friday, 5 pm to 7 pm, that can serve as a cheap alternative for dinner. Rates are $95/105 for a single/double. The *Quality Inn* (☎ 758 2200, 1 (800) 845 0648, fax 758 9009), 1043 Paseo del Pueblo Sur, has rooms in the $65 to $100 range and an indoor pool.

Centrally located right on the Taos Plaza, *La Fonda de Taos* (☎ 758 2211), 108 South Plaza, is a late 1930s hotel that looks like it has been left in a time warp. Though big, the lobby is eerily quiet, dark and dusty. It has great character and might be a good alternative to comparably priced chains on the strip. Even if you're not staying there, you might want to pay $3 to see a locked side room containing erotic paintings by DH Lawrence that were banned in England in 1929. The 24 rooms are small and musty. Doubles are $85, and suites of two double rooms with a shared bath sleeping four to six people are $120.

All of the five rooms at the *Neon Cactus* (tel 751 1258), 1523 Paseo del Pueblo Sur, are decorated in a particular movie-star theme. For instance, photos of Rita Hayworth and James Dean adorn the walls of two rooms, which are furnished with pieces from the '30s, '40s and '50s. Rates vary significantly depending on the season, with off-season rates as much as $50 less for the suites! The Casablanca room is $50 per night, the two suites are $125 for two or $145 for four, and the double rooms are $85. Rates include continental breakfast.

Six miles east of Taos Plaza on Hwy 64, *Taos Creek Cabins* (☎ 758 4715) rents five cabins with patios overlooking the creek for $60 to $100 with double occupancy all year, $10 for each additional person. A mile and a half further down Hwy 64 is *ShadyBrook* (☎ 751 1315), where you can rent an adobe casita with a fireplace, microwave and refrigerator for $75 to $110 a night – one night is free if you stay four nights. They have a little restaurant here where the chef will cook up anything you want, open from 8 am to 9 pm. A full breakfast is $3.50.

**B&Bs** There is a plethora of B&B accommodations in Taos and the surrounding area, and the differences among them are significant. The following are a few that are both reasonably priced and unique. Don't assume that a B&B is more expensive than a hotel. Most of the ones listed here are a very economical alternative to a strip motel. The Taos Bed and Breakfast Association (☎ 758 8245, 1 (800) 525 8267) can help find a place in advance, and it is especially helpful during peak season when many of the more desirable homes are booked.

The *Laughing Horse Inn* (☎ 758 8350, 1 (800) 776 0161), 729 Paseo del Pueblo Norte, 87571, is on Hwy 64 one-half mile north of the Taos Pueblo turnoff. In the '20s and '30s it was the home of Spud Johnson, publisher of a local magazine featuring work by DH Lawrence, Gertrude Stein and Georgia O'Keeffe, who were frequent guests. His quirky home, now more than 100 years old, has expanded to 10 rooms of various sizes plus a huge penthouse, most with shared bathrooms and some with a fireplace. The smaller ones have loft beds with the TV/VCR affixed to the ceiling. Singles are $42 to $52, and doubles are $49 to $65. Two guest houses with kitchen and fireplace are $120 for four people but can accommodate six for a little more. Rooms have VCRs, and the inn features a 400-tape VCR library, outdoor hot tub and loaner bikes. The kitchen is open to anyone who needs it, and there is an honor system for beer, wine, juice and snacks. The place is relaxed and friendly.

*El Rincón Bed & Breakfast* (☎ 758 4875), 114 Kit Carson Rd, 87571, is run by the daughter of Ralph Meyers, a well-known Taos figure from the early 20th century. His widow, 94-year-old Towena Martinez, continues to run the oldest trading post, now a store and eclectic museum of old Taos, 50 feet from the 100-year-old adobe home. Each room has a VCR and stereo, and many have fireplaces,

spas and refrigerators. They range from $59 for a double to $125 for a suite. Some of the rooms have waterbeds, and each one is done in antique furniture and Mexican tile. Breakfast is fruit, muffins and cold cereal by the fireplace in the winter or in the courtyard in the summer. There are no pretensions to this place, and you won't be disappointed by a generic bedroom at an exorbitant rate. The central location makes it easy to walk to nearby restaurants and galleries.

The *Willows Inn* (☎ 758 2558), at the corner of Kit Carson Rd and Dolan St, 87571, is run by Arkansas transplants Janet and Doug Camp, whose warmth and sincerity work to make this more like a home than an inn. A family-style hot breakfast and evening appetizers of wine and smoked trout, or something comparable, are included in the price, and Doug, an avid fisherman and guide, can direct you to local fishing and lend you his portable fly-tying table and tools. Listed on the National and State Historic Registers, the property was once the home and art studio of the late E Martin Hennings, a member of the Taos Art Society in the 1920s. The large adobe walls enclose an expansive lawn, towered over by two of the largest willows in North America, where Doug will snap your photo before you leave and then send it to you a few weeks later. There are five rooms, all with private baths, a fireplace and private entrance, for $95 each. Located a half mile from the Plaza, this is an especially nice place to stay in the summer, when the quiet gardens and grass are a welcome change from the high desert.

*Casa Milagros* (☎ 758 8001, 1 (800) 243 9334, fax 758 0127), 321 Kit Carson Rd, 87571, has five rooms for between $85 and $120, and a two-bedroom suite with kitchen, fireplace and double shower for $125 to $175, including a breakfast for two. Most rooms have a horno fireplace, and all have a down comforter and tasteful Southwestern decor. A couple blocks from Taos Plaza is *Casa Feliz* (☎ 758 9790), 137 Bent St, 87571, an adobe home listed on the National Register of Historic Places, which offers rooms from $85 to $110. Another option in the heart of town is *Casa Benavides* (☎ 758 1772), 136 E Kit Carson Rd, 87571. All rooms have a fireplace, private bath and antique furnishings, and rates include an afternoon tea with cookies and cakes, as well as a full breakfast. Rooms range from $95 for a double to $195 for a large room with two queen-size beds and a kitchen.

In nearby Arroyo Hondo, 12 miles north of town, two inexpensive B&Bs offer a unique Taos experience in rural solitude. *New Buffalo* (☎ 776 2015), 108 Lower Hondo Rd, 87513, is located on 80 acres in the Rio Hondo River Valley. A legendary commune in the 1960s that provided inspiration for the movie *Easy Rider*, it is run today as a B&B by Rick Klein, an original commune member, and his wife, Terry. A communal kitchen, a shared bath, five guest rooms decorated in Southwestern decor and a huge central kiva room with 12 skylights and winding stone steps are all suggestive of its former commune days. Breakfast is granola, fresh fruit and other healthy fare. Double rooms are $55, and the two-room suite, with loft and fireplace, is $65. Also available are teepees at $10 a person for dorm style (bring your own sleeping bag) or $20/40 for a private small/large one. The rate on private teepees is not per person, and one could put up to 12 in a large one. Camping anywhere on their land costs $12.50 for up to four people. Indoor kitchen facilities are available for rooms in the main house, and the teepees and tents have access to a solar shower, outhouse and outdoor kitchen. The New Buffalo is two miles from the confluence of the Rio Grande and Rio Hondo, where there are hot springs and access to the famous Taos Box rafting. Coming from Taos, turn left in Arroyo Hondo at the sign for the post office. Follow the paved road along the river, until it turns into a dirt road. you'll see signs for the New Buffalo one-third mile up the dirt road.

Another inexpensive rural option is *Mountain Light Bed and Breakfast*, (☎ 776 8474), PO Box 241, Taos, 87571. The two rooms are small and simple, but the house is perched on top of a hillside with an incredible 80-mile view over the valley and the Sangre de Cristo Mountain Range from the breakfast porch. This is a low-key place, with rooms from $35 to $48 for one person, $52 to $62 for two. A full breakfast of blue corn pancakes and eggs and use of a communal kitchen is included, but don't expect anything fancy here. In Arroyo Hondo turn right one-third mile past the post office road and look for the sign. It's best to call for directions!

### Places to Stay – top end

**Hotels** Parts of the *Taos Inn* (☎ 758 2233), 125 Paseo del Pueblo Norte, date to the 1600s, which is why it's on the National Register of Historic Places. The inn is probably the most upscale place in town. The cozy lobby of adobe archways, heavy wood furniture and a sunken fireplace is always busy, and there is live local music, from jazz and pop to classical, several nights a week. The Adobe Bar is packed on the weekends with locals and tourists alike. Stop for a drink or a snack. The rooms are, of course, decorated in a Southwestern motif, and the more expensive ones have a fireplace. Rates range from $85 to $160 all year long, except November and April when they are $75 to $115.

*Salsa del Salto* (☎ 776 2422) in El Prado on the way to Taos Ski Valley is expensive considering the size and decor of the rooms, which are unmemorable. Prices ranging from $85 to $160 include a gourmet breakfast and use of private tennis courts and a swimming pool. The giant stone fireplace in the sunny living room area is spectacular, and guests generally relax together over chips and salsa. Run by medal-winning skiers, this is really more of a B&B than a hotel.

With several rooms dating back to the early 19th century, *Taos Hacienda Inn* (☎ 758 1717, 1 (800) 530 3040), 315 Ranchitos Rd, is a rambling hacienda, completely enclosed by an adobe wall with huge cottonwoods in the courtyard. It's perched on a bit of a hill so you feel like you're far from town even though you're only a few blocks from the Plaza. The owners are from Aspen, and their focus is on luxury, but their efforts come across as a bit aloof and snobby. The public rooms are spacious, including a huge glassed-in breakfast room, but the bedrooms are rather small. Rates range from $85 to $185, including a full breakfast and snacks.

**Taos Ski Valley** There are about 20 lodges in and around the ski valley. Condominium rentals are available as well, and the easiest way to book one is through the Taos Valley Resort Association (see Taos Ski Valley above).

The lodges along the drive to the ski valley back up to the national forest, offering daily and weekly rates as well as a Ski Free package (from 24 November to 18 December and 27 March to 9 April) that includes lodging and ski passes. The *Anizette Inn* (☎ 776 2451, 1 (800) 446 8267), a quarter mile from the ski base, offers nightly rates that include a full breakfast and are based on occupancy, ranging from $95 for one person to $195 for six people in the winter, and from $45 to $75 in the summer. The Anizette's Ski Free package is $107 per couple. The *Columbine Inn* (☎ 776 1347), 1.8 miles from the slope, has quiet streamside suite rooms with a kitchen and fireplace for $145 a night, with doubles priced similarly to the Anizette Inn. The *Austing House Hotel* (☎ 776 2649, 1 (800) 748 2932, fax 776 8751) offers rooms for up to four people ranging from $95 to $150 during the ski season and from $50 to $85 during the summer. The Ski Free package ranges from $88 for a double and $155 for a room with four people, including passes for everyone.

There are three ski lodges at the ski base, and the differences between them are subtle. They all offer ski week packages, which include seven nights, six days of lift tickets, six morning lessons and three meals daily for seven days. Though all have better than generic rooms, many with fireplaces and refrigerators, the ambiance varies significantly. *Hotel Edelweiss*

(☎ 776 2301) is a small, cozy European-style hotel with newly renovated rooms. Doubles range from $65 to $150 all year, and ski week packages start at $1300. The *Inn at Snakedance* (☎ 776 2277, 1 (800) 322 9815, fax 776 1410) is the biggest of the three and is more like a big hotel than a ski lodge. Facilities include a mini spa with exercise equipment, a hot tub, a sauna and massage facilities, as well as a dining room and a bar overlooking the ski lifts. Summer rates are $75 for a double, and winter rates range from $115 in the Super Saver season to $210 in the holiday season. A meal package including lunch and dinner is available for $50 a day. Ski week packages range from $996 to $1398 per person. *Hotel St Bernard* (☎ 776 2251) generally offers only ski week packages, starting at $1320, but if it's slow they'll rent a room by the night. Call for rates.

### Places to Eat
Eating out in Taos can be disappointing, with some restaurants charging exorbitant prices for mediocre food. Try any of the open trailers along the road for a cheap, fast burrito or burger. Even the fanciest of places is casual, and restaurants are generally open until 9 or 10 pm.

**Coffee Shops** For an early cup of coffee and a donut, try *Daylight Donuts* (☎ 758 1156), 312 Paseo del Pueblo Sur. It's open Monday through Friday from 4 am to 1 pm, and until noon on Saturday, offering nothing but donuts and sausage gravy and biscuits.

The *Garden Restaurant* (☎ 758 9483), on the northwest corner of Taos Plaza, offers hearty portions of New Mexican fare for $7, standard eggs and pancakes for breakfast, an extensive sandwich menu at lunch, and steaks, stir fry, pasta and fish for dinner. Breakfast runs between $4 and $7, dinner between $7 and $12. This is a good place for a big meal at a reasonable price, but don't expect anything unique in decor or quality. They also have fresh-baked cookies, pies and breads to go. They're open from 7 am to 9 pm, seven days a week.

*Michael's Kitchen* (☎ 758 4178), 304C Paseo del Pueblo Norte Rd, is a busy breakfast spot for skiers and tourists, despite their claims that this is where the locals hang out. This place is always busy, and you'll likely find an early morning wait. Stop in for the biggest cinnamon roll you'll ever see (only $1.65) and a wide selection of hefty pastries. Breakfast includes the standard fare for between $4 and $7. Lunch and dinner offerings include sandwiches, burgers, New Mexican dishes, steaks and fish, with lunch in the $4 to $6 range and dinner under $12. Though the menu is extensive, the food is nothing special. It's open from 7 am to 8:30 pm.

The outdoor patio and grassy courtyard at *Cafe Tazza* (☎ 758 8706), 122 E Kit Carson Rd, is a pleasant place to enjoy an espresso and pastry. Menu items include homemade soups and tamales, and a wide selection of freshly ground coffee drinks in a bohemian atmosphere. Live entertainment consisting of locals playing folk-pop on acoustic guitars takes place on weekend evenings. It is open daily for breakfast and lunch from 8:00 am to 6 pm, Monday to Thursday and for dinner Friday to Sunday until 10 pm.

If you're looking for an interesting menu of freshly made sandwiches and salads, try the *Bent St Deli & Cafe* (☎ 758 5787), 120 Bent St. The emphasis here is on quality and variety, with the options of patio dining or takeout. The most expensive thing on the breakfast menu is the eggs Benedict for $5.75, and everything is a step above standard. With 21 sandwiches on the menu, including the Blue Ribbon BBQ for $5.50 and the Taos (turkey, green chile, bacon, salsa and guacamole rolled in a flour tortilla) for $6, you'll find what you want. It offers salads, including hummus, tabbouleh and Caesar. All lunches are under $7. For dinner there's pasta and a variety of unique chicken and fish dinners for between $10 and $12. Beer and wine are available, as well as award-winning desserts. Hours are Monday through Saturday from 8 am to 9 pm.

The *Mainstreet Bakery* (☎ 758 9610) on Guadalupe Plaza west of the main Plaza bakes bread for grocery stores in Santa Fe and Albuquerque. 'All organic – all natural . . . almost' is the motto in this simple place. It serves such fare as scrambled tofu and oatcakes, as well as a huge plate of eggs, beans and potatoes for under $5. Lunch is a burger or sandwich for $4 to $6 or the special – a bowl of black beans, green chile, red onions, tomatoes and cornbread for $3.95. Dinner runs under $10. It's quieter here, with more locals than tourists. Breakfast is served from 7:30 to 11:30 am, lunch noon to 2 pm and dinner 4 to 9 pm.

**Mexican & New Mexican** The newest rage among locals is *Fred's Place* (☎ 758 0514), 332 Paseo del Pueblo Sur. Before opening his restaurant, Fred spent months researching traditional recipes for standard New Mexican dishes. After talking to old Hispanic families in the area, as well as old timers of Taos Pueblo, and writing down their hints about not only what to cook, but how to cook, Fred opened his restaurant. His simple one-room place, reminiscent of old Mexico, has a small menu, but the quality is the highest in town. Everything is fresh and hearty. Try the carne adovada, slowly simmered pork in spicy red chile. Prices range from $3 to $7. It's open for lunch Monday through Friday from 11:30 am to 2:30 pm, and for dinner Monday through Saturday from 5 to 10 pm.

Though hotel staff may direct you to *El Patio de Taos* (☎ 758 2121), at the end of Teresina Lane north of the Plaza, you're better off stopping in for a drink and eating elsewhere. This restaurant's claim to fame is that it is the oldest building in Taos, built in the 1500s by Pueblo Indians, and is housed in a Taos Pueblo trading post. The decor is dripping with old Southwest, but the food is less than mediocre and overpriced – $9 for a small and forgettable burrito. It is, however, a good example of old architecture, and the kiva fireplace in the bar is a cozy spot for a drink.

*El Pueblo Cafe* (☎ 758 2053), 625 Paseo del Pueblo Norte, a no-frills cafe, is one of the few places in town open until 2:30 am

NEW MEXICO

on the weekends. Food is standard New Mexican fare, including traditional menudo and posole, in the $3 to $9 range. Beer and wine is available, and the portions are large. Open 6 am to 11:30 pm Sunday through Thursday, 6 am to 2:30 am Friday and Saturday.

**Italian** Perhaps the best restaurant in town, with prices much lower than some of the fancier places, is the *Trading Post Cafe* (☎ 278 5089), 4179 Hwy 68. Sit at the counter and watch the chefs utilize only the freshest ingredients in their northern Italian dishes. Scoop out a ladle of extra virgin olive oil to dip your bread in while you wait, and be assured that anything you order here will be delicious. Try the rosemary chicken, an oven-roasted half chicken with plenty for leftovers, for $8.95. If you're looking for a nice meal out, this is one of those places where all the pieces fall together; it's a better value than many of the more expensive restaurants in town and a favorite with locals. Housed in an old trading post, the decor is upscale and lively. The lunch menu runs in the $5 to $7 range, but expect to pay about $25 a person for a dinner with dessert and wine. It's open from 11:30 am to 2:30 pm for lunch and 5 to 9:30 pm for dinner.

The *Outback* (☎ 758 3112), located on Paseo del Pueblo Norte north of Allsup's convenience store and behind Video Casais, is a local favorite for pizza by the slice or whole. The menu includes calzones and unique pizza toppings like honey-chipotle chile sauce, Thai chicken and, of course, green chile. A slice costs between $2.50 and $4.25, and expect to pay $14 for a whole plain cheese pizza and up to $21 for some of the quirky gourmet pizzas. Salads and sandwiches, as well as beer and wine, are also available. Open Sunday through Thursday from 11 am to 9 pm, Friday and Saturday until 10 pm.

*La Luna* (☎ 751 0023), a quarter mile south of the Plaza at Pueblo Alegre Mall across from Smiths, serves traditional Italian specialties, including antipasto, 12 pasta specials, marinated shrimp and fresh mussels, pizzas baked in a wood-burning oven and lasagna. Lunch is Italian sandwiches and salads in the $5 to $7 range, and dinner runs from $6 to $10. To-go orders are also available. It's open for lunch Monday through Friday from 11:30 am to 2:30 pm, and for dinner Sunday through Thursday from 5:30 to 10 pm, Friday and Saturday from 5:30 to 11 pm.

One of the most elegant restaurants in town is *Villa Fontana* (☎ 758 5800), housed in an old home five miles north of Taos on Hwy 522. Northern Italian dishes focusing on locally picked mushrooms and seasonal game range from $14 to $25. It's open Monday through Saturday for cocktails at 4:30 pm, and dinner is served from 6 pm to closing.

**Continental** The *Apple Tree* (☎ 758 1900), 123 Bent St, is consistently excellent and reasonably priced considering the quality of the food, the creative menu and the historic adobe atmosphere. If you are looking for a delicious, upscale meal, this is a good bet. It is centrally located, cozy and relaxed, with impeccable service and ample servings. The dinner menu includes an appetizer of half a smoked trout for $6.95 and entrees of mango chicken enchilada for $13.95, vegetarian green curry for $9.95 and steak, lamb and pasta specialties. Lunch prices are considerably lower, with similar options. Expect to pay about $75 for a dinner for two, including appetizer, a bottle of wine and dessert. The Apple Tree has an extensive wine list and courtyard dining in the summer. Brunch in the $3 to $10 range is served Saturday from 11:30 am to 3 pm and Sunday. Lunch hours are Monday through Friday 11:30 am to 3 pm, and daily dinner hours are 5:30 pm to about 9:30. Reservations are recommended.

*Lambert's* (☎ 758 1009), 309 Paseo del Pueblo Sur, two long blocks south of Taos Plaza, is fancy by Taos standards, featuring American 'contemporary' gourmet and specializing in grill fare such as roast duck for $17, grilled salmon for $17 and pepper-crusted lamb for $18.50. Petite portions are available, for about $6 less. With its whitewashed walls and formal wait staff, this place tends to be a bit stuffy, but the food is excellent. It's open for lunch Monday through Friday from 11 am to 2 pm, and dinner every night from 5:30 to 9 pm.

Isolated in the hills nine miles south of town and offering incredible views of Taos Valley, *Stakeout Grill & Bar* (☎ 758 2042), 101 Stakeout Drive, is reminiscent of the cowboy West, specializing in steaks, including a New York strip for $16.50 and a 20-oz 'real cowboy steak' for $26.95. A vegetarian kabob at $9.95 and pasta at $12.95 are the cheapest items on the menu, with appetizers going for $7 to $9 and chicken, fish, duck, veal and seafood for $14 to $23. The food here is meat-and-potato style – the cuts are of excellent quality, but stay away from anything that sounds too fancy. Brunch is served Sunday from 11 am to 2 pm, May through October. Cocktails are served from 4:30, and dinner is from 5 to 10 pm. Come here for the views and a drink, but eat elsewhere if you're watching your budget! To get there, head south from the Plaza on Hwy 68 for eight miles. At the Stakeout sign on the left, go left on Stakeout Drive for one mile.

Inside the Taos Inn is *Doc Martin's* (☎ 758 1977), which has an extensive wine list and a creative menu of continental and Mexican cuisine, including seafood and game dishes. This is one of the most expensive restaurants in town, and reservations are recommended for dinner. It is open daily from 7:30 am to 2:30 pm and for dinner from 5:30 to 10 pm.

**Other Eateries** Offering six daily fresh beers that are brewed on the premises, *Esques, a Brew Pub* (☎ 758 1517), 106 Des Georges Lane, one-half block south of Taos Plaza, is a crowded hangout catering to locals and ski bums alike. A casual, two-room adobe, this is not only an excellent place for a nice cold beer – $3 a pint for such specialties as green chile beer and Dead Presidents Ale – but for cheap, fresh, hearty pub fare as well. Bangers and mashers, served with warm applesauce and

bread, is $6.50, and a huge burrito with whole wheat tortilla, two kinds of beans and salsa is $4. For $1 extra, get it smothered in vegetarian green chile brimming with zucchini and potatoes, also available by the cup for $2.50. Tuesday is sushi night. There is often live music such as banjo, acoustic guitar, jazz or conga drums. Hours are Monday through Thursday from 4 to 10:30 pm and Friday, Saturday and Sunday from noon to 10:30 pm.

The only tapas place in town is *Tapas de Taos Cafe* (☎ 758 9670), 136 Bent St, but it by no means offers the standard Spanish fare. A quirky little place, it serves an eclectic mix of New Mexican, Vietnamese and Italian food. You can get an interesting variety of appetizer portions, such as ceviche, pork and ginger potsticker, or spicy Vietnamese fried calamari for $4 to $7 each or a full dinner, including fajitas, capellini and a vegetable burrito for $6 to $13. Lunch costs a bit less and includes such dishes as bean thread noodles with shiitake mushrooms, ginger and scallions or enchiladas for $4 to $7. It's open for lunch Monday through Friday from 11 am to 3 pm, dinner 3 to 9:30 pm, and Saturday and Sunday for dinner only.

*Amigos Natural Foods Cafe and Deli* (☎ 758 8493), 326 Paseo del Pueblo Sur, has tofu burgers, salads and stir fry in the $3 to $8 range. Hours are 9 am to 7 pm, Monday through Saturday.

**Taos Ski Valley** On the way to Taos Ski Valley, the town of Arroyo Seco offers two excellent food options. Offering such treats as smoked trout, pâté and tiny bottles of extra virgin olive oil, as well as a wide selection of breads, imported cheeses, fruit and pastries, *Casa Fresen Bakery* (☎ 776 2969) is a gourmet deli in the middle of nowhere! Though the sandwiches tend be pricey ($4 to $7), you won't be disappointed. Box lunches are available, as well as a few hot entrees like green chile chicken pot pie and grilled panini sandwiches with gorgonzola, smoked salmon and sun-dried tomatoes. Stop in here to put together a picnic on your way to the ski slope or to the hiking trails of the Carson National Forest. It's open 7:30 am to 6 pm.

Another notable Arroyo Seco restaurant is the *Bistro* (☎ 776 1066), offering pizza from 11 am to 3 pm, with such toppings as ground buffalo and feta cheese for $11 and four course dinners for $25 served from 6 to 11 pm. This is not the place for vegetarians – the focus is on locally raised organic meats and game, including buffalo, venison, wild boar, duck and lamb. It's a cozy spot, and a welcome change from the hectic and crowded restaurants in Taos.

Food at the ski valley itself tends to be expensive. *Rhoda's* (☎ 776 2005) operates outdoor grills right at the base, offering burgers and chicken, and sandwiches and pasta are available inside. Expect to pay $5 to $15 for lunch. *Tim's Stray Dog Cantina* (☎ 776 2894) serves up some of the best green chile in New Mexico, as well as other pub fare, and is always busy with the ski crowd. Beans with green chile and a tortilla with a soda will run you $5, and Southwestern basics range from $4 to $7. It's open for breakfast at 7:30 am and serves until 9 pm. Stop by for an après ski beer or sit on the outdoor patio in the summer.

All the lodges offer comparable continental gourmet cuisine, but they haven't generally been known for delicious food or creative menus. However, the new owners at the *Hotel Edelweiss* offer an exceptional four-course dinner at a fixed price of $29, and the food is a big step above the others. They also have the only all-you-can-eat soup and salad bar at the slopes for $7.95.

### Entertainment

The *Storyteller Cinema* (☎ 758 9715) is at 110 Old Talpa Canon Rd. The *Taos Community Auditorium* (☎ 758 4677), 145 Paseo del Pueblo Norte, runs a summer film series as well as hosting a variety of theater and concert productions. Tickets are generally $10. Several restaurants and bars offer live music (see above).

### Things to Buy

Taos' history as a mecca for artists is evident in the huge number of galleries and studios in and around town. Unfortunately, there is also a lot of junk and a tourist industry of T-shirt and coffee mug shops, generally focused around the Plaza. Walk down Kit Carson Rd for some of the best galleries. You could easily spend an entire day wandering the streets, and a good rule to follow is that the places that look the least inviting – maybe dilapidated, with a handwritten sign tacked to the door – often have the most interesting work. The best way to explore the art community of Taos is to take the time to poke around, and beware of places with howling pink coyotes in the window!

The *Stables Art Center* (☎ 758 2036), 133 Paseo del Pueblo Norte, managed by the Taos Art Association, is next to the Community Auditorium and shows work of Taos artists. The building itself has a mysterious past. Arthur Manby, a wealthy entrepreneur and land developer who made many enemies in his acquisition of over 60,000 acres of land in the early 20th century, lived here, and his decapitated body was found in the house in 1929. The mystery of his murder is still unsolved. The Taos Art Association bought the property in 1953, and today it is a great source of information about the local art scene. Shows change monthly. The center is open in the winter from 10 am to 5 pm, and in the summer from 9 am to 7 pm.

*Twining Weavers* (☎ 758 9000), 135 Paseo del Pueblo Norte, is in the long, low adobe stables behind the Stables Art Center. It features hand-woven rugs, tapestries and pillows, as well as work in fiber, basketry and clay. Hours are Monday through Saturday from 10 am to 5 pm, Sunday noon to 5 pm.

*El Rincón Trading Post* (☎ 758 9188), 114 E Kit Carson Rd, features a great selection of Indian crafts and jewelry and Old West memorabilia. The store dates back to 1909 when German Ralph Meyers arrived, one of the first traders in the area. As of 1995 it is still run by his widow. Even if you're not in the market to buy anything, stop in here just to browse through the dusty museum of artifacts. It's open daily from 10 am to 6 pm.

If you're in the market for old medical objects, US military memorabilia or Art Deco lamps, stop in at *Maison Faurie Antiquités* (☎ 758 8455), 1 McCarthy Plaza. This is a great place to poke around because it is such an eclectic mix of antiques – basically anything that intrigued owner Robert Faurie – crammed into cabinets and shelves. It's open daily from 8 am to 9 pm.

*Franzetti Metalworks* (☎ 758 4784), 127 Bent St, was the first store to sell the light switch and plug covers, as well as toilet paper holders, that are now ubiquitous throughout New Mexico. This place has a great variety of shapes, like wolves, cats, cows and pigs, and ones that you won't find elsewhere. *Kilborn Pottery* (☎ 758 0135), 136 Paseo del Pueblo Norte, has interesting ceramic work with reduced prices on seconds.

*Nambe Mills* (☎ 758 8221), 216 Paseo del Pueblo Norte, sells a large selection of Nambeware, both first quality and seconds. Nambeware is modern-looking silver-colored dinnerware made of a unique alloy that allows you to use it in the oven or the freezer, and the dish will retain the heat or cold for hours. Each dish is individually made, and each is a bit different. Nambe originated in New Mexico and is now sold in department stores around the country.

### Getting There & Away
**Car** Taos is approximately 75 miles north of Santa Fe, and can be reached out of Española via Hwy 68 (the Low Road), or Hwy 76 (the High Road). Beware of crazy drivers on either of these routes, both of which are winding. Changes in elevation can result in dramatic differences in weather conditions.

**Bus** TNM&O, a subsidiary of Greyhound (☎ 758 1144, 1 (800) 231 2222), located at the Chevron food mart two miles south of town across the street from the chamber of commerce, has daily bus service from Albuquerque and Santa Fe, with stops at Pilar and Española. The cost from Santa Fe is $14.70/24 for one-way/roundtrip, and $19.95/39.90 from Albuquerque. Call for schedules and rates.

**Shuttle** Faust (☎ 758 3410 in Taos and ☎ 843 9042 from the Albuquerque Airport) and Pride of Taos (☎ 758 8340) offer shuttles from Albuquerque Airport to Taos for $35/65 one-way/roundtrip and to Taos Ski Valley for $40/75. They also offer services to Angel Fire, Red River, Santa Fe Airport, Lamy and Colorado, and pick up at motels. Prices vary according to season. Call for schedules and current rates.

### Getting Around
**Taxi** The two shuttle services (see above) are expensive and unreliable for local travel. Faust runs an on-call taxi service, from 7 am to 9 pm, with costs ranging from $7 for one to two people within the city limits, $30 one-way to Taos Ski Valley and $50 one-way to Red River. Call for schedules and current rates.

**Car Rental** At the Taos Municipal Airport (☎ 758 4995), 24662 Hwy 64 in Las Colinias, is Payless Rental Car (☎ 751 1110) and Rich Ford Rent-a-Car (☎ 758 9501). Jeep Trailways Rentals (☎ 754 6443) in Red River rents 4WD jeeps. Other major rental car agencies are located in Santa Fe and Albuquerque.

**Bicycle** Mountain and road bikes, as well as bike racks for your car can be rented through Gearing Up Bicycle Shop (☎ 751 0365), 129 Paseo del Pueblo Sur. Other stores that rent and service bikes are Hot Tracks Cyclery (☎ 751 0949), 729 Paseo del Pueblo Sur, and Native Sons Adventures (☎ 758 9342, 1 (800) 753 7559), 715 Paseo del Pueblo Sur. Native Sons Adventures also offers tours and shuttles. Maps and local information are available and rates vary.

**Hitchhiking** Though hitchhiking is dangerous anywhere, it is common to see people hitching to and from the ski valley.

NEW MEXICO

Use caution hitchhiking and women should not hitchhike alone.

## QUESTA

This tiny community is at the turnoff from Hwy 522 onto Hwy 38 to Red River. The immediate surroundings are unattractively barren, the result of mining and logging, although prettier country in the Carson National Forest to the east is just a few miles away.

The USFS Questa Ranger Station (☎ 586 0520, 758 6230), PO Box 110, 87556, has information about campgrounds in the Carson National Forest. Most are small and available on a first-come, first-served basis. The biggest is *Columbine*, five miles east on Hwy 38, with 27 sites at $8. There is drinking water but no showers or RV hookups. It is open from mid-May to mid-October.

There are a couple of simple motels. The best is the *Sangre de Cristo Motel* (☎ 586 0300) at the turnoff onto Hwy 38. Their *El Seville Restaurant* is open from 6 am to 8 pm. Also try *La Q Motel* (☎ 586 1814).

## RED RIVER

In the 19th century, gold was discovered in the hills surrounding Red River, and by 1905 there were 3,000 people, four hotels, 15 saloons and a thriving red-light district. The town developed a wild reputation, but by 1925 miners had left for golder pastures. Today the population is 350, surviving predominantly on tourism. Fortunately, the national forest prevents sprawling development and protects its Old West feel. The buildings look like they're out of a movie set. Small-town family fun is the focus here, though there are a couple of bars with live country music. You won't find a wild nightlife or the post-hippie and ski clientele characteristic of Taos.

### Orientation & Information

There are three streets running parallel to the river at the base of the ski slope – Rivers, Main and High – and you can walk anywhere within town. *Lifts West* (☎ 754 2778, 1 (800) 221 1859), 201 Main, is a

hotel complex in the center of town with a baseball park next door. Across the street is the chamber of commerce (☎ 1 (800) 348 6444). The police can be reached at 754 6166 or 911 for emergencies. A trolley service runs through the town, with free pickups at all the accommodations. Outdoor recreation is really the only thing to do here. The *Williams Trading Post* (☎ 754 2217) is a local institution and a general source of information on fishing and hiking.

### Activities

The area around Red River offers great **hiking** through the Carson National Forest's mountain meadows, lakes and streams. You can pick up trail maps at the chamber of commerce. Trails of two to 16 miles at all levels of difficulty weave through Columbine Canyon, including one to the top of Wheeler Peak. The trailhead for Red River Nature Trail, an easy two-mile trail with a 200-foot incline, is at the ski base. In the summer you can take a **mountain bike** up in the chair lift and ride down. Beaver Ponds and Middle Fork Lake Trails start at the end of Upper Valley Rd. You can either take an easy half-day hike to the Beaver Ponds, or park at the Middle Fork Trail lot and hike up two miles and 2000 vertical feet to a high mountain lake.

For **skiing**, Red River Ski Area (☎ 754 2223) has predominantly intermediate runs, and you won't find the high-terrain mountain trails that you do in Taos. It's a great place to come if you're just learning or if you find the intensity of Taos intimidating. Lift tickets are $33 for a full day, $24 for a half day, and a five-day package, including lift tickets, lessons and equipment, is $296. Call for other package rates. *Ski Rio* (☎ 586 9949) is north of Red River outside Costilla. With 1400 acres and 30 kilometers of groomed trails, the *Enchanted Forest* (☎ 754 2374) is New Mexico's biggest cross-country ski area. An all-day pass costs $9, and rentals are $10.50. For the three days before the full moon, they offer Moonlight Ski Tours. Go to *Miller's Crossing* (☎ 754 2375), 212

Red River is stocked with three species of trout.

Main, to book trips and arrange dropoffs. At the end of February, restaurants in town set up tables of desserts all along the trail system, and you can eat your way along during the Just Desserts Eat & Ski Festival.

The **fishing** in Red River is good due to the 20,000 German brown, cutthroat and rainbow trout that are annually stocked in the river and surrounding lakes. Talk to staff at Williams Trading Post for information. Brad Mider at *Fishin Buddies* (☎ 754 3150) will take you fishing for $100 to $150 a day or can just direct you where to go.

### Organized Tours

There is no shortage of outdoor adventure organizations in Red River, and they'll arrange any kind of trip you're looking for. Two that enjoy a good reputation are *Red Dawg* (☎ 754 2721) for snowmobiling trips and *Bitter Creek Guest Ranch* (☎ 754 2587, 1 (800) 562 9462) for horseback riding.

### Special Events

Red River, a half hour north of town, hosts Mardi Gras in the Mountains at the end of February to coincide with New Orleans' street festival, and on Memorial Day weekend, 6000 motorcyclists converge on the small town for one of the biggest biking weekends in the country.

### Places to Stay

Accommodations in Red River generally consist of motel-type lodges in town, cabins in the mountains and camping. The reasonably priced *Lodge at Red River* (☎ 754 6280) is probably the nicest place in town. This unique, centrally located landmark hotel has a cozy European feel lacking in the others. There is a bar and restaurant, with daily all-you-can-eat specials and home cooking for breakfast, lunch and dinner. Doubles are $58 in the summer and $68 in the winter. Singles are $39/42, and rooms accommodating groups of six or ten are also available. Call for ski package rates.

On two acres outside of town, the *Riverside* (☎ 754 2252), 201 E Main, offers quiet cabins with kitchens as well as double rooms for $50 to $70. *Copper King Lodge* (☎ 754 6210), 307 E River, has doubles and private cabins for $43 to $140 in the winter and $38 to $85 in the summer. The *Ponderosa Lodge* (☎ 754 2988) has doubles in the $40 to $75 range. Nestled up in the mountains, with a private fishing pond and stables, *Bitter Creek Guest Ranch* (☎ 754 1587, 1 (800) 562 9462)

---

## Pueblo Languages

From I539, when the Spanish explorers first encountered the Zuni, until I847, when the Taos Indians rebelled against the US government, the Pueblo Indians were harassed by invading foreign armies and missionaries. In spite of the 300 years of turmoil, they have successfully maintained their lifestyles, ceremonies and languages.

The languages spoken by the Pueblo people include Keresan and Tanoan. Tanoan includes dialects of Tewa, Tiwa and Towa. Many Pueblo Indians describe their language as an ancient tongue, and their elders say that the language was constructed according to the different vibratory levels of Mother Nature. According to their ancient ones of wisdom, the sounds of all native tongues are in an enormous ball of whirling energy that comes from an existence of goodness. Out of this whirling ball the Creator fashioned the different tongues, each with unique elements and each made from resonating qualities of goodness. Every tongue has its own vibration.

In Pueblo thought, the answer 'yes' is what created the blood of life. Their people were vibrations constructed by four processes described as descending, arising, purifying and relativity. Their language is the sound that fuses the descending and arising light in the crystallized meaning of time. Beyond the tongue, and beyond all sound, is silence. Silence is the root of all languages, because it is the pathway to the materialization of all concepts.

The Creator made us when He found that form could exist from sound. He made vibration, He made form, and He made our Mother and Father, the living universe.
– *Eagle/Walking Turtle* ■

---

offers doubles and cabins ranging from $65 to $125.

If you're looking for a B&B, try the *Copper Pig* (☎ 754 6132, 1(800) 454 5445), PO Box 302, Red River, 87558, which overlooks the town. All rooms have private baths, down comforters and feather beds, and rates include a full breakfast. Doubles are $80 to $110, and with a full dinner they're $100 to $135. There's a two-night minimum stay. requirement. A suite with a loft and hot tub goes for $60 a night at *Andie's B&B* (☎ 754 2274).

Bandanna Properties (☎ 754 2949), or *Red River Real Estate* (☎ 754 2459) can arrange the rental of a private home, or any other accommodations.

### Places to Eat

*Fat Daddy's* in Lifts West has a Chinese buffet for $8.95 Thursday to Sunday, as well as breakfast, steaks, sandwiches and New Mexican fare for under $11. Across the street at *Shotgun Willie's* (☎ 754 6505) you can get an all-you-can-eat mountain man breakfast for $3.99 or fast-food burgers and barbecue for $4 to $7. At the

*Lodge at Red River* (☎ 754 6280), a huge skillet breakfast is $5.50, or you can 'Build a Burger' for $5. Steaks, pork chops and Italian fare are also available at this simple, good place. *Sundance Mexican Restaurant* (☎ 754 2971) serves plates of beans and burritos and the like for under $10.

Waits are sometimes four hours long at the local steak saloon, *Texas Red's Steakhouse* (☎ 754 2964). It's a favorite with tourists looking for that taste of the Old West, and if there's no wait it's worth a stop. Expect to pay $10 to $20 for a steak, but they also have buffalo burgers and chicken fajitas for $6.50 and an extensive beer list. At the far end of town, *Brett's Homestead Steakhouse* (☎ 754 6136) is the locals' alternative to Texas Red's. Go to the *Black Crow Coffee House* (☎ 754 3150), 500 E Main, for a strong cup of coffee and pastries, with pasta and live music on the weekends. The owner, Nancy, always has time to chat and give tips on local things to do and places to stay and eat.

For boot-scooting to live country & western music Thursday through Sunday, go to the *Motherlode Saloon* (☎ 754 6280).

Another bar popular with locals is the *Bull O' the Woods* (☎ 754 2593), right next door to Motherlode, with a happy hour from 3 to 6 pm. Both places are hopping every night.

## ANGEL FIRE

Twenty-two miles east of Taos, the ski resort of Angel Fire has gained a reputation as condominium heaven. Though locals are making a great effort to develop a tourist clientele, the town grew too quickly, and there is no sense of history or even a quaint village. It just sprawls on the edge of a plateau, and a few monotonous restaurants and hotels and condos dot the hillside.

Bookings can be made through Resort Properties of Angel Fire (☎ 377 2312). The chamber of commerce (☎ 377 6661, 1 (800) 446 8117) is on the right as you drive into town. The *Angel Fire Ski Resort* (☎ 377 6401, 1 (800) 633 7463) has 60 trails, mostly for beginners and low inter-mediates, and the cost is $30 for a full day, $24 for a half. *Roadrunner Tours Ltd* (☎ 377 6416, 1 (800) 377 6416) rents skis and bikes and arranges outdoor trips, including snowmobile tours and overnight horseback riding trips.

The hub of activity is at *Legends* (☎ 377 6401, 1 (800) 633 7463), a huge hotel with a restaurant and bar at the base with double rooms for $90 to $130, or a three-day/three-night ski package including lift tickets for $387 to $440. Call for condo-minium and other package rates. The *Inn at Angelfire* (☎ 377 2504, 1 (800) 666 1949) is an unpretentious and informal ski lodge with family-style meals that offers daily rates for doubles, rooms sleeping eight and 12, and ski packages that include breakfast, dinner and lift tickets. Doubles are $90, and ski packages range from $100 to $130 nightly per person. A dorm room that sleeps up to 12 is $90 for the first four occupants and $20 for each additional one. Call for summer rates.

Try *Zebadiah's* (☎ 377 6358), Hwy 434, for a choice of eight half-pound burgers for under $5, barbecue for $7 to $11, New Mexican fare and steaks. With pool tables and occasional live music, this is the best place in town to hang out over a beer. It's open for breakfast everyday from 7 am to 10 pm, lunch from 11 am, and dinner until 9 pm on the weekdays and 10 pm on weekends.

NEW MEXICO

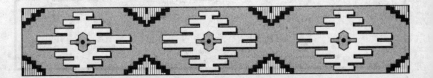

# Northwestern New Mexico

Much of this part of New Mexico is high desert, with starkly beautiful buttes and badlands pushing up against startlingly blue skies. As the visitor heads east from the Arizona state line, across the Continental Divide and toward the Rio Grande, the bare scenery eases into softer forest-clad mountains. The area is slashed by I-40, which carries traffic from Arizona to Albuquerque and beyond.

The area showcases some of the Southwest's most fabulous ancient Anasazi Indian ruins. Much of the land remains in the hands of Native Americans, with the Navajo, Zuni, Acoma and Jicarilla Apache Indian Reservations among those of most interest to visitors.

Within this scenic and interesting land, the juxtaposition of ancient and traditional with modern and technological can be

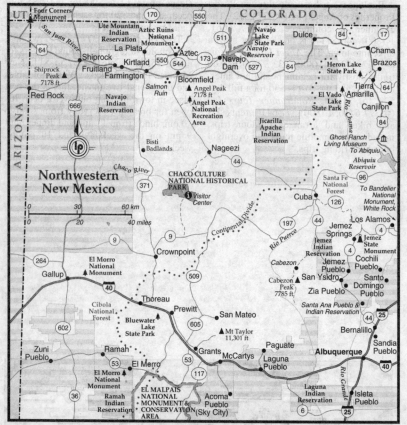

startling or thought-provoking. The fascinating 900-year-old Acoma Pueblo (also called 'Sky City'), one of the oldest continually inhabited communities in North America, is visible from your modern automobile as you speed along I-40.

Consider also the important archaeological sites of Bandelier National Monument. Here, ruins of Anasazi settlements and their barely accessible cliff dwellings lie a few miles away from the town of Los Alamos, famous as the site where the first atomic bomb was developed. Or look at Shiprock, a huge, strangely shaped butte of legendary religious importance to the Navajos – it's just 20 miles west of the tribally operated Navajo Mine, the largest open-pit mine in the New Mexico.

Other attractions abound. The Zuni Indian Reservation has attractive and unique jewelry – and a historically interesting church. Gallup is famous for its annual Inter-Tribal Indian Ceremonial, which has been featuring rodeos, dances, and native crafts and food for over 70 years. Less well known is the annual Northern Navajo Nations Fair, which has been held in Shiprock for almost as long. The Navajo Lake State Park features one of New Mexico's largest artificial lakes, which is excellent for fishing and other water sports. People enjoying rod and gun find good sport further east in the Chama area, where both Apache and non-Indian guides take customers to the best fishing and hunting spots. Railroad buffs revel in a nostalgic steam engine trip out of Chama on the Cumbres and Toltec Scenic Railroad. South of there is the wide open, crystal clear, dramatic country made famous by the paintings of Georgia O'Keeffe.

From cultural, scenic, archaeological and historical perspectives there is much to interest the visitor intent on spending a few days in this region. I begin the chapter in the far northwest, through Farmington and on toward Chama, Los Alamos and the Rio Grande. Then I trace the more frequently traveled I-40 corridor west of Albuquerque as it passes 'Sky City' and Gallup en route to the Navajo Indian Reservation and Arizona.

# The Farmington Area

The Anasazi left some magnificent sites here – foremost among them is Pueblo Bonito in the Chaco Culture National Historical Park, about two hours' drive south of Farmington. Many other Anasazi sites, referred to as 'outliers', dot the surrounding area. Aztec Ruins National Monument and Salmon Ruin are both a few miles from Farmington.

The area became the home of Navajos and Utes after the demise of the Anasazi. Today, the Navajo Reservation shares a very tiny boundary with Farmington. Around the beginning of the 19th century, Whites found the Animas River Valley to be a profitable beaver-trapping area (the animals were soon hunted into local extinction), but permanent Anglo settlement didn't happen until 1876, when ranchers arrived at the confluence of the Animas, San Juan and La Plata Rivers. The site became known as Farmingtown (the 'w' was later dropped), and the town developed into an agricultural center. The nearby towns of Aztec and Bloomfield were settled soon after. Aztec became the seat of San Juan County in 1891, but Farmington has since eclipsed it in size and economic importance.

The population was largely rural until the 1950s, when oil, gas and coal extraction began. Today, mining, agriculture and tourism all play an important part in the economy.

## FARMINGTON

Farmington boomed from a sleepy agricultural town of less than 4000 inhabitants in the 1950s to a mining center of about 25,000 by the 1960s. Today, with a population of around 40,000, Farmington is the largest town in northwestern New Mexico (and the Four Corners area) and offers plenty of facilities for the visitor – you could spend several nights here using the town as the base for excursions to the attractions described below. Hotel rates in

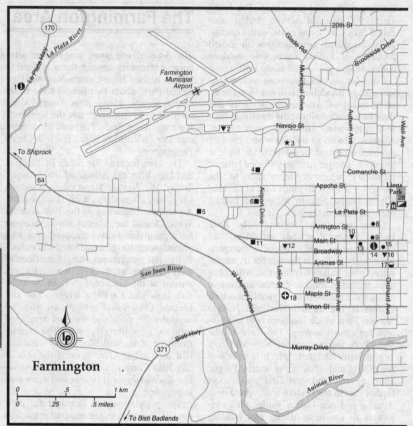

| | | | |
|---|---|---|---|
| 16 | KB Dillon's | 8 | Civic Center |
| 20 | Clancy's Pub | 9 | Farmington Magazine & Book Store |
| 22 | Los Rios Cafe | 13 | Totah Theater |
| 24 | La Fiesta Grande | 14 | Visitors Bureau |
| 25 | Golden Corral, Dynasty Chinese | 15 | Library |
| | Restaurant | 17 | TNM&O Bus Depot |
| 33 | Kettle Restaurant | 18 | Hospital |
| 37 | Rocky Mountain Rib Company | 19 | Post Office |
| | | 21 | Farmington Aquatic Center |
| **OTHER** | | 26 | Office Lounge |
| 1 | BLM | 27 | Family Funland |
| 3 | Police | 28 | Municipal Pool |
| 7 | Farmington Museum | 31 | Top Deck Lounge |

summer are cheaper than in the tourist centers of Cortez and Durango across the state line in Colorado. Also see the entries below under Aztec, Bloomfield and Chaco Culture National Historical Park and the section on northeastern Arizona and the Navajo Reservation for more ideas of things to do in the area.

Farmington's 5300-foot elevation results in a pleasant climate – average high and low temperatures are 91/60°F in July and 40/18°F in January. Annual rainfall is 7.5 inches and snowfall is 12.3 inches.

## Orientation & Information

The visitors bureau (☎ 326 7602, 1 (800) 448 1240), 203 W Main St, is next to the chamber of commerce. The BLM (☎ 327 5344) is at 1235 La Plata Hwy. The library (☎ 599 1270) is at 100 W Broadway. The post office (☎ 325 5047) is at 2301 E 20th St. The hospital (☎ 325 5011) is at 801 W Maple. The police (☎ 599 1000, or 911 in emergencies) are at 800 Municipal Drive.

## Farmington Museum

The city museum (☎ 599 1174 or 1179), 302 N Orchard Ave, showcases the pioneer history and the geology of the area. There is a children's gallery with fun hands-on exhibits and a variety of changing shows. Ask for a brochure describing some of Farmington's earliest buildings. Hours are noon to 5 pm Tuesday to Friday and 10 am to 5 pm on Saturday. Admission is free.

## Family Funland

This amusement park (☎ 324 0940), 200 Scott Ave, has kids' carnival rides, go-carts, miniature golf and other kid stuff. During the summer, hours are noon to 10 pm Monday to Friday and to later on weekends. During the school year, the park is open on weekends only.

## Horseracing

San Juan Downs racetrack (☎ 326 4551) is on Hwy 64 on the southeast side of town. There is thoroughbred and quarter horse racing at 1 pm on weekends and holidays from mid-April to Labor Day. There is also simulcast intertrack betting from other state racetracks throughout the year.

## Activities

New Mexicans head across the state line into Colorado to **ski** at Purgatory Ski Area (☎ 1 (303) 247 9000, 1 (800) 879 7874), which is about 80 miles north of Farmington north of Durango.

**Golf** 18 holes at Piñon Hills (☎ 326 6066), 2101 Sunrise Pkwy – this was rated the best regulation course in the state in *Golf Digest*'s 1991 and 1993 surveys. Or play nine holes at the Civitan par-27 course (☎ 599 1194), 2200 N Dustin Ave.

Farmington Recreation Center (☎ 599 1184), 1001 N Fairgrounds Rd, has 17 lighted tennis courts and five racquetball courts.

**Swim** indoors in the Olympic-size pool at the Farmington Aquatic Center (☎ 599 1167), 1151 N Sullivan Ave; or at Lions Pool (☎ 599 1187), 405 N Wall Ave. Or swim outdoors in summer at Brookside Park Pool (☎ 599 1188), 1901 N Dustin Ave. Brookside Park also offers basketball hoops, skateboarding areas, a playground and picnic tables.

If **windsurfing** is your sport, Morgan Lake on the Navajo Reservation about five miles southwest of Kirtland (15 miles southwest of Farmington) is a very popular area. Swimming is not allowed. Four Corners Windsurfing (☎ 598 6688), 128 County Rd 6675 in nearby Fruitland, has equipment.

## Special Events

Call the chamber of commerce for exact dates of all events. Rodeos are popular in Farmington. The biggest is the San Juan County Sheriff Posse Rodeo, which is held at the County Rodeo Ground (on Hwy 550 northeast of town) in early June. Locals say that the San Juan County Fair is New Mexico's largest county fair. It features a rodeo, chili cook-off, fiddlers' contest and plenty of other attractions. The fair is held in mid-August at McGee Park, southeast of town on Hwy 64. McGee Park is also the site of the Pro-Rodeo Roundup in early April.

The Invitational Balloon Festival features a balloon splash (in which hot-air balloonists dip their baskets in Farmington Lake) during Memorial Day weekend. The weekend also features other events such as tractor-pulls, river rafting, arts & crafts, entertainment and more. Freedom Days sees extensive celebrations on and around the Fourth of July. The Connie Mack World Series Baseball Tournament in mid-August features top amateur ballplayers and attracts scouts from college and professional teams. The seven-day event is held at Ricketts Ball Park, 1101 N Fairgrounds Rd. The Totah Festival, held over Labor Day weekend, has top-quality Native American arts & crafts both in juried competition and for sale by auction. Native American Days is held at the Animas Valley Mall, 4601 E Main, in late September. See Indian dances and browse the arts & crafts. A Holiday Arts & Crafts Fair is held at The Inn Best Western, 700 Scott Ave, during the last weekend in November and the first weekend in December.

## Places to Stay – camping

*Mom & Pop RV Park* (☎ 327 3200), 901 Illinois Ave (just off Hwy 64), has showers and charges $12 for sites with RV hookups and $4 per person in tents. There are 38 sites. The smaller *River Grove RV Park* (☎ 327 0974), 801 E Broadway, charges $11 for sites with RV hookups. The *Downs RV Park* (☎ 325 7094), 5701 Bloomfield Hwy, has showers, a laundry and tent sites for $10 and RV sites with hookups for $12. There is free primitive camping at Morgan Lake 15 miles southwest of Farmington.

## Places to Stay – bottom end

Hotel rates stay about the same year round, though there may be a slight increase during summer weekends with the influx of horseracing fans.

The cheapest places have simple but clean rooms with attached showers in the lower to mid-$20s. These include the *Zia Motel* (☎ 326 6614), 332 E Main St, the *Encore Motel* (☎ 325 5008), 1900 E Main St, and the *Bluffview Motel* (☎ 327 6231), 3700 Bloomfield Hwy.

The reliable bottom-end *Motel 6* chain has two hotels. One is at 1600 Bloomfield Hwy (☎ 326 4501), with rooms at $24/30 for singles/doubles, and the other is at 510 Scott Ave (☎ 327 0242), with rooms at $26/32. Both places have swimming pools and between them offer well over 200 rooms.

The *Farmington Lodge* (☎ 325 0233), 1510 W Main St, has very clean rooms with in-room coffee and a refrigerator. There is a pool, and the place is good value for $28/33 for singles/doubles. Another decent place at about this price is the *Basin Lodge* (☎ 325 5061), 701 Airport Drive. The *Super 8 Motel* (☎ 325 1813), 1601 Bloomfield Hwy, has a game room and 60 good-size rooms (some with waterbeds) for $29.88/38.88, which includes continental breakfast.

Other bottom-end hotels include the *Journey Inn* (☎ 325 3548), 317 Airport Drive, which has a pool, and the nearby *Sage Motel* (☎ 325 7501), 301 Airport Drive. Both have rooms starting in the $20s as do the *Apple Tree Inn* (☎ 326 1555), 5915 E Main St, and the *Redwood Lodge* (☎ 326 5521), 625 E Main St.

With the exception of the Motel 6s and Super 8 Motel, all the bottom-end places are quite small with 40 or less rooms.

## Places to Stay – middle

**Hotels** The hotels in this section are all quite large, with anywhere from about 70 to 150 rooms.

The *Days Inn* (☎ 327 4433), 2530 Bloomfield Hwy, has a pool, spa, restaurant and bar on the premises. Rooms are reasonably sized and there are some suites; rates are $40 to $60. The *Anasazi Inn* (☎ 325 4564), 903 W Main St, also has good rooms and a few suites in the same price range. There is a restaurant (Mexican and American food) and bar attached.

The town's best hotels are clustered around Scott Ave and Broadway. The *La Quinta Inn* (☎ 327 4706, fax 325 6583), 675 Scott Ave, has a pool, picnic and barbecue area and free coffee and continental breakfast. A 24-hour restaurant is next door. Attractive large rooms are in the $50s and lower $60s. The similarly priced *Comfort Inn* (☎ 325 2626, fax 325 7675), 555 Scott Ave, also offers a free continental breakfast and has a pool. It also has some suites for about $70.

The *Holiday Inn* (☎ 327 9811, fax 325 2288), 600 E Broadway, has a pool, spa, sauna and weight room. There is a sports bar with big-screen sports action to watch after your workout. The restaurant is open daily from 6 am to 2 pm and 5 to 10 pm – dinners are in the $8 to $16 range, and there is room service. Free transportation to and from the airport or bus station is available. All rooms are spacious and some have king-size beds. Rates are in the upper $50s and $60s.

**B&Bs** The modern *Silver River Inn* (☎ 325 8219), 3151 W Main St, 87499 (five miles west of downtown), overlooks the San Juan and La Plata Rivers. There is one suite featuring a private bath, kitchen, hot tub, queen-size bed and two twin day beds. Smoking and children under 12 are not permitted. Rates are about $70 for two and $90 for four people, including continental breakfast. Airport pickup and private car tours in the area can be arranged.

### Places to Stay – top end

The largest and fanciest place in town is Best Western's *The Inn* (☎ 327 5221, fax 327 1565), 700 Scott Ave. There is an attractive enclosed courtyard with trees, an indoor pool, spa, sauna, gym, game room, coin laundry, bar and restaurant with room service available 6 to 10 am and 5 to 10 pm. The 194 spacious rooms have refrigerators and queen- or king-sized beds and run $60 to $80 for singles and $70 to $90 for doubles. Free airport or bus station shuttles are available.

### Places to Eat

If you want a deliciously different breakfast, a change from the usual bacon and eggs, try *Something Special* (☎ 325 8183),

116 N Auburn Ave, open 7 am to 2 pm, Tuesday to Friday only. It also has very good set lunches and a variety of pastries and desserts. Any of the *hotel restaurants* listed above will provide a standard American breakfast for a reasonable price.

Continuing with out-of-the-ordinary breakfasts (and other meals), try the airport! *Señor Pepper's* (☎ 327 0436) is in the airport terminal – but what a difference from the bland, overpriced meals most people associate with airports! The restaurant is open from 5:30 am to 10 pm daily. The food has a strong Mexican flair and is a good value. Look past the buildings at the west end of the terminal parking area for views of Ship Rock, and walk over to the south side of the lot for views of Farmington spread out below.

Another decent Mexican restaurant is *La Fiesta Grande* (☎ 326 6476), 1916 E Main St, which has a salad bar as well as a Mexican buffet. It is open daily for lunch and dinner. *El Charro Cafe* (☎ 327 2464), 737 W Main St, is a small and homey Mexican restaurant open from 8 am to 9 pm daily, except Sunday (when it's open 9 am to 5 pm). Other Mexican places to try include *Los Hermanitos* (☎ 326 5664), 5915 E Main, and *Los Rios Cafe* (☎ 325 5699), 915 Farmington Ave.

For simple family dining, try the *Kettle Restaurant*, (☎ 326 0824), 685 Scott Ave, which is open 24 hours. For just lunch and dinner, *KB Dillon's* (☎ 325 0222), 101 E Broadway, has a Western decor and slightly pricey but tasty steak and seafood meals. The *Rocky Mountain Rib Company* (☎ 327 7422), 525 E Broadway, specializes in smoked and barbecued ribs and other meats. It is open daily for lunch and dinner. For cheaper steaks and less atmosphere, the *Golden Corral* (☎ 327 4162), 914 E Main St, is OK. For Chinese food, the *Dynasty* (☎ 326 2313), 930 E Main St, is decent.

*Clancy's Pub* (☎ 325 8176), 2703 E 20th St, calls itself an 'Irish cantina', and it's popular with young adults. A fine selection of imported beers is available to wash down a variety of hamburgers (up to one pounders!), sandwiches, Mexican food and pub grub. You can dine inside, where it's loud with rock music and interesting art covers the walls, or outside on their patio. Hours are 11 to 2 am daily, and prices are low to moderate.

About eight miles northeast of downtown (halfway to Aztec), along Hwy 550 on the north side, is the rustic and recommended *The Trough* (☎ 334 6176) – watch for it behind the large Country Palace night club. It is open daily for dinner (closed on Sundays). The menu features a wide selection of tasty meat and seafood dishes – the fish is flown in and fresh. Most entrees are about $15 to $20, though you'll spend up to $30 if your taste ranges to lobster.

### Entertainment
The big annual entertainment event is *Anasazi, the Ancient Ones* – a musical pageant performed from mid-June to late August most nights except Mondays. The show is at the outdoor amphitheater at Lion's Wilderness Park about three miles north of downtown along College Blvd. Some years, they alternate the pageant with a different performance – call the visitors bureau for an exact schedule. Shows are at 8 pm, and tickets are $10 for adults and $5 for children up to 18. For an extra $6, a Southwestern buffet dinner is served at 6:30 pm before the show. Tickets are available at the visitors bureau or at the door.

The local San Juan Stage Company (☎ 327 7477) presents plays and musicals throughout the year at the *Totah Theater*, 315 W Main St. The Civic Center Foundation for the Performing Arts (☎ 599 1145) presents off-Broadway performances at the *Civic Center*, 200 W Arrington St. Movie fans should check the four screens at the *Animas Cinema 4* (☎ 327 7856) in the Animas Valley Mall, 4601 E Main St.

For bar-oriented nightlife, *Clancy's Pub* (see Places to Eat) is popular. If you like bars on the wild side, head over to the *Country Palace* (☎ 334 6298), eight miles northeast of downtown on the north side of Hwy 550 – you can't miss it. They have a huge dance floor, live country music on weekends and an interesting clientele of bikers, cowboys, long-hairs, country music fans and the merely curious. Rather less wild but certainly popular, the *Office Lounge* (☎ 325 0046), 1809 E Main St, offers country & western and rock music and dancing most nights. The busiest place in town recently was the *Top Deck Lounge* (☎ 327 7385), 515 E Main St, usually with rock music and a cover charge of a few dollars.

### Things to Buy
Several trading posts in the Farmington area offer a variety of high-quality Indian crafts – the Navajo rugs are particularly good, but silver and turquoise jewelry, kachinas, basketware, sand paintings, ceramics and art are also popular buys.

Trading posts can teach you about the historical and cultural significance of these often expensive pieces. A top-quality Navajo rug can fetch several thousand dollars – do a little research before you buy (see the Navajo rugs aside in the section on Gallup). The best trading posts have museum-quality displays and, sometimes, demonstrations of how rugs or jewelry are made. The visitors bureau can tell you about dates of these.

Reliable trading posts are found along Hwy 64 west of town and include the Hogback Trading Company (☎ 598 5154), 3221 Hwy 64 in Waterflow (15 miles west of Farmington); Bob French's Navajo Rugs (☎ 598 5621), 3459 Hwy 64 in Waterflow; and Foutz Trading Company (☎ 368 5790) on Hwy 64 in Shiprock. The last also has a store in Farmington – the Foutz Indian Room (☎ 325 9413), 301 W Main St. Other stores are nearby on Main or Broadway, including Fifth Generation Trading Company (☎ 326 3211), 232 W Broadway, which specializes in Navajo sand paintings.

For books about the area, the best selection is at Farmington Magazine and Book Store (☎ 325 5562), 218 W Main St.

### Getting There & Away
**Air** The Four Corners Airport at the west end of town is reportedly the second busiest in the state. Mesa Airlines (☎ 326 3338,

1 (800) 637 2247) has several daily flights to and from Albuquerque, with connections to other New Mexican towns. America West Express (☎ 326 4494, 1 (800) 247 5692, 1 (800) 235 9292) has several flights a day to and from Phoenix (via Gallup), with connections to other Arizonan towns and nationwide destinations. United Express (☎ 326 4495, 1 (800) 241 6522) flies to Denver and other Coloradan cities. Four Corners Aviation (☎ 325 2867) provides local charter flights.

**Bus** TNM&O (☎ 325 1009), 101 E Animas St, has one or two buses a day to Albuquerque (a four-hour trip) with connections to most of the rest of New Mexico, Texas and Arizona. There are also one or two daily buses to Durango, Colorado. The morning bus continues to Grand Junction, Colorado, and connects with the Greyhound bus to Salt Lake City, Utah.

**Car Rental** The following companies rent cars (and vans or 4WDs) at the airport: Avis (☎ 327 9864, 1 (800) 331 1212); Budget (☎ 327 7304, 1 (800) 748 2540); Hertz (☎ 327 6093, 1 (800) 654 3131); and National (☎ 327 0215, 1 (800) 227 7368). Car rental is also available from Ugly Duckling (☎ 325 4313), 2307 E Main St, and Emergency Car Rental (☎ 327 2277), 1812 E 20th St. You can rent an RV from London's RV Rental (☎ 598 5177), 2035 Hwy 64 in Kirtland (eight miles west of Farmington).

### Getting Around
KB Cab (☎ 325 2999) has 24-hour taxi service in and around Farmington.

## AROUND FARMINGTON
### Mine Tours
The Navajo Mine (☎ 598 5861), 25 miles southwest of town on the Navajo Reservation, is the largest open-pit mine in the western USA. Free tours are offered at 10 am on Mondays. If mine tours are your thing, also call the San Juan Mine (☎ 598 5871), 15 miles west of Farmington, which has a 10 am tour on Wednesday, and the La

Plata Mine (☎ 599 4100), 20 miles north of Farmington, with a 10 am tour on Friday. All three mines produce coal used to fire the Four Corners Power Plant (☎ 598 8204) near Morgan Lake on the Navajo Reservation. The plant produces much of the energy for the Southwest and can be toured with two weeks' notice.

### Ship Rock
This 1700-foot-high volcanic plug rises eerily over the landscape and was an early landmark to White travelers, who named it after a fancied resemblance to a ship under sail. The rock lies 35 miles west of Farmington in Navajoland, and the Navajos, who didn't have much use for sailing ships, had a better name for it – *Tse Bitai*, meaning 'winged rock'. The rock figures in several Navajo legends and is sacred to the tribe, which is why climbing it is prohibited. You can see Ship Rock from Hwy 64, but better views are had from Hwy 666 and Indian Hwy 13, which goes almost to the base of it.

The Navajo community of **Shiprock**, 25 miles west of Farmington, is named after the rock. Shiprock hosts an annual Navajo Fair with a rodeo, powwow, parade, arts & crafts and contests, as well as traditional dancing, singing and food. This is perhaps the most traditional of the large Indian fairs and begins with the Night Way, a complex Navajo healing ceremony and *Yei Bei Chei* chant that lasts for several days. Parts of the ceremony are open to the general public, but photography and recording is strictly prohibited. (Photography is permitted at the non-ceremonial events such as the rodeo.) The fair is held in late September or early October, and information is available from the fair office (☎ 368 5108), the Farmington Chamber of Commerce and the Navajo Tourism Department in Window Rock, Arizona. Fair-goers should stay in Farmington – there are no motels in Shiprock.

### Bisti Badlands
'Bis-ti' is Navajo for 'badlands' and so the full name is slightly redundant. Some maps

Casa Rinconada at Chaco Culture NHP is one of the largest kivas in the Southwest. (RR)

Shoppers at the Indian Market in Santa Fe (TW)

International Balloon Festival, Albuquerque (RR)

Santa Fe's San Miguel Mission is the oldest church in New Mexico. (RRb)

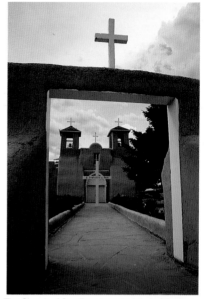

The Church of San Francisco de Asis in Ranchos de Taos is the subject of many artists' work. (RR)

Albuquerque's San Felipe de Neri Church dates to 1706. (RR)

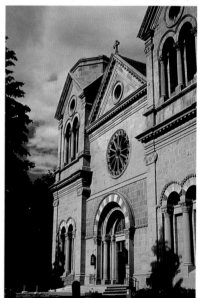

Archbishop Lamy began construction of the St Francis Cathedral in 1869. (AN)

refer to this area, about 35 miles south of Farmington along Hwy 371, as the Bisti Wilderness. The scenery here is barren but geologically interesting, with many eroded and colorfully pigmented formations – the best sights are along trails a couple of miles from the roads. The site is undeveloped BLM wilderness. Dirt roads lead a few miles east to the even more remote **De-Na-Zin Wilderness**. The Farmington BLM office has information.

### Mesa Verde National Park (CO)

Although Mesa Verde is in Colorado, about 40 miles north of the New Mexico state line, I mention it briefly because it is easily visited from Farmington and has the best known and most visited Anasazi cliff dwellings in the country. There are several important sets of ruins scattered throughout the park and visible from the road. Footpaths provide close-up access.

The park entrance fee is $5 per vehicle or $3 per person. Mesa Verde is open all year, but some roads and trails within the park are closed in winter. Some ruins can be seen year round and others only from about May to October, accompanied by a park ranger. During the summer, there are many ranger-led tours and other activities. Reservations and free tickets for these are usually required, especially during July and August.

Reserve ranger-led tours at the Far View Visitors Center (☎ 1 (303) 529 4543), 15 miles from the park entrance and open daily from 8 am to 5 pm May to September. The Chapin Mesa Museum (☎ 1 (303) 529 4475), 21 miles from the park entrance, has more extensive visitor information and is open daily from 8 am to 5 pm (to 6:30 pm in summer). Further information is available from the Superintendent, Mesa Verde National Park, CO 81330.

The *Morefield Campground*, four miles from the entrance, and the *Far View Lodge*, 15 miles from the entrance, are both operated by ARA Mesa Verde (☎ 1 (303) 529 4421), PO Box 277, Mancos, CO 81328. Campsites are available from May to mid-October and cost $8 for tents or $15.50

Anasazi ruins at Mesa Verde National Park – the Square Tower House

with RV hookups. There are showers, a coin laundry and a grocery store by the campground.

Lodge rooms are available from mid-April to late October and cost $84 from Memorial Day to Labor Day and $71 at other times. There are restaurants near the campground close to the Far View Visitors Center and in the lodge. ARA Mesa Verde also runs a variety of guided tours from May to mid-October. These range from three to six hours and cost $12 to $15 for adults and $5 for children – tickets are available at the lodge and campground.

The nearest towns with plentiful accommodations are Cortez, Colorado (10 miles), Durango, Colorado (36 miles), and Farmington (75 miles). Lonely Planet's *Rocky Mountain States* has more details.

### Ute Indian Reservations (CO)

The Ute Mountain Indian Reservation straddles the New Mexico-Colorado state

NEW MEXICO

line a few miles northwest of Farmington. The huge tribal park on the reservation features guided day and overnight camping tours and adventures with the chance to visit remote archaeological sites. Information is available from Ute Mountain Tribal Park (☎ 1 (303) 565 3751 ext 282, 1 (303) 565 8548, 1 (800) 847 5485).

The Southern Ute Indian Reservation is in Colorado but borders the New Mexico state line northeast of Farmington. During the summer, various dances and ceremonies are open to the public. Information is available from the Southern Ute Tourist Center (☎ 1 (303) 563 4531).

Both Towaoc and Ignacio have casinos with legal gambling.

### Durango-Silverton Railroad (CO)
There are historical narrow-gauge steam trains that run from Durango, Colorado (45 miles northwest of Farmington), to Silverton, Colorado, through beautiful forest and mountain scenery daily from May to October and on a limited basis from November to January. Reservations are a good idea – contact the railroad (☎ 1 (303) 247 2733), 479 Main Ave, Durango, CO 81301, for information.

### AZTEC
When early pioneers found extensive Indian ruins here, they mistakenly thought the site was related to the Aztec civilization in Mexico. Though the ruins proved to be Anasazi, the name stuck. The present town was founded in 1890 across the river from the ruins, and the old downtown sector has several interesting turn-of-the-century buildings. Main Ave and the parallel Church and Mesa Verde Avenues have dozens listed in the National Register of Historic Places. The Aztec Museum or the chamber of commerce have a leaflet describing the most important buildings. There are also antique and gift shops in the historic downtown area.

Aztec (population almost 6000) is the San Juan County seat. The town is 14 miles northeast of Farmington; Farmington has the nearest public transport.

### Information
The chamber of commerce (☎ 334 9551), 203 N Main Ave, is open on weekdays from 10 am to noon and 1 to 4 pm. The library (☎ 334 9456) and the police (☎ 334 6101, or 911 in emergencies) are both in the Aztec City Offices at 201 W Chaco St. The post office (☎ 334 6181) is on Llano St at S Main Ave.

### Aztec Ruins National Monument
This small 27-acre national monument tucked away on the north side of town contains important and unique Anasazi ruins. The main site was built in the early 1100s by a Chacoan group in a style similar to that at Chaco Canyon (see below). This was abandoned in the late 1100s, only to be reinhabited a few decades later by people from the Mesa Verde area, who added their own style of architecture to the site before they, too, abandoned it in the late 1200s. The main site is about 360 feet by 280 feet and includes some 400 rooms, of which the most important is the fully reconstructed Great Kiva – with an internal diameter of almost 50 feet, it is the largest reconstructed kiva in the country.

Despite the archaeological and cultural importance of the site, it receives much less visitation than the better known Chaco and Mesa Verde parks. For this reason alone, it is worth a stop. Inside the monument, a 400-yard trail takes visitors through the site and into the Great Kiva – guide booklets are available. Ranger-led tours are offered on summer mornings, and kiva talks are given in the afternoons.

Write to PO Box 640, Aztec, 87410 for more information about the monument. A visitors center (☎ 334 6174) and museum provide plenty of interpretive material at the entrance to the site. Hours are 8 am to 6 pm from Memorial Day to Labor Day and to 5 pm the rest of the year. It is closed on Christmas and New Year's Day. Admission is $2 per person or $4 per family; Golden Age, Access and Eagle passes are honored. There is a picnic area but no campground. There are three trading posts just outside the monument.

## Aztec Museum & Pioneer Village

This small but excellent museum (☎ 334 9829), 125 N Main Ave, features a varied collection of local Indian and early pioneering artifacts and is well worth a visit. It is housed in the old City Hall, built in 1940. Outside the museum is a small 'pioneer village' consisting of a dozen original or replica early buildings ranging from a church to a jail, a blacksmith shop to a bank. Hours are 9 am to 5 pm Monday to Saturday and 1 to 4 pm on Sunday from May 1 to Labor Day; the rest of the year hours are 10 am to 4 pm Monday to Satur-

day. Admission is $1; those over 60 or under 15 are free.

## Car Racing

Aztec Speedway (☎ 334 6629) resounds with the roar of automobile engines on Saturdays from April to September. Cars include hobby stock, street stock, mini sprints, winged 360, ASCS sprint cars and IMCA modifieds – I haven't a clue what these are, but if you are a stock-car racing fan I'm sure no explanation is needed. The track is half a mile south of town just off Hwy 544.

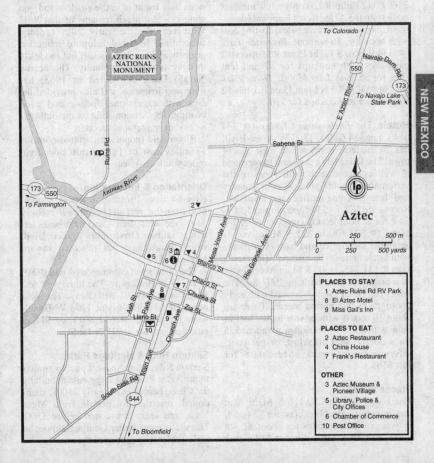

**Aztec**

PLACES TO STAY
1 Aztec Ruins Rd RV Park
8 El Aztec Motel
9 Miss Gail's Inn

PLACES TO EAT
2 Aztec Restaurant
4 China House
7 Frank's Restaurant

OTHER
3 Aztec Museum & Pioneer Village
5 Library, Police & City Offices
6 Chamber of Commerce
10 Post Office

NEW MEXICO

### Golf

Play nine regulation holes at Hidden Valley (☎ 334 3248), 29 Road 3025 (off South Side Rd – call for directions).

### Special Events

The annual Aztec Fiesta Days is held during the first weekend in June with games, arts & crafts, food booths and a bonfire – the burning of 'Old Man Gloom' celebrates the beginning of summer.

### Places to Stay

**Camping** *Aztec Ruins Rd RV Park* (☎ 334 3160), 312 Ruins Rd, is only a few minutes walk from the Aztec Ruins National Monument. There are 30 campsites, costing $10 with hookups, $6 without. *Riverside Park* (☎ 334 9456), S Light Plant Rd, offers 12 campsites with hookups for $7 and tent sites for $5. *San Juan Mobile Home Park* (☎ 334 9532), 305 N Light Plant Rd, has 12 campsites with hookups for $10.

**Hotels** The *Enchantment Lodge* (☎ 334 6143, fax 334 6146), 1800 W Aztec Blvd, has 20 modern rooms at the west end of town. The lodge has a pool and playground as well as picnic areas with views of the surrounding countryside. A coin laundry and free morning coffee are available. Rooms are $28 to $34 for a single, $34 to $44 for a double. Downtown, *El Aztec Motel* (☎ 334 6300), 221 S Main Ave, is about the same price and has seven rooms with kitchenettes. The historic *Miss Gail's Inn* (☎ 334 3452), 300 S Main Ave, 87410, is a brick structure built in 1907 as 'The American Hotel'. It is decorated with early photographs and period pieces. There are about 10 rooms with private baths, half of them with kitchenettes. Rates are about $55 for a double with breakfast, or get yourselves a room for a week, no breakfasts, for just $165.

### Places to Eat

*Frank's* (☎ 334 3882), 116 S Main Ave, serves a pretty good breakfast for $2 or $3, or you can get pancakes for about $1 – a good deal. They serve diner-style lunches as well. The *Aztec Restaurant* (☎ 334 9586), 107 E Aztec Blvd, serves decent Mexican and American fare from 5 am to 9 pm – prices are very reasonable. It may have entertainment on weekends. *China House* (☎ 334 8838), 104 S Main Ave, serves Italian food (just checking to see if you're paying attention!).

*The Trough* (see under Farmington) is about six or seven miles west of town.

## BLOOMFIELD

Settled in the 1870s, Bloomfield was notorious as a haunt of cattle rustlers and gun slingers – not much remains of that Wild West era. By the early 20th century, Bloomfield began developing irrigation projects and became a small but modestly thriving farming community. The nearby Navajo Dam, completed in 1963, has improved irrigation and also provided the area with exceptional fishing and good boating. The Salmon Ruin on the outskirts is another important attraction.

Bloomfield (population around 6000) is 13 miles east of Farmington and eight miles south of Aztec.

### Orientation & Information

Hwy 64 from Farmington enters Bloomfield from the west and becomes Broadway Ave – the main drag – and then bears left along Salmon Drive until Blanco Blvd, which heads east out of town toward Navajo Lake.

The chamber of commerce (☎ 632 0880) is at 224 W Broadway. The library (☎ 632 8315) is at 119 W Broadway. The post office (☎ 632 3050) is at 1108 W Broadway. The police (☎ 632 8011, or 911 in emergencies) are at 915 N 1st St.

### Salmon Ruin & Heritage Park

Salmon Ruin is an Anasazi pueblo similar to the Aztec Ruins – a large village built by the Chaco people in the early 1100s, abandoned, resettled by people from Mesa Verde and again abandoned before 1300. The site is named after George Salmon, an early settler who protected the area.

A self-guided trail winds through the site, which includes a large but unrestored kiva. There is a visitors center, museum, gift shop and picnicking area. The adjoining Heritage Park has the remains of the Salmon homestead and a variety of Indian cultural artifacts including petroglyphs, a Navajo hogan, an early Anasazi pithouse, a *tepee* (a conical tent used by Plains Indians) and a *wickiup* (a rough brushwood shelter).

Information is available from Salmon Ruin (☎ 632 2013), PO Box 125, 87413. The site is open daily from 9 am to 5 pm, except for New Year's Day, Thanksgiving and Christmas Day. Admission is $1 and 50¢ for children.

## Multi-Cultural Center
Changing exhibits and events highlight local art and history at this small museum (☎ 632 2840) at 330 S 2nd St.

## Angel Peak National Recreation Area
Along with Shiprock and Bisti, this is another area known for its desolate geological formations. There is a free campground with pit toilets but no water. The area is uncrowded and often empty. The turnoff for Angel Peak is 15 miles south of Bloomfield, then seven miles east along an unpaved road passable to cars.

## Places to Stay & Eat
For more comfortable camping than the free sites at Angel Peak, try Bloomfield's *KOA* (☎ 632 8339) at 1900 E Blanco Blvd. This campground has a few tent sites and about 70 RV sites for $13 to $17 and two Kamping Kabins for $22 double. There is a pool, playground, coin laundry and grocery store.

The simple *Bloomfield Motel* (☎ 632 3383), 801 W Broadway, offers standard rooms in the $30s – they give weekly discounts.

The best place to eat is the *Five Seasons Restaurant & Lounge* (☎ 632 1196), 1100 W Broadway, which serves American and Mexican lunches and dinners daily.

## Getting There & Away
Farmington has the nearest public transportation.

## NAVAJO DAM & NAVAJO LAKE STATE PARK
Built on the San Juan River, the Navajo Dam created Navajo Lake, which stretches over 30 miles northeast and across into Colorado. The lake offers excellent boating and fishing (for trout, bass, crappie and pike), and the San Juan River at the base of the dam has trout fishing that the locals call 'world class'.

## Orientation & Information
The state park is 23 miles east of Bloomfield or 25 miles east of Aztec. Information is available from Navajo Lake State Park (☎ 632 2278), 1448 NM 511 No 1, Navajo Dam, 87419. There is a visitors center at the park entrance, and day use is $3.

## Fishing
The tiny community of Navajo Dam (a few miles west of the park entrance at the intersection of Hwy 173 and Hwy 511) has several outfitters that provide fishing equipment and information and guide fishing trips. These include Born-n-Raised on the San Juan River, Inc (☎ 632 2194), Rizuto's Fly Shop (☎ 632 3893) and Four Corners Guide Service (☎ 632 3566, 1 (800) 669 3566). There are also outfitters and tackle shops in Farmington and Aztec – the chambers of commerce have lists. Note that the community of Navajo Dam is not synonymous with the dam itself, which is right by the park entrance on Hwy 539/511.

Fishing is by permit only, and there are catch and release and other regulations to protect the high quality of the fishing. Permit and regulation information is available from the state park, local outfitters, Abe's Motel & Fly Shop in Navajo Dam or the New Mexico Department of Game and Fish (☎ 827 7911).

## Places to Stay & Eat
**Navajo Dam** *Abe's Motel & Fly Shop* (☎ 632 2194) in Navajo Dam has standard

double rooms for $50 or $58 with a kitchenette. The place has 50 rooms, but they're often full with anglers – book well ahead. Abe's has RV campsites with hookups for about $10.

The eight-room San Juan River Lodge (☎ 632 1411), 1796 Hwy 173, has Rizuto's Fly Shop and a restaurant open from 6 to 9 am and 6 to 9 pm. The lodge prepares sack lunches. Rooms with two queen-size beds are $60/75 for singles/doubles and are sometimes booked up weeks ahead.

**Navajo Lake** The state park (☎ 632 2278) operates three campgrounds on the shores of the lake. The biggest is *Pine River*, which has tent sites for $7 and RV sites with hookups for $11. There is a visitors center with exhibits, a marina and boat launch, grocery store, playground and showers. Water-skiing is popular. Pine River is on the west shore of the lake just past the dam on Hwy 539/511.

*San Juan River Campground* has sites without hookups for tents or RVs for $7, and a boat launch area for canoes – this is the best place for river trout fishing. Fishing platforms designed for wheelchair access are available. There is drinking water but no showers. The campground is reached by crossing the San Juan River in the village of Navajo Dam and heading east. The lake is three miles downstream.

*Sims Mesa* has sites both with and without hookups for $11 and $7. There is drinking water (but no showers), a small visitors center, a boat launch and hiking trails. Sims Mesa is on the east shore of the lake and is reached by 18-mile-long paved Hwy 527, which goes north from Hwy 64, 32 miles east of Bloomfield. A shorter route is by unpaved roads leaving Hwy 539 just south of the dam. This is the least crowded campground.

## CHACO CULTURE NATIONAL HISTORICAL PARK

Massive, ancient, remote and spectacular Anasazi ruins are the reward at this park, if you can get there. All routes to the park involve over 20 miles of rough, unpaved road, which can become impassable after heavy rain – so think ahead. You need a whole day for a trip here, and it's not worthwhile unless you are interested in Anasazi ruins.

Although there is evidence of occupation dating from about the 5th century, most of the ruins here were built in the 10th and 11th centuries. At its height, Chaco is thought to have been home to between 2000 and 5000 inhabitants – archaeologists vary in their estimates. In the late 13th century, the Chaco dwellers, like all the Anasazi of the Four Corners area, disappeared – the precise reasons continue to baffle archaeologists.

The largest ruin is the huge **Pueblo Bonito**, four stories high and with 600 rooms and 40 kivas. The stonework is very fine (especially considering the tools – or the lack of them – that the builders had), and this is the 'type site' for the classic period of Chaco architecture. The excavated but not reconstructed great kiva at **Casa Rinconada** is one of the largest in the Southwest, larger than the reconstructed great kiva at the Aztec Ruins (described above). Apart from these two, there are several other major sites and many minor ones.

---

### Respecting Ancient Sites

Some ruins in Chaco Culture National Historical Park have been severely damaged. One such is the 'Sun Dagger', which consisted of three sandstone slabs arranged so that the sun shone through them to illuminate petroglyphs carved on nearby rocks – researchers found that solstice dates can be determined from the position of the sun on the petroglyphs. Unfortunately, visitation by researchers and others caused the slabs to shift, destroying their value as a calendar. The 'Sun Dagger' is now closed to the public (though a film of it can be seen in the visitors center).

The ruins are fragile, and visitors are asked to refrain from climbing on them. Vandals and souvenir hunters are also a problem – leave pottery fragments and stones where they lie. ■

None of the sites at Chaco have been fully reconstructed or restored. Some have been excavated and stabilized to appear as they would have a few hundred years ago, after abandonment but before being completely demolished by the ravages of weather, plants, animals and people. Some have been excavated and back-filled to keep them protected. Others have yet to be excavated.

Chaco was the center of a culture that extended far beyond the immediate area. Aztec and Salmon Ruin (see above) are among the best known of the outlying sites, but there are scores of others. These were linked to Chaco by roads, 30 feet wide and carefully constructed. Not much is visible of these roads today, but about 450 miles of them have been identified, and undoubtedly many more remain to be discovered. Clearly, this was a highly organized culture.

### Orientation & Information

A paved one-way loop road about eight miles in length passes near six of the most important sites. Many visitors arrive from the north and pass most of these sites en route to the visitors center, which is at the east end of the loop road. You'll probably get more out of your visit if you ignore the temptation to stop at every ruin you see and go first to the visitors center (☎ 786 7014), open daily from 8 am to 5 pm, or to 6 pm from Memorial Day to Labor Day. Orientation films are screened, and maps, brochures, books and information are available.

Note that facilities within the park are minimal – no food, gas or supplies are available. The nearest provisions are at Nageezi Trading Post, 26 miles from the visitors center.

The park is open all year and admission is $4 per vehicle. The ruins are closed from 30 minutes after sunset until 30 minutes before sunrise.

### Climate & When to Go

Late summer storms may temporarily close the roads to the ruins – call the visitors

Anasazi ruins at Chaco Culture NHP (CH)

center for road conditions after a storm. The elevation of over 6000 feet leads to very warm summer days and cool winter days. Winter nights commonly drop to the single digits and occasionally below 0°F. Snowfalls soften the landscape in winter but rarely close the roads.

### Things to See & Do

Apart from the self-guided auto loop tour, you can hike **backcountry trails** to see some more remote ruins, or to look down upon and see from a different perspective the ruins accessible by road. Free permits are required for backcountry trail use, and no overnighting is allowed there. Rattlesnakes have been reported basking on trails and in the ruins during hot summer days – watch your step.

Enquire in the visitors center about lectures and ranger-led **guided tours**, especially in summer.

## Places to Stay

There are no lodgings within the park. The *Gallo Campground*, 1.5 miles from the visitors center, is open all year on a first-come, first-served basis. It is sometimes full by noon in the summer, although there is a small overflow area along the road. Camping fees are $5 per site. There are toilets and picnic tables. Fireplaces are provided, but you must bring your own wood or charcoal. There is no water at the sites, but it is available in the visitors center (and nowhere else in the park). Trailers over 30 feet long cannot be accommodated.

The nearest lodging is the *Inn at the Post B&B* (☎ 632 3646), Nageezi Trading Post, 87037. Two rooms sharing a bath are about $55 double and a third room with a private bath is $65 double, including breakfast.

## Getting There & Away

From Nageezi, 37 miles southeast of Bloomfield on Hwy 44, turn right on unpaved Hwy 45 (also numbered 7800) for 11 miles to unpaved Hwy 57, then turn left for 15 miles to the visitors center. There are plans to open a new unpaved highway that would leave Hwy 44 about three miles southeast of Nageezi and enter the park from the east rather than from the north, thus passing the visitors center before the ruins. Check locally whether this road is open.

From the south, turn off I-40 in Thoreau and go north on Hwy 371 to Crownpoint (25 miles). Two miles north of Crownpoint, turn right on Hwy 9 (also marked 57) for 16 miles, then turn north for 20 miles on unpaved Hwy 57 to the park.

The above roads are signed. Other roads are marked on some maps, but these are unsigned, poorly maintained and I would not recommend them.

## JICARILLA APACHE INDIAN RESERVATION

The Apaches were comparatively late arrivals in the Southwest, migrating from the north in the 14th century. They were an aggressive group, taking advantage of the more peaceful Pueblo peoples who were already living here. Indeed, the Zuni Indian word *apachu* or 'enemy' led to the Apaches' present name. Jicarilla (pronounced hica-REE-ya) means 'little basket', reflecting their skill in basket weaving and other crafts.

Today, various Apache communities in the Southwest provide tourist attractions for visitors, although ranching, logging and mining are economically more important. In the case of the Jicarilla Reservation, Apache crafts and outdoor pursuits such as hunting, fishing and skiing all draw visitors. Almost 2000 Jicarilla Apaches live on the reservation.

## Orientation & Information

The tiny town of Dulce on Hwy 64 in the northern part of the reservation is the tribal capital. Ask anyone to point out the tribal offices. The administration office (☎ 759 3242), tourism department (☎ 759 3442) and the Game & Fish Department (☎ 759 3255) have tourist information. The tribal police (☎ 759 3222) are at Hawks Drive and Thunderbird.

Unlike at most other reservations, alcohol is available at the hotel and in the Apache House of Liquor. No permits or fees are needed to drive through the reservation. Photography is usually permitted.

## Things to See & Do

The **Jicarilla Arts & Crafts Museum** on Hwy 64 near the hotel has exhibits of various local crafts including baskets, beadwork, leather and feather work. There are occasional demonstrations. The museum's hours are erratic, but admission is free.

Anglers find that the eight lakes and the Navajo River are stocked with trout and provide good **fishing**. Hunters go after mule deer and elk from September to December. The Game & Fish Department requires that anglers and hunters obtain tribal licenses in addition to the more expensive state licenses. Tribal licenses are easily available at the Game & Fish office in Dulce. Staff there can also advise you about the best sites. Guided hunting and fishing trips are available.

**Cross-country skiing** trails are maintained in winter, and ski rentals are available.

## Special Events

The Little Beaver Roundup features a rodeo and several other events in mid to late July. The Goyiiya Fiesta, held on September 14 and 15 at Stone Lake (19 miles south of Dulce on Tribal Hwy J8), has a powwow and rodeo. The public is welcome. Other ceremonials are held throughout the year – call the tribal tourism department for details.

## Places to Stay & Eat

There are campgrounds by most of the fishing lakes. Several are easily accessible by car from Dulce.

The only hotel is a good one. The Best Western *Jicarilla Inn* (☎ 759 3663, fax 759 3170) has 42 pleasant rooms for about $50/60 single/double. Rates go up for the Little Beaver Roundup in July and down from January to May. The hotel has a restaurant, bar and big-money bingo as well as tourist information and a gift shop selling local crafts – ask them about the museum. They will make arrangements for you to ride on the Cumbres & Toltec Scenic Railroad (see Chama) – ask about their train package.

There is also a cafe in town – I didn't see it, but ask around.

# Chama to Española

East of the Jicarilla Apache Indian Reservation (see above), Hwy 64 joins Hwy 84, crosses over the Continental Divide and drops into the small community of Chama. This is the base for one of the most scenic train trips in the Southwest, as well as being a mecca for anglers, hunters and cross-country skiers.

South of Chama, the countryside becomes more characteristic of the classic, luminously lit landscapes favored by artists such as Georgia O'Keeffe, who lived in Abiquiu.

## CHAMA

This small town of 1250 inhabitants lies at a cool 7880 feet. Indians lived and hunted in the area for centuries, and Spanish farmers settled the Chama River Valley in the mid-1700s, but it was the arrival of the Denver & Rio Grande Railroad in 1880 that really put Chama on the map. Eventually, the railroad closed, but the prettiest part later reopened as the Cumbres & Toltec Scenic Railroad.

### Orientation & Information

Downtown Chama is on Hwy 17, 1.5 miles north of the so-called 'Y' junction (which is actually more like a T on its side) of Hwy 84/64 with Hwy 17. The main street is variously called Main St (though on maps it's officially Main Ave), Terrace Ave or Hwy 17. The area's attractions are spread out along Hwy 17, and along Hwy 84/64 for several miles south of the 'Y'.

The New Mexico Welcome Center (☎ 756 2235) at the 'Y' has general tourism information and maps about the whole state. The chamber of commerce (☎ 756 2306, 1 (800) 477 0149), 499 Main St, is open daily for local information. The post office (☎ 756 2240) is at 199 W 5th St. The clinic (☎ 756 2143) is at 211 N Pine St. The police (☎ 756 2319, or 911 in emergencies) are at 299 W 4th St.

The high elevation makes for a cooler climate. In July, temperatures range from a cool nighttime 40°F to 75°F in the daytime. In January, overnight temperatures drop well below 0°F with daytime temperatures about 32°F. Snowfall usually begins in October.

### Cumbres & Toltec Scenic Railroad

The coal-fired steam engine belches smoke and cinders, and some of the old semi-open carriages offer little protection from the elements, but this is part of the attraction. Railroad buffs enjoy the history, and others enjoy the magnificent scenery – it's a

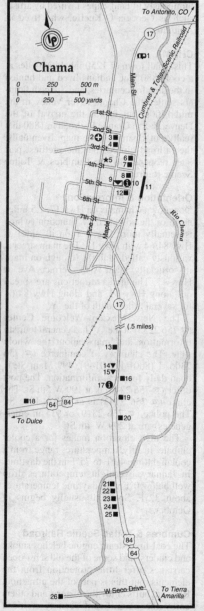

## Chama

0    250    500 m
0    250    500 yards

To Antonito, CO

Cumbres & Toltec Scenic Railroad

Main St

1st St
2nd St
3rd St
4th St
5th St
6th St
7th St

Pine
Maple

Rio Chama

≈ (.5 miles)

To Dulce

64  84

W Seco Drive

To Tierra
Amarilla

worthwhile train trip. This is both the longest (64 miles) and highest (over the 10,015-foot-high Cumbres Pass) narrow-gauge steam railroad in the USA. Some carriages are fully enclosed, but none are heated – bring warm clothes.

The train runs between Chama and Antonito, Colorado, every morning from Memorial Day to mid-October. The trip takes about six-and-a-half hours. You can take the full trip in either direction and return by van, or go by van and return by train. This costs $50 for adults and $26 for children 11 and under. You can also take the full trip and arrange your own return for $43 adults, $20 children, or only go to the

### PLACES TO STAY

1   Rio Chama RV Campground
3   Winters' Junction B&B
4   Gandy Dancer B&B
6   Jones House B&B
7   Foster Hotel
8   Chama Station Inn
12  Shamrock Hotel
13  Branding Iron Motel
16  DeMasters Lodge B&B
18  Twin Rivers Campground
19  Chama Trails Inn
20  Y Motel
21  Chama River Bend Lodge
22  Little Creel Lodge
23  Spruce Lodge
24  Elk Horn Lodge
25  El Meson Lodge
26  Oso Lodge B&B

### PLACES TO EAT

7   Foster Bar/Restaurant
10  Whistle Stop Cafe
13  Branding Iron Restaurant & Lounge
14  Viva Vera's Mexican Kitchen
15  High Country Restaurant & Lounge
24  Elk Horn Cafe

### OTHER

2   Clinic
5   Police and City Hall
9   Post Office
10  Chamber of Commerce, Cumbres Shopping Mall
11  Railroad Depot
17  New Mexico Welcome Center

NEW MEXICO

midpoint of Osier, Colorado, then return to your starting point for $32 adults, $16 children.

People over 60 receive a 10% discount, and advance reservations are recommended. To make reservations, call 756 2151 or write to PO Box 789, Chama, 87520, or contact the Colorado end at 1 (719) 376 5483, PO Box 668, Antonito, CO 81120. Carriages with wheelchair lifts are available with seven days' advance notice.

Next to the railroad depot is a **Narrow Gauge Railroad Museum** (☎ 756 2105) and a couple of gift shops selling railroad memorabilia. Ask at the chamber of commerce about their occasional fund-raising Moonlight Train Rides, which feature a barbecue at the pass.

Drinking alcohol and smoking are not allowed on the trains. There is a snack bar on board, and the train makes a lunch stop in Osier where you can buy lunch or bring your own picnic.

It is possible to get off at Osier and be picked up at a later date. This allows the option of backpacking and fishing in the San Juan Mountains. About 15 or 20 miles away (on foot) is the HI/AYH *Hi-Conejos River Hostel* (☎ 1 (719) 376 2518), which is remote and uncrowded. Beds are $8 for hostel members.

Antonito, Colorado, is smaller than Chama and offers fewer lodging possibilities. The basic *Park Motel* (☎ 1 (719) 376 5582) is near the station and has rooms for $23/33 for singles/doubles. Only a short walk into town is the *Narrow Gauge RR Inn* (☎ 1 (719) 376 5441, 1 (800) 323 9469) with rooms for $30/40. The best place to eat in Antonito is the *Dutch Mill Cafe*. See Lonely Planet's *Rocky Mountain States* for more details.

### Activities
You can **fish** in many lakes and streams year round (there is ice fishing in winter). Fly-fishing is good in many spots along the Chama River. Hunting season is September to December, but **hunting** season for elk runs from mid-September to mid-October.

Mule deer and bear are also hunted. Horseback packing and boating are favorite summer activities. During the long winter, cross-country skiing, snow shoeing and snowmobiling are very popular. Several outfitters in Chama provide guide and rental services – note that guided big-game hunting is expensive.

Chama Ski Service
  Snowshoes & cross-country skis (☎ 756 2492)
Dark Timber
  Fishing (☎ 756 2300)
DeMasters' Lodge
  Accommodations, snowshoes, cross-country skis, snowmobiles, horses and guides (☎ 756 2942, fax 756 2194)
Lone Pine Hunting & Outfitters
  Hunting, fishing, horses and guides, PO Box 314, Chama, 87520 (☎ 756 2992)
Reid Hollo Enterprises
  Horses (☎ 756 2685)

### Special Events
The Chama Chile Classic Cross-Country Ski Race is a big event with hundreds of competitors in 5 km and 10 km races. It is usually held on the weekend of Presidents Day (third Monday in February). There is also a hot-air balloon festival in February. A variety of concerts are presented in June during the Chama Valley Music Festival. Early August sees Chama Days with a rodeo, firefighters' water fight, chile cookoff and other festivities. The chamber of commerce can tell you of sailing regattas, harvest festivals and other events that occur without fixed dates.

### Places to Stay
The high season is the summer and fall. Rates are a few dollars less from about January to May, except during the ski race and balloon festival in February.

### Places to Stay – camping
*Rio Chama RV Campground* (☎ 576 2303), at the north end of town, is on the Chama River and has a view of a railroad bridge, so you can watch the steam train. Tent sites are $8.50, RV sites with hookups are $14,

and there are showers and picnic areas. It is open from mid-May to mid-October. *Twin Rivers Campground* (☎ 756 2218), on Hwy 84/64 west of the 'Y', charges $9 for tents and $13 for RVs with hookups. It has showers and a coin laundry. The *Chama River Bend Lodge* (see below) has RV sites with hookups for $12.50.

The campground at *Heron Lake State Park* has a few sites with partial hookups for $11 and about 100 sites without hook-ups for $7. There are bathrooms, drinking water, picnic areas and a visitors center. Day use is $3. Further information is available from the park (☎ 588 7470), PO Box 31, Rutheron, 87563.

### Places to Stay – bottom end
There is a paucity of cheap hotels in Chama. The old *Foster Hotel* (☎ 756 2296), opposite the train depot, was built in 1881 and hasn't had much renovation. Creaky rooms are about $35 (one bed) or $40 (two beds) for two people. Other simple places in this price range include the *Shamrock Hotel* (☎ 756 2416, 1 (800) 982 8679), 501 S Terrace Ave, also near the railroad depot, and the *Y Motel* (☎ 756 2166), 2450 S Hwy 84/64, near the 'Y'.

### Places to Stay – middle
**Motels & Lodges** The *Chama Trails Inn* (☎ 756 2156, 1 (800) 289 1421), 2362 S Hwy 17 by the 'Y', has an art gallery and 16 rooms with New Mexican decor starting in the low $40s for a double. Closer to town, the *Branding Iron Motel* (☎ 756 2162, 1 (800) 446 2650), 1511 S Hwy 17, has over 40 large motel rooms in the $50s and a restaurant.

The following places are found along the Rio Chama on Hwy 84/64 about a mile south of the Y, and all are within a short walk of good river fishing. The *Spruce Lodge* (☎ 756 2593), 2643 S Hwy 84/64, has a dozen rustic cabins starting at $41/43 for singles/doubles or $53 for a double with two beds and $5 for each extra person. A few cabins have kitchenettes. Nearby, the *Little Creel Lodge* (☎ 756 2382, 1 (800) 242 6259), 2631 S Hwy 84/64, has 16

cabins starting in the $40s. Cabins range from one to four rooms, and some have kitchens and/or fireplaces. They also provide corrals for your horses (the Lone Ranger stays here). The *Elk Horn Lodge* (☎ 756 2105, 1 (800) 532 8874), 2663 S Hwy 84/64, has two dozen pleasant motel rooms in the $40s and about 10 cabins with kitchenettes in the $50 to $70 price range. *Chama River Bend Lodge* (☎ 756 2264, 1 (800) 288 1371), 2605 S Hwy 84/64, has 15 motel rooms for about $48/54 for one or two beds, all queen- or king-size. There is an outdoor hot tub and RV hookups. The *El Meson Lodge* (☎ 756 2114) has 30 reasonably sized motel rooms starting at $49 a double.

In nearby Brazos, south of Chama and east of Hwy 84/64 on State Rd 512, the *Brazos Lodge* (☎ 588 7707) has cabins from one to four rooms ranging from $70 to $170. Cabins have a kitchenette and fireplace, and there is a hot tub. Also on this road is *Corkins Lodge* (☎ 756 2156, 1 (800) 289 1421), which has cabins sleeping two to four for $110 and a six-person cabin for $160. All have kitchens, smaller cabins have wood-burning stoves, and the large one has a fireplace. There is a swimming pool and access to private trout fishing on the Brazos River and on a lake on the property.

**B&Bs** The *Chama Station Inn* (☎ 756 2315), 423 S Terrace Ave, 85720, is opposite the railroad depot and offers eight rooms ranging from a standard double at $46 to a double with a queen-size bed and fireplace for $66. Nearby, the recommended *Gandy Dancer B&B* (☎ 756 2191, 1 (800) 424 6702), 299 Maple St, PO Box 810, 85720, has three attractive nonsmoking rooms in an early-1900s house with antiques. Dinners or box lunches are provided on request (in addition to a full breakfast). Rates are about $80 a double, and kids are welcome – the staff will arrange baby-sitting.

The *Jones House B&B* (☎ 756 2908), 311 Terrace Ave, PO Box 887, 87520, is in a 1920s adobe building with period furnishings. Three rooms with private bath are in the $70 to $80 range; two more with shared bath are about $50 to $60. There are two spas and a living room with books and board games. Smoking is not allowed. Also downtown, *Winters' Junction B&B* (☎ 756 2794), 241 Maple St, 85720, has two rooms, one with a queen-size bed for $75 and the other with a king-size for $85.

*DeMasters Lodge B&B* (☎ 756 2942, 1 (800) 288 1386, fax 756 2194), on Hwy 17 just north of the 'Y', PO Box 472, 87520, has five large rooms with queen- or king-size beds. There are both indoor and outdoor hot tubs, two large dining areas and a no smoking environment. Rates are $70 for a double with a complete breakfast or $55 without breakfast. Meals are available on request.

The *Oso Lodge B&B* (☎ 756 2954, 1 (800) 242 6259), 750 W Seco Drive (less than a mile off Hwy 84/64, two miles south of Chama), PO Box 808, Chama, 87520, is a favorite of sporting enthusiasts, only partly because it's owned by the famed father and son auto racers, Al Unser Sr and Jr. (Both men have won the Indianapolis 500 among many other racing honors.) The lodge has Western decor complete with stuffed *osos* (Spanish for 'bears'), free fishing on their lakes stocked with trout (guests need no permit because it's private property), a hot tub and local hunting and fishing information. Six large rooms with outdoor views rent for about $90 a double with breakfast in summer. Meals can be arranged, and winter discounts are offered.

Along the Brazos River about 12 miles south of Chama the *Casa de Martinez B&B* (☎ 588 7858), N Hwy 84, PO Box 96, Los Ojos, 87551, is an 1860s Spanish double adobe house that has been in the same family for four (or is it five?) generations. The atmosphere is homey, and the six rooms range from $55 to $90 a double – the most expensive room features a sitting room with a fireplace. Spanish is spoken, school-aged children are welcomed, and there is no smoking. Also in the Brazos area, near the end of State Rd 512, *Enchanted Deer Haven B&B* (☎ 588 7535,

1 (800) 619 3337), Tierra Amarilla, 87575, has two rooms with shared bath for $95 and two with private baths for $135. All rooms have queen- or king-size beds, and the larger rooms will sleep four – children are welcome. There is no smoking and a continental breakfast is served.

### Places to Stay – top end

The *Lodge at Chama* (☎ 756 2133), PO Box 127, 87520, is a huge luxury lodge in the San Juan Mountains near Chama. Guests fish from May to October, hunt from September to December and cross-country ski or ride snowmobiles from November to March. Hiking, wildlife viewing, photography and trail rides are other activities. There is a private elk and buffalo herd for hunting and photographing. Ten rooms and two suites are available; rates are close to $300 per person including all meals and some activities. Guided fly-fishing and hunting packages are available.

### Places to Eat

For inexpensive meals, I like *Viva Vera's Mexican Kitchen* (☎ 756 2557), 2209 S Hwy 17, which serves both Mexican and American food from 7 am to 8 pm daily. The *Whistle Stop Cafe* (☎ 756 1833) in the Cumbres Shopping Mall is convenient to the railroad depot. It is open from 7:30 am to 7:30 pm Monday to Saturday and serves American food – complete dinners start around $7. The *High Country Restaurant & Lounge* (☎ 756 2384), 2289 S Hwy 17, is the fanciest place, and the lounge looks like a Wild West saloon. Lunch and dinner is served in summer and fall, and only dinner in winter and spring. The budget conscious will find burgers and Mexican food – others may opt for steak and seafood with entrees from $13 to $20. There is also a salad bar.

Otherwise, your best bet is the hotel restaurants. Inexpensive and old-fashioned *Foster Bar/Restaurant* is open from 6 am till late – sometimes it offers a stage revue. The *Elk Horn Cafe* (☎ 756 2229), next to the Elk Horn Lodge, also offers reasonably priced breakfasts, lunches and dinners. The *Branding Iron Restaurant & Lounge*

NEW MEXICO

(☎ 756 2808), next to the Branding Iron Motel, is another reasonable choice.

### Entertainment

Apart from the occasional stage revue at the *Foster Bar & Restaurant*, you can try country & western dancing on weekends in *Ben's Lounge* (☎ 756 2922) on Hwy 17 a few hundred yards south of town.

### Getting There & Away

There is no public transport to or in Chama (apart from the scenic railroad).

### AROUND CHAMA
### Tierra Amarilla

This town, 15 miles south of Chama, is the county seat, although Chama offers many more visitor services. There are several century-old buildings to be seen in town. From here, scenic Hwy 64 heads east up over the Tusas Mountains to Taos – this road is closed by snow in winter.

A couple of miles north of TA (as it is locally known) is a turn to the east along State Rd 512 to scenic **Brazos Canyon**, where there are several places to stay. Between TA and Brazos, slightly west of Hwy 84/64, is the tiny village of Los Ojos. Here, visit **Tierra Wools** (☎ 588 7231), a weaving cooperative in a rustic, century-old building. Watch traditional weavers at work – hand spinning, dying and weaving rugs, hangings, ponchos and clothes. All the products are for sale.

### Heron Lake State Park

Eighteen miles southwest of Chama, this attractive lake park offers fishing, boating, camping and hiking. The fishing is excellent – a record-breaking 21-pound lake trout was caught here in 1993. Motorboats are limited to trolling speed, and sailing, canoeing and windsurfing are popular. Heron Lake Store (☎ 588 7436) has fishing gear, boat rental, a cafe and a grocery and liquor store. There is a short nature trail and a six-mile trail to El Vado Lake State Park (see below). In winter, locals ice fish and cross-country ski (along the El Vado Lake Trail).

The *Stone House Lodge* (☎ 588 7274) is about two miles from the lake and has cabins ($45 for one bedroom, $65 for two bedrooms), a cafe, grocery and tackle shop, and RV hookups.

### El Vado Lake State Park

This park is similar to Heron Lake, but in addition to fishing, boating, camping and hiking, water-skiing is also allowed. The campground has sites with no hookups for $7. There are bathrooms, drinking water, picnic areas and a playground. Day use is $3. Further information is available from the park (☎ 588 7247), PO Box 29, Tierra Amarilla, 87575.

*El Vado Ranch* (☎ 588 7354) is a couple of miles from the lake and has cabins with kitchenettes for $45 a double and $12 for each extra person. It also has RV hookups.

### CARSON NATIONAL FOREST

Although only a few miles east of Chama, the Carson National Forest cannot be easily reached from there. Hwy 64 between Tierra Amarilla (TA) and Taos crosses the forest, passing *Hopewell Campground* at 9800 feet, about 28 miles east of TA. This campground is open from May to October, has six free sites, toilets and no drinking water. In Tres Piedras, 50 miles east of TA, there is a ranger station (☎ 758 8678), PO Box 728, Tres Piedras, 87577.

Canjilon, three miles east of Hwy 84 on Hwy 115 and about 17 miles south of TA, has another ranger station (☎ 684 2486, 684 2489), PO Box 488, Canjilon, 87515. About 12 miles northeast of Canjilon on dirt roads, there are the *Canjilon Lakes Campgrounds* with 45 sites at 9900-feet elevation. There's drinking water, toilets and fishing. Sites are $5. It is open from May to September. Some 12 miles south of Canjilon, just off Hwy 84, is the *Echo Amphitheater Campground*, named after the natural red rock bowl in which it is located. The campground is open all year, has a free picnic site and short nature trail, drinking water, pit toilets and 20 campsites for $4.

Further information about the Carson

National Forest is available from the Supervisor (☎ 758 6200), PO Box 558, Taos, 87571.

## ABIQUIU & AROUND

The tiny community is famous as the place where Georgia O'Keeffe lived during most of her productive years. You can't visit her house, and there is no museum of her work here, so you have to use your imagination to try and see the surrounding countryside through her perceptive eyes. The attractive village plaza, which has a nice church and other old buildings, is worth a stop.

About three miles away is **Dar Al Islam**, a mosque that welcomes visitors. It comes as a surprise in this predominantly Native American and Christian land.

Seven miles west of town is **Abiquiu Dam & Reservoir** (☎ 685 4371). Surrounded by red rock and high-desert terrain, the reservoir is a beautiful spot for a swim. It also has a boat ramp, fishing for crappie, bass and trout, water-skiing, picnicking and a *campground* with showers open from mid-April to October. Campsites are $3 and $6 for a camper.

Just past the dam lies **Ghost Ranch Living Museum** (☎ 685 4312). Operated by the USFS, it is a living collection of indigenous plants and animals that have been hurt or abandoned. If they recover enough to survive on their own, they are returned to the wild. There is an excellent geological exhibit that explains the evolution of the nearby rock formations while you look through the telescope. You can see millions of years in the side of the rock! Interpretive trails are designed to teach you about the area's natural and cultural history – it's a worthwhile stop. The museum is four miles south of Echo Amphitheater on Hwy 84, or about 15 miles northwest of Abiquiu. Hours are 8 am to 4 pm daily from May to September, and Tuesday to Sunday during the rest of the year. Suggested donations are $2 for adults and $1 for seniors.

Ghost Ranch Conference Center (☎ 685 4333), just before the Living Museum, is a conference center with an ongoing dino-

Georgia O'Keeffe

saur excavation, and you can watch scientists painstakingly excavate dinosaur bones from locally quarried rock. There is also a small museum on local history and archaeology. This is where *City Slickers* was filmed, and it is a spectacular spot with hiking trails among the red rocks and grassy fields. Admission is free.

The only place to stay in Abiquiu is the nice-looking Abiquiu Inn (☎ 685 4378, 1 (800) 447 5621), Box A Hwy 84, Abiquiu, 87510. It has a dozen rooms ranging from rooms with one bed to rooms with two beds and a kitchen, all with private bath. Rates are $50 to $80, and advance reservations are advised. It runs a good and reasonably priced restaurant.

La Cocinita (☎ 685 4609), on Hwy 84 across from the Trujillo General Store, serves delicious homemade New Mexican food, burgers, and fresh fry bread every day from 10 am to 8 pm March through December. It doesn't look like much from the outside, but it's the best spot around for a good, inexpensive meal. You can buy food it to go at the walk-up window, or eat inside.

# Pajarito Plateau & Jemez Mountains

Covered with some of New Mexico's most rugged topography, this is a tough area to get around quickly. Massive volcanic explosions occurred just over a million years ago and blew an estimated 100 cubic miles (some authorities suggest 450 cubic miles) of ash and pumice into the air. (Compare this to the paltry 0.25 cubic miles ejected by the famous 1980 eruption of Mt St Helens in Washington State.) Eventually, the volcano collapsed in upon itself, leaving a tortured landscape of a massive caldera surrounded by fingerlike plateaus kicking off into what are now called the Jemez Mountains.

Hunter-gatherers lived in the area for thousands of years. The Rio Grande Anasazi (ancestors of today's Pueblo Indians) arrived by about 1200 AD and stayed for almost 400 years, leaving many ruins in the area – 7000 by one account. The most spectacular and important of these are preserved in Bandelier National Monument.

The rugged, out-of-the-way Pajarito Plateau area was the site chosen to develop the US atom bomb, and interested visitors can tour a fine museum explaining the history and research involved. In addition, the wild countryside provides challenging outdoor activities such as backpacking, cross-country skiing, fishing and hunting. Hwy 4, south of Los Alamos, gives a scenic view of the collapsed caldera.

## LOS ALAMOS

Los Alamos is named after a ranch built on the Pajarito Plateau by homesteaders in 1911. Seven years later, this became the Los Alamos Ranch School, an innovative place where rich young men were given a rounded education ranging from Homer to horseback riding.

In 1943, the US government took over the school and turned it into the top-secret headquarters of the Manhattan Project – the race to build the first atomic bomb was on. Over the next two years, the government poured $2 billion into the project headed by nuclear physicist J Robert Oppenheimer, who was assisted by many other brilliant scientists and the US military. On 16 July 1945, project scientists stood on a hillside near Los Alamos and watched the first atomic explosion several miles in the distance. Within a month, the USA dropped atomic bombs on Hiroshima and then Nagasaki, and Japan surrendered, essentially ending WW II.

Los Alamos continued to be clothed in secrecy until 1957, when restrictions on visiting were lifted. The Los Alamos Research Laboratory continues to be a major employer, with some 13,000 jobs throughout the state relying on the laboratory's existence. The town is the seat of Los Alamos County (New Mexico's smallest), and government jobs are an important part of the economy. There is a small but growing tourism industry, and Los Alamos has the lowest unemployment rate in the state. About 19,000 people live here.

The elevation is 7400 feet. Average high/low temperatures are 80/56°F in July and 40/19°F in January.

### Orientation & Information

Built on long thin mesas separated by steep canyons, Los Alamos has a confusing layout that takes a little bit of getting used to. The main entrance from the east is Hwy 502, which branches into the east-west streets of Canyon Rd, Central Ave and Trinity Drive – these are the main streets of town.

The chamber of commerce (☎ 662 8105), 2132 Central Ave, is in the Fuller Lodge (see before). Hours are from 8 am to 5 pm Monday to Friday. The library (☎ 662 8240, 662 8250) is at 1742 Central Ave. The local newspaper is the Los Alamos Monitor. The post office (☎ 662 2071) is next to the library. The hospital (☎ 662 4201) is at 3917 West Rd. The police (☎ 662 8222, or 911 in emergencies) are at 2500 Trinity Drive.

## Bradbury Science Museum

After the development of the atomic bomb, J Robert Oppenheimer, troubled by ethical issues raised by further development of nuclear weapons, left his post as museum director and was succeeded by Norris E Bradbury, after whom the museum is named. The well-organized displays, hands-on exhibits and audiovisual interpretations describe not only the history of the Manhattan Project but also nuclear research and defense technology up to the present.

Although the museum is educational and interesting, I found the overall experience to be creepy and unsettling – especially the sight of two young Japanese tourists intently examining duplicates of the Fat Man and Little Boy bombs dropped on Hiroshima and Nagasaki.

The museum (☎ 667 4444) recently moved to Central Ave and 15th St. It's open from 9 am to 5 pm Tuesday to Friday and from 1 to 5 pm Saturday to Monday (closed on holidays). Admission is free. Next door to the museum is the Otowi Station Museum Shop and Bookstore, which has a fine selection of science books and gifts.

## Fuller Lodge

This rustic log building was once the dining/rec room for the Los Alamos Ranch School and later for the scientists of the Manhattan Project. The lodge is now a national historic landmark and houses the chamber of commerce and two museums in the complex at 2132 Central Ave.

The **Los Alamos Historical Museum** (☎ 662 6272) has exhibits detailing the archaeological, historic and nuclear history of the area. Lectures and changing exhibits are featured, and there is a bookstore. The **Art Center** (☎ 662 9331) shows both local and national artists – some work is for sale. Hours for both museums are from 10 am to 4 pm Monday to Saturday and from 1 to 4 pm on Sunday. Hours may be extended in summer. Admission is free.

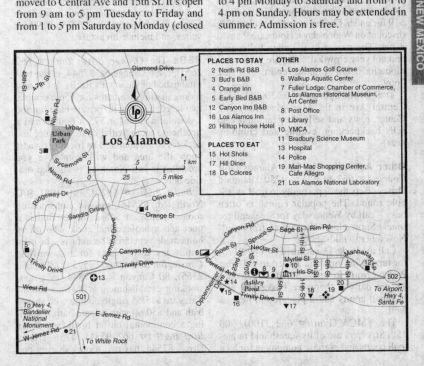

**PLACES TO STAY**
2 North Rd B&B
3 Bud's B&B
4 Orange Inn
5 Early Bird B&B
12 Canyon Inn B&B
16 Los Alamos Inn
20 Hilltop House Hotel

**PLACES TO EAT**
15 Hot Shots
17 Hill Diner
18 De Colores

**OTHER**
1 Los Alamos Golf Course
6 Walkup Aquatic Center
7 Fuller Lodge: Chamber of Commerce, Los Alamos Historical Museum, Art Center
8 Post Office
9 Library
10 YMCA
11 Bradbury Science Museum
13 Hospital
14 Police
19 Mari-Mac Shopping Center, Cafe Allegro
21 Los Alamos National Laboratory

## Activities

**Swimming** The Walkup Aquatic Center (☎ 662 7665, 662 8037), 2760 Canyon Rd, is the nation's highest Olympic-size pool. It has been the training ground of several Olympic medal-winning swimmers who claim the elevation helps them build endurance. The pool has public swimming from 12 to 8 pm Monday to Friday and from 10 am to 6 pm on weekends. Lane swimming is available in the morning. Entrance is $2.50 for adults, less for students and seniors. Multi-visit and other discounts are available.

**Skiing** Pajarito Ski Mountain (☎ 662 5725), about seven miles west of downtown, has five chair lifts servicing about 30 runs of which 40% are for experts and 35% are for intermediate skiers. Peak elevation is 10,440 feet, dropping to 9200 feet at the base. The resort is open on weekends and Wednesdays. Lift tickets are $31 for adults, $19 for under 12s and over 65s, with a 20% discount on Wednesdays. Hours are 9 am to 4 pm. The mountain is quite challenging and not very crowded; there are no accommodations. For a snow report, call 662 7669.

Trail Bound Sports (☎ 662 3000), at 771 Central Ave in the Mari-Mac Shopping Center, rents and sells ski gear (and also sells backpacking, cycling and climbing gear).

**Other Activities** The Los Alamos Golf Course (☎ 662 8139), at 4250 Diamond Drive, offers the opportunity to **golf** an 18-hole round. The popular course is often busy – call by Wednesday for weekend tee times. Snow closes the course from mid-November to mid-March.

Call the Parks Department (☎ 662 8170) for **tennis** information. The court at Urban Park on North Rd and 42nd St is open until 11 pm daily – there are basketball and handball courts and a playground here as well.

The YMCA Gym (☎ 662 3100), 900 15th St, offers use of its squash and raquetball courts and exercise equipment for $9 a day ($4.50 if you're staying at a local hotel or B&B).

The chamber of commerce can tell you about bowling, ice skating, archery and other sporting activities.

## Special Events

The main annual event is the Los Alamos County Fair & Rodeo held during 10 days in early to mid-August. Other events are scheduled throughout the year – call the chamber of commerce for information.

## Places to Stay

**Hotels** There are no cheap motels in town. The *Los Alamos Inn* (☎ /fax 662 7211, 1 (800) 279 9279), 2201 Trinity Drive, has a restaurant, lounge, pool and spa. Pleasant rooms are in the $60s and $70s. The *Hilltop House Hotel* (☎ 662 2441, fax 662 5913), 400 Trinity Drive, has a restaurant, lounge and pool. Some rooms have kitchenettes, and there are a few suites. Rates range from $70 to $85 for rooms or $100 to $190 for suites, and include breakfast.

**B&Bs** The *Orange Street Inn* (☎ 662 2651), 3496 Orange St, 87544, is the best established of the town's B&Bs. It has four rooms sharing two baths for $56 a double, two larger rooms with private bath for $66 a double, a suite for $75 a double and a 'treehouse room' with private entrance and deck for $75 a double. The friendly owners know the area and will even give you breakfast in bed. Smoking is allowed outside only.

*Bud's B&B* (☎ 662 4239), 1981 B/C North Rd, 87544, has six nonsmoking rooms starting at $45 a single. Bud is a poet and a professional cook who offers homemade vegetarian breakfasts – he even grinds his own wheat for his waffles! *Canyon Inn B&B* (☎ 662 9595, 1 (800) 662 2565), 80 Canyon Rd, 87544, is a nonsmoking establishment with four rooms. Rates are $45/55 single/double with shared bath and $50/60 with private bath, including a continental buffet breakfast. *Early Bird B&B* (☎ 662 9581), 4756 Trinity Drive, 87544, has two rooms sharing one bath for $50/65 single/double including full breakfast. *North Rd B&B* (☎ 662 3687, 1 (800) 279 2898), 2122 45th St, 87544, has two rooms and three two-room suites, most with private bath, for $48 to $65. Smoking is allowed outside only. All of these places give weekly discounts.

### Places to Eat

*Ashley's Restaurant & Pub* in the Los Alamos Inn is open daily from 6:30 am to 2 pm and 5 to 9 pm with dinner entrees in the $10 to $15 range. The slightly pricier *Trinity Sights Restaurant & Lounge* in the Hilltop House Hotel has good views and is open from 6:30 to 9:30 am, 11:30 am to 2 pm and 5 to 9 pm daily.

For a morning espresso jolt, head over to the *Cafe Allegro* (☎ 662 4040), 800 Trinity Drive (in the Mari-Mac Shopping Center). It has espresso, sandwiches, pastries and newspapers from 9:30 am to 6 pm Monday, from 8 am to 6 pm Tuesday to Friday and from 9 am to 2 pm on weekends. Good New Mexican fare is offered at *De Colores* (☎ 662 6285), 820 Trinity Drive. It is open from 11 am to 2 pm and 5 to 8 pm Monday to Saturday. For reasonably priced home-style cooking, try the *Hill Diner* (☎ 662 9745) at 1315 Trinity Drive. It is open 11 am to 2 pm and 5 to 8 pm on weekdays and 11 am to 8 pm on Saturdays. *Hot Shots* (☎ 662 2005), 2581 Trinity Drive, serves barbecue and other dishes from 11 am to 8 pm daily. It has a patio open in summer. The *Szechwan Chinese Restaurant* (☎ 662 3180), at 1504 Iris in the cinema mall, doesn't look like much but serves some of the best Chinese food in northern New Mexico.

### Getting There & Away

Ross Aviation (☎ 667 4521), 1040 Airport Rd (at the airport), has two flights daily (except Saturday) to and from Albuquerque. The fare is $60 one-way.

### Getting Around

Los Alamos Bus (☎ 662 2080) offers local bus service.

### WHITE ROCK

This small town is seven miles southeast of Los Alamos. It lies between the Tsankawi Ruins sector and main section of Bandelier National Monument. There is an area visitors center (☎ 1 (800) 444 0707) on Hwy 4 as you go through town.

The *Bandelier Inn* (☎ 672 3838, 1 (800) 321 3923), in the White Rock Shopping Center just off Hwy 4, has about 50 pleasant rooms in the $40s and $50s for singles and doubles, including continental breakfast. Most rooms have a microwave. Two-bedroom, two-bathroom suites with kitchen and living room are about $120.

For a meal, a few fast-food and other simple places are easily found. *Katherine's* (☎ 672 9661), 121 Longview Drive, is considered the best restaurant. It is open for lunch 11:30 am to 2:30 pm Tuesday to Friday and dinner 5:30 to 10 pm Tuesday to Saturday.

### BANDELIER NATIONAL MONUMENT

This monument is named after the Swiss-American explorer, Adolph Bandelier, who surveyed the ruins here in the 1880s. Almost 50 sq miles of rugged canyons are protected within the monument, and, apart from a short entrance road, Bandelier can be visited only on foot or horseback.

Unlike the Anasazi in the Four Corners region who mysteriously disappeared by about 1300 AD, the Rio Grande Anasazi inhabiting Bandelier lived here until about the mid-1500s, perhaps because of the moister climate. Several sites in Frijoles Canyon have been excavated and partially restored, including the large, oval-shaped ruin of Tyuonyi, which contained almost 400 rooms, and several ceremonial kivas. Many other ruins are found scattered in the backcountry, and Bandelier provides a fine destination for those interested in Anasazi ruins, backpacking or both.

### Orientation & Information

Hwy 4 follows the northern border of the monument to the entrance at the northeast corner. The road continues about four miles

Anasazi pots on display at Bandelier National Park Visitors Center (RR)

to the visitors center (☎ 672 3861) in Frijoles Canyon. It is open from 8 am to 5 pm daily and to 6 pm from Memorial Day to Labor Day and closed on Christmas Day. The visitors center has a slide show and a small museum interpreting the ruins. Restrooms are open 24 hours. There is a bookshop and snack bar and a nearby picnic area.

The bookshop sells trail maps and guidebooks, which can be obtained in advance from the Southwest Parks and Monuments Association (☎ 672 3861), HCR 1, Box 1, Suite 2, Los Alamos, 87544-9701. Information is also available from the Superintendent, Bandelier National Monument, HCR 1, Box 1, Suite 15, Los Alamos, 87544-9701.

Several trails leave from the visitors center into the Frijoles Canyon. Ranger-led walks and talks are offered during the summer.

Admission to the visitors center is free. Admission to the monument is $5 per carload or $3 per individual; Golden Eagle, Access and Age passes are honored. The monument trails are open from dawn to dusk.

### Frijoles Canyon Trail

This one-mile (one-way) trail heads roughly north from the visitors center and passes the major ruins. The first section is wheelchair accessible. A trail guidebook is available from the visitors center for $1. Sites along the trail include a big kiva, Tyuonyi and Long House Ruins, and cliff dwellings in the first half mile, which is fairly flat. The second half mile continues to the Ceremonial Cave, 140 feet above the canyon floor and reached by climbing four ladders – not recommended for people with a fear of heights. The Ceremonial Cave, which contains a kiva that may be entered, is a highlight of a visit to Bandelier.

### Falls Trail

This heads south from the visitors center and reaches two waterfalls, 1.5 and two miles away, and continues to the Rio Grande, 2.5 miles away. The trail passes Rainbow House Ruin along the way. A trail guide booklet is available.

### Tsankawi

This is an unexcavated ruin in a separate sector of the park, 11 miles north of the visitors center on Hwy 4 and two miles north of White Rock. There is a small sign and parking area. A steep two-mile trail leads to the ruins. The highlight here is the trail itself, which had been walked for centuries by the early inhabitants – their feet wore a trench into the soft rock, more than knee deep in places. From the ruins, which are on a mesa top, there are great views.

## Backpacking

About 70 miles of trails meander up, down and through the canyons of Bandelier, passing many ruins. Elevations range from 6000 to over 8000 feet, and the trails are steep. You should be in reasonable shape to hike them. Backpacking is allowed with a free permit available from the visitors center. No open fires are permitted. The trails are open year round but may be snow-covered in winter. Thunderstorms and heat are summer hazards, so spring and fall are considered the best backpacking seasons.

## Places to Stay

There are no lodges. *Juniper Campground*, 1.5 miles from the visitors center on foot or about four miles by car (near the monument entrance) offers about 100 sites, drinking water, toilets, picnic tables and fire grates, but no showers. The sites are open on a first-come, first-served basis from March to November and cost $6. The campground fills quickly, especially on weekends, so arrive early.

*Ponderosa Group Campground* is six miles west of the entrance station on Hwy 4 and has two sites open from mid-April to October. Group size must be between 10 and 50 individuals. The cost is $1 per person, and reservations are necessary – call the visitors center as far ahead as possible.

## JEMEZ SPRINGS & AROUND

Southwest of Los Alamos and west of Bandelier National Monument, the Jemez (pronounced HAY-mez) Mountains offer outdoor recreation opportunities, beautiful scenery, Jemez State Monument, Jemez Pueblo and more. Much of the land is within the Santa Fe National Forest. A ranger station is in the town of Jemez Springs. All these places are reached via Hwy 4, west, then south from Bandelier.

The tiny town of **Jemez Springs** has a few small hotels, several churches and monasteries, and also has a Santa Fe National Forest Ranger Station (☎ 829 3535) with information about camping, hiking, driving, hunting and other activities in the national forest. There are natural hot springs – you can take a dip at the **Bath House** (☎ 829 3303), which dates back to 1870 (it has been modernized). Entrance is $7 for a soak; massages are also offered for a fee, and a reservation is a good idea. Hours are 10 am to 8 pm.

Just over two miles north of the town, look for **Soda Dam** – strange mineral formations across Jemez Creek on the right side of the highway. The natural dam was formed by spring water heavily laden with minerals.

## Jemez State Monument

Once called Giusewa by the original inhabitants, the Jemez Pueblo Indians (see below), the monument now houses both Indian ruins and the ruins of a Spanish colonial church completed in 1622 – these are the main sights here. A worthwhile museum explains the significance and history of the area.

The monument is open daily from about 8 am to 5 pm – inclement weather may alter this. Admission is $2 for adults and $1 for children. The monument is off Hwy 4 just north of Jemez Springs. Call 829 3530 for further information.

## Jemez Pueblo

The Jemez were among the most active opponents of the Spanish during the Pueblo Revolt of the 1680s and 1690s, and they are the only people who speak the Towa language. Today, their pueblo, about 12 miles south of Jemez Springs, is closed to visitors except for their feast days on 2 August and 12 November, when there are ceremonial dances. Photography, recording and sketching are prohibited.

The scenery around and south of the pueblo is spectacular and intensely red. Red Rock, about three miles north of the pueblo, is the site of stalls selling local arts & crafts and food, especially on weekends. The Jemez are good potters.

The pueblo is in the middle of the extensive Jemez Indian Reservation, which the people use for agriculture, hunting and fishing. Two fishing areas open to the public are Holy Ghost Spring and Dragon-fly, about 18 and 24 miles north of San Ysidro on Hwy 44. Local rangers sell tribal permits, and the trout fishing is good. Further information is available from the Governor's Office (☎ 834 7359, fax 834 7331).

## San Ysidro

Hwy 4 ends here, at the intersection with Hwy 44, about five miles south of Jemez Pueblo. Gas and food is available. Head north on Hwy 44 to Cuba and on to Chaco and the Farmington area, or head southeast on Hwy 44 past Zia and Santa Ana Pueblos to the Rio Grande and Albuquerque.

### Places to Stay
**Camping** The Santa Fe National Forest operates many campgrounds in the area, most charging $6 a site and providing drinking water, toilets and picnic tables. They are open from May to October. Information is available from the ranger stations in Jemez Springs, Cuba, Española or Santa Fe.

The most accessible campgrounds are near La Cueva (the intersection of Hwy 4 with Hwy 126), nine miles north of Jemez Springs. Gas and food are available here. Two miles east of the intersection along Hwy 4 is the *Redondo* campground, and four miles further east on Hwy 4 is the *Jemez Falls* campground.

*San Antonio* is a USFS campground 1.5 miles west along Hwy 126. Eight miles further west along Hwy 126, *Fenton Lake* (☎ 829 3630), PO Box 555, Jemez Springs, 87025, is state-operated and provides year-round camping ($7), fishing and, in winter, cross-country skiing.

**Motels & B&Bs** In Jemez Springs, the *Jemez Mountain Inn* (☎ 829 3926) has eight rooms, two with kitchenettes, for about $40 a double. The *Laughing Lizard Motel* (☎ 829 3692) is similarly priced.

The *Dancing Bear B&B* (☎ 829 3336), PO Box 642, Jemez Springs, 87025, has three rooms. One with a shared bath is $45 a double, a second with an unattached private bath is $60 a double and a third room

with fireplace, private bath and river views is $90 a double. No smoking is allowed.

*La Cueva Lodge* (☎ 829 3814), nine miles north of Jemez Springs, has motel rooms for about $40.

### Places to Eat
In Jemez Springs, the *Laughing Lizard Cafe* (by the motel) offers good meals. The *Los Ojos Saloon* (☎ 829 3547) is an Old-West-style saloon that serves decent food. Also try *Deb's Deli* (☎ 829 3829).

The *Timber Ridge Restaurant* (☎ 829 3322), next to the La Cueva Lodge, serves home-style breakfast, lunch and dinner and is a popular spot for loggers, hunters, ranchers and state forest employees.

## CUBA
The 40-mile drive north of San Ysidro along Hwy 44 to Cuba is a very scenic one. The red-rock scenery is spectacular, and to the west, there are great views of 7785-foot Cabezon Peak – a volcanic plug rising over 2000 feet above the countryside. The base of the mountain can be reached by a dirt road leaving Hwy 44 to the west from near the Holy Ghost Spring in the Jemez Reservation. It's about a 10-mile drive passable to cars. Located along a scenic stretch of Hwy 44 at the intersection of Hwy 126, Cuba is a pleasant stop on the way to or from Chaco Canyon.

Settled over 200 years ago, Cuba is a small agricultural center and stopping place for travelers. It's about another 50 miles to Nageezi (the turnoff to Chaco Canyon).

The chamber of commerce (☎ 289 3705) is on the main street. The Santa Fe National Forest Ranger Station (☎ 289 3264), PO Box 130, Cuba, 87103, is on the right side of Hwy 44 as you arrive from the south.

The Sandoval County Fair & Rodeo is held annually in August.

### Places to Stay & Eat
Hwy 126 east of Cuba leads 11 miles to *Clear Creek* campground, operated by the USFS. There are pit toilets and fire grills but no drinking water. The campground is open from May to October and is free. A

couple of miles further on Hwy 126, *Rio Las Vacas* offers similar facilities. Hwy 126 continues about 15 miles to Fenton Lake (see Jemez Springs), but the dirt road is not passable after bad weather. It's a beautiful drive if you can get through. There are other campgrounds along the way, plus backpacking opportunities. Details are available from the forest ranger in Cuba. *Richard's RV Park* (☎ 289 3878) is on the main street in Cuba.

From south to north, you'll find the *Cuban Lodge Motel* (☎ 289 3269), the *Del Prado Motel* (☎ 289 3475) and the *Frontier Motel* (☎ 289 3474). Rooms start in the $20s. The *Cuban Cafe* (☎ 289 9434), 6333 Hwy 44 (opposite the Cuban Lodge Motel), serves good and inexpensive home-style meals all day long. *El Bruno's* (☎ 289 9429), in the middle of town, is a good choice for Mexican food.

### ZIA PUEBLO

Once home to some 6000 people, the pueblo was destroyed during the Pueblo Revolt of the 1680s. Now, only a few hundred people live here, and they are famous for their pottery. A stylized red sun motif on a yellow background, found on a Zia pot, has been incorporated into the state flag and is a well-known symbol of New Mexico. Zia pottery, with many other designs including, especially, a stylized roadrunner (bird) or a double rainbow, is available in the Zia Cultural Center and at many other outlets in New Mexico.

The annual ceremonial is on 15 August and the public may attend, but no photography, recording or sketching is allowed. The pueblo is about six miles southeast of San Ysidro off Hwy 44 (or 17 miles northwest of Bernalillo). Further information is available from the Zia Pueblo Governor's Office (☎ 867 3304, fax 867 3308).

### SANTA ANA PUEBLO

This pueblo, about eight miles southeast of Zia and eight miles northwest of Bernalillo, is reached by a two-mile gated road off Hwy 44. The gate is opened to the public only on the following feast days: 1 and 6

January, Easter, 24 and 29 June, 25 and 26 July and 25 to 28 December. Most of the tribe lives outside the pueblo in a modern village a couple of miles out of Bernalillo on Hwy 313. Here there is a crafts store open Tuesday, Thursday and Sunday. The tribe also operates the 27-hole Valle Grande Golf Course (☎ 867 9464) north of Bernalillo.

Further information is available from the Governor's Office (☎ 867 3301, fax 867 3395).

# I-40 West of Albuquerque

You can drive the 150 miles from Albuquerque to the Arizona border in a little over two hours, but don't. There is much to see along the I-40 corridor, and it's worth a couple of days at least. Two Indian pueblos are within sight of the freeway, and a third is a short drive away. The scenery is a mixture of red rock and black lava, with a couple of national monuments to showcase the highlights. Indian villages welcome tourists searching for unique arts & crafts. Anglo towns offer museums, lodging and a taste of the Wild West. And a national forest gives ample camping opportunities on tree-clad mountain slopes.

### LAGUNA PUEBLO

This Indian reservation (about 40 miles west of Albuquerque or 30 miles east of Grants) consists of six small villages. Although it was founded in 1699, it is the youngest of New Mexico's pueblos. The founders were escaping from the Spaniards and came from many different pueblos, and so the Laguna people have a very diverse ethnic background.

The Laguna Pueblo was built on a uranium-rich area, and the inhabitants were involved in the local post-WW II mining boom. Now, they are involved in a cleanup and reclamation program.

The pueblo is open daily from dawn to

dusk. Information about feast days and other matters is available from Laguna Pueblo (☎ 552 6654, 243 7616, fax 552 6007).

The **San José Mission** is visible from I-40. To get to it, take exit 114. Apart from visiting the mission, there is little to do in Laguna except on a feast day. The stone and adobe church was completed in 1705 and houses fine and interesting examples of early Spanish-influenced religious art painted by the Laguna people. It is open daily.

There is a growing pottery industry with ceramics being made in the Acoma style. Contact the tribal office about purchases.

## Special Events

Feast days are celebrated with dances, ceremonies, parades and sales of arts & crafts. The public may attend, but no photography, sketching or recording is permitted. The main feast days are two St Joseph's (San José) Days on 18 March and 19 September, St John's (San Juan) Day on 24 June, St Laurence's (San Lorenzo) Day on 10 August and Christmas Eve. Other days include Epiphany (6 January), St Peter and St Paul's Day (29 June), St Anne's Day (26 July), the Assumption (15 August), the Virgin Mary's Day (8 September), St Elizabeth's Day (25 September) and St Mary Margaret's (17 October).

The main feasts are held in Old Laguna, but some of the other feasts may be held in other pueblo villages.

## ACOMA PUEBLO

Also known as 'Sky City' because of it's mesa-top location, Acoma (pronounced AHK-ohma) is one of the most historic places on the continent. It vies with Taos Pueblo and Oraibi (on the Hopi Reservation in Arizona) for the title of oldest continuously inhabited settlement in North America – people have certainly lived here since the 12th century, although local legend claims that the first inhabitants arrived centuries earlier. Acoma Pueblo has had a long and often terrible history.

Several dozen residents live in Acoma

year round, although the village lacks electricity and running water. Most residents are elders who don't have to worry about getting kids to school. Many other people have temporary homes on the mesa, and hundreds more show up on ceremonial days. Most of the several thousand Keresan-speaking Acoma people live in one of the modern villages below the mesa, such as McCartys, Anzac and Acomita, all on the Acoma Indian Reservation.

The famous Acoma pottery is made from a very fine gray clay dug on the reservation. This clay enables ceramics to be made with extremely thin yet very strong walls, and Acoma pots are sought after by collectors. Good pots cost hundreds of dollars, and top-quality pieces run into the thousands. Note that some pots sold on the reservation are made from different clays, and although they have Acoma designs on them, they are cheaper and of inferior quality. Ask the salesperson what kind of clay has been used.

Call the Acoma Tourist Visitors Center (☎ 252 1139). The nearest accommodations is 27 miles away in Grants.

### Visitors Center & Museum

This is at the base of the Sky City mesa. A permanent museum exhibit called *One Thousand Years of Clay: Pottery, Environment and History* highlights the history of Acoma and showcases the local pottery. There is a snack bar selling Indian and American food, restrooms, parking lot, tour office and arts & crafts stalls. Hours are 8 am to 7 pm April to October and 8 am to 4:30 pm the rest of the year. Admission is free.

### Organized Tours

To climb to the Sky City, about 7000 feet above sea level and 357 feet above the surrounding plateau, you must go with a guide. Tours leave from the visitor's center frequently throughout the day, and the last tour is one hour before closing. Each tour is led by a knowledgeable Acoma guide who provides interesting narration and answers questions. The ascent of the mesa is made by bus and the descent is by bus or foot – your choice. The tour at the top lasts about an hour and is on foot.

In addition to seeing the ancient dwellings themselves, you can visit the fortress like **San Esteban del Rey Mission** built on the mesa top in the early 1600s – the heavy materials for its construction were carried up to the site. The views from here are seemingly endless.

Tours are given daily except for 10 to 13 July and either the first or second weekend in October, when the pueblo is closed to visitors. Tour fees are $6 for adults, $5 for those over 60, $4 for those 17 and under. Still-photography is permitted for a $5 fee (but not during special events). Video and movie cameras are not allowed.

### Special Events
No photography or recording of any kind is permitted during these events. Ceremonial dances and events should be observed only – please don't attempt to join in. For precise dates or information, call the visitors center. Sky City events include a Governor's Feast in February. Rooster pulls are held on San Juan's Day (24 June), St Peter and St Paul's Day (29 June) and Santiago's Day (25 July). (A rooster pull is a traditional tribal rain ceremony in which the boys and men of the pueblo literally pull a rooster apart.) There is a Harvest Dance on San Esteban Day (2 September), and Christmas festivities at the San Esteban Mission from 25 to 28 December.

In addition, outside of the Sky City, there are celebrations at Acomita and McCartys on Easter, at McCartys on Santa Maria Day (the first Sunday in May) and at Acomita on San Lorenzo's Day (10 August). An annual Arts & Crafts Fair is held during the summer at the visitors center.

### Getting There & Away
The visitors center is about 13 miles south of I-40 exit 96 (15 miles east of Grants) or I-40 exit 108 (50 miles west of Albuquerque). McCartys is near exit 96, and Acomita is near exit 102. There is no public transport.

## GRANTS & AROUND
Originally an agricultural center and railway stop founded in the 1880s, Grants experienced a major mining boom when uranium was discovered in 1950. After about 30 years, the boom went bust, but Grants discovered a new industry – tourism. The town has a fine mining museum and makes a good center for visits to, among other places, the El Morro and El Malpais National Monuments, and the Acoma and Laguna Pueblos.

### Orientation & Information
Santa Fe Ave (also called Business I-40 and Old Hwy 66) is the main drag through town and runs parallel and north of I-40 between exits 81 and 85.

The chamber of commerce (☎ 287 4802, 1 (800) 748 2142) is in the museum at 100 Iron St. The National Park Service El Malpais Information Center (☎ 285 5406), 620 E Santa Fe Ave, is open daily from 8 am to 4:30 pm and to 5 pm in summer. The Cibola National Forest Mount Taylor Ranger Station (☎ 287 8833), 1800 Lobo Canyon Rd, 87020, is open from 8 am to 4:30 pm, Monday to Friday. The library (☎ 287 7927) is at 525 W High St. The post office (☎ 287 3143) is at 120 N 3rd St. The hospital (☎ 287 4446) is at 1212 Bonita Ave. The police (☎ 287 4404 or 911 in emergencies) are at the corner of Roosevelt Ave and 1st St.

### New Mexico Mining Museum
Sharing the chamber of commerce building (see above), this is the only uranium-mining museum in the world (they say), and you can go underground and see what it was like to be a miner. Although the mine no longer operates because of decreased demand for this mineral, it's worth remembering that this is country's largest uranium reserve.

On the ground floor is a free museum of local Indian artifacts. Going below ground (by elevator in a miners' cage) costs $2 for ages 9 and up, and it's free for younger kids. Admission includes use of a 'sound stick', which provides a self-guided tour at your own pace. Groups can arrange live tour guides (ex-miners) by calling the chamber of commerce in advance. Hours are from 9 am to 6 pm Monday to Saturday and noon to 6 pm on Sunday, May to September. The museum closes at 4 pm from October to April.

### Bluewater Lake State Park
Camping and fishing for rainbow trout and catfish are the main attractions here. The 7400-foot elevation causes the lake to freeze hard in winter, when there is ice fishing. There is also a small playground,

grocery store, boat rental and water-skiing. Day use is $3. Information is available from Blue Water State Park (☎ 876 2391), PO Box 3419, Prewitt, 87045. The park is off exit 63 on I-40 (18 miles west of Grants) and then six miles south.

### Mt Taylor
This 11,301-foot peak is the highest in the area, and it is the southernmost of the four sacred mountains of the Navajo. Drivers can leave Grants heading northeast on paved Lobo Canyon Rd (Hwy 547) for about 13 miles to where it changes into

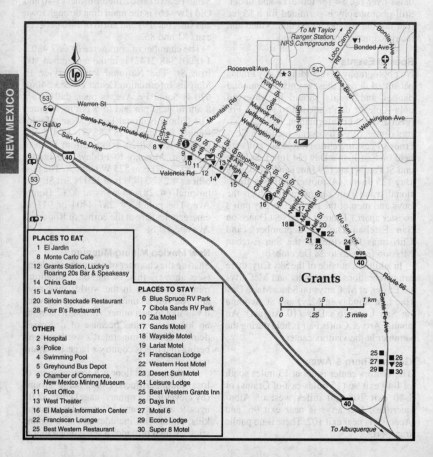

**PLACES TO EAT**
1  El Jardin
8  Monte Carlo Cafe
12  Grants Station, Lucky's Roaring 20s Bar & Speakeasy
14  China Gate
15  La Ventana
20  Sirloin Stockade Restaurant
28  Four B's Restaurant

**OTHER**
2  Hospital
3  Police
4  Swimming Pool
5  Greyhound Bus Depot
9  Chamber of Commerce, New Mexico Mining Museum
11  Post Office
13  West Theater
16  El Malpais Information Center
22  Franciscan Lounge
25  Best Western Restaurant

**PLACES TO STAY**
6  Blue Spruce RV Park
7  Cibola Sands RV Park
10  Zia Motel
17  Sands Motel
18  Wayside Motel
19  Lariat Motel
21  Franciscan Lodge
22  Western Host Motel
23  Desert Sun Motel
24  Leisure Lodge
25  Best Western Grants Inn
26  Days Inn
27  Motel 6
29  Econo Lodge
30  Super 8 Motel

**Grants**

0        .5        1 km
0    .25    .5 miles

gravel USFS Rd 239. Follow 239 and then USFS Rd 453 for another 3.3 miles to La Mosca Lookout at 11,000 feet, about a mile northeast of Mt Taylor's summit. It is possible to hike to the top of Mt Taylor, but check with the ranger station in Grants about trail conditions.

## Activities

You can **golf** at the nine-hole municipal golf course (☎ 287 9239), 1523 Horizon Ave in Milan (the western continuation of Grants), open from Tuesday to Friday. A new course is under construction east of town and should be open by the time you read this – ask at the chamber of commerce for directions. **Swim** at the public pool (☎ 287 7636), 551 Washington, open 1:30 to 5:30 pm daily. It costs $1.50. For **tennis,** call the parks department (☎ 287 7927) to ask about public courts and hours.

## Special Events

The Mt Taylor Quadrathlon (☎ 285 6969), held the second week in February, goes from Grants to Mt Taylor and combines cycling, running, cross-country skiing and snowshoeing. Individuals and teams of two to four athletes compete. Wild West Days features a PRCA rodeo, a parade, dancing, arts & crafts, food and fireworks on the Fourth of July or the closest weekend. The Oktoberfest, on the first Saturday in October, has a chili cook-off and various other foods and fun events.

## Places to Stay

The uranium boom produced many hotels – the bust left Grants with a surfeit of cheap hotel rooms that will delight the budget-conscious. Rates from about December to April may be a few dollars lower than the rest of the year.

## Places to Stay – camping

*Cibola Sands RV Park* (☎ 287 4376), on Hwy 53 half a mile south of I-40 exit 81, has a playground, store, showers and a coin laundry. The 54 sites are $10 for tents or $14 with RV hookups. *Blue Spruce RV Park* (☎ 287 2560) at exit 81 and *Lavaland*

*RV Park* (☎ 287 8665) at exit 85 both have tent and RV facilities next to I-40. Prices are about the same. There is tent and RV camping 20 miles west along I-40 at *Grants-West RV Park* (☎ 876, 2662) at exit 63 in Prewitt and at *St Bonaventure RV Park* (☎ 862 7885) 30 miles west at exit 53 in Thoreau.

The USFS (☎ 287 8833) operates the free *Lobo Canyon Campground*, eight miles northeast on Lobo Canyon Rd and then 1.5 miles east on unpaved USFS Rd 193. There are pit toilets and picnic facilities, but no water. The pleasantly wooded *Coal Mine Campground*, 10 miles northeast on Lobo Canyon Rd, has a nature trail, drinking water and flush toilets but no showers and costs $5. Both are open from mid-May to late October. The free, waterless *Ojo Redondo Campground* is about 20 miles west of town along unpaved USFS Rd 49 and USFS Rd 480. This is open all year, unless snow closes the road.

Eighteen miles west of Grants in *Bluewater Lake State Park*, a campground has a laundry and showers; tent sites are $7 and sites with RV hookups are $11.

## Places to Stay – bottom end

The cheapest place is the *Wayside Motel* (☎ 287 4268), 923 E Santa Fe Ave, which recently advertised rooms from $12 and up. Other cheap places include the *Franciscan Lodge* (☎ 287 4424), 1101 E Santa Fe Ave, which charges $18/20 for singles/doubles but may be noisy on weekends because of the adjoining bar; the *Lariat Motel* (☎ 287 2935), 1000 E Santa Fe Ave, with rooms for $19/22; the *Western Host Motel* (☎ 287 4418), 1150 E Santa Fe Ave, which has a pool and restaurant and charges $20/25; the *Zia Motel* (☎ 285 5610), 411 W Santa Fe Ave, with rooms for $22/25; and the *Desert Sun Motel* (☎ 287 4426), 1121 E Santa Fe Ave, which charges $23/26 and has larger rooms than most of the cheapest hotels.

The *Motel 6* (☎ 285 4607), 1505 E Santa Fe Ave, has a pool and charges $27/33 for standard rooms. With over 100 rooms, it is by far the largest bottom-end hotel. The

NEW MEXICO

recommended *Leisure Lodge* (☎ 287 2991), 1204 E Santa Fe Ave, has decent-looking rooms for $29/33 (one bed) or $38 (two beds). There is a pool.

### Places to Stay – middle
The *Sands Motel* (☎ 287 2996), 112 McArthur St, has good-size rooms, many with queen- or king-size beds and a refrigerator, in the low $40s for a double. The *Super 8 Motel* (☎ /fax 287 8811), 1604 E Santa Fe Ave, has a pool, hot tub, exercise room and continental breakfast included in the $36/40 (one bed) and $44 (two beds) rates. The *Econo Lodge* (☎ 287 4426, 1 (800) 424 4777), 1509 E Santa Fe Ave, is the town's largest hotel with 155 rooms in the $40s for a double, many with king-size beds. There is a pool, coin laundry, restaurant and lounge with room service and entertainment on weekends. The *Days Inn* (☎ 287 8883, fax 287 7772), 1504 Santa Fe Ave, has spacious, well-kept rooms with queen- and king-size beds in the $40s for a single and in the $50s for a double (one bed) or in the $60s to $70s (two beds).

The best hotel is the *Best Western Grants Inn* (☎ 287 7901, fax 285 5751), 1501 E Santa Fe Ave. Facilities include an indoor pool, hot tub, sauna, game room, coin and valet laundry, restaurant with room service and lounge with weekend entertainment and dancing. Large rooms have queen- or king-size beds, double wash basins, bathtubs, and refrigerators on request. Rates are $56 to $70 a single, $66 to $80 a double.

### Places to Eat
Locally popular *Grants Station* (☎ 287 2334), 200 W Santa Fe Ave, offers inexpensive family dining from 6 am to 11 pm daily. The menu is American with a few Mexican plates. Alcohol isn't served though you can get a beer at the adjoining Roaring '20s Bar. The 'Station' refers to the railroad (which is no longer in use for passengers), and there's plenty of railroad memorabilia.

The *Monte Carlo Cafe* (☎ 287 9250), 721 W Santa Fe Ave, serves reasonably priced and tasty Southwestern food in a traditional setting. Menu items range from stuffed chiles to Navajo tacos to steaks. They are open from 8 am to 10 pm daily, 9 am to 9 pm on Sunday. Homey and pleasant *El Jardin* (☎ 285 5231), 912 Lobo Canyon Rd, offers very good value, well-prepared Mexican food from 11 am to 8:30 pm Monday to Saturday. It is closed from 3 to 5 pm.

The *Four B's Restaurant* (☎ 285 6697), on Santa Fe Ave just north of I-40 exit 85, is open 24 hours. Featuring inexpensive American fare, it is convenient to the cluster of motels near that exit. Travelers with huge and uncritical appetites and slim budgets can try the *China Gate* (☎ 287 8513), 105 W Santa Fe, which features all-you-can-eat buffet lunches and dinners for about $5 and $6. The *Sirloin Stockade* (☎ 287 2576), 1140 E Santa Fe Ave, is open daily for lunch and dinner and has an all-you-can-eat smorgasbord lunch for under $6 as well as other reasonably priced and meaty food.

Decent steak and prime rib is served at *La Ventana* (☎ 287 9393), 110½ Geis St. Prices are around $15, although there are cheaper Mexican and chicken items. Seafood is also offered. Hours are 11 am to 10:30 pm daily except Sunday. The restaurant in the Best Western Grants Inn (☎ 287 7901) is also good. It's open from 6 to 10 am for breakfast and 5 to 9 pm for dinner.

### Entertainment
Catch a movie at the *West Theater* (☎ 287 4692), 118 W Santa Fe Ave. For a beer and some local color, try *Lucky's Roaring 20s Bar & Speakeasy* (☎ 287 2555), 218 W Santa Fe Ave. Weekend entertainment tends toward country & western music and dancing. Try the *Franciscan Lounge* (☎ 287 2345), 1109 E Santa Fe Ave, or the more tony lounge at the Best Western Grants Inn.

### Getting There & Away
Greyhound (☎ 285 6268), 1801 W Santa Fe Ave, has about five buses a day to Albuquerque (2.5 hours), Flagstaff, Arizona (three hours), and beyond.

## EL MALPAIS NATIONAL MONUMENT

El Malpais (pronounced el mahl-pie-ees and meaning 'bad land' in Spanish) is almost 200 sq miles of lava flows abutting adjacent sandstone. Five major flows have been identified, with the most recent 2000 to 3000 years old. Local Indian legend tells of 'rivers of fire', and prehistoric Native Americans may have witnessed the final eruptions.

The landscape is harsh but interesting. There are cinder cones and spatter cones, smooth *pahoehoe* lava and jagged *aa* lava, and a 17-mile-long lava tube system. Some lava caves contain permanent ice. Around the edges of the lava flows are sandstone formations, including New Mexico's largest accessible arch, and signs of previous dwellers in the area – petroglyphs, ruins and homesteaders' cabins.

### Information

El Malpais is a hodgepodge of NPS land, conservation areas and wilderness areas administered by the BLM, and private lands. Each area has different rules and regulations, and these change from year to year. There are no developed campsites or lodges. Backcountry camping is allowed, but a free permit is required. Consider visiting El Malpais Information Center in Grants (see above) before your visit. Also, you can stop by the El Malpais Ranger Station on Hwy 117 about 10 miles south of exit 49 on I-40. The station is open from 8:30 am to 5 pm daily. The area is open year round, and admission is free. Further information is available from the National Park Service, PO Box 939, or the BLM, PO Box 846, Grants, 87020.

### Things to See

On the east side of the monument Hwy 117 passes **Sandstone Bluffs Overlook** about 11 miles south of I-40. There is a picnic area with fine views of the lava flow. An interesting but rough hike (wear heavy shoes or boots) is the 7.5-mile (one-way) **Zuni-Acoma Trail**, which leaves from Hwy 117 a few miles further south. The trail crosses several lava flows and ends at Hwy 53 on the west side of the monument.

**La Ventana Natural Arch** is visible from Hwy 117, 17 miles south of I-40. Just beyond is another hiking trail.

County Rd 42 leaves Hwy 117 about 34 miles south of I-40 and meanders for about 40 miles through the BLM country on the west side of El Malpais. It passes several craters and lava tubes (reached by signed trails) and emerges at Hwy 53 near Bandera Crater. The road is unpaved, and high-clearance 4WD is recommended. Hikers need good boots on the rough lava and should carry a gallon of water per person per day. If entering lava tubes or caves beyond where daylight penetrates, you should carry three sources of light. The Park Service recommends wearing a hard hat. Go with a companion – this is an isolated area.

**Bandera Crater/Ice Cave** is 25 miles southwest of Grants on Hwy 53. The area is private property (☎ 783 4303) and costs $5 to visit, or $2.50 for children five to 11 years old. The area is surrounded by the national monument, and the Park Service is planning on incorporating it into the monument, in which case the fees may be dropped. A 1.5-mile trail leads part of the way up the Bandera Volcano. A trail a fifth of a mile long leads to the Ice Cave. Both trails are rough.

## EL MORRO NATIONAL MONUMENT

El Morro (Spanish for 'the headland'), is a 200-foot-high sandstone outcropping with a permanent pool of water at its base. This has made it a travelers' stopping place for thousands of years. In the 1200s, the Zuni people built a small pueblo on top of El Morro; the pueblo was abandoned around 1300. Today's Zuni call it *A'ts'ina* or the 'place of rock carvings'. The ancient inhabitants left many petroglyphs carved into the soft sandstone.

In 1605, Don Juan de Oñate left his name inscribed on El Morro – the first non-Native American carving – and Spaniards following him did the same. Anglos in the 1800s also carved evidence of their passing here until carving became illegal in 1906.

Visitors today can see the pueblo, the petroglyphs and the historical inscriptions.

## Orientation & Information

El Morro is 43 miles southwest of Grants. The park is open daily from 8 am to 7 pm from Memorial Day to Labor Day and to 5 pm the rest of the year. It is closed on Christmas Day. A visitors center has audio-visual and other displays, information, a bookshop and a picnic area. Rangers give talks during summer weekends. Admission is $4 per vehicle or $2 per person and Golden Eagle, Age and Access passes are honored.

Two self-guided trails leave the visitors center. The paved, half-mile-loop Inscription Rock Trail is wheelchair accessible and the unpaved, two-mile-loop Mesa Top Trail requires a steep climb to the pueblos. Guide booklets are available.

Further information is available from the Superintendent, El Morro (☎ 783 4226), Route 2, Box 43, Ramah, 87321-9603.

## Places to Stay & Eat

A nine-site NPS campground is a mile before the visitors center. There is drinking water and pit toilets. Fees are $5 per site on a first-come, first-served basis. The campground usually fills during summer weekends but rarely midweek.

*El Morro RV Park* (☎ 783 4612) has 34 sites on Hwy 53, about a mile east of El Morro. It is open from mid-March through November and charge $15 for sites with hookups or $9 for tents. There are showers, and a snack bar is open from 7 am to 8 pm. Two cabins rent for $35 a double. Hiking trails are nearby. A couple of miles further east is the cheaper *Tinaja Bar & Campground* (☎ 783 4349), which, as its name implies, has a bar. It is open from May to September.

The *Vogt Ranch B&B* (☎ 783 4362), PO Box 716, Ramah, 87321, is on Hwy 53, nine miles west of El Morro. This early-1900s ranch rents two rooms with private bath for about $70. Full breakfast is included, and dinner is available on request. The B&B is open from mid-April

to mid-December, and reservations are requested. The *Stagecoach Inn Restaurant* (☎ 783 4288) is a couple of miles further east in Ramah.

## ZUNI PUEBLO

The Zuni people speak a language different from all other Indian groups. The early Spaniards thought the pueblo was one of the legendary (and imaginary) 'seven cities of gold'. Although it was not a city of gold, today it is a premier jewelry-making center. The pueblo is 35 miles south of Gallup and has about 8500 inhabitants.

## Orientation & Information

Most main public buildings are stretched along Hwy 53, with side streets curving away into the pueblo. Photography is by permit only and is prohibited in some areas and for special events. Primitive camping requires a $3 permit from the tribal office. Most visitors stay in Gallup – Zuni has no hotels. There are a couple of cafes in Zuni. Information is available from the Zuni Tribal Office (☎ 782 4481, fax 782 2700).

## Our Lady of Guadalupe Mission

Walking from Hwy 53 to the mission

Zuni Pueblo

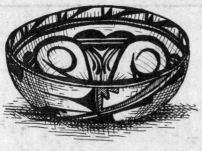

Zuni bowl

(☎ 882 4477) takes five minutes, and you pass Zuni stone houses and beehive-shaped mud ovens used for baking. The church dates from 1629, although it has been rebuilt twice since then. With its massive adobe walls and vigas, it is typical of Southwestern missions except that the interior features 24 superb, life-size paintings of kachinas by local artist Alex Seowtowa and sons Kenneth and Edwin. They began this project in 1970 and plan to finish in the mid-1990s. Photography is not allowed inside.

The church is open erratic hours from Monday to Friday and for 10 am mass on Sunday.

### Zuni Museum Project
This historical museum on Hwy 53 displays early photos and other tribal artifacts. Hours are supposedly 9 am to 4:30 pm on weekdays, but in reality they are very unpredictable.

### Special Events
This pueblo continues to allow non-Native Americans to its ceremonies, although they must adhere to appropriate etiquette, especially the no-photography rule. The most famous is the all-night *Shalako* ceremonial dance held in late November or early December.

In late August, the Zuni Tribal Fair features a powwow, local food and arts & crafts stalls. Other ceremonials occur on varying dates – ask at the tribal office.

### Things to Buy
The Zuni are famed worldwide for not only the high quality of their silverwork, but also because so many members of the pueblo are involved, in some way, with jewelry production. Their silverwork is inlaid with turquoise and a variety of other semiprecious stones from all over the world. The delicacy of the inlay is a hallmark of Zuni work. Other popular and relatively inexpensive purchases are Zuni fetishes – miniature animal carvings that the Zunis believe take on the spiritual nature of the animal itself. Miniature paintings, beadwork and pottery are also sold. You'll see several stores on Hwy 53 near the tribal offices.

## GALLUP
The Gallup Convention and Visitors Bureau proudly proclaims their town to be 'The Heart of Indian Country' and, indeed, Gallup is arguably the most 'Indian' of all off-reservation towns. It serves as the Navajo and Zuni peoples' major trading center, both for buying and selling. The supermarkets and shopping malls are crowded with Native Americans and, in turn, the many trading posts and arts & crafts galleries attract people from all over the world searching for the best of the local Indian rugs, jewelry, silverware, pottery, fetishes, kachinas, baskets, sand paintings and various other art forms. The visitors bureau estimates that 80% of Southwestern silver jewelry sold in the USA passes through Gallup.

Apart from fine shopping opportunities, visitors are attracted by the Inter-Tribal Indian Ceremonial – an annual six-day event that draws both Native American and non-Indian visitors. This is the biggest such affair in the Southwest and is well worth attending. And if you miss the Ceremonial, you can still see Indian dances performed nightly during the summer.

The Navajo Indian Reservation is the largest in the USA. The tribal capital at Window Rock, Arizona, is just 24 miles to the northwest, and so Gallup makes a good base from which to visit Navajoland.

NEW MEXICO

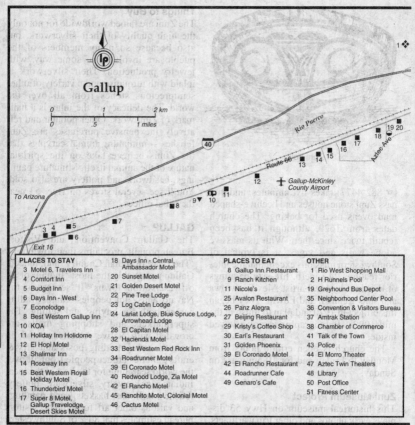

## Gallup

0    1    2 km
0    .5    1 miles

To Arizona

Rio Puerco

Route 66

Gallup-McKinley County Airport

Exit 16

| PLACES TO STAY | | PLACES TO EAT | OTHER |
|---|---|---|---|
| 3  Motel 6, Travelers Inn | 18  Days Inn - Central, Ambassador Motel | 8  Gallup Inn Restaurant | 1  Rio West Shopping Mall |
| 4  Comfort Inn | 20  Sunset Motel | 9  Ranch Kitchen | 2  H Runnels Pool |
| 5  Budget Inn | 21  Golden Desert Motel | 11  Nicole's | 19  Greyhound Bus Depot |
| 6  Days Inn - West | 22  Pine Tree Lodge | 25  Avalon Restaurant | 35  Neighborhood Center Pool |
| 7  Econolodge | 23  Log Cabin Lodge | 26  Panz Alegra | 36  Convention & Visitors Bureau |
| 8  Best Western Gallup Inn | 24  Lariat Lodge, Blue Spruce Lodge, Arrowhead Lodge | 27  Beijing Restaurant | 37  Amtrak Station |
| 10  KOA | 28  El Capitan Motel | 29  Kristy's Coffee Shop | 38  Chamber of Commerce |
| 11  Holiday Inn Holidome | 32  Hacienda Motel | 30  Earl's Restaurant | 43  Police |
| 12  El Hopi Motel | 33  Best Western Red Rock Inn | 31  Golden Phoenix | 44  El Morro Theater |
| 13  Shalimar Inn | 34  Roadrunner Motel | 39  El Coronado Motel | 47  Aztec Twin Theaters |
| 14  Roseway Inn | 39  El Coronado Motel | 42  El Rancho Restaurant | 48  Library |
| 15  Best Western Royal Holiday Motel | 40  Redwood Lodge, Zia Motel | 44  Roadrunner Cafe | 50  Post Office |
| 16  Thunderbird Motel | 42  El Rancho Motel | 49  Genaro's Cafe | 51  Fitness Center |
| 17  Super 8 Motel, Gallup Travelodge, Desert Skies Motel | 45  Ranchito Motel, Colonial Motel | | |
| | 46  Cactus Motel | | |

Although small areas of the reservation lie in Utah and New Mexico, the bulk is within Arizona.

As a town, Gallup dates back to 1881, when the Atchinson, Topeka & Santa Fe Railroad (then called the Atlantic and Pacific Railroad) reached that point. Before the railroad was built, there was a Wild West saloon here, a stopping place on the Overland Stagecoach route. The railroad workers used to come by here to pick up their paychecks – the story is that the paymaster's name was David Gallup, and the town took its name from him. Coal was discovered soon after the railroad arrived

and Gallup remained an important mining town until the middle of this century.

Today, Gallup (population about 20,000 inhabitants) is the seat of McKinley County. Its economy relies on trade and tourism.

### Orientation & Information

The famous old Hwy 66 is the main drag through town and runs east-west, parallel to and south of I-40, the Rio Puerco and the railway line. It is sometimes locally called 66 Ave.

The convention and visitors bureau (☎ 863 3841, 1 (800) 242 4282) is open

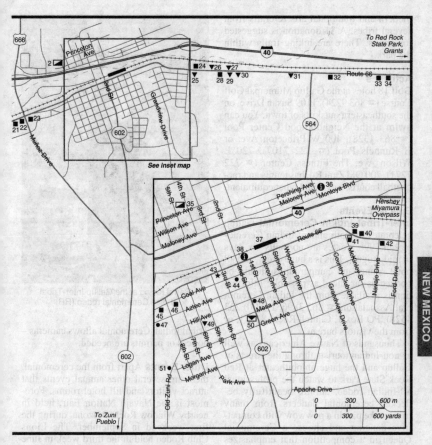

from 8 am to 5 pm daily in the summer and Monday to Friday in winter. The bureau is at 701 Montoya Blvd. Information is also available from 8:30 am to 5 pm Monday to Friday at the chamber of commerce (☎ 722 2228), 103 E Hwy 66, next to the Amtrak station. The library (☎ 863 1291) is at 115 W Hill. The local newspaper is the *Independent*. The post office (☎ 863 3491) is at 500 S 2nd St. The hospital (☎ 863 6832, 863 7000) is at 1901 Red Rock Drive. The police (☎ 722 4438 or 911 in emergencies) have a downtown office at 300 W Hwy 66. There is another police station (☎ 722 2231) at 451 State Rd 564.

The visitors bureau and the chamber of commerce have a free brochure detailing 19 downtown structure of historic and architectural interest built between 1895 and 1938. Look mainly along 1st, 2nd and 3rd Sts between Hwy 66 and Hill Ave.

### Red Rock State Park

Six miles east of town, this park features a museum and campground and is also the site of the annual Inter-Tribal Ceremonial and many other events (see below). The museum (☎ 722 6196) is open from 8:30 am to 4:30 pm Monday to Friday (hours are extended in summer), and features both modern and traditional arts & crafts from several tribes. A $1 donation is suggested for adults. There are hiking trails within the park.

## Activities

**Golf** 18 holes at the Gallup Municipal Golf Course (☎ 863 9224), 1109 Susan Drive, on the southeastern outskirts of town. You can **swim** at the Neighborhood Center Pool (☎ 863 1328), 400 W Princeton Ave, or H Runnels Pool (☎ 722 7107), 720 E Wilson Ave. The Fitness Center (☎ 722 7271), 700 Old Zuni Rd, has tennis and racquetball courts, a gym and other equipment.

## Special Events

**Inter-Tribal Indian Ceremonial** Gallup celebrates its 75th annual Indian Ceremonial in 1996 – dates are normally six days in mid-August. This is a huge event, and all hotel rooms and campgrounds should be booked as far ahead as possible. Information is available from the Indian Ceremonial Association (☎ 863 3896, 1 (800) 233 4528), PO Box 1, Church Rock, 87311, or from the visitors bureau.

Thousands of Native Americans as well as non-Indian tourists throng the streets of Gallup and the huge amphitheater at Red Rock State Park to watch the professional all-Indian rodeo, admire beautifully bedecked ceremonial dancers from many tribes, take part in a powwow with competitive dancing and choose a Ceremonial Queen in a competition that emphasizes both traditional and modern Native American customs. There is a huge non-mechanized parade, arts & crafts stalls and plenty of native food.

Costs of the events are very reasonable – the rodeo is about $8 for the afternoon, and an evening of dance performances is $12 in reserved seating or less for general admission. Children are half price. A $3 grounds admission (waived for rodeo and dance performance goers) gets you into the powwow, arts & crafts and food booths, as well as a variety of other performances. Photographers should note that, contrary to many Native American events, the Inter-

Barrel racing at the Gallup Inter-Tribal Indian Ceremonial rodeo (RR)

Tribal Indian Ceremonial allows cameras – no fees or permits are needed.

**Other Events** Apart from the ceremonial, there are several other annual events that attract visitors and fill hotel rooms. Foremost is the Navajo Nation Fair, held in nearby Window Rock, Arizona, during the first weekend in September. The Lions Club Rodeo held in the third week in June is the most professional and prestigious of several rodeos held throughout the year in the Gallup area. A Balloon Rally is held at Red Rock State Park during the first weekend in December – over 100 colorful hot-air balloons take part in demonstrations and competitions. Square dancers converge on Gallup in mid-April for their annual Fest-i-Gal.

## Places to Stay

It's a sellers market during Ceremonial week and other big events, and hotel prices can double then. Otherwise, there are plenty of hotel rooms available – this is a good base for budget travelers. Prices below reflect the normal summer rates – further discounts are possible during winter.

## Places to Stay – camping

The *KOA* (☎ 863 5021), 2925 W Hwy 66, has sites with hookups for $20 or $22 and Kamping Kabins for $27 from mid-April to mid-October. Discounts are available at other times. The campground has a coin laundry, swimming pool and recreation area, playground and grocery store. *Red Rock State Park Campground* (☎ 722 3839), PO Box 328, Church Rock, 87311, six miles east of downtown, is open year round and charges $8 for tents and $12 for hookups. There are showers, a coin laundry, and a grocery store. Both campgrounds have about 140 sites each.

## Places to Stay – bottom end

The following offer rooms beginning at about $20 or even less for most of the year, and the rooms are quite basic and often well worn. They are, however, fairly clean and provide hot showers – some even have kitchenettes. If staying for several days, ask for a discount. Driving west to east along Hwy 66, try *Sunset Motel* (☎ 863 3012), *Golden Desert Motel* (☎ 722 2231), *Log Cabin Lodge* (☎ 863 4600), *El Coronado Motel* (☎ 722 5510), *Redwood Lodge* (☎ 863 5411) and *Zia Motel* (☎ 863 4952). Along Coal St (west to east), you might also consider *Ranchito Motel* (☎ 863 6845) or *Cactus Motel* (☎ 863 6112).

If you're willing to spend a little more, the following, lining Hwy 66 west to east, are good possibilities: the *Shalimar Inn* (☎ 722 4493), which has shabby rooms but a popular bar; the *Thunderbird Motel* (☎ 863 3888), which has large rooms; the *Desert Skies Motel* (☎ 863 4485); the *Lariat Lodge* (☎ 722 5496); the *Arrowhead Lodge* (☎ 863 5111); or the *Hacienda Motel* (☎ 722 5900), 2510 E Hwy 66.

Among the best of the cheaper places are the popular (and often full) *Blue Spruce Lodge* (☎ 863 5211), 1119 E Hwy 66; the *Ambassador Motel* (☎ 722 3843), 1601

W Hwy 66, which has a pool; and the *Colonial Motel* (☎ 863 6821), 1007 Coal Ave. These all have rooms in the low to mid-$20s. Others in this price range are the *Budget Inn* (☎ 722 6631), 2806 W Hwy 66; *El Hopi Motel* (☎ 863 4172), 2305 W Hwy 66; and the *Pine Tree Lodge* (☎ 863 6861), 1115 W Hwy 66.

The *El Capitan Motel* (☎ 863 6828), 1300 E Hwy 66, has decent rooms in the upper $20s and lower $30s, as does the *Roadrunner Motel* (☎ 863 3804), 3012 E Hwy 66, which has a pool.

## Places to Stay – middle

*Motel 6* (☎ 863 4492), 3306 W Hwy 66, is convenient to the freeway and has a pool. Rooms are $32/38 for a single/double in summer, about $6 less during the rest of the year. Next door, the *Travelers Inn* (☎ 722 7765, fax 722 4752), 3304 W Hwy 66, has similar facilities and prices. The *Econolodge* (☎ 722 3800, 1 (800) 424 4777), 3101 W Hwy 66, has slightly nicer rooms. Officially they run in the $40s, but prices often drop to match the Motel 6 and Travelers Inn.

Other places with rooms in the $30s include the *Gallup Travelodge* (☎ 863 9301, fax 722 5933), 1709 W Hwy 66, which has a spa and a sauna, and the *Days Inn – Central* (☎ /fax 863 3891), 1603 W Hwy 66, which has a pool and includes continental breakfast. The *Roseway Inn* (☎ 863 9385, fax 863 6532), 2003 W Hwy 66, seems a reasonable deal and features a pool, spa, sauna, restaurant and bar.

Gallup's most interesting hotel is the historic *El Rancho* (☎ 863 9311, fax 722 5917), 1000 E Hwy 66. Opened in 1937, it quickly became known as the 'home of the movie stars'. Many of the great actors of the '40s and '50s stayed here – Humphrey Bogart, Katharine Hepburn and John Wayne to name just a few of dozens. The hotel fell on hard times in the '70s but was completely renovated and expanded in the late '80s, and it now features a superb Southwestern lobby, classy gift shop with top-quality arts & crafts, a reasonably priced restaurant and bar, and an eclectic selection of rooms – many with Western decor and named after the stars that stayed there. Rates range from about $38 to $56, and a few suites go for about $75 – a good deal, especially for those searching for a little nostalgia.

Other places with rooms in the $40s and $50s include the *Super 8 Motel* (☎ 722 5300, fax 722 6200), 1715 W Hwy 66, which has a pool, sauna, spa and coin laundry. The *Days Inn – West* (☎ /fax 863 6889), 3201 W Hwy 66, has similar amenities and includes continental breakfast, as does the *Comfort Inn* (☎ 722 0982, fax 722 2404), 3208 W Hwy 66.

### Places to Stay – top end
**Hotels** One Holiday Inn and three Best Westerns have the top-end wrapped up in Gallup – though, for my money, the El Rancho (above) is much more fun if not quite as modernly amenity-laden. Each of the hotels below has an indoor pool, sauna, spa, exercise area, coin laundry and comfortable, spacious rooms.

The *Holiday Inn Holidome* (☎ 722 2201, fax 722 9616), 2915 W Hwy 66, is the biggest place in town with over 200 rooms. The hotel has a restaurant with room service, coffee shop and lounge bar, as well as live music and country & western dancing. Open from 6 am to 10 pm, the restaurant is good and not overly expensive. Most rooms are in the $60s.

The Best Western *Royal Holiday Motel* (☎ 722 4900, fax 722 5100), 1903 W Hwy 66, has about 50 rooms in the $50s and $60s. The Best Western *Red Rock Inn* (☎ 722 7600, fax 722 9770), 3010 E Hwy 66, has rooms from $50 to $80, some with balconies. The Best Western *Gallup Inn* (☎ 722 2221, fax 722 7442), 3009 W Hwy 66, has a restaurant and bar with room service, and rooms from $60 to $90 during summer, somewhat less at other times. The Gallup Inn and the Holidome are considered the best in town.

**B&B** About 20 miles east of town at exit 44 on I-40 is the *Navajo Lodge B&B* (☎ 862 7553), Coolidge, 87312. They rent two cottages, each with kitchen, living room and bathroom, for about $75 a double including continental breakfast.

### Places to Eat
Food in Gallup is pretty much standard Western fare – steak and seafood, burgers and fries, and a sprinkling of Italian, Chinese, Mexican and New Mexican cooking. There are no restaurants specializing in Native American food though you find Navajo tacos offered on many menus.

Almost everybody seems to stop by the *Ranch Kitchen* (☎ 722 2537), 3001 W Hwy 66, which is open from 6 am to 10 pm daily (except Christmas) and has been serving Mexican and American food since the 1950s. Prices are reasonable, and the food is good. Another good and slightly cheaper family restaurant that has been operating for almost half a century is *Earl's Restaurant* (☎ 863 4201), 1400 E Hwy 66. If you prefer a smaller, mom & pop type place, try the *Roadrunner Cafe* (☎ 722 7309), 3014 E Hwy 66, which is open from 6 am to 9 pm daily and is inexpensive.

Very hungry travelers on a tight budget can try the all-you-can-eat specials offered from 11 am to 8 pm Monday to Saturday at the *Golden Phoenix* (☎ 863 3401), 2150 E Hwy 66. Fill up for under $5. Another all-you-can-eat place is the *Beijing Restaurant* (☎ 863 2654), 1321 E Hwy 66. Fancier Chinese food is served at the locally popular *Avalon Restaurant* (☎ 863 5072), 1104 E Hwy 66.

For more upscale dining, *Panz Alegra* (☎ 722 7229), 1201 E Hwy 66, is a good choice. The food is Mexican and tasty – the carne adovada (pork in very spicy sauce) is the house specialty. Italian and American meals are also served. It's not a fancy place, but it is locally popular and a good value. *Genaro's Cafe* (☎ 863 6761), 600 W Hill Ave, is a smaller place also serving decent Mexican food.

The better hotels offer good dining, especially the *El Rancho*, which is open from 6:30 am to 10 pm daily and offers very good-value daily specials as well as a la

## Rug Auction

The eastern Navajo community of Crownpoint, 25 miles north of Thoreau (exit 53 on I-80), is a great place to seek out Navajo rugs. On the third or fourth Friday of the month, a rug auction in the Crownpoint Elementary School attracts several hundred buyers, sellers and visitors. Rug previewing is from 3 to 6 pm and bidding is from 7 to 11 pm. It's standing-room only – arrive early.

Admission is free, and the several hundred available rugs sell from anywhere under $100 to over $2000. Prices are better than in stores – bring cash or checks for purchase. Many Navajos, often traditionally dressed, are in attendance, and other Native Americans sell crafts outside the school.

Information and dates are available from the Rug Weavers Association (☎ 786 5302), PO Box 1630, Crownpoint, 87313.

There is food and gas in Crownpoint, but nowhere to stay. Gallup is about a 90-minute drive away. ■

carte meals in the $10 to $15 range. The menu is a decent selection of Mexican and American fare. Similarly priced meals are served in *Nicole's* at the Holiday Inn, and at the Best Western Gallup Inn.

Night owls can grab a bite at *Kristy's Coffee Shop* (☎ 863 4742), 1310 E Hwy 66, or at the *Country Pride* (☎ 863 6801), in the Truckstops of America Plaza by exit 16 on I-40 west of town. Both places are open 24 hours.

### Entertainment

Local Native Americans perform social Indian dances at 7:30 pm nightly from Memorial Day to Labor Day at the *Red Rock State Park*. Shows are $5.

Catch a movie at the *Aztec Twin Theaters* (☎ 863 4651), 911 W Aztec Ave, or at the *El Morro Theater* (☎ 722 7469), 207 W Coal Ave.

*Talk of the Town* (☎ 722 3200), 808 E Hwy 66, has live music and dancing on weekends. Another popular dancing place with live variety music is the *Class Act* (☎ 863 2141) in the Rio West Shopping Mall on the northwest side of exit 20 off I-40. Country & western bands play at the lounge bar in the *Holiday Inn*.

### Things to Buy

Gallup has a huge selection – one of the biggest in North America – of stores selling Indian jewelry and other arts & crafts. The chamber of commerce provided me with a

list of over 60 arts & crafts shops, galleries, trading posts and pawnbrokers, and there are others. Check out as many as you can if you are seriously interested in getting top-quality goods at fair prices. The following selection is a few of the best-known reputable places, but many of the others are as good: Ellis Tanner Trading Company (☎ 722 7776), S Hwy 32 Bypass; OB's Indian America (☎ 722 5846), 3330 E Hwy 66; Richardson's Trading Company and Cash Pawn (☎ 722 4762), 222 W Hwy 66; and Tobe Turpen's Indian Trading Company (☎ 722 3806), 1710 S 2nd St.

### Getting There & Away

**Air** America West Express (☎ 1 (800) 247 5692, 1 (800) 235 9292) has direct flights to Farmington and Phoenix several times a day from the Gallup Airport at the west end of town. Mesa Airlines (☎ 722 5404, 1 (800) 637 2247) has several daily flights to Albuquerque. A cab to the airport is about $4 or $5 – call City Cab (☎ 863 6864).

**Bus** The Greyhound Bus Station (☎ 863 3761), 105 S Dean, has about five buses a day to Flagstaff (three hours 20 minutes) and Albuquerque (two-and-a-half hours) with connections to other cities.

The Navajo Transit System (☎ (602) 729 5458 in Window Rock, Arizona) has four buses Monday to Friday and three buses on Saturday from the Gallup Greyhound

Station to Window Rock (45 minutes). Schedules change, so call the numbers above to find the best connections.

**Train** The Amtrak Station, 201 E Hwy 66, has a daily evening train to Flagstaff, Arizona, continuing to Los Angeles, California, and a morning train to Albuquerque continuing on to Kansas City, Missouri, and Chicago, Illinois. Train tickets should be booked in advance through Amtrak (1 (800) 872 7245). There is no ticket agent at the Gallup station. Note that Amtrak provides an 'Indian Country Guide' who gives informative narration for the journey to or from Gallup – ask Amtrak about this.

# Northeastern New Mexico

Northeastern New Mexico is high plains country – grasslands stretching on to infinity. Many travelers speed through along I-40 or I-25 on their way to or from Albuquerque, oblivious to the area's fascinating history or geological landmarks. This is the area where some of the oldest Paleo-Indian artifacts have been found (at Folsom). The Santa Fe Trail provided a pioneering route through the area that would change Indian country forever. Here, 19th-century towns

with fascinating architecture evoke a real feel of the Wild West. And the vastness of the rolling plains hides surprises: volcanoes, the best scuba diving in the Southwest, superb fishing, dinosaur footprints and hot springs.

I begin by describing the area along I-40, continue north from Las Vegas to the Colorado border and then move to the farthest northeast corner of the state, abutting Colorado, Oklahoma and Texas.

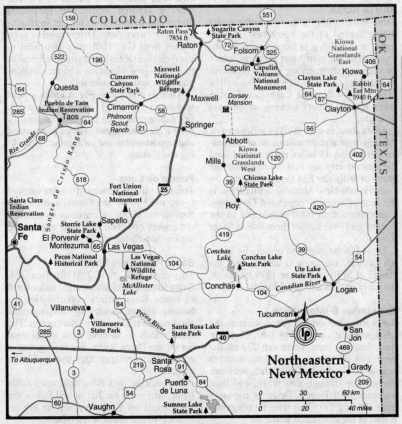

# I-40 East of Albuquerque

Santa Rosa, due east of Albuquerque, and Tucumcari, near the Texas state line, were once key stops along old Route 66, but today many travelers simply set their sites on the major cities. But they're bypassing many buildings of historical note, as well as a surprising number of small lakes that are ideal for boating, fishing and other water activities.

## SANTA ROSA

Santa Rosa's claim to fame is as the scuba diving capital of the Southwest. Admittedly, scuba diving is not a major Southwest attraction, and most travelers won't be carrying their diving gear with them. Nevertheless, Santa Rosa is also called 'The City of Natural Lakes', and these lakes interest divers seeking an unusual dive site.

Santa Rosa is on I-40, 114 miles east of Albuquerque and 59 miles east of Tucumcari. It is also 45 miles northwest of (and the nearest city to) Fort Sumner and the grave of Billy the Kid (see the chapter on southeastern New Mexico). Santa Rosa is the seat of sparsely populated Guadalupe County; less than 6000 people live in the county, and over half of them live in Santa Rosa.

Settled in the mid-19th century by Spanish farmers, the town is named after the chapel of St Rosa, built in 1879 by one of the early settlers and now in ruins.

### Orientation & Information

Santa Rosa lies on the Pecos River at the point where it's crossed by I-40. There are three freeway exits. From exit 273 (at the west end of town), the one main street begins as Coronado Drive, then becomes Parker Ave through downtown, and then becomes Will Rogers Drive as it passes exits 275 and 277. This main thoroughfare is part of the celebrated Route 66.

The chamber of commerce (☎ 472 3763), 486 Parker, has tourist information. The library (☎ 472 3101) is at 208 5th St. The local newspapers are *The Santa Rosa News* and *The Guadalupe County Communicator*. The post office (☎ 472 3743) is at 120 5th St. The hospital (☎ 472 3417) is at 535 Lake Drive. The police station (☎ 472 3605 or 911 in emergencies) is near the City Hall on 4th St.

### Blue Hole

This hole in the sandstone is fed by a natural spring flowing at 3000 gallons a minute, which keeps the water both very clear and pretty cool (about 61°F). The hole, a favored destination for scuba divers and swimmers, is 60 feet in diameter and 81 feet deep. Divers need to get a permit from City Hall; they also need to use their dive tables with extra care, because the 4600-foot elevation changes atmospheric pressure considerably.

Another dive site is **Perch Lake**, a short way south on Hwy 91, where a plane wreck lies submerged at 55 feet. Not far west of Blue Hole, **Park Lake** offers a playground and opportunities for swimming, picnicking and fishing.

### Puerto de Luna

This tiny village, which is 10 miles south of town, used to be the Guadalupe County Seat in the 1800s. Attractions include the old county courthouse, village church and various weathered adobe buildings.

### Santa Rosa Lake State Park

This state park (☎ 472 3110), Box 384, Santa Rosa, 88435, about eight miles north of Santa Rosa, offers opportunities for boating, fishing, picnicking, camping and a short nature trail by the visitors center. The lake, which is formed by a small dam across the Pecos River, has fishing that is reportedly excellent. Day use is $3 per vehicle.

To reach the park from downtown Santa Rosa, turn north on 2nd St and follow the signs (right on Eddy Ave, left on 8th St, under I-40 and north seven miles).

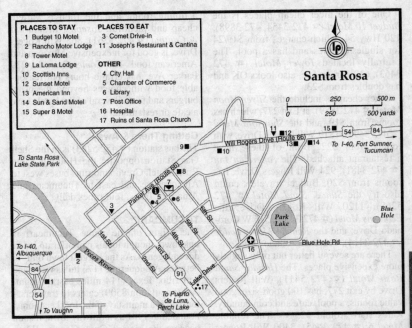

**Santa Rosa**

PLACES TO STAY
1 Budget 10 Motel
2 Rancho Motor Lodge
8 Tower Motel
9 La Loma Lodge
10 Scottish Inns
12 Sunset Motel
13 American Inn
14 Sun & Sand Motel
15 Super 8 Motel

PLACES TO EAT
3 Comet Drive-in
11 Joseph's Restaurant & Cantina

OTHER
4 City Hall
5 Chamber of Commerce
6 Library
7 Post Office
16 Hospital
17 Ruins of Santa Rosa Church

**NEW MEXICO**

### Special Events

Santa Rosa Days, celebrated annually over Memorial Day weekend, features a parade, entertainment, food booths, softball tournament, raft race and other sporting events.

The Annual Custom Car Show, held one weekend in August (usually the second one), attracts vintage and classic car enthusiasts as well as folks driving strange things on wheels. There's a parade, and live music and street dancing in the evening.

The third week in August sees Santa Rosa Fiestas, which includes local entertainment, a beauty-queen contest and crowning, and the bizarre annual Duck Drop, for which contestants buy squares and then wait for a duck suspended over the squares to poop – if the poop lands on your square, you win a cash prize.

### Places to Stay

**Camping** The *KOA* (☎ 472 3126), 2136 Will Rogers Drive, has tent sites for $13.50 and RV sites with hookups for $16.50.

Facilities include a coin laundry, showers, a cafe and swimming pool. The slightly cheaper *Donnie's RV Park* is across the street. *Ramblin' Rose RV Park* (☎ 472 3820) is on Hwy 54, southwest of town.

Just outside the city at *Santa Rosa Lake State Park*, there are two campgrounds: the Juniper Campground has primitive sites for $6 a night, and water is available; and the Rocky Point Campground has tent sites for $7 and RV sites with hookups for $11 or $13. Shelters and showers are available.

**Hotels** Santa Rosa has many inexpensive motels catering mainly to the I-40 traffic. The cheapest is the 'mom & pop' family-operated *La Mesa Motel* (☎ 472 3031), 2415 Will Rogers Drive, which charges $17 for two people. Motels charging $19 for two people include *La Loma Lodge* (☎ 472 3379), 763 Parker Ave, and the *Sunset Motel* (☎ 472 3762), 929 Will Rogers Drive.

One of the nicer cheap places is the *Budget 10 Motel* (☎ 472 3454, 472 3898), 120 Hwy 54, which charges from $19/24 for singles/doubles and has a pool. The centrally located *Tower Motel* (☎ 472 3463), 612 Parker Ave, also looks OK and has doubles from $23.

Other cheapies include the *Silver Moon Motel* (☎ 472 3889), at Exit 277, which has rooms from $19, and the *Shawford Motel* (☎ 472 3494), 1819 Will Rogers Drive, with rooms from $22. Both of these have a restaurant attached. The *American Inn* (☎ 472 3481), 924 Will Rogers Drive, has rooms from $20. Budget travelers could also try the *Sun & Sand Motel* (☎ 472 5268), 1120 Will Rogers Drive; the *Economy Motel* (☎ 472 3435), 516 W Coronado Drive; and the *Rancho Motor Lodge* (☎ 472 3414), 112 W Coronado Drive.

There are several better but only slightly more expensive places. The *Holiday Santa Rosa Motel* (☎ 472 5411), Will Rogers Drive by exit 277, has 100 good-size, good value rooms, a pool, cafe and coin laundry. Rates start around $25/30. The reliable *Motel 6* (☎ 472 3045), 3400 Will Rogers Drive, has 90 rooms and a pool. Rates vary from $25/31 to $30/36 depending on season and demand. The clean *Scottish Inns* (☎ 472 3466, 1 (800) 251 1962), 860 Will Rogers Drive, also has a pool, and some of its rooms have queen- or king-size beds. Rates are $27/31. Clean and somewhat bigger rooms are offered by the *Super 8 Motel* (☎ 472 5388), 2304 Will Rogers Drive, which has a coin laundry on the premises. Rates are $31.88/36.88.

The best place in town is the *Best Western Adobe Inn* (☎ 472 3446), Will Rogers Drive at exit 275, which has a pool, cafe and nice rooms with queen-size beds. Rates range from $38 to $48 for one person and $48 to $58 for two in the summer, a little less in winter.

### Places to Eat

Several places in town are worth a try. *Mateo's Family Restaurant* (☎ 472 5720), 500 W Coronado Blvd, is open daily from 6 am to 8 pm. It has a fast-food area and

a dining room, and the food is varied, cheap and plentiful. *Joseph's Restaurant & Cantina* (☎ 472 3361), 865 Will Rogers Drive, is good for inexpensive Mexican and American food. The *Comet Drive-in*, 239 Parker Ave, has erratic hours but reasonable food with choices beyond the usual burgers and fries. Several of the hotels have a cafe or restaurant.

### Getting There & Away

The bus station (☎ 472 5263) is in the Shell Gas Station opposite the Holiday Santa Rosa Motel. Greyhound runs buses west to Albuquerque and east to Tucumcari and Amarillo, Texas, four times daily.

### TUCUMCARI

The origin of the name Tucumcari is unknown, though locals can offer up half a dozen legends. As the biggest town on I-40 between Albuquerque (173 miles west) and Amarillo, Texas (114 miles east), Tucumcari (population 8500) caters to travelers – tourism is a mainstay of the local economy. Founded in 1901 as a railway town, it soon became the seat of Quay County. When Route 66 was opened in the 1920s, Tucumcari became an obligatory stop for travelers; today, with faster freeway speeds, many travelers simply drive on through. Nevertheless, there still are many inexpensive motels here, and signs advertise 'Tucumcari Tonight' for 300 miles in either direction along the interstate. This is a good and economical place to rest up.

### Orientation & Information

Tucumcari lies to the north of I-40 between exits 329 and 335. The main west to east thoroughfare between these exits is the old Route 66, now called Tucumcari Blvd through downtown. The principal north to south artery is 1st St, which intersects I-40 at exit 332.

The chamber of commerce (☎ 461 1694), 404 W Tucumcari Blvd, is open 9 am to 5 pm, from Monday to Friday. The library (☎ 461 0295) is at 602 S 2nd. The *Quay County Sun* is the local newspaper, that is published biweekly. The post office (☎ 461 0370) is at 222 S 1st. The hospital (☎ 461 0141) is at 301 Miel de Luna. The police (☎ 461 2160) are at 215 E Center.

## Tucumcari Historical Museum

This museum (☎ 461 4201), 416 S Adams, displays an eclectic mixture of local memorabilia, including thousands of items ranging from Indian artifacts to a barbed-wire collection. Several rooms are reconstructions of early Western interiors such as a sheriff's office, classroom and hospital room. Admission is $2 for adults and 50¢ for six- to 15-year-olds. Summer hours are 9 am to 6 pm, Monday to Saturday, and 1 to 6 pm on Sunday. During the rest of the year, they close one hour earlier and take Monday off.

## Ladd S Gordon Wildlife Preserve

At the east end of town, the preserve encompasses Tucumcari Lake, which attracts many overwintering ducks, geese and other water birds. The preserve is recommended for bird watchers. Ducks begin arriving in mid-October, and geese a month later. Though still under development, the preserve is open to visitors, who can reach it by taking a gravel road north of the Motel 6.

## Activities

Swimmers can cool off at the municipal pool (☎ 461 4582), 415 W Hines. The City Golf Course (☎ 461 1849) is on the west side of town.

## Special Events

**Piñata Festival** Held around the last weekend of June, this is the most important annual event. A *piñata* is a large model, usually made from decorated papier-mâché or cardboard, and then stuffed with candy and party favors. Children take turns pounding on the piñata with sticks until it breaks and the goodies spill. Children then scramble for handfuls. This is a festive Hispanic tradition.

Apart from showcasing the world's largest piñata, this festival features a rodeo,

parade, fiddling and band contests, sports events, dancing and general fun.

**Other Events** Arts & Crafts Fairs are held during weekends in early June and early December, and the **Quay County Fair** happens in August.

## Places to Stay – camping

The *KOA* (☎ 461 1841), a quarter mile east of exit 355, has tent sites for $14 and RV sites with hookups for $17. Facilities include showers, coin laundry, pool and playground. The *Mountain Rd RV Park* (☎ 461 9628), 1700 Mountain Rd, offers RV sites for $13.25 with hookups; tent campers can stay for $8. There are showers, a coin laundry and playground. *Owens RV Park*, on E Tucumcari Blvd, has RV sites for $9. There are showers and a laundry. You can also camp at *Conchas Lake State Park*, which has sites for $7 or $11 with RV hookups, and *Ute Lake State Park*, which offers two campgrounds with tent and RV sites for $7/11 (see Around Tucumcari below).

## Places to Stay – bottom end

There is no shortage of accommodations in Tucumcari, and the cheaper hotels offer very low prices – don't expect luxury and do shop around.

The cheapest is the old *Blue Swallow Motel* (☎ 461 9849), 815 E Tucumcari Blvd, which recently was advertising rooms for two for $10! (Since it was featured in a recent *Newsweek* article about Route 66, curiosity seekers may drive these prices up a few dollars – or force the owners to close their doors.) The *Americana Motel* (☎ 461 0431), 406 E Tucumcari Blvd, looks reasonable for $15.50/18.50. The *Buckaroo Motel* (☎ 461 1650), 1315 W Tucumcari Blvd, is one of the best cheapies; it charges $17/19 or $21 for rooms with kitchenettes.

The following establishments, all lining Tucumcari Blvd from east to west, charge from about $17/20 and some have a pool: the *Pony Soldier Motel* (☎ 461 9856), with king-size beds; the *Palomino Motel* (☎ 461 3622); the *Relax Inn* (☎ 461 3862),

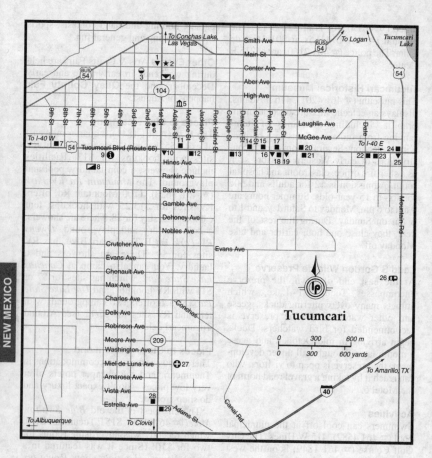

Tucumcari

with queen- and king-size beds; the *Townhouse Motel* (☎ 461 1340), with some king-size beds and kitchenettes; and *Redwood Lodge* (☎ 461 3635), with king-size beds.

The *Tucumcari Inn* (☎ 461 1133), 2000 W Tucumcari Blvd, offers rooms with king-size beds for $21/24; it has a game room. Clean rooms at the *Econo Lodge* (☎ 461 4194), 3400 E Tucumcari Blvd, are $21/30. The old standby, the *Motel 6* (☎ 461 4791), 2900 E Tucumcari Blvd, has decent rooms for $23/29. There is a pool. The *Friendship Inn* (☎ 461 0330, 1 (800) 424 4777), 315 E Tucumcari Blvd, has decent rooms for $22/27. Some rooms have king-size beds or waterbeds, and there is a pool and playground. The *Safari Motel* (☎ 461 3642), 722 E Tucumcari Blvd, has clean rooms for $24/28 and offers a coin laundry and pool.

## Places to Stay – middle
The following hotels charge about $30/35 for nice singles/doubles and all have queen- or king-size beds: *Howard Johnson's* (☎ 461 2747), 3604 E Tucumcari Blvd, provides continental breakfast; the *Royal Palacio Motel* (☎ 661 1212), at 1620 E Tucumcari Blvd, has a coin laundry; and the *Travelodge* (☎ 461 1401, 1 (800) 255 3050), 1214 E Tucumcari Blvd, has a pool. There is also the *Days Inn* (☎ 461 3158), 2623 S 1st.

The *Super 8 Motel* (☎ 461 4444, 1 (800) 800 8000), 4001 E Tucumcari Blvd, charges $31.88/36.88 and has an indoor pool, exercise room and coin laundry. The *Roadway Inn* (☎ 461 0360), 1023 E Tucumcari Blvd, charges from $32/38 and has some suites for $48; it has a pool and a coin laundry. The *Ramada Inn* (☎ 461 3140, 1 (800) 228 2828), 1302 W Tucumcari Blvd, is a good hotel with a pool, playground, coin laundry, restaurant and lounge. Rooms are about $45/55 in summer, less in winter. The adjoining restaurant is open from 6 am to 10 pm daily, offering a soup-and-salad bar as well as American and Mexican standards at affordable prices.

There are three Best Westerns in town (☎ 1 (800) 528 1234): the *BW Aruba Motel* (☎ 461 3335), 1700 E Tucumcari Blvd; the *BW Discovery Motor Inn* (☎ 461 4884), 200 E Estrella; and the *BW Pow Wow Inn* (☎ 461 0500), 801 W Tucumcari Blvd. All three have good rooms and a pool, coin laundry and decent restaurant. The *Aruba* charges about $38/45. The *Discovery* charges about $42/52 in summer, less at other times, and its restaurant is one of the best in town, with dinner entrees in the $8 to $15 range. There is a spa available, and some rooms have balconies. The *Pow Wow* charges about the same and has kitchenettes in some rooms. There is a lounge bar with entertainment on some nights.

The *Holiday Inn* (☎ 461 3780), exit 335 off I-40 on E Tucumcari Blvd, has good rooms costing between $50 and $85. Facilities include a pool, coin laundry, playground, restaurant and lounge.

## Places to Eat
*La Cita* (☎ 461 3930), 812 S 1st, earns praise for its Mexican food. It also serves inexpensive American food. Its hours are 11 am to 9 pm daily. Another inexpensive and reasonable Mexican/American cafe is *El Toro* (☎ 461 3328), 107 S 1st, open from 11 am to 7 pm daily. The *Golden Dragon* (☎ 461 2853), 1006 E Tucumcari Blvd, serves Chinese food from 11 am to 2:30 pm and 4 to 9:30 pm daily – it also sells meals to go.

*Denny's* (☎ 461 3094), 1102 E Tucumcari Blvd, and the *Terminal Cafe* (☎ 461 9649), at the truck stop at the west end of town, are both open 24 hours a day. *Dean's* (☎ 461 3470), 1806 E Tucumcari Blvd, is one of those fairly bland family restaurants that serves a little of everything – American, Mexican and Italian food for breakfast, lunch and dinner.

The better quality hotels have the best restaurants.

## Entertainment
The *Caprock Amphitheater* (☎ 576 2519), 21 miles east of Tucumcari, is where the New Mexico Outdoor Drama Association (☎ 576 2455, 576 2779) presents historical Western performances during weekends in

summer (Billy the Kid shows are the most popular). Barbecue dinners are available with the show. Dinners start at 6:30 pm, and shows start at 8 pm. Dinners cost $6/4.50 for adults/children under 13, and the show is $8/2.50. Children five and under go for free. The theater is eight miles south of the settlement of San Jon, 17 miles west of the Texas state line.

### Getting There & Away
Buses to Albuquerque and Amarillo, Texas, depart four times daily from the Greyhound Bus Terminal (☎ 461 1350), 118 E Center.

### AROUND TUCUMCARI
### Ute Lake State Park
This state park (☎ 487 2284), Box 52, Logan, 88426, is 26 miles northeast of Tucumcari or 3 miles west of the small village of Logan.

The 12-sq-mile lake is supposedly the second largest in New Mexico, and the fishing is outstanding – some of the best in the state. The lake is especially noted for its abundance of crappie and walleye. There is also boating, hiking, picnicking and camping. The Mine Canyon Entrance, a few miles southwest of Logan, leads to a boat ramp with no other facilities. The South Entrance (the main entrance) is via Hwy 540, which leaves Hwy 54 at the southwest side of Logan. The campground is near this entrance.

If you don't want to camp in the state park, the village of **Logan**, 23 miles northeast of Tucumcari on Hwy 54, is the nearest settlement to Ute Lake State Park.

The biggest place is *Ute Lake Motor Inn* (☎ 487 2245), off Hwy 540 west of Logan, which is near a boat ramp. In town, there is the *Fireside Inn Motel* (☎ 467 2247), the *Yucca Motel* (☎ 487 2272) and *BJ's Cafe & Motel* (☎ 487 2354).

The *Fireside Cafe* (☎ 487 9696) offers inexpensive American food. The *Road to Ruin* (☎ 487 9918) is a simple saloon in the middle of town. Whiskey is what the name refers to. Stop in for a beer, pool and darts, and talk to the locals about horses – or rather, *caballos*.

### Conchas Lake State Park
This park (☎ 868 2270), Box 976, Conchas Dam, Logan, 88416, is 32 miles northwest of Tucumcari on Hwy 104. The main attraction is excellent fishing, especially for walleye and crappie. Swimming, boating, golf, a children's playground, picnicking and camping are other attractions. *Conchas Lodge* (☎ 868 2988), at the south end of the lake, has a marina with boat rental, restaurant and lounge (weekend entertainment in summer), groceries and rooms in the lower mid-price range. Note that the dammed lake is subject to water level fluctuations, and boating may not always be possible.

If you are coming from the west on I-40, it is 24 miles north of exit 300 at Newkirk on Hwys 129 and 104. It is also 75 miles east of Las Vegas on Hwy 104.

# Las Vegas to Colorado

This stretch largely traces the route of the Santa Fe Trail. Las Vegas and Raton were both important centers of trade in the late 1800s, and both towns retain the flavor of that era in their many well-preserved buildings. The area is dotted with small lakes and canyons of breathtaking beauty. If you're looking for a bit of the Old West without a patina of consumer hype, this is the place.

### LAS VEGAS
Las Vegas is the largest and oldest New Mexican town east of the Sangre de Cristo Mountains. The area was inhabited mainly by Comanches until 15 Spanish families received a grant from the Mexican government to found Las Vegas in 1835. The importance of the town grew with the Santa Fe Trail, and when the US assumed possession in 1846, there were 1500 Spanish inhabitants.

The building of nearby Fort Union in 1851 and the arrival of the railroad in 1879 both spurred progress. Las Vegas was a rough and booming town, attracting cattle barons and cattle rustlers, outlaws and gun-slingers, and honest pioneers trying to make a living. During the late 1800s, Las Vegas was the most important city in New Mexico and many buildings were constructed. Historians claim that there are over 900 19th-century buildings in Las Vegas listed on the National Register of Historic Places.

Today, a majority of the inhabitants claim Hispanic heritage, and Las Vegas remains an important center for transportation, commerce and ranching. Tourism is playing an ever bigger role in the town's economy. Visitors come to savor the historic but uncrowded streets and to take advantage of the area's outdoor recreational opportunities. Las Vegas (population around 16,000) is 6436 feet above sea level and the seat of San Miguel County.

## Orientation & Information

Las Vegas is on I-25, 64 miles east of Santa Fe and 109 miles south of Raton. The main street is Hwy 85 or Grand Ave, which runs from northeast to southwest, paralleling the interstate.

The chamber of commerce (☎ 425 8631) is at 727 Grand Ave, in the same building as the City Museum. The Santa Fe National Forest Ranger Station (☎ 454 0560, 425 3535) is at 1926 7th St. The library (☎ 454 1403) is at 500 National St. The local newspaper is the *Las Vegas Daily Optic*. Los Artesanos Bookstore (☎ 425 8331), 220 Old Town Plaza, has an excellent selection of books on Las Vegas and the Southwest. The main post office (☎ 425 9387) is at 1001 Douglas St, and the branch post office (☎ 425 8341) is at 1900 Hot Springs Blvd. Recycle at the Recycling Depot (☎ 425 5568), 651 Commerce St. The hospital (☎ 425 6751) is at 1235 8th St. The police (☎ 425 7504) are at 6th St and University Ave.

## Historical Buildings

The chamber of commerce has detailed brochures describing walks in three historical districts. The historical center is the Old Plaza, at the intersection of S Pacific St and Bridge St. Look at the **Plaza Hotel** (built in 1880), which is still in use. To the right are the **Ilfeld Buildings** (the Los Artesanos Bookstore is in one of them), which were built and improved upon between 1867 and 1921. Next to the bookstore are the adobe **Dice Apartments**, parts of which predate the annexation by the USA in 1846. The **First National Bank** at the southeast corner of the plaza dates from 1880. Several more historical buildings are on and near the plaza and along Bridge St.

A few blocks east of the plaza on Bridge St is **Highlands University** (☎ 425 7511 or information office at 454 3497), established in 1893. Here, the Administration Building houses a huge New Deal (1930s) mural by Lloyd Moylan entitled *The Dissemination of Education in New Mexico*. Moylan made clever use of the rather odd-shaped walls at his disposal – his detailed studies of cultural change are painted on three high walls over a stairway, continuing up to arches on the second floor. Also on the campus, in the Ilfeld Auditorium, is a series of seven New Deal-era paintings entitled *Music is the Universal Language of Mankind* by Brooks Willis.

East of the university, Bridge St continues as National St. The **Carnegie Library** was built in 1903 and modeled after President Thomas Jefferson's home at Monticello, Virginia. This is the **Library Park** district, and there are many late-19th-century mansions along 5th and 6th between National and Washington Sts. It's also worth heading south on 6th to the **police station** (formerly City Hall) built in 1892. Further south is **Murphey's Drug**, built in 1898 and with a period interior.

## City Museum

Apart from the usual local historical artifacts, this museum (☎ 425 8726), 729 Grand Ave, features an exhibit about Teddy Roosevelt's Rough Riders, who fought in the 1898 Spanish-American War. Las Vegas was home to nearly half the Rough Riders. Hours are 9 am to 4 pm, Monday to Saturday. Admission is free.

## Storrie Lake State Park

Only four miles north of Las Vegas on Hwy 518, this state park (☎ 425 7278) Box 3157, Las Vegas, 87701, is popular with locals as well as visitors. The lake offers opportunities for boating, windsurfing and fishing, and there are picnic grounds, campsites, a playground and showers. Day use of the park is $3.

## Montezuma

This village, five miles northwest of Las Vegas on Hwy 65, is famous for the so-called **Montezuma Castle**, built as a luxury hotel next to the local hot springs. There were actually several hotels on the site, all destroyed by fire, and the present building was constructed in 1886. It lost money as a hotel, went through a number of ownership changes, and is now the **Armand Hammer United World College** (☎ 454 4258). The building is magnificent and can be toured on Saturdays in summer or by appointment.

The **hot springs** were named after the Aztec emperor who supposedly visited the springs in the early 1500s. The 130°F waters are reputed to have curative and therapeutic powers. There are changing rooms available; bathing is free.

## Gallinas Canyon

Beyond Montezuma, Hwy 65 climbs up to the attractive scenery of Gallinas Canyon in the Santa Fe National Forest. Six miles brings you to the village of **El Porvenir**, where there is the *Mountain Music Guest Ranch* (☎ 454 0565) with cabins for rent. Fishing and hiking are possible at the nearby USFS campgrounds. During the winter, the Gallinas River freezes, and there is ice-skating and cross-country skiing.

## Las Vegas National Wildlife Refuge

Five miles southeast of Las Vegas on Hwys 104 and 67, this 14-sq-mile refuge (☎ 425 3581), Route 1, Box 399, Las Vegas, 87701, has marshes, woodlands, grasslands and agricultural areas on which 262 species of birds have been recorded.

The refuge is open daily from dawn to dusk, and visitors can try a seven-mile drive and walking trails. The refuge ranger station, open from 8 am to 4:30 pm, Monday to Friday, has a bird list and information. Admission is free.

## Golf

The Municipal Golf Course (☎ 425 7711) is off Mills Ave at Country Club Drive.

## Special Events

Rails 'n Trail Days, held the first weekend in June, celebrates the town's history with train rides, a rodeo, country dancing, barbecue, historical reenactments (from shootouts to sheepshearing) and old-fashioned fun.

Las Vegas Fourth of July is a colorful mix of Hispanic and Anglo festivities: Mexican folk music and dancing, mariachi bands, parades, contests, arts & crafts, food stands and traditional fireworks displays. The event lasts up to four days.

The Southwest Culture Festival is a juried arts & crafts show held in the third week of July. Other events include lectures, demonstrations, slide shows and entertainment.

The San Miguel County Fair is held around the third weekend in August. The chamber of commerce has information about these and other events.

## Places to Stay – camping

The *KOA* (☎ 454 0180) is about four miles south of downtown just off exit 339 from I-25. Rates start at $12 for tent campers, a little more for RVs. Kamping Kabins are $22 a double. There are showers, a laundry, playground, pool and a recreation area. At Storrie Lake State Park, tent sites are $7, and sites with RV hookups are $11.

In Gallinas Canyon, you can throw up a tent at the *El Porvenir* and *E V Long* USFS campgrounds, where sites go for $6 per night. The campgrounds are open from May to October, water is available, and there is hiking and fishing nearby. Free dispersed camping is also possible. Villanueva State Park offers camping as well – tent sites cost $7, and RV sites with hookups are $11.

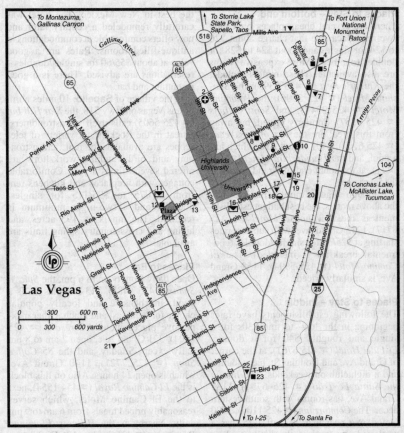

Las Vegas

NEW MEXICO

## Places to Stay – bottom end

There are several cheap places on Grand Ave near Baca Ave that charge about $20 to $24 for singles and about $24 to $28 for doubles (one bed). More expensive rooms are also available. These motels include: the *Knight's Rest* (☎ 425 9395); the *Sunshine Motel* (☎ 425 3506); the *Palomino Motel* (☎ 425 3548); and *Scottish Inns* (☎ 425 9357). Similarly priced, but away from this area, are the *Inn of Las Vegas* (☎ 425 6707), 2401 Grand Ave, which has a pool, and the *Thunderbird Motel* (☎ 454 1471), at the south end of Grand Ave near the interstate.

Although slightly more expensive than the above motels, the best budget establishment is the *Townhouse Motel* (☎ 425 6717), 1215 Grand Ave, with summer rates starting at $25/30 for singles/doubles (continental breakfast is included). The *El Camino Motel* (☎ 425 5994), 1152 Grand Ave, is similarly priced.

## Places to Stay – middle

The following establishments have rates beginning in the low- to mid-$30s for a single and roughly $40 for a double. *El Fidel Hotel* (☎ 425 6761), at the corner of Grand Ave and Douglas St, has a lounge and a nightclub on weekends. The *Inn on the Santa Fe Trail* (☎ 425 6791), 1133 Grand Ave, has rooms with southwestern decor. The *Comfort Inn* (☎ 425 1100), 2500 Grand Ave near exit 347 off I-25, has a pool and spa, and is the biggest place in town with over 100 rooms. The *Best Western Regal Motel* (☎ 454 1456), 1809 Grand Ave, has spacious rooms. The *Super 8 Motel* (☎ 425 5288) is at 2029 Grand Ave.

The *Carriage House* (☎ 454 1784), 925 6th St, is a B&B in a house dating from the 1890s. Its five rooms are furnished with antiques (many are for sale), and bathrooms are shared. Rates are a very reasonable $35/40 and include a full breakfast.

Las Vegas' best lodging is the *Plaza Hotel* (☎ 425 3591), 230 Old Town Plaza. Built in 1882, the elegant building overlooking the historical town plaza was then the best in New Mexico. The hotel was carefully remodeled a century later and now offers comfortable accommodations in antique-filled rooms. Rates are a good value at about $55/60 for singles/doubles – reservations are advised. There is a good restaurant and bar.

In the village of **Sapello**, 10 miles north of Las Vegas on Hwy 518, the *Star Hill Inn* (☎ 425 5605) calls itself 'an astronomers' retreat in the Rockies'. A variety of telescopes are available for rent, and astronomy and bird-watching workshops are offered several times a year. Comfortable cottages with fireplaces and kitchens rent from $65/75 to $95/115 for singles/doubles, and a two-night minimum is required. The inn is on 195 acres, and hiking and cross-country skiing trails are available.

## Places to Eat

Open daily from 6 am to 6 pm, the *Spic 'n Span* (☎ 425 6481), 713 Douglas St, is a good, inexpensive and locally popular choice for breakfast and lunch. Other inexpensive places include *Teresa's* (☎ 425 8104), 321 Grand Ave, open 7 am to 8 pm daily except Sunday, and the *85 Coffee Shop* (☎ 425 7721), 1140 Grand Ave, which is open 24 hours. Also on this block is the *El Camino Royal* (☎ 454 1554), next to the El Camino Motel, which serves reasonably priced meals from 6 am to 9 pm daily. Nearby is the *Hillcrest/Flamingo Restaurant* (☎ 425 7211), 1106 Grand Ave, which serves breakfasts and Mexican and American food at low to moderate prices from 6 am to 9 pm daily.

For good Mexican meals under $6, try the simple *Pancho's Cafe* (☎ 454 1936), 528 Grand Ave, open from 7 am to 9 pm daily (no alcohol is served). If you hanker after good Italian food, try *Gustavo's* (☎ 425 7080), 236 Mills Ave. For Chinese food, the place to go is the *Golden Dragon* (☎ 425 8522), 1336 Grand Ave. Both of these are open for lunch and dinner daily, and meals cost under $8.

*El Alto Restaurant* (☎ 454 0808), at the western end of Sapello St overlooking the city, is also called the 'supper club' because it's open only from 6 to 9:30 pm. Supposedly, El Alto is open daily, but it is often closed on Sunday and Monday nights. A Las Vegas institution, this restaurant is famous for its steak meals, all of which are priced under $15. Cheaper Mexican food is available, and there is a bar with music on some nights.

Though I found the service slow, another good choice is *El Rialto Restaurant* (☎ 454 0037), 141 Bridge St, which is in a late Victorian building in the historic center. It is locally popular and serves a wide range of meals from 10:30 am to 9 pm daily except Sunday.

The historic Plaza Hotel has the elegant *Landmark Grill* (☎ 425 3591), which is considered the best restaurant in town. It has reasonably priced breakfast and lunch from 7 am to 2 pm and has a delicious dinner menu available from 5 to 9 pm daily. Dinner reservations are a good idea.

### Entertainment
The *Serf Theater* (☎ 425 9857), 707 Douglas Ave, shows nightly movies. The *Bottle Shop Lounge* (☎ 454 0373), 1130 Grand Ave, has live country & western music and dancing from Wednesday to Saturday. The *Plaza Hotel Bar* sometimes has entertainment.

### Getting There & Away
**Bus** The bus terminal (☎ 425 8689), 508 7th St, has Greyhound and TNM&O buses to Raton, Santa Fe and beyond.

**Train** Amtrak (☎ 1 (800) 872 7245) runs a daily train to Chicago, Illinois, and to Los Angeles, California.

### AROUND LAS VEGAS
### Fort Union National Monument
Fort Union was established in 1851 to protect both Santa Fe and the Santa Fe Trail from Indian attack. It was the largest fort in the Southwest and was critical in mounting a defense against Confederate soldiers during the Civil War. It remained very important until the arrival of the railway in

1879. By 1891, the fort had been abandoned and, today, nothing remains except for a large area of crumbling walls in the middle of the grasslands. A visitors center provides an informative exhibit and display of area artifacts, and there is a self-guided tour of the ruins.

Fort Union National Monument (☎ 425 8025), Watrous, 87753, is 26 miles north of Las Vegas. Take I-25 to Watrous and Hwy 161 to Fort Union. Hours are 8 am to 5 pm daily (except Christmas and New Year's Day). Admission is $3 per vehicle or free with Golden Eagle, Age and Access Passes. There are picnic sites but nowhere to stay or camp.

### Villanueva State Park
This park (☎ 421 2957), Villanueva, 87583, lies in a red rock canyon on the Pecos River Valley. The valley was a main travel route for Indians and, in the 1500s, for the Spanish conquistadors. A small visitors center and self-guided trails explain the history. Other attractions include fishing, a playground, picnicking, camping and showers.

The park is 35 miles south of Las Vegas. Take I-25 south for 22 miles to Hwy 3; follow Hwy 3 south for 12 miles to the park entrance. Day use is $3.

En route to the park along Hwy 3 are the Spanish colonial villages of **Villanueva** and **San Miguel** (the latter with a fine church built in 1805). You'll also see the vineyards of **Madison Winery**; the tasting room (☎ 421 2299) is on Hwy 3 just north of I-25 – there are signs.

### SPRINGER
This small town (population 2000) was founded in 1879. It was the Colfax County seat from 1882 to 1897, when the seat was moved to Raton. Its main importance is as a center for the surrounding ranches, but there are some historical buildings and a museum worth visiting. Watch for herds of pronghorn antelope in this area.

Springer is 67 miles north of Las Vegas and 39 miles south of Raton, at the intersection of Hwy 56 to Clayton and Hwy 21 to Cimarron. The chamber of commerce is in the old Colfax County courthouse on Maxwell Ave, which is the main drag through town.

### Santa Fe Trail Museum
In the same building as the chamber of commerce, this museum (☎ 483 2341) displays the usual historical artifacts plus the only electric chair ever used in New Mexico.

### Dorsey Mansion
This two-story log mansion was built in 1878-1886 by cattle rancher and then Arkansas Senator Stephen Dorsey. It was the most opulent southwestern residence of its time and today it's still impressive. After a turbulent history as home, hospital, and hotel (not to mention post office, store and state monument), it is now privately owned – call ahead (☎ 375 2222) if you are interested in touring a grand historical building in the middle of nowhere. The mansion is 24 miles east of Springer on Hwy 56, then 12 miles north on a dirt road.

### Fishing
Five miles west of Springer, Springer Lake is famous for producing sizable pike and rainbow trout. Charette Lake, known for trout, is about 12 miles southwest of town (take the Hwy 569 exit from I-25).

### Places to Stay
There are three inexpensive motels in town. The best of the lot is the *Oasis Motel* (☎ 483 2777), 1001 Railroad Ave at the north end. Also try the *Broken Arrow Motel* (☎ 483 5555), which is near the freeway, and the avergae but adequate *Cozy Motel* (☎ 483 9963), 914 4th St. There are a few places to eat.

### Getting There & Away
Greyhound has a ticket office at 702 Maxwell (☎ 483 2649) and a station at 825 4th St (☎ 483 2379). There are two buses a day on the Raton to Las Vegas and Albuquerque line.

## CIMARRON
Cimarron is a historic Wild West town set in lovely country at the eastern base of the Sangre de Cristo Mountains. The area was the home of Ute and Apache Indians, prior to being settled in the 1840s by cattle baron Lucien Maxwell (see Fort Sumner State Monument). Cimarron became a stop on the Santa Fe Trail as well as being the first seat of Colfax County.

During the town's early decades, it was home to various gunslingers, train robbers, desperadoes, lawmen and other notable Western figures. Kit Carson, Buffalo Bill Cody, Annie Oakley, Clay Allison, Black Jack Ketchum, Wyatt Earp, Jesse James and Doc Holliday are just a few of the folks said to have passed through here. It was a wild town, with gunfights and murders commonplace – the old St James Hotel alone saw the deaths of 26 men within its walls.

Today, Cimarron is a quiet village of less than 1000 inhabitants. Several of the early buildings are still standing and warrant a visit.

Doc Holliday

## Orientation & Information

Cimarron is on Hwy 64, 41 miles southwest of Raton and 54 steep and mountainous miles east of Taos.

The chamber of commerce (☎ 376 2614, fax 376 2714), Box 604, 87714, on the main highway, is a good source of local information. There is a post office (☎ 376 2548), a clinic (☎ 376 2404) and police (☎ 376 2351).

## Historical Buildings

These lie south of the Cimarron River on Hwy 21, which heads south from Hwy 64 near the middle of town. Everything is within walking distance of the chamber of commerce.

The **Old Mill Museum** (☎ 376 2913) is in the Aztec Mill, built in 1864; it houses historical photographs and local memorabilia, notated by more informative signs than in most small country museums. There is an adobe house built during the same period nearby, and you may see buffalo grazing outside. The museum is open daily from June to August and on weekends in May and September. Admission is $2 or $1 for seniors, uniformed scouts and children under 12.

Across the street is the historic St James Hotel (see Places to Stay). Behind the St James is the Santa Fe Trail Inn, built in 1854, the old town plaza and well, and the Dahl Trading Post. South of the St James is Schwenk's Gambling Hall, the Well's Fargo Station and the old jail built in 1872.

## Philmont Scout Ranch

A working ranch (☎ 376 2281) about four miles south of Cimarron, this huge property (almost 220 sq miles) was donated to the Boy Scouts of America (BSA) by Waite Phillips, an Oklahoma oilman. Since 1938, well over half a million scouts have stayed here, camping, backpacking and learning outdoor skills.

The ranch headquarters is **Villa Philmonte**, a Spanish Mediterranean-style mansion completed in 1927. Guided tours are offered in the summer – call ahead for

hours. Nearby is the **Seton Memorial Library & Museum** with local frontier history and an exhibit of the works of E T Seton, first Chief Scout of the BSA. It is open daily from 8 am to 5 pm, June to August, and Monday to Saturday during the rest of the year. Admission is free.

Seven miles further south is the **Kit Carson Museum** in the village of Rayado. It is furnished in 1850s style, and interpreters in period costumes give guided tours daily from June to August. Admission is free.

## Special Events

Working cowboys compete in the annual the Fourth of July Rodeo. There are also fireworks and a parade.

Cimarron Days is held over Labor Day weekend and features arts & crafts, music and entertainment.

## Places to Stay

**Camping** *Rogers Mountain View RV Park* (☎ 376 2406), near the St James Motel, has RV sites. At *Cimarron Canyon State Park*, there is a $7 fee for campsites with water but no showers or RV hookups. Sites fill up quickly on weekends.

Northeast of Cimarron, Valle Vidal offers two campgrounds, *McCrystal Creek* (8100 feet) and *Cimarron* (9400 feet), both charging $7 per night and both with water but no showers or RV hookups. (Cimarron is closed in winter.) Dispersed and wilderness camping and backpacking are permitted. The nearest ranger stations are in Taos and Questa.

**Hotels & B&Bs** Cimarron is small and street signs are few. When you get to town, stop by the very helpful chamber of commerce (in the Cimarron Art Gallery) for directions to these hotels. If you wish to write to any of them, simply send correspondence marked 'General Delivery' (plus the 87714 zip code).

The best-known place is the *St James Hotel* (☎ 376 2664). It was first a saloon in 1873, a hotel in 1880 and then renovated in 1985. This was where many famous

NEW MEXICO

Westerners stayed, and the 13 historical rooms are named after them. These rooms are furnished with antiques and decorated in turn-of-the-century style – no TVs or phones. Rates vary from $45 for rooms with shared hall baths to between $65 and $80 for rooms with private baths. Most of the antique beds are doubles or twins; two rooms have modern queen-size beds. Visitors can see some of the rooms if they are not in use. A modern annex has new rooms with TVs and phones for $35/40 for singles/doubles.

There is a pool, coffee shop, a good restaurant and a cozy bar. Dinner entrees in the restaurant fall in the $10 to $20 range; while waiting for your food, see how many bullet holes you can count in the period pressed-tin ceiling.

For those seeking historical accommodations, another good choice is the *Casa de Gavilan* (☎ 376 2246). This comfortable B&B is in a 1908 white adobe house decorated with Southwestern antiques and art. There are six rooms with private bath; no smoking is permitted. Rates are $65 to $100 for two people including full breakfasts and evening appetizers and wine.

The *Santa Fe Trail Inn* (☎ 376 2916) is in one of the oldest buildings in town. Parts of the adobe structure date to the 1850s, and it became the National Hotel in the late 1800s. Later a private home, it now offers two rooms with bathrooms for $45 or $50. Two cabins, each with two bedrooms, bathroom and a fireplace, rent for $65 or $75. Continental breakfast is included; no smoking is permitted.

The *Cimarron House* (☎ 376 2616) is a modern house offering five rooms with king-size beds for $40/50 a single/double, including continental breakfast. Rooms have shared baths. There is an indoor pool. Again, no smoking is allowed. The *Kit Carson Inn* (☎ 376 2288) is a motel with 40 rooms, a pool, and an inexpensive restaurant open from 6 am to 8 pm. There is also a lively lounge bar. Rates are $35/40 for singles/doubles in summer, and cost less in winter.

### Places to Eat

Apart from the hotel restaurants, there is *Heck's Hungry Traveler* (☎ 376 2574), serving inexpensive Italian, Mexican and American food. The *Cimarron Art Gallery* (☎ 376 2614), which is also the chamber of commerce, sells all kinds of Southwestern art, souvenirs and fishing licenses; it also has an ice cream shop.

### Getting There & Away

TNM&O buses running between Raton and Taos stop twice a day. There is no bus stop, so flag buses down. Information is available from Cimarron Boot & Saddle Repair (☎ 376 2244).

## AROUND CIMARRON
### Cimarron Canyon State Park

This scenic steep-walled canyon begins 13 miles west of Cimarron and continues for seven miles along Hwy 64. You'll pass through it on the way to Taos. Several hiking trails leave from the three campgrounds (☎ 377 6271), Box 147, Ute Park, 87749, nestled along the Cimarron River. The trout fishing is reportedly excellent – so much so that possession of a fishing license is required to camp here.

### Valle Vidal

This beautiful mountainous and forested area in the northeastern corner of the Carson National Forest is the nearest national forest to Cimarron. Gravel roads

Mountain lions roam the remote Valle Vidal.

wind through remote countryside that contains a 2000-head elk herd, bear, mountain lion, deer, turkey and other wildlife. This is a good opportunity to see the fantastic scenery of the Sangre de Cristo mountains without encountering much traffic. Camping in two campgrounds, as well as dispersed and wilderness camping and backpacking are permitted (see Places to Stay).

Take Hwy 64 seven miles east of Cimarron and turn northwest on graveled USFS Rd 1950. It is about 20 miles to Valle Vidal, a further 20 through the area and a final 20 to Costilla (on Hwy 522, north of Questa).

## RATON

One of the most difficult sections of the Santa Fe Trail was the Raton Pass (7834 feet) in the foothills of the Rockies, now near the Colorado-New Mexico state line. The rocky pass had been in use by Indians and Spanish explorers for centuries before its increasingly frequent use by traders' wagons prompted local mountain man 'Uncle Dick' Wooton to make improvements. In 1866, Wooton dynamited a rough 'road' through the pass and set up a toll booth. Just south of the pass, wagon trains would rest and water at Willow Springs, which would become the site of the town of Raton.

The arrival of the railroad in 1879 prompted the founding of Raton, and it quickly grew into an important railway stop, and mining and ranching center. Many turn-of-the-century buildings have been preserved and can still be visited. Today, ranching and mining continue to be economically important, and the railway, along with the construction of I-25, has maintained Raton as a transport center. In addition, tourism is a growing industry. Travelers come to experience Raton's early Western ambiance, to bet at northeastern New Mexico's most popular racetrack and to visit the surrounding natural recreation areas.

Raton (population about 8000) is 6668 feet above sea level and the seat of Colfax County.

## Orientation & Information

Raton lies along I-25, about eight miles south of Raton Pass and the Colorado state line. The main north-south thoroughfare is 2nd St, which runs parallel to and just west of I-25. The main east-west street is Hwy 64/87, called Tiger Drive west of 2nd St and Clayton Rd east of 2nd St.

The chamber of commerce (☎ 445 3689), 100 Clayton Rd, is open from 8 am to 5 pm daily. The library (☎ 445 9711) is at 244 Cook Ave. The post office (☎ 445 2681) is at 245 Park Ave. The local newspaper is the *Raton Daily Range*. Recycle at RSS Enterprises (☎ 445 9282), 601 Kiowa Ave. The hospital (☎ 445 3661) is on Hospital Drive at the south end of town. The police station (☎ 445 2704) is at 224 Savage Ave.

## Historical District

The historical district lies along 1st, 2nd and 3rd Sts between Clark and Rio Grande Aves. This small area harbors over two dozen interesting buildings within easy walking distance. The Raton Branch of the American Association of University Women has produced a detailed brochure about the historical district, which is available from the chamber of commerce or the Raton Museum.

From the Raton Museum (see below), look over at the **Railway Station**, at 1st and Cook, which was built in 1903. Opposite the railway are several attractive buildings dating from the 1880s and 1890s. The yellow-painted brick **Marchiondo Building**, constructed in 1882, housed a dry goods store and post office. A block to the north, on 1st between Park and Clark, are the Veterans of Foreign Wars and Bennett's Transportation Buildings, which are the oldest in the district.

The **Shuler Theater** (☎ 445 5520), 131 N 2nd, was completed in 1915, and the elaborate European Rococo interior boasts excellent acoustics. In the foyer, eight New Deal (1930s) murals painted by Manville Chapman depict area history from 1845 to 1895. The theater is still in operation. Other New Deal murals can be seen in the

**library**, which was built in 1917 and was originally the post office, and in the present post office a block away. More New Deal art graces the historic **El Portal Hotel**, originally the Seaburg European Hotel constructed in 1904.

### Raton Museum

This museum of local history (☎ 445 8979) 218 S 1st St, is housed in the 1906 Coors Building. Hours (subject to change) are 10 am to 4 pm from Tuesday to Saturday during the summer and on weekends in winter. Admission is free.

### Sugarite Canyon State Park

This state park (☎ 445 5607), Box 386, Raton, 87740, has a visitors center, three lakes for fishing (license required) or boating (oars and electric motors only). It is in pretty meadows and forests in the foothills of the Rockies. Wild turkey and deer are sometimes seen in the area. The 7800-foot elevation provides cross-country skiing and skating in winter. Just east of town is the Sugarite Alpine Ski Area, where sledding is also possible.

### Horseracing

At the south end of town, La Mesa Park (☎ 445 2301) has horseracing every weekend and holiday from May to September and intertrack betting year round. Post time is 3 pm on Friday, 12:30 pm on Saturday, Sunday and holidays. General admission is free.

### Golf

The Municipal Golf Course (☎ 445 8113) is off Gardner Rd at the west end of Tiger Drive.

### Special Events

Apart from the horseracing season, the big event of the year is the Annual Arts & Crafts Fair, usually held the second weekend of August. While arts & crafts (both in juried contests and for sale) are the main focus, food stalls and other entertainment attract visitors. There is also a PRCA rodeo in late June.

### Places to Stay

During the May to September horseracing season, hotels are usually full on weekends and holidays, and prices may rise by $10 or so. (I give rates for non-racing weekends.) Call ahead or arrive by mid-afternoon to find a room at these times. Note that the hotel tax here is a hefty 12% – among the highest in the state.

### Places to Stay – camping

The *I-J & N Campground* (also known as the Hi-Lo) (☎ 445 3488), 1330 S 2nd, charges about $14 for an RV or tent space. The *Summerlan RV Park* (☎ 445 9536), near I-25 and Clayton Rd, charges about the same and allows tent campers. An RV park on S 2nd St opposite the El Rancho Motel offers spaces for $11 – but there was little action when I passed through.

At *Sugarite Canyon State Park*, a campground is open from May to October offering tent campsites for $7 and RV sites with hookups for $11. There is water but no showers. Get there by following Highway 72 out of town and then Highway 526 – it's about 10 miles and signed.

At *Maxwell NWR*, camping is often possible, but the sites are sometimes closed for waterfowl protection – call ahead.

### Places to Stay – bottom end

If you avoid the horseracing weekends, basic rooms at about $20/23 for singles/doubles can be had at the *Colt Motel* (☎ 445 2305), 1160 S 2nd, which is clean, well run and a good value. It does raise its prices about $10 for horseracing though. Similarly priced rooms are available at the *Crystal Motel* (☎ 445 2737), 1021 S 2nd; the *El Rancho Motel* (☎ 445 2291), 1005 S 2nd; the *Maverick Motel* (☎ 445 3792), 1510 S 2nd; the *Westerner Motel* (☎ 445 3101), 1460 S 2nd; the *Mesa Vista Motel* (☎ 445 3611), 726 E Cook; and the *Texan Motel* (☎ 445 3647), 201 Clayton Rd.

For just $3 or $4 more, try the *El Kapp Motel* (☎ 445 2791), 200 Clayton Rd, or the *Capri Motel* (☎ 445 3641), 304 Canyon Drive, both of which have small pools. Others in this price range include the

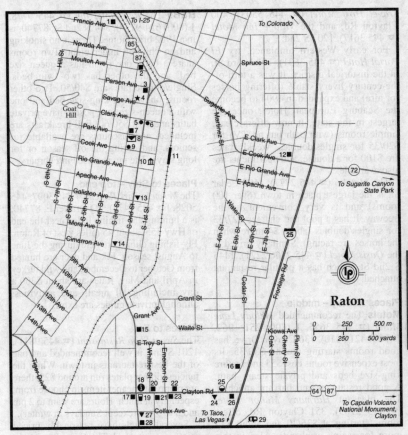

Raton

PLACES TO STAY
1   Capri Motel
2   Melody Lane Motel
3   Red Violet Inn
7   El Portal Hotel
12  Mesa Vista Motel
15  Crystal Motel & El Rancho
    Motel
16  Motel 6 & Super 8 Motel
17  Colt Motel
20  El Kapp Motel
21  Texan Motel
22  Best Western Sands
    Motel & Travel Host Motel

23  Harmony Manor Motel
26  Holiday Inn
28  Village Inn Motel
29  Summerlan RV Park

PLACES TO EAT
1   Capri Restaurant
13  El Matador
14  La Cosina
24  Domingo's Restaurant
27  Sweet Shop Restaurant

OTHER
4   Police
5   Raton Movie Theatre
6   Shuler Theater
8   Post Office
9   Library
10  Raton Museum (historic
    center)
11  Amtrak Station
18  Chamber of Commerce
19  Pioneer Bar
25  Bus Depot (behind
    McDonald's)

NEW MEXICO

*Travel Host Motel* (☎ 445 5503), 400 Clayton Rd, and the *Village Inn Motel* (☎ 445 3617), 1207 S 2nd.

For early Western ambiance, try *El Portal Hotel* (☎ 445 3631), 101 N 3rd St, in the historical district. It was a turn-of-the-century livery stable (offering horses for hire) and expanded in 1904 to become the Seaburg European Hotel, once the largest in the state. It now offers clean, simple rooms (with bath but no TV) for $20/35 for singles/doubles. Weekly rates are $100 for a double, and apartments are also available.

The *Motel 6* (☎ 445 2777), 1600 Cedar St, is the largest place in town (over 100 rooms) and is very convenient to the freeway. It has a pool and charges $27/33 for singles/doubles (about $4 more when the horses are racing). Similarly priced is the *Oasis Motel* (☎ 445 2766/2221), 1445 S 2nd St, which has a popular restaurant attached.

### Places to Stay – middle

**Motels** The recommended *Melody Lane Motel* (☎ 445 3655, 1 (800) 251 1962, 1 (800) 421 5210), 136 Canyon Drive, has good rooms starting around $30/35. Its most expensive rooms cost $55 and feature king-size beds and private steam bath. A good restaurant and bar are attached. The pleasant *Harmony Manor Motel* (☎ 445 2763), 351 Clayton Rd, offers rooms starting at $36/40 and about $14 more for racing weekends. Also in this price range is the *Robin Hood Motel* (☎ 445 5577), 1354 S 2nd, which has a pool, and the *Super 8 Motel* (☎ 445 2355), 1616 Cedar St.

The *Best Western Sands Motel* (☎ 445 2737, 1 (800) 528 1234), 300 Clayton Rd, has a pool, playground and restaurant. Spacious rooms with queen- or king-size beds are $65 during the summer season, less at other times. The *Holiday Inn* (☎ 445 5555, 1 (800) 255 8879), on Clayton Rd near I-25, has an indoor pool, a game room, a coin laundry and a good restaurant and lounge. Nice rooms run $63/73 for singles/doubles.

**B&Bs** The *Red Violet Inn* (☎ 445 9778, 1 (800) 624-9778), 344 N 2nd St, 87740, is in a 1902 brick home. There is no smoking and no children under eight. Two rooms share a bath; one room has a queen-size bed, and the other has two twin beds. Single/double rates are $40/50. Two other rooms, one with a king-size bed and one with a queen-size four-poster, have private baths and cost $50/60. Full breakfasts are included, and discounts are available for seniors, and during the off-season or for long stays. The inn is closed in February.

### Places to Stay – top end

The *Vermejo Park Ranch* (☎ 445 3097, 445 5028, fax 445 3474), PO Drawer E, 87740, is a hunting and fishing lodge near the end of Hwy 555, about 45 miles west of Raton. Fly-fishing clinics are held during the June to August season. Elk and deer are hunted from October to December, and wild turkey in April and May. Rates are about $300 a day including all meals and activities, although private guides are extra.

### Places to Eat

The *Sweet Shop Restaurant* (☎ 445 9811), 1201 S 2nd, is well recommended and one of the best restaurants in town. While the fanciest dinner plates run around $25, there are plenty of cheaper items to choose from, especially at lunch. Hours are 9 am to 2 pm and 5 to 9 pm (except Sundays in winter).

Several motels have reasonably priced restaurants attached. The *Capri Restaurant* (☎ 445 9755) is open from 7 am to 8 pm daily except Sunday, when it opens at 8 am. It has a varied menu (about $5 to $10), and the Italian food has been especially praised. The *Oasis Restaurant* is locally popular judging by the slew of pickups outside at breakfast time. The Melody Lane, Best Western Sands, and Holiday Inn Motels all have good restaurants.

For New Mexican food, try *La Cosina* (☎ 445 9675), 745 S 3rd, which has a homey atmosphere. The Mexican food is good at *El Matador* (☎ 445 9575), 445 S 2nd. Both places are reasonably priced.

Slightly more upmarket is *Domingo's* (☎ 445 2288), 1903 S Cedar St, which encourages you to enjoy the unusual decor of waterfalls, bridges and caves in the restaurant.

### Entertainment

Nightly movies are shown at the *Raton Movie Theater* (445 3721), at 2nd and Clark. Across the street, the historic *Shuler Theater* presents plays. The *Pioneer Bar*, at Clayton Rd and S 2nd, has live music on weekends and $1 beers at other times – a cheap but well-run local hangout.

### Getting There & Away

**Bus** Both Greyhound and TNM&O stop at the small bus station (☎ 445 9071) on Clayton Rd behind McDonald's. Several buses a day serve the route from Denver, Colorado, to Santa Fe (via both Taos and Las Vegas) and on to Albuquerque ($31 one-way). A bus leaves in the middle of the night for Clayton and Amarillo, Texas.

**Train** Amtrak (☎ 1 (800) 872 7245) stops at the historic railway station on 1st St. There is one train a day to Chicago and one daily to Los Angeles.

**Car** Hertz (☎ 445 3643) is at 303 S 2nd.

### AROUND RATON
#### Maxwell National Wildlife Refuge

This refuge (☎ 375 2331), Box 276, Maxwell, 87728, is 28 miles south of Raton along I-25 and three miles west of Maxwell. From Maxwell, take Hwys 445 and 505 – there are signs.

The refuge encompasses four sq miles of grass- and farmland around three lakes. It is managed for wintering waterfowl and upland game birds, and bird-watching is good from October through the winter. The burrowing owl and many other birds nest here in summer.

Camping is permitted, but call ahead because portions of the refuge are closed at times for waterfowl protection. Fishing is allowed.

# The Northeast Corner

The counties in this corner of the state are sparsely populated, and ranching is a mainstay of the economy. On some stretches of road, you may see more cattle than people or cars. But in these plains, the discovery of ancient bison bones and nearby arrowheads more than doubled estimates of how long humans have lived on this continent. And not far from that discovery, footprints of at least eight species of dinosaur were found. As you drive around the northeastern corner of New Mexico, keep your eyes peeled for wildlife, especially pronghorn antelope – I saw several large herds in the area around Folsom.

### CAPULIN VOLCANO NATIONAL MONUMENT

Ten thousand years ago, huge volcanic explosions spewed molten lava over the high plains. Cinders, ash and other debris piled up around the main vent, resulting in a symmetrical cone-shaped volcano rising 1000 feet above the surrounding plains. This is Capulin Volcano, the easiest to visit of several volcanoes in the area. It became a national monument in 1916.

The entrance to the Capulin Volcano National Monument (☎ 278 2201), Box 40, Capulin, 88414, is three miles north of the village of Capulin. (The village is 58 miles west of Clayton and 30 miles east of Raton on Hwy 87.) Near the entrance is a visitors center, open from 8 am to 8 pm from Memorial Day to Labor Day and 8:30 am to 4:30 pm during the rest of the year. Admission is $3 per vehicle (free with Golden Eagle, Age or Access passes). Informative audiovisual presentations are shown on request. Behind the visitors center, there is a short nature trail and picnic area.

From the visitors center, a two-mile road spirals up the mountain to a parking lot at the rim of the crater circles. A one-mile trail loops around the entire crater, which is 8182 feet at its highest point. Great views!

NEW MEXICO

## Folsom Man

A few miles north of Capulin Volcano is Folsom, the village near which the most important archaeological discovery in America was made. In 1908, George McJunkin, a local African-American cowboy, noticed some strange bones in Wild Horse Arroyo. Cowboy that he was, he knew that these were no ordinary cattle bones, and so he kept them, suspecting, correctly, that they were bones of an extinct form of bison. McJunkin told various people of his find, but it was not until 1926 to 1928 that the site was properly excavated, first by fossil bone expert Jesse Figgins and then by others.

Until that time, scientific dogma stated that humans had inhabited North America for, at most, 4000 years. Suddenly, facts about the continent's ancient inhabitants had to be completely revised. The 1926 to 1928 excavations showed stone arrowheads in association with extinct bison bones dated to 8000 BC, thus proving that people have lived here for at least that long. These Paleo-Indians became known as Folsom Man.

Thus the era of modern American archaeology began in Folsom in the late 1920s. More recent dating techniques have shown these artifacts to be 10,800 years old, among the oldest discovered on the continent, although it is clear that people have lived in the Americas for even longer

To learn more about George McJunkin and his incredible find, stop by the Folsom Museum, (☎ 278 2477) in the town of Folsom. It's open daily Memorial Day to Labor Day from 10 am to 5 pm. Otherwise, call for an appointment. ■

A one-third mile trail drops into the volcanic crater to the vent. Both trails are steep.

### Places to Stay & Eat

There is no camping in the national monument. The *Capulin Camp* (☎ 278 2921) at the Capulin gas station/store has RV hookups, tent spaces and showers. Des Moines, nine miles east of Capulin, has the *Central Motel* (☎ 278 2111) with clean and inexpensive rooms. Cafes are nearby – the *Sierra Grande Restaurant* (☎ 278 2721) looks OK.

### CLAYTON

Dinosaur tracks and the tracks of the Santa Fe Trail both contribute to the historical allure of the Clayton area. This high-plains region was the home of the Comanches and saw several Spanish expeditions, followed by intense Comanche-Spanish battles. It was part of the Spanish Empire until 1821, then part of Mexico, and finally annexed by the USA in 1848. Throughout this time, the Comanches retained a great amount of control in the area.

Clayton itself was founded in 1887 as a railway stop. By 1895 it had become the seat of Union County, and several turn-of-the-century buildings can still be seen in the historical downtown area. The infamous train robber Black Jack Ketchum was caught near here and hanged in Clayton in 1901 – the local museum tells the gruesome story.

Clayton (population about 3000), at 5050 feet above sea level, is at the center of Union County's cattle ranches and feedlots, and corn, wheat and sorghum are important crops. It is also near the Bravo Dome Carbon Dioxide Field, the world's largest natural deposit of carbon dioxide gas. The underground carbon dioxide deposit is injected into nearby oil fields, thus increasing oil production by 50% in some oil fields.

### Orientation & Information

The major thoroughfare is 1st St, which runs from northwest to southeast as Hwy 87. Hwy 56 intersects it as Monroe St to the west and Main St to the east.

The chamber of commerce (☎ 374 9253), 1103 S 1st St, is flanked by huge dinosaur monuments. The library (☎ 374 9423) is at 17 Chestnut St. The local newspaper is the *Union County Leader*. The post office (☎ 374 9541) is at 1 Walnut St. The medical center (☎ 374 8313) is at 314 N 3rd Ave. The police (☎ 374 2504) are at 112 N Front St.

## Herzstein Memorial Museum

This museum (☎ 374 9508), at 2nd and Walnut St, has interesting displays of local artifacts housed in the renovated Methodist Church, dating from 1919. The museum was dedicated in 1989, and there are plans to expand the exhibits. The museum is open on weekend afternoons year round and Friday and sometimes Thursday afternoons in the summer. Admission is free.

## Santa Fe Trail Landmarks

Distinctive Rabbit Ear Mountain (5940 feet) to the northwest of Clayton was a major Santa Fe Trail landmark. Historical markers on Hwys 406, 370 and 87 indicate where the trail crossed. The drive along Hwy 406 goes through the prairie of **Kiowa National Grasslands – East** (☎ 374 9652) before reaching McNees Crossing on the Santa Fe Trail, the site where two traders were ambushed and killed by Indians in 1828. Nearby is **Moses**, 22 miles northeast of Clayton, where a historic chapel stands

## Clayton Lake State Park

This state park (☎ 374 8808), Seneca, 88437, is the site of over 500 footprints of at least eight different species of dinosaur.

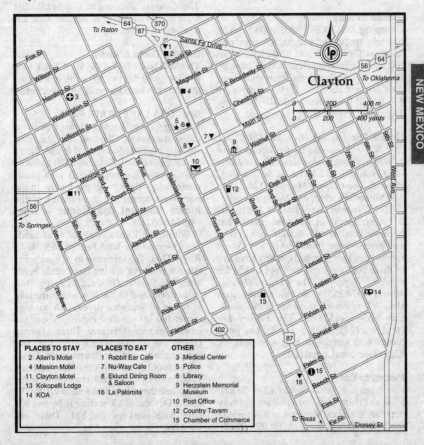

| PLACES TO STAY | PLACES TO EAT | OTHER |
| --- | --- | --- |
| 2  Allen's Motel | 1  Rabbit Ear Cafe | 3  Medical Center |
| 4  Mission Motel | 7  Nu-Way Cafe | 5  Police |
| 11  Clayton Motel | 8  Eklund Dining Room | 6  Library |
| 13  Kokopelli Lodge | & Saloon | 9  Herzstein Memorial |
| 14  KOA | 16  La Palomita | Museum |
| | | 10  Post Office |
| | | 12  Country Tavern |
| | | 15  Chamber of Commerce |

NEW MEXICO

A half-mile trail leads to the tracks and a walkway with interpretive signs. The low angles of early morning or late afternoon sunlight provide the best viewing.

Other attractions include fishing, boating and swimming in summer, watching migratory waterfowl in winter, picnicking and camping. Day use is $3. The park is 12 miles northwest of Clayton on Hwy 370. The Santa Fe Trail crosses Hwy 370 six miles north of the park.

### Golf
Clayton Golf Club (☎ 374 9957) is at the Air Park.

### Places to Stay
**Camping** *KOA* (☎ 374 9508), 903 S 5th St, has tent spaces for $12.50, RV sites with hookups for $14.50 and Kamping Kabins for $20. Facilities include a coin laundry, showers, playground and recreation area. At *Clayton Lake State Park*, tent sites are $7; it's $11 for sites with RV hookups. There are showers and a playground.

**Hotels** The *Mission Motel* (☎ 374 9890), 214 N 1st St, is one of the cheapest for $19/24 for singles/doubles. *Allen's Motel* (☎ 374 8099), 412 N 1st St, is also inexpensive. The *Clayton Motel* (☎ 374 2544), 422 Monroe St, charges $25/27.

The *Kokopelli Lodge* (☎ 374 2589), 702 S 1st, in operation since the 1940s, has been well maintained. Rooms vary in size, and prices range from $50 to $55. Some rooms have king-size beds; others have two or three bedrooms and cost $44 to $54 for three to six people. The *Clayton Holiday Motel* (☎ 374 2558), one mile northwest on Hwy 87, offers clean rooms with queen-size beds for $28/33. The *Luxury Inn* (☎ 374 8127), 1425 S 1st St, has good rooms with queen- or king-size beds for $32/42 including breakfast.

### Places to Eat
For breakfast *La Palomita* (374 2127), S 1st and Palm St, is open at 7 am and very popular; it serves Mexican and American food. The *Rabbit Ear Cafe* (☎ 374 9912),

402 N 1st St, is similar. The *Nu-Way Cafe* (☎ 374 9151), 117 Main St, is a mom-and-pop place downtown. It's open for breakfast and light snacks.

The *Eklund Dining Room & Saloon* (☎ 374 2551), 15 Main St, is the best place for lunches and dinners. It is housed in the historic Eklund Hotel, built in the 1890s but no longer functioning. The dining/saloon area is restored to the original old western style. Mexican dinners are well under $10, and American entrees fall in the $10 to $20 range.

### Entertainment
The *Country Tavern* (☎ 374 2413), 201 S 1st St, has a country & western band and dancing on weekends.

### Getting There & Away
TNM&O buses stop at the Shell Truck Stop (☎ 374 9300) on Hwy 87, south of town, on the daily run from Raton to Amarillo, Texas.

### CHICOSA LAKE STATE PARK
Harding County borders Union County to the southwest of Clayton. It is the most sparsely populated county in New Mexico – the telephone book lists about 450 numbers for the entire county. This is high-plains ranch land – open, vast and lonely. In the northwest corner are the prairies of the **Kiowa National Grasslands – West** (☎ 374 9652).

Within the Kiowa National Grasslands lies Chicosa Lake State Park (☎ 485 2424), Roy, 87743. The lake used to be a watering site for cowboys driving huge cattle herds along the famous Goodnight-Loving Trail in the 1860s and 1870s. Nowadays, the lake is prone to seasonal dryness. A visitors center has informative exhibits about the cowboy history of the area. There is fishing (sometimes), a playground, picnicking and camping in the middle of the prairie vastness.

The park is 9 miles north of Roy on Hwy 120. From Clayton, take Hwy 56 west for 39 miles, then Hwy 120 southwest for 36 miles. Day use is $3, tenting is $6 and RV sites with hookups are $11. There are showers.

# Southwestern New Mexico

This chapter covers the Rio Grande River Valley south of Albuquerque down to the Texas border, and then the area west of there to the Arizona state line. The Rio Grande Valley is, and always has been, the main thoroughfare through the area, and I-25 parallels it from Albuquerque south to Las Cruces, the largest city in southwestern New Mexico. In Las Cruces, I-25 joins I-10, which continues south into Texas or heads west into Arizona. Most travelers follow these routes to cruise through the region as quickly as possible, bent on reaching the more famous parts of New Mexico like Santa Fe and Taos. With fewer attractions than those areas, southwestern New Mexico still has much to offer travelers.

The first inhabitants of the area were hunter-gatherers of the Cochise culture, which dates from about 7000 BC. The Cochise gave rise to the Mogollon culture, which began to appear about 200 BC. The people lived in the mountains and valleys of the area and relied more on hunting and gathering than their Hohokam and Anasazi contemporaries, but eventually the Anasazi culture strongly influenced the Mogollon. The Mogollon left us with a number of archaeological ruins, of which the Gila (pronounced 'heela') Cliff Dwellings north of Silver City are the best known and most spectacular. They also left us with superb Mimbres black on white pottery that can be examined in several museums in the area. The Mogollon culture died out in the early 1300s – where the people went is a mystery.

The Pueblo Indians of the northern Rio Grande had a few southern outposts in the area. Late arrivals on the scene were Athapaskan-speaking Indians who arrived from the north soon after the disappearance of the Mogollon people. Among these late arrivals were the Apaches, who came to dominate southwestern New Mexico.

The most famous of the Apache leaders was Geronimo.

The Spaniards appeared in the 1500s. Cabeza de Vaca passed through the Las Cruces area in 1535, and Coronado marched north along the Rio Grande in 1540. By the 1600s, many of the pueblos had fallen under Spanish mission control to a greater or lesser extent, but the more nomadic Apaches remained free. The arrival of the Anglos in the 1800s changed that forever.

Today, with the exception of Las Cruces and Socorro, most of the towns in southwestern New Mexico are relatively young, dating to the late 1800s. Much of the southernmost part, around I-10, is part of the Chihuahuan Desert, where yucca and agave plants dominate the scene. This is ranching country, though the cattle are sparse. North of the desert, the countryside rises to the rugged mountains encompassed by the Gila National Forest. Here, opportunities for adventurous backpacking, fishing and hunting abound – this is wild country. The residents are few, and their livelihoods tend toward ranching, logging and some mining in the Silver City area.

The very wildness of the area is perhaps its greatest attraction, but visitors will also enjoy the Gila Cliff Dwellings National Monument, the Spanish architecture in the Las Cruces suburb of Mesilla, the quaint Victorian buildings in Silver City and the remnants of ghost towns near Lordsburg. The Bosque del Apache National Wildlife Refuge near Socorro offers unique bird-watching opportunities.

Many of southwestern New Mexico's small towns have annual country fairs and festivals, some of which are quite peculiar, such as the duck races in Deming. Most of these towns have small but interesting museums. And you'll certainly avoid most of the tourist crowds when you spend time in this area.

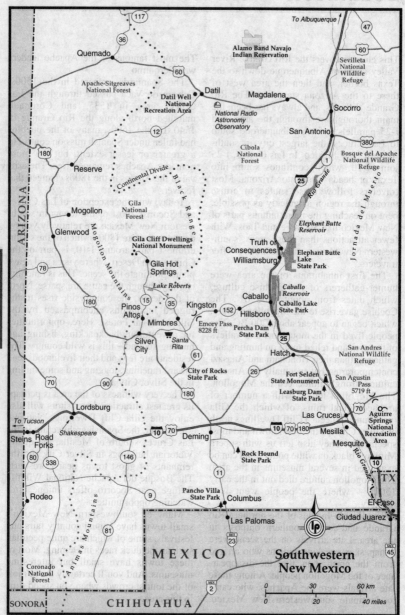

## Southwestern New Mexico

To Albuquerque

47

60

Sevilleta National Wildlife Refuge

Socorro

San Antonio

380

117

36

Quemado

60

Datil

Magdalena

Apache-Sitgreaves National Forest

Datil Well National Recreation Area

National Radio Astronomy Observatory

12

Bosque del Apache National Wildlife Refuge

1

25

Cibola National Forest

180

Reserve

Rio Grande

Continental Divide

Black Range

Gila National Forest

Elephant Butte Reservoir

Jornada del Muerto

Mogollon

Glenwood

Gila Cliff Dwellings National Monument

Truth or Consequences
Williamsburg

Elephant Butte Lake State Park

78

Gila Hot Springs

Lake Roberts

Caballo Reservoir

Caballo

Caballo Lake State Park

Kingston

152

Hillsboro

Pinos Altos

15

35

Emory Pass
8228 ft

Percha Dam State Park

ARIZONA

NEW MEXICO

180

Mimbres

Silver City

Santa Rita

61

Hatch

San Andres National Wildlife Refuge

City of Rocks State Park

26

Fort Selden State Monument

San Agustin Pass
5719 ft

Leasburg Dam State Park

Aguirre Springs National Recreation Area

90

70

Lordsburg

180

Las Cruces

70

To Tucson

Shakespeare

10

70

Deming

10

70

180

Mesilla

Mesquite

Steins

Road Forks

80

338

146

Rock Hound State Park

11

Rio Grande

10

TX

El Paso

Ciudad Juarez

Rodeo

9

Pancho Villa State Park

Columbus

Animas Mountains

81

Las Palomas

MEX 23

Coronado National Forest

MEXICO

Southwestern New Mexico

MEX 45

SONORA

CHIHUAHUA

MEX 2

0      30      60 km
0      20      40 miles

## SOCORRO

Socorro means 'help' in Spanish. The town's name supposedly dates to 1598, when Juan de Oñate's expedition received help from Pilabo Pueblo (now defunct). The Spaniards built a small church nearby, expanding it into the San Miguel Mission in the 1620s. After the Pueblo Revolt of the 1680s, Socorro was abandoned and the mission fell into disrepair, but it was renovated in the 1820s when the town was resettled by mainly Hispanic pioneers. It became an agricultural center and later, with the coming of the railroad in the 1880s, a major mining center and New Mexico's biggest town. The mining boom went bust in the 1890s, and the town returned to its agricultural base, but the growth surge of the late 1800s resulted in the many Victorian buildings that make the town architecturally interesting to visitors today.

Now the Socorro County seat, Socorro (population 9000) is 75 miles south of Albuquerque and 4585 feet above sea level. The New Mexico Institute of Mining and Technology offers post-graduate education and advanced research facilities, runs a mineral museum and, along with the government sector, plays a major part in the county's economy. The nearby Bosque del Apache refuge draws bird watchers, especially in winter.

### Orientation & Information

California St (Hwy 60/85), the main drag through town, runs north-south, parallel to and west of I-25. Major north-south streets are labeled SW or SE if they are south of Manzanares Ave and the plaza, NW or NE if they are north of it.

The chamber of commerce (☎ 835 0424), 103 Francisco de Avondo (just west of N California), PO Box 743, 87801, is open 8 am to 5 pm, Monday to Friday and 9 am to 12 noon on Saturday. Other good sources of regional information are Dana's Book Shop (☎ 835 3434), 203 Manzanares in the old Val Verde Hotel, which has a good selection of books about the Southwest, and Socorro News & Book Exchange (☎ 835 3361), 915 California NW, which offers the best local selection of magazines and used and rare books. The library (☎ 835 1114) is at 401 Park SW.

The post office (☎ 835 0542) is on the west side of the plaza. The hospital (☎ 835 1140) is on Hwy 60, southwest of town. The police (☎ 835 1883, or 911 in emergencies) are at 407 Center St.

### Historic Walking Tour

The chamber of commerce publishes a free quarterly *Socorro County Guidebook*, which includes a map of the historic downtown area within a few blocks of the plaza. Recently the guide described 60 sites, most dating from the last 30 years of the 19th century, some earlier. An early morning or evening stroll around the plaza area transports you back to the era of territorial New Mexico – and no throngs of tourists break the illusion.

The highlight of the walk is the **San Miguel Mission** (☎ 835 1620), three blocks north of the plaza. Although restored and added to several times, the mission still retains its colonial feel and parts of the walls date back to the original building. The mission is open daily, and admission is free.

### Mineral Museum

Thousands of minerals from around the world, fossils and other geological exhibits make this the state's largest mineral collection. The museum (☎ 835 5420) is on the campus of the New Mexico Institute of Mining & Technology (locally called 'Tech') on the northwestern outskirts of town; it is open from 8 am to 5 pm, Monday to Friday, and admission is free.

### Activities

**Golf** 18 holes at the par-72 New Mexico Tech Golf Course (☎ 835 5335), at the west end of the Tech campus. **Swim** at the pool (☎ 835 3091) at 1004 El Camino Real NW.

### Special Events

The Hilton Golf Tournament held the second weekend in June features a unique one-hole event – players tee off from the top of a mountain and golf through a makeshift 'course' in the desert to the hole, about 5 miles away and 3000 feet below. The San Miguel Fiesta during the first weekend in August features games, dances, food and crafts stalls outside the mission. The Socorro County Fair & Rodeo is held over Labor Day weekend. The Festival of the Cranes happens the third weekend in November and features special tours of Bosque del Apache, wildlife workshops and arts & crafts.

### Places to Stay – camping

*Socorro RV Park* (☎ 835 2234) is on the S Frontage Rd by exit 147 of I-25. Facilities include a pool, showers and coin laundry, and rates are $13 without hookups and $16 with.

Along Hwy 1 on the way to Bosque del Apache refuge, the *Birdwatchers RV Park* (☎ 835 1366) has sites with hookups for $14.50.

Also see below under Socorro to Quemado for more campgrounds as well as motel options.

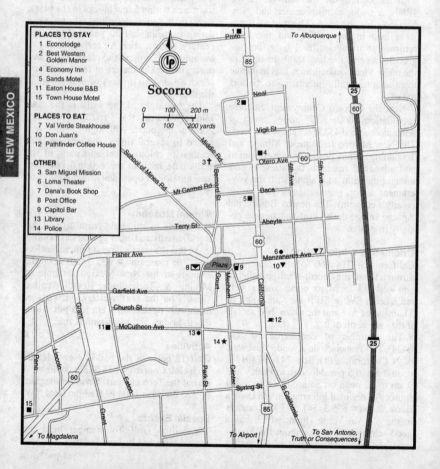

PLACES TO STAY
1  Econolodge
2  Best Western Golden Manor
4  Economy Inn
5  Sands Motel
11 Eaton House B&B
15 Town House Motel

PLACES TO EAT
7  Val Verde Steakhouse
10 Don Juan's
12 Pathfinder Coffee House

OTHER
3  San Miguel Mission
6  Loma Theater
7  Dana's Book Shop
8  Post Office
9  Capitol Bar
13 Library
14 Police

Socorro

To Albuquerque
To Magdalena
To Airport
To San Antonio, Truth or Consequences

## Places to Stay – bottom end

Rooms in the low $20s are available at the following, all of which are clean and reasonably well kept: the *Town House Motel* (☎ 835 4622), 803 Spring St; the *Sands Motel* (☎ 835 1130), 205 California NW; and the *Economy Inn* (☎ 835 4666), 400 California NE.

The *Motel 6* (☎ 835 4300), 807 S Hwy 85, is the town's largest motel with 123 rooms and a pool. Rates are $25/31 for singles/doubles. The *Vagabond Motel* (☎ 835 0276), 1009 California NW, has an inexpensive restaurant (American and Chinese food) and lounge bar, a pool and rooms for $27/32 for singles/doubles.

## Places to Stay – middle

**Hotels** The *San Miguel Motel* (☎ 835 0211, 1 (800) 548 7938), 916 California NE, has a pool, coin laundry and rooms with king-size beds for $37/44 for singles/doubles. The *Super 8 Motel* (☎ 835 4626, fax 835 3988), 1121 Frontage Rd NW, has a pool, spa and coin laundry, and standard rooms for $42.88/46.88 for singles/doubles.

The *Econolodge* (☎ 835 2500, fax 835 3261), 713 California NW, has comfortable rooms, a pool and spa. Rates include continental breakfast and run in the $40s. The 24-hour El Camino Restaurant and Lounge are next door. The Best Western *Golden Manor* (☎ 835 0230), 507 California NW, has a pool and a reasonably priced cafe (American and Mexican food) open from 6 to 10 am and 5 to 9 pm. Rooms with one bed are $43/49 for singles/doubles or $49/52 with two beds.

**B&Bs** The *Eaton House B&B* (☎ 835 1067), 403 Eaton Ave, PO Box 536, 87801, is in an 1880s adobe house furnished with antiques. The owners are birders and will arrange take-out breakfasts for pre-dawn departures. Five rooms with private baths rent for $75 to $105, depending on room and season. There is no smoking, and children under 14 are not allowed.

Ten miles south in San Antonio is the *Casa Blanca B&B* (☎ 835 3027),

13 Montoya St, PO Box 84, Socorro, 87801. This 1880 adobe farmhouse has two rooms sharing a bath for $45 a double and a third with a private bath for $55 a double, including continental breakfast. Rates may be lower if you arrive any other time than the winter birding season.

## Places to Eat

Unless you're in a hotel with breakfast, your best breakfast bet is probably one of the standard family restaurants like *Denny's* (☎ 835 2504), 913 California NW, or *Jerry's* (☎ 835 2255), 1006 California NE, which is open 24 hours.

Of Socorro's several Mexican restaurants, the cheerful, friendly and cheap *El Sombrero* (☎ 835 3945), 210 Mesquite, is a good bet. *Don Juan's* (☎ 835 9967), 118 Manzanares, does not serve beer but has pretty good food from 10 am to 9 pm, Monday to Friday. *Armijos's* (☎ 835 1686), 602 S Hwy 85, is also a local favorite.

Built in 1919, the historic (and now non-operational) Val Verde Hotel, was the center of the area's pre-WW II social life. Today it houses the *Val Verde Steakhouse* (☎ 835 3380), 203 Manzanares. The restaurant is pleasantly old-fashioned and serves good steak and seafood dinner entrees in the $10 to $17 range, more for lobster. It's open from 12 noon to 9 pm on Sunday and, on other days, from 11 am to 2 pm and 5 to 9 pm.

The *Pathfinder* (☎ 838 0034), 300 California SE, is a coffee house with a small art gallery, gift shop and occasional poetry readings.

## Entertainment

The *Loma Theater* (☎ 835 0965), 107 Manzanares, shows movies in a remodeled Victorian store.

Built in the 1890s, the funky old *Capitol Bar* (☎ 835 1193), 110 Plaza, is a good place for a beer in historical surroundings. The *Sports Page Night Club* (☎ 835 3556), 105 Francisco de Avando, has live bands and dancing on Thursday to Saturday nights – there is usually a cover charge of $2 to $5.

NEW MEXICO

NM Tech (☎ 835 5616) arranges a varied concert series with performances several times a year.

## Getting There & Away
Greyhound (☎ 835 9128), 1004 California NE (just behind Denny's) runs buses to Albuquerque at 4 am and 1 pm and to Las Cruces and El Paso, Texas, at 3:30 am and 4:30 pm (approximate times).

Socorro Roadrunner (☎ 835 1010) has four buses a day between Socorro and Albuquerque, currently leaving Socorro at 6 am, 11 am, 4 pm and 9 pm. They'll pick you up and drop you off at any address; the fare is $50 roundtrip.

## AROUND SOCORRO
## Bosque del Apache
## National Wildlife Refuge
This refuge protects almost 90 sq miles of fields and marshes that are a major wintering ground of many migratory birds, notably the very rare and endangered whooping cranes of which about a dozen winter here. In addition, you can see tens of thousands of snow geese, sandhill cranes and various other waterfowl. The migration lasts from late October to early April, but December and January are the peak viewing months and offer the best chance of seeing the whooping cranes. Year-round, about 325 species of birds and 135 species of mammals, reptiles and amphibians have been recorded here – this is a great destination for wildlife enthusiasts.

The visitors center (☎ 835 1828), PO Box 1246, Socorro, 87801, is open from 7:30 am to 4 pm from Monday to Friday, plus weekends in winter. It has restrooms and information. From the center, visitors can drive a 15-mile loop drive around the refuge. There are also hiking trails, and viewing platforms and towers. The refuge is open from one hour before sunrise to one hour after sunset, and admission is $2 per car. Golden Eagle, Access and Age passes and Duck Stamps (for duck hunters) are accepted.

Get there by leaving I-25 at San Antonio (10 miles south of Socorro) and driving eight miles south on Hwy 1 (or taking the San Marcial exit and driving 10 miles north on Hwy 1.

Visitors to Bosque del Apache often stop by the *Owl Bar Cafe* (☎ 835 9946) in San Antonio, the childhood home of Conrad Hilton, founder of the well-known hotel chain. It serves great burgers (their green chile cheeseburger is acclaimed) and is open from 8 am to 9:30 pm, Monday to Saturday. It is at the main intersection in town.

## SOCORRO TO QUEMADO
Hwy 60 west of Socorro goes through forests and high plains on its remote way to the Arizona state line, 140 miles away. Several interesting sites line this route.

### Magdalena
In the 1880s, Magdalena was the end of the trail for thousands of range animals – they were herded along what is now the Hwy 60 corridor from the west and shipped out from Magdalena on the railroad (now defunct). In 1919, a record-breaking 150,000 sheep and over 20,000 head of cattle were herded along the trail, which saw its last roundup in 1971.

Twenty-seven miles west of Socorro in the village of Magdalena, the Cibola National Forest Magdalena Ranger Station (☎ 854 2281), Hwy 60, 87825, is on the left as you arrive from Socorro. Get maps and camping/hiking/hunting information there. Three miles south of the ranger station is the ghost town of **Kelly** with a church and some mine-workings still visible. There are other ghost towns nearby – ask around for directions. The USFS *Water Canyon Campground* is six miles south of Hwy 60 along USFS Forest Rd 235 – the turnoff is 16 miles west of Socorro or 11 miles east of Magdalena. Open from April to October, the campground is free – bring drinking water.

You can stay at the *Inn of the Mountain Woman* (☎ 854 2757) or the *Western Motel* (☎ 854 2415), neither of which is very expensive. Grab a bite at the locally popular *Evett's* (☎ 854 2449) – fast food – or the *Ponderosa Cafe* (☎ 854 9916).

### The Very Large Array Telescope
The VLA is a group of over two dozen huge antenna dishes standing in the high plains about 20 miles west of Magdalena and easily visible from Hwy 60. The antennae combine to form an extremely powerful radio telescope used to probe the outer edges of the universe. A sign points the way to the visitors center at the National Radio Astronomy Observatory, four miles south of the highway, which is open from 8 am to sunset daily and free.

### Datil
Hwy 60 intersects with Hwy 12 at Datil, 43 miles west of Magdalena. (Hwy 12 is the route to Reserve, 60 miles to the southwest – see Silver City to Reserve). This was a major stopping point on the herding trail to Magdalena, but now it's just a small village with a store, gas station and cafe.

Just beyond the town is the signed *Datil Well National Recreation Area*, which has $5 camp sites, water and several miles of nature trails.

### Quemado
From Datil, Hwy 60 continues west 21 miles through the tiny settlement of Pie Town, where there is a cafe (which probably sells pies) and then a further 22 miles to Quemado. This ranching town of several hundred inhabitants has an Apache National Forest Ranger Station (☎ 773 4678), Quemado, 87829.

You can stay and eat at the *Largo Motel and Cafe* (☎ 773 4686) or *Allison's Chuck Wagon Inn & Restaurant* (☎ 773 4550). Or try the Mexican and American food at the funky and old-fashioned *El Sarape Cafe* (☎ 773 4620).

### TRUTH OR CONSEQUENCES
Originally called Hot Springs and built on the site of natural hot mineral springs in the 1880s, the town voted in 1950 to change its name to that of a famous 1940s radio and TV comedy program as a publicity and fund-raising gimmick, and it has been called Truth or Consequences (or, more often, T or C) since. The chamber of commerce or museum will fill you in on all the details of the name change.

T or C (population 7500) is the seat of Sierra County and a resort town for those wishing to use the hot springs or camp and fish in the three lakes/state parks nearby. The elevation here is 4260 feet above sea level.

### Orientation & Information
The chamber of commerce (☎ 894 3536), 201 Foch, is open from 9 am to 5 pm, Monday to Friday. The Gila National Forest Ranger Station (☎ 894 6677) is at 1804 N Date. The library (☎ 894 3027) is at 325 Library Lane. The post office (☎ 894 3137) is at 300 Main St. The hospital (☎ 894 2111) is at 800 E 9th St. The police (☎ 894 7111, or 911 in emergencies) are at 401 McAdoo St.

### Geronimo Springs Museum
This good museum (☎ 894 6600), 325 Main St, has plenty of local historical artifacts ranging from prehistoric Mimbres pots to beautifully worked cowboy saddles. Exhibits clarify the details of the famous 1950 name change. There are also mineral displays and local art. Hours are 9 am to 5 pm, Monday to Saturday, and 1 to 5 pm on Sundays. Admission is $1.50.

### Hot Springs
A gazebo outside the Geronimo Springs Museum shelters a natural spring in which Geronimo is said to have bathed. The mineral-laden waters have therapeutic properties, range in temperature from 98° to 110°F and have a pH of 7 (neutral). The commercial hot baths in town date from the 1920s and 1930s and look a little the worse for wear from the outside, though they are acceptably clean inside. Most charge about $2 for a hot bath (private, couple and family tubs available) or $20 and up for a massage. Either bring your own towels or rent them.

You might try the following establishments: Charles Motel & Bath House (☎ 894 7154), 601 Broadway, open 8 am to 5 pm daily (supposedly the hottest water in

town); Artesian Bath House & RV Park
(☎ 894 2684), 312 Marr Ave, open 7 am to
7 pm daily except Wednesday; Sierra
Grande Lodge & Health Spa (☎ 894 6976),
603 McAdoo; Indian Springs Apartments
and Pools (☎ 894 3823), 200 Pershing St
(natural pools with payment on the honor
system); Ye Olde Hot Springs Bath Haus,
Pershing and Austin Sts, open 7 am to
6 pm, Monday to Thursday, and to 8 pm on
Friday and Saturday.

### Callahan's Auto Museum
Cars from the 1920s to the 1960s are displayed here, along with automobile memorabilia. The museum (☎ 894 6900), 410
Cedar St, is open from 10 am to 5 pm,
Monday to Saturday, and admission is by
donation.

### Elephant Butte Lake State Park
New Mexico's largest lake is this 60-sq-
mile artificial one, formed in 1916 by
damming the Rio Grande. The state park is
five miles east of Truth or Consequences,
on the west shore of the lake. It is very
popular year round for all manner of water
sports and camping. Anglers go for bass,
catfish, pike, crappie and, below the dam,
trout. Desert Bass Fishing Guide Services
(☎ 744 5314) charges $190 a day for
guiding two anglers. The Elephant Butte
Resort Marina (☎ 744 5486) has a restaurant as well as several launching ramps,
boat rental, camping supplies and fishing
tackle and licenses. Other marinas nearby
include Rock Canyon (☎ 744 5462) and
Dam Site (☎ 894 2041). Water-skiing and
windsurfing are popular from April to
September.

A visitors center has exhibits inside and
a nature trail outside, and provides information. Facilities at the campground
include a playground, wheelchair-accessible showers, picnic and barbecue areas
and sites with and without hookups for $7
to $13. Day use is $3. Reach the lake by
heading east on Third St or north on Motel
Drive – follow the signs. Information is
available from the park (☎ 744 5421), PO
Box 13, Elephant Butte, 87935.

### Activities
**Golf** nine holes at the Municipal Golf
Course (☎ 894 2603), 685 W Marie, or the
Oasis Golf and Country Club (☎ 744 5224)
on Stagecoach Rd near Elephant Butte
Lake. **Swim** at the swimming pool (☎ 894
6151), 775 Daniels, which is open in the
summer.

### Special Events
The T or C Fiesta, held the first weekend in
May, celebrates the town's 1950 name
change – Ralph Edwards, host of the *Truth
or Consequences* program, has visited
every year since then. There is a rodeo, barbecue, parade and other events. The Sierra
County Fair has livestock and agricultural
displays during early September. Geronimo
Days, held the weekend before Columbus
Day, features Indian dancers, cowboy
poetry, fiddlers contests, gunfights and historical reenactments, cloggers and other
dancers, country & western, bluegrass, and
mariachi music, a procession and a bunch
of other Western stuff. The Old Time Fiddlers State Championship is held the following weekend.

### Places to Stay – camping
Caballo Lake State Park (see below), 20
miles south of Truth or Consequences, has
tent sites for $7 and RV sites with hookups
for $11. Facilities include showers and a
playground. *Cielo Vista RV Park* (☎ 894
3738), 501 S Broadway, has RV sites with
hookups for $11. There is a pool, spa and
coin laundry. *Artesian Bath House & RV
Park* (☎ 894 2684), 312 Marr Ave, has
inexpensive sites and hot springs. *Lakeside
RV Park & Campground* (☎ 744 5996), on
Country Club Blvd near the Oasis Golf and
Country Club, has tent and RV sites starting at $13.50. Facilities include showers,
coin laundry and an exercise room. Other
RV parks are found along Broadway (also
called Motel Drive) at the southwest end of
town. The *Lakeview KOA* (☎ 743 2811), a
quarter mile east of I-25 exit 63 (16 miles
south of T or C), has tent and RV sites from
$10 to $15, and they have a playground
and laundry. Also see state parks, above.

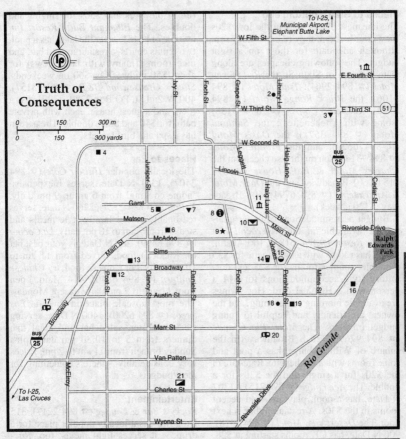

## Truth or Consequences

0 — 150 — 300 m
0 — 150 — 300 yards

**NEW MEXICO**

Ralph Edwards Park

Rio Grande

To I-25, Municipal Airport, Elephant Butte Lake

To I-25, Las Cruces

### PLACES TO STAY
- 4 Stout's Greasewood B&B
- 5 Motor Manor Motel & Apartments
- 6 Sierra Grande Lodge & Health Spa
- 12 Dude Motel & Apartments
- 13 Charles Motel & Bath House
- 16 Riverbend Hot Springs Resort
- 17 Cielo Vista RV Park
- 19 Indian Springs Apartments & Pools
- 20 Artesian Bath House & RV Park

### PLACES TO EAT
- 3 La Cocina
- 7 Chinese Lantern Restaurant

### OTHER
- 1 Callahan's Auto Museum
- 2 Library
- 8 Chamber of Commerce
- 9 Police
- 10 Post Office
- 11 Geronimo Springs Museum
- 14 Rocky's Bar & Lounge
- 15 Greyhound Bus Depot
- 18 Ye Olde Hot Springs Bath Haus
- 21 Municipal Pool

## Places to Stay – bottom end

The cheapest places start in the low $20s for a double room; they're basic and worn, although adequate for those on a tight budget. The following cheapies are along Date St north of Sixth St: the *Red Haven Motel* (☎ 894 2964); *Trail Motel* (☎ 894 3106); the *Black Range Motel* (☎ 894 2742); *Chateau Courts* (☎ 894 3138) (some with kitchenettes); the *Sunland Motel* (☎ 894 3571); the *Oasis Motel* (☎ 894 6629); and the *Frontier Motel* (☎ 894 7314). You might also check out the *Charles Motel & Bath House* (☎ 894 7154), 601 Broadway, and the *Dude Motel & Apartments* (☎ 894 6794), 608 Broadway ($120 a week).

Budget accommodations of better quality are available at the *Riverbend Hot Springs Resort* (☎ 894 6183), 100 Austin, which has rooms with a kitchenette for $35 a double, couples rooms for $25 and dormitory-style accommodations for $11 a person with a HI/AYH card. Hot springs are available morning and evening, and the owners are friendly and helpful to young budget travelers. The *Motel Rio Grande* (☎ 894 9769), 720 S Broadway (in the suburb of Williamsburg), has a pool and some rooms with a kitchenette. Rates are in the $20s for a single and the $30s for a double. The *Ace Lodge* (☎ 894 2151), 1302 N Date, has a pool, play area and decent rooms in the $30s. A restaurant/bar is next door. The *Desert View Motel* (☎ 894 3318), 906 N Date, has OK rooms starting at $28. The *Motor Manor Motel & Apartments* (☎ 894 3648), 595 Main, has rooms at similar prices. The *Super 8 Motel* (☎ 894 7888, fax 894 7883), 2151 N Date, has reasonable rooms for $36.88/46.88 for singles/doubles. The *Sierra Grande Lodge & Health Spa* (☎ 894 6976), 603 McAdoo, has recently reopened after remodeling.

## Places to Stay – middle

The Best Western *Hot Springs Motor Inn* (☎ 894 6665), 2270 N Date, has a pool, free coffee in the lobby and K-Bob's Restaurant next door. Large, pleasant rooms with queen- and king-size beds and double sinks run in the $40s and $50s for singles and doubles. The *Elephant Butte Resort Inn* (☎ /fax 744 5431), near the lake, has a pool, two tennis courts, a restaurant and bar, and nice rooms (many with lake views) for about $50 midweek or $60 on weekends. *Stout's Greasewood B&B* (☎ 894 3157), 400 W 2nd St, PO Box 2280, 87901, has a room and a guest house, each with private bath, for $40 and $50 a double. The garden has a spa and bird feeders.

## Places to Eat

The locally popular *Hilltop Cafe* (☎ 894 3407), 1301 N Date, serves inexpensive 'home cooking' from 6 am to 9 pm daily. *K-Bob's* (☎ 894 2127), 2260 N date, serves reasonably priced family-style meals and steaks from 7 am to 10 pm daily. *La Cocina* (☎ 894 6499), 280 N Date, is your best bet for Mexican food, served from 11 am to 10 pm daily. For Chinese food, try *Chinese Lantern* (☎ 894 6840), 414 Main, open from 11 am to 9 pm daily except Monday. The most upscale place in town is *Los Arcos* (☎ 894 6200), 1400 N Date, serving steaks, lobster, salad bar and local fish dinners from 5 to 10:30 pm daily plus Sunday brunch from 11 am to 2 pm. Prices vary considerably – there's something for most budgets.

## Entertainment

*Rocky's Bar & Lounge* (☎ 894 2217), 315 Broadway, is a locally popular place for a drink – it serves light meals, too. *Raymond's Lounge* (☎ 894 3830), 912 N Date, has a few pool tables.

## Getting There & Away

Greyhound (☎ 894 2369), 311 Broadway, runs several daily buses north and south along I-25.

## AROUND TRUTH OR CONSEQUENCES
### Caballo Lake State Park

Near the intersection of Hwy 152 and I-25, travelers can take a rest at Caballo Lake State Park (☎ 743 3942), PO Box 32, Caballo, 87931. The park has a marina

(☎ 743 3995) and campground. As with Elephant Butte Lake, Caballo Lake is an artificial lake resulting from a dam on the Rio Grande, and activities are similar. In addition, a few dozen bald eagles overwinter around the lake and can often be seen between October and February. The park is a mile east of exit 59 on I-25, 20 miles south of Truth or Consequences.

**Percha Dam State Park** is about three miles south of Caballo Lake State Park, which provides information about it. Camping facilities are similar, but there is no marina and fishing is mainly for catfish in the river.

## HATCH

Hatch is at the junction of Hwy 26 and I-25, 41 miles north of Las Cruces. Drivers rushing from Arizona to Albuquerque can take Hwy 26 between Deming and Hatch, thus avoiding Las Cruces and cutting about 55 miles from the trip.

Hatch is famous for being the center of the New Mexico's (and hence the USA's) chile growing region, and you can buy chiles, salsas, *ristras* (decorative strings and wreaths of chiles) and other chile products in one of several stores in this small town.

An annual chile festival is held over Labor Day weekend. Delicious meals and fresh and prepared chiles of all levels of spiciness are sold, and various country-fair type events take place. More information is available from the chamber of commerce (☎ 267 5050), 224 Elm. Food lovers might want to combine this festival with the nearby Hillsboro Apple Festival, held the same weekend.

**Hatch Museum** in the library (☎ 267 5132), 503 E Hall, is open from 9 am to 5 pm on Tuesday and Wednesday, noon to 6 pm on Thursday and 9 am to 1 pm on Friday and Saturday. Admission to the exhibits of local history is free.

The only hotel is the small and inexpensive *Village Plaza Motel* (☎ 267 3091), 608 Franklin. There is an RV park and a couple of cafes.

## LAS CRUCES

In 1535, Spanish explorers heading north from Mexico along the Rio Grande Valley passed through the Las Cruces area, recording that there were Indian villages nearby. Today there are few traces of those villages and of the many early travelers who passed through and camped in the area. In 1787 and again in 1830, Apaches killed bands of travelers camping here, and their graves were marked by a collection of crosses – hence the Spanish name of 'Las Cruces'.

There was no permanent settlement here until 1849, however. Several of the town's original buildings are still standing.

Adjacent to Las Cruces, the historic village of Mesilla was established in 1850 for Mexican settlers who wished to avoid becoming part of the USA after the Mexican-American War. Their hopes were, however, short-lived; in 1853, the USA bought Mesilla and many miles of land to the south and west in what became known as the Gadsden Purchase. Initially, Mesilla was a larger and more important town than Las Cruces, and the Hispanic plaza and surrounding streets contain many buildings from those early years, including a stagecoach stop for the Butterfield Overland Mail Company.

Today, Las Cruces has 63,000 inhabitants (it has grown fivefold since 1950), while Mesilla has only about 2000. Las Cruces is the Doña Ana County seat and New Mexico's second largest town. It is an important agricultural, industrial and academic center. Major crops are cotton, chile and pecans, and the nearby White Sands Missile Range provides many jobs. The New Mexico State University (NMSU) has some 15,000 students attending undergraduate, graduate and post-graduate programs.

The city is at 3890 feet in an attractive setting between the Rio Grande Valley and the strangely fluted Organ Mountains rising to the west. To the north lies the remains of Fort Selden and the adjacent Leasburg Dam State Park, where a small lake offers respite on hot days. To the east, two recreation areas lure bird watchers and outdoor enthusiasts. Despite several rather interesting annual events, there is no high/low season for hotels.

## Orientation & Information
The city lies roughly northwest of the intersection of I-25 and I-10 linking Arizona and Texas.

The chamber of commerce (☎ 524 1968), 760 W Picacho, 88005, and the Convention and Visitor's Bureau (☎ 524 8521, 1 (800) 343 7827), 311 N Downtown Mall, 88001, both provide visitor information. The BLM (☎ 525 4300) is at 1800 Marquess St. The library (☎ 526 1045) is at 200 E Picacho Ave. The local newspapers are the *Las Cruces Sun-News*, which runs both international and local news, and the *Las Cruces Bulletin*, which covers local community news. The main post office (☎ 524 2841) is at 201 E Las Cruces Ave. Las Cruces Recycles (☎ 527 7845) has information; bins are at Smith's, 2200 E Lohman; K mart, 1240 El Paseo Blvd; and other locations. The main hospital (☎ 522 8641, or 521 2286 for 24-hour emergencies) is at 2450 S Telshor Blvd. The police (☎ 526 0795, or 911 in emergencies) are at 217 E Picacho Ave.

## Historic Buildings
Check at the chamber or visitors bureau for brochures about local historical self-guided walks. Highlights include the old **Amador Hotel**, built in 1853 at Amador Ave and Water St, once the best hotel for many miles around and now a county office building. Built in 1877, the **Armijo House**, at Lohman and Main St, was the home of one of Las Cruces' most important families, and now it is the offices of a law firm. You can see a variety of turn-of-the-century buildings in the **Mesquite District** and the **Alameda District** a few blocks east and west of the Downtown Mall.

## Branigan Cultural Center
In the Downtown Mall at 500 N Water St, the center (☎ 524 1422) has a small but varied collection of local art, sculpture, quilts and historic artifacts. The center also arranges tours of the late 1800s **Log Cabin Museum** at Lucero and Main at the north end of the Downtown Mall. Hours are 9 am to 12 noon and 2 to 4:30 pm, Monday to Friday, 9 am to 3 pm on Saturday and 1 to 5 pm on Sunday. Admission is free.

## University Museum
The NMSU museum (☎ 646 3739), in Kent Hall at Solano Drive and University Ave, houses changing exhibits focusing on local art, history and archaeology. It's worth a look. Hours are 10 am to 4 pm, Tuesday to

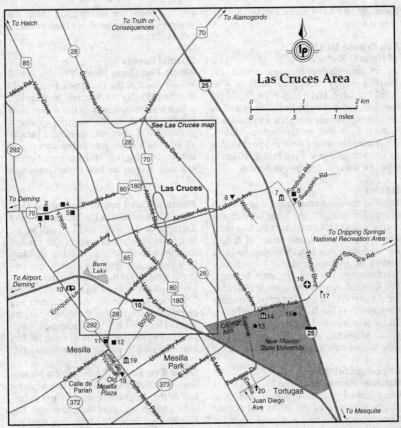

Las Cruces Area

| 0 | | 1 | | 2 km |
| 0 | .5 | | 1 miles | |

To Hatch

To Truth or Consequences

To Alamogordo

To Deming

To Airport, Deming

To Dripping Springs National Recreation Area

To Mesquite

See Las Cruces map

Las Cruces

Burn Lake

Mesilla

Mesilla Park

Old Mesilla Plaza

Tortugas

New Mexico State University

**NEW MEXICO**

## PLACES TO STAY

1. Budget Inn, Townhouse Motel
2. Royal Host Motel, Economy Inn
3. Western Inn
4. Desert Lodge, Paradise Motel
5. Imperial Sky Motel
8. Hilton
10. Bob Lilly's RV Park, Coachlight Inn
12. Mesón de Mesilla

## PLACES TO EAT

6. Nabe's Coffee Bar & Newsstand, Mesilla Valley Kitchen, Tegmeyer's Salad Works
9. Cattle Baron

18. La Posta, El Patio Restaurante & Cantina, Peppers, Double Eagle Restaurant

## OTHER

7. Las Cruces Museum of Natural History
11. Old West Brew Pub
13. Hershel Zohn Theater
14. University Museum
15. Pan American Center
16. Hospital
17. University Golf Course
19. Gadsden Museum
20. Church of Our Lady of Guadalupe

Saturday, and 1 to 4 pm on Sunday. Admission is free.

### Las Cruces Museum of Natural History

In an improbable location within the Mesilla Valley Shopping Mall at 700 S Telshor Blvd, this museum (☎ 522 3120) has both live and stuffed wildlife as well as other items loosely connected with natural history. Kids like the interactive exhibits. It's free and hours are noon to 5 pm Monday to Thursday, noon to 9 pm Friday, 10 am to 4 pm Saturday and 1 to 4 pm Sunday.

### Mesilla

Despite the souvenir shops and tourist-oriented restaurants, the Mesilla Plaza and surrounding blocks are a step back in time. The plaza is the obvious center of things, but wander a few blocks around to get a feeling of an important mid-19th-century Southwestern town of Hispanic heritage. For the Gadsden Purchase story and other local history, visit the **Gadsden Museum** (☎ 526 6293), on Barker Rd just off Hwy 28, a few hundred yards east from the plaza. Mesilla is about three miles southwest of downtown Las Cruces.

### Dripping Springs National Recreation Area

Once called the Cox Ranch and now jointly managed by the BLM and Nature Conservancy, this area is a good place for bird-watching in the Organ Mountains. Deer, coyotes and rock squirrels are often seen, and mountain lions are occasionally reported. Reach the area by heading east on University Ave, which becomes Dripping Springs Rd – it's about nine miles. Hours are 8 am to sunset; the Cox Visitor Center (☎ 522 1219) is open from 9 am to 5 pm; a nature trail is open from 8 am to 3 pm. Admission is $3 per vehicle, and there is a picnic area.

### Activities

You can **golf** at the NMSU course (☎ 646 3219) at University Ave and Telshor Blvd. Call the parks and recreation department

(☎ 526 0668) for information about the several swimming pools and tennis courts in Las Cruces.

### Special Events

**Whole Enchilada Fiesta** The city's best-known event is the Enchilada Fiesta, held the first Friday to Sunday in October, which features a variety of live music, food booths, arts & crafts, sporting events, a chile cookoff, carnival rides and a parade, all of which culminate in the cooking of the world's biggest enchilada on Sunday morning. Events are held in the Downtown Mall.

**Fiesta of Our Lady of Guadalupe** Held 10 to 12 December in the Indian village of Tortugas at the south end of Las Cruces, this fiesta involves drummers and masked dancers who accompany a statue of Mary in a procession from the church late into the first night. On the following day, participants climb several miles to 4914-foot Tortugas Mountain for mass; dancing and ceremonies continue in the village into the night. The Our Lady of Guadalupe Church (☎ 528 8171) is on Emilia St south of Tortugas Drive. The public is welcome.

**Other Events** The Southern New Mexico State Fair, held for six days in late September at the fairgrounds west of town, features a rodeo and other Western events. The Renaissance Arts and Crafts Fair, held the first weekend in November, features performers in 16th-century English garb as well as plenty of booths for shopping.

### Places to Stay – camping

In town, there's *Siesta RV Park* (☎ 523 6816), 1551 Avenida de Mesilla, with showers and a coin laundry. It charges $16 with full hookups and has a few less expensive tent sites. Cheaper places include *Bob Lilly's RV Park* (☎ 526 3301), 301 S Motel Blvd, (no tents) and *Dalmonts RV Trailer Corral* (☎ 523 2992), 2224 S Valley Drive.

The *Best RV Park* (formerly the KOA) (☎ 526 9030), 814 Weinrich Rd, is almost five miles west of the Rio Grande along

Picacho Ave. It has a pool, coin laundry, playground, grocery store, showers and Kamping Kabins for $23 a double, RV sites for $16 with hookups and tent sites for $15. Also look under Leasburg Dam State Park and Aguirre Springs, above.

### Places to Stay – bottom end

A number of cheap places are clustered along Picacho Ave between Motel Drive and Valley Drive. The nicest of these include the *Royal Host Motel* (☎ 524 8536), 2146 W Picacho, with a pool and rooms for $28/32 for singles/doubles; the *Economy Inn* (☎ 524 8627), 2160 W Picacho, with a pool and rooms for $25/30; and the *Desert Lodge* (☎ 524 1925), 1900 W Picacho, for $22/24.

Others with rates in the $20s along Picacho Ave from west to east include: the *Budget Inn* (☎ 523 0365); the *Townhouse Motel* (☎ 524 7733); the *Western Inn* (☎ 523 5399); the run-down *Paradise Motel* (☎ 526 5583); the *Imperial Sky Motel* (☎ 524 3591); and the *Desert Oasis Inn* (☎ 523 6958).

Other basic hotels with rooms starting in the $20s are scattered around town. These include: the *Bruce Motel* (☎ 526 1644), 800 S Main; the *Coachlight Inn* (☎ 526 3301), 301 S Motel Blvd; *Sands Motel* (☎ 524 7791), 1655 S Main; the *Dunes Motel* (☎ 523 4960), 2200 S Valley Drive; the *Villa Motel* (☎ 526 5573), 1785 S Main; and the *Century 21 Motel* (☎ 524 9626), 2454 N Main.

If you're willing to pay a little more, the best inexpensive motel is probably the *Motel 6* (☎ 525 1010, fax 525 0139), 235 La Posada Ln, with a pool, coin laundry and single/double rooms for $30/36.

### Places to Stay – middle

**Motels** The pleasant *A Day's End Lodge* (☎ 524 7753), 755 N Valley Drive, has a pool and rooms for about $35/40. The *Super 8 Motel East* (☎ 382 1490, fax 382 1849), 4411 N Main St, is one of the few Super 8s with a pool. Standard rooms are $37.88/41.88. In the same chain, *Super 8 Motel South* (☎/fax 523 8695), 245 La Posada Lane, has rooms for $38.88/44.88. The *Days Inn* (☎ 526 4441, fax 526 3713), 2600 S Valley Drive, has a restaurant (breakfast and dinner only), bar, indoor pool, sauna and coin laundry. Adequate rooms are $45/55 (though $35 rooms were offered recently).

The *Hampton Inn* (☎ 526 8311, fax 527 2015), 755 Avenida de Mesilla, is one of the closest hotels to Mesilla; it has a pool and nice rooms in the $50s (discounts for long stays). Continental breakfast is included, and there are coffee makers in each room. Nearby is *La Quinta* (☎ 524 0331, fax 525 8360), 790 Avenida de Mesilla, which has a pool and comfortable rooms in the $50s including continental breakfast. Opposite is the Best Western *Mesilla Valley Inn* (☎ 524 8603, fax 526 8437), 901 Avenida de Mesilla. It has a restaurant open from 6 am to 10 pm, room service, a bar with occasional entertainment, a pool and spa, a game room and a coin laundry. Double rooms are in the $50s.

Another Best Western charging in the $50s for a good-sized double is the *Mission Inn* (☎ 524 8591, fax 523 4740), 1765 S Main, which has a coffee shop and bar, a pool and playground. Breakfast is included in the rates. The *Plaza Suites* (☎ 525 5500), 301 E University Ave, has a one-bedroom suite with living room and kitchenette for $50 a double; two-bedroom suites are available. It has a pool.

**B&Bs** *Lundeen Inn of the Arts* (☎ 526 3327, 1 (800) 732 6025), 618 S Alameda Blvd, 88005, is a large, turn-of-the-century adobe house with 20 guest rooms and an art gallery. A few rooms have kitchenettes and all have private baths; some have neither phone nor TV. Rates range from $55 to $95 including full breakfast, kitchen privileges and an afternoon social hour. Elderhostel groups often stay here.

The *Mesón de Mesilla* (☎ 525 9212, fax 525 2380), 1803 Avenida de Mesilla, PO Box 1212, 88046, is a modern adobe house with 13 guest rooms furnished with antiques and all with private baths. Attractive gardens surround the house, which also

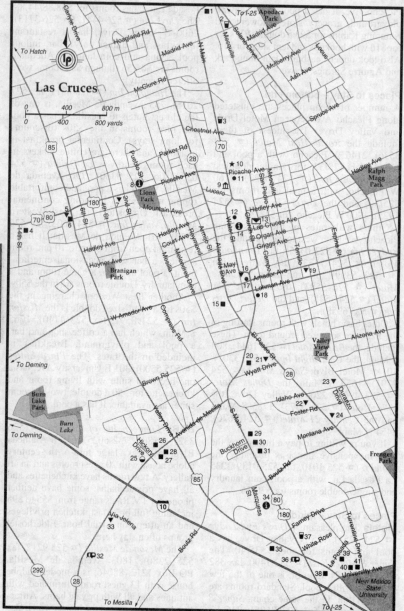

# Las Cruces

has a pool. You can borrow bicycles – it is only a short spin to the Mesilla Plaza. Rates range from $45 to $82 (rooms vary in size), including full breakfast in their good restaurant (see Places to Eat).

The *Hilltop Hacienda* (☎ 382 3556), 2520 Westmoreland, 88001, is seven miles north of town (call for directions). This modern Southwestern house has three rooms with shared bathrooms for $55 a double.

### Places to Stay – top end
The attractive *Holiday Inn* (☎ 526 4411, fax 524 0530), 201 E University Ave, is built to resemble a 19th-century Mexican village (if you ignore the indoor swimming pool!). Other facilities include a reasonably priced coffee shop, Western restaurant, old-fashioned saloon, room service, airport transportation and coin laundry. Double rooms fall in the $70 to $80 range.

The town's best and biggest hotel is the *Hilton* (☎ 522 4300, fax 521 7657), 705 S Telshor Blvd, which has a pool, spa and gym. There is also a restaurant with room service from 6 am to 10 pm, a bar with a variety of entertainment (jazz nights, top-40 dancing) and free airport transportation. Spacious rooms, each with a coffee maker, are in the $80 to $110 range, and a few more expensive suites are available.

### Places to Eat
**Las Cruces** A good place for breakfast is the Arroyo Plaza at 2001 E Lohman. Here, you'll find *Nabe's Coffee Bar & Newsstand* (☎ 523 9339) and the *Mesilla Valley Kitchen* (☎ 523 9311). Nabe's stocks the best selection of local and out-of-town newspapers and magazines, and serves breakfast from 7 to 11 am daily, and light meals, pastries and good coffee all day until midnight. The Mesilla Valley Kitchen is a popular breakfast and lunch spot, open from 6 am to 2:30 pm daily except Sunday (7 am to 1:30 pm). Both places have indoor and outdoor tables. In the same plaza, *Tegmeyer's Salad Works* (☎ 525 2332) offers an excellent self-serve soup and salad buffet for $5 at lunch or $5.50 at dinner. It is open from 11 am to 8:30 pm, Monday to Friday, and 11 am to 3 pm on weekends. There's another *Tegmeyer's* (☎ 525 2323) at 1300 El Paseo St.

A good, friendly and inexpensive family-style restaurant is *The Lantern* (☎ 524 1071), 1311 Avenida de Mesilla, which is open from 6 am to 8:30 pm daily except

Sunday (7 am to 8 pm). *Henry J's Gourmet Hamburgers* (☎ 525 2211), 523 E Idaho, is a flamboyant three-story house with huge windows and a '50s atmosphere. It has a salad bar as well as a good hamburger selection ranging from $3 to $5. Hours are 10:30 am to 10 pm daily. *My Brother's Place* (☎ 523 7681), 334 Main St, is popular for its New Mexican lunch specials, which draw downtown workers. It is open from 11 am to 9 pm, Monday to Thursday, and to 10 pm on Friday and Saturday. The nearby bars have plenty of pool tables and late-night action. *Fajitas* (☎ 523 6407), 600 E Amador, is in an attractive, century-old adobe house. Fajitas (broiled strips of beef, pork, chicken or shrimp served with tortillas and Mexican-style vegetables) cost around $10, and other cheaper Mexican meals are available. Hours are 11 am to 9 pm daily; it closes from 2 to 5 pm on weekdays.

Good steaks and seafood are served at the *Cattle Baron* (☎ 522 7533), 709 S Telshor, which is open daily from 11 am to 9:30 pm, Friday and Saturday to 10 pm. Most dinners cost from $10 to $20, and a kids' menu is available. *Cattleman's Steak House* (☎ 482 9051), 4401 N Main, is cheaper and convenient to the Super 8 Motel East. It is open from 11 am to 2 pm, Monday to Friday, from 5 to 10 pm, Monday to Saturday and from 11 am to 10 pm on Sunday. For Chinese food, a good choice is the *China Temple* (☎ 522 8770, 526 5210), 1401 El Paseo St. Open from 11 am to 9:30 pm daily, it features an all-you-can-eat lunch buffet until 2:30 pm on weekdays. For reasonably priced Japanese and 'New Oriental' dining, try unpretentious *Tatsu* (☎ 526 7144), 930 El Paseo Drive, which is open daily from 11 am to 9 pm, till 10 pm on Friday and Saturday. A good choice for Italian food is *Pullaro's* (☎ 523 6801), 901 W Picacho, which is open daily from 11 am to 2 pm and 5 to 9 pm. Nearby, *La Ristra* (☎ 523 0992, 523 0991), 1405 W Picacho, serves Mexican all-you-can-eat lunch buffets and full menu dinners from 11 am to 10 pm daily; mariachi bands occasionally play Thursday to Sunday.

**Mesilla** The *Mesón de Mesilla* (☎ 525 2380) restaurant (in the B&B) is a good one, serving lunch from 11:30 am to 2 pm on Wednesday, Thursday, Friday and Sunday, and dinner from 5:30 to 9:15 pm, Tuesday to Sunday. The varied continental menu changes often and most entrees run between $17 and $20. Sunday brunch is $14.95. Reservations are requested.

For Mexican and New Mexican cuisine, traditional Mesilla provides the appropriate setting. The most famous place is *La Posta* (☎ 524 3524), which is in an early 19th-century adobe house (predating the founding of Mesilla) on the east corner of the plaza. Once a Butterfield Stagecoach stop in the 1850s, the restaurant is now full of character. The current restaurant, which has been on the premises since the 1930s, is open from 11 am to 9 pm (9:30 pm on Fridays and Saturdays) daily except Monday. You can get a good Mexican dinner here for about $5 to $14 depending on your appetite.

Several other restaurants on the plaza serve equally good food – some people say even better, but in my mind, they are all good. *El Patio Restaurante & Cantina* (☎ 524 0982), a Mexican restaurant also housed in an early adobe building and in operation since the 1930s, has prices a touch lower than La Posta, and the bar attracts local jazz lovers. Hours are 11 am to 2 pm, Monday to Friday, and 5:30 to 9 pm (9:30 on Fridays and Saturdays); it's closed on Sundays. Plant-filled *Peppers* (☎ 523 4999), in modern pink and green pastels set off by old beams, serves a varied New Mexican cuisine in the $10 to $15 range. It is open from 11 am to 10 pm daily (9 pm on Sunday). Next door, the *Double Eagle Restaurant* (☎ 523 6700) is Mesilla Plaza's most upscale restaurant, offering continental and Southwestern cuisine in an elegant Victorian setting. It is open from 11 am to 10 pm daily and has dinner entrees in the $14 to $30 range.

### Entertainment

On Thursdays, *Las Cruces Bulletin* is a good source for local entertainment. *Las*

*Cruces Sun-News* runs daily cinema listings and a night-life guide in its *Que Pasa* Friday section. The main cinema complexes are *Cinema 8* (521 9355), in the Mesilla Valley Mall off Telshor south of Lohman; *Cinema 8* (522 7538) just north of the Mesilla Valley Mall; *Rio Grande Twin Theater* (526 2321), 213 N Main; and *Video 4* (523 6900), 1005 El Paseo Rd.

The reputable American Southwest Theater Company presents plays at the *Hershel Zohn Theater* (646 4515) in the NMSU campus. The Las Cruces Symphony (646 3709) plays at the NMSU *Pan American Center* (646 1420). Other campus cultural events take place here; call the special events director (646 4413) for information. The Las Cruces Community Theater (523 1200) performs in the *Downtown Mall*.

Several bars provide a varied nightlife. *Cowboys* (525 9050), 2205 S Main, is the best place for country & western music, both live and recorded. There's a big dance floor and a cover charge. Another popular country & western venue is *Tony Magee's Desert Sun* (523 5705), 1390 N Main. *Victoria's* (523 0440), 2395 N Solano Drive, features mariachi and Latin bands on weekends. *El Patio* (526 9943), next to the restaurant in Mesilla, has jazz acts midweek and rock or blues on weekends. The *Old West Brew Pub* (524 2408), 1720 Avenida de Mesilla, is a microbrewery with good beers; it is very popular among young people.

## Things to Buy

The Mesilla Plaza area has about 30 stores selling anything from Navajo rugs to the latest novels. Mainly, the stores sell souvenirs ranging from cheap and kitsch to expensive and excellent. Shoppers should allow several hours – good restaurants provide a respite from the consumer frenzy.

## Getting There & Away

**Air** Las Cruces has a small airport about eight miles west of downtown. Mesa Airlines (526 9743, 1 (800) 637 2247) runs several flights a day to Albuquerque.

El Paso International Airport, less than an hour away, has flights to all over the USA. See Bus below for transport to El Paso.

**Bus** Greyhound (524 8518, 1 (800) 231 2222) has an office behind the McDonald's Restaurant at 1150 Hickory Drive (just off Avenida de Mesilla north of I-10 exit 140). Two buses a day depart east to Roswell and beyond, 12 daily south to El Paso, six daily west to Tucson and Phoenix, Arizona, and California, and four daily north to Albuquerque and Denver, Colorado.

Las Cruces Shuttle Service (525 1784, 1 (800) 288 1784) has 12 vans a day from Las Cruces to the El Paso Airport. The one-way fare is $21 for one person or $30 for two people (and cheaper per person rates for larger groups). Roundtrip discounts are available. The service also runs three vans a day to Deming ($15 one-way) and Silver City ($25 one-way), also with group and roundtrip discounts. There is an extra $3 charge for pickup at your address, or call them for the nearest designated stop. Reservations are required.

## Getting Around

**Bus** Roadrunner Transit (525 2500) operates eight bus routes in Las Cruces (but not Mesilla). Buses run every 40 minutes from 6:30 am to 7:10 pm, Monday to Friday, and every 30 minutes from 9 am to 6 pm on Saturday. There is no Sunday service. Further information is available from the company from 8 am to 5 pm, Monday to Friday, or on any bus. Several routes pass the intersection of El Paseo St with Campo and Wyatt Drive, a few blocks south of the Downtown Mall.

There is no bus service to Las Cruces Airport – call a cab.

**Taxi** Checker Cab/Yellow Cab (524 1711) will take reservations and pick you up 24 hours a day.

## AROUND LAS CRUCES
### Fort Selden State Monument

Fort Selden was built in 1865 to protect travelers in the region. Buffalo soldiers

(African-American army units) were stationed here, and US General Douglas MacArthur spent some of his childhood at the fort. Closed in 1891, Fort Selden is now in ruins, but a small museum presents memorabilia, and an interpretive trail winds through the remains. Park rangers in period dress give demonstrations during summer weekends.

The monument (☎ 526 8911) is 15 miles north of Las Cruces (just west of I-25 exit 19). Daily hours are 9:30 am to 5:30 pm, 1 May to 15 September and 8:30 am to 4:30 pm at other times. They close on major holidays. Admission is $2 for those over 16.

Adjacent to Fort Selden, **Leasburg Dam State Park** offers camping and picnicking in desert scrub scenery. Leasburg Dam impounds a small lake offering limited boating, swimming and fishing, and there is a playground and play fort for kids. Water and showers are available.

The park (☎ 524 4068), PO Box 61, Radium Springs, 88054, is open year round. Day use is $3, camping is $7 or $11 with partial hookups. The 45 sites sometimes fill on weekends.

## Aguirre Springs National Recreation Area

About 20 miles east of Las Cruces, this BLM-managed scenic area on the east side of the Organ Mountains offers good birdwatching, strenuous mountain hiking, horse trails and primitive camping. Get there by driving east on Hwy 70, over the scenic **San Agustin Pass** (5719 feet; there is a pullout for views) to the signed Aguirre Springs road about two miles beyond the pass. It's about five miles to the campground along the steep and winding road (trailers over 22 feet not recommended), and the mountain views are worthwhile. Day use is free; the primitive campground costs $3 and has pit toilets and picnic tables but no drinking water.

## DEMING

Deming is on the northern edge of the Chihuahuan Desert, midway between Lordsburg and Las Cruces along I-10. Founded in 1881 as a railway junction town, it is now an agricultural center and the Luna County seat. Water for the farms and ranches comes from the invisible Mimbres River, which disappears underground about 20 miles north of town and emerges in Mexico. With about 12,000 inhabitants, it is the second largest town in southwestern New Mexico. A good museum and nearby state parks are the main year-round attractions for visitors. Deming has some unusual annual events, described below.

### Orientation & Information

Pine St is the main one-way east-to-west street, and one block to the south, parallel Spruce St is the main one-way west-to-east street. Spruce is also called Motel Drive.

The chamber of commerce (☎ 546 2674), 800 E Pine St, is open from 9 am to 5 pm daily. The library (☎ 546 9202) is at 301 S Tin. The post office (☎ 546 9461) is at 209 W Spruce. The hospital (☎ 546 2761) is at 900 W Ash. The police (☎ 546 3011, 546 3012, or 911 in emergencies) are at 700 E Pine.

### Deming Luna Mimbres Museum

Run by the Luna County Historical Society (☎ 546 2382), the museum is housed in what was once the National Guard Armory, built in 1916 at 301 S Silver St. Exhibits are varied, interesting and well displayed. See a superb doll collection, many Mimbres pots, several vintage cars, 1200 liquor decanters, beautiful homemade quilts, a Braille edition of *Playboy* and much more. Hours are 9 am to 4 pm daily except Sunday (1:30 to 4 pm); it is closed on Thanksgiving and 25 December. Admission is free, but I encourage contributions and a purchase at the gift shop.

### Rock Hound State Park

This park is known for its many semi-precious or just plain pretty rocks that can be collected – there is a 15 pound limit. The best rocks have been picked up, so you need a shovel and some rockhounding

Chuckwalla lizard

experience to uncover anything special, but beginners can try their luck and find something attractive. The best advice is to walk into the Little Florida Mountains for a while before beginning to look for rocks bearing, perhaps, agate, opal, jasper or quartz crystals.

The park is reached by heading south from Deming for five miles on Hwy 11, then turning east (there is a sign) on Hwy 141 for six miles to the park. Two miles before you reach the park, you'll see the **Museum and Rock Shop**, open from 9 am to 5 pm, Thursday to Tuesday. There is a $1 admission to the museum. The park has a 29-site campground. About two miles southeast of the main area is **Spring Canyon**, known for an introduced herd of wild Persian ibex, which you may catch a glimpse of if you are reasonably lucky. Other wildlife such as lizards, birds, rock squirrels and deer are often spotted here. Information is available from Rock Hound State Park (☎ 546 6182), PO Box 1064, Deming, 88030.

### Activities
**Golf** the 18-hole course (☎ 546 3023, 546 9481) at the east end of town. **Swim** at the municipal pool (☎ 546 4129) at 900 W Spruce.

### Special Events
### Great American Duck Races (GADR)
These duck races have been held annually on the fourth weekend in August for almost two decades. This is one of the most whimsical and popular festivals in the state, attracting tens of thousands of visitors. The main events are the duck races themselves – and this is serious business, with the world's largest duck race purse at stake ($10,000!). By strange coincidence, the surname of some of the best duck trainers is Duck. Robert and Bryce Duck's ducks took first and second place in the 1994 races. Other events during the GADR include the Tortilla Toss (winners toss tortillas over 170 feet), Outhouse Races, Best Dressed Duck contest, a rodeo, parade and fancy dress pageant. There are also hot-air balloons and food.

**Other Events** Additional local events include the Southwestern New Mexico State Fair, held for five days in late September/early October, which features a rodeo, livestock and produce judging, carnival, and arts & crafts. The rodeo and fairgrounds are at the east end of town. The Rock Hound Round-Up has been held annually in mid-March for over 30 years – this is your chance to buy, sell and learn more about the local gems, minerals and rocks. Sausage lovers won't want to miss the Czechoslovakian Klobase Festival held in mid-October.

### Places to Stay
Rooms are at a premium and prices rise during the duck races and the state fair, when you should make advance reservations. Otherwise, there is a good selection of reasonably priced accommodations in Deming.

### Places to Stay – camping
At *Rock Hound State Park* (see above), a 29-site campground has picnic areas, drinking water, showers and a playground. It is often full in winter. Day use is $3, camping is $7. *City of Rocks State Park* (see below) has secluded campsites ($7)

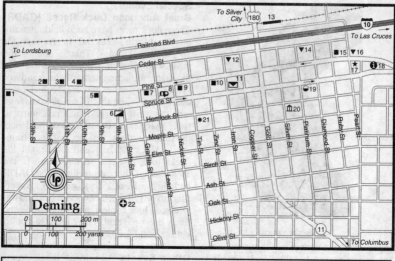

**Deming**

**PLACES TO STAY**

1  Best Western Mimbres Valley Inn
2  Budget Motel
3  Super 8 Motel, Western Motel
4  Wagon Wheel Motel
5  El Rancho Motel
7  Balboa Motel
8  Hitchin Post RV Park
9  Deming Motel
10  Butterfield Motel
15  Mirador Motel

**PLACES TO EAT**

12  Cactus Cafe

14  K-Bob's
16  La Fonda

**OTHER**

6  Municipal Swimming Pool
11  Post Office
13  Amtrak Station
17  Police
18  Chamber of Commerce
19  Greyhound Bus Depot
20  Deming Luna Mimbres Museum
21  Library
22  Hospital

that have picnic tables and firepits. A nature trail and cactus garden, playground, drinking water and showers are available. Also see Pancho Villa State Park below.

There are plenty of inexpensive RV parks in town – they are popular in winter. The best are the *Roadrunner RV Park* (☎ 546 6960), 2849 E Spruce, and the *Little Vineyard RV Park* (☎ 546 3560), 2901 E Spruce. Both have showers, pool, spa, recreation area, coin laundry and a few tent sites. Rates are $11 to $13 at the Roadrunner, $10 at the Little Vineyard. Other places are a little cheaper but are mainly geared to RVs – they include the *Hitchin Post*

*RV Park* (☎ 546 9145), 611 W Pine; the *Wagon Wheel RV Park* (☎ 546 8650), 2801 E Spruce; the *Dreamcatcher RV Park* (☎ 544 4004), 4004 E Spruce; and the *Sunrise RV Park* (☎ 546 8565), 2601 E Spruce.

### Places to Stay – bottom end

The *Belshore Motel* (☎ 546 2717), 1210 E Spruce, has a small pool and inexpensive restaurant; it doesn't look too bad for just $20 a double. With 30 rooms, it is the largest of the cheap places. Even cheaper and more basic-looking places include the *Hacienda Motel* (☎ 546 0817), 2909

E Spruce; the *Mirador Motel* (☎ 546 2795), 501 E Pine; and the *El Rancho Motel* (☎ 546 9254), 1010 W Pine. The *Budget Motel* (☎ 546 2787), 1309 W Pine, has a pool and looks OK at $20/23 for singles/doubles. The *Balboa Motel & Restaurant* (☎ 546 6473), 708 W Pine, also looks cheap.

The *Wagon Wheel Motel* (☎ 546 2681), 1109 W Pine, has pretty decent rooms for about $26 a double. The similarly priced *Deming Motel* (☎ 546 2737), 500 W Pine, also looks OK. Others at this price include the *Western Motel* (☎ 546 2744), 1207 W Pine, which has a cafe attached and the *Butterfield Motel* (☎ 544 0011), 309 W Pine. Each of these places has a pool.

### Places to Stay – middle
The *Motel 6* (☎ 546 2623), exit 85 off I-10, is Deming's largest hotel with 102 rooms at $26/32 for singles/doubles. It has a pool, as do the hotels below except for the *Super 8 Motel* (☎ 546 0481), 1217 W Pine, which has standard rooms for $35.88/40.88 for singles/doubles.

The following hotels have rooms in the $40 to $50 range. The *Chilton Inn* (☎ 546 8813, fax 546 7095), 1709 E Spruce, has a cafe open from 5:30 am to 9 pm. The Best Western *Mimbres Valley Inn* (☎ 546 4544), 1500 W Pine, has good sized rooms designed to give you a good night's sleep – many lack TVs and telephones. Free continental breakfasts are offered. The *Holiday Inn* (☎ 546 2661), exit 85 off I-10, has decent rooms and Fat Eddie's Restaurant open from 6 am to 10 pm – room service is available. There is a bar and a coin laundry. The *Grand Motor Inn* (☎ 546 2632, fax 546 4446), 1721 E Spruce, often gives discounts and has nice rooms. Its restaurant, one of the best in town, is open from 6 am to 9 pm or 10 pm in summer. It serves steak, seafood and Mexican meals and has a salad bar. Dinner entrees are in the $8 to $20 range.

### Places to Eat
Apart from the hotel restaurants, Deming offers the basic choice between a fast-food franchise or a Mexican-American restaurant. If you want the latter, try *La Fonda* (☎ 546 0465), 601 E Pine, open from 6 am to 9:30 pm daily, and the *Cactus Cafe* (☎ 546 2458), 218 W Cedar – there are a dozen others. Inexpensive family dining is available at *K-Bob's* (☎ 546 8883), 316 E Cedar, which is open from 7 am to 10 pm daily.

### Getting There & Away
**Bus** Greyhound (☎ 546 3881, 1 (800) 231 2222), at 300 E Spruce, has four daily buses westbound and three daily eastbound ones along I-10.

**Train** Amtrak (☎ 1 (800) 872 7245) has trains stopping at Deming on Tuesday, Thursday and Sunday at 3 pm bound for Tucson and Phoenix, Arizona, and Los Angeles, California. Trains for El Paso, Texas, and New Orleans, Louisiana, stop at 3 pm on Monday, Wednesday and Saturday.

### AROUND DEMING
### City of Rocks State Park
This park is 24 miles northwest of Deming (28 miles southeast of Silver City) along Hwy 180, then about five miles northeast on Hwy 61. Rounded volcanic towers make up this 'city', and the landscape is quite dramatic. You can camp among the towers in secluded sites. The park (☎ 536 2800), PO Box 50, Faywood, 88034, is open year round and charges $3 for day use.

### PANCHO VILLA STATE PARK
On 9 March 1916, the Mexican revolutionary and outlaw Pancho Villa, unhappy with the US government's support of his enemies, stormed across the border with between 500 and 1000 troops. He attacked US Army Camp Furlong and the town of Columbus (30 miles south of Deming and three miles north of the Mexican border), killing 18 people and burning several buildings before being pushed back into Mexico, having lost over 100 men. He was chased deep into Mexico by General John 'Black Jack' Pershing, who led US troops using both aircraft and motor vehicles – the first

NEW MEXICO

time that the USA used these in warfare. Villa, however, succeeded in eluding capture, and the USA hasn't undergone an invasion since.

Camp Furlong is long gone, and once bustling Columbus is now a sleepy village of some 600 inhabitants, but visitors often head there because of its unique history. The story of the invasion is described in a small museum housed in the restored 1902 US Customs House, which also serves as the park office. It's open from 8 am to 5 pm daily. A short film can also be viewed as can several buildings dating back to Camp Furlong days. There is also a desert botanical garden, picnic area, playground, campground with about 60 sites and showers, drinking water and fire pits. Rates are $3 for day use, $7 for camping or $11 with electrical hookups year round. The park is off Hwy 11 in 'downtown' Columbus. Further information is available from Pancho Villa State Park (☎ 531 2711), PO Box 224, Columbus, 88029.

### Columbus Historical Museum
This small museum (☎ 531 2620) is opposite the state park in the 1902 railway depot. Summer hours are 1 to 4 pm daily; call ahead in other months.

### Visiting Mexico
You can park your car on the US side of the border and walk across to Las Palomas, a village on the Mexican side. Curio shops and restaurants provide a taste of Mexico, and proprietors are happy to accept US dollars. You can cross the border 24 hours a day.

### Special Events
In town, the Columbus Festival features a parade, street fair and entertainment on the Saturday preceding Columbus Day (the second Monday in October). A commemorative ceremony is held on 9 March for those killed in the 1916 raid.

### Places to Stay & Eat in Columbus
*La Frontera RV Park* (☎ 531 2636) is on the north side of town along Hwy 11.

*Martha's House B&B* (☎ 531 2467, fax 531 2630), PO Box 587, 88029, is at Main and Lima Sts, two blocks east of Hwy 11. Five modern rooms with private bath, TV and balcony rent for $55 a double, including full breakfast. Dinners are served on request. Cheaper rooms, some with kitchenettes, are available at the *Sun Crest Inn* (☎ 531 2323) just off Hwy 11 in the center of Columbus. Nearby, the *Cafe Columbus* (☎ 531 2362) serves breakfast, lunch and dinner.

## SILVER CITY
At 5938 feet, Silver City is on the southern border of the mountainous Gila National Forest, 44 miles away from and almost 2000 feet above Lordsburg and the Chihuahuan Desert. Summer high temperatures in the upper 80°s F and winter lows in the 20°s F attract people to the area. The weather is generally sunny and fairly dry – July is the wettest month and May the driest.

The city's name tells the story – it was a mining town founded in 1870 after the discovery of silver in the area. The price of silver crashed in 1893, leading to the demise of the silver mining industry, but instead of becoming a ghost town like so many others, Silver City tapped another mineral wealth, copper, which is still mined today. Ranching is of some importance, and the city is the part-time home to over 2000 students at Western New Mexico University.

History is in evidence in the downtown streets, with their Victorian brick buildings and Wild West air. Billy the Kid spent some of his boyhood here, and a few of his haunts can be seen.

Today, Silver City (population 11,000) is the seat of Grants County and the gateway to outdoor activities in the Gila National Forest. Tourism has prompted the preservation of historical buildings – this town is more tourist-oriented than most in southwestern new Mexico. Locals sometimes call the town, simply, Silver.

North of Silver City, Hwy 15 heads through Pinos Altos and dead ends at the Gila Cliff Dwellings National Monument,

## Mines of Southwest New Mexico

The history of Silver City is closely linked to discoveries of minerals and the subsequent mining of them. If you happen to be in town over Labor Day weekend, you can attend dozens of events celebrating the town's mining heritage. Brochures available at the Silver City Chamber of Commerce detail mining tours of the area.

The best known of Silver's mines is the huge Phelps-Dodge Open Pit Mine constructed on the site of Old Tyrone, a then very modern mining town built in 1915 and abandoned a few years later when copper prices fell. The mine is 12 miles south of town along Hwy 90 – an observation point overlooks the mine 100 yards off the road to the west near mile marker 32. Free guided tours are offered Monday to Friday at 9 am – call 7:30 am to 4:30 pm, Monday to Friday, to reserve a spot (☎ 538 5331).

The Santa Rita Chino Open Pit Copper Mine, 14 miles east on Hwy 152, can be seen from an observation point on the highway. This huge mine is well over a mile wide and 1000 feet deep. Worked since 1800, it is the oldest active mine in the Southwest. ■

44 miles away. The road is scenic, mountainous, narrow and winding – allow a couple of hours to drive it. The section between Pinos Altos and Lake Roberts is not recommended for trailers over 22 feet.

To the east, Hwy 152 breaks off from Hwy 180 and heads to Emory Pass, beyond which you can take in good views of the Rio Grande country to the east. This route is scenic, but expect lots of hairpin bends.

### Orientation & Information

Hwy 180, the main east-west route, is sometimes called Silver Heights Blvd. Hwy 90 (Hudson St) enters from the south and intersects Hwy 180 north of downtown. The historic district lies west of Hudson St.

The chamber of commerce (☎ 538 3785, 1 (800) 548 9378), 1103 Hudson St, is open from 9 am to 5 pm, Monday to Friday. The Gila National Forest Ranger Station (☎ 538 2771) is at 2915 E Hwy 180. The library (☎ 538 3672) is at 515 W College Ave. The local newspaper is the *Silver City Daily Press*. The post office (☎ 538 2831) is at 500 N Hudson St. Bring your recyclables to Environmental Control Inc (☎ 538 2560), 714 N Bullard, which takes glass and plastic bottles, cans and cardboard from 8 am to 4 pm, Tuesday to Saturday. The hospital (☎ 388 1591) is at 1313 E 32nd St. The police (☎ 538 3723, or 911 in emergencies) are at 11th and Hudson St.

### Historic Downtown

Bullard St between Broadway and 6th is the heart of Victorian Silver City. (John Bullard opened the first silver mine here in 1870 – he died the next year in a fight with Apaches.) Main St, one block east of Bullard, used to be the main drag, but it was washed out in a series of massive floods, some up to 12 feet deep, beginning in 1895. Caused by runoff from logged and overgrazed areas north of town, the floods eventually cut 55 feet down below the original height of the street. Today, this gouged-out area has been turned into a city park called **'The Big Ditch'**. Brochures available at the chamber of commerce describe self-guided tours of the historic downtown area as well as driving tours in the surrounding countryside. If the chamber is closed, the brochures are usually in a box outside.

### Silver City Museum

The city museum (☎ 538 5921), 312 W Broadway, is in an elegant Victorian house built in 1881. Exhibits display Mimbres pottery and mining and household artifacts from Silver City's Victorian heyday. There are also changing exhibits, occasional lectures and a store selling Southwestern books and gifts. Hours are 9 am to 4:30 pm, Tuesday to Friday, and 10 am to 4 pm on weekends. Admission is free.

## Western New Mexico University Museum

The WNMU Museum (☎ 538 6386) houses the world's largest collection of Mimbres pottery, and has exhibits detailing local history, culture and natural history as well as changing shows. The gift shop specializes in Mimbres motifs – books, T-shirts, ceramics and posters. Lectures and other programs are occasionally presented.

The on-campus museum is reached along 12th or Alabama Sts. Hours are 9 am to 4:30 pm, Monday to Friday, and 10 am to 4 pm on weekends (closed on university holidays). Admission is free, but donations are welcomed.

### Pinos Altos

Seven miles north of Silver City along Hwy 15 lies Pinos Altos, established in 1859 as a gold mining town and briefly the county seat. Now it's almost a ghost town with only a few residents who strive to retain the 19th-century flavor of the place. Along Main St is a log cabin, originally built in 1866 as a school, which houses the **museum**. An opera house, restaurant, reconstructed fort and 1870s court house are also along Main St. A cemetery, turn-of-the-century church and other buildings are found on back streets.

### Activities

**Golf** at the 18-hole Scott Park Golf Course (☎ 538 5041), which is on the southeastern outskirts of town. You can play **tennis** there as well. **Swim** at the pool in the park at Silver and 32nd Sts, where there are also tennis courts.

**Bicycle** rental (about $15 a day) and camping equipment is available from Gila Hike & Bike (☎ 388 3222), 103 E College St, open 9 am to 5 pm, Monday to Saturday.

Various **outfitters** in the Silver City area can guide you on horseback, backpacking, hunting, fishing or 4WD trips. Several are listed under Lake Roberts and Gila Hot Springs, and also in the Silver City to Reserve section.

The Gila National Forest and Wilderness Area is rugged country of the sort that's perfect for backpackers, campers, hunters, anglers, cross-country skiers and other outdoor sports enthusiasts who are looking for challenging solitude. Contact the ranger station in Silver City for maps and detailed information. A recommended book is *The Gila Wilderness: A Hiking Guide* by John A Murray (UNM Press, Albuquerque, 1992). Several day hikes and a couple of overnight trips in this area are described in Parent's *The Hiker's Guide to New Mexico* (see Facts for the Visitor chapter).

### Special Events

Gila Bird and Nature Festival is held the last weekend in April. In early June, a PRCA rodeo happens during Wild Wild West Days, and later in June, the Tour of the Gila, one of the main bicycle stage races in the Southwest, comes to Silver City. Frontier Days on the Fourth of July has everybody in Western wear for a parade, dance, fireworks and other exhibits. A Cowboy Poetry Gathering takes place around the first or second

Pinos Altos hosts an annual rodeo during Wild Wild West Days in June.

weekend in August. Mining Days over Labor Day weekend celebrates the city's mining heritage with dozens of events.

### Places to Stay – camping

*KOA* (☎ 388 3351), 11824 E Hwy 180, is almost six miles east of town. It has a pool, playground and coin laundry, and charges $13.50 for tents and $17.50 with hookups. Cheaper RV camping is available at the following: *Silver City RV Park* (☎ 538 2239), Bennett and 13th Sts; *Logan's Mobile Haven & RV Park* (☎ 538 3331), 11072 W Hwy 180 (about two miles west of town); and *Continental Divide RV Park* (☎ 388 3005) north in Pinos Altos.

The Gila National Forest (☎ 538 2771) maintains the small *Cherry Creek* and *McMillan* campgrounds, about 12 and 14 miles north of town on Hwy 15. Neither have drinking water but both are free and open from April to October. Also see the areas east and north of Silver City below.

### Places to Stay – bottom end

There are no very cheap motels in Silver. *Hostelling International* (☎ 388 5485) is on the ground floor of the Carter House B&B (see below) and offers 22 dormitory style beds for $11 per person. Kitchen and laundry facilities are available. Reservations can be made with a credit card over the phone. Office hours are 8 to 10 am and 4 to 9 pm daily.

### Places to Stay – middle

**Motels** The *Copper Manor Motel* (☎ 538 5392), 710 Silver Heights Blvd, faces the *Drifter Motel* (☎ 538 2916), 711 Silver Heights Blvd. Both are under the same ownership, and both offer a pool and adequate rooms for $36/40 for singles/doubles with one bed, and a little more for two beds. The Copper Manor has a spa, and a restaurant and lounge open from 11 am to 10 pm. The Drifter restaurant, open from 6 am to 2 am, has a bar with live music (country & western, mainly) and dancing every night except Sunday.

The *Holiday Motor Hotel* (☎ 538 3711, 1 (800) 828 8291), 3420 E Hwy 180, has slightly nicer rooms for a few dollars more. It also has a pool, coin laundry and a restaurant open from 6 am to 9:30 pm. The *Super 8 Motel* (☎/fax 388 1983), 1040 E Hwy 180, charges $38.88/45.88 for one/ two people in standard rooms with one bed or $48.88 with two beds.

To experience a little of Silver City's history, stay at the restored *Palace Hotel* (☎ 388 1811), 106 W Broadway, 88061-5093. This hotel dates from 1882, and the 20 rooms vary considerably from small rooms with a double bed for $30 to two room suites with king- or queen-size beds for about $50, including continental breakfast. Rooms may have a shower, a bath tub or both. Some rooms have a refrigerator. The downtown location can be a little noisy on weekends.

The *Bear Creek Motel & Cabins* (☎ 388 4501) in Pinos Altos has 13 cabins, all with fireplaces and wood, some with kitchenettes and balconies. The mangers will lend you a gold pan if you want to try your luck in nearby Bear Creek. Rates start around $40.

At the intersection of Hwy 15 and 35 is the *Sapillo Crossing Guest Ranch* (☎ 536 3206), Route 11, Box 134, Silver City 88061, which has RV sites, a decent restaurant open at 7 am, a good gift shop, and 16 standard rooms with Western decor and private baths for $50 a double. There is no smoking in the rooms or restaurant. The ranch offers guided trail rides suitable for novices as well as experienced riders for $15 an hour or $65 for six hours including lunch. Longer pack trips can be arranged in advance.

**B&Bs** Built in 1906, the *Carter House B&B* (☎ 388 5485), 101 N Cooper St (near Broadway), 88061, houses a youth hostel downstairs (see above) and five rooms upstairs with private bath. Rates range from $48/54 to $59/65 for singles/doubles, including a buffet-style full breakfast.

The *Bear Mountain Guest Ranch* (☎ 538 2538, 1 (800) 880 2538), 2251 Bear Mountain Rd, PO Box 1163, 88062, is a large ranch house built in 1928 on 160 acres

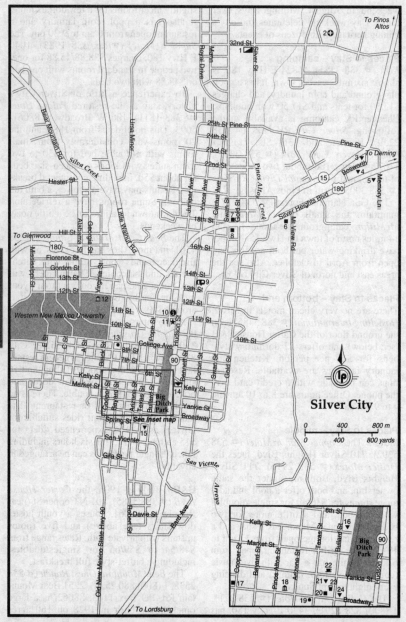

NEW MEXICO

**Silver City**

To Pinos Altos

To Deming

To Glenwood

To Lordsburg

0   400   800 m
0   400   800 yards

*See inset map*

Big Ditch Park

## PLACES TO STAY

| | |
|---|---|
| 6 | Super 8 Motel |
| 7 | Drifter Motel |
| 8 | Copper Manor Motel |
| 9 | Silver City RV Park |
| 17 | Hostelling International & Carter House B&B |
| 20 | Palace Hotel |

## PLACES TO EAT

| | |
|---|---|
| 3 | Mi Casita |
| 4 | Adobe Springs Cafe |
| 5 | Double Eagle Restaurant & Saloon |
| 8 | Red Barn Steak House |
| 15 | Jalisco Cafe |
| 16 | Silver Cafe |
| 21 | Black Cactus Cafe |
| 22 | AIR Espresso Bar & Gallery |
| 24 | Corner Cafe |

## OTHER

| | |
|---|---|
| 1 | Pool |
| 2 | Hospital |
| 10 | Chamber of Commerce |
| 11 | Police |
| 12 | WNMU Museum |
| 13 | Library |
| 14 | Post Office |
| 18 | Silver City Museum |
| 19 | Uncle Weldon's Cave |
| 23 | Buffalo Bar |

about three miles northwest of town (leave along Alabama St and follow the signs). A B&B since 1959, it has gained a well-deserved reputation among bird watchers and nature lovers as *the* place to stay in southwestern New Mexico. Rates start at $40/67 for singles/doubles with breakfast or $54/95 with all meals. There are suites sleeping five people ($125 with breakfast, $195 with all meals), and some rooms have kitchenettes. All have private baths. They also have six-day, five-night 'Lodge & Learn Programs' for $275 per person with all meals and classes on topics such as bird and plant identification, photography, local archaeology and history.

### Places to Eat

For good breakfasts and light meals throughout the day, the *Corner Cafe* (☎ 388

2056) at Bullard and Broadway is a good choice. It is open from 7 am to 8 pm, Monday to Friday, and 7 am to 6 pm on Saturday.

*AIR Espresso Bar & Gallery* (☎ 388 5952), 106 W Yankie St, is the place to go for a gourmet coffee and easy conversation. AIR? That's 'Artist in Residence' – enjoy the local art on the walls. It is open from 8 am to 5:30 pm daily except Friday. For a tasty breakfast or other meal with a New Mexican flavor, try the funky *Silver Cafe* (☎ 388 3480), 514 N Bullard, open from 7 am to 7:30 pm daily except Sunday. The *Adobe Springs Cafe* (☎ 538 3665), 1617 Silver Heights Blvd, is a more modern-looking and reasonably priced New Mexican restaurant open from 11 am to 9 pm, Monday to Friday, and 7 am to 9 pm on weekends.

You have a few choices for good Mexican food in town. The unpretentious but good *Jalisco Cafe* (☎ 388 2060), 100 S Bullard, is a local favorite; it is open from 11 am to 8:30 pm, Monday to Saturday. (It doesn't serve alcohol.) Another local favorite is *Mi Casita* (☎ 538 5533), 2340 Bosworth Drive, which serves huge plates for about $4 or $5. It is open from 11 am to 8 pm, Tuesday to Saturday.

This is cattle country. For a good steak, head over to the *Red Barn Steak House* (☎ 538 5666), 708 Silver Heights Blvd. Most steaks are in the $10 to $20 range, and the restaurant serves seafood and has a salad bar as well. The *Cucina Rustica* (☎ 538 3711), in the Holiday Motor Motel, has good Italian and continental dinners. The upscale *Black Cactus Cafe* (☎ 388 5430), 107 W Yankie St, serves New Mexican dinners from 5:30 to 9 pm, Thursday to Saturday, and Sunday lunch from noon to 4 pm.

The *Buckhorn Saloon* (☎ 538 9911), on Main St in Pinos Altos, offers fine dinners daily except Sunday from 6 to 10 pm (the saloon opens at 3 pm). Steaks, seafood and more are served in 1860s Wild West decor, and there is often live country music on Friday and Saturday. Most entrees are in the $10 to $20 range.

## Entertainment

The *Real West Cinema II* (☎ 538 5659) is at 11585 E Hwy 180 on the north side about five miles east of town – look hard for the sign or you'll miss it. Got kids in tow? Try *Uncle Weldon's Cave* (☎ 388 4256), 205 W Broadway, for mini-golf and other games.

The *Buffalo Bar* (☎ 538 3201), 201 N Bullard, has occasional dances with live or recorded music in the adjacent nightclub. Otherwise, it's your basic, not especially salubrious, western bar. Underage students frequent the nightclub because it has non-drinking nights – you can get a drink in the bar next door but can't bring it back into the nightclub. The *Double Eagle Restaurant & Saloon* (☎ 538 0100), 1740 E Hwy 180, has a small dance floor with Friday/Saturday night dancing. Also see the Buckhorn Saloon and Drifter Motel, above.

## Getting There & Away

**Air** The airport is 11 miles southeast of Silver City off Hwy 180. Mesa Air (☎ 388 4115, 1 (800) 637 2247) has three daily flights from Monday to Friday, one on Saturday and two on Sunday to and from Albuquerque. Roundtrip fares start at $119 with advance purchase and Saturday night stay-over requirements.

**Bus** Silver Stage Lines (☎ 388 2586, 1 (800) 522 0162) has vans leaving Silver City at 7 am and 2 pm for El Paso Airport, returning at 10:30 am and 5:30 pm. They'll pick you up, or you can catch one at Shadel's Bakery, across from the Buffalo Bar. They stop in Deming and Las Cruces. Las Cruces Shuttle Service (☎ 1 (800) 288 1784) has similar services leaving Silver City at 6:30 am and 3:30 pm, returning from El Paso at 10:45 am and 5:15 pm. They also have a van going to Las Cruces at 9 pm and returning at 4 am. Fares are $35 one-way to El Paso, Texas, and they'll pick you up. Discounts are available for roundtrips or for more than one person.

## Getting Around

Grimes Car Rental (☎ 538 2142) is at the Silver City airport. In town there is Taylor Car Rental (☎ 388 1800, 388 4848), 808 N Hudson, or Ugly Duckling Rent-a-Car (☎ 388 5813), 1960 E Hwy 180.

## AROUND SILVER CITY

### Lake Roberts Area

Lake Roberts is 25 miles north on Hwy 15 and then four miles east on Hwy 35. (The section of Hwy 15 between Pinos Altos and Lake Roberts is not recommended for trailers over 22 feet.) Managed by the New Mexico Department of Game and Fish (☎ 827 7882), the lake offers boating facilities and opportunities to fish for rainbow trout, catfish and smallmouth bass.

The Gila National Forest (☎ 536 2250) maintains *Mesa* and *Upper End* campgrounds at the northeast end of the lake, both with boat ramps and drinking water but no showers. Fees are $7. One campground may close in winter.

At the west end of the lake, the *Lake Roberts General Store & Cabins* (☎ 536 9929), Route 11, Box 195, Lake Roberts 88061, runs RV sites, coin-operated showers and laundry facilities. It has several cabins ranging from $35 a double to $70 for a cabin sleeping up to eight. All cabins have private bathrooms and kitchens with utensils. Guided hunting and pack trips are available with advance notice.

Hwy 35, which begins between Gila Hot Springs and Pinos Altos, provides an alternate but longer scenic route for returning from the Gila Cliff Dwellings to Silver. It continues east from the lake through the Mimbres Valley, passing the small *Rio Mimbres Lodge & RV Park* (☎ 536 9333) after about 15 miles and joining Hwy 152 about 10 miles further.

### Gila Hot Springs

Known and used by the area's Indians since ancient times, the hot springs are 38 miles north of Silver City within the *Gila Hotsprings Vacation Center* (☎ 536 9551, 536 9314), Route 11, Silver City 88061. The center has rooms with kitchenettes for $40/45 a double with one/two beds. Advance reservations are recommended.

An RV park with a spa and showers fed by the hot springs has sites for $12 with hookups and $9 without. A primitive campground next to hot pools has drinking water and toilets but no showers. Day use is $1 per person; camping is $2.50 per adult and kids are free. The center has a coin laundry, a snack bar, gift shop and a doll museum ($1 fee). Horses can be rented for $22 a day plus $50 a day if you want a guide. Guided fishing and wilderness pack trips can be arranged in advance for $70 to $105 per person per day, depending on group size. Trout fishing for hatchery-raised fish is best in spring on the Middle and West Forks of the Gila River, or year-round for wild fish in the backcountry. The East and Main Forks offer good bass fishing. Guided hunting trips and other outfitting services are also available.

The Gila River is two miles south of the hot springs. Two free Gila USFS *campgrounds* (no drinking water) are available on the north and south sides of the river where Hwy 15 crosses it. It is possible to float down the river from here to Turkey Creek, 45 miles away – contact the USFS for details. March and April are the best months.

### Gila Cliff Dwellings National Monument

The influence of the Anasazi on the Mogollon culture can clearly be seen in these cliff dwellings, which were occupied in the 13th century and are reminiscent of ones in the Four Corners Area. Aside from their historical value, the best thing about the ruins is their relative isolation which dissuades visitors that crowd many other Southwestern archaeological sites. A one-mile roundtrip self-guided trail climbs 180 feet to the dwellings set in cliffs overlooking a lovely forested canyon. Parts of the trail are steep and involve ladders.

The trail begins at the end of Hwy 15, two miles past the visitors center (☎ 536 9461), which has information, displays and a gift shop. From Memorial Day to Labor Day, the visitors center is open from 8 am to 5 pm and the trail from 8 am to 6 pm. At other times, the visitors center is open from 8 am to 4:30 pm and the trail from 9 am to 4 pm. The monument is closed on Christmas and New Year's Day. Admission is free. If you arrive any time other than the busy summer season, you can have the ruins to yourself, as I did one lovely October morning.

Between the visitors center and trailhead are two small campgrounds with drinking water, picnic areas and toilets. No food is available. They are free on a first-come, first-served basis and may fill on summer weekends. A short trail behind the campground leads to other, older dwellings.

Further information is available from the District Ranger, Route 11, PO Box 100, Silver City 88061.

### Historic Towns East of Silver City

Hwy 152 takes off from Hwy 180 about eight miles east of Silver City. It passes the mine at Santa Rita, and the turnoff for Hwy 35 and the Mimbres Valley before cresting the Black Range at Emory Pass, about 40 miles east of Silver City. Beyond the 8228-foot pass, there are good views of the drier Rio Grande country to the east. This is a scenic but slow road with plenty of hairpin bends.

**Kingston** The almost-ghost town of Kingston is a few miles beyond Emory Pass. Once a booming silver mining town with thousands of people, it now has about 30 full-time residents. You can stay here at the *Black Range Lodge* (☎ 895 5652), Star Rt 2, PO Box 119, 88042, which offers B&B accommodations in seven rooms, all with private bath and some with balconies. Rates are $40/50 for singles/doubles, and discounts for multi-night stays are offered.

**Hillsboro** This is another mining town of the late 1800s, about nine miles east of Kingston. Local agriculture revived the town after mining went bust, and today Hillsboro is known for its Apple Festival over Labor Day weekend. Fresh-baked apple pies, street musicians, arts & crafts and antique stalls attract thousands of visitors at this time.

Many of the town's old buildings are still in use and hence are well preserved. You can have a drink or stay in the *S Bar X Motel & Saloon* (☎ 895 5222), which has seven rooms at $24/28 for singles/doubles. The old saloon has been here since 1877 and offers live music on some weekends. Food is served here or in the cafe next door. The more recent *Enchanted Villa B&B* (☎ 895 5686), PO Box 456, 88042, has four rooms with shared bath, plus one with a private bath, for $40 to $60 a double. *Hillsboro General Store and Cafe* serves light meals daily except Tuesday. The *Hillsboro Orchard Bar-B-Q* (☎ 895 5642), at the west end of town, has good food but odd hours.

## SILVER CITY TO RESERVE

Hwy 180 northeast of Silver goes through remote and wild Gila country dotted with a few tiny communities. The Gila National Forest and Mogollon Mountains offer excellent opportunities for backpacking, hiking, camping and fishing.

### Glenwood & Mogollon

The little resort village of Glenwood is 62 miles northwest of Silver. Mogollon is a semi-ghost town, four miles north of Glenwood and then nine miles east on steep and narrow Hwy 159 – expect plenty of switchbacks. Tire chains may be needed on this road in winter.

Information is available from the Southern Catron County chamber of commerce (☎ 539 2721), PO Box 183, Glenwood, 88039. A small Gila National Forest Ranger Station (☎ 539 2481), PO Box 8, 88039, is a half mile south of town.

Hwy 174 goes east from Glenwood passing the **trout hatchery** (☎ 539 2461) after a half mile. Visitors are welcome. The **Catwalk** is 4.5 miles further – here, a trail up narrow Whitewater Canyon hugs the cliff suspended in a wire cage. It's a short but worthwhile hike with some steep spots. There is a USFS picnic area here.

Mogollon, once an important mining town, still has a few people living there,

offering 'antiques', snacks and various services such as licensed massages or hypnotherapy. Many buildings lie deserted and empty – it's a slightly spooky place.

Jim Mater of Gila Wilderness Tours (℅ 539 2424, 1 (800) 887 2453), 10 Catwalk Rd, offers 4WD tours of the area for a full day including lunch ($60 per person, $25 for teenagers, free for kids) or a half day tour for $25, $15 for teenagers. The tours go to Whitewater Canyon, Mogollon and other sites.

**Places to Stay & Eat** The USFS maintains the *Bighorn* campground in Gila National Forest, one mile north of Glenwood, with no drinking water or fee. It is open all year. Their similar *Willow Creek* campground is about 20 miles east of Mogollon and is closed in winter.

In Glenwood, the *Whitewater Motel* (☎ 539 2581) charges $31.50/35 for a single/double with one bed, more with two beds. The *Lariat Motel* (☎ 539 2361) has doubles starting at $32, or $42 for large units with kitchenettes. The best place is the *Los Olmos Guest Ranch* (☎ 539 2311), PO Box 127, Glenwood, 88039, which has a swimming pool, playground and local travel information. The ranch has 13 stone cabins. True to the remote location of the town, none has a telephone or TV (though all have private baths). Rates start at $45/65 for singles/doubles with breakfast, and dinners can be arranged.

Opposite the Lariat Motel is the *Blue Front Bar & Restaurant* (☎ 539 2561), which sells steaks and Mexican food. Near the Whitewater Motel, *Ellie's Country Kitchen* (☎ 539 2242) serves food from 7 am to 8 pm.

### Reserve

Reserve is on Hwy 12, seven miles east of Hwy 180 and 100 miles northwest of Silver. Founded in the 1870s, Reserve now has 600 residents and is the seat of Catron County, which only has some 3000 inhabitants itself, mainly ranchers, cowboys and loggers who particularly loathe federal government interference and environmentalists.

Recently, county officials passed a resolution urging every family to own a gun. This is about as close to the old Wild West as you'll get.

Information is available from the Catron County Chamber of Commerce (☎ 533 6458), PO Box 415, 87830. A Gila National Forest Ranger Station (☎ 533 6231) is in town. In emergencies, dial 911 or the Catron County Sheriff (☎ 533 6622, 533 6222).

The Catron County Fair and Rodeo is held in late August.

**Places to Stay & Eat** The *Rode Inn Motel* (☎ 533 6661) charges $35/40 for singles/doubles. Some rooms have kitchenettes. The slightly cheaper *Kountry Kitchen & Village Motel* (☎ 533 6600) has some RV sites and a cafe. The **Riverbend RV Park** is behind the Black Gold Service Station (☎ 533 6538). *Grandma T's* (☎ 533 6230) serves meals, or head over to *Uncle Bill's Bar* for a beer and burger.

## LORDSBURG & AROUND

Lordsburg was founded in 1880 as a railroad town during the construction of the Southern Pacific Railroad. Today, the small town (population 3000) is a minor ranching center and the seat of empty and arid Hidalgo County. Of particular interest to travelers are the two nearby ghost towns and the surrounding desert.

### Orientation & Information

The main drag through town is Motel Drive, which runs east-west, parallel to and north of I-10.

The chamber of commerce (☎ 542 9864), 208 Motel Drive, is open sporadically. At I-10 exit 20 at the west end of town, the New Mexico Welcome Center (☎ 542 8149) gives statewide information from 8 am to 5 pm daily. The library (☎ 542 9646) is at 208 E 3rd St. The local weekly newspaper is the *Lordsburg Liberal*. The post office (☎ 542 9601) is at 401 Shakespeare. The police (☎ 542 3505, or 911 in emergencies) are in the City Hall at 206 S Main.

### Shakespeare Ghost Town

Dating to 1856, Shakespeare was in turn a military commissary, a stagecoach stop and a boom-and-bust mining town that, at one time, housed nearly 3000 inhabitants – almost as many as Lordsburg today. Since 1935, Shakespeare has belonged to the Hill family, which has preserved several of the old buildings. The town is, therefore, private property, and visitors can enter only with educational and noncommercial guided tours.

Tours run on the second and fourth weekends of each month, as well as the Fourth of July and Labor Day weekends (no tours at Christmas). The 90-minute tours begin at 10 am and 2 pm and visit the interiors of eight buildings. Costs are $3 for adults, and $2 for children six to 12. Private tours can be arranged at other times. Four times a year, shootouts and other reenactments are held – call for details.

Further information is available from Shakespeare Ghost Town (☎ 542 9034), PO Box 253, Lordsburg, 88045. The town is 2.5 miles south of Lordsburg – the route is signed.

### Steins Railroad Ghost Town

Steins dates back to 1858 when it was a stagecoach stop. In 1880 the Southern Pacific Railroad built a depot here, and in the early 20th century, Steins had about 1000 residents. With the advent of diesel trains, Steins lost its importance, and Southern Pacific left in 1958. Many of the buildings were burnt down.

In 1988, Larry and Linda Links purchased the town, and they have been restoring it since. The couple gives guided tours and runs a gift/snack shop. You can walk around outside or ask in the store for a tour of 10 buildings filled with curios. Tours cost $1.50 for those 13 and older. They are open from 9 am to 6 pm daily except Thanksgiving and Christmas. The town is 15 miles west of Lordsburg at I-10 exit 3.

Further information is available from Steins Railroad Ghost Town (☎ 542 9791), PO Box 2185, Roadforks, 88045.

## Special Events

Land Sail Races are held on a dry lake bed six miles west of town at the end of March or beginning of April. Railroad Days, held over Memorial Day weekend, features model railroads, memorabilia and various train-related contests. The County Fair and Rodeo happens in August. Rockamania, held for three weeks in late February and early March, features a gem and mineral show and various related activities.

## Places to Stay – camping

*KOA* (☎ 542 8003), 1501 Lead St, charges $12.50 for tent sites and $17 with full hookups. It has a pool, playground and coin laundry. There are a couple of cheaper RV parks along Motel Drive that have seen better days.

## Places to Stay – bottom end

There are two *Motel 10*s. The one at 624 E Motel Drive (☎ 542 8850) charges $18.95 and up for basic but adequate rooms, while the one at 1202 S Pyramid (☎ 542 8872) has nicer rooms at $25.95 and up. The *Holiday Motel* (☎ 542 3535), 512 E Motel Drive, seems OK for $20.50/26 for singles/doubles. It has a small pool. The *Aloha Friendship Inn*

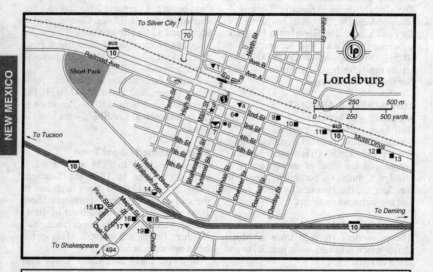

| PLACES TO STAY | | PLACES TO EAT |
|---|---|---|
| 9 | Holiday Motel | 1 | El Charro |
| 10 | Motel 10 | 4 | Soda Shoppe |
| 11 | Aloha Friendship Inn | 17 | Kranberry's |
| 12 | Best Western American Motor Inn | | |
| 13 | Oasis Inn | **OTHER** | |
| 15 | KOA | 2 | Amtrak Station |
| 16 | Best Western Western Skies Inn | 3 | Chamber of Commerce |
| | | 5 | City Hall, Police |
| 18 | Motel 10 | 6 | Coronado Theater |
| 19 | Super 8 Motel | 7 | Post Office |
| | | 8 | Library |
| | | 14 | Greyhound Bus Depot |

(☎ 542 3567), 816 E Motel Drive, is another adequate budget choice. Also try the *Oasis Inn* (☎ 542 9007), 1032 E Motel Drive.

### Places to Stay – middle

The *Super 8 Motel* (☎ 542 8882), 110 E Maple, offers standard rooms for $38.88/41.88 for singles/doubles. The Best Western *American Motor Inn* (☎ 542 3591, fax 542 3572), 944 E Motel Drive, has a pool, playground, lounge and restaurant open from 6:30 am to 9:30 pm. Rates are $39/44 for singles/doubles with one bed, $5 more with two beds, including full breakfast. The Best Western *Western Skies Inn* (☎ 542 8807, fax 542 8895), 1303 S Main, has a pool, and restaurants are close by. It charges $42/49 for singles/doubles, and the rooms are large with two queen-size beds.

### Places to Eat

My favorite is the *El Charro* (☎ 542 3400), 209 Southern Pacific Blvd, which serves tasty and inexpensive Mexican food (American too); it is open 24 hours. *Kranberry's Family Restaurant* (☎ 542 9400), 1401 S Main, serves standard American breakfasts, lunches and dinners.

The *Soda Shoppe* (☎ 542 9142), 330 E Motel Drive, is an old-fashioned soda fountain serving ice cream shakes, sundaes, malts, floats, splits and sodas – a nostalgic treat. You'll find it in the Medicine Shoppe of Lordsburg, built in 1929 on the location of Eagle Drug, itself built in 1889. It is open 9 am to 6 pm, to 8 pm in summer, and is closed on Sundays.

### Entertainment

The *Coronado Theater* (☎ 542 3702) is at 324 E 2nd St. The *Maverick Room* (☎ 542 9927), adjoining the El Charro restaurant, is a good place for a drink with the locals – they throw occasional dances.

### Getting There & Away

**Bus** Greyhound (☎ 542 3412, 1 (800) 231 2222) is at the McDonald's, 1105 S Main. It runs four daily buses westbound and three daily eastbound along I-10.

**Train** Amtrak trains (☎ 1 (800) 872 7245) stop in Lordsburg, just east of the intersection of Main and Motel Drive, on Tuesday, Thursday and Sunday at 4 pm bound for Tucson and Phoenix, Arizona, and Los Angeles, California. Trains for El Paso, Texas, and New Orleans, Louisiana, stop at 2 pm on Monday, Wednesday and Saturday.

### THE SOUTHWEST CORNER

The area south of Lordsburg is known as 'the boot heel' – look at the outline of the state map and you'll see why. The remoteness of this desert country is its own attraction for some people – most of the area is privately owned, so you'll have to do most of your exploring by car. A few tiny communities dot the landscape – Hachitas, Animas and **Rodeo**. This last has a small historic church on the main road. Inside is the **Chiricahua Art Gallery** (☎ 557 2225), open 10 am to 4 pm Monday to Saturday, which exhibits regional artists' work. The only place to stay is the *Rodeo RV Park* (☎ 557 2322), which charges $7.

NEW MEXICO

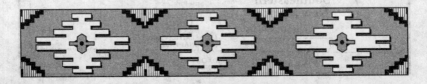

# Southeastern New Mexico

This chapter covers the southern half of New Mexico east of the Rio Grande River Valley. I begin at Carrizozo and travel down the lava fields of the Tularosa Valley area to Alamogordo and the stunning scenery of the world's largest gypsum sand dunes at White Sands National Monument. Then I continue to the Sacramento Mountains east of Alamogordo. The mountains provide a cool contrast to the searing desert sands, and the popular highland resorts of Cloud-croft and Ruidoso are described in detail. Then it's northeast to small historical villages – this is Billy the Kid country.

East of the Sacramento Mountains, the scenery flattens into the desolate tablelands of the *Llano Estacado* (Staked Plains) – no one can remember where the name comes from, though various suggestions are bandied about. Roswell, the largest town in the area and home to a superb museum, is on the western edge of the Llano Estacado.

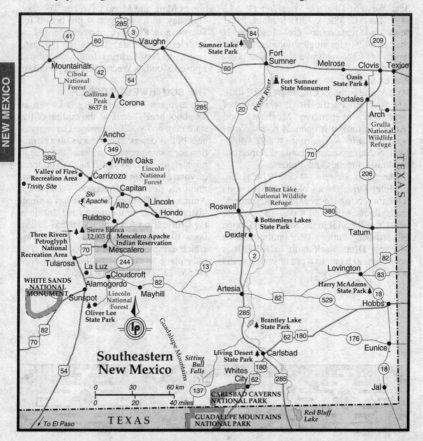

Southeastern
New Mexico

From Roswell, we go south to Carlsbad Caverns National Park, the most magnificent attraction in the area. Then it's northeast, through Hobbs to Clovis, famous as the center of one of the oldest Paleo-Indian cultures on the continent, and the historic Fort Sumner.

## CARRIZOZO

This small crossroads town at Hwys 380 and 54, just west of the Sacramento Mountains and 58 miles north of Alamogordo, has only about 1200 inhabitants but is the present seat of Lincoln County. Established in 1899, it was briefly an important railway town. Carrizozo lies at 5425 feet, surrounded by high desert and with Carrizo Peak (9650 feet) looming about nine miles to the east. While there are places to eat and stay in town, the most interesting sites lie outside town. Several small towns to the north are included in this area.

### Valley of Fires Recreation Area

Four miles to the west, this is the most interesting place to see in the area. At the site of the most recent lava flows in the continental USA, visitors can walk over a flow estimated to be 1500 years old, 47 miles long and up to 160 feet thick. Slowly, pioneering plants and animals have colonized this inhospitable terrain. It is thought-provoking to realize that some of the same lizard, snake and mouse species that exhibit melanism (dark coloration) here, where the lava is black, have adapted light coloration in response to the white gypsum of White Sands.

There is a three-quarter-mile self-guiding nature trail, as well as restrooms, picnic areas and camp sites. Entrance is $3 per vehicle for day use. The area is administered by the BLM(☎ 624 1790), Box 1857, Roswell, 88202.

### Trinity Site

Thirty-five miles west of Carrizozo, Trinity Site is where the first atom bomb was exploded. The test was carried out above ground and resulted in a quarter-mile-wide

crater and an eight-mile-high cloud mushrooming above the desert. This desolate area is fittingly called Jornada del Muerto (Journey of Death) and is overlooked by 8638-foot-high Oscura Peak (Darkness Peak on state maps). If you want to visit the remnants of this devastation (radiation levels are supposedly safe for brief visits), call the White Sands Missile Range (☎ 678 1134) or the Alamogordo Chamber of Commerce (☎ 437 6120). Only two public visits are allowed annually – on the first Saturdays in April and October.

### Places to Stay & Eat

Camping sites are available at Valley of Fires Recreation Area; they cost $6 to $11 for primitive sites to RV sites with hookups.

Most accommodations are clustered around the main highway intersection. The cheapest is the *Carrizozo Inn* (☎ 648 4006), which charges about $22 a single. The *Crossroads Motel* (☎ 648 2373) is about the same. The *Four Winds Motel* (☎ 648 2356) has doubles for $34.

The *Sands Motel & RV Park* (☎ 648 2989), S Hwy 54, is another possibility – though they were up for sale recently. Call ahead.

The *Four Winds Restaurant & Lounge* (☎ 648 2964) is at the intersection and serves meals from 6:30 am to 9:30 pm daily.

### Getting There & Away

TNM&O buses (☎ 648 2964) stop near the Four Winds Restaurant twice daily northbound and twice daily southbound on the Albuquerque to El Paso (Texas) run.

## NORTH OF CARRIZOZO
### White Oaks

This was a gold-mining center in the 1880s; now it's a ghost town with a small population and some interesting old buildings. Don't forget to look at the historic tombstones in the cemetery. Get there on Hwy 349, 11 miles northeast of Carrizozo.

## Ancho

This village is 22 miles north of Carrizozo (2.5 miles east of Hwy 54) and features **My House of Old Things** (☎ 648 2456), a small historical museum housed in eight rooms in the 1902 railway depot. It is open from 9 am to 5 pm daily, May to mid-October; adult admission is $2, and kids get in for 50¢.

## Corona

This village is 47 miles north of Carrizozo on Hwy 54, at the northern boundary of Lincoln County. There is a cheap motel and cafe. A few miles south of Corona, USFS Rd 161 and USFS Rd 144 lead nine and 11 miles respectively to Red Cloud Campground in the Cibola National Forest. This is at 7600 feet on the slopes of isolated **Gallinas Peak** (8637 feet), where there is a lookout. A small elk herd roams the Gallinas Range. The free campground is open from April to October but has no drinking water.

## WHITE SANDS NATIONAL MONUMENT

The white sands are huge dunes of gypsum covering several hundred sq miles. Gypsum is a chalky mineral used in making plaster of Paris and cement; the surrounding mountains contain vast quantities of the stuff. It gets dissolved by snowmelt and rainfall and washed down to Lake Lucero, in the southwest part of the monument. Here, the water evaporates, leaving solid gypsum that is blown northeast in dunes moving as fast as 20 feet per year. The landscape is a dazzling white sea of sand that visitors are encouraged to explore by vehicle or on foot.

Struggling to survive in this otherworldly environment are desert dwellers such as kangaroo mice, snakes and even toads. Some have evolved a lighter color to blend better with the background. Plants have a hard time growing in the shifting sands; a few that manage the trick of holding on include the yucca, the fourwing saltbush and the endearingly named rubber rabbitbush. These botanical acrobats tend to grow near the edges of the dunes – huge areas in the center of the dunes appear devoid of life.

### Information

White Sands National Monument (☎ 479 6124), Box 1086, Holloman Airforce Base, 88330-1086, is 16 miles southwest of Alamogordo. At the entrance there is a visitor center, open 8 am to 7 pm from Memorial Day to Labor Day, and to 4:30 pm the rest of the year. Here you'll find an informative museum, gift and bookshop and refreshments. There are ranger-led activities (talks, walks and audiovisual displays) several times daily in the summer.

From the visitor center, a 16-mile loop road leads into the heart of the dunes. The road is open from 7 am to sunset or till 11 pm on full-moon summer nights. There are many parking areas, and you are encouraged to climb and play in the dunes – but don't get lost! A one-mile loop 'nature trail' leaves from one of the parking areas; a 500-yard trail from another parking area leads to a backcountry campsite. Camping is by free permit only (obtain one from the visitor center), but there is no water – carry your own. There is no developed camping or other overnighting allowed in the monument. Picnic sites are at the end of the road. Rangers lead car tours to Lake Lucero periodically – call the visitor center for dates.

Because of tests at the nearby White Sands Missile Range, the road into the national monument is closed occasionally for a couple of hours – call ahead if your schedule is tight. Entrance fees are $4 per vehicle; Golden Eagle and Golden Age Passes are honored.

### ALAMOGORDO

This pleasant town of about 30,000 inhabitants lies at 4350 feet in the Tularosa Basin, with the Sacramento Mountains looming to the east. It is 207 miles south of Albuquerque and 68 miles northeast of Las Cruces. Alamogordo (Spanish for 'fat cottonwood') is a ranching and agricultural center and the Otero County seat. It is also the center of one of the most historically important space and atomic research programs in the country. The town is the best base from which to visit White Sands National Monument.

## History

Nomadic Indians began living in this area some 7000 years ago. Their descendants were the Jornada Mogollon people – ruins of one of their villages, about 1000 years old, can be seen at the Three Rivers Petroglyph National Recreation Area, 35 miles north of Alamogordo. The Mogollon people left mysteriously around the 13th century, and soon after, the Mescalero Apache settled here and became the dominant inhabitants. The Oliver Lee State Park area, 10 miles south of Alamogordo, was one of the Apache strongholds.

Spanish settlers founded La Luz, a village four miles north of Alamogordo, in 1705. Tularosa, 10 miles further north, was founded in 1863. The Spanish settlers and Apache Indians were constantly skirmishing throughout these years. An 1868 battle at Round Mountain (a few miles east of Tularosa) was one of the last major conflicts in the Alamogordo area. This led to the establishment of the nearby Mescalero Apache Indian Reservation, where many Apache now live.

Founded in 1898, Alamogordo itself was an important railroad town, although there are no longer train services here. The population, only 3000 in 1940, boomed with the development of local military bases, climaxing with the 16 July 1945 test explosion of the world's first atom bomb at Trinity Site. Nearby military sites such as Holloman Air Force Base, White Sands Space Harbor (a space shuttle landing site) and White Sands Missile Range continue to be an economic mainstay in the area.

## Orientation & Information

White Sands Blvd (also called Hwy 54, 70 or 82) is the main drag through town and runs north to south. I abbreviate this important thoroughfare to WSB below. Addresses on North WSB correspond to numbered cross streets (thus 1310 N WSB

is just north of 13th St); addresses from one block south of 1st St are S WSB.

The chamber of commerce (☎ 437 6120), 1301 N WSB, is open from 8:30 to 5 pm daily except Sunday, when hours are noon to 5 pm. The Lincoln National Forest Ranger Station is in the Western-style former Federal Building (☎ 437 6030), at 11th St and New York Ave, and is open from 7:30 am to 4:30 pm, Monday to Friday. The library (☎ 439 4140) is at 10th St and Oregon Ave. The local newspaper is the *Alamogordo Daily News*. The post office (☎ 437 9390) is at 900 Alaska Ave at 9th St. Recycle your cans at Basin Pipe & Metal (☎ 437 6272), just north of the Hwy 82/Hwy 70 intersection. The hospital (☎ 439 2100) is at 1209 9th St. The police (☎ 439 4300, or 911 in emergencies) are at 700 Virginia Ave at 7th St.

## Alameda Park & Zoo

The Alameda Park & Zoo (☎ 439 4290) is east of the chamber of commerce at 1321 N WSB. The zoo was established in 1898 as a diversion for railway travelers – it is the oldest zoo in the state. Small but well run, the zoo features exotics from all over the world, among them the endangered Mexican gray wolf. Hours are 9 am to 5 pm daily; admission is $2 for adults and $1 for both children and seniors. At the north end of the park is a newly established miniature railway exhibit. Call the Toy Train Depot (☎ 437 2855), 1991 N WSB, for more information. There are picnicking facilities in the park.

## Historical Museum

This small museum (☎ 437 6120), 1301 N WSB (next to chamber of commerce), focuses on local history. Hours are 10 am to 4 pm daily except Sunday, when the museum is open 1 to 4 pm. Admission is free.

## Historical Buildings

The historical center of town, east of N WSB along and just off 10th St, has many interesting buildings. Go to the attractive USFS building (formerly the Federal Building) at 11th and New York Sts to see Peter

Hurd's *Sun and Rain* frescoes, painted in the early 1940s as part of the New Deal art program.

### International Space Hall of Fame
This museum (☎ 437 2840, 1 (800) 634 6438 in New Mexico; 1 (800) 545 4021 elsewhere), a four-story-high glass museum nicknamed 'the golden cube', looms over the northeast side of town. Inside are exhibits about space research and flight – a must for anyone interested in the USA's research on the cosmos. The space center is open from 9 am to 5 pm daily (to 6 pm in summer).

Nearby is the **Tombaugh Space Theater**, which has the world's largest projector and shows excellent films, laser shows and multimedia presentations on a huge wraparound screen. Changing shows feature anything from the Grand Canyon to the dark side of the moon – there are several shows a day. Call the Hall of Fame for current showings. Adult admission is $3.75 for the theater, $2.25 for the Space Hall of Fame or $5.25 for both. Children six to 12 years old and seniors receive discounts, as do family groups. There are also special evening shows for $4; these are held daily in the summer and on weekends during the rest of the year.

Around the complex are gardens displaying a variety of rockets and astro-artifacts, including the grave of Ham, the first chimp in space. The center is reached from either Scenic Drive or Indian Wells Rd – there are many signs.

### Activities
Play golf at Desert Lakes Municipal Golf Course (☎ 437 0290), 2351 Hamilton Rd (south of town off Hwy 54); it has 18 holes and is open daily. Call the city Parks & Recreation Office (☎ 439 4142) for other suggestions.

### Places to Stay
There are plenty of motels and hotels stretching out along White Sands Blvd for approximately five miles, beginning in the south with the Holiday Inn and ending in the north with the Super 8 Motel. Don't forget that room tax is an additional 10%.

### Places to Stay – camping
The *KOA* (☎ 437 3003), 412 24th St, has many RV sites and a few tent sites and charges $15.50 for two people, $17.50 with hookups. Cheaper camping is at Oliver Lee State Park, 13 miles south, or Three Rivers, 35 miles north (see below). Both developed and free dispersed camping is available in the Lincoln National Forest – get USFS maps showing forest roads branching off from Hwy 82 east of Alamogordo.

### Places to Stay – Motels & Hotels
**Bottom End** The cheapest place is the *Alamo Inn* (☎ 437 1000), 1450 N WSB, which charges $21/27 and has a pool. The *Ace Motel* (☎ 437 5671), 2615 N WSB, charges $22/25. Both are basic places offering cheaper weekly rates.

For $22/25, the *Townsman Motel* (☎ 437 0210), 710 N WSB, and the *Budget 7 Motel* (☎ 437 9350), 2404 N WSB, are both adequate. A reasonable budget motel is the *Western Motel* (☎ 437 2922), 1101 S WSB, which charges $26/30 for queen-size beds, $3 or $4 more for king-size. The *Motel 6* (☎ 434 5970), 251 Panorama Blvd (behind the Holiday Inn), has a small pool and charges $24/30. The *All American Inn* (☎ 437 1850), 508 S WSB, has a pool, and at rates of $28/30, it's a fair value.

**Middle** The *Satellite Inn* (☎ 437 8454), 2224 N WSB, is a good value at $32/34. The inn is clean and has a pool. The *Super 8 Motel* (☎ 434 4205), 3204 N WSB, looks nice, has a laundry on the premises and charges $29/34, including continental breakfast. The *Days Inn* (☎ 437 5090), 907 S WSB, has a pool, laundry and a restaurant next door. Rooms are a fair value, beginning at $38 for one or two people.

The *Best Western Desert Aire Motor Inn* (☎ 437 2110), 1021 S WSB, is a good hotel, with a pool, spa, sauna, cafe and laundry. Comfortable rooms start at $47/52 including breakfast; you pay a little more for rooms with king-size beds and whirlpools.

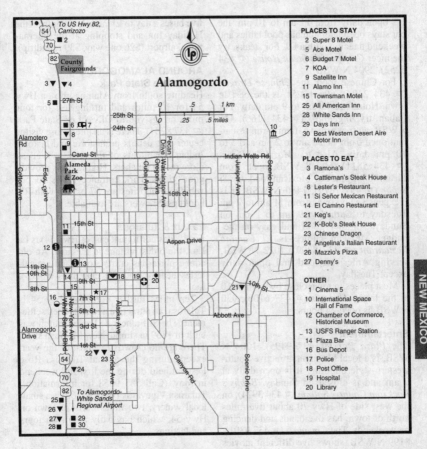

To US Hwy 82, Carrizozo

**Alamogordo**

County Fairgrounds

Alamotero Rd

Alameda Park & Zoo

Eddy Drive

Cotton Ave

Alamogordo Drive

New York Ave
White Sands Blvd

Alaska Ave

Florida Ave

Pecan Drive

Washington Ave

Oregon Ave

Cuba Ave

Juniper Ave

Scenic Drive

Indian Wells Rd

Canyon Rd

Canal St

25th St

24th St

27th St

18th St

Aspen Drive

15th St

13th St

11th St
10th St

9th St

8th St

7th St

5th St

3rd St

1st St

Abbott Ave

To Alamogordo-White Sands Regional Airport

0    .5    1 km

0    .25    .5 miles

**PLACES TO STAY**
2  Super 8 Motel
5  Ace Motel
6  Budget 7 Motel
7  KOA
9  Satellite Inn
11  Alamo Inn
15  Townsman Motel
25  All American Inn
28  White Sands Inn
29  Days Inn
30  Best Western Desert Aire Motor Inn

**PLACES TO EAT**
3  Ramona's
4  Cattleman's Steak House
8  Lester's Restaurant
11  Si Señor Mexican Restaurant
14  El Camino Restaurant
21  Keg's
22  K-Bob's Steak House
23  Chinese Dragon
24  Angelina's Italian Restaurant
26  Mazzio's Pizza
27  Denny's

**OTHER**
1  Cinema 5
10  International Space Hall of Fame
12  Chamber of Commerce, Historical Museum
13  USFS Ranger Station
14  Plaza Bar
16  Bus Depot
17  Police
18  Post Office
19  Hospital
20  Library

**NEW MEXICO**

Senior citizens and AAA members receive discounts. The *White Sands Inn* (☎ 434 4200, 1 (800) 255 5061), 1020 S WSB, is Alamogordo's newest motel and has prices and services comparable to the Desert Aire.

The *Holiday Inn* (☎ 437 7100), 1401 S WSB, is considered the best in town. It features a pool with a children's wading area, a laundry, a restaurant and a lounge bar. Rates begin at $70/78. AAA and senior discounts are available.

### Places to Eat

A good choice is *Ramona's* (☎ 437 7616), 2913 N WSB, open from 6 am to 10 pm

daily. It's locally popular for breakfasts (around $3 to $5) and has good homemade salsa to accompany the Mexican lunches and dinners (all under $10). Chimichangas are their specialty, but they serve American food too. Beer and wine is available. Another locally popular choice is *Lester's Restaurant* (☎ 434 3900), 2300 N WSB, which specializes in pancakes for breakfast. Steak, seafood, and Mexican food is served for lunch and dinner.

For lunches and dinners, *Keg's* (☎ 437 9564), 817 Scenic Drive, has a '60s decor and mainly American food (sandwiches, burgers and steaks) at reasonable prices.

It's open daily from 11 am to 10 pm; the bar stays open later and has pool tables and weekend dancing with a DJ. For steaks, try the nicer *Cattleman's Steak House* (☎ 434 5252), 2904 N WSB.

For Chinese food, the *Chinese Dragon* (☎ 434 2494), 606 1st St, is the best in town. Hours are 11 am to 9 pm daily. For Italian, try *Angelina's* (☎ 434 1166), 415 S WSB, an inexpensive, family-run restaurant open from 11:30 am to 2 pm and 5 to 10 pm daily. Also try *Mazzio's Pizza*, (☎ 434 5811), 600 S WSB, open from 11 am to 10 pm. For Mexican food, try *Si Señor* (☎ 437 7879), 1480 N WSB. It is inexpensive and open from 11 am to 9 pm Tuesday to Saturday, 9 am to 2 pm on Sunday. Another good and easy-on-the-budget Mexican choice is *El Camino Restaurant* (☎ 437 8809), 1022 N WSB, serving American food and open daily except Tuesday.

Most places in town close by 9 pm or 10 at the latest. *Denny's* (☎ 437 6106), 930 S WSB, is open 24 hours.

### Entertainment

The *Plaza Bar* (☎ 437 9495), 1004 N WSB, is a local bar in an attractive Southwestern-style building. It is open daily at 9 am and is closed on Sunday. *Bubby's Rock and Country Saloon* (☎ 434 3924), on the west side of Hwy 70 about five miles north of town, has live bands and dancing on weekends. The *Cinema 5* (☎ 437 9301), 3199 N WSB, shows five different movies daily.

### Getting There & Away

The White Sands Airport (☎ 437 9111) has four daily flights to Albuquerque with Mesa Airlines (☎ 1 (800) 637 2247) for $119 one-way and two flights daily to Las Cruces. Advance-purchase roundtrips are cheaper. Several car rental companies have offices at the airport and along WSB.

The TNM&O Bus Station (☎ 437 3050/1) is at 601 N WSB. There are several buses each day to Albuquerque, Roswell and El Paso, Texas. The fare to El Paso is $18. The El Paso Shuttle (☎ 437 1472) has

five buses a day to El Paso, leaving from the Holiday Inn and stopping at the international airport ($26 one way, $39 roundtrip).

## AROUND ALAMOGORDO
### Oliver Lee State Park

Heading south from Alamogordo on Hwy 54 for 10 miles and turning left for four miles brings you to Oliver Lee State Park (☎ 437 8284). There is an interesting visitor center that details prehistoric and historic Indian inhabitants of the area, as well as more recent ranchers. Hiking trails provide good views. Park entrance fee is $3 per vehicle. Campsites are $7 or $11 with RV hookups. Showers are available.

### La Luz & Tularosa

Four miles north (just east of Hwy 54) is La Luz, the oldest village in the area. An old adobe plaza has crafts stores and art galleries nearby, and the church is worth a look.

Ten miles further north on Hwy 54 is Tularosa, an attractive and unspoiled settlement. The St Francis de Paula Church was built in 1869 in simple New Mexican style. There are no crowds for most of the year, except during the annual Tularosa Rose Festival held during the first full weekend in May. (Call 585 9858 for information.) Tularosa Vineyards (☎ 585 2260) is a small local winery, two miles north of town on Hwy 54, which has daily afternoon tours and tastings.

### Three Rivers Petroglyph National Recreation Area

Continue north for 17 more miles on Hwy 54 and turn right for five miles to get to the Three Rivers Petroglyph National Recreation Area. A rough trail winds for almost a mile through a rocky outcrop where, about 1000 years ago, the Jornada Mogollon people inscribed some 20,000 carvings into the boulders. The elevated site gives good views of mountains to the east and the White Sands Monument glistening on the western horizon. Nearby is a pit house in a partially excavated village. The site is not as spectacular as other Southwestern ruins,

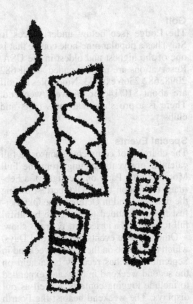

but it is quiet, uncrowded and worthwhile. There are six picnicking areas, water and restrooms. Overnight camping is allowed at no charge. There is no ranger station; call the Bureau of Land Management in Las Cruces (☎ 525 4300) for further information or to report vandalism or other problems. A dirt road continues about 10 miles beyond the petroglyph area to the Lincoln National Forest, where there is the Three Rivers Campground and trailhead.

## CLOUDCROFT

As you head east from Alamogordo on Hwy 82, you pass a road sign warning drivers to check brakes and gears because the road climbs 4315 feet in the next 16 miles. Cloudcroft is at a cool 9000 feet and provides welcome relief from the heat of the lowlands to the east. It is a village of about 650 people, many of whom work in tourism-related jobs.

Cloudcroft was founded in 1898 as a railroad town and, because of its cool elevation, soon became a vacation center for railroad employees. The railroad is long gone, but the vacationers remain. There are a few historic buildings from the turn of the century (walking around downtown is a little like walking onto a Western movie set), and the town has several gift shops, galleries and a cafe. The main attractions, however, are skiing in the winter and hiking and camping in the cool pine forests during the summer. Hunting is popular in the fall, as are tours to see the pretty fall colors. High up in the Sacramento Mountains, you may find yourself forgetting that you are in the US Southwest.

## Orientation & Information

Hwy 82 is the main drag through town, and most places are on this road or within a block or two of it.

The chamber of commerce (☎ 682 2733), Box 125, 88317, is on Hwy 82 and provides excellent tourist information. Summer hours are from 10 am to 5 pm daily except Sunday, when hours are 11 am to 3 pm. The Lincoln National Forest Cloudcroft Ranger Station (☎ 682 2551), Box 288, 88317, is on the southwest corner of Hwy 82 and Curlew Place. The post office (☎ 682 2431) is at 20 Curlew Place, just north of Hwy 82. The nearest hospital is in Alamogordo. In an emergency, call the Cloudcroft police (☎ 911 or (505) 682 2101). There is no public transport to Cloudcroft.

## Historic Buildings

Early Western architecture lines the west end of Burro Ave, where you will find the old wooden **First Baptist Church**. Cloudcroft's oldest church is the **Episcopal Church of the Ascension**, built around 1910 on the corner of Curlew Place and Chipmunk Ave. It is worth seeing this tiny log-cabin building that can only be described as cute.

## Sacramento Mountains Historical Museum

This museum (☎ 682 2932), on Hwy 82 opposite the chamber of commerce, displays turn-of-the-century buildings, farm equipment, household items and railroad memorabilia. Summer hours are 10 am to

4 pm Tuesday to Saturday, and 1 to 4 pm on Sunday. During the winter it is closed from Tuesday to Thursday. Admission is $1.

### Hiking

Hiking is one of the main summer activities, with outings ranging from short hikes close to town to overnight backpacking trips. Trails are open from April to November, though spring thaw and fall rain and snow can make them very muddy. Trails are snow-covered the rest of the year. Both the chamber of commerce and the USFS can provide descriptions of hikes and/or maps. Although trails are often fairly flat and easy, the 9000-foot elevation can make hiking strenuous if you are not acclimatized. The most popular easy hike is the 2.6-mile Osha Loop Trail, which leaves Hwy 82 from a small parking area opposite the old railroad trestle, one mile west of Cloudcroft.

### Skiing

This is the area's most popular winter sport. The newly renovated Snow Canyon Ski Area (☎ 682 2333, 1 (800) 333 7542), about two miles east of town on Hwy 82, is open from 8 am to 4 pm daily from mid-November to March. There are 25 runs designed mostly for beginning and intermediate skiers, so this is a suitable destination for the whole family. Lift tickets are $25/16 for adults/children (under 12). There are ski-rental packages (available for $12), lessons, a ski shop and a restaurant.

The golf course behind The Lodge (see Places to Stay) becomes a groomed cross-country skiing area in winter (☎ 682 2098, 682 2566 ext 373). Trail passes are $4, and ski rentals are $12. The Lodge also provides guided snowmobiling with rates beginning at $30/45 for singles/doubles per hour. Old-fashioned horse-drawn sleigh rides are also available from The Lodge; the price of a 30-minute ride for four people is $50.

Triple M's Snowplay Area (☎ 682 2205) is 4.5 miles south of Cloudcroft on the way to Sunspot. The area has snowmobile rentals, an ice-skating pond and skate rentals and slopes for inner-tubing.

### Golf

The Lodge (see below under Places to Stay) has a popular nine-hole course that is one of the highest and oldest in the USA. Reservations are recommended – call 682 2098, 682 2566 ext 373. Nine holes of golf are about $10/14 for midweek/weekend. There is a pro shop that rents carts and clubs.

### Special Events

The chamber of commerce sponsors a full calendar of events ranging from the Full Moon Skating Party on the night of a February full moon to an Oktoberfest during the first weekend in October. The Oktoberfest features guided tours of the beautiful fall foliage and a juried arts & crafts show.

Other notable events are Railroad Days, which used to be on the second weekend in September but has recently been held on the second weekend in May and expanded to include logging contests as well as rail displays. The weekend nearest the Fourth of July features the July Jamboree with arts & crafts, street dancing, food booths and cookouts and horseshoe pitching contests but no fireworks.

Cherries are produced in nearby High Rolls (between Cloudcroft and Alamogordo), and there is an annual Cherry Festival with cherry desserts being the major enticement. This is held on the third Sunday of June (Fathers' Day).

All these events and many others are free – call the chamber of commerce for a calendar. The center for most of these events is Zenith Park on Hwy 82.

### Places to Stay – camping

*Swallow Place RV Park* (☎ 682 6014) is at 104 Swallow Place, near downtown. It is a small place for RVs only. They have full hookups. A larger and more developed place is *Sugar Pines RV Park* at the southeast end of town. RV sites with hookups are about $14. Five miles north of town on Hwy 244 is the *Silver Springs RV Park* (☎ 682 2803), also with full hookups.

The Forest Service (☎ 682 2551) has several tent/RV campgrounds along Hwy

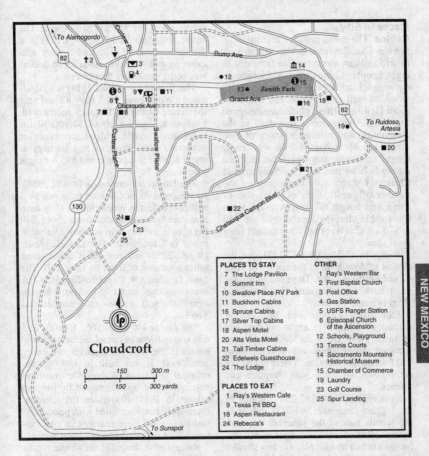

**Cloudcroft**

0    150    300 m
0    150    300 yards

**PLACES TO STAY**
7   The Lodge Pavilion
8   Summit Inn
10  Swallow Place RV Park
11  Buckhorn Cabins
16  Spruce Cabins
17  Silver Top Cabins
18  Aspen Motel
20  Alta Vista Motel
21  Tall Timber Cabins
22  Edelweis Guesthouse
24  The Lodge

**PLACES TO EAT**
1   Ray's Western Cafe
9   Texas Pit BBQ
18  Aspen Restaurant
24  Rebecca's

**OTHER**
1   Ray's Western Bar
2   First Baptist Church
3   Post Office
4   Gas Station
5   USFS Ranger Station
6   Episcopal Church
    of the Ascension
12  Schools, Playground
13  Tennis Courts
14  Sacramento Mountains
    Historical Museum
15  Chamber of Commerce
19  Laundry
23  Golf Course
25  Spur Landing

**NEW MEXICO**

244 to Ruidoso. Because of the elevation, all USFS campgrounds are open summer only (mid-May to mid-September). A half mile north from the intersection with Hwy 82, just east of Cloudcroft, you come to *The Pines*. Sites are $6; there is water but no showers. About 1.4 miles further north along Hwy 244 is the turnoff to USFS *Silver*, *Saddle* and *Apache* campgrounds, with sites for $7 a night. (Silver has good flat sites well suited to RVs.) Hot showers are available for $3 at the Silver area.

About a mile southeast of town on Hwy 130 is the USFS *Deerhead* campground

with $6 sites. There are also several campgrounds available for groups by reservation only. Free dispersed camping is also available.

The James Canyon National Forest Campground, which doesn't have water and is free, is 16 miles east of Cloudcroft and two miles west of the small village of Mayhill.

The *Rio Penasco RV Park* (☎ 687 3715) is in Mayhill, at the junction of Hwy 82 and 130. Mayhill has not much more than a store, gas station and 'the last bar for 72 miles'.

## Places to Stay

**Cabins** The most popular accommodations in Cloudcroft are cabins, which vary in size and can accommodate from one to eight people. Cabins usually include an equipped kitchen and a fireplace with wood, as well as the usual bed and bathroom facilities. These places are designed for families spending a few days in the mountains, and minimum stays of two nights are often required on weekends; longer minimum stays may be required during holiday periods, especially around Christmas. Rates vary depending on the number of guests, time of year, size of cabin and length of stay. Average rates for a cabin sleeping four people are $50 to $70 a night. Weekend reservations are a good idea.

*Buckhorn Cabins* (☎ 682 2421) are the closest to downtown at the corner of Hwy 82 and Swallow Place. There are 16 rooms; most have a kitchen and fireplace, and sleep two to eight people.

*Pine Crest Cabins* and *Tall Timber Cabins* (☎ 682 2301) are at the east end of town away from the main highway. Between them, there are seven cabins and four duplex units, each sleeping five or six people. All come with fireplace and kitchen.

*Spruce Cabins* (☎ 682 2381) is one of the biggest complexes, with 32 cabins in the woods behind the chamber of commerce. Most cabins sleep four or six and have a kitchen and fireplace; a few smaller units for two people are available, with a choice of kitchen or fireplace. Behind this complex is *Silver Top Cabins* (☎ 682 2396). These cabins have a fireplace and one, two or four bedrooms.

*Barn Door Cabins & RV Park* (☎ 687 2124) is to the east of Cloudcroft on Hwy 82, four miles before you reach the small village of Mayhill. Cabins with a fireplace are $35 for two people. There is a restaurant nearby (☎ 687 3662).

**Hotels** The *Aspen Motel & Restaurant* (☎ 682 2526) is a clean and simple motel at the east end of town on Hwy 82. It has 19 rooms going for $50 for two people. The small *Alta Vista Motel* (☎ 682 2221) is at the far east end of town and has six spacious rooms. All have one or more queen-size beds; some have fireplaces.

The *Summit Inn* (☎ 682 2814) is well situated a block away from Hwy 82 and near the center of things. Pleasant rooms with kitchenettes go for about $40/60/90 for two/four/six people. It also has cottages (or duplexes) with fireplaces and kitchens at about $75 for five people and $95 for eight people.

The *Edelweis Guesthouse* (☎ 682 2958), on the outskirts of Cloudcroft, is run by a realtor couple, the Wuerschings. They have a mobile home available from about $40 per couple and can help you buy a vacation home in Cloudcroft. The *Las Banderas* (☎ 682 2952) is a new B&B about seven miles southeast of town on Hwy 130. The *Spur Landing* (☎ 1 (800) 426 3365) has luxurious one- and two-bedroom houses next to the golf course – rates start around $100.

*The Lodge* (☎ 682 2566, 1 (800) 395 6343) stands out as one of the best historic hotels in the state and, indeed, the entire Southwest. It was built in 1899 as the original vacation lodge for railroad employees – it was destroyed by fire and rebuilt in 1911. Rooms in the antique, three-story hotel are filled with period furnishings; a 4th floor features an observatory with a copper dome and great views.

Rates start at about $75 for simple rooms with country decor and a double bed, or $85 for queen beds and antiques. A variety of suites for four go for $100 and up. The Honeymoon Suite (mirror-topped bed, whirlpool, champagne and antiques) and the Governor's Suite (the most elegant, where the rich and famous stay) go for about $185. There is also the Retreat, a four-bedroom mountain home for $295 (housing four people) and the *Lodge Pavilion*, an 11 room B&B in a restored building close to downtown, where rustic rooms go from $59 to $109.

The Lodge has a pool, sauna, hot tub and a nine-hole golf course.

## Places to Eat

Many people stay in places with kitchens, and there aren't many restaurants. *Ray's Western Cafe* (☎ 682 2817) at the west end of Burro Ave is a smoky, rustic, friendly and locally popular little place that is open for breakfast, lunch and dinner every day. Food is inexpensive. The *Texas Pit BBQ* (☎ 682 2307), on Hwy 82 near Swallow Place, caters to the many Texan visitors. Expect meaty dinners here. The *Aspen Motel* has a reasonable restaurant.

By far the best (and most expensive) food is served at the historic *Rebecca's* (☎ 682 3131) in The Lodge. The restaurant is named after a beautiful chambermaid who died in a lovers' dispute in the 1930s; her ghost supposedly haunts The Lodge. Daily dining is from 7 am to 10 pm (closed from 2 to 5 pm), and there is a Sunday brunch. Rebecca's features an outside deck and attractive mountain views; inside there is often piano or other entertainment. Dining is continental, and dinner entrees run from about $12 to $25 – reservations are recommended. Lunches are substantially cheaper.

## Entertainment

The *Red Dog Saloon* in The Lodge is great for a drink; hours are 5 to 12 pm Wednesday to Saturday, and it has live weekend entertainment. There is also *Ray's Western Bar* (☎ 682 9910) next to Ray's Cafe.

## AROUND CLOUDCROFT
### Sacramento Peak & Apache Point Observatories

One of the world's largest solar observatories is in Sunspot, 20 miles south of Cloudcroft. Take Hwy 130 for two miles and then follow paved USFS Rd 64 to the Sacramento Peak Observatory (☎ 434 7000). Guided tours are given on Saturdays, and self-guided tours are available during the rest of the week in summer. The Apache Point Observatory is also here. The drive to Sunspot is a high and scenic one, with the mountains to the east and White Sands National Monument visible to the west.

## MESCALERO APACHE INDIAN RESERVATION

The Apache were a nomadic people who arrived in this area about 800 years ago and soon became the enemies of the local Pueblo Indians. This enmity was exacerbated by the arrival of the Europeans. The Apaches, under pressure from European settlement and with their mobility greatly increased by the introduction of the horse, became some of the most feared raiders of the West. Many of the descendants of Geronimo, the most famous of the Apache warrior leaders, live in Mescalero.

Today, about 3000 Native Americans live on the 719-sq-mile reservation, which lies in attractive country south and west of Ruidoso. Despite the name of the reservation, the Apaches here are of three tribes: the Mescalero, the Chiricahua and the Lipan. Residents make a living from logging, ranching and tourism. The Ski Apache resort, lying just outside the reservation, is managed by the tribe.

NEW MEXICO

Apache leader Geronimo

## Information

The Tribal Council (☎ 671 4494/95), 106 Central, Box 176, Mescalero, 88340, is the best information source. The Tribal Museum is also here. Hours are 8:00 am to 4:30 pm Monday to Friday. Call for information about dancing and other cultural demonstrations. The village of Mescalero is 17 miles southwest of Ruidoso on Hwy 70.

## Special Events

The annual Apache Maiden's Puberty Ceremony takes place around the first weekend in July and attracts Indians and non-Indians. The traditional rites are held in Mescalero; photography is prohibited, and you should check with the tribal council about what you can actually see. Apart from the sacred rites of the Puberty Ceremony, there is a powwow, a rodeo, and arts & crafts demonstrations to which the public is welcome.

Dancing by other Indian tribes often takes place in Ruidoso on the Fourth of July, and photography is allowed there.

## The Inn of the Mountain Gods

This Apache-owned and operated conference center and resort is the most luxurious place to stay in southern New Mexico. Almost every imaginable activity is offered – for a price. Golf, tennis, swimming, fishing, hunting, boating, horseback riding, bicycling, shooting, archery, skiing, lawn games and a children's playground. Indoors, guests find more swimming and tennis, saunas and whirlpools, gambling (poker and bingo), a fine restaurant and a lounge serving alcohol, with live entertainment and dancing.

Large guest rooms, most with either balconies or patios and with great views, rent for a surprisingly modest $120 during the Memorial Day to Labor Day summer season. Rates are substantially less the rest of the year. An 18-hole round of golf costs $30; a fishing permit is $8; guided hunting trips cost several hundred dollars. Package deals are available for skiing, hunting, tennis and golf. Call the Inn (☎ 257 5141, 1 (800) 545 9011) for details or write

Box 269, Mescalero, 88340. The Inn is about three miles southwest of Ruidoso on Carrizo Canyon Rd.

If you are staying in Ruidoso, you are welcome to visit the inn to admire and use the facilities.

## RUIDOSO

This resort town of almost 5000 inhabitants lies at 6900 feet in the Sacramento Mountains. Its pleasant climate and forested surroundings attract people escaping the summer heat of Alamogordo, 46 miles to the southwest, and Roswell, 71 miles to the east, as well as many visitors from Texas.

During the summer, camping, hiking, horseback riding and fishing are the attractions. From early May to early September, the racetrack in nearby Ruidoso Downs has top-notch horseracing. During winter, the excellent Ski Apache resort attracts skiers from afar. Nearby is the Mescalero Apache Indian Reservation. Ruidoso capitalizes on these attractions; there are plenty of places to stay, many restaurants and gift stores – yet somehow the town manages to avoid the air of being a tourist trap.

## Orientation & Information

Ruidoso is a very spread-out town, with vacation homes tucked away on streets sprawling into the surrounding mountains. Hwy 48 from the north is the main drag through town. This is called Mechem Drive until it hits the small downtown area; then it becomes Sudderth Drive heading east to the Y-intersection with Hwy 70. Heading north for six miles on Mechem Drive brings you to the community of Alto, where more accommodations are available. The community of Ruidoso Downs (named after its racetrack) is actually a separate village just east of Ruidoso on Hwy 70. Both Ruidoso Downs and Alto are included under this Ruidoso section.

Tourist information is available at the chamber of commerce (☎ 257 7395, 1 (800) 253 2255), Box 698, 88345. It is at 720 Sudderth Drive. Summer hours are from 8:30 am to 5 pm Tuesday to Friday, from 9 am to 5 pm on Monday and Saturday, and 1 to 4 pm on Sunday. (On a recent visit I noted that the previous 15 people to have signed the guest book were from Texas – obviously Ruidoso is very popular with Texans.)

The Lincoln National Forest Smokey Bear Ranger Station (☎ 257 4095) is at 901 Mechem Drive, 88345. The library (☎ 257 4335) is at 501 Sudderth Drive. The post office (☎ 257 7120) is at 2959 Sudderth Drive. The Medical Center & Hospital (☎ 257 7381) is at 211 Sudderth Drive. The police (☎ 257 7365, or 911 in an emergency) are at 421 Wingfield St.

### Ruidoso Downs Racetrack

The Ruidoso Downs Racetrack (☎ 378 4431, 378 4140) is on Hwy 70 about 4.5 miles east of downtown Ruidoso. Ruidoso Downs is one of the major racetracks in the Southwest and operates from early May to early September Thursday to Sunday (and Monday on holidays). The All American Futurity is held at the end of the season on Labor Day – this is the world's richest quarter-horse race and is worth about $2.5 million. Post time is 1:15 pm on weekends and later on weekdays (call to confirm). General admission is free, parking is $3, and grandstand seats and boxes are available for $3.50 and up. Out of season, pari-mutuel betting is available for races across the USA, which are broadcast live to the sports theater. Good luck!

The **Museum of the Horse** (☎ 378 4142) is at the east end of the Ruidoso Downs Racetrack. The museum opened in 1992 under the auspices of the Hubbard Art Museum (also by the track) and has a fine display of over 10,000 horse-related items – anything from ancient Greek statues through Wild West stagecoaches to modern art. Artists such as Frederic Remington and Charles M Russell are featured. Hours are 9 am to 5:30 pm daily (though they may shorten off-season), and admission is $4 for adults, $2.50 for children.

### Skiing

The best ski area south of Albuquerque is **Ski Apache** (☎ 336 4356, 336 4565,

snow conditions 257 9001). It is 18 miles northwest of Ruidoso and is open daily from 8:45 am to 4 pm, late November to Easter. The Ski Shuttle (☎ 378 4456) will pick you up from any spot on Sudderth Drive or Mechem Drive if you call before 7:30 am.

Ski Apache is in the Lincoln National Forest and is operated by the Mescalero Apache Tribe. There are 50 runs between 9600 and 11,500 feet on the slopes of beautiful Sierra Blanca Peak (11,973 feet), the highest mountain in southern New Mexico. Novice runs comprise 25% of the mountain, intermediate 30% and advanced 45%; ski rental, instruction and several snack bars are available. With the state's only four-passenger gondola, plus eight chair lifts and a surface lift, there is a capacity for a stunning 15,300 skiers per hour, which means short lift lines. All-day passes are $35 for adults, or $22 for children 12 and under. There are many ski rental stores open on Mechem and Sudderth – shop around for the best deals.

### Hiking

Hiking is a popular summertime activity, with the 4.6-mile day hike from the Ski Apache area to the summit of Sierra Blanca Peak being especially popular. The summit, which lies within the Mescalero Apache Reservation, is over 2,000 feet higher than the Ski Apache parking lot and can only be reached by foot. Take Trail 15 from the small parking area just before the main lot, and follow signs west and south via trails 25 and 78 to Lookout Mountain (11,580 feet). From there an unnamed but obvious trail continues due south for 1.25 miles to Sierra Blanca Peak, which is marked as 11,973 feet on some maps and 12,003 on others.

Also from Ski Apache you can hike to Monjeau Lookout, 5.6 miles away. Begin with Trail 15 and then take Trail 25 (the Crest Trail) north until you reach USFS Rd 117 – the lookout is less than a mile away. The Crest Trail offers superb views and some sheltered camping areas (carry water). The ranger station in Ruidoso can supply maps and information for more adventurous trips.

## Other Activities
If you're looking for great views without a lot of exercise, try touring Sierra Blanca Peak during the non-skiing season. The peak offers several lookouts with stunning views – just drive up Ski Area Rd (532) from Alto. Along this road, you'll see signs for the Monjeau Lookout on USFS Rd 117, which also offers exceptional views to motorists.

**Horseback riding** is another option. Grindstone Stables (☎ 257 2241) on Grindstone Resort Drive near downtown has horses for rent, as does Buddie's Stable (☎ 258 4027), 707 Gavilan Canyon Rd.

For something completely different, try a **gold panning** tour offered by Lincoln County Gold Mining Company (☎ 257 4070), which has gold claims north of Alto.

**Fishing** is popular in season. The Rio Ruidoso runs through town and offers some good fishing opportunities, as do several lakes in the national forest.

You can play **golf** at Cree Meadows (☎ 257 5815), 301 Country Club Drive, Ruidoso's oldest golf course. The new links at the Sierra Blanca course (☎ 258 5330, 1 (800) 854 6571) opened in 1991 and has already gained a reputation as the best course in southern New Mexico. Reservations are recommended.

Go **swimming** at the town pool (☎ 257 2795), which features a water slide and is next to the library on Sudderth Drive.

## Special Events
The annual Ruidoso Art Festival, held during the last full weekend in July, attracts several hundred entrants, of whom only about 25% are selected. This is a top-quality juried event attended by thousands of browsing and buying visitors from all over the Southwest and beyond. There is a $3 admission.

The Aspenfest in the first weekend in October has a chili cook-off, a street festival and arts & crafts, all among the glorious colors of early fall. The fun continues with the Oktoberfest during the third weekend. This has a strong Bavarian theme with German food, beer and wine as well as professional polka and other dancing, oompah bands and public revelry. Admission is $5. The chamber of commerce has dates of other events.

## Places to Stay
There are many places catering to most budgets, though cheaper accommodation is the most limited. Travelers on a budget should avoid racing and holiday weekends, as well as weekends in the ski season, when even the cheaper hotels raise their prices by $5 or more. Reservations are recommended for these weekends if you want your choice of places to stay. Alternatively, form a group and rent a cabin or condo. The lowest rates are from after the Oktoberfest until Thanksgiving and from Easter to early May – when there isn't much going on.

## Places to Stay – camping
Commercial campgrounds in Ruidoso include *Blue Spruce RV Park* (☎ 257 7993), 302 Mechem Drive, where RV sites with hookups are $15. Another RV park is *Tall Pines* (☎ 257 5233), 1800 Sudderth Drive. The *River Ranch Campground* (☎ 378 4245), northeast of Ruidoso on Hwy 70, has RV sites with hookups for $19.50 and tent sites for $11.50. The *Circle B Campground* (☎ 378 4990), 2.5 miles northeast of Ruidoso Downs on Hwy 70, offers tent and RV sites with hookups for about $15. In Alto, the *Bonita Hollow Campground* (☎ 336 4325), is and has RV sites with hookups for $13.50 and tent sites for $9. All these places have showers available.

The Lincoln National Forest (☎ 257 4095) operates several campgrounds north of Ruidoso. All are open from May to September, and none have showers. *South Fork Campground* is near Bonito Lake and has fishing, hiking trails and drinking water. Take Hwy 48 11 miles north of Ruidoso, and turn left on USFS Rd 107 for five miles. There is a $6 fee.

The *Oak Grove*, *Skyline* and *Monjeau*

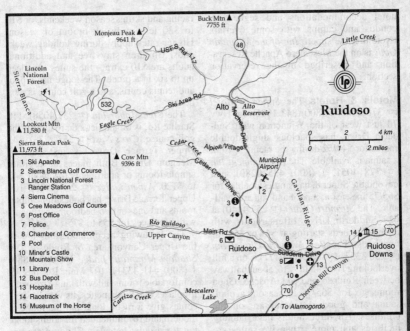

| 1 | Ski Apache |
| 2 | Sierra Blanca Golf Course |
| 3 | Lincoln National Forest Ranger Station |
| 4 | Sierra Cinema |
| 5 | Cree Meadows Golf Course |
| 6 | Post Office |
| 7 | Police |
| 8 | Chamber of Commerce |
| 9 | Pool |
| 10 | Miner's Castle Mountain Show |
| 11 | Library |
| 12 | Bus Depot |
| 13 | Hospital |
| 14 | Racetrack |
| 15 | Museum of the Horse |

NEW MEXICO

*Campgrounds* all have pit toilets but no drinking water nor fee (though this may change). Oak Grove is five miles west of Alto on the Ski Area Rd. Skyline is four miles along USFS Rd 117, which heads north one mile along Ski Area Rd. A mile beyond is the Monjeau Campground with four sites. These last three campgrounds are at 9000 feet or higher, so be prepared for cold camping. RVs longer than 16 feet are not recommended. Free dispersed camping is also allowed.

### Places to Stay – bottom end
The *Villa Inn Motel* (☎ 378 4471, 1 (800) 447 8455) is one of the better budget hotels. It is on Hwy 70 just west of the Y-junction with Sudderth Drive. It has 60 rooms beginning at $30/35 for a single/ double midweek, higher on weekends. Also good is the smaller *Apache Motel* (☎ 257 2986, 1 (800) 426 0616) at 344 Sudderth Drive, which has rooms ranging from about $32 and up for doubles – some

rooms have king-size beds or kitchenettes. The similarly priced *Pines Motel* (☎ 257 4334), 620 Sudderth Drive, is nicely situated by the river.

Another good budget choice is the *Innsbruck Lodge* (☎ 257 4071), 601 Sudderth Drive, with 42 rooms starting at $32. Also along Sudderth Drive, you'll find other reasonably priced places, such as: *Winners Inn Motel* (☎ 257 5886); *Alpine Lodge* (☎ 257 4423); *Stagecoach Motel* (☎ 257 2610); *Tomahawk Lodge* (☎ 257 4078); *The Holiday House* (☎ 257 4003); and *Twenty Nine Pines Hotel* (☎ 257 3204).

Other cheap places include the Economy Motel (☎ 378 4706), on Hwy 70 in Ruidoso Downs and Arrowhead Motel (☎ 257 4241), on Hwy 70 at the west end of town.

### Places to Stay – middle to top end
Many of the establishments below have a variety of units ranging from simple rooms to comfortable suites, all on the same premises. Descriptions begin with motel/

hotel accommodations and segue into condos and cabins with some overlap. (Note that the superb *Inn of the Mountain Gods* is on the Mescalero Apache Reservation and described in the reservation section.)

**Motels & Hotels** The *Super 8 Motel* (☎ 378 8180, 1 (800) 843 1991), on Hwy 70 just west of the Y-junction with Sudderth Drive, has spacious single/double rooms for $44/52 during the racing season; a sauna is available. The *Enchantment Inn* (☎ 378 4051, 1 (800) 435 0280), just beyond the Super 8, has singles/doubles for $65/75 in season; a pool and spa are available. The *Sitzmart Chalet* (☎ 257 4140) at 627 Sudderth Drive, offers rooms with queen-size beds starting at $41 or $54 for two beds. The *Best Western Chalet Inn* (☎ 258 3333, 1 (800) 477 9477) is on a hill overlooking Hwy 48 in Alto, about halfway between Ruidoso and Ski Apache. Good rooms go for $65/75 in season; a pool, sauna and good restaurant are on the premises. All three hotels have laundry facilities and more expensive suites are available. They drop their prices out of season.

The *Carrizo Lodge* (☎ 257 9131, 1 (800) 227 1224), on Carrizo Canyon Rd in the forest south of town, is in a building constructed in 1874. This historic hotel has long been an art center; it continues to host art schools and features a Southwestern art gallery. A pool, sauna, fitness center, restaurant and lounge are on the premises. Rooms begin at about $59; modern condos with fireplaces are more expensive.

The *Inn at Pine Springs Canyon* (☎ 378 8100, 1 (800) 237 3607) is on Hwy 70 on a hill opposite the racetrack – you can walk to the races. It has large rooms, attractive grounds and a spa. Rates are $70/80 in season and include continental breakfast; rates drop $20 out of season.

The *Village Lodge* (☎ 258 5442, 1 (800) 722 8779), 1000 Mechem Drive, has modern suites with king-size beds, kitchenettes, and living rooms with fireplaces. These are a good deal for $89 a double during most

racing and skiing season weekends, or $10 to $20 less midweek or out of season. Higher rates apply during holiday weekends. Children stay free and additional adults are $10 extra – the suites can sleep up to six in a pinch. The lodge has a pool and tennis courts, and a golf course is next door.

The *Cree Manor Inn* (☎ 257 4058), 110 Starlite Rd, is on a quiet side road near the golf course. *Cro's Nest* (☎ 257 2773), 143 Upper Terrace Drive, is just east of Mechem Drive. Both places have either simple rooms or apartments for about $40 to $120. *Aspen Lodge* (☎ 257 2978), 101 Upper Terrace Drive, has both simple motel rooms and one- or two-bedroom apartments with fireplaces for $55 to $75.

The following accommodations are in the Upper Canyon area of Ruidoso. The *Shadow Mountain Lodge* (☎ 257 4886, 1 (800) 441 4331), 107 Main Rd, has 19 comfortable rooms, all with king-size beds, fireplaces and kitchenettes. Its wooden balconies give a rustic look, but the lodge is modern and recommended for adults looking for a quiet getaway. Children are not encouraged – distinctive lodging for couples is the theme. Rates are about $84 for racing-season weekends and lower at other times.

The *Upper Canyon Inn* (☎ 257 3005, 1 (800) 551 3732), 215 Main Rd, has one-bedroom suites or two-bedroom cabins, all with kitchens and fireplaces. They'll lend you a fishing pole for use in the nearby river. Rates are $68 to $90.

**B&Bs** In the Upper Canyon is *KR&R B&B* (☎ 257 2940, 1 (800) 854 0697), 404 Main Rd. The cryptic name stands for Kearney's Rest & Relaxation Bed & Breakfast. This is a home built from rocks, unusual among the mainly wooden structures of the Upper Canyon. They'll serve you breakfast in bed if you'd like.

There are two small B&Bs north of Ruidoso. Neither allow smoking; both have private baths in all rooms. The *Sierra Mesa Lodge* (☎ 336 4515), Box 463, Alto 88312, is on Fort Stanton Rd in Alto, six miles north of Ruidoso. From Hwy 48 turn right and drive two miles on Fort Stanton Rd. The lodge has five rooms with different themes – the Victorian, French Country, Oriental, Country & Western and Queen Anne. All have queen-size beds. Rates are $80/90 for single/double, including breakfast (in bed if you wish) and afternoon tea. There is a hot tub and fireplace in the living room where guests and hosts gather. Children must be over 14, and there is no smoking.

*Monjeau Shadows* (☎ 336 4191), Bonito Rd, Nogal, 88341, is on Hwy 37, three miles north of the Hwy 48 intersection and another 13 miles north of Ruidoso. This Victorian-style B&B has four double rooms and a two-bedroom suite. The building is on several levels with a deck, a porch, bird feeders, a game room, a library and a pleasant 10-acre garden for walks. Rates are $75 double including breakfast and afternoon tea; dinner can be arranged.

**Condos** The *West Winds Lodge & Condos* (☎ 257 4031, 1 (800) 421 0691), 208 Eagle Drive, has accommodations ranging from simple motel rooms to luxury condos. It is close to the town center and a golf course, and has a hot tub and pool. Motel rooms with king-size (or two double) beds are $42 per double in racing and holiday seasons; doubles with kitchenettes and fireplaces are $54, and additional people are $10 extra. Out-of-season rates are up to $10 cheaper. Condos with one to three bedrooms, up to three baths and sleeping two to eight people, are $75 to $169 in season, $65 to $119 out of season. All condos have fireplaces and full kitchens. Ask for extended-stay discounts.

The *Vantage Point* (☎ 258 3100), 103 Rayman Buckner Drive, has comfortable condos on a quiet side street about three miles north of downtown. One-, two- or three-bedroom units all have fireplaces, kitchens, laundry facilities, and decks or patios. Rates are $60 to $90 for two to six people.

*Piñon Park Condominiums* (☎ 258 4129, 1 (800) 457 4666), 100 Jack Little Drive,

has luxurious, fully equipped and well-kept condos with two to five bedrooms, kitchen, fireplace, laundry, and private decks. Most have a game room and the largest ones have a hot tub. The condos are next to the links at Sierra Blanca Golf Course. Two-day minimum stays or four-day stays during holidays are required. These condos are among the best in town. Rates range from $85 to $250.

*Champions Run Condominiums* (☎ 378 8080) has fully equipped condos right next to the racetrack. There is a swimming pool and spa. *Fairway Meadows* (☎ 257 4019, 1 (800) 545 9013), 120 Lower Terrace Drive, has 24 condos with two bedrooms and two bathrooms, kitchens, fireplaces and laundry. It is next to the Cree Meadows Golf Course.

Many other condominium places in town charge from $60 to $200 depending on size and season. Many of them are most easily booked by reservation services whether you're staying for one night or an entire season. Condos and houses are the main offerings, though cabin rentals can also be arranged. Most of the following realtors can sell you a holiday home, too: *Four Seasons* (☎ 257 9171, 1 (800) 822 7654), *Gary Lynch Realty* (☎ 257 4011), *Century 21* (☎ 257 9057), *Lela Easter* (☎ 257 7313), *Coldwell Banker* (☎ 257 5111, 1 (800) 626 9213), and *Condotel* (☎ 258 5200, 1 (800) 545 9017).

**Cabins** Popular with skiers, *A-Frame Cabins* (☎ 258 5656), 1016 Mechem Drive, has a hot tub, pool and ski rental shop. Two- and three-bedroom cabins with fireplaces and kitchens rent for $65 to $110 for two to eight people. *Ponderosa Courts* (☎ 257 2631), 104 Laurel (just off Sudderth Drive), has cabins of various sizes. A small one-bedroom cabin with king-size bed and kitchenette is $35, and a large three-bedroom cabin with fireplace and kitchen goes for $75 for four people, $4 for each additional person.

The *Sierra Blanca Cabins* (☎ 257 2103, 258 9262), 217 Country Club Rd, are on the north side of the river a few blocks away from Sudderth Drive. These are 12 simple cabins with kitchenettes and fireplaces; there are picnic and children's play areas. Summer weekend and holiday rates in one-bedroom cabins are $68 to $76 for two to four people; two-bedroom cabins are $84 to $92 for four to six people.

*Casey's Cabins* (☎ 257 6355), 2640 Sudderth Drive, has 16 simple cabins with one to four bedrooms, some with fireplaces. Rates are $45 and up. *Apache Village* (☎ 257 2435), 311 Mechem Drive, has cabins with kitchens, fireplaces and some king-size beds for about $40 and up. Another reasonably priced choice is the *Idlehour Cabins* (☎ 257 2711), 100 Lower Terrace, a block away from Mechem. It has 12 two-bedroom cabins, with kitchens and fireplaces. *El Alto Lodge* (☎ 257 2521), 404 Mechem Drive, has cabins with fireplaces and kitchens for $55 to $80. *Starlite Cabins* (☎ 257 2255), 407 Mechem Drive, is also very affordable.

*High Country Lodge* (☎ 336 4321, 1 (800) 845 7265), Box 137, Alto, 88312, is on Hwy 48 a little south of the turnoff to Ski Apache. It has 32 two-bedroom cabins, each with kitchen, fireplace and porch. There is a pool, spa, sauna, game room and children's play area on the grounds. Rates are $99 to $125 for two to six people during weekends in season, substantially less at other times. Ask about discounts for extended stays.

*La Junta* (☎ 336 4361, 1 (800) 443 8423), Box 139, Alto, 88312, is one mile down a signed but unpaved road that heads west from Hwy 48, a quarter-mile north of the Ski Apache turnoff. At 7600 feet, La Junta is one of the highest accommodations in the Ruidoso area – cool in summer and snowy in winter. Ten different buildings are spread out over seven acres; each building has a Louisianian name such as Orleans or LaFourche, which reflects the origins of the owners. There are about 30 rooms, all with shared baths. Despite the lack of private baths, the friendly owners make this a popular place. Each building has a kitchen and fireplace. Doubles are about $79, while an entire building sleeping up to 12 is $200

a night – credit cards aren't accepted. Breakfast is available on request.

The following cabins are in the Upper Canyon area. *Riverside Cottages* (☎ 257 4753, 1 (800) 328 2804), 100 Flume Canyon Drive, just south of Main Rd, has five rustic cottages by the river. All are self-contained and have one or two bedrooms and a fireplace. Rates are $60 and up. *Ruidoso Lodge Cabins* (☎ 257 2510, 1 (800) 950 2510), 300 Main Rd, has eight cabins with one, two or three bedrooms. All come with kitchens, fireplaces and queen-size beds. Rates are about $79 to $130 for two to six people.

The *Dan Dee Cabins* (☎ 257 2165, 1 (800) 345 4848), 310 Main Rd, has 12 cabins with one, two or three bedrooms. They are nicely spread out over five acres, thus avoiding the cramped feel of some of the other nearby properties. All cabins have kitchens, fireplaces, queen-size beds and porches with charcoal grills. The cabins were constructed at various times beginning in the 1940s, and each is unique. There is a small children's playground. Rates are $77 to $125 for two to seven people in summer, $72 to $119 in winter and $62 to 104 out of season. Ask about multi-day discounts.

*Storybook Cabins* (☎ 257 2115), 410 Main Rd, has 10 spacious, well-maintained cabins, which are some of the better ones in the area. They have one to three bedrooms, queen- or king-size beds, fireplaces, kitchens, porches or decks and are set in attractive gardens. Summer and winter rates are $89 to $149 for one to three bedrooms. *Canyon Cabins* (☎ 257 2076), 416 Main Rd, has one- to three-bedroom cabins, some with king-size beds and all with the usual amenities. The largest cabin can supposedly sleep up to 14! Rates are $65 to $150 depending on occupancy, less out of season.

*Whispering Pine Cabins* (☎ 257 4311), 422 Main Rd, has small one-bedroom cabins with mini-kitchenettes for $55; larger one-bedroom cabins with full kitchens are $65; honeymoon cabins with oversize bath, luxurious furnishings and kitchenette are $72; and two-bedroom cabins with full kitchen cost $90. All feature king-size beds and fireplaces, and out-of-season discounts are available.

*Forest Homes Cabins* (☎ 257 4504), 436 Main Rd, offers one- to three-bedroom cabins with the usual amenities for $65 to $135 in season. *Sherwood Forest Cabins* (☎ 257 2424), 496 Main Rd, has 14 cabins renting from $70 to $120 in season. Apart from the usual amenities, there is a small indoor pool.

## Places to Eat

In accordance with its popularity as a year-round resort, Ruidoso has a large and varied selection of restaurants. A reasonable choice for breakfast is the *Log Cabin Restaurant* (☎ 258 5029), 1074 Mechem Drive, which is open daily from 6 am to 2 pm and 5 to 9 pm. For New Mexican breakfasts and lunches, the popular *Deck House* at 202 Mechem Drive is recommended for both food and decor. It is open from 7 am to 3 pm daily except Wednesday. Two relatively inexpensive steak houses open for breakfast, lunch and dinner are *K-Bob's Steak House* (☎ 378 4747), Hwy 70 at the Y-junction with Sudderth Drive, and *Cattleman's* (☎ 378 5423), 303 Hwy 70, in Ruidoso Downs.

For a breakfast buffet plus good Mexican food all day, try *Don Victor's* (☎ 257 9900), at the traffic circle at the west end of Sudderth Drive – it is particularly convenient for those staying in the Upper Canyon. Prices are reasonable. *Terraza Campanario* (☎ 257 4227), 1611 Sudderth Drive, is also good for Mexican and American food and serves breakfasts.

A couple of small restaurants cater to the light-lunch crowd. The *Hummingbird Tearoom* (☎ 257 5100), 2306 Sudderth Drive, is open for soup, salad and sandwich lunches from 11 am to 2:30 pm, Tuesday to Saturday. It stays open to 4 pm serving delectable desserts and, of course, afternoon tea. The *Blue Goose* (☎ 257 5271), 2608B Sudderth Drive, is behind the fashionable J Roberts clothing store. It is open daily in the summer from 11 am to 6 pm and serves sandwiches and lunch specials in a pleasant setting.

There are many more choices for lunch and dinner. The *Casa Blanca* (☎ 257 2495), 501 Mechem Drive, is open daily from 11 am to 10 pm. It serves Mexican food and hamburgers in a renovated Spanish-style house with a pleasant beer garden outside – musicians sometimes provide entertainment, and the crowd is lively. Happy hour runs from 2 to 6 pm. Prices for dinner entrees are under $10.

The *Flying J Ranch* (☎ 336 4330) is on Hwy 48 about 1.5 miles north of the Ski Apache turnoff in Alto. The Ranch is as popular for entertainment as for dining and features a 'Western village' with gunfights and pony rides for children. Doors open at 6 pm and a cowboy-style chuck-wagon dinner is served at 7:30 pm sharp (!) followed by a stage show of early Western music and melodrama at 8:15 pm. Reservations are requested – though if you have just pulled into town, you can probably mosey on down. The dinner is beef, beans, potatoes, biscuits and cake – cowboys didn't get menus on the trail and you won't either. On the other hand, there's plenty of food – and plenty of coffee or lemonade to wash it all down. The cost is $11 for adults, less for small children, and includes the entertainment. The Ranch is open Monday to Saturday from 1 June to Labor Day – private groups can make reservations from spring to fall.

OK – so you want something more elegant than beef and beans. At the opposite extreme is *Victoria's Romantic Hide-a-Way* (☎ 257 5440), 2103 Sudderth Drive in the Gazebo Shopping Center. This restaurant serves fine Italian food in a romantic ambiance; there are lace-curtained booths and a pleasant garden area as well as a special honeymoon section. Children are not allowed, and the cafe is no-smoking throughout. Another good choice for Italian food, as well as pizza and giant sandwiches, is *Michelena's* (☎ 257 5753), 2703 Sudderth Drive. This is the place to bring the kids or order takeout – it has a deck for dining. Prices are low to moderate. Hours are from 11 am daily – closing hours vary depending on demand.

The *Inncredible Restaurant* (☎ 336 4312), Hwy 48 in Alto, on the right just before the Ski Apache turnoff, is popular. Skylights and stained glass, cowboy art and a saloon all contribute to the Western ambiance. Steak, prime rib, seafood and pasta dishes are the main offerings, and there is a kids' menu. Dinner entrees run from about $8 to $18. Hours are 11:30 am to 10 pm daily – the lounge stays open later and features live entertainment on some nights.

The *Cattle Baron* (☎ 257 9355), 657 Sudderth Drive, is the best steak house in town and has excellent seafood as well. The decor is elegant but Southwestern – so you can wear your best finery or cowboy boots and hat and you'll fit in. The Western lounge is popular and deservedly so. Dinner entrees range from about $7 to $20 – lunches are much cheaper. Reservations are a good idea at both these restaurants.

The fanciest place in town is *La Lorraine* (☎ 257 2954), 2523 Sudderth Drive. The cuisine is French and well recommended. The decor is also French, and there is a courtyard for outdoor dining. Dinner entrees are in the $12 to $22 range; lunches cost about half that. Hours are 11:30 am to 2:30 pm for lunch Tuesday to Saturday and 5:30 to 10 pm for dinner Tuesday to Sunday, though it may open on Monday in the busy season.

## Entertainment

Going to the races is what Ruidoso is famous for, but there are plenty of other things to do. Another possibility is the *Miner's Castle Mountain Music Show* (☎ 257 6180), which claims to be the only show of its type west of Branson, Missouri. It's a Western variety show with country, bluegrass, polka, gospel, pop and Spanish music, as well as comedy routines and clowns. Admission is $10/6 for adults/children, and show time is 7:30 pm daily except Sunday. You can't miss the Disney-type castle on Hwy 70, about three-quarters of a mile west of the Y-junction with Sudderth Drive.

Two nightclubs with entertainment and dancing most nights are *Win, Place & Show* (☎ 257 9982), 2516 Sudderth Drive, and *The Winner's Circle* (☎ 257 9535), 2535 Sudderth Drive.

## Things to Buy

Shopping is a big attraction and not without reason; the various galleries and gift shops along Sudderth Drive and Mechem Drive have a wide selection of items ranging from cheap souvenirs to fine art. You may even find original work by some of the big names in New Mexican art such as Peter Hurd and Henriette Wyeth.

## Getting There & Away

The bus station (☎ 257 2660), 138 Service Rd, is just north of the 300 block of Sudderth Drive. TNM&O and Greyhound have buses headed to Alamogordo, Roswell and El Paso, Texas, several times a day.

Although Ruidoso has a small municipal airport, its facilities are only suitable for small planes. The nearest sizable airport is Sierra Blanca Regional Airport (☎ 336 8111, 336 8455) in Fort Stanton, almost 20 miles away. Mesa Air (☎ 1 (800) 637 2247) has flown there in the past but wasn't doing so recently. They do fly into Alamogordo and Roswell.

## SMOKEY BEAR HISTORICAL STATE PARK

Set in the village of Capitan, 20 miles east of Carrizozo and 20 miles north of Ruidoso, Capitan (population 800) has one claim to fame: Smokey Bear.

In 1950, a nearby fire burned 26.5 sq miles of forest. Firefighters found a burned black bear cub in the aftermath. They put the cub on a plane to Santa Fe, where he received medical care and recovered. He was named Smokey and became the focus of the USFS's highly visible anti-fire campaign. Slogans like 'Smokey's ABCs – Always Be Careful...with fire!' have been seen throughout national forests for decades. Smokey spent the rest of his life in Washington Zoo, where he died in 1976. He is buried in this state park.

Visitors can see the bear's grave and watch audiovisual programs about fire prevention in the visitor center (☎ 354 2748). There is a small botanical garden, children's playground, picnic area and gift shop. Overnight camping is not allowed; day use is 25¢ for adults. The park is on the main street through town.

Every Fourth of July there is a Smokey Bear Stampede with a parade, a rodeo, cookouts and other festivities.

### Places to Stay & Eat

Wilderness camping is possible in the Lincoln National Forest nearby; there are developed USFS campgrounds at Baca (15 miles east) and South Fork (20 miles west). South Fork has water and a $6 fee; it is open from May to September. To get there, take Hwy 48 south from Capitan. Baca has random camping and there is water – the season depends on whether USFS Rd 57 is open. The nearest ranger station is in Ruidoso.

In Capitan, the *Smokey Bear Motel* (☎ 354 2253) on the main road is the only place to stay. It is inexpensive but often full – call ahead. Carrizozo (20 miles west), Lincoln (13 miles east) and Ruidoso (22 miles south) offer hotels. The town has several restaurants.

### LINCOLN STATE MONUMENT

The tiny village of Lincoln (population about 100) is known as the scene of the Wild West gun battle that put Billy the Kid into legend and history books. Billy's story is that of a teenager turned outlaw, a kid tangled in a war between rival merchant and ranching interests. If you are a fan of Western history, a visit to Lincoln is a must. It is about 12 miles east of Capitan.

Lincoln was Mescalero Apache territory when Spanish settlers took control of it in the mid-1800s. Some 20 years later the settlement had grown from the simple tower (or *torreón*) of rocks settlers had erected to defend themselves to the small but booming town of Lincoln, the seat of Lincoln County. Lincoln's 400 inhabitants lived in adobe houses and shopped at Murphy's General Store – the only store in the region. This store made large profits by also providing supplies to nearby Fort Stanton. In 1877, competition arrived in the form of John Tunstall, an English merchant who built another general store.

To say that the merchants did not get along is an understatement. Within a year of his arrival, Tunstall was shot dead, allegedly by Murphy and his boys. Supporters of Tunstall wanted revenge, and the entire region erupted in what became known as the Lincoln County War. Tunstall's most famous follower was a wild teenager named Henry McCarty, alias William Bonney, soon to become known as Billy the Kid. Over the next months the Kid and his gang gunned down any of the Murphy faction that they could find, including Sheriff Pat Brady and other lawmakers. The Kid was captured or cornered a couple of times but managed some brazen and lucky escapes before finally being shot by Sheriff Pat Garrett near Fort Sumner in 1881.

The story has since been romanticized and retold many times in books, movies and songs. The consummate American outlaw, Billy the Kid has captured the imagination of the nation for over a century – often as a gunslinger fighting for what he thought was right rather than as a criminal desperado.

By the end of the century, the railway had come to nearby Carrizozo. Lincoln lost its country seat status and soon declined in political importance. Today the few remaining inhabitants of Lincoln have preserved the buildings of the 1880s, and the main street of town is a state monument.

A visit is a walk through time; modern influences such as neon-lit motels, souvenir stands and fast-food joints are not allowed to spoil the setting. There is a historical visitor center with an excellent museum and gift shop, as well as an introductory slide show that relates the Billy the Kid story in detail. You can walk through town and visit the torreón, the Tunstall Store (with a remarkable display of late 19th-century merchandise), the courthouse

Billy the Kid

where the Kid escaped imprisonment, the San Juan Mission, Drive Woods' house (built in 1882) and other buildings.

Each site has informative guides dressed in period costume who can answer your questions. All buildings are open from 9 am to 6 pm daily. Admission to the whole village is $4.50 for adults. Tickets are available from the courthouse at the west end of town or the historical center at the east end.

Information about Lincoln State Monument is available from the Lincoln County Heritage Trust (☎ 653 4025), the Lincoln State Monument (☎ 653 4372) and the Lincoln County Historical Society (☎ 653 4529).

**Special Events**

Old Lincoln Days festivities are held during the first full weekend in August. Musicians and mountain men, doctors and desperadoes wander the streets in period costume, and there are many activities and demonstrations of spinning, blacksmithing and other common frontier skills. Admission is included in the $4.50 fee for entrance to historic Lincoln. In addition, there is a folk pageant, 'The Last Escape of Billy the Kid'; adult admission is $3, children $1.

**Places to Stay & Eat**

Accommodations in town are limited and reservations are suggested. Lincoln Hospitality Group (☎ 653 4676), Box 27, 88338, can help. This group runs the *Casa de Patrón* B&B, built around 1860 and purportedly slept in by the Kid. Three historical rooms rent for $79, and two *casitas* (little homes) rent for $97. Breakfast is included, and dinner is available by prior arrangement. The owners sometimes arrange musical evenings.

The *Wortley Hotel* (☎ 653 4300), Box 96, is an adobe hotel built in 1872, which suffered fire damage in 1930 but was restored in 1960. Eight rooms each with a double brass bed and period furnishings rent for $60 to $65. A good restaurant is on the premises and available to the general public. Another possibility is the *Ellis Store* (☎ 653 4609), a 19th-century adobe house with three rooms for rent.

The *Eatery* on the main street sells snacks from 10 am to 5 pm daily. Otherwise, you have to head west to Capitan or 14 miles east to the town of Tinnie, where there is the *Silver Dollar* (☎ 653 4425), a distinguished old restaurant serving steak and seafood. This is the best restaurant in the area, charging $12 to $25 for dinner entrees. It is open for lunch and dinner Wednesday to Sunday, and reservations are suggested.

**ROSWELL**

Roswell is at the western edge of the dry plains known as the Llano Estacado. If you're driving east on Hwy 70/380 out of the Sacramento Mountains, enjoy the view. These are the last big mountains you'll see for awhile. The Llano Estacado is 3000 to 4000 feet in elevation.

The 'Staked Plains', extending east through Texas, were once home to millions of buffalo and many nomadic Native American hunters. White settlers and hunters moved in throughout the late 19th century. Between 1872 and 1874, some 3,700,000 buffalo were killed, an estimated 3.5 million by Whites. Within a few years, the Llano Estacado became desolate and empty, with only a few groups of Comanche mixed with other tribes roaming the plains, hunting and trying to avoid confinement on the reservation.

Roswell was founded in 1871. It became a stopping place for cowboys driving cattle along the Goodnight-Loving Trail from Texas to Colorado and the Chisum Trail to the west. The discovery of artesian water in 1890 caused the town to boom, and now the city is an important crossroads serving the ranching communities of southeastern New Mexico. It is also an important industrial center.

Roswell is the largest town in this part of the state and the seat of Chaves County. The county has a population of some 58,000, of which 47,000 live in Roswell – that ought to suggest how empty the surroundings areas are.

Summers are fairly hot, with many 90°F days, but it's a dry heat. Evenings cool down to pleasant temperatures. Winters can see an occasional snowfall that rarely lasts more than a day or two. For many travelers, Roswell is simply a convenient place to stop for a meal or a bed; however, excellent museums and thriving cultural life combined with the nearby wildlife refuge give ample reason to stop and explore.

### Orientation & Information

Most of Roswell is laid out as a grid. The main west-east drag through town is 2nd St, and the main north-south thoroughfare is Main St; where they intersect is the heart of downtown. All motels are on these two streets. Hwy 70 comes in on W 2nd St and turns left at Main St to head out of town to the north. Hwy 380 crosses town on 2nd St and Hwy 285 crosses town on Main St.

The chamber of commerce (☎ 623 5695, 623 5698), 131 W 2nd St, is the best source of tourist information. Hours are 9 am to 5 pm on weekdays. The library (☎ 622 7101) is at 301 N Pennsylvania Ave. The *Roswell Daily Record* is the local newspaper, which has been published since 1891. The main post office (☎ 622 3741) is at 415 N Pennsylvania Ave. The Eastern New Mexico Medical Center has a north facility (☎ 622 8170) at 405 W Country Club Drive and a south facility (☎ 622 1110) at S Main and Chisum Sts. The north facility is the main hospital for the region. The police (☎ 624 6770, or 911 in an emergency) are at 128 W 2nd St.

### Roswell Museum & Art Center

The excellent and well-organized Roswell Museum and Art Center (☎ 624 6744), 100 W 11th St, definitely deserves a visit. With 15 galleries, there is something here for everyone. A major focus is space research. Robert H Goddard, who launched the world's first successful liquid fuel rocket in 1926, spent over a decade carrying out rocket research in Roswell. His laboratory has been reconstructed at the museum, and a variety of early rocketry paraphernalia is on display. Also on display is the space suit that Harrison Schmitt, the New Mexican astronaut, wore on the moon during the Apollo XVII mission in 1972. Adjoining the museum is the **Goddard Planetarium**, with various multimedia shows – call for the current events.

Art galleries present changing exhibits of works by Peter Hurd, the famous Roswell painter, as well as many other Southwestern artists including Georgia O'Keefe. Hispanic and Chicano art is also exhibited, and there are fine bronzes on display. American Indian exhibits feature clothing, ceremonial items, pottery, basketwork and a growing collection of other artwork.

Shows change regularly, and the museum sponsors a variety of cultural events throughout the year; call for current information. The museum is open from 9 am to 5 pm daily except Sunday, when hours are 1 to 5 pm. Admission is free. There is a museum store.

### Chaves County Historical Museum

The Chaves County Historical Museum (☎ 622 8333), 200 N Lea, is housed in the 1910 mansion of local rancher James Phelp White, and it is in the National Register of Historic Places. The building is worth seeing; the inside has been carefully restored to its original early-20th-century decor with period furnishings, photographs and art. Changing exhibits include clothing, toys, crafts, typewriters, telephones and other memorabilia of the early 20th century. The museum is open from 1 to 4 pm on Friday, Saturday and Sunday, though special tours can be arranged. Admission is $2.

### General Douglas L McBride Military Museum

This museum is on the campus of the New Mexico Military Institute (☎ 622 6250), at N Main and College Blvd. Home to about 1000 high school and junior college cadets, the coed campus is considered one of the best military academies in the country. The institute was established in 1891, and the military Gothic architecture is impressive. The museum has displays on US military history with a focus on the contributions of New Mexicans. The campus is open to visitors and tours are offered by appointment. Admission to the museum is free; it is usually open from 9 am to 4 pm Monday to Friday, but the hours vary – call to check.

### UFO Museum & Research Center

In 1947 the Roswell newspaper reported a UFO crash near town. The military quickly closed the area and allowed no more information for several decades (although recently they claimed it was a balloon). Was it a flying saucer? The local Convention & Visitors Bureau suggests that Roswell's special blend of climate and culture attracted touring space aliens who wanted a closer look! Keep one eye on the sky.

Independent space travelers have been vacationing in Roswell since 1947.

Serious followers of UFO phenomena (not to mention skeptics or the merely curious) will want to visit the UFO Museum & Research Center (☎ 625 9495), 400 N Main, open from 1 to 5 pm daily. There are a variety of exhibits, a film-screening room, a research library and a gift shop. Admission is free.

### Spring River Park & Zoo

On the southeast corner of College and Atkinson, the Spring River Park & Zoo (☎ 624 6760) is a good place for younger children. Apart from the animals, there is a petting zoo, prairie-dog town, miniature train, antique carousel, kids' fishing pond, playground and picnic area. Zoo hours are 10 am till 8 pm every day; the concessions are open from 1 to 6 pm daily during the summer and on the weekends in spring and fall. Admission is free.

### Golf

The New Mexico Military Institute Golf Course (☎ 622 6250) on 19th St is open to the public, as is the Spring River Golf Course (☎ 622 9506) at 1612 W 8th St. Both have 18 holes.

### Special Events

The main annual event is the Eastern New Mexico State Fair (☎ 623 9411) held in the fairgrounds on Main and Poe Sts. The fair is usually in early October (occasionally late September) and features rodeo, carnival, livestock and agricultural competitions, arts & crafts, chili-eating contests, music and fun.

Also fun is Chaves County Dairy Day in early June. This features the Great Milk Carton Boat Race on Lake Van, 20 miles south of Roswell, as well as cheese sculpting contests, 36-foot-long ice-cream sundaes, games and sporting events. Start saving your milk cartons.

Roswell hosts quite a few other events throughout the year, including an air show and ballooning weekend in spring, a kite festival in May and a vintage car rally in September. Call the chamber of commerce for exact dates.

Prairie dogs don't bark, drool or bite.

### Places to Stay – camping

*Trailer Village Campgrounds* (☎ 623 6040), 1614 E 2nd, has RV sites with hookups for $14. A laundry is available. *Town & Country Mobile Estates* (☎ 624 1833), 333 W Brasher Rd, has tent and RV sites in the $11 to $16 range. Showers are available. Bottomless Lakes State Park is a good camping spot, which also has showers. Sites cost $7 or $11 with partial hookups.

### Places to Stay – bottom end

The cheapest motels charge about $25 to $35 for two people. These include the *Belmont Motel* (☎ 623 4522), 2100 W 2nd St; the *Hacienda Motel* (☎ 623 9425), 2331 N Main St, which has a pool, and *El Capitan* (☎ 622 9375), 1631 SE Main St.

A good choice for budget travelers is the *Budget Inn West* (☎ 623 3811), 2200 W 2nd St, and the *Budget Inn North* (☎ 623 6050, 1 (800) 752 4667), 2101 N Main St. Both places have simple but clean rooms, a pool and free coffee in the lobby. Rooms are about $27/31 for singles/doubles, but discounts ($26 for a double) are sometimes offered. Other places in this price range are

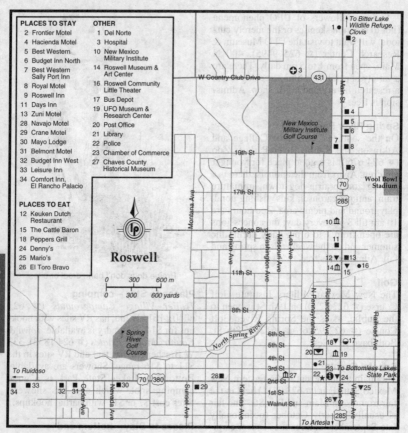

PLACES TO STAY
2   Frontier Motel
4   Hacienda Motel
5   Best Western
6   Budget Inn North
7   Best Western
    Sally Port Inn
8   Royal Motel
9   Roswell Inn
11  Days Inn
13  Zuni Motel
28  Navajo Motel
29  Crane Motel
30  Mayo Lodge
31  Belmont Motel
32  Budget Inn West
33  Leisure Inn
34  Comfort Inn,
    El Rancho Palacio

PLACES TO EAT
12  Keuken Dutch
    Restaurant
15  The Cattle Baron
18  Peppers Grill
24  Denny's
25  Mario's
26  El Toro Bravo

OTHER
1   Del Norte
3   Hospital
10  New Mexico
    Military Institute
14  Roswell Museum &
    Art Center
16  Roswell Community
    Little Theater
17  Bus Depot
19  UFO Museum &
    Research Center
20  Post Office
21  Library
22  Police
23  Chamber of Commerce
27  Chaves County
    Historical Museum

**Roswell**

the *Mayo Lodge* (☎ 622 0210), 1716 W 2nd St, the *Navajo Motel* (☎ 622 9220), 1013 W 2nd St, the *Crane Motel* (☎ 623 1293), 1212 W 2nd St, and the *Zuni Motel* (☎ 622 1930), 1201 N Main St.

Expect price increases during special events and holidays.

### Places to Stay – middle

The *Frontier Motel* (☎ 622 1400, 1 (800) 678 1401), 3010 N Main St, has good rooms with queen-size beds beginning at $32/36 for singles/doubles. Continental breakfast is included and there is a pool. The *Royal Motel* (☎ 622 0110, 1 (800) 423

3106), 2001 N Main St, is similar and has a kids' playground. Both hotels are a good value.

For just a few dollars more you can stay at the *Days Inn* (☎ 623 4021), 1310 N Main St, which has large rooms, a pool and hot tub, and a restaurant and includes a continental breakfast. The *Leisure Inn* (☎ 622 2575), 2700 W 2nd St, has spacious rooms and also has a pool and coffee shop. The *Comfort Inn* (☎ 623 9440), 2803 W 2nd St, charges $44/48 for comfortable single/double rooms, many with refrigerators. There is a pool and coffee shop, and a continental breakfast is included in the rates.

There are two Best Western hotels. The *El Rancho Palacio* (☎ 622 2721, 1 (800) 528 1234), 2205 N Main St, is the simpler one, though it does have a pool and spa. A restaurant is next door. Rates are about $40/42 for singles/doubles. The *Sally Port Inn* (☎ 622 6430, 1 (800) 528 1234), 2000 N Main St, is one of the two best hotels in town. A restaurant and covered swimming pool overlook a large courtyard. There is a gym, sauna and a lounge with entertainment and dancing on weekends. Both coin and valet laundries are available. Pleasant rooms with queen-size beds start at $53/63; some slightly pricier rooms with king-size beds and refrigerators are also available.

The other top hotel in town is the *Roswell Inn* (☎ 623 4920, 1 (800) 426 3052 in New Mexico, or 1 (800) 323 0913) at 1815 N Main St. This has a pool and restaurant. The lounge features complimentary hors d'oeuvres during the 5 to 7 pm happy hour and light entertainment most evenings. Southwestern and other art is found throughout the inn. Large rooms with queen- or king-size beds are $55/62; suites with king-size beds and refrigerators start at $95.

### Places to Eat

Fast-food, pizza and chain restaurants predominate. The restaurants at the Sally Port and Roswell Inns attract diners who aren't staying at the hotels.

Apart from the above, your best bet for an early breakfast is the *Keuken Dutch Restaurant* (☎ 624 2040), 1208 N Main St. It is open daily from 6 am to 10 pm and serves inexpensive American food with a Dutch twist.

Several places serve Mexican and American food. *Peppers Grill* (☎ 623 1700), 500 N Main St, is casual, inexpensive and popular. *Mario's* (☎ 623 1740), 200 E 2nd St, is good and a little more upmarket. Both are open daily for lunch and dinner till 9 pm, or 10 pm on Friday and Saturday.

Two other Mexican restaurants stand out. *Los Ranchos* (☎ 622 9545), 911 E 2nd St, is

inexpensive and good. It is open till 9 pm. *El Toro Bravo* (☎ 622 9280), 102 S Main St, has a few regional New Mexican dishes mixed in with the mainly Mexican offerings. Prices are low to moderate. It is open for lunch from Monday to Friday and for dinner (until 9 pm) Monday to Saturday.

For moderately priced steaks and seafood, try the *Cattle Baron* (☎ 622 2465), 1113 N Main St, or *Cattleman's Steak House* (☎ 623 3500), 2010 S Main St.

If you are hungry at 3:49 am, try *Denny's* (☎ 623 5377), 200 N Main St, open 24 hours. There's another Denny's at 2200 N Main St (☎ 622 9960).

### Entertainment

The *Roswell Symphony Orchestra* (☎ 623 5882), 3201 N Main St, has been performing since 1960. The main season is October to April, but other concerts may be scheduled throughout the year. Other orchestras play here by invitation. Call for dates.

The *Roswell Community Little Theater* (☎ 622 1982), 1101 N Virginia Ave, has also been around for many years and performs several plays throughout its September to June season.

The *Del Norte* (☎ 623 5139), 2800 N Main St, and the *Cinema 4* (☎ 623 9139), 4501 N Main St in the Roswell Shopping Mall, show movies.

### Getting There & Away

**Air** Roswell Industrial Air Center (☎ 347 5703) is at the south end of Main St. Mesa Air (☎ 347 5501 at the airport, 1 (800) 933 6372) has eight non-stop flights to and from Albuquerque every weekday, fewer on weekends. It also has two or three flights a day to Carlsbad, Hobbs and Dallas/Ft Worth, Texas.

**Bus** The Greyhound and TNM&O Bus Depot (☎ 622 2510, 622 2511), 515 N Main St, is open from 6 am to 6 pm and 9 to 11 pm daily. Buses leave for Carlsbad ($15) and Albuquerque ($28) twice a day. There are also buses to Portales, Clovis, Las Cruces and Santa Fe. Buses to Texas go to Amarillo, Lubbock and El Paso.

## Getting Around

A brand new bus service (☎ 624 6766) runs throughout the city and to the airport. Fares are 75¢. Hertz (☎ 347 2211), Avis (☎ 347 2500) and National (☎ 347 2323) all have car rental offices at the airport.

## AROUND ROSWELL
### Bottomless Lakes State Park

Bottomless Lakes State Park (☎ 624 6058), Box 120, 88201, is Roswell's most popular outdoor attraction. Seven lakes provide relief from the summer heat with swimming, fishing, windsurfing, scuba diving, canoeing, walking, bird-watching, picnicking and camping. A visitor center near the entrance provides information about which activities are permitted in which lake.

Day use is $3 per car, and camping is permitted. To get to the park, drive 10 miles east of Roswell on Hwy 380, then five miles south on Hwy 409 (there are signs).

### Dexter National Fish Hatchery

The fish hatchery (☎ 734 5910) is 20 miles southeast of Roswell on Hwy 2 (take Hwy 285 southbound and look for signs). This hatchery is especially important for the study of rare and endangered southwestern fish species. Visitors are welcome.

### Bitter Lake National Wildlife Refuge

The 38-sq-mile Bitter Lake National Wildlife Refuge (☎ 622 6755), Box 7, 88202, is particularly known for wintering water birds. The heart of the refuge is six man-made lakes totaling 1.2 sq miles. Tens of thousands of ducks, geese and sandhill cranes are found here from October to March, with mid-November to early December being peak times. The snow geese are particularly abundant and spectacular.

In the summer, a variety of birds remain to nest including the threatened snowy plover and the endangered least tern – special protection for the tern means you probably won't get to see it, but there are plenty of other species to observe. Over 300 have been recorded and a bird list is available. Also keep your eyes open for

horned toads, snakes and other reptiles as well as deer, rabbits and coyotes.

The refuge is about 15 miles northeast of Roswell. Follow the signed roads from either Hwy 380 or 285/70. Hours are from one hour before sunrise to one hour after sunset – camping is not permitted. An 8.5-mile self-guided auto tour is available, with plenty of stops and lookouts. The ranger station is open from 7:30 am to 4 pm Monday to Friday; a booth by the entrance has bird lists, maps, and information at other times. Admission is free.

## ARTESIA

Artesia is a crossroads town about halfway between Roswell and Carlsbad, and halfway between Cloudcroft and Hobbs. During the late 1800s there were only a few buildings here, huddled around a spring in the middle of the dry Llano Estacado. Artesia came into being in 1903, when an artesian well was dug to irrigate the area. Twenty years later, another well yielded oil, and Artesia became an important agricultural and industrial town.

Artesia (elevation 3400 feet) has a population of some 12,000 people. It is the home of New Mexico's largest petroleum refinery, and the oil industry provides many jobs.

### Orientation & Information

Artesia is the crossroads of the west-east Hwy 82 (Main St in town) and the north-south Hwy 285 (1st St). Most businesses are on these streets.

The chamber of commerce (☎ 746 2744) is at 408 W Texas Ave. The library (☎ 746 4252) is at 306 W Richardson Ave. Local events are reported in the *Artesia Daily Press*. The post office (☎ 746 4412, 748 3558) is at 201 N 4th St. The hospital (☎ 748 3333) is at 702 N 13th St. The police (☎ 746 2703 or 911) are at 305 N 7th St.

### Artesia Historical Museum & Art Center

The Artesia Historical Museum & Art Center (☎ 748 2390), 505 W Richardson Ave, in an early Artesia house. Built in 1904, the museum and is noted for the

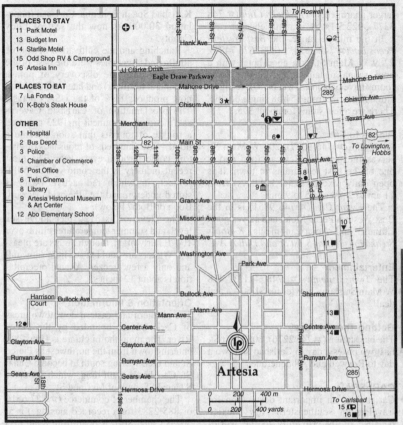

**PLACES TO STAY**
11  Park Motel
13  Budget Inn
14  Starlite Motel
15  Odd Shop RV & Campground
16  Artesia Inn

**PLACES TO EAT**
7  La Fonda
10  K-Bob's Steak House

**OTHER**
1  Hospital
2  Bus Depot
3  Police
4  Chamber of Commerce
5  Post Office
6  Twin Cinema
8  Library
9  Artesia Historical Museum
   & Art Center
12  Abo Elementary School

cobblestones used to embellish the outside walls. Local artists have their work displayed here, and there is an exhibit of local historical artifacts. Hours are from 8 am to noon and 1 to 5 pm Tuesday to Saturday (except holidays). Admission is free.

### Abo Elementary School

This elementary school (☎ 748 2755), 1802 Center Ave, is built underground and serves as a nuclear fallout shelter for the community. It is supposedly the first underground school in the USA and can be visited during school days (it is closed in the summer).

### Places to Stay

For camping, try the *Ponderosa RV Park* (☎ 746 3209) at 3204 W Main St, or the *Odd Shop RV & Campground* (☎ 748 3779) is at 1502 S 1st St. *Brantley Lake State Park* (see under Carlsbad) about 30 miles south also has camping.

The best cheap hotel is *Artesia Inn* (☎ 746 9801, 1 (800) 682 4598), 1820 S 1st St. It has a swimming pool and clean rooms for about $30/35 single/double. The *Starlite Motel* (☎ 746 9834), 1018 S 1st St, is similar but lacks a pool. The *Park Motel* (☎ 746 3561), 612 1st St, has a pool and gives discounts for long stays. It has some

**NEW MEXICO**

larger apartments. The *Budget Inn* (☎ 748 3377), 922 S 1st St, is a little cheaper.

In the middle range, the *Best Western Pecos Inn* (☎ 748 3324, 1 (800) 676 7481), 2209 W Main St, is a good hotel with a pool, sauna, restaurant and lounge. Some rooms have balconies, wet bars or refrigerators. Rates are from $51/58 single/double. There are a few suites for about $95.

## Places to Eat
*La Fonda* (☎ 746 9377), 206 W Main St, serves inexpensive Mexican food and is one of the best restaurants in town. It is open daily (except major holidays) from 11 am to 2 pm and 5 to 9 pm.

The *Kwan Den* (☎ 746 9851) is in the Best Western Pecos Motel and serves good Chinese and American meals. *K-Bob's Steak House) is at S 1st St and Dallas Ave.

## Entertainment
The *Twin Cinema* (☎ 746 4112), 418 W Main St, shows movies for $1.50 – a real deal!

## Getting There & Away
The bus station (☎ 746 2276), 608 N 1st St, has two buses a day to Carlsbad and two a day to Roswell and Albuquerque.

## CARLSBAD
Carlsbad is an important destination for travelers in southeastern New Mexico because of its proximity to the world-famous Carlsbad Caverns, about 25 miles away. The caverns are described later; this sections deals with the city of Carlsbad.

Carlsbad is on the Pecos River, about 30 miles north of the Texas state line. Apache and Comanche Indians inhabited this dry area before the Europeans arrived. Several Spanish expeditions traveled through on exploratory trips along the Pecos in the 16th and 17th centuries. By the late 1800s, cowboys were driving huge herds of cattle along the Pecos River Valley; a local rancher, Charles B Eddy, founded the town in 1888. Originally named Eddy, it was renamed Carlsbad because local mineral springs reminded the inhabitants of the

Karlsbad Spa in Bohemia. Carlsbad (population 30,000) is now the seat of Eddy County.

Ranching and the cultivation of cotton, alfalfa and vegetables were the base of the economy until the discovery of potash (a mineral fertilizer) and later, oil. Carlsbad now produces 85% of the USA's potash. The proclamation of Carlsbad Caverns as a national monument in 1923 attracted a trickle of tourists that soon became a flood – now hundreds of thousands of visitors come through every year. The most recent industry is the controversial WIPP project, in which radioactive waste is stored underground (see the aside Hazard, Boon or Both? below).

The elevation is 3120 feet above sea level, and summer temperatures climb over 100°F fairly often, though nights are pleasant. Winters are cool but see little snow fall and only a few freezes. Annual precipitation is about 12 inches.

## Orientation & Information
The northern and eastern downtown areas of Carlsbad are bounded by the Pecos River. The main thoroughfare is Hwy 285, entering town from the northwest as Pierce St and then veering south to become Canal St, Carlsbad's main drag, which becomes S Canal St south of Mermod St.

The chamber of commerce (☎ 887 6516 or 885 2283 for a recorded message) is at 302 S Canal St. It is open from 8 am to 5 pm Monday to Friday but usually has brochures available from a dispenser by the door. The National Parks Information Center (☎ 885 8884), 3225 National Parks Highway (at the south end of town), has information on both Carlsbad Caverns National Park and Guadalupe Mountains National Park, just across the state line in Texas. It is open from 8 am to 4:30 pm daily. The Lincoln National Forest Guadalupe Ranger Station (☎ 885 4181) is in the Federal Building on the northeast corner of Halagueno and Fox Sts.

The *Carlsbad Current-Argus* is the local daily. The library (☎ 885 6776) is on the northwest corner of Halagueno and Fox

Sts. The post office (☎ 885 5717) is at 301 N Canyon. The Guadalupe Medical Center (☎ 887 4100), 2430 W Pierce, is the main hospital. The police (☎ 885 2111 or 911) are at 405 S Halagueno St.

### Driving Tour

The chamber of commerce provides a *Discover Carlsbad Scenic Drive* brochure that covers the tour in detail. It begins at the west end of the Bataan Bridge, which is where Greene St crosses the Pecos River. 'Discover Carlsbad' markers point the way, and informative signs describe the sights. The tour follows Park Drive and Riverside St along the Pecos River waterfront, then loops through the Living Desert State Park on Skyline Drive, takes Church and Pate Sts back to town, and finishes by driving along Pierce and Canal Sts to the town center.

### Living Desert State Park

The Living Desert State Park (☎ 887 5516) is on Skyline Rd (off Hwy 285 northwest of town). For me, this is the premier attraction in the town and definitely deserves a visit if you are interested in natural history. The park is spread out over the Ocotillo Hills on the northwestern outskirts of town and exhibits the wildlife of the Chihuahuan Desert. Well-marked trails wander through

Golden eagle

the park and take the visitor past wildlife enclosures and through natural looking gardens. This is a great place to see and learn about cacti and coyotes, gopher snakes and golden eagles, and wildlife with evocative Southwestern names such as agave, javelina, ocotillo and yucca. Black bear, pronghorn antelope, mountain lion and buffalo can also be seen. The view of the Pecos River Valley below is an added bonus.

Although this is a state park, there are none of the usual state park facilities – no picnicking nor camping. There is a visitor center and gift shop. The park is open daily except Christmas Day. Hours are 8 am to 6:30 pm from May 15 to Labor Day, 9 am to 3:30 pm during the rest of the year. Admission is $3, children under six are free, and admission stops one hour before closing.

### Carlsbad Museum & Art Center

The Museum & Art Center (☎ 887 0276), 418 W Fox St, displays mastodon and cameloid bones, Apache artifacts, pioneer memorabilia, art from the Taos school and local arts & crafts. See the large and dramatic The *Jicarilla Apache Trading Post* painted in the 1930s by LaVerne Nelson Black under New Deal sponsorship. Hours are from 10 am to 6 pm daily except Sunday. Admission is free.

### Lake Carlsbad

A system of dams and spillways maintains a constant water height on the Pecos River for a two-mile section north of the Bataan Bridge. This river-lake area provides various amusements.

At the north end of Park Drive is **Port Jefferson** (☎ 887 0512). Boats are available for hire and water skiing is popular. The **Carlsbad Riverfront Park** nearby offers picnicking, playgrounds and an adjacent beach and swimming area with water slides and diving boards.

Across the river from the park (via a footbridge) is the **Presidents Park Amusement Village** (☎ 887 0512), 711 Muscatel Ave, with carnival rides, a narrow-gauge train ride and other attractions. Hours are from 5 to 10 pm Monday to Friday, Memorial Day to Labor Day, and from 1 to 10 pm on weekends from March to October. Near the amusement village is the **Lake Carlsbad Golf Course** (☎ 885 5444) with 18 holes and a pro-shop. It is open from 6:30 am to dusk daily except Tuesday.

### WIPP Visitor Center
The WIPP (Waste Isolation Pilot Plant) Visitors Center was set up to explain the project, which stores nuclear waste underground near Carlsbad. The center demonstrates how the waste is disposed and tries to emphasize the project's safety. The visitor center (☎ 234 7200), 101 E Greene St, is open from 8 am to 4 pm Monday to Friday. See the aside below.

### Eddy County Courthouse
This historic building at Canal and Mermod Sts was constructed in 1891 and remodeled in 1939. The Southwestern touches are worth a look: the cattle brands of the most important local ranches are carved into the door frames, and the interior ceilings boast heavy beams and ornate iron chandeliers.

---

### Hazard, Boon or Both?
The Waste Isolation Pilot Plant (WIPP) is a controversial project to dispose of nuclear waste in underground salt beds near Carlsbad. Proponents point out that the project brings jobs and strengthens Carlsbad's economy. Opponents of the project are concerned that a transportation accident could cause incalculable damage to New Mexico. The waste comes from the Los Alamos area and has to travel across almost the entire state to reach Carlsbad – how can the waste be transported absolutely safely over such a long distance? And how long can it remain harmlessly buried? As you walk around Carlsbad, you'll see stickers on car bumpers and store windows opposing or supporting WIPP. ■

---

### Family History Center
The Family History Center (☎ 885 1368), 1200 W Church, is an international genealogical research facility affiliated with the Salt Lake Library. Visitors are welcome to research their family tree. Hours are from 10 am to 4 pm Tuesday to Friday and from 6 to 7 pm on Tuesday and Wednesday.

### Brantley Lake State Park
This state park (☎ 457 2384) is about 18 miles north of Carlsbad and 30 miles south of Artesia. There is fishing, boating, picnicking and camping. Day use is $3, and camping is possible.

### Special Events
Alfalfafest, Carlsbad's annual country fair, is held the second weekend in October. Apart from the usual parade, food booths, music, dancing and arts & crafts displays, the festival features plenty of old-fashioned, country-style events that are a lot of fun. Try your skill in the water balloon and 'cow chip' tossing competitions, or watch three-legged, tractor, outhouse and duck races – it's all here.

There is also an annual hot-air balloon competition in the first week of September.

### Places to Stay – camping
South of Carlsbad is *Carlsbad RV* (☎ 885 6333), 4301 National Parks Hwy, has a pool, laundry, playground and showers. Sites are $12 or $16.50 with hookups. Also try *Midcity Trailer Park* (☎ 887 6220), 1701 S Canal, and *Windmill Grocery & RV Park* (☎ 885 9761), 3624 National Parks Hwy. *Brantley Lake State Park* (see above) has tent sites for $6 and sites with RV hookups for $11. Showers are available.

### Places to Stay – bottom end
The cheapest place is the *El Rey Motel* (☎ 887 5331), 3515 National Parks Highway, which has basic doubles from $21. The *La Fonda Motel* (☎ 885 6242), 1522 S Canal St, has good rooms with queen-size beds and a refrigerator for $24/28 for singles/doubles. There is a pool. The *Economy Inn* (☎ 885 4914), 1621 S

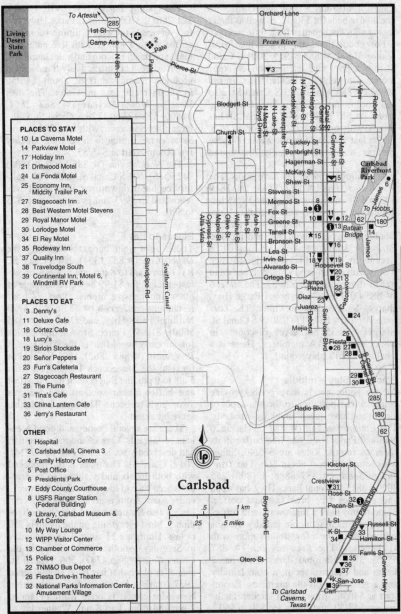

**NEW MEXICO**

**PLACES TO STAY**
10  La Caverna Motel
14  Parkview Motel
17  Holiday Inn
21  Driftwood Motel
24  La Fonda Motel
25  Economy Inn,
    Midcity Trailer Park
27  Stagecoach Inn
28  Best Western Motel Stevens
29  Royal Manor Motel
30  Lorlodge Motel
34  El Rey Motel
35  Rodeway Inn
37  Quality Inn
38  Travelodge South
39  Continental Inn, Motel 6,
    Windmill RV Park

**PLACES TO EAT**
 3  Denny's
11  Deluxe Cafe
16  Cortez Cafe
18  Lucy's
19  Sirloin Stockade
20  Señor Peppers
23  Furr's Cafeteria
27  Stagecoach Restaurant
28  The Flume
31  Tina's Cafe
33  China Lantern Cafe
36  Jerry's Restaurant

**OTHER**
 1  Hospital
 2  Carlsbad Mall, Cinema 3
 4  Family History Center
 5  Post Office
 6  Presidents Park
 7  Eddy County Courthouse
 8  USFS Ranger Station
    (Federal Building)
 9  Library, Carlsbad Museum &
    Art Center
10  My Way Lounge
12  WIPP Visitor Center
13  Chamber of Commerce
15  Police
22  TNM&O Bus Depot
26  Fiesta Drive-in Theater
32  National Parks Information Center,
    Amusement Village

**Carlsbad**

0        .5        1 km

0    .25    .5 miles

Canal St, also has a pool and rooms with queen-size beds for $30/32, as well as larger rooms with kitchenettes for a little more.

For about the same price, the *Royal Manor Motel* (☎ 885 3191), 2001 S Canal St, has a pool and refrigerators in some rooms. The centrally located *La Caverna Motel* (☎ 885 4151), 223 S Canal St, also has rooms for $22/24. The *Driftwood Motel* (☎ 887 6522), 844 S Canal St, has rooms with queen-size beds for $22/25. These last two lack pools. Most of these cheaper hotels offer weekly discounted rates.

The following hotels all have pools. The *Stagecoach Inn* (☎ 887 1148), at 1819 S Canal St, has a big playground for children, a spa and rooms with queen- or king-size beds. A coin laundry is available. Double rooms are about $40 and up. The *Parkview Motel* (☎ 885 3117), 401 E Greene St, has a playground and nice rooms with queen- and king-size beds and free in-room coffee for $28/37. The *Motel 6* (☎ 885 0011), 3824 National Parks Hwy, charges $32/38, less in winter. The *Lorlodge Motel* (☎ 887 1171), 2019 S Canal St, charges $30/35 but gives discounts in winter and to AAA members. There is a small children's playground.

### Places to Stay – middle

All the better hotels have pools, provide courtesy transportation to the bus depot or airport and have queen- and king-size beds. The *Continental Inn* (☎ 887 0341), 3820 National Parks Hwy, has free coffee in its spacious rooms. Rates are $35/40. Suites with waterbeds cost about $60. The *Travelodge South* (☎ 887 8888, 1 (800) 255 3050), 3817 National Parks Hwy, has a spa and provides free breakfast and coffee. Some rooms have a microwave and refrigerator, and there is a coin laundry. Rooms start at $48/52 or a few dollars more with kitchenettes. The *Rodeway Inn* (☎ 887 5535), 3804 National Parks Hwy, has a sauna and exercise room, a coin laundry and a restaurant on the premises. Rooms start at $40/43; rooms with kitchen facilities are $48/50, and suites are $50 to $60.

The *Quality Inn* (☎ 887 2861, 1 (800) 321 2861), 3706 National Parks Hwy, is a full-service hotel with a dining room and coffee shop, a lounge with live entertainment and dancing, coin and valet laundries, a gift shop and attractively landscaped grounds. Rooms start at about $46/56 in summer and less in winter. The *Best Western Motel Stevens* (☎ 887 2851, 1 (800) 528 1234), 1829 S Canal St, is the largest hotel in town, with over 200 rooms. Services are similar to those at the Quality Inn. Rooms start at $45/55.

The *Holiday Inn* (☎ 885 8500, 1 (800) 742 9586), 601 S Canal St, is the only full-service hotel downtown. The hotel was renovated in 1993 and rates are about $75 to $80.

### Places to Eat

Those on a tight budget should try the *Deluxe Cafe* (☎ 887 1304), 224 S Canal St. It is open 5 am to 8 pm and features breakfast specials for $1.99 as well as a range of other inexpensive items. Two 24-hour restaurants are *Jerry's* (☎ 885 6793), 3720 National Parks Hwy, and *Denny's* (☎ 885 5600), 810 W Pierce St. Another choice for an early breakfast is the *Stagecoach Restaurant* (☎ 885 2862), 1801 S Canal St (next to the Stagecoach Inn). Open from 5 am to 9 pm, the Stagecoach has breakfast and buffet dinner specials and features Texas-style barbecue. The better hotels also serve breakfast.

There are several homey and good Mexican restaurants. One of the most popular, and deservedly so, is *Lucy's* (☎ 887 7714), 701 S Canal St. The place is often packed with both locals and visitors, so reservations aren't a bad idea, especially on weekends. Apart from a great Mexican menu, Lucy's also features a steak bar and grill for dinner. Most everything on the menu is $10 or less. Hours are 11 am to 10 pm Monday to Saturday. Another good choice is the *Cortez Cafe* (☎ 885 4747), 506 S Canal St, a smaller place that has been around since 1937 (that's a long time for southeastern New Mexico). It is open from 11 am to 2 pm and from 4 to 8 pm, Wednesday to

Sunday. For the ravenous traveler, *Señor Peppers* (☎ 887 0866), 834 S Canal St, has an all-you-can-eat Mexican lunch buffet. The restaurant is open from 11 am to 9 pm Monday to Saturday and from 11 am to 2 pm on Sunday. *Tina's Cafe* (☎ 885 4239), 3122 San Jose Blvd, also has homemade Mexican food.

*Furr's Cafeteria* (☎ 885 0430), 901 S Canal St, recently advertised all-you-can-eat lunches for $4.99 and dinners for $5.00 Monday to Friday. It has a good selection of other inexpensive meals. It is open daily from 11 am to 8 pm.

There are a couple of steak houses that offer seafood and fried chicken as well. The *Sirloin Stockade* (☎ 887 7211), 710 S Canal St, serves most meals for under $10 and features an all-you-can-eat soup, salad and dessert 'Smorgas Bar' for $5.50. It is open from 11 am to 9 pm daily, and to 10 pm on Fridays and Saturdays.

For Chinese dinners, try the *China Lantern Cafe* (☎ 885 3450), 3400 National Parks Hwy. This has been here since 1952, which is a good sign. Hours are 4:30 to 9 pm, Tuesday to Saturday.

The better hotels all have good restaurants. The best in town is the *Flume* at the Best Western Motel Stevens. American food is served in an elegant but informal Western ambiance. Dinner entrees range from $8 to $17. The Flume is open daily from 5:30 am to 10 pm.

### Entertainment

See the hotel lounges (above) for entertainment ideas. One of the liveliest bars in town is *My Way Lounge* (☎ 887 0212), 223 S Canal St in front of the La Caverna Motel. The wood-beam, rustic interior houses pool tables and a dance floor with live country & western and rock bands most nights of the week.

The *Fiesta Drive-in Theater* (☎ 885 4126), San Jose Blvd and Fiesta St, has three screens, giving you the chance to experience a form of American entertainment that has almost disappeared – the drive-in movie. The concession stand offers a range of fast food (not just candy and popcorn), so you can eat here and make a night of it. For indoor movies, go to the *Mall Cinema 3* (☎ 885 0777), 2322 W Pierce St.

The *Carlsbad Community Theater* (☎ 887 3157), on National Parks Hwy about five miles south of downtown, has regular dramatic performances.

### Getting There & Away

**Air** Carlsbad's Cavern City Airport (☎ 885 5236) is about six miles south of town. Mesa Air (☎ 885 0245 at the airport or 1 (800) 637 2247) has several direct flights a day to Albuquerque, Hobbs and Roswell.

**Bus** The Bus Depot (☎ 887 1108), 1000 S Canyon St, has a TNM&O bus to White City (for Carlsbad Caverns) at 9:40 am daily. The fare is $3.25. Buses also go to Hobbs, Roswell, Albuquerque and El Paso, Texas.

### Getting Around

Hertz (☎ 887 1500 at the airport, 1 (800) 654 3131) has rental cars. McCausland Aviation (☎ 885 5236) and Rent a Car (☎ 887 1500) have planes and cars to charter and rent. Both are at the airport. MOM'S Carwash (☎ 885 1183), 521 S Canal St, rents used cars – guaranteed clean.

## CARLSBAD CAVERNS NATIONAL PARK

Carlsbad Caverns has its skeptics. Who in their right mind would drive for hours across the desert just to see a cave? Once visitors see the caverns, however, even the most skeptical are impressed. This is one of the greatest cave systems in the world, and a visit is, without a doubt, a highlight of a journey through the Southwest.

The geological explanations for the cave system's existence are easy enough to understand and write about but very difficult to grasp in a realistic sense. The concepts are staggering. Carlsbad Caverns are in the Guadalupe Mountains, which began to be deposited as an underwater reef in a great inland sea 250 million years ago.

NEW MEXICO

Then the sea evaporated, leaving salt and gypsum deposits. Erosion and uplift began to uncover the reef, and rainwater percolating through it started to dissolve some of the limestone within. This process is continuing today, and thus, Carlsbad Caverns is referred to as a living cave system.

Indian people knew of the caves and left paintings near the entrance, but the steepness of the entrance precluded any in-depth exploration until the early 20th century. Then, local cowboys discovered bat dung (guano) deposited in the cave mouth by the millions of bats inhabiting the cave. People began mining the guano, which is a valuable fertilizer.

One of the miners, Jim White, began venturing further into the cave and emerged with tales of huge rooms full of incredible geological formations. Slowly, word of his exploits filtered out, and tourists began to visit the caverns. The earliest visitors were lowered into the cave in buckets – a far cry from today's system of elevators and walkways. In 1923, Carlsbad Caverns was proclaimed a national monument; it became a national park in 1930.

The park covers some 74 sq miles and includes almost 80 caves – the visitor gets to see only a small fraction of the entire system. Even this small fraction is huge by any standards. The normal walking tour from the cave mouth is three miles long and goes through an underground chamber called, with simple understatement, the Big Room. It is 1800 feet long, 255 feet high and over 800 feet below the surface. Several other tours are available. If you are pressed for time, you can descend by elevator, glimpse some of the underground highlights and return to the surface within a couple of hours. However, there is enough to keep you occupied for a couple of days or more.

The park's second most important attraction is the Mexican free-tail bat colony, but only those visitors who are around at dusk or dawn from April to October can appreciate it. During the rest of the year the bats winter in Mexico. The colony once numbered several million, but pesticide use diminished the colony to about a quarter of a million. (Pesticides kill insects, bats eat insects and, after eating thousands of poisoned bugs, the bats themselves become poisoned.) Today, with some degree of control of overpesticide use, the colony shows some signs of recovery, and current population estimates range from 300,000 to 500,000 bats.

There is also a visitors center which has information, a museum, a cafe, a gift shop and bookstore.Within the park you'll find a short nature trail, a nine-mile scenic drive and overnight backpacking.

## Orientation & Information

The park entrance is immediately west of White's City. The main cavern and visitor center are seven miles away along a winding mountain road lined with limestone cliffs in which cave entrances can be seen. Information is available at the National Parks Information Center in Carlsbad or at the visitor center (☎ 785 2232) in the park. To listen to a 24-hour recorded message about the caverns, call 785 2107.

The park is open from dawn till dusk, and admission is free. To enter the cavern, however, there is a $5 fee for adults and a $3 fee for children ages six to 15. (Golden Eagle Passes do not apply to these entrance fees; Golden Age or Access Pass holders are eligible for a 50% discount). All cave entrance fees are collected at the visitor center, open from 8 am to 7 pm June to August and from 8 am to 5:30 pm the rest of the year. The cavern is open from 8:30 am to 6:30 pm in summer and until 5 pm in winter – ticket sales stop 90 minutes before the cavern is closed. When you pay your entrance fee, you get an informative brochure with maps and detailed park information. Everything is closed on Christmas Day.

If you want to try the 50-plus miles of hiking trails, topographic maps are available at the visitor center. A one-mile nature trail starts outside the visitor center, and a 9.5-mile scenic loop drive begins nearby – no trailers or large vehicles allowed. There is a picnicking area.

Carlsbad caverns RR)

## Cave Tours

The main cavern is usually visited in one of two ways – the Red Tour or the Blue Tour. Both tours are self-guided and begin at the visitor center where you can rent a radio (for 50¢) to guide you on your way. In addition, special guided tours are sometimes available.

Underground temperatures are a constant 56°F, so a light sweater is appropriate. Smoking is not permitted anywhere underground. Food and drink are not allowed except in the underground lunchroom, which serves fast food, sandwiches and snacks. There are restrooms here. (The Park Service is considering closing the underground lunchroom because food particles are attracting creatures that don't belong in the cave system.)

Pets are not allowed underground, but kennels are available at the surface for a $3.50 fee. Children's strollers are not allowed – a nursery is available at the surface (for a $5 fee) if you don't want to bring your child underground (children under six are allowed on the Red and Blue Tours only). Much of the Red Tour is accessible to wheelchairs. Touching any of the formations or stepping off the designated trails is prohibited.

**Red Tour** This is the most popular tour. It begins with a 755-foot elevator descent from the visitor center to the main cavern,

followed by a 1.25-mile underground walk through the Big Room. The entire walk is paved and lit, and park rangers wander around to answer questions. The cavern and geological formations tower around you, and the views are splendid. This tour visits the best known formations and sites. A short cut allows you to take just half of the tour. The return is via the elevator.

**Blue Tour** This tour begins with a short walk from the visitor center to the main entrance of the cavern. From here, a steep trail hairpins down into the depths of the cave (wear good shoes for walking). It is a 1.75-mile descent, passing through the huge Main Corridor and into a number of smaller, scenic underground rooms. The Blue Tour then connects with the Red Tour route, thus making a three-mile trip in all. The return is via the elevator. Because of the extended length, Blue Tour ticket sales stop three hours before the cavern closes.

**Organized Tours** Ranger-led tours of the Red and Blue Tour routes are available in the winter when visitation is lower; during the summer, there are simply too many visitors for guided tours of the main routes.

For the adventurous, ranger-led tours to some of the lesser known areas are offered. These tours are not on paved trails, and participants are required to wear hard hats and headlamps (furnished by the Park Service). Be prepared to scramble and get a little muddy. Some of the tours are with candle lanterns to give participants an idea of what it must have been like to be an early explorer.

Tours are currently offered to Left Hand Cave, Lower Cave and the Cave of the White Giants. Most tours take about four hours and are limited to 12 participants. Two or three tours are offered daily in the summer. Advance reservations can be made by phone, but if you arrive at 8 am you'll often find space on a tour the same day, particularly midweek. The cost is $5 for adults and $3 for children six to 15 years old. Children under six are not permitted on the special tours. These fees also include the Blue or Red Tours, so you can spend the entire day underground.

Tours are also offered to Spider Cave, which one ranger described as 'down and dirty'. This one costs $10 for adults and $6 for children six to 15 years old.

**Other Caves** The above tours are all in or just off the main cavern. You can also visit **New Cave**, which is a 23-mile drive from the visitor center. New Cave is unlit and unpaved and can be visited only on ranger-led tours. You must furnish your own flashlight and transportation. The tour is limited to 25 people and is fairly strenuous. Children under six are not permitted. The tour costs $6 for adults and $3 for children, and does not include entrance to the main cavern. Entrance fees must be paid at the visitor center where you get directions for the 23-mile drive. From the New Cave parking lot it is a very steep half-mile climb to the cave mouth followed by a 1.25-mile hike through the cave. The tour lasts about 2.5 hours and reservations are recommended. Tours are offered most days during the summer and weekends during the rest of the year.

The awe-inspiring and very beautiful **Lechugilla Cave** was discovered in 1986. With a depth of 1593 feet and a length of about 60 miles it is the deepest and fourth largest cave in North America. Exploration is still continuing. See the March 1991 *National Geographic* magazine for superb photos. Visits to Lechugilla are for experienced cavers with technical equipment only. Typical visits last 24 to 36 hours and some last several days – permits are required from the National Park Service, which allows very limited numbers of cavers to enter for exploration, surveys or scientific study.

**Bat-Watching**
The colony of almost half a million Mexican free-tail bats inhabiting Carlsbad Cavern is a great attraction. The bats spend the day inside the cave (you can't see them) and come out at dusk. Rangers give interpretive lectures at the amphitheater by the cave's mouth while hundreds of visitors watch the bats emerge over a period of 30 minutes to two hours – it is quite a sight. The time of emergence depends on the weather (storms force the bats to stay inside). The visitor center can usually predict fairly accurately what time the bat flight will occur. From October to April the bats are in Mexico.

Every year in August, the Park Service has a Bat Flight Breakfast. This costs $5 and happens from 5 to 7 am. After breakfast, you get to watch the bats come swooping back into the cave. The fee also allows you into the cavern on the Red or Blue Tour. Call the park to find out the exact date. You can see the dawn arrival of the bats on other days too – the park is open, though the visitor center is closed till 8 am.

**Places to Stay & Eat**
There is no accommodation or car/RV overnighting within the park, although overnight backpacking trips into the desert backcountry are allowed by permit (which is free). Everything must be packed in, including water. Ask at the visitor center about trails.

Although many visitors to the caverns stay twenty miles north in the city of Carlsbad, the closest indoor accommodations to the park are in White's City, named after Jim White, the first serious explorer of Carlsbad Caverns. Basically a hotel complex rather than a city, White's City is at the entrance to the Carlsbad Caverns National Park.

Best Western runs the *Park Entrance RV Park*, which charges $16 for tent or RV sites with hookups. There are showers, a laundry, and pool and hot tub privileges at the local Best Western motels. The *Best Western Cavern Inn* and the *Best Western Guadalupe Inn* (☎ 785 2291, 1 (800) 228 3767) have large rooms for $75. They also manage the *Walnut Canyon Motel* across the street, which has smaller rooms for $52. There are two swimming pools, two hot tubs and a coin laundry.

Near these places to stay are a small grocery store, a post office, gift shops, and the Million Dollar Museum, which claims to have 30,000 Western items on display and charges visitors $2.50 to see them. From White's City to the caverns is a seven mile drive.

The town's two restaurants, *Fast Jack's* and the *Velvet Garden Restaurant* (both at ☎ 785 2291) serve fast food, and steak and seafood, respectively.

## Entertainment
The *Velvet Garter* in White's City has a saloon with swinging doors to swagger (stagger?) through. *Granny's Opera House* has old-fashioned melodrama (be prepared to cheer the heroine, boo the villain and throw popcorn at the enemy) most nights during the summer.

## Getting There & Away
Almost all visitors to the caverns come by car. There is a daily bus from Carlsbad or El Paso (Texas) to White's City with TNM&O. There is an airstrip at White's City for private aircraft. The folks at the Best Western in White's City have vans to pick you up at the airport or to take you to the caverns.

## GUADALUPE MOUNTAINS
This southeastern extension of the Sacramento Mountains continues through southeastern New Mexico and across into western Texas. The northern part of the range is in the Guadalupe District of New Mexico's Lincoln National Forest. South of the Texan state line, these mountains form the Guadalupe Mountains National Park. The eastern foothills of these mountains are in the Carlsbad Caverns National Park.

The Guadalupe Mountains are remote and fairly dry. Camping and hiking are the main activities, and fishing and hunting is allowed in the national forest area. Parts of the Guadalupe Mountains are an exposed reef (the Capitan Reef) that was formed 250 million years ago. Today, geologists continue to find numerous fossils of ancient sea creatures throughout the reef area.

## Lincoln National Forest
The Guadalupe District of the Lincoln National Forest encompasses 285,000 acres and ranges in altitude from 3500 to 7600 feet, allowing for a varied wildlife population. There are few roads, however, and facilities are quite primitive.

The main attraction here is **Sitting Bull Falls**, about 50 miles from Carlsbad. There are waterfalls, swimming holes and a picnic area but no campground. The area is open from April to November. The falls are reached either by taking Hwy 285 north of Carlsbad for 12 miles and then heading west on Hwy 137 and 276 or by taking Hwy 62/180 south of Carlsbad for about 10 miles and taking Hwy 408 west to 137 and 276. Follow the signs. These are unpaved roads in good enough condition for cars most of the year.

Hwy 137 also continues south to Rim Road 540 and Five Points Vista view point on the way to the Guadalupe Mountains National Park in Texas. Dispersed camping is allowed throughout the national forest. Further information and maps are available at the National USFS Ranger Station in Carlsbad.

## Guadalupe Mountains National Park (TX)
This national park is 55 miles south of Carlsbad and 110 miles east of El Paso, Texas. Although the park is entirely in Texas, the northern boundary is the New Mexican state line, and the closest access is from New Mexico. If you've driven this far to see Carlsbad Caverns, you might want to see this national park as well.

The main activities are hiking and backpacking. Unlike many other Southwestern national parks, there is no scenic drive. The park is crossed in the far southeastern corner by Hwy 62/180, and there is a visitor center here. When I stopped by one foggy and slightly drizzly August day, I was the only visitor – when you consider the hordes of visitors thronging most national parks in August, you realize that this is a park for the seeker of remote wilderness. Guadalupe Mountains National Park is an island in the Chihuahuan Desert and contains Guadalupe Peak (8749 feet), the highest point in Texas.

The main visitor center (☎ (915) 828 3251), Box 400, Salt Flat, TX 79847-9400, is open from 7 am to 6 pm in the summer, shorter hours in winter. The center offers a small museum, slide show, maps and books, and all the information you'll need. Admission to the park is free.

There is no food or lodging in the park, though there are two campgrounds. *Pines Springs Campground*, next to the visitor center, has water and restrooms but no showers. Campfires are prohibited. Camping is $5 a night, and the campground is rarely full except during some summer weekends. *Dog Canyon Campground*, at the far north of the park, is reached via Hwy 137 from New Mexico. This campground has similar services but no fee.

The McKittrick Canyon Visitor Center is about halfway between the New Mexican state line and the main visitor center. This center is open from 6 am to 6 pm in the summer and gives access to McKittrick Canyon, one of the most scenic hiking areas in the park. Both day and overnight hikes are accessible from here.

Both visitor centers and campgrounds give access to the 80 miles of hiking trails in the park. Backcountry camping is allowed in designated campsites with a permit, which can be obtained for free from the visitor centers. Water is available at some backcountry campsites – talk to rangers for details.

The nearest lodging is in White's City and Carlsbad (35 and 55 miles northeast) or in Van Horn, Texas, 75 miles south.

## HOBBS

Hobbs is named after James Hobbs, a Texan settler who built the first house here in 1907. Cattle ranching and the cultivation of alfalfa, cotton, grain and vegetables were economic mainstays until oil was discovered in 1928. Although cattle and agriculture are still important, Hobbs is now the center of New Mexico's largest oil field.

Hobbs is 69 miles east of Carlsbad or 77 miles west of Artesia. The drive is through the flat ranch lands (formerly grasslands) of the Llano Estacado. The horizontal landscape is punctuated frequently by seesaw-like pumps, stolidly forcing oil to the surface. Texan pioneers, cattle ranches, oil fields – Hobbs is only three miles from the Texan state line and feels equally Texan and New Mexican.

With a population of over 30,000, Hobbs is the largest town in Lea County (population 55,000).

### Orientation & Information

Hobbs' main west-east drag is Hwy 62/180, which is Marland Blvd. The main north-south thoroughfare is Hwy 18, called Del Paso St downtown and running into Bender Blvd and Lovington Hwy north of town. To the south, Hwy 18 heads toward the small oil communities of Eunice and Jal. Neither Hwy 62/180 nor Hwy 18 is a simple straight line – see the map.

The chamber of commerce (☎ 397 3202), 400 N Marland Blvd, has information about Hobbs, as well as Lovington and Lea County. It is open from 9 am to 5 pm Monday to Friday. The library (☎ 397 9328) is at 509 N Shipp Drive. The post office (☎ 393 2912) is at 119 W Taylor St. The Lea Regional Hospital (☎ 392 6581) is at 5419 Lovington Hwy. The police (☎ 397 9265 or 911) are at 316 N Dalmont St. For general food and clothes shopping, try the Bel Air Shopping Center at the intersection of Bender and Del Paso.

### Lea County Cowboy Hall of Fame & Western Heritage Center

The Hall of Fame & Western Heritage Center (☎ 392 1275, 392 4510 ext 371) is at 5317 Lovington Hwy on the campus of New Mexico Junior College. Prominent local ranchers and rodeo cowboys are honored here with commemorative plaques and displays of their personal memorabilia. There are also exhibits of local Indian culture, pioneer history and natural history. Hours are 1 to 5 pm Wednesday to Saturday or by appointment (call ahead – hours have changed several times in the past few years). Admission is free.

## Thelma A Webber
## Southwest Heritage Room
The Heritage Room (☎ 392 6561 ext 314) is in the Scarborough Memorial Library at the College of the Southwest, 6610 Lovington Hwy. Artifacts of local history ranging from Paleo-Indian through pioneering cowboy to early oil exploration are the focus of this small museum. Hours are 8 am to 9 pm from Monday to Thursday, 8 am to 5 pm on Friday and 9 am to 1 pm on Saturday during the school year. During the summer break, hours are 8 am to 5 pm Monday to Friday. The museum is closed on holidays. Admission is free.

## Safari Ostrich Farms
Cattle ranching's newest competitor is ratite ranching, a small but growing industry in the Southwest. Ratites are flightless running birds with a flat breastbone and include the African ostrich, Australian emu and South American rhea, all of which can be seen at this farm. The Ostrich Farms (☎ 393 4920) are at 2700 Brand Drive, off Hwy 62/180 northeast of Hobbs. Tours are available.

## Harry McAdams State Park
The Harry McAdams State Park (☎ 392 5845) is just off the Lovington Hwy, about seven miles northwest of downtown Hobbs. There is a picnic area and children's playground, and a small area museum in the visitor center. Day use is $3 per carload; overnight camping is $7 or $11 with hookups. Showers are available.

## Confederate Air Force Museum
The Confederate Air Force Museum (☎ 392 5342) is at Lea County Airport on Carlsbad Hwy. This collection of WW II aircraft in flying condition is in a hangar at the airport and can be visited daily from 8 am till sunset. If the hanger is closed, call airport security (☎ 393 9915). Admission is free.

## Linam Ranch Museum
The Linam Ranch Museum (☎ 393 4784, 393 2766) is on Carlsbad Hwy eight miles west of town. This collection of local turn-of-the-century Indian and pioneer artifacts can be visited by appointment only. Watch for a group of buildings on the south side of the road near a Big Red Bull sign. The museum is the stone building.

## Gliding
Hobbs' weather is ideal for soaring and gliding, and the town is the home of the National Soaring Foundation (☎ 392 6032) and the Soaring Society of America (☎ 392 1177). You can take joy rides or lessons at the Hobbs Industrial Airpark. The airpark is behind Harry McAdams State Park and is not the commercial Lea County Airport.

## Other Activities
For **swimming** try the public pools at Humble Park (☎ 397 9337), 700 N Grimes, and Heizer Park (☎ 397 9316), 215 E Castle (0.8 miles south of Marland Blvd on Cochran St).

Play **golf** at the Ocotillo Golf Course (☎ 397 9297), adjacent to Harry McAdams State Park.

## Special Events
Mexican Independence Day is celebrated during the Cinco de Mayo (5 May) festival every year in the City Park with parades, Mexican food booths, and arts & crafts.

The National Soaring Glider Championships take place annually in July.

## Places to Stay – camping
The *Oriole Courts RV Park* (☎ 397 2551), 615 N Marland Blvd, is a small RV campground charging $11 for sites with hookups. Camping is available at *Harry Mc-Adams State Park*; see above.

## Places to Stay – bottom end
There are plenty of inexpensive places to stay – prices may rise during the Glider Championships or the Lea County Fair in nearby Lovington, but generally these hotels are a good value.

The *Desert Hills Motel* (☎ 393 9196), 129 E Marland Blvd, offers a swimming pool and hot tub. Single rooms start at $19;

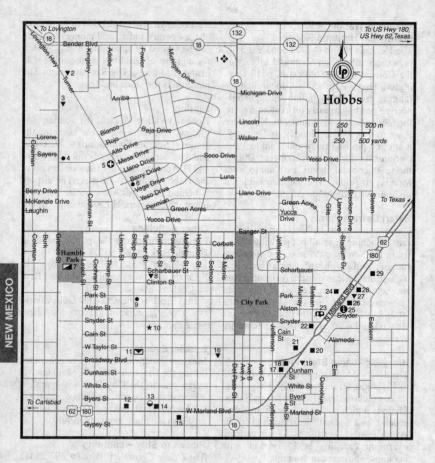

| PLACES TO STAY | | |
|---|---|---|
| 12 | La Posada Motel | |
| 14 | Lamplighter Motel | |
| 15 | Palms Inn | |
| 17 | Desert Hills Motel | |
| 18 | Rose Motel | |
| 20 | Best Western Leawood | |
| 21 | Executive Inn, Sands Motel | |
| 22 | Inn Keepers | |
| 23 | Oriole Courts RV Park | |
| 24 | Zia Motel | |
| 26 | Hobbs Motor Inn | |

| 28 | Sixpence Inn |
|---|---|
| 29 | Super 8 Motel |

**PLACES TO EAT**

| 2 | Western Sizzlin' Steak House |
|---|---|
| 3 | Cattle Baron |
| 8 | The Griddle |
| 16 | La Fiesta |
| 19 | Mi Won Chinese Restaurant |
| 21 | Sirloin Stockade Restaurant |
| 27 | Kettle Restaurant |

| OTHER | | |
|---|---|---|
| 1 | Bel Aire Shopping Center | |
| 4 | Community Players Playhouse | |
| 5 | Hospital | |
| 6 | Broadmoor Theater | |
| 7 | Pool | |
| 9 | Library | |
| 10 | Police | |
| 11 | Post Office | |
| 13 | Bus Terminal | |
| 25 | Chamber of Commerce | |

doubles with a king-size bed are $25. The *Executive Inn* (☎ 397 6541), 211 N Marland Blvd, offers free coffee and has nice rooms starting at $30/40 for singles/doubles. The *Sixpence Inn* (☎ 393 0221), 509 N Marland Blvd, has rooms sleeping up to four people for $25 – a good deal for budget travelers. There is a pool as well. The *Sands Motel* (☎ 393 4442), 1300 E Broadway, has rooms for $19/25. Fax and copy machines are available. The *Super 8 Motel* (☎ 397 7511, 1 (800) 800 8000), 722 N Marland Blvd, offers free coffee and has rooms beginning at about $28/32, as well as more expensive suites. The *Zia Motel* (☎ 397 3591), 619 N Marland Blvd, has nice rooms for $23/26. There is a pool.

The following three hotels charge about $18/25 for singles/ doubles: *Palms Inn* (☎ 393 6166), 315 E Marland Blvd (with a pool), *Rose Motel* (☎ 393 2020), 1223 E Broadway, and *Western Holiday Motel* (☎ 393 6494), 2724 W Marland Blvd. Other cheap places include *La Posada Motel* (☎ 393 2762), 210 W Marland Blvd, and the *Lamplighter Motel* (☎ 397 2406), 110 E Marland Blvd, which has a pool and offers weekly rates beginning at $80.

### Places to Stay – middle

All the hotels listed in this section have a swimming pool and feature queen- or king-size beds. The *Hobbs Motor Inn* (☎ 397 3251, 1 (800) 635 8839 outside New Mexico, 1 (800) 624 5937 in New Mexico), 501 N Marland Blvd, has a restaurant and lounge with live music and dancing on weekends. Rooms are about $37/42 for singles/doubles. The *Best Western Leawood* (☎ 393 4101, 1 (800) 528 1234), 1301 E Broadway, has rooms for $39/44 and includes breakfast. One of the newer good hotels in Hobbs is *Inn Keepers* (☎ 397 7171, 1 (800) 628 40740), 309 N Marland Blvd. Continental breakfast is included in the rates of $36/40 for singles/doubles.

### Places to Eat

There are plenty of fast-food places. *The Griddle*, 710 N Turner St, is open from 6 am to 2 pm for early breakfasts and lunches.

The *Kettle Restaurant* (☎ 397 0663), 505 N Marland Blvd, is open 24 hours.

*La Fiesta* (☎ 397 1235), 604 E Broadway, has been around since 1957 serving inexpensive Mexican lunches and dinners. The *Mi Won Chinese Restaurant* (☎ 393 7644), 1518 E Marland Blvd, has a daily all-you-can-eat lunch buffet.

The best place in town is the *Cattle Baron* (☎ 393 2800), 1930 N Grimes St, serving steak and seafood; there is also a lounge. Hours are from 11 am to 9:30 pm daily except Friday and Saturday, when they serve till 10:00 pm. Dinner entrees are in the $10 to $20 range; lunches are much cheaper. A cheaper place for steak and seafood is the *Sirloin Stockade* (☎ 393 0306) at 1406 E Broadway. Open daily from 11 am to 9 pm, this one has an all-you-can-eat smorgasbord during the week. Also good is *Western Sizzlin' Steak House* (☎ 393 7608), 2022 N Turner, which serves homemade rolls.

### Entertainment

Movies are screened at the *Broadmoor Theater* (☎ 397 2603), 1400 N Turner, and the *Cinema Three* (☎ 392 3988), 1609 Joe Harvey Blvd.

The *Community Players Playhouse* (☎ 393 0676), 1700 N Grimes, presents plays several times a year. There are also three nightclubs in town.

### Getting There & Away

**Air** Lea County Airport (☎ 393 4943, 393 9915) is five miles west of downtown. Mesa Airlines (☎ 393 1327 at the airport, 1 (800) 637 2247) has two or three flights a day to Albuquerque and Carlsbad.

**Bus** The bus terminal (☎ 397 3535) is at 400 S Turner. TNM&O has one bus a day to Lovington, continuing into Texas, and two buses a day to Carlsbad, continuing to El Paso, Texas.

### Getting Around

City Taxi (☎ 393 5151) gets you around. National (☎ 393 6424, 393 2010) has rental cars at the airport.

## LOVINGTON

Although Hobbs is the largest and most important town in Lea County, Lovington, 22 miles northwest of Hobbs, is the county seat. The town is named after Robert Florence Love, around whose homestead the town was founded in 1908. Agriculture was Lovington's economic mainstay until 1950 when oil was found a few miles to the northeast. Now, oil and natural gas are Lovington's most important industries. The town has a population of 9500.

### Orientation & Information

Hwy 18 (Main St downtown) runs north-south and is the most important thoroughfare. Hwy 82 (Ave D downtown) is the main east-west intersection.

The chamber of commerce (☎ 396 5311) is at 1535 N Main St. The library (☎ 396 3144) is at 119 S Main St. The post office (☎ 396 2300) is at 203 E Ave D. The local newspaper is the *Lovington Daily Leader*. The police (☎ 396 2811 or 911) are at 213 S Love St. The hospital (☎ 396 6611) is at 1600 N Main St.

### Lea County Historical Museum

The historical museum (☎ 396 4805) is housed in an old hotel at 103 S Love St. Local pioneer artifacts are on display.

### Special Events

Call the chamber of commerce about any of the following county events. The Lovington Auto Show, featuring tractors, vintage and model cars, is held at the Lea County Fairgrounds during the first half of April. The Country & Bluegrass Music Festival is held on the courthouse lawn in July.

The Fourth of July is celebrated in Chaparral Park with entertainment all day, highlighted by the World's Greatest Lizard Race with dozens of reptilian racers competing for trophies. There are traditional fireworks in the evening.

The annual Lea County Fair & Rodeo (☎ 396 5344) is one of the biggest county fairs in New Mexico and is over 60 years old. It is held at the county fairgrounds

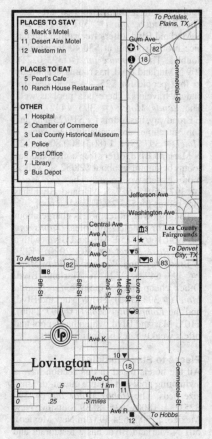

PLACES TO STAY
8  Mack's Motel
11  Desert Aire Motel
12  Western Inn

PLACES TO EAT
5  Pearl's Cafe
10  Ranch House Restaurant

OTHER
1  Hospital
2  Chamber of Commerce
3  Lea County Historical Museum
4  Police
6  Post Office
7  Library
9  Bus Depot

Lovington

during the second week in August. There's a top-notch PRCA rodeo as well as a huge variety of livestock and agricultural events ranging from swine judging and sheep shearing to a flower show. There are also parades, dances, a fiddlers contest, food booths, arts & crafts and much more.

The annual Southeastern New Mexico Arts & Crafts Show draws exhibitors from neighboring states during the first weekend in November. The annual Electric Light Parade features dozens of floats covered with Christmas lights parading through downtown after dark on the last weekend of November.

## Places to Stay

The *Desert Aire Motel* (☎ 396 3623), 1620 S Main St, charges $20 for a double room. The *Western Inn* (☎ 396 3635), 2212 S Main St, has a swimming pool and charges $24 for doubles. The hotel offers long-term discounts and has some rooms with kitchenettes. *Mack's Motel* (☎ 396 2588), 805 W Ave D, is similar.

The best in town is the *Lovington Inn* (☎ 396 5346), 1600 W Ave D (at the corner of 17 St). There is a pool, a decent restaurant and a lounge with dancing. Rates are $36 for a double.

## Places to Eat

The *Ranch House Restaurant* (☎ 396 4130), 1318 S Main St, is reasonably priced. It is open for breakfast, lunch and dinner, and offers American and Mexican food. *Pearl's Cafe* (☎ 396 2067), 318 S Love St, serves home-style breakfasts and lunches. The *Pioneer Steak House* (☎ 396 2348), 2510 S Main St, is locally popular for lunch and dinner. The restaurant in the Lovington Inn is also good.

## Getting There & Away

The bus station (☎ 396 4501), 913 S Main St, has one or two buses a day eastbound into Texas or southbound to Hobbs and Carlsbad.

## PORTALES

This pleasant college town (population 13,000) is the home of Eastern New Mexico University (ENMU). With almost 4000 students, the university contributes a great deal to the atmosphere and cultural life of the town. There are several museums in and around Portales. The town lies at just over 4000 feet at the northern end of the Llano Estacado.

Because of the relatively deep water table, Portales was a very small town until the drilling of deep wells in the 1940s enabled agriculture to expand. Today, agriculture forms the base of the economy. Wheat, milo (a form of sorghum), corn, cotton and peanuts are the main crops. Portales produces more Valencia peanuts than anywhere in the world – peanut farming and peanut butter manufacturing are big business. Cattle ranching is also important, as is ENMU, which employs over 500 people.

## Orientation & Information

Portales is 19 miles southwest of Clovis and 91 miles northeast of Roswell on Hwy 70 (this parallels the railway; there are no passenger services). Getting around can be confusing. Hwy 70 is a divided road downtown, running southwest to northeast on W 2nd St and northeast to southwest on W 1st St. Downtown streets run southwest to northeast, while avenues run southeast to northwest. Things get complicated away from the old downtown, where avenues change to run north-south and streets to east-west. Study the map.

Tourist information is available from the Roosevelt Chamber of Commerce (☎ 356 8541), 200 E 7th St at Abilene Ave. Information about Eastern New Mexico University is available on campus (☎ 562 1011). The *Portales News-Tribune* is the local daily newspaper. The library (☎ 356 3940) is at 218 S Ave B. The post office (☎ 356 4781) is at 116 W 1st St (inside, check out the New Deal mural entitled *Buffalo Range* painted in 1938). The hospital (☎ 356 4411) is at 1700 S Ave O. The police (☎ 356 4404, or 911) are at 1700 N Boston Ave.

## Eastern New Mexico University Museums

There are several museums on the campus that don't have fixed hours, so call ahead. **Roosevelt County Historical Museum** (☎ 562 2592) is on the southeast side of Hwy 70 near the ENMU administration buildings. The main focus is pioneer and early settlement history, though archaeology and Indian history are also represented. While you're nearby, take a look at the interesting New Deal murals in the administration building (☎ 562 2123).

The **Jack Williamson Science Fiction Collection** is in the University Library (☎ 562 2624), south of the administration building. Williamson used to teach at

ENMU and authored dozens of sci-fi novels and stories. His manuscripts and his letters to sci-fi writers Robert Heinlein and Ray Bradbury can be inspected. The library also has a New Deal mural.

The **Miles Museum** (☎ 562 2651) south of the library in Roosevelt Hall, has a geology display. Also in the same building is the **Natural History Museum** (☎ 562 2723), which focuses on local wildlife.

### Blackwater Draw Museum

The Blackwater Draw Museum (☎ 562 2202), on Hwy 70 about seven miles northeast of downtown, is next to the important Blackwater Draw archaeological site (☎ 356 5235). It was here, in the 1930s, that arrowheads and other artifacts of Paleo-Indian culture discovered at this site proved that people were living here at least 11,000 years ago. This led scientists to the realization that people had been living in the Americas several thousand years earlier than previously estimated.

For the average tourist, there's not much to see, but archaeology buffs will want to make a stop and tour the site. A small museum exhibits Clovis arrowheads (named after the nearby town) and has an interpretive display.

During the summer, the museum is open from 10 am to 5 pm Monday to Saturday, noon to 5 pm on Sunday. During the rest of the year, it is daily open except Monday. Admission is $2 for adults and $1 for children and seniors. On the fourth Sunday of each month admission is free. The archaeological site is a quarter mile from the museum. Summer hours are the same as the museum. In spring and fall the site is open on weekends only, weather permitting; it is closed from November to February.

### Windmill Collection

A private collection of over 60 windmills, some of them dating to the 1870s, can be seen in a field off Kilgore Ave, three-quarters of a mile south of 3rd St at the east end of town. The private collection, owned and curated by Bill Dalley, is the largest windmill collection in the USA.

### Oasis State Park

This state park (☎ 356 5331), Box 144, 88130, provides outdoor recreation for the residents of Portales and Clovis. There is a small lake (the oasis) for fishing surrounded by cottonwood trees and sand dunes. Picnicking and camping are available. Day use is $3. Get there by taking Hwy 70 two miles northeast of Portales, then Hwy 467 north for about six miles.

### Grulla National Wildlife Refuge

Although administered from Texas, the Grulla National Wildlife Refuge (☎ (806) 946 3341) is in New Mexico. Drive 16 miles east of Portales on Hwy 88 to the village of Arch, then three miles south. This is a wintering site for various waterfowl, including sandhill cranes.

### Special Events

Heritage Days are held in late May – there is a rodeo and other contests, a parade and entertainment. The Roosevelt County Fair is held in mid-August and features agricultural and livestock shows. The rodeo and fairgrounds are at the north end of Boston Ave.

The big annual event is the Peanut Valley Festival, usually held around the third weekend in October. Apart from arts & crafts and entertainment, the festival features nutty events such as burying students in a tank full of peanuts (for charity), peanut cooking and craft contests, and peanut olympics. The festival is over 20 years old.

### Places to Stay – camping

The *Wagon Wheel Campground* (☎ 356 3700) has RV and tent sites about four miles northeast of downtown on Hwy 70. Oasis State Park offers primitive campsites for $6 or $7 and sites with partial RV hookups are $11. There are showers.

### Places to Stay

The *Super 8 Motel* (☎ 356 8518), 1709 W Hwy 70, has rooms with queen-size beds starting at $39.88. Morning coffee is available in the lobby, and there is a small

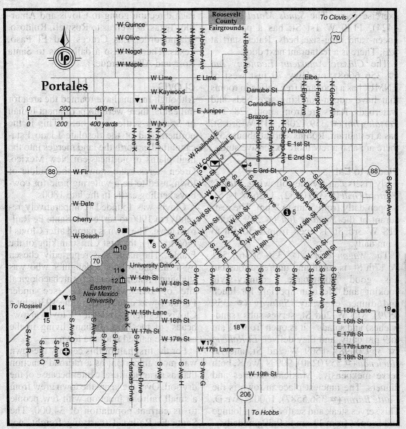

Portales

W Quince
W Olive
W Nogol
W Maple

N Ave B
N Ave A
N Main Ave
N Abilene Ave

N Boston Ave

Roosevelt
County
Fairgrounds

To Clovis

70

W Lime          E Lime

W Kaywood
W Juniper       E Juniper

▼1

Danube St
Canadian St
Brazos

N Elgin Ave
N Fergo Ave
N Globe Ave

0    200    400 m
0    200    400 yards

W Ivy

N Ave K
N Ave J

Elbe
Amazon
N Chicago Ave
E 1st St
E 2nd St

88

W Fir

W Railroad E
W Commercial E

2
3
4

▼

E 3rd St

88

S Elgin Ave
S Kilgore Ave

W 1st St
W 2nd St

6

S Main Ave
S Abilene Ave
S Chicago Ave
S Dallas Ave

W Date
Cherry
W Beach

9 ■
▼8
⌂10

W 3rd St
W 4th St
S Ave D
S Ave C
W 5th St
W 6th St
W 7th St
W 8th St

5 ℹ

S 9th St
S 10th St
W 11th St
W 12th St

70

University Drive
11 ●
12 ⌂
W 14th St
W 14th Lane

Eastern
New Mexico
University

S Ave F
S Ave E
S Ave D
S Ave C
S Ave B
S Ave A
S Main Ave
S Abilene Ave
S Globe Ave

W 14th St

To Roswell

▼13
■14
15

S Ave K
W 15th Lane
W 15th St
W 16th St

18▼

E 15th Lane

19 ●

E 16th St
E 17th St
E 17th Lane
E 18th St

S Ave R
S Ave Q
S Ave P
S Ave O
S Ave N
S Ave M
S Ave L
16 ✚

W 17th St
W 17th Lane

▼17

Utah Drive
Kansas Drive
S Ave J
S Ave I
S Ave H
S Ave G

W 19th St

206

To Hobbs

NEW MEXICO

### PLACES TO STAY
6   Portales Inn
9   Sands Motel
14  Classic American
    Economy Inn
15  Super 8 Motel

### PLACES TO EAT
1   La Hacienda Restaurant
6   Portales Restaurant
8   Subway Sandwiches
9   Mark's Eastern Grill
13  El Rancho Restaurant
17  Wagon Wheel Restaurant

18  Cattle Baron Restaurant

### OTHER
2   Tower Theater
3   Post Office
4   Bus Depot
5   Chamber of Commerce
7   Library
10  Historical Museum
11  University Library
12  Miles Museum,
    Natural History Museum
16  Hospital
19  Windmill Collection

exercise room. The *Sands Motel* (☎ 356 4424), 1130 W 1st St, has a pool and queen- and king-size beds. Rates start at $23. There is a restaurant next door.

The *Classic American Economy Inn* (☎ 356 6668), on Hwy 70 just west of ENMU, has a pool and free coffee in rooms that have queen- or king-size beds and waterbeds. Rates are from about $28. The *Portales Inn* (☎ 359 1208), 218 W 3rd St, has a restaurant. Rooms start at about $32; there are also a few more expensive suites.

### Places to Eat

Early risers can try the following. *Mark's Eastern Grill* (☎ 359 0952), 1126 W 1st St, is open daily from 5 am to 9 pm. The restaurant at the *Portales Inn* (☎ 359 1208), 218 W 3rd St, is open from 6:30 am to 8 pm daily.

The *Wagon Wheel* (☎ 356 5036), 521 W 17th St, is small and unpretentious but has good homemade, country-style cooking and Mexican specials for lunch and dinner everyday. *Subway* (☎ 359 0579), 815 W 2nd St, serves subs (sandwiches) and salads – it is open from 11 am to 9 pm daily, and they deliver. *El Rancho* (☎ 359 0098), 1609 W 2nd St, and *La Hacienda* (☎ 359 0280), 909 N Ave K, both serve inexpensive Mexican lunches and dinners. The fanciest place in town is the *Cattle Baron* (☎ 356 5587), 1600 S Ave D. This serves steak and seafood, has a lounge and is open from 11 am to 9:30 pm daily.

### Entertainment

The *College of Fine Arts* at ENMU presents theater and symphony events several times a year. Call the promotions office (☎ 562 2500) or the theater (☎ 562 2710, 562 2711) for information.

The *Tower Theater* (☎ 356 6081), 101 N Ave A, shows movies.

### Getting There & Away

The nearest scheduled commercial air service is in Clovis. The private Portales Airport (☎ 478 2863) is west of town.

The bus depot (☎ 356 6914) is at 215 E 2nd St. TNM&O has three buses a day in

each direction going to Clovis and Amarillo, Texas, as well as to Roswell, Ruidoso, Alamogordo, Las Cruces and El Paso, Texas. There is also a daily bus to Santa Rosa and Albuquerque.

## CLOVIS

Although Indians have roamed the area for millennia, there were no permanent Indian or Spanish settlements here. This is the northern end of the desolate Llano Estacado; further north the land merges into the high plains of northeastern New Mexico. Green Acres Lake, now in the middle of town, used to be a watering hole for cowboys herding cattle in the late 1800s.

Clovis was founded (comparatively recently) in 1906 to serve as a Santa Fe Railroad town. The town is named after Clovis I (466 to 511), the first Christian king of the Franks. The name was reportedly chosen by a railroad official's daughter who was studying French. The nearby archaeological site of Blackwater Draw (see under Portales) was discovered in the 1930s by a Clovis resident, and the 'Clovis arrowheads' of the Paleo-Indians living in the area were named after the town.

For the first half of this century the town was more important as a railroad junction than as an agricultural center because of the dry soil. Over the years the town grew from a small railroad junction with few people to its current population of 34,000. The Santa Fe Railroad (carrying freight, not passengers) continues to be an economic mainstay; however, the drilling of deep wells in the 1950s improved agriculture tremendously. Grain, alfalfa, corn, wheat and peanuts are all important, as is livestock. The nearby Cannon Air Force Base is also economically vital and provides an estimated 10% of the jobs in Clovis.

### Orientation & Information

Hwy 60/84 is the main east-west thoroughfare and is called Mabry Drive, 1st St and 3rd St as it goes through town and on to Texas, only nine miles to the east. Most motels are on Mabry Drive. Prince St is the main north-south cross street and becomes

Hwy 70 southbound and Hwy 209 northbound. Main St is the most historic street.

The chamber of commerce (☎ 763 3435) is at 215 N Main St. The library (☎ 769 7840) is at 701 N Main St. The *Clovis News Journal* is the local newspaper. The post office (☎ 763 5556) is in the Federal Building. Recycle at Clovis Recycling (☎ 762 2333), which is on the corner of Prince St and Brady Ave. The hospital (☎ 769 2141) is at 2100 N Thomas St at 21st St. The police (☎ 769 1921 or 911 in emergencies) are at 217 W 4th St.

### Historic Buildings
Sections of Main St are cobbled, and several interesting early buildings are found along it. Some of this important downtown street looks like part of a 1940s Western movie set. Built in 1919 the **Old Lyceum Theater** (☎ 763 6085), 411 N Main St, was the site of regular performances until its closure in 1974. It has since been refurbished and has occasional performances. Tours of its ornate vaudeville interior are available on request; call or ask at the barber shop next door.

The nine-story **Hotel Clovis**, topped by statues of Indian heads, is at 1st and Main Sts. When it was built in 1931, it was the highest building in New Mexico and retained that status until 1953. It has been closed for some years and is available for sale. Want to buy a historic 100-room hotel? Renovation costs are estimated at $2 million. Up the street at 4th St and Mitchell (a block west of Main) is another 1931 building, formerly the post office, then the county library until 1990. It houses a 48-by-111-inch oil mural of Clovis in the 1930s painted under government New Deal sponsorship. The future of this building is uncertain – ask at the chamber of commerce about seeing the building and mural.

The town's oldest surviving house (☎ 763 6505) was built in 1907; it is seen at the Curry County Fairgrounds (☎ 763 6502) at 600 S Norris St. The house contains a small museum that is open during the annual county fair and at other times by appointment.

### Norman Petty Studios
These recording studios are famous as the place where several early rock & roll artists made their names. Foremost among these was Buddy Holly, who recorded here in the 1950s, as well as Roy Orbison, Buddy Knox, Jimmy Gilmer and Roger Williams. Beatle Paul McCartney bought the rights to Buddy Holly's music in 1976 and was instrumental in renovating the old studio in 1986.

The old studio, 1313 W 7th St, can be toured by appointment (call the chamber of commerce) and is open during the annual Clovis music festival. It is a minor mecca for fans of early rock & roll. The Petty family still operates a studio in Clovis.

### Hillcrest Park & Zoo
Hillcrest Park, at 10th & Sycamore Sts, has a swimming pool, gardens, picnic areas, tennis courts and the Municipal Golf Course (☎ 769 7871). It also houses Hillcrest Zoo (☎ 769 7873), with a petting zoo and about 500 animals. Hours are 9 am to 6 pm daily except Monday; admission is $1.

### Eula Mae Edwards Museum
This museum is on the campus of the **Clovis Community College** (☎ 769 2811), 417 Schepps Blvd. A small collection of prehistoric and Indian artifacts is displayed, and there is an art gallery. Admission is free – call for current hours.

### Livestock Auctions
Cattle are auctioned every Wednesday in a livestock auction (☎ 762 4422), 504 S Hull St, drawing buyers from Texas, Kansas, Oklahoma and Arizona. In a good year about 70,000 head are sold for a total value of well over $30 million. Major horse auctions are held quarterly. Ranchers and cowboys, slow-moving cattle and fast-talking auctioneers – this is a good glimpse of the American West.

NEW MEXICO

### Ned Houck Park

Six miles north on Hwy 209, Ned Houck Park (☎ 389 5146) has fishing, archery, motorbike dirt tracks and picnic grounds. It also has the **Pappy Thornton Farm Museum**, which displays turn-of-the-century farm implements, a windmill and a ranch house.

### Texico

This is a small town on the New Mexico/Texas state line, nine miles east of Clovis. There is a New Mexico welcome center (☎ 482 3321), 336 Hwy 60/70/84, with maps and information. The annual festival is Texico-Farwell Border Days held around the last weekend of July. There is a rodeo, a parade, arts & crafts and a barbecue.

### Special Events

Pioneer Days occurs annually around the first weekend in June. It features an excellent PRCA rodeo, a parade, a fiddlers contest, a chili cook-off, dancing and athletic events including an outhouse race along Main St.

The Music Festival, with its special emphasis on '50s rock & roll and tours of the old Norman Petty Studios, also features a balloon rally, a '50s classic car parade and, of course, dancing. This all happens around late August or early September.

Also around this time is the Curry County Fair, with livestock and agricultural exhibits, a tractor pull, food booths, square dancing and a carnival.

The Cannon Air Force Base (☎ 784 3311), six miles west of town, holds an open house in September.

### Places to Stay – camping

The *Campground of Clovis* (☎ 763 6360), 4707 W 7th St, is 3.5 miles west of downtown. Tent sites start at $12.50; RV sites with hookups start at $16. There are showers, a laundry room and a playground.

In the past, overnight camping has been permitted at *Ned Houck Park* (see above). *Oasis State Park* (see under Portales) is 18 miles away (take Hwy 60/84 west for three

miles, then Hwy 467 south for 13 miles to the signed access road).

### Places to Stay – bottom end

Clovis has the best hotel selection that you'll find in the area.

The *Westward Ho Motel* (☎ 762 4451), 616 E 1st St, is the closest to downtown and charges from $21 a single. The reliable *Motel 6* (☎ 762 2995), 2620 Mabry Drive, charges $25/31 for singles/doubles and has a pool. Similarly priced rooms are available at the *Kings Inn* (☎ 762 4486), 1320 Mabry Drive, and at the *Pioneer Inn Motel* (☎ 769 0870), 1700 Mabry Drive.

The *Days Inn* (☎ 762 2971), 1720 Mabry Drive, is a good value with singles ranging from $27 to $32 and doubles from $33 to $38. The motel has a pool, pleasant rooms and complimentary coffee. Other possibilities in this price range include the *Bishops Inn* (☎ 769 1953), 2920 Mabry Drive, and the *Sands Motel* (☎ 763 3439), 1400 Mabry Drive. The Bishops Inn has a pool, and the Sands Motel has refrigerators in the rooms.

### Places to Stay – middle

The *Comfort Inn* (☎ 762 4591), 1616 Mabry Drive, has nice singles/doubles from $34/43. The *Best Western La Vista* (☎ 762 3808), 1516 Mabry Drive, is similarly priced. This one also has a few rooms with refrigerators and a suite for about $60. The *Clovis Inn* (☎ 762 5600, 1 (800) 535 3440), 2912 Mabry Drive, costs a few dollars more and includes a complimentary breakfast. It has some rooms with kitchenettes and a few suites. All three of these hotels have a swimming pool and queen-size beds.

The *Holiday Inn* (☎ 762 4491), 2700 Mabry Drive, is the most expensive hotel and provides the greatest range of facilities. There are two swimming pools and a sauna, a restaurant and lounge bar, and a game area. Many rooms have refrigerators; both queen- and king-size beds are available. Rates are around $50/60 for singles/doubles.

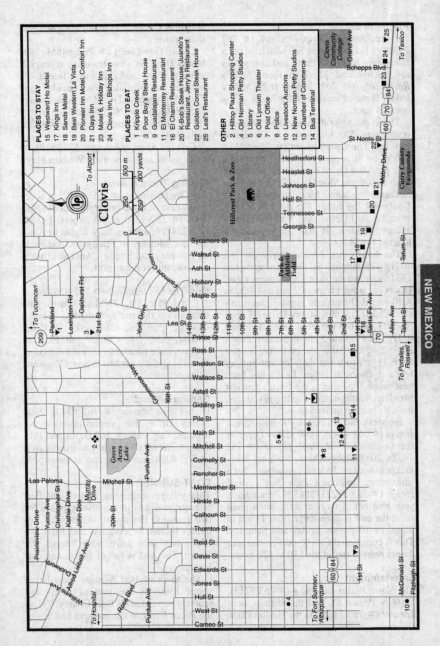

**PLACES TO STAY**
15 Westward Ho Motel
17 Kings Inn
18 Sands Motel
19 Best Western La Vista
20 Pioneer Inn Motel, Comfort Inn
21 Days Inn
23 Motel 6, Holiday Inn
24 Clovis Inn, Bishops Inn

**PLACES TO EAT**
1 Kripple Creek
3 Poor Boy's Steak House
9 Guadalajara Restaurant
11 El Monterrey Restaurant
16 El Charro Restaurant
20 K-Bob's Steak House, Juanito's Restaurant, Jerry's Restaurant
22 Golden Corral Steak House
25 Leal's Restaurant

**OTHER**
2 Hilltop Plaza Shopping Center
4 Old Norman Petty Studios
5 Library
6 Old Lyceum Theater
7 Post Office
8 Police
10 Livestock Auctions
12 New Norman Petty Studios
13 Chamber of Commerce
14 Bus Terminal

NEW MEXICO

## Places to Eat

For breakfast, try *Kripple Creek* (☎ 762 7399), 2417 N Prince St, which is open from 6 am to 11 pm daily and also serves sandwiches and Mexican food. *Jerry's Restaurant* (☎ 762 2081), 1620 Mabry Drive, features breakfasts for $1.99 – it is open 24 hours.

There are several inexpensive Mexican restaurants. The following are all recommended. The *Guadalajara* (☎ 769 9965), 916 W 1st St, is open for lunch from 11 am to 2 pm Monday to Friday and for dinner from 5 to 9 pm Monday to Saturday – the restaurant has a nice Mexican ambiance. *El Charro* (☎ 769 1345), 805 E 1st St, is open from 11 am to 2 pm and 5 to 9 pm daily except Sunday. It has all-you-can-eat lunches for $4.89.

The family-run *El Monterrey* (☎ 763 4031), 118 Mitchell St, has been here since 1931, so must be doing something right! Hours are from 11 am to 2 pm and 4:30 to 8:30 pm daily except Sunday. *Juanito's* (☎ 762 7822), 1608 Mabry Drive, is open from 11 am to 9 pm from Tuesday to Saturday and 11 am to 2 pm on Sunday. *Leal's* (☎ 763 4075), 3100 Mabry Drive, is open from 11 am to 9 pm daily except Sunday when it closes at 8 pm. Leal's has been here since 1957 and is the town's fanciest Mexican restaurant; despite this status, most dishes are under $10.

For steak and seafood, try *K-Bob's Steak House* (☎ 763 4443), 1600 Mabry Drive, or the *Golden Corral Steak House* (☎ 762 7422), 2018 Mabry Drive. Both are fairly inexpensive, family-style restaurants. For a little more ambiance *Poor Boy's Steak House* (☎ 763 5222), 2115 N Prince St, is your best bet. This restaurant has a good salad bar and is open daily from 11 am to 9 pm, or 10 pm on Friday and Saturday. This is considered Clovis' best restaurant.; dinner entrees run in the $10 to $20 range.

## Entertainment

The *North Plains Cinema 4* (☎ 763 7713), 2809 N Prince St, and the *Hilltop Twin Theater* (☎ 763 7876), in the Hilltop Plaza Shopping Center at 21st and Main Sts, both show movies.

*Clovis City Limits* (☎ 762 6485), 3800 Mabry Drive, is a bar featuring country & western music and dancing – free dance lessons are available on Tuesday and Thursday nights. The *Boot Hill Lounge and Nightclub* (☎ 762 5562), 4400 Mabry Drive, also has country & western bands and a dance floor.

*Caprock Amphitheater* (☎ 576 2519), 49 miles north, hosts historical Western Plays.

## Getting There & Away

**Air** Clovis Airport (☎ 763 4712) is seven miles east of town on 21st St. Mesa Airlines (☎ 389 1230 at the airport, 1 (800) 637 2247) has three daily flights to Albuquerque Monday to Friday and one flight on Saturday and Sunday. Aircraft charters are available at the airport.

**Bus** The bus terminal (☎ 762 4584) is at 1st and Pile Sts. TNM&O buses pass through on the run to Amarillo (Texas), Clovis, Portales, Roswell, Ruidoso, Alamogordo, Las Cruces and El Paso (Texas), three times a day in each direction. There is also a daily bus to Santa Rosa and Albuquerque.

## Getting Around

High Plains Shuttle (☎ 762 8343), 2700 Mabry Drive, has airport-to-downtown shuttles. City Cab (☎ 762 6050) and JMS Taxi (☎ 769 6000) can get you around. Avis (☎ 762 4084) has rental cars at the airport.

## FORT SUMNER

This village sprang up around old Fort Sumner, and it is in the history books for two reasons: the disastrous Bosque Redondo Indian Reservation and Billy the Kid's last showdown with Sheriff Pat Garret. The area is full of Indian and outlaw history.

The town of Fort Sumner (population about 1500) is the seat of small and sparsely populated De Baca County. It is on the Pecos River in the northern reaches of the Llano Estacado and has an economy based on agriculture and tourism.

## Orientation & Information

Hwy 60 runs east-west through town, where it is called Sumner Ave – this is the main thoroughfare, and most places of interest lie along it. Hwy 84 to Santa Rosa leaves Sumner Ave northbound on 4th St – this is the major north-south cross street. Fort Sumner is 84 miles north of Roswell, 45 miles southwest of Santa Rosa and 60 miles east of Clovis.

The chamber of commerce (☎ 355 7705), 509 Sumner Ave, has tourist information. (When I called them recently, the De Baca General Hospital answered my call. 'Oh, we're taking calls for the chamber', they said, and provided me with the information I wanted. This is not a big town.)

Aficionados of outlaw history can contact their ilk through the Outlaw Gang (☎ 355 9935) in Taiban, 11 miles east of Fort Sumner. The library (☎ 355 2832) is at 509 N 7th St. The De Baca General Hospital (☎ 355 2414) is at 500 N 10th St. The post office (☎ 355 2423) is at 622 N 5th St. The Fort Sumner Sheriff's Office (☎ 355 2405, for emergencies call 911) is located in the basement of the courthouse at 514 Ave C.

## Billy the Kid Museum

The Billy the Kid Museum (☎ 355 2380), 1601 E Sumner Ave, has over 60,000 privately owned items on display. Obviously, there's more here than just a Billy the Kid exhibit – there are Indian artifacts and items from late-19th- and early-20th-century local life. Hours are from 8:30 am to 5 pm daily, mid-May to mid-September. The museum is open Monday to Saturday for most of the rest of the year, except January and February. Admission is $2.

## Fort Sumner State Monument

The state monument (☎ 355 2573) is two miles east of Fort Sumner on Hwy 60, then four miles south on Hwy 272. The original Fort Sumner was built here in 1862 as an outpost to fight the Apache tribe and the Confederate Army around the time of the Civil War. After driving the Confederates south, the troops turned all their forces on the Indians.

The battles that followed were cruel and bloody, involving broken treaties and several massacres. Many Apache fled to Mexico – the rest were herded into a desolate strip of land near the fort known as Bosque Redondo. The Navajo were soon forced to join the Apache, walking the deadly 'Long March' from Canyon de Chelly, almost 400 miles to the west.

By the end of 1864, about 9000 Navajos and 500 Apaches had been herded into the Bosque Redondo Reservation, where the federal government hoped to convert them to farmers. In 1968, General Sherman declared it a failure; the reservation was not sustainable because the land was harsh and unsuitable for intensive agriculture. After four years of starvation and deprivation, the surviving Indians were allowed to return to their homelands.

The fort was then purchased by Lucien Maxwell, one of the richest ranchers of the period, who turned it into a palatial ranch. His son, Peter, inherited the spread in 1875. Billy the Kid was visiting here in 1881 when he was shot and killed by Sheriff Pat Garrett.

Unfortunately, the original fort no longer stands, but a visitor center has excellent interpretive exhibits and historical artifacts. The emphasis here is on Indian and pioneer history, and rangers in period costumes present demonstrations on weekends. Hours are 9:30 am to 5:30 pm except Tuesday, Wednesday and national holidays. Admission is $1 for adults and free for children. No camping is allowed.

## Old Fort Sumner Museum

This museum is near the state monument. There is more local history here, with an emphasis on Billy the Kid. The graves of the Kid and Lucien Maxwell are behind the museum. The Kid's tombstone is protected by an iron cage – 'souvenir hunters' keep stealing it. Entrance to the museum is another $1.

NEW MEXICO

## De Baca County Courthouse

The courthouse (☎ 355 2601), 514 Ave C, was built in 1930. The 2nd floor has three walls of murals depicting *The Last Frontier*, painted by Russell Vernon Hunter in 1934 as part of President Franklin Roosevelt's New Deal domestic reforms. These can be viewed during business hours.

## Sumner Lake State Park

The state park (☎ 355 2541), Box 125, 88119, is around a man-made lake formed by the damming of the Pecos River. The lake is locally popular for fishing, swimming, boating, water-skiing and beautiful sunsets. There is a picnic area, playground and campground.

Admission is $3 per vehicle for day use. Get there by taking Hwy 84 north for 11 miles, then Hwy 203 west for six miles.

## Special Events

Old Fort Days are held during the second weekend in June. They feature various athletic events, including a tombstone race in which contestants must negotiate an obstacle course while lugging an 80-lb tombstone. The purse for the winner is $1000. Other attractions are a rodeo, a parade, a mock gunfight, a barbecue and arts & crafts displays.

The De Baca County Fair is held in the last week in August. Call the chamber of commerce for details on both events.

## Places to Stay & Eat

Camping is available at Sumner Lake State Park (see above), which charges $7 for camping, $11 for sites with partial hookups. There is water but no showers.

There are only two simple and fairly inexpensive motels: the *Coronado Motel* (☎ 355 2466), 309 W Sumner Ave, and the *Oasis Motel* (☎ 355 7414), 1700 E Sumner Ave.

Restaurants are also limited. Try *Rodeo Cafe* (☎ 355 9986), 112 E Sumner Ave, for cheap Mexican lunches and dinners. Opposite, *Dariland* (☎ 355 2337), 113 E Sumner Ave, serves burgers and shakes. There is also *Fred's Restaurant & Lounge* (☎ 355 7500), at 1408 E Sumner Ave.

## Getting There & Away

The Fort Sumner Bus Station (☎ 355 7745), 1018 Sumner Ave, has a daily TNM&O bus in each direction between Albuquerque and Clovis (continuing to Lubbock, Texas).

# GLOSSARY

**adobado** – marinated meat used in Mexican cooking; often grilled.

**adobe** – sun-dried brick of clay and straw; used to build houses in many pueblos. The style is imitated in buildings throughout the Southwest.

**Anasazi** – Navajo for 'the Ancient Ones', or 'enemy ancestors', prominent Pueblo culture that flourished in the Southwest until the 14th century. Today's Pueblo Indians, including the Zuni and Hopi, are descendants of the Anasazi.

**Anglo** – a term used by Native Americans, sometimes perjoratively, to denote non-Hispanic Whites.

**ATV** – all-terrain vehicle.

**bolo** – a necktie made of a piece of cord or leather held in place by an ornamental fastener, often set with a semiprecious stone.

**BRO** – Backcountry Reservation Office, Grand Canyon National Park's NPS center for issuing permits.

**caliche** – a naturally occurring nitrate-rich fertilizer used in the Southwest.

**canyoneering** – exploring the bottom of a canyon on foot. Levels of difficulty range from pleasant afternoon jaunts to spending weeks exploring and camping on the canyon floor.

**casa** – Spanish for house or home.

**casita** – Spanish for little house. Many of the better New Mexican and Arizonan hotels offer casitas, which are generally separate, small adobe units, each with a private entrance and often with fireplaces.

**cerveza** – Spanish for beer.

**chiggers** – a bedbug-like mite, the bite of which leaves severe, itchy welts.

**Chihuahua** – northern Mexican state adjacent to New Mexico.

**Craftsman-style** – style of architecture developed during the Arts & Crafts Movement, a reaction to the perceived shoddiness of machine-made goods in the late 19th and early 20th centuries. This style of architectural and furniture design is typified by simple, functional designs, handcrafted in traditional materials such as clay, porcelain tiles, wood and stone.

**drive-in** – a movie theater or a diner where customers stay in their cars while they watch a movie, or order food or eat. A drive-in theater is essentially a parking lot facing a huge movie screen. The soundtrack is audible either via small speakers or the radio. A drive-in diner may provide trays that hang off the car's windows. Both are becoming anachronisms.

**DUP** – Daughters of Utah Pioneers, an organization of female descendants of the original Utah pioneers which runs history museums throughout the state.

**efficiencies** – furnished, short-term flats or apartments with private bathrooms and kitchenettes.

**fetish** – a handcarved object that represents the spirits of animals or of natural phenomena, common in all Southwestern Native American cultures. The Zuni in particular are noted for their elaborate fetish carvings.

**fry bread** – a specialty of Southwest Indians. This bread is formed into rounds, deep-fried and served hot and sometimes topped with honey as a dessert, or with meat, beans and vegetables in Navajo tacos.

**GCA** – Grand Canyon Association, a private, environmentally active organization that publishes books, maps, trail guides and videos on the Grand Canyon. The GCA also runs the Grand Canyon Field Institute, which offers classes in the national park. Its profits benefit the park.

**heishi** – beads carved from shells and

turquoise and often strung into necklaces by Pueblo Indians.

**HI/AYH** – Hostelling International/American Youth Hostels, a term given to hostels affiliated with Hostelling International, which is managed by IYHF (International Youth Hostel Federation).

**horno** – Spanish for oven; a conical outdoor oven built of adobe.

**kachina** – a powerful supernatural being that figures prominently in Pueblo religions, especially that of the Hopi. During some ceremonies dancers in costume become mediums for the kachinas and, for the duration of the dance, are invested with their powers. Kachina also refers to the carved dolls that are representations of Kachina spirits.

**kiva** – a circular, windowless, usually underground chamber originally built by the Anasazi and Mogollon cultures. Anthropologists first assumed kivas were strictly ceremonial chambers, but now they concede that kivas also had daily purposes. Later Pueblo Indians built and used kivas for ceremonies and other purposes. Kivas in today's pueblos are not open to the public. Reconstructed kivas can be entered at Bandelier and Aztec Ruins National Monuments.

**LDS** – Latter-Day Saints, from the formal name of the Mormon Church, the Church of Jesus Christ of Latter-Day Saints.

**luminaria** – weighted paper bags containing votive candles. On holidays, especially Christmas, the candles are lit and the bags placed in a row along a building's front walkway and ledges.

**mariachi** – music (similar to the polka) that originated in western Mexico for weddings at the turn of the century. It was introduced to the Southwest, Texas and California by migrant workers.

**metate** – a concave stone on which Native Americans and Hispanics grind grain using a hand-held 'mano' stone.

**microbrewery** – any brewery that produces under 10,000 barrels of beer a year.

Usually the beer will be unpasteurized and closer to European-style beer in its flavor than typical American commercial Pilsners.

**moradas** – lodges in which the Penitente Brotherhoods of New Mexico and southern Colorado practiced their once secretive rites, including self-flagellation.

**Navajo taco** – fry bread smothered in pinto beans, spicy meat and toppings similar to those on a tostada.

**New Deal** – a series of economic reforms and work projects initiated by Franklin Roosevelt in 1933 to create jobs and increase US productivity during the Great Depression, which began in 1929 and lasted throughout the 1930s and ended with the beginning of WW II.

**NHS** – National Historic Site.

**NPS** – National Park Service.

**NRA** – National Recreation Area.

**NWR** – National Wildlife Refuge.

**Penitente Brotherhood** – a once secretive Roman Catholic religious group with mainly Hispanic followers that formerly practiced such rites as self-flagellation and fasting.

**petroglyph** – an ancient rock carving or an inscription on a rock.

**pictograph** – a picture or symbol representing a word rather than a sound, usually drawn or painted on a rock.

**piñon** – a pine tree that flourishes throughout the western USA and Mexico that produces an edible nutlike seed, called a pine nut.

**PRCA** – Professional Rodeo Cowboys Association, an organization based in Colorado Springs, Colorado, that coordinates and sanctions rodeos throughout the West.

**presidio** – a fortress built by the Spanish before the turn of the 19th century. They were used throughout the Southwest to garrison troops affiliated with the missions.

**pueblo** – a Native American village permanently constructed in adobe or stone.

**Pueblo** – a designation of 25 Native American tribes, including the Zuni and Hopi, that have descended from the Anasazi.

Their pueblos, made up of permanent multistory stone structures, are found in an area extending from northeastern Arizona to the Rio Pecos in New Mexico and from Taos on the Rio Grande, in the north, to a few miles below El Paso, Texas. Most Pueblo villages are divided into two clans, one commonly known as the Summer People and the other as the Winter People.

**pullout** – an area on the shoulder of rural roads and highways for short-term stopping or for allowing faster vehicles to pass.

**res** – slang for reservation, frequently used by Native Americans.

**reservation** – sovereign land owned by a Native American tribe, as designated in treaties with the US government. Typically, the land is in a remote location, the soil is agriculturally inferior and other resources are scarce.

**retablos** – altarpieces or religious pictures.

**river running** – rafting, white-water rafting, kayaking or canoeing on rivers.

**Route 66** – US Hwy 66 was commissioned in 1926 to link Los Angeles with Chicago, 2448 miles away. Route 66 gave Americans their first taste of automobile populism, as California became easily accessible to anyone with a car. Route 66 has since been replaced by interstate highways.

**santos** – carved wooden religious figurines used in small Catholic shrines, including those of the Penitente Brotherhood.

**sipapu** – in Zuni tribal legend, early ancestors came up through four successive underworlds to reach this world. The entrance they emerged through is called the *sipapu*. Kivas often have a symbolic sipapu dug in the floor.

**Smokey the Bear** – an orphaned black bear cub found by USFS workers after a huge forest fire in 1950. Smokey was used by the Forest Service as a 'goodwill ambassador' to educate people about the dangers of forest fires. Smokey died in 1976 but lives on in advertisements in the form of a gruff black bear in blue jeans and a forest worker's peaked camp hat, admonishing campers that 'Only *YOU* can prevent forest fires!'

**Sonora** – northern Mexican state adjacent to Arizona.

**sopaipilla** – pillow-like, deep-fried flatbread often served with honey – a favorite in the Southwest and similar to Native American fry bread.

**sub sandwich** – a long sandwich on a French roll, loaded with meat, cheese, lettuce, tomato (or other vegetables) and condiments. Also known as a hero, hoagie or poor boy.

**trogon** – a colorful tropical bird from Costa Rica that winters in Arizona and New Mexico.

**USFS** – United States Forest Service, a division of the Department of Agriculture that implements policies on federal forest lands according to the principles of 'multiple use', which permit timber cutting, watershed management, wildlife management, and camping and recreation.

**USGS** – United States Geological Survey, an agency of the Department of the Interior responsible for detailed topographic maps of the entire country, among other things. Available at outdoor-oriented businesses, USGS maps are popular with hikers and backpackers as they are sometimes the only maps to backcountry areas.

**vigas** – wooden beams used to support the roof of pueblo villages. Vigas are added to modern adobe houses for decoration.

**WPA** – Works Progress Administration, a New Deal program set up in 1935 to increase employment through a series of public works projects, including road and building construction, beautification of public structures (especially post offices) and the publication of a well-respected series of state and regional guidebooks.

**Yei Bei Chei** – a nine-day Navajo healing ceremony that takes place in winter.

**zia symbol** – a stylized sun motif used in Zia Pueblo pottery; the Arizona state symbol.

# Appendix I – Climate Charts

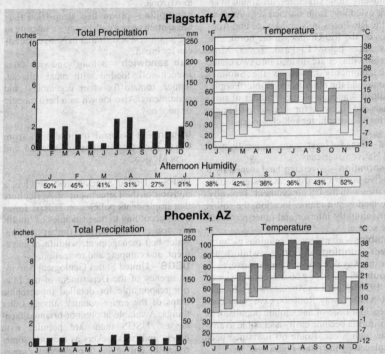

## Flagstaff, AZ

**Total Precipitation**

**Temperature**

**Afternoon Humidity**

| J | F | M | A | M | J | J | A | S | O | N | D |
|---|---|---|---|---|---|---|---|---|---|---|---|
| 50% | 45% | 41% | 31% | 27% | 21% | 38% | 42% | 36% | 36% | 43% | 52% |

## Phoenix, AZ

**Total Precipitation**

**Temperature**

**Afternoon Humidity**

| J | F | M | A | M | J | J | A | S | O | N | D |
|---|---|---|---|---|---|---|---|---|---|---|---|
| 34% | 28% | 24% | 17% | 14% | 12% | 21% | 24% | 23% | 24% | 28% | 34% |

## Tucson, AZ

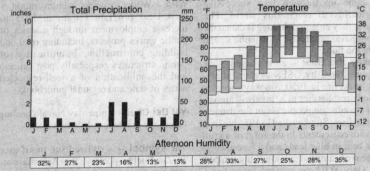

**Total Precipitation**

**Temperature**

**Afternoon Humidity**

| J | F | M | A | M | J | J | A | S | O | N | D |
|---|---|---|---|---|---|---|---|---|---|---|---|
| 32% | 27% | 23% | 16% | 13% | 13% | 28% | 33% | 27% | 25% | 28% | 35% |

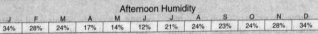

924

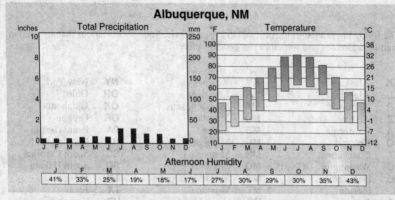

## Albuquerque, NM

| | inches | Total Precipitation | mm | °F | Temperature | °C |

### Afternoon Humidity

| J | F | M | A | M | J | J | A | S | O | N | D |
|---|---|---|---|---|---|---|---|---|---|---|---|
| 41% | 33% | 25% | 19% | 18% | 17% | 27% | 30% | 29% | 30% | 35% | 43% |

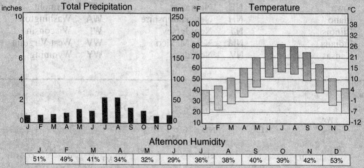

## Santa Fe, NM

### Afternoon Humidity

| J | F | M | A | M | J | J | A | S | O | N | D |
|---|---|---|---|---|---|---|---|---|---|---|---|
| 51% | 49% | 41% | 34% | 32% | 29% | 36% | 38% | 40% | 39% | 42% | 53% |

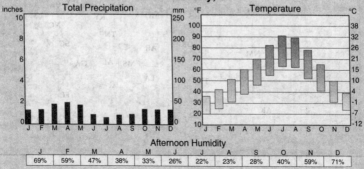

## Salt Lake City, UT

### Afternoon Humidity

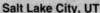

| J | F | M | A | M | J | J | A | S | O | N | D |
|---|---|---|---|---|---|---|---|---|---|---|---|
| 69% | 59% | 47% | 38% | 33% | 26% | 22% | 23% | 28% | 40% | 59% | 71% |

# Appendix II – State Abbreviations

The following is a list of the official US Postal Service state abbreviations that are used in mailing addresses and sometimes in general reference.

| | | | | | |
|---|---|---|---|---|---|
| **AK** | Alaska | **KY** | Kentucky | **NY** | New York |
| **AL** | Alabama | **LA** | Louisiana | **OH** | Ohio |
| **AR** | Arkansas | **MA** | Massachusetts | **OK** | Oklahoma |
| **AZ** | Arizona | **MD** | Maryland | **OR** | Oregon |
| **CA** | California | **ME** | Maine | **PA** | Pennsylvania |
| **CO** | Colorado | **MI** | Michigan | **RI** | Rhode Island |
| **CT** | Connecticut | **MN** | Minnesota | **SC** | South Carolina |
| **DC** | Washington, DC | **MO** | Missouri | **SD** | South Dakota |
| **DE** | Delaware | **MS** | Mississippi | **TN** | Tennessee |
| **FL** | Florida | **MT** | Montana | **TX** | Texas |
| **GA** | Georgia | **NC** | North Carolina | **UT** | Utah |
| **HI** | Hawaii | **ND** | North Dakota | **VA** | Virginia |
| **IA** | Iowa | **NE** | Nebraska | **VT** | Vermont |
| **ID** | Idaho | **NH** | New Hampshire | **WA** | Washington |
| **IL** | Illinois | **NJ** | New Jersey | **WI** | Wisconsin |
| **IN** | Indiana | **NM** | New Mexico | **WV** | West Virginia |
| **KS** | Kansas | **NV** | Nevada | **WY** | Wyoming |

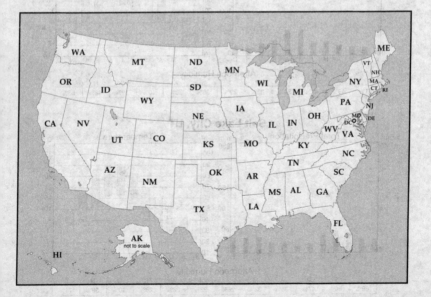

# Index

## MAPS

## TEXT

Maps are in **bold** type.

Abajo Mountains (UT)  348
Abbey, Edward 320
Abiquiu (NM) 783
accommodations 83-88
Acoma Pueblo (NM) 792-793
Aguirre Springs National
    Recreation Area (NM)850
air travel
    air passes 93, 99-100
    to/from abroad 96-103
    within the USA 92-94, 104
Ajo (AZ) 639-640
Alamo Lake State Park (AZ) 466
Alamogordo (NM) 868-872
Albuquerque (NM) 676-699,
    **677, 679, 682, 686-687**
    entertainment 697-698
    getting around 699
    getting there & away 699
    places to eat 691-697
    places to stay 686-691
    things to see 678-684
Algodones Sand Dunes (AZ) 476
Alpine (AZ) 586-588
Alta (UT) 137, 145, 146
Altamont (UT) 213
Anasazi Indians 16-17, 264, 529, 554, 676, 784
Anasazi ruins
    Arizona 553-556
    Colorado 769
    New Mexico 700, 731, 770, 772-773, 774-776, 787-789
    Utah 314, 349-350, 353, 356
Ancho (NM) 868
Angel Fire (NM) 759
Angel Peak National Recreation
    Area (NM) 773
Antelope Island State Park (UT) 133

Apache Indians 17, 21, 776-777, 831
    Reservations 579-581, 592-593, 877-878
Apache Lake (AZ) 597
Apache Trail (AZ) 596
archaeological sites
    Arizona 558-560, 583-584, 593-594, 596, 635
    New Mexico 682-683, 700, 710, 729-730, 772-773, 774-776, 797-798, 861, 872-873, 912
    Utah 214, 221, 226-228, 254-255, 260-261, 271, 288-289, 347
Arches National Park (UT)
    326-330, **327**
Arcosanti (AZ) 498-499
Arivaca (AZ) 636
Arizona 359-668, **362-363, 441, 478, 539, 567, 599**
    economy 34, 365
    history 361-365
Arizona State University
    377-378
Artesia (NM) 894-896, **895**
Ash Fork (AZ) 538
astronomy
    Arizona 516, 517, 608, 637-638, 641
    New Mexico 837, 870, 877, 889
atomic research 18, 684, 707, 785, 867
Aztec (NM) 770-772, **771**

Baker Dam Reservoir (UT) 289
Bandelier National Monument
    (NM) 787-789
Bandera Crater/Ice Cave (NM)
    797

baseball 475, 627, 698, 765
bats 902, 904
Bear Lake (UT) 207-209
Bear River Migratory Bird
    Refuge (UT) 194
Beaver (UT) 266-269, **267**
Belen (NM) 703
Benson (AZ) 648
Bernalillo (NM) 700
Bicknell (UT) 319
Big Cottonwood Canyon (UT)
    138-139
Big Lake (AZ) 584
Billy the Kid 23, 671, 887, 919
Biosphere 2 (AZ) 630-631
bird-watching
    Arizona 455-456, 466, 502, 611-612, 641, 651-652, 664, 665
    New Mexico 811, 816, 827, 836, 844, 850, 894
    Utah 133, 134, 165-166, 186, 194, 199, 205, 206, 214, 235, 238, 261, 299, 309
Bisbee (AZ) 656-660, **658**
Bisti Badlands (NM) 768-769
Bitter Lake National Wildlife
    Refuge (NM) 894
Blanding (UT) 349-351, **350**
Bloomfield (NM) 772-773
Blue Hole (NM) 808
Bluewater Lake State Park (NM)
    794
Bluff (UT) 355-356
Bonanza (UT) 221
Bonneville Salt Flats (UT)
    231-232
Bonney, William 887
books 60-65
Bosque del Apache National
    Wildlife Refuge (NM) 836
Bottomless Lakes State Park
    (NM) 894

# Lonely Planet online
## ⟶ travels in cyberspace

Now anyone can browse the latest online information in the **Lonely Planet Travel Centre** on the Internet's World Wide Web. All that's needed is access to the Internet and a Web browser like Netscape or Mosaic.

Lonely Planet's main goal is to give travelers the latest information about the places covered in the guidebooks, and the Internet provides the most efficient means for doing this. Travelers can now get up-to-the-minute news about their destinations!

The **Travel Centre** is also a great planning tool for those who haven't quite decided where they want to go – continents and countries can be explored by way of interactive maps instead of wading through stacks of books – and new destinations are being added regularly.

The **Lonely Planet Travel Centre** currently has seven main menu selections:

- **destinations:** travel profiles of individual countries from LP guidebooks, including full-color clickable maps and photos
- **postcards:** messages and advice from travelers
- **on the road:** tall tales and true stories from Lonely Planet authors and photographers
- **detours:** a sampling of travel destinations well off the beaten track
- **health:** a complete health checklist for travelers for use both prior to departure and while on the road
- **propaganda:** a complete list of Lonely Planet guidebooks and travel-related information
- **what's new:** the latest additions to the Lonely Planet title list and Web site

The URL for the **Lonely Planet Travel Centre** is **http://www.lonelyplanet.com**

# Lonely Planet TV Series & Videos

Lonely Planet travel guides have been brought to life on the TV screen and on video. Like the guidebooks these shows are based on the joy of independent travel – looking honestly at some of the most exciting, picturesque and frustrating places in the world. Each program is presented by one of three travelers from Australia, England and the USA. These travelers are not presented as experts, guides or reporters. Rather, they are engaging storytellers who become fellow traveling companions as the viewer is drawn into the travel experience.

Lonely Planet videos encourage the same approach to travel as Lonely Planet travel guides – get off the beaten track, be informed about where you're going, get to know the people you are visiting and have fun!

Lonely Planet videos are available in bookstores and video outlets and are being broadcast globally.

*Video destinations include:*
**Alaska; Australia (Southeast); Brazil (Northeast); Ecuador & the Galapagos Islands; Indonesia; Jamaica; Japan (Tokyo to Taiwan); Ruta Maya (Yucatan, Guatemala & Belize); Morocco; North India (Varanasi to the Himalayas); Pacific Islands; Vietnam; Zimbabwe, Botswana & Namibia**

*Coming in 1996:*
**the Arctic (Norway & Finland); Baja California; Chile & Easter Island; China (Southeast); Costa Rica; East Africa (Tanzania & Zanzibar); Great Barrier Reef (Australia); Israel & the Sinai Desert; Papua New Guinea; the Rockies (USA); Syria & Jordan; Turkey.**

*The Lonely Planet television series is produced by:*
**Pilot Productions**
Duke of Sussex Studios
44 Uxbridge Street
London W8 7TG U K

*Lonely Planet Videos are distributed by:*
**IVN Communications Inc**
2246 Camino Ramon
San Ramon, California 94583, USA
107 Power Rd, Chiswick
London WH 5PL, UK

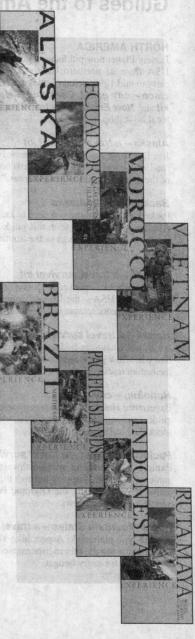

# Guides to the Americas

## NORTH AMERICA

Lonely Planet now publishes a growing list of guidebooks to the USA from its northern California office. Upcoming titles for early to mid 1996 include *Los Angeles – city guide, San Francisco – city guide, California & Nevada – a travel survival kit* and *New England – a travel survival kit;* check with your local bookshop.

### Alaska – a travel survival kit
Jim DuFresne has traveled extensively through Alaska by foot, road, rail, barge and kayak, and tells how to make the most of one of the world's great wilderness areas.

### Backpacking in Alaska
Packed with everything you need to know to safely experience the Alaskan wilderness on foot, this guide covers the most outstanding trails, from Ketchikan in the Southeast to Fairbanks near the Arctic Circle.

### Canada – a travel survival kit
This guidebook is packed with facts on this huge country to the north of the USA – the Rocky Mountains, Niagara Falls, ultramodern Toronto, remote villages in Nova Scotia and much more.

### Hawaii – a travel survival kit
No matter what your budget, this guide gives inside information that will allow you to explore Hawaii's sights – whether on or off the beaten track.

### Honolulu – city guide
Experience Honolulu's intriguing variety of attactions using this guide, from sampling a phenomenal selection of Asian cuisines to snorkeling at Hanauma Bay.

### Pacific Northwest – a travel survival kit
Explore the secrets of the Northwest with this indispensable guide – from island hopping through the San Juans and rafting the Snake River to hiking the Olympic Peninsula and discovering Seattle's best microbrews.

### Rocky Mountain States – a travel survival kit
Whether you plan to ski Aspen, hike Yellowstone or hang out in sleepy ghost towns, this indispensable guide is full of down-to-earth advice for every budget.

# CENTRAL AMERICA & THE CARIBBEAN
## Baja California – a travel survival kit
For centuries, Mexico's Baja peninsula – with its beautiful coastline, raucous border towns and crumbling Spanish missions – has been a land of escapes and escapades. This book describes how and where to escape in Baja.

## Central America on a shoestring
Practical information on travel in Belize, Guatemala, Costa Rica, Honduras, El Salvador, Nicaragua and Panama. A team of experienced Lonely Planet authors reveals the secrets of this culturally rich, geographically diverse and breathtakingly beautiful region.

## Costa Rica – a travel survival kit
A gold-medal winner of SATW's Lowell Thomas Travel Journalism Awards, this bestselling guidebook offers complete coverage of Costa Rica. Sun-drenched beaches, steamy jungles, smoking volcanoes, rugged mountains and dazzling birds and animals – it's all here!

## Eastern Caribbean – a travel survival kit
Powdery white sands, clear turquoise waters, lush jungle rainforest and a laid-back pace make the islands of the Eastern Caribbean an ideal destination for divers, hikers and sun-lovers. This guide will help you to decide which islands to visit and includes details on inter-island travel.

## Guatemala, Belize & Yucatán: La Ruta Maya – a travel survival kit
Climb a volcano, explore the colorful highland villages or laze your time away on coral islands and Caribbean beaches. The lands of the Maya offer a fascinating journey into the past which will enhance appreciation of their dynamic contemporary cultures. This guide is a medalist in SATW's Lowell Thomas Travel Journalism Awards.

## Mexico – a travel survival kit
The unique blend of Indian and Spanish cultures, a fascinating history and hospitable people make Mexico a travelers' paradise.

# SOUTH AMERICA
## Argentina, Uruguay & Paraguay – a travel survival kit
Discover some of South America's most spectacular natural attractions in Argentina; friendly people and beautiful handicrafts in Paraguay; and Uruguay's wonderful beaches.

### Bolivia – a travel survival kit
From lonely villages in the Andes to ancient ruined cities and the spectacular city of La Paz, Bolivia is a magnificent blend of everything that inspires travelers.

### Brazil – a travel survival kit
From the mad passion of Carnival to the Amazon – home of the richest ecosystem on earth – Brazil is a country of mythical proportions. This guide has all the essential travel information.

### Chile & Easter Island – a travel survival kit
Travel in Chile is easy and safe, with possibilities as varied as the countryside. This guide also gives detailed coverage of Chile's Pacific outpost, mysterious Easter Island.

### Colombia – a travel survival kit
Colombia is a land of myths – from the ancient legends of El Dorado to the modern tales of Gabriel García Márquez. The reality is beauty and violence, wealth and poverty, tradition and change. This guide shows how to travel independently and safely in this exotic country.

### Ecuador & the Galápagos Islands – a travel survival kit
Ecuador offers a wide variety of travel experiences, from the high cordilleras to the Amazon plains – and 600 miles west, the fascinating Galápagos Islands. Everything you need to know about traveling around this enchanting country is covered in this guide.

### Peru – a travel survival kit
The lost city of Machu Picchu, the Andean altiplano and the magnificent Amazon rainforests are just some of Peru's many attractions. All the travel facts you'll need can be found in this comprehensive guide.

### South America on a shoestring
This practical guide provides concise information for budget travelers and covers South America from the Darien Gap to Tierra del Fuego.

### Trekking in the Patagonian Andes
The first detailed guide to this region gives complete information on 28 walks and lists a number of other possibilities extending from the Araucanía and Lake District regions of Argentina and Chile to the remote icy tip of South America in Tierra del Fuego.

### Venezuela – a travel survival kit
From the beaches along the Caribbean coast and the snow-capped peaks of the Andes to the capital, Caracas, there is much for travelers to explore. This comprehensive guide is packed with 'first-hand' tips for travel in this fascinating destination.

**Also available: *Brazilian* phrasebook, *Latin American Spanish* phrasebook, *USA* phrasebook and *Quechua* phrasebook.**

# PLANET TALK

## Lonely Planet's FREE quarterly newsletter

We love hearing from you and think you'd like to hear from us.

**When...** is the right time to see reindeer in Finland?
**Where...** can you hear the best palm-wine music in Ghana?
**How...** do you get from Asunción to Areguá by steam train?
**What...** is the best way to see India?

Every issue is packed with up-to-date travel news and advice including:

- a letter from Lonely Planet founders Tony and Maureen Wheeler
- travel diary from a Lonely Planet author – find out what it's really like out on the road
- feature article on an important and topical travel issue
- a selection of recent letters from our readers
- the latest travel news from all over the world
- details on Lonely Planet's new and forthcoming releases

To join our mailing list contact any Lonely Planet office (addresses below).

*Also available: Lonely Planet T-shirts. 100% heavyweight cotton (S, M, L, XL)*

## LONELY PLANET PUBLICATIONS

**Australia:** PO Box 617, Hawthorn 3122, Victoria
☎ (03) 9819 1877   **fax** (03) 9819 6459   **e-mail** talk2us@lonelyplanet.com.au

**USA:** Embarcadero West, 155 Filbert Street, Suite 251, Oakland, CA 94607
☎ (510) 893 8555, toll-free (800) 275 8555  **fax** (510) 893 8563
   **e-mail** info@lonelyplanet.com

**UK:** 10 Barley Mow Passage, Chiswick, London W4 4PH
☎ (0181) 742 3161 **fax** (0181) 742 2772   **e-mail** 100413.3551@compuserve.com

**France:** 71 bis rue du Cardinal Lemoine, 75005 Paris
☎ 1-46 34 00 58   **fax** 1-46-34-72-55   **e-mail** 100560.415@compuserve.com

**World Wide Web:** http://www.lonelyplanet.com

# Lonely Planet Guidebooks

Lonely Planet guidebooks cover every accessible part of Asia as well as Australia, the Pacific, South America, Africa, the Middle East, Europe and parts of North America. There are five series: *travel survival kits*, covering a country for a range of budgets; *shoestring guides* with compact information for low-budget travel in a major region; *walking guides; city guides* and *phrasebooks*.

## Europe

Baltic States & Kaliningrad
Baltic States phrasebook • Britain
Central Europe • Central Europe phrasebook
Czech & Slovak Republics • Dublin
Eastern Europe • Eastern
Europe phrasebook • Finland
France • Greece • Greek phrasebook
Hungary • Iceland, Greenland & the Faroes
Ireland • Italy • Mediterranean Europe
Mediterranean Europe phrasebook
Poland • Prague • Russian phrasebook
Scandinavian & Baltic Europe
Scandinavian Europe phrasebook
Slovenia • Switzerland • Trekking in Greece
Trekking in Spain • USSR • Vienna
Western Europe • Western Europe phrasebook

## North America

Alaska • Backpacking in Alaska
Baja California • Canada • Hawaii • Honolulu
Mexico • Pacific Northwest
Rocky Mountain States • Southwest

## Central America

Central America • Costa Rica
Guatemala, Yucatán & Belize: La Ruta Maya
Eastern Caribbean • Latin American
Spanish phrasebook

## Africa

Africa • Arabic (Moroccan) phrasebook
Central Africa • East Africa
Kenya • Morocco • North Africa
South Africa, Lesotho & Swaziland
Swahili phrasebook
Trekking in East Africa • West Africa
Zimbabwe, Botswana & Namibia

## South America

Argentina, Uruguay & Paraguay
Bolivia • Brazil • Brazilian phrasebook
Chile & Easter Island • Colombia
Ecuador & the Galápagos Islands
Peru • Quechua phrasebook
South America • Trekking in the
Patagonian Andes • Venezuela

# Mail Order

Lonely Planet guidebooks are distributed worldwide. They are also available by mail order from Lonely Planet, so if you have difficulty finding a title please write to us. US and Canadian residents should write to Embarcadero West, 155 Filbert St, Suite 251, Oakland CA 94607, USA ; European residents should write to 10 Barley Mow Passage, Chiswick, London W4 4PH; and residents of other countries to PO Box 617, Hawthorn, Victoria 3122, Australia.

## North-East Asia

Beijing • China • Mandarin Chinese phrasebook • Hong Kong, Macau & Canton • Cantonese phrasebook Japan • Japanese phrasebook Korea • Korean phrasebook • Mongolia Mongolian phrasebook North-East Asia • Seoul • Taiwan Tibet • Tibet phrasebook • Tokyo

## The Middle East

Arab Gulf States
Arabic (Egyptian) phrasebook
Egypt & the Sudan
Iran • Israel • Jordan &
Syria • Middle East
Trekking in Turkey
Turkey • Turkish
phrasebook • Yemen

## Indian Subcontinent

Bangladesh • India
India travel atlas
Trekking in the Indian
Himalaya • Hindi/Urdu
phrasebook • Karakoram
Highway • Kashmir,
Ladakh & Zanskar
Nepal • Nepali phrasebook
Trekking in the Nepal Himalaya
Tibet phrasebook
Pakistan • Sri Lanka
Sri Lanka phrasebook

## South-East Asia

Bali & Lombok • Bangkok • Cambodia
Ho Chi Minh • Indonesia
Indonesian phrasebook • Jakarta
Laos • Lao phrasebook
Malaysia, Singapore & Brunei
Myanmar (Burma) • Burmese phrasebook
Philippines • Pilipino phrasebook
Singapore • South-East Asia
Thailand • Thai phrasebook
Thai Hill Tribes phrasebook
Thailand travel atlas
Vietnam • Vietnamese
phrasebook

## Islands of the Indian Ocean

Madagascar & Comoros
Maldives & Islands of the
East Indian Ocean
Mauritius, Réunion & Seychelles

## Australia & the Pacific

Australia • Australian phrasebook
Bushwalking in Australia • Fiji • Fijian phrasebook
Islands of Australia's Great Barrier Reef • Melbourne
Micronesia • New Caledonia • New Zealand
Tramping in New Zealand • New South Wales
Outback Australia • Papua New Guinea
Bushwalking in Papua New Guinea
Papua New Guinea phrasebook
Rarotonga & the Cook Islands • Samoa
Solomon Islands • Sydney • Tahiti & French Polynesia
Tonga • Vanuatu • Victoria • Western Australia

## The Lonely Planet Story

Lonely Planet published its first book in 1973 in response to the numerous 'How did you do it?' questions Maureen and Tony Wheeler were asked after driving, bussing, hitching, sailing and railing their way from England to Australia.

Written at a kitchen table and hand collated, trimmed and stapled, *Across Asia on the Cheap* became an instant local best seller, inspiring thoughts of another book.

Eighteen months in South-East Asia resulted in their second guide, *South-East Asia on a shoestring*, which they put together in a backstreet Chinese hotel in Singapore in 1975. The 'yellow bible', as it quickly became known to backpackers around the world, soon became *the* guide to the region. It has sold well over half a million copies and is now in its 8th edition, still retaining its familiar yellow cover.

Today there are over 160 Lonely Planet titles in print – books that have that same adventurous approach to travel as those early guides; books that 'assume you know how to get your luggage off the carousel' as one reviewer put it.

Although Lonely Planet initially specialized in guides to Asia, they now cover most regions of the world, including the Pacific, South America, Africa, the Middle East and Europe. The list of *walking guides* and *phrasebooks* (for 'unusual' languages such as Quechua, Swahili, Nepali and Egyptian Arabic) is also growing rapidly.

The emphasis continues to be on travel for independent travelers. Tony and Maureen still travel for several months of each year and play an active part in the writing, updating and quality control of Lonely Planet's guides.

They have been joined by over 50 authors, 110 staff – mainly editors, cartographers and designers – at our office in Melbourne, Australia, at our US office in Oakland, California, and at our European office in Paris; another six at our office in London handle sales for Britain, Europe and Africa. Travelers themselves also make a valuable contribution to the guides through the feedback we receive in thousands of letters each year.

The people at Lonely Planet strongly believe that travelers can make a positive contribution to the countries they visit, both through their appreciation of the countries' culture, wildlife and natural features, and through the money they spend. In addition, the company makes a direct contribution to the countries and regions it covers. Since 1986 a percentage of the income from each book has been donated to ventures such as famine relief in Africa; aid projects in India; agricultural projects in Central America; Greenpeace's efforts to halt French nuclear testing in the Pacific; and Amnesty International.

Lonely Planet's basic travel philosophy is summed up in Tony Wheeler's comment, 'Don't worry about whether your trip will work out. Just go!'.

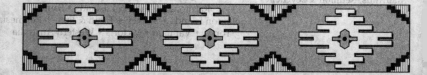